THE LAW

of

LANDLORD AND TENANT
IN SCOTLAND

by

G. CAMPBELL H. PATON, Q.C., M.A., LL.B.

*Reader in Scots Law, University
of Edinburgh*

and

JOSEPH G. S. CAMERON, M.A., LL.B., W.S.

*formerly Lecturer in Conveyancing,
University of Edinburgh*

Published under the auspices of

THE SCOTTISH UNIVERSITIES LAW INSTITUTE

W. GREEN & SON LTD.

1967

First published 1967

Printed in Great Britain
by
The Central Press (Aberdeen) Ltd.
Aberdeen

THE LAW OF LANDLORD AND TENANT
IN SCOTLAND

CONTENTS

PART I
LEASES IN GENERAL

PART II
STATUTORY LEASES

PREFACE

This volume comprises a restatement as at 30th April 1966 of the Law of Scotland regarding the relationship of Landlord and Tenant. Part I deals with what may be termed the Common Law section of the subject, albeit in places impinged upon by the Legislature. It is a striking tribute to the soundness and stability of Scots Law in this sphere that since 1916—when Sir John Rankine published the third edition of his classic work on the *Law of Leases in Scotland*—there have been few decisions in the Courts and comparatively few statutory developments, while on some points on which Sir John Rankine gave his valuable opinion there has been neither a decision nor a statute. Social, economic and political changes in the country in general have rendered it unnecessary to deal at length with certain subjects, *e.g.* mining leases, which are now virtually unknown. In regard to Part II, however, which deals with Statutory Leases, the law is modern; in many places it is complex and confusing and in some instances liable at any moment to statutory repeal or alteration. It seems to be highly desirable, to put it mildly, that the blessing of a codification of the law relating to some at least of these statutory leases should take place at the earliest possible date: it is, therefore, good news to learn that the Rent Acts, so far as applying to Scotland, may be consolidated in one Act applying to Scotland in the near future (First Report of Scottish Law Commission and First Programme of the Commission on Consolidation and Statute Law Revision).

Subjects such as Valuation and Rating and Reparation in relation to landlord and tenant have not been dealt with, as it is felt that these are adequately covered in other works.

An Addendum of authorities reported between 1st May 1966 and 31st December 1966 inclusive is given on pages ix, x, xi and xii.

The book is a joint work, J. G. S. Cameron, however, being primarily responsible for Part I and G. C. H. Paton for Part II. In such a vast and complicated field of law it has not been practicable to set out all the authorities, but it is hoped that none of the essential ones have been omitted.

We desire to record our warm thanks to Professors J. M. Halliday and G. L. F. Henry, who each read a large part of the book either in M.S. or in proof and kindly made a number of most valuable suggestions.

We also desire to acknowledge our indebtedness to the kind assistance of Mr. K. G. Barr, LL.B., Advocate, who helped us with Chapter IX, Mr. J. A. D. Hope, LL.B., Advocate, who not only checked the references in Chapters XVIII to XXI but also revised Chapter XX in the light of the Rent Act 1965, passed after the Chapter had been written, and Mr. A. L. McNicoll, Town Clerk Depute, Edinburgh, who went over Chapter XXII.

The Index and the Tables of Cases and of Statutes have been prepared by Mr. J. M. Pinkerton, LL.B., Advocate, and we are grateful to him for having undertaken this laborious task.

Among those who assisted so capably in the typing of what some-times must have been somewhat indecipherable manuscript, we must especially thank Mrs. L. S. Wilson, Miss C. B. Murray, Mrs. C. M. Cameron, M.A., Miss E. C. Cameron, Miss M. B. Weightman and Mrs. A. E. Easton. A word of gratitude is also due both to the printers and to the publishers for their helpful co-operation and for all that, as usual, they have so capably and efficiently done towards the production of the volume.

G. C. H. P.

J. G. S. C.

EDINBURGH, 1967.

N.B. It has not been thought necessary to include a bibliography of works cited, many of which are very well known. Suffice it to say that a reference to Rankine is, unless otherwise indicated, to the 3rd edition of his work on *Leases* and a reference to Bell is, again in the absence of indication to the contrary, to the 10th (and last) edition of his *Principles,* while in the case of his *Commentaries* (cited as *Comm.*) it is to the 7th (and last) edition.

ADDENDUM

As stated in the Preface, the law in the text and the footnotes is set out as *reported* up to and including 30th April 1966. While the book was passing through the press, a number of decisions and other matters were reported and a note of these up to 31st December 1966 is accordingly given here:

CONSTITUTION AND PROOF OF THE CONTRACT

P. 23   *Informal Leases for more than One Year—Proof of Verbal Agreement.*

A purchaser, having made a probative offer to purchase a house, which was not accepted in writing, took entry and founded on his subsequent actings, including extensive meliorations, which were known to the seller. *Held* that the purchaser was entitled to an unrestricted proof of his averments and was not restricted to proving the informal contract of sale by the writ or oath of the seller. *Observed*, following Gloag, *Contract*, 2nd ed., 46-47, that when *rei interventus* is relied upon in cases where parties have been in negotiation for a contract, and one of them has acted, and been known to and allowed to act, on the mistaken assumption that the negotiations had reached the point of a complete contract, the actings may be evidence that agreement has been actually reached; moreover, proof of *rei interventus* is not limited to writ or oath. *Dicta* of Lord Macmillan in *Mitchell* v *Stornoway Trustees*, 1936 S.C. (H.L.) 56, at p. 66 criticised. *Errol* v *Walker*, 1966 S.L.T. 159.

The conclusion reached by the Court in *Errol* v *Walker, supra*, so far as it affects leases, seems to be that proof of an alleged lease can rest on the writ of the party seeking to uphold the contract together with actings of that party amounting to *rei interventus*. This is an extension of the doctrine of *rei interventus* and is criticised in "*Rei Interventus* Reconsidered", 11 J.L.S. 263.

REMOVINGS

Pp. 265, *Period of Notice to Quit.* Rent Act 1957, s. 16. Where the notice
273   is to be given "not less than four weeks" before the date when it is to take effect, this is to be reckoned as including the first and excluding the last day. *Schnabel* v *Allard*, [1966] 3 All E.R. 816.

AGRICULTURAL HOLDINGS ACTS

P. 318 1949 Act, ss. 25, 26; 1958 Act, s. 3.
Notice to Quit. Circumstances where the withholding of consent to a notice to quit would cause greater hardship to the landlord.

Forbes v *Darling*, 1965 S.L.C.R. App. 139. Where financial hardship is not alleged by either party, relative hardship connected with the farming operations of both parties should be the decisive factor. *Davies* v *Barber*, 1965 S.L.C.R. App. 133.

Agricultural Holdings Act 1948, s. 25 (1) (d); 1958 Act, s. 3 (2).
Held in England under these Acts that " hardship " in that context is not limited to hardship referable to the possession or use of the holding and its meaning is unlimited. Consent to a notice to quit can thus be given where the greater hardship to the landlord is due to his financial situation or, on his death, that of his widow and his estate. *Bailey* v *Purser* [1967] 1 All E.R. 188.

CROFTERS ACTS

Pp. 393, *Subjects.* A lease of a croft which included runrig subjects was
405   held not to be void from uncertainty because the individual rigs could not be identified. *Walker* v *Forestry Commission*, 1965 S.L.C.R. App. 58.

Ibid. In view of the Court's own records and other facts, an area of ground let by a landlord was held not to be in fact part of the common grazings. *MacDonald* v *Secretary of State for Scotland*, 1965 S.L.C.R. App. 46.

Ibid. Pertinent of subjects. A right of access over a footpath through a township as a pertinent of a croft was held not to have been proved by a crofter. *Stewart* v *Secretary of State for Scotland*, 1965 S.L.C.R. App. 45.

P. 449   1955 Act, s. 12.
Resumption. A landlord was held entitled on certain conditions to resume parts of a croft which he had used for many years as a joiner's business. *Russell* v *Murray* (No. 2), 1965 S.L.C.R. App. 101.

Ibid. An application to resume for county council housing was rejected for lack of evidence to support it. *Portman Estates* v *Renwick*, 1965 S.L.C.R. App. 100.

Ibid. Resumption of part of a croft for a distillery warehouse was held reasonable. *Morrison* v *MacLachlan*, 1965 S.L.C.R. App. 95.

P. 450   *Resumption of common grazing.* Where part of a croft was resumed for the construction of a new trunk road, the landlord was held liable for the maintenance of fencing thereby rendered necessary. *Macpherson* v *Achintee Shareholders*, 1965 S.L.C.R. App. 98.

Pp. 454, 1955 Act, s. 14; 1961 Act, s. 6.
461
Renunciation. On an application for compensation, a counter-claim by the landlord for deterioration was held to be incompetent. *MacLennan* v *Botley,* 1965 S.L.C.R. App. 113.

P. 453 *Ibid.* The value of a dwellinghouse must be based on the economic potentialities of the holding to an incoming tenant. *Aird* v *Secretary of State for Scotland,* 1965 S.L.C.R. App. 111.

P. 453 1961 Act, s. 6 (2).
The open market value of permanent improvements was fixed at nil where the croft was remote and a tenant was unlikely to be found. *Anderson's Exr.* v *Blance,* 1965 S.L.C.R. App. 117.

P. 462 *Succession. Intestacy.* Where the heir-at-law had not claimed the tenancy of a croft on his father's death, it was held that the heir-at-law of a younger son, who had occupied the croft until his own death, was entitled to the tenancy. It was observed that the landlord did not need to have recognised the younger son as tenant. *MacIver* v *MacIver,* 1909 S.C. 639 followed. *MacDonald* v *Fraser,* 1965 S.L.C.R. App. 51.

P. 471 1961 Act, s. 9 (3).
Reorganisation Schemes. Observations made by the Land Court as to the assessment of compensation and the fixing of rents. *Nicolson* v *Hughson,* 1965 S.L.C.R. App. 159.

P. 473 1955 Act, s. 22 (1); 1961 Act, s. 14 (1). See S.I 1966 No. 471.

P. 486 1961 Act, s. 4 (1).
Land Court. Where an application to renounce a tenancy in order to get a right to a conveyance of a dwellinghouse is refused on the ground that the Commission is not satisfied that it is in the general interests of the community to grant it, the Land Court cannot interfere, if the Crofters Commission have properly applied themselves to the particular and general considerations which are their statutory province, the matter being one of policy. *Mackenzie* v *Crofters Commission,* 1966 S.L.T. (Land Court) 13, 1965 S.L.C.R. App. 56.

RENT RESTRICTIONS ACTS

P. 587 1965 Act, s. 20 (1) (b).
The Court's discretion to rescind or vary an order for possession made before the 1965 Act came into force applies to all Court Orders, including consent orders: the fact that the order is a consent order is a relevant factor, but evidence must be given of the

behaviour of the parties and the circumstances of the agreement. *Mouat-Balthasar* v *Murphy* [1966] 3 All E.R. 477, approving *Barton* v *Fincham* and *Rossiter* v *Langley* but disapproving *Wellesley* v *White*.

P. 616 1957 Act. s. 12 (6).

It is proposed to revive this subsection in relation to Scotland in the Housing (Financial Provisions) (Scotland) Bill 1966 : the sub-section provided, in relation to a furnished house, that where rent is payable weekly under any contract to which the Rent of Fur-nished Houses Control (Scotland) Act 1943 applies, it shall be the duty of the landlord to provide a rent book or other similar docu-ment for use in respect of the dwelling, containing particulars of the rent and of the other terms and conditions of the contract; and if, at any time after the expiry of two months from the commencement of the 1957 Act, the landlord fails to comply with the requirements of this subsection, he and any person who on his behalf demands or receives rent under the contract shall in respect of each week in which the failure occurs or continues be guilty of an offence and liable on summary conviction to a fine not exceeding £10.

Pp. 554, 561 1965 Act, ss. 17 (1), 27 (3) (b).

Fair Rent. Held by the First Division on appeal from a Rent Assess-ment Committee that, in the circumstances of the case, the installing by way of replacement of a sink unit, a W.C. basin and a fireplace —without the landlord's consent and in order to conform with the tenant's standards of comfort etc.—amounted to " repairs " and not " improvements "—and was, therefore, to be considered, and not disregarded, in assessing the " fair rent ". The Court followed *Morcom* v *Campbell-Johnson,* [1956] 1 Q.B. 106 at 115 *per* Denning, L.J. that the test of improvement or repair under the Acts of 1920 and 1939 was that if the facts amounted only to replacement, even if modernisation was involved, this was under these Acts " repair ". *Stewart's J.F.* v *Gallaher,* 1967 S.L.T. 52.

TENANCY OF SHOPS ACTS

P. 629 S. 3 (2).

Premises used to repair boots and shoes but also for the sale of articles displayed there, the sales being a minor but substantial part of the tenant's income, were held to be a shop. *Oakes* v *Knowles,* 1966 S.L.T. (Sh. Ct.) 33.

NOTE (*a*) the Housing (Scotland) Act 1966, which came into force on 1st April 1967 and which consolidates almost entirely the statute law regarding housing in Scotland.

(*b*) Pp. 210 note 20 and 211 note 21, National Insurance Act, 1959, s. 11 (1) is now National Insurance Act 1965, s. 61 (1).

TABLE OF CASES

b

TABLE OF STATUTES

xlv

TABLE OF STATUTORY INSTRUMENTS &c.

Part 1

LEASES IN GENERAL

CHAPTER I

NATURE OF THE CONTRACT OF LEASE

Historical Background. A discussion of the sources and origins of the contract of lease in Scotland and of its relationship, if any, with the contract of location in other legal systems is not within the scope of this work; for such a discussion the reader is referred elsewhere.[1] What follows is merely a brief historical sketch.[2]

Originally there was no sharp distinction between leases and feus; and the dispositive clauses of some old feu charters contain phrases now regarded as peculiar to leases. The Act of 1457 c. 71, which was passed to encourage feu farm tenure, contains such terms as " tennant, upon setting of feu ferme ", and " assedation " in relation to a feu.[3] Even Stair, speaking about two centuries later, apparently viewed feu farm as perpetual location.[4] At common law a lessee, though protected against the lessor and his representatives for the duration of his lease, had no protection against the singular successors of the lessor. Feudal principles did not allow a right in land to be effectual against singular successors without sasine, and thus leases were often clothed with the specious form of charter and sasine in an attempt to give the lessee the real right.[5] To alleviate the position of poor tenants the Leases Act 1449 laid down that a lease should be enforceable by the lessee against the singular successors of the lessor, provided certain conditions were fulfilled, one of them being that the lessee should have entered into possession of the subjects of the lease. By entering into possession the lessee publishes the fact of his lease to the world in general and to singular successors in particular, and after the passing of the Act the practice of taking sasine on a tack fell into disuse,[6] although the feudal origin of tacks remains of some relevance.[7] After the Act the form

---

[1] Ross, *Lectures,* 2nd ed., II, 457; Hunter, *Landlord and Tenant,* 4th ed., I, 1; Grant, *Economic History of Scotland,* Chapters II, III, VI and VII; Grant, *The Social and Economic Development of Scotland before 1603,* Section II, Chapter IV; *Register of Brieves 1286-1386* (Stair Society, Vol. 10) 20-21—it was not usual in early times for the King to grant leases, *ibid.,* p. 21.

[2] Adapted from article by H. H. Monteath, " Heritable Rights ", in *Introduction to Scottish Legal History* (Stair Society, Vol. 20) 193; and Report of Scottish Leases Committee 1952 Cmd. 8656.

[3] The Act of 1457 c. 71 was repealed by the Statute Law Revision (Scotland) Act 1906; the word " tenant " is still widely, if improperly, used in common parlance to denote an occupier, even if he happens to be the owner.

[4] II, 3, 34.

[5] Craig, *Jus Feudale* II, 7, 28.

[6] Craig, *op. cit.,* II, 7, 27, writing at the end of the 16th century, speaks of sasine as being unnecessary, but still in common use on leases for a fixed term of years, especially in the northern part of the country.

[7] *Millar* v *M'Robbie,* 1949 S.C. 1 *per* L.P. Cooper.

of lease changed from a unilateral grant to the bilateral form of contract which it now normally takes. The Leases Act 1449, as subsequently interpreted and enlarged by judicial decisions, remains the basis of our law of leases. It was designed for the benefit of people working the land, which was then virtually the only lettable subject, but in course of time it quickly came to be applied to urban property, and generally to adjuncts of land capable of being treated as separate feudal tenements; and leases not protected by the Act cover an even wider range of property.

A new means of securing a lease against a purchaser came with the Registration of Leases (Scotland) Act 1857, which provided that certain long leases could be recorded in the Register of Sasines, and, once recorded, be effectual against the singular successors of the granter, even although the tenant had not taken possession. Although recorded in the Register of Sasines, registered leases are distinct from feu rights so recorded, since a lease does not give the lessee a right of property in the subjects let, but only a right of possession, and so a recorded lease is not a feudal title. A further development came with the Long Leases (Scotland) Act 1954, which provided that certain long leases of dwelling houses, whether or not registrable under the 1857 Act, could at the request of the tenant be converted into feus upon certain conditions.

At common law a lease is a contract, and parties may import into it such conditions as they think fit. However, in the 19th and 20th centuries inroads into the freedom of parties to contract as they like have been made by a mass of legislation, such as the bodies of statutes making up the Rent Restriction Acts, the Agricultural Holdings Acts, the Crofters and Small Landholders Acts, and also the Tenancy of Shops (Scotland) Acts 1949-1964, the Housing (Scotland) Act 1962 Sections 25 and 26 and the Rent Act 1965. Most of the provisions of those Acts are designed for the protection of tenants, and they provide a statutory code for the security of tenure of tenants and their succession on their deaths as well as regulating the incidence of repairs and improvements to the subjects to which they apply; in many cases such provisions cannot be overridden even by express provision in a lease.

An essential principle of a lease is that, however long its duration, it confers only a temporary right on the tenant, and so on its expiry the land and any erections thereon revert to the landlord, who is the true owner.

With the exception of leases for a year or less, leases must be in writing. However, if neither party gives due notice to end the lease at the expiry of its term, a new lease will be inferred by tacit relocation on the same conditions as the old for the same period if the original lease was for less than one year, or for a further year if the original was for more than one year. The result is that a very great number of leases for quite short periods are in effect continued in existence over very long periods by the implied consent of the parties.

Definition and Terms. A Lease is a contract of location by which the use of land or any other immoveable subject is let for a period of time to the lessee in consideration of a determinate rent or duty to be paid or performed to the lessor either in money, the fruits of the ground or services.[8] The term " Lease " is used for both the contract itself or the right created by it. The analogous contract in the case of moveables is the contract of Hire. There is a growing modern practice of letting out furniture to hotels and offices on contracts which are called " leases "; this is an incorrect use of the word " lease " and such a contract, the subject of which is moveable, should be called a " hire ". In a lease the lessor is usually called the landlord, and the lessee the tenant. In older times a lease was commonly called a tack and the tenant was called the tacksman; the contract of lease was also referred to as assedation, and the verb " to set " was used in place of the more modern word " let ". If the consideration in a lease takes the form of a period-ical payment, it is called a rent, or, in the case of minerals, a royalty or lordship; if it takes the form of a lump sum, it is called a grassum or foregift. If the granter is himself the tenant under another lease, the contract is usually termed a Sublease, the granter is called the principal lessee or principal tenant and the grantee is called the sublessee or subtenant.

ESSENTIALS OF LEASE AT COMMON LAW

Cardinal Elements. Essentially a lease is a purely personal contract between the landlord and tenant. In certain circumstances the contract of lease has been invested by statute[9] with the quality of a real right, and for this purpose a lease must satisfy certain conditions. Those statutory requirements which a lease must satisfy so as to confer a real right are more exacting than those which a contract must satisfy so as to become a lease at common law. However, from the above definition it will appear that the four cardinal elements of a lease are (1) the parties to the contract with *consensus in idem* between them, (2) heritable subjects let, (3) a consideration for the let and (4) a period of time for which the subjects are let. The mere fact that the contract is called a lease and that the parties are referred to as landlord and tenant does not make the contract a lease if one or more of the cardinal elements are missing.[10]

Consensus in Idem. Mere negotiations are not enough. The parties to the contract must reach agreement as to the subjects, consideration and period.[11] Although they may have settled any two of them, yet, if

---

[8] Erskine, II, 6, 20; Hume, *Lectures,* II, 56; Hunter, *op. cit.,* I, 79; Rankine, *Leases,* 3rd ed., 1.
[9] Leases Act 1449.
[10] *Brand* v *Bell's Trs.* (1872) 11 M. 42; *Mann* v *Houston,* 1957 S.L.T. 89.
[11] *Gray* v *Edinburgh University,* 1962 S.C. 157; see also *Temperance Permanent Building Society* v *Kominek,* 1951 S.L.T. (Sh. Ct.) 58.

no mention is made of one of them, or if upon mention of it the parties
have differed and have separated without coming to an agreement, then
there is no binding lease: thus, if the granter has bound himself in
writing to give a person a lease but without mentioning the rent or the
duration, and if this defect cannot be supplied by circumstances or by
inference from what has passed between them, there is no lease: a court
cannot fix a rent or a term of years.[12]

Rent. The rent need not be a definite sum of money. It may be
illusory or nominal, it may be in the form of fruits[13] or services,[14] it
may be expressly set off against interest or other debt due by the landlord
to the tenant, or it may be wholly or partially discharged.[15] The rent
may take the form of or be included in an annuity for the granter's
life.[16] If, however, no provision is made for a rent, the contract is not
a lease. Thus, where the owner of a garage, in consideration of a lump
sum of £200, let it for a period of ten years by an agreement providing
that no rent should be payable, but that the grantee had the right to
terminate the contract, in which event the owner was to pay him a
sum equivalent to £20 for each unexpired year, it was not only held that
the agreement was not capable of conferring a real right against the
granter's singular successor, but it was observed that by reason of the
omission of an essential part of the contract the agreement was not a
lease at all.[17] Where the prospective tenant was willing to pay a reasonable or fair market rent, it was held that there was no *consensus in idem*
as to rent, and that consequently no lease had been concluded.[18] A personal right of occupancy free of rent established by minute of agreement
is not a lease.[19] An agreement for the supply of electricity whereby an
occupier was to pay the proprietors an annual sum based on a percentage
of the capital expended on the property by the proprietors was in the
circumstances held not to be a lease and the payment was not a rent.[20]
However, where the parties have entered into the relationship of landlord
and tenant, the Court has been willing to presume that the parties had
intended that the rent should be the annual value or market rent.[21]

[12] Hume, *Lectures,* II, 57.
[13] The Conveyancing (Scotland) Act 1924 s. 12, which abolished feuduties payable
in grain, etc., applies only to feus.
[14] The Tenures Abolition Act 1746 ss. 21 and 22 expressly saved leasehold services
provided for in writing and also services due by tenants to mills.
[15] *Laird of Mellerstains* v *Haitlie* (1591) Mor. 15165; *Lundy* v *Smith of Lundy*
(1610) Mor. 15166; *Ross* v *Blair* (1627) Mor. 15167; *Sinclair* v *M'Beath* (1788)
Hume 773; Bell § 1198; Hume, *Lectures,* II, 59; Rankine 114.
[16] *Thomson* v *Thomson* (1896) 24 R.269; *Thomson* v *Thomson & Co.* (1899) 1 F.
1134.
[17] *Mann* v *Houston,* 1957 S.L.T. 89.
[18] *Gray* v *Edinburgh University,* 1962 S.C. 157.
[19] *Wallace* v *Simmers,* 1960 S.C. 255.
[20] *Bo'ness Town Council* v *Assessor for Linlithgowshire,* 1907 S.C. 774; but see
Glasgow Tramway and Omnibus Co. Ltd. v *Glasgow Corporation* (1897)
24 R. 628.
[21] *Young* v *Cockburn* (1674) Mor. 11624; *Glen* v *Roy* (1882) 10 R. 239.

Period. The term need not be definite. A lease may be granted for an indefinite period, until the occurrence of an event or even in perpetuity.[22] The Court sustained a tack which bore to endure " perpetually and continually as long as the grass groweth up and the water runneth down ".[23] The fact that the duration is not expressed in the agreement is not necessarily fatal. Where the lease is complete but for the date of entry, the Court may assume that the date of entry is the date of the concluded agreement.[24] When no duration has been specified in a contract and the parties have entered into the relationship of landlord and tenant, the lease may be construed to be for one year only; or if the lease implies a longer duration, then for the most limited term which the words admit, even though the tenant may have been in possession for a considerable time.[25] Parole evidence may be admitted to prove the parties' intention as to the length of the lease.[26] However, the absence from a lease of any mention of an ish may indicate that the parties' intention was that it was not to be a lease but merely a revocable licence.[27] Thus an agreement for the supply of water so long as the granter continued to pump it from his pit took the form of a lease in all respects, except that there was no provision for an ish; it was held that there was no lease on account of the absence of an ish, especially as the granter might at any time put an end to it by ceasing to pump.[28]

The want of an ish was discussed at length in *Gray* v *Edinburgh University*.[29] The proprietors of a building entered into negotiations to lease it to Edinburgh University, who stated their wish to take the subjects at a reasonable or fair market rent. No agreement was reached as to duration, and the University did not enter into possession. In an action against the University the proprietors contended that the negotiations for a lease, when the parties were agreed as to the subjects and rent, would infer a lease for one year. It was held that, since there was no *consensus in idem* either as to rent or as to duration, no lease had come into existence. The Court went on to discuss the circumstances in which a lease for one year might be implied, and came to the conclusion that such a presumption could only arise when the relationship of landlord and tenant had already come into existence. The Court found it impossible to hold that, unless there was express agreement to take possession or implied agreement evidenced by actual taking of possession, the law will compel a prospective tenant, who has either disagreed with his

[22] *Crichton* v *Lord Ayr* (1631) Mor. 11182; 15191; *Campbell of Auchinbreck* v *M'Lauchlan* (1748) Mor. 15248; Bell § 1194; Hume, *Lectures,* II, 58; Rankine 115.
[23] *Carruthers* v *Irvine* (1717) Mor. 15195.
[24] *Christie* v *Fife Coal Co.* (1899) 2 F. 192.
[25] *Redpath* v *White* (1737) Mor. 15196, *Clark* v *Lamont* 27 Jan. 1816 F.C.; Bell § 1194; Rankine, 115.
[26] *M'Leod* v *Urquhart* (1808) Hume 840; *Russell* v *Freen* (1835) 13 S. 752; *Wilson* v *Mann* (1876) 3 R. 527.
[27] Rankine, 115.
[28] *Dunlop & Co.* v *Steel Co. of Scotland* (1879) 7 R. 283.
[29] 1962 S.C. 157.

prospective landlord as to the duration of the lease or has not yet reached the stage of discussing that topic, to take possession for a year. The exception in favour of a lease for one year is a practical step to meet an emergency situation arising where there is agreement that the tenant is to have possession, and what it does is to put a time limit on that possession.[30]

LEASE DISTINGUISHABLE FROM OTHER CONTRACTS

Feu. Leases were originally granted in the form of charters by the proprietor without any written obligation signed by the tenant, but because no deed which was not subscribed by himself could bind the tenant, leases came to be drawn as mutual contracts.[31] However, the obligations of a vassal are based principally on tenure, while those of a tenant are based purely on contract. Even now there is little practical difference between a long lease and a feu,[32] especially as a perpetual lease is competent. The distinction is often mainly theoretical. A lease is essentially personal, although in certain circumstances it gives a real right, whereas the main purpose of a feu is to give the vassal a real right. A leasehold right is not equivalent to a feu right,[33] and a purchaser may resile from his bargain, if unknown to him the subjects turn out to be leasehold instead of feudal.[34]

Sale. A lease may normally be distinguished from a sale in that in the case of a lease the property in the subjects let does not pass to the tenant, although the tenant may be entitled to the fruits. Thus an agreement whereby turnips might be consumed on the ground but not removed was thought to be a lease rather than a sale in the same way as a lease of a park for grazing.[35] On the other hand an agreement for the supply and consumption of steam was thought to be a sale rather than a lease.[36] It is, however, difficult to apply this distinction in the case of a mineral lease, which is in effect, if not in form, an out and out sale of the subjects let, or part of them, and not merely of the fruits.[37] Generally, however, mineral leases are treated as leases, and the law of leases is applied to them, subject to certain specialities.[38] A power to trustees to grant leases has been held not to import a power to grant leases of minerals not

[30] *Gray* v *Edinburgh University,* 1962 S.C. 157, *per* L.J.C. Thomson at p. 165.
[31] Erskine, 11, 6, 20.
[32] *Buchanan's Trs.* v *Pagan* (1868) 7 M.1.
[33] *Edmond* v *Reid* (1871) 9 M. 782.
[34] *M'Connell* v *Chassells* (1903) 10 S.L.T. 790 (O.H.); *Fleming* v *Boswell,* 1948 unreported, referred to in Report of the Scottish Leases Committee, 1952 Cmd. 8656, para. 48, 1948 C.L. 4378.
[35] *Ferguson* v *Fyffe* (1868) 6 S.L.R. 68.
[36] *Clark* v *Stewart* (1872) 10 S.L.R. 152; see *infra,* p. 75.
[37] *Brand & Sons* v *Bell's Trs.* (1872) 11 M. 42; *Mungall* v *Bowhill Coal Co.* (1900) 2 F. 1073; *M'Cosh* v *Assessor for Ayrshire,* 1945 S.C. 260; *Collective Securities Co.* v *Assessor for Ayrshire,* 1946 S.C. 244.
[38] *Gowans* v *Christie* (1873) 11 M. (H.L.) 1; see *infra,* p. 76.

previously worked or let.[39] The position of a purchaser of land, who is paying the price by instalments and who is not to receive a conveyance from the seller until all the instalments are paid, has been distinguished from that of a tenant.[40]

Family Settlement. In certain cases a family settlement taking the form of a lease has been held not to be a proper lease, and has been refused the interpretation which a lease would have had.[41] On the other hand, a family arrangement whereby a business was transferred by the proprietor to his sons in return for an annuity, was held to be in part equivalent to a lease, although it did not expressly bear to be a lease, and although it did not follow that the relationship of the parties was only that of landlord and tenant.[42]

Contract of Service. Tied House. Where an employee is given the occupancy of a house belonging to his employer, the contract may not be one of lease, but the occupancy may be merely an adjunct of a contract of service, usually termed a "service occupancy". The house is often called a "tied house". Many classes of employees, farm-workers, industrial workers, caretakers, teachers, managers, company directors and members of various professions are given the possession of houses as part of their remuneration, and in that event it may be implied that on the employment ceasing, the occupancy also comes to an end. In some cases the conditions of the employee's tenure of the house may be regulated not by a missive of let, but by the conditions of his employment. In other cases the employee is given the occupancy of a house for a fixed rent, and in that event it should be stated expressly whether the occupancy is to terminate on the employment ceasing.[43]

In the absence of express provision the nature of the occupancy must be decided upon the particular circumstances of each case. A service occupancy will be inferred only if the occupation is necessary to the service, not where the service is merely a precondition to the occupancy.[44] In other words, where the occupation is necessary for the performance of services, and the occupier is required to reside in the house in order to perform those services, the occupation being strictly ancillary to the performance of the duties which the occupier has to perform, the occupation is that of a servant and not of a tenant. The residence must be ancillary and necessary to the performance of the servant's duties, and

---

[39] *Campbell* v *Wardlaw* (1883) 10 R. (H.L.) 65; *Nugent's Trs.* v *Nugent* (1898) 25 R. 475.
[40] *Caledonian Railway Co.* v *Morrison* (1898) 25 R. 1001; see also *Lowe* v *Gardiner*, 1921 S.C. 211 and *Cook* v *Wylie*, 1963 S.L.T. (Sh.Ct.) 29.
[41] *Stevenson* v *Love* (1842) 4 D. 1322.
[42] *Thomson* v *Thomson* (1896) 24 R. 269, explained in *Thomson* v *Thomson & Co.* (1899) 1 F. 1134.
[43] Rankine, 595.
[44] Fraser, *Master and Servant*, 3rd edn., p. 7.

unless he is required for that purpose to reside in the house, and not merely as an arbitrary regulation on the part of the master, a service occupancy will not be inferred.[45]

In some cases it is a very difficult question of mixed fact and law as to whether the relationship is one of tenancy or service. Where the terms of the service contract were exceptional, it was held that a gardener's occupancy of a cottage belonging to his former employers was a proper tenancy.[46] Similarly the occupancy of a baker, who paid his employer a small rent for one of three houses, which his employer found for him and which he was informed " went with the job ", although he was not told his occupation would cease with his employment, was held to be a lease and not a service occupancy, the grounds of the decision (following Mr. Justice Mellor's *dictum* above) being that it mattered nothing to the efficiency of the baker's duty whether he lived in that particular house or elsewhere.[47] On the other hand, where there was deducted from a teacher's salary an amount equal to the annual value of the Education Authority's house occupied by him, it was held that the contract was one of service, and not of lease.[48] The question whether a particular right is a service occupancy or a lease is of importance in determining the rights of parties when the employment comes to an end; and also in deciding whether the employee has security of tenure under the Rent Restriction Acts.[49] In ordinary circumstances the occupation by a servant of a house belonging to the master and in the master's civil possession is an occupation for the benefit of the master at least as much as it is for the benefit of the servant.[50] Thus, where the house is a tied house, the employer on the termination of the employment is entitled to vacant possession of the subjects. If the servant refuses to leave the house, the master has the remedy of a summary application for ejection.[51] This applies not only on the resignation of the employee, but also on his dismissal, whether such dismissal is justified or not, as he no longer has any title to possession of the subjects.[52] Even where the employment has been terminated by neither the master nor the servant, but by some outside agency, such as a national emergency, the right of occupancy comes to an end and the employee or his family may be ejected.[53] However, it is now provided by statute that it is unlawful for an owner to enforce against a service occupier except by proceedings in court, his right to recover possession of premises let as a dwelling.[54]

---

[45] *Dictum* of Mellor, J. in *Smith* v *Seghill Overseers*, [1875] L.R. 10 Q.B. 422, approved by L.P. Cooper in *M'Gregor* v *Dunnett*, 1949 S.C. 510.
[46] *Dunbar's Trs.* v *Bruce* (1900) 3 F. 137.
[47] *M'Gregor* v *Dunnett*, 1949 S.C. 510.
[48] *Pollock* v *Assessor for Inverness-shire*, 1923 S.C. 693.
[49] *Marquis of Bute* v *Prenderleith*, 1921 S.C. 281; see *infra*, p. 520.
[50] *Cairns* v *Innes*, 1942 S.C. 164 *per* L.P. Normand at p. 171.
[51] *Whyte* v *School Board of Haddington* (1874) 1 R. 1124.
[52] *Scott* v *M'Murdo* (1869) 6 S.L.R. 301; *James Gibson & Son Ltd.* v *Gibson* (1899) 36 S.L.R. 522.
[53] *Cairns* v *Innes*, 1942 S.C. 164.
[54] Rent Act 1965, s. 32 (2); see *infra*, p. 251.

When miners were in the habit of occupying for many years houses belonging to a colliery company, not under missives of let, but under general regulations applying to all employees of the company, stating that the houses were to be leased only during the period of employment, which was terminable upon fourteen days' notice, it was held that for rating purposes the houses were let for less than one year.[55]

Right in Security.   Attempts used to be made to dress up a security transaction in the garb of a lease. Where a lease of a ship-building yard was entered into in an attempt to create a security over moveables by means of hypothec, but no change of possession took place, it was held that the relationship of landlord and tenant never truly existed, and that the contract was not a true lease.[56] Similarly a " minute of lease " of pawnbroking premises together with its stock of pledges, providing that the granter should cede possession to the grantee upon a certain event, was held not to be a lease, but an ineffectual attempt to create a security over moveable property.[57] On the other hand, a lease granted in security of advances made under a trust deed for creditors, the granter remaining in possession as manager for the trustee, was held to be a lease and the granter's continued possession to be as agent for the trustee.[58] The test in such cases will be the degree of effective possession given to the alleged tenant. The granter of an *ex facie* absolute disposition, who remains in possession of the security subjects, does not divest himself of his reversionary right, and his position is not that of a tenant,[59] but he may by his actings put himself in the position of a tenant.[60]

Joint Adventure.   A lease may be scarcely distinguishable from an agreement of joint adventure when the profits are to be shared between the owner and the occupier of ground on which some joint operation is carried on.[61] It is not uncommon for the owner and occupier to join in exploiting the minerals. Where such a contract, taking the form of a lease, contained a clause giving the proprietor the option of taking a share of the profits instead of the stated rent, it was held that the contract was a proper lease.[62]

Right of Occupation.   It is not uncommon for a person to be allowed to occupy the property of another free of rent, and, as has been seen, if there is no rent and if no rent is contemplated by the parties, there is

[55] *Mags. of Buckhaven & Methil* v *Wemyss Coal Co. Ltd.,* 1928 S.C. 66.
[56] *Heritable Securities Investment Association Ltd.* v *Wingate Co.'s Tr.* (1880) 7 R. 1094.
[57] *Paterson's Tr.* v *Paterson's Trs.* (1891) 19 R. 91.
[58] *Macphail & Son* v *M'Lean's Tr.* (1887) 15 R. 47.
[59] *Cf. Caledonian Railway Co.* v *Morrison* (1898) 25 R. 1001.
[60] *Paton* v *Turnbull* (1875) 12 S.L.R. 383.
[61] *Miller* v *Walker* (1875) 3 R. 242.
[62] *Beresford's Tr.* v *Assessor for Argyllshire* (1884) 11 R. 818.

no lease.[63] However, there is a presumption against such a right of occupation,[64] and there have been cases involving special circumstances in which a person in occupation of another's property has been presumed to occupy as a tenant, and, although no direct obligation to pay rent has been proved, to be bound to pay the annual value of the subjects to the proprietor.[65]

Precarious Possession. When property is occupied without any shadow of title, the possession of the occupier is termed "precarious" and an action of ejection is therefore competent.[66]

Licence. Where a right of occupation is not gratuitous, it is sometimes difficult to distinguish it from a proper lease. The term "personal licence" is sometimes used in a wide sense to include leases which are not valid against singular successors, but the term is used here as a convenient name for a contract, falling short of a lease, whereby not the heritage itself but the right to use a particular part of it or to put a particular part of it to some use is granted. Provided that such a licence has *consensus in idem*, it is not rendered ineffectual as between the contracting parties merely because it is not a lease, but of course it would be of no avail against a purchaser. The distinction is important not only in questions between the grantee and singular successors of the granter, but also in questions with the granter, for example as to whether the right is assignable, whether there is an implied warrandice to the grantee, or whether the landlord's hypothec is available, and in questions of valuation and rating. The concept of personal licence does not seem to have been accepted until comparatively recently. An agreement to take for a rent water pumped from a pit so long as the pumping continued was, because it was not a sale, held to be the only other possible thing, namely a lease without an ish and so terminable by a party on reasonable notice.[67] Such an unusual contract would perhaps be termed a licence nowadays, but the legal effect would be the same. In each case the question whether a particular contract is a lease or a licence depends on the express terms of the agreement or on the customary relation set up by it or both taken together.[68] In most cases the question turns on the degree of possession given to the grantee.

The distinction between a lease and a licence has been considered in a series of valuation cases. A contract whereby a city corporation granted to a tramway company the exclusive right to use carriages with

---

[63] *Supra,* p. 6; *Wallace* v *Simmers,* 1960 S.C. 255.

[64] *Young* v *Cockburn* (1674) Mor. 11624.

[65] *Glen* v *Roy* (1882) 10 R. 239; *Evans* v *Harkness* (1890) 17 R. 931.

[66] *Lowe* v *Gardiner,* 1921 S.C. 211; *Asher* v *M'Leod,* 1948 S.C. 55; *Christie's Trustees* v *Munroe,* 1962 S.L.T. (Sh. Ct.) 41; *Cook* v *Wylie,* 1963 S.L.T. (Sh. Ct.) 29; see *infra,* p. 284.

[67] *Dunlop & Co.* v *Steel Co. of Scotland* (1879) 7 R. 283; Gloag, *Contract,* 2nd ed., 302.

[68] Rankine, 2.

flange wheels on the corporation's tramways for the period of 23 years on condition *inter alia* that the company should pay interest on the sum expended by the corporation in making the tramways and certain other payments and expenses, was held to be a lease of a heritable subject, and not merely a licence to use carriages on certain streets.[69] On the other hand an agreement between a city corporation, which had constructed an aerodrome, and a company conducting a school for pilots, whereby the company were allowed the use of the landing ground and of the terminal buildings and certain other facilities on certain conditions, including payment to the corporation of an annual sum, was held not to be a lease, but a privilege to use the subjects jointly with other users.[70] The terms of a letter by a farmer, by which for a full rent he granted for a number of years the right of shooting over a farm, of which he was a tenant, were held not to confer the right of possession which a lease would have conferred, and merely gave a personal licence to shoot.[71] Where a railway company in return for merely nominal payments granted to the proprietors of lands adjoining the embankments the right to kill rabbits and preserve game on the embankments, the company's object being to prevent damage to the embankments and to protect itself from claims for damages from adjoining tenants, it was held that such grants did not confer the degree of occupation necessary for leases of heritable subjects.[72] An agreement between the executive committee of a national exhibition and amusement caterers, whereby spaces in the exhibition grounds were allocated to the caterers for the purpose of erecting exhibits in consideration of *inter alia* a share in the profits, was held not to be a lease, but merely an agreement allocating a portion of the land for a particular use.[73]

Several cases have involved the use of advertising sites. An agreement between a hotel proprietor and a firm of billposters, by which for an annual payment the former permitted the latter to affix an advertisement board to a part of his premises to be afterwards determined, the right to continue for three years and to be terminable on three months' notice, was held to be an ordinary lease at a yearly rent of the portion of ground on which the board was erected.[74] A similar agreement whereby a railway company granted to an advertiser the use of a board fixed in a station for a yearly payment was held to be a lease.[75] An agreement, whereby a railway company granted to a firm of advertising agents the exclusive right of fixing hoardings to the company's property, the sites of the hoardings being under the control and disposal of the advertising

[69] *Glasgow Tramway & Omnibus Co. Ltd.* v *Glasgow Corporation* (1897) 24 R. 628.
[70] *Magistrates of Perth* v *Assessor for Perth and Kinross,* 1937 S.C. 549.
[71] *Inland Revenue* v *Anderson,* 1922 S.C. 284.
[72] *L.M.S. Railway Co.* v *Assessor of Public Undertakings,* 1937 S.C. 773.
[73] *Popular Amusements Ltd.* v *Assessor for Edinburgh,* 1909 S.C. 645.
[74] *Wilson & Co.* v *Assessor for Kincardineshire,* 1913 S.C. 704.
[75] *L.N.E. Railway Co.* v *Assessor for Glasgow,* 1937 S.C. 309.

agents, was held to constitute a lease of the sites.[76] On the other hand, where a firm of advertising contractors, who had been granted the right to display advertisements in post offices, entered into a written contract with a company, whereby the firm undertook to display for three years the company's advertisements in moveable frames on the walls or in the windows of a certain number of post offices for payment of a fixed annual sum for each advertisement and for the hire of each frame, and subject to the approval of the Postmaster-General, the contract was held to be not a lease of heritage, but a licence to use the spaces.[77]

One test in such cases is whether the possession of any piece of heritage is ceded by the alleged lessor to the alleged lessee.[78] If possession is given, the question is whether the possession is intended to be exclusive or only partial. If the right to possession is exclusive, the contract may be a lease; but if it is only partial, the contract will be merely a licence. This is well illustrated by two cases involving lock-up garages. In the first case,[79] premises belonging to two motor garage businesses each consisted of *inter alia* a large number of separate lock-ups let for varying periods to private car owners at rents which included water, heating, light, washing facilities, etc.; each occupant had a key, but in each case the garage company concerned reserved a right of access for inspection and cleaning; the occupants were expected to and in most cases did obtain supplies from the garages, which derived a considerable part of their profits from this fact; in the case of one garage most of the lock-ups opened on to a street; in the other case they could only be entered through the garage premises. It was held that the contract in each case was not a lease, but merely a contract for the use of defined portions of the premises for a limited purpose. The *ratio* of the case was that there was no independent occupation by the occupants. In the second case,[80] the proprietor of a piece of ground erected a number of wooden lock-ups, each with its own key, which he let as garages to car owners under a verbal agreement whereby he received a weekly or daily payment, and either party could terminate the arrangement at a week's notice; the proprietor was not a mechanic and no services were given, although the occupiers were entitled to use free of charge a wash bed and a wooden shed. It was held that the garages were let to the occupiers as tenants, and that they were not subjects in which the occupiers had merely the right to accommodate their cars. The *ratio* was that each occupier during the period of his let had exclusive possession.

[76] *L.M.S. Railway Co.* v *Assessor for Public Undertakings*, 1937 S.C. 773.
[77] *U.K. Advertising Co.* v *Glasgow Bag-Wash Laundry*, 1926 S.C. 303; Gloag, *Contract*, 2nd ed., 164; see Armour, *Valuation for Rating*, 3rd ed., 142-144 and 191-194.
[78] *U.K. Advertising Co.* v *Glasgow Bag-Wash Laundry*, *supra*, per L.P. Clyde at p. 306.
[79] *Broomhill Motor Co.* v *Assessor for Glasgow*, 1927 S.C. 447.
[80] *Chaplin* v *Assessor for Perth*, 1947 S.C. 373.

Possession is not always the sole criterion in distinguishing between a lease and a licence. An agreement taking the form of a lease and giving exclusive possession to the grantee may yet fail to qualify as a lease and be reduced to the status of a personal licence on account of some other defect, such as the want of a rent.[81]

Local Authority Housing. The provision of housing by Local Authorities is regulated generally by the Housing Acts,[82] which prescribe some of the conditions under which houses subject to the Acts may be let. It may, however, be a question of circumstances whether or not an arrangement for the occupancy of a particular house is a normal lease or is subject to the Housing Acts.[83]

[81] *Mann v Houston,* 1957 S.L.T. 89.
[82] Housing (Scotland) Acts 1950-1965.
[83] *Glasgow Corporation v Assessor for Glasgow,* 1943 S.C. 276.

CHAPTER II

CONSTITUTION AND PROOF OF THE CONTRACT

Necessity for Writing. The general rule governing the constitution of contracts relating to heritable property is that such contracts, being *obligationes literis,* must be entered into in writing, and that the writing must be probative.[1] This rule, derived from feudal conveyancing, which required a real right to be constituted in writing, applies to leases with the important exception mentioned below, that leases for not more than one year do not require to be in writing.[2]

FORM OF WRITING

Bilateral Contract. No particular form of writing is required to constitute the contract. A lease is essentially an agreement between two parties, and as such it should logically take the form of a bilateral contract embodied in one document and signed by both parties. Such a document, which must be probative, is preferably, but not necessarily, signed in duplicate by both parties, each of whom retains one signed copy as a record of the agreement. More often perhaps, only one document is signed by both parties and is kept by one party, the other party receiving an unsigned copy as his record of the agreement.[3] In either of those situations the practice is for the landlord's agent to prepare the lease; the principal signed document is retained by or on behalf of the landlord, and the tenant is given the duplicate signed document or the unsigned copy, as the case may be. As the contract is a mutual one, no questions of delivery arise, and it does not matter who keeps the lease.[4] If there is a discrepancy between the duplicates, both copies may have to be looked at, and parole evidence admitted.[5]

Agreement to Lease. Frequently, however, no such bilateral contract is signed, and the terms agreed between the parties are not reduced to a single document. Thus, the contract may be contained in two or more writings, each of them being attested or holograph of the granter or of his authorised agent; commonly the writings are adopted as holograph by the granter or his agent, these being equivalent to holograph

---

[1] The Subscription of Deeds Act 1681; *Paterson v Paterson* (1897) 25 R. 144.
[2] Erskine, III, 2, 2; Bell § 1188; Hume, *Lectures,* II, 59; Rankine, 100. But see four old cases of verbal leases for any length of time in *Sheriff Court Book of Fife 1515-1522* (Scottish History Society, 1928), pp. 59, 60, 104 and 212.
[3] *Brown v College of St. Andrews* (1851) 13 D. 1355.
[4] *Robertson's Trs. v Lindsay* (1873) 1 R. 323.
[5] *Grant v Sinclair* (1861) 23 D. 796.

writings for this purpose. That frequently happens when the agreement is allowed to rest on missives consisting of an offer or promise to grant or take a lease, holograph of one party or his agent, and an acceptance, holograph of the other party or his agent, although the parties may originally have intended that their agreement should be reduced to a single formal document. Such missives are often to be found on a single piece of paper, as where a holograph acceptance is endorsed on a holograph offer to grant or take a lease. More rarely, where lands are let by auction, the missives may consist of a signed minute written on signed articles of roup. The missives may consist of a mere promise to grant or take a lease, or of a promise not to remove a tenant before a given term, duly accepted. In such cases, it is a question of circumstances whether the execution of a formal deed is a condition precedent to a concluded bargain, and, if necessary, the Court will remit to a conveyancer to adjust the terms of a formal contract.[6] Where a written offer to take a lease was met by a general acceptance also in writing with the words " subject to lease drawn out in due form ", and there was no doubt as to the meaning of the parties, it was held that a bargain had been concluded, and that if the parties would not concur in drawing up a lease, the Court would remit to a conveyancer to draw one with the usual clauses; the words " subject to lease drawn out in due form " did not import a condition into the acceptance, but merely required a formal lease to be prepared to give effect to binding missives.[7]

In all those cases, if there is a concluded agreement to lease properly authenticated, and the parties allow the bargain to rest on it, it is as effectual as if it had been reduced to a single formal lease, whether or not the parties originally intended to embody their contract in a more formal document. An agreement to lease is as effective as a lease. It does not matter whether the writing embodying the contract is called a " lease ", " minute of agreement ", " minute of lease ", " missive of let ", or any other title; the effect is the same. The rule that writing is necessary applies not only to the final contract, if there is one, but also to the preliminary missives; unless and until there is a writing probative of both parties, there is no obligation on either side, and either party may resile, even though the party resiling is the one who has executed a probative writing.[8]

Articles of Lease. It is the practice in large agricultural and mineral estates and also in large blocks of urban property to embody in a document called " Articles of Lease ", " Estate Regulations " or " Conditions of Let", or some such title, the conditions under which the re-

---

[6] Rankine, 101-102, and authorities cited there; see also *Sweet & Maxwell* v *Universal News Services* [1964] 2 Q.B. 699.
[7] *Erskine* v *Glendinning* (1871) 9 M. 656.
[8] *Goldston* v *Young* (1868) 7 M. 188 (missives of sale).

spective subjects are to be let.[9] The various conditions in this document can be adopted in whole or in part or subject to modification into each particular lease. This not only ensures uniformity, but, by having printed sets of articles, much needless repetition is avoided in the actual lease. These articles may be annexed and signed as relative to the lease, or failing that, they should be identified by being docqueted and signed by the parties as relative to the lease and a copy given to the tenant, but failure to sign them does not necessarily prevent their adoption.[10] Obviously if it is intended that they should be incorporated in a particular lease, this should be done expressly.[11]

Leases Defective in Form. As will be seen, a lease for more than a year not constituted by probative writing may in certain circumstances be cured by the actings of parties. Thus, *rei interventus,* that is actings on the faith of an improbative agreement, will serve to set up a lease which is verbal or improbative, provided it can be proved either by writing, however informal or even later in date than the agreement, or by the oath of the defender.[12] There is a somewhat confusing doctrine which distinguishes between contracts requiring to be constituted in probative writing—*obligationes literis*—on the one hand, and contracts which require writing for their proof—*in modum probationis*—on the other hand.[13] In addition there is a distinction between the mode of constituting *obligationes literis* that are defective in form and the mode of proving them. In *Walker* v *Flint*,[14] which held that a verbal lease for a term of years followed by *rei interventus* could be *proved* by writ or oath, the opinion was expressed that such a lease could be *constituted* by verbal agreement followed by *rei interventus*.[15] In practice this distinction may not be of great importance, as the constitution of a lease is not of much value, unless it can be proved.

Probative Unilateral Obligations. Where there is an offer fixing the terms of a lease probative only of the landlord, there is authority for the proposition that the mere fact of the tenant entering into possession with or without other acts falling short of *rei interventus,* is sufficient to constitute a lease, or at least prove its acceptance.[16] The same rule seems to apply in cases where only the tenant has signed an offer or lease and this has been followed by actings not amounting to

---

[9] *E.g.* see *Encyclopaedia of Scottish Legal Styles,* Vol. 6, Nos. 150 and 151.
[10] Rankine, 108-109.
[11] *Maclaine* v *Stewart* (1898) 36 S.L.R. 233; affd. 1889 (H.L.) 37 S.L.R. 623.
[12] *Walker* v *Flint* (1863) 1M. 417.
[13] *Paterson* v *Paterson* (1897) 25 R. 144; for a criticism of this doctrine see Walker, *Evidence,* 84; Smith, *A Short Commentary,* 802-803.
[14] (1863) 1 M. 417.
[15] *Per* L. J. C. Inglis at p. 421.
[16] *Arbuthnot* v *Campbell* (1793) Hume 785; *Arbuthnot* v *Reid* (1804) Hume 815; *M'Pherson* v *M'Pherson* 12 May 1815 F.C.; *Gray* v *Low* (1859) 21 D. 293; *Carlyle* v *Baxter* (1869) 6 S.L.R. 425; Rankine, 101.

rei interventus.[17] In such cases of unilateral obligations in writing, the person who receives the offer is entitled to hold the offerer bound immediately on receipt of the offer, and shows his own intention by his conduct.[18] Reference is merely made here to a number of older cases involving attempts to set up without the help of *rei interventus* leases for more than a year from offers, obligations and promises not probative of both parties.[19]

LEASES FOR NOT MORE THAN ONE YEAR

Constitution and Proof. An important exception to the general rule requiring probative writing is that leases for not more than one year may be constituted either verbally or by writing which is not probative.[20] No supporting *rei interventus* is required to constitute the contract.

Proof of such a lease is allowed *prout de jure,* whether or not possession has followed on the verbal agreement or informal writing.[21] In the same way, a promise of a year's lease or a promise not to remove a sitting tenant for a year can be proved by parole evidence.[22] Where the tenant alleges a verbal lease of one year, and the landlord alleges a shorter and unusual period such as seven months, this may have the effect of putting the onus of proof on the landlord.[23] *A fortiori,* proof of a lease for less than one year is competent by reference to the oath of parties.[24] Although documentary evidence of a lease for a year or less is unnecessary, if such evidence is available as well as parole evidence, it will depend on the circumstances whether the document was intended to exclude further enquiry into the terms of the bargain or can be regarded as part of the evidence, but normally the character of the document will betray itself.[25] The giving of arles or earnest money seems to be of little value as evidence of the constitution of a lease.[26] If a lease is constituted verbally, its terms may from time to time be altered by verbal agreement, which in turn may be proved by parole evidence.[27] There is a distinction between a verbal lease for a year and a lease, originally in writing, continuing from year to year by tacit

---

[17] *Ross* v *Ross* (1805) Hume 573; *Duke of Gordon* v *Carmichael* (1800) Hume 805; *Ballantine* v *Stevenson* (1881) 8 R. 959.
[18] Rankine, 102.
[19] Rankine, 101/102 and authorities cited there.
[20] Rankine, 116 and authorities cited there; Hume, *Lectures,* II, 60.
[21] *Jackson* v *Graham* (1705) Mor. 12413. The Act of Sederunt of 16th July 1532 permitted a year's tack to be proved by witnesses: see *Acta Dominorum C. et S. (Stair Society,* Vol. 14) No. 101.
[22] *Charters* v *M'Duff* (1567) Mor. 8397; *Fraser* v *Leslie* (1581) Mor. 12405; *Lord Monteith* v *Tenants* (1582) Mor. 8397.
[23] *Gibson* v *Adams* (1875) 3 R. 144.
[24] See *Stewart* v *Leith* (1766) Mor. 15178.
[25] Rankine, 117 and authorities cited there.
[26] *Ibid.*
[27] *Morrison* v *Campbell* (1842) 4 D. 1426; *Macfarlane* v *Mitchell* (1900) 2 F. 901; *Nairn Station Hotel Ltd.* v *Macpherson* (1905) 13 S.L.T. 456 (O.H.).

relocation; in the latter case the better view appears to be that alterations are not provable by parole.[28]

Duration of Verbal Leases. The term "verbal lease" has sometimes been used by writers to denote not only a lease made by word of mouth, but also a lease constituted by writings which fall short of being probative,[29] but in this work "verbal" is limited to its literal meaning, that is, oral.

It has been said that a verbal lease for a period of more than one year is not binding even for one year, because the terms are adjusted at the commencement of a course of years and are probably unsuitable for a shorter period.[30] If parties verbally agree on a lease for twenty years, their bargain is certainly not binding for the twenty years, and it is doubtful if it is binding even for one year. The reason is obvious: the rent, mode of management and whole other mutual prestations of parties have been arranged and adjusted on the notion of a lease for twenty years and are therefore probably quite unsuitable to a single year's possession. This doctrine is perhaps not settled law, and a distinction was drawn between leases on which possession had followed and those where possession had not followed and matters were entire. Thus, a tenant under a verbal lease for a period of years, on which he had never possessed, was held entitled to resile.[31] Where, however, the tenant had entered into possession under a verbal lease for a period of years, the lease was said to be binding on both parties and the tenant must pay the rent; and there is a series of old cases suggesting that a verbal lease for a period of years was binding for one year only, and that either party was entitled to resile at the end of each successive year, on giving proper notice.[32] There was difference of judicial opinion in a case where it was held that a verbal agreement to take furnished lodgings for sixteen months at a certain rate per month, which had been followed by possession, but by no other *rei interventus,* could not be proved by parole evidence, even to the extent of establishing a contract for one year;[33] it was not, however, decided whether, if such a verbal agreement were proved by writ or oath, it would be valid even for one year. It seems quite illogical that a lease not valid for several years should be valid for a year merely because there is a rule that leases for a year or less need not be in writing, and there must be many circumstances where a person is willing to take or grant a lease for a term of years when he would not agree to a lease for a year. The fact

[28] Rankine, 117.
[29] Rankine, 116.
[30] Hume, *Lectures,* II 60; Rankine, 118; Gloag, *Contract,* 2nd ed., 163; opinions of L.J.C. Patton in *Fowlie* v *M'Lean* (1868) 6 M. 254 at p. 256, and of L.P. Normand in *Pollock* v *Whiteford,* 1936 S.C. 402 at p. 409.
[31] *Skene* (1637) Mor. 8401.
[32] Rankine 118; see opinion of Lord Benholme in *Fowlie* v *M'Lean, infra,* at p. 257.
[33] *Fowlie* v *M'Lean* (1868) 6 M. 254.

that the law recognises the validity for one year of a verbal lease for
a period of years followed by possession must be merely an emergency
remedy to obviate the hardship caused to both parties by a removal at
a broken term, and it is very convenient to allow the lease to run on
till the end of the year and to give it such effect.[34] In such cases, a party
may have a claim of damages, not for breach of an unproved contract,
but for actual loss sustained in good faith in consequence of unjustifiable
representations and inducements made by the other.[35] Similarly, improvements may not be sufficient to set up a lease for years, even if
they found a claim for compensation. The question in such cases is
whether there are stipulations in the lease for a term of years incompatible
with a one year's lease.[36]

Where a tenant alleged a verbal agreement for a lease of five years
followed by possession and *rei interventus* and also an interim agreement
for a yearly tenancy, it was held that he could prove the averment of a
five years' lease only by writ or oath, but that he could prove the yearly
tenancy *prout de jure*.[37]

INFORMAL LEASES FOR MORE THAN ONE YEAR

Constitution. Although leases for more than one year should be constituted only by writing probative of both parties, it very often happens
that possession of the subjects is both given and taken and important
rei interventus takes place on the faith of a bargain without any formally authenticated written lease. For example, there may be a written
offer signed by the landlord, but not holograph of him, and there may
or may not be a written acceptance by the tenant, but, if on the faith
of the improbative offer possession has followed and the lease has been
acted upon, both parties will be bound for the whole of the duration
expressed in the imperfect writing; so in many such cases a defective
lease is validated and rendered binding on both parties by *rei interventus*.
So common is this and so numerous are the reported cases on the
subject, that one may wonder whether in practice the majority of leases
have never been reduced to formal writings.

The practical effect of *rei interventus*—or, it may be, of *rei interventus*
and homologation combined—is not only to exclude the plea of *locus
poenitentiae* on the part of the party who has allowed the other to act
on the faith of the contract, but equally it operates as a bar to resiling
on the party who has chosen to act upon it.[38] The result is to make a
defective lease as effective as if it had been probative in the first place.
" If things have been done on the faith of the agreement and in pur-

---

[34] Rankine, 119; *cf. Gray* v *Edinburgh University,* 1962 S.L.T. 173 *per* L.J.C.
Thomson at p. 176.
[35] *Heddle* v *Baikie* (1846) 8 D. 376, explained in *Allan* v *Gilchrist* (1875) 2 R. 587.
[36] Rankine, 119.
[37] *Gibson* v *Adams* (1875) 3 R. 144.
[38] *Bathie* v *Lord Wharncliffe* (1873) 11 M. 490.

suance of it, that is to say, if the agreement has been followed by *rei interventus,* there is a rule of law to this effect, that an improbative writing combined with *rei interventus* shall be sufficient. The operation of *rei interventus* is sometimes expressed as a bar to *locus poenitentiae,* but the practical effect is that it perfects the contract. Further, a verbal lease for a period of years followed by *rei interventus* will be sufficient. The mode of proving the verbal agreement, however, is another matter ".[39] Following the foregoing opinion, it may be said that, failing a document probative of both parties, a lease for a period of years may be constituted by a verbal or improbative written agreement followed by *rei interventus.*

Thus whether parties have intended to reduce their agreement to a formal written contract or not, the operation of *rei interventus* may complete the bargain for them, and it may happen that the details of the contract so inferred may differ from what the parties originally had in mind or might have inserted in their formal contract.

Proof. However, a verbal agreement or informal document is of little value, unless its existence can be proved. " The *rei interventus* may be proved, of course, by parole evidence, and in general can only be proved in that way. But with regard to the verbal bargain, I think it is quite fixed that that can only be proved in one or other of two ways. The first mode is by writing. There is nothing anomalous in saying that a verbal bargain may be proved by writing; for there may be writing enough to prove, though not to constitute, the bargain. The other mode is by oath ".[40] Thus, the two elements required to prove an informally constituted lease for a period of years are (a) a verbal or improbative written agreement, which is provable only by the writ or oath of the defender, and (b) conduct of the parties amounting to *rei interventus,* which is provable *prout de jure.*[41] The function of the writ in this context is not to constitute the agreement but to instruct its existence, but this distinction is one that is lost sight of in several *dicta,* if indeed it is of importance. In every case the two elements, namely, proof of the agreement by writ or oath, and proof of the *rei interventus,* must be looked at together, as an *unum quid,* the force and relevancy of each being only to be judged with reference to the other; they must be correlative.[42] Unless the informal agreement can be proved, no amount of *rei interventus* can set it up; and it is useless to prove an informal agreement, unless *rei interventus* has followed on it.

Proof of Verbal Agreement. When *rei interventus* is put forward in support of a lease resting on improbative writings, such as an offer

---

[39] *Walker* v *Flint* (1863) 1 M. 417 *per* L.J.C. Inglis at p. 421.
[40] *Ibid.*
[41] *Gowans' Trs.* v *Carstairs* (1862) 24 D. 1382; *Walker* v *Flint, supra.*
[42] Rankine, 120.

signed by only one party, the question is simply whether the actings averred are sufficient to constitute *rei interventus;* but when it is put forward in support of an alleged verbal agreement, the further question arises as to how the verbal agreement, if disputed, is to be proved. Parole evidence of the verbal agreement is excluded, and proof is limited to the writ or oath of the defender, and it follows that if a pursuer rests his case on a verbal agreement followed by *rei interventus,* and the verbal agreement is not admitted, he must prove the agreement by the writ of the defender, or by referring it to his oath.[43] A successful proof of *rei interventus,* if allowed, would leave his case deficient, because it would establish only that the verbal agreement was fully binding, if it was ever entered into; it would not establish that there ever was a verbal agreement. Therefore proof of *rei interventus* in such cases will not be allowed, unless the fact of agreement is admitted or an offer is made to prove it by the writ or oath of the defender.[44] Thus where a tenant averred that he was in possession under a verbal lease for three years, and that he had incurred expenditure on the subjects in reliance on the agreement and with the knowledge and permission of the landlord, it was held that proof of the alleged lease was limited to the landlord's writ or oath.[45] In many cases involving verbal leases there may be no writ.

Proof by Writ. The nature of the writ, which will be accepted as evidence of a verbal agreement or improbative agreement and as opening up the way to a proof of *rei interventus,* varies with the circumstances of each case, and no very definite rules can be laid down. The writ need not form part of the constitution of the contract.[46] The writ may be that of a factor to the party denying the contract.[47] For this purpose the contents of the writ are of more importance than the formality of its execution. The writ need not be probative; the statutory rules as to the authentication of writings apply to the constitution of contracts where writing is obligatory, not to the manner in which contracts may be proved, nor to writings used in evidence to prove a fact.[48] The writ in such cases may be neither holograph nor tested, the want of a signature by one party is not always an objection, it is not necessary that there should be writing by both parties, and it is immaterial that the writ is in a slovenly or irregular form, or even that it is deficient in mentioning an essential part of the bargain; but the writ must be such

[43] *Neil* v *Earl of Cassilis* 22 Nov. 1810 F.C.; *Gowans' Trs.* v *Carstairs* (1862) 24 D. 1382; *Walker* v *Flint* (1863) 1 M. 417; *Paterson* v *Earl of Fife* (1865) 3 M. 423; *Gibson* v *Adams* (1875) 5 R. 144; Gloag, *Contract,* 2nd ed., 175.
[44] *Gowans' Trs.* v *Carstairs* (1862) 24 D. 1382; Gloag, *op. cit.* 175.
[45] *Walker* v *Flint* (1863) 1 M. 417.
[46] *Emslie* v *Duff* (1865) 3 M. 854.
[47] *Ibid.*
[48] Gloag, *op. cit.* 175; Smith, *A Short Commentary,* 803; Walker, *Evidence,* 311.

as can reasonably be held to have been intended as evidence of a concluded bargain and so executed.[49] Some of the terms of the agreement
may be proved by one writ, and some by another.[50]

Types of Writ. The writ may have been intended to be the formal
contract embodying the terms of lease, but the signature of one or both
of the parties may not have been properly authenticated, or one or both
parties may have initialled it instead of signing it in full, or one of the
parties may not have signed it at all, or the date or testing clause may
have been omitted or a notarial execution may have been faulty.[51] Even
an engrossed lease signed by neither party might be accepted as evidence.[52] The writ may be a preliminary one, originally intended to be
superseded by a more formal deed, but allowed by neglect or otherwise
to remain the only writ embodying the agreement. Thus missives or
articles of roup, improperly signed or unsigned by one party, or even
an advertisement followed by an offer or an acceptance have been
admitted in evidence.[53]

Drafts. Drafts have very frequently been admitted as evidence.[54]
Thus, an unsigned draft drawn by the landlord, proved to have been
adjusted by both parties, and returned to the landlord, was accepted as
good evidence of the verbal contract; there was also written corroboration of the transaction in entries in a rental book, but it was questioned
whether such corroboration was necessary.[55] Where the draft is the only
document embodying the terms of the contract, the supervening *rei interventus* is the best evidence of the parties' intention not to regard the
draft as merely a preliminary document.[56] In *Wight* v *Newton*,[57] at the
date on which the tenant took possession a draft lease had been prepared and its whole terms agreed, with the exception of a repairs clause
objected to by the tenant, and the tenant had subsequently been in
occupation for three years; in an action raised by the tenant to have a
formal lease executed the landlord maintained that, as no concluded
contract in terms of the draft had been come to, the tenant was possessing on a yearly tenancy; it was held that the draft lease, mutually
approved in all its terms with the exception of the repairs clause and
followed by entry and possession, constituted a valid contract of lease
for a period of years, and that the tenant was entitled to a lease in
terms of the draft, but with the omission of the repairs clause, which
the Court declined to insert in the absence of proof of the parties' agree-

---

[49] Hume, *Lectures,* II, 64-67.
[50] *Wilson* v *Mann* (1876) 3 R. 527.
[51] Rankine, 121, and authorities cited there.
[52] *Girdwood* v *Wilson* (1834) 12 S. 576 *per* Lord Moncreiff (L.O.).
[53] Rankine, 122.
[54] *Grieve* v *Pringle* (1797) Mor. 5951; *Campbell* v *Dougal* (1813) Hume 861.
[55] *Bathie* v *Lord Wharncliffe* (1873) 11 M. 490.
[56] Rankine, 122.
[57] 1911 S.C. 762.

ment. That was not a case[58] of missives containing the cardinal elements of a lease and requiring to be filled in by the Court inserting the usual and necessary clauses,[59] because all the conditions of the lease were agreed on with the one exception; nor was it a case in which terms, provable only by writ or oath, were demanded that were neither usual nor necessary.[60] Of course, if the bargain is finally embodied in a completed lease, a mere draft intended as such, though signed, will not let in *rei interventus* to qualify the bargain.[61]

Copies. The rules applying to the admissibility of drafts apply to copies, notarial copies, copy drafts and unsigned minutes.[62] A document purporting to be a copy of a lease and containing all the essentials of a lease, found in its proper chronological order in an estate lease book and not signed by the parties in terms of the law except for the " mark " of the tenant attested by two witnesses, was held to be a sufficient basis for *rei interventus* and to have been set up as a valid contract of lease by the fact that the tenant and his successors subsequently possessed the subjects in accordance with the stipulations contained in it.[63] It would appear from the judicial opinions expressed in that case, and from the fact that a " mark " is of no legal effect in Scotland, that the same decision would have been reached had the copy not been marked and witnessed. It was also held in that case that the copy so marked and witnessed and supported by *rei interventus* was a " specific agreement in writing " within the meaning of the Act in question.[64]

Memoranda by Landlord. Writings by the landlord either in his estate books or elsewhere, although they may not be accepted as constituting a written lease (and even this has been questioned[65]), may be accepted as a basis for *rei interventus*.[66] In such cases the distinction is made between a writing, however irregular and unshapely, which appears to have been intended as the permanent agreement, on the one hand, and a brief note or occasional memorandum by the landlord for his own private use or some transient and incidental mention of terms of lease in a writing intended for some quite different purpose, on the other hand.[67] In most of the cases where such memoranda have been accepted, the memoranda have been semi-public in character affecting a large number of tenants, such as the rent-roll of a large estate or notes of

---

[58] *Ibid., per* Lord Ardwall at p. 771, explained by Rankine, p. 123.
[59] *Cf. Erskine* v *Glendinning* (1871) 9 M 656. *supra,* p. 17.
[60] *Paterson* v *Earl of Fife* (1865) 3 M. 423; see *infra,* p. 28.
[61] *Infra,* p. 36.
[62] Rankine, 123.
[63] *Wares* v *Duff-Dunbar's Trs.,* 1920 S.C. 5.
[64] Crofters Holdings (Scotland) Act 1886 s. 8 (c).
[65] *Earl of Dalhousie* v *Crokat* (1868) 6 M. 659.
[66] For many examples see Rankine 123-126 and cases cited there.
[67] *Maxwell* v *Grierson* (1812) Hume 849; Rankine 125.

simultaneous negotiations with a large number of tenants.[68] Some of the many examples are : — a letter by the husband of a proprietrix giving a list of farms, rents, durations of leases, etc., sent to the surveyor of taxes for the purposes of a valuation roll,[69] an unsigned holograph note by the landlord retained by him giving the names of several tenants, farms and rents,[70] entries in a rental book along with advertisements of several lots,[71] and letters passing between a landlord and his son and his factor taken along with the son's notebook and the factor's list, relating to proposed leases of several houses in a village.[72] Sometimes the existence of a lease may be proved by several separate writs, from all of which the terms of the agreement have to be gleaned. Thus, the existence and import of a lease were in one case held to be instructed by a letter from a tenant, then sitting from year to year, who was also the landlord's factor, asking leave to carry out operations which would occupy a period of years, a written approval signed, but not holograph, of the landlord, a letter from the landlord's agents to the tenant stating the ish, an advertisement of sale of the estate showing the ish and rent, and entries in the cash book of the factor, docqueted by the landlord and audited.[73] On the other hand, mere entries in a factor's accounts and collection lists of rents paid, not giving details of the endurance, along with receipts for rents were not sufficient to instruct a long lease.[74]

Writ of Factor. The writ of the landlord's factor or other agent is equivalent to the writ of the landlord himself, provided of course that the factor has the authority to bind his principal, the scope of his authority being in each case a question of fact provable by parole evidence.[75] Thus, informal letters between law agents negotiating the terms of a lease and an engrossed lease signed by the tenant, followed by acts on the part of the tenant made on the faith of the contract, were not sufficient a basis for *rei interventus,* where the landlord's agent had no authority to grant leases and it was not proved that the landlord knew of the tenant's actings.[76]

Receipt for Rent. A simple receipt for rent by itself is not a sufficient foundation, because it does not indicate the duration of the lease.[77]

---

[68] Rankine, 125.
[69] *Emslie* v *Duff* (1865) 3 M. 854.
[70] *Earl of Aboyne* v *Ogg* (1810) Hume 847.
[71] *Campbell* v *M'Kinnon* (1867) 5 M. 636, affd. (1870) 8 M. (H.L.) 40 (Tobermory case).
[72] *Sellar* v *Aiton* (1875) 2 R. 381.
[73] *Wilson* v *Mann* (1876) 3 R. 527.
[74] *Craig* v *Bell* (1871) 10 M. 8.
[75] *Sinclair* v *Caithness Flagstone Co.* (1880) 7 R. 1117 *per* L.P. Inglis at p. 1120; (1881) 8 R. (H.L.) 78 *per* Lord Watson at p. 90; Rankine, 121 and other cases cited there.
[76] *Danish Dairy Co.* v *Gillespie,* 1922 S.C. 656.
[77] *Maxwell* v *Grierson* (1812) Hume 849; *Gowan's Trs.* v *Carstairs* (1862) 24 D. 1382; Walker, *Evidence* 311.

However, there is little doubt that a receipt for rent, prepared and signed by the landlord or his authorised agent and setting forth that the footing on which the rent is paid is a lease for a period of years, would nowadays be held to be a writ sufficient to let in proof of *rei interventus*.[78]

Oath Instructing Agreement. If there is no writ to instruct the existence of a verbal or informal lease upon which *rei interventus* has proceeded, proof is limited to a reference to the oath of the party who denies its existence.[79] For this purpose an admission on record has the same effect as a reference to oath, and an agreement may be proved partly by one and partly by the other.[80] Without *rei interventus*, however, an admission on record or by reference to oath is valueless, because it does not take the place of the essential writing, but is merely an admission of a contract from which the party admitting it has the right to withdraw.[81] " That which proves the verbal agreement is oath of party; but that which gives it validity and prevents resiling is the subsequent acting on it ".[82] *Dicta* in certain cases which appear to indicate that an *obligatio literis* may be referred to oath must be read as partial statements of the law and as being made on the assumption that *rei interventus* was, or could have been averred, in which case proof of the contract by writ or oath would have been permissible.[83] Thus, where there are no averments of *rei interventus*, a landlord is not permitted to prove by reference to the tenant's oath an oral agreement to increase the rent under a written lease; and a lease being an *obligatio literis* can not be established partly by writing and partly by oath.[84] The defender's admission must be taken as it stands and along with any qualifications he may attach to it.[85] Where a tenant in possession on a verbal lease for nineteen years sued the landlord for damages for breach of an obligation, also verbal, to carry out certain improvements, the landlord admitted the verbal lease on record, but denied the obligation; it was held that the obligation was part of the constitution of the lease and could only be proved by the landlord's writ or oath, and, as the tenant could not have proved the existence of the lease by parole evidence, neither could he prove the obligation which he alleged was contained in it.[86] As a reference to oath without *rei interventus* is futile, the Court should satisfy itself as to the relevancy and sufficiency of the averments

---

[78] Rankine, 125-126.
[79] *Gowan's Trs.* v *Carstairs* (1862) 24 D. 1382; *Walker* v *Flint* (1863) 1 M. 417; Rankine, 126.
[80] *Paterson* v *Fife* (1865) 3 M. 423; Walker, *Evidence*, 310.
[81] Gloag, *Contract*, 2nd ed., 176; Walker *Evidence*, 86.
[82] *Walker* v *Flint*, *supra per* Lord Benholme at p. 422.
[83] Walker, *Evidence*, 87.
[84] *Perdikou* v *Pattison*, 1958 S.L.T. 153.
[85] Gloag, *op. cit.*, 176.
[86] *Paterson* v *Earl of Fife* (1865) 3 M. 423; Gloag, *op. cit.*, 176.

of *rei interventus* before allowing the reference.[87] The importance of formality in allowing a reference to oath was discussed in the case cited.[88]

Exclusion of Parole. Where the existence of a lease, on which *rei interventus* has followed, is proved by writ or oath or judicial admission, the whole stipulations of the lease have to be proved by one or more of those means, and it is not permissible to instruct by parole evidence any stipulations which are not contained in it.[89] So, where a verbal agreement to sublet was followed by possession and acts amounting to *rei interventus,* and its terms were subsequently embodied in an exchange of informal letters, it was held incompetent to prove by parole evidence that it was an express condition of the verbal sublease that the subtenant should take the subjects *tantum et tale* as the granters held them from the principal landlord, the letters containing no reference to such a condition.[90] A tenant was unable to prove by parole evidence the existence of a repairs clause, to which the landlord objected and which the tenant alleged formed part of a draft lease, on which *rei interventus* had proceeded.[91]

Questions with Singular Successors. Any written lease, however informal or improbative, on which *rei interventus* has followed, may be made effectual against not only the original parties, but also singular successors of the granter, that is if it complies with the other requirements of the leases Act 1449.[92] This is probably also true of a verbal lease proved by writ.[93] However, singular successors are not affected by anything less than writing, and it would be useless to try to set up against a purchaser a verbal lease provable by oath or admission on record.[94]

REI INTERVENTUS

Nature. If the existence of an informally executed bargain can be proved by writ or oath, an imperfect lease may be rendered effective if the subsequent actings of parties amount to *rei interventus.* The nature of *rei interventus* is best understood from Bell's definition: " *Rei Interventus* raises a personal exception which excludes the plea of *locus poenitentiae.* It is inferred from any proceedings not unimportant on the part of the obligee, known to and permitted by the obligor to take place on the faith of the contract as if it were perfect; provided they are unequivocally referable to the agreement and productive of alteration of circumstances, loss or inconvenience, though not irretrievable ".[95] Much has

[87] Rankine, 126.
[88] *Pollock* v *Whiteford,* 1936 S.C. 402.
[89] *Paterson* v *Earl of Fife* (1865) 3 M. 423; Rankine, 126.
[90] *Downie* v *Laird & Sons Ltd.* (1902) 10 S.L.T. 28 (O.H.).
[91] *Wight* v *Newton,* 1911 S.C. 762.
[92] *Infra,* p. 104.
[93] *Wilson* v *Mann* (1876) 3 R. 527 *per* L.J.C. Moncreiff at p. 532.
[94] Rankine, 126.
[95] Bell § 26.

been written elsewhere about the doctrine of *rei interventus,* but as probably the greater part of the law on the subject has been derived from cases involving leases, it is not inappropriate to deal with the subject at some length in this work.

The circumstances inferring *rei interventus* vary with each case, but the most usual situation is that of a tenant, who, to the knowledge of the landlord, has spent money on improvements, claiming that he did so by virtue of a verbal lease for a period of years, while the landlord claims that such expenditure was consistent with a verbal lease for one year; the tenant has to prove the verbal agreement by writ or oath, but may prove the *rei interventus* by parole evidence; if the tenant can prove that his expenditure is directly ascribable to a lease for a period of years and if the other facts are strong enough, then the landlord is barred from resiling. In such a case the tenant is the obligee and the landlord the obligor, but a lease being a mutual contract with obligations on either side, the proceedings of either party or both may be founded upon as *rei interventus;* but there is perhaps more difficulty in relying on the landlord's actings than on the tenant's; for in many cases it can be argued that the landlord's expenditure may have been for the benefit of the property in general and not ascribable to the particular tenant's lease.[96]

The *rei interventus* may consist of actings or abstention from action.[97] It may be proved by parole evidence.[98] The actings must be " known to and permitted by the obligor ", be " unequivocally referable to the agreement " and be " productive of alteration of circumstances, loss or inconvenience ". Those three elements must all be proved and the averments must be specific enough to show that the actings satisfied those conditions.[99]

" Known to and Permitted ". The actings must be " known to and permitted " by the other party to take place on the faith of the agreement as if it were binding. The knowledge and permission required do not necessarily involve actual cognisance and conscious permission of everything done on the faith of the agreement;[1] it is enough if the actings are such as would naturally be expected to follow on the agreement,[2] but not if they are too remote.[3] Knowledge of an agent, who has authority to permit the acts, is equivalent to knowledge of the landlord himself.[4] Where a landlord's law agent without his authority negoti-

---

[96] *Skene* (1637) Mor. 8401; Rankine, 127.
[97] *Danish Dairy Co.* v *Gillespie,* 1922 S.C. 656.
[98] *Walker* v *Flint* (1863) 1 M. 417 at 421.
[99] *Gardner* v *Lucas* (1878) 5 R. 638; *Buchanan* v *Harris and Sheldon* (1900) 2 F. 935 per L.P. Balfour at p. 939; *Danish Dairy Co., supra;* Gloag, *Contract,* 2nd ed., 173; Walker, *Evidence* 312.
[1] Rankine, 127.
[2] *Gardner* v *Lucas* (1878) 5 R. 638; Walker, *Evidence,* 313.
[3] *Gardner* v *Lucas, supra.*
[4] *Forbes* v *Wilson* (1873) 11 M. 454.

ated the renewal of a lease by informal letters between law agents, and it was not proved that the landlord was aware of the tenant's payment of the expenses of the lease and their abstention from looking for other premises, the landlord was allowed to repudiate the agreement.[5]

" Unequivocally Referable ". The proceedings founded upon as inferring *rei interventus* must be " unequivocally referable " to the prior agreement, that is, they must be consistent with and unable to be explained except by the prior agreement. Mere acts of ordinary tenancy are not sufficient, if they can be ascribed to a yearly lease or to some agreement other than the one relied on. Thus, if the tenant alleges a verbal agreement of lease for a number of years, it may not be enough for him to prove possession, payment of rent and even ordinary cultivation, as those acts may equally well be ascribed to a lease for not more than one year, for which a verbal lease is sufficient.[6] Such acts are probably not sufficient to validate a merely verbal lease for a period of years.[7] In such circumstances what is required to constitute *rei interventus* is the doing of acts, which from their nature can be explained only by a contract for a period of more than one year. A verbal agreement to take lodgings for sixteen months followed by possession, but by no other *rei interventus,* could not be proved *prout de jure* even to the extent of establishing a lease for one year, and it was questioned whether, if such an agreement were proved by writ or oath, it would be valid even for one year.[8] In an early case it was held that although ordinary improvements in the way of better culture and management of the lands were not by themselves sufficient *rei interventus* to set up a verbal bargain for a term of years; yet the other proceedings founded on, that is erecting a building, were only referable to a bargain for a term of years, and would not have been permitted, unless the bargain was to be implemented.[9] Expenditure or improvements by the tenant which would be improvident on a yearly tenure may be held to have been done in reliance on an informal agreement for a lease for a term of years.[10]

Mere Possession. While it is true that mere possession is not enough without *rei interventus* to constitute a verbal lease for a period of years, where there are documents, which, though informal, contain the requisites of a lease, possession following on them and attributable to them can only be taken up as for the full term of years contained in the informal lease, the effect of such possession being to put the documents

---

[5] *Danish Dairy Co.* v *Gillespie,* 1922 S.C. 656.
[6] *Philip* v *Gordon Cumming's Exrs.* (1869) 7 M. 859; *Buchanan* v *Nicoll,* 1966 S.L.T. (Sh. Ct.) 62; Rankine, 128; Walker, *Evidence,* 312.
[7] *Supra,* p. 20.
[8] *Fowlie* v *M'Lean* (1868) 6 M. 254.
[9] *Macrorie* v *Macwhirter* 18 Dec. 1810 F.C.
[10] *Bathie* v *Lord Wharncliffe* (1873) 11 M. 490; Gloag, *op. cit.,* 174.

in the same position as if they had been formally executed.[11] Thus two years' possession by tenants on a lease for fifteen years, signed by the landlord but not by the tenants, bound the tenants for the whole term.[12] One year's possession on a lease for nineteen years, signed by the tenant and retained but not signed by the landlord, bound the landlord.[13] A draft lease for nineteen years followed by possession for three years was held to constitute a valid lease.[14] If a new lease has been arranged by informal writings with a tenant in possession under a lease about to terminate, his continued possession may be held attributable to the new lease and not to tacit relocation on the old lease.[15] Thus, continued possession (without other *rei interventus* founded on in the judgment) validated informal missives for a new lease of three years and the plea of tacit relocation was excluded.[16] It is often difficult to ascertain from the cases in which possession was held to validate a lease to what extent other acts of *rei interventus* were taken into consideration. The function of mere possession has been explained[17] thus:—*first*, to clinch a bargain, already perfected on the landlord's side;[18] *second*, to infer acceptance of an improbative offer, where the only alternative, possible or pleaded, is tacit relocation;[19] *third*, to help in converting a personal into a real right;[20] and *fourth*, to perfect an assignation.[21]

It is obvious that the acts relied upon as *rei interventus* must occur after the informal lease,[22] but they need not come after the writ or oath instructing the agreement.[23] The *rei interventus* may take place before possession on the informal contract is possible, as where the possession is under an existing lease about to expire, and the *rei interventus* follows an imperfect contract for a new lease.[24] However, the *rei interventus* must be ascribable to the particular agreement in question, and not to some other agreement that may have supervened, or to a prior agreement.[25] Thus, where there was a binding agreement for the renewal of a lease and the tenant alleged an additional verbal agreement, it was held that the acts he founded on were ascribable to the lease and not to the verbal agreement.[26] Actings on the part of tenants provided for in a formal lease, which had been reduced on the

---

[11] *Buchanan* v *Harris & Sheldon* (1900) 2 F. 935 *per* Lord Adam at p. 939.
[12] *Macpherson* v *Macpherson* 12 May 1815 F.C.
[13] *Ballantine* v *Stevenson* (1881) 8 R. 959.
[14] *Wight* v *Newton*, 1911 S.C. 762.
[15] *Sutherland's Tr.* v *Miller's Tr.* (1888) 16 R. 10; *Macfarlane* v *Mitchell* (1900) 2 F. 901.
[16] *Buchanan* v *Harris & Sheldon* (1900) 2 F. 935.
[17] Rankine, 128.
[18] *Supra*, p. 18.
[19] *Sutherland's Tr.; Macfarlane; Buchanan*, all *supra*.
[20] *Infra*, p. 110.
[21] *Infra*, p. 160.
[22] Rankine, 127; Walker, *Evidence*, 312.
[23] *Emslie* v *Duff* (1865) 3 M. 854 *per* Lord Ardmillan at p. 860.
[24] *Murdoch* v *Moir* 18 June 1812 F.C.
[25] Rankine, 127.
[26] *Philip* v *Gordon Cumming's Exrs.* (1869) 7 M. 859.

grounds of fraud, could not be ascribed to a prior informal agreement, which they sought to enforce.[27] Where a landlord failed to establish by *rei interventus* the constitution of a written lease never signed, the tenant was able to show that his possession could equally well be ascribed to a prior verbal lease.[28]

The *rei interventus* should have a sufficiently clear and distinct relation to the terms of the alleged contract.[29] The actings need not be done precisely in terms of provisions in the lease, but, if they are, then there is less possibility of ascribing them to any other motive than implementing the lease.[30]

"*Loss or Inconvenience*". The actings must be productive of some loss or inconvenience to the party who acts on the faith of the agreement. The extent of the loss must depend on the circumstances.[31] A large expenditure by a tenant on improvements would indicate that it was made in pursuance of a lease for a long period rather than of a yearly lease.[32]

Facts Amounting to Rei Interventus. Normally the *rei interventus* consists of possession followed by expenditure on improvements or alterations made by the tenant to the subjects of the lease. The improvements and alterations include manuring, liming, enclosing, making dykes, planting trees, erecting buildings and other similar proceedings. However, each case will depend on its own circumstances, the main factors being the nature of the property, the amount and expense of the improvements or alterations, the rent and the alleged duration.[33] A typical case is that of a draft lease for nineteen years adjusted between but not signed by the parties, followed by the tenant taking down ruined cottages so that the landlord might use the materials in terms of the draft, driving tiles for drainage, and importing lime and manure at her expense.[34] Similarly a binding lease for twenty-nine years was held to have been constituted by a written offer from the tenant stating the rent and ish, combined with circumstances both before and after its date including the tenant at his own expense forming an avenue, referred to in the offer.[35]

Apart from improvements or alterations, other acts[36] which either alone or in conjunction with others have constituted *rei interventus* include subletting with the knowledge of the landlord;[37] abstention by

---

[27] *Gardner* v *Lucas* (1878) 5 R. 638.
[28] *Pollock* v *Whiteford*, 1936 S.C. 402.
[29] *Bathie* v *Lord Wharncliffe* (1873) 11 M. 490, *per* L.P. Inglis at p. 495.
[30] *Ibid.,* p. 496.
[31] See Walker, *Evidence*, 313.
[32] *Walker* v *Flint* (1863) 1 M. 417; *Bathie* v *Lord Wharncliffe* (1873) 11 M. 490.
[33] Rankine, 128-9 and examples given there.
[34] *Bathie* v *Lord Wharncliffe* (1873) 11 M. 490.
[35] *Forbes* v *Wilson* (1873) 11 M. 454.
[36] Rankine, 130 and examples given there.
[37] *Bell* v *Goodall* (1883) 10 R. 905.

the tenant from looking for other accommodation;[38] paying a grassum;[39] and paying a rent considerably larger than that which was payable under an existing lease in pursuance of a general treaty for new leases between the landlord and many tenants on the estate.[40] Paying an increased rent after the natural close of a lease does not necessarily amount to *rei interventus,* as this can equally well be ascribed to a yearly lease;[41] but paying an increased rent for several years may be sufficient.[42]

It was not decided whether a tenant's abstention from giving statutory notice of his intention to terminate a lease in consequence of an informal agreement for a new lease at a reduced rent was sufficient *rei interventus* to validate such agreement.[43]

Proceedings on the part of the landlord may amount to *rei interventus,* as where he abstains from efforts to find another tenant.[44] The hypothetical example has been given of a landlord removing a " To Let " notice from a house following an informal agreement to let it; if the tenant knows that this has been done and does not immediately intimate his desire to resile, but allows the landlord to lose the opportunity of reletting the house, he cannot resile later.[45] Similarly, where the tenant of a hotel maintained the contract of lease until it was too late for the landlords to apply for a licence for themselves, it was held that there was sufficient *rei interventus* to bar the tenant from resiling.[46]

ADMISSIBILITY OF EXTRINSIC EVIDENCE

General Rule. It is a general rule that, where a lease, like any other contract, has been entered into in writing, it is incompetent to add to, contradict or qualify its terms by parole evidence.[47] Thus the tenant under a written lease cannot prove by parole evidence that it had been arranged that he was to get possession of ground not included in the boundaries prescribed in the lease.[48] Similarly, the landlord may not prove by parole evidence that subjects were included by mistake in a formal lease.[49] It was held incompetent to lead parole evidence to show that the statement in a lease that certain buildings had been valued at a certain sum on entry was incorrect,[50] or to add a condition to the landlord's power of resumption in a written lease.[51] It is incompetent

---

[38] *Danish Dairy Co.* v *Gillespie,* 1922 S.C. 656.
[39] *Macrorie* v *Macwhirter* 18 Dec. 1810 F.C.
[40] *Earl of Aboyne* v *Ogg* (1810) Hume 847; Hume, *Lectures,* II, 66.
[41] Rankine, 130.
[42] *Sellar* v *Aiton* (1875) 2 R. 381.
[43] *Sutherland's Tr.* v *Miller's Tr.* (1888) 16 R. 10.
[44] *Sutherland & Co.* v *Hay* (1845) 8 D. 283 (a year's lease only).
[45] *Ibid.* per Lord Medwyn.
[46] *Nairn Station Hotel Ltd.* v *Macpherson* (1905) 13 S.L.T. 456 (O.H.).
[47] *Lawson* v *Murray* (1825) 3 S. 536.
[48] *Carmichael* v *Penny* (1874) 11 S.L.R. 634; *Gregson* v *Alsop* (1897) 24 R. 1081; see also *Earl of Ancaster* v *Doig* 1960 S.C. 203.
[49] *Earl of Fife's Trs.* v *Duncan* (1824) 3 S. 178 (N.E. 241).
[50] *Lawson* v *Murray* (1825) 3 S. 536.
[51] *Sharp* v *Clark* (1807) Hume 577.

to introduce parole evidence as to a verbal agreement implying obligations by either party not provided for in the written lease: for example an obligation on the tenant to pay the cost of cultivation of a previous tenant not mentioned in the lease,[52] or an obligation on the landlord to repair fences, although the lease put the obligation on the tenant.[53] Similarly it is incompetent to prove a verbal promise alleged to have been made by either party at the time of the lease being signed.[54] Moreover, as has been seen, where the lease founded on is informal and has had to be proved by writ or oath, proof of *rei interventus* will not be allowed to contradict its terms.[55] Proof that the written contract does not express the agreement of the parties is not entirely excluded, but is limited to the writ or oath of the party seeking to maintain the terms of the written contract.[56]

The rule that parole evidence will not be admitted to contradict the express terms of a written lease is illustrated by a modern case.[57] Parties entered into a formal probative lease of a café for a term of five years at a particular rent; three years later the landlord brought an action against the tenants averring that there had been an oral agreement entered into *unico contextu* with the lease, providing for the payment to the landlord of a sum equal to what he expended by way of owners' rates and property tax each year; the landlord contended that either the oral agreement was a collateral one and could be set up by parole evidence, or alternatively that proof before answer *habili modo* should be allowed, so that his right of reference to the tenants' oaths might be preserved. It was held (firstly) that the effect of the oral agreement being to alter an express stipulation as to one of the essentials of the lease, it was not a collateral agreement and so could not be proved by parole evidence, and (secondly) that, as the oral agreement related not to the proof but to the constitution of a lease, which being an *obligatio literis* could not be established partly in writing and partly by oath, a reference to oath was not competent. The element of *rei interventus* was not involved. In other words in the case of an *obligatio literis* the rules of evidence demand proof of *rei interventus* before allowing a proof of the agreement by writ or oath.[58]

Exceptions. Parole evidence will be admitted to supply an obvious omission from a lease. Thus the endurance of a lease shown by *rei interventus* to be a lease for a period of years was supplied by parole

---

[52] *Alexander* v *Gillon* (1847) 9 D. 524.
[53] *M'Gregor* v *Strathallan* (1862) 24 D. 1006.
[54] *Glasgow Magistrates* v *Macfait* (1755) Mor. 12341; *Maxwell* v *Burgess* (1773) Mor. 12351.
[55] *Supra,* p. 28.
[56] *Sharp* v *Clark* (1807) Hume 577; *Sinclair* v *MacBeath* (1869) 7 M. 934; *Stewart* v *Clark* (1871) 9 M. 616; Hume, *Lectures,* II, 71.
[57] *Perdikou* v *Pattison,* 1958 S.L.T. 153.
[58] For a full discussion of this case see A. I. Phillips " Collateral Agreements " in I *Conv. Rev.,* 116.

evidence.[59] Where the contract has to be inferred out of two or more documents, the difficulty may arise whether the writs contain or were intended to contain the whole bargain, but the rule seems to be that the Court, if satisfied that a valid contract has been established and that it is a lease for a period of years, will admit parole evidence to supply an obvious omission.[60] Where a two years' lease of heritable subjects for use as a bulb-growing establishment was concluded by informal letters without specifying the date of entry, and possession had followed, parole evidence was admitted to prove the date of entry.[61] It is quite a common and recognised practice in a lease to describe the extent of the subjects let by reference to a previous tenancy; this does not mean that the terms of the description are ambiguous; it merely means that one has to go to extrinsic evidence to find out what in fact the previous tenant had.[62] If, however, the writings themselves do not suggest the need of supplement, it is competent to qualify their terms only by writ, which must be subsequent to the contract, of the party proposing to maintain it, or by an admission or a reference to his oath, along with *rei interventus*.[63]

The general rule excluding parole evidence applies only in a question with a party who maintains the terms of the written lease. If he admits that it does not accurately represent the agreement of the parties, parole evidence is of course allowed to prove what the real agreement is.

When the question is not as to the contents of the lease or their meaning, but as to its validity, parole evidence is admissible. Thus, there is no restriction on the methods of proof of the scope of the granter's authority[64] or proof of fraud, essential error, illegality or blunders in draftsmanship.[65] As with other contracts, parole evidence will be admitted to clear up a latent ambiguity in a lease, to show the circumstances surrounding the parties at the time when the lease was made, if this is relevant, to prove a collateral agreement under certain circumstances or to show that a term in a lease has a technical meaning.[66] Also an authoritative opinion has been stated to the effect that a lease may be modified by proof of a universal and clear custom in regard to a matter on which the lease is silent.[67]

---

[59] *M'Leod* v *Urquhart* (1808) Hume 840, as explained by L. P. Dunedin in *M'Allister* v *McGallagley*, 1911 S.C. 112 at p. 117.
[60] Rankine, 110.
[61] *Watters* v *Hunter*, 1927 S.C. 310.
[62] *Earl of Ancaster* v *Doig*, 1960 S.C. 203 *per* L.J.C. Thomson at p. 209; contrast *Gregson* v *Alsop* (1897) 24 R. 1081.
[63] *Philip* v *Gordon Cumming's Exrs.* (1869) 7 M. 859; *Stewart* v *Clark* (1871) 9 M. 616.
[64] *Dodds* v *Walker* (1822) 2 S. 81 (N.E. 73).
[65] See Walker, *Evidence*, 269-270.
[66] See generally Gloag, *Contract*, 2nd ed., Chapter XX; Walker, *Evidence*, Chapter XXI.
[67] *Stewart* v *Maclaine* (1899) 37 S.L.R. 623 (H.L.) *per* Lord Shand at p. 626; see also *Buchanan* v *Riddell* (1900) 2 F. 544.

Prior Communings. On the principle of *Inglis* v *Buttery*,[68] where a contract of lease has been drawn up in a formal and probative form, not only is parole evidence excluded, but also evidence of all prior communings whether verbal or written is excluded, unless it is expressly incorporated or unless there has been an error in the deed.[69] So, an obligation by a landlord to carry out fencing and drainage provided for in an earlier informal agreement but not mentioned in the written lease was disregarded.[70]

Where a formal lease was not executed until two years after a tenant's entry (although it bore to be retrospective), and a dispute arose about the rent for the period prior to the date of execution of the lease, it was held competent to admit evidence of an informal agreement governing the period in question; the landlord was not attempting to modify or contradict the terms of the formal lease for the period after its execution.[71]

Subsequent Alteration of Written Contract. It can be stated with more confidence than is usually possible in making general statements, that where the relations of parties are regulated by a formal written contract, the averment that the contractual provisions have been altered by a subsequent verbal agreement cannot be proved by parole evidence.[72] Where one party abides by the terms of a written lease, and the other avers that the terms of the lease were subsequently altered by verbal agreement, not only is parole evidence of the verbal alteration inadmissible, but a reference as to the agreement to the oath of the other party is incompetent, unless there are also averments of actings consequent on the verbal agreement inferring *rei interventus* or homologation.[73] Thus, without relevant averments of actings a tenant under a written lease cannot prove by parole evidence an agreement to reduce the rent specified in the lease,[74] or an agreement that a building he was bound to erect might be made of materials other than those specified in the lease.[75]

However, there is no reason why parties to a lease or their successors should not agree to make any alterations on its terms or to authorise a breach. Such agreement may of course be embodied in formal writing. However, if such agreement has been made by informal writ or verbally, and one party to the knowledge of and without objection from the other has proceeded to act on the faith of the lease as altered, such action

---

[68] (1878) 5 R(H.L.) 87 (ship-repairing contract).
[69] *Earl of Fife's Trs.* v *Duncan* (1824) 3 S. 178 (N.E. 241); *Mackintosh* v *May* (1895) 22 R. 345; *Gregson* v *Alsop* (1897) 24 R. 1081; Gloag, *Contract*, 2nd ed., 367; Gloag & Henderson, *Introduction to the Law of Scotland*, 6th ed., 113.
[70] *Norval* v *Abbey*, 1939 S.C. 724.
[71] *Korner* v *Shennan*, 1950 S.C. 285.
[72] Gloag, *Contract*, 2nd ed., 391.
[73] Walker, *Evidence*, 304-305.
[74] *Riddick* v *Wightman* (1790) Hume 776; *Gibb* v *Winning* (1829) 7 S. 677; *Rattray* v *Leslie's Tr.* (1892) 19 R. 853.
[75] *Skinner* v *Lord Saltoun* (1886) 13 R. 823.

may amount to *rei interventus* and bar the right of the other party to depart from the altered terms.[76] This principle of innovation by verbal agreement was given expression in *Wark* v *Bargaddie Coal Co.*[77] In this case a written contract of a lease of coal prohibited the tenants from working coal within fifteen feet of the boundaries. The landlord alleged that this stipulation had been broken by the tenants and raised an action to compel them to restore a wall or barrier of coal of the thickness stipulated and to interdict them from further working in this barrier. The tenants alleged that the landlord had at their request consented verbally to allow them to work through the adjacent coal. They averred various matters which, they maintained, involved *rei interventus* and inferred the landlord's consent and acquiescence. The landlord admitted knowledge of what had occurred, but denied consent and acquiescence. The Court of Session considered that two questions were involved, and held (firstly) that it was incompetent to prove by parole evidence such a relaxation or departure from an important provision of a written lease, and (secondly) that no facts were averred sufficient to infer acquiescence. However, the House of Lords reversed this decision, and Lord Chancellor Chelmsford said that although the two things separately, that is, verbal agreement to depart from the terms of the written lease and subsequent acquiescence might be of no avail, yet the two taken together might be sufficient to let in parole evidence. Much confusion has been caused by that *dictum* in so far as it implies that a verbal agreement to vary, in contrast with a verbal agreement constituting, a lease, may be proved by parole evidence, and it has received some criticism.[78] The decision in *Wark* has been explained to mean that, where there are averments of acquiescence in operations inconsistent with the terms of the written contract, they may be admitted to proof; and that, if it appears that the acquiescence was the consequence of a previous arrangement, it is then competent to prove that arrangement.[79] Again, the decision has been stated to amount to no more than that if a landlord authorises something to be done in contravention of a written lease, the tenant is not liable as for a breach of contract.[80] The landlord's consent to a deviation from a lease in the past does not imply an agreement to alter the terms of the lease, and mere acquiescence in acts which would be a breach of the original terms of the contract can at the most bar a claim for damages for breach of contract, but can confer no sanction for the future.[81] In other words, the acquiescence operates only while it continues.[82]

[76] *Bargaddie Coal Co.* v *Wark* (1856) 18 D. 772, revd. (1859) 3 Macq. 467, 21 D. (H.L.) 1; *Kirkpatrick* v *Allanshaw Coal Co.* (1880) 8 R. 327.
[77] *Supra.*
[78] See Walker, *Evidence*, 306.
[79] *Sutherland* v *Montrose Shipbuilding Co.* (1860) 22 D. 665 *per* L.J.C. Inglis at p. 673.
[80] *Carron Co.* v *Henderson's Trs.* (1896) 23 R. 1042 *per* Lord M'Laren at p. 1054.
[81] *Carron Co.* v *Henderson's Trs., supra.*
[82] *Callander* v *Smith* (1900) 8 S.L.T. 109.

The chief difficulty in such cases is to determine what kinds of acts are sufficient to infer the acquiescence which may let in a general proof.[83] The question arose in *Kirkpatrick* v *Allanshaw Coal Co.*[84] The landlord raised an action against the tenant of a coalfield for a half year's rent, and the tenant's defence was that the landlord in order to enable the tenant to resist the demand of his workmen for an increase in wages had verbally agreed to reduce the rent by a third, and that the tenant had on the faith of this agreement resisted the demands of the workmen and shut up the colliery for two months. A majority of the First Division refused to allow a proof of the tenant's averments, holding that, to let in proof of a verbal agreement to alter a written contract followed by acts acquiesced in, the acts in question must be acts amounting to a contravention of the provisions of the written contract, and not merely be acts done in reliance on the verbal alteration but which could have been lawfully done without it; the facts alleged were not inconsistent with the original lease. There must be inconsistency between the original contract on the one hand and both the verbal agreement and the acts inferring acquiescence on the other hand.

The rules as to innovation of the terms of a written lease have been summarised as follows:—[85] " (1) A lease may have its provisions varied by a subsequent agreement expressed in a probative writing. That is of course clear. (2) The same result may follow from an improbative written agreement followed by *rei interventus;* or from a verbal agreement proved by writ or oath and followed by *rei interventus.* The rule so far is the same as in the constitution of contracts relating to heritage.[86] (3) A lease may also be altered by a verbal agreement proved by parole, if followed by actings contrary to the lease and in pursuance of the agreement. At least it may be so to the effect of justifying or barring challenge of the particular acts done.[87] (4) Apart from express agreement, written or verbal, consent to a particular contravention may be implied from knowledge and non-objection, that is to say, from acquiescence on the part of the landlord and such acquiescence may be proved by parole.[88] (5) Apart also from express agreement, a lease may be altered *rebus ipsis et factis,* that is to say, it may be altered both for the past and for the future by acts of the parties necessarily and unequivocally importing an agreement to alter, and such acts may be proved by parole ".[89] This last method which relies on Lord Chancellor Chelmsford's *dictum* in *Wark* is possibly effective only where the acts done with the approval

[83] Gloag, *Contract,* 2nd ed., 396.
[84] (1880) 8 R. 327 (diss. Lord Shand).
[85] *Carron Co.* v *Henderson's Trs.* (1896) 23 R. 1042 *per* Lord Kyllachy (L.O.) at p. 1048.
[86] *Gowans' Trs.* v *Carstairs* (1862) 24 D. 1382; *Walker* v *Flint* (1863) 1 M. 417; *Gibson* v *Adams* (1875) 3 R. 144.
[87] *Bargaddie Coal Co.* v *Wark* (1859) 3 Macq. 467, 21 D. (H.L.) 1; *Kirkpatrick* v *Allanshaw Coal Co.* (1880) 8 R. 327.
[88] *Bargaddie Coal Co., supra.*
[89] *Ibid.*

and consent of the landlord make it impossible without unreasonable loss to revert to the scheme of the lease, and where the past permission or tolerance necessarily implies consent for the future;[90] of necessity the actings relied on for this purpose must be at variance with the terms of the written contract, and they must be more compelling than those required to establish *rei interventus* or homologation.[91]

The distinction will be noticed between on the one hand a verbal agreement constituting a lease, which verbal agreement may be proved only by writ or oath, and on the other hand a verbal agreement altering the terms of a lease, which verbal agreement may in limited circumstances be proved by parole evidence. However, if the verbal agreement altering the terms of the original lease is of an unusual or innominate character, such as where a tenant averred that the landlord had promised on certain conditions to repay all money lost during the course of the lease, proof will be limited to writ or oath; this was not a case of alteration of a written contract by parole agreement, but the constitution of an original and independent agreement by parole.[92]

Proof of Reduction of Rent. Parole evidence has occasionally been admitted to prove a verbal agreement for a permanent reduction of rent. It was admitted in a case involving an alteration from a grain to a money rent supported by receipts for eleven years' rent inconsistent with the original lease.[93] Normally, however, if the evidence of the agreement is only parole, the actings relied upon can equally well be attributed to an abatement allowed from year to year as to a permanent reduction, and proof by parole evidence alone has been rejected in several cases.[94] A reduction in rent may be proved by a reference to the landlord's oath.[95] It may also be proved by informal writings followed by *rei interventus.* Thus a permanent reduction all over an estate has been established by a letter from the landlord to his factor acted on for a number of years.[96] However, the writ must clearly state that the reduction is to be permanent.[97] A return made by the landlord for valuation purposes is not conclusive of a permanent reduction of the rent specified in a lease.[98]

EXPENSES OF PREPARATION

In the absence of any arrangement to the contrary, the practice is for each party to pay his own solicitor's expenses for preparing the

[90] *Carron Co.* v *Henderson's Trs., supra, per* L.P. Robertson at p. 1053; Rankine. 113.
[91] Walker, *Evidence,* 307.
[92] *Garden* v *Earl of Aberdeen* (1893) 20 R. 896.
[93] *Baillie* v *Fraser* (1853) 15 D. 747.
[94] *Riddick* v *Wightman* (1790) Hume 776; *Grant* v *Watt* (1802) Hume 777; *Law* v *Gibsone* (1835) 13 S. 396; *Turnbull* v *Oliver* (1891) 19 R. 154.
[95] *Gibb* v *Winning* (1829) 7 S. 677.
[96] *Lindsay* v *Webster* (1841) 4 D. 231.
[97] *Dickson* v *Bell* (1899) 36 S.L.R. 343.
[98] *Rattray* v *Leslie's Tr.* (1892) 19 R. 853.

lease. The landlord pays for any plan. The cost of any search is borne by the party under obligation to produce it. Any stamp duty or recording dues are borne by the grantee.[99] The Cost of Leases Act 1958 provides that, notwithstanding any custom to the contrary, a party to a lease shall, unless the parties agree otherwise in writing, be under no obligation to pay the whole or any part of any other party's solicitor's costs of the lease;[1] a " lease " includes a sublease or an agreement for a tenancy or sub-tenancy, and " costs " includes fees, charges, disbursements (including stamp duty), expenses and remuneration.[2]

[99] Table of Fees for Conveyancing and General Business approved by The Council of the Law Society of Scotland, 1964, Chapter VI.
[1] Costs of Leases Act 1958, s. 1.
[2] Ibid., s. 2.

CHAPTER III

PROROGATION AND RENEWAL OF THE CONTRACT

It frequently happens that a tenant obtains a new lease of the same subjects on the same or similar conditions. When the transaction merely amounts to an extension of the period of the old lease without altering the other conditions and the new lease begins after the lapse of the old, the old lease is said to be prorogued; where the new lease begins before the lapse of the old or alterations are made in the rent or other conditions, the old lease is said to be renewed.[1] There is, however, no important distinction between prorogation and renewal, and the word "renewal" is commonly used for either transaction. In each case the substance of the transaction is a new lease entered into between the landlord and the sitting tenant.[2]

As between the tenant and the lessor or his representatives the main question that will arise is whether the new lease is validly constituted. Although the old lease may be used to explain the new one, the new lease must be constituted in accordance with the rules for the constitution of leases generally. Just as a lease may be set up by informal writings followed by *rei interventus,* so also may a lease be renewed or prorogued in that way.[3] A letter from the landlord to a liferent tenant binding himself at the end of the liferent lease to renew it in favour of the tenant's son at the first term of Whitsunday after its expiration was held binding on the lessor's representatives without proof of express acceptance.[4] A written obligation by an heir of entail in possession to accept a renunciation and to grant a new lease, followed by *rei interventus* and possession, was held to bind a succeeding heir of entail like any other singular successor.[5] In several cases continued payment of rent and possession following upon informally concluded negotiations for a renewal have been held to be ascribable to the new lease and not to tacit relocation on the old lease.[6] However, the landlord was not bound by negotiations for a renewal, where he had signed, but not delivered, the new lease, and the tenant had failed to pay a stipulated grassum.[7] And acts which would be *rei interventus* if referable to an alleged renewal may lose

---

[1] Ross, *Lectures,* 2nd ed., II, 500.
[2] Rankine, 148.
[3] *Barr* v *Turner* (1904) 12 S.L.T. 369; *Nairn Station Hotel Ltd.* v *Macpherson* (1905) 13 S.L.T. 456 (O.H.).
[4] *Wilson* v *Henderson* (1823) 2 S. 428 (380).
[5] *Campbeltown Coal Co.* v *Duke of Argyll,* 1925 S.C. 668.
[6] *M'Kenzie* v *M'Kenzie* (1799) Hume 801; *Sutherland's Tr.* v *Miller's Tr.* (1888) 16 R. 10; *Buchanan* v *Harris and Sheldon* (1900) 2 F. 935; *Macfarlane* v *Mitchell* (1900) 2 F. 901.
[7] *Hamilton* v *Duke of Queensberry's Exrs.* (1833) 12 S. 206.

their value if they take place during the currency of the old lease.[8] If, however, a personal contract of renewal is instructed, and cannot be enforced against a singular successor, the granter and his representatives will be liable in damages.[9]

The question may arise whether the new lease and the old lease, taken together, are to be regarded as a single lease or as two separate contracts. This will depend on the circumstances and particularly on the date on which the agreement for prorogation or renewal was made. Where parties executed on the same day a two years' lease of shootings and also an agreement for a lease of ten years of the same subjects to commence at the expiry of the first, it was thought that the two contracts stood on a different footing and did not together constitute one lease for twelve years, and it was questioned whether the prorogation of a lease during its currency was effectual against a singular successor of the granter.[10]

Questions with singular successors of the landlord may arise from the rule that possession is necessary to complete the real right of the tenant.[11]

Options to Renew. A lease may contain a clause giving the tenant an option to renew the lease on its expiry. Strictly speaking, this is a right of prorogation,[12] but it is normally called a right of renewal. Such an option must be exercised by the tenant before the expiry of the lease.[13] Where a landlord let premises to a tenant for twenty years under a lease providing that the tenant should have the option of renewing the lease from time to time on the same terms, if he so desired, the lease expired without the option being exercised by the tenant, who remained in occupation; it was held that after the expiry of the lease a tenancy had continued from year to year by tacit relocation, that one of the implied terms of tacit relocation was that either party could terminate the lease at the end of the year by giving notice, and that accordingly the tenant's option to renew the lease for 20 years had flown off, being quite inconsistent with the right of the landlord under a lease from year to year.[14]

[8] *Brown* v *Ogilvie* (1822) 1 S. 316.
[9] Rankine, 149.
[10] *Birkbeck* v *Ross* (1865) 4 M. 272 *per* Lord Barcaple (L.O.) at p. 276.
[11] *Infra,* p. 112.
[12] Rankine, 148.
[13] *Commercial Union Assurance Co. and Others,* 1964 S.L.T. 62.
[14] *Ibid. per* L.P. Clyde at p. 63.

CHAPTER IV

PARTIES TO THE CONTRACT

General. The granter of a normal lease is the proprietor or landlord, who is often called the lessor; the grantee becomes the tenant, often called the lessee. As a general rule the granter must be the proprietor of the subjects let, but he may be an administrator for the proprietor such as an attorney or factor, in which case his right to grant a lease is generally measured solely by the terms of his written mandate. Again, the granter of the lease may be proprietor only in a limited sense such as a trustee, liferenter, bondholder in possession, etc. Generally, at common law a lease by a limited owner ended with his ownership, but there are now many exceptions to this rule. A person, who is himself a tenant, may by granting a sublease become a lessor with the rights and duties of a landlord in relation to the subtenant; again, the subtenant may grant a further sublease in favour of another party and so on. However, although the granter of a sublease is not himself the proprietor of the subjects, he derives his right ultimately from the proprietor. The same person may therefore be both a tenant in relation to his landlord and a landlord in relation to his tenant.

A lease is a contract and the general rules governing capacity to contract apply to leases. In this chapter we shall consider the capacity to contract of, and the disabilities affecting, various types of person with particular reference to the contract of lease.

GRANTERS

Title. The granter of a lease must be either the proprietor of the subjects let, or one who is entitled to the full use and possession of the subjects, such as a liferenter, or one who is entitled to administer the subjects, such as a trustee.[1] In the case of a lease which happens to be a sublease, the sublessor is one who is entitled to the full use and possession of the subjects by virtue of a lease granted by the proprietor in his favour. The right to grant a lease flows from ownership.

By accepting a lease the lessee *prima facie* acknowledges the lessor's right to grant it, and this may debar him from maintaining that the granter is not the proprietor.[2] " It is a universally true proposition that a tenant accepting a lease from anyone cannot challenge the title of his

---

[1] Bell § 1181.
[2] *Eliott's Trs.* v *Eliott* (1894) 21 R. 858; *Cunninghame* v *Assessor for Ayrshire* (1895) 22 R. 596; *Sinclair* v *Hughes,* 1954 S.L.T. (Sh. Ct.) 64.

landlord ".[3] This, however, does not prevent a tenant from showing that he is not bound by a lease which does not bind the true proprietor.[4]

An action of damages may lie against someone who has leased subjects to which he has no right or title in respect of loss or injury caused by the tenant's operations, as where a superior wrongfully let minerals, the working of which caused damage to the surface.[5]

Infeftment. The proper title of the granter of a lease who is proprietor of the subjects is his infeftment,[6] and he is usually referred to as " heritable proprietor ". Where the granter is not infeft, it has been said that the lease does not confer an effectual or permanent right, though it might be made perfect by the granter's subsequent infeftment, provided no mid-impediment has intervened.[6] If the lessor's title, though unimpeached at the time of the lease being granted, is reduced later, the lessee's title will fall with it. Thus a lease granted by trustees was reduced, where the trust deed under which they acted was reduced.[7] If the lessor's title was never more than inchoate, a lease granted by him will fall when his own title is reduced. Thus a lease by the purchaser of subjects under missives, which were later reduced, was not an effectual contract and could not be enforced against the lessee.[8] Before a landlord can enforce a lease there must be combined in his person two elements, namely, the real right to the lands and the personal obligation to grant the lease or to enforce it.[9] It follows that a lease by someone whose title is bad is invalid, and can not even be cured by being assigned by him to the true owner. Thus, where the title of a *bona fide* possessor of land, although *ex facie* regular and completed by infeftment, was reduced by the true owner during the currency of a lease and he assigned the lease to the true owner, it was held by a majority that the assignation was of no effect as the granter had nothing to assign; and it was observed that the rule which precludes a lessee from impugning the title of the lessor applies only when the lessee in a question with the lessor is maintaining some right or claiming some benefit under or in respect of the lease, not when he is renouncing or repudiating it.[10] From the two cases just referred to it will be observed that a lease granted by a person whose title is bad may be impugned not only by the person claiming to be proprietor but also by the lessee, and that such a lease not binding on the true owner cannot be homologated by him.

It may be asked how far the mere lack of infeftment of the granter affects the validity of a lease. Infeftment is said to be the " proper "

---

[3] *Reid's Tr.* v *Watson's Trs.* (1896) 23 R. 636 *per* Lord Young at p. 643.
[4] *Reid's Tr.* v *Watson's Trs., supra.*
[5] *Thomson* v *Wilson's Trs.* (1895) 22 R. 866.
[6] Bell § 1181.
[7] *Macniven* v *Murray* (1847) 9 D. 1138.
[8] *Weir* v *Dunlop & Co.* (1861) 23 D. 1293 (the rubric is inaccurate).
[9] *Ibid., per* L.J.C. Inglis at p. 1298.
[10] *Reid's Tr.* v *Watson's Trs.* (1896) 23 R. 636 (diss. Lord Young).

title of the granter,[6] but is it essential? If the granter of a lease is the true proprietor, but is not infeft, there is no doubt that the lease which he has granted will be validated *accretione* in the event of the proprietor completing his title by infeftment. Thus where a proprietor who was uninfeft granted a tack, and later after becoming infeft granted a disposition, the right of the tacksman was by the operation of accretion preferred to that of the disponee.[11] In the same position would be someone having right by a personal title which he can make real by expeding a notice of title in his favour under the Conveyancing (Scotland) Act 1924,[12] (including a beneficiary nominated by executors under the Succession (Scotland) Act 1964)[13] or even someone having only a personal right such as an unserved heir under the Conveyancing (Scotland) Act 1874.[14] There can be little doubt that a lease granted by a purchaser under missives, whose title is subsequently completed and is not challenged, is perfectly valid. Accretion cannot be pleaded by the lessee if the subjects let by an uninfeft proprietor have been acquired by someone who does not represent the true owner, such as a purchaser from a former infeft owner or a creditor of a former infeft owner adjudging his debtor's land, or a fiar at the termination of the granter's liferent. An executor is *eadem persona cum defuncto* and therefore cannot repudiate a lease granted by the deceased while uninfeft, but it is said that a mid-impediment may occur to interrupt the operation of accretion; the lessor may die or become bankrupt before taking infeftment in the subjects and the right of the lessee may be defeated by a singular successor or a trustee in bankruptcy or anyone not bound to represent the lessor.[15] However, in all those cases it is perhaps not so much the lack of infeftment which might destroy the lease, but a defect in the granter's right of ownership which, though perhaps unimpeached at the time of granting the lease, is nevertheless impeachable for some reason.

What happens if a lease is granted by an uninfeft proprietor and is capable of being validated *accretione* by the granter's subsequent infeftment, but the granter does not in fact become infeft? An uninfeft proprietor has no real right himself and so cannot confer one upon his lessee. The lease is contractually binding upon the granter and his personal representatives, as they take his estate subject to the obligations incumbent on him. However, a singular successor, such as a purchaser or someone adjudicating the landlord's interest, is in a different position.[16] He acquires a real right, and so is bound to recognise only the real rights

[11] *Neilson* v *Menzies* (1671) Mor. 7768.
[12] s. 4.
[13] s. 15 (2).
[14] s. 9.
[15] Bell § 1181; Rankine, 47-48; *Encyclopaedia of the Laws of Scotland,* Vol. 9, 154.
[16] See Chapter VII.

of others. Thus, while an uninfeft proprietor can grant a valid lease, it will not be good against a singular successor.[17]

Conversely, mere infefment of the granter does not protect the lease if the granter's title is reduced.

Limited Title. A lease binding on singular successors may be granted not only by the absolute proprietor, but by one having a limited title. A proprietor's right to lease his heritage remains unaffected by his granting a bond and disposition in security, as the fee is still with the proprietor. Nothing short of a real transference of title will deprive the proprietor of his right to grant a lease, which will be valid in questions with third parties acting in good faith, unless the lease amounts to an alienation of the subjects or is not granted in the ordinary course of administration.[18]

Effect of Diligence, Insolvency, etc. An inhibition, the purpose of which is to prevent the owner of heritage from alienating it or burdening it with debt to the prejudice of the inhibiting creditor, does not affect a lease granted after the inhibition in ordinary course for a fair rent and normal duration. Where, however, a lease is granted for a grassum in place of a rent, or for an inadequate rent or for an unusually long duration or gives unusually extensive rights to the tenant, it may amount to an alienation and so be struck at by an inhibition.[19] Similarly, an action of adjudication, the purpose of which is to attack heritable property for debt, may render the subjects litigious and prevent future voluntary alienations, but it will not affect a lease granted in ordinary course for a fair rent and normal duration.[20]

Insolvency of the granter of a lease does not affect its validity if the lease is granted in ordinary course, unless it is challengeable either as an illegal preference under the Bankruptcy Act 1696, or as a gratuitous alienation under the Bankruptcy Act 1621, such as a lease made by a father in the knowledge of his insolvency to his son for an inadequate rent.[21] Similarly, the subsequent sequestration of the granter does not affect the validity of a fair and just lease already granted by him. However, as the administration of a bankrupt's affairs passes on his sequestration to his trustee, a lease cannot be granted by the owner after the date of the first deliverance. A trustee in sequestration who takes possession of the heritable estate of the landlord renders himself liable to implement the conditions of the lease at least to the extent of the rents received by him,[22] and he will be bound by an agreement

---

[17] *Ritchie* v *Scott* (1899) 1 F. 728, discussed *infra*, p. 53.
[18] *Encyclopaedia of the Laws of Scotland,* Vol. 9, 154.
[19] Rankine, 51.
[20] Rankine, 51-52.
[21] *Gorrie's Trs.* v *Gorrie* (1890) 17 R. 1051.
[22] *Harvie* v *Haldane* (1833) 11 S. 872.

made by the landlord in ordinary course such as an agreement for abatement of rent.[23] A trust deed for creditors, duly intimated, divests its granter of his whole estate for the purposes of the trust, and he cannot thereafter grant a valid lease, except in so far as he does so with the concurrence of the trustee. Decree in an action of maills and duties transfers to a heritable creditor the right to grant leases of the security subjects, and after the decree the debtor cannot grant a valid lease.[24]

Particular Granters—Trustees. The powers of trustees have not been strictly defined. In the first instance, they will have such powers as may have been expressly or impliedly conferred on them by the trust deed. If no such power is conferred on them, it is clear that at common law they are entitled to perform ordinary, necessary acts of administration, and that the granting of a lease of ordinary duration is an act of normal trust administration.[25] There is the possibility of defeasance in the event of the trust coming to an end before the stipulated ish.[26] By statute trustees are empowered to grant leases of any duration (including mineral leases) of the heritable estate or any part thereof and to remove tenants, provided that such acts are not at variance with the terms of the trust deed.[27] They may also make abatement or reduction, either temporary or permanent, of the rent or other consideration stipulated in any lease and accept renunciations of leases.[28] Trustees are not entitled to use their statutory powers should these powers tend to defeat or confuse the purposes of the trust, and their statutory power of granting leases may be restricted by implication. A prohibition against selling or disposing of the trust estate was held to preclude trustees from granting a lease for 99 years, even although the lease was on terms advantageous to the trust.[29] Whereas there is no limit to the duration of a lease which trustees are empowered by statute to grant, it may be at variance with the terms and purposes of the trust to grant a lease for a term longer than the duration of their own office, if they are to hand over the estate to the fiar on the death of a liferenter. On the other hand, a lease for 999 years was held to be properly granted, as it was not at variance with the terms and purposes of the trust.[30]

In the case of minerals a distinction is made between mines worked or let in the testator's lifetime on the one hand and mines opened after his death on the other. As a general rule, trustees are presumed to have

[23] *Lindsay* v *Webster* (1841) 4 D. 231.
[24] Bell § 1185.
[25] McLaren, *Wills and Succession,* 3rd ed., II, 1181 § 2194.
[26] Rankine, 41.
[27] Trusts (Scotland) Act 1921 s. 4.
[28] *Ibid.*
[29] *Petrie's Trs.* v *Ramsay* (1868) 7 M. 64.
[30] *Birkmyre* (1881) 8 R. 477.

power to grant leases only of minerals worked at the commencement of the trust; but where the intention of the truster is clearly to treat his land as a mineral estate, then the trustees are presumed to have power to let unworked minerals.[31] The distinction is based on the fact that a lease of minerals is really equivalent to a sale. Thus an express power of sale will normally imply power to grant a mineral lease.[32]

Even if a transaction such as the granting of a lease should be at variance with the terms and purposes of the trust, it is provided that the Court of Session may on the petition of the trustees under any trust other than one constituted by Act of Parliament authorise them to grant the lease on the Court being satisfied that such an act is expedient for the execution of the trust.[33] Further, where trustees have entered into a transaction permitted by the Trusts (Scotland) Act 1921, such as the grant of a lease, the validity of such a lease is not challengeable by the lessee or any other person on the ground that it is at variance with the terms and purposes of the trust, provided that, where the trustees are acting under the supervision of the Accountant of Court, his approval is obtained.[34] The effect of this is that the need for a petition under the 1921 Act[33] is now largely obviated. The right of a beneficiary to raise an action against a trustee in respect that such a lease is a breach of trust is, however, not affected,[35] and such a petition may sometimes be advisable for the protection of the trustees.

For the purpose of the statutory powers of trustees, the term " trustee " includes *inter alia* any trustee under any trust, whether nominated, appointed, judicially or otherwise, or assumed, whether sole or joint, and whether entitled or not to any benefit under the trust or remuneration for his services, and includes any trustee *ex officio*, executor nominate and executor dative.[36]

Tutors, Curators, Judicial Factors, Etc. The definition of " trustee " also includes any tutor, curator, and judicial factor.[37] " Judicial factor " means any person holding a judicial appointment as a factor or curator on another person's estate.[38] Both a father as tutor at common law and a mother as tutrix under the Guardianship of Infants Act 1886 of a pupil child come within the definition of " trustee ".[39] Judicial factors act under the supervision of the Accountant of Court. All those persons have the same statutory power as trustees to grant leases of any

---

[31] *Wardlaw* v *Campbell* (1883) 10 R. (H.L.) 65; *Dick's Trs.* v *Robertson* (1901) 3 F. 1021; *Ranken's Trs.* v *Ranken,* 1908 S.C. 3; *Naismith's Trs.* v *Naismith,* 1909 S.C. 1380.
[32] *Naismith's Trs.* v *Naismith, supra.*
[33] Trusts (Scotland) Act 1921, s. 5.
[34] Trusts (Scotland) Act 1961, s. 2.
[35] *Ibid.*
[36] Trusts (Scotland) Act 1921, s. 2; Succession (Scotland) Act 1964 s. 20.
[37] Trusts (Scotland) Act 1921 s. 2.
[38] Trusts (Scotland) Act 1921 s. 2, as amended by Trusts (Scotland) Act 1961 s. 3.
[39] Guardianship of Infants Acts 1925 s. 10.

duration, but, as in the case of trustees, the question whether the exercise of such powers, including the granting of a lease, is or is not at variance with the terms and purposes of the trust must always be considered.[40] Although there may be no trust deed, the terms and purposes of a person's appointment may be ascertained from the circumstances.[41] Whether a tutor, curator or judicial factor may at his own hand grant a lease for a period longer than the duration of his own office will depend on the circumstances, the nature of the property, and the interests of the ward.[42] For example, the tutor of a pupil child wishing to grant a lease of his ward's property to endure beyond the ward's attainment of age may feel it prudent to seek special power,[43] but on the analogy of the case cited such a petition may be dismissed as unnecessary.[44] However, so far as the lessee and persons other than the ward are concerned, it is unnecessary to obtain special power if the consent of the Accountant of Court is obtained.[45]

In the case of agricultural holdings special power is given to the Sheriff to appoint a tutor, curator or other guardian to a landlord or tenant who is a pupil or minor or is of unsound mind.[46]

Pupils and Minors. A pupil has no power to contract, and his tutor or tutrix would grant a lease on his behalf.

A minor with curator would grant a lease with his curator's consent; a lease without the curator's consent would be void. Whether he has a curator or not, a minor is not entitled to dispose of his heritage gratuitously, although he may dispose of it by will;[47] and possibly a long lease amounting to an alienation of his property without adequate consideration would be void.

In all cases leases granted by or on behalf of pupils and minors would be voidable until the expiry of the *quadriennium utile* on proof of lesion.

Liferenter. In modern times heritage held for the liferent of some person is normally held by trustees, who would grant any necessary leases and account to the liferenter for the rents. However, it sometimes happens that trust machinery is not employed, and the liferenter is in possession having taken infeftment in favour of himself in liferent and in favour of another in fee. Such a liferent is known as a " proper liferent " and any leases are granted by the liferenter.[48] A proper liferenter's feudal title should be complete either by virtue of his original infeftment in the case of a liferent created by reservation to himself or

---

[40] *Leslie's J.F.,* 1925 S.C. 464.
[41] *Ibid.*
[42] *Douglas* (1867) 6 M. 178.
[43] Under Trusts (Scotland) Act 1921 s. 5.
[44] *Cunningham's Tutrix,* 1949 S.C. 275.
[45] Trusts (Scotland) Act 1961 s. 2.
[46] Agricultural Holdings (Scotland) Act 1949 s. 84.
[47] Succession (Scotland) Act 1964 s. 28.
[48] See *Miller* v *Inland Revenue* 1928 S.C. 819 *per* Lord Sands at p. 837.

4

by infeftment if it is a liferent created by someone else in his favour.[49] Even where there is trust machinery, a liferenter may be empowered by the trust deed to grant leases. A proper liferent whether created by reservation or constitution may be created in a deed which defines the power of the liferenter to grant leases. In the absence of such express power the liferenter is entitled to let the lands for the duration of his own life, and a lease of land for a period of years granted by him subsists until the term of Whitsunday following his death.[50] Even a liferenter by reservation has no power to grant a lease to be effective beyond his own lifetime.[51] If he wishes to let for a fixed term which may outlast his own life, he must obtain the consent of the fiar.[52] Where a widow was given the liferent of a landed estate " with absolute control and management " thereof and " without any interference from the heir ", it was held that her power of leasing was no greater than that of an ordinary liferenter, and that she could not grant agricultural leases of nineteen years.[53]

As a liferenter's right is purely usufructuary, difficulties arise where the subjects of the liferent include timber or minerals. A liferenter is entitled to windfalls and ripe wood, but cannot normally grant a lease conferring a right to the tenant to cut growing timber except for some purpose essential to good management of the estate.[54] Like a trustee, a liferenter may have the right to work or let a mine in operation at the beginning of his liferent, but is presumed not to be entitled to open a new mine or let the minerals of an unopened mine.[55]

Fiduciary Fiar. A fiduciary fiar may apply to the Court of Session for any of the powers competent to trustees at common law or under the Trusts (Scotland) Act 1921, or he may apply for the appointment of trustees to administer the property.[56] A fiduciary fiar with such power, or the trustees so appointed, may thus grant leases to the same extent as ordinary trustees.[57]

Fiar. A fiar of trust property subject to a direct liferent cannot grant an effectual lease without the consent of the liferenter,[58] but there would be no objection to a lease to take effect after the liferenter's death. If the liferenter is not yet in immediate enjoyment, as in the case of a provision granted in a marriage contract by a husband to a

[49] Bell § 1181; *Miller* v *Inland Revenue*, 1930 S.C. (H.L.) 49, *per* Lord Dunedin at p. 56.
[50] *Thomson* v *Merston* (1628) Mor. 8252; Bell § 1183; Rankine, 79.
[51] *Fraser* v *Middleton* (1794) Mor. 8256.
[52] Bell § 1057.
[53] *Fraser* v *Croft* (1898) 25 R. 496.
[54] Rankine, 80.
[55] *Wardlaw* v *Campbell* (1882) 9 R. 725, (1883) 10 R. (H.L.) 65; see *supra*, p. 47.
[56] Trusts (Scotland) Act 1921 s. 8.
[57] *Encyclopaedia of the Laws of Scotland*, Vol. 9, 161.
[58] Rankine, 78.

wife to take effect only on the husband's death, the latter is not restricted in his power of leasing.[59] And any leases granted by the husband will continue in force notwithstanding his own death and the beginning of his wife's liferent.[60] But it is essential to the validity of such leases that they are granted *in bona fide*, and the wife's eventual liferent is not affected by leases which are not acts of ordinary administration or are granted to defraud her of her rights.[61]

Debtor under Bond and Disposition in Security. The normal form of bond and disposition in security leaves the granter with full powers of ordinary administration, so long as he is not in default. His right to grant leases may be restricted in a back letter, but, apart from any such limitation, he has power to grant ordinary leases which will bind the bondholder.[62] He may grant mineral leases. However, the creditor is not bound by a lease granted by the debtor which is not an act of ordinary administration, such as a lease of minerals of long duration and containing exceptional clauses which viewed together are unfairly favourable to the tenant and so impair the bondholder's security.[63] Nor is the bondholder bound by an agreement between the proprietor and the tenant restricting the use to be made of other subjects.[64] The creditor has a right to reduce any lease subsequently granted which impinges on his security.[65]

Bondholder in Possession. By the Heritable Securities (Scotland) Act 1894 a creditor in possession may at his own hand grant leases of the security subjects or part thereof for a period of not more than seven years.[66] Also the Sheriff of the county may empower a creditor in possession to lease the subjects for more than seven years, but not more than twenty-one years for property in general and thirty-one years for minerals. The application to the Sheriff must set forth the name of the proposed tenant, the duration and conditions of the proposed lease, and the Act provides for service of the application on the proprietor of the security subjects and for such other intimation and enquiry as the Sheriff may think proper. If satisfied that a lease for a longer duration than seven years is expedient the Sheriff may approve the lease on the terms and conditions proposed or on such modified conditions as may appear to him to be expedient.[67]

---

[59] *Ibid.*
[60] *Countess of Moray* v *Stewart* (1772) Mor. 4392, 2 Pat. 317; Rankine, 78.
[61] *Laing* v *Denny* (1827) 5 S. 903; Rankine, 78 and other cases cited there.
[62] *Edinburgh Entertainments Ltd.* v *Stevenson*, 1926 S.C. 363 (*ex facie* absolute disposition).
[63] *Reid* v *M'Gill*, 1912 2 S.L.T. 246.
[64] *Mackenzie* v *Imlay's Trs.*, 1912 S.C. 685.
[65] *Edinburgh Entertainments Ltd.* v *Stevenson*, *supra*.
[66] s. 6.
[67] s. 7.

If the creditor is in possession with the consent of the debtor, he need not raise an action of maills and duties to take advantage of those statutory provisions.[68] A heritable creditor in possession is not precluded from granting a lease of one part of the security subjects which conflicts with the provisions of a lease of another part, granted by the debtor while he was still in possession.[69]

It may be noted that while the Act gives to a creditor wishing to obtain possession a summary remedy for removing a proprietor in personal occupation of the property,[70] and that this remedy extends to removing a person in occupation by the mere permission of the proprietor,[71] it gives no right to the creditor to remove tenants, with whom his only remedy is the action of maills and duties raised against the debtor.[72]

Ex Facie Absolute Disposition. In the transaction of loan effected by means of the *ex facie* absolute disposition the creditor receives a disposition or other conveyance of the security subjects granted by or with the consent of the debtor. This disposition will be recorded by the creditor in the Register of Sasines with the result that in questions with third parties not having notice of the nature of the transaction the creditor is *ex facie* the absolute proprietor of the subjects. The true position is revealed by a minute of agreement, personal bond or other form of back letter, either bilateral or unilateral, containing *inter alia* an obligation by the creditor to reconvey the subjects to the debtor on repayment of the loan. This back letter is not normally recorded and therefore does not affect third parties not having notice of it, although as between debtor and creditor it may regulate the right of either of them to grant leases.

Lease by Granter of Ex Facie Absolute Disposition. Normally the debtor is left in possession of the security subjects either by express provision in the back letter or by the tacit consent of the creditor. In these circumstances the power of the debtor to grant leases appears from the reported cases to depend partly on whether or not he was himself infeft before the disposition in favour of the creditor was granted, and partly whether the debtor had any mandate from the creditor to grant leases. In one case, A, who was the infeft proprietor of certain subjects, conveyed them to B by an *ex facie* absolute disposition, qualified by an unrecorded back letter, which declared that if A failed to repay a loan, B should have full right of property in the subjects. A, who remained in possession, later granted a lease. The lease was held to be

[68] *Mackenzie* v *Imlay's Trs.,* 1912 S.C. 685.
[69] *Ibid.*
[70] Heritable Securities (Scotland) Act 1894 s. 5.
[71] *Inglis' Trs.* v *Macpherson,* 1911 2 S.L.T. 176.
[72] Heritable Securities (Scotland) Act 1894 s. 3.

valid on the ground that the fact that A had been allowed to remain in possession implied a mandate from the *ex facie* absolute disponee to A to grant a lease.[73] It has been said that that decision might equally well have been reached on the ground that the debtor's original infeftment entitled him to grant a lease. "The principle is that a security in this form, being merely a security after all in substance, although in form a disposition absolute, does not divest the granter even feudally, and he is therefore in a position to deal with his own estate by virtue of his own original title, and requires no other right or authority, so long as he leaves his creditor's security unimpaired."[74] In similar circumstance a lease granted by a debtor originally infeft was upheld on the grounds (a) that the lease was not reducible merely because A had divested himself and that the back letter was not recorded, (b) that in virtue of the radical right remaining in him, A had power to grant leases, provided he did not depreciate B's security, and (c) that, in any event, A had an implied mandate from the creditor to grant leases, and that the mandate had not been recalled or exceeded.[75] It has been observed that such an implied mandate is personal to the debtor and is not transmissible, for example, to a trustee for his creditors.[76]

The commonest case nowadays is where A purchases subjects with the aid of a loan from B, who receives a disposition in his favour granted by the seller with A's consent. In these circumstances A, not having been infeft, has no radical or reversionary right to the property, and his ability to grant leases may depend on his having an implied mandate from the creditor to do so. In *Ritchie* v *Scott*[77] A remained in possession for some years and then granted a trust deed for creditors. Subsequently with the concurrence of his trustee he granted a lease of part of the security subjects. In an action at the instance of B, the lease was reduced on the grounds that any implied mandate by the creditor came to an end on the granting of a trust deed and that the debtor never having been infeft in the subjects had no right or title to grant the lease. Lord Kinnear remarked, "The difference between a debtor infeft, who dispones his estate to creditors by an absolute disposition but really in security, and that of the defender, who had never had at any time a right of property in the subjects, is very material indeed."[78] His remarks have since received approval, but in a case where the lessor had been infeft originally, and it was his remarks in support of a lease granted by such a lessor which received particular approval.[79]

The position of a lease by a debtor, not originally infeft, who has consented to an *ex facie* absolute disposition is not at all clear. Accord-

---

[73] *Abbot* v *Mitchell* (1870) 8 M. 791.
[74] *Ritchie* v *Scott* (1899) 1 F. 728 *per* Lord Kinnear at p. 736.
[75] *Edinburgh Entertainments Ltd.* v *Stevenson*, 1926 S.C. 363.
[76] *Ritchie* v *Scott, supra, per* Lord Kinnear at p. 735.
[77] *Supra.*
[78] *Ibid., per* Lord Kinnear at p. 736.
[79] *Edinburgh Entertainments Ltd.* v *Stevenson, supra.*

ing to Lord Kinnear's *dictum* in *Ritchie* v *Scott,* the granter of an *ex facie* absolute disposition qualified by an unrecorded back letter retains a perfectly valid and sufficient title to dispose of the property in any way, provided he does not impair the security. A security in this form, being merely a security in substance, does not even divest the granter feudally, and he is therefore in a position to deal with his property by virtue of his own original title; and his original infeftment is his title to grant a lease. So far, few would quarrel with this view, but Lord Kinnear went on to say that the right to deal with the estate in this way depends entirely on the original title on which the security is merely a burden, and therefore the doctrine will not support a lease granted by a purchaser, who merely consented to an *ex facie* absolute disposition being granted to the creditor, and who had no original title, but merely a *jus crediti.*

Probably the principle to be deduced from the cases[80] is that whether or not the debtor was originally infeft in the security subjects before they were conveyed to the creditor, if the creditor leaves the debtor in possession, then he holds him out as proprietor and gives him a mandate, either express or implied, to grant leases, which will hold good against the creditor.[81] If the tenant does not know the true position and accepts the lease in good faith, he is safe against challenge by the creditor or his singular successors, provided that the lease satisfies the requirements for conferring a real right on him.[82] However, the mandate is personal to the debtor and is not assignable;[83] and such a mandate is revocable, apparently even verbally.[84] The creditor is entitled to challenge a lease granted by the debtor, if its terms are outwith the scope of the mandate and so diminish the value of the creditor's security, but a lease of a shop for twenty-five years has been held to be an act of ordinary administration.[85] In practice, the creditor will ensure that the power of the debtor to grant leases, if allowed at all, is limited.

Where a proprietor grants a lease and subsequently conveys the property by *ex facie* absolute disposition, that of course does not impair the lease; nor does it of itself affect the proprietor's title to sue in a removing.[86]

Lease by Ex Facie Absolute Disponee. So far as third parties are concerned, if the back letter is not recorded, the creditor is the infeft proprietor, and as such he may grant a valid lease to anyone who takes it

[80] For a discussion of the cases on the legal effect of an *ex facie* absolute disposition see Professor J. M. Halliday, "The *Ex Facie* Absolute Disposition", in I *Conv. Rev.,* 5.
[81] Burns, *Conveyancing Practice,* 4th ed., 487.
[82] *Infra,* p. 104.
[83] *Ritchie* v *Scott* (1899) 1 F. 728.
[84] Burns, *Conveyancing Practice,* 4th ed., 487.
[85] *Edinburgh Entertainments Ltd.* v *Stevenson,* 1926 S.C. 363.
[86] *Infra,* p. 254.

in good faith. The position between debtor and creditor is regulated by the back letter, and therefore the creditor will not normally be able to grant a lease until he has taken possession on the debtor's default. Where a debtor who had granted an *ex facie* absolute disposition was left in possession after his sequestration, it was held that in the circumstances of the case he had lost his radical right of ownership and had become a tenant of the creditor.[87]

Heir of Entail.[88] In the absence of express provision in the deed of entail, an heir of entail in possession may grant leases of ordinary duration. If he exceeds his power, there is an illegal alienation of the entailed estate and the lease is voidable. The Montgomery Act,[89] Rosebery Act,[90] and Rutherford Act,[91] and Entail Amendment Act 1882 all contain provisions as to leases which may be granted by an heir of entail in possession. Generally, such a lease may be granted at a fair rent for a period not exceeding twenty-one years of agricultural lands, and thirty-one years of minerals. A grassum is incompetent. A lease of a mansion-house, or policies, or of the home farm of an estate may not be granted for a period beyond the lifetime of the granter.[92] However, a lease of the mansion-house, offices, gardens and policies granted by an heir of entail in possession continues until the next term of Whitsunday or Martinmas occurring not less than three months after his death; the rent from the date of death to the termination is payable to the succeeding heir.[93] A lease of shootings over an entailed estate has been held to be ineffectual after the death of the granter, but this conclusion may have been reached as much upon a consideration of the Leases Act 1449 as upon any other ground.[94] The general rule of law with regard to a permissible lease of land subject to the fetters of an entail is that the period must not be excessive, the rent must be fair, and a grassum must not be taken. If this rule is contravened in any particular, the lease will be reducible at the instance of a subsequent heir of entail.[95]

Questions have arisen as to whether obligations in leases, or agreements relative thereto, undertaken by an heir of entail are binding on subsequent heirs of entail, or only on the personal representatives of the granter. If improvement obligations are such as could have been charged by the granter on the entailed lands, the subsequent heirs of entail are

---

[87] *Paton* v *Turnbull* (1875) 12 S.L.R. 383.
[88] As entails are relatively unimportant in modern times, the following paragraphs are adapted from *Encyclopaedia of the Laws of Scotland,* Vol. 9, 164-165. Reference is made generally to Rankine, 54-78.
[89] Entail Improvement Act 1770.
[90] Entail Powers Act 1836.
[91] Entail Amendment Act 1848.
[92] Entail Powers Act 1836 s. 1.
[93] Entail (Scotland) Act 1914 s. 6.
[94] *Pollock Gilmour & Co.* v *Harvey* (1828) 6 S. 913; *Birkbeck* v *Ross* (1865) 4 M. 272; see *infra,* p. 105.
[95] Statutes cited *supra.*

liable to implement the obligations.[96] On the other hand, such obligations as could not have been charged on the entailed lands by the granter when the obligations became prestable, had the granter survived till then, are not enforceable against a succeeding heir in possession, but will be enforceable against the personal representatives of the granter of the obligations.[97] The distinction is illustrated in certain sheep stock cases.[98]

Joint Proprietors. All the joint or *pro indiviso* proprietors of heritable property must concur in the granting of a lease thereof.[99] Thus, while one of two owners of land might shoot over it himself or allow a third party to shoot over it, it was held that he was not entitled to grant to a third party a lease of the shootings for a rent.[1] Where one only of two *pro indiviso* proprietors bears to grant a lease there is no room for the operation of *rei interventus* against the other proprietor who has not been a party to the letting.[2] Similarly all proprietors must concur in sequestration for rent or in an action of removing.[3]

If one of several *pro indiviso* proprietors of subjects let grants a bond and disposition in security embracing his share, the bondholder may recover by an action of maills and duties the debtor's proportion of the rent, if the tenant and co-proprietors consent, and the debtor has no title to object, as that would be in derogation of his own assignation of the rents.[4] It appears that a tenant cannot be compelled to pay his rent in fractions to several proprietors, and that one such proprietor is not entitled to sue for the whole rent or any part of it without the consent of his co-proprietors.[5]

The distinction between joint property and common property has been discussed in a case involving a lease granted by two burghs of property owned by them in common.[6]

Attorneys, Factors, Commissioners, etc. The powers of factors, attorneys and other agents depend wholly on the scope of their mandates, which should be in writing, as gathered from the deed itself or by necessary implication according to the general rules of agency.[7] Thus a commission to " input and output " tenants empowers the commissioner to grant leases and there is no implied restriction to leases for

---

[96] Entail Amendment (Scotland) Act 1878 ss. 1 and 2.
[97] *Ibid.*
[98] *Gardiners* v *Stewart's Trs.,* 1908 S.C. 985; *Gillespie* v *Riddell,* 1909 S.C. (H.L.) 3; *Riddell's Exrs.* v *Milligan's Exrs.,* 1909 S.C. 1137.
[99] *Campbell* v *Campbell* 24 Jan. 1809 F.C.; *Higgins* v *Lanarkshire Assessor,* 1911 S.C. 931.
[1] *Campbell* v *Campbell, supra.*
[2] *Barr* v *Turner* (1904) 12 S.L.T. 369 (O.H.).
[3] *Infra,* pp. 215 and 256.
[4] *Schaw* v *Black* (1889) 16 R. 336.
[5] *Ibid., per* Lords Kinnear and Shand.
[6] *Mags. of Banff* v *Ruthin Castle Ltd.,* 1944 S.C. 36.
[7] Rankine, 45.

one year only; but power to "output" covers only removings.[8] The
duration of a lease granted by a commissioner is not limited by the
endurance of the commission.[9] The power to grant leases, of course,
falls with the termination of the factory, but it may be advisable to
intimate its termination to the parties concerned.[10]

It is doubtful whether a factor can without express power grant a
lease.[11] It has been decided that a solicitor, even though he may be
employed to collect the rents and to attend to the repairs of a property,
has no general authority to grant leases on behalf of his client, and that
the existence of such an authority must be proved by the person founding on it;[12] thus a landlord was held to be entitled to refuse to implement
a contract of lease concluded between his solicitors and the tenant's
solicitors.[13] Parole evidence is admissible to determine the scope of an
agent's authority to grant a lease.[14] The onus of proving that an agent
has power to insert a particular condition in a lease prepared by him
lies on the person alleging that he is so empowered.[15]

A factor having general power to grant a lease is presumed to have
power to alter or modify its terms.[16] Although parole evidence may be
let in to prove an agent's authority to abate rent, the actual agreement
of abatement must be by the agent's writ.[17]

Companies, Partnerships, etc. In the case of a partnership or unincorporated body which cannot be vested in heritable property in its
social name, a lease should be granted by the trustees or individuals
who are infeft in the property for behoof of the firm or body, and the
consent of the firm or body should be taken.

Otherwise, bodies whether incorporated or not may grant leases, but
care should be taken that the transaction is not *ultra vires* of the granter.
A lease granted by a company whose memorandum of association does
not contain the power is void.

Local Authorities. Local authorities may let any land belonging to
them (a) without any consent for a term not exceeding seven years, or
(b) by public roup for a term exceeding seven years,[18] and this applies
to land forming part of the common good of the burgh.[19] A 99 years'
lease of property forming part of the common good of two burghs was

[8] Rankine, 46.
[9] *Ibid.*
[10] *Heddrington* v *Book* (1724) Mor. 4047.
[11] Rankine, 46.
[12] *Danish Dairy Co. Ltd.* v *Gillespie,* 1922 S.C. 656.
[13] *Ibid.*
[14] *Dodds* v *Walker* (1822) 2 S. 81 (N.E. 73).
[15] *Dallas* v *Fraser* (1849) 11 D. 1058.
[16] *Grant* v *Sinclair* (1861) 23 D. 796.
[17] *Dickson* v *Bell* (1898) 6 S.L.T. 47 (O.H.).
[18] Local Government (Scotland) Act 1947, s. 165, as amended by Town and
Country Planning (Scotland) Act 1959, s. 27.
[19] Local Government (Scotland) Act 1947, s. 171.

reduced after the lapse of some 30 years because certain procedure required by statute to be carried out before its grant had been omitted.[20] Similarly a local authority or government department may be empowered to deal with property only in a particular way or to let it only at a fixed rent.[21]

New Towns. The development corporation established for the purposes of a new town may let land in such manner and subject to such conditions as they may consider expedient for the development of the new town, but they may not grant leases for more than 99 years without the consent of the Secretary of State for Scotland.[22]

Glebes. At common law a lease by a minister of part of his glebe land was limited by the duration of his own incumbency, and the tenant's possession was terminated by induction of a new minister.[23] On his translation or death, the rent for the period, to which the crop sown at the termination of his incumbency applied, belonged to him or his representatives.[24] By statute[25] a minister might with the approval of the heritors and presbytery and subject to certain conditions grant leases without grassum of part of his glebe for any term not exceeding 11 years. Also authority might be obtained from the Court of Teinds to let a glebe on a building lease for any term not exceeding 99 years.[26] However, by the Church of Scotland (Property and Endowments) Act 1925 the property in all glebes has been transferred to the Church of Scotland General Trustees, and judicial permission to grant leases is no longer necessary.

The Crown. The management of Crown lands, as distinct from the personal property of the monarch, is vested in the Crown Estate Commissioners. The Commissioners have power to grant leases of Crown lands for not more than one hundred years.[27] No person dealing with the Commissioners need enquire as to the extent of their authority or the observance of any restriction on the exercise of their powers.[28] Crown leases of salmon fishings are quite common.

GRANTEES

General. A lease normally narrates that in consideration of a certain rent the lessor lets the subjects to the lessee. Frequently the element

20 *Mags. of Banff* v *Ruthin Castle Ltd.,* 1944 S.C. 36.
21 *Glasgow Corporation* v *Assessor for Glasgow,* 1943 S.C. 276.
22 New Towns Act 1946, s. 5.
23 *M'Callum* v *Grant* (1826) 4 S. 527.
24 *Taylor* v *Stewart* (1853) 2 Stuart 538.
25 Glebe Lands Act 1866 s. 3.
26 *Ibid.,* s. 5.
27 Crown Estate Act 1961 s. 3.
28 *Ibid.,* s. 1 (5).

of *delectus personae*[29] is present and the landlord may be interested in restricting the right of the tenant to assign his lease or sublet the subjects or to dispose of his lease after his death. Normally the lease contains an exclusion of assignees and of subtenants. A lease is heritable in the succession of the lessee, and prior to the passing of the Succession (Scotland) Act 1964 descended to his heirs. Whether or not there was an express destination to heirs, the lease would pass on the lessee's death intestate to his heir-at-law, unless heirs were expressly excluded. Now, however, as a result of the assimilation of heritage and moveables,[30] a lease, apart from one expressed to be for the duration of the tenant's life only, vests in his executors, to whom certain powers are given.[31] The landlord may wish to exclude the exercise of such powers by limiting the lease to the lifetime of the tenant.

Sometimes a cautioner joins in a lease to guarantee due performance of the tenant's obligations. He will be personally liable to the landlord, but the other remedies of the landlord will be available only against the tenant.

Effect of Diligence, Insolvency, etc. A lessee's power to accept a lease is not affected by diligence or insolvency, but, if he has been sequestrated or has granted a trust deed, he may require the co-operation of his trustee.

A tenant's power to sublet, assign or renounce may be affected by inhibition, adjudication, or insolvency. An inhibition has no effect against a renunciation granted because the lease is already at an end.[32] If a lease excludes assignees and subtenants, an inhibition does not prevent the tenant from renouncing it in favour of the landlord.[33] All leases are adjudgeable, unless assignees are expressly excluded or unless there is a special exclusion of adjudgers or other creditors; and if the exclusion of assignees contains an exception in favour of such as the landlord may approve, the landlord may withhold approval and so exclude adjudication.[34] An assignation, renunciation or sublease may be struck at by the Bankruptcy Acts 1621 and 1696 in the same way as a lease by the proprietor.[35]

Particular Grantees—Trustees. The power of trustees to take leases depends on the powers expressly conferred on them by the trust deed, and failing such express powers it will depend on the terms and purposes of the trust. There is no general statutory power to trustees to take leases and the taking of a lease upon certain terms may amount to an

[29] *Infra*, p. 149.
[30] Succession (Scotland) Act 1964 s. 14.
[31] *Ibid.*, s. 16; *infra* p. 180.
[32] Rankine, 53.
[33] *Fraser* v *Marquis of Abercorn* (1835) 14 S. 77.
[34] Rankine, 54.
[35] *Paterson's Tr.* v *Paterson's Trs.* (1891) 19 R. 91.

act or investment outwith their powers. Trustees, however, have statutory power to acquire with funds of the trust estate " any interest in residential accommodation " reasonably required to enable them to provide a suitable residence for occupation by any of the beneficiaries.[36] The wording of the section would appear to cover not only a purchase, but also the taking of a lease, of such property. The interest is to be acquired for residential rather than investment purposes, but it may be provided for any of the beneficiaries. Such a lease is not challengeable by the lessor or any other person (apart from a beneficiary) on the ground that the act is at variance with the terms and purposes of the trust.[37]

A power to enter into a lease for other than residential occupation, although not expressly conferred in the trust deed, may be implied from the existence of other powers. Thus, if a testator directs his trustees to carry on his business, that would seem to imply power to continue to hold the business premises on lease or even power to take on lease other premises clearly necessary or advantageous to the business.[38] It will depend on the circumstance of each case whether the trustees are justified in binding the trust estate by taking a lease, but generally they can, and are bound to, do what they can for the benefit of the estate within the limits set by the intention of the truster and by the rules of necessary or ordinary administration and provided they do not act as *auctores in rem suam*.[39]

Executors, Tutors, Curators, Judicial Factors, etc. The rules applying to such persons are broadly the same as those applying to trustees.

Pupils and Minors. The rules applying to pupils and minors taking leases are the same as those applying to their granting leases.

Joint Lessees. A lease may be granted in favour of more than one individual as joint tenants. Apart from the capacity of the parties to enter into the contract, a lease to joint tenants may involve questions of rights and liabilities *inter se* and with the landlord, and the question of succession to the tenants' interest in the lease, etc.

As the tenant's obligations in a lease are obligations *ad facta praestanda*, it follows that in the absence of provision to the contrary each of the joint tenants is liable *in solidum* for implement of all the obligations, including payment of rent; and this also applies to obligations arising as a result of tacit relocation.[40] The fact that one of two lessees does not occupy the subjects does not exempt him from liability for the

[36] Trusts (Scotland) Act 1961, s. 4.
[37] *Ibid.*, s. 2.
[38] *Encyclopaedia of the Laws of Scotland*, Vol. 9, 175.
[39] Rankine, 45.
[40] *Brown* v *Paterson* (1704) Mor. 14629.

non-observance of conditions by the other.[41] Each joint tenant is entitled to insist on joint possession and management, although the subjects are partly agricultural and partly mineral.[42] Each tenant has a distinct right to his *pro indiviso* share which he can transmit by assignation to a third party, if assignation is not excluded;[43] and if he dies intestate his interest in the lease passes to his own executors, unless there is provision to the contrary.[44] On the other hand a lease may be granted in favour of two lessees and the survivor, and in this event the predeceaser's share will accrue to the survivor.[45] The fact that a lease has been taken by two persons jointly does not prevent the representatives of the predeceaser from proving that the moveables on the farm belong wholly to him.[46] Nor did it prevent one of two *ex facie* joint tenants from claiming that he had the whole real interest in a farm, at least after he had lodged in process an assignation in his favour by the other tenant.[47] Where there was a destination in a lease in favour of two persons and the survivor and the tenants bound " themselves and their respective heirs, executors and successors, all conjunctly and severally, renouncing the benefit of discussion to pay " the rent to the landlord, it was held that on the death of one of the tenants, although the lease passed to the survivor, the predeceaser's representatives became jointly and severally liable with the survivor for the rent until the termination of the lease.[48] In this case the wording of the obligation to pay rent displaced the general presumption that an obligation to pay rent is only meant to attach to those persons who are for the time being in right of the lease as tenants.[49] If joint tenants have not bound themselves and their heirs, executors and successors jointly and severally and if the lease by its terms passes to the survivor, the representatives of the predeceaser will be liable only for rent up to the date of death. If a tenant who is bound along with his representatives to pay the rent assigns his lease with the landlord's consent, the representatives are not bound to pay rent becoming due after the assignee takes possession.[50] The addition of such words as " jointly and severally " in such cases is regarded as implying that the tenant and his representatives are to continue liable along with those succeeding as assignees; the words " without the benefit of discussion " have no meaning in such circumstances.[51]

---

[41] *Sutherland* v *Robertson* (1736) Mor. 13979.
[42] *Dickson* v *Dickson* (1821) 1 S. 117, (1823) 2 S. 462.
[43] *Gray* v *Rollock* (1570) Mor. 4246.
[44] *Dickson* v *Dickson, supra.*
[45] *Gray* v *Rollock, supra; Macalister* v *Macalister* (1859) 21 D. 560.
[46] *Kilpatrick* v *Kilpatrick* (1841) 4 D. 109.
[47] *Middle Ward of Lanark District Council* v *Marshall* (1896) 24 R. 139.
[48] *Burns* v *Martin* (1887) 14 R. (H.L.) 20; see *Dundee Police Commissioners* v *Straton* (1884) 11 R. 586 (feuduty).
[49] *Burns* v *Martin, supra, per* Lord Watson at p. 24; *Skene* v *Greenhill* (1825) 4 S. 25.
[50] *Skene* v *Greenhill, supra.*
[51] *Burns* v *Martin, supra, per* Lord Watson.

A lease to two tenants providing for an irritancy on the bankruptcy of the tenants does not without special provision fall on the bankruptcy of only one of them.[52] Sequestration of the estate of one of two joint tenants is not an abandonment of the lease entitling the landlord to damages for breach of contract, where the landlord exercises an option to irritate the lease, provided that the other tenant, being solvent, is willing to carry on.[53]

Special Destination. Questions have arisen in the past with regard to the interpretation of leases to joint tenants with destinations in favour of heirs. Distinctions were made between (a) a lease to two lessees and their heirs, (b) a lease to two lessees and the survivor and their heirs and (c) a lease to two lessees in conjunct fee and liferent and their heirs.[54] In all those cases the rule holds that the destination will be read as part of a contract, and will not be governed by the special rules which are applicable to destinations in dispositions of land and which result from the feudal principles that the fee cannot be *in pendente* and that in the case of spouses the husband is *dignior persona.*[55] Where the meaning of the destination as it stands is not questioned, but the action is brought to determine that the lease was really granted for behoof of one of the lessees[56] or of a third party,[57] this is really an attempt to prove a trust, and the only admissible evidence will be the writ or oath of the party maintaining the *prima facie* interpretation of the words used.[58]

The terms " liferent " and " fee " which were at one time commonly used with regard to the tenants' interest in a lease are anomalous, difficult to understand and inappropriate.[59] The words " whom failing " occurring in a lease should not be construed in the same way as in a destination of heritable property or a testamentary writing.[60]

Companies, Partnerships, etc. A lease may be granted in favour of a company incorporated under the Companies Acts, if its memorandum contains the power. On the company going into liquidation the lease may be brought to an end by the landlord, if there is no right to assign it;[61] the liquidator is an administrator for the purpose of winding up and not a trustee in the sense of the Bankruptcy Acts.[62]

---

[52] *Young* v *Gerard* (1843) 6 D. 347.
[53] *Buttercase and Geddie's Tr.* v *Geddie* (1897) 24 R. 1128.
[54] Rankine, 84-86.
[55] *Macalister* v *Macalister* (1859) 21 D. 560; *Marquis* v *Prentice* (1896) 23 R. 595.
[56] *M'Vean* v *M'Vean* (1864) 2 M. 1150.
[57] *Seth* v *Hain* (1855) 17 D. 1117.
[58] Rankine, 84.
[59] *Macalister* v *Macalister* (1859) 21 D. 560.
[60] *Ibid.*
[61] *Campbell* v *Calder Iron Co.* (1805) Bell *Comm.*, I, 78 (7th ed.); *Marquis of Breadalbane* v *Whitehead & Sons* (1893) 21 R. 138.
[62] *Bank of Scotland* v *Liquidators of Hutchinson, Main & Co. Ltd.*, 1914 S.C. (H.L.) 1.

Although a partnership or unincorporated body may not be vested in feudal property in its own name, it is capable of receiving a lease in its social name,[63] but, it is said, this does not apply if the name is merely a descriptive one.[64] However, as a corporation or firm trading under a descriptive name can sue or be sued in the Sheriff Courts without the addition of the names of the individual members,[65] it is difficult to see why the grant of a lease, not being a feudal investiture, should not be taken in its descriptive name. Practice varies, but it would seem desirable in the case of a partnership, whether the title is a social one or a descriptive one, to take the lease in favour of the individual partners and the survivors and survivor as trustees for the firm (and for the partners thereof present and future, if that is the intention), and to take them all bound jointly and severally along with the firm itself for the implement of the tenants' obligations.[66] Any partner of a firm may bind it by accepting a lease in the firm's name, provided he does so within the scope of the partnership business, and the benefit of the lease will accrue to the partnership as a whole, whatever the motives of the partner were in obtaining it.[67] One partner should not acquire for himself subjects held on lease by the firm or by the partners as trustees for the firm, as this is not consistent with the *uberrimae fides* required of partners; should he do so, he will be held to be a trustee for himself and his co-partners.[68] It is a question of circumstances whether one partner has authority to bind the firm. One partner in a contract of joint adventure to run a music hall was held personally liable for the rent under a lease of a circus concluded by his partner in the firm's name for the purpose of the venture for the remainder of the period of actual occupation, even after the partnership was dissolved; it was not necessary to decide whether his partner had authority to bind the firm for the whole term of years specified in the lease;[69] it was questioned whether one of several joint adventurers has implied authority to enter into a lease for any period, so as to bind his co-adventurers.[70]

In the case of a lease to a firm or unincorporated company, its dissolution by bankruptcy, death, mutual consent or other cause brings the lease to an end, if assignees are excluded.[71] So also a lease to the partners of a company for behoof of themselves and future partners was held not to be inconsistent with a clause excluding assignees without the consent of the landlord, and the lease came to an end on the sequestration of the

---

[63] *Dennistoun, Macnair & Co.* v *M'Farlane* (1808) Mor. App. *voce* "Tack" 15; *Murray* v *Hogarth* (1835) 13 S. 453; Bell § 357.
[64] Rankine, 86; *Encyclopaedia of the Laws of Scotland*, Vol. 9, 171.
[65] Sheriff Courts (Scotland) Act 1907, First Schedule, para. 11.
[66] *Encyclopaedia of the Laws of Scotland*, Vol. 9, 171; see also *Encyclopaedia of Scottish Legal Styles*, Vol. 6, 183.
[67] Rankine, 86-87, and authorities cited there.
[68] *Encyclopaedia of the Laws of Scotland*, Vol. 9, 171.
[69] *Cooke's Circus Buildings Co. Ltd.* v *Welding* (1894) 21 R. 339.
[70] *Ibid.*
[71] *Campbell* v *Calder Iron Co., supra.*

company.[72] The death of one of the partners of a firm terminates a lease, unless there is a survivorship clause, because in theory the firm has become a new legal person, whereas the lease was taken in the name of the trustees for the former firm.

A joint tenancy does not necessarily create a partnership whether or not the tenants share any profits made by the use thereof,[73] but a partnership may be inferred, if the additional element of control of a business is present.[74] There is no necessary connection between the endurance of the partnership and of a lease forming part of its assets.[75] If part of the term of the lease is unexpired at the dissolution of the partnership and the lease is assignable, it is a partnership asset and should be distributed as such.[76] Where a firm or company has been dissolved and the partners cannot agree as to the disposal of a lease, it should be sold; this is true even if the lease is not taken *socio nomine*, provided it is held for the benefit of the firm.[77] Thus where partners in a company have in the course of business obtained a lease in favour of themselves as individuals and their assignees or sublessees, and the company is later dissolved by the death of a partner, the survivor is bound to concur with the representatives of the deceased in the sale of the lease as a company asset.[78] Similarly where a lease was taken in the joint names of two individuals intending to enter into partnership, and that purpose was broken off, it was held that one party was not entitled to resist an application for the sale of the lease and for his removal from the premises.[79]

[72] *Walker* v *M'Knight* (1886) 13 R. 599.
[73] Partnership Act 1890, s. 2 (1).
[74] *Stewart* v *Buchanan* (1903) 6 F. 15.
[75] Rankine, 87.
[76] *Ibid.*
[77] *Ibid.*
[78] *Aitken's Trs.* v *Shanks* (1830) 8 S. 753.
[79] *M'Whannell* v *Dobbie* (1830) 8 S. 914.

CHAPTER V

SUBJECTS OF THE CONTRACT

Introduction. The proper subjects of the contract of lease are land and other corporeal heritable property, such as buildings.[1] It is immaterial whether the land is held by feudal, allodial or other tenure. Rights closely connected with land such as fishings, game and water can be made the subjects of leases. Timber growing on land and the minerals beneath it are sometimes made the subjects of contracts taking the form of leases, although it has been frequently maintained that a temporary right to take minerals or timber is more of an executory sale than a lease.[2] Even moveable articles situated in or on heritable property can be leased along with the heritage itself, as in the case of a furnished let of a house. Moreover, there is sometimes little distinction in form or fact between the lease of a furnished house or hut, which is clearly heritable, and the " lease " of a furnished caravan, which, although it may be stationary, is clearly moveable. Strictly, the latter contract would be one of hire.

It may be useful to discuss the various types of lease and the nomenclature used in the course of considering the different subjects of a lease. The respective classes of lease discussed in this chapter are not mutually exclusive, and the various classes tend to impinge on one another. The subjects and types of leases are of infinite variety and embrace such diverse contracts as the let of a village hall for an evening, and the lease of a brewery or golf course for 999 years.[3]

TYPES OF LEASES

Long Leases. Long leases of land, particularly for building purposes, were commonly granted in some parts of Scotland as an alternative to feus. Apart from such building leases, there may be long leases of ground with buildings already erected thereon or even of flats in tenements. In modern times long leases of office accommodation are quite common.

A feature of a long lease, whether registrable under the Registration of Leases (Scotland) Act 1857 or not, is that the tenant under the lease is virtually the proprietor, while the landlord is in a position similar to that of a superior. In many cases the rent or tack duty under a

[1] Rankine, 89.
[2] *Ibid.,* and cases cited there; *Inland Revenue* v *Belhaven's Exrs.,* 1925 S.C. 635.
[3] For examples of rights forming the subject-matter of leases not dealt with in this Chapter, see Chapter I and also *Encyclopaedia of Scottish Legal Styles,* Vol. 6, Nos. 174-182.

long lease will bear no relation to the actual annual value of the subjects, especially in the case of a building lease, where the main value of the subjects is in the buildings erected by the lessee after the lease has been granted. Such a tenant is in a very different position from a tenant under a lease of ordinary duration. He can normally assign or sublet without the consent of the landlord, and for practical purposes during the subsistence of the lease he enjoys all the advantages of a feuar, so far as the surface of the ground is concerned.[4] Under the Lands Valuation (Scotland) Act 1854[5] a tenant under a lease of over 21 years, or 31 years in the case of minerals, was for the purposes of that Act deemed to be the proprietor of the subject let.[6] He would appear in the valuation roll as proprietor. Thus the tenant under a lease for 99 years of a piece of ground, on which his author had built a house, was held to be " proprietor " and " owner " within the meaning of the Valuation Acts, and so was not entitled to recover from the landlord the owner's proportion of the local rates paid by him.[7] Owners' rates were abolished, and Sec. 6 of the Lands Valuation (Scotland) Act 1854 was repealed, both of them by the Valuation and Rating (Scotland) Act 1956, and the special significance of the periods of 21 or 31 years has disappeared for valuation purposes; but the problem may arise as to whether tenants under long leases should be entered in the valuation roll as proprietors.[8] Prior to the latter Act the rent under a long lease was not necessarily assessed as the annual value of the subjects, but it could and still can afford some evidence of its value.[9]

The term " long lease " is normally applied only to urban subjects, or at any rate not to agricultural leases even of very long duration. The period which may render the lease " long " varies for different purposes: for the purpose of the Lands Valuation (Scotland) Act 1854 it was 21 years, or 31 years for minerals, for the Registration of Leases (Scotland) Act 1857 it is 31 years, and for the Long Leases (Scotland) Act 1954 it is 50 years; for the purpose of the Entail Amendment Act 1848 it was held to mean leases of a duration beyond ordinary administration.[10]

Ground Leases.[11] The term " ground lease ", while not a *nomen juris* of Scots Law, has been used to describe a type of long lease, whereby vacant ground is leased to a tenant, who may erect buildings on it by virtue of a direction or an express or implied permission to do so contained in the lease. If the purpose is building, it is sometimes

[4] *MacBain* v *Gordon* 1917 S.C. 185, *per* Lord Salvesen at p. 193.
[5] s. 6.
[6] *M'Laren* v *Clyde Navigation Trustees* (1865) 4 M. 58.
[7] *MacBain* v *Gordon, supra.*
[8] See Armour, *Valuation for Rating*, 3rd ed., 179 for a discussion of this point.
[9] *Ibid.*, 275.
[10] *Farquharson* (1870) 9 M. 66.
[11] Reference is made generally to Report of the Scottish Leases Committee, 1952 Cmd. 8656.

called a " building lease ". The duration of such leases varies, but they were commonly granted for a period of 99 years, being the permitted period under the Montgomery Act,[12] which first empowered heirs of entail to grant building leases before they were permitted to grant feus; but longer periods such as 999 years are commonly found. Many of such leases were granted in the 18th and 19th centuries, but they are comparatively rarely granted nowadays, at least for residential purposes. They were more common in the Counties of Lanark, Ayr, Dumfries and Renfrew than in other parts of Scotland. They were often granted because there was some obstacle to feuing, such as prohibition of subinfeudation or restrictions in an entailed estate, or the subjects might be burgage property; also a lease may have been cheaper than a feu charter, or landowners may have thought they could retain more control of the ground by leasing than by feuing; again, some landlords or their factors may have felt more familiar with the English system of leasehold than with the indigenous feudal system, although the tack, long or short, has a perfectly respectable Scottish ancestry. By no means all the long or ground leases which are registrable are actually recorded in terms of the Registration of Leases Act 1857.

The similarity between such ground leases of very long duration and feus is marked, but cannot be taken too far.[13] The rent or tack duty tends to be in the same range. In addition to the rent there is sometimes a casualty, such as a double tack duty on the succession of an heir and the full annual rental upon an assignation to singular successors, as where it was provided in a lease for 354 years that an heir was liable for double the tack duty, but an assignee or singular successor was liable for a full year's rent of what the subjects should be worth at the time.[14] Such casualties in leases were not affected by the Feudal Casualties (Scotland) Act 1914, although the Court of Session is empowered to provide by Act of Sederunt for the redemption and extinction of such casualties on the analogy of the provisions of that Act.[15] Meanwhile, therefore, leasehold casualties will still apply in leases not converted into feu rights either by agreement or under the Long Leases (Scotland) Act 1954. The similarity to a feu of a lease for 999 years renewable in perpetuity at the option of the tenant, the rent being £1 : 13 : 10½ with a duplicand on each removal, has been commented on; but it was held by the Lord Ordinary that, where in a contract for the sale of heritable property the seller agreed to give the purchaser a feudal title, but was able only to give an assignation of the unexpired portion of the lease, he did not implement his side of the bargain.[16]

[12] Entail Improvement Act 1770.
[13] *Supra*, p. 8.
[14] *Crawford* v *Campbell*, 1937 S.C. 596.
[15] Feudal Casualties (Scotland) Act, s. 23.
[16] *Fleming* v *Boswell*, 1948 C.L. 4378, narrated in Report of the Scottish Leases Committee, 1952, *supra*, para. 48; see also *M'Connell* v *Chassels* (1903) 10 S.L.T. 790 (O.H.).

At the end of the lease, however far off, provided it is not perpetual, the buildings, although erected by the tenant, will revert to the landlord.

Investment Leases.[17] During this century, the practice has grown up of commercial undertakings obtaining the use of additional working capital by the sale of their premises to financial companies such as insurance, investment or property companies, and then receiving leases of the same premises; or, instead of paying the price for a particular property which it wishes to acquire, a commercial undertaking may arrange for a financial company to buy it and to grant it a lease. The purchase price paid by the financial company to the commercial undertaking or to the seller represents the value of the buildings as well as of the ground, and the rent charged to the commercial undertaking represents an annual yield on the outlay. In very recent times it has become common for property companies to develop property for the purpose of leasing it to commercial undertakings. Frequently the property company finances the operation by borrowing from an insurance company, to whom it grants a heritable security over the property. The growing use of such leases is largely an import from England, perhaps at least partly because one or other of the parties may be controlled from south of the Border by people who prefer to use formulae with which they are familiar; but in particular cases there may also be economic or fiscal reasons which make it desirable for a commercial undertaking to be the tenant rather than the proprietor of its premises. Such leases are sometimes called " investment leases ", and they are most commonly used for shops, factories and office accommodation. Obviously these leases must be granted for long terms, usually for more than 21 years and sometimes much longer. Generally, however, the landlord will not wish to grant too long a lease at a fixed rent. The rent will be substantial, as the buildings are already erected, unlike the rent in a ground lease of a vacant plot. The tenant may assume responsibility for all repairs, insurance and even feuduty—in fact all the normal liabilities of an owner. It is apparently rare for such leases, which tend to be lengthy and to use the language of English rather than Scots Law, to be recorded in the Register of Sasines, although there is no reason why they should not be so recorded, provided they comply with the requirements of the Registration of Leases Act 1857. For a typical example of an investment lease see the case cited.[18]

Tenancies at Will.[19] The term " tenancy at will " is not a technical term in Scots Law, but it has been used for convenience to describe a

[17] Reference is made generally to Report of the Scottish Leases Committee, 1952, *supra.*
[19] Reference is made generally to Report of the Scottish Leases Committee, 1952, *supra.*
[18] *Littlewoods Mail Order Stores Ltd.* v *Assessor for Edinburgh,* 1953 S.C. 200.

practice found still to subsist in certain parts of Scotland, particularly in fishing and rural villages of the North-east coast, in Highland villages, and in a mining village in Lanarkshire. The builder of a house rents from the landowner the ground on which he builds it, and he may or may not be issued with an informal acknowledgment of the position. A house changes hands by means of a simple receipt, and not by a conveyance or assignation. The purchaser (or assignee) and the seller (or cedent) attend on the estate factor and intimate the sale, whereupon the new tenant's name is entered in the rental book. There are certain rights of succession. If the new tenant fails to pay his rent, the house reverts to the landowner, who sells it and so recovers the arrears of rent. For rating purposes the tenant at will is treated as both owner and occupier. The holding is perhaps more akin to a feudal holding than to a lease, but the right is infinitely more precarious than a feu. Those tenancies at will are similar to the obsolete rental rights or kindly tenancies or " kyndnes ",[20] but one difference seems to be that, in the case of the " kyndnes", assignation and subletting were excluded by the nature of the right, while the tenants-at-will appear to have certain, if limited, rights of alienation.[21]

Kindly Tenants of Lochmaben.[22] A somewhat similar, but stronger, right is that of the Crown's Kindly Tenants of the Four Towns of Lochmaben, who with a romantic and somewhat litigious history behind them, have been held to possess as proprietors " according to every criterion by which property can be ascertained ". Entry in the rental book of the King's steward is accepted as the badge of ownership, transmissions *inter vivos* or by succession being entered in the roll without formal writ. They cannot be removed so long as they pay their rent, and they are at liberty to alienate either redeemably or irredeemably, being treated generally as proprietors.[23] It has, however, become customary in transmissions on sale or in security to use deeds in normal feudal form and to have them recorded in the Register of Sasines, in order to make their titles marketable outside the district. The Kindly Tenants also have ownership of salmon fishing in a stretch of the River Annan, not confined to the water *ex adverso* their own lands.[24] Commissioners of Fishing for the Royal Four Towns have recently been

[20] Bell, § 1279; Rankine, 152-154.
[21] Rankine, 153, but see Report of the Scottish Leases Committee, 1952, *supra*, para. 80.
[22] See H. H. Monteath " Heritable Rights " in *Introduction to Scottish Legal History* (Stair Society Vol. 20), 195.
[23] Rankine, 153-154.
[24] *Royal Four Towns Fishing Association* v *Assessor for Dumfriesshire*, 1956 S.C. 379. Lord Patrick at p. 385 gives a concise review of the nature and history of the Kindly Tenants. See also Ross, *Lectures*, 2nd ed., II, 474, 478-81; 21 *J.R.*, 323.

incorporated having statutory powers in respect of certain fishings in that river.[25]

Rural and Urban Leases. An important distinction is drawn between rural tenements on the one hand and urban tenements on the other. The distinction does not depend so much on the situation of the subject in the country or the town as on its nature. Where the main subject let is the use of the *solum,* its produce and what is naturally on it or below it, the lease is a Rural Lease. Where the main subject let is the use of the *superficies,* or what has been placed on the surface by the art of man, such as buildings of all kinds, the lease is an Urban Lease. The addition of an accessory to the main subjects of the lease makes no difference. Thus the existence of a farmhouse does not make the farm less of a rural tenement; and the existence of an area or garden does not make a villa less urban than a factory.[26] The distinction is particularly important in determining whether or not a lease may be assignable,[27] the liability for repairs and maintenance,[28] the terms for payment of rent[29] and who is entitled to it, and the method of giving notice of removal.[30]

Rural Leases—Arable and Pastoral. A rural lease may be of a farm or of land to be used for agricultural purposes, and important questions may depend on whether the farm land is to be regarded as arable or pastoral. It must be one or the other. It has been held in a series of cases that the produce cannot be divided according as it is derived from arable or pastoral portions of the farm, and that the criterion for judging whether a farm is arable or pastoral is to ascertain the sources from which the profits are mainly derived.[31] In other words, whether a farm is arable or pastoral depends on which of the two qualities predominates at the time when the question arises, even where (there being in the lease a prohibition against ploughing up) arable farming might have been more profitable than pastoral.[32] In the Portmore case it was held that the question fell to be determined according to the general character of the occupation which the tenant *de facto* had at the time when the question arose, and that a farm was none the less a pastoral farm because a part of it was under the plough, the preponderating proportion being in grass.[33] There is no authority to

---

[25] Royal Four Towns Fishing Order Confirmation Act 1965.
[26] Rankine, 174, and institutional writers cited there.
[27] *Infra,* p. 150.
[28] *Infra,* p. 131.
[29] *Infra,* p. 139.
[30] *Infra,* p. 272.
[31] *Petley* v *M'Kenzie* (1805) Hume 186; *Campbell* v *Anstruther* (1836) 9 Sc. Jur. 163; *M'Clymonts* v *Cathcart* (1848) 10 D. 1489; *Mackenzie's Trs.* v *Somerville* (1900) 2 F. 1278.
[32] Rankine, 342-343.
[33] *Mackenzie's Trs.* v *Somerville* (1900) 2 F. 1278 (Portmore case).

show what would be the result of improvements, which during the
currency of a lease turned a pastoral farm into an arable one, or the
converse case of laying down a large part of a farm in grass; but it
would appear from the *dicta* in the Portmore case that the actual state
of the farm when the question arose would alone be looked at, rather
than the essential character of the ground.[34] The effect of miscropping
by ploughing up land required to be left in pasture may also cause
difficulty.[35]

Apart from farms and ground let for agricultural or grazing purposes, leases may be granted of woodlands, fields and ground of all
kinds for allotments,[36] market gardens or other horticultural purposes,
or simply for sport, pleasure or amenity.

Urban Leases. Probably most leases are what are sometimes called
" occupation leases ",[37] that is, leases not of vacant ground, but of ground
with buildings already erected thereon as residential or business
premises, or it may be of a flat in a tenement or even of a room in a
house. The duration of the let may be as short as a few days or may
be several years. In many cases dwellinghouses are held on yearly
missives continuing by tacit relocation; in other cases the lease may
have originally been granted for a short period, but the house may
have been affected by the Rent Restriction Acts.

Furnishings and Services.[38] In either urban or rural leases, the
subjects let may include not only the bare heritable subjects, but also
moveable property. In accordance with the common law obligation to
deliver to the tenant the subject let in a state fit for the purpose for
which it was let, or in accordance with an express obligation, the
landlord is in many cases bound to provide along with the bare premises
(such as a dwellinghouse or a farm with buildings, etc.), certain usual or
stipulated appurtenances. If these are and remain moveable, they may
be classed under the most general designation as furnishings; this
includes furniture in houses, fittings in shops, machinery in mines and
factories, and steelbow in farms. If, being originally definite moveable
objects, they have, either at the inception or during the currency of
the lease, been affixed to the premises, they are known as landlord's
fixtures in the narrower sense of the term. In each case the furnishings
or fixtures (with the exception of steelbow) remain the property of the
landlord. On the other hand, if the tenant provides and stocks or
furnishes the premises with articles, animate or inanimate (known as
plenishing), which are and remain moveable, these continue to be his

[34] *Ibid., per* Lord Adam at p. 1282 and Lord Maclaren at p. 1286.
[35] *Bairds* v *Harper* (1865) 3 M. 543.
[36] *Infra*, p. 633.
[37] Report of the Scottish Leases Committee, 1952, *supra.*
[38] See Rankine, 286-287.

property, subject to the right of the landlord to attach them by hypothec. If, however, the tenant affixes definite moveable objects to premises let, the legal effect sometimes is that he is not entitled to remove them at the expiry of the lease, but must leave them with the landlord without consideration. They are then included in the term landlord's fixtures in the wider sense of the word. If the tenant is entitled to sever and remove under certain conditions objects annexed to the premises, they are known as tenant's fixtures.

When not only heritable property, but along with it property which is at the date of the contract or delivery, and is intended to remain, moveable, is handed over to a tenant, the contract is logically divisible into two parts: (1) an ordinary contract of lease as regards heritable property and (2) as regards the moveable property, either a letting to hire, if it is to be returned *in specie* at the ish, or a loan of the nature of *mutuum,* where the *ipsa corpora* cannot, or are not intended to, be returned at the ish, but an equivalent delivered over instead. Examples of a combined contract of lease and hire are furnished houses, shops containing loose fittings, mines and factories with moveable machinery, and bowing of cows. The only example of a contract of lease and loan is a steelbow farm.

The matter is still further complicated where, in a contract of lease and hire, there is hire not only of corporeal moveables, but also of services. This is the case of lodgings and also of factories with machinery and steam-supply. In dealing with these complex subjects the law directs, first, that the general rules of location (letting to hire) or loan shall apply, but second, that the special rules which govern that sort of location which is called lease shall in some cases dominate over the more general principles applicable to all location.[39]

Bowing of Cows. This is a mixed contract of lease and hiring still or at one time found in certain parts of Scotland whereby the proprietor or tenant of a farm let to a " bower " the " bowing " or produce of a dairy of a specified number of milch cows along with the pasturage of specified fields. The cows remain the property of the lessor, who unless it is stipulated otherwise takes the risk of deaths or casualties rendering the cows unfit to yield milk. It will suffice to refer to the authorities cited.[40]

Steelbow. This is, or was, a mixed contract of lease and loan applying to stock and goods lent by the landlord of a farm to the tenant at the beginning of a lease, the tenant being under an obligation to return a like quantity at his outgoing. The custom is probably obsolete,

---

[39] *Ibid.*
[40] Hunter, *Landlord and Tenant,* 4th ed., I, 358-359; Rankine, 290-291; *Encyclopaedia of the Laws of Scotland,* Vol. 9, 247.

although the word survives in agricultural leases to denote straw and manure to be left at the termination. It will suffice to refer to Rankine and the authorities cited there.[41]

PARTICULAR SUBJECTS

After a discussion of the various classes of lease, the next topic is a consideration of some particular types of subjects let.

Furnished Dwellinghouses. Perhaps most leases granted nowadays are leases of furnished houses. Usually the term is for a few weeks or months, but it may extend for a period of years. Many of such leases are verbal, or if committed to writing rest on missives. There are really two contracts inseparably bound together—a let of the house and a hiring of the furniture. The let of the house is the more important, and the combined contract takes the form of a lease and is invariably treated as such. In some cases it is thought desirable in the lease to allocate the consideration between the rent proper and payment for the use of the moveable property,[42] but if this is done, the landlord's hypothec will give security for the rent only.[43] The rent is almost invariably payable in advance, because, the property being furnished, the tenant will not bring in sufficient of his own moveables for the landlord to attach for arrears of rent. In all cases it is an elementary precaution to prepare an inventory of the moveable items; otherwise the onus would be on the landlord to prove that a particular item of furniture was handed over to the tenant in good condition. Where the lease provides that the parties shall sign an inventory and this is not done, such failure is probably only a breach of a condition of the lease, and not a breach of a suspensive condition.[44] The tenant will be taken bound to replace breakages, etc.

For rating purposes the landlord of furnished premises has always been regarded as the occupier of the heritable property. A peculiarity of a furnished let is the very general, if not universal, understanding that in the absence of provision to the contrary the landlord pays the rates and taxes in respect of his tenant's occupancy.[45] " Such a usage has nothing to do with the liability for public burdens in a question between the occupier and the rating authority. It is concerned solely with the ultimate incidence of these burdens as between landlord and tenant and with the implied obligation of relief which the landlord of certain subjects incurs in a question with his tenant, unless the

---

[41] Rankine, 291-292.
[42] *Encyclopaedia of Scottish Legal Styles,* Vol. 6, No. 131. See Finance Act 1958 s. 35 (exemption from stamp duty on hire of moveables).
[43] *Catterns* v *Tennent* (1835) 1 Sh. & Macl. 694 (correct the rubric, which states the opposite of what was decided).
[44] *Steuart* v *Neilsons* (1864) 2 M. 817; *Elliott* v *Erickson,* 1960 S.L.T. (Sh. Ct.) 28.
[45] *Aitken* v *Harper* (1865) 4 M. 36; *Macome* v *Dickson* (1868) 6 M. 898.

lease otherwise provides."[46] The usage was not affected by the Valuation and Rating (Scotland) Act 1956.

In the absence of provision to the contrary, the tenant will pay for the fuel he consumes, but the lease should state who is to pay for such items as the telephone rental, although if the lease does not mention a telephone, presumably the tenant should pay. In some cases, especially in flatted dwellinghouses, whether furnished or unfurnished, the lease may include the provision of such services as hot water, electricity, central heating, the labour of porters, cleaners etc.[47]

In the absence of provision to the contrary, a tenant may move furniture from one room to another,[48] and may remove pictures from the walls and store them in the house, if no damage is caused by removing and storing them.[49]

Furnished leases involve *delectus personae*, and therefore a power to the tenant to sublet or assign the lease is not presumed, but requires express stipulation. [50]

Lodgings. Individual rooms in a house may be let to tenants either furnished or unfurnished. Where, however, rooms are let furnished along with such services as attendance, cooking and washing, the transaction is probably a contract of lease, service and hire combined. Normally in such cases the degree of control over the subjects given to the lodger is too small to confer the status of lease on a transaction which is more akin to the keeping of a hotel or boarding house. In the case of lodgings a formal contract is rarely, if ever, entered into, and the matter is usually allowed to rest on a verbal agreement or at the most on an exchange of letters. The duration of the lodging, and the stipulated period of notice, if any, are often short, for example weekly, or for such period as the rent is agreed to be payable, and the contract can be readily terminated in the event of dispute. On the other hand, the term of lodging and the period of notice may depend on the nature of the subjects and the class of lodger. Where a student was proved to have engaged boarding-house accommodation in advance for a university term, and did not take it, it was held in the particular circumstances of the case that he was liable to his landlady for loss caused to her; the rent was payable weekly in advance, but the extent of his liability was not decided.[51]

In England a lodger has a right to the use of the doorbell, the knocker, the skylight of the staircase and the water closet, unless it has been stipulated otherwise.[52]

[46] *Sturrock* v *Murray,* 1952 S.C. 454 *per* L.P. Cooper at p. 457.
[47] For stamp duties on such leases, see Sergeant, *Stamp Duties,* 3rd ed., 130.
[48] Rankine, 288.
[49] *Miller* v *Stewart* (1899) 2 F. 309 (diss. Lord Young); *infra,* p. 137.
[50] Rankine, 175.
[51] *Smith* v *Fogg* (1963) Sheriff Court (Aberdeen) not reported.
[52] Woodfall, *Landlord and Tenant,* 26th ed., I, 13.

Business Premises. Shops, restaurants, public houses, hotels, factories and other premises used for business, trade or manufacturing are frequently the subjects of leases. Where fittings or machinery are included, the same rules apply as to furnished houses, and there should obviously be a detailed inventory of the moveable property.[53]

Leases of shops have the special protection of the Tenancy of Shops (Scotland) Acts 1949-1964.[54] One effect of this legislation has been to discourage proprietors from giving short leases of shops.

Steam, Water and Machinery. Sometimes business premises are let along with the supply of steam for use by the tenant as a source of power or heat, or with a supply of water, hot or cold, for industrial purposes. A lease may also include the use of machinery. In the case of steam, it is probably made by the landlord in adjoining property occupied by him, and it may be surplus to his own requirements. This may have been commoner in older times, but the practice of supplying steam or hot water to a tenant is not unknown nowadays. Sometimes the commodity may be supplied in the absence of a lease of heritage, in which case the contract is not really one of lease;[55] where, however, the letting of the supply of steam or water is combined with a lease, the latter is regarded as the principal contract and the former as accessory.[56] If the two contracts are inseparable and indivisible, the law of leases applies to the whole, and the rent and hire, if combined in one sum, are regarded as rent.[57] Where, however, the rent for the heritage and the payment for the steam or water supply are separate, the law of leases applies only to the subjects for which the rent is payable, that is, to the heritage; it follows that the landlord's hypothec is not available for arrears of the hire.[58] An omission to include in a formal lease an alleged verbal agreement to supply steam for heating was held to be provable only by the oath of the landlord, or by his writ subsequent to the lease.[59] For further cases involving such contracts reference is made to the authorities cited.[60]

The grant of a water supply unconnected with a lease of heritage may be so extensive as to amount to a lease. This is probably the case where the water is in its natural state, as where a landed proprietor granted a 999 years lease to a company of "the command of all the water on his lands" with power to lead in water from other lands and to make dams, etc.[61] On the other hand, an agreement taking the form

---

[53] *Steuart v Neilsons* (1864) 2 M. 817; *Elliott v Erickson,* 1960 S.L.T. (Sh. Ct.) 28.
[54] *Infra,* p. 628.
[55] *Auld v Baird* (1827) 5 S. 264 (N.E. 246); Rankine, 289.
[56] *Wilson v Norris* 10 March 1810 F.C.; *Wilson v Pollock* (1827) 6 S. 3.
[57] *Catterns v Tennent, infra,* per Lord Brougham at p. 717.
[58] *Catterns v Tennent* (1835) 1 Sh. & Macl. 694 (correct the rubric).
[59] *Stewart v Clark* (1871) 9 M. 616.
[60] *Walker v Turnbull* (1843) 5 D. 1334; *Kilmarnock Gas Co. v Smith* (1872) 11 M. 58; *Sawers v M'Connell* (1874) 1 R. 392; Rankine, 91 and 289-290.
[61] *Swan's Trs. v Muirkirk Iron Co.* (1850) 12 D. 622.

of a lease and providing for the supply of waste water pumped from a coalpit at an annual rent was held not to be a lease merely because of the lack of an ish, and it was remarked that a lease of water or water power was quite well known.[62] The supply by a gas company to the tenant of ground belonging to them of ammoniacal liquor and tar was treated as one of the subjects of the lease,[63] but perhaps the contract should have been regarded as a sale.[64] In England a contract for the supply of power to tenants of a mill was held not to be part of a lease.[65]

Where the consideration payable depends on the quantity of steam or water supplied, the contract, it is submitted, is one of sale.

Minerals. The transaction by which minerals are let for mining or quarrying is called a lease and normally receives effect as such, although its purposes are essentially different in character from those of a lease of the surface of the ground, or of buildings on the surface, in that the subjects which are let are in reality sold to the mineral tenant. A contract for the removal of colliery dross from a bing at a fixed rate per ton was held to be a sale and not a lease.[66] Mineral leases are not so common since the nationalisation of coal, and this branch of the subject is perhaps not so important as it once was. However, minerals other than coal are commonly let, and even the National Coal Board has limited power to grant licences to work certain coals and such licences may provide for payments " in the nature of rent ".[67]

The consideration in a mineral lease is akin to a price payable by instalments in respect of subjects sold with gradual delivery,[68] and quite logically the consideration frequently depends on the quantity of the substance mined or quarried, rather than being a fixed rent. Thus, the rent may take the form of an agreed proportion payable in kind of the minerals taken. Nowadays, however, it usually is a lordship or royalty based on the quantity or sometimes the quality of the minerals taken; and it may be a " sliding scale " royalty depending on the market price or selling price of the mineral from time to time.[69] Payment by way of royalties is an obvious protection to the tenant in case the mineral runs out, but normally the landlord stipulates for an alternative fixed minimum rent. It used to be common for a lease of coal to provide for the delivery to the landlord of a certain amount of free coal, if required.[70]

Normally it is the minerals alone which are let to the mineral tenant, and not the surface of the ground. Different minerals may be let to

[62] *Dunlop & Co.* v *Steel Co. of Scotland* (1879) 7 R. 283.
[63] *Kilmarnock Gas Light Co.* v *Smith* (1872) 11 M. 58.
[64] Gloag, *Contract*, 2nd ed., 628.
[65] *Bentley* v *Metcalfe* [1906] 2 K.B. 548.
[66] *Inland Revenue* v *Lord Belhaven and Stenton's Exrs.*, 1925 S.C. 635.
[67] Coal Industry Nationalisation Act 1946, s. 36.
[68] Rankine, 74.
[69] Rankine, 314; *Encyclopaedia of Scottish Legal Styles*, Vol. 6, Nos. 166 and 167.
[70] *Inland Revenue* v *Baillie*, 1936 S.C. 438.

separate tenants at the same time. Thus, the surface may well be let to an agricultural tenant and the minerals to one or more mineral tenants. Sometimes the surface is let to the mineral tenant for purposes ancillary to the mining, and in this event there is usually a provision for a normal rent in addition to the lordship or royalty.[71] Sometimes different minerals are let to the same tenant under the same lease, which may stipulate for a different royalty for each substance. A lease may provide for a fixed rent either in addition to or in place of a specified royalty, and the parties may agree on a brief trial period before the fixed rent is to begin. A lease sometimes contains a " shorts clause ", giving the landlord a fixed rent in the event of royalties falling below a certain annual sum, and entitling the tenant to take in a subsequent year a quantity of the mineral free of royalty to make up his deficiency. A landlord, who has been induced by erroneous returns furnished by the tenant to accept for several years a fixed rent in place of royalties, is not barred from re-covering arrears of royalties.[72] Care should be taken to specify exactly on what the royalty is to be based. Where it was provided in a lease that, in the event of the " annual output " from a mineral field exceeding a certain amount, a royalty should be paid on the total quantity put out and removed from the lands, it was held that in view of the wording used " annual output " applied to the whole mineral brought to the surface, although the royalty was payable only on the part thereof removed from the lands.[73] The landlord's hypothec extends to lordships and royalties, as well as to fixed rents, because they are equally the return or consideration given for the occupation of the subjects let.[74]

A mineral lease should specify clearly the subjects let by giving a detailed description of the mineral or minerals to be worked. The question whether a particular sort of seam of minerals is included in the description in a lease is a question of fact.[75] Reference is made to the undernoted authorities for the meaning of such words as " mines, minerals and quarries ".[76]

The duration of a mineral lease is usually fairly long, but it is common to provide for breaks at definite intervals in case the minerals fail or become difficult to work profitably.[77] Even if such a break is provided for in a lease, a tenant is not entitled to reduce it between breaks on the ground that the minerals cannot be worked to profit.[78] In the absence of stipulation, the general rule is that a mineral tenant is not entitled

[71] *Dixon's Trs.* v *Church's Trs.* (1894) 21 R. 441.
[72] *Simpson's Asylum Trs.* v *Gowans* (1874) 11 S.L.R. 309.
[73] *Dalgleish* v *Fife Coal Co.* (1892) 30 S.L.R. 58.
[74] *Liquidators of Linlithgow Oil Co. Ltd.* v *Earl of Rosebery* (1903) 6 F. 90.
[75] *Gillespie* v *Russel* (1854) 17 D. 1; (1856) 18 D. 677; (1857) 19 D. 897; (1859) 21 D. (H.L.) 13, 3 Macq. 757.
[76] *Borthwick-Norton* v *Gavin Paul & Sons*, 1947 S.C. 659, and cases cited there; Halsbury's *Laws of England*, 3rd ed., Vol. 26, 320.
[77] *Shotts Iron Co.* v *Deas* (1881) 8 R. 530; *Waddell's Trs.* v *Monkland Iron Co.* (1885) 13 R. 237; *Ebbw Vale Steel Co.* v *Wood's Tr.* (1898) 25 R. 439.
[78] *Gowans* v *Christie* (1871) 9 M. 485; (1873) 11 M. (H.L.) 1; *Fleeming* v *Baird & Co.* (1871) 9 M. 730.

to abandon his lease on the grounds of unprofitability or difficulty of working[79] falling short of a complete exhaustion of the mineral.[80]

Mineral leases usually contain special provisions as to such matters as the mode of working, surface damages, support and restoration of the ground at the termination.[81] The right of the surface owner to support may be modified by the terms of his title or by agreement, and the mineral owner or his tenant may thus be entitled to lower the surface on payment of damages, or even without paying damages.[82] Apart from express agreement, a surface owner's compensation is probably measured as at the date of the breach of obligation of support, not at the date of lease.[83] Sometimes a mineral lease provides that the landlord may resume possession if dissatisfied with the tenant's mode of working. In such a case the landlord is not bound to state the cause of this dissatisfaction; where the tenants refuse to move, the landlord is entitled to damages for breach of contract, but not to violent profits; and the tenants are entitled to a reasonable time to make arrangements for ceding possession.[84] Where an agreement authorised a mineral tenant to erect all necessary buildings and provided for the execution of a formal tack " containing all clauses usual and necessary ", it was held that the tenant was entitled to the insertion of a clause empowering him to remove his buildings at the end of the lease, unless the landlord took them over at valuation.[85]

Woods and Timber. As in the case of minerals, the transaction by which the right to cut timber is given is commonly called a lease, but in reality it is more in the nature of a sale. The contract should define the type and age of trees which the tenant is entitled to cut, and sometimes power is given to erect a sawmill. The landlord's hypothec does not apply to leases of timber;[86] and for this and other reasons it is doubted whether timber itself (unlike minerals) can properly be the subject of a lease.[87] The right to take timber may, however, be an adjunct of a lease of the land on which the timber grows, as where a woodland is let with express power to take timber.

Shooting and Fishing. Salmon Fishings. As salmon fishings are separate feudal tenements, there never has been any doubt as to whether

---

[79] *Edmiston* v *Preston* (1675) Mor. 15172; *Gray* v *Hog* (1706) 4 B.S. 635; *Dixon* v *Campbell* (1824) 2 Sh. App. 175.
[80] *Wilson* v *Mader* (1699) Mor. 10125; *Murdoch* v *Fullerton* (1829) 7 S. 404.
[81] Rankine, 445-453; for the general law of support, see Rankine, *Land-Ownership*, 4th ed., Ch. xxviii.
[82] *Buchanan* v *Andrew* (1873) 11 M. (H.L.) 13; *Bank of Scotland* v *Stewart* (1891) 18 R. 957; *Anderson* v *M'Cracken Bros.* (1900) 2 F. 780; *Pringle* v *Carron Co.* (1905) 7 F. 820.
[83] *Neill's Trs.* v *Wm. Dixon Ltd.* (1880) 7 R. 741.
[84] *Houldsworth* v *Brand's Trs.* (1875) 2 R. 683; (1876) 3 R. 304; (1877) 4 R. 369.
[85] *Wilson* v *Douglas* (1868) 7 M. 112.
[86] *Muirhead* v *Drummond* (1792) Bell, *Comm.*, II, 28.
[87] But see Hunter, *Landlord and Tenant*, 4th ed., 273-276.

the right to take salmon by legal means may be leased by the proprietor thereof. A lease of salmon fishings is protected by the Leases Act 1449.[88] In many cases the proprietor is the Crown, which through the Crown Estate Commissioners is in the habit of granting leases of the salmon either to the riparian or littoral owners, or to other parties.[89] The taking of oysters and mussels is probably in the same situation as salmon fishing.

In granting either a conveyance or a lease of salmon fishings the granter sometimes reserves to himself the right to fish, and it is a question in each case whether this retained right is a right capable itself of being leased[90] or merely a privilege personal to the granter.[91]

Game and Sporting Leases. The granter of a lease of shootings, salmon fishings or other fishings must be either the proprietor of the lands, or the person in possession of a right of shooting or fishing over them, which is not a mere personal privilege. The holder of a mere servitude of pasturage has no right to lease the sporting rights,[92] nor has one of several proprietors of common property without the consent of the others.[93]

At common law the right of killing game belongs to the owner of the ground, and he may pursue game over his own land, even if it is let to a tenant. He is not, however, entitled to enter the policies of a house let by him as a residence.[94] The right of killing game may be made an adjunct, express or implied, of a lease of land. However, an ordinary agricultural lease without clear implication is not presumed to carry rights of fishing.[95] Similarly, an agricultural lease even for a period as long as 999 years is not presumed to carry the right of shooting game.[96] In England an agricultural lease carries the sporting rights over the subjects unless they are expressly reserved.[97] On the other hand, a building lease of a quarter of an acre for 99 years was held to exclude effectually the landlord's right of shooting, as the purpose of the lease was inconsistent with that right.[98]

Formerly it was thought that, as shootings and fishings (other than of salmon) were not feudal tenements, they could not be leased, and a grant of these rights was regarded as a mere personal privilege.[99] In fact, it was considered unsportsmanlike to make a profit out of killing

[88] *Infra,* p. 105.
[89] *Lovat* v *Macdonell* (1868) 6 M. 330; *Stephen* v *Lord Advocate* (1878) 6 R. 282.
[90] *Gemmill* v *Riddell* (1847) 9 D. 727.
[91] *Duke of Richmond* v *Duff* (1867) 5 M. 310.
[92] *Forbes* v *Anderson* 1 Feb 1809 F.C.
[93] *Campbell* v *Campbell* 24 Jan. 1809 F.C.
[94] *Graham* v *M'Kenzie* (1810) Hume 641; *M'Douall* v *Caird* (1869) 6 S.L.R. 583.
[95] *Copland* v *Maxwell* (1871) 9 M. (H.L.) 1.
[96] *Welwood* v *Husband* (1874) 1 R. 507.
[97] Woodfall, *Landlord and Tenant,* 26th ed., 812.
[98] *Welwood* v *Husband, supra, per* Lord Shand (L.O.), but the Inner House, while not deciding this point, expressed a contrary view.
[99] *Pollock, Gilmour & Co.* v *Harvey* (1828) 6 S. 913.

game in a fair sportsmanlike manner.[1] However, in cases decided during the 19th century it came to be recognised that a grant of sporting rights, although not necessarily a lease having the protection of the Leases Act 1449, was nevertheless a true lease for a variety of purposes,[2] including valuation of lands.[3] In some of these cases buildings were let along with the sporting rights, but the incorporeal right of fishing or shooting was the principal right, and the other right merely accessory. It has now been laid down in a series of decisions that a right of shootings need not be a mere personal franchise, but that what the tenant receives is a right of occupation of land, as much as in the case of an agricultural tenant; it is for a different purpose, but it is none the less a right of occupation; the shooting tenant goes on to the land for the purpose of shooting game, just as the agricultural tenant goes on for the purpose of tilling the ground.[4] However, a distinction, narrow as it may be, has been drawn between a lease of the right to shoot game conferring a limited right of occupation of the ground, and perhaps of buildings and certain services for the purpose of the lease[5] on the one hand, and a lease of land for the purpose of shooting game on the other hand; and this distinction may be of use in determining whether the lease is protected by the Leases Act 1449. If the grant implies no right of occupation of the ground, then it may not be a lease at all, but merely a licence. The terms of a particular grant of a right to shoot or trap rabbits has been held not to be a lease, but a personal licence.[6] The precise nature of such a right as rabbit-trapping, for which the rent may take the form of a royalty according to the number of animals caught, has not been judicially determined.[7] Thus the grant of a right of shooting or fishing may fall into one of three categories:—(a) a lease of salmon fishings, or a lease of a deer forest for stalking, both valid in questions with singular successors of the granter,[8] (b) a lease, but not valid against singular successors,[9] and (c) a privilege falling short of a lease, and therefore not communicable.[10]

It is common in a sale or lease to reserve a right of sporting to the granter, and the question whether such a reserved right is itself a lease

---

[1] *Earl of Aboyne* v *Innes,* 22 June 1813 F.C.; (1819) 6 Pat. 444; Hume, *Lectures,* IV, 265.
[2] *Macpherson* v *Macpherson* (1839) 1 D. 794; *Sinclair* v *Lord Duffus* (1842) 5 D. 174; *Menzies* v *Menzies* (1861) 23 D. (H.L.) 16; *Crawfurd* v *Stewart* (1861) 23 D. 965; *Farquharson* (1870) 9 M. 66; *Stewart* v *Bulloch* (1881) 8 R. 381.
[3] See Armour, *Valuation for Rating,* 3rd ed., 63-71 for a discussion of the rating of shootings and fishings.
[4] *Stewart* v *Bulloch, supra,* per L.P. Inglis at p. 383.
[5] See *Encyclopaedia of Scottish Legal Styles,* Vol. 6, Nos. 169-185.
[6] *Inland Revenue* v *Anderson,* 1922 S.C. 284.
[7] *L.M.S. Railway Co.* v *Assessor for Public Undertakings,* 1937 S.C. 773, *per* Lord Robertson at p. 783.
[8] *Gemmill* v *Riddell* (1847) 9 D. 727; *Farquharson* (1870) 9 M. 66.
[9] *Birkbeck* v *Ross* (1865) 4 M. 272.
[10] *Inland Revenue* v *Anderson, supra.*

or merely a licence depends entirely on its terms.[11] A right of fowling[12] over a particular estate was in a series of decisions interpreted as permitting the shootings to be let, whether or not the lessees were the tenants of the dominant estate and also as permitting sale of the game, if the right of shooting was exercised in such a way as not to encroach unreasonably on the owner's concurrent right of shooting.[13] Normally, however, a reserved right of sporting is narrowly construed. A reservation of deer created in a feudal grant was held not to be a right of stalking, but merely a right to deer which might be captured or killed on the land.[14] Even a right of salmon fishing may not always be lettable, as is illustrated by two similar but contrasting cases. In one case, the proprietor of a salmon fishing let it, but reserved to himself " and his heirs and successors " and to the proprietor of the lands and " to those having their authority " the right of angling with the rod, it being provided that the catch was to belong to the lessee; it was held that the wording of the reservation showed that it was not a mere personal privilege, but was a right communicable by lease.[15] In the other case, the proprietor of an estate sold the salmon and other fishings in a river but reserved to himself and his successors in the lands the privilege of fishing with the rod for amusement only; it was held that in the absence of proof of more extensive use, the reservation, although a perpetual heritable right, was merely a privilege personal to the proprietor of the land for the time being, and not a right which he was entitled to delegate or communicate to any other person.[16]

Normally a game lease does not take the form of a lease of the land itself, but gives to the tenant the exclusive right of shooting, or fishing, on the lands described, but without prejudice to such rights as the agricultural tenants may have by statute or common law to kill deer, hares and rabbits for the protection of their crops. The lease should specify what kinds of birds, animals or fish may be taken and by what means they may be killed. It may prescribe a limit to the number of animals to be shot, and usually the tenant is taken bound to exercise his rights in a fair and sportsmanlike manner and to leave a fair stock of game on the land at the termination of the lease.[17] In the case of fishing, the grant is normally limited to fishing with a specified number of rods on the river.[18] The tenant of shootings may be required to keep down vermin, and may also undertake not to increase the stock of game unduly so as to increase damage by the game to the agricultural tenant's crops.

[11] Rankine, 502.
[12] *privilegium et libertas aucupandi.*
[13] *Earl of Aboyne* v *Innes* (1819) 6 Pat. 444; *Marquis of Huntly* v *Nicol* (1858) 20 D. 374; *Marquis of Huntly* v *Nicol* (1896) 23 R. 610.
[14] *Hemming* v *Duke of Athole* (1883) 11 R. 93; see also *Carnegie* v *Lord Kintore* (1829) 8 S. 251.
[15] *Gemmill* v *Riddell* (1847) 9 D. 727.
[16] *Duke of Richmond* v *Duff* (1857) 5 M. 310.
[17] *Encyclopaedia of Scottish Legal Styles,* Vol. 6, Nos. 169-173.
[18] *Tuke* v *Maclachlan* (1899) 7 S.L.T. 244 (O.H.).

6

The lease will normally contain a clause binding the tenant to relieve the landlord of claims at the instance of the agricultural tenant. The term of lease may vary from a season or part of a season to a large number of years. With the right there may be given dwellinghouses, furniture, boats, vehicles, ice-houses, etc., and the services of ponies, keepers, beaters and domestic servants with arrangements for their payment and dismissal. It is usual for the rent to be paid in advance.[19] This is probably because the landlord has no right of hypothec, as the tenant brings on to the land none of his possessions, which could be attached for failure to pay rent. A petition brought immediately after the shooting season for sequestration of a tenant's effects contained in a house let with the shootings was refused in the absence of proof of custom.[20]

The tenant is entitled to the game he has contracted for under his lease. Thus where a tenant took a lease of a deer forest advertised as such, which was found to be frequented in the shooting season only by hinds and not by stags, it was held that this did not exclude proof that he had entered into the lease under essential error, although he had had the ground inspected by his own gamekeeper.[21] Similarly, where a proprietor let " the exclusive right of shooting over " a grouse moor with fishing and mansion-house " all as lately occupied by " the former tenant, and it was found that the former tenant had in fact shared part of the shooting with another party, it was held that the tenant had not got exclusive possession, and he was entitled to a reduction of rent by way of damages.[22]

Relations with Agricultural Lease. As has been seen, it is possible for the same ground to be let concurrently to an agricultural tenant and to a sporting tenant. Strictly speaking, there is no contractual relationship between the two, and any claim by one against the other would be founded on delict.[23] Apart from that, there is no direct action of one against the other. An agricultural tenant may suffer not only damage to his crops, stock and fencing by the sporting tenant's pursuit of the game (which might found a direct claim for reparation), but also damage caused by the depredations of the game itself; the sporting tenant may suffer loss by the agricultural tenant's failure to keep down vermin. Their rights are founded on contract with the landlord and it is to him that each must look for redress. Thus, where a farm tenant sued both his landlord and the game tenant in respect of damage caused by rabbits, it was held that the landlord alone was liable.[24]

---

[19] *Butter* v *Foster*, 1912 S.C. 1218.
[20] *Fraser* v *Patrick* (1879) 6 R. 581.
[21] *Wemyss* v *Campbell* (1858) 20 D. 1090.
[22] *Critchley* v *Campbell* (1884) 11 R. 475.
[23] *Inglis* v *Moir's Tutors* (1871) 10 M. 204.
[24] *Ibid.*

The whole question of the rights of the agricultural tenant against his landlord on account of game is reserved for a later chapter,[25] but it may be said here that when a claim arises at the instance of his agricultural tenant, the landlord may well have a right of relief against the sporting tenant arising out of the latter's lease. An example of this is to be found in two cases which were tried together—an action by the agricultural tenant against his landlord in respect of damage to crops caused by an excessive stock of game and rabbits and an action of relief by the landlord against the sporting tenant. It was observed that the liability of each tenant to the landlord depended on the contract, express or implied, between the respective parties, and that where the sporting tenant did not come individually into contact with the agricultural tenant, there could be no direct right of action by the latter against the former.[26] It was also held that, even although the sporting lease contained no provision on the point, the sporting tenant was liable to the landlord in relief, as there was an implied condition that the stock should not be unduly increased.[27] This practically assumes that in every game lease there is an express or implied condition that the shooting tenant shall be liable to relieve the landlord of all claims on account of the stock of game being unreasonably high; but the principle of *Byrne* v *Johnson* was questioned in a case, which, however, is distinguishable because the game lease contained an express obligation to relieve the landlord of claims made by the tenant for damage sustained from game.[28] Where the game lease regulates the right of relief, the principle of *Byrne* v *Johnson* does not have the effect of extending the tenant's liabilities beyond what is expressed in his lease, and so a sporting tenant was not liable for damage where the agricultural tenant had not claimed. Any claim by the tenant or claim of relief by the landlord on the ground of damage by game must be intimated timeously.[29]

Delectus personae is implied in a sporting lease, and therefore the tenant has no implied power to assign or sublet without the landlord's permission.[30] Where a lease of shootings in Scotland was drawn in English form and executed in England, the tenant claimed that English law, which implied a power of subletting, should apply; it was, however, held that in the absence of the contrary intention being expressed, the lease must be interpreted according to Scots law and accordingly the power of subletting was not implied.[31]

---

[25] Chapter XVIII.
[26] *Kidd* v *Byrne*, and *Byrne* v *Johnson* (1875) 3 R. 255.
[27] *Byrne* v *Johnson, supra.*
[28] *Eliott's Trs.* v *Eliott* (1894) 21 R. 858. Lord M'Laren's criticism at p. 863 of the decision in *Byrne* v *Johnson* is *obiter.*
[29] *Broadwood* v *Hunter* (1855) 17 D. 340, 1139, (1856) 18 D. 574; *Eliott's Trs., supra.*
[30] *Earl of Fife* v *Wilson* (1864) 3 M. 323 *per* Lord Kinloch at 324; *Mackintosh* v *May* (1895) 22 R. 345.
[31] *Mackintosh* v *May, supra.*

Rabbits. Rabbits are not game,[32] and at common law an agricultural tenant has a limited right, unless the lease provides otherwise, to kill them for the protection of his crops.[33] The right could at common law be taken away from the tenant by reservation in the lease.[34] As rabbits are not game, the right is not taken from the tenant by reserving to the landlord the exclusive right to the game.[35] The tenant may employ others to kill rabbits on his verbal instruction.[36] Although rabbits are not game, a lease of " the whole game and shooting of every description " was presumed to include rabbits; so, apart from the Ground Game Act, it is probable that neither the landlord nor anyone on his behalf may shoot rabbits during the subsistence of such a game lease without the tenant's permission. However, as a result of that Act the landlord of a game lease, if he is occupier of the ground, does not deprive himself of the right to shoot ground game,[37] defined by the Act as being hares and rabbits.[38]

Kelp Shores. The right to cut seaweed for the manufacture of kelp (a source of soda and iodine) is a right distinct from that of the agricultural or pastoral tenant of seaside land and is not presumed to have been let with these lands. The right may be granted separately, and leases of kelp shores were at one time common,[39] and they may well be granted in modern times when the chemical uses of seaweed are being exploited once more.

Other Subjects. Other subjects of leases which were of greater importance in earlier times than now are Mills, Multures, Railways, Ferries,[40] Tolls, Dues, Rents and Feuduties and it will suffice to refer to Rankine and the authorities cited there.[41]

---

[32] *Moncrieff* v *Arnott* (1828) 6 S. 530.
[33] *Fraser* v *Lawson* (1882) 10 R. 396; *Crawshay* v *Duncan,* 1915 2 S.L.T. 13.
[34] *Richardson* v *Maitland* (1897) 24 R. (J.) 32.
[35] *Jack* v *Nairne* (1887) 14 R. (J.) 20.
[36] *North and George* v *Cumming* (1864) 3 M. 173.
[37] Ground Game Act 1880, s. 2.
[38] *Ibid.,* s. 8.
[39] *Campbell* v *Campbell* (1795) Mor. 9646; *Sinclair* v *M'Beath* (1788) Hume 773; Hume, *Lectures,* II, 59; Rankine, 91.
[40] *Encyclopaedia of Scottish Legal Styles,* Vol. 6, 177.
[41] Rankine, 89-92.

CHAPTER VI

LEASE AS A PERSONAL CONTRACT

Application of Law of Contract. At common law a lease is a personal contract, and, as such, is governed by the general law of Contract. It is not within the scope of this work to discuss the law of Contract, for which the reader is referred to the standard work.[1] However, a few principles of the law of Contract particularly applicable to leases, not dealt with elsewhere in this work, are discussed here. It should be borne in mind that the law of Landlord and Tenant forms only a small section of the law of Contract, which is constantly being developed. The cases affecting leases are neither numerous, nor are many of them particularly modern, and those cited in this chapter should be regarded as illustrative of the contractual element in leases rather than as modern authorities of the law of Contract.

Consent. There must be *consensus in idem* between the parties; that is, both parties must have reached agreement not only to enter the contract but also agreement as to its terms.[2] If no agreement to enter into the lease is established between the parties, then there is no contract. This usually occurs where there have been negotiations for a lease, but one of the parties has refused to sign it on account of failure to agree one or more of its conditions; then no lease has come into existence.[3] The same applies where an informal contract has been followed by possession or supporting *rei interventus;*[4] the informal documents must show *consensus in idem.*[5] However, it is no objection if the absence of true agreement is merely formal, provided there is no doubt as to the meaning of the parties.[6]

It has already been seen that the parties must reach agreement on the cardinal elements of a lease, that is, the subjects, the consideration and the period.[7] If a bargain has been completed by the acceptance of a missive containing the cardinal elements subject to "the usual and necessary clauses", these clauses and no others will be introduced into the extended lease (by a remit to a conveyancer if necessary) and

---

[1] Gloag, *Contract,* 2nd ed.
[2] *Gray* v *Edinburgh University,* 1962 S.L.T. 173; *supra,* p. 5.
[3] *Dallas* v *Fraser* (1849) 11 D. 1058.
[4] *Cairns* v *Gerrard* (1833) 11 S. 737; *Fraser* v *Brebner* (1857) 19 D. 401; *Duke of Hamilton* v *Buchanan* (1877) 4 R. 328, (1878) 5 R. (H.L.) 69.
[5] *East Kilbride Development Co.* v *Pollok,* 1953 S.C. 370 (O.H.) (sale).
[6] *Steuart* v *Neilsons* (1864) 2 M. 817; *Erskine* v *Glendinning* (1871) 9 M. 656; Rankine, 95.
[7] *Supra,* p. 5.

neither of the parties can resile on the ground that they cannot agree on the limited terms; these terms may be such as are imported by an extensive, universal and clear custom, but a fairly general usage cannot import a clause whose wording materially varies.[8] Thus, where parties had entered into missives of lease which contained the essential terms of a lease but no reference to the estate regulations usually incorporated in leases by the proprietor, it was held that the tenant was not entitled to the benefit of provisions in the regulations as to the taking over of sheep stock, although there was evidence that it was the invariable custom of the district to insert such provisions in leases.[9]

Consent Improperly Obtained. To the same extent as in the case of other contracts, the absence of true consent may be shown, if a party has been induced to enter into a lease in error or by improper means, such as force and fear, fraud and misrepresentation.

Fraud, Misrepresentation. A lease obtained by improper means is voidable, and may be reduced by either the landlord or the tenant, who has been induced to sign it.[10] Most cases concern statements made by one party before or at the time when the contract was made. Statements made by a tenant may have induced the landlord to grant him a lease on favourable terms.[11] More frequently, cases concern statements made by the landlord, such as in advertisements of the subjects to let. If such statements turn out to be incorrect and have not been embodied in the lease, the tenant will have no claim of warrandice, and he must rely on reducing the contract on the grounds of misrepresentation. It is, however, not always easy to determine whether a particular statement is a representation or a term of the contract; sometimes it may be both, and the tenant may have the choice of reducing the lease on the ground of misrepresentation or of suing for damages for breach of contract.[12]

Neither party is bound to warrant every representation made to the other in negotiating for a lease, or to reveal everything that might weigh with the other in deciding whether or not to contract. It used to be said that to found a reduction on the ground of misrepresentation there must be proof not merely of concealment or of false representation but also of fraudulent misrepresentation.[13] A more modern view, however, has been that a contract is voidable if induced by misrepresentation, whether innocent or fraudulent, on the principle that a man

---

[8] Rankine, 95.

[9] *Maclaine* v *Stewart* (1898) 36 S.L.R. 233, (1899) 37 S.L.R. (H.L.) 623.

[10] *M'Neillie* v *Cowie* (1858) 20 D. 1229; *Beresford's Trs.* v *Gardner* (1877) 4 R. 363, 885, 1091, (1878) 5 R. 638.

[11] *Beresford Trs., supra; Drummond* v *Douglas & Co.* (1851) 23 Sc. Jur. 648.

[12] Compare two cases with similar facts—*Earl of Wemyss* v *Campbell* (1858) 20 D. 1090 (reduction) and *Critchley* v *Campbell* (1884) 11 R. 475 (damages); see also *Gregson* v *Alsop* (1897) 24 R. 1081; *Brodie* v *M'Lachlan* (1900) 8 S.L.T. 145.

[13] *Campbell* v *Boswall* (1841) 3 D. 639; Rankine, 96.

has no right to insist on a contract which he could not have obtained if he had not led the other into error by misrepresenting the facts.[14] The fact that a party has entered the contract in error would seem more important than the means by which it was induced, so far as regards a ground of reduction.

A mere expression of opinion, although it may turn out to be unfounded, and although the other party may have relied on it, is not misrepresentation, if the opinion be honestly held; but it is clearly fraudulent to state an opinion which one does not hold, or to express a definite opinion on a point, on which the state of one's mind is complete ignorance, if the intention is to induce the other party to act upon it.[15] The question whether a particular statement is to be read as a mere opinion or as a definite assertion may often be a narrow one. Although no absolute rules can be laid down, there is a tendency to hold that a statement on a point on which parties have equal means of information is to be read as a mere expression of opinion, especially if in the circumstances a reasonably prudent man would have investigated the matter for himself.[16] Thus, in agricultural leases the acreage and stock-carrying capacity of a farm, or in mineral leases the extent and quality of the minerals, are matters on which an intending lessee should satisfy himself, and very considerable discrepancies between the statements made by the lessor and the actual facts may be regarded as mere expressions of opinion.[17] A tenant, who averred that he had entered into a lease of a farm on the faith of statements in an advertisement to the effect that it was capable of maintaining a certain number of sheep and cattle, was held not to have been entitled to rely on the advertisement.[18] Where a tenant under a mineral lease claimed the right to abandon it on the ground that the minerals were not sufficient to pay the cost of working, and founded on a representation by the landlord that there was a large stratum of freestone capable of being worked for profit, it was held that statements of this kind were expressions of opinion, and, even though erroneous, formed no ground for reducing the lease.[19]

Conversely, an intending tenant is under no obligation to reveal to the lessor that he has good reason to believe that the land has a greater value than the lessor suspects.[20] On the other hand, alleged misrepresentation by mineral tenants, who had definite knowledge of the

---

[14] Gloag, *op. cit.*, 471; Gloag & Henderson, *Introduction to the Law of Scotland*, 6th ed., 69; but see Smith, *A Short Commentary on the Law of Scotland*, 833-835, and Gow, *Mercantile and Industrial Law of Scotland*, 58-60.

[15] Gloag, *op. cit.*, 462.

[16] *Ibid.*

[17] *Oliver v Suttie* (1840) 2 D. 514; *Campbell v Boswall* (1841) 3 D. 639; *M'Pherson v Campbell's Trs.* (1869) 41 Sc. Jur. 634.

[18] *Hamilton v Duke of Montrose* (1906) 8 F. 1026.

[19] *Gowans v Christie* (1871) 9 M. 485, (1873) 11 M. (H.L.) 1.

[20] *Gillespie v Russel* (1856) 18 D. 677, (1857) 19 D. 897, and (1859) 21 D. (H.L.) 13.

existence of a valuable mineral, of which the landlord was unaware, was held to be relevant in an action by the landlord to have a lease reduced on the ground of fraud.[21]

Error. A contract may be reduced on the ground of essential error.[22] Where a tenant took a lease of a deer forest advertised as such, but it turned out that during the shooting season it was frequented only by hinds, not stags, although his gamekeeper had inspected the land, he was allowed an issue to try whether the subjects were a deer forest and whether he had entered the contract under essential error as to its subjects.[23] On the other hand, in the absence of misrepresentation, a mere error in the quality of the subjects leased is apparently not a ground for an action of reduction.[24]

Personal Bar. Homologation. The right of a party to challenge a lease on the ground that his consent has been improperly obtained may be lost by *mora* or homologation. Thus, possession and payment of rent for a number of years may bar an action of reduction on the ground of misrepresentation as to the quality of minerals or the carrying capacity of a farm.[25]

Acceptance of rent by the landlord implies his recognition of a sublessee or assignee,[26] but only if the rent is paid by the sub-tenant or assignee in that capacity and the landlord is aware of it;[27] for in those cases all that is required to be proved is that the landlord does not exercise his power to object to the subletting or assignation.[28] On the other hand, where the landlord cannot get rid of a tenant without a process of reduction, acceptance of rent does not amount to homologation,[29] but merely excludes recourse against the tenant for the value of his possession.[30] Conversely, payment of rent by a tenant may have the effect of barring a counter-claim against his landlord.[31]

Homologation by itself will probably not validate an informally constituted contract, but it is very frequently associated with *rei interventus* and the homologation may form one of the facts which, taken together, constitute the *rei interventus*.[32] The distinction is sometimes narrow, but it has been explained that a contract between A and B has been homologated when A has recognised an informal or voidable

---

[21] *Ibid.*
[22] Gloag, *op. cit.*, Chapter XXVI.
[23] *Earl of Wemyss* v *Campbell* (1858) 20 D. 1090.
[24] *Hamilton* v *Duke of Montrose* (1906) 8 F. 1026.
[25] *Rig* v *Durward* (1776) Mor. 5672; *Grieve* v *Rutherford's Trs.* (1871) 9 S.L.R. 60.
[26] *Maule* v *Robb* (1807) Hume 835; *Hay* v *M'Tier* (1806) Hume 836; *Aglionby* v Watson (1809) Hume 845; Hume, *Lectures,* IV, 96.
[27] *Earl of Elgin* v *Walls* (1833) 11 S. 585.
[28] Rankine, 99.
[29] *Aglionby* v *Watson, supra,* per Lord Glenlee.
[30] Rankine, 99.
[31] *Broadwood* v *Hunter* (1855) 17 D. 340; *Emslie* v *Young's Trs.* (1894) 21 R. 710.
[32] E.g. *Bathie* v *Lord Wharncliffe* (1873) 11 M. 490; *Nairn Station Hotel Ltd.* v *Macpherson* (1905) 13 S.L.T. (O.H.).

contract as binding on him; it is validated by *rei interventus* when A has allowed B to act on the faith that the informal obligation is binding.[33]

Pacta Illicita. A lease entered into for the purpose of promoting an illegal or immoral purpose would be unenforceable. There are no Scottish cases, but in England a landlord was refused an action of recovery of rent where he knew that the house was to be used by the tenant for the purpose of prostitution or keeping a mistress, or where the purpose of the lease—a particular method of boiling tar—was prohibited by statute.[34] However, the fact that a contract contains an illegal provision does not necessarily make the whole contract unenforceable, if the illegal provision is severable. Thus, where in an agricultural lease the tenant renounced the right to kill ground game, it was held that, although the renunciation was illegal under the Ground Game Act 1880 sec. 3, the lease was not avoided.[35]

There is no reason why one should not contract with a person with whom one has an immoral or illegal relationship, if that is not the purpose of the contract. A lease granted on favourable terms to trustees for the granter's mistress was not reducible merely on account of the relationship of the parties.[36]

Certain leases may be struck at by statute. For example, it is provided by the Burgh Police (Scotland) Act 1892 that the conviction of any person of occupying or managing a brothel shall *ipso facto* void and terminate any lease of the house or building used for that purpose from and after the date of the conviction without prejudice to the legal right of the owner for the current year's rent.[37]

Delivery. As a lease is a mutual contract, the obligations on each party are incurred by signature, and there is no need for delivery, nor does it matter in whose custody the actual document is. So, where a lease was signed in duplicate by a landlord and tenant, it was held that the contractual relationship was fully established without any delivery of the actual copies by either party; the agent for the landlord, in whose hands both copies were, refused to deliver a copy to the tenant, unless he found security for the fulfilment of his obligations under the lease; it was held that this was quite ineffectual, as in the ordinary case a mutual contract requires no delivery and whoever holds the document holds it for all the parties and against all the parties.[38]

---

[33] Gloag, *op. cit.,* 175, note 1.
[34] Woodfall, *Landlord and Tenant,* 26th ed., 485.
[35] *Stanton* v *Brown* [1900] 1 Q.B. 671.
[36] *A.* v *B.,* 21 May 1816 F.C.; reversed on another ground and reported as *Hamilton* v *Waring* (1820) 6 Pat. 644.
[37] Burgh Police (Scotland) Act 1892 s. 403.
[38] *Robertson's Trs.* v *Lindsay* (1873) 1 R. 323.

Principles of Construction. As a lease is a mutual contract containing correlative rights and obligations, it must be construed as a whole, each clause being taken in conjunction with all the others and with the common and statutory law of the land. Moreover, it must be so read as to bring out the intention of the parties, so far as that appears on the face of the contract, when thus interpreted, along with such extraneous evidence as may competently be adduced.[39] The Courts have no bias either for or against the landlord or the tenant; and the only presumption admissible seems to be the general maxim that a deed shall be construed *contra proferentem,* that is, against the party who drew a deed to which the other merely consented.[40] The doctrine that leases are *stricti* (even *strictissimi*) *juris* was imbedded in our jurisprudence at a time when a grant of a lease was regarded as a favour to a follower rather than as a commercial transaction, and the only traces it has left behind are to be found in the rule of *delectus personae.*[41]

It is well to recall that a lease *is* a contract, and that the parties are free to make any lawful bargain they like, fair or unfair.[42] The Court has no equitable jurisdiction to restrict a party's right expressed in a lease. Thus, the Court will not interfere with a right of resumption, merely because it seems to be unfair,[43] nor with the landlord's enforcement of an irritancy clause, unless he makes an oppressive use of his power.[44]

The *ejusdem generis* rule of construction has been applied to leases in several cases.[45]

Law Applicable. The *lex loci situs* applies, and in the absence of any indication to the contrary, the presumption is that a lease of Scottish heritage is to be construed according to Scots law. Where a lease of shootings in Scotland was drawn in England by an English solicitor in English form and was signed in England, it was held that, as there was nothing in its terms to show that the parties intended the lease to be construed according to English law, it fell to be construed according to Scots law; in consequence an exclusion of subtenants was implied.[46]

Mutuality of Contract. As a lease is a mutual contract, both parties to it are bound by it or neither.[47] Thus, both parties must sign it, or if

---

[39] Rankine, 98.
[40] *Johnson* v *Gordon* (1805) Hume 822 *per* L.P. Campbell.
[41] Rankine, 98.
[42] *Edinburgh Corporation* v *Gray,* 1948 S.C. 538 *per* L.P. Cooper at p. 545.
[43] *Stewart* v *Lead* (1825) I W. & S. 68; *Edinburgh Corporation* v *Gray, supra,* *per* L.P. Cooper, disapproving Hunter, *Landlord and Tenant,* 4th ed., II, 214.
[44] *Per* L.J.C. Inglis in *Stewart* v *Watson* (1864) 2 M. 1414 at p. 1420; L.J.C. Thomson in *M'Douall's Trs.* v *Macleod,* 1949 S.C. 593 at p. 599; *infra,* p. 232.
[45] *Glasgow Corporation* v *Glasgow Tramways Co.* (1897) 24 R. 628, revd. (1898) 25 R. (H.L.) 77; *The Admiralty* v *Burns,* 1910 S.C. 531; *Crichton Stuart* v *Ogilvie,* 1914 S.C. 888; *Turner* v *Wilson,* 1954 S.C. 296; *Piggott* v *Robson,* 1958 S.L.T. 49; *infra,* p. 242.
[46] *Macintosh* v *May* (1895) 22 R. 345.
[47] Rankine, 97; Gloag, *op. cit.,* 407.

they are more than two, all must sign it.[48] The general rule that both parties to a lease are bound by all its terms applies even where it is provided that one party may have the option of rescinding the contract, as where there is a break in favour of one party only.

There is a general presumption that a lease is to be regarded as a whole, that the obligations on either side are given in consideration of each other and that failure by one party to perform his side of the bargain will justify the other in withholding performance of the obligations incumbent on him. Thus, material failure on the part of the landlord to give full possession to the tenant will give the tenant grounds for reducing the lease, if *restitutio in integrum* is still possible, or, failing reduction, a claim of damages, while a minor failure will entitle the tenant to an abatement in rent.[49] If the landlord fails to a sufficiently material extent to carry out repairs or improvements which he has undertaken, the tenant may abandon his lease and, depending on the circumstances, also claim damages.[50] Short of abandoning the lease, the tenant may withhold his rent, unless the lease excludes that right.[51] If his loss exceeds the rent withheld, he may also claim damages, but a tenant who has obtained an award of damages cannot also retain the rent in respect of them.[52] Similarly, a party is not entitled to take benefit by a mutual contract and at the same time repudiate its conditions. So it was held that a tenant, who refused to implement a condition of the lease that she should reside on a farm, had, notwithstanding the absence of any irritancy clause, forfeited her right to the lease.[53] One party cannot found on the other's breach, if he himself is in breach of his side of the lease.[54]

In cases where the incidence of contractual obligation is interfered with by statute, the principle of mutuality is so far recognised that it will be inferred that, if a statute declares that one party to the contract is bound, or is free to resile, a corresponding obligation or right to resile will be inferred in the other party.[55] Thus, the right of a lessee, which at common law was a mere personal right against the lessor, being protected by the Leases Act 1449 against singular successors, it was

[48] *York Buildings Co.* v *Baillie* (1724) Mor. 8435; *Hamilton* v *Buchanan* (1877) 4 R. 328, (1878) 5 R. (H.L.) 69; but see *Hamilton* v *Smith* (1738) Mor. 9168.
[49] *Webster* v *Lyell* (1860) 22 D. 1423; *Kilmarnock Gas Light Co.* v *Smith* (1872) 11 M. 58; *Guthrie* v *Shearer* (1873) 1 R. 181; Rankine, 208; Gloag, *op. cit.*, 628; *infra*, p. 127.
[50] *Lyons* v *Anderson* (1886) 13 R. 1020; *M'Kimmie's Trs.* v *Armour* (1899) 2 F. 156; *Dickie* v *Amicable Property Investment Building Society*, 1911 S.C. 1079; *Mullen* v *Dunbarton County Council*, 1933 S.C. 380; Gloag, *op. cit.*, 628; *infra*, p. 131.
[51] *M'Donald* v *Kydd* (1901) 3 F. 923; *Earl of Galloway* v *M'Connell*, 1911 S.C. 846; *John Haig & Co.* v *Boswall-Preston*, 1915 S.C. 339; *Fingland & Mitchell* v *Howie*, 1926 S.C. 319; *Skene* v *Cameron*, 1942 S.C. 393; *infra*, p. 141.
[52] *Fingland & Mitchell* v *Howie*, *supra*; *Christie* v *Wilson*, 1915 S.C. 645.
[53] *Edmond* v *Reid* (1871) 9 M. 782.
[54] *Macnab* v *Willison*, 1960 S.L.T. (Notes) 25; *British Transport Commission* v *Forsyth* (1963) 79 Sh. Ct. Rep. 97; but see *Wilson-Clarke* v *Graham* (1963) 79 Sh. Ct. Rep. 113.
[55] Gloag, *op. cit.*, 409.

held on the principle of mutuality that the lessee was bound to the singular successor in certain obligations he had undertaken in the lease.[56]

Unity of Contract. There is a general presumption that a contract is to be regarded as a whole, that the obligations undertaken by one party are the counterparts of obligations undertaken by the other. There is no ground for separating the parts of the contract into independent obligations, so that one party can refuse to perform his part of the contract and yet insist on the other performing his part; the unity of the contract must be respected.[57] Where a landlord enforced a clause entitling him to bring the lease to an end because of the tenant's failure to pay rent, it was held that the tenant could not insist on a clause in the lease by which the landlord undertook to take over the sheepstock at the tenant's " awaygoing ".[58]

The obligations presumed to be correlative do not need to be *inter naturalia* of a lease. In such cases there is a general presumption that the reason why the parties have not recorded their agreements in separate documents is that they intended them to be interdependent.[59] Two parties entered into a minute of agreement for the lease of a hotel and it was stipulated that the tenant should take over the furniture and stock at valuation; in terms of the agreement the tenant consigned £200 in joint names to account of the price, but before taking over the furniture and stock, he intimated that he did not intend to fulfil the agreement; in an action for delivery of the endorsed deposit receipt it was held that the tenant, having declined to carry out his part of the contract, could not call on the landlord to fulfil his obligations until the latter had an opportunity of constituting his claim of damages.[60] Where a lease gave a tenant an option to purchase the subjects during the currency of the lease and provided for an irritancy in the event of an assignation, the tenant assigned his lease without the landlord's consent, but the landlord did not enforce the irritancy; it was held that the tenant could not validly exercise his option to purchase while he was in breach of a material condition of the lease.[61]

However, it is only a presumption that a contract is indivisible, and it is competent to prove that the provisions of a lease are not interdependent. There is nothing to prevent two separate contracts being recorded in the same deed, and it is then a question of construction whether they are interdependent or not.[62] Even when there is clearly one contract, some of its provisions may be independent obligations.

---

[56] *Hall* v *M'Gill* (1847) 9 D. 1557.
[57] See *Turnbull* v *M'Lean* (1874) 1 R. 730 (sale of goods).
[58] *Marquis of Breadalbane* v *Stewart* (1904) 6 F. (H.L.) 23.
[59] *Gloag, op. cit.,* 595.
[60] *Dingwall* v *Burnett,* 1912 S.C. 1097.
[61] *Penman* v *Mackay,* 1922 S.C. 385.
[62] *Pendreigh's Trs.* v *Dewar* (1871) 9 M. 1037, approved in *Marquis of Breadalbane* v *Stewart* (1904) 6F. (H.L.) 23.

Where a tenant undertook to expend on repairs the sum of £200 to be repaid at the end of the lease, it was held that, although the tenant had incurred an irritancy by having become bankrupt and was therefore materially in breach of his lease, his right to repayment of the sum he had laid out was an independent stipulation, which was not affected by the fact that the other provisions of the lease had not been implemented; he was, therefore, entitled to recover the sum when the lease would naturally have expired; his right to recover it was conditional upon his performance of a correlative obligation to expend it on repairs, and not on the obligation to fulfil all the conditions of the lease.[63] It is doubtful whether a tenant, by offering to give up one part of a lease which has become unenforceable and by paying the full rent, can save the rest from reduction.[64]

General arbitration clauses in contracts are in a special category and are normally presumed to be severable from the main contract, the theory being that the counterpart and consideration for which one party renounces his right to go to the Court is a similar renunciation by the other party.[65] It was, however, concerning a particular arbitration clause in a lease that the general rule of unity of contracts was stated thus: — " The obligation to refer not having reference to any matter merely extrinsic, or which can be regarded as in any proper sense foreign to the proper object of the lease, but on the contrary constituting an express condition of the contract and necessary to its extrication, according to the *modus operandi* intended and bargained for from the first, it must receive effect as a stipulation entirely inseparable from the whole substance of the right ".[66] The main exceptions to this rule, apart from general arbitration clauses, are stipulations for which particular counter-stipulations can be found to be expressed or implied in the lease;[67] then the stipulation and counter-stipulation may be severable from the lease itself.

Conditions. The question may arise whether a particular provision of a lease is a term of the contract or is a condition necessary to the constitution of the contract. In the former case failure to comply with it amounts to breach of contract; in the latter case the effect of failure to satisfy the condition is that there is no concluded contract.

Where a written offer to take a lease was met by a general acceptance also in writing with the words " subject to lease drawn out in due form ", it was held that a binding contract had been concluded by the offer and acceptance, and that, if the parties would not concur in drawing a lease,

[63] *Ibid.*
[64] Opinions in *Earl of Galloway* v *Duke of Bedford* (1902) 4 F. 851; Gloag, *op. cit.*, 411.
[65] Gloag, *op. cit.*, 596.
[66] *Montgomerie* v *Carrick* (1848) 10 D. 1387, *per* Lord Ivory at p. 1392.
[67] *Pendreigh's Tr.* v *Dewar* (1871) 9 M. 1037.

the Court would remit to a conveyancer to draw one.[68] Where a lease
of minerals provided that certain items of machinery were to be taken
over by the tenant " conform to inventory of same hereunto appended,
and signed by both parties as relative hereto " and no inventory was
prepared and signed, it was held that the contract was complete, although
no inventory had been prepared, this provision amounting to an obligation on each party to concur in drawing up an inventory and not a condition suspensive of the contract.[69] Similarly, where a lease of a furnished
house referred to an inventory of contents, which was to be prepared
and made part of the agreement and signed by both parties, it was held
that the landlord's failure to prepare an inventory did not entitle the
tenant to maintain that no valid lease had been entered into.[70]

Where it was a condition of the granting of a lease that the tenant
should find security for the due performance of his obligations and he
failed to do so, it was held that there was no concluded lease.[71]

Running with the Lands. At common law a lease is essentially a
personal contract binding the original landlord and original tenant and
their representatives. If the lease is assignable, it remains binding in a
question between the original landlord and the tenant's assignees and
successors; and to the extent that the landlord and his successors can
enforce its ordinary conditions, such as the obligations to pay rent and
to keep the subjects in repair, whether expressed in the lease or implied
by law, the lease may be said to " run with the lands ". However, at
common law the lease does not bind the landlord's singular successors.
As will be seen in the next chapter, when a lease meets the requirements
of the Leases Act 1449, the lease itself and its ordinary conditions do
bind the singular successors of the landlord. Conversely, if there ever
was any doubt about the matter, it was held that, where the Leases Act
applies, a singular successor of the landlord has a title to enforce the
obligations of the lease against the tenant.[72] Thus, the contract runs with
the lands, and its terms are binding on the persons who are landlord
and tenant respectively from time to time. This is true not only of the
obligations expressed in the lease, but also of those that may be implied
by law,[73] or inferred from a custom of the district.[74]

However, singular successors are not generally bound by private
agreements between the original landlord and tenant not appearing in
the lease itself. Where a landlord during the currency of a lease gave
the tenant a letter undertaking to give him £200 for improvements he
had carried out, it was held that the letter, being " altogether extrinsic ",

[68] *Erskine* v *Glendinning* (1871) 9 M. 656.
[69] *Steuart* v *Neilsons* (1864) 2 M. 817.
[70] *Elliot* v *Erickson*, 1960 S.L.T. (Sh. Ct.) 28.
[71] *Cairns* v *Gerrard* (1833) 11 S. 737.
[72] *Hall* v *M'Gill* (1847) 9 D. 1557.
[73] *Huber* v *Ross*, 1912 S.C. 898.
[74] *Bell* v *Lamont*, 14 June 1814 F.C.

did not bind the landlord's singular successor and did not justify the tenant in retaining his rent in a question with a trustee for the landlord's creditors.[75] Similarly, an undertaking by a landlord contained in a letter separate from the lease itself to grant a new lease did not bind a purchaser.[76] However, where a letter from the landlord expressly stated that his tenant was to get a reduction in his rent until the expiry of the lease, this was held to bind a purchaser, presumably because the letter altered an essential term of the contract and was regarded as part of the lease itself.[77] *Page v Strains*

Where an unusual obligation is given in a lease to a tenant and is specially reserved in a disposition to a purchaser, the latter will be bound by it.[78]

Real and Personal Conditions. The next chapter will discuss the requirements which a contract of lease must satisfy before it binds a singular successor of the landlord. However, on the assumption that a particular lease does bind a singular successor, the question arises as to which of its conditions are *real* and bind singular successors of either party, and which of its conditions are *personal* and do not bind them. In fact most of the cases are concerned with whether or not conditions bind the singular successors of the landlord; few of them are concerned with the successors of the tenant.

While the ordinary and essential conditions of a lease will run with the lands,[79] there may be certain obligations undertaken by the original parties which are purely personal and which affect only them and their personal representatives. The general rule is that only those conditions which are *inter naturalia* of a lease run with the lands.[80] This appears to mean that in order to bind a singular successor the condition must be one commonly occurring in the type of lease concerned; thus, while an obligation to grant a feu charter, contained in a lease for 999 years, was held not to bind a singular successor of the landlord, the result might have been different, had there been proof that an obligation of this kind was customary in leases of such duration.[81] Apart from the ordinary conditions as to rent, possession and repairs, which obviously transmit to singular successors, any other conditions, which are not foreign to the proper object of the lease but which constitute conditions of the contract and are necessary to it, will bind a singular successor.[82]

Conditions which have been held to transmit against singular successors of the landlord include:—obligations to compensate the tenant

[75] *Turner v Nicolson* (1835) 13 S. 633.
[76] *Jacobs v Anderson* (1898) 6 S.L.T. 234.
[77] *Page v Strains* (1892) 30 S.L.R. 69.
[78] *Findlay v Stuart* (1890) 29 S.L.R. 15 (O.H.).
[79] *Montgomerie v Carrick* (1848) 10 D. 1387.
[80] *Bisset v Mags. of Aberdeen* (1898) 1 F. 87; Gloag, *op. cit.*, 234.
[81] *Bisset, supra, per* Lord Moncreiff, at p. 90.
[82] *Montgomerie v Carrick* (1848) 10 D. 1387.

for improvements;[83] an obligation to put buildings and fences in good repair;[84] a right to sink pits;[85] a clause referring all disputes to arbitration, the clause being essential to the contract;[86] rights of pasturage, quarrying stone and taking peats in long leases granted in the course of founding a new town at Tobermory;[87] an obligation to abate the rent, provided it is clearly intended to apply for the whole term of the lease,[88] even if contained in a separate document modifying the original lease;[89] an agreement to give effect to a permanent change in the method of paying the rent;[90] an implied obligation not to derogate from the grant by carrying on operations in the landlord's own adjacent property having an injurious effect on the tenant's business;[91] and an obligation on the landlord to take over at valuation an acclimatised sheep stock left by the tenant in terms of the lease.[92]

Conditions which have been held not to transmit against singular successors include:—a right of a farm tenant to take peat from a moss in another part of his landlord's estate;[93] a provision for the abatement or retention of rent in consideration of personal services rendered by the tenant to the landlord,[94] although such services may take the place of rent and render the lease itself good against a singular successor;[95] provisions for the retention of rent in satisfaction of some private debt by the landlord to the tenant unconnected with the lease;[96] an obligation in a 999 years' lease to grant a feu charter on demand;[97] obligations to pay for improvements or repairs which have become liquid debts;[98] an obligation to pay a fixed sum, if the tenant should leave the subjects in good repair at the end of the lease, on the ground that a condition, which resolved itself into payment of a sum of money, does not bind singular successors;[99] an obligation to pay for improvements on the

---

[83] *M'Doual* v *M'Doual* (1760) Mor. 15259; *Arbuthnot* v *Colquhoun* (1772) Mor. 10424, 15220; *Morison* v *Patullo* (1787) Mor. 10425; *Fraser* v *Maitland* (1824) 2 Sh. App. 37; *Stewart* v *M'Ra* (1834) 13 S. 4; *Stewart* v *Campbell* (1834) 13 S. 7; *Stewart* v *Dunmore's Tr.* (1837) 15 S. 1059.
[84] *Barr* v *Cochrane* (1878) 5 R. 877; *Waterson* v *Stewart* (1881) 9 R. 155.
[85] *Montgomerie* v *Carrick, supra.*
[86] *Ibid.*
[87] *Campbell* v *M'Lean* (1867) 5 M. 636, (1870) 8 M. (H.L.) 40.
[88] *Riddick* v *Wightman* (1790) Hume 776; *Grant* v *Watt* (1802) Hume 777; Hume, *Lectures,* IV, 77.
[89] *Page* v *Strains* (1892) 30 S.L.R. 69.
[90] *Baillie* v *Fraser* (1853) 15 D. 747.
[91] *Huber* v *Ross,* 1912 S.C. 898.
[92] *Gillespie* v *Riddell,* 1908 S.C. 628, affd. 1909 S.C. (H.L.) 3. (The point of the case was that such an obligation for special reasons did not bind an heir of entail.)
[93] *Duncan* v *Brooks* (1894) 21 R. 760, opinion of Lord Young at p. 764.
[94] *Ross* v *Sutherland* (1838) 16 S. 1179.
[95] *Lundy* v *Smith* (1610) Mor. 15166.
[96] Bell §§ 1201, 1202; Hume, *Lectures,* IV, 76-77.
[97] *Bisset* v *Mags. of Aberdeen* (1898) 1 F. 87.
[98] *Cumine* v *Bayley* (1856) 19 D. 97; *Walker* v *Masson* (1857) 19 D. 1099.
[99] *Swan & Sons* v *Fairholme* (1894) 2 S.L.T. 74 (O.H.).

expiry of a lease, postponed until the expiry of a new lease, on the ground that the claim became liquid on the expiry of the old lease.[1]

Obligations to grant renewals have sometimes been held to bind singular successors, but the position is far from clear. A right of renewal was sustained in one case,[2] which has since been doubted,[3] and in a second case which seems to have been decided on the ground that the singular successor had homologated the tenant's right.[4] The answer probably depends on the length of the particular lease and whether obligations of renewal are frequently inserted in leases of that nature and duration.[5]

Obligations which would be binding on a singular successor of the landlord may fail to bind an heir of entail, not because they are exceptional or personal obligations not *inter naturalia* of the lease, but because they would contravene the fetters of the entail.[6] Thus, before it was permitted by statute an obligation to pay for improvements was held not to bind a succeeding heir of entail,[7] and before the passing of the Entail (Scotland) Act 1914 obligations to take over sheep stocks were held unenforceable against a succeeding heir.[8]

Conditions held to have been enforceable by the landlord include: — the right to the delivery of minerals in addition to rent;[9] a right to damages for miscropping;[10] the right to damages for disrepair;[11] and the right to exercise a break.[12]

Title to Sue. Actions by Third Parties. A lease being a personal contract, the only persons affected by the contract are the granter on the one hand and the tenant for the time being on the other hand. When the lease satisfies the requirements of the Leases Act 1449 or of the Registration of Leases (Scotland) Act 1857, there is a continual contractual relationship which runs with the lands between the granter and his successors and the tenant and his successors. Apart from the landlord and tenant for the time being or their personal representatives, no one has a title to sue or may be sued in respect of the contract, except in so far as he may be a party to it, such as a cautioner. For example, no person other than the landlord has a title to enforce an exclusion of

[1] *Purves' Trs.* v *Traill's Tr.*, 1914 2 S.L.T. 425 (O.H.); but see *Buchanan* v *Taylor*, 1916 S.C. 129. See Gloag, *op. cit.*, 234.
[2] *Wight* v *Hopetoun* (1763) Mor. 10461.
[3] *Bisset* v *Mags. of Aberdeen, supra, per* Lord Trayner, at p. 89.
[4] *Scott* v *Straton* (1772) 3 Pat. 666.
[5] Opinion of Lord Moncreiff in *Bisset, supra*, at p. 90.
[6] *Panton* v *Mackintosh*, 1908 S.C. 647 (O.H.) *per* Lord Kyllachy, referred to in *Gillespie* v *Riddell, infra*.
[7] *Moncrieff* v *Tod & Skene* (1825) 1 W. & S. 217.
[8] *Gardiners* v *Stewart's Trs.*, 1908 S.C. 985; *Gillespie* v *Riddell*, 1908 S.C. 628, affd. 1909 S.C. (H.L.) 3; *Riddell's Exrs.* v *Milligan's Exrs.*, 1909 S.C. 1137.
[9] *Walpole* v *Beaumont* (1780) Mor. 15249.
[10] *Carnegie* v *Guthrie* (1866) 5 M. 253.
[11] *Hall* v *M'Gill* (1847) 9 D. 1557.
[12] *Infra*, p. 243.

assignees or subtenants;[13] and no person other than the tenant can sue
on the warrandice in a lease, and that only against the landlord.[14]

To enable a third party to sue on a contract made by two parties there
must be a *jus quaesitum tertio*, that is, the third party must establish that
the two contracting parties intended to confer on him a right to sue.[15]
There have not been many cases involving leases.[16] Where a lease of
minerals bound the tenants to pay compensation to the landlord or his
tenants or feuars for any damage due to subsidence, it was held that a
feuar from the landlord under a subsequent feu contract, which excluded
recourse against the superior, had a title to sue the tenants.[17] The question has not arisen whether one lessee may enforce against a neighbouring co-lessee restrictions contained in the latter's lease (for example,
building conditions contained in a long lease) on the ground of similarity
of conditions and mutuality of interest,[18] but there seems no reason why
this should not be possible, if there is reference to a common plan or
a stipulation in each long lease that the same restrictions are to be
imposed in all the others.

Actions by Landlord or Tenant. More frequently the question has
arisen as to what extent a landlord or a tenant has a title to sue third
parties or may be sued by third parties. A landlord has no *jus quaesitum
tertio* in a contract between his tenant and a third party merely on the
ground that fulfilment of the contract might result in improvement of
the subjects.[19] Thus, a landlord could not require his tenant to account
for a sum of money he had received by way of compensation for damage
done by a third party.[20]

A tenant comes in place of his landlord as occupier of the lands,
and *qua* occupier he may become involved in rights and obligations with
third parties. His title to sue in any particular matter depends on his
interest. There never has been any doubt as to an occupying tenant's
title to sue for declarator, damages, interdict, removing or restitution in
so far as his interest extends or otherwise to protect his holding.[21] Thus,
in an action of interdict by a tenant of a farm to prevent pollution of a
stream by neighbouring tenants, it was held that, as he was the assignee
of the landlord's title in so far as it was necessary for his own protection
in the subjects let, he had the same right as the landlord to maintain

13 *Infra*, p. 154.
14 *Infra*, p. 130.
15 Smith, *A Short Commentary on the Law of Scotland*, 780–784; Gloag, *op. cit.*,
   234 *et seq.* See also an article " *Jus Quaesitum Tertio* " in 1956 *J.R.*, 3.
16 *Wood* v *Moncur* (1591) Mor. 7719; 1 B.S. 126; *Craigie* v *Reid* (1807) Hume
   830; both these cases are unsatisfactory as authorities, Rankine, 579–580.
17 *Dryburgh* v *Fife Coal Co.* (1905) 7 F. 1083.
18 See *Hislop* v *M'Ritchie's Trs.* (1881) 8 R. (H.L.) 95 (feu).
19 *Peddie* v *Brown* (1857) 3 Macq. 65, *per* Lord Chancellor Cranworth at p. 71
   (*obiter*).
20 *Peddie* v *Brown*, *supra*.
21 Rankine, 710.

the purity of the stream, and accordingly he had a good title to pursue the action.[22]

There is no doubt that the landlord and the tenant may both sue together in the same action, if it involves the rights and interests of both.[23]

Relations with Superior. The principle that the tenant may pursue actions to vindicate his right under his lease was held to extend to the determination of rights of ownership where the form of action was one of declarator of the tenant's right to act under a lease. A proprietor granted a lease of minerals in certain lands, which had been feued by his predecessor and of which he was superior; the mineral tenants raised an action against the feuars for declarator that they had the exclusive right to work the minerals in the lands feued; the feuars defended on the ground that the minerals had passed to them by their feu charters before the present proprietor had granted the lease; it was held (by a majority) that the tenants did have a title to sue based on the fact that they were simply seeking to vindicate their rights under their lease.[24]

However, it is only so far as necessary for that purpose that a tenant has a title to sue. He cannot challenge the validity or enforceability of his landlord's feudal grant. Land was feued for the purpose of building a roadhouse, and the feu disposition contained a clause forbidding the erection of other buildings without the superior's consent; subsequently new owners granted a 20 years' lease to tenants, who proposed to build an extension, and the superiors refused consent except upon payment of £1,000 by way of an inducement; in an action by the tenants for declarator that they were entitled to proceed without the consent of the superiors, the tenants averred *inter alia* that the vassals (their landlords) had given their consent by a letter dated after the raising of the action; it was held (reversing the Outer House judgment) that the tenants had no title to sue, (1) because they were not vindicating their rights under the lease, but were modifying a feu disposition to which they were not parties, and (2) because upon their own averments they did not have permission from the vassals to erect the additional building at the time when the action was raised.[25] The first ground was sufficient for the decision:—" A vassal may give to a tenant some of the bundle of rights comprised in the *dominium utile* of the land, but he cannot give the tenant a right to sue for the determination of the rights and conditions of the vassals' grant from the superior. The present action is not a vindication of the tenant's rights under his lease. No-one is challenging

22 *Fleming* v *Gemmill,* 1908 S.C. 340.
23 *Jolly* v *Brown* (1828) 6 S. 872; *Young* v *Cunningham* (1830) 8 S. 959; *Paton* v *Hunter* (1875) 12 S.L.R. 305; *Baird & Co.* v *Kilsyth Feuars* (1878) 6 R. 116; Rankine, 711.
24 *Baird & Co.* v *Kilsyth Feuars, supra.*
25 *Eagle Lodge Ltd.* v *Keir & Cawder Estates Ltd.,* 1964 S.L.T. 13.

them. It is an attempt to secure a modification of the conditions of a feudal grant by the superior to the vassal contained in a deed to which the tenants are not parties. I can find no justification in principle or in authority for such an action ".[26]

The superior cannot interfere with the terms of a lease. Where a vassal under a feu charter containing a clause of pre-emption granted a tack for 19 years renewable for successive periods of 19 years, it was held that the lease could not be deemed to be an alienation, and that the superior could not prevent the completion of the lease, much less reduce it.[27] A lease, of course, is not proof against irritancy of the feu.[28]

Payment of Rent. The forms which rent may take have already been considered.[29] The ordinary rules relating to the extinction of obligations apply to the modes of payment of rent.[30] The persons entitled to receive the rents are the landlord, his executors or other representatives, his creditors and his assignees to the rents.[31] Payment must be made by the tenant to the person whom he honestly and reasonably believes to be the person entitled thereto.[32] Thus, a tenant who pays his rent prematurely may have to pay again to a party to whom the subjects have been sold,[33] though not to the landlord's trustee in bankruptcy.[34] The landlord in possession of the estate at the term when the rent falls due is the person entitled to exact it from the tenant, and the tenant has no concern with any question of accounting between the landlord and the previous proprietor or his representatives.[35]

Apocha Trium Annorum. This is a legal presumption in favour of payment raised by the production by a debtor of three consecutive discharges of periodical payments such as interests, feuduties, rents and salaries.[36] Where the tenant can produce three separate written unqualified receipts for consecutive termly (not necessarily yearly) instalments of rent, there is a presumption that all prior instalments have been paid.[37] Although the payments must be periodical, usually yearly or half-yearly, it seems reasonable in the absence of authority to suppose that receipts for instalments for shorter periods would be sufficient.[38] The presumption which " is mainly inferred from the reiteration of discharges without reservation, which no prudent man is presumed to do ",[39]

[26] *Ibid., per* L.P. Clyde at p. 16.
[27] *Lumsden* v *Stewart* (1843) 5 D. 501.
[28] Rankine, 133.
[29] *Supra*, p. 6.
[30] Gloag, *op. cit.*, Chap. XXXIX.
[31] Rankine, 317-318.
[32] Bell, § 560.
[33] *Lady Traquair* v *Houatson* (1667) Mor. 10024; Bell, § 562.
[34] *Davidson* v *Boyd* (1868) 7 M. 77; Bell, § 562.
[35] *Lennox* v *Reid* (1893) 21 R. 77.
[36] Erskine, III, 4, 10; Bell, § 567; Gloag, *op. cit.*, 718.
[37] Rankine, 320.
[38] Rankine, 321.
[39] Stair, I, 18, 2.

is not raised by a single receipt covering three or more consecutive instalments.[40] Discharges by a singular successor do not raise any presumption that earlier instalments due to the previous landlord have been paid.[41] Receipts by successive factors do not raise the presumption.[42] The presumption is one which may be rebutted,[43] probably nowadays by parole evidence.[44]

Prescription. The Triennial Prescription introduced by the Prescription Act 1579 applies *inter alia* to actions of debt for house-maills not founded on written obligations.[45] If such an action is not pursued within three years, the creditor must prove the debt by the debtor's writ or oath. " House-maills " has been held to include the rent of a house on a verbal lease, not the rent of a farm or glebe.[46] By the terms of the Act the prescription does not apply to written leases. The years of the landlord's minority are not deducted, nor is the running of the prescription affected by citation.[47] The prescription is interrupted by diligence.[48]

The Quinquennial Prescription established by the Prescription Act 1669 also applies *inter alia* to rents. The Act provides that rents not pursued within five years after the tenant has left must be proved by reference to the tenant's writ or oath.[49] Rural as well as urban leases are affected.[50] The Act applies both to verbal leases (where the triennial prescription would apply) and also to written leases.[51] In terms of the Act the years of the landlord's minority are to be deducted. The prescription is excluded by action or diligence within the five years.[52] The years of prescription are stated not to begin to run until the tenant leaves, and so where a tenant purchased the subjects and remained in possession, it was held that the rents for the period, during which he was a tenant, had not prescribed.[53]

The effect of both the triennial and quinquennial prescriptions is not to extinguish the obligation, but to put upon the landlord the onus of proving the constitution and subsistence of the debt and to limit the

---

[40] Dickson, *Evidence*, 3rd ed., I, 177; *Gloag, supra;* Walker, *Evidence*, 58.
[41] *Master of Corstorphine* v *Tenants* (1636) Mor. 11396; *Gray* v *Reid* (1699) Mor. 11399; Gloag, *op. cit.*, 719; Walker, *Evidence*, 58.
[42] Dickson, *op. cit.*, I, 180; Walker, *Evidence*, 58.
[43] *Hunter* v *Lord Kinnaird's Trs.* (1829) 7 S. 548.
[44] *Cameron* v *Panton's Trs.* (O.H.) (1891) 18 R. 728 (annuity); *Stenhouse* v *Stenhouse's Trs.* (O.H.) (1899) 36 S.L.R. 637 (annuity); Gloag, *op. cit.*, 718; Walker, *Evidence*, 58.
[45] Bell, § 628; Napier, *Prescription*, 714 *et seq.;* Millar, *Prescription*, 115 *et seq.;* Gloag, *op. cit.*, 741 *et seq.*
[46] *Ross* v *Fleming* (1627) Mor. 12735; *Cumming's Trs.* v *Simpson* (1825) 3 S. 545; Gloag, *op. cit.*, 742; Dickson, *Evidence,* 3rd ed., 487; Walker, *Evidence*, 147.
[47] *Brown* v *Brodie* (1709) Mor. 11150 (minority); *Campbell* v *McNeill* (1799) Mor. 11120 (citation).
[48] Gloag, *op. cit.*, 744.
[49] Bell, § 634; Napier, *Prescription*, 813 *et seq.;* Millar, *Prescription*, 155 *et seq.;* Gloag, *op. cit.*, 746.
[50] *Boyes* v *Henderson* (1823) 2 S. 190 (N.E. 169).
[51] *Nisbet* v *Baikie* (1729) Mor. 11059.
[52] Gloag, *op. cit.*, 746.
[53] *Johnston's Exrs.* v *Johnson* (1897) 24 R. 611.

mode of proof to the writ or oath of the tenant.[54] The oath, and probably the writ, must be of the tenant himself, and not of his manager, however exclusive the management may have been.[55]

Confusion. Where the same person is both creditor and debtor in the same obligation, it may be extinguished by the merger of interests known as confusion.[56] The obligation extinguished by this means is a debt, and so, while the same person is landlord and tenant, the obligation to pay rent does not come into existence. On the other hand, a continuing right, such as a feu or lease, is not invariably extinguishable *confusione.* In such cases confusion does not operate either payment or discharge; it prevents the possibility of a debt arising; it extinguishes the *jus crediti;* from the moment that the inconsistent characters of debtor and creditor are combined in the same person, both debtor and creditor cease to exist; there is no longer any debt or any relation of debtor and creditor at all.[57] Thus, where the lessee in a long lease had purchased the subjects, which had been let to him, it was held in a question involving the amount of composition due to his superior that, while he was both owner and tenant of the same subjects, he could not owe rent to himself and that each term's rent was extinguished *confusione* during the union of rights; the question whether the lease itself was extinguished *confusione* was not decided.[58] Where the merger takes place through the acquisition by the landlord of the tenant's interest, there can be little doubt that the lease is extinguished and will not revive.[59] Where it is the tenant who acquires the land, for example by purchase or succession, confusion would seem to operate.[60] The lease cannot revive by the act of the purchaser or his successors and, if they again let the lands, a new lease is required.[61] It has been suggested that the only question remaining is as to the effect of a reduction of the owner's title by the lessor or someone in his right, when the lease might revive.[62]

[54] Gloag, *op. cit.,* 744 and 746.
[55] *Bertram & Co.* v *Stewart's Trs.* (1874) 2 R. 255; Rankine, 322.
[56] Erskine, III, 4, 23; Bell, § 580; Gloag, *op. cit.,* 725.
[57] *Motherwell* v *Manwell* (1903) 5 F. 619, *per* Lord Kinnear at p. 631 (feu).
[58] *Lord Blantyre* v *Dunn* (1858) 20 D. 1188; Gloag, *supra.*
[59] Rankine, 525.
[60] Opinion of Lord Deas in *Lord Blantyre* v *Dunn, supra,* at p. 1200; *Campbell* v *M'Kinnon* (1867) 5 M. 636, but this point was not raised in the House of Lords, *Campbell* v *M'Lean* (1870) 8 M (H.L.) 40; Rankine, 525; but see *Earl of Zetland* v *Glover Incorporation* (1868) 6 M. 292, affd. (1870) 8 M. (H.L.) 144; Gloag, *op. cit.,* 727.
[61] Rankine, 525; *Encyclopaedia of the Laws of Scotland,* Vol. 4, 890.
[62] Rankine, 525; but see opinion of Lord Deas in *Lord Blantyre* v *Dunn, supra.*

Chapter VII

LEASE AS A REAL RIGHT

Leases Act 1449. Leases may be divided into two groups, viz., (1) leases valid only against the granter and his representatives, and (2) leases valid also against the singular successors of the granter. At common law a lease was merely a personal contract binding on the lessor and his representatives, but not on his singular successors, such as purchasers or creditors who were not parties to the contract. A singular successor of the landlord could therefore put out a tenant or demand a higher rent. This situation was altered by the Leases Act 1449, which stated, " It is ordained for the safetie and favour of the puir people that labouris the ground, that they, and al utheris that hes taken or sall take landes in time to cum fra lordes, and hes termes and zeires thereof, that suppose the lordes sell or annaly that land or landes, the takers sall remain with their tackes, unto the ischew of their termes, quhais handes that ever thay landes cum to for siklike maill as they tooke them for." The Act, which endowed the personal contract of lease with a completely new character, is said to be the oldest ordinance to that effect in any European system of law.[1] The Act, which bears the impress of a political compromise between the conflicting interests of the great feudal landowners and the peasantry, " remains to this day the basis of our law of leases—the Scottish answer to the English ' term of years ' ".[2]

The Act itself is very brief, but it has received interpretation wider than its exact terms. For example, it has been held to protect not only the poor husbandmen for whom it was intended, but also the tenants of urban subjects irrespective of their means.[3] The effect of the Act is to give a tenant under a lease to which it applies security of tenure in a question with a singular successor of the granter. This is commonly called a " real right ", but it is not a real right in the sense of a feu right; a contract of lease, although it has some of the privileges of a real right, does not substantially differ from a mutual contract.[4]

Parties against whom Protection is Given. As at common law a lease was already effective against the landlord's representatives, the Act expressly applies when the landlord sells or alienates the subjects,

[1] Hume, *Lectures,* IV, 73; see also *ibid.,* II, 56.
[2] Lord Cooper, *Selected Papers 1922-54,* 284; see also Grant, *Social and Economic Development of Scotland before 1603, 255 et seq.* The Act has also been described as the *Magna Carta* of Scottish agriculturists in Menzies' *Lectures on Conveyancing,* 1900 ed., 899-900.
[3] Hume, *Lectures,* IV, 83, commenting on and contradicting Erskine, II, 6, 27.
[4] *Edmond* v *Reid* (1871) 9 M. 782 *per* Lord Cowan at p. 785.

that is, it operates against singular successors, who have been judicially held to include purchasers, creditors, heirs of entail, and the Crown as *ultimus haeres*. However, a lease which was improperly granted will confer no protection. Thus a lease granted by a liferenter terminates on his death, and is ineffectual against the fiar, and a lease granted by an heir of entail outwith his power can be reduced by a succeeding heir. A lease is not proof against irritancy of the feu by the superior.[5]

Requisites for Protection. Many a lease is perfectly valid in a question with the granter or his representatives, but ineffective against his singular successors. To have the protection of the Act a lease must satisfy certain requirements. The Act itself says that it is for the benefit of a person remaining in possession of land under a lease specifying a rent and an ish. There is also the old common law requirement that a lease for more than one year must be in writing. Therefore the conditions required to bring a lease within the scope of the Act of 1449 are, (a) that the subject must be land, (b) that the lease, if for more than one year, must be in writing, (c) that it must have a definite ish, that is, a date for the termination of the contract, (d) that it must specify a rent, and (e) that there must be possession by the tenant. Further, as has been seen, there is the requirement that the granter must be infeft, although the lack of infeftment may be cured by accretion.[6]

The Act has been very liberally interpreted in favour of tenants. The story of the Highland Clearances would have been a happier one, if only the unfortunate crofters had held tacks. The Act may apply not only to the lease itself but to a particular right conferred by the lease, such as a stipulation that the tenant may retain his rent,[7] or to an adjunct or pertinent given by the lease, such as a right of pasturage.[8] Such a right or privilege itself does not necessarily require to be capable of being the subject of a lease binding on singular successors; " many things may be let as pertinents which a singular successor cannot take away, although he might not have been bound by a lease which let only these things themselves ".[9] On the other hand it may happen that a lease enjoying the protection of the Act contains subsidiary obligations which do not bind singular successors, especially if such obligations are not *inter naturalia* of the lease.[10]

Illustrations of the applicability of the Act to various types of leases and stipulations can be seen in the series of Tobermory cases.[11] These arose out of leases granted, around 1790, by the British Fisheries Society

---

[5] Rankine, 133.
[6] Burns, *Conveyancing Practice*, 4th ed., 607; *supra*, p. 44.
[7] Bell, § 1202; Hume, *Lectures*, IV, 76
[8] *Campbell* v *M'Lean* (1870) 8 M. (H.L.) 40.
[9] *Campbell* v *Mackinnon* (1867) 5 M. 636 *per* Lord Deas at p. 651.
[10] *Duncan* v *Brooks* (1894) 21 R. 760; *Bisset* v *Mags. of Aberdeen* (1898) 1 F. 87.
[11] *Campbell* v *Mackinnon* (1867) 5 M. 636; *Campbell* v *M'Lean* (1870) 8 M. (H.L.) 40.

of building lots for 99 years renewable for ever on payment of a grassum with certain privileges.

(a) *Subjects Must Be Land.* The Leases Act 1449 speaks only of " landes ", but it has long been held to apply to urban as well as rural subjects.[12] Within the term " lands " there are included all those subjects which are adjuncts of land called *fundo annexa,* or " all heritable subjects capable of such open and continuous possession as may naturally suggest to a singular successor the existence of a lease ",[13] such as land, houses, mills, minerals, quarries, ferries, harbours, salmon fishings, etc. On the other hand, a lease of the right to services, and a lease of the right to collect rents or feuduties do not transmit against singular successors, as they are not feudal tenements or do not involve occupation of land.[14]

Trout fishings and shootings have been commonly held not to come under the Act, as they are mere incidents of the ownership of the land and are not capable of being made the subject of separate ownership by infeftment.[15] A previous chapter[16] discussed the distinction between a mere personal licence to take game falling short of a lease, on the one hand, and the grant of a right to take game involving a degree of occupation of the ground, qualifying as a lease on the other hand. Here, however, different considerations arise, and the question is whether a particular contract, being a lease, qualifies for the protection of the Leases Act of 1449. It is possible to detect a distinction between a lease of land for the purpose of shooting or fishing on the one hand, and a lease of shootings or fishings without express use of the land on the other hand. Irrespective of the growing importance of game leases generally, it was held (following the decision in *Pollock*[17]) that a two years' lease of shootings, including two shooting lodges and a keeper's house, was ineffectual against a singular successor, even though the latter at the time of purchasing the estate knew of its existence.[18] It was, however, questioned whether the same principle would apply to a lease of a deer forest, where all other use of land is excluded and the sporting tenant is the sole tenant.[19] It had previously been suggested, but not decided, that a lease of shootings for 19 years could bind a succeeding heir of entail.[20] Those questions were to some extent answered in a petition by an heir of entail seeking authority to grant a 19 years' lease of a deer forest to trustees for Queen Victoria; the lease was not merely

---

[12] *Waddell* v *Brown* (1794) Mor. 10309; *M'Arthur* v *Simpson* (1804) Mor. 15181; Hume, *Lectures,* IV, 83.
[13] *Campbell* v *Mackinnon, supra, per* Lord Deas at p. 651.
[14] Rankine, 135-136.
[15] *Pollock, Gilmour & Co.* v *Harvey* (1828) 6 S. 913.
[16] *Supra,* p. 80.
[17] *Pollock, Gilmour & Co.* v *Harvey, supra.*
[18] *Birkbeck* v *Ross* (1865) 4 M. 272.
[19] *Ibid., per* Lord Barcaple at p. 275.
[20] *Earl of Fife's Trs.* v *Wilson* (1859) 22 D. 191 *per* Lord Ardmillan at p. 198.

a lease of shootings; it was a lease of a large tract of ground embracing a power to shoot, but not limiting the use or occupation, although only a small part of the ground was fit for any other use; the power was granted, and it is therefore clear that a valid lease of land may be granted for sporting purposes.[21] One judge went so far as to express his opinion that the progress of society and the practice of the country had placed shootings in the common category of property and had given to leases of shootings the proper character of leases generally and that therefore a lease of shootings without the land would bind a succeeding heir of entail.[22] However, a contrary view, also by way of *obiter*, has been expressed in the House of Lords;[23] and a lease of trout fishings without a grant of land has been held not to come within the ambit of the 1449 Act, one of the several grounds of the decision being that trout fishing was not a feudal tenement.[24] If the contract is a mere licence to take game and is not a lease, it obviously does not have the protection of the Leases Act 1449.

From the foregoing decisions it would seem that much will depend on how the lease is worded. If it is expressed to be a lease of shootings and/or fishings other than salmon fishings with the use of land or buildings ancillary thereto, it may not be protected by the Act.[25] If it takes the form of a lease of land or buildings for the purpose of shooting or fishing, it will probably have the protection of the Act.[26] It seems to be easier for a lease of shootings, which normally demands a more extensive contract and use of land, to come within the ambit of the Leases Act 1449 than a lease of fishings other than of salmon. Whether or not a lease of shootings without the land is protected has never been expressly decided since *Pollock*, but it would not be surprising if that decision were reversed if the question were to come before the Court.[27]

A tenant's right to take peats from a peat-moss was thought not to be protected by the Leases Act.[28]

(b) *Writing.* Although the Act itself does not say so, a lease for more than one year must be in writing, if it is to qualify for the protection of the Leases Act.

A lease for a year or less does not require the solemnity of writing, and such a lease, though verbal, would be effective against singular successors. However, a verbal lease for a single year of subjects sold

[21] *Farquharson* (1870) 9 M. 66.
[22] *Farquharson, supra,* per Lord Kinloch at p. 75.
[23] *Per* Lord Hatherley in *Campbell* v *M'Lean* (1870) 8 M. (H.L.) 40 at p. 44.
[24] *Earl of Galloway* v *Duke of Bedford* (1902) 4 F. 851, (Lord Kinnear at p. 865 following *dicta* of L.P. Inglis in *Patrick* v *Napier* (1867) 5 M. 683).
[25] As in *Birkbeck* v *Ross* (1865) 4 M. 272.
[26] As in *Farquharson* (1870) 9 M. 66.
[27] *Macpherson* v *Macpherson* (1839) 1 D. 794; *Menzies* v *Menzies* (1861) 23 D. (H.L.) 16; *Stewart* v *Bulloch* (1881) 8 R. 381; Menzies, *Lectures on Conveyancing,* 1900 ed., 900; Tait, *Game Laws,* 2nd ed., 34.
[28] *Duncan* v *Brooks* (1894) 21 R. 760.

before the intended date of entry under the lease would not be effective against a purchaser; nor would a verbal agreement as to the length of notice under a verbal lease for a year bind the purchaser, if the effect were to be to prolong the lease beyond one year.[29]

A verbal lease for more than one year, even though established by the oath of the granter plus possession and *rei interventus,* does not come within the purview of the Act, and so is ineffectual against the singular successors of the landlord.[30] Apart from that, the general rules for the constitution of leases apply to leases enjoying the benefit of the Act, and if the writing is sufficient to bind the granter, it will bind his singular successors.[31] Thus the writing need not be probative, if it is supported by *rei interventus.*[32] Verbal agreements qualifying the terms of a lease are ineffectual against a singular successor, who has not consented to or homologated them.[33]

An option to a tenant under a lease for one year to demand a lease for a term of years is not effective, unless exercised before the sale to a purchaser.[34]

(c) *Definite Ish.* In the discussion of the cardinal points of a lease, it was seen that the absence of mention of the duration might render the lease void on the ground of absence of *consensus in idem,* although in some circumstances an ish could be inferred.[35] However, so far as the Leases Act is concerned, a lease to be effective against singular successors must have an ish. The Act is expressed to be in favour of such tenants as have " termes and zeires ", who are entitled to " remaine with their tackes unto the ischew of their termes ". The Act has been interpreted to apply however long the period may be, provided it is definite.[36] Thus a lease in perpetuity, or for an indefinite term, such as for " as long as the grass grows and water runs ", though perfectly valid in a question with the granter or his personal representatives,[37] is not binding on his singular successors.

Although the Act requires a definite ish, it does not require a fixed ish. The lease may be given for a liferent or successive liferents, but it must provide that it is to come to an end on the occurrence of an event which is bound to happen. However, difficulties arise when a lease is granted for a definite term followed by an indefinite term. There have been two cases where a lease, granted for a fixed period of 19 years and to be renewable for successive periods of 19 years for ever

---

[29] Hume, *Lectures,* IV, 74.
[30] Bell, § 1187.
[31] Bell, § 1190.
[32] *Wilson* v *Mann* (1876) 3 R. 527; *Buchanan* v *Harris and Sheldon* (1900) 2 F. 935.
[33] Hume, *Lectures,* IV, 77.
[34] *Clark* v *Farquharson* (1799) Mor. 15225.
[35] *Supra,* p. 7.
[36] Bell, § 1194; Hume, *Lectures,* IV, 77-79; Rankine, 139-143.
[37] *Carruthers* v *Irvine* (1717) Mor. 15195.

or indefinitely, has been enforced against a singular successor.[38] In those cases there was the element either of special knowledge on the part of the purchaser plus an obligation to warrant the lease, or of homologation of the lease on the part of the purchaser. However, the principle of those cases was at least partly approved in a third case where leases of building lots granted in Tobermory for 99 years renewable for ever on payment of a grassum were in a question with the singular successor of the lessor held to be valid leases for the first 99 years; but the question remained whether the singular successor was under any obligation to grant renewals at the end of that period.[39] It may be concluded that where a lease is granted for a definite period followed by an indefinite period, it will come within the Act, but only for the definite period. The ish may be treated as definite, although a period of years is not stated, provided the period can be determined, as with leases granted for the lifetime of the granter or grantee or even someone else.[40]

Some difficulty in construing the Leases Act may arise where the term is definite and yet amounts to a lease in perpetuity. Is there any limit to the duration of the lease for the purpose of the Act? At one time there was some doubt as to whether leases for extremely long periods were good,[41] and a lease for 2,400 years was held to be outwith the Act, but that may have been because the rent was elusory.[42] Many of the old cases concerned entails, where leases were annulled as being alienations. It can be said with certainty that leases for normal periods will be good against singular successors; that liferent leases or leases terminating with a liferent will be effectual; that building leases for such reasonable terms as to indemnify the expense will be protected; and that mining leases may be greatly prolonged.[43] A lease for 1,140 years was held good against the Crown, which was the singular successor,[44] and nowadays building leases of 99 or 999 years are not uncommon, and there is no doubt that they are valid against singular successors, although not necessarily recorded under the Registration of Leases Act 1857. The question is now largely academic in view of the 1857 Act. This provides that a lease to which the Act applies, if good against the granter, shall be good against his singular successors, so that it will not matter if a registered lease contains no definite ish.

An obligation by the landlord in a 999 years' lease to give a lessee a feu charter on demand was held not binding on a singular successor of the landlord as not being *inter naturalia*.[45]

---

38 *Wight* v *Earl of Hopetoun* (1763) Mor. 10461; *Scott* v *Straiton* (1771) Mor. 15200.
39 *Campbell* v *M'Kinnon* (1867) 5 M. 636; affd. *Campbell* v *M'Lean* (1870) 8 M. (H.L.) 40.
40 *Thomson* v *Thomson* (1896) 24 R. 269.
41 Rankine, 142.
42 *Alison* v *Ritchie* (1730) Mor. 15196.
43 Bell, § 1195.
44 *Lord Advocate* v *Fraser* (1762) 2 Pat. 66.
45 *Bisset* v *Mags. of Aberdeen* (1898) 1 F. 87.

(d) *Definite Rent.* The Leases Act 1449 speaks of " siklike maill as they took them for ", and this has been interpreted to mean that there must be a definite rent.[46] The Act does not apply where there is no rent at all, in which case there is no lease.[47] Nor does it apply where the rent is elusory, but as there has been no judicial interpretation of elusoriness in this connection, the practical result is that a rent of some kind is essential. In questions with singular successors there must under the statute be a rent payable to the proprietor of the land; and that rent must stand undischarged as some equivalent for the possession of which the purchaser of the land is deprived.[48] A tack let for an elusory tack duty and for an endurance of 2,400 years was found not good against singular successors.[49] While the rent must not be elusory or nominal, there is no requirement that it must be a fair and equal rent.[50] A grassum alone is not sufficient.[51] However, if there is a rent, the singular successor cannot complain that it is made elusory on account of a grassum having been paid at the beginning of the lease, nor can he demand that the amount of the grassum should be apportioned over the whole term of the lease and added to the rent.[52]

Rent is normally a sum of money either specified or capable of being ascertained, or it may be a certain amount of grain, minerals or other fungibles; or it may take the form of services to be rendered by the tenant to the landlord, for example to shoe horses and mend ploughs.[53] The money value of the grain may be ascertained from the fiars' prices, or there may be other means of converting the value of goods or services into money, either indicated in the lease or otherwise. The rent or part of it may, for example, represent a percentage, like interest, of capital expenditure to be expended by the landlord on improvements; or a percentage of such expenditure incurred by the tenant may mitigate the rent. If the consideration so ascertained is definite, the lease will have the protection of the Act.[54]

A consideration has been regarded as definite, where the lease provided for the retention of the rent by the lessee in security of improvements by him or pending fulfilment of an obligation incumbent on the landlord in connection with the lease, and such a right of retention is effective against singular successors.[55] In such cases neither creditors nor purchasers can complain, since they have means of knowing the

---

46 Bell, § 1199; Hume, *Lectures,* IV, 75-77; Rankine, 144-147.
47 *Supra,* p. 6.
48 Bell, § 1199.
49 *Alison* v *Ritchie* (1730) Mor. 15196.
50 Hume, *Lectures,* IV, 77.
51 *Mann* v *Houston,* 1957 S.L.T. 89.
52 Bell, § 1201; Rankine, 144.
53 *Lundy* v *Smith* (1610) Mor. 15166.
54 Bell, §§ 1203-1205; Rankine, 144-145.
55 *Stewart* v *M'Ra* (1834) 13 S. 4; *Montgomerie* v *Carrick* (1848) 10 D. 1387 at p. 1396.

position.[56] However, the same is not true where such an obligation is not contained in the lease.[57]

Once a fixed rent has been specified in a lease, a stipulation either in the lease itself or subsequent to it for the retention of rent for a reason unconnected with the lease, such as in satisfaction of a separate debt, or in payment of interest or services, is purely a personal contract and is not itself transmissible against a singular successor.[58] He may sue for the full rent, if it is specified in the lease, but the rent is not elusory, and there is no reason to suppose that the lease itself does not hold good against a singular successor.[59]

Where the owner of a garage let it for a period of 10 years for a single payment of £200, of which a proportion would be returnable for any unexpired period in the event of earlier termination, it was held not only that the occupier was not protected by the Leases Act 1449 against a singular successor of the landlord because of the absence of a rent, but also that the contract was not a lease at all.[60] Similarly, a right of occupation by a third party free of rent created in a minute of agreement was held not to be a lease, but merely a personal right which could not be made into a real right under the Act.[61]

The Registration of Leases Act 1857 provides that registered leases, if good against the granters, shall be effectual against singular successors; so that where the Act applies it will not matter if a rent is elusory.

(e) *Possession.* The Leases Act 1449 operates in favour of lessees " that has taken or sall take landes ", that is, in favour of lessees who have taken possession of the subjects let. Tacks were originally constituted by charter and sasine, but since the fifteenth century the only appropriate legal method of perfecting a lessee's right as against the singular successors of the landlord has been by possession.[62] No substitute for possession has been recognised except registration of long leases under the Registration of Leases Act 1857.[63] Without possession the tenant is merely the personal creditor of the lessor.[64] The principle is that in order to confer a real right on the tenant against third parties there must be some form of publication, and it is by entering into possession that the tenant publishes the fact of his lease to the world in general and to singular successors in particular, in the same way as a personal title to land is made real by registration or an assignation of an incor-

---

[56] Bell, § 1202.
[57] *Turner* v *Nicolson* (1835) 13 S. 633.
[58] *Ross* v *Blair* (1627) Mor. 15167; *Ross* v *Duchess of Sutherland* (1838) 16 S. 1179.
[59] Rankine, 145-146.
[60] *Mann* v *Houston,* 1957 S.L.T. 89.
[61] *Wallace* v *Simmers,* 1960 S.C. 255.
[62] Bell, § § 1209-1211; Hume, *Lectures,* IV, 79-83; Rankine, 136-139.
[63] *Infra,* p. 114.
[64] *Millar* v *M'Robbie,* 1949 S.C. 1 *per* L.P. Cooper at p. 6.

poreal moveable right is perfected by intimation. Even the most formal lease does not give any possessory interest in the land, which it purports to let, until the proposed lessee enters into possession, actual or constructive.[65] Assignation of a lease plus intimation to the landlord is not sufficient.[66] Leases in competition with each other must be very rare, but a posterior lease, on which possession has followed, is preferable to a prior lease, on which there has been no possession.[67]

A lease will be defeated, if the lessee does not take possession before a singular successor of the landlord completes his title by infeftment; if the tenant has not taken possession by then, the lessor is no longer able to confer possession on him.[68] This rule applies even where the delay in taking possession is no fault of the tenant, and a lease containing a postponed date of entry, such as one to commence after a certain event like the redemption of a security or the death of the granter, is ineffectual, if a singular successor of the granter takes infeftment before the lessee takes possession.[69] In *Millar* v *M'Robbie*[70] entry under a lease was to be Whitsunday, but before that date the landlord sold the subjects to a purchaser who recorded his title on 21st April, and the tenant had not and could not have converted his personal right into a real right by taking possession under the lease; it was held that the purchaser could repudiate the lease. The purchaser had raised his action before becoming infeft, but this did not matter.[71]

For the nature and types of possession reference is made to the undernoted authority.[72] The possession required in connection with leases must be actual possession appropriate to the nature of the subjects, but it may be either natural or civil; a tenant possessing by his subtenant possesses as effectually as if he were in occupation himself.[73] The rules applicable to possession in this context are the same as those for possession supporting *rei interventus,* and may be illustrated partly from the same cases.[74] A lease constituted by informal writ and *rei interventus* (including possession) is good against a singular successor, whether or not the latter is aware of the *rei interventus.*[75] The possession must be under the lease in question and after the date of entry fixed by it,[76] and some effect has been given to a lease, later reduced,

[65] *Hutchinson* v *Ferrier* (1852) 1 Macq. 196 *per* Lord Truro at p. 208.
[66] *Grant* v *Adamson* (1802) Hume 810; *infra*, pp. 160 *et seq.*
[67] *Kerr* v *Lord Ramsay* (1620) Mor. 15227; *M'Millan* v *Gordon* (1627) Mor. 15229.
[68] *Fraser* v *Laird of Pitsligo* (1611) Mor. 15227; *Wallace* v *Harvey* (1627) Mor. 15229.
[69] *Hamilton* v *Tenants* (1632) Mor. 15230; *Johnson* v *Cullen* (1676) Mor. 15231.
[70] 1949 S.C. 1.
[71] *Ibid., per* L.P. Cooper at p. 8.
[72] Rankine, *Land-Ownership*, 4th ed., 3-7.
[73] Bell, § 1211.
[74] *E.g., Wilson* v *Mann* (1876) 3 R. 527; *Buchanan* v *Harris & Sheldon* (1900) 2 F. 935.
[75] *Wilson* v *Mann, supra.*
[76] *Earl of Fife's Trs.* v *Wilson* (1859) 22 D. 191; Bell, § 1210; Hume, *Lectures,* IV, 81.

on which possession had followed.[77] If possession begins on a verbal or informal lease, and the term of entry under the written lease has not yet arrived, a singular successor will not be affected by the written lease; and, if an unexpired lease at its close is to be followed by a new one, which is written out and executed by the parties, possession under the old lease will not validate the new one.[78]

Questions sometimes arise between the tenant and the singular successors of the landlord upon the prorogation or renewal of an existing lease. The difficulty is to determine whether the tenant's possession during the period between the agreement for a prorogation or renewal and the natural termination of the existing lease is to be ascribed to that lease or to the new one, and the question will arise if a singular successor acquires his right during that period.[79] If an unexpired lease is at its close to be followed by a new one, the tenant's possession during the interval will normally be ascribed to the old lease, and therefore will not validate the new lease as against a singular successor of the landlord.[80] It makes no difference if the prorogation is endorsed on the original lease.[81] Where a tenant had obtained successive leases, one to start after another had terminated, his possession under an earlier lease did not validate a later one in a question with a singular successor.[82] The fact that the singular successor may be aware of the prorogation or renewal makes no difference.[83]

Similarly, an obligation to renew an existing lease at its termination at the option of the tenant does not bind a singular successor, if the latter's right emerges before the tenant takes possession under the new lease.[84] In such cases there is also the element of the tenant being free to decline the new lease, if he wishes, with the result that apart from the question of possession such an arrangement will not be regarded as a completed contract, and although binding on the original landlord will not bind his successor. So, where parties on the same day entered into a lease of shootings for two years and also a minute of agreement, stating that the tenant should become tenant of the same shootings for a period of ten years from the termination of the first lease on the same terms, but at an increased rent and subject to the power of the tenant to renounce the second lease, it was held that the minute of agreement was not a lease but merely an obligation to grant one in the future, and

---

[77] *Eliott's Trs.* v *Eliott* (1894) 21 R. 858; Bell, § 1210.
[78] *Pratt* v *Abercromby* (1858) 21 D. 19; Bell, § 1210.
[79] Bell, § 1210; Hume, *Lectures,* IV, 81-82; Rankine, 149-151.
[80] *Scot* v *Graham* (1769) Mor. 15220.
[81] Hunter, *Landlord and Tenant,* 4th ed., I, 492.
[82] *Drum* v *Jamieson* (1602) Mor. 15209; *Maxwell* v *Tenants* (1630) Mor. 15215; *Cranston's Crs.* v *Scott* (1757) Mor. 15218.
[83] *Johnston* v *Monzie* (1760) 5 B.S. 877; *Birkbeck* v *Ross* (1865) 4 M. 272.
[84] *Dalrymple* v *Hepburn* (1737) Mor. 9444; *Jacobs* v *Anderson* (1898) 6 S.L.T. 234 (O.H.).

so was not effectual against a supervening singular successor of the landlord.[85]

However, it is possible for a lease to be prorogated or renewed before its termination so as to be effectual against singular successors. This can probably be accomplished by a new lease being granted upon the renunciation of the original lease;[86] then possession cannot be ascribed to anything but the new lease. There is authority for holding that it may be done without a renunciation, provided that it is clear that the possession is to be on the new lease from its date;[87] if there is a change of rent, this would indicate that possession is on the new lease;[88] and even without a change of rent there may be special circumstances to indicate that possession is on the new lease.[89]

The possession founded on must be exclusive, but questions have arisen in distinguishing between the possession of outgoing and incoming tenants with regard to different crops or parts of the farm.[90] A lease of an arable farm granted in December 1947 provided that the incoming tenant was to get access to the land for certain purposes on 1st March 1948, which was the date of removal of the outgoing tenant from the green crop, but it expressly provided that the date of entry was Whitsunday 1948; meanwhile, the farm was sold with entry on 29th February to a purchaser, whose title was recorded on the 21st April; it was held that the tenant's occupation in March and April took place only by virtue of a limited licence before he obtained true and legal entry under his lease, and so was ineffectual against the singular successor of the landlord.[91] This is an example of a tenant, having a personal right which could not be converted into a real right until his term of entry, being defeated by a purchaser having a real right. The same result would arise in the case of a registrable lease, as the Registration of Leases (Scotland) Act 1857 provides that a lease recorded before the date of entry is ineffective.[92]

The lands which are the subject of the lease must be viewed as a *unum quid,* as the subject of a lease is one and indivisible, and it is impossible to describe a person who is exercising the limited right of certain parts as being in possession of the whole; as the taking of sasine upon a medieval tack could only have been performed when the new tenant replaced the old at the date of entry, so a new tenant cannot begin to possess until the end of the old tenant's lease.[93]

[85] *Birkbeck* v *Ross* (1865) 4 M. 272.
[86] *Per* Lord Barcaple (L.O.) in *Birkbeck* v *Ross* (1865) 4 M. 272 at p. 276.
[87] *Per* Lord Barcaple, *ibid.; Richard* v *Lindsay* (1725) Mor. 15217.
[88] *Neilson* v *Menzies* (1671) Mor. 15231; Bell § 1210.
[89] *Montgomerie* v *Vernon* (1895) 22 R. 465.
[90] See *Wight* v *Earl of Hopetoun* (1863) 1 M. 1074; (1864) 2 M. (H.L.) 35.
[91] *Millar* v *M'Robbie,* 1949 S.C. 1.
[92] s. 2.
[93] *Millar* v *M'Robbie, supra,* per L.P. Cooper at pp. 7 and 8, following House of Lords *dicta* in *Wight* v *Earl of Hopetoun, supra.*

Registration of Leases. An equivalent to possession was given by the Registration of Leases (Scotland) Act 1857. This Act will be dealt with more fully in a later chapter.[94] Here it will suffice to say that it applies to probative leases for 31 years or more of subjects not exceeding 50 acres in extent (except in the case of minerals, for which there is no limit in area). Such a lease, if it is valid in a question with the granter, is, on being recorded in the Register of Sasines at or subsequent to the date of entry mentioned therein, effectual against any singular successor whose infeftment is later than the date of such registration.[95] The registration of such a lease, or other writ permitted by the Act, completes the right under it to the effect of establishing a preference in virtue thereof as effectually as if the grantee or party in his right had entered into actual possession of the subjects leased at the date of registration thereof.[96] The dates of registration determine the preference of writs *inter se*.[97]

Registration is stated to be equivalent to possession, but it is no stronger than possession, so that in a competition between a recorded lease and a lease complying with the Act of 1449 and possessed on, but not recorded, the priority would depend on which took place first, the recording or the possession.[98]

The principal effect of the Act is that a registrable lease, once recorded, is valid in a question with a singular successor, although there may be no rent and no definite ish, and although the lessee may not have entered into possession.

Questions with Purchasers. Warrandice. How far does knowledge of a lease bar a singular successor of the landlord from taking exception to it? In *Wight* v *Earl of Hopetoun*[99] a lease granted for two periods of 19 years with an obligation on the granter, his heirs and successors to renew it after that time from 19 years to 19 years in all time coming upon the tenant's paying a certain sum as grassum at each renewal was found binding on a singular successor; the lease should probably not have conferred protection under the Leases Act 1449, having no definite ish, but the *ratio* of the judgment appears to have been that the purchaser had accepted a disposition of the lands subject to an express exception of this very tack, and containing an express assignation of the disponer's interest under it with right to quarrel the tack on any ground not inferring warrandice, which a reduction by the disponee certainly would have done, and was thus personally barred from objecting.[1] The purchaser was not bound to warrant the lease, but once he recorded

---

[94] Chapter VIII.
[95] s. 2.
[96] s. 16.
[97] s. 12.
[98] Rankine, 139.
[99] (1763) Mor. 10461, 15199.
[1] Hume, *Lectures*, IV, 78; Rankine, 140, approved by L.P. Clyde in *Mann* v *Houston*, 1957 S.L.T. 89 at pp. 93-94, but see Lord Sorn's opinion at p. 95.

his title he was barred by personal exception from challenging the lease on any ground which would open the door to the tenant claiming recourse against the seller under the warrandice clause in the lease.[2] In *Scott* v *Straiton*[3] a lease granted for successive periods of 19 years was upheld against a singular successor, but the ground of the decision was homologation, the landlord and his ancestors having allowed the lease to stand for some 100 years.[4]

However, mere knowledge does not constitute personal bar. A purchaser may be aware that a right is claimed over the subjects, and that the seller has by contract bound himself to observe it; he is not thereby under any obligation to treat it as binding him as a singular successor.[5] Thus, there have been a series of cases where the purchaser's knowledge of a sporting lease, valid against the granter, did not bar the purchaser from claiming that it was not protected by the Leases Act 1449.[6] " If a lease of game is not effectual against a purchaser, it is difficult to see how that essential invalidity can be cured by the purchaser's knowledge. In that view, the granting of such a lease to subsist against singular successors was an attempt to create a real, though temporary, right in the lands, which the law refuses to recognise, and which therefore a purchaser is entitled to ignore ".[7] Similarly, the purchaser's knowledge of the prorogation of an unexpired lease did not prevent him from objecting to it on the ground that no possession had followed on the prorogation,[8] and the purchaser's knowledge of a sublease permitted by the seller did not bind the purchaser.[9]

In *Mann* v *Houston*,[10] where an agreement was held not to be a lease protected by the Leases Act 1449 for want of a definite rent, and not to be a lease at all for want of one of the essential elements of a lease, the fact that the purchaser had notice of the right of occupancy both in the missives and also in his disposition, which expressly excepted the current leases from the warrandice, did not prevent him from reducing it. Similarly, the purchaser's knowledge of a right of occupancy created by a minute of agreement, falling short of a lease, granted by a previous owner did not bind the purchaser.[11]

Where there is a subsisting lease, the form of the warrandice clause in the disposition by seller to purchaser is usually something like this: " And I grant warrandice, but excepting therefrom the current leases and the rights of possession of tenants and occupiers, without prejudice,

[2] Per L.P. Clyde in *Mann* v *Houston, supra,* at p. 94; but see Bell, § 1194 and Craigie, *Heritable Rights,* 1013.
[3] (1771) Mor. 15200; affd. (1772) 3 Pat. 666.
[4] Hume, *Lectures,* IV, 78; Rankine, 140.
[5] Gloag, *Contract,* 2nd ed., 232.
[6] *Pollock, Gilmour & Co.* v *Harvey* (1828) 6 S. 913; *Birkbeck* v *Ross* (1865) 4 M. 272.
[7] Lord Barcaple (L.O.) in *Birkbeck* v *Ross, supra,* at p. 276.
[8] *Johnston* v *Monzie* (1760) 5 B.S. 877.
[9] *Jacobs* v *Anderson* (1898) 6 S.L.T. 234 (O.H.).
[10] 1957 S.L.T. 89.
[11] *Wallace* v *Simmers,* 1960 S.C. 255.

however, to the right of my said disponee to quarrel or impugn the
same on any ground at law not inferring warrandice against me ".[12]
Does the purchaser by accepting and recording a disposition containing
a warrandice clause in those terms bar himself *personali exceptione* from
impugning a lease? The question is discussed at some length in *Mann*
v *Houston*[13] where the *ratio* of *Wight* v *Earl of Hopetoun*[14] was considered, but it should be noted that the opinions expressed do not agree,
and in any case are not necessary to the decision of *Mann* v *Houston*,
as the agreement in question was found not to be a lease. It is probable
that a clause in those terms applies only to leases protected by the.
Leases Act 1449, as there is no need to except other leases; that the effect
of the clause is merely to regulate the position between seller and purchaser, and cannot enable a tenant with only a personal right to enforce
his lease against a purchaser; that the purchaser is giving a counter-
stipulation or counter-warrandice that he will not challenge a lease on
any ground which will involve a claim by the tenant against the seller
for breach of warrandice in the lease; that the remedy for breach of
warrandice or breach of this counter-warrandice is damages; and that
the purchaser by accepting warrandice in the above terms is merely
undertaking to relieve the seller of any personal claim, which the tenant
may have under the warrandice in his lease in the event of the purchaser successfully impugning his lease.[15]

In any event it may be asked whether the exception of leases from
the warrandice clause, although it is normally inserted *ob majorem
cautelam*, serves any purpose at all.[16] Where there is a lease valid
against a singular successor, failure to except it from the warrandice in
the purchaser's disposition does not constitute a breach of that warrandice.[17] A purchaser who wishes to ensure that there are no leases will
not rely on the warrandice clause, but will stipulate for entry with
vacant possession.

[12] *E.g.,* see *Encyclopaedia of Scottish Legal Styles,* Vol. IV, Nos. 248, 300 and
    331; Burns, *Conveyancing Practice,* 4th ed., 348.
[13] *Supra.*
[14] (1763) Mor. 10461, 15199, where, however, there was the additional element of
    an assignation to the purchaser of the seller's rights under the lease and there
    may have been other elements such as acceptance of rent; Hume, *Lectures,* IV,
    78; Rankine, 140.
[15] *Mann* v *Houston, supra,* opinion of Lord Sorn at p. 95.
[16] Bell, *Lectures on Conveyancing,* 3rd ed., 644.
[17] *Lothian & Border Farmers Ltd.* v *M'Cutcheon,* 1952 S.L.T. 450.

STATUTORY PROVISIONS RELATING TO LONG LEASES

General Background. Long leases of land, particularly for building purposes, were commonly granted in some parts of Scotland as an alternative to feudal grants. As has been seen,[1] a feature of such a long lease, sometimes called a ground or building lease, is that the tenant is regarded as being in the position of proprietor, while the landlord is in a position similar to that of a superior. The rent is frequently related to the value of the ground before the buildings were erected thereon by the tenant, as in the similar case of a feudal grant of a vacant piece of ground. On the other hand, long leases were sometimes given of ground with buildings already erected thereon and even of flats in tenements, in which case the rent was related to the market rent at the time of letting. In either case, although the tenant under a long lease is virtually the proprietor, nevertheless he is not proprietor for all purposes and a lease does not confer so strong a right as a feu.[2] In particular, a tenant suffers from two main disadvantages, which do not trouble a feuar or true proprietor.

The first disadvantage is that to satisfy the Leases Act 1449 and so to acquire a real right in the subjects let, the tenant must have possession. If he does not enter into possession, he runs the risk of his right being defeated by a purchaser or other singular successor of the landlord. This necessity of taking possession applies not only to the original tenant but also to anyone to whom he may assign his lease by way of sale or security. A feuar may use his property as a security for borrowed money by granting a bond and disposition in security or *ex facie* absolute disposition in favour of the lender, and may then continue to occupy the property. At common law a tenant cannot borrow on the security of buildings without giving possession to his creditor; the only way in which a creditor can obtain a real right in a question with the landlord is by taking actual possession of the security subjects following an assignation of the lease. This state of affairs was to some extent remedied, so far as long leases are concerned, by the Registration of Leases (Scotland) Act 1857, the principal effect of which was to make it possible to record certain leases in the Register of Sasines, and so to render them valid without possession; this enables the original lessee or a subsequent assignee, whether a purchaser or creditor, to make his right real by registration instead of by possession.

---

[1] *Supra,* p. 65.
[2] *Supra,* p. 67.

The second disadvantage suffered by a tenant is that a lease is essentially a temporary right, and so on its expiry the land itself and all the buildings thereon must revert to the landlord. A feu is essentially a perpetual right. On the other hand, a lease, however long, must have an ish, if it is to confer security of tenure under the Leases Act 1449, and upon that ish, however far away it may be, the lands and buildings must revert to the landlord.

This situation was to some extent modified by the Long Leases (Scotland) Act 1954, the principal effect of which was to give tenants under certain existing long leases the right to demand feu charters upon certain conditions.

REGISTRATION OF LEASES

The Registration of Leases (Scotland) Act 1857, which has since been amended and extended,[3] provides that it shall be lawful to record in the Register of Sasines certain leases of land and heritages, whether executed before or after the passing of the Act. In order to be registrable under the Act the lease must comply with certain requirements:—

(1) It must be probative.[4] The absence of probative writing cannot be supplied by *rei interventus*.[5]

(2) It must be of a duration of not less than 31 years;[6] or it must contain an obligation on the granter to renew it from time to time for fixed periods, or upon the termination of a life or lives, or otherwise, so that it will endure for a period of 31 years or more.[7] It has been asked whether a break, which might reduce the term of a lease to less than 31 years would disqualify it,[8] but this seems unlikely on the analogy of the case cited.[9]

(3) The area of the subjects let must not exceed 50 acres, except in the case of a lease of mines or minerals, for which there is no limit.[10]

(4) Except for a lease of burgage property and for a lease executed before 10th August 1857 or in terms of an obligation to renew contained in a lease dated before that date, the lease to be registrable must set forth the name of the lands of which the subjects let consist or form part and also the extent of the land,[11] unless the lease itself contains either a particular description or a description by reference of the subjects let and there is endorsed on the lease and recorded with it a probative declaration signed by the landlord and lessee stating that the extent of the subjects

---

[3] Registration of Leases Amendment Act 1877, s. 1; Conveyancing (Scotland) Act 1924, ss. 4 and 24; Long Leases (Scotland) Act 1954, ss. 26 and 27; and Succession (Scotland) Act 1964, Sched. 3.
[4] 1857 Act, s. 1.
[5] *Infra*, p. 121.
[6] 1857 Act, s. 1.
[7] *Ibid.*, s. 17.
[8] Burns, *Conveyancing Practice*, 4th ed., 388.
[9] *Fleming* v *Middle Ward of Lanarkshire* (1895) 23 R. 98 (compensation for compulsory acquisition).
[10] 1857 Act, s. 18.
[11] *Ibid.*, s. 18; Burns, *Conveyancing Practice*, 4th ed., 388.

does not exceed 50 acres.[12] Where a lease has already been recorded before 1st September 1954 without stating the name or extent of the subjects, the recording is not to be invalid if the lease contains a particular description or a description by reference; and any future deed relating to the land may be recorded, if and only if it contains a declaration that the extent of the land let under the lease does not exceed 50 acres, or if such a deed has already been recorded since 1st September 1954.[13]

(5) Registration must take place at or subsequent to the term of entry.[14] Registration before the date of entry would be ineffectual against a singular successor of the landlord acquiring his right before that date.[15]

The writs which may be registered under the Registration of Leases (Scotland) Act 1857 are leases complying with that Act, as amended by the Long Leases (Scotland) Act 1954, and also assignations either absolute[16] or in security,[17] translations of assignations in security,[18] extract decrees of adjudication or of sale,[19] notarial instruments or notices of title,[20] discharges and renunciations[21] and extract decrees of reduction.[22] If a lease was registered for preservation before the 1857 Act, an extract may be used in recording for publication, viz., extracts from the Books of Council and Session and Sheriff Court or Burgh Books, and also Commissary Records prior to 1809.[23] Where a lease registrable under the 1857 Act has not been recorded in the Register of Sasines and cannot be found, it is possible to record a copy in the Register of Sasines in its place, if there is endorsed on the copy and recorded with it a probative declaration by the landlord and lessee for the time being; and the lease is deemed to have been recorded on the date of the recording of the copy.[24] Provision is also made for the event of the landlord's failure to sign such a declaration.[25]

No set form of lease is prescribed, and any lease complying with the requirements of the Act may be recorded, whether it was granted before or after the Act. Forms of assignations, bonds and assignations in security, notarial instruments, translations of assignations in security, renunciations and discharges of bonds and assignations in security are given in the Schedules of the 1857 Act. Moreover, the Conveyancing

[12] Long Leases (Scotland) Act 1954, s. 27.
[13] *Ibid.*, s. 27.
[14] 1857 Act, s. 2.
[15] See *Millar* v *M'Robbie*, 1949 S.C. 1 (possession before term of entry on an unrecorded lease), *supra*, p. 113.
[16] 1857 Act, s. 3.
[17] *Ibid.*, s. 4.
[18] *Ibid.*, s. 6.
[19] *Ibid.*, s. 10, as amended by Conveyancing (Scotland) Act 1924, s. 24 (7).
[20] 1857 Act, s. 8, as amended by Succession (Scotland) Act 1964, Sched. 3; and Conveyancing (Scotland) Act 1924, s. 24.
[21] 1857 Act, s. 13.
[22] *Ibid.*, s. 14.
[23] *Ibid.*, s. 19.
[24] 1954 Act, s. 26.
[25] *Ibid.*, s. 26.

(Scotland) Act 1924[26] provides that the forms given by that Act for dispositions of land and the creation or transfer of rights in security over land may be adopted with modifications for the constitution, transmission, restriction and discharge of securities over leases and the completion of title to leases and to securities over leases. The forms provided by the 1857 Act are illustrative only and need not be rigidly adhered to.[27]

The effect of registration is that all registrable leases valid in a question with the granters thereof and recorded at or subsequent to the date of entry mentioned therein are by virtue of such registration effectual against any singular successor in the subjects whose infeftment is later than the date of such registration.[28] The recording in the Register of Sasines of a lease or other writ permitted by the Act completes the right under it to the effect of establishing a preference in virtue thereof as effectually as if the grantee or party in his right had entered into actual possession of the subjects of the lease or other writ at the date of registration thereof.[29] The dates of registration determine the preference of writs *inter se*.[30]

So far as assignations are concerned, the Act provides that any party in right of a lease, which has been duly recorded, may, in accordance with the provisions of the lease, and not otherwise, assign it in whole or part by assignation in the form provided; and the recording of such assignation shall fully and effectually vest the assignee with the right of the granter in such lease to the extent assigned, provided that such assignation shall not prejudice the right of hypothec or other rights of the landlord.[31] The wording of the section makes it quite clear that a lease may be assigned only if there is power to do so in the lease; normally in a long lease the power to assign is unlimited, but it is perfectly competent to impose restrictions for business or other reasons although there is some doubt as to the competency of prohibiting assignation in a very long lease.[32]

Registration is stated to be the equivalent of possession, but it does not prevail over actual possession. If the holder of a lease, which has been recorded, gives an assignation to one person, and thereafter gives an assignation to another person, and neither assignee enters into possession, the second assignee who registers his assignation first is preferred to the first assignee who merely intimates his assignation to the lessor;[33] but the assignee who enters into possession before the other records his assignation will prevail.[34]

26 s. 24.
27 *Rodger* v *Crawford* (1867) 6 M. 24; *Crawford* v *Campbell*, 1937 S.C. 596.
28 1857 Act, s. 2.
29 *Ibid.*, s. 16.
30 *Ibid.*, s. 12.
31 *Ibid.*, s. 3.
32 *Bain* v *M'Kenzie* (1896) 23 R. 528 *per* Lord Kinnear at p. 533; *infra*, p. 152.
33 *Rodger* v *Crawford* (1867) 6 M. 24.
34 *Ibid., per* Lord Neaves at p. 31.

The 1857 Act expressly provides that except for the purposes of the Act it is not necessary to record any registrable lease, but that all such leases which should under the existing law prior to the Act have been valid and effectual against a singular successor shall, though not recorded, be valid and effectual against such singular successor as well as against the granter.[35] Thus, if a tenant under a long lease complying with the Leases Act 1449 has possession, there is no need for him to record his lease (assuming that it is registrable) in order to make his right real. The effect of registration is equivalent to, but no higher than, possession, [36] and so a lessee or assignee in possession in respect of a lease complying with the Leases Act 1449, although it had not been registered, will hold the subjects let against a lessee or assignee of the same subjects holding a writ registered later in date than the date of possession. Thus the holder of a registered lease under the Act is not in so strong a position as the holder of a recorded conveyance such as a feu charter, with whom *bona fide* parties can deal on the faith of the records.[37]

The holder of an improbative long lease fortified by *rei interventus* cannot make use of the 1857 Act, which permits only probative leases to be registered.[38] He must rely on possession to make his right real.[39]

The recording of a lease is not equivalent to feudal infeftment, and it is incorrect to use the words "infeft" and "infeftment" in relation to recorded leases.[40] The inapplicability of feudal principles to recorded leases was discussed in a case involving a claim by a landlord for the payment of casualties on the entry of assignees.[41] A purchaser of heritable property can resile, if it turns out that unknown to him the property is held by leasehold tenure, even although the lease is for as long as 999 years.[42]

It may be noted that some leases can be registered and so be made effectual against singular successors, although they would not have had the protection of the 1449 Act as, for example, leases in perpetuity, leases granted for elusory rents, as well as leases on which no possession has followed.

LEASEHOLD SECURITIES

The Registration of Leases (Scotland) Act 1857 for the first time made securities over leases possible without possession of the subjects

[35] 1857 Act, s. 2.
[36] *Ibid.*, s. 16.
[37] Rankine, 189.
[38] 1857 Act, s. 1.
[39] *Wilson* v *Mann* (1876) 3 R. 527.
[40] Conveyancing (Scotland) Act, 1924, s. 24 (1).
[41] See opinion of Lord Jamieson (L.O.) in *Crawford* v *Campbell*, 1937 S.C. 596, although his decision was reversed on other grounds.
[42] *M'Connell* v *Chassels* (1903) 10 S.L.T. 790 (O.H.); *Fleming* v *Boswell* (O.H.) 1948 C.L. 4378, mentioned in Report of Scottish Leases Committee, 1952 Cmd. 8656, para. 48.

having to be given to the lender. As will be seen later,[43] a lease at common law cannot easily be made the security for a debt, because the only method by which a creditor can normally perfect his security is by taking possession. An assignation not followed by possession does not make the assignee's right real. The commercial desirability of rendering the tenant's interest under the lease a suitable subject for security for borrowed money was the main reason for the 1857 Act, but, as has been seen, the Act has by no means been made use of only for the purposes of security.

The Act makes it lawful for a recorded lease, if it so permits, to be assigned in security for the payment of borrowed money, or of annuities, or of provisions to wives or children, or in security of cash credits or other legal debt or obligation, by an assignation in security in the form provided, the recording of which shall constitute a real security over the lease to the extent assigned;[44] and such assignations in security are transferable by translations.[45] The form of assignation in security provided by the Act includes a power of sale.[46] The creditor or party in right of such assignation in security, without prejudice to any power of sale therein, is entitled on six months' default of payment of capital or interest to apply to the sheriff for a warrant to enter into possession of the subjects.[47] It is, however, provided that a creditor in right of an assignation in security, although recorded, shall not incur personal liability to the landlord, unless or until he enters into possession.[48]

The form of assignation in security provided by the Act[49] is illustrative only, and need not be rigidly adhered to.[50] It has been held that it is perfectly competent to constitute a security over a lease by an *ex facie* absolute assignation qualified by a back letter.[51] Where that method was adopted and was followed by an assignation back to the tenant's trustees on repayment of the loan, and both assignations were recorded but neither was intimated to the landlord, it was held that the landlord could not exact two casualties which he was entitled under his lease to claim on the " entry " of assignees; the opinion was expressed that if necessary it would have been competent to found on the back letter as showing the true nature of the transaction.[52] The same case contains a discussion of the Act and the inapplicability of feudal principles to it.[53] An *ex facie* absolute assignation qualified by a back

---

[43] *Infra*, p. 160 *et seq.*
[44] 1857 Act, s. 4.
[45] *Ibid.*, s. 6.
[46] *Ibid.*, Sched. B.
[47] *Ibid.*, s. 6.
[48] *Ibid.*, s. 6.
[49] *Ibid.*, s. 4, and Sched. B.
[50] *Rodger* v *Crawford* (1867) 6 M. 24.
[51] *Crawford* v *Campbell*, 1937 S.C. 596.
[52] *Crawford* v *Campbell*, 1937 S.C. 596.
[53] *Ibid.*, opinion of Lord Jamieson (L.O.).

letter (unlike an *ex facie* absolute disposition of land) is moveable in the succession of the creditor.[54]

The form of *ex facie* absolute assignation commonly used is modelled on the form of absolute assignation provided by the Act.[55] It may be a simple assignation by the lessee to his creditor, or where the lessee is purchasing the property and obtaining a loan at the same time, it may be an assignation by the cedent with the consent of the purchaser in favour of the creditor.

A creditor under a bond and assignation in security of a lease is not entitled to poind the ground,[56] nor to raise an action of maills and duties.[57] However, he has his power of sale[58] and his right to enter into possession.[59]

A creditor lending on the security of leasehold subjects must ensure that there is no limitation on the power of assignation and that the duration of the unexpired portion of the leases exceeds the duration of the loan. The lease itself must, of course, have been recorded; if not recorded, it is valueless as a security. As recording is no stronger than possession,[60] a creditor should ensure that there is no prior assignation of all or part of the subjects completed by possession but not by registration, the existence of which is not disclosed in the Register. Although an assignation in security is solely a creature of the statute and was intended to be recorded, it nevertheless contains words which would operate as an assignation at common law, and the wording of Section 16 suggests that possession on an assignation in security might be equivalent to registration.

CONVERSION OF A LEASE INTO A FEU

Upon the expiry of a lease the ground and all the buildings thereon revert to the landlord, notwithstanding the fact that the tenant may have erected the buildings at his own expense, or may have paid the full value of the buildings on acquiring the lease. When making a lease for a period like 99 years, the parties may not have had this in immediate contemplation. However, a large number of leases for 99 years were granted last century, many of them shortly after the 1857 Act. Thus a large number were due to expire about the middle of the twentieth century in a period of greatly increased property values and shortage of housing, thereby causing considerable hardship. Moreover, as has been seen,[61] a leasehold right is inferior to a feu right, and a

---

[54] *Stroyan* v *Murray* (1890) 17 R. 1170.
[55] 1857 Act, s. 3 and Sched. A, as amended by Conveyancing (Scotland) Act 1924 s. 24.
[56] *Luke* v *Wallace* (1896) 23 R. 634.
[57] *Dunbar* v *Gill*, 1908 S. C. 1054.
[58] 1857 Act, Sched. B; Conveyancing (Scotland) Act 1924, s. 24.
[59] 1857 Act, s. 6.
[60] *Ibid.*, s. 16.
[61] *Supra*, p. 67.

tenant under a lease, however long, even if it is a perpetual one, is unable to confer on a purchaser a full right of property in the subjects. Also, long leases were regarded in some quarters as something of an anomaly in Scottish conveyancing, especially as many of them were originally granted because the more orthodox feudal grant was for some reason incompetent. For those social and technical reasons, after temporary legislation,[62] the Long Leases (Scotland) Act 1954 was passed to enable tenants under certain long leases of residential property to have them converted into feus. Such a practice was not entirely new, and prior to the 1954 Act many landlords were willing on certain terms to give to their tenants feudal writs in place of long leases that had expired or were approaching expiry.

The Long Leases (Scotland) Act 1954 provides that where any property was let under a lease granted before 10th August 1914 for a period of not less than 50 years, and such property, or a part thereof, was occupied as a private dwellinghouse forming his usual residence by the lessee under such lease, or by the sub-lessee under a sub-lease for a period of not less than 50 years, such lessee or sub-lessee (both referred to as the " occupying lessee ") might give notice to the landlord requiring him to grant a feu right of the property or part thereof.[63] The significance of the date 10th August 1914 is that this was the date of the passing of the Entail (Scotland) Act 1914, by which the last restriction on the power of an heir of entail to grant feus was removed. Presumably, long leases granted since then were arranged by choice and not by compulsion, although it may be noted that it was not until 1938 that existing prohibitions of subinfeudation were finally removed.[64]

The notice requiring the landlord to grant a feu must have been given to the landlord before 1st September 1959.[65]

The term " lessee " means any person for the time being holding the interest of lessee under a lease and includes the person holding the right of reversion to a lease assigned *ex facie* absolutely.[66]

The property may include any garden, yard, garage, outhouse or pertinent belonging to and occupied with a dwellinghouse forming the lessee's or sub-lessee's usual residence.[67] The Act applies if part of the property is used for business, trade or professional purposes other than for the sale of exciseable liquor for consumption on the premises.[68]

The term " occupying lessee " is extended to include trustees holding the interest of lessee in the lease of a house occupied by a person beneficially interested in the house,[69] and the trustees of any religious

---

[62] Long Leases (Temporary Provisions) (Scotland) Act 1951; Leasehold Property Act and Long Leases (Scotland) Act Extension Act 1953.
[63] 1954 Act, s. 1.
[64] Conveyancing (Scotland) Act 1938, s. 8.
[65] 1954 Act, s. 1 (2).
[66] *Ibid.*, s. 1 (4) (a).
[67] *Ibid.*, s. 1 (4) (b).
[68] *Ibid.*, s. 1 (4) (c).
[69] *Ibid.*, s. 2 (a).

denomination holding that interest, where the occupier is a minister or missionary.[70] The term also extends to include a person acquiring the interest of lessee by inheritance, where the house is occupied by a member of the lessee's family residing with him at his death.[71] The procedure under the Act was not open to anyone acquiring interest as lessee on or after 10th May 1951[72] otherwise than by inheritance.[73] Special provision was made where the landlord was a local authority, government department or development corporation.[74]

Special provision was made for the case of landlords who had acquired their interest between 1st January 1939 and 9th May 1951 with a view to personal occupation or development of the property.[75]

The Act provided for the calculation of sums to be paid to the landlord in consideration of the grant of a feu right, according as the lease had at the date of the notice 100 years or less to run,[76] or more than 100 years to run;[77] for payments to intermediate landlords in the case of sub-leases,[78] and for payments to heritable creditors of the landlord.[79]

The Act furnished a form of feu contract of the subjects containing a renunciation by the lessee of the lease, and, in the case of a sub-lease, a renunciation by each intermediate landlord as well as by the occupying lessee.[80] The position of heritable creditors of the lessee holding *ex facie* absolute assignations or bonds and assignations in security was safeguarded.[81]

Leases expiring between 1st September 1954 and 1st September 1959 were to have effect as if the expiry date had been Whitsunday, 1960,[82] subject to the right of the occupying lessee to adhere to the proper expiry date.[83] During that period any option to the landlord to terminate a lease was postponed till Whitsunday 1960.[84]

The Act provided rules for determining the duration of a lease, where the lease contained an obligation on the landlord to renew, where the duration was dependent upon the endurance of a life, or lives, and where the landlord had an option to terminate.[85] It also

[70] *Ibid.*, s. 2 (b).
[71] *Ibid.*, s. 2 (c).
[72] The date of passing of the Long Leases (Temporary Provisions) (Scotland) Act 1951.
[73] 1954 Act, s. 3.
[74] *Ibid.*, s. 4.
[75] *Ibid.*, s. 5.
[76] *Ibid.*, s. 7.
[77] *Ibid.*, s. 8.
[78] *Ibid.*, s. 9.
[79] *Ibid.*, s. 10.
[80] *Ibid.*, ss. 11-13.
[81] *Ibid.*, ss. 14 and 21.
[82] *Ibid.*, s. 15.
[83] *Ibid.*, s. 16.
[84] *Ibid.*, s. 17.
[85] *Ibid.*, s. 18.

provided rules for determining the rent, where it was wholly or partly payable otherwise than in money.[86]

It may be noted that the application of Part I of the 1954 Act is not confined to recorded leases, or leases capable of being recorded, under the Registration of Leases (Scotland) Act 1857.[87]

Lastly, the provisions of the 1954 Act relating to the conversion of a lease into a feu now apply only in cases where a notice was given to the landlord before 1st September 1959. There may still be cases where the notice has been given and the conversion procedure has not yet been completed. The Act also remains a useful guide for the terms and conditions on which other long leases of residential property may be converted into feus by the agreement of the parties. It is believed that no great use has been made of the Act, but that leases are from time to time renounced in exchange for feudal grants by mutual agreement.

[86] *Ibid.,* s. 19.
[87] Part II of the 1954 Act consisting of Sections 26 and 27 operates as an extension of the provisions of the Registration of Leases (Scotland) Act 1857.

CHAPTER IX

THE RIGHTS AND OBLIGATIONS OF LANDLORD
AND TENANT

Introduction. Without special mention in a lease, certain rights and obligations are imposed or inferred by law in a contract of lease.

LANDLORD'S OBLIGATIONS

Giving Full Possession of the Subjects as Let. The landlord's primary obligation is to ensure that the whole of the subjects as let are available to the tenant at the date of entry expressed or implied[1] in the lease.[2] The landlord must, therefore, communicate to the tenant his rights to remove or eject third parties in possession of the subjects or he may be compelled to exercise these rights on the tenant's behalf.[3] Any material failure on the landlord's part in the performance of this obligation will give the tenant grounds for reducing the lease, if *restitutio in integrum* is still possible, and for claiming damages;[4] while a minor discrepancy will at most entitle the tenant to an abatement of rent.[5] Thus, where in the lease of a country house certain store-rooms were retained by the landlord without express reservation in the lease itself, the tenant was not entitled to abandon the lease on this account.[6]

Apart from any restrictions upon possession expressed in the lease or implied from its character, the tenant will be entitled to the exclusive possession of the subjects, free from any encroachment on the part of the landlord.[7] The landlord of a furnished house, however, has certain rights in regard to locking cupboards, wardrobes, desks, etc.[8]

While the possession which has to be given need not involve possession of every right which the landlord has had in relation to the subjects,[9] it will, however, involve the possession of rights appurtenant to the lease, where these are essential to its purposes.[10] Where necessity

---

[1] *Seton* v *White* (1679) Mor. 15173.
[2] Stair, I, 15, 6; Bankt, II, 9, 21; Ersk., II, 6, 39; Hume, *Lectures*, II, 71; Hunter, *Landlord and Tenant*, 4th ed., II, 178 *et seq.*; Rankine, 200 *et seq.*; *Seaforth's Trs.* v *Macaulay* (1844) 7 D. 180; *Tennent's Trs.* v *Maxwell* (1880) 17 S.L.R. 463.
[3] Ersk., II, 6, 28; Rankine, 200.
[4] Rankine, 208.
[5] Gloag, *Contract*, 2nd ed., 628; *Kilmarnock Gas Light Co.* v *Smith* (1872) 11 M. 58; *Guthrie* v *Shearer* (1873) 1 R. 181.
[6] *Webster* v *Lyell* (1860) 22 D. 1423.
[7] *Baxter* v *Paterson* (1843) 5 D. 1074.
[8] *Miller* v *Wilson*, 1919 1 S.L.T. 223 (O.H.).
[9] Ersk., II, 6, 22; *Laird of Touch* (1664) Mor. 15252; *Colquhoun* v *Watson* (1668) Mor. 15253.
[10] Bell, § 1224 (2); Hunter, *op. cit.*, II, 186; Rankine, 206; *Weir* v *Glenny* (1832) 10 S. 290; *Galloway* v *Cowden* (1885) 12 R. 578.

or the purposes of a lease require it, rights of positive servitude may be held to have been created in favour of the subjects over neighbouring land retained by the landlord, since such servitudes can be created by implied grant, and the landlord is taken to have bound himself not to derogate from his own grant.[11]

Breach of the landlord's obligation can also occur where possession is not given timeously, and while the Court may regard a delay of a day or two as immaterial,[12] delay of twenty days in one case,[13] and a month in another,[14] was held to be sufficient to entitle the tenant to abandon the lease.

Maintenance of the Tenant in Possession.[15] The essence of this obligation is to be found in the absolute[16] warrandice which will be implied in any lease in the absence of express stipulation to the contrary. The tenant's title is warranted at the date of entry, and the landlord is precluded from any action which may encroach upon the tenant's possession throughout the period of the lease.[17] This limitation placed upon the landlord can also be stated in terms of the principle that a granter may not derogate from his own grant.[18]

Total[19] or partial eviction from the subjects must be shown by the tenant before breach of the obligation is established.[20] Partial eviction, which entitled a tenant to damages in the form of an abatement of rent, was held to have occurred where the tenant of a farm found that members of the public were entitled under the common good of a burgh to certain fishing rights affecting his farm.[21]

There are, however, certain clearly defined limits placed by the law upon the scope of the landlord's obligation. In the first place, a preliminary question may arise as to whether a particular encroachment upon possession is covered by warrandice, and where possession is referable to a collateral licence and not to the lease itself, the warrandice will not apply.[22] Also, it may be clear that a tenant has knowingly

[11] Rankine, 206; *Huber v Ross*, 1912 S.C. 898 *per* L.P. Dunedin at p. 912.
[12] *Drummond v Hunter* (1869) 7 M. 347 *per* Lord Barcaple at p. 350; *Tennent's Trs. v Maxwell* (1880) 17 S.L.R. 463.
[13] *Brown v Maxwells* (1633) Mor. 3109.
[14] *Drummond v Hunter* (1869) 7 M. 347.
[15] Hume, *Lectures,* II, 71; Rankine, 213 *et seq.*
[16] *Middletons v Yorstoun* (1826) 5 S. 162; *Middletons v Megget* (1828) 7 S. 76.
[17] *Murray v Douglas* (1837) 15 S. 890; *Gibson v Stewart* (1894) 21 R. 437; *Fisken v Wells* (1915) 31 Sh. Ct. Rep. 239; *cf. Blanche v Wainstein* (1923) 39 Sh. Ct. Rep. 228.
[18] *Shawsrigg Fireclay Co. v Larkhall Collieries* (1903) 5 F. 1131, *per* Lord Trayner at p. 1138; *Huber v Ross,* 1912 S.C. 898 *per* L.P. Dunedin at pp. 910-911; Gloag, *op. cit.,* 297. The general principle is stated in *Caledonian Rly. Co. v Sprot* (1856) 19 D. (H.L.) 3, 2 Macq. 449.
[19] As, *e.g.,* in *Menzies v Duke of Queensbury's Exrs.* (1832) 11 S. 18.
[20] *Dougall v Magistrates of Dunfermline,* 1908 S.C. 151, especially *per* Lord Ardwall at p. 160.
[21] *Dougall v Magistrates of Dunfermline, supra; Brown v Brown* (1826) 4 S. 489 *per* L.P. Boyle at p. 490.
[22] *Burnet v Stewart* (1863) 1 M. 524.

taken the risk of a possible defect in his landlord's title, as, for example, in respect of a disputed piece of ground adjacent to the subjects of lease;[23] or that a limitation upon the title should have been known to both parties at the date of the lease,[24] for the tenant is put upon his enquiry and the landlord is under no obligation to disclose every burden which may exist.[25] Secondly, where possession has been lost through the tenant's own fault, there can be no claim against the landlord. Thus, a tenant had no relevant claim where, due to his own failure to take protective measures, third parties had encroached upon a privilege of pasture on a common which was an appurtenant to his farm.[26] Thirdly, the landlord cannot be held responsible for the unlawful acts of third parties even though they are also tenants of his,[27] unless he can be shown to have been a party to such acts.[28] Lastly, it has also been held that no liability will attach to the landlord where possession is lost as a result of *damnum fatale* or supervenient legislation,[29] and, though there has been a tendency to apply the terminology of eviction in such cases,[30] this practice has been expressly disapproved;[31] but, as will be seen, if the eviction is total or substantial, the tenant may be entitled to abandon his lease without further liability for rent on the principle of *rei interitus*.

Difficult cases may arise where the interference with a tenant's possession occurs as a result of operations carried on by his landlord on a neighbouring property. While it is clear that nothing in the nature of a negative servitude can be created by implication in favour of the subjects leased over other property belonging to the landlord,[32] nevertheless it has been held that the landlord's duty in such a case is more onerous than that of a neighbouring proprietor.[33] Hence by an application of the principle that a landlord may not derogate from his own grant, the landlord is precluded from conducting operations on his property which may result in structural damage or material, physical and tangible injury to the subjects leased.[34] It is of no significance that the operations may have been carried out with all possible care and skill.[35] In the leading case on this subject, where a photographer, who was tenant of a top flat in a tenement which he used for business purposes,

[23] *Kinloch* v *Fraser* (1829) 7 S. 819.
[24] *Gordon* v *Ruxton* (1797) Hume 798; *Reid* v *Shaw* (1822) 1 S. 371.
[25] *Symington* v *Cranston* (1780) Mor. 16637.
[26] *Stewart* v *Wand* (1838) 16 S. 408.
[24] *Gordon* v *Ruxton* (1797) Hume 798; *Reid* v *Shaw* (1822) 1 S. 371.
[28] *Gardner* v *Walker* (1862) 24 D. 1430, *per* L.P. McNeill at p. 1434.
[29] *Goldie* v *Williamson* (1796) Hume 793; *Holliday* v *Scott* (1830) 8 S. 831; *Tay Salmon Fisheries* v *Speedie*, 1929 S.C. 593; *Mackeson* v *Boyd*, 1942 S.C. 56; *Lentran Estates* v *Cross* (1958) 46 S.L.C.R. 28.
[30] *Tay Salmon Fisheries* v *Speedie, supra,* per L.P. Clyde at p. 601; but *cf. per* Lord Sands at p. 604.
[31] *Mackeson* v *Boyd*, 1942 S.C. 56, *per* L.P. Normand at p. 61.
[32] *Huber* v *Ross*, 1912 S.C. 898, *per* L.P. Dunedin at p. 909.
[33] *Huber* v *Ross, supra.*
[34] *Ibid., per* L.P. Dunedin at p. 912.
[35] *Huber* v *Ross, supra;* Rankine, 218.

9

sued his landlord in respect of various types of damage alleged to have occurred as a result of structural alterations by the landlord to a lower flat, a distinction was made between damage due to vibration or dust and damage due to noise or occasional obstruction to access.[36] It was held by the majority,[37] that only the former type of damage, involving physical and tangible injury to the subjects, was recoverable. The damage complained of must affect the premises and not merely the occupants, and must be material and not merely a source of temporary inconvenience.[38]

The landlord's obligation does not require him to restore subjects to their former state where through accident they have been actually or constructively destroyed,[39] nor does it preclude him from carrying on business in a neighbouring property in competition with his tenant.[40]

Implied Warrandice that the Subjects are Reasonably Fit for the Purposes of the Lease.[41] Though this implied obligation is stated in rather general terms, its application in practice is limited to artificial structures,[42] such as houses or outbuildings on the subjects of lease, and the standard of the landlord's obligation in this respect is variously defined in relation to urban or agricultural leases. The obligation does not apply to minerals in a mineral lease.[42]

In the case of urban subjects, houses, offices, shops and stores must be reasonably habitable and tenantable and in a wind and watertight[43] condition.[44] Breach of this obligation would justify a tenant in refusing to enter,[45] or in claiming a reduction of rent. " Wind and watertight " has been defined as meaning " wind and watertight against what may be called the ordinary attacks of the elements, not against exceptional encroachments of water due to other causes ".[46] There is, however, a variable element in the application of this standard, " since the extent of this obligation will vary according to the value and rental of the subjects and the reasonable requirements of a tenant who hires a house of given accommodation and rental ".[47] But a landlord is clearly in

---

[36] *Huber* v *Ross, supra,* at p. 913.
[37] Lord Johnston dissented—*ibid.,* at p. 917.
[38] *Ibid., per* L.P. Dunedin at p. 912.
[39] *Walker* v *Bayne* (1815) 6 Pat. 217, 3 Dow 233; *cf.* Housing (Scotland) Act, 1962, s. 25 (2b), *infra,* p. 134.
[40] *Craig* v *Miller* (1888) 15 R. 1005 (Whole Court).
[41] Ersk., II, 6, 39 and 43; Hume, *Lectures,* II, 71; Bell, § 1253; Rankine, 240-241: Gloag, *op. cit.,* 315 *et seq.*
[42] Rankine, 241.
[43] *E.g. Reid* v *Baird* (1876) 4 R. 234; see *Gosskirk* v *Edinburgh Railway Station Access Co.* (1863) 2 M. 383.
[44] *Wolfson* v *Forrester,* 1910 S.C. 675, *per* L.P. Dunedin at p. 680, and *per* Lord Johnston at p. 681.
[45] *Brodie* v *McLachlan* (1900) 8 S.L.T. 145; *cf. Anderson* v *Watson* (1894) 2 S.L.T. 293.
[46] *Wolfson* v *Forrester,* 1910 S.C. 675 *per* L.P. Dunedin at p. 680; *cf. Reid* v *Baird, supra.*
[47] *Mechan* v *Watson,* 1907 S.C. 25, *per* Lord McLaren at p. 28.

breach of his obligation where a house is infested with beetles and cockroaches,[48] or where the drains and water supply are completely inadequate,[49] though such inadequacy is to be measured in terms of ordinary efficiency for the purpose, and not in relation to the best methods of drainage which may be available.[50] Thus, a landlord was not liable in damages where a flour-store, the subject of the lease, was equipped with a thirty-year-old drainage system which flooded when an outside drain became choked.[51] Where the sufficiency of a store is in question, the standard to be applied is sufficiency on the basis of reasonable use by the tenant, having regard to the general and recognised practice in the particular trade concerned.[52] Where urban subjects are concerned, there is authority that there is no warranty implied that the subjects will always remain fit for the purposes of the lease.[53]

In an agricultural lease the obligation is to put buildings on a farm in a proper state of repair,[54] and to provide sufficient buildings to enable the tenant to cultivate the land.[55] It is also implied that the buildings provided should be capable of lasting for the length of the lease if used with ordinary care by the tenant.[56] While an existing water supply must be put into proper repair by the landlord,[57] he does not thereby undertake that this will continue to be adequate.[58]

The landlord's obligation in respect of the condition of the buildings and fences provided is more onerous than that of an outgoing tenant who is not liable for defects due to natural decay or fair wear and tear.[59] A landlord will have to replace buildings where renewal becomes necessary on account of inadequacies produced by natural decay.[60]

Obligation in Relation to Repairs. (a) *Urban Leases.*[61] Once the tenant is in possession the landlord is bound to repair any defect which makes the premises less than wind and watertight or not in tenantable repair.[62] It has been held that the spread of damp from the foundations

---

[48] *Kippen* v *Oppenheim* (1847) 10 D. 242.
[49] *Tennent's Trs.* v *Maxwell* (1880) 17 S.L.R. 463.
[50] *N.B. Storage Co.* v *Steele's Trs.*, 1920 S.C. 194, *per* Lord Dundas at pp. 204-206.
[51] *N.B. Storage Co., supra.*
[52] *Glebe Sugar Refining Co.* v *Paterson* (1900) 2 F. 615.
[53] *Sandeman* v *Duncan's Trs.* (1897) 4 S.L.T. 336, *per* Lord Kyllachy; affd. 5 S.L.T. 21.
[54] Bankt., I, 20, 10; Ersk., II, 6, 39; Bell, § 1253; *cf.* Agricultural Holdings (Scotland) Act, 1949, s. 5; *infra,* p. 301; *Buchanan* v *Stark* (1776) 5 B.S. 515; *Barclay* v *Neilson* (1878) 5 R. 909.
[55] *Barclay* v *Neilson, supra, per* L.P. Inglis at p. 911.
[56] Rankine, 250; Gloag, *op. cit.,* 316.
[57] *Christie* v *Wilson,* 1915 S.C. 645.
[58] *Russell* v *Sime* (O.H.), 1912 2 S.L.T. 344; *Reid* v *Bremner* (1928) 44 Sh. Ct. Rep. 251.
[59] *Davidson* v *Logan,* 1908 S.C. 350; *cf.* Agricultural Holdings (Scotland) Act, 1949, s. 5.
[60] *Davidson* v *Logan, supra.*
[61] *Cf.* the statutory obligations under the Housing (Scotland) Acts, 1950, s. 3, and 1962, ss. 25, 26 and 27, "the implied repairs provision". See *infra,* p. 133.
[62] Bankt., I. 20, 50; Ersk., II, 6, 43; Hume, *Lectures,* II, 73; Glegg, *Reparation,* 4th ed., 445/6; *Marianski* v *Jackson* (1872) 9 S.L.R. 480; *Dickie* v *Amicable Property Investment Society,* 1911 S.C. 1079.

of a house was not a breach of the landlord's obligation.[63] But in any event this obligation is not a warranty,[64] for the landlord "is in no breach as to this part of his bargain till the defect is brought to his notice and he fails to remedy it ",[64] and consequently " he is not bound to inspect the premises periodically in order to see what their condition is when he has no reason to suspect or believe that they are other than they should be ".[65]

The landlord is entitled to a reasonable time in which to repair defects of which the tenant gives notice;[66] after such a period of time the tenant will be able to resile from the lease and claim damages where material defects have not been rectified,[67] or to claim an abatement of rent where the defects are of less importance.[68] Where there were dangerous defects in the drainage system of a house, it was held that it was unreasonable for the landlord to take two months to have these put in order.[69] If, however, no action is taken by the landlord, and the tenant remains in occupation of the subjects with full knowledge of the defect, any injury sustained as a result of this is the tenant's own responsibility,[70] unless he has remained because of the landlord's assurance that the premises are safe,[71] or that repairs will be carried out immediately.[72] Similarly, a tenant can have no claim against his landlord when the damage stems from a defect in the construction of the house which would be obvious to the tenant at the time of entering into the lease,[73] since " the law does not hold a landlord of house property to be in the position of an insurer of the safety of his tenants ".[74]

The obligation to repair does not extend to cases where the defect is due to the tenant's own negligence,[75] the act of a third party,[76] or *damnum fatale.*[77]

---

[63] *McGonigal* v *Pickard,* 1954 S.L.T. (Notes) 62, *per* Lord Mackintosh.
[64] *Wolfson* v *Forrester, supra, per* L.P. Dunedin at p. 680; Glegg, *op. cit.,* 446; *McKimmie's Trs., infra.* See too *Euman's Trs.* v *Warnock* (1930) 46 Sh. Ct. Rep. 164 as regards the statutory provision.
[65] *Hampton* v *Galloway and Sykes* (1899) 1 F. 501, *per* Lord Trayner at p. 507.
[66] *McKimmie's Trs.* v *Armour* (1899) 2 F. 156, *per* Lord McLaren at p. 162, and *per* Lord Kinnear at p. 162.
[67] Gloag, *op. cit.,* 605; Glegg, *op. cit.,* 447; *McKimmie's Trs.* v *Armour, supra; Scottish Heritable Security Co.* v *Granger* (1881) 8 R. 459; *Dickie, supra; Proctor, infra.*
[68] Gloag, *op. cit.,* 629.
[69] *Scottish Heritable Security Co.* v *Granger, supra.*
[70] *Webster* v *Brown* (1892) 19 R. 765, *per* Lord Trayner at p. 768; *Russell* v *Macknight* (1896) 24 R. 118; *McManus* v *Armour* (1901) 3 F. 1078; *Proctor* v *Cowlairs Co-op. Society,* 1961 S.L.T. 434 (O.H.).
[71] *Caldwell* v *McCallum* (1901) 4 F. 371.
[72] *Shields* v *Dalziel* (1897) 24 R. 849; *McKinlay* v *McClymont* (1905) 43 S.L.R. 9; *Grant* v *McClafferty,* 1907 S.C. 201; *Mullen* v *Dunbarton County Council,* 1933 S.C. 380; Walker, *Delict,* 352; Glegg, *op. cit.,* 446. See *Proctor, supra.*
[73] *Mechan* v *Watson,* 1907 S.C. 25; *Davidson* v *Sprengel,* 1909 S.C. 566.
[74] *Mechan* v *Watson, supra, per* Lord McLaren at p. 28.
[75] *Cf. Hardie* v *Black* (1768) Mor. 10133; *McLellan* v *Ker* (1797) Mor. 10134.
[76] *Lyons* v *Anderson* (1886) 13 R. 1020; *Allan* v *Roberton's Trs.* (1891) 18 R. 932; *N.B. Storage Co.* v *Steele's Trs.,* 1920 S.C. 194.
[77] Bell, § 1253; Rankine, 242.

A landlord's common law obligations in relation to the condition of the property at the date of entry and during the currency of the lease have been modified by statute and extended in certain respects in relation to some classes of urban property. In general, these statutory obligations apply " notwithstanding any stipulation to the contrary "[78] in the lease. The basic statutory obligation is now contained in section 3 of the Housing (Scotland) Act, 1950, which governs " letting for human habitation . . . at a rent not exceeding £26 ". Leases of more than three years' duration upon terms that the tenant shall put the property into tenantable condition are expressly excluded from the ambit of the section.[79] Where the section is applicable, it is made an implied condition of the lease that the house is at the commencement of the tenancy " in all respects reasonably fit for human habitation " and an undertaking is also to be implied that the landlord will maintain the property in this condition during the lease. The statutory standard of " fitness for human habitation " is expanded by the Housing (Scotland) Act, 1962,[80] where reference is made to eleven detailed types of defect[81] and it is provided that a house shall be determined unfit for human habitation if and only if it is defective in one or more of these matters. The first of these, " general state of repair ", is in very broad terms. The statutory criterion has been interpreted as implying that : " If the state of repair of a house is such that by ordinary user damage may naturally be caused to the occupier, either in respect of personal injury to life or limb or injury to health, then the house is not in all respects reasonably fit for human habitation ".[82] Thus, where the daughter of a tenant was injured as a result of putting her hand through a cracked pane of glass in a bathroom door (which had been cracked for over six years), it was held that the pursuer must have used exceptional force in opening the door, and that her action was not " ordinary user " of

---

[78] Housing (Scotland) Act, 1950, s. 3 (1); cf. Housing (Scotland) Act, 1962, s. 27— the Sheriff is given power to authorise variation of the statutory obligations by s. 27 (1).

[79] s. 3 (1) proviso.

[80] s. 24 (1).

[81] (a) General state of repair;
(b) structural stability;
(c) freedom from dampness;
(d) natural lighting;
(e) air space;
(f) ventilation;
(g) adequacy and accessibility of water-supply;
(h) adequacy and accessibility of sanitary and other conveniences;
(i) drainage;
(j) condition of paving and drainage of courts, yards or passages, and
(k) facilities for storage, preparation and cooling of food and for the disposal of waste water.

[82] Morgan v Liverpool Corporation [1927] 2 K.B. 131 per Atkin L.J. at p. 145, approved in Summers v Salford Corporation [1943] A.C. 283; and followed by Lord Milligan in Haggerty v Glasgow Corporation, 1964 S.L.T. (Notes) 95 at p. 96.

the door.[83] It has also been held that the statutory undertaking does not amount to a guarantee on the part of the landlord that the house will never become unfit for human habitation,[84] and that it must be established that the landlord was aware that a defect existed before he can be held to be in breach of his obligation[83]—notwithstanding that the Housing (Scotland) Act, 1950,[85] gives the landlord a right of inspection upon twenty-four hours' notice in writing to the tenant or occupier.[86]

Further statutory provisions apply in the case of urban leases[87] for a period of less than seven years, where in virtue of the Housing (Scotland) Act, 1962,[88] an " implied repairs provision " is to be a necessarily implied term of the contract between the parties,[89] unless the Sheriff authorises the inclusion of provisions in the lease modifying this obligation.[90] This obligation on the part of the landlord does not, however, relieve the tenant of his duty to use the premises in a proper manner,[91] nor does it require the landlord to rebuild the subjects where they have been destroyed as the result of *damnum fatale*.[92] The standard of repair required is expressly referred to the age, character and prospective life of the house concerned, and the locality in which it is situated.[93] The landlord is also given a right to inspect the subjects upon giving the occupier the required twenty-four hours' notice in writing of his intention to do so.[94]

(b) *Rural Leases.* Although a landlord is obliged to put buildings and fences in tenantable repair at the date of entry, he is not obliged to make ordinary repairs of maintenance to these during the course of the lease, since these are to be regarded as mere accessories of the subjects of lease, and are not the principal counterpart of the tenant's

---

[83] *Haggerty* v *Glasgow Corporation, supra.*

[84] *Euman's Trs.* v *Warnock, supra; McKeown* v *Woodrow Anderson and Others* (1933) 49 Sh. Ct. Rep. 240; *MacDougall* v *McAllister* (1935) 51 Sh. Ct. Rep. 89; and see *Haggerty, supra.*

[85] s. 3 (2).

[86] *cf. Morgan* v *Liverpool Corporation, supra.*

[87] and not agricultural tenancies—Housing (Scotland) Act, 1962, s. 26 (4). Only leases granted after 3rd July 1962 are affected—s. 26 (1).

[88] ss. 25 and 26.

[89] s. 26 defines the leases covered by s. 25 as: (a) a lease for less than seven years; (b) a lease determinable by the landlord before the expiry of seven years from its commencement. A lease is treated as one for seven or more years if the landlord cannot so determine it and if the tenant can renew it for a period which combined with the original period is seven or more years. A lease of a house within the ambit of the Agricultural Holdings (Scotland) Act 1949 is not covered—s. 24 (4), nor is a new lease to an existing tenant, or to a former tenant who has remained in continuous possession after the termination of his lease, unless s. 25 could have applied or did apply to the former lease—s. 26 (3). Where part of the term of the lease is prior to the date of granting it, the lease is treated as one for the period starting on the date of granting—s. 26 (5). Lease includes sublease—s. 28.

[90] s. 27 (1).

[91] s. 25 (2a).

[92] s. 25 (2b).

[93] s. 25 (3).

[94] s. 25 (4).

obligation to pay rent.[95] The landlord is, however, responsible for carrying out extraordinary repairs to the property where these have become necessary due to natural decay and involve some element of renewal going beyond mere maintenance.[96]

Obigation to Relieve the Tenant in Respect of Rates. Where there is no stipulation to the contrary in a lease of a furnished house, the landlord is impliedly bound to relieve the tenant in respect of rates.[97]

TENANT'S OBLIGATIONS

Entry into Possession. The tenant is under an obligation to enter into possession of the subjects at the date of entry,[98] which can be enforced by specific implement, and he will be liable for any material damage which occurs to the subjects through neglect as a result of non-entry.[99] Provided that the landlord is ready to put the tenant in possession of the subjects at the date of entry, his delay in performing some of his other obligations will not excuse the tenant from the obligation of entering into possession.[1] Thus, a tenant in an agricultural lease is liable in damages for failure to enter into possession even though the landlord has delayed in repairing houses, fences or drains, since these are only accessories to the main subjects.[1] Nor is a tenant excused from his obligation by the fact of a former tenant remaining in possession of the subjects after the date of entry, since it would be open to him to require the landlord to enter him in possession at that time.[2]

" The date of entry should always be expressed ".[3] Where this has not been done, the date is that of the lease.[4] " If parties enter into a contract for a lease complete in all its details but without any statement of the commencement of the lease, the necessary reading of the contract is that it is a lease from the time at which it is made, subject, in the case of an agricultural lease, to those specialities which the sequence of cultivation of an arable subject makes necessary and which affect both entry and ish ".[5] The date may be the following term of Whitsunday or Martinmas.[6] The date of entry may be in advance of the date of lease

---

[95] Bankt., I, 20, 10; *cf. Fletcher* v *Henderson* (1933) 49 Sh. Ct. Rep. 25.
[96] *Johnstone* v *Hughan* (1894) 21 R. 777; *cf.* Agricultural Holdings (Scotland) Act, 1949, s. 5 (2) (a).
[97] *Sturrock* v *Murray*, 1952 S.C. 454, applying *Macome* v *Dickson* (1868) 6 M. 898; *supra*, p. 73.
[98] Stair, II, 9, 31; Bankt., II, 9, 21; Ersk., II, 6, 39; Hume, *Lectures*, II, 75; Bell, § 1222; Rankine, 233; *Lord Randifuird* v *Crombie* (1623) Mor. 15256; Gloag, *op. cit.*, 656.
[99] *Mathieson* v *Nicolson* (1819) 2 Mur. 141; *cf. Smith* v *Henderson* (1897) 24 R. 1102.
[1] *Duncan* v *McDougal* (1796) Hume 792.
[2] *Lisk* v *Rob* (1674) 1 B.S. 715.
[3] Rankine, 338.
[4] *Ibid.;* Stair, II, 9, 30.
[5] *Christie* v *Fife Coal Co.* (1899) 2 F. 192 *per* L.J.C. Macdonald at p. 197. See also Burns, *Conveyancing Practice,* 4th ed., 607.
[6] Rankine, 338; Stair, *supra;* Ersk., II, 6, 24; Menzies, *Lectures on Conveyancing,* 1900 ed., 908.

if, for instance, there is a verbal agreement allowing entry prior to the date of the lease. " It frequently happens that, on account of entry having been taken, or possession retained, in consequence of a verbal agreement, the lease is dated later than the term of entry. It is then usual in the lease to declare that the entry was so taken ' notwithstanding the date hereof '. The lease will then be construed as if it had been executed at the actual date of entry, in so far as any other construction would leave any clause in it insensible ".[7] In the case of an arable farm, the time or date is usually Whitsunday, and this is so notwithstanding that the lease itself gives the date in regard to land in crop as Martinmas after Whitsunday, or Martinmas.[8] In the case of pastoral farms it is usually Whitsunday. Grass parks may be let for a season only and the date is then the commencement of that season. Where the lease is one of a house, it is normally Whitsunday or Martinmas, particularly if the lease is one for more than a year.[9]

Where the date is Whitsunday or Martinmas, the term day is the last whole day of the preceding period. The Removal Terms (Scotland) Act, 1886,[10] has given a uniform time in the case of houses, shops and other buildings including houses or buildings let with land for agricultural purposes: it provides that in such lets, in the absence of express stipulation to the contrary, where the date is Whitsunday or Martinmas it is at noon on 28th May or 28th November respectively, or noon on the following day where the 28th day is a Sunday.

Retention of Possession. As the tenant impliedly undertakes that he will retain possession of the subjects, the landlord has a right to expect that the subjects will have the benefit of care and use over the period of the lease, and that they will not deteriorate due to neglect.[11] Thus, a tenant who left a house unoccupied for a month in winter, and who neglected to take any steps to have the house aired and fired, was held liable to the landlord in respect of damage due to burst pipes.[12] However, the tenant's obligation to possess does not oblige him to reside personally on the subjects leased.[13]

Where the tenant is in breach of this obligation, the landlord may be entitled to bring the lease to an end, or to sue for damages in respect

---

[7] Rankine, 338, who cites in support of the practice the *Juridical Styles* and Ross, *Lectures,* and in support of the construction *Foulis* v *McWhirter* (1841) 3 D. 343, and *Ramsay* v *Howison,* 1908 S.C. 697. This plain and obvious interpretation of the literal meaning of the words in the clause—long accepted in practice—apparently (and, with respect it is submitted, unjustifiably) caused difficulty to the judges of the Second Division in *Korner* v *Shennan,* 1950 S.C. 285.

[8] Rankine, 339.

[9] *Ibid.,* 340.

[10] s. 4. See *infra,* p. 263.

[11] Rankine, 233-4; *Mickel* v *McCoard,* 1913 S.C. 896; *cf. Blair Trust* v *Gilbert,* 1940 S.L.T. 322, affd. 1941 S.N. 2, where the condition was express.

[12] *Mickel* v *McCoard, supra.*

[13] Rankine, 234, and *Lauder* v *Bagley's Contract* [1893] 3 Ch. 4, there cited.

of deterioration of a house[14] due to neglect, or of the good-will of an inn after it had been closed for several months.[15] It would also be open to the landlord to compel the tenant to resume possession of the subjects according to the minimal standards prescribed by law; but where a lease of a shop is concerned, the tenant cannot be compelled to carry on business, though he must furnish the shop, keep fires in it, and air it.[16]

No Inversion of Possession.[17] The tenant may not invert the possession by treating the subjects in a way which is outwith the scope of the lease.[18] Thus, it was held to be inversion for the tenant of a farm to use the outbuildings to accommodate stage-coach horses,[19] and for the tenant of a grain-mill to use it for grinding sawdust,[20] a change of use of the mill which made a material change in the insurance risk of the subjects.[21] In two cases where tenants proposed to introduce railway systems on the subjects, the landlords were granted interdict, since the operation of these railways had no connection with the original purposes of the leases;[22] and where land was let for occupation by a priest, the tenant was not entitled to put up wooden huts on the property to house other tenants who had been evicted.[23]

The tenant of a shop may be entitled to hold occasional auction sales there,[24] and to place a temporary sign outside the shop advertising a bargain clearance sale,[25] even though no express power to do so is given by the lease. He may, however, be guilty of inversion if he attaches permanent showcases to the outside walls of the shop, so that they project from the building.[26] It is probably not inversion of possession for a tenant to attach a signboard containing his name and designation as shopkeeper to the front of the shop.[27] The tenant of a furnished house is entitled to move furniture or pictures in the house to suit his own requirements as occupant,[28] provided that this is done carefully,[29] and that everything is replaced at the end of the tenancy.[30] The landlord

---

[14] *Smith* v *Henderson, supra; Mickel* v *McCoard, supra.*
[15] *Graham* v *Stevenson* (1792) Hume 781.
[16] *Whitelaw* v *Fulton* (1871) 10 M. 27; Gloag, *op. cit.*, 656.
[17] Hume, *Lectures*, II, 76; Rankine 236; *Duke of Argyle* v *McArthur* (1861) 23 D. 1236, per L.J.C. Inglis at p. 1240.
[18] *Duke of Argyle* v *McArthur, supra; Mercer* v *Esk Valley Rly. Co.* (1867) 5 M. 1024; *Galbraith's Tr.* v *Eglinton Iron Co.* (1868) 7 M. 167; *Leck* v *Merryflats Patent Brick Co.* (1868) 5 S.L.R. 619; *Bayley* v *Addison* (1901) 8 S.L.T. 379 (O.H.); *Thompson* v *Ford* (1946) 62 Sh. Ct. Rep. 60.
[19] *Duke of Argyle* v *McArthur, supra.*
[20] *Bayley* v *Addison, supra.*
[21] *Ibid.*, per Lord Stormonth Darling at p. 381.
[22] *Leck* v *Merryflats Patent Brick Co., supra; Mercer* v *Esk Valley Rly. Co., supra.*
[23] *Kehoe* v *Marquess of Lansdowne* [1893] A.C. 451.
[24] *Keith* v *Reid* (1870) 8 M. (H.L.) 110.
[25] *Morrison* v *Forsyth*, 1909 S.C. 329.
[26] *British Linen Bank* v *Purdie* (1905) 7 F. 923.
[27] *Ibid.*, per Lord Stormonth Darling at p. 926.
[28] *Miller* v *Stewart* (1899) 2 F. 309; *supra*, p. 74.
[29] *Ibid.*, per L.J.C. Macdonald at p. 312.
[30] *Ibid.*, per Lord Moncreiff at p. 315.

might, however, be entitled to interdict, " if it could be proved that there was any serious risk of injury to the furniture or pictures if removed ".[30] It has been held that it is an inversion of possession for a tenant to commit suicide in furnished lodgings.[31]

Inversion would arise from a course of conduct on the part of the tenant rather than from isolated acts. The question would be whether the tenant's conduct involved a departure from the sort of occupation contemplated by the parties when they entered into the lease,[32] " looking at the whole circumstances of the case . . . and the *bona fides* of the transaction ".[33] A tenant is not necessarily limited in his occupation to the extent and nature of the use which he has in fact enjoyed from the beginning of the lease, provided that a proposed increase or change in use is covered by the original terms of the lease. Where the terms of a lease gave an iron company the " use " of a water-course, it was held that they were entitled to use it as a navigable canal, although their use of the water-course for the preceding fifty years had merely been as a means of conveying water to the iron-works.[34] Inversion may be aggravated if a permanent alteration to the structure of the subjects is involved,[35] as where a tenant cut through the joists of the building to insert a boiler and furnace for ham curing, the lease having been granted to him in the capacity of provision merchant.[36]

The landlord may lose his right to object to an inversion of possession through acquiescence.[37] Thus, a landlord was not entitled to interdict his tenant from using part of a shop as a dwelling house, since the tenant had been doing this for a period of more than three years, and the premises had been entered in successive Valuation Rolls on this basis.[38]

Use of Reasonable Care in the Management of the Subjects. Apart from the rules as to inversion of possession, the tenant is bound to use reasonable care in his management of the subjects and will be liable to make good any damage attributable to his negligence in this respect.[39] In an agricultural lease the obligation will amount to conforming to the

---

[31] *A.* v *B.'s Trs.* (1906) 13 S.L.T. 830.
[32] *Gordon* v *Crawford* (1825) 4 S. 95; *Keith* v *Reid, supra.*
[33] *Keith* v *Reid, supra,* per Lord Colonsay at p. 118.
[34] *Swan's Trs.* v *Muirkirk Iron Co.* (1850) 12 D. 622.
[35] *British Linen Bank* v *Purdie, supra.* Cf. *Morrison* v *Forsyth, supra; Muir* v *Wilson* (1822) 1 S. 444; *Leck* v *Fulton* (1854) 17 D. 408.
[36] *Leck* v *Fulton, supra.*
[37] *Skene* v *Maberly* (1822) 1 S. 347; *Moore* v *Munro* (1896) 4 S.L.T. 172.
[38] *Moore* v *Munro, supra.*
[39] Ersk., II, 6, 43; Hume, *Lectures,* II, 77-78; *McLellan* v *Ker* (1797) Mor. 10134; *Smith* v *Henderson* (1897) 24 R. 1102; *Mickel* v *McCoard,* 1913 S.C. 896. Cf. Housing (Scotland) Act, 1950, s. 162; and Housing (Scotland) Act, 1962, s. 25 (2a).

rules of good husbandry, though these will vary according to the usual practice of the part of the country in which the lands are situated.[40] Where specific rules of management are detailed by the parties in a lease, the tenant fulfils any obligation of management by observance of these and no further obligation is to be implied.[41] The tenant of a store or warehouse may be liable in damages for injury to the premises caused by overloading the building beyond the general and recognised practice of the particular trade, provided that the building was originally fit for the purpose for which it was let.[42]

Payment of Rent. Though rent will normally be the subject of express stipulation in a lease, a tenant who has entered into possession will be impliedly bound to pay the landlord a fair rent in return for the use and possession of the subjects.[43] " The presumption is that the party in possession is liable to pay the real worth of the subjects occupied; . . . an occupant . . . though no direct obligation to pay rent is proved, is bound to pay the annual value of the subject, the onus lying on him to show that he got it for less or . . . for nothing at all ".[44]

Rent may fall to be paid at the legal or at a conventional term. The distinction is important in arable or pastoral leases both in succession to the landlord and the tenant, and in the sale of a farm to a landlord. The legal terms control apportionment in succession. The legal terms at which rent must be paid by the tenant will vary according to the character of the subjects let, though it may be agreed, and it is common practice, to state the term conventionally in the deed and so to accelerate or postpone payment to a date before or after the legal term[45] by providing for forehand—that is where it is payable before the legal term— or backhand rents in the lease.[46] Rent is often conventionally postponed in arable farms. Legal term is " a shorthand way of expressing the common law term, or terms fixed by the common law as those which will regulate if there is no paction to the contrary. The fixing of these is a recognition by law of what has been so long custom as to have become law ".[47] In the case of an agricultural lease, although the payment of

---

[40] Stair, II, 9, 31; Bankt., II, 9, 21; Ersk., II, 6, 39; Hume, *Lectures,* II, 84; Rankine, 415; *Maxwell* v *McMurray* (1776) 5 B.S. 515. *Cf.* Agricultural Holdings (Scotland) Act, 1949, s. 12, which gives the tenant freedom of cropping; and s. 28, as amended by 1958 Act, Schedule I para. 38, which entitles the landlord to obtain a certificate of bad husbandry from the Land Court in certain circumstances; and ss. 57 (1) and 58, which determine his rights to compensation at the termination of the lease. See *infra,* pp. 314, 346-7.

[41] *Stark* v *Edmondstone* (1826) 5 S. 45.

[42] *Glebe Sugar Refining Co.* v *Paterson* (1900) 2 F 615; *cf. Corrie, Mackie and Co.* v *Stewart* (1882) 22 S.L.R. 350.

[43] *Young* v *Cockburn* (1674) Mor. 11624; *Wilson* v *Pollock, Gilmour and Co.* (1827) 6 S. 3; *Ogilvie* v *Boath* (1868) 5 S.L.R. 231; *Glen* v *Roy* (1882) 10 R. 239.

[44] *Glen* v *Roy, supra, per* L.J.C. Moncreiff at p. 240.

[45] *Wigan* v *Cripps,* 1908 S.C. 394, *per* Lord Low at p. 400; Rankine 342.

[46] Rankine, 343.

[47] *Baillie* v *Fletcher,* 1915 S.C. 677 at pp. 699-700 *per* Lord Johnston. The terms were first fixed as to arable and later extended to pastoral subjects, *ibid.,* at p. 699.

rent by the tenant will generally have to be made half-yearly at Whitsunday or Martinmas, referable to the possession which he has had under the lease, the calculation of the periods at which rent is impliedly due is specifically related to the crop which the tenant is able to enjoy.[48] A distinction is made between arable and pastoral farms, and a farm which has both of these elements is classified as either arable or pastoral according to whether the arable or pastoral element is the more important in the income of the farm.[49] In the lease of an arable farm, since the separation of the crop will have occurred prior to Martinmas, a new tenant's possession of the subjects is deemed to begin at that date, even though he may have had entry to the farm house and buildings at an earlier date, e.g. Whitsunday; the first payment of rent, that is, for the first half of a crop and year, falls due at the Whitsunday following the sowing of the crop, and the second at Martinmas after reaping. Although there is an apparent anomaly where the tenant possesses a part of the subjects prior to the period for which his first payment of rent is strictly referable, this anomaly is removed if the lease is considered in its entirety, since the tenant will quit that part of the subjects at a correspondingly earlier date, while his payment of rent will continue until separation of the waygoing crop.[50] In the case of a pastoral farm, the lease generally runs from Whitsunday to Whitsunday, and the first payment of rent falls due at the date of entry for the possession following that term, since the crop is at that time ready for the tenant's enjoyment.[51] The remaining instalment of the year's rent will be legally due at Martinmas after the crop is consumed and this payment is also taken to be referable to the tenant's possession of the grass crop during the summer—his subsequent possession of the subjects during the winter and spring being " thrown in as an unimportant accessory " for which no rent is payable.[52] It follows from this that in the case of a pastoral farm where rent is payable according to the legal terms, at the termination of the lease the tenant will be entitled to continue in occupation of the subjects for the six months following the term of Martinmas on which payment of the last half of his last year's rent is made.[53] An example of a conventional term in an arable farm would occur if entry is to the houses and buildings at Whitsunday but to the land at Martinmas and the first year's rent is payable as to one half at Martinmas and as to the other half six months thereafter; the rent would then be payable conventionally forehand. It would be backhand

---

[48] Generally, Rankine 342, and *Baillie* v *Fletcher,* 1915 S.C. 677 at p. 683 *per* L.P. Strathclyde.
[49] *McClymonts* v *Cathcart* (1848) 10 D. 1489; *Mackenzie's Trs.* v *Somerville* (1900) 2 F. 1278; *supra,* p. 70.
[50] *Wigan* v *Cripps,* 1908 S.C. 394, *per* Lord Low at p. 400.
[51] *Baillie* v *Fletcher,* 1915 S.C. 677.
[52] *Ibid., per* L.P. Strathclyde at 686, quoting Lord Kyllachy in *Mackenzie's Trs., supra.*
[53] *Ibid., per* Lord Johnston at p. 701.

if the first year's rent were payable one half at Lammas or Martinmas a year later and the second half six months thereafter.[54]

In the case of urban property, rent runs from day to day.[55] It is usually in practice paid—and it is normally so provided for in the deed—in equal parts twice a year at Whitsunday and Martinmas and, unless there is express provision to the contrary, annual rents are for the period from 28th May or 28th November. In the case of small dwellinghouses, however, the period for which the rent is made payable is particularly important.

Retention of Rent. The tenant is not relieved of his obligation to pay rent simply because the quantity and value of the subjects do not come up to his expectation, though his obligation may be modified in a case of partial *rei interitus*.[56] In certain circumstances the tenant's obligation to pay rent may be suspended and he will be entitled to retain the rent until an abatement of rent has been allowed and its amount fixed.[57] This right of retention stems from the recognition of the mutuality of the various obligations of landlord and tenant under the lease, since even the landlord's apparently liquid claim for rent is only enforceable when he has fulfilled his own obligations under the lease.[58] Thus, " rent is not liquid in the sense that a sum due by bond is. It is a matter of contract in consideration of something to be done. It is paid for possession of the subjects let. If the tenant says he has not got entire possession, that is a good answer to the claim for rent."[59] Retention can then occur in cases where the tenant has for some reason without his own fault, failed to obtain possession of the whole subjects,[60]

---

[54] See *e.g., Butter v Foster,* 1912 S.C. 1218; and also *Kintore v McGregor,* 1917 1 S.L.T. 270 (O.H.), where rent legally due at Whitsunday 1915 was made conventionally payable nine months later at Candlemas 1916. In *Baillie v Fletcher* the rents were in fact made conventionally payable six months backhand. In pastoral farms, Rankine says at 343, forehand rent is scarcely conceivable unless the majority view in *Baillie* is accepted, that the rent runs from Whitsunday to Whitsunday and then forehand is normal.

[55] *Butter v Foster,* 1912 S.C. 1218 at pp. 1224-5 *per* Lord Johnston. So too in leases of shootings—*Maxwell's Trs. v Scott* (1873) 1 R. 122.

[56] Stair, I, 15, 2; *Gowans v Christie* (1873) 11 M. (H.L.) 1, *per* Lord Selborne (Ld. Ch.), at p. 4. See *infra.*

[57] Gloag, *op. cit.,* 628; *Kilmarnock Gas Light Co. v Smith* (1872) 11 M. 58; *Guthrie v Shearer* (1873) 1 R. 181; *Dougall v Magistrates of Dunfermline,* 1908 S.C. 151.

[58] Gloag, *op. cit.,* 628; *Graham v Gordon* (1843) 5 D. 1207; *Munro v McGeoghs* (1888) 16 R. 93; *Sivright v Lightbourne* (1890) 17 R. 917; *McDonald v Kydd* (1901) 3 F. 923; *Earl of Galloway v McConnell,* 1911 S.C. 846; *John Haig and Co. v Boswall-Preston,* 1915 S.C. 339; *Fingland and Mitchell v Howie,* 1926 S.C. 319; *Euman's Trs. v Warnock* (1930) 46 Sh. Ct. Rep. 164. *Cf. Drybrough v Drybrough* (1874) 1 R. 909; *Muir v McIntyres* (1887) 14 R. 470 (accidental destruction).

[59] *Graham v Gordon, supra, per* Lord Fullerton at p. 1211, approved *per* L.P. Inglis in *Munro v McGeoghs, supra,* at p. 94; *Fingland and Mitchell, supra.*

[60] Note 57 *supra,* and *Muir v McIntyres, supra; Duncan v Brooks* (1894) 21 R. 760.

or where the landlord is in a material[61] breach of his obligations in respect of the state of repair of the subjects.[62]

In certain circumstances an offer by the landlord to execute the necessary repairs may preclude the tenant's claim to retain rent.[63] The Court may make it a condition of the tenant's retention of rent that consignation in Court takes place.[64] An otherwise valid claim for retention may be lost by an intervening payment of rent without reservation of the tenant's rights in respect of damages.[65]

Obligation to Plenish. In cases where the right of hypothec still exists there is a correlative liability on the tenant's part to stock the premises to such an extent as will make the full right of hypothec practically available.[66]

Obligations in Relation to Repairs.[67] In addition to the specific liability to indemnify the landlord for damage to the subjects as a result of negligence, the tenant in an agricultural lease comes under an obligation to keep buildings and fences in repair and to leave them at his removal in the same state of tenantable repair as he received them.[68] This obligation is not, however, as onerous as that of a landlord putting subjects in a tenantable state at the beginning of a lease, since the tenant is not liable to make good damage resulting from natural decay or fair wear and tear.[69] Nor is the tenant liable where damage is due to *damnum fatale* or to some essential defect in structure.[70]

Effect of Rei Interitus upon the Obligations of Landlord and Tenant. Where without the fault of either the landlord or the tenant the subjects of lease are destroyed through *damnum fatale*,[71] or can be regarded as being constructively destroyed, as where they have been

---

[61] *Davie* v *Stark* (1876) 3 R. 114, *per* L.J.C. Moncreiff at p. 1119; *Macdonald* v *Kydd* (1901) 3 F. 923, *per* Lord Moncreiff at p. 928; *cf. Humphrey* v *Mackay* (1883) 10 R. 647.

[62] Gloag, *op. cit.*, 629; *Graham* v *Gordon, supra; Munro* v *McGeoghs, supra; Sivright* v *Lightbourne, supra; Fingland and Mitchell* v *Howie*, 1926 S.C. 319; *Marshall's Trs.* v *Banks*, 1934 S.C. 405. *Cf. Skene* v *Cameron*, 1942 S.C. 393, where the tenant's right of retention was excluded by contract; *supra*, p. 91.

[63] *Cf. McRae* v *Macpherson* (1843) 6 D. 302.

[64] *Clark* v *Finlay* (1823) 2 S. 480; *Cumming* v *Williamson* (1842) 4 D. 1304.

[65] *Stewart* v *Campbell* (1889) 16 R. 346.

[66] Bell, § 1273; Rankine, 399; *infra*, p. 212.

[67] Note the obligations under the Agricultural Holdings (Scotland) Act, 1949, s. 5. See *infra*, p. 301.

[68] Bankt. I, 20, 10, II, 11, 21; Ersk., II, 6, 38; Bell, § 1253; Rankine, 251; *Whites* v *Houston* (1707) Mor. 15258. *Cf.* Agricultural Holdings (Scotland) Act, 1949, s. 5 (2) (b).

[69] Hume, *Lectures*, II, 80; *Mossman* v *Brocket* (1810) Hume 850; *Davidson* v *Logan*, 1908 S.C. 350. See Bell, § 1254 for definition of " fair wear and tear ". It is often provided in a lease that liability for fair wear and tear is excepted. See II. *Conv. Rev.*, 187.

[70] Hume, *Lectures*, II, 80; Bell, § 1254; *Mossman* v *Brocket, supra*.

[71] *Duff* v *Fleming* (1870) 8 M. 769.

requisitioned under statutory authority,[72] the relationship and obligations of landlord and tenant will come to an end. Thus, where the subjects have been destroyed by fire,[71] or where they have been requisitioned by military authorities,[73] or made into a zone for aerial gunnery and bombing practice,[74] the tenant will be entitled to abandon the lease. Destruction of a part of the subjects may be enough if the part in question was essential for the purposes for which the premises were let.[75]

However, " a case of destruction is not made out by showing that the premises have been made uncomfortable . . . (or) . . . unsuitable for the purpose of the lease for a short time . . . When such a calamity as a fire . . . has accidentally occurred a tenant may reasonably be called on to submit to considerable inconvenience as the natural and often necessary consequence; and if the injury to the premises be short of destruction, and the damage may be repaired within such a time that the term ' considerable inconvenience ' would fairly describe all the tenant has to undergo, he is not entitled to throw up his lease but is . . . bound to give his landlord an opportunity of having the damage repaired, insisting as he is no doubt entitled to do, that no time shall be lost in having the premises restored to their former condition."[75] In the particular case in question, the premises though damaged by fire had always remained fit for use for the tenant's business.[76] Where a part of the subjects let has been destroyed, the tenant may be entitled to an abatement of rent.[77] It is settled that the doctrine of *rei interitus* does not apply where it is merely the purpose for which the subjects were let that has become impossible, and thus that a tenant is not entitled either to an abatement of rent,[78] or to rescission of the lease,[79] where, for example, the licence of a hotel, the subject of the lease, has been revoked, or the imposition by legislation of a close season has proved injurious to a salmon fishery.[80]

The landlord is under no obligation to rebuild subjects which have been destroyed by *damnum fatale,* and though in such a case the general maxim *res perit suo domino* will apply, " the meaning of this is that where there is no fault anywhere, the thing perishes to all concerned; that all who are interested constitute the *dominus* as to this purpose ".[81] So the loss in such a case will be divided between the landlord, who will lose his rent, and the tenant, who will lose possession.

[72] *Tay Salmon Fisheries Co.* v *Speedie,* 1929 S.C. 593; *Mackeson* v *Boyd,* 1942 S.C. 56.
[73] *Mackeson* v *Boyd, supra.*
[74] *Tay Salmon Fisheries Co.* v *Speedie, supra.*
[75] *Allan* v *Markland* (1882) 10 R. 383, *per* Lord Shand at pp. 389-390.
[76] *Allan* v *Markland, supra.*
[77] *Muir* v *McIntyres* (1887) 14 R. 470, especially *per* L.P. Inglis at pp. 472-3; *Sharp* v *Thomson,* 1930 S.C. 1092.
[78] *Donald* v *Leitch* (1886) 13 R. 790.
[79] *Hart's Trs.* v *Arrol* (1903) 6 F. 36.
[80] *Holliday* v *Scott* (1830) 8 S. 831.
[81] *Bayne* v *Walker* (1815) 3 Dow 233, *per* Lord Eldon (Ld. Ch.) at p. 245.

MANAGEMENT OF PREMISES

It is usual to stipulate in the lease of a shop or business premises that the landlord on the one hand will not set up or allow to be set up by another tenant a rival trade on adjacent premises and that on the other hand the tenant will not set up a trade that is noxious or a nuisance or set up a particular trade. In the lease of a house which is intended by the lease to be used as a private dwellinghouse, it is also common to prohibit the setting up of any trade or business, *e.g.*, a boarding house or a hotel. The interpretation of such conditions or restrictive covenants is a matter of the ordinary interpretation of contracts, and the point has arisen in the case of feu charters and feu contracts.

Each case will depend on its own terms. The cases in recent times in regard to leases have been very few and it seems sufficient here to refer to the examples given in the undernoted authorities,[82] to which may be added the case of *Randall Ltd.* v *Summers*.[83] In that case the tenants were sellers of boots and shoes and the lease provided that the landlord was not to let any other shop in the same property for a " business of similar nature ". It was held that there was no breach of that stipulation where the landlord let to a firm of naval outfitters whose business included the selling of men's boots, mainly to naval officers but also to civilians, and whose lease provided that the shop was to be used " exclusively for the purpose of their business ".

A clause binding the tenant to a particular mode of management or to pay an additional rent by way of penalty does not entitle him to deviate from that mode and to pay additional rent.[84] Thus, where the tenant in a 999 years' lease was taken bound to pay an additional rent of £10 for infringing a prohibition against keeping a public house, it was held that the prohibition was absolute and that he had not the option of contravening it upon payment of the additional rent.[85]

REMEDIES OF LANDLORD AND TENANT

It may be useful to give here a short summary of the respective remedies of a landlord and of a tenant for breach by the other party of the obligations in a lease.

Remedies of Landlord. For recovery of rent a landlord has all the ordinary remedies of a creditor, *e.g.*, a petitory action for the rent as a debt due to him, the various forms of diligence such as arrestment,

---

[82] Rankine, 439-445; Woodfall, *Landlord and Tenant*, 26th ed., 548-553, 584-603; Gloag, *op. cit.*, 12, 401. In the case of a landlord, see *e.g.*, *Davie* v *Stark, infra.*
[83] 1919 S.C. 396.
[84] *M'Kenzie* v *Craigies*, 18 June 1811 F.C., affd. (1815) 6 Pat. 117; *M'Kenzie* v *Gilchrist*, 13 Dec. 1811 F.C.; Hunter, *Landlord and Tenant*, 4th ed., II, 500.
[85] *Gold* v *Houldsworth* (1870) 8 M. 1006.

poinding, adjudication and inhibition and also the process of sequestration in bankruptcy. If there is a cautioner or guarantor of the rent he can proceed against him in the ordinary way. In addition, he can under his right of hypothec sequestrate and, if need be, sell the goods and effects covered by that right. The landlord can also claim by a multiple-poinding if there is a competition as to the right to the rent. A clause of consent to registration for preservation and execution also enables the landlord, following a decree for registration, to give a six days' charge on such a decree,[86] and thus to execute summary diligence.[87] A charge for arrears of rent under deduction of what is recoverable under the hypothec has been held not to be void for uncertainty.[88] The landlord has also a remedy by irritancy, either in accordance with statute or under a clause in the lease.[89]

If he is a heritable creditor—not, however, a creditor under an *ex facie* absolute disposition[90]—he can use an action of maills and duties. This action, at one time the action for payment of rents,[91] has long in practice been "competent only to a heritable creditor who, having a security title to the rents, seeks to enforce his right to exact from the tenants payment of their rents as against the proprietor or civil possessor of the ground, to whom the tenants would, apart from the decree, pay the rents."[92] The tenant need not be called as a party.[93] The decree secures that the tenant will pay the rent only to the heritable creditor and enables him to enter into possession and enforce payment from the tenant to himself. And he can use sequestration for rent. Even without such a decree the creditor can enforce payment by intimating the assignation of rents to the tenant and then raising an ordinary action.

In respect of breach by the tenant of any of the other obligations of the lease—that is, those other than payment of rent—the landlord may be entitled to rescind the lease and claim damages against the tenant. It is not decided if an obligation to perform a specific act can be enforced by summary diligence.[94] Irritancy is also a remedy in cases of breach of stipulations other than as to rent where such is provided for in the lease.[89]

Remedies of Tenant. If there is a breach by the landlord of an obligation incumbent upon him under the lease, the tenant may retain

---

[86] Titles to Land Consolidation (Scotland) Act, 1868, s. 138. There is a similar provision in the Registration of Leases (Scotland) Act, 1857, for a clause in such a lease.
[87] See Menzies, *Lectures on Conveyancing*, 1900 ed., 183 *et seq.;* Bell, § 68, *Comm.* I, 4.
[88] *Martin* v *Forbes* (1824) 3 S. 275.
[89] See *infra,* p. 228.
[90] *Scottish Heritable Securities Co.* v *Allan Campbell and Co.* (1876) 3 R. 333 *per* L.P. Inglis at 340-1.
[91] Rankine, 360-1.
[92] Bell, § 922; *Scottish Heritable Securities Co., supra.*
[93] Heritable Securities (Scotland) Act, 1894, s. 3.
[94] See *Hendry* v *Marshall* (1878) 5 R. 687, where L.P. Inglis thought that it was competent; Graham Stewart, *Diligence*, 415-6.

the rent on the basis of the correlative nature of mutual obligations.[95] If the breach consists of a failure to carry out repairs then, assuming the landlord knew or ought to have known of the need for the repairs, the tenant may carry them out at his own expense and deduct the cost from the rent.[96] If, for instance, the landlord has failed, where there is no protective provision in the lease, to repair damage to the property that has not resulted from any event amounting to *damnum fatale* or its accidental destruction, then damages may be claimed in an ordinary action, but the landlord's attention must have been drawn by the tenant to the need for the repair,[97] and if the landlord offers to repair he must be given a reasonable time to take action.[98] If the breach of the lease by the landlord is material, the tenant can rescind the contract or throw up the lease or abandon the subjects or even obtain a suspension of the lease combined possibly with an action of damages.[99] He can, if he chooses, simply claim damages. The right to rescind or throw up the lease will arise if the breach or failure is of sufficient materiality in law or there is a refusal by the landlord to act.[1] Each case will depend on its own facts. So where the landlord of a shop undertook in a lease that there would be no competing business in a neighbouring shop but he opened a shop whose trade was competitive and the tenant, therefore, said he would give up the lease before its due termination and refused to pay the last term's rent, it was held that the tenant was justified in the steps he had taken as the breach was of a material stipulation.[2] On the other hand, the opinion was expressed[3] that a breach by the landlord of a provision (which there was in that case) that the shop was to be fitted with gas fittings at the landlord's expense would not be material and so justify rescission of the contract.

Provisions or stipulations as to the character or quality of work to be performed are material and, where the obligation is defectively performed, it will depend on the degree of the defective performance whether the breach will justify rescission.[4] It has been held[5] that in a lease for a term of years, the tenant cannot abandon the subjects or throw up the lease because in the early years of the lease the landlord has failed to carry out repairs or alterations and that his remedy is at that stage confined to damages or possibly retention of the rent. If the contract becomes impossible of performance because of *rei interitus* or

---

[95] Rankine, 326 *et seq*. See *supra*, p. 90 *et seq*.
[96] Ersk., II, 6, 43; Gloag and Henderson, *Introduction to the Law of Scotland*, 6th ed., 119.
[97] *Sandeman* v *Duncan's Trs.* (1897) 4 S.L.T. 336, 5 S.L.T. 21; Gloag, *op. cit.*, 605.
[98] Gloag, *op. cit.* 605.
[99] Rankine, 326; Gloag, *op. cit.*, 605; Gloag and Henderson, *op. cit.*, 119; *Burns* v *McNeil* (1898) 5 S.L.T. 289.
[1] Gloag, *op. cit.*, 603-5.
[2] *Davie* v *Stark* (1876) 3 R. 1114. See *supra*, p. 91.
[3] *Ibid.* at 1119 *per* L.J.C. Inglis.
[4] Gloag, *op. cit.*, 605.
[5] *Todd* v *Bowie* (1902) 4 F. 435.

some event short of destruction of the subject that prevents performance, the lease is avoided or discharged and damages cannot be recovered from the landlord. If the breach results in partial eviction then the tenant may be entitled to abandon the lease or at least is entitled to a corresponding abatement of rent.[6]

[6] *Muir* v *McIntyres, supra; Sharp* v *Thomson, supra.*

CHAPTER X

ASSIGNATION AND SUBLETTING

Introduction. Although a lease is by nature a personal contract, the interest of either party to it can be transmitted to another. This chapter is mainly concerned with whether and to what effect a tenant may transfer his interest to another *inter vivos*, that is by assigning his lease or subletting the subjects of the lease. The next chapter is concerned with the devolution of the tenant's interest in a lease as a result of death. It will be seen in both cases that there may be certain limitations upon the transmissibility of the tenant's interest.

Transfer of Landlord's Interest. Before the transmissibility of the tenant's part of the lease is considered, it will suffice to deal briefly with the transfer of the landlord's interest. There is no *delectus personae* of the lessor, and the tenant cannot object to a new landlord. There is no restriction on the power of the landlord to transfer his interest in a lease to another, nor is any procedure necessary to effect a transfer other than the change of ownership of the subjects. The landlord's interest in the lease and his right to enforce it are incidents of ownership; they pass with ownership and cannot be divorced from ownership. Infeftment may be necessary to give a title to pursue an action to enforce the landlord's rights,[1] but the lack of infeftment does not affect his rights and in any event can be cured by accretion.

When the subjects of a lease are sold, the original landlord, and his executors after his death, remain liable for all personal conditions,[2] and any other obligations which do not transmit against his singular successors, such as obligations undertaken by an heir of entail in possession, are not binding on his successor.[3] Whether the original landlord remains liable for real conditions,[4] that is obligations which do transmit, is not fully settled;[5] but the law probably is that he and his executors remain liable for all obligations to pay money, such as an obligation to pay for improvements executed by the tenant before the transfer,[6] but that only the purchaser is liable for normal real conditions such as the obligation for upkeep and repairs.[7]

---

[1] *Infra,* p. 254.
[2] *Supra,* p. 94.
[3] *Gardiner* v *Stewart's Trs.,* 1908 S.C. 985; *Riddell's Exrs.* v *Milligan's Exrs.,* 1909 S.C. 1137.
[4] *Supra,* p. 95.
[5] Gloag and Henderson, *Introduction to the Law of Scotland,* 6th ed., 375.
[6] *Walker* v *Masson* (1857) 19 D. 1099; *Swan & Sons* v *Fairholme* (1894) 2 S.L.T. 74 (O.H.); *Purves' Trs.* v *Traill's Tr.,* 1914 2 S.L.T. 425 (O.H.); *supra,* p. 96.
[7] Gloag and Henderson, *op. cit.,* 375.

Distinction between Assignation and Subletting. An assignation of a lease is a transfer by the tenant (who may be either the original lessee or an assignee) of his interest in a lease to another person called the assignee, who becomes the new tenant. The granter or cedent ceases to have any further interest in the lease, and his place is taken by the assignee, who thereupon stands in the same relation to the landlord as that in which the cedent stood. A sublease is a lease granted by a tenant of all or part of the subjects leased to him, with the result that he remains the tenant of his own landlord and becomes the landlord of the subjects which he has leased to his subtenant. The essential difference between assignation and subletting is that in the former the granter ceases to be tenant of his landlord, whereas in the latter the granter of the sublease continues to be tenant of his landlord.[8] In the case of assignation there is only one subsisting contract of lease, and there are only two parties in the relation of landlord and tenant to each other. In the case of sublease there are two contracts of lease and three parties, landlord, tenant, and subtenant.

Power to Assign or Sublet. If he has his landlord's consent, a tenant may always assign his lease or sublet the subjects. If he cannot obtain the landlord's consent, he may assign or sublet only so far as he has power to do so in his lease. The power may be expressed or implied, although in many cases it is expressly excluded. In so far as it is not expressly excluded, the tenant has power to assign or sublet only in cases where the doctrine of *delectus personae* does not apply. The power of alienation is excluded unless by a grant, either express or arising out of qualities in the contract deemed by necessary legal implication to include that power; this rule is founded on the doctrine that leases are *stricti juris,* and involve a *delectus personae*.[9] In England the position is the reverse; the right to assign or sublet is always implied, although it may be expressly excluded.[10]

Delectus Personae. The doctrine of *delectus personae,* whereby it is assumed that the landlord deliberately chooses a particular tenant for his personal qualities such as his financial standing, his agricultural skill or his personal habits, still survives to a limited extent, and, in the absence of express provision, may determine whether a tenant may assign his lease or sublet the subjects leased to him without the consent of the landlord.[11] Where the doctrine applies, the theory is that a landlord may object to an assignee or subtenant on the ground that, whereas he had chosen the original tenant, the assignee or subtenant

---

[8] *Trotter* v *Dennis* (1770) Mor. 15282; *Skene* v *Greenhill* (1825) 4 S. 25 (N.E. 26); Rankine, 171.
[9] Hunter, *Landlord and Tenant,* 4th ed., I, 236; Rankine, 172.
[10] Woodfall, *Landlord and Tenant,* 26th ed., 29, 840.
[11] Hume, *Lectures,* IV, 88-89; Rankine, 172.

is not the type of person he would have chosen for a tenant. Whether or not the doctrine applies depends on the nature of the subjects let.

The doctrine applies only to voluntary alienations and does not exclude the tenant's heirs,[12] or his legal or judicial assignees such as adjudgers and trustees in sequestration, or possibly quasi-judicial assignees such as trustees under trust deeds for creditors and managers for creditors.[13] An express exclusion of the tenant's creditors is effective,[14] and it is always possible expressly to exclude his assignees, subtenants and legatees.[15]

Leases to which the Doctrine Applies. Apart from a few exceptions, it is presumed that *delectus personae* applies.

In a tenancy of rural subjects it is presumed that the tenant is selected for personal reasons, and therefore in the case of a farm lease of ordinary duration, whether arable or pastoral, the tenant may not assign or sublet his holding without the express consent of the landlord.[16] The origin of this principle was the interest of the landlord to prevent powerful, and possibly unfriendly, persons from obtaining possession of the landlord's land, which they might try to retain by force; also the landlord had an interest in choosing tenants capable of rendering him military service.[17] In modern times the landlord has an interest in his lessee's agricultural skill and desirability as a neighbour.

Delectus personae is implied in sporting leases, perhaps more than in any other kind of lease, and accordingly it is incompetent for the tenant of a shooting or fishing lease to sublet or assign without the landlord's permission, even although the occupancy of a house may be involved.[18] There has been no decision as to the assignability of a mineral lease, although the question has been considered, and the opinion expressed that a mineral lease for 31 years is not assignable, such a period not being considered an extraordinary duration for minerals.[19] The doctrine also applies to a lease of a furnished house, because a furnished lease includes the hire of furniture, and the combined contract cannot be assigned;[20] also a landlord usually has considerable interest in the type of person who is using articles of an intimate nature such as furniture, crockery, etc.

---

[12] *Thomson* v *Watson* (1750) Mor. 10337; *Tailfer* v *McDougall* (1811) Hume 857; Hume, *Lectures,* IV, 88; Rankine, 157.
[13] Stair, II, 9, 6; Hume, *Lectures,* IV, 89; Bell, § 1216; Rankine, 177; Wood, *Lectures on Conveyancing,* 436; Burns, *Conveyancing Practice,* 4th ed., 608.
[14] *Elliot* v *Duke of Buccleugh* (1747) Mor. 10329; *Cunningham* v *Hamilton* (1770) Mor. 10410; Hume, *Lectures,* IV, 90.
[15] *Kennedy* v *Johnstone,* 1956 S.C. 39.
[16] *Ibid.,* per L.P. Clyde at p. 43.
[17] Bell, §§ 1214 *et seq.*
[18] *Earl of Fife* v *Wilson* (1864) 3 M. 323 *per* Lord Kinloch (L.O.) at p. 324; *Macintosh* v *May* (1895) 22 R. 345.
[19] *Duke of Portland* v *Baird & Co.* (1865) 4 M. 10 *per* L.J.C. Inglis at p. 16 and Lords Cowan and Neaves at pp. 19 and 22; Rankine, 175-176.
[20] Hume, *Lectures,* IV, 89; Rankine, 175.

Leases to which the Doctrine Does Not Apply. No *delectus personae* is implied in leases of unfurnished urban subjects for a term of years, and the tenant may therefore assign or sublet unless expressly prohibited from doing so.[21]

There may, however, be circumstances which infer that a particular lease of urban property is not assignable. In an early case of a lease of a shop for a year the Court held by a majority that in the circumstances there was no power to sublet,[22] but it now seems certain that for this purpose there is no distinction between a lease for less than a year and a lease for more than a year.[23] In a lease by the proprietor of a village of an inn and bakehouse with the exclusive right of selling spirits and bread, the greater part of the rent was declared to be for the monopoly conferred; it was held that though the subjects were urban, the contract must be read as a whole, and its provisions showed that it was personal to the particular lessee.[24] This case was distinguished from the lease of a shop with the goodwill of a business, which would be assignable on the ground that it would involve no continued obligation on the tenant as to goodwill.[25]

While the tenant of urban property has an implied power to sublet without obtaining the consent of the landlord, it does not follow that the landlord impliedly consents to each particular sublet.[26]

No *delectus personae* is implied in rural leases of unusual duration, and the tenant may therefore assign or sublet in the absence of provision to the contrary.[27] There are no recent cases on this point. Farm leases of 19 or 21 years have been held to be of ordinary duration and therefore not assignable;[28] 38 years has been held to be an unusual duration.[29] There has been no decision on a duration of between 21 and 38 years, but it is probable that no *delectus personae* would be implied because of the " almost universal prevalence " of leases for 19 or 21 years.[30]

A lease for the tenant's life is of unusual duration and is assignable.[31] Similarly a lease for the lessee's term of office, such as to a minister for the period of his incumbency is of unusual duration and is assignable.[32] There is no decision on the ordinary duration of mineral leases, but see the case cited.[33]

[21] *Aitchison* v *Benny* (1748) Mor. 10405; *Hatton* v *Clay & M'Luckie* (1865) 4 M. 263; *Robb* v *Brearton* (1895) 22 R. 885; Hume, *Lectures,* IV, 89; *Bell,* § 1274.
[22] *Gordon* v *Crawford* (1825) 4 S. 95.
[23] Rankine, 175.
[24] *Earl of Elgin's Trs.* v *Walls* (1833) 11 S. 585.
[25] *Ibid., per* Lord Glenlee at p. 590.
[26] *Dalrymple's Trs.* v *Brown,* 1945 S.C. 190.
[27] *Simpson* v *Gray & Webster* (1794) Mor. 15294; Hume, *Lectures,* IV, 95.
[28] *Alison* v *Proudfoot* (1788) Mor. 15290; *Earl of Cassilis* v *Macadam* (1806) Mor. App. *voce* Tack 14.
[29] *Simpson* v *Gray & Webster* (1794) Mor. 15294.
[30] Rankine, 173.
[31] Hume, *Lectures,* IV, 89, 95; Rankine, 173.
[32] *Pringle* v *M'Lagan* (1802) Hume 808.
[33] *Duke of Portland* v *Baird & Co.* (1865) 4 M. 10 at pp. 16, 19 and 22.

Express Exclusion of Assignees and Subtenants. In cases where the doctrine of *delectus personae* does not apply, the tenant's power to assign his lease or sublet the subjects may be expressly excluded in the lease. It is normal practice to insert a clause excluding assignees and subtenants not only in a lease where *delectus personae* is not implied, if only to keep out a man of straw, but also where it would be implied. Such a clause will be strictly construed. An exclusion of assignees does not imply an exclusion of subtenants,[34] and conversely it has never been doubted that a prohibition of subletting does not imply an exclusion of assignees.[35] In England a prohibition of subletting will prevent an assignment, but a prohibition of assignment does not always prevent a sublet.[36]

A common form of express exclusion is " excluding assignees and subtenants ". An exclusion expressed in such general terms will operate to exclude not only voluntary but also judicial or legal assignees, such as adjudgers and trustees in sequestration, and quasi-judicial assignees, such as trustees and managers for creditors,[37] so that it is unnecessary to exclude them expressly,[38] although this is commonly done.[39] In contrast to this, it has been noted that an exclusion of assignees inferred from *delectus personae* excludes only conventional and not judicial or quasi-judicial assignees.[40] A destination in a lease to the partners of a firm as trustees for the firm and the partners present and future was held not to be inconsistent with an express exclusion of assignees, and the lease therefore came to an end on the sequestration of the firm.[41] It would therefore seem that a prohibition of assignation in a lease to a partnership may well affect the power to assign it to assumed partners.[42]

It has been said that, where a lease is of such duration as to amount to an alienation, an express exclusion of assignees like an implied exclusion would be ineffectual,[43] but in view of the modern popularity of leases of business premises for very long terms, it is thought that the duration would have to be extremely long before an express exclusion would be ignored, if at all.

An express exclusion of assignees fortified by an irritancy in the event of the tenant's bankruptcy overrides the common law rule that he who sows a crop is entitled to reap it.[44]

---

[34] *Trotter* v *Dennis* (1770) Mor. 15282.
[35] Rankine, 172, 177.
[36] Woodfall, *Landlord and Tenant*, 26th ed., 576.
[37] *Elliot* v *Duke of Buccleuch* (1747) Mor. 10329; *Dewar* v *Ainslie* (1892) 20 R. 203; Bell § 1218.
[38] Rankine, 177.
[39] *Encyclopaedia of Scottish Legal Styles,* Vol. 6, Nos. 140 and 146.
[40] *Supra,* p. 150; Rankine, 177.
[41] *Walker* v *M'Knight* (1886) 13 R. 599.
[42] *Walker* v *M'Knight, supra; Bristol Corporation* v *Westcott* (1879) 12 Ch. D. 461; Woodfall, *Landlord and Tenant,* 26th ed., 581.
[43] *Bain* v *M'Kenzie* (1896) 23 R. 528 *per* Lords M'Laren and Kinnear at pp. 532 and 533.
[44] *Chalmer's Tr.* v *Dick's Tr.,* 1909 S.C. 761; see also *infra,* p. 197.

"Without Consent". Many variations in the clause restricting assignation and subletting are possible, and they will receive effect according
to their terms.[45] Where assignees and subtenants are prohibited with
the addition of such words as " without the consent in writing of the
landlord " or " unless specially approved by the landlord ", these words
have no effect in qualifying the exclusion; and it has been held in a
long line of cases that the landlord is entitled to refuse to accept an
assignee without giving any reason.[46] Such words do not detract in any
way from the landlord's power of arbitrary veto, and the landlord is
entitled to the strictest interpretation of them. Where under such a clause
a lease was assigned with the landlord's consent, it was held incompetent for the assignee to retrocess it to the original tenant without the
consent of the landlord.[47] Where a lease provided that assignees must
be approved of by the landlord or grant security for payment of the
rent and performance of other obligations, it was held that the onus
was on the cedent to offer, not on the landlord to demand, security, in
order to bring the alternative into force, and that the cedent was never
relieved of the original obligations contained in the lease.[48] Where a
shop was let to a tenant excluding assignees except such as might be
approved by the landlord, different opinions were expressed as to
whether a trustee under a trust deed for creditors was an assignee of the
tenant or a manager for him entitled to remain in possession.[49] The mere
fact that the landlord has not taken steps to object to an assignee or
subtenant in possession will not necessarily be held to imply that he has
given his consent to the assignation or subletting.[50]

It is fairly common nowadays to attempt to compromise between
the landlord's arbitrary power to veto any assignation or sublet without
giving his reasons on the one hand and complete freedom of choice of
assignee or subtenant on the other hand; this is done by providing that
assignation or subletting is to be permitted only with the consent of the
landlord " which consent shall not be unreasonably withheld ". This
phrase seems to be an importation from England, where there is a body
of law on the subject,[51] but the exact meaning of it has never had to
be determined by a Scottish Court, perhaps because of the reasonableness and flexibility of the phrase itself.[52]

---

[45] *Kennedy* v *Johnstone*, 1956 S.C. 39.
[46] *Muir* v *Wilson*, 20 Jan. 1820 F.C.; *Wight* v *Earl of Hopetoun* (1855) 17 D. 364;
  Gray v *Low* (1859) 21 D. 293; *Duke of Portland* v *Baird & Co.* (1865) 4 M. 10;
  Marquis of Breadalbane v *Whitehead & Sons* (1893) 21 R. 138.
[47] *Ramsay* v *Commercial Bank of Scotland* (1842) 4 D. 405.
[48] *Gemmel* v *Low* (1823) 2 S. 563 (N.E. 486).
[49] *Dewar* v *Ainslie* (1892) 20 R. 203.
[50] *Duke of Portland* v *Baird, supra; Marquis of Breadalbane* v *Whitehead &
  Sons, supra.*
[51] Landlord & Tenant Act 1927, s. 19 (1); Woodfall, *Landlord and Tenant,* 26th
  ed., 566 *et seq.*
[52] Rankine 179; Gloag, *Contract,* 2nd ed., 302. For discussion of this subject and
  a review of the English cases see II *Conv. Rev.,* 41.

Attempts to Evade Exclusion.   Where there is an exclusion of assignees and subtenants or either of them, the Court will intervene to prevent a covert assignation or sublease taking the guise of a different kind of transaction.[53] Thus a landlord was able to reduce a trust deed by his tenant whereby a trustee had been put in possession.[54] Similarly, an arrangement whereby a third party obtained possession of a farm on condition that he should cultivate it free of charge to the tenant was reduced.[55] An arrangement whereby a tenant of a shop had removed his goods and had given occupation to a person alleged to be merely his shopkeeper was held to be a device to evade an express exclusion of assigning and subletting.[56] A deed taking the form of a factory and commission whereby a tenant gave a factor unlimited power of management in consideration of certain advances was held to cloak an assignation, and therefore incurred an irritancy.[57] It is, however, a question of fact whether a trustee for creditors is an assignee or a manager for the tenant;[58] or whether an occupier is a subtenant or a servant.[59]

Enforceability.   The exclusion of assignees and subtenants may be fortified by an irritancy clause, which, if enforced, will bring the lease to an end, and being a conventional irritancy it cannot be purged.[60] If there is no irritancy clause, an assignation is of no effect and the lease remains with the cedent, or a sublease will be reducible at the option of the landlord; and an action of damages will lie for any damage suffered by the landlord, but the lease itself will not be brought to an end.[61]

The right of objecting to an assignation or sublease, where such is prohibited either expressly or impliedly, is personal to the landlord, and neither the tenant nor any other party can object to an assignation not vetoed by the landlord.[62] But where testamentary trustees of the tenant tried to take possession under a lease with a clause excluding subtenants and assignees and the landlord had repudiated this claim, the heir was held to have a title to sue without the landlord's concurrence.[63] No-one can object to the use the landlord makes of his power.[64]

Where a tenant has granted an assignation or sublease in breach of an express prohibition, he may eject the grantee as one having no title to possess, but he cannot found his action on a notice to remove

[53] Hume, *Lectures,* IV, 90-92; Rankine, 179-180.
[54] *Porter* v *Paterson* (1813) Hume 862.
[55] *Hamilton* v *Sommerville* (1855) 17 D. 344.
[56] *Hatton* v *Clay & M'Luckie* (1865) 4 M. 263.
[57] *Lyon* v *Irvine* (1874) 1 R. 512.
[58] *Dewar* v *Ainslie* (1892) 20 R. 203; *Mess* v *Sime's Tr.* (1898) 1 F. (H.L.) 22.
[59] *Philipps* v *Humber* (1904) 6 F. 814; for " service occupancies " see p. 9, *supra.*
[60] *Lyon* v *Irvine, supra; Pickard* v *Reid,* 1953 S.L.T. (Sh. Ct.) 5; *infra,* p. 232.
[61] Rankine, 180.
[62] *Hay* v *Wood* (1801) Mor. 15297; *Dobie* v *Marquis of Lothian* (1864) 2 M. 788; Hume, *Lectures,* IV, 92; Bell, § 1218.
[63] *Murdoch* v *Murdoch's Trs.* (1863) 1 M. 330.
[64] *Dobie* v *Marquis of Lothian, supra.*

based on the assignation, because the law will not enforce directly what it has prohibited.[65]

Acceptance by Landlord of Assignee or Subtenant. Where assignees or subtenants are excluded, either expressly or by implication, the landlord's right to object to an assignee or subtenant may be renounced expressly or by acquiescence.

The landlord may expressly waive his veto by consenting in the assignation or sublease itself. If his consent is required and given on one occasion, it remains necessary on subsequent occasions.[66] He may renounce his right of veto conditionally, although it was held in an early case that in doing so he is not entitled without the consent of the parties to impose more ample conditions in his own favour.[67] However, it seems to be clear that the landlord can make what arrangement he pleases with the assignee and no one else can object to the terms agreed between them.[68] So where an assignation took place through the tenant's sequestration, the tenant had no title to object to conditions agreed on between the assignee and the landlord, involving a renunciation of the lease.[69].

Where the landlord is entitled to object to an assignation or sublease and does not expressly consent in the assignation or sublease or elsewhere, his consent can sometimes be inferred, if his conduct amounts to acquiescence.[70] What amounts to acquiescence by the landlord is always a question of circumstances.[71] Acceptance by the landlord from an assignee or subtenant of one term's rent is not enough to infer acquiescence; there must be some act on the part of the landlord clearly inferring his acceptance of the assignee as tenant or of the subtenant as such. It is essential that the landlord be aware of the assignation or sublease.[72] Acquiescence was held to be established by enquiries made by a landlord as to the character and substance of a subtenant before he took possession, by occupation for over 10 years, by payment of rent to the landlord by the subtenant on his own account, and by his being allowed to remain after the principal tenant had absconded.[73] Open and undisturbed possession for several years and receipts for rent, acknowledged to have been paid by the occupier *qua* subtenant, taken along with a factor's letter as to when the rent was to be paid, were sufficient to show acquiescence.[74] On the other hand a letter from the

[65] *Macdonald* v *Mackenzie,* 1949 S.L.T. (Sh. Ct.) 80 (sublease of a croft without landlord's consent prohibited by statute).
[66] *Ramsay* v *Commercial Bank of Scotland* (1842) 4 D. 405.
[67] *Irvine* v *Valentine* (1793) 3 Pat. 287.
[68] *Dobie* v *Marquis of Lothian, supra.*
[69] *Ibid.*
[70] Hume, *Lectures,* IV, 96; Rankine, 180, 192; Rankine, *Personal Bar,* 82.
[71] *Gray* v *Low* (1859) 21 D. 293.
[72] *Dalrymple's Trs.* v *Brown,* 1945 S.C. 190.
[73] *Hay* v *M'Tier* (1806) Hume 836.
[74] *Maule* v *Robb* (1807) Hume 835; Hume, *Lectures,* IV, 96.

landlord to an occupier requesting him " as my subtenant " to take action against unlawful peat-cutting was quite consistent with a yearly or precarious tenancy and was not a recognition of a sublease for years.[75] Acceptance of rent from a subtenant, who was also cautioner in the principal lease was not proof of acquiescence in the sublease, especially as the receipts were not in his favour.[76] The fact that possession has been given to an assignee with the knowledge of the landlord and without objection on his part is an important element and could in the absence of other evidence be conclusive, but, where the facts show beyond question that the landlord did not intend to accept the assignee and intimated the contrary intention, the mere absence of objection to the possession of the assignee is not conclusive.[77] Even when subletting is not excluded, as in a lease of urban property where the tenant has implied power to sublet, it does not follow that the landlord has acquiesced in a sublease of which he has no knowledge.[78] For the purpose of the Rent Acts consent of the landlord must be an actual consent given expressly or impliedly by a landlord, who knew of the sublease.[79]

Express Power to Assign and Sublet. A clause expressly permitting the tenant to assign or sublet may be inserted in a lease where such power would be impliedly excluded by law. The power may be given by granting the lease in favour of the tenant and his assignees and sub-lessees. A power to sublet does not imply a power to assign, and a power to assign does not include a power to sublet.[80]

In the case of commercial subjects express power is sometimes given to assign a lease to other persons carrying on the same kind of business as the original lessees.[81] Such a clause may be necessary to entitle a lessee to assign his lease to a partnership of which he is a member, to a partner he has assumed, or to a limited company taking over his business. Without such a power it would be incompetent, if the landlord objected, for one partner to assign his interest to another.[82] A lease to the partners of a firm for behoof of themselves and future partners is not inconsistent with a clause excluding assignees without the consent of the landlord.[83]

Implied Power to Assign and Sublet. The power to assign or sublet is implied in cases where there is no element of *delectus personae*. These

[75] *Fraser* v *Fraser* (1833) 11 S. 565.
[76] *Earl of Elgin's Trs.* v *Walls* (1833) 11 S. 585.
[77] *Lord Elphinstone* v *Monkland Iron and Coal Co. Ltd.* (1886) 13 R. (H.L.) 98; *South West Farmers Ltd.* v *Gray,* 1950 S.L.T. (Sh. Ct.) 10; *Pickard* v *Reid,* 1953 S.L.T. (Sh. Ct.) 5.
[78] *Dalrymple's Trs.* v *Brown,* 1945 S.C. 190.
[79] *Dalrymple''s Trs.* v *Brown, supra.*
[80] Rankine, 172-173.
[81] *Encyclopaedia of Scottish Legal Styles,* Vol. 6, No. 183.
[82] Rankine, 177.
[83] *Walker* v *M'Knight* (1886) 13 R. 599.

are unfurnished urban leases and leases of unusual duration.[84] The fact that the tenant has implied power to assign or sublet without the consent of his landlord does not, however, mean that there is an implied consent of the landlord to every assignation or sublet.[85]

ASSIGNATION

Nature. The interest of the tenant in a lease is an asset, and if it is assignable, he can dispose of it either for onerous consideration or gratuitously. Leases were originally personal rights, and although they were heritable in succession, the proper method of transferring them has always been by assignation and not disposition.[86] When a lease is assigned, the assignation transfers to the assignee the original tenant's right to the lease, and the lease itself, from a specified date to the termination of the lease. The assignee is entitled to possess the whole subjects of the lease on the same terms as the cedent and comes under the same obligations to implement the provisions of the lease, including payment of rent.

It may be noted here that at common law assignations are almost invariably transfers of the whole subjects of let; there seems to be no reported cases involving part of the subjects in a lease. However, the Registration of Leases (Scotland) Act 1857 provides for partial assignations, which are quite common where the subjects of the lease come to be possessed separately.[87]

Form of Assignation. Apart from assignations of leases registrable under the Registration of Leases (Scotland) Act 1857, there is no statutory form. The style books contain few styles of assignation,[88] and in practice the statutory form, suitably adapted, is often used for unregistered leases. As in the case of a lease itself, the assignation requires no *voces signatae*, provided that the intention to assign is unequivocally expressed.[89] The assignation may briefly narrate the main provisions of the lease; it states the consideration, if any, for the assignation, and the granter assigns and makes over to the assignee the granter's whole interest in the lease for the remainder of its term under declaration that the assignee is to be bound to pay the rent to the landlord and perform the other prestations in the lease; a date of entry is stated; and the cedent may undertake to relieve the assignee of byegone rents and other stipulations. Where the landlord's consent is necessary, as where

---

[84] *Supra*, p. 151.
[85] *Dalrymple's Trs. v Brown*, 1945 S.C. 190, *per* L.P. Normand at p. 192.
[86] *Blair v Blair* (1849) 12 D. 97 *per* Lord Moncreiff at p. 115.
[87] 1857 Act, ss. 3 and 4; Scheds. A and B; Conveyancing (Scotland) Act 1924, Sched. J (note 2).
[88] *Jur. Styles*, 6th ed., 560; *Scots Style Book*, I, 434; *Encyclopaedia of Scottish Legal Styles*, Vol. 6, No. 162.
[89] *Kinninmont v Paxton* (1892) 20 R. 128.

assignation is expressly or impliedly excluded, his consent may be incorporated in the deed.

The granter may grant warrandice from his own facts and deeds only as regards the landlord's power to grant the lease and absolute warrandice as regards his own title to it, and in the absence of expression this will be the degree of warrandice implied.[90] In a lease of extraordinary duration there is perhaps no reason why the cedent should not grant absolute warrandice.[91] Under the Registration of Leases Act the words " I grant warrandice " in an assignation of a registered lease have the same meaning as in a conveyance of land.[92]

The word " dispone " is not and never has been appropriate in an assignation of leasehold property.[93]

Constitution and Proof of Assignation. The rules applying to the constitution and proof of leases apply generally to assignations. Thus, an assignation was reduced where the docquet of a justice of the peace, who had notarially executed an assignation for the cedent, was reduced because it was not holograph.[94] It is incompetent to prove an assignation by parole evidence alone.[95] Informal writings have been sufficient to instruct an agreement between a tenant and assignee whereby the assignee undertook to take over the tenant's obligations and the tenant undertook to assist in obtaining the landlord's consent to the assignation, but the contract was not a completed assignation but merely a bargain between a tenant and a third party not binding the landlord.[96] Similarly a decision that parole evidence was incompetent to prove a contract involving the sale of a business on the ground that it was a transfer of a lease was reversed presumably because the agreement was really a bargain *in re mercatoria.*[97]

Uncompleted Assignations. Before the assignation from cedent to assignee becomes effective, the terms of the transfer must be fulfilled. Thus, an assignation by an elderly farmer of his lease in favour of the husband of one of his nieces upon certain conditions was rendered ineffective by the death of the assignee before he had been accepted by the landlord and before he could fulfil his part of the agreement.[98] A mere offer to assign does not prevent the offerer from carrying into effect the conditions of his lease, the implement of which the landlord is entitled to demand; thus, an arbitration award fixing the rent pronounced before the assignee accepted the offer was binding on him.[99]

90 Bell, *Lectures on Conveyancing,* 3rd ed., 1208; *Encyclopaedia of the Laws of Scotland,* Vol. 15, 521.
91 Bell, *op. cit.,* 1208.
92 Registration of Leases (Scotland) Act, 1857, s. 20.
93 *Blair* v *Blair* (1849) 12 D. 114 *per* Lord Moncreiff at p. 115.
94 *Irvine* v *M'Hardy* (1892) 19 R. 458.
95 *Barbour's Trs.* v *Halliday* (1883) 20 S.L.R. 673.
96 *Kinninmont* v *Paxton* (1892) 20 R. 128.
97 *Moncrieff* v *Seivwright* (1896) 33 S.L.R 456.
98 *Smith* v *Riddell* (1886) 14 R. 95.
99 *Robertson* v *Boyd & Winans* (1885) 12 R. 419.

Completion of Assignee's Title. (a) *As between Cedent and Assignee.*
In conformity with the general law of personal obligations the right of
the assignee of a lease in a question with the cedent is completed by
delivery of the assignation.[1]

(b) *As between Assignee and Landlord.*   In a question with the landlord the title of the assignee is completed by intimation of the assignation.[2]
Leases are primarily personal rights, and so in a competition between
two *bona fide* onerous assignees, the landlord is entitled until intimation
to transact with the cedent ignoring the assignee, and is bound to prefer
the party who first intimates his assignation and to put him in possession.[3] It seems to be sufficient that the assignation be *bona fide,* onerosity
being merely one important element in evidence of good faith. Intimation in some form is necessary for the purpose of establishing privity
of contract between the landlord and assignee. This is particularly true
in the case where the right assigned is already subject to a sublease
because the assignee can have no physical possession.[4]

By the Transmission of Moveable Property (Scotland) Act 1862[5]
(the relevant section of which does not appear to be confined to moveable rights)[6] formal intimation of an assignation may be made by (1)
a notary public delivering a certified copy of the assignation to the landlord, in which case a certificate of intimation by the notary is sufficient
evidence, or (2) the holder of the assignation or his agent transmitting
a certified copy by post to the landlord, whose written acknowledgment
thereof is sufficient evidence of intimation. The Act expressly covered
any form of intimation that was already in use. Neither the old form of
notarial intimation in use before 1862 nor intimation in statutory form are
solemnities, and the law accepts in certain cases other forms of notice or
evidence of notice which are regarded as equivalent, *e.g.* (1) a probative
acknowledgment by the landlord of the assignee's right; (2) citation in an
action by the assignee against the landlord; (3) a charge or citation on any
diligence against the landlord; (4) production of the assignation in court in
an action between them.[6] Mere private knowledge of the assignation does
not amount to intimation, although this puts the recipient of the
knowledge in bad faith,[7] nor parole evidence of actual notice, nor a
reference to the landlord's oath, nor evidence of a promise to recognise
the assignee.[8] Registration for preservation is not equivalent to intimation. Recording in the Sasine Register for publication is equivalent to
intimation, but this is practicable only in the case of assignations of
registered leases.

[1] Erskine, III, 5, 3.
[2] *Burnet* v *Frazer* (1673) Mor. 13470.
[3] *Yeoman* v *Elliot & Foster,* 2 Feb. 1813 F.C.; *Inglis & Co.* v *Paul* (1829) 7 S. 469
per opinion of majority at p. 473.
[4] *Wallace* v *Campbell* (1750) Mor. 2805 at p. 2811.
[5] s. 2.
[6] Rankine, 182.
[7] *Bouack* v *Croll* (1748) Mor. 1695.
[8] Rankine, 182.

Although entering into possession is the method by which the assignee establishes his right with the world at large, it is not an alternative to intimation, and it would seem that in a question with the landlord the assignee must also intimate his assignation to him in some way.

(c) *As between Assignee and Third Parties.* While it had long been settled than an assignee's title to a lease might be completed by intimation to the landlord in a question with the landlord himself and his representatives,[9] it was questioned whether such intimation alone was effective against the landlord's singular successors, or against creditors or subsequent assignees, or whether in addition possession was required to make the assignee's right real.[10] The difficulty did not arise so much where the possession was in the hands of subtenants and it was the principal lease which was assigned, as physical possession by the assignee was impossible, but he could exercise civil possession by such means as intimation to the subtenants and collection of rents.[11] The difficulty arose more in assignations of leases not burdened with subleases, where physical possession by the assignee was not impossible.[12] Most of the cases arose out of attempts to create a right of security over a lease resulting in a competition between the assignee and the cedent's general creditors. An intimated assignation merely undertaking to give possession at a future date or subject to a condition, but not followed by possession, was held incapable of competing with a subsequent assignation on which possession had followed.[13] Where a company granted to a bank an assignation, which was intimated to the landlord and the bank granted a sublease to the company, who remained in possession and paid the rents, it was held that the assignation was not effectual against creditors, although the question of the efficacy of intimation without possession was not decided.[14]

In the leading case,[15] a sublessee granted an assignation, which was intimated to the principal tenant before the granter's sequestration, but not to the tenants of the granter until after his sequestration, and no possession physical or civil was taken by the assignee; it was held by a majority of the Court that possession was necessary to complete the assignation in a question with the cedent's trustee in bankruptcy, that civil possession could easily have been obtained by intimation to the cedent's lessees before the sequestration, and that such intimation, coming after the sequestration, was too late. " In a question with the singular successors of the landlord and the tenant or his assignee, a tack is a real right by force of the Statute 1449; and therefore it is incomplete

[9] *Yeoman* v *Elliot & Foster*, 2 Feb. 1813 F.C.; *Inglis & Co.* v *Paul* (1829) 7 S. 469 *per* opinion of majority at p. 473.
[10] *Wallace* v *Campbell* (1750) Mor. 2805, 15282; Hume, *Lectures*, IV, 97-99.
[11] *Grant* v *Adamson* (1802) Hume 810.
[12] Rankine, 182-185.
[13] *Kennedy* v *Forsyth* (1829) 7 S. 435.
[14] *Brock* v *Cabbell* (1822) 2 S. 52 (N.E. 54); (1830) 8 S. 647; (1831) 5 W. & S. 476.
[15] *Inglis & Co.* v *Paul* (1829) 7 S. 469.

unless possession, natural or civil, has been obtained ".[16] Nothing has occurred to shake the general principle laid down by the majority in *Inglis & Co.* v *Paul*, founded as it was on abundant analogy, sound legal principle and obvious convenience,[17] and the principle has been followed in several other cases where an assignation of a lease in security has been held to be ineffectual without possession or intimation to subtenants.[18]

Where a company assigned certain mineral leases together with the moveables and plant on the ground to trustees for debenture holders, the assignations were intimated to the landlords, but the assignees took no steps to enter into possession of the subjects; on the company going into liquidation, it was held that the debenture holders had no preference as regards the leasehold (or the moveable) property, as no possession had followed on the assignations.[19] " The assignation of the leases, with no possession following upon it, creates no right whatever in the assignee except a mere personal claim against the granter of the assignation. It may give him a very good personal claim to be put in possession of the subjects assigned, and the granter of the assignation may have no answer to such a claim when it is made, but till possession is actually obtained there is no real right, and no security created in favour of the assignee whatever. At one period of our law this might have been the subject of contention, but for the last half century it has been settled by the well known case of *Cabbell and Brock* and a series of cases connected with it, that an assignation of a lease without possession is quite unavailing as a real security ".[20]

Whether or not there has been a change of possession is a question of fact, depending on the circumstances of each case. An assignation by a father to his son aged 16 for the purpose of taking advantage of a provision prolonging a lease of his farm followed by intimation to the landlord, the substitution of the son's name for his father's on the carts, in the landlord's rental books and for the purpose of taxes, public burdens and sales of produce, was upheld against the father's creditors, although the father had continued to manage the farm while the son served an apprenticeship to a Writer to the Signet.[21] If the property is in the occupation of the subtenants, the assignee cannot of course take physical possession, but he can do the equivalent, that is intimate his assignation to the subtenants and collect the rents.[22] Where an assignee did not take possession, but left the cedent in possession of part of the subjects, and intimated the assignation to the landlord and to the subtenants and collected the rents from some of them, it was questioned

[16] *Ibid.*, majority opinion at p. 473.
[17] Rankine, 186.
[18] *Hamilton's Tr.* v *Stewart* (1830) 8 S. 799; *Benton* v *Craig* (1864) 2 M. 1365; *Mess* v *Sime's Tr.* (1898) 25 R. 398; affd. (1898) 1 F. (H.L.) 22.
[19] *Clark* v *West Calder Oil Co.* (1882) 9 R. 1017.
[20] *Ibid.*, per L.P. Inglis at p. 1024.
[21] *Miller* v *Duncan* (1825) 4 S. 48 (N.E. 49).
[22] *Wallace* v *Campbell* (1750) Mor. 2805; Bell *Comm.*, I, 64.

whether such acts would amount to possession so as to give the assignee a real right to the whole lease.[23] An application by trustees for debenture holders for authority to sell the subjects of their security, which they had never possessed, was not sufficient.[24]

Competition between Assignations.　It is clear from the foregoing paragraphs that, in the event of a competition between assignees, the assignee who first takes possession of the subjects is preferred.[25] If a tenant first assigns to one person, who merely intimates his assignation to the landlord, and then to another, who enters into the natural possession, the preference in this competition for the real right is with the latter, who first forms a real connection with the subjects.[26] However, the second assignee must be in good faith: if he is aware of a prior assignation he cannot by taking possession first prevail over the prior personal right.[27]

Effect of Assignation.　In order that an assignation be valid there must be no exclusion of assignees in the lease, or if there is such an exclusion, it must be waived by the landlord expressly or impliedly.[28]

The effect of a completed assignation of a lease is that the assignee is substituted for the cedent or tenant and succeeds to the cedent's rights and obligations under the lease. Unless provision is made to the contrary, the landlord on accepting the assignee as tenant renounces all claims against the cedent apart from rent. After an assignation of a lease has been regularly executed and duly intimated to and acquiesced in by the landlord, and the assignee admitted into possession the obligation of the cedent for rents is limited to those prior to the possession of the assignee.[29] Lord Watson has stated the position thus;—" According to the Law of Scotland, the assignation of his lease by a tenant who has power to assign has the effect of making the assignee sole tenant from the time he obtains possession of the subject of the lease, and of discharging the cedent from future liability to the landlord ";[30] and again, " It must be presumed that an obligation to pay rent is only meant to attach to those persons who are for the time being in right of a lease as tenants. In *Skene* v *Greenhill* a tenant, who had expressly bound himself ' his heirs, executors and successors' for payment of the rent, assigned the lease with the assent of the landlord, and it was held

[23] *Wright* v *Walker* (1839) 1 D. 641.
[24] *Clark* v *West Calder Oil Co.* (1882) 9 R. 1017.
[25] *Inglis & Co.* v *Paul, supra; Kennedy* v *Forsyth, supra; Brock* v *Cabbel, supra,* Hamilton's Tr. v *Stewart, supra; Benton* v *Craig, supra; Clark* v *West Calder Oil Co., supra; Mess* v *Sime's Tr., supra.*
[26] Hume, *Lectures* 4, 98.
[27] *Rodger* v *Fawdry,* 1950 S.C. 483 (purchaser recording disposition in Register of Sasines in knowledge of prior missives).
[28] *Supra,* p. 155.
[29] *Skene* v *Greenhill* (1825) 4 S. 25 (N.E. 26).
[30] *Lord Elphinstone* v *Monkland Iron & Coal Co. Ltd.* (1886) 13 R. (H.L.) 98 at p. 102.

that the cedent and his representatives were under no obligation to pay rents becoming due after the assignee entered into possession. A tenant may, however, engage that he and his representatives shall remain bound along with his successors in the lease, and if he contracts in terms which, according to their just construction, imply that he has undertaken that responsibility to the lessor, the stipulation must receive effect. Had the obligation in *Skene v Greenhill* been laid on the tenant and his heirs, executors and successors 'all conjunctly and severally', I think the decision would have been different, because in that connection the words which I have added, 'all conjunctly and severally', plainly import that the tenant and his representatives are to remain liable for rent along with the persons succeeding to the lease as assignees ".[31] There is nothing to prevent a tenant under an assignable lease, which proves unprofitable, from escaping liability for future rent by assigning it to a man of straw.

A lease may contain an express provision to the effect that the original tenant should remain liable for performance of the prestations even after assignation. Thus two leases of minerals by the same landlord to the same tenant contained an exclusion of assignees and subtenants except upon condition that the tenant should remain liable for the rents and prestations and " implement of all the stipulations " contained in them; the tenant, having assigned the leases, became divested of all right under them and ceased to be tenant, although he remained liable for the rent, and it was held that he had merely a personal right of relief against the assignees for the rent due to the landlord; conversely, the landlord had only a personal claim against the cedent and could invoke the ordinary remedies of a landlord against the assignees whom he had accepted.[32]

Arrears of Rent. An assignee becomes liable not only for rents accruing from the date of his possession, but probably also for arrears of rent due for the possession of his cedent.[33] Thus the acceptance by a trustee for creditors of an assignation of a tenant's lease renders the trustee liable for payment of byegone rents, the arrears being an inseparable burden on the assignation of a lease.[34] Similarly, a trustee in sequestration, having adopted a lease, becomes liable to pay in full the arrears of rent on the principle that an assignee, whether voluntary or judicial, who takes possession of lands under a lease, renders himself liable for arrears of rent.[35] Where there is a sublease, the possession of the subtenant following an assignation of the principal lease is considered as being for the assignee and not for the cedent, with the result

---

[31] *Burns v Martin* (1887) 14 R. (H.L.) 20 at p. 24; Gloag, *Contract*, 2nd ed., 263-4, 417.
[32] *Gray's Trs.* v *Benhar Coal Co. Ltd.* (1881) 9 R. 225.
[33] *Turnbull* v *Scot* (1626) Mor. 15273; *Bannatine* v *Scot* (1632) Mor. 15274; Gloag & Henderson, *Introduction to the Law of Scotland*, 6th ed., 374.
[34] *Ross* v *Monteith* (1786) Mor. 15290; *M'Gregor* v *Hunter* (1850) 13 D. 90.
[35] *Dundas* v *Morison* (1857) 20 D. 225; *infra*, p. 196.

that the assignee cannot argue that he has not obtained legal possession; he is therefore liable for byegone rents.[36]

In so far as the assignation is prohibited by the lease and the landlord's consent has not been obtained, the cedent remains liable for payment of rent and the other obligations of the lease.[37]

Questions may arise between cedent and assignee involving matters other than performance of the obligations in the lease. The cedent may reduce an assignation on the ground of essential error, but only if he offers to make *restitutio in integrum*.[38] The assignee may have a claim against the cedent under the warrandice in the assignation.[39] In such cases the ordinary rules of the law of contract apply.

Further Assignations. There may be any number of assignations of a lease. Where a lease has changed hands more than once, a reference in the lease itself to " assignees " is not confined to the first assignee.[40] An assignation back to someone who has assigned a lease may be called a retrocession. The person to whom a lease is retrocessed, even if he is the original tenant, is in the same position as an ordinary assignee. Thus, if the landlord's consent is necessary for an assignation, it is also necessary for a retrocession.[41]

SUBLETTING

Nature. A sublease, although it is granted by someone who is himself a tenant and not proprietor, is none the less a lease, and is governed generally by the same rules.[42] The sublease may be of the whole subjects of the principal lease or of only part. It may be for the remainder of the term of the principal lease or for only part. A sublease of the whole subjects for the whole remaining term of the principal lease is not to be confused with an assignation. It is possible for a subtenant to grant a sublease, and so on in the same way as a feuar or subfeuar of land may himself grant subfeus.

The rules which apply to the constitution and proof of leases in general apply also to subleases. Similarly the requirements necessary to constitute a lease as a real right apply to subleases. The Registration of Leases (Scotland) Act 1857 applies equally to subleases. The general rules governing assignation and subletting apply also to a subtenancy.

Form of Sublease. The contract takes the form of a lease, and it may not be apparent that it is in fact a sublease. The principal tenant granting the sublease lets the subjects to the subtenant, who binds

---

[36] *Paton* v *Couston* (1674) Mor. 15274.
[37] *Gemmel* v *Low* (1823) 2 S. 563; *Ramsay* v *Commercial Bank* (1842) 4 D. 405.
[38] *Hay* v *Rafferty* (1899) 2 F. 302.
[39] *Hardy* v *Willson* (unreported) 1950 C.L. 4877 (O.H.).
[40] *Murray* v *Torrie* (1776) 5 B.S. 516.
[41] *Ramsay* v *Commercial Bank, supra.*
[42] Rankine, 190.

himself to pay the rent to the granter and to perform the other obligations contained in the sublease.

Like an ordinary lease, a sublease should contain an obligation of warrandice by the granter to the subtenant. If no such obligation is expressed, absolute warrandice will be implied.[43] The warrandice under the principal lease may be assigned to the subtenant.[44]

A sublease may and frequently does refer to the principal lease, a copy of which may be delivered to the subtenant. It is certainly desirable that the existence and contents of the principal lease should be brought to the notice of the subtenant. This might help to defeat a claim by the subtenant under the warrandice clause. Frequently obligations conceived in favour of the principal tenant incumbent on the landlord under the principal lease are assigned to the subtenant in the sublease, and the subtenant may bind himself to implement and fulfil and to relieve the original tenant of the whole stipulations and obligations incumbent on the tenant under the principal lease, excepting the payment of the principal rent.[45] However, there must be many a sublease where it is not considered necessary to mention the principal lease or the fact that the transaction is a sublease; for example, in a short lease, furnished or unfurnished, of subjects already held under a lease.

The principal landlord may well be a party to a sublease, particularly where his consent to the subletting is necessary because of an exclusion of subtenants. If he is a party to the sublease, the grounds of his being one should be clearly expressed. Sometimes it is provided that the subrent should be paid direct to the principal landlord to the extent of the rent in the principal lease and that the principal tenant should remain bound for its payment; or the landlord may declare the principal tenant free and take the subtenant bound for payment of the rent in the principal lease.[46] If the effect of the sublease is to free the original tenant of all liabilities in a question with his landlord, the transaction becomes an assignation,[47] and the distinction can become quite narrow where the subjects and period of the principal lease and sublease are identical.

Limitation of Sublease. The various conditions and restrictions contained in the principal lease should be reflected in the sublease. The granter of the sublease cannot confer on his subtenant any greater right than he has under his own principal lease, although of course he can give less. Obviously, the extent of the subjects sublet cannot exceed the extent of those let under the principal lease. Most important in practice,

---

[43] *Middleton* v *Yorstoun* (1826) 5 S. 162 (N.E. 148); *Middleton* v *Megget* (1828) 7 S. 76; *Downie* v *Laird* (1902) 10 S.L.T. 28 (O.H.).
[44] *Dick* v *Taylor's Trs.* (1831) 10 S. 19.
[45] *Jur. Styles*, 6th ed., I, 558; *Encyclopaedia of Scottish Legal Styles*, Vol. 6, Nos. 141 and 142.
[46] See note to *Jur. Styles, supra,* at p. 560.
[47] Rankine, 192.

the duration of the sublease cannot exceed that of the principal lease.
A sublease granted for the " remaining duration " of the principal lease
expires at the natural termination of the principal lease, and if the
principal lease is reduced before then, the subtenant is entitled to damages.[48] However, there was no claim for damages, where the sublease
bound the subtenant to remove when required on the principal lease
being reduced, and the sublease gave no express warrandice.[49] Where a
tenant under a principal lease for 19 years sublet a farm " to the end of
my own lease " and the original landlord took advantage of a break
in the principal lease after 10 years and evicted the subtenant, it was held
that on a sound construction of the sublease the original tenant merely
undertook to give the subtenant the same tenure which he himself enjoyed.[50] If no term is stated in the sublease, it will probably be presumed
that both it and the principal lease will terminate together.[51]

Completion of Subtenant's Right. Where subletting is competent,
how does the subtenant complete his right in a question with the
original tenant and third parties? So far as the granter is concerned,
the sublease itself is sufficient, and as it is a mutual contract like the
principal lease, delivery is not necessary. So far as third parties are concerned, a sublease just like a principal lease or assignation requires the
seal of real possession, and is in itself an imperfect transaction until
followed by possession.[52] Normally there is no need to intimate the
sublease to the principal landlord.[53] So far as the principal landlord is
concerned, the right of the subtenant is completed by possession with
reference to the sublease. Thus, where subletting is not excluded or is
acquiesced in, a subtenant in possession under a sublease to which the
Leases Act 1449 applies or a subtenant having a registered sublease is safe
against not only the granter of the sublease and his singular successors,
but also against the original landlord and his singular successors. A subtenant in possession is secure against the principal landlord and his singular successors, even if the original tenant abandons the lease or renounces
it in favour of the principal landlord, unless his possession was originally ascribed to some other right than the sublease and the fact that it
is now ascribed to the sublease has not been intimated to the landlord.[54]
The possession of the subtenant is, however, unavailing against a reduction of the principal lease, and, where a principal lease by an heir of

---

[48] *Middleton* v *Yorstoun* (1826) 5 S. 162 (N.E. 148); *Middleton* v *Megget* (1828)
    7 S. 76.
[49] *Laidlaw* v *Wilson* (1830) 8 S. 440.
[50] *Logan* v *Weir* (1872) 9 S.L.R. 268.
[51] Rankine, 191.
[52] Hume, *Lectures,* IV, 100; Bell, § 1212.
[53] *Underwood* v *Richardson* (1824) 3 S. 336 (N.E. 238); *Marston* v *Underwood*
    (1827) 5 S. 200 (N.E. 185); but see *Earl of Morton* v *Tenants* (1625) Mor. 15228;
    Bell, *Leases,* 3rd ed., 363.
[54] *Earl of Morton* v *Tenants* (1625) Mor. 15228; Bell, Leases, 3rd ed., 362-3.

entail was reduced as being *ultra vires,* a sublease fell with it.[55] *Maxwell v Queensberry's Exrs.*[55] was the test case which decided the fate of many " Queensberry leases ", and the decision in the Court of Session and its reversal by the House of Lords gave rise to much litigation between Queensberry tenants, their subtenants and the landlords.[56] Further, the possession of the subtenant is ineffectual against the exercise of a power of resumption in the principal lease,[57] or against any irritation of the principal lease.[58]

On the other hand, possession on a sublease known to and permitted by the proprietor may amount to *rei interventus* and cure an informal principal lease.[59]

Effect of Sublease. (a) *As between Landlord and Principal Tenant.* As already stated, the granter of a sublease remains the tenant of his landlord, and their relationship is unchanged.

(b) *As between Principal Tenant and Subtenant.* The general law of leases applies to a sublease, and the parties to it have with regard to each other the same rights, duties and remedies as they would have had, if it had been a principal lease. The subtenant has to pay the rent to the principal tenant, unless this is otherwise provided for in the sublease. The principal tenant becomes liable to his subtenant to implement the obligations incumbent on him contained in the sublease.

The sublease itself is the sole measure of the relationship of the parties. While conditions of the principal lease can be imported into a sublease and so become enforceable as between tenant and subtenant, any conditions not so imported will not apply as between tenant and subtenant. Thus, where a sublease contained no express assignation of an option to renew, it was held that the sublessee had no right to a renewal.[60] Similarly, where a tenant, whose lease prohibited the sale of spirits, granted a sublease which did not refer to this restriction, it was held that he could not enforce the conditions of his own tenure against his subtenant.[61]

In consequence of the absolute warrandice expressed or implied in the sublease, the subtenant, who is evicted by reason of the principal lease being reduced before its natural termination, will have a claim for damages or diminution of rent against the principal tenant.[62] Thus, where a landlord exercised his right of resumption in the principal lease,

[55] *Maxwell* v *Duke of Queensberry's Exrs.* (1827) 5 S. 935 (N.E. 869); revd. (1831) 5 W. & S. 771.
[56] *E.g. Middleton* v *Yorstoun, supra; Hutchison* v *Queensberry's Exrs.* (1828) 6 S. 849; *Middleton* v *Megget, supra; Laidlaw* v *Wilson, supra; Dick* v *Taylor's Trs., supra; Smyth* v *Rogerson* (1832) 10 S. 433.
[57] *Downie* v *Laird & Sons Ltd.* (1902) 10 S.L.T. 28 (O.H.).
[58] *Grant* v *Morton* (1789) 3 Pat. 145.
[59] *Bell* v *Goodall* (1883) 10 R. 905.
[60] *Robertson* v *Player* (1876) 4 R. 218.
[61] *Fergusson* v *Brown* (1902) 9 S.L.T. 341 (O.H.).
[62] *Middleton* v *Yorstoun* (1826) 5 S. 162 (N.E. 148); *Middleton* v *Megget* (1828) 7 S. 76; *Dick* v *Taylor's Trustees* (1831) 10 S. 19.

a subtentant was held entitled to be indemnified against loss occasioned by her premature removal.[63] It is, of course, possible expressly to exclude such a warrandice claim.[64] Where a tenant, whose lease was liable to be reduced, granted a sublease with an obligation on the subtenant to remove when the principal lease was reduced and without any express warrandice, it was held that there was no implied warrandice as to the duration.[65] Warrandice from fact and deed in a sublease may import an obligation on the tenant to communicate to the subtenant a proportion of the damages claimed from the landlord under his own warrandice clause.[66] Where there has been no eviction, no such claim lies.[67]

 (c) *As between Landlord and Subtenant.* There is no privity of contract between the principal landlord and the subtenant, and as a general rule no right of action lies between them arising out of the sublease as such. The warrandice in the principal lease, however the clause is expressed, can be enforced against the landlord only by the principal tenant and his heirs and assignees. Where a tenant under a lease in favour of him and his heirs, assignees and subtenants and containing an obligation of warrandice in favour of him and his " aforesaid " sublet a farm with warrandice but without assigning the warrandice in the principal lease, it was held that the word " aforesaid " did not imply warrandice by the landlord to a subtenant and that the latter had no title to sue in a direct action of damages against the landlord.[68] The subtenant must first claim against the principal tenant under the warrandice expressed or implied in his sublease, and, if the subletting was not excluded, the principal tenant can recover from the landlord under his warrandice.[69] The subtenant's claim against the tenant may be expressly excluded, and he will have no claim against the landlord.[70]

Landlord's Remedies. If the landlord's consent to a sublease is necessary but has not been obtained expressly nor inferred by acquiescence, the landlord may at any time eject the subtenant as a possessor without a valid title, sue for violent profits and proceed under his hypothec.[71] In a criminal case[72] a tenant of an unfurnished house under a lease, which prohibited subletting without the consent of the landlord, sublet it without such consent and furnished it with her own furniture; later, having decided to give up her own tenancy, she gave her subtenants sufficient notice of termination, removed her furniture and returned the keys to the landlord's factors; it was held that

[63] *Downie* v *Laird & Sons Ltd.* (1902) 10 S.L.T. 28 (O.H.).
[64] *Hutchison* v *Duke of Queensberry's Exrs.* (1828) 6 S. 849.
[65] *Laidlaw* v *Wilson* (1830) 8 S. 440.
[66] *Smyth* v *Rogerson* (1832) 10 S. 433.
[67] *Watson* v *Turner* (1831) 9 S. 687.
[68] *Maxwell* v *Duke of Queensberry's Exrs.* (1831) 5 W. & S. 771.
[69] *Dick* v *Taylor's Trs.* (1831) 10 S. 19.
[70] *Hutchison* v *Duke of Queensberry's Exrs.* (1828) 6 S. 849.
[71] Rankine, 198.
[72] *Paterson* v *Robertson*, 1944 J.C. 166, 1945 S.L.T. 31.

the subtenants, who returned and re-entered the house and occupied it in spite of the factor's warning to remove were no better than squatters, and that their conviction under the Act in question[73] was justified. Where, however, the landlord's consent has been obtained, he has to wait until the termination of the principal lease to eject the subtenant, who has no defence to such an action;[74] but a subtenant who has received no warning may not be ejected summarily.[75]

Although there is no contractual relationship between landlord and subtenant, the landlord can enforce rights against the subtenant indirectly but effectively. He always has available the weapon of irritancy, which can be used for any breach by the subtenant of conditions of the principal lease. Thus, the landlord can oust the subtenant by irritating the principal lease, and this has been held to apply even although the subtenant has not been called in the action.[76] However, it seems desirable that the subtenant should be called in an action of reduction by the landlord against the principal tenant, at least if the landlord was a party to the sublease or has knowledge of it; but the fact that he was not called seems no bar to a subsequent reduction of the sublease itself.[77] Conversely, in an action of ejection by a landlord against a subtenant under a lease excluding subtenants, it was held that the principal tenant should have been called.[78]

By virtue of his hypothec under the principal lease the landlord may sequestrate goods of a subtenant for rent due to him by the principal tenant.[79]

Competition between Assignations and Subleases. What happens when a tenant grants an assignation of his lease to one person and a sublease of the same property or part of it to another? The key is always possession. It has already been seen that if the tenant assigns to one person, who merely intimates it to the landlord, and then assigns to another who assumes natural possession, then the preference is with the *bona fide* assignee who first forms a real connection with the subjects by taking possession.[80] In the same way, if a subtenant takes possession before an assignee, then the subtenant is preferred, and the assignee's right is burdened with the sublease and he must be content to receive the subrents, his author's remaining interest in the subjects.[81] If the assignee takes possession before the subtenant, the assignation will prevail, and the sublease will be valueless. Where the original tenant first sublets to one person who takes possession, and then assigns to

[73] Trespass (Scotland) Act 1865.
[74] *Robb* v *Menzies* (1859) 21 D. 277.
[75] *Robb* v *Brearton* (1895) 22 R. 885.
[76] *Grant* v *Morton* (1789) 3 Pat. 145.
[77] Bell, *Leases*, 3rd ed., 470-471; Rankine, 193.
[78] *Morison* v *Grant* (1895) 11 Sh. Ct. Rep. 201.
[79] *Steuart* v *Stables* (1878) 5 R. 1024, *infra*, p. 208.
[80] *Supra*, p. 162.
[81] *Grant* v *Adamson* (1802) Hume 810; Hume, *Lectures*, IV, 98-99.

another his right as principal tenant, the assignation is of the surplus rent only and the cedent has no further interest; the assignee completes his real right by exercising civil, if not physical, possession, that is, by intimation to the subtenant and uplifting the rents.[82]

Interjection of Tenancy. The normal course of events leading to a subtenancy is that A, the proprietor of land, has granted a lease to B, who thereafter grants a sublease to C. A is B's landlord and B becomes landlord to C. Suppose, however, events do not take place in that order; suppose that in the first place A has granted a lease or leases direct to C and perhaps to other tenants, and that for some reason he wishes to achieve the same result as in the first example; can be then interject a lease in favour of a third party B, so that B becomes the landlord of C? In England it is possible for a landlord to assign his " reversion " to a lease of tenanted subjects so as to establish a relationship of tenure between the assignee of the reversion and the tenant; a second lease validly granted by the lessor during the currency of a prior lease vests the reversion to the first lease in the lessee under the second lease, although the second lease may be for a shorter term than the first.[83] Attempts have been made to do this in Scotland, but it seems to be a clear principle of our law that when a proprietor has granted a lease to a tenant, he cannot interpose another party as tenant so as to degrade the first lessee into the position of a subtenant.[84] Similarly, a superior cannot interject a midsuperior between him and his vassals without their consent.[85]

Where a father granted to his son a lease of lands, which were let to several tenants, and empowered him to raise the rents and generally to exercise the power of landlord, it was remarked that such a grant was not a lease of lands at all, but a lease of the power to act as landlord.[86] Such a lease is really a lease of rents, which at one time was quite common. Not being a lease of land and not involving the occupation of land, it does not come within the scope of the Leases Act 1449.[87] It has, however, been suggested that on an analogy with the English system an interposed lease might be recognised in Scotland in a question with a singular successor, if it covered a larger area than the original leases, so that possession of part of it was possible, and if its term was longer than that of the original leases, so that possession was possible at some future date.[88] It is thought, however, that a lease including subjects already tenanted would be held not to be a lease at all *quoad* the tenanted subjects, but merely an assignation of the rents thereof.

---

[82] *Wallace* v *Campbell* (1750) Mor. 2805 at p. 2811; Bell, *Comm.* I, 64.
[83] Woodfall, *Landlord and Tenant,* 26th ed., 2.
[84] *Wilson* v *Wilson* (1859) 21 D. 309 *per* L.J.C. Inglis at p. 312.
[85] Erskine, II, 5, 4; Menzies, *Lectures on Conveyancing,* 1900 ed., 644.
[86] *Bruce* v *Assessor for Zetland* (1882) 10 R. 34.
[87] Erskine, II, 6, 27; III, 5, 5; *Encyclopaedia of the Laws of Scotland,* Vol. 9, 61.
[88] II *Conv. Rev.,* 216.

Apart from succession and bankruptcy, there are only two ways of
transferring the interest of a landlord: one is by a disposition or other
conveyance of the ownership of the subjects; and the other, falling short
of a conveyance, is by assigning the rents. The rents may be assigned
in a security deed giving the creditor the right to an action of maills and
duties, or they may be carried in a personal assignation of rents. Such
a personal assignation probably does not now confer the right to maills
and duties and is only effective for so long as the property belongs to
the granter.[89]

[89] Bell, *Comm.* I, 793.

CHAPTER XI

SUCCESSION

THE interests in a lease held by the landlord and tenant respectively
may descend or pass to other persons on the occasion of death or
bankruptcy. This chapter is mainly concerned with the succession to
the tenant's interest upon his death. The next chapter will deal with the
effect of the tenant's bankruptcy. It is necessary only to deal very briefly
with the succession to the landlord's interest.

Succession to the Landlord. So far as the landlord is concerned,
his interest in the lease on his death passes with the ownership of the
land itself either under his will or on his intestacy, and his successor
may enforce its conditions against the tenant. If the tenant has acquired
a real right, he may enforce the lease itself and all its real and personal
conditions[1] against the landlord's executors, who are his personal
representatives.

Succession to the Tenant. Introduction. It has always been possible to exclude the devolution of a lease on the tenant's death by
making it a lease for the tenant's lifetime only or for the duration of his
tenure of an office. Such a lease terminates automatically on the tenant's
death or on his vacating the office, and there is no question of any
successor acquiring it.[2] An example of a lease given for the duration of
an office is one granted to a minister during his incumbency, but this
must be rare nowadays. Such a lease is to be distinguished from a service
occupancy, which is not a lease.[3] However, liferent leases are not uncommon as a device to ensure that the subjects will revert to the landlord
on the tenant's death. At common law such a lease cannot be bequeathed,
and on intestacy it does not fall to the heir-at-law. Moreover, a liferent
lease is excluded from the provisions of the Succession (Scotland) Act
1964, as it is not included in the estate of a deceased person.[4]

Apart from leases restricted to the tenant's life or tenure of office,
the subject of the tenant's succession is the right to possess the subjects
of the lease for the remainder of its duration on the same terms and
conditions as they were possessed by the deceased tenant.

The common law has passed through various stages from a time
when a lease, although for a fixed term of years, terminated on the

---

[1] *Supra,* p. 95.
[2] *Tennent* v *Tennent* (1760) Mor. 13845; *Gordon* v *Michie's Trs.* (1794) Mor.
13851; *Stewart* v *Grimmond's Reps.* (1796) Mor. 13853.
[3] *Supra,* p. 9.
[4] See ss. 16 (1), 36 (2).

death of the tenant, unless his heirs were expressly called in the lease, to a period when a lease could be bequeathed, if it was assignable, and fell to the heir-at-law, if it was not assignable. Whether it was assignable or not, it fell to the heir-at-law on intestacy. Certain limited powers of bequest have been given by statutes to tenants of agricultural holdings,[5] small landholders,[6] and crofters;[7] and a measure of protection, not amounting to a power of bequest, was given to the families of tenants under leases controlled by the Rent Acts.[8] Finally, there was enacted the Succession (Scotland) Act 1964, which, besides altering the law of succession on intestacy, slightly extended the tenant's power of bequest and gave to the tenant's executors important new administrative powers in relation to leases.

The succession to a lease depends in the first place on whether any provision has been made in the lease itself or can be implied from its nature as to its devolution on the tenant's death. Such provision may take the form of a special destination in the lease, or it may take the form of an express or implied power of bequest given to the tenant. In the second place, in the absence of a special destination or of a validly exercised power of bequest, the lease will devolve on the heir, if the tenant died before 10th September 1964, or on his executor representing the persons entitled to succeed on intestacy, if the tenant died on or after that date.[9]

Special Destinations. Not only the tenant's power of bequest, but also the succession of the heir-at-law at common law, or of the persons entitled to succeed on intestacy under the Succession (Scotland) Act 1964, may be excluded wholly or partially by a special destination in the lease itself, such as, " to A and B " with words of survivorship or to "A and B in conjunct fee and liferent ".

In such cases, the destination will be read as part of a contract and will not be governed by the special rules governing destinations in conveyances of heritage which result from the principles that the fee cannot be *in pendente* and that the husband is the *dignior persona*.[10] Where the meaning of the destination as it stands is not questioned, and the action is brought for the purpose of showing that the lease was really granted for the benefit of one of the lessees or of a third party, this is really an attempt to prove a trust, and the only admissible evidence will be the writ or oath of the party maintaining the *prima facie* interpretation of the words used.[11] A special destination may also be contained

---

[5] *Infra,* p. 356.
[6] *Infra,* p. 425.
[7] *Infra,* p. 461.
[8] *Infra,* p. 594.
[9] Succession (Scotland) Act 1964 ss. 14, 16.
[10] Rankine, 84-86; *supra,* p. 62.
[11] *Seth* v *Hain* (1855) 17 D. 1117; McLaren, *Wills and Succession,* 3rd ed., II, 1049-50, 1062.

in an assignation of a lease, if assignation is not excluded. Whether contained in the lease itself or in an assignation, the special destination may be subject to evacuation.[12] However, there is strong presumption against evacuation, as the destination is normally contractual as between the tenants.[13]

If the lease is granted to A and B, or to A and B and their heirs or successors, without words of survivorship, then on the death of the predeceaser his share of the lease devolves on his successors and not on the survivor.[14] This applies even where the parties are husband and wife.[15]

If the lease is to A and B and the survivor and their heirs or successors, there is accretion to the survivor.[16] If the predeceaser grants an *inter vivos* assignation of his share to a third party, the predeceaser's interest on his death accresces to the survivor.[17] This rule applies even where the tenants are husband and wife, and the heir of the surviving spouse succeeds.[18] The rule is not affected by divorce.[19] A destination in an assignation of a lease of 99 years to spouses in conjunct fee and to the survivor of them in fee did not carry the lease to the survivor where the destination had been effectively evacuated.[20]

If the lease is in favour of A and B in conjunct fee and liferent and to their heirs or successors, the right of each appears to be a full half share burdened by the liferent of the other,[21] but the terms " fee and liferent " are anomalous when used with regard to leases.[22]

It is quite competent for a lease to provide for a destination-over after the death of a tenant, but when such words as " whom failing " are used, they should not be construed in the same way as in a destination in a will or in a disposition of heritage.[23]

In cases where special destinations are used, it is sometimes necessary to discriminate between words inferring a destination and words intended merely to define the duration of the lease.[24] A lease to a party and his heirs-male for 19 years and for the lifetime of his second son was held not to extend the lease for the second son's life after the expiry of 19 years.[25] If it is intended to exclude the right of the heirs on intestacy to succeed, the intention should be made unmistakably

[12] *Walker* v *Galbraith* (1895) 23 R. 347.
[13] *Fleming* v *Fleming* (1800) Mor. App. *voce* Implied Will 1.
[14] *Douglas* v *Graham* (1566) Mor. 4245; *Dickson* v *Dickson* (1821) 1 S. 117, (1825) 2 S. 462; Rankine, 84.
[15] *Forrester* v *Milligan* (1830) 8 S. 992.
[16] Bell, *Leases*, 3rd ed., 122.
[17] *Gray* v *Rollock* (1570) Mor. 4246; *Lidderdale* (1627) Mor. 4247.
[18] *Laird of Craigmillar* v *Nisbet* (1638) Mor. 6089; *Boyd* v *King's Adv.* (1749) Mor. 4205.
[19] *Countess of Argyle* v *Tenants* (1573) Mor. 327.
[20] *Walker* v *Galbraith* (1895) 23 R. 347.
[21] Bell, *Comm.*, I, 62.
[22] *Macalister* v *Macalister* (1859) 21 D. 560 *per* L.J.C. Inglis at p. 564; *Marquis* v *Prentice* (1896) 23 R. 595.
[23] *Macalister, supra; Marquis, supra.*
[24] Rankine, 161.
[25] *Dunn* v *Dunn* (1835) 13 S. 590.

clear.[26] A lease to a person for his life and for the life of any of his sons, to whom he might assign it, was held to go to the eldest son as heir in the absence of nomination of a younger son.[27] A lease for 38 years and the lifetime of the person having right at the termination thereof " either as heir or assignee " was held to have come to an end on the death of the original tenant, who survived the fixed period.[28]

Power of Bequest in Lease. At common law the question whether or not a particular lease can be bequeathed by the tenant depends on whether or not the lease is assignable. A bequest of a lease is considered equivalent to a voluntary assignation, and so a tenant under a lease prohibiting assignation has no power to bequeath it. Certain statutes give a limited power of bequest in the case of agricultural subjects where assignation is expressly or impliedly prohibited, and now there is a limited power of bequest in the case of leases of all kinds of subjects, where there is an *implied* condition excluding assignation.[29] In most cases, therefore, it is necessary to ascertain whether a particular lease is assignable.

Implied Power. The principles governing the assignability of leases have already been outlined,[30] and it will suffice to state here that as a general rule, if a lease contains an express exclusion of assignees or if *delectus personae* is implied from the nature of the lease, then it cannot be assigned or be made the subject of a valid bequest; if it contains no express exclusion of assignees and if no *delectus personae* is implied, then it can be assigned or bequeathed. In the absence of express provision, therefore, rural leases, sporting leases, and furnished leases cannot be bequeathed; on the other hand, urban leases and other leases of extraordinary duration can be bequeathed.

Express Power. The foregoing general rule may be overridden by express provision in the lease. An express power to assign entitles the tenant to select his successor *mortis causa* or *inter vivos*.[31] Without being fully assignable *inter vivos* a lease may contain a power of bequest either in general terms or more commonly for the purpose of avoiding the bad effects of succession by a plurality of successors, like heirs-portioners, or by a minor or *incapax,* or for the purpose of benefiting the tenant's family as a whole.[32]. Thus, the lease may empower the

[26] *Crichton* v *Lady Keith* (1857) 19 D. 713; Rankine, 161.
[27] *Fraser* v *Fraser* (1805) Hume 819.
[28] *Carnegy* v *Scott* (1822) 1 Sh. App. 114.
[29] Succession (Scotland) Act 1964, s. 29 (1); *infra,* p. 179.
[30] See Chapter X.
[31] Hunter, *Landlord and Tenant,* 4th ed., I, 225, 237; *Kennedy* v *Johnstone,* 1956 S.C. 39 *per* L.P. Clyde at p. 43.
[32] Rankine, 162.

tenant to nominate as his successor one of his family,[33] or even to bequeath the lease to any one person.[34]

Although it is of importance to a tenant to have the power of regulating the succession to his lease, a destination in a lease expressed in general terms such as " to A and his heirs ", or " executors " or " successors ", confers no power of bequest, if assignees[35] are expressly excluded. The addition of " heirs " is unnecessary.[36] The addition of " executors " or " successors " is treated *pro non scripto*.[37] A destination in an assignation will not prevail over an exclusion of assignees in the lease itself.

Express Exclusion. Except in the case of crofts and agricultural subjects, it is always possible to exclude the succession of the heirs by making the lease a liferent one, and the heirs of a liferent tenant have no right of succession.[38] It is competent also for the landlord to reserve power in a lease to resume possession of the subjects after the death of the tenant, and, where a lease empowered him to do so, if he should be dissatisfied with the conduct of the tenant's representatives, it was held that he was not bound to state the reasons for his dissatisfaction.[39] The right of the heir to succeed may be made subject to a condition, but, if so, only the landlord has a title to enforce it.[40]

It is possible in a lease expressly to exclude a legatee,[41] but only if a statute does not make such an exclusion invalid.[42] It was not possible to exclude the heir-at-law of a tenant dying before 10th September 1964, nor is it now possible to exclude an intestate heir chosen by the executor by virtue of his statutory power,[43] unless the lease is limited to the tenant's life or duration of office, or unless it contains a special destination.

Taking up Bequest. If the legatee wishes to take up the succession he must, because he is an assignee, enter into possession of the subjects, and it is advisable, and, in the case of some leases, it is obligatory to intimate the bequest to the landlord.[44] If the legatee declines to take up

[33] *Deuchar* v *Minto* (1798) Mor. 15295; *Stewart* v *Pirie* (1832) 11 S. 139.
[34] *Irvine* v *Fiddes* (1827) 5 S. 534 (N.E. 502).
[35] *Deuchar* v *Minto supra; Cunningham* v *Grieve*, 8 March 1803 F.C., Mor. 15298, (1804) 4 Pat. 571, (1805) Mor. App. *voce* Tack 9, (1806) 6 Pat. 16; *Lowden* v *Adam*, 21 Nov. 1805 F.C., Mor. App. *voce* Tack 10; *Bain* v *Mackenzie* (1896) 23 R. 528; Hume, *Lectures*, IV, 93.
[36] *Thomson* v *Watson* (1750) Mor. 10337; Bell, § 1219.
[37] Rankine, 158-159.
[38] *Supra*, p. 172.
[39] *Houldsworth* v *Brand's Trs.* (1875) 2 R. 683; see also *Guild* v *McLean* (1897) 25 R. 106; *Jackson's Trs.* v *William Dixon Ltd.* (1901) 3 F. 782.
[40] *Fraser* v *Fraser* (1831) 9 S. 849.
[41] *Kennedy* v *Johnstone*, 1956 S.C. 39.
[42] See Agricultural Holdings (Scotland) Act 1949 s. 20, as enlarged by Succession (Scotland) Act 1964, Sched. 3.
[43] Under Succession (Scotland) Act 1964, s. 16 (2).
[44] *Grant's Trs.* v *Arrol*, 1954 S.C. 306; Crofters Holdings (Scotland) Act 1886, s. 16; Agricultural Holdings (Scotland) Act 1949, s. 20; Succession (Scotland) Act 1964, Sched. 2.

the lease, that will let in the heir-at-law at common law, or, in the case of deaths on or after 10th September 1964, the executor representing the intestate heirs. Again, it is advisable to intimate to the landlord the fact that the legatee renounces the succession.[45]

No Power of Bequest. In the absence of a special destination or of a validly exercised power of bequest, the lease will at common law devolve on the heir-at-law, or, if the tenant died on or after 10th September 1964, on his executor as representing the intestate heirs.[46]

It is still necessary to consider the common law not only because it regulates the succession to leases held by tenants dying before 10th September 1964 and the succession to crofts,[47] but also because much of the law governing the rights and duties of the heir-at-law is applicable to the person now entitled to succeed to a lease on intestacy.

Common Law. It had long been established that a tenant under a lease containing or implying an exclusion of assignees had no power at common law to bequeath his interest under the lease to his executors, trustees or any other person.[48] The landlord could not be compelled to accept the legatee as tenant. Thus, a lease, being heritable in succession, went on the death of the tenant, whether testate or intestate, to the heir-at-law.

Originally it was thought that the doctrine of *delectus personae*[49] operated to prevent anyone succeeding in the event of the tenant dying during the currency of the lease, and in that event the practice was for the subjects to revert to the landlord. However, it was not in the interests of landlords to insist on this rigid interpretation, because, as long as it was adhered to, the tenant could not be expected to lay out any expenditure on upkeep or improvement of the subjects, and the change in practice must probably be ascribed to this consideration more than to any other cause.[50] Where the tenant under a 15 years' lease of a salt-pan died, his heir, although not expressly mentioned in the deed, was held entitled to succeed, and the Court observed that the contrary view was consistent only with cases recorded two centuries before.[51] It is now well established that at common law the heir-at-law of the tenant succeeds even in the absence of any express destination to heirs.[52] If a lease is assigned and the assignee dies, the heir of the assignee succeeds to the lease, although he may not be expressly mentioned in the assignation.[53] The heir of an heir also succeeds.[54]

---

45 *Grant's Trs.* v *Arrol, supra.*
46 Succession (Scotland) Act 1964, s. 14 (1).
47 *Ibid.*, s. 37 (1) (b).
48 *Kennedy* v *Johnstone*, 1956 S.C. 39 *per* L.P. Clyde at p. 43.
49 *Supra*, p. 149.
50 Hume, *Lectures*, IV, 88.
51 *Thomson* v *Watson* (1750) Mor. 10337.
52 Bell, § 1219.
53 *Tailfer* v *M'Dougall* (1811) Hume 857.
54 Rankine, 157.

12

Although a lease is heritable, it transmits at common law to the heir of the deceased tenant by mere survivance. No service or other procedure has ever been required.[55] Procedure by general service or writ of acknowledgment was provided for long leases by the Registration of Leases (Scotland) Act 1857,[56] but these facilities (now repealed)[57] did not transmit the right, but were merely steps whereby the heir completed title to secure a real right.[58]

In the case of heirs-portioners, it has been stated on the analogy of heritable property that the eldest heir-portioner succeeds to the lease as her *praecipuum* subject to her accounting to the others,[59] or, if no division is possible, it will go to them all *pro indiviso*.[60] However, the principle of *praecipuum* seems only to regulate the division of an estate between heirs-portioners *inter se*.[61] The fact that most leases expressly exclude heirs-portioners and state that the eldest is to succeed, suggests that in the absence of words to the contrary heirs-portioners are entitled to share the lease, at least so far as the landlord is concerned, and in that event to avoid division it is probable that the eldest has a *praecipuum*.[62] A destination to heirs, excluding heirs-portioners, is equivalent to a declaration that the eldest shall succeed without division.[63] A lease is not mentioned as comprised in "*praecipuum*" in the leading case on heirs-portioners.[64] The *pro indiviso* share of each heir-portioner does not accresce to the survivors, but descends to her own heirs.[65] It has been held that where heirs-portioners succeeded as liferenters in a lease provided to a man "during his lifetime and that of his heirs", this was limited to the life of his immediate heirs; and so the death of one of the heirs-portioners put an end only to her *pro indiviso* share,[66] either because the surviving sister could only succeed to the lapsing share by succession and not by accretion,[67] or because there could be no division of an indivisible subject and the lease endured so long as any immediate heir of the original tenant was in life.[68]

Succession (Scotland) Act 1964. A detailed study of the provisions of the Act would be out of place in this work, and the reader is referred to the work cited.[69] What follows is a brief outline of its main provisions so far as they affect leases.

[55] Erskine, III, 8, 77; Bell, § 1680; Bell, *Leases,* 3rd ed., 399; McLaren, *op. cit.,* I, 99.
[56] ss. 7 and 8; Bell, § 1680.
[57] Succession (Scotland) Act 1964, s. 34 (2).
[58] McLaren, *supra.*
[59] Bell, § 1659; Rankine, 159; *Encyclopaedia of the Laws of Scotland,* Vol. 9, 90.
[60] *Young* v *Gerard* (1843) 6 D. 347; Bell, § 1219.
[61] Sandford, *Law of Succession,* I, 28.
[62] *Duff* v *Lady Keith* (1857) 19 D. 713; *Pratt* v *Abercromby* (1858) 21 D. 19.
[63] *Duff, supra; Pratt, supra.*
[64] *Callander* v *Harvey,* 1916 S.C. 420.
[65] Bell, § 1219.
[66] *Tweeddale* v *Dods* (1821) unreported, but commented on by Sandford, *supra.*
[67] Bell, § 1219.
[68] Sandford, *supra; Rankine, 160.
[69] Meston, *Succession (Scotland) Act 1964.*

The Act assimilated heritage and moveables for the purpose of the succession to the intestate estate of a person dying on or after 10th September 1964,[70] and laid down new rules for the division of intestate estates.[71] The estate of a deceased person is defined to include " the interest of a tenant under a tenancy or lease which was not expressed to expire on his death ", where such interest was held by the deceased immediately before his death.[72] For the purposes of the Act " lease " includes a sublease and " tenancy " includes a subtenancy.[73] The word " tenancy " is not defined. The Act does not affect the succession to or the devolution of the tenancy of any croft within the meaning of the Crofters (Scotland) Act 1955 Sec. 3 (1).[74] On the death of a tenant the lease falls to the executor representing the testate or intestate heirs.[75] Thus, apart from crofts, the status of heir-at-law has been rendered obsolete, so far as leases are concerned.[76]

Further, the Succession (Scotland) Act 1964 gives tenants a limited power of bequest by providing that a bequest by a tenant of his interest under a tenancy or lease to any one of the persons who, if the tenant had died intestate, would be, or would in any circumstances have been, entitled to succeed to his intestate estate by virtue of the Act shall not be treated as invalid by reason only that there is among the conditions of the tenancy or lease an implied condition prohibiting assignation.[77] This does not empower a tenant to bequeath his lease, if it contains an express prohibition of assignation, nor is he empowered to bequeath it to more than one person; but if such a prohibition is merely an implied one, then he may bequeath it to any *one* of the persons entitled to succeed to his intestate estate; to this limited extent he may select his

[70] *Ibid.,* s. 1.
[71] *Ibid.,* ss. 2-6.
[72] *Ibid.,* s. 36 (2).
[73] *Ibid.,* s. 36 (1).
[74] *Ibid.,* s. 37 (1) (b).
[75] *Ibid.,* s. 14 (1).
[76] The Act assimilates heritage and moveables for the purpose of intestate succession (s. 1 (1)), and so it is quite definite that, for the purpose of intestate estates, the status of heir-at-law has been abolished, except in the case of crofts, titles of honour etc. (s. 37 (1) (a)). Has it been abolished for testate cases? So far as ordinary heritable property was concerned, the heir-at-law had no rights except on intestacy, but he did have rights even in testate cases to a lease excluding assignees, as he took it not by succession but by destination. The Act assimilates heritage and moveables *for the purpose of administration and winding up,* and vested both in the executor to be administered and disposed of *according to law* (s. 14 (1)); but this does not amount to assimilation for the purpose of the substantive rules of succession. The Act provides that any reference in other statutes to the heir-at-law shall be construed as a reference to the persons entitled by virtue of the Act to succeed on intestacy to any part of the estate of the deceased (Sched. 2); but this does not amount to general abolition of the heir-at-law. Perhaps, however, this question is merely academic. In testate cases the lease will go to the legatee, if the deceased had power under the Act to bequeath it; if he did not have power, the lease will not be the subject of a valid bequest (s. 16 (2) (a)), and by implication the lease will fall into intestacy and will devolve according to the new rules, which apply to so much of the estate as is undisposed of by testamentary disposition (s. 36 (1)).
[77] *Ibid.,* s. 29 (1).

successor. The special provisions relating to bequest of agricultural leases contained in the Crofters' Holdings (Scotland) Act 1886 and the Agricultural Holdings (Scotland) Act 1949 are not prejudiced, but are slightly enlarged.[78]

The Succession (Scotland) Act 1964 also provides that, where the tenant himself has not made a valid bequest of his interest under a lease, or, if such a bequest has been made and is either not accepted by the legatee or in the case of an agricultural lease[79] is declared null and void under the Crofters' Holdings (Scotland) Act 1886 or the Agricultural Holdings (Scotland) Act 1949, then the executor is entitled to transfer the interest in the lease to any one of the persons entitled to succeed to the tenant's intestate estate or to claim legal rights or the prior rights of a surviving spouse out of the estate, notwithstanding any express or implied condition prohibiting assignation; but the executor is not entitled to transfer it to anyone else without the landlord's consent.[80] For the purposes of this section " lease " includes tenancy.[81] It will be noted that this section gives to the executor a wider power than the power of bequest given to the tenant himself by the same Act. The executor may select the successor to a lease from a slightly wider class of beneficiaries, and may do so in the face of an express, as well as an implied, prohibition;[82] the tenant may select his own successor only from his intestate heirs and then only in the face of an implied, and not an express, prohibition.[83]

Other provisions of the Act relating to an executor's powers with regard to leases will be dealt with later.[84]

Legal and Prior Rights. Legal Rights. Terce and courtesy were never due out of leases, because leases are not feudal rights.[85] The same applies to leases registered under the Registration of Leases (Scotland) Act 1857. In any event those rights are not exigible out of the estate of any person dying on or after 10th September 1964.[86]

However, the rights of *jus relicti, jus relictae* and legitim are still competent (a) where the deceased died intestate, after the prior rights of a surviving spouse on intestacy in the dwelling house and furniture[87] and to the financial provision on intestacy[88] have been satisfied out of the estate,[89] and (b) in all cases where the deceased died testate. For

[78] *Ibid.*, s. 29 (2) and Sched. 2.
[79] Within the meaning of the Small Landholders (Scotland) Acts 1886 to 1931 and the Agricultural Holdings (Scotland) Act 1949.
[80] Succession (Scotland) Act 1964, s. 16 (2).
[81] *Ibid.*, s. 16 (9).
[82] *Ibid.*, s. 16.
[83] *Ibid.*, s. 29.
[84] *Infra*, pp. 189, 190.
[85] Erskine, II, 9, 49; Bell, §§ 1598, 1605; McLaren, *op. cit.*, 1, 92, 96.
[86] Succession (Scotland) Act 1964, s. 10 (1).
[87] *Ibid.*, s. 8.
[88] *Ibid.*, s. 9.
[89] *Ibid.*, s. 10 (2).

the purpose of calculating legal rights, the distinction between heritable and moveable property is preserved, and as *jus relicti, jus relictae* and legitim are exigible from the net moveable estate only and as leases are heritable, those rights are not exigible from leases. However, as stated above, an executor is empowered to transfer a lease to any one of the persons entitled to claim legal rights.[90]

Prior Rights of Spouse on Intestacy. The Succession (Scotland) Act 1964 introduced new rights in favour of the surviving spouse of a person dying intestate on or after 10th September 1964, and these can affect leases in two ways:—(a) a lease may itself be the subject of the right and (b) a lease may be transferred by the executor to a surviving spouse entitled to claim a prior right.

Right to Lease of House. Where an intestate estate includes a relevant interest in a dwelling house, in which the surviving spouse was ordinarily resident at the time of the intestate's death, the surviving spouse is entitled to that interest, if its value does not exceed £15,000. If its value exceeds that figure, the surviving spouse is entitled to the sum of £15,000 in lieu.[91]

There are two other exceptional cases where the spouse is not entitled to the relevant interest in the dwelling house itself, but to a sum equal to its value. The first exception is where the dwelling house forms part only of the subjects comprised in one tenancy or lease, under which the deceased was the tenant.[92] The result of this exception is that a landlord cannot be compelled to accept a surviving spouse as tenant of only part of the subjects of a lease. The other exception is where the relevant interest forms the whole or part of subjects, an interest in which is comprised in the intestate estate and which were used by the intestate for carrying on a trade, profession or occupation, and the value of the estate as a whole would be likely to be substantially diminished, if the dwelling house were disposed of otherwise than with the assets of the trade, profession or occupation.[93]

" Relevant interest " is defined to mean the interest of an owner or the interest of a tenant subject in either case to any heritable debt secured over the interest.[94] " Tenant " means a tenant under a tenancy or lease (whether of the dwelling house alone or of the dwelling house together with other subjects), but not a tenancy to which the Rent and Mortgage Interest Restriction Acts 1920 to 1939 apply.[95] " Dwelling house " includes a part of a building occupied (at the date of death of the intestate) as a separate dwelling, including any garden or portion of ground attached

[90] *Ibid.*, s. 16 (2).
[91] *Ibid.*, s. 8.
[92] *Ibid.*, s. 8 (2) (a).
[93] *Ibid.*, s. 8 (2) (b).
[94] *Ibid.*, s. 8 (6) (d).
[95] *Ibid.*, s. 8 (6) (d).

to, and usually occupied with, the dwelling house or otherwise required for its amenity or convenience.[96]

If the intestate had a relevant interest in more than one dwelling house, the surviving spouse is given six months to decide which to choose,[97] the only requirement being that the surviving spouse must have been ordinarily resident therein at the date of death.[98] Provision is made for the determination by arbitration of the value of the relevant interest in a dwelling house.[99]

The general effect as applied to leases is that if a tenant of a dwelling house (other than one subject to the Rent Restriction Acts) dies intestate leaving a surviving spouse, such spouse is entitled to succeed to the lease subject to certain exceptions when he or she must take cash instead. It does not matter if the lease is not assignable, as special power is given to the executor to transfer in satisfaction of prior rights.[1] Where the deceased intestate had a relevant interest in more than one dwelling house, the surviving spouse would normally choose the more valuable. It should be noted that what the surviving spouse is entitled to is the relevant interest, not the dwelling house itself. As the value of a lease of property is normally less than the value of a similar property, the surviving spouse would normally choose the house which the deceased owned in preference to the lease of another house of which the deceased was merely the tenant.

LEGAL CHARACTER OF SUCCESSOR

Legatee. A person, to whom a lease is bequeathed by virtue of an express or implied power of bequest or by virtue of a statutory power of bequest, does not simply take the lease as part of the deceased tenant's succession. The legal character of the legatee is that of a voluntary assignee.[2] Thus, where a long lease provided for a small casualty to be paid on the succession of every heir or lineal descendant of a deceased tenant and for a much larger payment on the entry of every assignee or singular successor, it was held that the larger sum was payable by the tenant's trustees to whom he had bequeathed his estate in trust for behoof of his children.[3] A bequest of a lease is not exactly like a demise of property, but operates much more in the way of an assignation;[4] and it has been questioned whether the right, which the testator enjoyed under a lease, is to be regarded in all respects as if it is an item of property forming part of the testator's estate, either to be taken up by the legatee or to fall into intestacy.[5]

[96] *Ibid.*, s. 8 (6) (a).
[97] *Ibid.*, s. 8 (1).
[98] *Ibid.*, s. 8 (4).
[99] *Ibid.*, s. 8 (5).
[1] *Ibid*, s. 16 (2).
[2] *Crawford* v *Livingstone's Trs.*, 1938 S.C. 609.
[3] *Ibid.*
[4] *Grant's Trs.* v *Arrol*, 1954 S.C. 306 *per* Lord Sorn at p. 312.
[5] *Ibid.*

Possession by the legatee may not always be sufficient, at any rate if the possession can be ascribed to any reason other than the bequest. A tenant under a lease of urban property (to which the Rent Acts applied), continued from year to year by tacit relocation, bequeathed his whole estate to his widow, who continued to possess the subjects until her own death, but did not intimate the bequest to the landlord; in an action by the landlord for the ejection of the son of the marriage who had resided in the subjects since before his father's death, it was held (1) that, as the bequest had never been intimated to the landlord, the widow's occupation could not be attributed to the bequest by her husband, but to her statutory right of tenancy as widow, and (2) that her failure to exercise the contractual right transmitted to her did amount to a failure in the original tenant's succession resulting in intestacy; and that accordingly the son had no right, either statutory or contractual, to remain in occupation.[6] It is therefore advisable for a legatee to intimate the bequest to the landlord, and, of course, if the lease is an agricultural one, he must do so.[7]

Heir-at-Law. The heir-at-law of a tenant who died before 10th September 1964 could succeed to a lease in one of two situations. The first occurred on the intestacy of the tenant, and the heir took a lease, which the deceased had power to, but did not dispose of by will. The second situation occurred not only in intestate cases but in all cases where the tenant did not have the power to dispose of the lease by will. In the second situation the heir-at-law did not succeed in his capacity as the person succeeding to the heritable estate on intestacy, but in a special capacity, and this rendered the heir-at-law's position as regards leases a somewhat anomalous one.

It had been settled that the heir-at-law, who at common law succeeded to a lease of ordinary duration containing an exclusion of assignees, did so not by right of succession to the deceased tenant, but in his own right *ex lege* or by force of the destination expressed or implied in the contract with the landlord.[8] Where a tenant under a 19 years' lease of urban property, granted to him and his heirs excluding assignees and subtenants, died, it was held that the heir, who took up the lease, did not incur passive representation for the debts of his predecessor, because he took the lease, not as representing his ancestor, but in his own right.[9] " The father's right of tenancy terminated with his life. He had no power to assign the lease; he had no power to nominate an heir, because it has been decided, and cannot now be disputed, that where assignees are excluded and the heir is admitted by the terms of the lease, it must be taken by the heir of line. And therefore there was nothing in the father

---

[6] *Ibid.*; but this would not now be the position in view of the rights given to a " second successor " by the Rent Act 1965, s. 13.
[7] Crofters Holdings (Scotland) Act 1886, s. 16; Agricultural Holdings (Scotland) Act 1949, ss. 20 and 21; amended by Succession (Scotland) Act 1964, Sched. 2.
[8] *Macalister* v *Macalister* (1859) 21 D. 560; Bell, § 1219; Rankine, 166.
[9] *Bain* v *Mackenzie* (1896) 23 R. 528.

under this contract of lease at any time except the interest which it gave him during his own life ".[10]

The foregoing principle applied where there was a destination expressed in favour of " heirs " or " successors " or where such a destination was not expressed but merely implied, and also where the heir took the lease in the character of heir of provision, as in a lease to "A, whom failing B ".[11] A testator, who was tenant under six leases of salmon fishings, in five of which the destination was to the tenant and his heirs and in the other to the tenant, assignees and subtenants being excluded in all cases, died leaving a will, in which he bequeathed a share of residue to his heir-at-law in full satisfaction of legitim and other legal claims; it was held that the leases did not form part of the testator's succession, and that the heir-at-law took them in his own right by force of the destinations in the leases; and that accordingly he neither forfeited the testamentary provision in his favour nor was bound to collate the value of the leases in the event of his claiming legitim.[12] While this principle may have been true of a lease of ordinary duration, it may not have applied to a lease of such duration that it amounted in law to an alienation, when the exclusion of assignees would be ineffectual.[13]

At common law a lease is heritable in succession, and it was for long thought that the heir-at-law succeeding to a lease, whether containing an exclusion of assignees or not, must collate the lease as a condition of his sharing the moveable estate.[14] Apparently this view was based on the analogy of an heir of entail, who as a condition of sharing the moveable fund had to collate the heritage to which he succeeded as heir of entail.[15] It is to be noted that the question of collating a lease might arise not only in intestate cases, where the tenant failed to bequeath his lease, assuming that he had power to do so, but also in testate cases, where he had no power of bequest over a lease excluding assignees. It was questioned whether there was any common fund, where assignees were excluded in the lease and there was no power of bequest, because then the heir at law did not take the lease as part of his ancestor's succession, and was not in the same position as an heir of entail, who was an heir of provision.[16]

---

[10] Ibid., per Lord Kinnear at p. 532.
[11] Macalister, supra.
[12] Paterson's J.F. v Paterson, 1956 S.L.T. 223.
[13] Bain v Mackenzie, supra, obiter dicta of Lords M'Laren and Kinnear at pp. 532 and 533.
[14] M'Feggan v Murray (1805) Hume 887; Stewart v M'Naughton (1824) 3 S. 351 (N.E. 250); Robertson (1841) 3 D. 345; Mitchell (1847) 10 D. 148; Bell, § 1912; McLaren, Wills and Succession, 3rd ed., I, 151; Fraser, Husband and Wife, 1050.
[15] Gilmour v Gilmour, 13 Dec. 1809 F.C.; Johnston v Johnston (1814) Hume 290; Anstruther v Anstruther (1836) 14 S. 272; (1836) 2 Sh. & Macl. 369; Marquis of Breadalbane v Marquis of Chandos (1836) 14 S. 309; (1836) 2 Sh. & Macl. 377.
[16] Rankine, 170, following Bain v Mackenzie (1896) 23 R. 528; but see Bell, § 1922.

Finally, it was settled that a lease excluding assignees need not be collated.[17]

Statutory Successor. As regards deaths on or after 10th September 1964, questions may arise as to the legal character of persons succeeding to leases by virtue of the Succession (Scotland) Act 1964.

A person, to whom a tenant by virtue of his statutory power[18] has bequeathed a lease containing an implied exclusion of assignees, will be in the same position as a legatee. So also is a legatee of a lease of agricultural subjects.[19] The tenant had power, if only a statutory power, to assign the lease and to nominate his successor.

On the other hand, where there has been no bequest, the executor, in whom there is vested an interest in a lease containing an express or implied prohibition of assignation, takes the lease by force of statute. Any person to whom the executor may transfer it by virtue of his administrative power,[20] would seem to be in a similar position to an heir-at-law,[21] but taking the lease by force of statute and selection by the executor.

The rules governing the incidence of the liability for debts between particular parts of a deceased's estate have not been altered.[22] The position now is that the executor of a deceased tenant will normally pay all his debts from the whole estate. If he does not pay debts due from the leasehold subjects, that will be reflected in the value at which the assignee selected by the executor takes over the lease to account of his share.

The question of collation *inter haeredes* does not arise in respect of deaths on or after 10th September, 1964.

Adoption of Lease. A lease may contain onerous obligations on the tenant, and no person is obliged to take up the succession to it any more than he is bound to take up the succession to any other property. Also, with the exception of leases of normal duration excluding assignees, a person taking up a lease rendered himself liable for the deceased's tenant's debts. By the Conveyancing (Scotland) Act 1874 an heir-at-law was not liable for the debts of his ancestor beyond the value of the estate to which he succeeded.[23] Although the heir-at-law acquired a personal right to the heritable property, including a lease, by mere survivance,[24] he was not liable for his predecessor's debts, unless he completed his title or took possession of the lands and so incurred

---

[17] *Paterson's J.F.* v *Paterson, supra;* see article in 1964 S.L.T. (News) 61 criticising this decision.
[18] Succession (Scotland) Act 1964, s. 29 (1).
[19] Crofters Holdings (Scotland) Act 1886, s. 16; Agricultural Holdings (Scotland) Act 1949, s. 20; as amended by Succession (Scotland) Act 1964, Sched. 2.
[20] Succession (Scotland) Act 1964, s. 16 (2).
[21] *Supra.*
[22] Succession (Scotland) Act 1964, s. 14 (3).
[23] Conveyancing (Scotland) Act 1874, s. 12, repealed by Succession (Scotland) Act 1964, s. 34 (2).
[24] Conveyancing (Scotland) Act 1874, s. 9, repealed by Succession (Scotland) Act 1964, s. 34 (2).

what was known as passive representation.[25] There is no longer any
specified time for deliberation, but an heir is still entitled to six months
before any action of constitution may be brought against him.[26] Possession by the heir during that period by cultivating the land and other
acts of management will not necessarily be regarded as indicating an
intention to take the lease, but it is prudent to let the landlord know
that the possession is merely tentative; if his actings are more than acts
of ordinary administration, they will indicate an intention to take up
the lease.[27]

When an heir or other successor takes possession of the subjects of a
lease, he should communicate to the landlord the footing on which possession is taken, because his actings, if equivocal, may be founded on
as showing an intention of taking up the lease on one hand, or of
abandoning it on the other.[28] The intention to take up a lease, and
the intention to abandon it, may each be proved not only by express
words but also tacitly by the party's conduct, and abandonment has
been inferred from the heir's conduct in several cases. Sometimes it is
a question of fact whether the persons in possession are only managers
for the heir or are pretended tenants.[29] Long delay on the part of the
heir in claiming possession was not enough to infer abandonment, if the
heir was abroad and ignorant of the destination in the lease.[30]

The foregoing paragraph applies also to the case of a tenant dying
on or after 10th September 1964, except that it is not the heir-at-law
who is involved. If the succession is intestate, it is the executor who will
decide whether to adopt the lease or to invoke his statutory power of
terminating it.[31] If there has been a valid bequest by the deceased tenant,
the legatee will decide whether to adopt it.

Acceptance by Landlord. Where assignation is excluded and not
permitted by statute, the landlord may object to a bequest by the tenant.[32]
The landlord, however, may expressly agree to, or tacitly acquiesce in,
an alteration of a destination or in a bequest by the tenant.[33] The
heir-at-law at common law or the executor representing the intestate
heirs under the Succession (Scotland) Act 1964 may challenge a deed

---

[25] *Fenton Livingstone* v *Crichton's Trs.,* 1908 S.C. 1208.
[26] Bell, § 1638.
[27] Rankine, 167.
[28] *M'Gavin* v *Sturrock's Tr.* (1891) 18 R. 576; *Moncrieffe* v *Ferguson* (1896) 24
R. 47.
[29] *Munro* v *Munro* (1825) 4 S. 328 (N.E. 231); *Watt* v *Duff* (1852) 14 D. 879;
Wilson v *Stewart* (1853) 16 D. 106; *Gray* v *Low* (1859) 21 D. 293; *Forbes* v
Ure (1856) 18 D. 577.
[30] *Crichton* v *Lady Keith* (1857) 19 D. 713.
[31] *Infra,* p. 189.
[32] *Deuchar* v *Minto* (1798) Mor. 15295; *Cunningham* v *Grieve,* 8 March 1803 F.C.,
Mor. 15298, (1804) 4 Pat. 571, (1805) Mor. App. *voce* Tack 9, (1806) 6 Pat.
16; *Lowden* v *Adam,* 21 Nov. 1805 F.C., Mor. App. *voce* Tack 10; *Gray* v *Low*
(1859) 21 D. 293; *Colquhoun's Trs.* v *Purdie,* 1946 S.N. 3; *Grant's Trs.* v
Arrol, 1954 S.C. 306. See Hume, *Lectures,* IV, 93.
[33] *Darroch* v *Rennie,* 8 March 1803 F.C., Mor. 15301; *Gray* v *Low, supra.*

or bequest excluding him from the succession on various grounds, but he cannot do so on the ground of the exclusion of assignees in the lease, that objection being personal to the landlord.[34] If the landlord fails to challenge it, the bequest becomes secure by acquiescence. A successful challenge by the landlord does not have the effect of cancelling the lease, but only of letting in the succession of the heir-at-law or executor representing the intestate heirs. Once the landlord has repudiated the bequest, not necessarily by legal action, the heir-at-law or the executor representing the intestate heirs has a title to pursue an action of declarator of his right to the lease without the concurrence of the landlord in the action.[35]

It is not competent for the heir-at-law at common law nor for an intestate heir, to whom the executor transfers a lease, to relinquish possession and put someone else in his place, without the consent of the landlord.[36] If he is under a disability and a manager is appointed to take charge, the question may arise whether the arrangement amounts to a prohibited assignation or a *bona fide* arrangement for the management of the subjects.[37]

Abandonment of Lease. At common law, if the heir declined to take up the lease, and it had not yet come to its natural termination, the lease reverted to the landlord, who might relet the subjects. On general principles of contract the landlord had a claim against the tenant's personal representatives for any arrears of rent outstanding at his death.

The liability of the representatives for future rent had not been satisfactorily decided. In one case where both the heir and the executor refused to take up the lease for the remainder of its term, the question arose as to the liability of the executor for loss sustained by the landlord through non-implement of the contract.[38] The Lord Ordinary described such a claim as not an action for damages strictly or properly so called, but as an action for liquidated rent expressly covenanted to be paid, and all that the defender could claim was that the landlord should deduct whatever he could fairly make from the subjects, which had been thrown back to him. A court of seven judges to which the case eventually went, although finding the executor liable, proceeded upon the ground that the question was *res judicata* between the parties, and reserved their opinion on the general question. There can be little doubt that the Lord Ordinary was right, although there was no proper review of the question.[39] The measure of damages in such a case would appear to be the rent due to the natural ish, suitably discounted and under deduction of rents actually received from reletting the subjects.[40]

---

[34] *Hay* v *Wood*, 8 Dec. 1801 F.C., Mor. 15297; Bell, § 1218.
[35] *Murdoch* v *Murdoch's Trs.* (1863) 1 M. 330.
[36] *Gray* v *Low* (1859) 21 D. 293.
[37] *Lyon* v *Irvine* (1874) 1 R. 512.
[38] *Bethune* v *Morgan* (1874) 2 R. 186.
[39] *Strathdee* v *Paterson* 1913 1 S.L.T. 498 (O.H.); Rankine, 168.
[40] *Bethune* v *Morgan, supra, per* Lord Gifford at pp. 188-189.

There may be other obligations on the tenant remaining unfulfilled at the time of his death, such as repairs and improvements, and his representatives will be liable to implement these, or failing implement to compensate the landlord for any loss.[41] At common law the executor could not claim the lease as of right, although the landlord might accept him, nor could the executor be compelled by the landlord to take up the lease. Possibly, if the landlord insisted against the executor, equity would require him, as a condition of so insisting, to receive the executor as tenant.[42] While an offer by the tenant's executors to take up the lease would be a good answer to an action of damages for breach of the lease so far as depending on discontinued possession, it could be rejected by the landlord and was no answer to a claim which became due at a removing.[43] Although normally a lease is so worded that the tenant and his " heirs, executors and representatives " or his " heirs, executors and successors " are expressly bound to pay the rent and to perform the tenant's obligations, the omission of these words did not detract from the liability of the executors in cases where the heir renounced the lease. Where the heir renounced, the executors were bound if the tenant was bound.[44]

The effect of an obligation imposed on the tenant " and his heirs, executors and successors (or representatives) " jointly and severally has already been considered.[45]

In the case of a tenant dying on or after 10th September 1964, the risk of a lease being abandoned had been greatly diminished by the statutory power given to an executor to transfer a lease.[46] In default of a valid and effective bequest of a lease, the executor is empowered to select a successor from among the persons entitled to succeed to the intestate estate or to claim legal or prior rights, and, notwithstanding any express or implied exclusion of assignees, the landlord is compelled to accept such a nominee. There is some likelihood that in the deceased's family there will be someone interested in carrying on the lease, which was not always possible when only the heir-at-law had any right in the matter at common law. Moreover, a lease comprised in the estate of a deceased tenant now vests in his executor by virtue of confirmation.[47] If there is no valid bequest of the lease or if the executor does not select a successor, the executor may take up the lease for the purpose of administering it according to law.[48] In any event, it is the executor who will be liable *qua* executor to the landlord for any arrears of rent outstanding at the tenant's death or for any other obligations on the tenant then remaining unfulfilled. A claim by the landlord for damages in

[41] *Scott's Exrs.* v *Hepburn* (1876) 3 R. 816.
[42] *Bethune* v *Morgan, supra.*
[43] *Scott's Exrs.* v *Hepburn, supra;* Rankine, 169.
[44] *Scott's Exrs.* v *Hepburn, supra.*
[45] *Supra,* p. 61.
[46] Succession (Scotland) Act 1964, s. 16 (2).
[47] *Ibid.,* ss. 14 (1) and 16 (1).
[48] *Ibid.,* s. 14 (1).

respect of premature termination by reason of the tenant's death will normally arise only in the event of the executor invoking his statutory power of termination.[49]

Statutory Power of Termination. The Succession (Scotland) Act 1964 introduced new provisions enabling a lease to be terminated in cases where it might otherwise have had to be abandoned.[50] Irrespective of the provisions of a lease or of any statutory or other provision, the lease may be terminated either by the executor or by the landlord (a) if the executor is satisfied that he cannot dispose of it according to law and so informs the landlord, or (b) if the lease is not in fact disposed of within a certain period; the period is one year or such longer period as may be fixed by agreement or failing agreement by the Sheriff on the summary application by the executor, the period running from the date of death[51] (except for an agricultural lease being the subject of a petition to the Land Court when the period runs from the date of the determination or withdrawal of the petition or application).[52] Due notice of determination must be given by the landlord or executor, the period for other than agricultural subjects being six months, without prejudice to any enactment prescribing a shorter period of notice for the lease in question.[53]

The new statutory power to terminate a lease is not to prejudice any claim by any party to a lease for compensation or damages in respect of the termination of the lease or any rights under it; but any award of compensation or damages in respect of such termination by the executor is enforceable against the executry estate and not against the executor personally.[54]

Leases vested in Executors. The Succession (Scotland) Act 1964 provides that the whole estate of a person dying on or after 10th September 1964 (whether testate or intestate) shall vest by virtue of Confirmation in the executor who shall administer and dispose of it according to law.[55] The estate vested in the executor includes any interest being the interest of a tenant under a lease which is comprised in the estate of a deceased person.[56] The Act makes special provision for account to be taken of the fact that a lease is vested in an executor only *qua* executor with regard to breaches of the conditions of a lease.[57] In the case of agricultural leases, the Land Court is not to make an

---

[49] *Ibid.*, s. 16 (5).
[50] *Ibid.*, s. 16 (3).
[51] *Ibid.*, s. 16 (3) (a).
[52] *Ibid.*, s. 16 (3) (b).
[53] *Ibid.*, s. 16 (4).
[54] *Ibid.*, s. 16 (5).
[55] *Ibid.*, s. 14 (1).
[56] *Ibid.*, s. 16 (1).
[57] *Ibid.*, s. 16 (7).

order for removal under the Small Landholders and Agricultural Holdings (Scotland) Act 1931,[58] nor is an arbiter to make an award in favour of the landlord under the Agricultural Holdings (Scotland) Act 1949,[59] unless satisfied that it is reasonable that it should be made, having regard to the fact that the lease is vested in the executor in his capacity as executor.[60] In the case of non-agricultural leases, the Court shall not grant decree in an action of removing against the executor for a breach of a condition of the lease, unless satisfied that the condition alleged to have been breached is one which it is reasonable to expect the executor to have observed, having regard to the fact that the lease is vested in him in his capacity as an executor.[61]

Where an agricultural lease is the subject of a valid bequest by the deceased, the fact that the interest is vested in the executor does not affect the detailed provisions in favour of legatees contained in the Crofters' Holdings (Scotland) Act 1886 and the Agricultural Holdings (Scotland) Act 1949.[62]

Transfer by Executor. It has already been seen that the Succession (Scotland) Act 1964 specially empowered the executor to transfer an interest in a lease to any one of a limited class of beneficiaries, notwithstanding that the lease contains an express or implied condition prohibiting assignation, but not to transfer the interest to any other person without the consent of the landlord.[63] He may of course transfer such a lease to anyone with the landlord's consent, and of course he may transfer a lease to anyone if there is no prohibition. The deceased himself may have exercised an express or implied power of bequest or he may have exercised his statutory power of bequest in the face of an implied prohibition.[64] In all those cases the executor may affect the transfer by the normal method of assignation. Alternatively, if the lease is to be transferred to a person in satisfaction of legal rights or prior rights, to a person entitled to share in the estate by virtue of the Act or to a person entitled to take the lease under any testamentary disposition of the deceased, the executor may effect a transfer by endorsing on the Confirmation (or certificate of confirmation in respect of the lease) a docket in that person's favour.[65]

Ultimus Haeres. In the absence of heirs, the Crown succeeds to a lease as *ultimus haeres,* but this is inferred by analogy from heritable property in general and most of the cases refer to bastardy.[66] The Crown

[58] 1931 Act, s. 3.
[59] 1949 Act, ss. 27 (2) and 25 (2) (f).
[60] Succession (Scotland) Act 1964, s. 16 (6).
[61] *Ibid.,* s. 16 (7).
[62] *Ibid.,* s. 16 (8).
[63] *Ibid.,* s. 16 (2).
[64] *Ibid.,* s. 29 (1).
[65] *Ibid.,* s. 15 (2).
[66] Erskine, III, 10, 2-4; Bell, § 1669; McLaren, *Wills and Succession,* 3rd ed., I, 79-80; II, 763.

is not, properly speaking, an heir, but is treated in all respects as one, except that it does not satisfy the definition of an heir in a special destination; it is not kept out by an exclusion of assignees, and this rule is not affected by the fact that it cannot possess of itself, but must pass on the right to a donatary, who therefore succeeds as an heir in right of the Crown and not as an assignee.[67] The right of the Crown as *ultimus haeres* to succeed to any estate, to which no person is entitled is expressly saved by the Succession (Scotland) Act 1964.[68]

Choice of Law. Leases, being heritable or immoveable property according to Scots Law, devolve according to the *lex loci situs*,[69] and so the succession to a lease of subjects situated in Scotland is governed by the law of Scotland, notwithstanding the domicile of the deceased. The Succession (Scotland) Act 1964 did not alter any rule as to the choice of law.[70]

[67] Bell, *supra;* McLaren, *supra;* Rankine, 160.
[68] Succession (Scotland) Act 1964, s. 7.
[69] *Mackintosh* v *May* (1895) 22 R. 345.
[70] s. 37 (2).

Chapter XII

BANKRUPTCY

Bankruptcy of Landlord. The effect of insolvency on the power to grant leases has already been considered, and it has been seen that the subsequent sequestration of the granter does not affect the validity of a fair and just lease granted by him.[1] An adjudger or trustee in sequestration on the landlord's estate is a singular successor of the landlord, and the security of the tenant's tenure depends on whether the tenant has a real right to his lease under the Leases Act 1449.[2]

A trustee in sequestration is bound by the real conditions of the lease, including an agreement for abatement of rent.[3] A trustee, who takes possession of the landlord's heritable estate and so adopts the lease, renders himself liable to implement any obligations incumbent on the landlord to the extent of the rent received by him, but not to any greater extent.[4] The trustee's primary duty, however, is to realise the estate, and if he proceeds to sell the subjects and does not take up and adopt the lease, the trustee incurs no liability for special obligations such as repairs, and the tenant can only rank on the bankrupt's estate in respect of a claim for damages.[5] Where a landlord resumed portions of subjects in a lease and paid the tenant annual compensation, which exceeded the rent, it was held on the landlord's sequestration that the tenant had no preferred ranking for the difference, but only an ordinary ranking on the landlord's estate.[6]

The trustee has no higher right than the landlord would have had, and a tenant who has prepaid his rent to the landlord before the latter's sequestration cannot be compelled to pay it again to the trustee.[7]

On the principle that a debt incurred after the bankruptcy cannot be compensated by a debt due before it, a tenant cannot set off a debt due to him by his landlord against the rent becoming due for his occupation after the landlord's bankruptcy.[8] However, he can set off such a debt against arrears of rent.[9] If there is an express stipulation that the tenant shall have the right to retain his rent against a debt, it would seem that

[1] *Supra*, p. 46.
[2] See Chapter IV.
[3] *Lindsay* v *Webster* (1841) 4 D. 231.
[4] *Harvie* v *Haldane* (1833) 11 S. 872.
[5] *Harkness* v *Rattray* (1878) 16 S.L.R. 117.
[6] *Bertram* v *Guild* (1880) 7 R. 1122.
[7] *Davidson* v *Boyd* (1868) 7 M. 77.
[8] Goudy, *Bankruptcy*, 4th ed., 559.
[9] *Ibid.;* Rankine, 326.

the tenant may plead compensation, if he is sued before he is legally interpelled by the publication of the sequestration.[10]

Bankruptcy of Tenant. Effect on Lease. The bankruptcy of the tenant does not itself annul a lease, except in the case of a lease to a firm or unincorporated company from which assignees are excluded.[11] The tenant, though bankrupt, may still continue in possession, provided he pays the rent regularly and performs the other obligations of the contract.[12] It has been held that, where sequestration of the tenant of an urban subject let on a year's lease occurred in the middle of the term, the bankrupt could not be sued for the balance of the rent subsequent to the date of sequestration although he continued in possession,[13] but this decision has been questioned.[14] Neither the insolvency of a tenant, nor his notour bankruptcy, nor sequestration for rent, nor his judicial sequestration, nor the granting of a trust deed for creditors gives the landlord a right to annul a lease, unless there is a stipulation to that effect.[15] An implied exclusion of assignees does not affect the position.[16] A lease may contain an express exclusion of assignees, but this is construed as giving the landlord an option to refuse to consent to an assignation to a trustee in sequestration, and it cannot be founded on by the bankrupt.[17]

Irritancy. A lease, however, may contain an express provision to the effect that, in the event of the tenant becoming notour bankrupt, allowing a poinding and sale to take place, granting a trust deed for creditors, or, though no such trust conveyance is executed, possessing the subjects only nominally or through a manager for others than himself, the lease shall in the option of the landlord become null and void and the landlord shall be at liberty summarily and without any declarator or irritancy or other process to resume possession.[18] There are many variants of the clause, but, however it is worded, the option to terminate rests with the landlord alone.[19] Further, even although the tenant has been sequestrated, the existence of such a clause does not dispense with the necessity for giving notice to remove.[20] The landlord must exercise his option within a reasonable time.[21] If he irritates the lease, it is held

[10] *Campbell of Auchinbreck's Crs.* v *M'Lauchlan* (1748) Mor. 1736; Hume, *Lectures*, IV, 76-77; Goudy, *op. cit.*, 559; Rankine, 326.
[11] *Supra* p. 63.
[12] *Crawford* v *Maxwell* (1758) Mor. 15307; Bell, *Comm.*, 7th ed., I, 76.
[13] *Fraser* v *Robertson* (1881) 8 R. 347.
[14] Goudy, *Bankruptcy*, 4th ed., 368.
[15] Rankine, 542.
[16] *Supra* p. 150.
[17] *Dobie* v *Marquis of Lothian* (1864) 2 M. 788.
[18] *Encyclopaedia of Scottish Legal Styles*, Vol. 6, No. 146.
[19] *Kinloch* v *Mansfield* (1836) 14 S. 905; *Bidoulac* v *Sinclair's Tr.* (1889) 17 R. 144.
[20] *Waugh* v *More Nisbett* (1882) 19 S.L.R. 427.
[21] *Tennent* v *Macdonald* (1836) 14 S. 976; *Lindsay* v *Hogg* (1855) 17 D. 788; *Bidoulac* v *Sinclair's Tr.*, *supra*; Rankine, 543.

13

to have been terminated by the landlord in exercise of his option, and therefore he is not entitled to damages for breach of contract;[22] but he is entitled to damages if he does not irritate and the lease is given up by the bankrupt tenant or his trustee.[23]

There is no difficulty in ascertaining whether an irritancy has been incurred, when the fact on which it is founded is a trust deed, notour bankruptcy, sequestration in bankruptcy, or landlord's sequestration.[24] However, difficulty may arise when the irritancy is merely founded on the tenant's "insolvency".[25] Difficulties may also arise if there is a plurality of tenants.[26] Where a lease to two joint tenants provided for an irritancy in the event of either of them being sequestrated, and one of them was sequestrated, while the other, being solvent, offered to go on with the lease, it was held that the landlord having refused to accept this offer and having irritated the lease, could not claim damages for diminution of rent, as it had been terminated by the landlord by his own option.[27]

Where a lease provided that on its expiry the landlord should pay the tenant a specified sum expended on improvements, and the landlord enforced a conventional irritancy on the tenant's bankruptcy and resumed possession, it was held that, notwithstanding the premature termination by the tenant's bankruptcy, the landlord by the terms of the contract had to pay him that sum;[28] and a minority opinion was expressed that the landlord, having taken advantage of the conventional irritancy, was bound to pay the sum at once.[29] It was later held, where in similar circumstances the landlord accepted a renunciation from the tenant and his trustee, that the landlord was bound to pay the full sum at once without discount, as, by accepting a renunciation, the landlord had agreed that that should be taken as the termination of the lease for all purposes.[30]

Vesting in Trustee. The act and warrant of confirmation in favour of a trustee in sequestration transfers to and vests in him the whole heritable estate (including leases) belonging to the bankrupt for behoof of the creditors absolutely and irredeemably as at the date of the sequestration to the same effect as if a decree of adjudication subject to

[22] *Walker's Trs.* v *Manson* (1886) 13 R. 1198; *Bidoulac* v *Sinclair's Tr., supra.*
[23] *Kinloch* v *Mansfield, supra; Bidoulac* v *Sinclair's Tr., supra.*
[24] *Forbes* v *Duncan,* 2 June 1812 F.C.; *Hall* v *Lady Grant* (1831) 9 S. 612; *Stewart* v *Watson* (1864) 2 M. 1414; *Buttercase & Geddie's Tr.* v *Geddie* (1897) 24 R. 1128.
[25] *Hog* v *Morton* (1825) 3 S. 617 (N.E. 433); *Moncrieff* v *Hay* (1842) 5 D. 249; Goudy, *Bankruptcy,* 4th ed., 15-16; Rankine, 544.
[26] *Tennent* v *Macdonald* (1836) 14 S. 976; *Young* v *Gerrard* (1843) 6 D. 347; *Burns* v *Martin* (1887) 14 R. (H.L.) 20.
[27] *Buttercase and Geddie's Tr.* v *Geddie* (1897) 24 R. 1128.
[28] *Pendreigh's Tr.* v *Dewar* (1871) 9 M. 1037.
[29] *Ibid.,* per Lord Kinloch at p. 1043.
[30] *Walker's Trs.* v *Manson* (1886) 13 R. 1198.

no reversion had been pronounced in his favour.[31] It has long been settled that a lease, in which assignees are only impliedly excluded, may be attached by adjudication.[32] A lease containing an express exclusion of assignees is not adjudgeable,[33] but the effect of a clause of exclusion is that the lease passes to the trustee, subject to the right of the landlord to object.[34]

It is not entirely clear whether a trustee under a trust deed for creditors is a voluntary assignee or a legal assignee.[35] It has already been seen that an implied exclusion of assignees excludes only voluntary assignees and not quasi-judicial assignees,[36] while an express exclusion on the other hand does exclude quasi-judicial assignees.[37] The following paragraphs are intended to apply to a trustee under a trust deed for creditors as well as to a trustee in a judicial sequestration. The bankrupt's estate having vested in him, the questions arise as to whether the trustee wishes to adopt the lease, and, if so, whether the landlord can be compelled to accept him.

Adoption of Lease. If assignees and subtenants are excluded, the landlord cannot be compelled to accept the trustee as tenant. The only method of carrying on the lease would be for the trustee to arrange with the bankrupt to carry on as tenant.[38] Actual possession by the tenant is indispensable, but temporary non-residence is not enough to infer abandonment of possession.[39] If assignation is excluded, but subletting is not excluded, the trustee may obtain a sublease.[40] The trustee can always ask for an assignation or sublease from the bankrupt and take the chance of the landlord objecting to it or enforcing an irritancy.[41] It is always possible for the landlord to waive his objection, either conditionally or unconditionally,[42] and the tenant has no title to object.[43]

If the trustee wishes to adopt the lease, he does so by possessing the subjects and paying the rent. He may also obtain an assignation from

---

[31] Bankruptcy (Scotland) Act 1913, s. 97. See also *White* v *Stevenson*, 1956 S.C. 84 where it was held that a trustee in sequestration was entitled to eject a bankrupt proprietor from his house (*infra*, p. 285).
[32] *Elliot* v *Duke of Buccleuch* (1747) Mor. 10329.
[33] *Supra*, p. 152.
[34] *Dobie* v *Marquis of Lothian* (1864) 2 M. 788; *supra*, p. 154.
[35] Wood, *Lectures on Conveyancing*, 436; Burns, *Conveyancing Practice*, 4th ed., 608.
[36] *Supra*, p. 150.
[37] *Supra*, p. 152.
[38] *Laird* v *Grindlay* (1791) Mor. 15294; *Earl of Galloway* v *M'Hutcheon* (1807) 5 Pat. 169; *Dobie* v *Marquis of Lothian, supra; Lyon* v *Irvine* (1874) 1 R. 512; Hume, *Lectures*, IV, 90 *et seq.;* Rankine, 696.
[39] *Durham* v *Henderson* (1773) Mor. 15283; *Earl of Dalhousie* v *Wilson* (1802) Mor. 15311; *Young's Trs.* v *Anderson* (1809) Hume 843; *Sydserf* v *Todd*, 8 March 1814 F.C.; *Roberts* v *Wallace* (1843) 5 D. 760; *Lyon* v *Irvine, supra;* Hume, *Lectures*, IV, 92; Rankine, 696.
[40] Rankine, 696.
[41] *Ibid.*
[42] Rankine, 696-697.
[43] *Dobie* v *Marquis of Lothian, supra.*

the tenant. He is never bound to take up the lease any more than he is obliged to take up any other contract of the bankrupt.[44] If he does so, he is treated as an assignee of the bankrupt and renders himself personally liable to the landlord for the performance of all the tenant's obligations under the lease.[45] This liability extends to arrears of rent,[46] except to any extent that these may have been waived by the landlord,[47] and to future rents.[48] The liability is not confined to the extent of the bankrupt's funds in his hands.[49] It is no answer to claim that he adopted the lease in ignorance of the existence of arrears nor to prove that bills had been granted for the arrears, if these bills have not been paid.[50] The reason for holding the trustee personally liable is that, if he remains in possession longer than is necessary to ascertain what is the value of the property, that is, as the assignee of a bankrupt, he renders himself liable to the covenants of the lease.[51] The trustee, however, may make a bargain with the landlord to the effect that he is not to incur personal liability or that his liability is to be limited in some way.[52]

It is always a question of circumstances whether the trustee has in fact adopted the lease, that being an act of extraordinary administration.[53] He is entitled to a reasonable time to consider the question, and temporary intromissions with the subjects for the purpose of realising the bankrupt's effects will not readily be construed as precluding ultimate renunciation.[54] Thus, if the bankrupt is tenant of agricultural subjects, the land may be tilled and sown by the trustee or the crop reaped, and such acts are done by the trustee in the course of realising the estate and do not amount to an adoption of the lease.[55] Mere occupation of the subjects by the trustee without any other indication of the intention to adopt the lease will give the landlord a claim against him only for the value of his occupation and any loss or damage caused by it.[56] If, however, the subjects are retained for a considerable time and under circumstances which are incapable of any other construction, the lease will be held to have been taken up.[57] If a trustee invokes a provision of the lease in the tenant's favour, such as calling on the landlord to take over

---

[44] *Kirkland* v *Cadell* (1838) 16 S. 860 at p. 881.
[45] *Cuthill* v *Jeffrey,* 21 Nov. 1818 F.C.; *Dundas* v *Morison* (1857) 20 D. 225; *supra* p. 163.
[46] *Nisbet & Co's. Tr.* (1802) Mor. 15268; *Laing* v *Duff* (1845) 7 D. 556; *Dundas* v *Morison, supra.*
[47] *Maclean's Tr.* v *Maclean's Tr.* (1850) 13 D. 90.
[48] Rankine, 698.
[49] *Fairlie* v *Nelson* (1821) 1 S. 242 (N.E. 211).
[50] *Dundas* v *Morison, supra.*
[51] Per Lord Wynford in *Gibson* v *Kirkland & Sharpe* (1836) 6 W. & S. 340 at p. 350; *Kirkland* v *Cadell, supra,* at p. 881.
[52] *M'Lean's Tr.* v *M'Lean's Tr., supra; Munro* v *Fraser* (1858) 21 D. 103; *Dobie* v *Marquis of Lothian* (1864) 2 M. 788.
[53] Goudy, *Bankruptcy,* 4th ed., 283; Rankine, 698-699.
[54] *M'Gavin* v *Sturrock's Tr.* (1891) 18 R. 576; *Imrie's Tr.* v *Calder* (1897) 25 R. 15.
[55] *Kirkland* v *Cadell* (1838) 16 S. 860 at p. 881; *M'Gavin* v *Sturrock's Tr., supra.*
[56] *Stead* v *Cox* (1835) 13 S. 280; *Richardson* v *Scott* (1835) 13 S. 972; *Lord Strathmore's Trs.* v *Kirkcaldy's Trs.* (1853) 15 D. 752.
[57] *Gibson* v *Kirkland & Sharpe, supra.*

sheep stock, that will necessarily infer adoption.[58] Acceptance by a trustee under a trust deed for creditors of an assignation of a lease followed by possession and cultivation was held to imply adoption of the lease and personal liability for rent; although the landlord had acceded to the trust deed, he was entitled not merely to receive a dividend out of the bankrupt's estate, but to claim the whole rent from the trustee, who had rendered himself personally liable therefor as tenant.[59] It is obvious then that a trustee, who possesses or intromits with the subjects of a lease, should indicate clearly to the landlord the footing on which he does so.

Abandonment of Lease. If, instead of adopting a lease, the trustee abandons it, and the tenant does not remain in possession, the landlord is entitled to claim and rank for damages for any loss caused by the abandonment. The measure of damages is normally the difference between the old rent and the new rent or annual value for the remaining years of the lease, subject to discount for immediate payment of a divident out of the bankrupt's estate and other contingencies.[60] It has already been stated that the landlord is not entitled to claim damages, if he has invoked an irritancy clause. Where, however, a trustee wrote a letter to the landlord, quoting the irritancy clause and intimating that he and the tenant intended to remove, this was held to amount to a renunciation on the trustee's part and was not an exercise of the landlord's option to irritate; therefore a claim for damages on the bankrupt's estate was not excluded.[61]

Growing Crops. It is a general rule of law that he who sows a crop is entitled to reap it.[62] Accordingly, a trustee in sequestration is entitled to dispose of a crop sown by the bankrupt tenant.[63] This, however, is a right which may be modified or taken away by express agreement between the landlord and tenant that the former should be entitled to certain crops.[64] It may also happen that, as a result of an arrangement made by the tenant, the crop, which he has sown, does not belong to him, as where a potato crop belonged to a joint adventure formed by a farmer and a potato merchant; in that event the trustee was not entitled to dispose of the crop and could claim that the property in the crop was in the landlord.[65]

---

[58] *Craig's Tr.* v *Malcolm* (1900) 2 F. 541.
[59] *Moncrieffe* v *Ferguson* (1896) 24 R. 47.
[60] *Bidoulac* v *Sinclair's Tr.* (1889) 17 R. 144; *Ebbw Vale Steel Co. Ltd.* v *Wood's Tr.* (1898) 25 R. 439.
[61] *Bidoulac* v *Sinclair's Tr., supra.*
[62] Erskine, II, 1, 26.
[63] *Chalmer's Tr.* v *Dick's Tr.,* 1909 S.C. 761; *M'Kinley* v *Hutchison's Tr.,* 1935 S.L.T. 62.
[64] *Moncreiff* v *Hay* (1842) 5 D. 249; *Chalmer's Tr.* v *Dick's Tr., supra.*
[65] *M'Kinley* v *Hutchison's Tr., supra.*

It would appear that before it is reaped a crop is *pars soli*, but that the tenant who sowed it has a right to reap and remove it when it is ripe. If any diligence is done on the basis that the crop is *pars soli* which would defeat the tenant's right to remove it, then the creditor who has done diligence is preferred to a subsequent assignee of the tenant's right. If, however, the tenant has validly assigned the right to remove the crop before steps are taken to attach it as *pars soli*, then the assignee is preferred.[66]

Claims. Balancing of Accounts. A stipulation in a lease against removal of the crop before payment of rent gives the landlord no effectual security or preference in a question with the tenant's creditors, while the tenant remains in possession,[67] nor does a provision that the tenant shall hand over his stock at valuation to the landlord enable the latter to claim a preference for arrears of rent on the tenant's bankruptcy.[68] The question whether upon a premature termination due to bankruptcy the landlord may or may not set off arrears of rent due to him against sums due to be paid by him on taking over articles at the end of a lease turns mainly on the questions (1) whether prior to the first deliverance in sequestration or perhaps to some other date, at which the tenant's insolvency has been brought home to the landlord, there has been such concourse of debit and credit as the doctrine of balancing accounts in bankruptcy demands, (2) whether the lease has or has not to be invoked by or on behalf of the ordinary creditors, and (3) whether the landlord has entered into possession before the critical date.[69] It will suffice here to cite some of the authorities.[70] Where a lease is prematurely terminated by the tenant's bankruptcy, he has in the absence of express provision no claim for compensation for improvements to the subjects by which the landlord is *lucratus*.[71]

An ascertained claim by a landlord for damages in respect of his bankrupt tenant's failure to keep the subjects in repair may be set off against money in his hands due to the tenant.[72]

---

[66] See *dicta* in *Chalmer's Tr.* v *Dick's Tr., supra,* criticised in *M'Kinley* v *Hutchison's Tr., supra,* but followed in *Trinity House of Leith* v *Mitchell & Rae Ltd.,* 1957 S.L.T. (Sh. Ct.) 38.
[67] *Stewart* v *Rose* (1816) Hume 229; *M'Gavin* v *Sturrock's Tr.* (1891) 18 R. 576.
[68] *M'Lean's Tr.* v *M'Lean's Tr.* (1850) 13 D. 90.
[69] Rankine, 701.
[70] *Taylor's Trs.* v *Paul* (1888) 15 R. 313; *Davidson's Tr.* v *Urquhart* (1892) 19 R. 808; *Smith* v *Harrison & Co's. Tr.* (1893) 21 R. 330; *Jaffray's Tr.* v *Milne* (1897) 24 R. 602; *Torrance* v *Traill's Trs.* (1897) 24 R. 837; *Hart* v *Baird* (1897) 5 S.L.T. 172 (O.H.); *Craig's Tr.* v *Malcolm* (1900) 2 F. 541; *Forbes' Tr.* v *Ogilvy* (1904) 6 F. 548; Goudy, *Bankruptcy,* 4th ed., 559-560; Rankine, 701-703.
[71] *Walker* v *M'Knights* (1886) 13 R. 599.
[72] *Munro* v *Fraser* (1858) 21 D. 103.

CHAPTER XIII

LANDLORD'S RIGHT OF HYPOTHEC

Nature of Right. In addition to his ordinary remedies as a creditor, a landlord has a special remedy for the recovery of rent due to him, in the form of a right in security without possession of the subjects over which it extends. This right is implied by law and is called a right of hypothec. It is a tacit or legal hypothec, and is the chief example of such in Scots Law, another example being the hypothec of the superior for his feu duty.

Bell in his *Commentaries*[1] says the right " has been sometimes called a right of property; sometimes a mere hypothec, originating from a tacit contract. But without pretending to determine precisely whether the origin of the right is to be referred to the one or to the other principle (neither, perhaps, being fully adequate to account for all the effects), it may be represented as a right of hypothec, convertible by a certain legal process into a real right of pledge ". It may indeed be aptly classed as " a real right in security ",[2] implied by law as between landlord and tenant over subjects allowed to remain in the tenant's (or debtor's) possession. The right is *inter naturalia* of a lease, but it has been excluded by statute in the case of certain leases. It represents a right to have retained upon the subjects let, and to recover from those in whose possession they are, if they have been removed in breach of the right, the produce of the subjects or other articles and effects which are upon them. The process whereby the right of hypothec is converted into a real right is known as the landlord's sequestration (or sequestration for rent) as distinct from ordinary or mercantile sequestration. Expediency and the common advantage of the parties alone justify the existence of the right, says Rankine,[3] and these co-exist only where the origin is in a custom known to everyone and where the ordinary use and enjoyment of what is hypothecated is not affected.

The origin of the right lies in the Roman Law, and from that law it was incorporated into Scots common law through France or Holland by the early 17th century;[4] the earliest reported cases, at any rate, are in 1611 and 1623.

---

[1] II, 27.
[2] *Encyclopaedia of the Laws of Scotland*, Vol. 8, 1.
[3] 367.
[4] Rankine, 366; Hume, *Lectures*, IV, 8 *et seq.*; Bell, *Comm.*, II, 27 and authorities cited by Bell for the history of the right.

Extent of Right. Leases under which Competent. The right extends to all leases of urban subjects, that is, dwellinghouses (except certain small dwellinghouses), shops, factories and warehouses, mines, quarries and fisheries.[5] In leases of certain small houses[6] in burghs and urban districts of counties (in burghs of under 10,000 population and urban districts of counties only if adopted by a special resolution of the town council or the county council) the right is excluded by the House Letting and Rating (Scotland) Act, 1911[7] from all bedding material and all tools and implements of trade used or to be used by the occupier or any member of his family as the means of his or her livelihood in the dwellinghouse and all such further furniture and plenishing as the occupier may select to the value of £10 according to the sheriff officer's inventory or valuation.

At common law the right did not exist in a contract of wood cutting, which was really an ordinary sale with payment by instalments,[8] nor in a lease of water power or of steam power.[9] If, however, two leases of power and of mill were one and indivisible for one lump rent, the hypothec existed for both.[10] The right exists in mineral leases.[11] The right does not apply in leases of ferries, customs and other such rights but probably exists in game rents, if the lands themselves are let as a deer forest or mainly or solely for sport.[12]

While at common law the landlord had a right of hypothec in the case of leases of agricultural subjects,[13] though it was slightly restricted by an Act in 1867,[14] the effect of the Hypothec Abolition (Scotland) Act, 1880, has been that there are hardly any agricultural or pastoral leases still affected by the right. To all intents and purposes the right is now excluded in agricultural leases and a large body of case law that had grown up in regard to those leases is now of historical interest only.[15] Under the Act of 1880[16] the right of hypothec was abolished as from

---

[5] Rankine, 366, 370. See at common law also, Hume, *Lectures,* IV, 23 *et seq.;* Hunter, *Landlord and Tenant,* 4th ed., II, 355.

[6] If the population is less than 20,000, having a gross annual value of £10 or less; if over 20,000 and not exeeding 50,000, at £15 or less; and if over 50,000, at £21 or less; plus in each case 25 per cent. under the Rent Restrictions Act 1920; hotels, inns and houses let with land for agricultural or horticultural purposes or let in conjunction with a shop, workshop, stable or byre, are excluded. House Letting and Rating (Scotland) Act 1911, s. 1, as amended by Valuation and Rating (Scotland) Act 1956, s. 37.

[7] s. 10. This right to select applies only in the case of and after a sequestration for rent, *McLachlan's Trs.* v *Croal,* 1928 S.L.T. (Sh. Ct.) 42, 44 Sh. Ct. Rep. 354.

[8] *Muirhead* v *Drummond* (1792) unreported; Bell, *Comm.,* II, 28.

[9] *Catterns* v *Tennent* (1834) 12 S. 686, 1 Sh. & Macl. 694, where, as Rankine (289, 371) points out, the rubric gives the exact opposite of what was decided.

[10] *Catterns* v *Tennent, supra.*

[11] Rankine, 379.

[12] Rankine, 371.

[13] Erskine, II, 6, 56; Bell, § 1233.

[14] Hypothec Amendment (Scotland) Act; Bell, § 1235.

[15] See, for some at least of these cases, Bell, §§ 1233 *et seq., Comm.,* II, 27 *et seq.;* Hume, *Lectures,* IV, 8-23.

[16] s. 1.

4th November, 1881, in all leases of subjects let for agriculture or pasture exceeding two acres in extent. The right was, however, continued in leases, bargains or writings current at 4th November, 1881. Lawns, parks and policies, used for rearing stock or raising crops and not let for such purpose and intended only as accessory to a house, are probably still subject to the right, though the question may turn on the circumstances.[17] The right exists in nursery or market gardens and is not affected by the 1880 Act, these being neither agricultural nor pastoral either in ordinary language or in terms of the later Agricultural Holdings (Scotland) Acts.[18]

Thus, the right is at the present time virtually confined to urban leases, that is, to leases of buildings in town or country, to which the 1911 Act does not apply.

Parties Having or Entitled to Exercise the Right. A person who is in the position of a landlord and entitled to demand rent may exercise the right of hypothec. Thus, the landlord himself is entitled; so also is his assignee to the rent, so far as the cedent was entitled;[19] a heritable creditor infeft and in possession,[20] and the holder of an *ex facie* absolute disposition;[21] an adjudger infeft and using diligence to get possession;[22] and a cautioner for rent, having got an assignation in relief on paying the rent,[23] but a third party other than a cautioner paying the rent can require an assignation, only if it is clear that the landlord will not be prejudiced.[24] A liferenter in possession (but not the fiar) can exercise the right,[25] though in a case where the subjects of the liferent were under lease when the liferent commenced and the rents were to be paid during the lease to the fiar, who was burdened with an annuity to the liferenter in lieu of the rents, it was held that the fiar and not the liferenter was entitled.[26] Where there is more than one person as landlord, as *pro indiviso* owners or joint owners, the right belongs to them as a body.[27] Where the landlord holds the lands let on two different tenures for two different parts of the lands and there is one lease, moveable property on both parts may be sequestrated.[28]

It is essential to the right of hypothec that there be a *bona fide* relationship of landlord and tenant—a true lease—and not some device or part of some device adopted to create a security over moveable

[17] Rankine, 372.
[18] *Ibid.*
[19] Erskine, II, 6, 56.
[20] *Railton* v *Muirhead* (1834) 12 S. 757; *Robertson's Trs.* v *Gardner* (1889), 16 R. 705.
[21] *Scottish Heritable Security Co.* v *Allan, Campbell and Co.* (1876) 3 R. 333.
[22] Bell, § 1243.
[23] Bell, §§ 1238, 1243; *Guthrie and McConnachy* v *Smith* (1880) 8 R. 107.
[24] Bell, § 557; *Guthrie, supra, per* L.P. Inglis at p. 111.
[25] Rankine, 369.
[26] *Zuill* v *Buchanan* (1833) 11 S. 682.
[27] *Stewart* v *Wand* (1842) 4 D. 622.
[28] *Meek* v *Smith* (1832) 10 S. 652.

property that would not otherwise be recognised.[29] Thus, where the lease was in reality only part of a security transaction, being a lease back to the debtor or borrower at an enhanced rent, and all payments of rent were to be ascribed to payment of interest and instalments of principal, the parties being thus only nominally landlord and tenant, it was held that the lenders had no hypothec over the borrower's property, when on the borrower's bankruptcy they sequestrated the moveables as falling under a landlord's hypothec. It was also an attempt to create a security over moveables without possession and a fraud on the Scottish bankruptcy laws.[30]

Subjects Covered. In considering this matter, there are two aspects: (i) the nature of the subject, (ii) the ownership of the subject. The subjects are generally called the *invecta et illata.*

(i) In an urban dwellinghouse, the subjects covered by the hypothec are all furniture, books, pictures, plate and any other moveable property brought into the house by the tenant.[31] Cash, bonds, bills and other documents of debt are not included, probably, Rankine thinks, because they are not part of the plenishing: they do not increase the tenant's visible wealth in the house.[32] Wearing apparel, at least if necessary and proper clothing, is not regarded as included;[33] and tools of trade also are excluded, where they are such as are absolutely necessary to enable the tenant to gain a living.[34] While Rankine[35] thinks they must be of small value in order to be protected, he admits there are Sheriff Court cases to the contrary which he cites; and the leading case[36] in ordinary sequestration would seem to support these Sheriff Court cases. In commercial, industrial or similar premises such as a shop, warehouse, factory or mill, the subjects include furnishings, utensils, machinery and instruments of trade, manufactures of the tenant or third parties and materials intended to be made up into articles and goods in stock (the stock in trade) for sale or hire.[37] Business books are not included to the extent of allowing the landlord to levy the debts.[38] In the case of a mine or quarry, the produce or minerals output or excavated, and probably

[29] Gloag and Irvine, *Rights in Security,* 160, 233.

[30] *Heritable Securities Investment Association* v *Wingate and Co.'s Tr.* (1880) 7 R. 1094.

[31] Bell, § 1276, *Comm.,* II, 29; Hume, *Lectures,* IV, 26 says that in a let of a coachhouse and stable it covers the tenant's carriages and horses: this would apply *mutatis mutandis* to a garage in the 20th century.

[32] Rankine, 373-4; Bell, § 1276, *Comm.,* II, 30.

[33] Bell, § 1276. See Hume, *Lectures,* IV, 23, that the *family's* wearing apparel is included, but Bell, *Comm., supra,* disagrees.

[34] Gloag and Henderson, *Introduction to the Law of Scotland,* 6th ed., 372.

[35] Rankine, 374.

[36] *Macpherson* v *Macpherson's Tr.* (1905) 8 F. 191.

[37] Bell, § 1276. *E.g.,* in a billiard saloon, the table and fittings. *Nelmes and Co.* v *Ewing* (1883) 11 R. 193. See Hume, *Lectures,* IV, 26-7.

[38] Bell, § 1276.

the machinery and implements,[39] and in the case of a fishery the boats and tackle and other utensils and the produce are included.[40] The right is, as already indicated, virtually abolished in agricultural and pastoral subjects, but where it does still apply, the subjects are the produce and the stock, that is, in dairy farms the stock and the cheese, in pastoral farms the stocking and crop, if any, and in arable farms the crop and stocking. It covers crops or fruits of every kind, natural or industrial.[41] Household furniture or furnishings and agricultural implements are excluded, as also are (unless they are brought on the premises in fulfil-ment of a specific obligation in the lease) imported manures, lime, drain tiles, feeding stuffs and other material, not being the produce of or made on the farm or lands and not at the time incorporated with the soil or consumed or otherwise applied to the purpose for which such matter has been procured.[42] It is thought that tenant's fixtures in these agricultural subjects are included on the ground that the term " agricul-tural implements " in the 1867 Act cannot be confined to produce and stocking.[43] In pastoral subjects all fruits of the soil are included, that is, fruits preserved which may be retained or recovered and not grass which is in course of daily consumption.[44] In the case of horticultural subjects such as orchards, nursery gardens and market gardens the ordinary common law rules apply and thus implements and produce and tenant's fixtures are included.[45]

(ii) The general rule is that a person cannot pledge property of which he is not the owner. It is presumed also from possession that articles on the premises belong to the tenant. The property of children of the tenant, of his guests, of his servants and of his lodgers is excluded in accordance with the general rule.[46] In any event, such property is not normally part of the ordinary plenishing, but comprises specific personal items. If, of course, furniture materially different and more various is brought in by a lodger, it may be held that he is really a subtenant,[47] and if most or the major part of the furniture is owned by a third party, such as a lodger, then the hypothec may apply to it, if it is, for example,

---

[39] *Weir's Exrs.* v *Durham* (1870) 8 M. 725; *Lindsay* v *Earl of Wemyss* (1872) 10 M. 708; *Marquis of Breadalbane* v *Tobermory Salt Quarry Co.* (1917) 33 Sh. Ct. Rep. 154.

[40] Hume, *Lectures,* IV, 23.

[41] Hume, *Lectures,* IV, 19-20; Bell, § 1235; *Comm.,* II, 28-9.

[42] Hypothec Amendment (Scotland) Act 1867, s. 6; Bell, *supra.*

[43] Rankine, 381.

[44] Rankine, 383.

[45] *Ibid.*

[46] Hume, *Lectures,* IV, 24; Bell, *Comm.,* II, 29; *Bell* v *Andrews* (1885) 12 R. 961. See *Henderson* v *Young, infra.* See proposal to limit hypothec to goods which are the property of the tenant and hence to exclude from it the goods of others, including subtenants, Fourteenth Report of the Law Reform Committee for Scotland, 1964 Cmd. 2343, para. 41; 1964 S.L.T. (News) 149.

[47] Rankine, 378. The goods of a subtenant are included in respect of his own rent and also, if the sublease is unauthorised, the rent of the principal tenant, his landlord. See *infra,* p. 208 and *Blane* v *Morison* (1785) Mor. 6232.

given to the tenant to enable him to furnish a boarding house,[48] though it would not apply if the lodger has taken the furniture there for his own convenience.[49] Apart from such instances, however, the right of hypothec has been held to extend to property of which the tenant is not owner and which does not belong to someone in the house, on the theory of presumed consent of the owner, evidenced by his giving possession to the tenant, a theory which has been attacked by Rankine[50] as "unsatisfactory" but as one to be followed "without too close a scrutiny into the principles". Thus, property which has been let on hire to the tenant is covered, especially if it is the whole furniture of a house that is let on hire or if a substantial part of it has been hired; for then it is presumed also that the person who let out the property estimated this risk in his charge for the hire, while the landlord was regarding as security the furnishing as a whole and would have demanded more furnishing of the premises, if he had thought that his hypothec was not covered.[51] It has been doubted whether in such cases where the whole furniture is on hire (or hire-purchase) notice to the landlord prior to the placing in the house frees the property from hypothec.[52] Single articles on hire such as a piano, or a sewing machine, so far as they were not of the nature of ordinary furniture, were in some earlier Sheriff Court cases held to be excluded, where there was a known custom to hire out such articles as part of a business,[53] but this exemption is no longer supported by the authorities.[54]

Hire purchase goods are in the same position as being subject to hypothec.[55] Single articles let on hire purchase are as much subject as those hired.[56]

---

[48] *Johnstone's Exrs.* v *Wilson*, 1913 1 S.L.T. 378 (Sh. Ct.).
[49] *Maclachlan* v *Wilson*, 1913 1 S.L.T. 378 (Sh. Ct.).
[50] Rankine, 375. See Bell, § 1276, *Comm.*, II, 31.
[51] Bell, § 1276; Hume, *Lectures*, IV, 24, who calls it a deviation from principle, if it is the law, for convenience and it is assumed that the hirer consents.
[52] Rankine, 375, citing but questioning Sheriff Court cases in favour of exemption from hypothec.
[53] Bell, § 1276.
[54] That they are not excluded was the opinion in *Penson* v *Robertson*, 6 June 1820 (Hume, *Lectures*, IV, 24) and it was assumed that the law was so in *McIntosh* v *Potts* (1905) 7 F. 765, and it was the view in some later Sheriff Court cases noted by Rankine at 376 and in *Caldwell* v *Drake* (1915) 31 Sh. Ct. Rep. 298 (a piano on hire purchase), while in *Edinburgh Albert Buildings Co.* (*infra*) Lord President Strathclyde regarded *Penson* as correctly decided. Rankine himself, in the light of these views (excluding, of course, that of the Lord President in 1917) of the Courts, came to change his previous view that they were exempt, though he thought the point was still arguable. See *Smith Premier Typewriting Co.* v *Cotton* (1907) 14 S.L.T. 764. Gas fires supplied by a local authority to a tenant under an agreement called "on hire purchase system" were held subject to hypothec as the agreement was a sale by instalments and not a hire. *Cunningham* v *Greenock Corporation* (1928) 44 Sh. Ct. Rep. 139.
[55] *Rudman* v *Jay*, 1908 S.C. 552.
[56] Gloag and Henderson, *Introduction to the Law of Scotland*, 6th ed., 372; *Caldwell* v *Drake, supra.*

If the hiring is occasional and transient, for example, chairs or articles for a party, these articles are not included.[57] In the case of a furnished letting an additional article, such as a piano got on hire, is not included.[58]

The foregoing rules apply alike to the tenant of a house or a tenant of a shop, warehouse, factory or mill.[59]

Where furniture has been deposited with the tenant of a house or gratuitously lent to him, it may be held to be subject to the hypothec, notwithstanding the absence of consideration, even if it be a single article or if the deposit or lending be a casual event. The case of deposit or gratuitous loan raises " a question of greater difficulty ", says Bell.[60] In *Cowan* v *Perry*[61] furniture was lent and put in with hired furniture, but was held exempt on the ground that the hired furniture sufficed. On the other hand, in *Wilson* v *Spankie*[62] furniture was allowed by creditors of a bankrupt tenant to remain for a few weeks in the house, and it was held subject to the hypothec on the ground that the credit for the rent was prolonged on the continued possession of the tenant as under a hypothec assented to by the creditors. Where, however, the tenant had absconded and the furniture had been sold under Crown diligence, but the buyer (a friend) allowed the tenant's wife and family to use it for nine months, it was held[63] not to be subject to hypothec, the Court, however, refusing to decide the general point. The furniture remained exempt even for current rent, the landlord being aware of the situation. The question seems to be one of the whole circumstances of each case, as the undernoted Sheriff Court cases seem to show.[64]

In the case of a shop, warehouse, factory or mill, goods may be there on sale or return; if so, they are probably subject to the hypothec.[65]

[57] *Adam* v *Sutherland* (1863) 2 M. 6, *per* Lord Deas.
[58] *Edinburgh Albert Buildings Co.* v *General Guarantee Corporation*, 1917 S.C. 239, where, however, the rent was payable in advance, and on the facts the landlord could not have relied on the piano as security.
[59] See *Smith* v *Lorenzo Po and Capaldi*, 1931 S.L.T. (Sh. Ct.) 31, 47 Sh. Ct. Rep. 141, where automatic slot and gaming machines, commonly found in similar shop premises and used for customers' amusement, which were the only effects of value in the premises, were held to fall under the hypothec. See Rankine, 378.
[60] *Comm.*, II, 30. See Bell, § 1276.
[61] 31 Jan. 1804 (Hume, *Lectures*, IV, 24; Bell, *Comm.*, II, 31).
[62] 17 Dec. 1813 F.C.; Hume, *supra*. The case was approved by the Lord President in *Bell* v *Andrews*, *supra*.
[63] *Adam* v *Sutherland* (1863) 2 M. 6.
[64] *Ross* v *Irwin* (1912) 28 Sh. Ct. Rep. 347, where furniture lent to the tenant was the principal and only valuable part of the plenishing and it was held subject to hypothec; *Boni* v *McIver* (1933) 49 Sh. Ct. Rep. 191, where articles (about a third of the value of the plenishing) lent to the tenant were also held subject to hypothec, for, being such a large part of the plenishing, the landlord must have allowed possession to be continued on the faith of them; *Henderson* v *Young*, 1928 S.L.T. (Sh. Ct.) 30, where certain furniture had been brought into a house by a young married couple who had been lodging for a brief period in the house, and it was held exempt as not having been brought in as a replacement for any of the tenant's furniture. See Rankine, 376-7.
[65] *Macdonald* v *Westren* (1888) 15 R. 988. See *Lawsons Ltd.* v *Flint* (1915) 31 Sh. Ct. Rep. 236, *sub nom. Lawsons* v *Avon India Rubber Co.*, 1915 2 S.L.T. 327 (Sh. Ct.), where goods were held covered.

Goods may also be deposited or lent for sale or hire by the tenant, who may or may not have to perform some work or repair upon them: such goods generally are considered not to be covered.[66] So with the goods and effects of travellers in a hotel or an inn.[67] Goods given to a tenant for exhibition or repair or as a sample are not included.[68] If, however, the goods have been given or entrusted to the tenant for sale or are the tenant's property, they can be sold until sequestration, and a *bona fide* purchaser of them is protected until that event;[69] though, if goods purchased from the tenant are left on the premises, for example, for the convenience of the buyer and are there at the date of the sequestration and so have not been delivered to the buyer, they are subject to the hypothec,[70] but delivery to the buyer of goods sold thus would exclude the right.[71] Goods in stock, Rankine thinks,[72] are not covered by hypothec, even if sold after sequestration, and to prevent dilapidation of the security the premises should be closed on a judicial warrant or the sequestrated goods removed. If the goods entrusted for sale are in large quantities in proportion to the rest of the goods in the shop, they may be held subject to the hypothec.[73]

Where there is hired property subject to hypothec on the premises, the owner of it should on a sequestration apply to the Sheriff Court to grant warrant to sell subject to his property being sold last, or should ask the judge of the roup to put his property up for sale only after the debtor's own property has been sold.[74]

Rent Secured. The purpose of the hypothec is to secure payment of rent.[75] In the first place, " rent " covers not only the rent laid down in the lease but may also include other items under the lease, for example, interest on a capital sum being outlay by the landlord on " old " improvements, which is regarded as rent under the Agricultural

---

[66] See Rankine, 378-9. Hume, *Lectures,* IV, 27, thinks that where work has to be done on articles deposited for hire, the landlord can only detain till payment of the hire for the particular articles.

[67] Bell, § 1276, *Comm.,* II, 31; Hume, *Lectures,* IV, 24.

[68] *Pulsometer Engineering Co.* v *Gracie* (1887) 14 R. 316 (exhibition); *Smith Premier Typewriting Co.* v *Bruce* (1936) 52 Sh. Ct. Rep. 11 (exhibition as sample); *Lawsons Ltd.* v *Flint* (1915) 31 Sh. Ct. Rep. 312 (*do.*).

[69] Rankine, 379. Hume, *Lectures,* IV, 27, thinks that a single article cannot be taken even after a sequestration and that the tenant can sell it.

[70] *Ryan* v *Little,* 1910 S.C. 219. The Sale of Goods Act 1893, s. 61, reserves the landlord's right of hypothec.

[71] *Wyld* v *Robertson* (1832) 10 S. 538.

[72] 379, citing Hunter, *Landlord and Tenant,* 4th ed., II, 380; More's *Notes,* 83.

[73] Hunter, *supra;* Rankine, *supra,* who, while thinking that trade custom might play a part, considers it would be necessary to prove fraud or gross negligence in letting down the stock in hand, and knowledge of the depositor or entruster.

[74] Rankine, 376.

[75] Bell, §§ 1233, 1277.

Holdings (Scotland) Act.[76] Other items are said to be open to doubt.[77] In the case of a lease of mines or quarries the hypothec covers fixed rent or royalties.[78]

In the second place, one year's rent due or current is covered.[79] Each year's rent is secured successively.[80] Thus, arrears are not included,[81] nor is rent for a year during no part of which the articles are on the premises.[82] And this principle applies equally to monthly as to yearly lets.[83] So in agricultural subjects the livestock are held hypothecated for the rent of each year successively.[84] Agricultural produce (crops and manure) is hypothecated for the year of which it is the produce, irrespective of the term of payment of rent.[85] In the case of horticultural subjects there seems to be no authority as to the duration of the hypothec, but it is suggested by Rankine[86] that the analogies apply according to the circumstances, depending on whether the produce, like arable crops, are annual or at shorter intervals, or whether, like livestock, they need several years to be fit for market.

Sequestration must be used within three months from the last term of payment, otherwise the hypothec falls.[87] Thus, the right to each year's rent must be made effectual by sequestration within three months after the last term of payment. When this has been done, the effect is to give the landlord full preference. It does not matter that the effects are not sold until later than the three months, provided that there is no undue delay, and that there is nothing amounting to abandoning of the proceedings.[88] The three months' rule was laid down for livestock in agricultural subjects as far back as 1726.[89] Even where the conventional terms of payment in agricultural subjects are postponed, the rule still applies that hypothecation is for the rent of each year. In practice, it is usual (" and prudent ")[90] to apply for sequestration in respect of *invecta* and stocking for payment of the rent actually due and also in security of the rent to become due at the next term. Thus, there are

---

[76] Agricultural Holdings (Scotland) Act 1949, s. 40 and see 1923 Act, s. 3 (3); Connell, *Agricultural Holdings (Scotland) Act*, 5th ed., pp. 28-29. See *Callander* v *Smith* (1900) 8 S.L.T. 109, *per* Lord Kyllachy.
[77] Bell, § 1239; *e.g.*, pactional rent on divergence from prescribed management. Cf. *Robertson* v *Clerk* (1842) 4 D. 1317, and *Witham* v *White* (1866) 38 Sc. Jur. 586. Hume, *Lectures*, IV, 22, says that a claim of damages for breach of prestations other than rent is not covered.
[78] *Liquidators of Linthlithgow Oil Co.* v *Earl of Rosebery* (1903) 6 F. 90.
[79] Bell, §§ 1249, 1277, *Comm.*, II, 32; Hume, *Lectures*, IV, 12, 26; *Young* v *Welsh* (1833) 12 S. 233.
[80] *Ibid.*
[81] *Ibid.*
[82] *Thomson* v *Barclay* (1883) 10 R. 694; *Sawyers* v *Kinnair* (1897) 25 R. 45.
[83] *Ingram* v *Singer Co.* (1910) 26 Sh. Ct. Rep. 156.
[84] *Crawford* v *Stewart* (1737) Mor. 6193, 10531; Bell, *Comm.*, II, 32.
[85] Bell, § 1239, *Comm.*, ii, 32; Hume, *Lectures*, IV, 12.
[86] Rankine, 385.
[87] Bell, §§ 1240, 1277, *Comm.*, II, 32; Hume, *Lectures*, IV, 25.
[88] Hume, *Lectures, supra; McLeod* v *Thomson's Crs.* (1805) Hume, 226.
[89] *Hepburn* v *Richardson* (1726) Mor. 6205. The Act of 1867, s. 4, introduced the limit for produce.
[90] Rankine, 385.

three months to secure the rent of the past year and also the rent of the current year. In the case of crops, however, these are only covered for the rent for the year in which the crop is raised.[91]

Effect of Sublease. This has to be looked at from three points of view: (a) as between the original landlord and the subtenant; (b) as between the tenant and the subtenant; and (c) as between the original landlord and the tenant.

(a) There is no privity of contract between the landlord and a subtenant.[92] If the landlord has not consented to or recognised or acknowledged the sublease, his right of hypothec is not affected by the existence of the sublease, and he can attach the subjects on the premises let for payment or in security of the rent of the principal tenant.[93] It is immaterial that the subtenant has paid his rent to the tenant.[94] Moreover, the landlord's right extends as against a purchaser from the subtenant, or an arrester of funds due by the subtenant to the tenant, or the tenant himself,[95] unless there has been undue delay.[96] Where only part of the subjects in the principal lease is sublet, the subtenant's effects are none the less subject to the landlord's hypothec for the full amount of the principal tenant's rent, and it is immaterial that he has paid all the rent that he is due under the sublease to the tenant.[97] If payment is made to the landlord by the subtenant after he has paid the rent to the tenant, the subtenant cannot, in the absence of an agreement to assign, require an assignation of the hypothec, unless the landlord's own rights would not be prejudiced.[98] If, however, the landlord has agreed to the sublease, or in a case where the sublease is permitted by law, the landlord's hypothec only secures payment to him of the rent due by the subtenant to his landlord or, probably, paid before the stipulated term of payment.[99] The rent must have been asked from him by the landlord before he has paid it to the tenant, that is, his own immediate landlord.[1] The subtenant cannot be asked to pay again,[2] but Rankine thinks that, if he has paid before the proper term, he may be called on to pay again.[3] There may be a clause providing that the subtenant is to be

---

[91] Bell, § 1239.
[92] *Supra* p. 168.
[93] Bell, § 1237, *Comm.*, II, 31; Hume, *Lectures*, IV, 18. In agricultural subjects hypothec was not affected by a sublease—*Steuart* v *Stables* (1878) 5 R. 1024.
[94] *Ibid.*
[95] *Fowler* v *Cant* (1630) Mor. 6219 (purchase); *Countess Traquair* v *Cranstoun* (1667) Mor. 6221 (arrester).
[96] *Ross* v *Williamson* (1817) Hume 232. See Hume, *Lectures*, IV, 20.
[97] Rankine, 399; *Lord Salton* v *Club* (1700) Mor. 1821, 6224; Erskine, II, 9, 63. *Cf.* Bell, *Comm.*, II, 32.
[98] *Steuart* v *Stables* (1878) 5 R. 1024.
[99] Bell, § 1237.
[1] *Blane* v *Morison* (1785) Mor. 6232. Hume, *Lectures*, IV, 18-9; Bell, *Comm.*, II, 32; Rankine at 398 doubts if the rule in *Blane* can be applied in cases other than where there is *express* authority.
[2] *Ibid.*
[3] Rankine, 398.

liable for the principal rent, and in that event the landlord has full powers.[4]

(b) Where there is power to sublet or where subletting is permitted, the tenant has a hypothec for payment or in security of the rent due under the sublease; and an assignation of all the landlord's remedies is implied under that power.[5] Where a sublease had expired and the landlord granted a lease to the subtenant and the tenant sequestrated for the last term's rent under the original sublease, it was held that this sequestration was preferable to a sequestration by the landlord for the first term of his lease to the subtenant.[6]

(c) The tenant must have paid the rent or must find security for the rent due by him to his landlord to the full amount before he can sequestrate the subtenant's effects.[7] If he has not paid all the principal rent and is still the tenant, he thus cannot sequestrate in competition with his landlord, unless he has at least found security for the rent which he is due.[8] The landlord must, of course, act fairly. If he gives up his sequestration of the subtenant's effects and gives time to the subtenant, then the tenant is freed. But the landlord may abandon sequestration of the subtenant's effects without discharging the principal tenant, and the latter is entitled himself to sequestrate as against the subtenant or on payment adopt the landlord's sequestration.[9]

Assignation of Hypothec. Where a cautioner pays the rent to the landlord, the landlord must assign to the cautioner the right of hypothec. Sequestration after the assignation gives the cautioner a preferable right to any sequestration by the landlord for the next term's rent.[10] Where a person who is not a cautioner, *e.g.,* a subtenant after paying the tenant, pays the rent to the landlord, he can get an assignation, in the absence of a contract to that effect, provided that the landlord has no interest to refuse it, that is, only where the landlord will not be prejudiced.[11]

Effect of Tenant's Bankruptcy. This is dealt with in the next paragraph.

Competition between Hypothec and other Rights.

(i) The landlord's right of hypothec is preferable to any private diligence; that is, to all unprivileged creditors of the tenant, poinding or arresting his effects, who are, therefore, limited to subjects not covered

[4] Bell, *Comm.,* II 32; *McLachlan* v *Sinclair* (1897) 13 Sh. Ct. Rep. 362.
[5] Hume, *Lectures,* IV, 19; Bell, *Comm.,* II, 31.
[6] *Christie* v *McPherson,* 14 Dec. 1814 F.C.; Bell, *Comm.,* II, 32.
[7] *Stevenson* v *Cooper* (1822) 1 S. 345.
[8] *Ibid.*
[9] Bell, § 1237.
[10] *Stevenson* v *McCulloch* (1821) 1 S. 27; Bell, *Comm.,* II, 33.
[11] *Steuart* v *Stables, supra; Guthrie and McConnachy* v *Smith* (1880) 8 R. 107.

14

by the hypothec.[12] They can poind subjects covered by the hypothec in order to secure any reversion, but they cannot remove or sell them, and are liable to an interdict if they threaten to proceed.[13] A landlord, who has entered into possession on the death of a tenant insolvent before his mercantile sequestration and has concurred with the trustee in referring to arbitration the valuation of certain articles taken over under the lease, can set off against the arrears of rent the amount of that valuation.[14] A conventional hypothec, however, cannot be created.[15] If a creditor sells a substantial part of the effects, he will incur liability for the whole rent; it is not enough for him to say that what is left is sufficient to secure the rent.[16] The landlord has also no preference under his hypothec in respect of arrears not covered by the hypothec.[17]

(ii) The landlord's right is also preferable to that of the trustee in the tenant's mercantile sequestration[18] and to that of a liquidator in a company's liquidation.[19] Thus, an ordinary sequestration or liquidation has no effect on the right to sequestrate under the hypothec. This, however, is qualified by certain preferable claims in an ordinary sequestration or liquidation. In bankruptcy[20] certain debts are preferable:— local rates due at the date of sequestration and having become due within twelve months before that date; all assessed taxes, National Defence Contribution and income tax assessed on the tenant up to April 5th next before that date not exceeding a year's assessment; wages or salary of any clerk or servant for services rendered to the bankrupt during four months before that date and not exceeding £200 to anyone; wages of any workman or labourer in respect of services rendered due two months before that date and not exceeding £200 to anyone; contributions payable by the bankrupt as employer under the National Insurance Act, 1946, and the National Insurance (Industrial Injuries) Act, 1946, and compensation under the National Service Act, 1948; and any sums due at the relevant date (the award of sequestration) from the bankrupt on account of tax deductions for the previous twelve months next before that date and any payment in lieu of national insur-

---

[12] *Philips* v *Easson* (1807), Hume 228; Hume, *Lectures,* IV, 24.
[13] *Wyllie* v *Fisher,* 1907 S.C. 686.
[14] *Davidson's Tr.* v *Urquhart* (1892) 19 R. 808; *Torrance* v *Traill's Trs.* (1897) 24 R. 837.
[15] *McGavin* v *Sturrock's Tr.* (1891) 18 R. 576.
[16] *MacKersy* v *Edinburgh Loan Co.* (1912) 29 Sh. Ct. Rep. 28; *Miller* v *Rankin* (1881) 2 Guth. 276.
[17] *Tulloch* v *Willoughby D'Erseby* (1835) 14 S. 198.
[18] Bankruptcy (Scotland) Act 1913, s. 115. See *Hardie* v *Adamson* (1923) 39 Sh. Ct. Rep. 229, where the landlord had sequestrated under his hypothec after the tenant's ordinary sequestration but before the trustee had been confirmed in his appointment.
[19] Companies Act 1948, s. 327; *Anderson's Tr.* v *Donaldson and Co.,* 1908, S.C. 38.
[20] Bankruptcy (Scotland) Act 1913, s. 118, as amended by Companies Act 1947, ss. 91 and 115, and National Insurance Act 1946, ss. 55 (2), 79 (j), National Insurance (Industrial Injuries) Act 1946, s. 90 (j), National Service Act 1948, Finance Act 1952, s. 30 (6), and National Insurance Act 1959, s. 11 (1).

ance contributions payable on termination of a person's employment before or by effect of death or the award of sequestration. There are similar preferences in the case of liquidation of a company.[21]

(iii) Purchasers as intromitters are subject to the landlord's preferable right, and must restore what they have removed or pay its value in name of rent.[22] A plea that sufficient goods are left will depend on whether the rent is due or is only current.[23] In order to be protected, the purchase must be followed by delivery;[24] a sale, where sequestration occurs before removal of the goods, thus gives no preference to the buyer, even though the right of property has passed at the sale. And, to be protected, the sale must be in bulk in open market, not a sale by sample.[25] Agricultural produce is in a special position by statute, as it is exempt if *bona fide* bought for its fair marketable value from a tenant and removed and paid for or *bona fide* bought at a public auction from a tenant or anyone having his authority to sell after seven days' written notice of intention to sell given to the landlord or those entitled to the rent or his agent or factor, provided sequestration has not been obtained and registered before lapse of the notice.[26] This does not apply, however, to produce which the tenant may not sell or remove or produce affected by a registered sequestration before its removal and payment of the price or after that notice.[27] Ignorance of the fact that the rent has not been paid does not protect a purchaser from the right of hypothec.[28]

Certain rights, however, are preferable to hypothec. (i) The rights of the Crown. Crown process of diligence gives the Crown a preference, the law in this respect following the law of England.[29] This preference applies, unless, before the commencement of the Crown proceedings, the tenant's effects have been sold under sequestration and the sale procedure fully carried out;[30] and it applies even if the Crown proceedings are commenced before warrant has been issued under the sale procedure authorising the sheriff clerk to pay to the landlord the amount

---

[21] Companies Act 1948, s. 319, as amended by Finance Act 1952 and National Insurance Act, 1959, *supra*.
[22] *Swinton* v *Seton* (1627) Mor. 6218; *Hay* v *Elliot* (1639) M. 6219; *Scot* (1678) Mor. 6223; *McGhie* v *Mather* (1824) 3 S. 337 (N.E. 239); Hume, *Lectures,* IV, 24. See *Fitzgerald* v *Simpson* (1922) 38 Sh. Ct. Rep. 160, where the buyer of stock and property was held liable in payment of rent for the half year before his term of entry. And in *McLachlan's Trs.* v *Croal*, 1928 S.L.T. (Sh. Ct.) 42, 44 Sh. Ct. Rep. 354, the buyer was held as a *bona fide* buyer liable to restore or repay the sum paid to the tenant; he was not liable for the whole of the rent in arrears at the time of purchase but only for arrears to the extent of the price paid.
[23] Rankine, 395; Hume, *supra*.
[24] See *Ryan* v *Little*, 1910 S.C. 219. Hume, *supra*.
[25] Erskine, II, 6, 60; Bell, § 1242; *Comm.*, 11, 34.
[26] Hypothec Amendment (Scotland) Act 1867, s. 3. See *McLachlan's Trs.*, *supra*.
[27] *Ibid*.
[28] *Barns* v *Allan* (1864) 2 M. 1119 *per* L.P. McNeil at p. 1125.
[29] Hume, *Lectures,* IV, 27-8; Bell, *Comm.*, II, 34, 52-3; *Ogilvie* v *Wingate* (1792) 3 Pat. 273.
[30] *Robertson* v *Jardine* (1802) Mor. 7891.

due to him out of the sale price.[31] Exactions of a public nature statutorily declared preferable to private debts are not included in this preference.[32] (ii) The superior's hypothec in respect of his feu duty, a lease being always under the burden of feu duty.[33] The superior can sequestrate; he can also raise an action of poinding the ground or a personal action against the tenant as intromitter limited to the feu duties during the tenant's possession.[34] If the tenant has *bona fide* paid the rent to the landlord, then the superior has no claim on the tenant. (iii) Deathbed and funeral expenses of the tenant.[35] The claim must be fair and reasonable. It applies notwithstanding that sequestration has begun before the tenant's death and that there has been an order to pay the proceeds of the sale of the effects to the landlord, from whom they can be recovered.[36]

Plenishing Order. Under the right of hypothec, but probably only where the subject was let to be *domus instructus*,[37] there is an obligation upon the tenant to provide with stock-in-trade, to furnish or to plenish the premises let suitably, that is, to the extent which is adequate to make the landlord's right fully and practically available.[38] The landlord can insist on this stocking, furnishing or plenishing, notwithstanding that the premises are denuded in consequence of the removal and sale by him under the hypothec for a previous term's rent.[39] While the tenant of a shop must thus stock it sufficiently, he need not open it and carry on business in it, unless this is stipulated in the lease.[40] The right applies in rural as well as urban subjects.[41]

The landlord enforces his right by a plenishing order in the Sheriff Court proceeding on an Initial Writ.[42] The order requires the tenant to stock or plenish the subjects to an amount sufficient to afford security for the current year's rent or to find caution for that rent, and orders, failing either of these steps, summary ejection of the tenant to the effect that the landlord may enter and possess, and grants authority to the landlord to relet and apply the rent from the reletting in payment of the rent due, to remove the effects that are there to neutral custody, and to open shut and lockfast places. The time, which should be fixed, is in the

---

[31] *The King* v *Johnston,* 1809, unreported; Hume, *Lectures,* IV, 28-9; Bell, *Comm.,* II, 53-4, 406-7. See Rankine, 387, that this is the accepted practice.
[32] *Campbell* v *Edinburgh Parish Council,* 1911 S.C. 280. But in *Hutton* v *Grant,* 1913 1 S.L.T. 468, the preference was held to include telephone rent-charge.
[33] Erskine, II, 6, 63; Bell, § 698; *Yuille* v *Lawrie* (1823) 2 S. 155.
[34] Rankine, 388; *Anderson's Trs.* v *Donaldson,* 1908 S.C. 38.
[35] Bankruptcy (Scotland) Act 1913, s. 118 (5); *Rowan* v *Bar* (1742) Mor. 11852; *Drysdale* v *Kennedy* (1835) 14 S. 159.
[36] Bell, §§ 1241, 1277, 1403; *Rowan* v *Bar, supra.*
[37] Rankine, 399 note.
[38] Bell, § 1273.
[39] *Macdonald* v *Mackessack* (1888) 16 R. 168.
[40] *Whitelaw* v *Fulton* (1871) 10 M. 27.
[41] Rankine, 400.
[42] Dobie, *Law and Practice of Sheriff Courts in Scotland,* 425, *Styles in Use in Sheriff Courts,* 369-70.

Sheriff's discretion. The Sheriff can order reletting but Rankine considers[43] that in reletting the landlord must not make such arrangements as unreasonably to exclude *locus poenitentiae*.

The effect of the order is not to terminate the lease but to allow the landlord to relet. Thus the tenant, if in breach of his obligation during the currency of the lease, and where the subjects have not been relet so that his reinstatement is consistent with the new siutation, can offer to pay up the arrears and to plenish and then require reinstatement to be given to him.[44]

Right of Retention under Hypothec.   The landlord may prevent the tenant or any other party from displenishing the premises under a right which he has by law of retention or detention of the effects on the subjects of his hypothec.[45] He may thus insist on the tenant retaining on the subjects the *invecta et illata*. He enforces this right by interdict in the Sheriff Court against the tenant and all others acting for him or under his instructions, prohibiting the sale or removing of, or interference in any way with, the *invecta et illata* or any part of them, so far as subject to hypothec, until caution is found.[46] It also may prevent poinding by creditors.

The extent of the landlord's right of retention depends on whether the rent is actually payable or is not actually payable. If the landlord takes steps after the term of payment, the right covers such plenishing as is in value equivalent to a full year's rent. Unless a poinding creditor proves that enough has been left by him to satisfy the full year's rent, he will be liable as an intromitter;[47] it is not a defence that he acted legally and *bona fide* consumed the fruits.[48] If sufficient effects are not left, the rent, being due and payable, must be paid, and an offer of caution is not sufficient.[49] The landlord need not assign his right to the rent and his hypothec.[48] If, however, the landlord takes steps before the term of payment, that is, before the rent is actually payable, the whole effects must be left, and this even though the tenant is neither in arrears nor *vergens ad inopiam* but is solvent.[50] It is not sufficient for the tenant to say that enough goods have been left to meet the rent or hypothec.[51] The landlord can insist on the whole effects being left until he gets security for payment of the rent. Where sufficient security is found or offered in answer to an application for interdict, then the application must state clearly the acts sought to be forbidden and allege

[43] Rankine, 401.
[44] *Wright* v *Whitelaw* (1875) 3 R. 68.
[45] Erskine, II, 6, 58; Bell, § 1239, *Comm.*, II, 32.
[46] Dobie, *Law and Practice, supra*, 427, 482 *et seq., Styles, supra*, 231-2.
[47] *Lord Polwarth* (1642) Mor. 6221; *Rutherford* v *Scott* (1736) Mor. 6226; *Philips* v *Easson* (1807) Hume 228.
[48] *Ruthven* v *Arbuthnot* (1673) Mor. 6222.
[49] *Crawford* v *Stewart* (1737) Mor. 10531.
[50] *Preston* v *Gracie* (1845) 7 D. 942.
[51] *Ibid.*

displenishing contrary to good management.[52] A third party may remove or poind the goods, provided that caution or assignation of the rent, interest and penalties is offered;[53] and this, it is thought,[54] covers the tenant as well as creditors. In this case the landlord must assign his right to the rent and hypothec.[55] It has been held that an action for the rent is irrelevant *quoad* contractors where they had removed the effects of a tenant who had not paid his rent.[56]

" Corollary to and not wider than the right of retention " is the landlord's right to recover the *invecta et illata,* if they have been already removed.[57] At one time he could recover them *brevi manu,* but he must now get a warrant for their return from the Sheriff Court.[58] Intimation must be made to the tenant and any party in whose custody the effects are, unless there is some very special reason stated in the judgment, such as where there has been a clandestine removal and it would defeat the purpose of the measure.[59] The warrant gives authority to search for and carry back the effects to the house, from which they have been removed, to be sequestrated, inventoried and secured.[60] If a third party has removed *invecta et illata,* he incurs liability as an intromitter to pay the rent at least up to the value of the effects he has removed, and he may even be liable for the whole rent in exceptional circumstances.[61]

If the landlord took the effects without a warrant after the property in them has passed under a poinding or *ex intervallo,* he is liable to a counterclaim for damages of the nature of spuilzie, but he can claim the rent against anyone wrongfully intromitting with the property.[62]

Both the right of retention and the right of recovery are exceptional measures, and both interdict and warrant are got *periculo petentis* so that, if the statements, upon which the Court has been led to grant interdict or the warrant, are not true[63] or if there is a real dispute in regard to the rent, so that exceptional measures are thus not necessary,[64] the landlord will be liable in damages. If the tenant has given information for the inventory, he is not entitled to allege later that there were some irregularities.[65]

If there has been fraudulent bankruptcy involving the clandestine removal of sequestrated effects, there may be liability, at common law or under the Bankruptcy (Scotland) Act, 1913, to the criminal law.[66]

---

[52] *Cathcart* v *Sloss* (1864) 3 M. 76, 521.
[53] *Crawford, supra.*
[54] Rankine, 392, *Cathcart, supra. Cf. Lord Salton* v *Club* (1701) Mor. 1821, 6216.
[55] *Crawford, supra.*
[56] *Bell* v *Boyd and Sons* (1936) 52 Sh. Ct. Rep. 228.
[57] Rankine, 392.
[58] Dobie, *Law and Practice, supra,* 425.
[59] *Ibid.*
[60] *Ibid.;* Dobie, *Styles, supra,* 473-4.
[61] *Steuart* v *Peddie* (1874) 2 R. 94.
[62] *Park* v *Cockburn* (1676) Mor. 6203.
[63] *Jack* v *Black,* 1911 S.C. 691; *Shearer* v *Nicoll,* 1935 S.L.T. 313.
[64] *Gray* v *Weir* (1891) 19 R. 25.
[65] *Taylor* v *McKnight* (1882) 9 R. 857; *McDonald* v *Grant* (1903) 11 S.L.T. 575.
[66] s. 178; Rankine, 393; Macdonald, *Criminal Law,* 5th ed., 2, 107-8.

Sequestration. By the process known as landlord's sequestration, the landlord can put his real right of hypothec into force by attaching specific subjects and making his right a real right over them. His right of hypothec is converted into a real right of pledge.[67] It is the diligence by which the right is made effective by attaching specific subjects, but if this process of sequestration does not suffice to meet his claim, it must be followed by a sale of the subjects or effects, from the proceeds of which the landlord will receive the amount due to him or, at least, a proportion of it.

Sequestration must be commenced within the time limit of the hypothec.[68] The process is, by practice, confirmed by decision in the Court of Session, competent only in the Sheriff Court.[69] It must be raised too in the Sheriff Court of the county where the subjects are situated.[70] It is, in the light of the foregoing well-established practice and decision, therefore, incompetent in the Court of Session.

The process may also be used *currente termino* in security of rent not yet due, as the hypothec covers not only rent due but current rent.[71] It is common to combine conclusions for rent past due and for rent growing due; and this should generally be done, as it is probably incompetent to convert the one process into the other.[72] Any articles covered by the hypothec can be sequestrated in security. Sequestration in security will, however, only be granted on cause shown, for it is a process of considerable severity as against the tenant. Thus, there must be specific averments that the tenant is *vergens ad inopiam,* or is removing effects or displenishing the subjects in breach of the hypothec, or that in some other way the landlord's right is prejudiced or affected.[73] The process in security is at the landlord's risk, and so, if the rent is duly paid on the due date, the proceedings are at the landlord's own expense.[74] Where rent was payable in advance, viz., on 15th May, but the commencement of the period of possession was on 28th May, in respect of which the rent was exigible, it was held competent to sequestrate before 28th May, when the rent was not paid on 15th May.[75]

Procedure in Sequestration.[76] The Writ asks the Court to sequestrate and to grant warrant to officers of the Court to inventory and secure

---

[67] Bell, *Comm.,* II, 33.
[68] Bell, § 1245.
[69] *Duncan* v *Lodijinsky* (1904) 6 F. 408.
[70] See Dobie, *Law and Practice, supra,* 422.
[71] Bell, *Comm.,* II, 33; *Encyclopaedia of Scots Law,* Vol. 8, 11.
[72] Bell, § 1245; Rankine, 401, 386.
[73] *Donald* v *Leitch* (1886) 13 R. 790; *Duffy* v *Gray* (1858) 20 D. 580; *McLaughlan* v *Reilly* (1892) 20 R. 41; Hume, *Lectures,* IV, 16.
[74] *Nicol* v *Mercer* (1902) 10 S.L.T. 142 (Sh. Ct.), 18 Sh. Ct. Rep. 253.
[75] *Henderson* v *Huzzard* (1934) 50 Sh. Ct. Rep. 300; Dobie, *Law and Practice, supra,* 425.
[76] See Sheriff Courts (Scotland) Act 1907, Rules 104-109; Dobie, *Law and Practice, supra,* 423 *et seq., Styles, supra,* 446 *et seq.;* Lewis, *Sheriff Court Practice,* 8th ed., 260-264.

the whole stock, fittings, furniture, goods and other effects, so far as subject to the hypothec, in security and for payment of rent due (and usually also current rent) with interest etc., and thereafter to grant warrant to sell by public roup the whole or so much of the effects sequestrated as will pay the rent, interest and expenses, and to order payment out of the proceeds or any consigned sum to the landlord; and also a crave for a plenishing order, should the sale produce less than is necessary for the hypothec; and, if hypothecated effects have been removed before the date of the Writ, warrant to search for, take possession of and carry back these effects. Warrant for sequestration etc. may include, where such is necessary, authority to open shut and lockfast places in order to carry out the warrant. In order to ensure the safety and security of the effects, a suitable fit person (a judicial manager) may be authorised to take charge of the sequestrated effects, or the tenant may be ordered to give caution that they will be made forthcoming.

The warrant to sequestrate is granted at once on presentation of the Writ, that is, on the landlord's *ex parte* statement,[77] and this authorises the inventorying of the effects and orders service of the Writ and answers to be lodged. The effects are inventoried and valued by a sheriff officer in the presence of one witness.[78] The officer must visit the lands, which is in accordance with " invariable practice ".[79] The inventory is the only legal evidence and is conclusive evidence of what has been sequestrated, and anything not in the inventory is not attached.[80] The landlord cannot use the effects in carrying on the business which the tenant carried on.[81]

Where the tenant is aware that sequestration proceedings are going to be taken and wishes to be heard, he may lodge a caveat and, if he does, he will be heard before the warrant is given.[82] He may also, where sequestration is being threatened, apply for and get interdict, if he wishes issues that have arisen between himself and the landlord to be decided, without waiting for the landlord to act.[83] In both these cases caution or consignation will be ordered by the Court as a condition of the hearing or the interdict.[84]

---

[77] Hume, *Lectures,* IV, 15; Dobie, *Law and Practice, supra,* 424.
[78] See *Lochgilphead Town Council* v *McIntyre* (1943) 59 Sh. Ct. Rep. 179, where it was held that it was unnecessary to appraise each article in a sequestration in the Ordinary Court.
[79] Rankine, 403.
[80] *Horsburgh* v *Morton* (1825) 3 S. 596; *Lamb* v *Grant* (1874) 11 S.L.R. 672. See *Marquis of Breadalbane* v *Tobermory Slate Quarry Co.* (1917) 33 Sh. Ct. Rep. 154, where the warrant authorised the inventorying of the tenant's *whole* effects so far as falling under the hypothec, irrespective of their value in relation to the rent sued for.
[81] *Lindsay* v *Earl of Wemyss* (1872) 10 M. 708.
[82] Dobie, *Styles, supra* 67; Lewis, *op. cit.,* 262.
[83] *Ibid.*
[84] *Ibid.*

If a third party's effects have been taken, he can appear in the process and claim them,[85] either by lodging a minute craving allowance to appear and recall of the sequestration in regard to his effects—this has been held the proper course for him to take[86]—or by an ordinary Writ.[87] Where the article is a hired one, the owner should apply for the reservation of the article until the tenant's goods have been disposed of and, if he does not do so, he cannot claim damages against the landlord, even if he has intimated that the article is his own.[88] A third party may insist on the tenant's goods being sold first.[89]

Recall of Sequestration. The Court will recall the sequestration, if caution is found for the rent or consignation of it is made, or on payment of it with expenses.[90] Caution includes the expenses of process.[91] Where the sequestration has been in security only and payment is made at the proper time, recall will be granted, but the landlord must pay his own expenses.[92] Sequestration may be recalled *de plano*, if, *e.g.*, the sum sued for is not true rent, or the rent is for a longer period than that of the tenant's tenure[93] or is for a subject never possessed by the tenant[94] or justly abandoned, without such delay as involves liability for rent.[95] Recall should be made by interlocutor of the Sheriff.[96]

Breach of Sequestration. After they have been inventoried, the effects are *in manibus curiae*. They cannot be removed or intermeddled with without judicial authority and, if anyone—tenant, purchaser or another creditor—does so, he incurs certain liabilities. Breach of the sequestration is a contempt of court, a delict or a quasi-criminal offence.[97] As such, it is cognisable in the first instance only by the Sheriff Court but may be dealt with by the Court of Session incidentally.[98] The guilty party incurs liability for all loss and damage caused by the breach to the landlord and such penalties as the Court may impose. Where there has been a deliberate breach by the tenant, the Court may summarily imprison him until the goods are restored or caution is found or con-

---

[85] *Lindsay, supra; Hoare* v *Mackay* (1905) 13 S.L.T. 588; *McIntosh* v *Potts* (1905) 7 F. 765.
[86] *McKechnie* v *Duke of Montrose* (1853) 15 D. 623.
[87] *Jack* v *Waddell's Trs.,* 1918 S.C. 73, where in the case of a poinding interdict after decree for sale was held competent. See Rankine, 403. When warrant to sell is *granted,* interdict is the proper course, Dobie, *Law and Practice, supra,* 428.
[88] *McIntosh, supra.*
[89] *Ibid.*
[90] *Galloway* v *McPherson* (1830) 8 S. 539; *Renfrew* v *Hall* (1901) 4 F. (J.) 27; *Stalker* v *Somerville* (1901) 4 F. (J.) 31; Dobie, *Law and Practice, supra,* 427.
[91] *Clark* v *Duncan* (1833) 12 S. 158.
[92] *Gordon* v *Suttie* (1836) 14 S. 954.
[93] *Tennent's Trs.* v *Maxwell* (1880) 17 S.L.R. 463.
[94] *Guthrie* v *Shearer* (1873) 1 R. 181. *Cf. Tennent's Trs., supra.*
[95] *Campbell* v *Boswall* (1839) 1 D. 1023.
[96] *Kippen* v *Oppenheim* (1846) 8 D. 957.
[97] Bell, § 1244; Hume, *Lectures,* IV, 15.
[98] *Muir* v *Downie* (1839) 2 D. 166.

signation is made.[99] It was held that the taking of sequestrated grain for farm servants or for the use of stock or horses was not a breach.[1] If the breach is by a third party and he was not party to any fraud, he will be ordered to restore the goods, if they are still in his power, and to pay damages; or to pay the rent with damages in respect of the landlord's loss either to the full extent thereof or up to the value of what has been removed.[2] A person poinding furniture (who ought to know of the right of hypothec) must inquire whether the seller is a tenant in arrear of rent; otherwise he will be *in mala fide*.[3] While ignorance of the sequestration by one in charge of the later roup or sale of the goods may be, it has been held,[4] a defence, Rankine questioned the soundness of this view.[5] If the third party knew of the sequestration and is thus *in mala fide,* he is liable for the whole rent.[6]

Damages for Wrongful Sequestration. Where the sequestration has been executed improperly or oppressively, *e.g.,* without a title to do so or where it was not reasonably necessary, as where the tenant is solvent and has counter claims against the landlord or there is an error as to the rent which is secured, or where a warrant to carry back effects was got in a case where the tenant had openly removed effects and before the rent was payable, or where it has been executed without regard to the tenant's interests, *e.g.,* where there has been gross inventorying beyond the amount necessary to pay the rent or where successive sequestrations have been needlessly used, the landlord will be liable in damages for wrongful sequestration.[7] The issue, says Rankine,[8] is purely a jury question, and no useful proposition of law can be laid down. The sequestration does not require to be reduced before damages can be claimed.[9]

Sale. This is the second step in sequestration. A separate warrant is obtained from the Sheriff for this purpose, and it must be executed by an officer of court or another person appointed by the Sheriff. The sale is by public roup or auction.[10] It has to be reported to the Court

[99] Hume, *supra; Goldie* v *Oswald* (1839) 1 D. 426.
[1] *McGlashan* v *Duke of Athole,* 29 June 1819 F.C.; *Gordon* v *Suttie, supra.* Probably this applies to domestic servants, Rankine, 405.
[2] Bell, § 1244; *Jack* v *McCaig* (1880) 7 R. 465; *McNaughton* v *Underwood* (1910) 27 Sh. Ct. Rep. 74; *Frame* v *Mills and Co.* (1909) 25 Sh. Ct. Rep. 236; *Mackersy* v *Edinburgh Loan Co.* (1912) 29 Sh. Ct. Rep. 28.
[3] *Jack* v *McCaig, supra.*
[4] *Laing* v *Robertson* (1829) 7 S. 335.
[5] Rankine, 405-6, as being inconsistent with cases of purchasers and with, in certain sorts of moveables, universal knowledge of the risk run by intromitters of hypothec.
[6] *Jack* v *McCaig, supra.*
[7] See, *e.g., Gray* v *Weir* (1891) 19 R. 25. *Cf. McLaughlan* v *Reilly* (1892) 20 R. 41; *Jack* v *Black,* 1911 S.C. 691; *McLeod* v *MacLeod* (1829) 7 S. 396; *Robertson* v *Galbraith* (1857) 19 D. 1016; *Steuart* v *Peddie* (1874) 2 R. 94; *McIntosh* v *Potts* (1905) 7 F. 765; *Gray* v *Smart* (1892) 19 R. 692.
[8] Rankine, 406.
[9] *McLeod* v *McLeod, supra.*
[10] Dobie, *Styles, supra,* 467.

within fourteen days and the landlord must lodge the roup rolls or certified copies of them and a state of debt.[11] The Sheriff may order the gross proceeds of the sale to be consigned. The next step is for the accounts to be taxed and the sale approved, and the landlord is then paid in full, or *pro tanto* if not enough is realised.[12] Where the landlord is paid in full, the balance, if any, is paid to the tenant less expenses, commissions and discounts on payments made by bill. This balance can be attached by ordinary diligence by creditors of the tenant, including the landlord.[13] Where sequestration has been in security only, warrant of sale will be granted only when the term of payment has arrived and is bygone, in the case of *invecta et illata;*[14] but, in the case of crop and stock, these may be sold before the term.[15] This was said to be because, while *invecta et illata* do not change much in price, crop and stock are subject to fluctuations in price and are expensive or troublesome to keep.[16] Liability for breach of sequestration may also occur in connection with a sale. Thus, where a grossly unnecessary amount of goods has been sold and the sale carried out in such a manner that a fair price cannot be got for the goods, the landlord is liable in damages for the wrongful use of sequestration.[17]

Whether the landlord is liable for the proceedings of the auctioneer at the sale is an undecided issue.[18]

Small Debt Cases. There are special forms of procedure in the Sheriff Small Debt Court where the rent or balance of rent does not exceed £50.[19] The procedure covers sequestration for current rent or in security.[20] It is sufficient if the term's rent does not exceed £50 without regard to the rent for the *cumulo* period. Breach of sequestration in such small debt cases involves summary punishment by a fine or imprisonment as for contempt of court. There is also liability in terms of the ordinary law. Where irregularities occur before decree in the small debt court, an action of damages is not allowed, since this would really represent an appeal from that court, which is not permitted.[21] Warrant can

---

[11] *Ibid.*
[12] *Ibid.*
[13] *McFarlane* v *Forrester* (1823) 2 S. 505; *Aitken* v *McKay* (1905) 22 Sh. Ct. Rep. 47; *Gatherer* v *Muirhead* (1909) 25 Sh. Ct. Rep. 357.
[14] *Wells* v *Proudfoot* (1800) Hume 225; *Duffy* v *Gray* (1858) 20 D. 580; Hume, *Lectures,* IV, 26.
[15] *Grant* v *Sherris* (1784) Mor. 6201; *Dow* v *Hay* (1784) Mor. 6202; Hume, *Lectures,* IV, 21.
[16] Rankine, 401. In modern times *invecta et illata* do, unfortuantely, change in price in the upward direction.
[17] See, *e.g., McLeod* v *McLeod, supra; Robertson* v *Galbraith, supra; McIntosh* v *Potts, supra.*
[18] See *Robertson, supra.*
[19] Small Debt (Scotland) Act 1837, ss. 5, 20; Sheriff Courts (Scotland) Act 1907, ss. 42, 43; Sheriff Courts (Civil Jurisdiction and Procedure) (Scotland) Act 1963.
[20] Sheriff Courts (Scotland) Act 1907, s. 43.
[21] *Crombie* v *McEwan* (1861) 23 D. 333.

be obtained to eject the tenant from displenished premises and to re-let them.[22]

Register of Sequestrations.   A sequestration must be registered in a Register kept by the Sheriff Clerk or other court officer having the custody of the records of the court where it has been granted in, or as nearly as may be in, a prescribed form.[23] This register can be inspected by any person on payment of a certain fee.[24]

Forfeiture of Hypothec.   The right of hypothec may be lost by the landlord as to any particular term's rent not only by the lapse of time for enforcement of it by sequestration but also by personal bar through undue delay in proceeding with the sale of the goods.[25] Abandonment may also be implied, if the landlord acquiesces in circumstances which are inconsistent with the hypothec existing for the time being.[26] If the landlord takes a bill for the rent or allows a poinding creditor to sell on condition that from the proceeds of the sale the rent will be paid, this will not, however, generally be treated as amounting to abandonment.[27] But a summons of sequestration does not infer abandonment of a claim to arrears of rent due for an earlier period.[28]

[22] Small Debt Amendment (Scotland) Act 1889, s. 6.
[23] Hypothec Amendment (Scotland) Act 1867, s. 7, as amended by the Statute Law Revision Act, 1893.
[24] *Ibid.*
[25] Bell, *Comm.,* II, 32.
[26] Rankine, 411.
[27] *Swinton* v *Stewart* (1776) 5 Bro. Supp. 477.
[28] *Findlay* v *Shanks* (1929) 46 Sh. Ct. Rep. 70.

CHAPTER XIV

TACIT RELOCATION

THE Roman Law doctrine of tacit relocation, whereby certain contracts, although entered into for a definite period of time, require notice of termination, applies in Scotland to leases, contracts of partnership and contracts of service. So far as a lease is concerned, tacit relocation amounts to a constructive renewal of the contract, if effective steps have not been taken to terminate it at its natural expiry or at a specified break. In England this doctrine is not followed, and no steps are required to determine a lease at its expiry date.[1] However, a somewhat similar effect is achieved from " holding over ", whereby a tenant continuing in possession after the expiry of a lease for years may be taken to hold upon such of the terms of the former lease as are consistent with a yearly tenancy.[2]

Effect. If neither party has given due notice of his intention to terminate the lease at its ish, the parties are by their silence assumed to have agreed that the lease should be prolonged.[3] The lease then continues upon the same terms as before, except as to duration. Irrespective of the nature of the subjects let, if the lease is for one year or longer, it is continued for a further period of one year, and so on from year to year, until due notice of termination is given by one of the parties; if the lease is for less than one year, it is continued successively for that period until due notice is given.[4] The first part of this rule as to the duration of the tacit relocation is amply vouched; the latter part is implied therein and in the nature of the right.[5] Part of the law is now based on statute: the Sheriff Courts (Scotland) Act, 1907,[6] with regard to lands exceeding two acres in extent held under a probative lease specifying a term of endurance, and the Agricultural Holdings (Scotland) Act, 1949,[7] with regard to agricultural holdings, both provide that a lease for a year or more shall in default of notice be renewed by tacit relocation for one year and thereafter from year to year.

Tacit relocation may apply whether the lease was originally constituted by formal writing or informally with the aid of *rei interventus.*[8]

[1] Woodfall, *Landlord and Tenant*, 26th ed., 910.
[2] *Ibid,* 1044.
[3] Hume, *Lectures*, IV, 101.
[4] Erskine, II, 6, 35; Bell, § 1265.
[5] Rankine, 602, and authorities cited there.
[6] s. 34, *infra* p. 267.
[7] s. 3, *infra* p. 301.
[8] *Buchanan* v *Harris & Sheldon* (1900) 2 F. 935.

The legal effect of tacit relocation is " that all the stipulations and conditions of the original contract remain in force, in so far as these are not inconsistent with any implied term of the renewed contract ".[9] Where a lease for more than one year has been continued by tacit relocation, one of those implied terms is that during the tacit relocation either party may terminate the lease at the end of a year by giving the requisite notice. It follows from this that an option to the tenant contained in the lease to demand a further lease for a period of years is quite inconsistent with the landlord's right to bring the continued lease to an end at the end of a year, and so such an option cannot be validly exercised after tacit relocation has set in.[10]

It is perhaps misleading to speak of a lease being " renewed " by tacit relocation. In the general theory of the doctrine there is ample support for the view that, while in every case there is a new contract implied from the tacit assent of parties to a continuance of the relationship, it does not follow that there is a new lease; from the first there is inherent in the bargain an implied agreement that, whatever may be the stipulated period of endurance, that period may be extended by tacit agreement of the parties.[11] Tacit relocation is therefore to be distinguished from prorogation and renewal;[12] they imply the making of a new lease by agreement; tacit relocation implies the prolongation of an existing one by tacit consent. However, tacit relocation is not an indefinite prolongation of a lease; it is the prolongation each year of the tenancy for a further year (that is if the lease was for a period of years), if the actings of the parties show that they are consenting to this prolongation.[13] As in all contracts, a tacit relocation or reletting must be based on consent, and in the case of tacit relocation the law implies that consent, if all parties are silent on the matter.[14]

Tacit relocation comes into operation immediately after the last date on which notice to terminate may competently be given, and both parties are bound by the new contract of lease, whether the tenant continues in possession or not.[15] Accordingly, even if the tenant quits the subjects at the end of a lease, he remains liable in the same way as if he had remained in possession.[16] However, a cautioner's liability comes to an end with the lease and is not expanded by a prolongation of the lease through tacit relocation.[17]

[9] Per Lord Watson in Neilson v Mossend Iron Co. (1886) 13 R. (H.L.) 50 at p. 54 (partnership).
[10] Commercial Union Assurance Co. Ltd. & Others, 1964 S.L.T. 62.
[11] Per L.J.C. Cooper in Douglas v Cassilis & Culzean Estates, 1944 S.C. 355 at p. 361.
[12] Supra, p. 41.
[13] Per L.P. Clyde in Smith v Grayton Estates Ltd., 1960 S.C. 349 at p. 354.
[14] Ibid.
[15] Robertson & Co. v Drysdale (1834) 12 S. 477.
[16] M'Intyre v M'Nab's Trs. (1831) 5 W. & S. 299.
[17] Bell, § 1265; Rankine, 413, 602.

Subjects. Tacit relocation applies to subjects of all kinds, but it is not an absolute rule that all leases require notice of termination. Leases of land let for less than one year for grazing or mowing, these uses being essentially seasonal, do not require notice, and there is no room for tacit relocation.[18] Similarly, no notice is required to terminate a lease of a furnished house for a definite period less than one year nor a lease of fishings or shootings merely for the season.[19] Where an employee occupies a house as part of his remuneration under a contract of service, there is no lease,[20] and he cannot plead tacit relocation upon his employment coming to an end.[21]

If separate subjects are let at a *cumulo* rent any notice to terminate the lease must cover all the subjects. So, where a house and shop were let together under the one lease, it was held that a notice to quit only the shop was ineffectual and did not prevent tacit relocation operating in respect of both subjects.[22]

The nature of the subjects regulates the length of the notice required.[23]

Parties. The right to found on tacit relocation is not lost by the death of the party entitled to claim it.[24] Thus, where a tenant already possessing on tacit relocation died within forty days before the term of Whitsunday without having received due notice, it was held that his heir had the benefit of tacit relocation to the same effect as the tenant would have had if he had survived.[25] Conversely, it is no bar to tacit relocation that the party having an interest to prevent it is incapacitated from doing so by death, insanity or minority.[26]

Notice. In order that the plea of tacit relocation may be excluded, it is necessary that due notice of termination be given by one party to the other. This rule has for long applied, even where the lease provides that the tenant is to remove at the ish without warning or process of removing.[27] The form and period of notice to be given by the landlord will be discussed more fully later.[28] Where notice is given by the tenant, the period must be the same as that required of the landlord.[29]

---

18 Agricultural Holdings (Scotland) Act 1949, s. 2 (1); *Macharg* (1805) Mor. App. *voce* Removing 4; *Secretary of State for Air* v *Davidson* (1950) 66 Sh. Ct. Rep. 59; *Roberts* v *Simpson* (1954) 70 Sh. Ct. Rep. 153; *Mackenzie* v *Laird,* 1959 S.L.T. 268; Hume, *Lectures,* IV, 111; Rankine, 599.
19 Gloag, *Contract,* 2nd ed., 733; Gloag and Henderson, *Introduction to the Law of Scotland,* 6th ed., 144.
20 *Supra,* p. 9.
21 *Young, Ross, Richardson & Co.* v *Paton* (1808) Hume 582; *MacArthur* v *MacMaster* (1894) 2 S.L.T. 137 (O.H.).
22 *Gates* v *Blair,* 1923 S.C. 430; but see opinion of Lord Selborne in *Ld. Adv.* v *Drysdale* (1874) 1 R. (H.L.) 27 at p. 36.
23 See Chapter XVII.
24 Gloag, *Contract,* 2nd ed., 735.
25 *Hume* v *M'Leod's Reps.* (1808) Hume 583.
26 Rankine, 599.
27 Hume, *Lectures,* IV, 113; Rankine, 556.
28 See Chapter XVII.
29 *M'Intyre* v *M'Nab's Trs.* (1831) 5 W. & S. 299.

Except in the case of urban subjects, the notice must be in writing.
It was for long the familiar practice for either the landlord or the
tenant of urban subjects to intimate verbally his intention not to allow
tacit relocation to occur,[30] provided that the other party was made
aware of his intention.[31] The Sheriff Courts (Scotland) Act, 1907,[32] enacted that where houses with or without land attached not exceeding
two acres in extent (and certain other subjects mentioned in the section)
are let for a year or more " notice of termination of tenancy shall be
given in writing to the tenant by or on behalf of the proprietor or to
the proprietor by or on behalf of the tenant "; and further, that such
notice shall entitle the proprietor to apply to the Sheriff for a warrant
for summary ejection in common form against the tenant. It has been
held that the provision in the Sheriff Courts (Scotland) Act, 1907, as to
notice being given in writing applies only when the procedure for
summary ejection is being followed.[33] Thus the provisions of that statute
do not affect the common law rule that in urban subjects the plea of
tacit relocation may be excluded by verbal or informal notice given by
either party.

Where there is a subtenant, the landlord in order to exclude the
plea of tacit relocation must give notice to the principal tenant as well
as to the subtenant, unless the subtenant has been recognised by the
landlord and the principal tenant has given up natural possession and
is no longer bound for the rent.[34] In the normal case where the principal
tenant has sublet the subjects and remains liable for the rent to the
landlord, the principal tenant must receive notice.[35] Tacit relocation
would seem to operate in favour of a principal tenant, who has given
up natural possession but who remains in civil possession by collecting
the subrents.[36] Where a principal tenant, but not the subtenant, had
received due notice of termination, it was held that the subtenant could
not be summarily ejected, but opinion was expressly reserved as to
whether his continued possession could found a plea of tacit relocation
for him;[37] it is difficult to see how it could found such a plea, the principal tenant's right having come to an end.[38] There is obviously no need
to give notice to a subtenant, where subletting is excluded and the landlord has not recognised him.[39]

---

[30] *Tait* v *Sligo* (1766) Mor. 13864; *Gilchrist* v *Westren* (1890) 17 R. 363; *Hood* v
    N.B. Railway Co. (1895) 3 S.L.T. 196 (O.H.); Hume, *Lectures,* IV, 110.
[31] *Gilchrist* v *Westren* (1890) 17 R. 363.
[32] s. 37.
[33] *Gillies* v *Fairlie* (1920) 36 Sh. Ct. Rep. 6; *Craighall Cast-Stone Co.* v *Wood
    Bros.,* 1931 S.C. 66; *infra* p. 273.
[34] Hume, *Lectures,* IV, 105-106; Rankine, 599.
[35] *Thomson* v *Harvie* (1823) 2 S. 581 (N.E. 498); Hume, *Lectures,* IV, 105.
[36] Rankine, 600.
[37] *Robb* v *Brearton* (1895) 22 R. 885.
[38] Rankine, 600.
[39] Hume, *Lectures,* IV, 106.

Formality of Notice. It has already been seen that the notice founded upon as excluding tacit relocation must be made timeously.[40] However, it is not entirely clear whether the notice required to prevent the operation of tacit relocation requires the same degree of formality as the notice which a landlord would have to give as a preliminary to an action of removing. For example, would a technical error in preparing a notice, making it ineffective to found an action of removing at the landlord's instance,[41] be useless to found upon as excluding tacit relocation? Can an invalid notice of removal be ignored? It has been held that a notice affecting only part of subjects let does not prevent tacit relocation operating for the whole subjects,[42] but this seems to lose sight of the principle that tacit relocation is based on tacit consent.[43]

This question was raised in cases involving a plurality of tenants or landlords. Where there were two or more tenants, notice given by one of them was held to be sufficient, if it could be shown that he had the authority of the others; but opinions were reserved on the general question whether all the joint tenants must concur in giving notice in order to avoid tacit relocation.[44] One of two or more joint proprietors could give notice of termination, if it could be shown that he had the authority of the others, which authority could be proved by parole evidence; but again the question whether notice by one such *pro indiviso* proprietor is sufficient to prevent the operation of tacit relocation was not decided.[45] Thus, both in the case of joint tenants and in the case of joint landlords opinions differed as to whether one of them could at his own hand by giving notice exclude tacit relocation or whether all must concur. It would seem an oppressive rule that demanded that one of two or more joint tenants or joint landlords should remain bound by a lease after its natural termination, merely because one or more of his co-obligants failed to concur with him in giving notice.[46] The theory of tacit relocation is that silence on the part of landlord or tenant implies that the other party is entitled to assume that the lease is continued by consent; but, if one of two joint tenants, so far from being silent, has spoken, and that without ambiguity, to the contrary effect by giving notice of termination, there would appear to be no room for the application of the theory on which tacit relocation depends.[47] For the contrary view that all joint tenants or joint landlords must concur it was argued that, if only one tenant or landlord had given notice, the notice was invalid, effect could not be given to an invalid notice, and therefore tacit reloca-

---

40 *Supra,* p. 223.
41 *Rae* v *Davidson,* 1954 S.C. 361.
42 *Gates* v *Blair,* 1923 S.C. 430.
43 Gloag, *Contract,* 2nd ed., 734 (note 3).
44 *Graham* v *Stirling,* 1922 S.C. 90.
45 *Walker* v *Hendry,* 1925 S.C. 855.
46 Opinion of L.P. Clyde in *Graham* v *Stirling, supra,* at p. 106.
47 Opinion of L.J.C. Alness in *Walker* v *Hendry, supra,* at p. 875.

15

tion took place.[48] However, the difficulty has now been resolved by a
decision, that, since tacit relocation was based on the implied consent
of all the parties to a lease, a notice of removing by one of two joint
tenants was sufficient to exclude tacit relocation and to terminate the
lease.[49] There were three possible constructions to put on the notice :
the first, that it terminated the tenancy so far as one tenant was concerned was rejected as it would convert the lease into a totally different
contract; the second was that it terminated the contract altogether; the
third was that coming from only one tenant it was invalid and inept;
the third construction ignored the meaning of tacit relocation which is
based on the implied consent of all the parties to the lease.[50] There seems
little doubt that notice given by one of two or more joint landlords would
be equally effective to exclude tacit relocation.

Tacit Relocation Excluded. There is room for the doctrine only
when the parties are silent and allow the lease to expire without notice.
Where a tenant gave notice of his intention to remove at the expiry of
his lease, but did not do so on account of illness, it was held that his
continued posssesion could not be founded on tacit relocation, but rendered him liable to violent profits as one possessing without any title.[51]
Tacit relocation is automatically excluded by the parties entering
into a new lease either for a year, which may be verbal, or for more than
one year;[52] and this has been held even in special circumstances, where
the tenant continued to pay the old rent.[53] In several cases continued
payment of rent and possession following upon informally concluded
negotiations for a renewal have been ascribed to the new lease and not
to tacit relocation on the old lease.[54] Where a landlord intimated an
increase of rent and the tenant replied that he would not pay it, but
did not give notice to terminate the lease and remained in possession, it
was held that he must be taken to have assented to the new terms and
that tacit relocation was excluded.[55]
Either party may bar himself from founding on tacit relocation. Thus
a tenant, who, by making an application to the Crofters' Commission,
tried to put it beyond the landlord's power to bring his tenancy to an
end, was held to be barred from pleading tacit relocation, as tacit relocation implies tacit consent.[56] A tenant, who abandons his lease or does

---

[48] Opinion of Lord Anderson in *Walker* v *Hendry, supra,* at p. 883; *cf. Gates* v
Blair, 1923 S.C. 430.
[49] *Smith* v *Grayton Estates Ltd.,* 1960 S.C. 349.
[50] *Ibid.,* per L.P. Clyde at p. 354, following the *dicta* of L.P. Clyde in *Graham* v
Stirling, supra, and L.J.C. Alness in *Walker* v *Hendry, supra.*
[51] *Tod* v *Fraser* (1889) 17 R. 226.
[52] *Blain* v *Ferguson* (1840) 2 D. 546; *Morrison* v *Campbell* (1842) 4 D. 1426;
Rex & Co. v *Boyd,* Oban Sheriff Court not reported (1949) C.L. 4775.
[53] *Montgomerie* v *Vernon* (1895) 22 R. 465.
[54] *M'Kenzie* v *M'Kenzie* (1799) Hume 801; *Sutherland's Tr.* v *Miller's Tr.* (1888)
16 R. 10; *Buchanan* v *Harris & Sheldon* (1900) 2 F. 935.
[55] *M'Farlane* v *Mitchell* (1900) 2 F. 901.
[56] *MacArthur* v *MacMaster* (1894) 2 S.L.T. 137 (O.H.).

not retain natural or civil possession after its ish, cannot found on tacit relocation.[57] Where a tenant died before the ish and his heir made no attempt to interfere with the farm, which was managed by his younger brothers, it was held that there was no room for tacit relocation in favour of the heir, who had not taken possession and had had no contact with the landlord.[58]

Objection Excluded. Either party may bar himself from objecting to a plea of tacit relocation. If a landlord, after giving notice to quit, takes no further steps and allows the tenant to remain in possession, the inference is that the parties have agreed to depart from the notice and that tacit relocation will come in.[59] Where, however, the landlord of a dwellinghouse affected by the Rent Acts has served a notice to quit, acceptance of rent for not more than three months from the expiry of the notice is not deemed to prejudice any right to possession.[60] Mere lapse of time on the part of the landlord in enforcing a decree of removing is not sufficient to let in tacit relocation, but there may be circumstances where delay beyond a reasonable time will infer tacit relocation.[61] If a tenant, who has given notice, continues in possession without disturbance by the landlord, the parties may be presumed to have changed their purpose and the tacit relocation will revive.[62] Where a tenant of grain lofts left grain there and it was found that there was no compulsion on him to do so, it was held that his continued possession barred him from founding on a letter giving up the premises and that he was liable for a further year's rent as a result of tacit relocation.[63]

A party, who has received inadequate notice from the other without objection and has allowed the other to act on the assumption that it was sufficient, may be barred from founding on the inadequacy.[64] Either party may be barred from objecting to a plea of tacit relocation by having paid or accepted rent in respect of a period after the termination of the lease.[65] Most of the authorities, however, are cases of notices being held ineffectual for the purpose of founding an action of removal by the landlord.[66]

---

[57] Rankine, 600.
[58] *Wilson* v *Stewart* (1853) 16 D. 106.
[59] Erskine, II, 6, 35; *Milner's Curator Bonis* v *Mason*, 1965 S.L.T. (Sh. Ct.) 56.
[60] Increase of Rent and Mortgage Interest (Restrictions) Act 1920, s. 16 (3); *infra*, p. 516.
[61] *Taylor* v *Earl of Moray* (1892) 19 R. 399.
[62] Erskine, II, 6, 35.
[63] *Robertson & Co.* v *Drysdale* (1834) 12 S. 477.
[64] *Gordon* v *Bryden*, 13 Jan. 1803 F.C., Mor. 13854; *Dunlop* v *Meiklem* (1876) 4 R. 11; Hume, *Lectures,* IV, 109.
[65] Rankine, 601.
[66] *Infra*, p. 279.

CHAPTER XV

IRRITANCY

Introduction. An irritancy is the forfeiture or determination of a right consequent upon an omission to comply with, or an act done in contravention of, the express or implied conditions upon which the particular right is held.[1] An irritancy may arise by force of law as an implied term of the contract in respect of failure to implement an essential condition, and this is termed a legal irritancy.[2] An irritancy may also arise as a result of express agreement in the contract and this is known as a conventional irritancy.[3] Frequently a conventional irritancy is merely a copy of a legal irritancy.

In the event of a breach of the contract of lease by the tenant, the landlord is entitled to raise an action of damages for the breach.[4] Alternatively, if the lease infers an irritancy, either legal or conventional, the landlord has the option of terminating the lease.[5] If he exercises this option, he cannot both irritate the lease and claim damages for premature termination,[6] unless he expressly reserves his right to damages.[7] Normally an irritancy clause expressly gives the landlord the option of bringing the lease to an end in the event of certain events occurring;[8] sometimes, however, without expressly giving the landlord the option of terminating the lease, the clause may merely state that, in the event of certain events occurring, the lease shall *ipso facto* become null and void.[9] In whatever way the lease is expressed, it is construed as giving the landlord an option to bring the lease to an end, which he may or may not exercise, and not as giving the defaulting tenant a right to abandon it.[10] The landlord must take overt steps to exercise his option, and an irritancy clause does not dispense with the necessity for giving notice of his intention to invoke it.[11] The remedy of irritancy is open to the landlord, only if there is an irritancy implied by law, or if there is an irritant clause expressed in the lease.

---

[1] *Encyclopaedia of the Laws of Scotland,* Vol. 8, 968; Gloag, *Contract,* 2nd ed., 665.
[2] *Ibid.*
[3] *Ibid.*
[4] *Kinloch* v *Mansfield* (1836) 14 S. 905; Rankine, 532.
[5] *Bidoulac* v *Sinclair's Tr.* (1889) 17 R. 144; Gloag, *op. cit.,* 668.
[6] *Walker's Trs.* v *Manson* (1886) 13 R. 1198; *Buttercase & Geddie's Tr.* v *Geddie* (1897) 24 R. 1128; *Bidoulac* v *Sinclair's Tr., supra*; Gloag, *op. cit.,* 669.
[7] *Walker's Trs.* v *Manson, supra.*
[8] *Buttercase & Geddie's Tr.* v *Geddie, supra.*
[9] *Bidoulac* v *Sinclair's Tr., supra.*
[10] *Kinloch* v *Mansfield, supra; Bidoulac* v *Sinclair's Tr., supra.*
[11] *Waugh* v *More Nisbett* (1882) 19 S.L.R. 427.

Legal Irritancies. The irritancies which are implied by law rest partly on common law, but mainly now on statute.

(1) Common Law. Before 1756 there was at common law an implied legal irritancy where a tenant had failed to pay rent for two successive years.[12] This remedy is analogous to the irritancy *ob non solutum canonem* implied in feu rights.[13] A distinction seems to have been drawn between a default for two years, which implied an absolute irritancy, and a default for a lesser period, in which event the tenant to avoid removing could pay up the arrears and find caution.[14] This common law irritancy applied principally to agricultural subjects, but there seems to be no reason why it should not extend to other subjects;[15] it has been held to apply to urban subjects.[16] The irritancy was enforceable by means of an extraordinary action of removing in the Court of Session.[17]

(2) Act of Sederunt, 1756. The common law irritancy was largely confirmed and slightly altered by the Act of Sederunt of 14th December, 1756,[18] which, however, applies only to agricultural, including pastoral, subjects.[19] This provides that where a tenant has irritated his tack by suffering two years' rent to be in arrear, it shall be lawful for the landlord to declare the irritancy before the Sheriff, and to insist in a summary removing before him; and it shall be lawful for the Sheriff to find the irritancy incurred and to decern in the removing.[20] It also provides that, where the tenant is one full year's rent in arrear or deserts his possession and leaves the ground unlaboured, the Sheriff may ordain the tenant to find caution for the arrears and for five future crops or for the remainder of the lease, if less than five years, and, failing caution, to remove him summarily.[21] Thus, the Act of Sederunt brought the irritancy within the jurisdiction of the Sheriff, substantially re-enacted the common law distinction between arrears of two years, which incurred an irritancy, and arrears of one year, in respect of which the landlord could only demand caution;[22] and it extended the remedy of caution to the case of desertion of the subjects by the tenant.

The provisions of the Act of Sederunt were modified and altered by the Hypothec Abolition (Scotland) Act, 1880, which reduced the periods for which an irritancy was incurred and caution could be demanded to

---

[12] Hume, *Lectures*, IV, 116-117; Rankine, 532-533.
[13] *Regiam Majestaten* (Stair Soc. Vol. II), 206-207; Rankine, 533.
[14] *Alexander* v *Jackson* (1744) Mor. 15306; Hume, *Lectures*, IV, 117.
[15] Rankine, 533.
[16] *Halyburton* v *Cunningham* (1677) Mor. 13801.
[17] *Nisbet* v *Aikman* (1866) 4 M. 284 (in which Lords Cowan and Benholme at pp. 289 and 290 explain Erskine II, 6, 50).
[18] Printed in Codifying Act of Sederunt 1913, L. 15; Hume, *Lectures*, IV, 118-124; Rankine, 533-535; Ross, *Lectures*, 2nd ed., II, 540, et seq.
[19] *Wright* v *Wightman* (1875) 3 R. 68; Rankine, 533.
[20] s. 4; Ross, *op. cit.*, II, 544.
[21] s. 5; Ross, *op. cit.*, II, 545.
[22] *Morton* v *Murray's Reps.* (1793) Mor. 13872; *Urquhart* v *Mackenzie* (1824) 3 S. 84 (N.E. 56); *M'Allister* v *Sprot* (1825) 4 S. 353 (N.E. 357); *Mackenzie* v *Mackenzie* (1848) 10 D. 1009; *Oliver* v *Weir's Trs.* (1870) 8 M. 786.

one year and six months respectively.[23] However, so far as agricultural
holdings are concerned, it has been provided by successive statutes, now
embodied in the Agricultural Holdings (Scotland) Act, 1949, that the
procedure of the Act of Sederunt shall not apply in any case where the
procedure for the removal of a tenant for non-payment of rent is competent.[24] Thus, as the Act of Sederunt relates only to agricultural subjects,
it must be regarded as virtually obsolete, although not repealed.

(3) House Letting and Rating (Scotland) Act, 1911. The fact that
the common law irritancy is available in the case of urban subjects is
of little practical importance as jurisdiction is limited to the Court of
Session, and in any event more summary remedies are available to a
landlord who by virtue of his right of hypothec can demand security
for rent from the tenant under pain of removing.[25] However, a statutory
irritancy for non-payment of rent in the case of small houses was introduced by the House Letting and Rating (Scotland) Act, 1911,[26] whereby,
if the occupier of a small dwelling-house shall at any time be in arrear
with his rent for not less than seven days, the owner may give him twenty-
eight days' notice to quit.[27]

(4) Agricultural Holdings (Scotland) Act, 1949. For agricultural
subjects the remedy given by the Act of Sederunt of 1756 has been virtually superseded by the Agricultural Holdings (Scotland) Act, 1949,[28]
whereby, if six months' rent is due and unpaid, the landlord may raise
an action in the Sheriff Court for the removal of the tenant at the next
term of Whitsunday or Martinmas, unless the arrears are paid or caution
found for the arrears and for one further year's rent.[29]

Purging. It is a general principle that a legal irritancy, although incurred, may be purged by payment of the arrears of rent before decree
is extracted in the action taken to enforce it.[30] So an irritancy incurred
under the Act of Sederunt of 1756 could be purged by payment of the
arrears or by the desertion ceasing before the decree was extracted, and
the same principle applies to the other legal irritancies both at common
law and statute.[31] After decree has been extracted, purgation comes too
late.[32]

Conventional Irritancies. Irritancy clauses in leases usually relate
to failure to pay rent, prohibited assignation and the insolvency of the

---

[23] ss. 2 and 3.
[24] Agricultural Holdings (Scotland) Act 1949, s. 19 (3); *Fletcher* v *Fletcher* (1930)
   47 Sh. Ct. Rep. 336.
[25] *Supra,* p. 212.
[26] s. 5.
[27] *Infra,* p. 271.
[28] s. 19.
[29] *Infra,* p. 355.
[30] Rankine, 538; Gloag, *op. cit.,* 665.
[31] Rankine, 538-539.
[32] Rankine, 539.

tenant, but any lawful condition of the contract may be fenced with an irritancy clause for the purpose of giving the landlord the option of terminating it upon a breach of that condition by the tenant.

Non-Payment of Rent. The object of this clause is sometimes to curtail, or even to prolong,[33] the period of arrears after which a legal irritancy would be implied, or to simplify the procedure for enforcing the irritancy, but most usually the object is to ensure that the irritancy is not purgeable. So far as agricultural subjects are concerned, the Agricultural Holdings (Scotland) Act 1949[34] provides a fairly adequate remedy for non-payment of rent, while for urban subjects the landlord's hypothec gives an effective weapon to the landlord. However, it is usually desirable to include the clause in urban as well as agricultural leases, and it would seem practically essential in cases where the hypothec does not normally apply, for example, leases of furnished houses and sporting subjects. The irritancy is available only when there are arrears for the specified period at the date of raising the action.[35]

Prohibited Assignation and Subletting. The right of the landlord to object to assignations and subleases where the lease contains an exclusion of assignees and subtenants has already been considered.[36] The exclusion may be fenced with an irritancy clause, the object of which is not only to prevent the assignation or sublet but to cut down the right of the cedent. So where the tenant of a farm under a lease containing an irritancy in the event of his assigning it granted, in consideration of a loan, a deed of factory and commission giving the factor an unlimited power of management, it was observed that, if the deed was in fact an assignation, the irritancy so incurred could not be purged.[37]

Insolvency. The effect of an irritancy in the event of the insolvency or the equivalent of the debtor has already been discussed.[38]

Other Grounds. Failure to possess or stock the subjects is frequently made the ground of an irritancy.[39] An irritancy for failing to conduct a public house properly or doing anything which might endanger the continuance or renewal of the licence was held to be enforceable, but not to have been incurred in the circumstances of the case.[40] Where, however, it was provided that an irritancy was to be incurred if " in the opinion of " the landlord the tenant should so misconduct or neglect

[33] *Ogilvie* v *Duff* (1834) 12 S. 857.
[34] s. 19.
[35] *Hog* v *Morton* (1825) 3 S. 617.
[36] *Supra*, p. 154.
[37] *Lyon* v *Irvine* (1874) 1 R. 512.
[38] *Supra*, p. 193.
[39] *Stuart* v *Warnocks* (1883) 20 S.L.R. 863 (O.H.).
[40] *Noble* v *Hart* (1896) 24 R. 174.

the business as to endanger the licence, the irritancy was held to have
been incurred; and it was also decided that the landlord was not bound
to give reasons for his opinion, the tenant having made no relevant averment of fraud or *mala fides*.[41] A clause in a long lease providing for
an irritancy in the event of the subjects being used as a public house
was held to be enforceable.[42]

Commonly the irritancy clause in a lease provides that it is to
operate, if the tenant fails to pay his rent for a specified period, or shall
become insolvent or the equivalent, " or shall commit a breach of any
further term or condition of the lease ".[43] In the case of agricultural
subjects, the irritancy may extend to failing to reside personally on the
farm, failing to maintain an adequate stock, and failing to cultivate
according to the rules of good husbandry.

Purging of Conventional Irritancies. A conventional irritancy, once it
has been incurred, cannot be purged by payment of the arrears of rent or
by remedy of any other breach on which the landlord founds.[44] There is
some ground for holding on the analogy of feus[45] that, if a conventional
irritancy is a mere copy of a legal irritancy,[46] it may be purged by payment
before extract of the decree enforcing the irritancy, but even such an irritancy cannot be purged if it is accompanied by an express clause excluding the power to purge.[47] At one time it was not entirely clear whether a
conventional irritancy for non-payment of rent in terms other than those
implied by law was purgeable,[48] but the weight of opinion was against
purgation.[49] However, apart from cases where the conventional irritancy
is merely a copy of a legal one, it has been finally established that a
conventional irritancy cannot be purged.[50] In the case in question, a
farm lease provided for an irritancy in the event of the tenant failing
to pay his rent within three months after it became due; the tenant having failed to pay the half year's rent due at Whitsunday and the rent
being still unpaid in October, the landlord, having previously given
notice of his intention, brought an action for declarator that the tenant
had incurred an irritancy and for an order ordering him to remove; on
9th November the tenant paid the arrears of rent and thereafter lodged
defences on the ground that the irritancy had been purged by payment

---

[41] *Guild* v *M'Lean* (1897) 25 R. 106.
[42] *Lord Belhaven and Stenton* v *Chassels* (1904) 12 S.L.T. 290 (O.H.); *cf. Gold* v
   Houldsworth (1870) 8 M. 1006 (pactional rent).
[43] *Encyclopaedia of Scottish Legal Styles,* Vol. 6, No. 146.
[44] Rankine, 547-548. See Gloag, *op. cit.,* 665-6
[45] *Lockhart* v *Shiells* (1770) Mor. 7244; *Tailors of Aberdeen* v *Coutts* (1840) 1
   Rob. App. 296; *Duncanson* v *Giffen* (1878) 15 S.L.R. 356; *Maxwell's Trs.* v
   Bothwell School Board (1893) 20 R. 958.
[46] *Hogg* v *Hogg* (1780) 2 Pat. 516.
[47] *Finlayson* v *Clayton* (1761) Mor. 7239; *Hog* v *Morton* (1825) 3 S. 617; *Earl of
   Elgin* v *Whittaker and Street* (1902) S.L.T. 375 (O.H.).
[48] Gloag, *op. cit.,* 667.
[49] Hume, *Lectures,* IV, 123; Bell, §§ 1248-1249; Hunter, *Landlord and Tenant,*
   4th ed., II, 142; Mackay, *Court of Session Practice,* II, 98; Rankine, 347.
[50] *McDouall's Trs.* v *MacLeod,* 1949 S.C. 593.

of the rent, the irritant clause being merely a remedy for non-payment; after an exhaustive review of the authorities,[51] the Court held that, as the parties to the lease had bargained that failure of punctual payment should irritate the lease, payment after the action had been raised could not affect the bargain, and that the landlord was entitled to decree. It was observed that a different decision might have resulted had the landlord made a misuse or an oppressive use of his powers, or where the stipulation in the lease as to the effect of non-payment of rent was merely an expression of the common or statutory law.[52]

The Court has intervened to prevent a misuse of the irritancy, for example, when there was an excusable error as to whether each of several lessees was liable for the whole or only part of the rent, or where the tenant had been wrongfully ousted from possession, or where payment had been offered to the landlord.[53] More recently, however, irritancies other than those incurred by failure to pay rent have been regarded as coming under the principle that a party who has agreed to an irritancy must submit to its enforcement. Irritancies incurred on insolvency are strictly enforced, as their purpose is to give the landlord power to terminate a lease to a tenant whose financial status is unsatisfactory. Irritancies incurred on the ground of admitted insolvency are not rendered unenforceable by the tenant settling with his creditors.[54] Where a lease provided that, if the tenant by allowing the rent to run into arrear should suffer sequestration at the landlord's instance to be applied for and awarded against him, the lease was to terminate at the option of the landlord, it was held that, as the conventional irritancy was not the mere expression of a legal one, the tenant could not purge the irritancy by paying the arrears.[55] It was observed that the Court will not interfere in cases of conventional irritancies, unless there is abuse or oppression, as, for example, if the landlord takes advantage of the irritancy by instant sequestration without notice to the tenant.[56] A tenant, who had incurred an irritancy by granting a deed equivalent to an assignation, contended that he could purge the irritancy by withdrawing the deed;[57] " the answer to that, and a good one it is, is that conventional irritancies are not purgeable, and that there is nothing in this case to take it out of that rule ".[58]

Enforcement of Irritancy. Apart from cases where the Court may exercise an equitable jurisdiction to allow a tenant in default to purge

---

[51] *Ibid., per* L.J.C. Thomson at p. 599, Lord Mackay at p. 603, and Lord Jamieson at p. 616.
[52] *Ibid., per* L.J.C. Thomson at p. 603.
[53] Rankine, 548 and older cases cited there.
[54] *Gordon* (1805) Mor. App. *voce* Tack 11; *Hall* v *Grant* (1831) 9 S. 612; *Tennent* v *Macdonald* (1836) 14 S. 976.
[55] *Stewart* v *Watson* (1864) 2 M. 1414, approved in *M'Douall's Trs.* v *MacLeod, supra;* Gloag, *op. cit.,* 668. See Hume, *Lectures,* IV, 123.
[56] *Ibid., per* L.J.C. Inglis at p. 1420.
[57] *Lyon* v *Irvine* (1874) 1 R. 512; Gloag, *op. cit.,* 668.
[58] *Ibid., per* L.P. Inglis at p. 518.

an irritancy in exceptional circumstances and on the ground of oppression,[59] it is generally accepted that, if the parties have agreed to an irritancy, the Court will enforce it, and that considerations of hardship are irrelevant.[60] This is a simple and strict question of contract and it is altogether incompetent for the Court to enter into any question as to whether the landlord has made a hard bargain with his tenant or not.[61] An attempt has been made to draw a distinction between an irritancy, which is a fair condition of the lease and an irritancy which is penal,[62] but the distinction is non-existent, as every irritancy runs the risk of being penal.[63]

Although a landlord, who has enforced an irritancy clause, is precluded from claiming damages for premature termination of the lease,[64] he is probably not barred from claiming damages for breaches of other conditions.[65] Most of the authorities involve irritancy on the ground of bankruptcy, but even then, there seems no reason why irritancy at the landlord's instance, while precluding damages for premature termination, should preclude damages for any prior breaches.[66]

In order to enforce an irritancy the landlord must discharge his own obligations under the lease.[67] Enforcement of an irritancy, however, may, extinguish the right of the tenant to enforce obligations on the landlord. Thus, the termination of a lease on account of non-payment of rent precluded the tenant from requiring the landlord to implement an obligation to take over sheep stock at valuation at the "waygoing".[68] It is a general rule of law that he who sows a crop is also entitled to reap it; however, an irritancy clause may be expressed in terms wide enough to deprive the tenant or his trustee in sequestration of the crop which he has sown.[69] Without a clause forfeiting the crop to the landlord the enforcement of an irritancy would not deprive the tenant of his crop.[70]

Procedure. It is not within the scope of this work to discuss the procedure to be followed in an action of irritancy,[71] but a brief outline may be given of its nature and form.

[59] *Stewart* v *Watson* (1864) 2 M. 1414, *per* L.J.C. Inglis at p. 1420.
[60] *Moncrieff* v *Hay* (1842) 5 D. 249; *Chalmers Tr.* v *Dick's Tr.*, 1909 S.C. 761.
[61] *Moncrieff* v *Hay, supra, per* Lord Moncreiff at p. 259.
[62] *Scott* v *Wotherspoon* (1829) 7 S. 481; *Horn* v *M'Lean* (1830) 8 S. 329.
[63] Rankine, 547.
[64] *Supra,* p. 228.
[65] *Alan's Tr.* v *Allan & Sons* (1891) 19 R. 215.
[66] Gloag, *op. cit.,* 669.
[67] *Macnab* v *Willison,* 1960 S.L.T. (Notes) 25.
[68] *Marquis of Breadalbane* v *Stewart* (1904) 6 F. (H.L.) 23; contrast the effect of a break, *infra,* p. 244.
[69] *Chalmers' Tr.* v *Dick's Tr.*, 1909 S.C. 761.
[70] *M'Kinley* v *Hutchison's Tr.*, 1935 S.L.T. 62, in which *dicta* in *Chalmers' Tr.* v *Dick's Tr.*, to the effect that growing crops are *partes soli* are criticised; but these *dicta* were followed in *Trinity House of Leith* v *Mitchell and Rae,* 1957 S.L.T. (Sh. Ct.) 38.
[71] See Mackay, *Manual of Practice,* 377-378; Maclaren, *Court of Session Practice,* 649; Dobie, *Sheriff Court Practice,* 25 and 415-416.

Legal and conventional irritancies do not become effective without a decree of extraordinary removing, unless the tenant is willing to remove. A notice of removing is not appropriate in an extraordinary removing,[72] but the tenant is entitled to receive distinct intimation of the landlord's intention to bring the lease to a premature end.[73] This rule applies even where the lease itself provides that in the event of the irritancy being incurred the lease shall *ipso facto* become null and the tenant obliges himself to remove without warning or process of removing.[74] The facts founded on by the landlord as constituting the breach, if not admitted, must be proved, and, even if they are admitted, the question as to time of removal may be a matter within the discretion of the Court.[75] An action of interdict is not an appropriate method of enforcing an irritancy,[76] although interim interdict has been granted in special circumstances.[77]

The landlord must exercise his option to terminate within a reasonable time, but surrender of his rights will not be readily inferred.[78] Where an irritancy had been incurred by a tenant assigning his lease, and the landlord did not at once elect to terminate it but drew the tenant's attention to the contravention and entered into negotiations, which ultimately proved abortive, for an increase of rent from the assignee, it was held that the tenant could not validly exercise an option to purchase the subjects, when by assigning the lease he was in breach of one of its material conditions, and that the landlord's right to irritate had not been waived, but was merely in reserve.[79]

Declarator. It is common to combine an action of removing on the ground of irritancy with one of declarator that the irritancy has in fact been incurred. At one time it was thought to be the general rule that irritancies whether legal or conventional must be judicially declared,[80] although it had been held that a conventional irritancy in a lease on the bankruptcy of the tenant was enforceable without a declarator.[81] For a long time the Sheriff's jurisdiction in matters of heritable right and title was in abeyance and resort had to be made to the Court of Session for a

---

[72] *Pickard* v *Reid*, 1953 S.L.T. (Sh. Ct.) 5; *infra*, p. 279.
[73] *Waugh* v *More Nisbett* (1882) 19 S.L.R. 427.
[74] *Supra*, p. 228.
[75] *M'Niven* v *Murray* (1847) 9 D. 1138; *Williamson* v *Johnstone* (1848) 11 D 332; *Stewart* v *Watson* (1864) 2 M. 1414; *Lyon* v *Irvine* (1874) 1 R. 512.
[76] *Rankine* v *M'Lachlan* (1864) 3 M. 128.
[77] *Chalmers' Tr.* v *Dick's Tr.* (1908) 16 S.L.T. 105.
[78] *Tennant* v *M'Donald* (1836) 14 S. 976; *Lindsay* v *Hogg* (1855) 17 D. 788; *Bidoulac* v *Sinclair's Tr.* (1889) 17 R. 144.
[79] *Penman* v *Mackay*, 1922 S.C. 385.
[80] Bell, *Leases*, 3rd ed., 414.
[81] *Gordon* (1805) Mor. App. *voce* Tack. 11; *Forbes* v *Duncan*, 2 June 1812 F.C.; Hume, *Lectures*, IV, 92; Hunter, *Landlord and Tenant*, 4th ed., II, 134; Rankine, 546; Maclaren, *Court of Session Practice*, 749.

declaration of a heritable right;[82] however, the extension of the jurisdiction of the Sheriff Court to include matters of heritable right[83] generally makes it immaterial, on the question whether a removing without declarator of irritancy is competent, whether the case depends in that Court or the Court of Session.[84] There are certainly many extraordinary removings in which declaratory conclusions are both appropriate and expedient, and whenever the questions as to the legality of the irritancy or its existence are sufficiently serious as to make it expedient and necessary in the opinion of the Court (Court of Session or Sheriff Court) that they should be made the subjects of express declaratory conclusions, then the Court is entitled to insist on declarator, and will do so, to the effect of treating the action as incompetent, unless or until proper declaratory conclusions are brought before it; it will be seen, however, that the grounds on which this practice rests are grounds not of absolute legal competency or incompetency, but of convenience and high expediency.[85] No declaratory conclusions are necessary, if the irritancy is instantly verifiable; there is, therefore, no inflexible rule based upon legal principle which renders declaratory conclusions necessary.[86] In the case in question the ground of the irritancy was non-payment of rent, increased by an improbative minute of agreement acted upon by the parties, and the lease contained the usual provision that the landlord might after due notice for payment hold it as void and null without the necessity of declarator or process of law; it was held that, although a declarator of irritancy would have been appropriate and convenient, the circumstances of the case were not such as to render the action incompetent in its absence, and that the fact that the minute of agreement was improbative and required proof of *rei interventus* did not make a declarator of its validity necessary.[87]

Where the fact on which irritancy depends is admitted or is instantly verifiable, such as judicial sequestration, notour bankruptcy, landlord's sequestration or the granting of a trust deed for creditors, and the lease contains the usual provision that declarator or other process of law shall be unnecessary, an action of removing without declaratory conclusions is perfectly adequate; if the lease does not expressly dispense with a declarator, it is probably sufficient if there is a provision for *ipso facto* nullity.[88] If, however, the fact on which the irritancy depends is not admitted and requires proof, for example " insolvency ", or if there is any question as to the validity of documents constituting the lease or

[82] *Register of Brieves* 1286-1386 (Stair Soc. Vol. 10) 32; *Encyclopaedia of the Laws of Scotland*, Vol. 13, 540-541; Dobie, *Sheriff Court Practice*, 25.
[83] By Sheriff Courts (Scotland) Act, 1877 (repealed) and Sheriff Courts (Scotland) Acts, 1907-1913.
[84] *Duke of Argyll* v *Campbeltown Coal Co.*, 1924 S.C. 844 *per* L.P. Clyde at pp. 850-851.
[85] *Ibid., per* L.P. Clyde at p. 851.
[86] *Ibid., per* Lord Sands at p. 853.
[87] *Duke of Argyll* v *Campbeltown Coal Co., supra.*
[88] Rankine, 546.

setting forth the conditions alleged to have been broken, declaratory conclusions, if not necessary, are advisable.[89]

It is incompetent for the tenant to plead a counter-claim of damages against an action of declarator of irritancy with a conclusion for removing.[90]

Sometimes an irritancy is fortified by a clause in which the tenant consents that summary diligence shall pass thereon for removing him from the subjects in the event of the irritancy being enforced by the landlord.[91]

[89] *Duke of Argyll* v *Campbeltown Coal Co., supra;* Rankine, 547; Dobie, *Sheriff Court Practice,* 416.
[90] *Macnab* v *Nelson,* 1909 S.C. 1102.
[91] *See Hendry* v *Marshall* (1878) 5 R. 687; Graham Stewart, *Diligence,* 415-416.

Chapter XVI

TERMINATION BY AGREEMENT

Introduction. A lease may be brought to an end before its stipulated ish (termination) by the agreement of the parties to it. This result may be achieved by mutual consent at the time of bringing it to an end, where the tenant decides to renounce the lease with his landlord's approval; or the possibility of a premature termination may have been pre-arranged in the lease itself, if an option has been given to one or both of the parties to break the lease.

Renunciation. Renunciation is the method by which the tenant gives up his lease. The circumstances in which he may abandon his lease in the event of a material breach of the conditions of the lease on the part of the landlord have already been considered.[1] The rules as to the abandonment of a lease by the tenant's heir[2] and the circumstances in which the executor of a deceased tenant or the landlord may terminate a lease[3] have also been considered. Under the present heading there will be discussed the effect of a renunciation, which is agreed to or acquiesced in by the landlord.

Form of Renunciation. Where the landlord consents to the tenant giving up the lease, the proper method of effecting the arrangement is by the tenant granting a deed called a Renunciation in favour of the landlord. The deed normally provides for the discharge of the landlord's and tenant's claims against each other.[4] It may be a bilateral deed signed by both parties, or it may be a unilateral deed signed only by the tenant, but the landlord will be bound by acceptance of it.[5] The renunciation may sometimes be granted not by the tenant himself but by someone deriving right through him, for example, a trustee in sequestration or a trustee for creditors, and many of the authorities involve the element of insolvency.[6] In the case of registered leases the statutory form of renunciation is a unilateral deed granted by the tenant in favour of the landlord, who may record it in the Register of Sasines.[7] Apart from registered leases, no particular form of renunciation is required other

---

[1] *Supra*, p. 146.
[2] *Supra*, p. 187.
[3] *Supra*, p. 189.
[4] *Encyclopaedia of Scottish Legal Styles*, Vol. 6, No. 164.
[5] *Walker's Trs.* v *Manson* (1886) 13 R. 1198.
[6] *Williamson* v *Johnstone* (1848) 11 D. 332; *Walker's Trs.* v *Manson, supra; Bidoulac* v *Sinclair's Tr.* (1889) 17 R. 144.
[7] Registration of Leases (Scotland) Act 1857, s. 13 and Sch. G, amended by Conveyancing (Scotland) Act 1924, s. 24 (5).

than that it must be clear and explicit.[8] It is evident that a written renunciation is desirable, as, even although the parties have verbally agreed that the lease should be given up, either party may change his mind, so long as matters remain entire.[9] However, where there is no written renunciation, the actions of the parties may be such as to support a verbal agreement: for example, if in pursuance of a verbal bargain of renunciation the landlord or a new tenant has obtained possession of the subjects, or if the tenant has received payment of the price, if any, stipulated for his renunciation.[10] Where a tenant delivered his lease to his landlord along with an improbative renunciation and later died, the fact that his heir did not demand possession was held to be sufficient *rei interventus* to support the improbative renunciation, in spite of the fact that other members of the tenant's family had remained in possession.[11] Possibly, if in pursuance of a verbal agreement the tenant comes to the landlord and redelivers to him his written lease expressly for him to dispose of it at his pleasure, this will bind the tenant.[12]

Implied Renunciation. Even without any express bargain, written or verbal, a renunciation may be inferred from conduct of the parties plainly implying that it is their final intention that the lease should be terminated, as where the tenant leaves the subjects and the landlord possesses them either by himself or by another tenant without interference for a number of years.[13] Renunciation may also be inferred from facts and circumstances inconsistent with the continued existence of the lease in question, such as the granting of a new lease differing materially from the old.[14]

Acceptance. Not only should the renunciation itself be properly in writing, but, if it is unilateral, it is desirable that the landlord's acceptance should also be in writing, usually embodying a discharge of the tenant's obligations. Acceptance, however, may be proved by conduct inconsistent with the maintenance of the lease, such as by the landlord taking possession,[15] or by his recording a renunciation of a registered lease. Where there was a question as to whether a renunciation had been accepted, it was held that the landlord was entitled to apply for a judicial inspection of the premises which the tenants were bound to keep in repair, as, if the tenants were right in maintaining that an agreement for renunciation had been reached, the landlord might lose his claim to have the repairs carried out.[16]

8 Bell, § 1271; *Strachan* v *Hunter,* 1916 S.C. 901 (break).
9 Hume, *Lectures,* IV, 115.
10 *Ibid.*
11 *Milne* v *Forbes* (1830) 8 S. 990; Rankine, 523.
12 Hume, *Lectures,* IV, 115.
13 *Taylor* v *Maxwell* (1728) Mor. 14310; Hume, *Lectures,* IV, 115-116.
14 Rankine, 524.
15 Rankine, 523.
16 *Lees* v *Marr Typefounding Co.* (1877) 4 R. 1088.

Discharge of Claims. Normally the renunciation or acceptance will specify the extent to which mutual claims are to be discharged. An express acceptance by a landlord, if made without reservation, has the effect of discharging the landlord's and tenant's claims *inter se*.[17] Where a tenant, after a renunciation of his lease had been accepted by the landlord, raised an action of damages against him for loss suffered as a result of floods, for which he alleged the landlord to have been responsible, it was held that, although he had given notice of his claim before he renounced his lease, the landlord's acceptance of the renunciation implied a discharge of all claims competent to him against the landlord.[18] Very precise words will be required to instruct an exception to this rule, especially if the claim is by the landlord for damages for breach of the tenant's obligation to possess the subjects.[19] Where a lease gave a landlord an option to irritate it upon the tenant's bankruptcy, and the landlord accepted from the tenant and his trustees under a trust deed for creditors a renunciation bearing that the rights of the parties were reserved and that the landlord should " in no way be prejudiced by accepting this renunciation in place of terminating the lease ", it was held that on a construction of the deed of renunciation the landlord had not reserved a right to claim damages.[20] Where, however, a landlord, in allowing the testamentary trustees of a tenant an abatement of the arrears of rent at his death, reserved the right to claim the full sum in the event of future rents not being paid punctually, and subsequently entered into an agreement for a renunciation, expressly reserving the landlord's claims, it was held that, the rent not having been punctually paid, the landlord could still claim the abated rent.[21]

In the case of an agricultural holding it has been held that a renunciation by the tenant, accepted by the landlord, does not bar the tenant from recovering compensation for unexhausted improvements.[22]

There is a distinction between a *de facto* renunciation or abandonment by the tenant and a renunciation or abandonment by agreement. Where a lease provided for an irritancy in the event of the tenant's bankruptcy, and his trustee in sequestration wrote to the landlord that in pursuance of the irritancy clause the tenant and the trustee were removing, and it was later arranged that the trustee should continue in possession until the next term of Whitsunday and be personally liable for the rent till then, and the landlord relet the subjects to another tenant for a reduced rent, it was held that the trustee's letter was a mere *de facto* renunciation without anything following on the landlord's

---

[17] *Jenkins* v *Younger* (1825) 3 S. 639; *Waterson* v *Stewart* (1881) 9 R. 155; Rankine, 523.
[18] *Lyons* v *Anderson* (1886) 13 R. 1020, opinions of L.J.C. Moncreiff and Lord M'Laren at pp. 1024 and 1025.
[19] Rankine, 523; *cf.* effect of irritancy, *supra*, p. 234.
[20] *Walker's Trs.* v *Manson* (1886) 13 R. 1198.
[21] *Scott-Chisholme* v *Brown* (1893) 20 R. 575.
[22] *Strang* v *Stuart* (1887) 14 R. 637.

part importing a waiver of his rights; moreover, as the landlord had not exercised his option to irritate the lease, he was not precluded from ranking for a claim for loss of rent.[23]

Other Effects. Frequently a renunciation is followed by a lease to new tenants, and questions may arise out of arrangements made between the outgoing and incoming tenants.[24] The renunciation and the new lease may form a tripartite contract entered into by the landlord and the old and the new tenants.[25]

Sometimes a renunciation is granted conditionally or in consideration of some payment by the landlord to the tenant. Where a renunciation is to take effect at a future date on condition of payment by the landlord of a fixed sum, the landlord's bankruptcy gives the tenant the choice of holding to the lease or claiming in the sequestration.[26] Where a tenant renounced one of two farms to his landlord on condition of receiving the surplus rents under a new lease of one farm and then assigned the surplus rents to trustees, who intimated the assignation to the landlord, it was held that the landlord could not retain the surplus rents in security of arrears of rent due for the other farm.[27]

A renunciation of a principal lease does not affect the principal landlord's remedies against a subtenant. Where a tenant had unlawfully sublet and then renounced his own lease, the landlord brought an action of ejection against the subtenant; the subtenant argued that upon the renunciation the landlord's right against him was no higher than that of the tenant on the principle *assignatus utitur jure auctoris* and that an action of ejection was incompetent, but it was held that the action was competent, the subtenant being without a title.[28]

Capacity of Parties. Trustees have a general statutory power to accept renunciations of leases, where such acts are not at variance with the terms and purposes of the trust.[29] Trustees, however, have no general power to grant renunciations, and it used to be common for trustees to petition the Court for power to renounce farm leases.[30] A trustee who adopts the lease of a deceased tenant becomes personally bound by its conditions, and it would seem that no judicial authority is necessary for him to give up a lease.[31] The special power of an executor of a tenant to terminate a lease has already been discussed.[32] Tutors, curators

[23] *Bidoulac* v *Sinclair's Tr.* (1889) 17 R. 144. See *supra,* p. 228.
[24] *Nivison* v *Howat* (1883) 11 R. 182; *Convery* v *Summerlee Iron Co.* (1884) 12 R. 191.
[25] *Convery* v *Summerlee Iron Co., supra.*
[26] Rankine, 524.
[27] *Stephenson's Trs.* v *Marquis of Tweeddale* (1823) 2 S. (N.E. 169).
[28] *Paramount Gowns (Scotland) Ltd.* v *Fraser,* 1949 C.L. 4770.
[29] Trusts (Scotland) Act 1921, s. 4.
[30] Rankine, 526.
[31] *Ibid.*
[32] *Supra,* p. 189.

16

and judicial factors probably require judicial authority to renounce leases.[33]

It is thought that one of two or more joint tenants cannot at his own hand renounce the lease before its termination,[34] although by giving notice of its termination he may prevent tacit relocation operating.[35]

Total Resumption. A lease may be brought to an end by the landlord exercising a power expressly reserved to him in the lease to resume possession of the whole of the subjects let. Such a power is really a break in favour of the landlord and differs from partial or piecemeal resumption. A power of resumption for particular purposes such as planting, building, feuing or letting on building leases, is fairly common. The *ejusdem generis* rule applies to such a provision;[36] the opinion has been expressed that the generality of the power must be limited by reference to the purpose and scope of the contract and that the landlord cannot take back ground to such an extent or for such purposes as would prevent the tenant from making a profitable use of the remainder for the purpose for which it was let.[37]

The power of total resumption is discussed more fully under the next heading.

Breaks. A lease may provide that it may be brought to an end before its natural termination. Breaks are common in leases of long duration, especially where the contract appears at the outset to be of uncertain commercial value to either party, such as a lease of minerals,[38] or where the personal convenience of the parties is concerned, as in a lease of a farm or dwellinghouse.

Breaks may be stipulated in favour of either party or both. Where the break is in favour of the landlord, it is a reserved power of total resumption of the subjects let; where it is in favour of the tenant, it gives him an option to renounce the lease. A break in favour of the landlord differs from an irritancy, which he can only invoke in the event of a breach of a condition. A break in favour of a tenant differs from a clause sometimes found in a mineral lease providing for the termination of the contract upon the mine becoming unworkable to a profit.[39] Whether the break is in favour of the landlord or the tenant, it is normally to be exercised only at one or more stipulated points of time, although sometimes power is given to the landlord to resume at any time,[40] and in

[33] *Young* v *Gerard* (1843) 6 D. 347; *Buttercase & Geddie's Tr.* v *Geddie* (1897) 24 R. 1128; Rankine, 526.
[34] *Graham* v *Stirling*, 1922 S.C. 90 *per* Lord Skerrington.
[35] *Smith* v *Grayton Estates Ltd.*, 1960 S.C. 349; *supra*, p. 226.
[36] *Admiralty* v *Burns*, 1910 S.C. 531; *Turner* v *Wilson*, 1954 S.C. 296; *Piggott* v *Robson*, 1958 S.L.T. 49.
[37] *Admiralty* v *Burns*, *supra*, *per* Lord Kinnear at p. 539; Gloag, *Contract*, 2nd ed., 403.
[38] *Supra*, p. 77
[39] *Fleeming* v *Baird & Co.* (1871) 9 M. 730; Rankine, 527.
[40] *E.g.*, *Earl of Rosebery* v *Brown*, 7 March 1811 F.C.

a furnished lease it is not uncommon to provide that either party may break it at any time on giving, say, one month's notice. An uninvoked provision for a break in favour of a tenant differs from a right of renewal, which gives the tenant the option to demand a new lease only upon the termination of the old.[41]

It is important to make it clear whether the break is intended to be in favour of the landlord or the tenant; otherwise the Court may have to determine the meaning of an ambiguous or defective clause.[42] The clause should also specify the time or times at which the party is to exercise it, and by what method he is to intimate his intention to the other party. Sometimes a break in favour of the landlord may provide for a cash consideration to be paid to the tenant.[43] Sometimes, as an alternative to a break, there may be a provision for a readjustment of rent.[44] Where a break is provided for, the party exercising his option is not required to give his reasons for doing so.[45] There is little doubt that, unless the clause is qualified in some way, the option to break transmits to singular successors of the landlord.[46]

The party wishing to exercise his right to break the lease should give notice of his intention to do so in the manner laid down by the lease,[47] and the notice must be given timeously.[48] The notice must be clear and explicit.[49] The Court may have to decide whether the terms of a letter by one party to the other are to be construed as indicating his intention to break the lease.[50] Where it is the landlord who is taking advantage of a break and there is no provision in the lease for the length of notice, a reasonable time must be given to the tenant to remove.[51] If the tenant fails to remove, the landlord's remedy is an action of removing with or without declaratory conclusions.[52]

As the power to break depends entirely on express provision in the lease itself, problems seldom arise, and there are few authorities. It will suffice to mention only a few cases. Where the subjects of lease providing for mutual breaks at certain specified times were compulsorily

---

[41] *Supra*, p. 42.
[42] *Johnston* v *Gordon* (1805) Hume 822; *Grants* v *Sinclair* (1861) 23 D. 796; Rankine, 528.
[43] *Encyclopaedia of Scottish Legal Styles*, Vol. 6, No. 139 (c).
[44] *Wallace* v *Tacksmen* (1715) 5 B.S. 7; Rankine, 527.
[45] *Earl of Rosebery* v *Brown*, 7 March 1811 F.C.; *Stewart* v *Rutherford* (1863) 35 Sc. Jur. 307; *Houldsworth* v *Brand's Trs.* (1875) 2 R. 683, (1876) 3 R. 304, (1877) 4 R. 369.
[46] *Murray* v *Brodie* (1806) Hume 825; *Ross* v *M'Finlay* (1807) Hume 832; *Davidson* v *Girvan* (1838) 16 S. 1125.
[47] *Guild* v *M'Lean* (1897) 25 R. 106.
[48] *Fraser's Trs.* v *Maule & Son* (1904) 6 F. 819.
[49] Bell, § 1271.
[50] *Strachan* v *Hunter*, 1916 S.C. 901; *Ritchie* v *Lyon* (1940) 56 Sh. Ct. Rep. 39.
[51] *Sharp* v *Clark* (1807) Hume 577; *Wilson* v *Campbell* (1839) 2 D. 232; *Houldsworth* v *Brand's Trs.*, *supra*; *Guild* v *M'Lean*, *supra*.
[52] *Granger* v *Geils* (1857) 19 D. 1010; *Houldsworth* v *Brand's Trs.*, *supra*; see *Duke of Argyll* v *Campbeltown Coal Co.*, 1924 S.C. 844 (irritancy) *supra*, p. 235; Rankine, 530.

acquired, it was held that the lease should be valued for the purpose
of compensation on the footing of a lease for its full term subject to a
deduction for the contingency of its being brought to an end at an
earlier date.[53] Where a tenant under a five years' lease containing a
mutual break at the end of the third year sought a remit to a man of
skill to examine the fences, and then the landlord before the hearing of
the appeal availed himself of the break, it was held that the proposed
remit was useless and inappropriate, although its object was to preserve
evidence of the condition of the fences.[54] Where a lease was terminable
on six months' notice by the landlord, or on three months' notice by
the tenant, who on giving such notice was to be entitled to remove his
materials, it was held that, the landlord having given due notice, it
was unnecessary for the tenant to do so in order to remove the
materials.[55] Where the break is mutual, only one party need exercise it.

The question whether a subtenant, on being put out by the principal
landlord exercising a break in the tenant's lease, is entitled to damages
from the tenant depends on whether the sublease was intended to cover
the whole period of the principal lease or to give possession only so
long as the tenant held the land; he would probably be entitled to
damages if it were the tenant who took advantage of the break.[56]

It has been held that the words " natural expiry " used in a lease
include the termination of the tenancy by one of the parties taking
advantage of a break.[57]

[53] *Fleming* v *District Committee of Middle Ward of Lanarkshire* (1895) 23 R. 98.
[54] *Jenkins* v *Gascoigne,* 1907 S.C. 1189.
[55] *Laing* v *Stevenson* (1848) 11 D. 142.
[56] Rankine, 532.
[57] *Cassilis & Culzean Estates* v *Dunlop's Trs.,* 1941 S.N. 60 (O.H.); contrast the
effect of irritancy, *supra,* p. 234.

CHAPTER XVII

REMOVINGS

Introduction. " By far the largest number of questions in the law of leases have arisen in connection with the termination of the contract ".[1] Unfortunately this is also the most confusing branch of the subject, at least partly because of the names used for the different forms of remedies. It is, therefore, necessary to define some of the terms used in this chapter.

In its more general sense the word " Removing " is the technical term for the relinquishment of possession by a tenant, whether of his own free will or not, and whether during the lease or at its termination.[2] In this sense a removing may take place not only at the stipulated ish, but also prematurely by a rescinding of the contract,[3] by destruction of the subjects,[4] by abandonment by the tenant,[5] by termination by the executors of a deceased tenant,[6] by irritancy,[7] by renunciation,[8] by the exercise of a break,[9] by reduction of the contract by a third party[10] and by the contract being rendered null by statute.[11] A removing may be either voluntary or compulsory from the point of view of the tenant.[12]

Where the removing is premature, that is, taking place at a time earlier than the most remote date contemplated by the contract, it is termed an Extraordinary Removing. A voluntary extraordinary removing may result from the tenant's taking advantage of a breach of contract on the part of the landlord setting the tenant free if he wishes; or it may take the form of a renunciation, requiring the agreement of both parties, or of a break in favour of the tenant. A compulsory extraordinary removing may result from the landlord's taking advantage of an irritancy or of a break in his favour. An extraordinary removing may have originally been voluntary but have become compulsory, as where a tenant has renounced his lease and then refuses to remove.

Where the removing takes place at the most remote ish contemplated by the contract, it is termed an Ordinary Removing. If at the termination of the lease the tenant quits without demur, his removing is voluntary, and nothing needs to be done except to settle any outstanding claims

---

[1] Rankine, 511.
[2] *Ibid.*
[3] *Supra,* p. 146.
[4] *Supra,* p. 142.
[5] *Supra,* p. 146.
[6] *Supra,* p. 189.
[7] *Supra,* p. 228.
[8] *Supra,* p. 238.
[9] *Supra,* p. 242.
[10] *E.g.,* for want of capacity or lack of infeftment; see Chapter IV.
[11] *Supra,* p. 89.
[12] Rankine, 511.

between the parties. If, however, the tenant declines to quit voluntarily, the landlord must resort to an Action of Removing.

In its stricter sense, the word " Removing " refers to the process of law whereby a landlord seeks to reinforce his tenant's obligation to relinquish possession.[13] Thus an action of extraordinary removing is the landlord's means of enforcing an irritancy, a break in favour of the landlord or a renunciation granted to him by the tenant. An action of ordinary removing is the remedy for use against a tenant who does not give up possession at the ish.

Ordinary removings were also divided into Solemn Removings and Summary Removings. Solemn removings were actions brought under the Act 1555 c. 39 Anent Warning of Tenants (now repealed)[14] or the Act of Sederunt of 14th December, 1756; summary removings were those brought neither under the Act nor the Act of Sederunt, and less formal notice was required.[15] The distinction is of little importance nowadays, and the term " summary removings " usually denotes the statutory process for removing tenants of subjects let for less than one year.[16]

Distinction between Removing and Ejection. Although the terms " Removing " and " Ejection " are frequently used interchangeably, they are not synonymous, and there is an important distinction between them. As indicated above, an Action of Removing is the process whereby a landlord recovers possession from a tenant. An Action of Ejection, on the other hand, in its original sense is the process by which a proprietor of heritable property recovers possession of it from someone who is occupying it without any right or title, *i.e.* a possessor *vi, clam aut precario.*[17] In this sense ejection has nothing to do with tenants and is not exclusively a landlord's remedy. Ejection, however, has acquired a secondary meaning as the process whereby a landlord recovers possession from a tenant whose title has been cut down judicially. In this sense it applies to the act of the Sheriff in carrying out a decree of removing issued by the Court of Session either under the Act of 1555 c. 39 or in a few other rare cases at common law; to the final stages of an action of removing in the Sheriff Court, where the decree of removing contains a warrant of ejection; and to cases where the process is brought merely to enforce a decree of removing already obtained in the Sheriff Court and where the extract warrant *de plano* authorises the officers of Court to eject the defender summarily.[18] The process of ejection, therefore, has two main meanings, *viz.,* (a) an independent substantive action, by which

---

[13] *Ibid.*
[14] The Act of 1555 c. 39 was repealed by the Statute Law Revision (Scotland) Act, 1964, Schedule 1.
[15] *Infra,* p. 260.
[16] Sheriff Courts (Scotland) Act 1907, s. 38 and First Schedule, Rules 115 to 122; *infra,* p. 270.
[17] Rankine, 593; Rankine, *Land-Ownership,* 4th ed., 8 *et seq.*
[18] *Campbell's Trs.* v *O'Neill,* 1911 S.C. 188, in which Lord Johnston at p. 191 outlines the history of Ejection as a remedy against tenants; Rankine, 592-593.

a person having no right to occupy heritable property, or whose right has terminated, is put out without necessity of any previous process of removing,[19] and (b) the purely accessory proceedings, by which a decree of removing or the equivalent is carried into effect, where the occupant of subjects refuses or delays to quit possession.[20]

That was substantially the position until the passing of the Sheriff Courts (Scotland) Act 1907, which provided in certain cases for a " summary warrant of ejection "[21] and for a " warrant for summary ejection in common form ".[22] In both cases the word " ejection " was used in relation to forms of process which at common law were of the nature of removings.[23] The same Act also provided new remedies in certain cases for removing or " ejecting " tenants without application to the Court[24] or without a decree of removal.[25]

Difficulties arising from Distinction. In many cases there is the practical difficulty of determining whether the particular occupier is a tenant or an occupier without a title. This difficulty arises where there is no written lease and where for some reason the origin of the possession is obscure or its nature is not easy to determine. It is necessary for the pursuer to select as his remedy either an action of removing or an action of ejection, depending on his view of the nature of the defender's occupancy. The selection of the wrong remedy may be fatal to his case.[26] Moreover, where it is not easy to determine whether or not the defender has a title to occupy the subjects, the difficulty arises as to whether or not notice of removing must be given. The danger on the one hand is that, if notice is not given on the footing that the defender has no title, the action may be held to be incompetent, and on the other hand, if notice is served on a person who has no title to occupy, this may be held as implying the acknowledgement of a title.[27] " The distinction between ejection and removing is deeply rooted in the principles and in the history of the law of Scotland, but the fact that these remedies (appropriate as they respectively are to circumstances essentially different, but by no means readily distinguishable) must be sought by separate forms of process, is, under the conditions of modern times, productive of misunderstanding and even of miscarriage. Unhappily, this occurs in a department of law where simplicity and certainty of procedure are urgently desirable, and would not be difficult of attainment, if the atten-

19 *Infra*, p. 284.
20 *Infra* p. 283.
21 s. 36; *infra*, p. 269.
22 s. 37; *infra*, p. 269.
23 *Infra*, p. 266.
24 s. 34; *infra*, p. 267.
25 s. 35; *infra*, p. 268.
26 See Second Report of the Law Reform Committee for Scotland on the procedural law relating to actions of removing and actions of ejection, 1957 Cmnd. 114, para. 7.
27 *Ibid.*, para. 14.

tion of the Legislature were called to it ".[28] Attention has been drawn to this difficulty on at least one occasion,[29] but nothing has been done, although the Legislature has found time to enact many provisions of a political and social nature affecting the rights of landlords and tenants.

Removing as a Process of Law.   Much of this chapter is concerned with Removing in its stricter sense of the process by which a tenant, whose right of occupation has come to an end either prematurely or at the termination of his lease, is judicially warned to remove from the subjects. The substantive law of irritancies, renunciations and breaks has already been discussed, and it now remains to study the procedure by which the landlord may enforce the tenant's obligation to quit the subjects as a result thereof, as well as his obligation to remove at the natural termination of the lease.

Exclusive Remedy.   A sitting tenant can be dispossessed only by a process of removing or " ejection ".[30] A landlord is not entitled to take the law into his own hands and put the tenant out without due process of law.[31] Where the tenant is in possession of an *ex facie* valid title, the landlord is not entitled to adopt a *brevi manu* method to compel him to leave, even if it is clear that the lease was obtained by fraudulent statements and for improper purposes.[32] If a landlord has been induced to enter into a lease by misrepresentation and fraud, the law does not leave him helpless, since it is open to him to have the contract rescinded, and in a case of emergency a summary remedy may be given.[33] It was held in a case of service occupancy[34] that a proprietor might eject a servant *brevi manu* from a house after his dismissal for insolence, but such an ejection has been made unlawful by statute.[35] A dismissed servant may be removed by an action of ejection, and an action of removing is not necessary.[36] A subtenant, who has received no warning to remove, cannot be ejected summarily by the proprietor.[37]

Neither interdict nor suspension and interdict is an appropriate remedy against a tenant in possession.[38] Thus, interdict cannot be used to enforce an irritancy, to prevent an assignation nor to prevent a tenant,

[28] *Lowe* v *Gardiner*, 1921 S.C. 211, *per* L.P. Clyde at p. 216.
[29] See Recommendations of Second Report of the Law Reform Committee, *supra*, p. 11; *infra*, p. 287.
[30] Rankine, 512.
[31] *Fairbairn* v *Miller* (1878) 15 S.L.R. 705.
[32] *Brash* v *Munro & Hall* (1903) 5 F. 1102
[33] *Ibid., per* Lord Moncreiff at p. 1105.
[34] *Supra*, p. 10.
[35] *Scott* v *M'Murdo* (1869) 6 S.L.R. 301, noticed by L.P. Normand in *Cairns* v *Innes*, 1952 S.C. 164 at p. 171; but see Rent Act, 1965, ss. 30 and 32, *infra*, p. 249.
[36] *Sinclair* v *Tod*, 1907 S.C. 1038; *Cairns* v *Innes, supra*.
[37] *Robb* v *Brearton* (1895) 22 R. 885.
[38] Rankine, 512.

who alleges tacit relocation, from continuing to cultivate.[39] Where, however, a tenant after being dispossessed, returns or threatens to return to the subjects, interdict is the appropriate remedy;[40] and interdict may be employed against third parties alleging a right to use land which is let.[41] Where a tenant sought an interdict to prevent his landlord advertising the subjects and taking steps to remove him, interim interdict was granted as regards the advertisements, but not the removing.[42]

Wrongous Ejection. If ejection takes place without order of law, a claim of damages for wrongous ejection arises at common law.[43] Thus, if a landlord without due process of law seizes his tenant's furniture or throws it into the street, he may render himself liable to a civil claim for damage done to the furniture, expenses incurred in the ejection and loss of trade, if any, besides *solatium* for wounded feelings.[44] The pursuer must show that he was in possession.[45] Applying for and obtaining an illegal warrant of ejection, even although not executed, has been held to be a ground of damages, though slight.[46] It is not lawful to eject a tenant during the night.[47] Landlords or their agents have been found liable in damages for rendering the subjects uninhabitable by removing a roof or door.[48] On the other hand, there will be no claim of damages, if the tenant has already been ousted from possession or has voluntarily left the subjects.[49]

Rent Act 1965. In order to combat the practice of Rachmanism[50] found to exist in certain English cities, important new provisions were enacted by the Rent Act 1965, Secs. 30 and 32, both of which apply with modifications to Scotland. The general aim is the protection of occupiers of residential premises from " harassment " and eviction and tenants of dwellings from eviction without due process of law. Those

---

[39] *Borrows* v *Colquhoun* (1854) 1 Macq. 691; *Rankin* v *M'Lachlan* (1864) 3 M. 129; *Johnston* v *Thomson* (1877) 4 R. 868.
[40] *Johnston* v *Thomson, supra; Baillie* v *Mackintosh* (1882) 19 S.L.R. 352; *Boswell's Trs.* v *Pearson* (1886) 24 S.L.R. 32.
[41] *Macleod* v *Davidson* (1886) 24 S.L.R. 69.
[42] *Arneil* v *Paisley Town Council*, 1948 S.L.T. (Notes) 46 (O.H.).
[43] Rankine, 592.
[44] *Russel* v *Clerk* (1749) Mor. 15265; *Douglas* v *Walker* (1825) 3 S. 534 (N.E. 370).
[45] *Macdonald* v *Duchess of Leeds* (*Macdonald* v *Chisholm*) (1860) 22 D. 1075; *Gordon* v *Smith*, 1947 S.L.T. (Notes) 51 (O.H.).
[46] *Bisset* v *Whitson* (1842) 5 D. 5.
[47] *Macgregor* v *Viscount Strathallan* (1864) 2 M. 1339.
[48] *Bissett* v *Whitson, supra; Brash* v *Munro & Hall* (1903) 5 F. 1102.
[49] *Tait* v *Paton* (1825) 4 S. 208 (NE. 211); *Anderson* v *Abel* (1854) 16 D. 796.
[50] The word was coined by journalists after Peter Rachman, named in House of Commons as a landlord who exploited tenants; see definition in " Rachmanism —A Lawyer's View ", 107 *Solicitors Journal*, 670:—" to exploit the housing shortage in an unlawful manner or by unlawful means; to disguise the ownership of properties by multifarious ownerships and interrelated companies; to use and threaten force and terrorise tenants (especially statutory); to adopt unlawful means of expelling such tenants from their homes ".

sections embrace dwellinghouses generally, and are not confined to premises affected by previous legislation or by other provisions of the Rent Act 1965. It is accordingly appropriate to discuss those two sections of the 1965 Act here.

Unlawful Eviction and Harassment of Occupier. The Rent Act 1965, Sec. 30, provides that it shall be a criminal offence for any person unlawfully to deprive the residential occupier of any premises of his occupation of the premises or any part thereof or to attempt to do so, unless he proves that he believed, and had reasonable cause to believe, that the residential occupier had ceased to reside in the premises.[51] If any person, with intent to cause the residential occupier of any premises either (a) to give up the occupation of the premises or any part thereof or (b) to refrain from exercising any right or pursuing any remedy in respect of the premises or part thereof, does acts calculated to interfere with the peace or comfort of the residential occupier or members of his household or persistently withdraws or withholds services reasonably required for the occupation of the premises as a residence, he shall be guilty of an offence.[52] A person guilty of an offence under this section shall be liable to a fine or a term of imprisonment or both.[53] Where an offence under the Act is committed by a body corporate, special provision is made for punishing its officers as well as the body corporate.[54] The provisions of the section are expressly stated to be without prejudice to any liability or remedy to which an offender may be liable in civil proceedings.[55]

A " residential occupier " is defined as a person occupying premises as a residence, whether under a contract or by virtue of any enactment or rule of law giving him the right to remain in occupation or restricting the right of any other person to recover possession of the premises.[56] In addition to various classes of tenants protected, controlled or regulated by the Rent Acts, the definition of " residential occupier " is wide enough to cover (a) an ordinary contractual tenant, (b) a licensee, lodger or service occupier, (c) a former unprotected tenant (*e.g.* under a furnished tenancy), against whom the landlord may not exercise his right of possession except by Sec. 32 of the 1965 Act, (d) a former service occupier, whose contract of service has expired, and who is also protected by Sec. 32 and, if employed in agriculture, by Sec. 33 and possibly also (e) the deserted wife of a tenant or licensee.[57]

It will be noted that " any person ", not merely the landlord or owner, may be guilty of the offence, and that the deprivation of occupa-

---

[51] s. 30 (1).
[52] s. 30 (2).
[53] s. 30 (3).
[54] s. 44.
[55] s. 30 (4).
[56] s. 30 (5).
[57] Bramall, *Rent Act 1965*, 2-074 (contrast the position of a deserted wife under s. 32, *infra*). Also those protected under the Reserve &c. Forces Act 1951.

tion must be achieved or attempted "unlawfully".[58] Although the acts
of harassment prohibited by Sec. 30 (2) need only be "calculated" to
interfere with peace and comfort, so that no specific intent to interfere
need be proved, there must be a specific intent to cause the occupier
to quit or to refrain from exercising a right or remedy.[59] "Exercising
any right" would appear to cover the use of any shared accommodation,
the use of a shared garden or passage over a right of way.[60] "Pursuing
any remedy" would appear to cover the bringing by the occupier of
legal proceedings to establish a right or to recover money overpaid,
prosecution for an offence under the 1965 Act or the Rent Acts, recourse to a Rent Tribunal under the Rent of Furnished Houses Control
(Scotland) Act 1943, or recourse, to the rent officer or rent assessment
committee under the 1965 Act.[61] There is no definition in the Act of
the services which may not be withdrawn or withheld, but Sec. 30 (2)
applies only to those reasonably required, not necessarily to those provided in the contract or otherwise.[62]

Prohibition of Eviction without due Process of Law. The Rent Act
1965, Sec. 32, provides that, where any premises have been let as a
dwelling under a tenancy which is not a protected tenancy within the
meaning of Part III of the Act and (a) the tenancy (referred to as the
"former tenancy") has come to an end, but (b) the occupier continues
to reside in the premises or part of them, it shall not be lawful for the
owner to enforce against the occupier, otherwise than by proceedings
in the Court, his right to recover possession of the premises.[63] For this
purpose, a person who, under the terms of his employment, had exclusive
possession of any premises otherwise than as a tenant, shall be deemed
to have been a tenant, and the expression "let" and "tenancy" shall
be construed accordingly.[64] "The owner" of premises means the person who, as against the occupier, is entitled to possession, and "the
occupier" means any person lawfully residing in the premises or part
of them at the termination of the former tenancy.[65] This makes it clear
that protection against eviction is available to the former tenant, any
member of his family and any lawful subtenant.[66] The word "lawfully"
would seem to exclude from the protection of this section a subtenant,
where subletting is prohibited.[67] Sec. 30 applies where the owner's right
to recover possession arises on the death of a tenant under a statutory

---

[58] *Ibid.*, 2-071.
[59] *Ibid.*, 2-072.
[60] *Ibid.*
[61] *Ibid.*
[62] *Ibid.*
[63] 32 (1). See s. 33 as to agricultural employees.
[64] 32 (2).
[65] 32 (3).
[66] Bramall, *op. cit.*, 2-078.
[67] *Ibid.*

tenancy.[68] This protects an occupier when either he is not entitled to a transmission or two transmissions have taken place.[69]

The general effect of Sec. 32 is to prohibit the eviction without a Court order of any occupier under a tenancy, which has come to an end, but not a " protected tenancy ".[70] It is expressly provided that Sec. 32 is not to affect any rule of the law of Scotland prohibiting the securing of possession otherwise than by due process of law.[71] It has already been seen that at common law it is incompetent to evict a tenant without due process of removing, and that eviction *brevi manu* or wrongous ejection gives rise to a " civil claim of damages ".[72] The Court is the Sheriff Court.[73] Prior to 1965, the Sheriff had virtually exclusive jurisdiction in removings.[74] Thus Sec. 32 made very little change so far as Scotland is concerned apart from the inclusion of occupiers under service occupancies within the term " tenant ".[75] At common law it was normally necessary to raise an action of ejection against a servant to oust him from subjects occupied by him by virtue of a service occupancy after the termination of his employment.[76] It was, however, held that the ejection of a coachman *brevi manu* from a house after his dismissal for insolence was an act legal and competent for his master to take;[77] the effect of Sec. 32 is to render such ejection unlawful for the purpose of Sec. 30 (1).[78] The employee must have " exclusive possession " of the premises before Sec. 32 operates.[79]

The term " let as a dwelling " may be construed in the same way as in the earlier Rent Acts.[80] " Continues to reside " appears to require personal residence of the occupier and not, for example, occupation by a deserted wife.[81] Continuous residence since the termination of the tenancy is probably essential.[82]

TITLE TO SUE IN REMOVINGS

Where Pursuer is Lessor. If the party suing is the granter of the lease, he is entitled to sue no matter how defective his title may be, and the tenant is not entitled to impugn the lessor's title.[83] On the same prin-

[68] s. 32 (4).
[69] Bramall, *op. cit.*, 2-078.
[70] Protected tenancies for this purpose are tenancies to which the various statutes listed in the Rent Act 1965, s. 34 apply; but see the exception in s. 32 (4).
[71] s. 32 (5).
[72] *Supra*, p. 248.
[73] s. 35 (1) (b).
[74] *Infra*, p. 283.
[75] s. 32 (2).
[76] *Cairns* v *Innes*, 1942 S.C. 164.
[77] *Scott* v *M'Murdo* (1869) 6 S.L.R. 301.
[78] s. 32 (5); Bramall, *op. cit.*, 2-078a.
[79] Bramall, *op. cit.*, 2-077.
[80] *Ibid.*
[81] *Ibid.*
[82] *Ibid.*
[83] *Earl of Hamilton* v *Crawford* (1583) Mor. 13784; *Earl of Arran* v *Crawford* (1583) Mor. 14023; *York Building Co.* v *Carnegie* (1764) Mor. 4054; *Butter* v *M'Donalds* (1769) Mor. 11999; *Penman* v *Martin* (1822) 1 S. 523; Hume, *Lectures*, IV, 107; *Rankine*, 513.

ciple, a tenant could not impugn his lessors' title to grant the lease when they sued him for damages for deterioration.[84] This rule has been applied, where the lessor at the time of granting the lease was the principal tenant of the subjects;[85] where the lessor at the date of the lease was an undischarged bankrupt left in possession of the subjects;[86] and where the lessor was a bondholder, although it was not averred that she was a creditor in possession.[87] The principle that the tenant cannot challenge his lessor's title applies only where the lessee in a question with the lessor or someone deriving right from the lessor is maintaining some right or claiming some benefit under or in respect of the lease, not where he is renouncing or repudiating the lease.[88] A lessee is not entitled to demand production of the lessor's title for the purpose of ascertaining whether the lease is a valid security.[89]

It is, however, competent for the tenant to show that the lessor's title to sue has been lost by a divestiture of the subjects;[90] but, where the tenant's defence resolves itself into a declarator of the right of property, an action of removing is not the proper place to try the question.[91] If it is not disputed that the lessor has divested himself, as by granting a disposition to the purchaser, he clearly has no title to sue in an action of removing. A mere assignation of the rents, however, does not deprive the lessor of his title to sue, as he has not divested himself of the ownership.[92] In a somewhat complicated case A, when he became bankrupt, was in possession of an inn let to him verbally by the proprietor; his trustee sold his right to B and granted an assignation of rents, but A continued in possession until his death; B raised an action of removing against A's widow, in which he averred that he was proprietor, founding on the assignation as his title; in his answers to a suspension of the decree of removing, B averred that he had sublet the subjects verbally to A after obtaining the assignation. It was held by a majority that B had set out in the removing no title to sue, and that the Court was bound to do in the suspension what the Sheriff ought to have done in the removing. In the removing there was averred only a title of owner, which was in fact contradicted by the assignation.[93]

Ex Facie Absolute Dispositions. The existence of an *ex facie* absolute disposition, truly granted in security of a loan, sometimes gives

---

[84] *Eliott's Trs.* v. *Eliott* (1894) 21 R. 858; *supra*, p. 43.
[85] *Dunlop & Co.* v *Meiklem* (1876) 4 R. 11.
[86] *King* v *Wieland* (1858) 20 D. 960.
[87] *Sinclair* v *Hughes*, 1954 S.L.T. (Sh. Ct.) 64.
[88] *Weir* v *Dunlop & Co.* (1861) 23 D. 1293; *Reid's Tr.* v *Watson's Trs.* (1896) 23 R. 636, *per* Lord Trayner at p. 648; *supra*, p. 44.
[89] *Denniston Macnayr & Co.* v *M'Farlane* (1808) Mor. App. *voce* Tack 15.
[90] *Lady Essilmont* v *Tenants* (1582) Mor. 13783; *Maxwell* v *Tenants*, and *Lord Nithsdale* v *Tenants* (1627) Mor. 13788.
[91] *King* v *Wieland*, *supra*.
[92] *Wilson* v *Wilson* (1859) 21 D. 309.
[93] *Sinclair* v *Leslie* (1887) 14 R. 792; Rankine, 514.

rise to difficulties. Such a disposition, if completed by infeftment, has been held to be a divestiture sufficient to displace the title to sue, although the point is in some doubt.[94] In one case the pursuer in an action of removing set forth as his title to sue a feu contract in favour of a firm, of which he was the sole surviving partner, and admitted that a creditor of the firm had been infeft in the subjects upon an *ex facie* absolute disposition qualified by a back letter. It was held by a majority that the pursuer had not averred a sufficient title to sue.[95] The opinion was expressed, however, that, if the pursuer had distinctly set forth that the substantial right of property was in him as sole surviving partner of the firm, that would have been sufficient, notwithstanding the feudal divestiture.[96] The opinion was also expressed that, had it been stated that the defender was in possession under a title, though personal, flowing from the pursuer, she could not be listened to in objecting to the title of her own author.[97] Where a proprietor of subjects, who had herself granted an *ex facie* absolute disposition, which she produced along with the back letter, sued in an action of ejection, it was held that she was still feudally vested in the radical right to the subjects and could exercise all rights of ownership subject to the concurrence of the creditors, who had concurred in the action.[98] Where a tenant pleaded that his lessor had after the date of the lease divested himself by consenting to an *ex facie* absolute disposition to a building society, it was held that, as the pursuer was the actual lessor, the tenant could not impugn his title, although it appeared that the landlord never had been infeft.[99] Where, however, the title of the tenant did not flow from the pursuer, the granting of an *ex facie* absolute disposition by the pursuer, who had not been infeft, deprived him of his title to sue.[1] It would seem therefore that an infeft proprietor, who grants a lease and thereafter an *ex facie* absolute disposition does not lose his title to sue (a) because the tenant, who has accepted a lease from him, cannot impugn his title, and (b) because he retains his radical right on the subjects. If the landlord who granted the lease had never been infeft, he still has a title to sue, as the tenant cannot impugn his title.

Where Pursuer is not Lessor.   Where the landlord pursuing an action of removing is not the original lessor, he must as a general rule be infeft.[2] Where an action of removing is brought by a party other than the one from whom the title of the party sought to be dispossessed is said to have

[94] Rankine, 514.
[95] *Traill* v *Traill* (1873) 1 R. 61.
[96] *Ibid.,* per L.J.C. Moncreiff and Lord Neaves at pp. 63 and 65.
[97] *Ibid.,* per Lord Cowan at p. 63.
[98] *Barclay* v *Miller* (1921) 37 Sh. Ct. Rep. 96.
[99] *Fraser* v *Sharp,* 1957 S.L.T. (Sh. Ct.) 14.
[1] *Kerr* v *Young* (1920) 36 Sh. Ct. Rep. 184.
[2] *Walker* v *Hendry,* 1925 S.C. 855; Erskine, II, 6, 51; Hume, *Lectures,* IV, 107; Rankine, 515.

flowed, there must be infeftment in the person of the pursuer.[3] A decree obtained while the pursuer was uninfeft is not validated by his subsequent infeftment.[4] There are said to be two exceptions to the general rule: where the pursuer derives his title by judicial sale,[5] and where the conclusion for removing is subordinate to a declarator.[6]

Originally it had been held that the pursuer had to be infeft at the time of giving the warning to remove,[7] but later it came to be recognised that the lack of infeftment could be remedied before the case was called,[8] although some doubt remained as to whether it could be remedied during the course of the action.[9] It has however, been finally established that infeftment prior to the notice is not essential, although it must be obtained before decree in the action of removing.[10] Thus, as the law stands at present, a proprietor of tenanted subjects, who is not the granter of the lease, must obtain infeftment before decree in the action passes. It is perhaps worth drawing attention to the anomaly that such a person need not be infeft in order to grant a disposition to a purchaser.[11] It has been seen that properly a lessor should be infeft in order to grant the lease itself.[12]

If infeftment cannot be taken by a purchaser before he raises an action of removing, it is competent to conjoin the seller with him.[13] It has also been held that, where missives of sale have been concluded providing for entry at a future date, the seller has a title to sue until that date.[14] It probably follows that a purchaser in that position cannot give a valid notice of removal and that he cannot found on a notice given by the seller, unless it has been expressly assigned to him.[15] As infeftment in the person of the pursuer of an action of removing is essential, unless he granted the lease, a pursuer with a defective title cannot obtain a good title by sisting as joint pursuer a person with a good title.[16]

It is the landlord in possession at the time when the rent is legally due who has a good title to sue for removal and payment of rent, and

---

[3] Per Lord Cowan in Traill v Traill (1873) 1 R. 61 at p. 64.
[4] Scott v Fisher (1832) 10 S. 284.
[5] Lord Advocate v Ardnamurchan Tenants, 5 B.S. 570; Alexander v Dornoch Tenants (1773) 5 B.S. 571.
[6] Tennent v M'Donald (1836) 14 S. 976.
[7] Stevenson v Stevenson (1623) Mor. 13268.
[8] Campbell v M'Kellar (1808) Mor. App. voce Removing 5.
[9] Scott v Fisher, supra; Rankine, 516.
[10] Walker v Hendry, supra; see opinion of L.J.C. Alness at p. 869 et seq. for an outline of the history of this point.
[11] Second Report of the Law Reform Committee for Scotland, 1957 Cmnd. 114, para. 17.
[12] Supra, p. 44.
[13] Ferguson v Morison (1802) Mor. 13806; Hume, Lectures, IV, 108.
[14] Grandison v Mackay, 1919 1 S.L.T. 95 (O.H.).
[15] Hunter, Landlord and Tenant, 4th ed., II, 24; Grant v Bannerman (1920) 36 Sh. Ct. Rep. 59; James Grant & Co. Ltd. v Moran, 1948 S.L.T. (Sh. Ct.) 8; George M. Brown Ltd. v Collier, 1954 S.L.T. (Sh. Ct.) 98; see Burns, Conveyancing Practice, 4th ed., 174.
[16] Kerr v Young (1920) 36 Sh. Ct. Rep. 184; cf. Symington v Campbell (1894) 21 R. 434 (purchase of ship).

the tenant has no concern with any question of accounting between him and the previous proprietor or his representatives.[17]

Limited Owners. Special rules apply where the landlord's title is not absolute. Thus, where there are two or more joint proprietors, all of them must concur in the action of removing, no matter how small the interest of any of them may be,[18] unless it can be shown that the mandate of one of them extends to the removal of tenants in right of leases obtained from him.[19] The rule against impugning the granter's title does not apply here.[20] Notice given by one of two joint landlords is insufficient, but it is competent to prove that he had the approval of the other.[21] Both of them, however, must concur in the action. Any co-adjudger may proceed alone, if he is ready with a more solvent tenant or one offering a higher rent.[22]

Fiar and liferenter must concur in a removing, if the lease was granted by them or their common author.[23] Trustees have statutory power to remove tenants, and this applies to executors-nominate, executors-dative, tutors, curators and judicial factors.[24] An attorney, factor or commissioner requires express power in writing, and a power to grant leases does not necessarily imply a power to remove tenants.[25]

Lessees. In the case of a sublease, if the principal tenant suing in a removing is the granter of the sublease, the subtenant like any other tenant cannot impugn his own lessor's title however defective it may be.[26] The principal tenant may without his own landlord's consent remove a subtenant to whom he has let the subjects, even although the landlord's consent may originally have been required to make the sublease effectual.[27] Where the principal tenant, who is pursuing a removing, is not himself the lessor, infeftment has no application, and he may sue without producing the lessor's infeftment,[28] provided that he has the character of tenant of the subjects.[29] His title to sue a removing is not lost until a decree of removing has been obtained against him by his own landlord, and a decree of reduction of his own lease is apparently not sufficient to alter the state of possession.[30] An action of removing by a tenant against

[17] *Lennox* v *Reid* (1893) 21 R. 77.
[18] *Murdoch* v *Inglis* (1679) 3 B.S. 297; *Grozier* v *Downie* (1871) 9 M. 826.
[19] *Grozier* v *Downie, supra.*
[20] Rankine, 517.
[21] *Walker* v *Hendry,* 1925 S.C. 855.
[22] *A* v *B* (1680) Mor. 2448; *Halliday* v *Bruce* (1681) Mor. 2449; Rankine, 517.
[23] *Buchanan* v *Yuille* (1831) 9 S. 843, (1833) 11 S. 682.
[24] Trusts (Scotland) Act 1921, ss. 2 and 4 (c); Trusts (Scotland) Act 1961; s. 3; Succession (Scotland) Act 1964, s. 20; see *supra,* p. 47.
[25] *York Building Co.* v *Carnegie* (1764) Mor. 4054; Rankine, 518.
[26] *Supra,* p. 252.
[27] *M'Ilreavie* v *Smith* (1810) Hume 851.
[28] *Pringle* v *Tenants* (1629) Mor. 13792.
[29] *Anderson* v *Yule* (1610) Mor. 13786.
[30] *Innes* v *Allardyce* (1822) 2 S. 93 (N.E. 85); Rankine, 519.

a subtenant is not the proper place for the landlord to raise questions of heritable right, and the removing will be allowed to proceed in spite of his intervention.[31] The character of lessee must *bona fide* exist in the pursuer, and the Court may have to enquire into his title to ascertain whether he is in fact a lessee or merely a factor for another, who is alleged not to have authorised the proceedings,[32] or whether the subjects are included in the lessee's own lease.[33]

Questions have sometimes arisen as to the power of a lessee of subjects to remove either a former tenant of the same subjects or a tenant or possessor not holding of him as lessor, but of someone else, such as the proprietor.[34] The lessee must have authority to remove tenants.[35] The authority may be an express power " to output and input tenants "; or it may be implied from its duration, for example, if the lease is for the lessee's life or for more than 19 years, even although the lessee has not been in possession, or in the case of a shorter lease if the lessor or lessee has been in possession.[36] Otherwise the lessee must proceed by declarator and removing.[37] In the absence of authority to remove tenants, a pursuer has no title to remove an occupier from subjects, of which the pursuer is neither tenant nor proprietor.[38] It is doubtful whether in any circumstances a yearly tenant under a verbal lease may pursue an action of removing.[39]

Defenders. Where a lease is held jointly by two or more tenants, the pursuer in an action of removing must call them all in the action, whether they are in possession or not, if he intends to remove them all,[40] but it is quite competent to put out certain *pro indiviso* lessees and to allow the others to remain in possession.[41]

As regards assignees and subtenants, the Act of Sederunt of 14th December, 1756,[42] provided that, in the case of an assignation not intimated to the landlord or a sublet, the warning given to or process used against the principal tenant should be effectual against assignees and subtenants and should be sufficient ground for ejecting them.[43] Where an assignee's right has been intimated to the landlord, or a

[31] *Shirlaw* v *Wilson* (1823) 2 S. 561 (N.E. 485).
[32] *Johnston* v *Dickson* (1831) 9 S. 452.
[33] *Ritchie* v *Dickson* (1857) 19 D. 949.
[34] *E.g., Winans* v *Mackenzie* (1883) 10 R. 941 (removal of cottars from a tenanted estate).
[35] Rankine, 519.
[36] *Gentle* v *Henry* (1747) Mor. 13804 (new tenant removing former tenant).
[37] Rankine, 519.
[38] *Cameron* v *Robertson* (1867) 39 Sc. Jur. 256 (crofters removing a cowherd who occupied subjects direct from proprietor).
[39] *Ibid.*
[40] *Macdonald* v *Macdonald* (1807) Hume 580; *Macdonald* v *Sinclair* (1843) 5 D. 1253.
[41] Stair, II, 9, 43, and IV, 26, 10; Rankine, 520.
[42] Printed in Codifying Act of Sederunt, 1913 L. 15.
[43] s. 3; see Ross, *Lectures,* 2nd ed., II, 544; Hume, *Lectures,* IV, 105; Rankine, 520-521.

17

subtenant has been recognised by the landlord, the assignee or subtenant is the proper person to be called as defender, and notice given to the principal tenant is not enough.[44] If the landlord has no knowledge of the assignation, or has not recognised a subtenant, it is necessary to call the cedent or principal tenant, and a decree against him is sufficient.[45] It is wise, however, to call all possessors on whatever title as defenders in an action of removing, and there is no advantage in separating the instance.[46] If an assignee or subtenant is in possession in defiance of an express or implied exclusion, the landlord may remove the intruder without calling his author.[47]

Husband and Wife. A spouse, who is the owner or tenant of the matrimonial home, may eject the other spouse from it, and consistorial considerations are irrelevant to a question which is purely patrimonial.[48] Where one spouse has let subjects to the other spouse as tenant, the first spouse is entitled to remove or eject the other in the same way as any other tenant.[49]

PROCEDURE IN REMOVINGS PRIOR TO SHERIFF COURT (SCOTLAND) ACT 1907

A brief sketch of the historical development of the process of removing will suffice for the purpose of this work, but fuller accounts will be found in the authorities cited below.[50] It is still necessary to understand the procedures in use immediately before the passing of the Sheriff Court (Scotland) Act 1907, as the Act does not render them incompetent.

No Obligation to Remove. If the lease does not contain an obligation on the tenant to remove voluntarily at the end of the lease, and if the tenant has not subsequent to the lease granted any such express obligation, the removing must nowadays be effected by the interposition of judicial authority.[51] This, however, was not always so.

---

[44] *Lady Lawriston* v *Tenants* (1632) Mor. 13810; *Duke of Queensberry* v *Barker*, 7 July 1810 F.C.; *Robb* v *Brearton* (1895) 22 R. 885.
[45] Act of Sederunt, 14 December 1756, s. 3; *Thomson* v *Harvie* (1823) 2 S. 581; *Wilson* v *Campbell* (1839) 2 D. 232.
[46] Rankine, 521.
[47] *Ibid.*
[48] *Colquhoun* v *Colquhoun* (1804) Mor. App. *voce* Husband and Wife 5; *MacLure* v *MacLure*, 1911 S.C. 200; *Millar* v *Millar*, 1940 S.C. 56; *Labno* v *Labno*, 1949 S.L.T. (Notes) 18; *Scott* v *Scott* (1948) 64 Sh. Ct. Rep. 119; *Donachie* v *Donachie* (1948) 64 Sh. Ct. Rep. 120; *Macpherson* v *Macpherson*, 1950 S.L.T. (Sh. Ct.) 24; *Lawson* v *Lawson* (1950) 56 Sh. Ct. Rep. 207; *McLeod* v *McLeod*, 1958 S.L.T. (Sh. Ct.) 31.
[49] *Millar* v *Millar, supra.*
[50] Balfour, *Practicks* (Stair Society ed.), 456-464; Ross, *Lectures*, 2nd ed., II, 509, *et seq.*; Hume, *Lectures*, IV, 101-115; Hunter, *Landlord and Tenant*, 4th ed., II, 25-75; Rankine, 550-558; see also *Campbell's Trs.* v *O'Neill*, 1911 S.C. 188, *per* Lord Johnston at p. 193, and *Walker* v *Hendry*, 1925 S.C. 855, *per* L.J.C. Alness at p. 869.
[51] Hunter, *op. cit.*, 39.

Originally a tenant was put out by force of arms, and this used to lead to violence, if the tenant resisted, although there were two early enactments, which attempted to make the removing of a tenant a more peaceful process.[52] Before 1555, the landlord would call at the tenant's house and intimate verbally that he must remove upon the second day after Whitsunday, and he would break a wooden dish or platter as a symbol that all agreement and connection between him and the tenant was at an end. If the tenant did not remove by the third day after the term, he was forcibly ejected.[53] This procedure, very effective from the point of view of the landlord, was abrogated by the Act of 1555 c. 39 anent Warning of Tenants, from which our present law of removings may be said mainly to derive, although some of its solemnities appear to have been already in use.[54] Its main requirement was that a written precept or warning must be given to the tenant forty days before Whitsunday. Strict rules were laid down for execution of the precept and for the form of action to follow on the tenant's failure to remove.[55]

The Act of 1555 c. 39 was rendered practically obsolete by the Act of Sederunt of 14th December, 1756,[56] which gave the landlord the choice of proceeding by precept under the Act of 1555 or of bringing an action of removing before the Judge Ordinary, that is the Sheriff, which action had to be called at least forty days before Whitsunday.[57] The term of Whitsunday remained the only date against which the process could be raised until the passing of the Sheriff Courts (Scotland) Act 1853.[58] This Act laid down that it should be competent to raise a summons of removing at any time, provided there was an interval of forty days between the date of execution of the summons and the term of removal. The 1853 Act was repealed by the Sheriff Courts (Scotland) Act 1907.[59] The Act of 1555 c. 39 was finally repealed by the Statute Law Revision (Scotland) Act 1964.

Obligation to Remove. A simpler procedure was available where the tenant was under an express obligation to remove without warning or process of law. Such an obligation was (and is) literally construed and enforced, in the sense that warning was unnecessary and that the landlord might apply for summary removing in all cases where the obligation, whether contained in the lease or otherwise instructed, was dated within the year of removal.[60] If there were more than one term of re-

---

[52] Act 1469, c. 34 and Act 1546, c. 3 (both were repealed by the Statute Law Revision (Scotland) Act 1906; Hunter, *op. cit.,* II, 39-40.
[53] Ross, *op. cit.,* II, 509-514; Hunter, *op. cit.,* II, 39.
[54] *Ibid.,* 40.
[55] Rankine, 551-552.
[56] Printed in Codifying Act of Sederunt, 1913, L. 15.
[57] s. 2.
[58] s. 29.
[59] s. 52.
[60] Rankine, 555.

moving, it was sufficient that the date was within the year preceding the earliest of them.[61]

By the Act of Sederunt of 14th December, 1756, it was provided that the landlord might obtain letters of horning and charge the tenant thereon forty days before Whitsunday in the last year of the lease.[62] This remedy was virtually superseded in practice by the Sheriff Courts (Scotland) Act 1853,[63] but this latter Act was repealed by the Sheriff Courts (Scotland) Act 1907,[64] which substituted somewhat similar provisions.[65]

An obligation to remove may take the form of a clause of removal contained in the lease itself or of a separate letter of removal.[66] A mere verbal obligation to remove cannot be proved by parole evidence,[67] but it has been held that a verbal promise to remove, made near the termination of a lease, could be proved by the tenant's oath.[68] Where the clause of removal occurs in the lease itself, it obliges the tenant to flit and remove with his family and goods at the expiry of the lease and that without previous warning or process of law.[69] An addendum to the effect that the tenant is to pay an increased rent for occupation beyond the prescribed term is read in favour of the landlord, and not as a licence to the tenant to stay on at the increased rent.[70]

FORMS OF ACTION

The Act of Sederunt of 14th December, 1756, has not been repealed, and the forms of actions provided by it are still competent, although they have been to some extent superseded by subsequent legislation.[71] Ordinary removings falling under either the Act of 1555 c. 39, now repealed, or the Act of Sederunt required forty days' judicial warning and were termed "solemn removings". Removings, which fell under neither enactment but were regulated by common law, or later enactments were termed "summary removings".[72] The chief examples of summary removings were (a) removings from urban property, where 40 days' written notice was not, and is not, always required,[73] (b) removings from certain subjects let for less than one year, formerly under the Sheriff Courts (Scotland) Act 1838[74] and now under the Sheriff Courts

---

[61] *Ibid.*
[62] s. 1.
[63] ss. 30 and 31.
[64] s. 52.
[65] s. 35; *infra*, p. 268.
[66] Rankine, 554-555.
[67] Hume, *Lectures,* IV, 114; Rankine, 554.
[68] *Edmonston* v *Bryson* (1744) Mor. 12415, 13884.
[69] *E.g., Encyclopaedia of Scottish Legal Styles,* Vol. 6, Nos. 133, 144, *etc.*
[70] *Cross* v *Muirhead* (1813) Hume 860; *Campbell* v *M'Laurin* (1814) Hume 864.
[71] By Sheriff Courts (Scotland) Act, 1853, which was itself repealed by the Sheriff Courts (Scotland) Act 1907, s. 52.
[72] Hunter, *Landlord and Tenant,* 4th ed., II, 42; Rankine, 558; Lewis, *Sheriff Court Practice,* 8th ed., 266.
[73] *Infra,* p. 263.
[74] Repealed by the Sheriff Courts (Scotland) Act 1907, s. 52.

(Scotland) Act 1907,[75] and (c) removings in cases where the tenant had bound himself to remove.[76] The distinction between solemn and summary removings is of little or no significance nowadays.

The Sheriff Courts (Scotland) Act 1907 provides certain new procedures for removing tenants. It deals only with ordinary removings and its provisions do not render any of the former procedures incompetent.[77] In view of the multiplicity of remedies available, it may be useful to list here the following forms of action of removing which, with the exception of the first, still survive : —

(A) *Ordinary Removings*[78]

　　(1) *Act 1555 c. 39.* An action in the Court of Session or Sheriff Court to obtain a decree of removing followed by an application to the Sheriff to eject. The Act of 1555, for long obsolete, has at last been repealed, and this remedy is of historical interest only.[79]

　　(2) *Act of Sederunt 14th December, 1756, Sec. (1).* Letters of horning, where the tenant is bound by his lease to remove without warning. This form is virtually obsolete.[80]

　　(3) *Act of Sederunt 14th December, 1756, Sec. (2).* An action of removing called before the Sheriff forty days before the term of Whitsunday. This form is virtually obsolete.[81]

　　(4) *At Common Law.* An action of removing or of declarator and of removing in common form in the Court of Session or Sheriff Court. This was always available for urban subjects.

　　(5) *Sheriff Courts (Scotland) Act 1907, Sec. 34.* The registration and extract, six weeks after the date of the last ish, of a probative lease of lands exceeding two acres specifying a term of endurance.

　　(6) *Sheriff Courts (Scotland) Act 1907, Sec. 35.* The operation by diligence of a letter of removal.

　　(7) *Sheriff Courts (Scotland) Act 1907, Sec. 36.* A summary warrant of ejection, where the tenant of lands exceeding two acres, holding without a written lease, has received six months' notice to remove.

　　(8) *Sheriff Courts (Scotland) Act 1907, Sec. 37.* A warrant for summary ejection in the case of lets for a year or more, where the subjects let are houses, or are, generally speaking, subjects other than lands of two acres or more.

---

[75] s. 38.
[76] *Supra,* p. 259.
[77] s. 34.
[78] See Second Report of the Law Reform Committee for Scotland, 1957 Cmnd. 114, para. 5.
[79] *Per* Lord Johnston in *Campbell's Trs.* v *O'Neill,* 1911 S.C. 188 at p. 192. The Act was repealed by the Statute Law Revision (Scotland) Act 1964, Schedule 1.
[80] Second Report of the Law Reform Comittee, *supra,* para. 5.
[81] *Ibid.*

(9) *Sheriff Courts (Scotland) Act 1907, Sec. 38.* A summary
    application for removing, where the let is for a shorter period
    than one year.

(B) *Extraordinary Removings*[82]

(10) *At Common Law.* (a) An action of irritancy in the Court
     of Session against a tenant two years in arrear with his rent.
     This was largely superseded by the Act of Sederunt of 14th
     December, 1756. (b) An action of irritancy or declarator of
     irritancy to enforce a conventional irritancy such as non-
     payment of rent or breach of a condition of the lease. The
     Sheriff Court now has concurrent jurisdiction with the Court
     of Session.[83]

(11) *Act of Sederunt 14th December, 1756, Sec. 4.* An action of
     irritancy in the Sheriff Court where the tenant of agricultural
     subjects is two years in arrear with his rent. This is virtually
     obsolete.[84]

(12) *Act of Sederunt, 14th December, 1756, Sec. 5.* An action in
     the Sheriff Court to ordain a tenant, who is one year in
     arrear or deserts possession and leaves the ground un-
     laboured, to find caution. This is virtually obsolete.[85]

(13) *Agricultural Holdings (Scotland) Act 1949, Sec. 19.* An
     action in the Sheriff Court to remove a tenant of agricultural
     subjects, who is six months in arrear with his rent.

(14) *House Letting and Rating (Scotland) Act 1911, Sec. 5.* A
     summary application in the Sheriff Court or burgh police
     court for removing the occupier of a small dwellinghouse,
     who is seven days in arrear with his rent.

REMOVAL TERMS

Period of Notice. To prevent the operation of tacit relocation, the
party wishing to bring a lease to an end at its natural termination must
give timeous notice to the other party.[86] Moreover, in order to found an
action of removing, the landlord must have given timeous notice to the
tenant or have received timeous notice from the tenant. The notice is
variously called " notice of removing ", " notice to quit ", " warning ",
" letter of removal ", etc.

Although the degree of formality of the notice to be given for the
purpose of excluding tacit relocation may not in all cases be so great
as that of a notice to be used as the preliminary to an action of remov-

[82] See Chapter XV.
[83] Sheriff Courts (Scotland) Act 1907, s. 5 (4); *supra*, p. 229.
[84] *Supra*, p. 229.
[85] *Ibid.*
[86] *Supra*, p. 223.

ing,[87] the same considerations apply to the period of such notice. Where it is the tenant who gives notice, he must give the same period of warning as would have been required of the landlord.[88] The period of notice and the manner in which it is given depend partly on the nature of the subjects let and partly on the length of the lease. If no date of termination is stated in the lease, certain presumptions apply, and, in the absence of indication to the contrary, the ish of a lease for a term of years would be an anniversary of the date of entry.[89] In the case of a shorter lease, the ish would normally be presumed to be the same day of the month as the entry. A difficulty in practice is that there may be no record of when entry originally took place.

(1) *Urban Subjects.* At common law the rules as to removings from urban subjects depended on the custom of the locality where the buildings were situated.[90] Normally, but not invariably, the removal term was Whitsunday.[91] In the case of subjects in a burgh, the practice was for the burgh officer to chalk the most patent door of the building in the presence of one witness forty days before the term of removing, whether it was Whitsunday or Martinmas.[92] Chalking is probably still sufficient without other intimation to the tenant, and an acknowledgement by the tenant that intimation has been made to him timeously is equivalent to chalking.[93] The proper, but not the only, evidence of this " peace-warning ", as it is called, is the execution by the officer.[94] It was not necessary that warning should be given on the premises, provided that it was made to the tenant either by personal service or at his dwelling-house.[95] Similar rules applied to houses outside burghs.[96] Normally nowadays the warning is given by a notice of removal sent by either party to the other by registered post[97] or recorded delivery service.[98]

The term of removal and period of notice are now mainly regulated by the Removal Terms (Scotland) Act 1886. This provides that where under any lease the term of entry to, or removal from, a house is a term of Whitsunday or Martinmas, then, in the absence of stipulation to the contrary, the tenant shall, notwithstanding any usage to the contrary,

---

[87] *Supra,* p. 225.
[88] Rankine, 597.
[89] See *supra,* p. 135, for presumptions as to date of entry.
[90] Rankine, 559.
[91] The Act of 1469, c. 34, referred to the incasting and outcasting of tenants at Whitsunday and Martinmas; the solemnities of the Act of 1555, c. 39, and the Act of Sederunt of 14th December, 1756, which provided for notice to be given before Whitsunday, were not required for urban subjects.
[92] Erskine, II, 6, 47.
[93] *Encyclopaedia of the Laws of Scotland,* Vol. 12, 452.
[94] *Scott* v *Boyd* (1829) 7 S. 592; *Robb* v *Menzies* (1859) 21 D. 277, *per* Lord Deas at p. 282; Ross, *Lectures,* 2nd ed., II, 551.
[95] *Scott* v *Cook* (1886) 24 S.L.R. 34.
[96] Rankine, 561.
[97] Removal Terms (Scotland) Act 1886, s. 6.
[98] Recorded Delivery Service Act 1962, s. 1.

enter to, or remove from, the house at noon on 28th May, if the term
is Whitsunday, or at noon on 28th November, if the term is Martinmas,
or on the following day if the term falls on a Sunday.[99] In all cases where
warning is required forty days before a Whitsunday or Martinmas term of
removal, the warning must be given forty days before 15th May and 11th
November respectively.[1] If the house (other than a dwellinghouse or
building let along with land for agricultural purposes) is let for any
period not exceeding four months, notice must be given as many days
before the ish as shall be equivalent to at least one third of the full
period of the lease,[2] provided that in no case shall notice of removal be
given less than 28 days before the date on which it is to take effect.[3]
It is also provided by the Removal Terms (Scotland) Amendment Act
1890 (which applies to contracts of service) that, notwithstanding anything
in the latter Act, in all cases where warning of removal from a house is
required forty days before a Whitsunday or Martinmas term of removal,
such warning shall be given forty days before 15th May and 11th November respectively.[4] It has been held that this provision applies only to a
house occupied under a lease and not to a house occupied under a
contract of service.[5]

The effect is that, in the absence of provision to the contrary, where
the removal term is the 28th day of May or November, the period of
warning on either side must be calculated to the 15th and 11th days of
those months respectively. Thus, where a tenant wishing to exercise a
break at Whitsunday by giving six months' notice gave notice on 27th
November, it was held that he had not done so timeously.[6]

Special statutory provisions regulate the period of notice to be given
in the case of houses to which the House Letting and Rating (Scotland)
Act 1911 applies.[7] It will suffice to say that, notwithstanding the date of
entry, all lets of small dwellinghouses to which the Act applies, except
those for a shorter period than one month, shall terminate and shall be
terminable only at noon on the 28th day of a month, or when that day is
a Sunday, on the Monday following, and all lets of small dwellinghouses
for less than one month shall terminate and be terminable at noon on a
Monday.[8]

The Rent Act 1957 provides that no notice to quit any premises let
as a dwelling shall be valid, unless it is given at least four weeks before

---

[99] s. 4.
[1] s. 4; *Temperance Permanent Building Society* v *Kominek,* 1951 S.L.T. (Sh. Ct.)
58.
[2] s. 5.
[3] Rent Act 1957, Schedule 6, para. 28.
[4] s. 2.
[5] *Stewart* v *Robertson,* 1937 S.C. 701.
[6] *Fraser's Trs.* v *Maule & Son* (1904) 6 F. 819.
[7] *Supra,* p. 200.
[8] House Letting and Rating (Scotland) Act 1911, s. 3.

the date on which it is to take effect.[9] This provision is not confined to controlled tenancies.[10]

(2) *Agricultural Subjects.* At common law a lease of agricultural subjects normally runs from and to the term of Whitsunday or Martinmas.[11] The provisions of the Removal Terms (Scotland) Act 1886 with regard to the terms of entry to and removal from houses apply to a dwellinghouse or building let along with land for agricultural purposes,[12] but not to the land itself. Thus, unless other dates are specified in the lease, the removal date from the lands is 15th May or 11th November, and the removal date from the buildings is 28th May or 28th November, but the period of notice is calculated to the 15th May or 11th November. Parties may put their own interpretation on the words " Whitsunday " and " Martinmas " used in a lease,[13] but, where the lease has been entered into on or after 1st November, 1948, " Whitsunday " and " Martinmas " mean respectively 28th May and 28th November.[14] The period of notice required for agricultural subjects and the manner of giving it will be more fully discussed in a later chapter.[15]

(3) *Other Subjects.* Where the tenant has not bound himself to remove by writing, dated and signed within twelve months of the term of removal, or where there is more than one ish, within twelve months of the ish first in date, an action of removing may be raised by the landlord at any time, provided—(a) In the case of a lease of lands exceeding two acres for three years or more, notice of not less than one year nor more than two years is given.[16]

(b) In the case of leases of lands exceeding two acres, whether written or verbal, held from year to year or under tacit relocation, or for any other period less than three years, notice of not less than six months is given.[17]

(c) In the case of houses let with or without land attached not exceeding two acres in extent as also of mills, fishings, shootings and all other heritable subjects except land exceeding two acres in extent, and let for a year or more, notice of not less than forty days is given.[18] Apart from being a preliminary to an action of removing at the instance of the landlord, notice of termination in the case of these subjects may be given by the tenant to the landlord.[19] It is also provided in the case of these

[9] Rent Act 1957, s. 16.
[10] *Ibid.*, s. 25 (1).
[11] *Supra*, p. 136.
[12] ss. 3 and 4.
[13] *Hunter* v *Barron's Trs.* (1886) 13 R. 883.
[14] Agricultural Holdings (Scotland) Act 1949, s. 93 (1).
[15] *Infra*, p. 310.
[16] Sheriff Courts (Scotland) Act 1907, First Schedule, Rule 110 (a).
[17] *Ibid.*, Rule 110 (b).
[18] *Ibid.*, Rule 110 (c).
[19] *Ibid.*, s. 37.

subjects that, where the ish is Whitsunday or Martinmas, the notice must be given at least forty days before 15th May or 11th November.[20]

(4) *Letter of Removal.* An action of removing may be raised at any time, provided the tenant has bound himself to remove by writing, dated and signed within twelve months of the term of removal, or, where there is more than one ish, of the ish first in date.[21] It seems that the writing need not be holograph or tested.[22] It has been held that writing must be something different from the lease itself, and that consequently an obligation to remove in the lease is not equivalent to such a writing.[23]

SHERIFF COURTS (SCOTLAND) ACT 1907

The procedure in ordinary removings now usually followed is that of the Sheriff Courts (Scotland) Act 1907 Secs. 34-38 and Rules 110-122. The exact procedure depends partly on the nature of the subjects and partly on the period of the let. The Act deals only with ordinary removings, and its provisions do not render any former procedure incompetent;[24] nor does it deal with an action of ejection of persons without title. The principal effects of the Act so far as removings are concerned may be summarised as follows—[25]

(1) It defines cases in which no application to the Courts for removing or ejection is necessary. Here the Act adopts, with alterations, the procedure originally provided by the Sheriff Courts (Scotland) Act 1853, which the 1907 Act repeals. (2) It defines certain cases in which action forty days before the ish, *i.e.* solemn removing, is unnecessary. (3) It provides rules and forms as to the notice to be given and for the procedure to be followed in actions of removing under different conditions. These rules and forms may be used in actions of removing in common form and are not exclusive to the new procedures introduced by the Act. Thus, as has been seen, the provisions of Rule 110 may be applied to ordinary removings generally.[26]

Some of the provisions of the 1907 Act are by no means clear, and it has been said that the Act has " thrown the whole matter, which was by no means devoid of confusion at any rate, into still greater confusion."[27] One of the most confusing features of the Act is the use of the word " ejection " (which properly means the action for recovering possession from one who has no title to possess, such as an occupier *vi, clam aut precario*) in relation to forms of process for recovering possession from tenants.[28] Thus Sec. 36 provides for a " summary warrant of ejection " and

---

[20] *Ibid.,* s. 37.
[21] *Ibid.,* Rule 110.
[22] Dobie, *Sheriff Court Practice,* 412.
[23] *Cesari* v *Anderson* (1922) 38 Sh. Ct. Rep. 137.
[24] s. 34.
[25] Lewis, *Sheriff Court Practice,* 8th ed., 266.
[26] *Supra,* p. 265.
[27] *Per* Lord Johnston in *Campbell's Trs.* v *O'Neill,* 1911 S.C. 188 at p. 192.
[28] Second Report of the Law Reform Committee for Scotland on the procedural law relating to actions of removing and ejection, 1957 Cmnd. 114, para. 4.

Sec. 37 for a " warrant of summary ejection " in certain cases. It may have been the intention of the framers of the Act that actions brought under Secs. 36 and 37 should be regarded as ejections and not removings, but it has been decided that an action taken under Sec. 37, though an " ejection " in name, is a " removing " in fact.[29]

(1) *Ejection without Application to Court for Removing or Ejection*: —
    (a) *Lands exceeding two acres. Probative Lease. 1907 Act, Sec. 34.* Where lands exceeding two acres in extent are held under a probative lease specifying a term of endurance with or without an obligation on the tenant to remove without warning, an action of removing may be unnecessary, if notice to remove has been given. The previous notice has to be given in writing (a) where the lease is for three years or more, not less than one year and not more than two years before the termination, and (b) where the lease is from year to year (including lands occupied by tacit relocation) or for any other period less than three years, not less than six months before the termination of the lease (or where there is a separate ish as regards lands and houses or otherwise, before the ish first in date). If such notice is given, the lease or an extract thereof from any Court books has the same effect as an extract decree of removing obtained in an ordinary action at the instance of the landlord against the lessee or any party in possession. Such lease or extract with authority in writing signed by the landlord or his factor or solicitor is sufficient warrant to any sheriff officer or messenger-at-arms of the sheriffdom in which the lands are situated to eject the party in possession at the expiry of the term or terms of endurance of the lease.[30] The notice under Sec. 34 shall be as nearly as may be in the Form H.[31]

If written notice is not given in terms of Sec. 34, the lease is renewed by tacit relocation for another year and thereafter from year to year.[32] Removal or ejection in virtue of Sec. 34 is not competent after six weeks from the last ish in date.[33] Nothing in Sec. 34 affects the right of the landlord to remove a tenant who has been sequestrated or who has incurred an irritancy or other liability to remove by non-payment of rent.[34] The provisions as to notice do not apply to stipulations entitling the landlord to resume land for building, planting, feuing or other purposes, nor do they apply to subjects let for less than a year.[35] Nothing in the Act is to be construed to prevent proceedings under any lease in common form.[36]

It seems clear that the above provisions apply whether the lands alone are let or the lease is of lands over two acres in extent along with

[29] *Campbell's Trs.* v *O'Neill, supra; Mackay* v *Menzies,* 1937 S.C. 691.
[30] Sheriff Courts (Scotland) Act 1907, s. 34.
[31] *Ibid.,* First Schedule, Rule 111.
[32] s. 34.
[33] *Ibid.*
[34] *Ibid.*
[35] *Ibid.*
[36] *Ibid.*

houses.[37] The provision that the notice must be given not less than six months before the earliest of more than one ish would appear to apply to all leases coming under the section, not merely to those for less than three years.[38] The provision that, if written notice is not given in terms of the Act, tacit relocation ensues would appear to supersede any conventional stipulation in the lease itself dispensing with, or providing for the length or manner of notice.[39]

(b) *Lands exceeding two acres. Letter of Removal. 1907 Act, Sec. 35.* Where a tenant in possession of lands exceeding two acres, whether with or without a written lease, grants a letter of removal, either at the time of entering the lease or at any other time, either holograph or attested by one witness, such letter has the same effect as an extract decree of removing, and shall be a sufficient warrant for ejection with the same effect as is provided with regard to a lease or extract, that is, by Sec. 34. Such a letter of removal is operative against its granter or party in his right within the same time, that is, not later than six weeks from the last ish in date, and in the same manner after notice to remove in terms of Sec. 34. Where the letter of removal is dated and signed within twelve months before the date of removal or before the first of more than one ish, no notice need be given by either party to the other.[40] The letter of removal may be in the terms of Form I.[41]

Alternative of Ordinary Action. It has been seen that in cases falling under the Sheriff Courts (Scotland) Act 1907, Secs. 34 and 35, no process of removing or ejection is necessary, but that the tenant may be ejected without a decree of Court. The landlord, however, is not bound to use the shorthand methods given by those sections, and, in cases where there is a real dispute, it may be more convenient to have the matter brought into court by an ordinary action of removing, under which, if decree is granted, the defender will be ordained to flit and remove under pain of ejection.[42] It appears that the provisions of Secs. 34 and 35 are so drastic, and their operation so fraught with hazard to any who seek to invoke them that they are very seldom, if ever, used.[43]

It has already been seen that an action of removing may be raised at any time, provided the tenant has bound himself to remove by writing, dated and signed within twelve months of the term of removal, or, if there is no such writing, provided there has been given notice of specified

[37] Dobie, *op. cit.*, 410.
[38] *Montgomerie* v *Wilson*, 1924 S.L.T. (Sh. Ct.) 48; Rankine, 566-567; Dobie, *op. cit.*, 410.
[39] *Duguid* v *Muirhead*, 1926 S.C. 1078 (O.H.), *per* Lord Constable at pp. 1082-3; Dobie, *op. cit.*, 410; but see *Viscountess Cowdray* v *Ferries*, 1918 S.C. 210, *per* Lord Johnston at p. 210 (*obiter*).
[40] Sheriff Courts (Scotland) Act 1907, s. 35.
[41] *Ibid.*, First Schedule, Rule 111.
[42] Dobie, *Sheriff Court Practice*, 412.
[43] Rankine, 571; Second Report of the Law Reform Committee for Scotland, 1957 Cmnd. 114, para. 5.

duration depending on the nature of the subjects and the length of the lease.[44]

(2) Application for Warrant to Eject without Decree

(a) *Lands exceeding two acres. No Written Lease and no Letter of Renewal. 1907 Act, Sec. 36.* Where lands exceeding two acres in extent are occupied by a tenant without a written lease, and the tenant has not granted a letter of removal, the lease may be terminated by written notice given by or on behalf of one party to the other not less than six months before the termination of the tenancy. Such notice entitles the proprietor, in the event of the tenant failing to remove, to apply for and obtain a summary warrant of ejection against the tenant.[45] The notice under Sec. 36 shall be as nearly as may be in the Form H.[46]

It appears that the summary warrant of ejection under Sec. 36 is identical with the warrant for summary ejection provided for under Sec. 37.[47] The application is made by initial writ craving summarily to eject the defender and it is treated as an ordinary cause; technically the action is one of removing, and the tenant is entitled to state such defences as would have been open to him in a removing.[48]

(b) *Holdings not exceeding two Acres let for One Year or more. 1907 Act, Sec. 37.* In all cases where houses, with or without land attached, not exceeding two acres in extent, lands not exceeding two acres in extent let without houses, mills, fishings, shootings, and all other heritable subjects (except land exceeding two acres in extent) are let for a year or more, notice of termination shall be given in writing by or on behalf of one party to the other. The notice must be given at least forty days before 15th May when the termination is Whitsunday, and at least forty days before 11th November when the termination is Martinmas. Such a notice " shall not warrant summary ejection " but, whether given to or by or on behalf of the tenant, it shall entitle the proprietor to apply to the Sheriff for " a warrant for summary ejection in common form " against the tenant.[49] Notices under Sec. 37 shall be as nearly as may be in the Form J which may be used by either party.[50]

The application is made by initial writ craving warrant summarily to eject the defender, and, despite the use of the word " ejection ", the action is technically an action of summary removing.[51] The tenant is entitled to state such defences as would have been open to him in an action of removing; the whole meaning of Sec. 37 is simply to cut out

---

[44] Sheriff Courts (Scotland) Act 1907, First Schedule, Rule 110; *supra*, p. 265.
[45] Sheriff Courts (Scotland) Act 1907, s. 36.
[46] *Ibid.*, First Schedule, Rule 111.
[47] Dobie, *Sheriff Court Practice*, 413.
[48] *Ibid.; cf. Campbell's Trs.* v *O'Neill*, 1911 S.C. 188.
[49] Sheriff Courts (Scotland) Act 1907, s. 37.
[50] *Ibid.*, First Schedule, Rule 112.
[51] Rankine, 573; Dobie, *Sheriff Court Practice*, 413.

the action of removing, substitute the mere notice, and then allow the objections to be stated in the " ejection " instead of in the removing.[52]

The section does not provide for the event of the termination date not being a term of Whitsunday or Martinmas, but apparently notice should in any case be given forty days before the date of termination.[53] Where a landlord gave written notice to the tenant to remove at the term of Whitsunday without specifying whether that meant the 15th or the 28th of May, and the tenant held a lease for which the term of removal by virtue of the Removal Terms (Scotland) Act 1886 was 28th May, it was held that the notice was not rendered bad, as the tenant could not be turned out before the 28th, and there was no proposal to turn him out before that date.[54] A notice given and received on 5th April (the fortieth day before 15th May) was held not to have been given timeously.[55]

(3) *Summary Removings. Subjects let for less than One Year. 1907 Act, Sec. 38.* Where houses or other heritable subjects are let for a shorter period than one year, the proprietor or his factor or any other person authorised to pursue a process of removing may present to the Sheriff a summary application for removing, and a decree pronounced in such summary cause shall have the full force and effect of a decree of removing and warrant of ejection.[56] In the absence of express stipulation, the period of notice is (a) where the let does not exceed four months, as many days before the ish as is equal to at least one-third of the full period of let, and (b) where the let exceeds four months, forty days before the ish, provided that in no case shall notice of removal be given less than twenty eight days before the date on which it is to take effect.[57]

Those provisions have been modified in the case of houses falling under the House Letting and Rating (Scotland) Act 1911,[58] generally described as " small dwelling-houses ", and which fall to be treated as subjects let for less than one year. Notice to terminate the let of a small dwelling-house on the day on which a payment of rent falls due may be given by either party, and shall be given in accordance with the provisions of the Sheriff Courts (Scotland) Act 1907, but shall expire only at noon on the day on which that payment of rent falls due, unless that is a Sunday, in which case it will expire at noon on the following day.[59] The period of notice is (a) forty days for a let of more than three months, or (b) if the let is for three months or less, at least one third of the period of let, but in no case shall the notice be given less than twenty eight days before the

---

[52] *Campbell's Trs.* v *O'Neill,* 1911 S.C. 188; *Mackay* v *Menzies,* 1937 S.C. 691; Rankine, 573; Dobie, *op. cit.,* 414.
[53] Rankine, 573; Dobie, *op. cit.,* 414.
[54] *Campbell's Trs.* v *O'Neill, supra.*
[55] *M'Leod* v *George* (1933) 49 Sh. Ct. Rep. 302.
[56] Sheriff Courts (Scotland) Act 1907, s. 38, First Schedule, Rule 115.
[57] *Ibid.,* s. 38, as amended by Rent Act 1957, Sixth Schedule, para. 29.
[58] *Supra,* p. 200.
[59] House Letting and Rating (Scotland) Act 1911, s. 4.

date on which it is to take effect.[60] If the occupier is in arrear with his rent for not less than seven days, the owner may give him twenty eight days' notice to terminate the let.[61] Provision is also made for a summary application for removing to the Sheriff or other court exercising jurisdiction in summary removings, and a decree pronounced on such summary application has the same effect as a decree of removing and warrant of ejection.[62]

No form of notice is prescribed by either Act for use in cases to which this procedure applies, but in practice Form J of the 1907 Act suitably adapted is used,[63] but it is certainly not compulsory.[64] It must be in writing.[65] The Sheriff Courts (Scotland) Act 1907 provides a special form of initial writ, warrant and decree and generally regulates the procedure to be followed in summary removings under Sec. 38.[66]

Save as explained below, an action for summary removing brought under the Sheriff Courts (Scotland) Act 1907, Sec. 38, is conducted and disposed of in the summary manner in which proceedings are conducted under the Small Debt Acts and is not subject to review.[67] This excludes even the limited right of appeal to the High Court of Justiciary competent in small debt cases,[68] but it may not exclude review by suspension, if it is averred that the lease is for a year or more.[69] If the defender finds caution for violent profits, or if such caution is dispensed with, he is entitled to lodge written answers,[70] in which event the action proceeds as an ordinary one of removing and is subject to review in common form.[71] The Sheriff has a discretionary power in the course of the proceedings to determine whether such an action shall proceed as an ordinary or as a summary cause, no matter in which form it was initiated.[72]

In the case of a summary application for removing brought under the House Letting and Rating (Scotland) Act 1911, it is provided that in any burgh, where the Sheriff Court is the only court exercising jurisdiction in summary applications, an application in respect of a small dwelling house may be presented in the burgh police court, where the same pro-

---

[60] Ibid., s. 4, as amended by Rent Act 1957, Sixth Schedule, para. 30.
[61] Ibid., s. 5, as amended by Rent Act 1957, Sixth Schedule, para. 30.
[62] House Letting and Rating (Scotland) Act 1911, s. 6 (1).
[63] Lewis, Sheriff Court Practice, 8th ed., 273; Dobie, Sheriff Court Practice, 406.
[64] Barr & Sons Ltd. v Muncie (1923) 39 Sh. Ct. Rep. 50; British Transport Commission v Miller, 1955 S.L.T. (Sh. Ct.) 40.
[65] Aitken v Morris (1922) 38 Sh. Ct. Rep. 70.
[66] First Schedule, Rules 115-122.
[67] Sheriff Courts (Scotland) Act 1907, First Schedule, Rule 119, as amended by Sheriff Courts (Scotland) Act 1913, Second Schedule.
[68] Lovell & Son v Macfarlane, 1949 J.C. 123.
[69] Robertson v Thorburn, 1927 S.L.T. 562 (O.H.); Dobie, op. cit., 406.
[70] Sheriff Courts (Scotland) Act 1907, First Schedule, Rule 121, as amended by Sheriff Courts (Scotland) Act 1913, Second Schedule.
[71] Ibid., Rule 122. It may be noted here that when the 1907 Act came into operation there was no "common form" of appeal in actions of removing, review being only by way of suspension. Normal rights of appeal in removings were first provided by the Act of Sederunt of 12th July 1938 (see infra, p. 287).
[72] Sheriff Courts (Scotland) Act 1907, s. 48; Purves v Graham, 1924 S.C. 477, per Lord Hunter at p. 483.

cedure is to be followed as in the Sheriff Court.[73] In any summary application no delay beyond forty eight hours is to be granted by the sheriff or magistrate to the occupier of a small dwelling-house, unless on cause shown, or on caution for, or consignation of, the rent due being found.[74]

The procedure is available only against a tenant, not a squatter, but would apparently be available in the case of a house let during employment but terminable on notice.[75] The procedure was allowed in one case where the relationship of landlord and tenant was found not to have been set up, but the action finally proceeded as an ordinary cause.[76]

NOTICE OF REMOVING

A notice of removing may be given for one or both of two purposes, namely, to prevent the operation of tacit relocation,[77] and as a foundation for an action of removing. There are different forms of notice for use in different circumstances, most of them provided by the Sheriff Courts (Scotland) Act 1907, and the variety of forms are productive of confusion and uncertainty.[78] Certain of the forms may be used by the tenant as well as the landlord. An action of removing at the landlord's instance may sometimes be founded on a notice given by the tenant. The period of notice has already been discussed.[79]

Urban Subjects. The rules as to warning in the case of urban subjects have long been different from, and much less strict than, those which apply in the case of rural subjects.[80] At common law an informal notice, which may even be verbal, suffices in the case of a let of an urban subject,[81] and a formal peace warning is unnecessary.[82] Although some authorities seem to apply this relaxation to all urban leases,[83] most *dicta* have limited it to verbal leases or yearly tenancies.[84]

---

[73] House Letting and Rating (Scotland) Act 1911, s. 6 (1).
[74] *Ibid.*, s. 6 (2).
[75] *Mags. of Buckhaven and Methil* v *Wemyss Coal Co.*, 1928 S.C. 66; *Earl of Eglinton* v *M'Luckie*, 1944 S.L.T. (Sh. Ct.) 21; Lewis, *op. cit.*, 386; Dobie, *op. cit.*, 405.
[76] *Oban Town Council* v *Erwin*, 1945 S.L.T. (Sh. Ct.) 27.
[77] *Supra*, Chapter XIV.
[78] See Second Report of the Law Reform Committee for Scotland, 1957 Cmnd. 114, para. 8.
[79] *Supra*, p. 262.
[80] *Per* Lord Curriehill in *Robb* v *Menzies* (1859) 21 D. 277 at p. 281.
[81] *Gilchrist* v *Westren* (1890) 17 R. 363; Hume, *Lectures*, IV, 110; Rankine, 597; *supra*, p. 224.
[82] *Tait* v *Sligo* (1766) Mor. 13864; *Jack* v *Earl of Kelly* (1795) Mor. 13866; *Hood* v *N.B. Railway Co.* (1895) 3 S.L.T. 196 (O.H.).
[83] In *Gilchrist* v *Westren*, *supra*, the lease was a written one for seven and a half years and it was the tenant who gave the verbal notice; see Hume, *Lectures*, IV, 110, and Rankine, 597, who speak of verbal leases generally.
[84] *Morris* v *Allan* (1839) 1 D. 667; *Gillespie* v *Fairlie* (1920) 36 Sh. Ct. Rep. 6; *Craighall Cast-Stone Co.* v *Wood Bros.*, 1931 S.C. 66, *per* L.P. Clyde and Lord Morison at pp. 68 and 69. In those cases and in *Hood* v *N.B. Railway Co.*, *supra*, where it was the landlord who gave the verbal notice, the tenancies were yearly ones.

What is clear is that this old familiar practice was not affected by the Sheriff Courts (Scotland) Act 1907, Sec. 37, which requires written notice, but only for the simplified procedure provided by that section;[85] nor is it affected by Rule 110 of that Act, which relates to actions of removing in ordinary form, but which does not make written notice mandatory.[86] Thus, a verbal notice by the tenant of urban subjects of his intention to remove has been held a sufficient foundation for an action of removing in ordinary form at the instance of the landlord.[87] Similarly, verbal or informal notice given by the landlord has been held to be sufficient.[88] There are two Sheriff Court decisions to the effect that the calling of an action of removing from urban subjects forty days before the term is sufficient notice in itself.[89]

Although the provisions of the Sheriff Courts (Scotland) Act 1907 do not abrogate the procedure in use before the passing of the Act,[90] and therefore written notice of removal from urban subjects may not always be essential, it is only prudent to give such notice, and it is normal to use Form J for notices both by the tenant and the landlord,[91] and there is nothing incompetent in an action following upon such statutory notice proceeding in ordinary form.[92] The difficulty of proving the giving or receipt of a verbal notice is obvious.[93]

In the case of dwellings, however, the common law practice whereby written notice may not always be essential has been modified by the Rent Act 1957, Sec. 16: this provides that no notice by a landlord or a tenant to quit any premises let as a dwelling shall be valid unless given not less than four weeks before the date on which it is to take effect.

Agricultural Subjects. In the case of land let for agricultural purposes, the Agricultural Holdings (Scotland) Act 1948 provides that notice by the landlord to the tenant shall be given either (a) in the same manner as notice of removal under the Removal Terms (Scotland) Act 1886; or (b) in the form and manner prescribed by the Sheriff Courts (Scotland) Act 1907; and such notice shall come in place of the notice required by the latter Act.[94] The 1949 Act itself prescribes the period of notice;[95] the 1886 Act regulates only the manner of giving notice;[96]

---

[85] *Supra*, p. 224.
[86] *Gillies* v *Fairlie, supra.*
[87] *Gillies* v *Fairlie, supra; Craighall Cast-Stone Co.* v *Wood Bros., supra.*
[88] *Grant* v *Bannerman* (1920) 36 Sh. Ct. Rep. 59; *Ld. Advocate* v *Dykes* (1921) 37 Sh. Ct. Rep. 133.
[89] *Green* v *Young* (1919) 35 Sh. Ct. Rep. 201; *Kerr* v *Young* (1920) 36 Sh. Ct. Rep. 184; see Dobie, *Sheriff Court Practice*, 414.
[90] Sheriff Courts (Scotland) Act 1907, s. 34; Lewis, *Sheriff Court Practice*, 8th ed., 267.
[91] Sheriff Courts (Scotland) Act, 1907, First Schedule, Rule 112.
[92] *Per* L.P. Dunedin in *Campbell's Trs.* v *O'Neill*, 1911 S.C. 188 at p. 198; *Reid* v *Anderson* (1920) 36 Sh. Ct. Rep. 11; Dobie, *op. cit.*, 414.
[93] *Glass* v *Klepczynski*, 1951 S.L.T. (Sh. Ct.) 55.
[94] Agricultural Holdings (Scotland) Act 1949, s. 24 (4).
[95] *Infra*, p. 310.
[96] *Infra*, p. 278.

18

and the 1907 Act prescribes the form of notice. It has been held (by a majority) that, despite the wording of the 1949 Act, Sec. 24 (4), the landlord is not given a choice of either the manner prescribed by the 1886 Act or the form and manner prescribed by the 1907 Act, but that the form of the notice to quit must conform with the 1907 Act.[97] The result is that, where the land exceeds two acres in extent, written notice must be given in terms of Form H of the 1907 Act,[98] or, where the land does not exceed two acres in extent, in terms of Form J to that Act.[99]

The Agricultural Holdings (Scotland) Act 1949, prescribes no form for the notice to be given by the tenant to the landlord, and a simple letter by the tenant is sufficient, so long as it unequivocally bears to be notice of the tenant's intention to quit the subjects.[1]

Other Subjects. Apart from urban subjects, where the notice may be verbal or at least informal, and agricultural subjects, where the forms of the Sheriff Courts (Scotland) Act 1907 are obligatory, the 1907 Act provides forms which may or must be used depending on the circumstances.

In actions of removing in ordinary form, as distinct from the special procedures introduced by the 1907 Act, Rule 110 prescribes no form for the notice to be given by landlord or tenant, nor does it even require the notice given by the landlord to be in writing. Apart from urban subjects, however, notice always had to be in writing. Form H would normally be used by the landlord for subjects exceeding two acres,[2] and Form J for subjects not exceeding two acres.[3] A tenant would use Form I[4] in which to bind himself within twelve months of the ish to remove; this obligation must be in writing;[5] however, those forms are not obligatory in actions of removing in common form.[6] Conversely, although notice has been given in one of those statutory forms, the action following thereon may be in ordinary form and need not be one of the special statutory procedures.[7]

The notice required to be given by the landlord for the purpose of the action of ejection without application to the Court where the subjects exceed two acres, provided by the 1907 Act, Sec. 34, *shall* be as

[97] *Rae* v *Davidson*, 1954 S.C. 361.
[98] Sheriff Courts (Scotland) Act 1907, First Schedule, Rule 111.
[99] *Ibid.*, Rule 112; Dobie, *Sheriff Court Practice* 409; but see Connell, *Agricultural Holdings (Scotland) Acts*, 5th ed., 131, where it is said that Form H is obligatory.
[1] Connell, *op. cit.*, 17.
[2] Sheriff Courts (Scotland) Act, 1907, First Schedule, Rule 111.
[3] *Ibid.*, Rule 112.
[4] *Ibid.*, Rule 111.
[5] *Ibid.*, Rule 110.
[6] *Gillies* v *Fairlie* (1920) 36 Sh. Ct. Rep. 6; *Grant* v *Bannerman* (1920) 36 Sh. Ct. Rep. 59; *Kirk* v *Aitchman* (1929) 45 Sh. Ct. Rep. 317; *Ritchie* v *Lyon* (1940) 56 Sh. Ct. Rep. 39; Lewis, *op. cit.*, 269; see also the authorities cited with regard to urban subjects, *supra*, pp. 272-3.
[7] Per L.P. Dunedin in *Campbell's Trs.* v *O'Neill*, 1911 S.C. 188 at p. 198; *Reid* v *Anderson* (1920) 36 Sh. Ct. Rep. 11; Dobie, *op. cit.*, 414.

nearly as may be in terms of Form H, and the letter of removal to be given by the tenant for the same purpose under Sec. 35 *may* be in terms of Form I.[8]

The notice required to be given by the landlord for the purpose of the application for warrant to eject without decree, where the subjects exceed two acres and there is no written lease, provided by the 1907 Act, Sec. 36, *shall* be as nearly as may be in terms of Form H.[9] The notice to be given by the landlord for the purpose of a similar application, where subjects not exceeding two acres are let for a year or more, provided by the 1907 Act, Sec. 37, *shall* be as nearly as may be in terms of Form J; and this form *may* also be used for a notice by the tenant to the landlord.[10]

No notice is prescribed by the 1907 Act, Sec. 38, for the purpose of summary removings from subjects let for less than one year; in practice Form J is used for proceedings both under that Act[11] and under the House Letting and Rating (Scotland) Act 1911,[12] but no special form is obligatory.[13]

Where a tenant of a shop, on whom a valid notice to quit had been served, obtained a renewal of the tenancy for a further year under the Tenancy of Shops (Scotland) Act 1949, it was held that the landlord must serve a fresh notice in order to terminate the renewed tenancy.[14]

Contents of Notice. Where a special form of notice of removing has been made obligatory, such as a notice to quit agricultural subjects and a notice required to found one of the special procedures introduced by the Sheriff Courts (Scotland) Act 1907, the Act provides that the notice of removal to be given by the landlord shall be as nearly as may be in one or other of the forms provided.[15] Both Forms H and J are addressed to the tenant or party in possession with his designation and address, requiring him to remove from the subjects, which are described, at a term or terms of removal. Form H also requires a reference to the lease, which should be described, or to a letter of removal or otherwise as the case may be; Form J does not have this requirement. While slight deviations from those forms may be ignored,[16] it is essential to include the above elements, and any material departure from the prescribed form will render the notice invalid.[17] In certain circumstances

---

[8] Sheriff Courts (Scotland) Act 1907, First Schedule, Rule 111.
[9] *Ibid.*, Rule 111.
[10] *Ibid.*, Rule 112.
[11] *Ibid.*, Rule 112.
[12] *Ibid.*, s. 4.
[13] *Barr & Sons Ltd.* v *Muncie* (1923) 39 Sh. Ct. Rep. 50; *British Transport Commission* v *Miller,* 1955 S.L.T. (Sh. Ct.) 40.
[14] *White* v *Paton* (1953) 69 Sh. Ct. Rep. 176, disapproving *Hill* v *M'Caskill's Trs.* (1951) 67 Sh. Ct. Rep. 128.
[15] Sheriff Courts (Scotland) Act 1907, First Schedule, Rules 111 and 112.
[16] *Rutherford* v *Oswald,* 1945 S.L.T. (Sh. Ct.) 9.
[17] *Scott* v *Livingstone,* 1919 S.C. 1; *Rae* v *Davidson,* 1954 S.C. 361; see also *Johnston* v *Pettigrew* (1865) 3 M. 954, *per* Lord Cowan at p. 962 for the meaning of such words as " as nearly as may be ".

a notice to quit agricultural subjects must state the reason why the notice is given.[18]

The notice must explicitly require the tenant to remove. It is not sufficient merely to intimate the termination of the tenancy or the landlord's intention to resume possession.[19] A notice in conditional terms is inept,[20] but, provided the notice is unconditional and unequivocal, it is not necessarily rendered invalid by the addition of a statement that the tenant may continue for a further period,[21] or of a clause giving him an option to purchase the subjects.[22]

The notice must specify the term, or, if there are separate subjects let for different periods, the terms, at which the tenant is required to remove.[23] Form H envisages the date of removal to be a legal term and does not require the exact date, but Form J requires the terms of Whitsunday and Martinmas to be explained by the addition of the exact day of the month. Where the words " being the twenty-eighth day of May " were omitted from a notice timeously given to a tenant, where Whitsunday by virtue of the Removal Terms (Scotland) Act 1886, meant 28th May, the notice was held to be valid;[24] the tenant had an Act of Parliament to explain the meaning of " Whitsunday ", and suffered no prejudice, but a similar omission might have had a different result had the proposal been to turn the tenant out on the 15th and not the 28th May.[25] Similarly, a notice was held to be valid, where it omitted the words " term of Whitsunday ", but required the tenant to remove on 29th May, the 28th being a Sunday.[26] The insertion of the wrong date, such as Whitsunday instead of Martinmas,[27] or 15th May instead of 28th May, will render the notice invalid.[28] Similarly, a notice is invalid if it specifies a date before that up to which the rent has been paid in advance.[29]

The subjects must be described. Obviously there must be no ambiguity as to the subjects from which removal is required.[30] A notice given to the tenant under a verbal lease of a cottage on a farm with garden, byre and field, which ran " I beg to serve formal notice to quit

[18] Agricultural Holdings (Scotland) Act 1949, s. 25 (2); *infra*, p. 315.
[19] *Patten* v *Morison* (1919) 35 Sh. Ct. Rep. 252; *Core* v *Gray* (1920) 36 Sh. Ct. Rep. 113; *Richards* v *Cameron* (1946) 62 Sh. Ct. Rep. 106; *George M. Brown Ltd.* v *Collier*, 1954 S.L.T. (Sh. Ct.) 98 (all Form J).
[20] *Murray* v *Grieve* (1920) 36 Sh. Ct. Rep. 126.
[21] *Watt* v *Findlay* (1921) 37 Sh. Ct. Rep. 34.
[22] *Naysmith* v *Maxwell* (1925) 41 Sh. Ct. Rep. 318.
[23] Rankine, 566; for agricultural subjects let for different periods see *Montgomerie* v *Wilson*, 1924 S.L.T. (Sh. Ct.) 48.
[24] *Campbell's Trs.* v *O'Neill*, 1911 S.C. 188, *per* L.P. Dunedin and Lord Kinnear at pp. 198 and 200.
[25] *Ibid.*
[26] *Temperance Permanent Building Society* v *Kominek*, 1951 S.L.T. (Sh. Ct.) 58.
[27] *Earl of March* v *Dowie* (1754) Mor. 13843.
[28] *Macdonald* v *Cameron* (1916) 32 Sh. Ct. Rep. 261; *Anderson* v *Scott* (1939) 55 Sh. Ct. Rep. 143; *James Grant & Co. Ltd.* v *Moran*, 1948 S.L.T. (Sh. Ct.) 8.
[29] *Peters* v *Symons*, 1953 S.L.T. (Sh. Ct.) 65.
[30] *Cameron* v *Ferrier* (1912) 28 Sh. Ct. Rep. 220; *Birrell & Hay* v *Thomson* (Sheriff Court) 1948 C.L. 4437.

at Whitsunday (28th May), 1918, as I shall be requiring the cottage for an employee ", was held to be invalid for want of a sufficient description for the purpose of a warrant for summary ejection.[31] It has already been seen that, where separate subjects are let together for a single rent, a notice to quit one of them is insufficient to prevent the operation of tacit relocation.[32] Where separate subjects are let together for separate rents, an action of removing in respect of one of them may proceed on a notice covering all of them.[33]

When Form H is the prescribed form of notice, there is the further requirement that the notice must refer to the lease, letter of removal, or otherwise as the case may be. Thus, where a notice to the tenant to quit agricultural subjects let under a probative lease complied with Form H in all respects, except that it omitted to refer to and describe the lease, it was held (by a majority) to be invalid on this mere technical ground.[34] Where there is a letter of removal by the tenant, there would appear from a strict interpretation of Form H to be no need to refer to the lease itself. If there is no written lease and no letter of removal, it is clearly impossible to refer to either. Form H, however, contains an alternative in the words " or otherwise as the case may be ". Accordingly, where subjects were let by informal writings supported by *rei interventus*, it was held that a notice not referring to the lease, but specifying the subjects as " presently possessed and used by you " and signed by a solicitor as agent for the landlord " by whom said land and houses are sublet to you ", was sufficient.[35]

Forms H and J do not specifically require mention of the name of the party on whose behalf the notice is given. There are conflicting Sheriff Court decisions as to whether this is necessary when the notice is given by his agent or by an officer.[36] It may be signed by law agents in the firm's name.[37]

When it is the tenant who gives notice, he may do so in terms of Form I or Form J, but these forms are not made obligatory.[38] Moreover, as has been seen, even Forms H and J are not obligatory, except where required by statute in the case of agricultural land and the special procedures of the Sheriff Courts (Scotland) Act 1907.[39] In all cases where a statutory form is not made obligatory, the essence of a notice of removal, whether by the landlord or the tenant, is that it must be a

---

[31] *Scott* v *Livingstone*, 1919 S.C. 1.
[32] *Gates* v *Blair*, 1923 S.C. 430; *supra*, p. 223.
[33] *Falconer* v *Chisholm's Trs.*, 1925, S.N. 16; this point was not raised on appeal, 1925 S.C. 742.
[34] *Rae* v *Davidson*, 1954 S.C. 361.
[35] *Watters* v *Hunter*, 1927 S.C. 310.
[36] *Grant* v *Bannerman* (1920) 36 Sh. Ct. Rep. 59; *M'Lauchlin* v *Mowat* (1920) 36 Sh. Ct. Rep. 116; *Seggie* v *Haggart*, 1926 S.L.T. (Sh. Ct.) 104.
[37] *Rutherford* v *Oswald*, 1945 S.L.T. (Sh. Ct.) 9; *Cullen* v *Niekerk* (1952) 68 Sh. Ct. Rep. 220.
[38] Sheriff Courts (Scotland) Act, 1907, First Schedule, Rules 111 and 112; *Strachan* v *Hunter*, 1916 S.C. 901 (break); *Ritchie* v *Lyon* (1940) 56 Sh. Ct. Rep. 39.
[39] *Supra*, p. 275.

definite and unconditional intimation enabling the other to know exactly
his position.[40]

It cannot be said to be entirely clear whether an informal notice
given by the landlord may be sufficient to prevent tacit relocation and
yet be insufficient to found an action of removing.[41] If, however, tacit
relocation does not come into operation, that in itself can found an
action of removing; this may happen where the tenant has by his
actings barred himself from objecting to an inadequate notice of
removal.[42]

Manner of Giving Notice. Removal notices under the Sheriff Courts
(Scotland) Act 1907, Secs. 34, 35, 36, 37 and 38 may be given by a
messenger-at-arms or sheriff officer, or by letter sent by registered post
or recorded delivery service, signed by the person entitled to give notice
or by his solicitor or factor, posted at any post office within the United
Kingdom in time to admit of its being delivered at the address thereon
on or before the last date upon which notice must be given, addressed
to the person entitled to receive it, and bearing his address at the time,
or if that is unknown, his last known address.[43] The foregoing provision
is identical with a provision in the Removal Terms (Scotland) Act 1886,
Sec. 6 (which applies only to houses other than those let with agricultural land) except that the 1886 Act does not permit the notice to be
delivered by a messenger-at-arms or sheriff officer. Service effected by
the landlord through the ordinary post or by hand is not sufficient.[44] If
the notice is given by messenger-at-arms or sheriff officer, it must apparently be served by delivery.[45] The Citation Amendment (Scotland) Act
1882 does not apply to notices of removing, although it does apply
to citation in the ensuing action.[46]

Evidence of Notice. A certificate of notice given by means of Form
H or letter of removal given by Form I dated and endorsed on the
lease or extract, or upon the letter of removal, and signed by the
messenger-at-arms or sheriff officer, or by the person giving notice or
his solicitor or factor, or an acknowledgement endorsed thereon by the
party in possession or his agent, is sufficient evidence that notice has
been given; provision is also made for the case where there is no lease.[47]

---

[40] Bell, § 1271; *Craighall Cast-Stone Co.* v *Wood Bros.,* 1931 S.C. 66. See also
　Murray v *Grieve* (1920) 36 Sh. Ct. Rep. 126; *Ritchie* v *Lyon, supra.*
[41] *Supra,* p. 225.
[42] *Blain* v *Ferguson* (1840) 2 D. 546; *Dunlop & Co.* v *Meiklem* (1876) 4 R. 11.
[43] Sheriff Courts (Scotland) Act, 1907, First Schedule, Rule 113, as extended by
　Recorded Delivery Service Act 1962, s. 1.
[44] *Department of Agriculture for Scotland* v *Goodfellow,* 1931 S.L.T. 388; *Hay*
　v *Anderson,* 1949 S.L.T. (Sh. Ct.) 20; *Glass* v *Klepczynski,* 1951 S.L.T. (Sh.
　Ct.) 55.
[45] Lewis, *Sheriff Court Practice,* 8th ed., 269.
[46] s. 3.
[47] Sheriff Courts (Scotland) Act 1907, First Schedule, Rule 114.

A certificate of notice given by means of Form J, dated and endorsed upon a copy of the notice or letter, signed by the party sending the notice, is sufficient evidence that notice has been given.[48]

Action of Extraordinary Removing. Where the landlord wishes to remove his tenant before the natural termination of the lease, the process is one of extraordinary removing. It is provided by the Sheriff Courts (Scotland) Act, Sec. 34 that nothing " herein contained " shall be construed to prevent proceedings under any lease in common form. This has been interpreted as meaning that extraordinary removings are not affected by any part of the 1907 Act,[49] and none of the special procedures of that Act apply to them. For an extraordinary removing no notice requires to be given,[50] but an action of removing in ordinary form has to be raised. The usual reason for raising the action is to enforce a legal or conventional irritancy,[51] and, as has been seen, where it is a conventional irritancy that is being enforced, the action of removing is preferably combined with a declarator of the irritancy, although this is not always necessary.[52] The Sheriff Court now has concurrent jurisdiction with the Court of Session in all actions of declarator of irritancy, but in questions of heritable right and title where the value of the subjects exceeds £50 a year or £1,000 of capital, either party may require the case to be remitted to the Court of Session.[53]

Prescription and Personal Bar. It will suffice to mention here only two special defences to an action of removing. Firstly all actions proceeding on warning, spuilzies and ejections shall prescribe in five years, if they are not wakened in that time, minorities being excepted.[54] The older triennial prescription of notices of removing has long been obsolete.[55]

The other is that the landlord who has served a notice of removal on his tenant may, by accepting rent after the term of removal, find himself barred from founding on the notice.[56]

VIOLENT PROFITS

Introduction. Violent profits are so called because they are such profits as are due by and for violent or illegal possession of property, as distinct from ordinary profits such as the rent of property in the

[48] *Ibid.*

[49] Dobie, *Sheriff Court Practice*, 415; Lewis, *Sheriff Court Practice*, 8th ed., 267.

[50] *Pickard* v *Reid*, 1953 S.L.T. (Sh. Ct.) 5.

[51] *Supra*, Chapter XV.

[52] *Duke of Argyll* v *Campbeltown Coal Co.*, 1924 S.C. 844; *supra*, p. 235.

[53] Sheriff Courts (Scotland) Act 1907, s. 5 (4).

[54] Prescription Act 1669, as explained by Prescription Act 1685; Millar, *Prescription*, 159; Rankine, 579.

[55] The obsolete Act of 1579 c. 82 was repealed by Statute Law Revision (Scotland) Act 1964, Schedule 1.

[56] *British Transport Commission* v *Miller*, 1955 S.L.T. (Sh. Ct.) 40; *Coatbridge Town Council* v *Tamburrino*, 1958 S.L.T. (Sh. Ct) 4; *Milner's Curator Bonis* v *Mason*, 1965 S.L.T. (Sh. Ct.) 56; Gloag, *Contract*, 2nd ed., 735.

lawful occupation of a tenant.[57] They are penal damages instituted as a special deterrent against a tenant retaining possession unwarrantably; for whatever is done without proper warrant or authority is, by the law, accounted violence.[58]

In Removings and Ejections. By immemorial custom in burghs violent profits are estimated at double the rent.[59] In the case of other subjects they are the greatest profit that the landlord could have made either by possessing them himself or by letting them to others, as well as compensation for all the damage which they may have suffered at the hands of the wrongful possessor.[60] In other words, violent profits embrace all that the landlord could have made of the subjects, if he had been in possession, and all the damage done to the subjects by the tenant.[61] Nowadays, questions as to violent profits arise only in connection with actions of removing and ejection, and in this more restricted sense they are the profits due in respect of the tenant's or occupier's possession after he ought to have removed.[62] The title to demand violent profits is the same as that required of the landlord to pursue the action of removing itself.[63] It appears that violent profits fell to the heir of a deceased landlord rather than to his executor, but in the case of a death on or after 10th September 1964 they will fall to the executor.[64] An action for violent profits, being an action of spuilzie, is subject to the triennial prescription introduced by the Prescription (Ejections) Act 1579. The Act has been interpreted as meaning not that actions for reparation for unwarrantably taking away moveables or possessing land are incompetent unless pursued within three years, but that the privilege enjoyed by the pursuer of proving the extent of his injury by his own oath is cut off, if the action is not brought within three years.[65]

Caution for Violent Profits. The requirement that a defender in an action of removing should find caution for violent profits, if his defence is not instantly verifiable, was first introduced by the Act of 1555 c. 39, now repealed,[66] and then in the Ejection Caution Act 1594, which is still extant. It was substantially repeated in the Act of Sederunt of 10th

[57] Stair, II, 9, 44; IV, 29, 2.
[58] Erskine,, II. 6, 54; Rankine, *Law of Land-Ownership in Scotland*, 4th ed., 23; Walker, *Delict*, 937.
[59] Erskine, II, 6, 54; *Macdonald* v *Macdonald* (1906) 22 Sh. Ct. Rep. 11.
[60] *Morton & Co.* v *Colquhoun & McFarlane* (1783) Mor. 13893; Erskine, II, 6, 54; Rankine, *Law of Land-Ownership in Scotland*, 4th ed., 23.
[61] *Per* L.P. Inglis in *Gardner* v *Beresford's Trs.* (1877) 4 R. 1091 at p. 1092.
[62] Erskine, II, 6, 54; *Encyclopaedia of the Laws of Scotland*, Vol. 15, 499.
[63] *Damitson* v *Mags. of Linlithgow* (1582) Mor. 16459; *Ross* v *Lady Fowlis* (1595) Mor. 16459; *Underwood's Tr.* v *Bell* (1831) 9 S. 334; *Macdonald* v *Macdonald* (1905) 21 Sh. Ct. Rep. 5.
[64] Erskine, II, 6, 48. See Succession (Scotland) Act 1964, s. 14 (1).
[65] *Constable of Dundee* v *Laird of Strathmartin* (1587) Mor. 11067; *Baillie* v *Young* (1835) 13 S. 472; Erskine, III, 7, 16; Napier, *Prescription*, 711; Millar, *Prescription*, 115; Walker, *Delict*, 1003.
[66] By Statute Law Revision (Scotland) Act 1964, Schedule 1.

July 1839, Sec. 34, later abrogated.[67] If the defender did not instantly verify his defence, but made averments requiring proof or argument, such as that he was possessing by tacit relocation, or had not been given sufficient warning, he had to find caution for violent profits before he was heard on his defence.[68] If, however, the landlord had himself to prove something to establish his title to sue, both parties stood in the same situation, and he could not demand caution.[69]

Until 1907, unless a tenant could instantly verify a defence excluding the action, he was compelled to find caution, and, if he failed to do so, decree was pronounced against him. It is now provided in the case of subjects let for a year or more, that, if any action of ordinary removing is defended, the Sheriff *may* order the defender to find caution for violent profits.[70] Such an order will not be made, if it appears that the defender has an instantly verifiable defence to the action.[71] So far as summary removings are concerned, the defender is entitled to give in written answers, only if he has found caution or it has been dispensed with,[72] and then the case proceeds as an ordinary action.[73] Thus, the Sheriff now has discretion to require or dispense with caution both in the case of leases for a year or more and in the case of leases for less than a year. He has no power to order caution, unless the action is defended.[74]

The motion for caution should be made as soon as appearance is entered,[75] and if an order for caution is made and not implemented, decree of removing or ejection may be granted at once.[76] The interlocutor ordering caution is only appealable with leave.[77]

Caution in Extraordinary Removings. Whether caution for violent profits may be demanded in actions of extraordinary removings depends on the circumstances. It was held in an early case that it could not be demanded, unless stipulated for.[78] There was some divergence of opinion as to whether the Act of Sederunt of 10th July 1839, Sec. 34, applied to actions of irritancy and removing on the ground of non-payment of rent or bankruptcy.[79] The right to demand caution for violent profits rests on

[67] This Act of Sederunt depended on the Sheriff Courts (Scotland) Act 1838, which was repealed by the Sheriff Courts (Scotland) Act 1907; see *Inglis Trs.* v *Macpherson,* 1910 S.C. 46.
[68] *Johnstone* v *Maxwell's Trs.* (1845) 7 D. 1066; *Robb* v *Menzies* (1859) 21 D. 277.
[69] *St. Clare* v *Grant* (1687) Mor. 13893; *Oliver* v *Weir's Trs.* (1870) 8 M. 786, *per* Lord Cowan at p. 788.
[70] Sheriff Courts (Scotland) Act 1907, First Schedule, Rule 110.
[71] *Milne* v *Darroch* (1937) 53 Sh. Ct. Rep. 3.
[72] Sheriff Courts (Scotland) Act 1907, First Schedule, Rule 121 (as amended by Sheriff Courts (Scotland) Act 1913).
[73] *Ibid.,* Rule 122.
[74] *Blythswood Friendly Society* v *O'Leary,* 1966 S.L.T. (Sh. Ct.) 64.
[75] *King* v *Wieland* (1858) 20 D. 960.
[76] Dobie, *Sheriff Court Practice,* 417.
[77] *Jack* v *Carmichael* (1894) 10 Sh. Ct. Rep. 242; *Buchanan* v *Dickson* (1934) 51 Sh. Ct. Rep. 41.
[78] *Douglas* v *Idington* (1628) Mor. 13892.
[79] *Ross* v *Duff* (1899) 15 Sh. Ct. Rep. 227; *Burton* v *Mechie* (1903) 21 Sh. Ct. Rep. 63.

the fact that the lease has come to an end, and in an extraordinary removing the fact that the irritancy may first have to be proved may exclude the demand, although there may come a stage in the action when the demand may be let in.[80] On the other hand, in the usual cases of removing founded on irritancy, the absence of receipts for rent or the production of the deliverance awarding sequestration would let in the demand.[81] As the Sheriff Courts (Scotland) Act 1907 deals only with actions of ordinary removings, the discretion given to the sheriff to require or dispense with caution does not apply to extraordinary removings. The matter rests on common law and established practice. Caution for violent profits in extraordinary removings should not be confused with the caution for rent provided for in actions of irritancy under the Act of Sederunt of 14th December 1756, Sec. 5.[82]

Liability for Violent Profits. The fact that a defender has not been required to find caution for violent profits does not necessarily mean that he is not, or may not eventually be found to be, liable for violent profits.[83] Liability on a final determination is one thing, and liability to find caution beforehand is a totally different thing, which cannot be imposed except by virtue of some statutory enactment or long established practice.[84] Conversely, a tenant, who has been required to find caution, does not necessarily have to pay violent profits, if he loses the case. He is liable for them only if and for so long as he has been acting in bad faith, and the onus of proof of *mala fides* is on the landlord.[85]

Bona Fides. The tenant will be liable for violent profits only for such time as he was fully aware that he had no legal title to remain in the subjects.[86] If and for so long as he has been possessing the subjects in good faith, he is not liable for more than the rent.[87] It may happen that a tenant's possession, originally in good faith, continues in bad faith. The point of time at which the transition from good to bad faith takes place depends on the circumstances of each case, and many of the authorities have been cases arising as a result of the right of the tenant having been reduced after appeal.[88] The following rules have been stated: " First, when the possession has commenced in good faith, it lies with the true owner to show when it ceased to be so, before

[80] *Oliver* v *Weir's Trs.* (1870) 8 M. 786, *per* Lord Neaves at p. 789.
[81] Rankine, 582.
[82] *Supra,* p. 229; *Cossar* v *Home* (1947) 9 D. 617 (where the distinction seems to have been ignored); *Mackenzie* v *Mackenzie* (1848) 10 D. 1009; *Oliver* v *Weir's Trs., supra.*
[83] *Houldsworth* v *Brand's Trs.* (1876) 3 R. 304.
[84] *Per* Lord Kinnear in *Inglis' Trs.* v *Macpherson,* 1910 S.C. 46 at p. 49.
[85] *Carnegy* v *Scott* (1827) 6 S. 206, *per* L.J.C. Boyle at p. 208.
[86] Hunter, *Landlord and Tenant,* 4th ed., II, 526; Rankine, 583; *Encyclopaedia of the Laws of Scotland,* Vol. 15, 503.
[87] *Brisbane's Trs.* v *Lead* (1828) 7 S. 65.
[88] *E.g.,* the Queensberry leases, reduced by the House of Lords; see authorities in Rankine, *Law of Land-Ownership in Scotland,* 4th ed., 81-83.

the right to demand violent profits can prevail; secondly, when possession has been continued during a litigation regarding the title of the possessor, it is sufficient to support the possessor's plea of *bona fides* that he had *probabilis causa litigandi;* and third, that the principle is equally applicable, whether the possession be challenged in respect of want of title in the possessor's author, or in respect of the nature and conditions of his own right ".[89] It may be added that the transition from *bona fides* to *mala fides* must be taken as having occurred at some stage of a judicial process, not through private intimation,[90] and that a tenant who has begun his defence in good faith may after an adverse decision be held to be in bad faith and liable for violent profits from that date.[91]

PROCEDURE IN SHERIFF COURT

Jurisdiction. Apart from the long obsolete procedure under the Act 1555 c. 39,[92] the only occasions on which the Court of Session will grant a decree of removing are where a conclusion for removing follows, is ancillary to, and carries into effect conclusions for declarator or reduction. With the charge on such a decree for removing, the function of the Court of Session comes to an end, and the ejection is left to be carried out by the Sheriff.[93] Thus, the Sheriff Court now has exclusive jurisdiction in ordinary removings, including the special procedure introduced by the Sheriff Courts (Scotland) Act 1907. The Sheriff Court has concurrent jurisdiction with the Court of Session in extraordinary removings within certain limits,[94] but even in these cases the ejection ancillary to the removing is left to the Sheriff. If, however, the action of removing involves something that the Sheriff cannot try, for example, proving the tenor of a lost lease, the case will have to be transferred to the Court of Session.[95]

Decree of Removing. In the Sheriff Court a decree of removing may be extracted after seven or fourteen days, depending on the circumstances, or at such earlier time as the Sheriff may allow.[96] The decree should be carried out at once; delay in putting the decree into execution may infer waiver on the part of the landlord,[97] but a delay of three weeks after the

[89] *Per* L.J.C. Moncreiff in *Houldsworth* v *Brand's Trs.* (1876) 3 R. 304 at p. 310.
[90] Rankine, 583.
[91] *Duke of Buccleuch* v *Hyslop* (1824) 2 Sh. App. 43; *Innes* v *Duke of Gordon's Exrs.* (1830) 4 W. & S. 305; *Carnegy* v *Scott* (1830) 4 W. & S. 431; *Encyclopaedia of the Laws of Scotland,* Vol. 15, 504.
[92] Repealed by Statute Law Revision (Scotland) Act, 1964, Schedule 1.
[93] *Per* L.P. Dunedin in *Campbell's Trs.* v *O'Neill,* 1911 S.C. 188 at p. 197; Rankine, 586.
[94] *Supra,* p. 235.
[95] *Raeside* v *Mattocks,* 1953 S.L.T. (Sh. Ct.) 27.
[96] Sheriff Courts (Scotland) Act 1907, First Schedule, Rule 85. The Act of Sederunt of 10th July 1839, s. 113, under which a decree of removing could be extracted after forty-eight hours, was abrogated by the repeal by the 1907 Act of the Sheriff Courts (Scotland) Act 1838.
[97] Rankine, 588.

term was held not to have this effect.[98] The defender is charged to remove on forty eight hours' warning under pain of ejection.[99] If the charge is not obeyed, the Sheriff Officer can carry out the ejection without further recourse to the Court.[1] The period of charge is fixed, and is not related to the circumstances of a particular case, although there often are circumstances, such as the nature of the defence and of the legal questions involved, which would make it reasonable to postpone the date on which the decree should operate.[2]

EJECTION AS AN INDEPENDENT ACTION

Introduction. Where a person is in occupation of heritable subjects without any right or title to possess them, the legal method of dispossessing him is an action of ejection in the original sense of a substantive and not merely an accessory process.[3] This remedy is a normal incident of land-ownership and may be exercised either by the proprietor or a person legally entitled to the possession of the land. It has nothing particularly to do with leases, although it frequently happens that the parties have been in the relationship of landlord and tenant.

There is no process of removing and there is no need for any warning. In this sense it is frequently called " summary ejection ". The action proceeds as an ordinary cause, but craves the summary ejection of the defender.[4] The procedure is the same as a removing, except that no charge is necessary on the decree, and the extract warrant *de plano* authorises the officers summarily to eject the defender.[5] The action comes within the common law jurisdiction of the Sheriff, and is not specially dealt with by the Sheriff Courts (Scotland) Act 1907.[6]

No Title to Possess. To justify this form of action, the defender must either never have had a title to occupy the subjects, or any such title must have been judicially terminated.[7] It has been repeatedly held that an action of ejection cannot be used, unless the occupier is in possession by fraud, force or precarious possession, that is, he must possess *vi, clam aut precario.*[8] Thus, it cannot be used against a purchaser under missives, who has not paid the price;[9] a defender, who has obtained an *ex facie* valid

[98] *Taylor* v *Earl of Moray* (1892) 19 R. 399.
[99] Sheriff Courts (Scotland) Extracts Act, 1892, s. 7 (4).
[1] *Ibid.*
[2] Second Report of the Law Reform Committee for Scotland, 1957 Cmnd. 114, para. 11.
[3] *Supra*, p. 246.
[4] Dobie, *Sheriff Court Practice*, 417.
[5] Sheriff Courts (Scotland) Extracts Act 1892, Schedule, Form 9.
[6] Lewis, *Sheriff Courts Practice*, 8th ed., 277; Dobie, *op. cit.*, 417.
[7] *James Gibson & Son Ltd.* v *Gibson* (1899) 36 S.L.R. 522.
[8] *Hally* v *Lang* (1867) 5 M. 951, *per* Lord Deas at p. 954; *Scottish Property Investment Company Building Society* v *Horne* (1881) 8 R. 737, *per* L.P. Inglis at p. 740; *Walker* v *Kerr*, 1917 S.C. 102; *Lowe* v *Gardiner*, 1921 S.C. 211, *per* Lord Cullen at p. 218; *Ford* v *Cameron* (1949) 65 Sh. Ct. Rep. 31; *Jarvie* v *Lonsdale* (1949) 65 Sh. Ct. Rep. 189; *Buist* v *Hogarth*, 1954 S.L.T. (Sh. Ct.) 13; *Cook* v *Wyllie*, 1963 S.L.T. (Sh. Ct.) 29.
[9] *Lowe* v *Gardiner, supra; Christie's Trs.* v *Munroe*, 1962 S.L.T. (Sh. Ct.) 41.

lease;[10] or a subtenant, who has received no warning to remove.[11] In such cases, so long as the " unnecessary and confusing distinction" between ejection and removing remains, the appropriate remedy is an action of removing.[12] An action of ejection is not a proper method of trying a question of right to possession and, therefore, if the defender has a right or title to occupy the subjects, an action of removing must be raised; but it is not a valid objection to an action of removing that the defender has no title to occupy and that an action of ejection would have been competent and appropriate.[13] A closing order does not in all circumstances terminate a tenancy,[14] and an action of ejection at the instance of the landlord has been held to be incompetent.[15]

Against whom Ejection Used. The persons against whom the process of ejection is available include the following:—(a) the heir of a liferent tenant, subject to the rule *messis sementem sequitur;*[16] (b) a squatter occupying without any title;[17] (c) an employee, whose occupancy of the premises is incidental to his employment, on the termination of his employment;[18] (d) a proprietor in personal occupation of lands disponed in security, who is in default of payment of interest or principal,[19] but a liferenter is not a proprietor in this sense,[20] nor is this remedy available to the holder of an *ex facie* absolute disposition qualified by a back letter;[21] and (e) a bankrupt in occupation of property vested in his trustee in sequestration.[22] There is also a special case of ejection being used against a tenant, not in order to terminate his right of possession, but to suspend it temporarily, until he fulfils an obligation to furnish the subjects in implement of a decree in sequestration for rent proceedings.[23]

A process of ejection is not merely a process of diligence, but is a process in which questions either of fact or of law can be determined; it

[10] *Scottish Supply Association* v *Mackie,* 1921 S.C. 882.
[11] *Robb* v *Brearton* (1895) 22 R. 885.
[12] Per L.P. Clyde in *Lowe* v *Gardiner, supra,* at p. 216 and in *Scottish Supply Association* v *Mackie, supra,* at p. 888.
[13] *Nisbet* v *Aikman* (1866) 4 M. 284; *Marquis of Breadalbane* v *Cameron,* 1923 S.L.T. (Sh. Ct.) 6; *Earl of Eglinton* v *M'Luckie,* 1944 S.L.T. (Sh. Ct.) 21; Dobie, *Sheriff Court Practice,* 417.
[14] *Ferguson* v *Pittman,* 1958 S.L.T. (Sh. Ct.) 18.
[15] *Syme* v *Kirkpatrick,* 1956 S.L.T. (Sh. Ct.) 71. An action of removing would probably have been incompetent also, *ibid.*
[16] *Gordon* v *Michie's Reps.* (1794) Mor. 13851; *Stewart* v *Grimmond's Reps.* (1796) Mor. 13853; Hume, *Lectures,* IV, 112; Rankine, 593-594.
[17] *Macdonald* v *Duchess of Leeds* (*Macdonald* v *Chisholm*) (1860) 22 D. 1075; *Hally* v *Lang* (1867) 5 M. 951; *Macdonald* v *Watson* (1883) 10 R. 1079; Rankine, 596.
[18] *Whyte* v *School Board of Haddington* (1874) 1 R. 1124; *J. Gibson & Son* v *Gibson, supra; Dunbar's Trs.* v *Bruce* (1900) 3 F. 137; *Sinclair* v *Tod,* 1907 S.C. 1038; *Cairns* v *Innes,* 1942 S.C. 164.
[19] Heritable Securities (Scotland) Act 1894, s. 5; *Hutchison* v *Alexander* (1904) 6 F. 532.
[20] *Scottish Union and National Insurance Co.* v *Smeaton* (1904) 7 F. 174.
[21] *Scottish Property Investment Company Building Society* v *Horne* (1881) 8 R. 737.
[22] *White* v *Stevenson,* 1956 S.C. 84.
[23] *Macdonald* v *Mackessack* (1888) 16 R. 168; *supra,* p. 212.

is not made incompetent by the fact that a question of law is involved,[24] provided the defender's averments are relevant.[25]

Caution for Violent Profits. It has been held that a heritable creditor, in ejecting a proprietor under the Heritable Securities (Scotland) Act 1894, Sec. 5, is not entitled to require the debtor to find caution for violent profits.[26] There were two grounds for this decision. The first was that the Sheriff Courts (Scotland) Act 1907 had, by repealing the Sheriff Courts (Scotland) Act 1838, abrogated the Act of Sederunt of 10th July 1839, Sec. 34, which made it imperative in actions of removing and in summary applications for ejection for the defender to find caution, and had instead given the Sheriff power to dispense with caution in summary removings.[27] The second ground was that there is no authority in the 1894 Act for holding that a heritable creditor is entitled in a process of ejection to require the defender to find caution for violent profits; and that it does not follow that a creditor has all the rights which a landlord has in an action of removing.[28]

How far that decision can be extended to actions of ejection by persons other than heritable creditors is not entirely clear, and it leaves open the question whether caution for violent profits can competently be demanded in an action of ejection against, say, a squatter.[29] It would be an anomalous situation which placed a squatter in a more favourable position than a tenant, and in a series of Sheriff Court cases it has been decided, not without some hesitation, that caution for violent profits can be required of a defender in an action of ejection.[30] This view, however, is at least partly based on authorities which support general liability for violent profits, and there never has been any doubt that an occupier without a title can be found liable for them;[31] but liability to find caution beforehand is a totally different thing, and cannot be imposed except by virtue of some statutory enactment or long established practice.[32]

---

[24] *Whyte* v *School Board of Haddington, supra; Cairns* v *Innes, supra; Asher* v *Macleod,* 1948 S.C. 55.

[25] *South West Farmers Ltd.* v *Gray,* 1950 S.L.T. (Sh. Ct.) 10.

[26] *Inglis' Trs.* v. *Macpherson,* 1910 S.C. 46.

[27] See Lord Kinnear's opinion at p. 49, which refers to the Sheriff Courts (Scotland) Act 1907, s. 38 and First Schedule, Rule 121, before this Rule was amended by the Sheriff Courts (Scotland) Act, 1913.

[28] *Per* Lords Kinnear and Johnston at p. 50.

[29] Second Report of the Law Reform Committee for Scotland, 1957 Cmnd. 114, para. 16.

[30] *Glasgow Lock Hospital* v *Ashcroft,* 1949 S.L.T. (Sh. Ct.) 58; *Fife County Council* v *Hatten,* 1950 S.L.T. (Sh. Ct.) 13; *Thomson's Trs.* v *Harrison* (1958) Sh. Ct. Rep. 77; *Cheshire* v *Irvine,* 1963 S.L.T. (Sh. Ct.) 28.

[31] *Cromar* v *Duke of Gordon* (1830) 8 S. 353; *Robb* v *Menzies* (1859) 21 D. 277, *per* Lord Deas at p. 282; *Houldsworth* v *Brand's Trs.* (1876) 3 R. 304, *per* L.J.C. Moncreiff at p. 310; Stair, II, 9, 44; Erskine, II, 6, 54; Bell, § 1268 c; Rankine, 581; Gloag and Henderson, *Introduction to the Law of Scotland,* 6th ed., 490.

[32] *Per* Lord Kinnear in *Inglis' Tr.* v *Macpherson, supra,* at p. 50, see also Dobie, *op. cit.,* 417, where it is stated that caution for violent profits cannot be demanded in an action of ejection.

It has been held that the remedy of caution for violent profits cannot be granted in the course of a remedy which is neither itself an action of removing nor one designed for bringing under review a decree in an action of removing.[33]

REVIEW BY COURT OF SESSION

Until 1936, there was an important distinction between decrees of removing and decrees of ejection in the manner in which they could be reviewed by the Court of Session. It had long been the rule, founded on the Court of Session Act 1825,[34] that the only method by which a tenant, ordered to remove by a decree of an inferior court, could have it reviewed was by way of suspension.[35] The rule was held to apply also to the case of a " summary ejection " under the Sheriff Courts (Scotland) Act 1907 on the ground that such an action was in substance a removing.[36] It applied to an action of removing where the tenant claimed the protection of the Rent Restrictions Acts.[37] It did not apply to an interlocutory judgment allowing a proof in an action of removing.[38] On the other hand, in actions of ejection of persons without a title review was and still is by way of appeal.[39]

The distinction was removed by an Act of Sederunt of 12th July 1938, the effect of which was to repeal the Court of Session Act, Sec. 44 and to render decrees of removing of tenants appealable from the Sheriff Court to the Court of Session in the same way as in ejections and ordinary actions, suspension of decrees of removings being no longer competent.[40] The position is now regulated by Rule of Court No. 267,[41] which provides that notwithstanding any provision in any Act of Parliament to the contrary, the Rules shall apply to all appeals from any interlocutor, judgment or determination (including decrees of removings) pronounced by any inferior court (other than the Land Court), which may competently by submitted for review to the Court of Session.

REPORT OF THE LAW REFORM COMMITTEE

Reference has frequently been made in this chapter to a Report of the Law Reform Committee for Scotland on the procedural law relating to actions of removing and actions of ejection.[42] The Report, which does not deal with agricultural holdings, draws attention to some of the anoma-

---

[33] M'Donald v Buist (O.H.) 1950 C.L. 4959.
[34] Court of Session Act (Judicature Act) 1825, s. 44.
[35] Campbell's Trs. v O'Neill, 1911 S.C. 188.
[36] Ibid.
[37] Kemp v Ballachulish Estate Co., 1933 S.C. 478; Mackay v Menzies, 1937 S.C. 691.
[38] Stirling v Graham, 1920 S.C. 4.
[39] Clark v Clarkes (1890) 17 R. 1064; Barbour v Chalmers (1891) 18 R. 610; Robb v Brearton (1895) 22 R. 885; Campbell's Trs. v O'Neill, supra.
[40] Lewis, Sheriff Court Practice, 8th ed., 279; supra, p. 271.
[41] Rules of Court, 1965, enacted by Act of Sederunt, 10th November, 1964.
[42] Second Report of the Law Reform Committee for Scotland, 1957 Cmnd. 114.

lies and difficulties in the law of removings and ejections, and there seems to be no better way of closing the chapter than by referring to the recommendations made by the Report.[43]

[43] *Forms of Action*
1. There should be provided one form of action for use in all cases where it is desired to recover possession of heritable property from an occupier. Where there was a lease for a year or more the action should be originated in the Sheriff's Ordinary Court, and in all other cases in the Small Debt Court. In the Small Debt Court the form of writ should be the same as in the Sheriff's Ordinary Court. (Paragraphs 8, 9, and 10.)

Operation of Decree
2. In all decrees for recovery of possession of heritable property the Court should fix the date upon which the decree is to become effective. (Paragraph 11.)

Notices of Removing
3. Where there is a let the notice should be in writing, and a single form should be provided. (Paragraph 12.)
4. In the case of a let for a year or more the period of notice of removing should be forty days, but in the case of all other lets the period of notice should be fourteen days or the period of let, whichever is the shorter, these periods to apply in the absence of any express stipulation in a lease for a longer period of notice. (Paragraph 13.)
5. It should be made clear that the service of a notice of removing should not be held to imply the recognition of any title in the person on whom the notice is served. (Paragraph 14.)

Date of Termination of Lets
6. All annual lets (whether by tacit relocation or otherwise) should be presumed to terminate at 15th May (without prejudice to the Removal Terms (Scotland) Act, 1886), unless the contrary appears, the onus of rebutting the presumption being placed on the party who maintains the contrary. (Paragraph 15.)

Caution for Violent Profits
7. In all actions for recovery of possession of heritable property it should be competent for the Sheriff in his discretion to order the defender to find caution for violent profits. (Paragraph 16.)

Title to Sue
8. It should be competent for any person having a right to heritable property by a title not completed but capable of being completed to take a decree for recovery of possession. (Paragraph 17.)

Part II

STATUTORY LEASES

Chapter XVIII

THE AGRICULTURAL HOLDINGS ACTS

Introduction

History. The purpose of the Agricultural Holdings Acts has been to
secure fairness to tenant farmers and to encourage efficient farming and
the maintenance at a high standard of the fertility of the land and, in the
case of the latest Acts, to ensure that the landlord receives a proper
economic rent. The Acts are " really in the interests of both landlord and
tenant as well as of the community at large, to whose advantage it is that
the arable land of Scotland shall be cultivated to the best advantage ".[1] So
far as the tenant is concerned, this has been achieved by giving security
of tenure to the tenant and providing him with compensation for improvements which he has made on the land. At common law the tenant had no
claim for compensation for improvements, even though the lease ended
before its due termination, unless there was a clause in the lease to that
effect,[2] though it was usual to provide in the lease for compensation for
unexhausted manures. It was presumed that in making the improvements
the tenant had expected and intended to reap the benefit and recoup himself during the remainder of the lease.[3] But, if there was no such clause,
the tenant, without a breach of the rules of good husbandry, could in the
latter years of his lease overwork and denude the land and leave it
unproductive for the early years of his successor's lease. So far as the
landlord is concerned, his position has been protected under the latest
Acts in regard to the amount of the rent and the termination of the lease
should the tenant die. All this, however, has only been brought about
by a series of statutes dating from 1883.

The first Act was that of 1883.[4] Prior to this there had been very
few statutory developments affecting agricultural tenants, and though
some provisions, as in the Leases Act 1449, had been in their interests, the
law generally had not been favourable towards tenants. This Act of
1883 introduced a right to compensation for certain scheduled improvements, made provision for arbitration of claims, for a right of the tenant
to bequeath the lease to anyone he pleased, for a right of the tenant to
fixtures, and it forbade contracting out of its terms. These were important
and basic innovations. The Act was amended in relation to procedure

---

[1] *Earl of Galloway* v *McClelland,* 1915 S.C. 1062 at 1099-1100, *per* Lord Salvesen, adopted by L.J.C. Cooper in *Turnbull* v *Millar,* 1942 S.C. 521. See
Rankine, 269.
[2] Rankine, 259.
[3] *Walker* v *McKnight* (1886) 13 R. 599.
[4] Agricultural Holdings (Scotland) Act 1883.

in 1889,[5] and again in 1897[6] as to market gardens, giving market gardeners rights to compensation additional to those which they and other agricultural tenants had under the 1883 Act. It was further amended in regard to arbitration in 1900.[7] Another Act was passed in 1906,[8] which was to come into operation only on 1st January, 1909, but it did not take effect, as all the Acts were repealed and consolidated in an Act in 1908,[9] though all orders, Acts of Sederunt, instruments, consents, etc., given or made under the prior Acts were to have effect as if done under the 1908 Act.[10]

The 1908 Act introduced several important principles. Not only did it simplify arbitration procedure, providing that notwithstanding an agreement in the lease for two arbiters and an oversman claims for compensation should go to a single arbiter, but it gave to the tenant a right to compensation for damage by game or for unreasonable disturbance, that is, if the lease was terminated without good and sufficient cause and for reasons inconsistent with good estate management, and a certain freedom of cropping, notwithstanding any restrictions in the lease, and it added to the types or classes of improvements for which compensation was to be payable to the tenant. It also provided that where there was a stipulation for payment of higher rent or other liquidated damages no more could be recovered than the damage actually suffered, unless in a few exceptional cases such as the prohibition of the breaking of permanent pasture. Provision was made for a record of the holding, that is, of the condition of the buildings, fences, gates, roads, drains, ditches and the cultivation of the holding, if either party required it. In *Brown* v *Mitchell* the Lord President (Dunedin) said,[11] on disturbance, referring to a provision in the 1908 Act (which is no longer operative) that the tenant must aver that the landlord had terminated the lease without good and sufficient cause for reasons inconsistent with good estate management. The Act was not intended to give fixity of tenure but compensation for capricious disturbance by a landlord in capriciously ending the lease. There might be perfectly good reasons—and Parliament had obviously so intended— for getting rid of a tenant that were not strictly agricultural reasons, that were indeed inconsistent with such reasons, e.g., that the rent was too low or that the tenant was making the farm a headquarters of bad company. And a low rent was inconsistent with good estate management.

A short Act of 1910[12] amended the arbitration simplification in the 1908 Act in respect of way-going valuations,[13] excluding valuations of

---

[5] Agricultural Holdings (Scotland) Act 1889.
[6] Market Gardeners Compensation (Scotland) Act 1897.
[7] Agricultural Holdings Act 1900.
[8] Agricultural Holdings Act 1906.
[9] Agricultural Holdings (Scotland) Act 1908.
[10] s. 36.
[11] 1910 S.C. 369 at 384. He affirmed his view in the House of Lords in *Viscountess Cowdray* v *Ferries*, 1919 S.C. (H.L.) 27 at 31.
[12] Agricultural Holdings (Scotland) Amendment Act 1910.
[13] 1908 Act, s. 11.

sheep stocks, etc., the property of the outgoing tenant agreed under the lease to be taken over by the landlord or the incoming tenant and questions as to the ascertainment of the sum under the agreement whether or not these valuations and questions were under the lease referred to arbitration. Further amendments in 1920[14] and 1921[15] followed. The 1920 Act related *inter alia* to compensation for disturbance, giving substantial rights to compensation for disturbance even where the disturbance was not unreasonable, and also giving rights to compensation for an increase in the value of a holding by the adoption of a special standard or system of farming, while it widened the scope of a record of a holding to include improvements and fixtures and buildings which the tenant was entitled to remove and extended the date when the record had to be made, and it further extended the scope of arbitration in claims for compensation, introducing a panel of arbiters and provided for compensation to a landlord for deterioration of a holding. The 1921 Act, a short one, gave explanations of certain provisions of the 1920 Act.

Then came the next consolidation Act in 1923.[16] This Act *inter alia* gave compensation for improvements even though the tenant was bound by the lease to make improvements,[17] and compensation for disturbance was payable unless the landlord brought himself within one of the exceptions in the Act. It also increased the scope of arbitration. A short amending Act in 1923[18] provided for the serving of notices, etc., where there was a change of landlord. Next came the 1931 Act,[19] which amended the law as to claims for compensation for improvements, also as to compensation for temporary pasture and in regard to the matters to be referred to arbitration. It provided for a reference to the Land Court instead of to arbitration, for the situation where part of a holding is resumed without notice and for the application by a landlord of sums recovered by him under a fire insurance policy where the tenant is liable for the whole or part of the premiums. The next Act is the 1948 Act,[20] which was followed by a consolidating Act in 1949,[21] and this 1949 Act, which repealed the prior Acts of 1923 and 1931, and an Act in 1958[22] are the now ruling Acts. The 1949 Act extended the tenant's security of tenure and rights to compensation, the 1958 Act on the other hand aided the landlord, secured him as far as possible in an economic rent, restricted the tenant's succession rights and increased the powers of the Land Court. Finally the Succession (Scotland) Act 1964 made important changes in relation to the succession to holdings.

[14] Agriculture Act 1920.
[15] Agriculture (Amendment) Act 1921.
[16] Agricultural Holdings (Scotland) Act 1923.
[17] It thus reversed *Earl of Galloway* v *McClelland*, 1915 S.C. 1062.
[18] Agriculture (Amendment) Act 1923.
[19] Small Landholders and Agricultural Holdings (Scotland) Act 1931.
[20] Agriculture (Scotland) Act 1948.
[21] Agricultural Holdings (Scotland) Act 1949.
[22] Agriculture Act. See Reserve &c. Forces Act 1951; Rent Act 1965.

In this chapter when "the Act" is referred to it is the 1949 Act unless otherwise indicated, and any statement in reference to that Act applies notwithstanding the 1958 Act unless the contrary is indicated.[23]

1949 Act. General. It is still necessary in some instances to refer to the Acts repealed by the 1949 Act. Thus, the provisions of the 1949 Act as respects rights of landlords and tenants to compensation, including apportionment where a holding is divided, and the payment and recovery of compensation do not apply, but certain of the older Acts (those between 1923 and 1948[24]) apply where the tenant has quitted the holding before the commencement of the 1949 Act on 24th November 1949 or where he quits it thereafter in consequence of a notice to quit given by him or the landlord before 1st November 1948 or in consequence of a renunciation of the tenancy in pursuance of a written agreement made before that date.[25] There is a general saving clause in the 1949 Act[26] and regulations having effect for the purpose of certain provisions of the 1948 Act in force on 24th November 1949 and certain directions under the 1923 Act or an Act repealed by that Act if in force on 24th November 1949 are continued in force and so far as they could have been done under a corresponding provision of the 1949 Act have effect as if done under that corresponding provision.[27] Any document referring to a former Act relating to agricultural holdings or an enactment repealed by the 1908 Act is, so far as it or its operation is material for the purposes of the repealed Acts,[28] so far as they are continued in force under the 1949 Act,[29] to be construed in like manner as if the Act had not been passed and otherwise is construed as referring to the corresponding provision of the 1949 Act.[30]

Subject to the provisions of the Act[31] which otherwise expressly provide, nothing in the Act is to prejudicially affect any power, right or remedy of a landlord, tenant or other person, vested in or exercisable by him by virtue of any other Act or law, or under any custom of the country, or otherwise, in respect of a lease or other contract, or of any improvements, deteriorations, away-going crops, fixtures, tax, rates, teind, rent or other thing.[32] As the consulted judges observed in *Brodie*

---

[23] The following are the chief works on the various Acts prior to the 1948 Act: Cameron, *Agricultural Holdings Act 1883* (1886); Connell, *Agricultural Holdings Acts 1883-1900* (1901, 1909); Do., *Agricultural Holdings Acts* (1923, 1928, 1938); Johnston, *Agricultural Holdings Acts* (1883, 1884, 1885, 1891, 1901, 1909); Reid, *Agricultural Holdings Act 1923* (1923); Rankine, *Leases*, 3rd ed., 268 *et seq.*, 748 *et seq.* On the 1949 and 1958 Acts the works of Connell, *supra*, 5th ed. (1961).

[24] s. 98; Schedule Eight.

[25] s. 98. See too s. 99 (6).

[26] s. 99 (1).

[27] s. 99 (2) (3).

[28] Schedule Eight.

[29] s. 98.

[30] s. 99 (7).

[31] *e.g.*, ss. 12 (2), 68 (1).

[32] *Ibid.*, s. 100.

v *Ker*,[33] this provision re-affirms the salutary rule that the right of the subject to invoke the common law courts of the country for the decision of any question properly falling within their jurisdiction can only be excluded by express provision or clear implication in a contract or statute.

But in interpreting the present Act it is dangerous to refer to provisions of older Acts now repealed. " We were presented in the course of debate with several arguments based upon the earlier Agricultural Holdings Acts. The Act of 1883 was thrice amended—in 1897, 1900 and 1906—and the whole of these statutes were then replaced by the consolidating Act of 1908. This Act in its turn was amended in 1910, 1920 and 1921, and consolidation again took place in 1923. There has been a further amending Act in 1931. In the course of these legislative vicissitudes, the detailed phraseology of the sections and their order in the statutory scheme have more than once been varied, and the changes, which are more than verbal, must be regarded as deliberate and significant. In these circumstances—to quote the words of Lord Watson in *Bradlaugh* v *Clarke* (1883, 8 App. Cas. 354 at p. 380):—' It appears to me to be an extremely hazardous proceeding to refer to provisions which have been absolutely repealed, in order to ascertain what the legislature meant to enact in their room and stead '. I propose therefore to concentrate upon the Act of 1923 ".[34]

Consents and Agreements in writing. A written consent or a written agreement under the Act, if signed by the parties or anyone authorised by them, is not open to objection because it is not executed in accordance with the Acts about execution of deeds in Scotland.[35] It need not be tested or holograph.

Notices. The Act contains provisions as to service of notices or other documents under the Act.[36]

Termination. This means in relation to a tenancy " the termination of the lease by reason of effluxion of time or from any other cause ".[37] The phrases " termination of the tenancy " and " termination of the lease " have generally the same meaning.[38]

Subjects. The subjects of the legislation are agricultural holdings, and the definition of such has varied. The present definition of a holding is a very wide one, namely " the aggregate of the agricultural land comprised in a lease not being a lease under which the said land is let to the tenant during his continuance in any office, appointment or employment

[33] 1952 S.C. 216 at 224.
[34] *Turnbull* v *Millar*, 1942 S.C. 521 at 533, *per* L.J.C. Cooper.
[35] s. 85.
[36] s. 90.
[37] s. 93 (1).
[38] See *infra*, p. 306, note 29.

held under the landlord ",[39] and " agricultural land " is defined as " land used for agriculture which is so used for the purpose of a trade or business[40] and includes any other land which, by virtue of a designation of the Secretary of State under sub-section 1 of section 86 of the Agriculture (Scotland) Act 1948, is agricultural land within the meaning of that Act ",[41] while " agriculture " is defined as including " horticulture, fruit growing, seed growing, dairy farming and livestock breeding and keeping, the use of land as grazing land, meadow land, osier land, market gardens and nursery gardens, and the use of land for other agricultural purposes and agricultural shall be construed accordingly ".[37] Farming of land includes the carrying on in relation to the land of any agricultural activity[42] and the use of land for agriculture includes, in relation to land forming part of an agricultural unit, any use of the land in connection with the farming of the unit.[43]

There may be a single contract of tenancy but if a second contract is expressly stated to be subsidiary or supplemental to or by way of variation of the main contract, the contract of tenancy may be the original contract as so modified.[44]

A holding may include, if the lease makes it part of the subjects let, the use, along perhaps with others including the landlord, of hill land for grazing.[45]

It has been held in England[46] that an allotment need not be of any particular size to be an agricultural holding; but it is essential that it is used for the growing of fruit or vegetables for the purposes of a trade or business. So a holding may be of only quarter of an acre,[47] and even if the dwellinghouse is of much greater value than the land, both may be treated as forming a holding.[48] In another case[49] it was laid down that for the Act to apply the lease or tenancy as a whole must be in substance one of agricultural land, the term " aggregate " referring to the definition " agricultural " in the Act, and it was thus held that a lease of seven acres and three cottages was one of an agricultural holding, notwithstanding that none of the cottages was occupied by persons engaged in agriculture. So a small non-agricultural element is

---

[39] ss. 1 (1), 93 (1).
[40] It has been held in England that land is used for agriculture and is so used for the purposes of a trade or business if the use is agricultural even if that is for the purposes of a trade or business which is not agricultural, and so a letting for grazing to the owner of a riding school, though it included a use for the purposes of the school which was not an agricultural business, came within the Act. *Rutherford* v *Maurer* [1962] 1 Q.B. 16.
[41] s. 1 (2).
[42] s. 93 (3).
[43] s. 93 (4).
[44] *Blackmore* v *Butler* [1954] 2 Q.B. 171, *per* Somervell, L.J., at 177.
[45] See *Earl of Ancaster* v *Doig*, 1960 S.C. 203.
[46] *Stevens* v *Sedgeman* [1951] 2 K.B. 434.
[47] *Malcolm* v *McDougall*, 1916 S.C. 283.
[48] *Malcolm, supra; Hamilton* v *Duke of Hamilton's Trs.*, 1918 S.C. 282.
[49] *Howkins* v *Jardine* [1951] 1 K.B. 614. See *Monson, infra.*

immaterial, as, for example, a porter and ale licence.[50] The definition of a holding in the 1949 Act is, however, wholly different from the definitions in the previous Acts and contemplates a contract of tenancy which comprises in part agricultural land and in part land which is not agricultural. There is no scope for the argument that the primary or dominant user is the test. So an inn and eleven acres of agricultural land used as such have been held to be a holding.[51] It has been observed[52] that *Howkins*[53] decided that the definition of a holding in the Act does not, in the case of a composite or mixed holding, work a severance into agricultural land and non-agricultural land. So where the lease was of a shop, conservatory, greenhouses, store rooms and some open ground described as a cultivated stockgarden and 65 per cent. of the turnover was in respect of the sale of cut flowers, pot plants, shrubs, and wreaths (only one-fifth of that representing the value of the raising of plants and shrubs) and 35 per cent. represented the purchase and sale of such things as seed potatoes and fertilisers, the subjects were used for a retail shop and the raising of products was ancillary, and thus the land was not as a whole used for agriculture.[54] And it has been held that a dwellinghouse may be land used for agriculture and thus a holding, it being a question of fact and degree in each case.[55] So if the house is let as a farmhouse for use in connection with a farm it will be a holding, and a cottage for a farm worker may be a holding.[55]

A "market garden" is defined as "a holding, cultivated, wholly or mainly, for the purpose of the trade or business of market gardening".[56] Under earlier Acts, where the definition was in the same terms, a holding wholly under raspberries was held to be a market garden[57] and on the other hand a lease of buildings and ground for the purpose of growing bulbs, an experimental bulb growing establishment, was held not to be one of a holding.[58] Land used as an orchard, with rhubarb and other crops grown underneath the trees, the fruit and crops being sold, was held in England to be a market garden.[59]

Persons. The parties concerned are landlord and tenant. "Landlord" is defined as "any person for the time being entitled to receive the rents and profit or to take possession of any agricultural holding" and as including "the executor, administrator, assignee, heir-at-law, legatee, disponee, next-of-kin, guardian, *curator bonis* or trustee in bankruptcy of a landlord".[60] Where a tenant sublets his holding he is a landlord

[50] *Taylor* v *Fordyce*, 1918 S.C. 824.
[51] *Dunn* v *Fidoe* [1950] 2 All E.R. 685.
[52] *Monson* v *Bound* [1954] 3 All E.R. 228.
[53] *Supra.*
[54] *Monson, supra.*
[55] *Blackmore* v *Butler* [1954] 2 Q.B. 171.
[56] s. 93 (1).
[57] *Grewar* v *Moncur's C.B.*, 1916 S.C. 764.
[58] *Watters* v *Hunter*, 1927 S.C. 310.
[59] *Lowther* v *Clifford* [1927] 1 K.B. 130.
[60] s. 93 (1).

vis-a-vis his tenant; and there is nothing in the Act which gives a subtenant a right to remain in possession on the proper termination of the
tenancy in accordance with the ordinary provisions of the law.[61] The
definition covers heritable creditors in possession, liferenters and such
like.[62] The term "assignee" was under the 1923 Act held to include a
third party who intends to buy from the landlord and takes possession
before the missives are complete.[63] A landlord, whatever his estate or
interest in the holding, may for the purposes of the Act give any
consent or make any agreement or do or have done to him any act as if
he were absolute owner,[64] that is, the owner or person capable of
disposing by disposition or otherwise of the fee simple or *dominium
utile* of the whole interest of or in land, although the land or his interest
therein is burdened, charged or encumbered.[65] If the landlord is a pupil
or a minor or is of unsound mind, not having a tutor, curator or other
guardian, the sheriff, on the application of any person interested, may
appoint for the purposes of the Act a tutor or a curator to him, and
may recall the appointment and appoint another tutor or curator if and
as the occasion requires.[66] The Act applies to Crown lands, lands
belonging to Her Majesty in right of the Crown[67] and lands belonging
to a Government Department or held on behalf of Her Majesty for
the purposes of any Government Department, in both cases subject
to any prescribed modifications.[68] Where land belongs to Her Majesty
in right of the Crown, for the purposes of the Act the Crown Estate Commissioners or other proper officer or body having charge of the
land for the time being or, if there is no such officer or body, such
person as Her Majesty may appoint in writing represents Her Majesty
and is deemed to be landlord.[69] Anything which the Act requires or
authorises to be done by, to or in respect of, a landlord may be done
by, to or in respect of any agent of his.[70]

The term "tenant" means "the holder of land under a lease and
includes the executor, administrator, assignee, heir-at-law, legatee,
disponee, next-of-kin, guardian, *curator bonis,* or trustee in bankruptcy,
of a tenant".[71] A tenant will presumably include a subtenant, and a
principal tenant will then be the landlord. The "Acts recognised only

---

[61] *Sherwood* v *Moody* [1952] 1 All E.R. 389.
[62] *Waddell* v *Howat,* 1925 S.C. 484.
[63] *Cunningham* v *Fife County Council,* 1948 S.C. 439. But see *Secretary of State
for Scotland* v *Prentice,* 1963 S.L.T. (Sh. Ct.) 48.
[64] s. 80.
[65] s. 93 (1).
[66] s. 84.
[67] s. 86 (1).
[68] s. 86 (2).
[69] s. 86 (1); Crown Estate Acts 1956, 1961. But the Crown has no interest to
grant a lease of requisitioned land for it has no legal interest in the land. It
can only exercise powers incidental to its possession, such as giving a licence
to use. *Finbow* v *Air Ministry* [1963] 2 All E.R. 647.
[70] s. 93 (7).
[71] s. 93 (1). A trustee for creditors cannot claim compensation. *Christison's
Trs.* v *Callender Brodie* (1905) 8 F. 928.

one type of tenant, and that is the tenant who can claim the benefit of the statutory provisions in favour of agricultural tenants."[72] If accepted by the landlord, trustees of a deceased tenant may be " tenants " within Acts and in the ordinary case a trust title does not affect their right to claim any of the statutory benefits under the Acts. The trust title is *res inter alios acta.* The trustees undertake full liability as tenants and can claim full benefits as such without any limitations by the fact of their trustee character.[73] The lease may exclude expressly legatees, executors and assignees, and such a clause will, of course, override the statutory definition.[74] What is a lease under the Act is dealt with in the next paragraph. If the tenant is a pupil or a minor or is of unsound mind and has not a tutor, curator or other guardian, the sheriff may appoint one for the purposes of the Act and may recall the appointment and appoint another person.[75] The Act applies with any prescribed modifications where the tenant is a Government Department or holds his interest on behalf of Her Majesty for the purpose of any Government Department.[76]

Anything which the Act requires or authorises to be done by, to or in respect of the tenant may be done by, to or in respect of the tenant's agent.[77]

The designations of landlord and tenant continue to apply to parties until the conclusion of any proceedings taken under or in pursuance of the Act in respect of compensation for improvements or under any agreement made in pursuance of the Act.[78] While proceedings initiated against a landlord who satisfies the statutory definition will, until they are concluded, bar a claim from being pursued against any other person, the proceedings must be judicial proceedings, *e.g.,* the initiation of an arbitration under the Act.[79] Thus, intimation of an intention to claim or the actual making of a claim or negotiations are not proceedings under the Act.[80] And the person who is owner, that is, entitled to receive the rents, at the termination of the tenancy when the tenant quits, is the person who must pay the compensation, even though the notice to quit office was given to or by a prior owner. This is the view taken in England having regard to the definition of " landlord ".[81] In a Scottish case[82] where the change of ownership occurred simultaneously with the termination of the lease, the purchaser entering into posssession and the tenant quitting on the termination of the lease on the same day.

---

[72] *Dalgety's Trs.* v *Drummond,* 1938 S.C. 709 at 718, *per* L.P. Normand.
[73] *Dalgety's Trs., supra.*
[74] *Kennedy* v *Johnston,* 1956 S.C. 39. See *infra,* p. 357.
[75] s. 84.
[76] s. 86 (2).
[77] s. 93 (7).
[78] s. 93 (6).
[79] *Waddell* v *Howat,* 1924 S.L.T. 684 at 687, *per* Lord Constable; *Dale* v *Hatfield Chase Corporation* [1922] 2 K.B. 282, *per* Scrutton, L.J., at 298.
[80] *Waddell, supra,* at 687.
[81] *Bradshaw* v *Bird* [1920] 3 K.B. 144; *Dale, supra.*
[82] *Waddell* v *Howat,* 1925 S.C. 484.

it was held that there the selling owners were the landlords and the obligation to pay compensation did not pass to the purchaser. They alone were landlords at the termination when the tenant quitted. The relevant time in the case of improvements is that particular date.

Lease. "Lease" means "a letting of land for a term of years, or for lives, or for lives and years, or from year to year".[83] With certain exceptions the letting cannot, without the prior approval of the Secretary of State for Scotland, be for less than from year to year. Where under a lease entered into on or after 1st November 1948 any land is let to a person for use as agricultural land for a shorter period than from year to year and the circumstances are such that if he were a tenant from year to year he would in respect of the land be the tenant of an agricultural holding, then, unless the letting was approved by the Secretary of State before the lease was entered into, the lease takes effect with necessary modifications as if it were one from year to year; this does not, however, apply in regard to a lease of land (a) entered into, whether or not the lease expressly so provides, in contemplation of the use of the land only for grazing or mowing during some specified period of the year, or (b) granted by a person whose interest in the land is that of a tenant under a lease which is for a shorter period than from year to year and which has not taken effect as above as a lease from year to year.[84] Where seasonal lets were given of a grass park for grazing purposes, to endure so long as the landlord held the tenancy of part of a house belonging to the tenant, and the period of each year during which the land was to be used for grazing was not fixed by dates, it was held[85] that the use of land for grazing or mowing was essentially seasonal and leases for such purposes were seasonal, and that fixed or specific dates for the beginning and the end of such leases were not necessary. A specified period of the year need not have definite terminal dates. "Grazing season" and "seasonal let" were here well-known terms and it was common practice not to specify dates. And a let for mowing from 1st November to 30th October—for 364 days—was held to be a let for a specified period of the year.[86] A tenancy for eighteen months is not an interest less than a tenancy from year to year nor one for a term of two years or upwards; "year to year" is a tenancy known to the law by that expression and there is nothing in the Act that entitles a court to construe it as one from year to year as enlarged by the Act.[87] A letting for eighteen months creates a greater interest than a tenancy from year to year which is terminable at the end of the first year.[87] But a tenancy for a year has been held to be an interest less than a tenancy

[83] s. 93 (1).
[84] s. 2 (1).
[85] *Mackenzie* v *Laird,* 1959 S.C. 266.
[86] *Reid* v *Dawson* [1955] 1 Q.B. 214.
[87] *Gladstone* v *Bower* [1960] 2 Q.B. 384.

from year to year;[88] and a letting "for six months" periods was held to be a lease for at least a year.[89]

Tacit Relocation. The tenancy of a holding, instead of ending on the expiry of the stipulated[90] endurance of the lease, is held to be continued by tacit relocation for another year and thereafter from year to year, unless notice to terminate the tenancy under the Act[91] has been given by either party to the other.[92] Notice from one of two joint tenants of a holding occupied by tacit relocation is sufficient to stop the running of tacit relocation and to terminate the tenancy.[93] Tacit or implied consent or silence by all parties is necessary for prolongation by tacit relocation and if one of joint tenants gives notice the necessary consent is not present for tacit relocation to operate. The Statute[94] does not alter the common law in this respect.

The effect of tacit relocation is that there is a prolongation each year of the tenancy for a further year. There is not really a new tenancy created at all. The old contract remains: it is prolonged.[95] While there is a new contract implied from the tacit consent of parties to the continuation of the relationship it does not follow that there is a new lease to which the doctrine of tacit relocation is applicable. It is from the outset inherent that there is implied agreement that the stipulated period of endurance may be extended by tacit agreement of parties.[96] It is not an indefinite prolongation of a lease but a prolongation each year of the tenancy for a further year if parties' actings show that they are consenting to this. It is based on consent which is implied if all are silent.[97] This is important in compensation provisions.

Fixed Equipment. There is deemed to be incorporated in every lease entered into on or after 1st November 1948[98] an undertaking by the landlord that at the commencement of the tenancy or as soon as is reasonably possible thereafter he will put the fixed equipment on the holding into a thorough state of repair, and will provide such buildings and other fixed equipment as will enable an occupier reasonably skilled in husbandry to maintain efficient production as respects both the kind of produce specified in the lease or, failing such a specification, in use to

[88] *Bernays* v *Prosser* [1963] 2 Q.B. 592.
[89] *Rutherford* v *Maurer* [1962] 1 Q.B. 16.
[90] This would include a "break" and if there is no stipulated endurance the lease is implied as yearly.
[91] s. 24.
[92] ss. 3 (1), 24 (1).
[93] *Smith* v *Grayton Estates*, 1960 S.C. 349.
[94] s. 3 (1).
[95] *Cowe* v *Millar*, 1923, not reported, *per* L.P. Clyde, quoted in *Connell*, 5th ed., pp. 107, 130 and accepted in *Douglas, infra* and *Smith, supra.*
[96] *Douglas* v *Cassillis and Culzean Estates*, 1944 S.C. 355, *per* L.P. Normand at 361. In *Mackenzie* v *Macgillivray*, 1921 S.C. 722, the lease was held to continue on its own express terms and not by tacit relocation.
[97] *Smith, supra, per* L.P. Clyde at 354.
[98] s. 5 (6).

be produced on the holding and the quality and quantity thereof, and will during the tenancy effect such replacement or renewal of the buildings or other fixed equipment as may be rendered necessary by natural decay or by fair wear and tear.[99] Fixed equipment is defined[1] in the Act as including " any building or structure affixed to land and any works on, in, over or under land, and also includes anything grown on land for a purpose other than use after severance from the land, consumption of the thing grown, or of produce thereof, or amenity, and, without prejudice to the foregoing generality, includes the following things, that is to say—(a) all permanent buildings, including farm houses and farm cottages, necessary for the proper conduct of the agricultural holding; (b) all permanent fences, including hedges, stone dykes, gate posts and gates; (c) all ditches, open drains and tile drains, conduits and culverts, ponds, sluices, flood banks and main water courses; (d) stells, fanks, folds, dippers, pens and bughts necessary for the proper conduct of the holding; (e) farm access or service roads, bridges and fords; (f) water and sewerage systems; (g) electrical installations including generating plant, fixed motors, wiring systems, switches and plug sockets; and (h) shelter belts ". There is also deemed to be incorporated in such a lease a provision that the tenant's liability for maintenance of fixed equipment extends only to a liability to maintain the fixed equipment on the holding in as good a state of repair (natural decay and fair wear and tear excepted) as it was in immediately after it was put in repair by the landlord, or in the case of equipment provided, improved, replaced or renewed during the tenancy as it was in immediately after it was so provided, improved, replaced or renewed.[2] But landlord and tenant may make an agreement, after the lease has been entered into, by which one party undertakes to execute on behalf of the other party, and either wholly at his expense or wholly or partly at the other party's expense, any work which the other party must under the lease execute to fulfil his obligations under the lease.[3] Any question regarding the liability of either party under these provisions is determined by arbitration.[4] The arbiter's award has effect as if the terms and provisions specified and made in it were contained in a written agreement entered into between the landlord and the tenant and having effect as from the making of the award or such later date as the award provides.[5] A clause in a lease entered into on or after 1st November 1948 requiring payment by the tenant of the whole or a part of a fire insurance policy premium in respect of any fixed equipment on the

[99] s. 5 (2) (a). Whatever the terms of the lease in this connection, the landlord must carry out the provisions of s. 5 (2): *Secretary of State for Scotland v Sinclair* (1960) 48 S.L.C.R. 10.
[1] s. 93 (1).
[2] s. 5 (2) (b).
[3] s. 5 (3).
[4] s. 5 (5).
[5] s. 6 (4).

holding is null and void.[6] Any question as to liability is referred to arbitration.

References to the terms, conditions or requirements of a lease or of an agreement relating to a holding are construed as including references to any obligations, conditions or liabilities imposed by the custom of the country in respect of the holding.[7]

Nothing in the 1949 Act is to be construed as repealing the provisions[8] of the 1940 Act,[9] which excluded the operation of the 1923 and 1931 Acts in relation to certain tenancies.[10]

Holdings without Written Lease. Where in respect of the tenancy of a holding there is no written lease embodying the terms of the tenancy or if there is such a lease (1) entered into on or after 1st November 1948 or (2) entered before then and now expired and continued by tacit relocation and having no provision for one or more of the matters specified in Schedule Fifth or having a provision that is inconsistent with that Schedule or the provisions of the Act[11] anent liabilities for provision and maintenance of fixed equipment or for payment of insurance premiums, either party may notify the other requesting him to enter into such a lease, containing provision for all of these matters or a provision not consistent with that Schedule or these provisions[11] of the Act, as the case may be.[12] If no such lease is concluded within six months after the giving of such notice, the terms of the tenancy are to be referred to arbitration,[12] and the arbiter must by his award specify the terms of the existing tenancy and, in so far as they do not provide for all the matters specified in Schedule Fifth or make provision inconsistent with that Schedule or the provisions[11] of the Act, must make such provision

---

[6] s. 5 (4). See s. 23.

[7] s. 93 (5).

[8] s. 26. This applied to a contract of tenancy for a term not exceeding four years beginning after 21st March, 1940, and before the end of the war period (the period for which the Emergency Powers (Defence) Act 1939, is in force) if it provides for the cultivation of land as arable land and, where immediately before the beginning of that term the land consisted of permanent pasture, for the sowing by the tenant of permanent grass seeds along with the last or waygoing crop; and if immediately before 21st March, 1940, and thereafter till the beginning of that term the land was not being used for agricultural purposes or was being so used in pursuance of a letting that was not a contract of tenancy within the 1923-1931 Acts or the land consisted of permanent pasture and was occupied by the landlord. And where as regards a contract made before 21st March, 1940, and after 2nd September, 1939, the landlord satisfies an arbiter appointed under the Acts that the Acts would not apply because of the foregoing provision if references to 2nd September, 1939, were substituted for references to 21st March, 1940, and that parties meant that these Acts should not apply, then the Acts do not apply to the contract of tenancy. The 1940 Act was extended by the 1943 Act (the Agriculture (Miscellaneous Provisions) Act 1943, s. 14) to eight years, and where the contract had ended before the end of the war period and a new contract for a term not exceeding four years had been made, the 1940 Act was by s. 14 to apply to it.

[9] Agriculture (Miscellaneous War Provisions) Act 1940.

[10] 1949 Act, s. 99 (8).

[11] s. 5.

[12] s. 4 (1).

for those matters as appears to him to be reasonable.[13] He may include in his award any further provisions not inconsistent with the provisions of the Act relating to the tenancy as may be agreed between landlord and tenant.[14] The arbiter's award has effect as if the terms and provisions specified and made in it were contained in a written agreement between the landlord and the tenant and having effect as from the date of the award or such later date as the award specifies.[15] The matters specified in Schedule Fifth are the names of the parties, particulars of the holding referable to a map or plan sufficiently describing the fields, etc. as to identify the holding, the term or terms for which the holding or parts of it is or are let, the rent and the dates on which it is payable, an undertaking by the landlord to reinstate or replace any building damaged by fire if this is necessary to manage the holding in accordance with the rules of good estate management, and (except where he is a Government Department or someone representing the Crown or has made with the Secretary of State's approval provision for defraying the cost) to insure such buildings to their full value against fire; and an undertaking by the tenant to return to the holding the full equivalent manurial value of harvested crops grown for consumption on the holding that have been destroyed by fire so far as such return is necessary for farming in accordance with the rules of good husbandry and (except where the tenant is a Government Department or has with the Secretary of State's approval made other provision) to insure to their full value against fire all dead stock on the holding and all harvested crops grown on the holding for consumption on the holding.

Form and Execution of Leases. It has been held that a " lease in writing " within the meaning of the Act need not be in the form of a probative writ; thus, a lease constituted in improbative writings passing between landlord and tenant which had become binding on them by *rei interventus* or homologation was a " lease in writing " under the Act.[16]

Transfer of Liability for Maintenance. Where liability for the maintenance or repair of any item of fixed equipment is transferred from tenant to landlord under the foregoing provisions for a lease, the landlord may within the prescribed[17] period beginning with the date on which the transfer takes effect require that there be determined by arbitration, and paid by the tenant, the amount of any compensation which would have been payable[18] in respect of any previous failure of the tenant to discharge his liability had the tenant quitted the holding on the termination

[13] s. 4 (2).
[14] s. 4 (3).
[15] s. 6 (4).
[16] *Grieve & Sons* v *Barr*, 1954 S.C. 414.
[17] That is, under Regulations.
[18] Under s. 57.

of his tenancy at the date on which the transfer takes effect.[19] Similarly, where the liability has been transferred from landlord to tenant, then any claim by the tenant, if he so requires within the prescribed period, is to be determined by arbitration and any amount under the award to be paid by the landlord is to be paid to the tenant by the landlord.[20] The arbiter's award is to have effect as if the terms and provisions specified and made in it were contained in a written agreement between the landlord and the tenant and having effect as from the making of the award or such date as the award provides.[21]

Variations of Terms of Tenancy or Lease as to Permanent Pasture. Where under a lease entered into before or after the commencement of the Act—24th November 1949—there is provision for maintenance of specified land or a specified proportion of the holding as permanent pasture, the landlord or the tenant may by written notice to the other demand a reference to arbitration of the question whether it is expedient, in order to secure the full and efficient farming of the holding, that the amount of land required to be maintained as permanent pasture should be reduced.[22] The arbiter may in his award direct that the lease shall have effect subject to such modifications of the provisions as to the land to be maintained as permanent pasture or to be treated as arable land and as to cropping as he specifies.[23] If he directs a reduction of the area to be so maintained, he may order that the lease is to have effect as if it provided that on quitting the holding on the termination of the tenancy the tenant should leave as permanent pasture or as temporary pasture sown with seeds mixture of such kind as he (the arbiter) specifies, such area (in addition to the area required by the lease as modified by the direction to be maintained as permanent pasture) as he specifies.[24] The area required to be left must not exceed the area by which the land required by the lease to be maintained as permanent pasture has been reduced by his direction.[24]

The 1949 Act is not to be construed[25] as repealing the provision of the 1943 Act[26] under which occupiers of agricultural land who have ploughed up land consisting of permanent pasture under directions under Defence Regulations and thus incurred liability or obligation by contract, custom or rule of law to sow it again or pay increased rent, damages, etc. or suffer forfeiture for the ploughing or the failure to sow again had this obligation or liability extinguished. Land was to be deemed arable land after the ploughing and to have been such at all material times.[27] But

[19] s. 6 (1).
[20] s. 6 (2).
[21] s. 6 (4).
[22] s. 9 (1) as amended by 1958 Act, Schedule First, Part II, para. 32.
[23] s. 9 (2) (a) as amended, *supra.*
[24] s. 9 (2) (b) as amended, *supra.*
[25] s. 99 (8).
[26] s. 15.
[27] s. 15 (1).

20

this is not to apply to land comprised in a contract of tenancy to which the provisions of the 1940 Act apply except as directed by an arbiter.[27]

Variation or Addition of Terms not to Affect Continuance of Lease. A lease is not brought to an end and neither party can bring proceedings to terminate it or, except by joint consent, can treat it as ended by the fact that a new term has been added or that any terms have been varied or revised under the Act.[28] This includes a variation of the rent.[29]

PROVISIONS REGARDING RENT

Variation of Rent. Either party, whether or not the lease was entered into before or after the commencement of the Act, may by written notice served on the other demand a reference to arbitration of the question of " what rent should be payable in respect of the holding as from the next ensuing day on which the tenancy could have been determined by notice to quit given at the date of demanding the reference ".[30] The rent must be fixed by arbitration before or shortly after the term stated in the notice for the section is " clearly looking forward " and contemplating " a rent, commencing at the date when the notional notice to quit would terminate the tenancy, and fixed before that term is reached ". So a notice given in November 1962 asking for arbitration as to the rent from Martinmas 1963 followed by submission only in mid-1964 was held spent and void.[30a] But a reference cannot be demanded in such circumstances that any increase or reduction of rent would take effect as from a date earlier than the expiration of five years from the latest in time of three dates—(1) the commencement of the tenancy; (2) the date as from which there took effect a previous increase or reduction of rent whether under this provision of the Act[30] or not; and (3) the date as from which there took effect a previous direction under the section that the rent should continue unchanged.[31] For the purposes of this provision certain increases or reductions are to be disregarded: an increase or reduction by an arbiter in an arbitration[32] as to the terms of the tenancy[33] or as to liability for fixed equipment;[34] an increase in respect of certain

---

[28] 1949 Act, s. 10.
[29] *Ibid., supra*, p. 306. " Termination " in relation to a tenancy means the termination of the lease by reason of effluxion of time or from any other cause, s. 93 (1). Termination of the lease may not always be the same as termination of the tenancy. Connell, *op. cit.*, p. 203.
[30] s. 7 (1).
[30a] *Graham* v *Gardner*, 1966 S.L.T. (Land Ct.) 12. The same view has been taken in England under an equivalent section in *Sclater* v *Horton* [1954] 2 Q.B. 1. In *Graham* the court reserved the question whether the new rent could be determined within a reasonable period after the notional notice to quit would become effective provided arbitration began before that time.
[31] s. 7 (3).
[32] s. 6 (3).
[33] Under s. 4.
[34] Under s. 5 (5).

improvements by the landlord;[35] and a reduction in respect of dispossession of the tenant of part of the holding.[36]

Where a tenant had demanded a reference to arbitration as to the amount of the rent and parties jointly agreed to go to arbitration before the Land Court, the argument that the Court was not entitled to vary the rent in the absence of a change of circumstances between the date of the lease and the date of the hearing before the Court was rejected, and it was held that the fixing of the rent by an arbiter was not under the Act, the terms of which were clear and unqualified, restricted to where a change of circumstances was established.[37]

The rent properly payable is the rent at which, having regard to the terms of the tenancy, other than those relating to rent, the holding might reasonably be expected to be let in the open market by a willing landlord to a willing tenant, there being disregarded, in addition to the items mentioned next, any effect on rent of the fact that the tenant who is a party to the arbitration is in occupation of the holding.[38] The items mentioned which the arbiter is to disregard in fixing the rent are: (1) any increase in the rental value of the holding due to improvements executed wholly or partly at the expense of the tenant (whether or not the expense has been or will be reimbursed by a grant out of moneys provided by Parliament) without any equivalent allowance or benefit made or given by the landlord in consideration of their execution, and if the improvement was not executed under an obligation imposed on the tenant by the lease,[39] while the continuous adoption by the tenant of a standard or system of farming more beneficial to the holding than that required by the lease, or, in so far as no system is so required, than the normal system on comparable holdings in the district, is regarded as an improvement executed at the tenant's expense;[40] and (2) any improvement executed by the landlord in so far as he has received, or will receive, grants out of moneys provided by Parliament in respect of the improvement (the rent is not to be fixed higher than would have been properly payable if these improvements had not been so executed);[39] and (3) any benefit that may accrue to the tenant from the Agricultural Marketing Act 1931, e.g., by production of milk.[41] The

---

[35] s. 8 (1), (2).
[36] s. 34.
[37] *Cowane's Hospital Patrons* v *Rennie*, 1959 S.L.T. (Notes) 76.
[38] 1958 Act, s. 2, amending 1949 Act, s. 7 (1). See observations on fixing open market rents in *Crown Estate Commissioners and Gunn* (1961) 49 S.L.C.R. App. 173. And see too *Secretary of State for Scotland* v *Young* (1960) 48 S.L.C.R. 31 that in fixing rents the court requires evidence of the "open market rent" of comparable subjects, as between willing landlord and willing tenant. New rents for four holdings, it was held, should be fixed according to the open market rents of similar holdings: *Secretary of State for Scotland* v *Sinclair* (1962) 50 S.L.C.R. 6.
[39] 1949 Act, s. 7 (2) (a).
[40] *Ibid.*, s. 7 (4).
[41] *Ibid.*, s. 7 (2) (b). The relief in respect of rates also referred to here does not now apply, as agricultural land no longer enters the Valuation Roll; Valuation and Rating (Scotland) Act 1956, s. 7.

rent must not be fixed at a lower amount because of any dilapidation or deterioration of, or damage to, fixed equipment or land caused or permitted by the tenant.[42] In fixing the rent, the arbiter, it has been suggested,[43] should consider the rent that would be paid " by a new tenant with reasonably adequate means and capable of farming to good advantage," and in that connection the general state of agriculture and the trend of prices. And it has been held that in fixing the rent the arbiter must have evidence of the open market rent of comparable subjects, that is the rent as between a willing landlord and a willing tenant.[44] " Market prices are the result of freedom of contract and of competition and the direction is now to fix a rent at open market value. In the *Encyclopaedia of the Laws of Scotland* Sheriff Dickson says— '. . . the fair value of an article is the highest price which it will bring on free exposure in the open market.' . . . the Court must have in mind not what any particular tenant (or class of tenant) can make of the holding but what the productive potentiality of the holding as an agricultural subject could be expected to realise in the open market."[45]

Where it appears to an arbiter acting under a reference as to the terms of the tenancy that by reason of any provision he is required to make in his award it is equitable that the rent be varied, he may vary the rent accordingly.[46] And similarly, in a reference in respect of the liability of landlord or tenant as to the maintenance of fixed equipment, the arbiter may for the same reason vary the rent.[46]

Right of Landlord to Increased Rent. In certain cases the landlord can demand that the rent be increased, in respect of certain improvements carried out by him on the holding before or after the commencement of the Act. He can serve a notice in writing on the tenant within six months of the completion of the improvement requiring the rent to be increased as from the completion of the improvement, or, where it was completed before 1st November 1948, as from that day, by an amount equal to the increase in the rental value of the holding attributable to the carrying out of the improvement, but where any grant has been made to the landlord for the improvement out of monies provided by Parliament (*e.g.,* the Hill Farming Act 1946) the increase in rent is reduced proportionately.[47] The improvements referred to are (a) those carried out at the request of, or in agreement with, the tenant; (b) those carried out in pursuance of an undertaking given by the landlord under certain provisions of the 1923 Act[48] or the 1949 Act[49]; (c) those carried out in compliance with a direction by the Secretary of State under

---

[42] *Ibid.*, s. 7 (2) (c). See Connell, *op. cit.*, 5th ed., p. 107.
[43] Connell, *supra*, pp. 7-8.
[44] *Secretary of State for Scotland* v *Young, supra.*
[45] *Ibid.*, at 33.
[46] s. 6 (3).
[47] s. 8 (1).
[48] s. 3 (3), (6) (b).
[49] s. 52 (3).

powers conferred on him by or under any Act; (d) those carried out in accordance with a provision in that behalf included in a hill farming land improvement scheme approved under the Hill Farming Act 1946, at the instance or with the consent of the tenant; or (e) works for the supply of water to the holding executed in pursuance of directions by the Agricultural Executive Committee for the area under Defence Regulations or of a scheme approved by the Committee.[50] Where the landlord has executed on the holding works of the nature of fixed equipment which are required to be executed or similar works at the request of or in agreement with the tenant, these works are regarded as improvements.[51] No increase, however, can be made if before 1st November 1948 the landlord and the tenant have agreed on an increase in rent or other benefit to the landlord in respect of the improvement, or if before that date any sum became payable under the 1923 Act[52] (that is, interest on expenditure or improvements made by the landlord under Schedule First, Part II of that Act) or the 1943 Act[53] (that is, interest on the landlord's expenditure on works for water supply) or the Hill Farming Act 1946,[54] in respect of the cost of executing it.[55] And where interest on the cost of works for water supply, or rent in respect of an improvement under (d) above was payable under the 1923 Act or the 1946 Act before 1st November 1948, or became payable under these provisions after that date by agreement between the parties made before that date, it remains recoverable though these provisions were repealed by the Agriculture (Scotland) Act 1948.[56] Where an improvement has been affected by any authorised operations under the Opencast Coal Act 1958—operations carried out for or incidental to the fulfilment of working coal by opencast operations or restoring land affected by such working—the increase in rental value of the holding attributable to the carrying out of the improvement is to be assessed as if those operations in so far as affecting the improvement had not been carried out.[57]

Right of Tenant to Reduction of Rent. The tenant is entitled to a reduction of rent[58] where the tenancy of part of a holding held on a tenancy from year to year terminates by reason of a notice to quit[59] given[60] for the purpose of adjusting the boundaries between agricultural units or amalgamating such units or parts thereof or with a view to the use of land to which the notice relates for any of the following

---

[50] s. 8 (1).
[51] Agriculture (Safety, Health and Welfare Provisions) Act 1956, s. 125.
[52] s. 3 (3).
[53] s. 9.
[54] s. 9, as amended by Livestock Rearing Act 1951, s. 1 (2) (b).
[55] s. 8 (2).
[56] s. 8 (3).
[57] Opencast Coal Act 1958, s. 14 (8) (a).
[58] s. 34.
[59] See as to notice to quit, *infra*, pp. 311 *et seq.*
[60] s. 32 (1).

purposes[61] (and the notice states that it is given for that purpose or with a view to any such use as the case may be):

(a) the erection of farm labourers' cottages or other houses with or without gardens;

(b) the provision of gardens for farm labourers' cottages or other houses;

(c) the provision of allotments;

(d) the provision of small holdings under the Small Landholders (Scotland) Acts 1886 to 1931, or of such holdings as are mentioned in section sixty-four of the Agriculture (Scotland) Act 1948;

(e) the planting of trees;

(f) the opening or working of any coal, ironstone, limestone, brick-earth, or other mineral, or of a stone quarry, clay, sand, or gravel pit, or the construction of any works or buildings to be used in connection therewith;

(g) the making of a watercourse or reservoir;

(h) the making of any road, railway, tramroad, siding, canal or basin, or any wharf, pier, or other work connected therewith.

He is also entitled to a reduction where the landlord resumes possession of a part of the holding under a provision in the lease reserving right to the landlord to resume possession of a part for certain specific purposes.[58] The amount of the reduction in either case, which is determined by arbitration, is proportionate to that part of the holding and in respect of any depreciation of the value to the tenant of the residue of the holding caused by the severance or the use made of the part severed.[58] In the case of resumption by the landlord, the arbiter is to take into account any benefit or relief allowed to the tenant under the lease in respect of the resumed land.[58]

Variation of the rent does not affect the continuance of a lease.[62]

NOTICE OF TERMINATION OF TENANCY

Notice to Quit. Written notice of intention to terminate a lease or tenancy must be given not less than one year and not more than two years before the termination of the lease.[63] And it is not competent to contract out of this rule.[63] If notice is not given, the lease is renewed by tacit relocation for another year, and so on from year to year,[63] and the period of notice in such cases is the same, *viz.,* not less than one year and not more than two years.[64] The provisions of the Sheriff Courts (Scotland) Act 1907 regarding removings have effect subject to the provisions of section twenty four of the 1949 Act.[65]

---

[61] s. 32 (2). See *Secretary of State for Scotland* v *Prentice,* 1963 S.L.T. (Sh. Ct.) 48.
[62] s. 10. See *supra,* p. 306.
[63] s. 24 (1).
[64] s. 24 (2).
[65] s. 24 (3). See Rent Act 1965, s. 30.

There is a statutory form of notice to quit to be given by the landlord, that is under the Sheriff Courts (Scotland) Act 1907,[66] and it must be as nearly as possible in that form.[67] The manner of giving the notice must be as in the Removal Terms (Scotland) Act 1886 or the 1907 Act.[68] Notice by ordinary post has been held in Scotland not enough,[69] but it has been recently decided in the English Courts that a notice under the Act (the equivalent English Act) is validly served if in fact it is delivered to the persons to whom it is addressed whether or not sent by registered post.[70] There is no form of notice to be given by the tenant, who can thus intimate his intention to remove by a letter.

The statutory provisions as to notice do not apply to a notice given under a power reserved in the lease for the landlord to resume land for building, planting, feuing, or other purposes[71] not being agricultural purposes,[72] nor to subjects let for less than year not being a lease that takes effect as from year to year under the Act.[72] The landlord may be able, if the lease provides to that effect, to resume without notice.[73] Power to resume may apply to the whole of the holding.[74]

In a lease of a dwellinghouse or building let along with land for agricultural purposes, if the term of entry or removal of a tenant is Whitsunday or Martinmas, then, in the absence of contrary express stipulation, the term of removal is, despite any contrary custom or usage, noon at 28th May or noon at 28th November respectively, or, if either

---

[66] Form H.
[67] *Rae and Cooper* v *Davidson*, 1954 S.C. 361—failure to incorporate a reference to the lease was held fatal though the tenants were not prejudiced; see here L.J.C. Thomson's review of the history. See also *Watters* v *Hunter*, 1927 S.C. 310.
[68] s. 24 (4).
[69] *Department of Agriculture for Scotland* v *Goodfellow*, 1931 S.C. 556.
[70] *Re Poyser & Mills' Arbitration* [1964] 2 Q.B. 467. Here notice had been sent by recorded delivery service before the Recorded Delivery Service Act 1962, came into operation.
[71] See *Pigott* v *Robson*, 1958 S.L.T. 49; and *Turner* v *Wilson*, 1954 S.C. 296, where it was held on a clause in a lease that this did not cover the case where the landlord wanted to resume in order to farm himself. In *Glencruitten Trs.* v *Love*, 1966 S.L.T. (Land Ct.) 5 two adjoining farms had each a dwellinghouse and steading. They were let to a tenant excluding one of the dwellinghouses. The lease reserved power to the landlord to resume any part of the land for any purpose other than agriculture. It was held that the landlord could not resume the steading adjoining the excluded dwellinghouse in order to use it in connection with that house for this would be contrary to the good faith of the lease—such resumption never obviously having been contemplated by the parties —and the steading being an essential part of the subjects let. In so deciding the court followed not only the general principle laid down by Lord Salvesen in *The Admiralty* v *Burns*, 1910 S.C. 531 at 542, but also the opinion of Lord Young in *Trotter* v *Torrance* (1891) 18 R. 848 at 854, where he questioned whether a right to resume ten acres of an arable farm extended to resumption of a dwelling-house or steading premises.
[72] s. 24 (6) as amended by 1958 Act, Schedule First, Part II, para. 34.
[73] *Kininmonth* v *British Aluminium Co.*, 1915 S.C. 271.
[74] *Alston's Trs.* v *Muir*, 1919 2 S.L.T. 8.

day is a Sunday, on the following day at the same hour, but notice is necessary before 15th May or 11th November respectively.[75]

Notice given before a tenancy begins is ineffective; so where notice was given to determine the tenancy on 29th September 1960 and on 27th September of that year another notice was given to quit on 29th September 1961, the second notice indicated that a new protected tenancy had been created, the first notice having been valid, and having been served before the new tenancy began was ineffective.[76]

Unless the context otherwise requires, Whitsun and Martinmas are 28th May and 28th November respectively.[77]

A landlord can always remove a tenant whose estate is sequestrated under the Bankruptcy (Scotland) Act 1913 or who by failure to pay rent or otherwise has incurred an irritancy of his lease or other liability to be removed.[78]

Where landlords or tenants are joint holders notice by one is sufficient,[79] but it is advisable that all act.

Provision is made in the 1949 Act as to the service of a notice to the effect that such is duly given or served if delivered to the party or left at his proper address[80] or sent to him by post in a registered letter,[81] which now includes the modern recorded delivery service,[82] and in the case of an incorporated company or body, given to or served on the secretary or clerk of the company or body[83] at its registered or principal office.[84]

Notice to Quit Part of a Holding. In a year to year tenancy, including one renewed by tacit relocation, a notice to quit part of a holding is not invalid because it relates only to part if it is given for the purpose of adjusting the boundaries between agricultural units or amalgamating such units or parts thereof, or with a view to the use of the land for certain specified purposes,[85] *i.e.*, the erection of farm labourers' cottages or other houses with or without gardens; the provision of gardens for such cottages or other houses; the provision of allotments; the provision of small holdings under the Small Landholders (Scotland) Acts 1886-1931 or of certain other holdings;[86] tree planting; the opening or working

---

[75] Removal Terms (Scotland) Act 1886, which does not apply to land let for agricultural purposes.
[76] *Lower* v *Sorrell* [1963] 1 Q.B. 959.
[77] 1949 Act, s. 93 (1).
[78] s. 24 (5). See 1963 S.L.T. (News) 69 at 70.
[79] *Smith* v *Grayton Estates*, 1960 S.C. 349, following dicta in *Graham* v *Stirling*, 1922 S.C. 90 and *Walker* v *Hendry*, 1925 S.C. 855.
[80] s. 90 (1)—that is, the last known address, s. 90 (3).
[81] s. 90 (1). This relates to proof of service, Connell, *op. cit.*, p. 194.
[82] Recorded Delivery Service Act 1962.
[83] s. 90 (2).
[84] s. 90 (3).
[85] s. 32 (1). See *Stewart* v *Moir*, 1965 S.L.T. (Land Ct.) 11, where the notice not merely did not state that it was for any of those purposes, but did not state any purpose at all.
[86] As under Agriculture (Scotland) Act 1948, s. 64.

of any coal, ironstone, limestone, brickearth or other mineral, or of a stone quarry, clay, sand or gravel pit, or the construction of any works or buildings to be used in connection with such opening or working; the making of watercourses or reservoirs; or the making of any road, railway, tramroad, siding, canal or basin, or any wharf, pier or other work connected therewith.[87] The notice must expressly state that it is given for that purpose or with a view to that use.[85] And if the landlord gives such a notice for any of these purposes, the tenant may, within twenty-eight days after the giving of notice or after the time when it is determined that it has effect, where proceedings are necessary, accept the notice as one to terminate the tenancy of the entire holding, by serving a written counter-notice[88] on the landlord and the notice has then effect accordingly.[89] Where a landlord of grazings which were let sold the greater part to the Forestry Commission for the planting of trees but continued to let the remainder to the tenant, it was held that the Forestry Commission could not give by themselves notice to quit their area: it was necessary for them to have the collaboration of the landlord.[90] In a later case[90a] it was pointed out that the validity of the notice given in *Prentice* (which had been given under Section 32 and was thus not challenged as relating to part only of a holding) had been challenged on the ground that it had not been given by the landlord of the holding whereas in this later case the notice relating in fact to part of a holding was not given in terms of that section, no purpose being stated. In this later case the holding was one of four separate parks, each with a different owner. The owners of two of the parks gave notice as to their respective parks but only one of them applied for consent to the notice. It was held that the notice by this owner was invalid as relating to part only of a holding held on a year to year tenancy; and the Court went on to express its opinion that the application was incompetent in any event as seeking consent to the operation of a notice relating to lands in part not owned by the applicant owner.

Security of Tenure

Where notice to quit the holding or part of it has been duly served upon him, the tenant may, within one month of the giving of the notice, serve on the landlord a written counter-notice[91] requiring that a certain provision[92] of the Act shall apply to the notice to quit, and in that

---

[87] s. 32 (2). See *Secretary of State for Scotland* v *Prentice*, 1963 S.L.T. (Sh. Ct.) 48 (tree planting).

[88] Under s. 25 (1) *infra*. See *Hamilton* v *Lorimer* (1959) 47 S.L.C.R. 7.

[89] s. 33.

[90] *Secretary of State for Scotland* v *Prentice*, *supra*.

[90a] *Stewart* v *Moir*, 1965 S.L.T. (Land Ct.) 11.

[91] See as to the serving of notices, *supra*, p. 311. And note that the tenant can serve on the original landlord unless or until he is notified that the original landlord has ceased to be so and has also received notice of the name and address of the new landlord, s. 90 (4).

[92] s. 25 (1), as amended by 1958 Act, Schedule First, Part II, para. 35.

event the notice to quit is not to have effect unless the Land Court consents to the operation of the notice;[92] but this does not apply where[93]

(b) the notice to quit relates to land being permanent pasture which the landlord has been in the habit of letting annually for seasonal grazing or of keeping in his own occupation and which has been let to the tenant for a definite and limited period for cultivation as arable land on the condition that he shall, along with the last or waygoing crop, sow permanent grass seeds;

(c) the notice to quit is given on the ground that the land is required for a use, other than for agriculture, for which permission has been granted on an application made under the enactments relating to town and country planning, or for which (otherwise than by virtue of any provision of those enactments) such permission is not required;[94]

(d) the Land Court, on an application in that behalf made not more than nine months before the giving of the notice to quit, was satisfied in relation to the holding that the tenant was not fulfilling his responsibilities to farm in accordance with the rules of good husbandry, and certified that it was so satisfied; the landlord may apply to the Land Court for a certificate that the tenant is not fulfilling his responsibilities to farm in accordance with the rules of good husbandry,[95] and the Land Court if satisfied that the

---

[93] s. 25 (2), as amended, *supra.* Subsection (a) was deleted by 1958 Act.

[94] See *Jones* v *Gates* (1954) 1 All E.R. 158, where it was held that a field (which the landlord said he intended to sell as a sports ground) was not " required " for a use referred to in the subsection as the landlord had not used it as such and was not in negotiation at the time: his mere statement was not enough, any more than the prospect of use by a " prospective purchaser " not identified and maybe non-existent. See *Min. of Agriculture, Fisheries and Food* v *Jenkins* [1963] 2 Q.B. 317.

[95] The Rules of Good Husbandry (s. 93 (2), Agriculture (Scotland) Act 1948, Schedule Sixth) are as follows:—

(1) For the purposes of this Act (the 1948 Act), the occupier of an agricultural unit shall be deemed to fulfil his responsibilities to farm it in accordance with the rules of good husbandry in so far as the extent to which and the manner in which the unit is being farmed (as respects both the kind of operations carried out and the way in which they are carried out) are such that, having regard to the character and situation of the unit, the standard of management thereof by the owner and other relevant circumstances, the occupier is maintaining a reasonable standard of efficient production, as respects both the kind of produce and the quality and quantity thereof, while keeping the unit in a condition to enable such a standard to be maintained in the future.

(2) In determining whether the manner in which a unit is being farmed is such as aforesaid regard shall be had, but without prejudice to the generality of the provisions of the last foregoing paragraph, to the following:—

(a) the maintenance of permanent grassland (whether meadow or pasture) properly mown or grazed and in a good state of cultivation and fertility;

(b) the handling or cropping of the arable land, including the treatment of temporary grass, so as to maintain it clean and in a good state of cultivation and fertility;

(c) where the system of farming practised requires the keeping of livestock, the proper stocking of the holding;

(d) the maintenance of an efficient standard of management of livestock;

tenant is not fulfilling his said responsibilities, shall grant such a certificate;[96]

(e) at the date of the giving of the notice to quit the tenant had failed to comply with a demand in writing served on him by the landlord requiring him within two months from the service of the demand to pay any rent due in respect of the holding, or within a reasonable time to remedy any breach by the tenant, which was capable of being remedied, of any term or condition of his tenancy which was not inconsistent with the fulfilment of his responsibilities to farm in accordance with the rules of good husbandry;[95]

(f) at the date of the giving of the notice to quit the interest of the landlord in the holding had been materially prejudiced by the commission by the tenant of a breach, which was not capable of being remedied in reasonable time and at economic cost, of any term or condition of the tenancy which was not inconsistent with the fulfilment by the tenant of his responsibilities to farm in accordance with the rules of good husbandry;[95]

(g) at the date of the giving of the notice to quit the tenant was a person who had become notour bankrupt or had executed a trust deed for behoof of his creditors.

In notices to quit under these six sub-heads it is a condition of the notice being effective that it state the reason for which it is given, that is, it must specify the statutory basis for the exclusion of the tenant's right to give a counter-notice.[97]

(e) as regards hill sheep farming in particular:—
    (i) the maintenance of a sheep stock of a suitable breed and type in regular ages (so far as is reasonably possible) and the keeping and management thereof in accordance with the recognised practices of hill sheep farming;
    (ii) the use of lug, horn or other stock marks for the purpose of determining ownership of stock sheep;
    (iii) the regular selection and retention of the best female stock for breeding;
    (iv) the regular selection and use of tups possessing the qualities most suitable and desirable for the flock;
    (v) the extent to which regular muirburn is made;
(f) the extent to which the necessary steps are being taken—
    (i) to secure and maintain the freedom of crops and livestock from disease and from infestation by insects and other pests;
    (ii) to exercise systematic control of vermin and of bracken, whins, broom and injurious weeds;
    (iii) to protect and preserve crops harvested or in course of being harvested;
    (iv) to carry out necessary work of maintenance and repair of the fixed and other equipment.
The duty to farm in conformity with these rules is one owed to the nation and is also an express condition of all agricultural leases in Scotland (1963 S.L.T. (News) 69).

[96] s. 28, as amended by 1958 Act, Schedule First, Part II, para. 38.
[97] See *Cowan* v *Wrayford* [1953] 2 All E.R. 1138, where a notice was held bad as it alleged failure to remedy breaches but the period for remedying them had not expired. Where remedying of the breach of a condition that the tenant

Notice to Quit given to Successor or Legatee. If a notice to quit is given by a landlord to a tenant who has acquired right to the lease by virtue of the Succession (Scotland) Act 1964 Section 16 or as a legatee[98] the provisions as to a counter notice &c.[99] do not apply,[1] if, where the lease has expired or has less than two years to run of its stipulated endurance, the landlord terminates the tenancy by notice to quit not earlier than the term (that is, the term of outgoing stipulated in the lease or the corresponding term in any succeeding year), following the first anniversary of the tenant's acquiring right as heir or legatee and not later than the term next occurring after the second anniversary of that date;[1] or if, where the lease has more than two years to run of its stipulated endurance, the landlord gives notice when it becomes legally competent for him to serve the notice to quit.[1]

The notice must always bear to be given in pursuance of the relevant sub-section.[1] If the successor or the legatee acquires right to the lease within seven years of the passing of the 1958 Act, that is before 1st August 1965, he is given an extra year's grace to the second anniversary.[2]

Notice and Counter-Notice. The counter-notice must be so expressed as to indicate a clear intention to invoke the right given by the Act, and a mere letter saying " I don't intend to go " and that the writer will appeal is not within the Act as showing an intention to require that the provision of the Act should apply.[3] The reason must be stated in the notice;[4] and the notice must be clear and unambiguous.[5] The exception must be stated as the reason for the notice. The landlord " should put his cards on the table and all his cards on the table " and must state the situation as he understands it clearly.[6] It has been held sufficient to refer in the notice to reasons as in the paragraphs of the Act,[7] the paragraph being identified,[8] or to state the reasons in a letter along with the notice.[9] A notice to quit is not made invalid merely by stating in addition to a good reason one that is bad;[10] if it gives a valid reason (which must be considered at the date when the notice is delivered to the tenant) it does not become a bad notice because it also gives a

---

reside personally was demanded, no period of time, it was held, need be specified for compliance. *Morrison-Low* v *Howison,* 1961 S.L.T. (Sh. Ct.) 53 at 57. Where there is a failure to remedy only one of several breaches, then unless by the application of the *de minimis* rule, consent is not necessary: *Price* v *Romilly* [1960] 3 All E.R. 429.

[98] In terms of 1949 Act, s. 20.
[99] *Ibid.,* s. 25 (1).
[1] 1958 Act, s. 6 (3), as amended by Succession (Scotland) Act 1964, Sch. 2, para. 23. See as to this subsection and its problems, 1959 S.L.T. (News) 162-5.
[2] *Ibid.,* s. 6 (4).
[3] *Mountford* v *Hodkinson* [1956] 2 All E.R. 17.
[4] *Budge* v *Hicks* [1951] 2 K.B. 335.
[5] *Cowan* v *Wrayford, supra.*
[6] *Macnab of Macnab* v *Anderson,* 1957 S.C. 213, *per* L.J.C. Thomson at 217.
[7] *In re Digby and Penny* [1932] 2 K.B. 491.
[8] *Hammon* v *Fairbrother* [1956] 2 All E.R. 108: so the adding of reasons as an act of courtesy does not bring the notice within s. 25 (2).
[9] *Turton* v *Turnbull* [1934] 2 K.B. 197.
[10] *French* v *Elliott* [1959] 3 All E.R. 866.

bad reason, and is not affected thereby.[10] Subsections (e) and (f) *supra* are mutually exclusive, and thus, where a landlord served first a notice demanding under these two subsections the remedying of the breach of conditions specified, some of which were remediable, and later served a notice to quit in terms of the two subsections, it was held[11] that the tenant was entitled to fair notice or clear indication of whether the alleged breaches came under the one or the other subsection. The two were completely distinct and in scope and mode of operation very different. Where the notice was under (c) *supra* and there was in fact no purchaser or person who wished to use the land for purposes other than agriculture, namely, as a sports ground, it was held the land was not required for use other than agriculturally.[12] With reference to (e) and (f) *supra* it has been held[13] that the right of a landlord under a lease to execute repairs at his own hand and charge the cost to the tenant— such a conventional remedy—falls to be read as an addition to, or supplementary to, and not as in substitution for, the obligation imposed on the tenant under the lease and for the remedies implied by law in the circumstances. Because he is entitled to do the repairs himself at the tenant's expense he has not disentitled himself from founding on the tenant's failure to do them in the first place. An extra remedy stipulated for in the landlord's favour cannot have the effect of destroying his other remedies. An arbiter on a reference to arbitration following notice to quit under (e) cannot in such procedure found on the principle of mutuality and treat the notice as invalid because the landlord is in breach of his obligations under the lease.[14] Again under (d) *supra* only removing at the earliest at the ish is covered and so, unless where there is tacit relocation, it is available as a ground only for a very limited period.[15] The landlord can, however, dispossess the tenant before the term if the rules are contained in the lease and breach of them is made a conventional irritancy. It does not necessarily involve an irremediable breach. The landlord can probably prevent further deterioriation of the holding during the period before the tenancy terminates by interdict where the acts are those of commission by the tenant. And he can in any event avoid founding on that sub-section by alleging material prejudice under (f). Sub-sections (e) and (f) do not apply where compliance with a condition of the lease is inconsistent with the rules of good husbandry; probably the landlord must show the condition is not inconsistent with the rules.[16] In relation to (e) a notice to remedy breaches is not wholly invalidated because the period of time allowed in the notice

---

[11] *Macnab, supra.* See also *Budge, supra.*
[12] *Jones* v *Gates* [1954] 1 All E.R. 158.
[13] *Halliday* v *Fergusson & Sons,* 1961 S.C. 24. See also *Allan's Tr.* v *Allan & Sons* (1891) 19 R. 215.
[14] *Wilson-Clarke* v *Graham,* 1963 S.L.T. (Sh. Ct.) 2.
[15] *Macnabb* v *Anderson,* 1955 S.C. 38, *per* Lord Patrick at 44.
[16] See 1963 S.L.T. (News) 69-71. *Cp. Macnabb, supra, per* Lord Russell at 44.

later becomes unreasonable in respect of some of the breaches; the landlord can still rely on the other breaches.[17]

The Land Court must consent[18] to the operation of a notice to quit if, but only if, they are satisfied[19] as to at least one of the following matters, being a matter or matters specified by the landlord in his application for the Court's consent—

(a) that the carrying out of the purpose for which the landlord proposes to terminate the tenancy is desirable in the interests of good husbandry as respects the land to which the notice relates, treated as a separate unit;[20] or

(b) that the carrying out thereof is desirable in the interests of sound management of the estate[21] of which the land to which the notice relates forms part or which that land constitutes; or

(c) that the carrying out thereof is desirable for the purposes of agricultural research, education, experiment or demonstration, or for the purposes of the enactments relating to smallholdings or such holdings as are mentioned in section sixty-four of the Agriculture (Scotland) Act 1948, or allotments; or

(d) that greater hardship would be caused by withholding than by giving consent to the operation of the notice;[22] or

(e) that the landlord proposes to terminate the tenancy for the purpose of the land being used for a use, other than for agriculture, not falling within paragraph (c) of sub-section (2) of section twenty five as above stated.[23]

---

[17] *Shepherd* v *Lomas* [1963] 2 All E.R. 902.

[18] Appeal to the Court of Session is not competent: *Davidson* v *Chiskan Estate Co.* (1952) 40 S.L.C.R. 41.

[19] The landlord must lead evidence though the tenant does not appear: *McLellan* v *McGregor*, 1952 L.C., Stirling (R.N. 44).

[20] See *Eastern Angus Properties* v *Chivers & Sons* (1960) 48 S.L.C.R. 1 at 3; both parties were limited companies. The interests of good husbandry are not the same as the rules of good husbandry. Connell, *op. cit.*, 5th ed., 138 and cases cited. The test thus seems here to be primarily one of the landlord's interest, and it has been suggested that the view in *Eastern Angus Properties* (*supra*) that the landlord must aver and prove bad husbandry by the tenants is erroneous as the essential issue is that the landlord's purposes are in the interests of good husbandry: 1963 S.L.T. (News) 71-2.

[21] See 1959 S.L.T. (News) 160. See too *Gibson* v *McKechnie* (1961) 49 S.L.C.R. 11, also *Davidson, supra,* where a landlord with no agricultural experience could not terminate in order to instal a manager.

[22] The onus of proof of greater hardship is on the landlord. *Mackenzie* v *Tait* (1951) 39 S.L.C.R. 3; *McLaren* v *Lawrie*, 1964 S.L.T. (Land Ct.) 10. See examples of failure by landlord to prove greater hardship in *Eastern Angus Properties, supra; Gibson, supra.* In *Longair* v *Reid* (1960) 48 S.L.C.R. 34, a landlord aged 73 with no home who wished to live personally on the holding was held to have proved greater hardship; and greater hardship was also held established in *Mitchell* v *Fraser* (1961), 49 S.L.C.R. App. 176; and in *McBay* v *Birse*, 1965 S.L.T. (Land Ct.) 10, where too a plea that some parcels of land in the notice were not let to the tenant, consent being sought as to the rest only, was held incompetent.

[23] s. 26 (1) as substituted by the 1958 Act, s. 3 (2) (3). See also Opencast Coal Act 1958, s. 14 (6), (9). Practical research with agricultural chemicals is a use other than for agriculture: *Dow Agrochemicals* v *E. A. Lane (North Lynn)* 1965, 115 L.J. 76. It was held that " a fair and reasonable landlord would not insist on

Notwithstanding that the Land Court are satisfied as to one of the matters, they must withhold consent " if in all the circumstances it appears to them that a fair and reasonable landlord would not insist on possession ".[23] Where consent is given, the Land Court may impose such conditions as appear to the Court requisite for securing that the land to which the notice relates will be used for the purpose for which the landlord proposes to terminate the tenancy.[24] Where on an application by the landlord the Land Court is satisfied that by reason of any change of circumstances or otherwise any such condition ought to be varied or revoked the Court must vary or revoke it.[25] Where the Court has imposed a condition to secure that the land will be used for the purpose for which the landlord has proposed to terminate the tenancy and it is proved on an application to the Court by the Crown that the landlord has not complied with the condition or has acted in contravention of it, the Land Court may impose a penalty on the landlord of an amount not exceeding two years' rent of the holding at the rate current immediately before the termination of the tenancy, or, if the notice to quit related to part only of the holding, an amount not exceeding the proportion thereof as the Court considers attributable to the part.[26]

Where the tenant serves a counter-notice, the landlord must apply to the Land Court for consent within one month of the service of the counter-notice.[27] A tenant who has received a notice to quit may require any question which may arise in connection with the notice under Section 25 (2) of the Act to be determined by arbitration under the Act, and, if so, he must notify the landlord to that effect within one month after service on him of the notice to quit,[28] and if the arbiter's award is such that the relevant provisions of the Act[29] would have applied to the notice to quit had a counter-notice been served under these provisions,[29] the period for serving it is extended to one month from the issue of the award.[28] The effect of requiring arbitration or of an application to the Court for consent is to suspend the operation of the notice until the issue of the award or of the Court's decision.[30] If the Court's decision giving consent or the award is issued later than six months before the date when the notice to quit is expressed to take effect, the Court may on application not later than one month after the issue of the decision or award postpone the operation of the notice for a period

possession " in a case where he applied for consent to part of the holding being used " for forestry purposes " and the success of this project was problematical. *Carnegie* v *Davidson*, 1966 S.L.T. (Land Ct.) 3.

[24] s. 26 (5). See Reserve &c. Forces Act 1951; 1958 Act, *infra*, paras. 45-6.
[25] s. 26 (6), as amended by 1958 Act, Schedule First, Part II, para. 36.
[26] s. 30 (1), as substituted by 1958 Act, Schedule First, Part II, para. 40.
[27] s. 27 (1), as substituted by 1958 Act, Schedule First, Part II, para. 37. See *supra*, p. 316, as to a successor of legatee.
[28] s. 27 (2), as substituted by 1958 Act, Schedule First, Part II, para. 37.
[29] s. 25 (1), as amended by 1958 Act, Schedule First, Part II, para. 35.
[30] s. 27 (3), as substituted by 1958 Act, Schedule First, Part II, para. 37.

not exceeding twelve months.[31] Where a second notice to quit was served about three weeks after the first one and it stated the same reason as the first and added a new one, and the tenant had before service of the second one required arbitration as to the first one which had not yet been determined, it was held that the operation of the second notice was not suspended pending the arbiter's award, for if two concurrent notices were given for different reasons and arbitration was required as to one only, the other remained effective.[32]. Where the reference to arbitration has been made to determine any question that has arisen under (f), the arbiter must not make an award in favour of the landlord where the tenancy is vested in an executor unless he is satisfied that it is reasonable that it should be made, having regard to the fact that the interest is vested in the executor in his capacity as executor.[33]

Effect of Notice to Quit where Holding Agreed to be Sold. Where notice to quit a holding has been given by the landlord to the tenant and while the notice is still current a contract for the sale of the landlord's interest in the whole or a part of the land is made,[34] the landlord and the tenant may make a written agreement whether the notice remains in force or ceases to be of effect, but it must be entered into within three months of the making of the contract of sale.[35] The validity of the notice is not affected merely because the operation of it is under the agreement conditional. If they do not make such an agreement within the three months, the landlord must within fourteen days from the making of the contract, or, where the notice expires within those fourteen days, before the expiry of the notice give written notice to the tenant of the making of the contract,[36] and before expiry of the notice to quit the tenant may not later than one month from receipt by him of the notice of making of the contract notify the landlord in writing that he elects that the notice remain in force.[37] If the landlord and the tenant do not make such an agreement or the tenant does not notify the landlord to the above effect the notice to quit is of no effect unless the landlord has failed duly to give notice of the contract and the tenant quits in consequence of the notice.[38]

Notice to Quit to Subtenant. Where the tenant has been given notice to quit and in consequence he gives notice to quit to a subtenant, the subtenant cannot avail himself of the provisions of the Act,[39] which do

---

[31] s. 27 (4), as substituted by 1958 Act, Schedule First, Part II, para. 37.
   See *e.g., Graham* v *Wilson-Clarke* (1962) 50 S.L.C.R. 35.
[32] *French* v *Elliott* [1959] 3 All E.R. 866.
[33] Succession (Scotland) Act 1964, s. 16 (6).
[34] s. 31 (1).
[35] s. 31 (2).
[36] s. 31 (2) (a).
[37] s. 31 (2) (b).
[38] s. 31 (3).
[39] s. 25 (1), as amended by 1958 Act, Schedule First, Part II, para. 35.

not apply to the notice to the subtenant, but if the tenant serves a counter-notice on the landlord under the Act[39] he must also serve on the subtenant written notice that he has served the counter-notice, and the subtenant is entitled to be a party to any proceedings before the Land Court for their consent to the notice to quit.[40] If the notice by the landlord to the tenant does not have effect, the notice to the subtenant also does not have effect.[41] A notice to quit part of a holding which is accepted by the tenant as one to quit the whole is treated as one to quit the whole holding.[41]

COMPENSATION PROVISIONS

Compensation for Disturbance. The landlord has to pay compensation for disturbance to his tenant where a tenancy of a holding terminates because either the tenant receives a notice to quit from the landlord or the tenant gives a counter-notice that he accepts a notice duly given to quit part of the holding as one to quit the entire holding, and in consequence of the notice or counter-notice the tenant quits the holding.[42] The compensation is not payable[43] where operation of the notice to quit is excluded under certain provisions of the Act.[44] Where the tenancy terminates because of a counter-notice and the part of the holding affected by the landlord's notice together with any part of the holding affected by any previous notice as is validated under the Act[45] is less than one-quarter of the area of the original holding or of a rental value less than one-quarter of the rental value of the original holding, and the holding as proposed to be diminished is reasonably capable of being farmed as a separate holding, compensation is not payable except as to the part of the holding to which the notice relates.[46] Where the tenant has lawfully sublet the whole or a part of the holding, and in consequence of a notice to quit from his landlord becomes liable to pay compensation to his subtenant, he is not debarred from recovering compensation merely because, owing to his not being in occupation on the termination of the tenancy, he does not quit the whole or the part of the holding.[47] Compensation under the Act is in addition to any other compensation to which the tenant may be entitled.[48] It is not payable[49] to a successor whose interest is terminated by the Land Court on the landlord's application,[50] and almost certainly is not payable too where the tenant is removed for non-payment of rent.[51]

[40] s. 27 (6), as substituted by 1958 Act, Schedule First, Part II, para. 37.
[41] s. 27 (5), as substituted by 1958 Act, Schedule First, Part II, para. 37.
[42] s. 35 (1).
[43] s. 35 (1), proviso.
[44] *Viz.*, s. 25 (2) (b), (d), (e), (f), (g); see *supra* at pp. 314-5.
[45] s. 32. See *supra*, p. 312.
[46] s. 35 (4).
[47] s. 35 (3).
[48] s. 35 (5).
[49] s. 21 (5), as substituted by Succession (Scotland) Act 1964, Schedule 2, para. 22.
[50] s. 21 (2), (3) as substituted by Succession (Scotland) Act 1964, Schedule 2, para. 22.
[51] s. 19.

21

It is essential that the tenant must have quitted the holding at the time specified in the notice, for the language and the provisions of the Act " plainly imply that the quitting of possession shall take place at or immediately after the termination of the tenancy ".[52] The notice need not be a valid one if it is accepted by the tenant.[53]

The amount of compensation is " the amount of the loss or expense directly attributable to the quitting of the holding which is unavoidably incurred by the tenant upon or in connection with the sale or removal of his household goods, implements of husbandry, fixtures, farm produce or farm stock on or used in connection with the holding ",[54] and includes " any expenses reasonably incurred by him in the preparation of his claim for compensation (not being expenses of an arbitration to determine any question arising under (the) section) ".[54] It has been held that a difference in quantity between grain as ascertained by arbiters under the lease on valuation and as actually threshed and delivered was not a loss " directly attributable " to the quitting of the holding but was one due to error of the arbiters in underestimating the quantity. The use of the term " directly " shows that what must be sought is the immediate cause —the *causa causans*—of the loss, and here that was error by the arbiters.[55] There is a loss " unavoidably incurred " where there is a difference between the prices obtained at a displenishing sale for stock and implements and their value to the tenant unsold.[56] The price realised at a displenishing sale is not conclusive of value to the tenant, and so where the going-concern value of a sheep stock to which the tenant was entitled was not realised on sale but only the break-up value, the difference between these values was held to be such a loss.[57]

The compensation is an amount equal to a year's rent of the holding at the rate at which rent was payable immediately before the tenancy terminated without the tenant having to make proof of any such loss or expenditure as is mentioned above.[58] " Rent " is defined[59] as the rent after deduction of such an amount as, failing agreement, the arbiter finds equivalent to the total of (a) the amount payable by the landlord in respect of the holding for the year of termination (the year in which the tenancy was terminated) by way of public rates, taxes, or assessments or other public burdens, the charging of which would entitle him

---

[52] *Hendry* v *Walker*, 1927 S.L.T. 333, *per* Lord Constable at 337.
[53] *Westlake* v *Page* [1926] 1 K.B. 298; *Kestell* v *Langmaid* [1950] 1 K.B. 233.
[54] s. 35 (2). Where a landlord had resumed, in terms of the lease, an acre in order to feu it as a site for a house it was held that the tenant could not, in the absence of express provision in the lease, claim compensation on the basis that he was entitled to use the area for a caravan site. The Acts did not give any right to use holdings for ancillary occupations. The court reserved their opinion whether a prohibition of " camping " in a lease included caravans: *Sinclair* v *Secretary of State for Scotland*, 1966 S.L.T. (Land Ct.) 2.
[55] *Macgregor* v *Board of Agriculture*, 1925 S.C. 613.
[56] *Barbour* v *McDouall*, 1914 S.C. 844.
[57] *Keswick* v *Wright*, 1924 S.C. 766.
[58] s. 35 (3), proviso (a).
[59] s. 35 (2).

to relief under the Income Tax Act 1952;[60] and (b) the amount (if any) recovered from the landlord in respect of that year under the Local Government (Scotland) Act 1929.[61] This last-mentioned item referred to a right of an occupier of agricultural land and heritages occupying under a lease entered into prior to 1st June 1928, to recover on 15th May in each year from the landlord by retention of rent a sum equal to the owner's share of rates for the year beginning on 16th May 1930 multiplied by two and a half times. It would seem that " public taxes " etc. is confined to local rating or taxes, income tax being one on income and not on property.[62] The scope of the term " rent ", whether including other payments, has not been determined. Stipend is not a valid deduction.[63]

The amount of one year's net rent as compensation is the minimum. The maximum is two year's net rent,[64] but the tenant cannot claim more than the minimum unless he has given to the landlord not less than one month's notice of the sale of his household goods, implements of husbandry, fixtures, farm produce and farm stock on or used in connection with the holding and has afforded the landlord a reasonable opportunity of making a valuation thereof.[65] Where a tenant gave notice of intention to claim compensation and then sold, without any further notice, stock and implements by public roup, he was held[66] to have given the landlord a " reasonable opportunity ", for the words of the Act do not necessarily imply that the tenant must take any active step until the landlord seeks the opportunity; he does not need to notify the landlord that he will have a reasonable opportunity. There is no duty on the tenant to do anything. Where, therefore, the tenant's loss and expense directly attributable to the quitting of the holding unavoidably incurred on or in connection with the sale or removal of his household goods etc. exceeds a year's rent, he can claim up to the maximum amount, apparently without the deductions where the claim is limited to the minimum.[67] If the tenant seeks to prove loss in excess of a year's rent but does not even establish as much as the loss of a year's rent he can still recover the minimum.[68]

Rights of compensation conferred by the 1949 Act are in lieu of such rights conferred by any former Act relating to holdings.[69]

[60] s. 95. The 1949 Act had the words " owner's rates or of any other public " but owner's rates were abolished by the Valuation and Rating (Scotland) Act 1956, s. 16, as from 16th May 1957, and that Act, s. 44, Schedule Seventh, Part III, repealed the words " owner's rates or of " and " other ".
[61] s. 47 (1).
[62] *Edinburgh Corporation* v *Lord Advocate*, 1923 S.C. 112.
[63] *Masterton* v *Board of Agriculture* 1924, not reported, where this was conceded.
[64] s. 35 (2), proviso (c).
[65] s. 35 (2), proviso (b).
[66] *Barbour* v *McDouall, supra.*
[67] Connell, *op. cit.,* 5th ed., p. 23.
[68] *McHarg* v *Speirs*, 1924 S.C. 272.
[69] s. 99 (10).

Compensation for Damage by Game. Where a tenant of a holding has sustained damage to his crops from game, the right to kill and take which is not vested in him or in anyone claiming under him other than the landlord and which he has not written permission to kill, he is entitled to compensation from his landlord for the damage if it exceeds in amount 1/- per acre of the area over which it extends.[70] " Game " is defined as " deer, pheasants, partridges, grouse and black game ".[71] Damage from game includes where the damage has been done by game, in the particular case black game, from a neighbouring estate, and even during the " close " season.[72] On the analogy of a decision on the terms of a lease before the first Act, where the damage exceeds 1/- per acre the full amount is recoverable without deduction of the first shilling.[73]

In order that the tenant may recover compensation, he must give written notice to the landlord as soon as may be after the damage was first observed by him and he must give a reasonable opportunity to the landlord to inspect the damage, in the case of damage to a growing crop before it is begun to be reaped, raised or consumed, and in the case of damage to a crop reaped or raised before it is begun to be removed from the land.[74] Written notice of the claim and particulars of it must also be given to the landlord within one month after the expiry of the calendar year (that is, 1st January to 31st December), or such other period of twelve months as may be substituted therefor by agreement of parties, in respect of which the claim is made.[75] Where written notice was given before the expiry of the calendar year it was held to have been competently given.[76] The Act merely prescribes a time limit on the expiry of which the claim prescribes if the notice and particulars have not been given.[77] The words mean " before the end of " one month or " not later than " the end of one month.[76] Where the right to kill and take game is vested in someone other than the landlord, the landlord is entitled to indemnification by that other person against all claims for compensation under the Act.[78] The landlord has thus a claim of relief.

The amount of compensation is, in default of agreement, determined by arbitration.[79] and any question arising about the landlord's claim of relief is determined by arbitration.[78]

If the tenant has permission from the landlord to kill any " game " defined in the Act and his crops are damaged by that particular species or kind of " game ", he is not entitled to compensation. So where he had written permission to kill deer, and deer damaged his crops, he could

[70] s. 15 (1).
[71] s. 15 (4).
[72] *Thomson* v *Earl of Galloway*, 1919 S.C. 611.
[73] *Roddan* v *McCowan* (1890) 17 R. 1056.
[74] s. 15 (1), proviso (a).
[75] s. 15 (1), proviso (b).
[76] *Earl of Morton's Trs.* v *Macdougall*, 1944 S.C. 410.
[77] *Earl of Morton's Trs., supra, per* L.J.C. Cooper at 413.
[78] s. 15 (3).
[79] s. 15 (2).

not claim compensation.[80] The basis of the legislation is the protection
of the tenant by permission to kill or the provision of compensation,[81]
and the word " game " is used distributively in the section.

The tenant has, of course, at common law the right to kill ground
game—hares and rabbits—and his position as regards protection against
damage by such is further safeguarded by the Ground Game Act 1880,
giving him the statutory right to kill such animals.

Rights to compensation conferred by the 1949 Act are again here
in lieu of rights to compensation conferred by any former Act relating
to holdings.[82]

The Agricultural Act 1948 Section 43 (1) gives an occupier of a
holding a right to kill deer on land other than moorland or unenclosed
land and it is also provided by Section 52 that nothing in the part of
that Act where that provision occurs is to preclude a right to compensation for damage which he would have had if that provision had not
been made. It has been held that the 1949 Act is a consolidating Act,
and though repealing the 1923 Act provision on compensation did not
intend to alter the rights to compensation given by the 1923 Act and
hence a tenant who had not permission in writing to kill game had a
right to compensation for damage done by deer to crops.[82a] The right
given by the 1948 Act is in addition to and does not derogate from
the right to compensation for damage done. " Such an additional right
cannot affect a right to compensation which (the tenant) would otherwise have had even if that additional right would have operated as a
bar to compensation in the pre-existing law."[82b]

Compensation for Improvements. Improvements which are classified
as Old or New, according to the date when they were begun, and are
also classified according to whether consent of or notice to the landlord
is necessary are contained in the First, Second and Third Schedules of
the Act (in the case of market gardens there are also certain special
or additional improvements in the Fourth Schedule). Those in the First
Schedule are " new improvements ". The First, Second and Third
Schedules apply to farms and market gardens. These three Schedules
are each further classed into Parts I, II and III. The improvements in
Part I comprise permanent improvements, those in Part III temporary
improvements, those in Part II drainage, formation of silos, road and
bridge making, water courses, permanent fences, reclaiming of waste
land, provision of sheep dipping accommodation and repairing and
renewal of embankments against floods, etc., and, further, in the case

[80] *Ross* v *Watson*, 1943 S.C. 406.
[81] *Ross, supra, per* L.J.C. Cooper at 418-9.
[82] s. 99 (10).
[82a] *Lady Auckland* v *Dowie*, 1965 S.L.T. 76, affirming 1964 S.L.T. (Land Ct.) 20.
The 1923 Act provision was in s. 11 (1) which is virtually identical with s. 15 (1)
of the 1949 Act.
[82b] *Ibid., per* Lord Wheatley at p. 80.

of new improvements, the erection of hay or sheaf sheds, provision of fixed threshing mills, barn machinery at fixed dairying plant, improvement of permanent pasture, sewage disposal and necessary repairs to fixed equipment (not being repairs which the tenant is bound to carry out).

Old Improvements. A tenant is entitled at the termination of his tenancy and on quitting the holding to compensation from his landlord for what are called " old improvements " carried out by him.[83] If, however, the improvement is one that he was required to carry out under the terms of the tenancy he cannot get compensation for it if the lease was entered into before 1st January 1921.[83] Where under the lease alternative methods of cropping were allowed, one producing an improvement, the other not doing so, and the tenant chose the former, it was held[84] that he could claim compensation, for he was not bound to choose that method. He had a choice and was not contractually required to carry out that one, to choose that method of cropping and thus to execute the improvement. Where an owner had sold his lands at the same time as the tenant quitted them, it was held[85] that the selling owner was the landlord under the Act and the obligation of compensation did not transmit.[86]

An " old improvement " is a 1923 Act improvement or a 1931 Act improvement;[87] a 1923 Act improvement is an improvement, specified in the Second Schedule of the 1949 Act, begun before 31st July 1931, while a 1931 Act improvement is one specified in the Third Schedule of the 1949 Act, begun at or after 31st July 1931 and before 1st November 1948.[88] The amount of compensation is " such sum as fairly represents the value of the improvement to an incoming tenant ".[89] In the case of feeding stuffs, the meaning of " manurial value " is the value of the manurial constituents thereof before the feeding stuff was consumed and no compensation is payable for feeding stuffs where they are included in dung not applied to the land.[90] In cases of difficulty the value can only be measured by the addition of value to the holding as a whole.[91] The tenant's right to claim compensation under any custom, agreement or otherwise in lieu of the foregoing compensation is not prejudiced by the Act.[92] The 1949 Act[93] is not to be construed as repealing the provision of the 1943 Act[94] in terms of which, where

[83] s. 37 (1).
[84] *Gibson* v *Sherret*, 1928 S.C. 493.
[85] *Waddell* v *Howat*, 1925 S.C. 484.
[86] *Waddell, supra.*
[87] s. 36 (2).
[88] s. 36 (1).
[89] s. 38.
[90] *Brown* v *Mitchell*, 1910 S.C. 369.
[91] *Mackenzie* v *Macgillivray*, 1921 S.C. 722 at 731, *per* L.P. Clyde.
[92] s. 37 (2). See s. 42, *infra.*
[93] s. 99 (8).
[94] ss. 15 (3), 19 (d).

a tenant, in order to comply with directions under Defence Regulations, has made an improvement by way of removal of tree roots, boulders or stones or other like obstacles to cultivation, whether in arable or other land, that improvement is deemed to be one under the 1931 Act First Schedule Part III, this, however, not applying to land to which the provisions of the 1940 Act apply.[95]

In the case of certain " old improvements ", neither the landlord's consent nor notice to him is necessary.[96]

In the case of certain old improvements, however, compensation is not payable unless before they are carried out the landlord has consented in writing to their being carried out, either unconditionally or on terms as to compensation or otherwise agreed on between him and the tenant,[97] and in the latter event the compensation under the agreement replaces the statutory compensation.[98] The improvements referred to here are 1923 Act improvements specified in Part I of the Second Schedule of the 1949 Act or 1931 Act improvements specified in Part I of the Third Schedule of the 1949 Act.[99] The consent need not be in a formal or probative deed.[1] It has been suggested that compensation for such improvements is not payable where the lease was entered into on or after 1st January 1921, even when the tenant contracted to make the

[95] 1943 Act, s. 15 (4).
[96] Second and Third Schedules, Part III.
[97] s. 39 (1).
[98] s. 39 (2).
[99] s. 39 (1), Schedule Second, Part I : —
    1. Erection, alteration, or enlargement of buildings.
    2. Formation of silos.
    3. Laying down of permanent pasture.
    4. Making and planting of osier beds.
    5. Making of water meadows or works of irrigation.
    6. Making of gardens.
    7. Making or improvement of roads or bridges.
    8. Making or improvement of watercourses, ponds, wells, or reservoirs, or of works for the application of water power or for supply of water for agricultural or domestic purposes.
    9. Making or removal of permanent fences.
   10. Planting of hops.
   11. Planting of orchards or fruit bushes.
   12. Protecting young fruit trees.
   13. Reclaiming of waste land.
   14. Warping or weiring of land.
   15. Embankments and sluices against floods.
   16. Erection of wirework in hop gardens.
   17. Provision of permanent sheep dipping accommodation.
   18. In the case of arable land the removal of bracken, gorse, tree roots, boulders, or other like obstructions to cultivation.
    Schedule Third, Part I : —
    1. Erection, alteration or enlargement of buildings.
    2. Laying down of permanent pasture.
    3. Making and planting of osier beds.
    4. Making of water meadows or works of irrigation.
    5. Making of gardens.
    6. Planting of orchards or fruit trees.
    7. Protecting young fruit trees.
    8. Warping or weiring of land.
    9. Making of embankments and sluices against floods.
[1] s. 85.

improvements.[2] Where the landlord under the lease gave his consent to the planting of fruit bushes and the erection of sheds and the lease provided that compensation could be claimed if it was claimed before a certain date (the expiry of the lease) in respect of the bushes, but no compensation was to be paid for the sheds, and the tenant could remove the sheds and, if no compensation was claimed, the bushes before the expiry of the lease, it was held[3] that he was entitled to make this condition, and the tenant not having fulfilled it was not entitled to compensation, and the prohibition of compensation for the sheds was not invalid. The section does not allow the landlord to contract out but allows the tenant to contract into the right to obtain such compensation. Parties are free to negotiate any bargain they please as to compensation and any other matter relative to the making of the improvements and the effect of its execution on their respective rights and obligations, provided no term of the bargain infringes any provision of the Act or is otherwise unlawful. The landlord can refuse his consent if he likes. If conditions are prescribed, no intention in the Act to circumscribe these can be deduced; the landlord is master of the situation. There is no good reason in equity or in policy, said Lord Wark,[4] why landlord and tenant should not be left to make their own bargain. If the tenant is expressly permitted, as opposed to being obliged, by a written lease to make some of these improvements, this is probably " consent in writing ".[5]

In the case of a certain other old improvement under the 1923 Act (*viz.* drainage, specified in the 1949 Act Second Schedule Part II) compensation is not payable unless the tenant not more than three nor less than two months before he began to carry out the improvement, gave to the landlord written notice under the 1923 Act[6] of his intention to carry it out and of the manner in which he proposed to carry it out, and unless in addition parties agreed on the terms as to compensation or otherwise on which the improvement was to be made or, if there was no such agreement and the tenant did not withdraw the notice, the landlord did not exercise his right under the 1923 Act[6] to carry out the improvement himself within a reasonable time.[7] If he did not do the work within a reasonable time, the tenant could do it himself and claim compensation. Landlord and tenant may agree by the lease or otherwise to dispense with notice, and in that event the foregoing provision is not applicable.[8] Knowledge of the landlord or his factor or acquiescence or even an agreement which was without reference to the Act but in accordance with estate custom by either of them to the

[2] Connell, *op. cit.*, 5th ed., p. 153.
[3] *Turnbull* v *Millar*, 1942 S.C. 521.
[4] *Turnbull, supra,* at 550.
[5] Connell, *op. cit.*, 5th ed., p. 26.
[6] s. 3.
[7] 1949 Act, s. 40 (1).
[8] s. 40 (1), *proviso*.

tenant's scheme of drainage was held not to imply dispensing with the notice.[9] It has been held[10] that such an agreement need not be in writing, but the Court in a later case reserved their opinion on this point.[9] There is a similar provision[11] in regard to certain old improvements under the 1931 Act (those specified in the 1949 Act Third Schedule Part II)[12] except (1) that the tenant's notice must be not more than six months nor less than three months before he began to carry out the improvement; (2) that, where the landlord gave notice of objection and the matter was, under the 1931 Act,[13] referred for determination by the Department of Agriculture for Scotland in the case of the period before 4th September 1939, and in the case of the period commencing on that day the Secretary of State for Scotland,[14] the Department or the Secretary of State must be satisfied that the improvement should be carried out and it was carried out in accordance with the directions (if any) given by the Department or the Secretary of State as to the manner in which it was to be carried out; and (3) that the provision as to these 1931 Act improvements is not applicable not only where parties agreed by lease to dispense with notice but also where the improvement consists of drainage which was carried out by the tenant in order to comply with directions under Defence Regulations but which he was not required to do under the terms of the tenancy. If landlord and tenant agreed, whether after notice under the 1923 Act or by agreement to dispense with such notice, on the terms of compensation for the improvement, then the compensation payable under that agreement is substituted for compensation under the Act.[15]

In the case of old improvements in the form of repairs to buildings, being buildings necessary for the proper cultivation or working of the holding, other than repairs which the tenant is himself under obligation to execute[16] and which are included in the Parts of the Schedules specifying improvements for which the consent of or notice to the landlord of their execution is not necessary for a claim for compensation, it is

[9] *Barbour* v *McDouall,* 1914 S.C. 844.
[10] *Hamilton Ogilvy* v *Elliot* (1905) 7 F. 1115.
[11] s. 40 (2).
[12] Schedule Third, Part II : —
    10. Drainage.
    11. Formation of silos.
    12. Making or improvement of roads or bridges.
    13. Making or improvement of watercourses, ponds or wells, or of works for the application of water power or for the supply of water for agricultural or domestic purposes.
    14. Making or removal of permanent fences.
    15. Reclaiming of waste land.
    16. Repairing or renewal of embankments and sluices against floods.
    17. Provision of sheep dipping accommodation.
    18. The provision of electrical equipment other than moveable fittings and appliances.
[13] s. 28 (2).
[14] s. 40 (4).
[15] s. 40 (3). See s. 42.
[16] Second Schedule, Part II, para. 29 and Third Schedule, Part III, para. 29.

provided[17] that compensation is not to be payable unless before beginning to execute the repairs, the tenant gave to the landlord written
notice under the 1923[18] or the 1931[19] Acts of intention to execute the
repairs with particulars thereof and the landlord did not exercise his
rights under these Acts to execute the repairs himself within a reasonable time after receipt of the notice.

If a written agreement, which does not need to be formal or probative, was made before 1st January 1921, under which " fair and
reasonable " compensation, having regard to the then existing circumstances, was secured to the tenant for an old improvement specified in
Part III of the Second or Part III of the Third Schedule of the Act,
that compensation is substituted for the statutory compensation under
the 1949 Act as respects that improvement.[20] It has been held that it
is for the arbiter to decide whether it is " fair and reasonable ", but
his decision may be reviewed by the Court. If it is, as is usual, embodied
in a formal lease there is a strong presumption that it is " fair and
reasonable ".[21] A party seeking to repudiate the agreement must con-
descend particularly on the provisions objected to and the reasons why
it is alleged that the compensation is not " fair and reasonable ".[21] There
is often a scale annexed to the agreement and this scale must be looked
at as a whole.[22]

Although the laying down or the leaving at the termination of the
tenancy of temporary pasture[23] was in breach of the terms of the lease
or of any agreement made by the tenant regarding the method of
cropping the arable lands, he is entitled to compensation for an old
improvement under the 1931 Act in laying down temporary pasture
with clover, grass, lucerne sainfoin, or other seeds sown more than two
years prior to the termination of the tenancy, in so far as the value of
the temporary pasture on the holding at the time of quitting exceeds
the value of the temporary pasture at the commencement of the tenancy[24]
for which the tenant did not pay compensation.[25] It has been suggested[26]
that the temporary pasture at the commencement of the tenancy must
have been sown more than two years prior to the commencement.
Second year's grass is usually sown more than two years before the
tenancy terminates and is " temporary pasture ".[27] The pasture must

[17] s. 41.
[18] First Schedule, para. 29.
[19] First Schedule, para. 30.
[20] s. 42.
[21] Bell v Graham, 1908 S.C. 1060. See also Brown v Mitchell, 1910 S.C. 369.
[22] Brown, supra.
[23] Pasture includes meadow: s. 93 (1).
[24] See Findlay v Munro, 1917 S.C. 419, per Lord Salvesen at 426-7 and Lord
    Guthrie at 428 that constructively a sitting tenant who enters a new lease takes
    over from himself—it is the commencement of the lease under which he was
    occupying when he quitted. See also Earl of Galloway v McClelland, 1915 S.C.
    1062, per Lord Johnston at 1082.
[25] s. 43; Schedule Third, para. 28.
[26] Connell, op. cit., 5th ed., p. 35.
[27] Earl of Galloway, supra, per Lord Johnston at 1083.

have been laid down after the passing of the 1931 Act on 31st July 1931.[28] The arbiter in assessing the amount of compensation therefor must take into account any injury to, or deterioration of, the holding due to the breach of the lease except in so far as the landlord has recovered damages in respect of such injury or deterioration.[29] This applies only to temporary pasture laid down after the passing of the 1931 Act,[30] whether or not the lease was made before or after the passing of the Act. Conflicting views were expressed[31] whether leaving pasture that might have been broken up was equivalent to " laying down " pasture; Lord Anderson considered that it was, but Lord Salvesen and Lord Guthrie held the contrary opinion.

Compensation is not payable for an old improvement carried out on land which when it was begun was not a holding within the 1923 Act and would not have fallen to be treated as such by virtue of Section thirty-three of that Act.[32]

In assessing the amount of compensation under the Act there has to be taken into account (a) any benefit which the landlord has given or allowed to the tenant in consideration of the tenant carrying out the improvement, whether or not expressly stated in the lease to be so given or allowed, and (b) in the case of manuring (that is, any of the improvements specified in paragraphs 25-27 of the Second and Third Schedules of the Act[33]), the value of the manure required by the lease or custom to be returned to the holding in respect of any crops grown on and sold off or removed from the holding within the last two years of the tenancy or other less time for which the tenancy has endured, not exceeding the value of the manure which would have been produced by the consumption on the holding of the crops so sold off or removed.[34] Manuring is defined[35] as the application to land of purchased artificial or other purchased manure, or the consumption on the holding by cattle, sheep or pigs or by horses other than those regularly employed on the holding of corn, cake or other feeding stuff not produced on the holding or of corn proved by satisfactory evidence to have been produced and consumed on the holding. Apart from the terms of the lease nothing is taken into account in respect of the waygoing crop, and it is not usual for the outgoing tenant to return manure in respect of it. Where the improvement is by the addition of lime and a contribution has been made in respect of it under the Agriculture Act 1937,[36] the contribution

---

[28] 1931 Act, s. 40.
[29] 1949 Act, s. 43.
[30] See 1931 Act, s. 40, that compensation for any improvement made or begun before 31st July, 1931, shall be such as if that Act had not been passed.
[31] *Findlay, supra.*
[32] s. 44 (4).
[33] s. 44 (5).
[34] s. 44 (1). See s. 62, *infra,* p. 341, by which a ploughing grant is treated as benefit.
[35] s. 44 (5), referring to Second and Third Schedules, paras. 25 to 27.
[36] Part I.

is taken into account in assessing compensation under the 1949 Act or a custom or an agreement, as a benefit allowed to the tenant in consideration of carrying out the improvement.[37] And where the improvement consists of drainage which was carried out by the tenant for the purpose of complying with directions given under Defence Regulations but which he was not required to carry out by the terms of the tenancy, then, in assessing compensation under the Act, if it is shown to the satisfaction of the assessor that the improvement consisted of, or was wholly or in part the result of or incidental to, operations in respect of which a grant has been made or is to be made to the tenant out of monies provided by Parliament, this grant is also to be treated as a benefit and the compensation reduced to such an extent as the assessor thinks appropriate.[38] It was held[39] that the mere non-termination of a lease was not a " benefit ", but if the landlord had proved prolongation of the tenancy in respect of an undertaking to execute the improvements the Court indicated that that might have been held to be a " benefit ". A contractual right to take two white crops in succession off land which had lain three years in grass was regarded as not being a " benefit ";[40] and acceptance of a lower rent in respect of obligations in the lease to apply manures was held also not to be a benefit as not specially allowed.[41]

Where the tenant has remained in the holding during two or more tenancies, e.g., successive leases or tenancies from year to year, he can still claim compensation for old improvements notwithstanding that they were not carried out during the tenancy on the termination of which he quits the holding but were effected during the previous lease or year.[42] A sitting tenant constructively takes over any improvements every time the lease is renewed.[43] It is suggested that a change in the rent or the conditions of the tenancy or resumption of part of the farm would not affect the application of this rule, and that a material reduction in the area of the subjects let would not affect the application in relation to improvements in the remaining part.[44]

Where an improvement was made or begun before 1st January 1909, the date of commencement of the 1908 Act, or made on a holding held under a lease other than a year to year lease current on 1st January 1884, the compensation is such (if any) as could have been claimed if the 1923-1948 and 1949 Acts had not been passed, but the procedure for ascertaining and recovering the compensation is that under the 1949 Act and the amount is payable, recoverable and chargeable as if it were

[37] s. 44 (2).
[38] s. 44 (3).
[39] Mackenzie v Macgillivray, 1921 S.C. 722.
[40] Findlay, supra, per Lord Salvesen at 426 and Lord Guthrie at 428.
[41] McQuater v Fergusson, 1911 S.C. 640.
[42] s. 45.
[43] See note, p. 330, supra.
[44] Connell, op. cit., 5th ed., p. 162.

compensation under the Act.[45] If, in case of an old improvement, the tenant has, on entering into occupation of the holding, with the written consent of the landlord and under an agreement made before 1st November 1948, paid to an outgoing tenant any compensation payable under or in pursuance of the 1923-1948 or the 1949 Acts in respect of the whole or part of such an improvement, or if he has, in the case of an old improvement of the kind specified in Part III of the First Schedule of the 1949 Act (that is, temporary improvements), with the written consent of the landlord and in pursuance of an agreement made after 1st November 1948 paid to an outgoing tenant compensation payable under these Acts in respect of the whole or a part of such an improvement, he can, on quitting the holding, claim compensation for the whole or the part of the improvement as the outgoing tenant could have done had he remained tenant and quitted the holding at the time when the tenant quits it.[46] The consent does not require to be in a formal or probative form.[47] Agreements by the incoming tenant with the landlord to pay to an outgoing tenant compensation or to relieve the landlord of such are, with certain exceptions, null and void.[48]

It is not decided whether the tenant can claim where manurial improvements, for example, have been made by a sub-tenant.[49]

New Improvements. A tenant is entitled at the termination of the tenancy and on quitting the holding to compensation from his landlord for what are called " new improvements " carried out by him,[50] but if the lease was entered into before 1st January 1921 he is not entitled to compensation for any improvement he was bound to carry out under the terms of the tenancy.[51] The tenant's right to claim compensation under a written agreement in lieu of any statutory compensation for a new improvement is not prejudiced by the Act.[52] A " new improvement " is an improvement specified in the First Schedule of the Act, begun on or after 1st November 1948, whether or not the tenant entered into occupation of the holding before or after that date.[53] The amount of compensation is " such sum as fairly represents the value of the improvement to an incoming tenant ".[54] In ascertaining this figure there must be taken into account any benefit under a written agreement given or allowed to the tenant by the landlord in consideration of carrying out the improvement, and any grant out of monies provided by Parliament

[45] s. 96.
[46] s. 46. See Opencast Coal Act 1958, s. 24, *infra,* p. 339.
[47] s. 85.
[48] s. 11. See *infra,* p. 337.
[49] See Connell, *op. cit.,* 5th ed., p. 24.
[50] s. 48 (1).
[51] s. 48 (1), *proviso.*
[52] s. 48 (3).
[53] s. 47 (1), (2).
[54] s. 49 (1).

which has been or will be made to the tenant in respect of the improvement,[55] *e.g.* under the Hill Farming Act 1946. It will be noted that the benefit in the case of new improvements in contrast to the case of old improvements must be under a written agreement; and that manuring is not taken into account in regard to new improvements.

In the case of certain new improvements it is not necessary for notice to be given to the landlord or for his consent to be obtained.[56]

In the case of certain new improvements,[57] however, it is necessary, in order that compensation may be payable, that before the improvement is carried out the landlord has given written consent to its carrying out, either unconditionally or on terms as to compensation or otherwise agreed on between him and the tenant.[58] The consent need not be in a formal or probative deed.[59] Where the consent is given on terms as to compensation agreed on, the compensation payable under the agreement is substituted for that under the Act.[60] If the tenant is expressly permitted to execute some of the improvements under a written lease, this may be consent in writing.[61]

[55] s. 49 (2). See s. 62, *infra*, p. 341, by which a ploughing grant is treated as a benefit.

[56] Schedule First, Part III:—
24. Protecting fruit trees against animals.
25. Chalking of land.
26. Clay burning.
27. Claying of land.
28. Liming of land.
29. Marling of land.
30. Eradication of bracken, whins or broom growing on the holding at the commencement of the tenancy and, in the case of arable land, removal of tree roots, boulders, stones, or other like obstacles to cultivation.
31. Application to land of purchased manure (including artificial manure).
32. Consumption on the holding of corn (whether produced on the holding or not) or of cake or other feeding stuff not produced on the holding by (a) horses, cattle, sheep or pigs, or (b) poultry folded on the land as part of a system of farming practised on the holding.
33. Laying down temporary pasture with clover, grass, lucerne sainfoin or other seeds, sown more than two years prior to the termination of the tenancy, in so far as the value of the temporary pasture on the holding at the time of quitting exceeds the value of the temporary pasture on the holding at the commencement of the tenancy for which the tenant did not pay compensation.

[57] Schedule First, Part I:—
1. Laying down of permanent pasture.
2. Making of water-meadows or works of irrigation.
3. Making of gardens.
4. Planting of orchards or fruit bushes.
5. Warping or weiring of land.
6. Making of embankments and sluices against floods.
7. Making or planting of osier beds.
8. Haulage or other work done by the tenant in aid of the carrying out of any improvement made by the landlord for which the tenant is liable to pay increased rent.

[58] s. 50 (1). See *Turnbull* v *Millar*, 1942 S.C. 521. *Supra*, p. 328.
[59] s. 85.
[60] s. 50 (2).
[61] Connell, *op. cit.*, 5th ed., p. 26.

In the case of certain other new improvements,[62] the tenant must not less than three months before he begins to carry out the improvement notify the landlord in writing of his intention to carry it out and the manner in which he proposes to carry it out, otherwise compensation is not payable.[63] If such notice is given, then the landlord and the tenant may agree in writing as to the terms regarding compensation or otherwise on which the improvement is to be carried out, and in that event the compensation so agreed is substituted for the statutory compensation.[64] It is open to the landlord and the tenant, by the lease or otherwise, to agree in writing that notice is not necessary: such an agreement may provide for anything that may be provided by an agreement as to the terms of compensation, etc., and, if it does, will be as valid and effective as an agreement as to the terms of compensation, etc.[65]

Where, however, the landlord within a month of receipt of notice from the tenant notifies the tenant in writing that he objects to the carrying out of the improvement or the manner in which the tenant proposes to carry it out, compensation is not payable,[66] but the tenant may apply to the Land Court for approval of the carrying out of the improvement; the Court may refuse its approval or may approve unconditionally or on such terms as to the reduction of the compensation

---

[62] Schedule First, Part II:—
9. Land drainage.
10. Construction of silos.
11. Making or improvement of farm access or service roads, bridges and fords.
12. Making or improvement of watercourses, ponds or wells, or works for the application of water power for agricultural or domestic purposes or for the supply of water for such purposes.
13. Making or removal of permanent fences, including hedges, stone dykes and gates.
14. Reclaiming of waste land.
15. Renewal of embankments and sluices against floods.
16. Provision of stells, fanks, folds, dippers, pens and bughts necessary for the proper conduct of holding.
17. Provision or laying on of electric light or power, including the provision of generating plant, fixed meters, wiring systems, switches and plug sockets.
18. Erection, alteration or enlargement of buildings and making or improvement of permanent yards, loading banks and stocks.
19. Erection of hay or sheaf sheds, sheaf or grain drying racks, and implement sheds.
20. Provision of fixed threshing mills, barn machinery and fixed dairying plant.
21. Improvement of permanent pasture by cultivation and reseeding.
22. Provision of means of sewerage disposal.
23. Repairs to fixed equipment, being equipment reasonably required for the efficient farming of the holding, other than repairs which the tenant is under an obligation to carry out.
Note that the landlord's consent is not, in the case of new improvements, needed for the erection, alteration or enlargement of buildings.
[63] s. 51 (1).
[64] s. 51 (2).
[65] s. 51 (3).
[66] s. 52 (1).

that would be payable if the Court approved unconditionally or as to other matters, as appear to the Court to be just.[67] If the Court approves of the carrying out of the improvement, the landlord, within a month of receipt of the Court's decision, may notify the tenant in writing that he will himself carry out the improvement.[68] If, however, the landlord either does not give this notice or gives it and the Court later, on the tenant's application, holds that the landlord has not carried out the improvement within a reasonable time, the tenant may do it himself and will be entitled to compensation as if the landlord had not given notice of objection, and any terms of approval will have effect as if contained in a written agreement between landlord and tenant.[69]

Although the laying down or the leaving at the termination of the tenancy of temporary pasture was in breach of the terms of the lease or of any agreement by the tenant as to the mode of cropping the arable lands, the tenant is none the less entitled to compensation for the laying down of the temporary pasture with clover, grass, lucerne sainfoin, or other seeds, sown more than two years prior to the termination of the tenancy, in so far as the value of the temporary pasture on the holding at the time of quitting exceeds the value of the temporary pasture on the holding at the commencement of the tenancy[70] for which the tenant did not pay compensation; but in ascertaining the amount of compensation the arbiter must take into account any injury to or deterioration of the holding due to the breach except in so far as the landlord has recovered damages in respect of it.[71]

The tenant is entitled to compensation for new improvements where he has remained in the holding during two or more tenancies, notwithstanding that the improvements were not carried out during the tenancy on the termination of which he quits the holding.[72] If, on entering into occupation of the holding, the incoming tenant under a written agreement[73] with his landlord by which he undertakes to pay to the outgoing tenant (up to a maximum stated in the agreement) any compensation payable by the landlord under or in pursuance of the 1923-1948 or the 1949 Acts in respect of an improvement of the kind specified in the First Schedule Part III[74] or to refund to the landlord up to that maximum any compensation payable by the landlord, has paid to the outgoing tenant or refunded to the landlord any compensation payable by the landlord under or in pursuance of these Acts in respect of the whole or part of a new improvement, then on his quitting the holding he can claim compensation for the improvement or part of it in like manner

[67] s. 52 (2), as amended by 1958 Act, Schedule First, Part II, para. 41.
[68] s. 52 (3), as amended, *supra.*
[69] s. 52 (4), as amended, *supra.*
[70] See note 24, p. 330, *supra.*
[71] s. 53; Schedule First, para. 33. See also *Earl of Galloway, supra, per* Lord Johnston at 1082.
[72] s. 54.
[73] See s. 11 (2).
[74] See note 56, *supra,* p. 334.

as the outgoing tenant would have been entitled had he remained tenant and quitted when the tenant quits.[75] If in any other case the tenant on entering paid to the landlord any amount for the whole or a part of a new improvement, then, subject to any written agreement between the landlord and the tenant, he can when he quits claim compensation for the whole or the part of the improvement, as he would have been entitled to claim had he been tenant when the improvement was carried out by him.[76]

Improvements under Repealed Acts. Compensation for an improvement made or begun before 1st January 1909 (the date of commencement of the 1908 Act) or made on a holding held under a lease, other than a lease from year to year current on 1st January 1884, is such amount, if any, as could have been claimed if the 1923-1948 and the 1949 Acts had not been passed. The procedure for ascertainment and recovery, however, is that provided by the 1949 Act and the amount so ascertained is payable, recoverable and chargeable as if it were compensation under the 1949 Act.[77] Thus, some of the repealed Acts remain in force for the limited purpose of determining the compensation claimable and the conditions under which it is payable. The rights to compensation conferred by the 1949 Act are, however, in lieu of rights of compensation conferred by any former Act relating to holdings.[78]

Agreements in Relation to Compensation. An agreement made after 1st November 1948 by an incoming tenant with the landlord by which the former undertakes to pay to an outgoing tenant any compensation payable by the landlord under or in pursuance of the 1923-1948 or 1949 Acts in respect of improvements or to refund to the landlord any such compensation paid by the landlord to the outgoing tenant is null and void;[79] but this does not apply to a written agreement between the incoming tenant and the landlord by which the former undertakes to pay to the outgoing tenant, up to a maximum stated in the agreement, any compensation payable by the landlord under or in pursuance of these Acts in respect of the whole or part of temporary improvements specified in the 1949 Act[80] or to refund to the landlord up to that maximum any compensation so payable that the landlord has paid to an outgoing tenant.[81]

[75] s. 55 (1).
[76] s. 55 (2).
[77] s. 96.
[78] s. 99 (10).
[79] s. 11 (1).
[80] Schedule First, Part III. See note 56, *supra*, p. 334.
[81] s. 11 (2).

22

Compensation to Successor Tenant. A tenant who after 1st August 1958 has acquired right to a lease as the successor of the former tenant or as a legatee[82] is not deprived, on quitting in pursuance of a notice to quit,[83] of a right to compensation for an improvement under the First Schedule Part II of the 1949 Act[84] carried out between 1st November 1948 and 1st August 1958 merely because of the failure of the person who carried it out to notify the landlord in terms of the 1949 Act[85] of his intention to carry it out;[86] but a claim cannot be made unless the Land Court on his application (1) are satisfied that, if notice had been given, the landlord would not have given a notice of objection[87] or, if he had, the Secretary of State would not have withheld his approval of the carrying out of the improvement, and (2) authorise the claim.[88] The compensation payable in this case is not to exceed either such sum as fairly represents the value of the improvement to an incoming tenant or such sum as is equal to the capital cost less a tenth of such cost for each complete year that has elapsed between the completion of the carrying out of the improvement and the tenant's quitting of the holding, whichever is the less.[89]

Power of Secretary of State to Vary Schedules. After consulting those who appear to him to represent the interests of landlords and tenants the Secretary of State may vary the First and the Fourth Schedules by order.[90] His order must be contained in a statutory instrument, which must be approved by resolution of each House of Parliament.[91] The order may provide as to the operation of the Act in relation to tenancies current when the order takes effect in such way as appears to the Secretary of State just having regard to the variation, but the right of a tenant to claim, for an improvement begun before the order was made, compensation that he would but for the order be entitled to claim is not affected by the order.[92]

Application to Crown Land. The Crown Lands Act 1927,[93] under which the Commissioners of Crown Lands could pay out of capital the cost of carrying out certain improvements and other works, applied to compensation payable by the Commissioners for certain new improve-

82 Under s. 20.
83 Under 1958 Act, s. 6 (3).
84 See note 62, *supra*, p. 335.
85 Under s. 51.
86 1958 Act, s. 6 (5).
87 Under s. 52.
88 1958 Act, s. 6 (5), *proviso* (a).
89 *Ibid.*, s. 6 (5), *proviso* (b).
90 s. 79 (1).
91 s. 79 (3).
92 s. 79 (2). See Opencast Coal Act 1958, ss. 26, 28.
93 s. 15.

ments[94] or market garden improvements[95] begun on or after 1st November 1948 as the Act applies to the cost specified[93] therein.[96] Any compensation payable by the Commissioners under Part III of the First, Second and Third Schedules was paid as part of the expenses of management of the land revenues of the Crown.[96] These provisions are repealed.[96]

Effect of Crofters Act 1955 etc.[97] The Crofters Act 1955[98] provides that nothing in the Act affects the provisions of the 1949 Act as to payment to an outgoing tenant of compensation for improvements, but compensation is not payable under the 1949 Act for any improvements[99] for which compensation is payable under the 1955 Act.[1] When, however, any improvements are valued under the 1949 Act with a view to payment of compensation to a crofter, the valuation is made by the Land Court unless landlord and crofter otherwise agree in writing.[99]

Under the Opencast Coal Act 1958,[2] where there has been a compulsory rights order in favour of the National Coal Board—an opencast site order or a storage site order—if before the date of entry there have been carried out improvements qualifying for compensation,[3] whether begun before or after 1st November 1948, or a special system of farming,[4] then at the end of the period of occupation, if he has lost the benefit of any improvements or of a special system of farming, the tenant is entitled to compensation as if his tenancy had ended and he had quitted at the end of the period of occupation. All the provisions of the 1949 Act then apply as to the making of claims, the calculating and recovering of compensation, etc., with amendments as to the time for giving notice of intention to claim and as to the time for settling claims;[5] but this is subject to deductions[6] in respect of the amount of compensation due to the landlord in respect of deterioration, etc. of the holding,[7] excluding the part of the holding not covered by the order. Any provisions as to making the right to compensation depend on notice or the making of a claim are disregarded.[8] Where again agricultural land is occupied by the National Coal Board in the exercise of rights under a compulsory rights order compensation is payable by the Board to the tenant for certain improvements[9] (those where consent or notice are not needed) carried

[94] Schedule First, Parts I and II. See notes 57, 62, *supra*, pp. 334-5.
[95] Schedule Fourth, paras. 1, 2, 5. See *infra*, p. 360.
[96] 1949 Act, s. 86 (3), repealed by Crown Estate Act 1961, Third Schedule.
[97] See *infra*, pp. 443 *et seq.*
[98] s. 14 (10).
[99] See *infra*, p. 454.
[1] that is, under s. 14 (10).
[2] s. 24 (1), (2), (3).
[3] Under Schedule First, Parts I and II. See notes 57, 62, *supra*, pp. 334-5.
[4] Under s. 56. See *infra*.
[5] Opencast Coal Act, s. 24 (6).
[6] *Ibid.*, s. 25 (1).
[7] Under 1949 Act, ss. 57, 58, *infra*.
[8] Opencast Coal Act, s. 25 (2).
[9] *Ibid.*, s. 26 6), and Schedule Fourth, Part IV, which is in the same terms as Schedule Fourth, Part III of the 1949 Act—*infra*, p. 361—with the substitution of " land " for " holding ".

out by the tenant before the date of entry under the order.[10] The amount of compensation is the sum payable under the 1949 Act had the tenant quitted at the date of entry.[11]

Compensation for Continuous Adoption of Special Standard of Farming. Where a tenant proves that the value of a holding to an incoming tenant has been increased during his tenancy by the continuous adoption of a standard of farming or a system of farming which has been more beneficial to the holding than the standard or system required by the lease, or, in so far as no system of farming is required by the lease, than the system normally practised on comparable holdings in the district, the tenant when he quits the holding can obtain compensation from the landlord, namely, " such compensation as represents the value to an incoming tenant of the adoption of that standard or system ".[12] The tenant must give written notice to the landlord of his intention to claim compensation not later than one month before the termination of the tenancy, and a record[13] of the condition of the fixed equipment on the holding and of the cultivation of the holding must have been made.[14] Compensation is not, therefore, payable in respect of any matter arising before the date of the record or, if there has been more than one record during the tenancy, before the date of the first record.[14] The tenant, however, cannot recover in virtue of these provisions for an old or a new improvement or an improvement to which the market gardens provisions of the Act apply any compensation which he could not otherwise have recovered.[15] In assessing the compensation, due allowance must be made for any compensation agreed or awarded for an old or a new improvement which has caused or contributed to the benefit.[16] The term " high farming " is the term colloquially used for this matter, but it is not a legal term for a claim under the Act.[17]

Compensation in relation to Parts of Holdings. If a tenancy of part of a holding terminates because of a notice to quit that part, given for the purpose of adjusting the boundaries between agricultural units or

[10] *Ibid.*, s. 26.
[11] *Ibid.*, s. 26 (3).
[12] 1949 Act, s. 56 (1).
[13] See *infra*, p. 353.
[14] s. 56 (1), *proviso.*
[15] s. 56 (3).
[16] s. 56 (2). Prior to the 1923 Act the effects, though the manurial value was exhausted, of the application of feeding stuffs consumed on or manures applied to a holding were too remote for a claim for compensation; there was no claim allowed for cumulative fertility. The 1923 Act, s. 9, allowed a claim for those effects but nothing of the nature of cumulative fertility is allowed in assessing compensation for improvements.
[17] See Connell, *op. cit.*, 5th ed., p. 168. In *Brodie-Innes* v *Brown*, 1917 1 S.L.T. 49, the Court held the phrase in an arbiter's award " continuous good farming " during the whole tenancy whereby the fertility of the farm was greatly increased was *ultra vires* and could not be explained away in the absence of joint averment of interpretation of it.

amalgamating agricultural units or parts thereof, or with a view to the use of the land for certain purposes—the notice stating that it is so given—or if the landlord resumes possession of part of the holding in terms of the lease, the provisions of the Act as to compensation apply as if that part were a separate holding which the tenant has quitted in consequence of a notice to quit.[18] Where the landlord has resumed possession of part of a holding under the lease, then in assessing compensation for the tenant the arbiter must take into account any benefit or relief allowed to the tenant under the lease in respect of the resumed land.[19] If land in a lease is not a " holding " only because it includes land, called " non-statutory land ", which because of the nature of the buildings on it or the use to which it is put would not, if separately let, be an " agricultural holding ", the provisions as to compensation for disturbance or for improvements apply, unless it is otherwise agreed in writing, to the part of the land other than the non-statutory land as if it was a holding.[20]

Compensation where Holding is Divided. Where a holding has become vested in more than one person in several parts and there has been no apportionment of the rent payable by the tenant either with his consent or under any Act, the tenant can require that any compensation payable to him under the Act shall be determined as if the holding had not been divided; the arbiter, where necessary, must apportion the amount of compensation awarded between those persons who constitute the landlord, any additional expenses of the award due to the apportionment being directed to be paid by those persons in such proportions as the arbiter determines.[21]

Compensation in respect of Ploughing Grants. Where a tenant of a holding has received payment of a ploughing grant under the Agricultural Development Act 1939[22] or has applied or is to apply for such a payment, then, in assessing compensation under the Act or by custom or agreement, if it is shown to the assessor's satisfaction that the improvement or cultivations in respect of which compensation is claimed were wholly or partly the result of or incidental to the operations by virtue of which the grant became payable, the grant must be taken into account as if it were a benefit allowed to the tenant in consideration of carrying out the improvement or cultivations, and the compensation must be reduced to the extent considered appropriate by the assessor.[23]

[18] s. 60 (1).
[19] s. 60 (1), *proviso.*
[20] s. 60 (2).
[21] s. 61.
[22] Part IV.
[23] s. 62.

Exclusion of Compensation for Ploughing-up of Permanent Pasture.
Notwithstanding anything in the Act or in any custom or agreement, a
tenant cannot recover compensation in respect of anything done under
an order[24] directing ploughing up of permanent pasture;[25] and in
assessing compensation to the outgoing tenant where there has been
such ploughing up, the value per acre of any tenant's pasture (that is,
pasture laid down at the tenant's expense or paid for by him on entering
the holding[25]) comprised in the holding is taken as not exceeding the
average value per acre of the whole of the tenant's pasture comprised
in the holding on the termination of the tenancy.[25]

Exclusion of Compensation for Certain Improvements.   Compensation is not payable for (a) an old improvement specified in the Second
Schedule, Part III or the Third Schedule, Part III of the Act or (b) a
new improvement specified in the First Schedule, Part III, if carried out
for certain purposes of the 1923 Act[26] or for the purpose of provisions
of the 1949 Act,[27] both relating to returning to the holding of the manurial
value of crops sold or removed in breach of custom, lease or agreement
or the protection of the holding from injury or deterioration due to the
system of cropping.[28]

" Substituted " Compensation. In the case where this is allowed in
respect of temporary improvements it must be " fair and reasonable ".[29]   In other cases[30] it has been suggested that it is enough that it
is not nominal or illusory.[31] It was held that the tenant was not deprived
of his right to claim compensation and the clause was valid where in a
lease a clause allowed the landlord to treat in his option certain expenditure on improvements and repairs as a deduction from the statutory
compensation.[32]

Termination of Interest of Successor. Where the interest of the successor of the tenant is terminated by the Land Court[33] on an application by the landlord, that termination is treated as the termination of the
tenancy for the purpose of the compensation provisions, other than, of
course, compensation for disturbance, which is not payable in that event.[34]

---

[24] Under s. 9 (2) (b). See p. 305.
[25] s. 63 (1), as amended by 1958 Act, Schedule First, Part II, para. 42.
[26] s. 35 (1), *proviso.*
[27] s. 12 (1), *proviso.* See *infra,* p. 350.
[28] s. 63 (2).
[29] s. 42. See as to " substituted " compensation, *supra,* p. 330.
[30] ss. 39, 40, 48, 50, 51.
[31] Connell, *op. cit.,* 5th ed., p. 40.
[32] *Young* v *Oswald,* 1949 S.C. 412.
[33] s. 21 (3) as substituted by Succession (Scotland) Act 1964, Schedule 2, para. 22.
[34] s. 21 (5) as substituted by Succession (Scotland) Act 1964, Schedule 2, para. 22.

Compensation where Tillage, etc. under Directions. There are provisions in the 1943 Act,[35] which the 1949 Act is not to be held to have repealed,[36] giving a tenant—where directions have been given to him affecting during the last twelve months of the tenancy the cultivation, management or use of the holding—on the termination of the tenancy in respect of tillage or manuring done to comply with the directions and contrary to or exceeding that in the lease or custom such compensation as fairly represents the value thereof or of the excess to an incoming tenant; compensation for his services and expenses in laying down the crop or the excess part as may be determined by arbitration is to be paid by the landlord to the tenant for growing crops sown under directions contrary to or in excess of the lease or custom, and the crops are to be the landlord's property.

Market Gardens. There are special provisions about compensation in such cases.[37]

Contracting out of Statutory Compensation. This subject is dealt with at the end of the section on compensation payable to landlords.[38]

Charges by Tenant on Holding in Respect of Compensation. Where on or after 1st November 1948 a sum has become payable to a tenant in respect of compensation by the landlord and the landlord has not discharged that liability within a month after the date when the sum became payable, the Secretary of State, on the tenant's application and after not less than fourteen days' notice of his intention to do so to the landlord, may create a charge on the holding, or on the lease if the landlord is lessee of a holding under a registered lease,[39] for the payment of the sum.[40] The Secretary of State may make a charging order in favour of the tenant charging and burdening the holding or the lease as the case may be with an annuity to repay the sum and the expenses of the order and of recording it in the Register of Sasines.[41] Certain provisions of the Water (Scotland) Act 1946[42] are as modified to apply to the charging order.[43] The charge on a holding or a lease is not to be treated as a contravention of any prohibition against charging or burdening in the deed or settlement under which the holding is held.[43]

Charge by Improvement Company. A company incorporated by Parliament or under the Companies Act 1948 which has power to advance

---

[35] ss. 15 (2), 19 (d).
[36] ss. 99 (8).
[37] See *infra*, p. 360.
[38] See *infra*, p. 348.
[39] Registration of Leases (Scotland) Act 1857.
[40] s. 70 (1).
[41] s. 70 (2).
[42] s. 55 (2), (4)-(10).
[43] s. 70 (3).

money for the improvement or for the cultivation and farming of land may advance money on a charging order duly made and recorded under the 1949 Act on whatever terms and conditions are agreed to by the company and the person entitled to the order.[44]

Charge by Landlord on Holding in Respect of Compensation or Improvement. If on or after 1st November 1948 a landlord who is not absolute owner of the holding has (a) paid to the tenant in respect of compensation for an old or a new improvement or for disturbance the sum due to the tenant under the Act or under custom or agreement, or (b) himself defrayed the cost of an improvement proposed to be made by the tenant, he may apply to the Secretary of State, who may, after giving not less than fourteen days' notice to the absolute owner, make a charging order in favour of the landlord, charging and burdening the holding with an annuity to repay the amount of the compensation or the cost of the improvement along with the expenses of obtaining the charging order and recording it in the Register of Sasines.[45] Certain provisions of the Water (Scotland) Act 1946[42] are as modified to apply.[45] The annuity so constituted is a charge on the holding specified in the order and ranks after all prior charges heritably secured on the holding,[46] and the charge is not treated as a contravention of any prohibition against charging or burdening in the deed or instrument under which the holding is held.[47]

Application by Heir of Entail of Entailed Monies for Improvement. Where entailed land is sold under the Entail Acts, the price, when it is entailed estate under these Acts, may be applied by the heir in respect of the rest of the estate or of any other estate belonging to him and entailed on the same series of heirs, in payment of any expenditure and expenses incurred by him in pursuance of the Act for carrying out or paying compensation for certain kinds of improvements,[48] or in discharge of any charge with which the estate is burdened under the Act in respect of that improvement.[49]

Hill Farming Improvements. The Act is applied[50] to improvements for which provision is made by an approved hill farming land improvement scheme as it applies to other improvements.[51] Where a tenant has

---

[44] s. 83.
[45] s. 82 (1).
[46] s. 82 (2).
[47] s. 82 (3).
[48] Second Schedule, Parts I and II, and Third Schedule, Parts I and II, in relation to old improvements, and First Schedule, Parts I and II, in relation to new improvements.
[49] s. 81. It is suggested that this provision does not apply where compensation is agreed on by parties. Connell, *op. cit.,* 5th ed., p. 190.
[50] s. 94; Schedule Seventh, substituting a new s. 9 of the Hill Farming Act 1946.
[51] Hill Farming Act 1946, s. 9 (1).

carried out on the holding an improvement specified in the First Schedule, Parts I or II, in accordance with provisions in such a scheme for the carrying out of the improvement and for the tenant's being responsible for doing the work, being provisions included in that scheme at the instance or with the consent of the landlord, then in the case of an improvement in Part I the landlord is to be deemed to have consented as under the Act[52] in relation to the improvement, and in the case of an improvement in Part II the tenant is to be deemed to have given notice as under the Act[53] in relation to the improvement and the landlord deemed to have received the notice and to have given no such notice to the tenant as is mentioned in the Act[54] objecting to the carrying out of the improvement or the manner in which it is proposed by the tenant to carry out the work.[55]

Any agreement as to compensation or otherwise between landlord and tenant regarding the improvement is to have effect as if on the terms stated[56] in the Act.[55]

If the Secretary of State withholds or reduces an improvement grant in regard to an improvement on the ground that the work has been badly done, he may direct that any right conferred by the Act[57] to have the rent increased is not to be exercisable in regard to that improvement, or is to be exercisable only to such extent as is specified in his direction; any such direction given after the right has been exercised is retrospective, and any excess rent must be repaid.[58]

In assessing the amount of compensation under the Act or custom or an agreement, if it is shown to the assessor's satisfaction that the improvement or cultivations in respect of which the compensation is claimed was or were wholly or partly the result of or incidental to work in respect of the cost of which an improvement grant has been paid or will be payable, then the cost of the grant must be taken into account as if it were a benefit allowed to the tenant in consideration of carrying out the improvement or cultivations, and therefore compensation is reduced to the extent that the assessor thinks appropriate.[59]

COMPENSATION TO THE LANDLORD

The foregoing paragraphs have dealt mainly with the claims of the tenant to compensation, but the landlord has equally rights to compensation if the tenant has not been, to put it broadly, a good tenant farmer.

Compensation for Deterioration of Parts of a Holding. When the tenant quits a holding on the termination of the tenancy, the landlord is

---

[52] s. 50.
[53] s. 51.
[54] s. 52.
[55] Hill Farming Act 1946, s. 9 (2).
[56] 1949 Act, s. 50 or s. 51 as the case may be.
[57] Hill Farming Act, s. 8.
[58] *Ibid.*, s. 9 (3).
[59] *Ibid.*, s. 9 (6).

entitled to compensation in respect of any dilapidation or deterioration of, or damage to, any part of the holding or anything in or on the holding due to the tenant's non-fulfilment of his responsibilities to farm in accordance with the rules of good husbandry.[60] The landlord must, not later than three months before the termination of the tenancy, give written notice to the tenant of his intention to claim compensation, otherwise it is not recoverable.[61] There must too be a record[62] of the holding in order to found a claim by the landlord.[63] That is, compensation cannot be recovered in any case where the lease was entered into after 31st July 1931 or under and in accordance with any lease entered into on or after 1st November 1948, unless during the tenant's occupancy a record of the condition of the fixed equipment on and the cultivation of the holding has been made under the Act,[62] or in respect of any matter arising before the date of the record or, if more than one record has been made during the occupancy, before the date of the first such record; if, however, landlord and tenant agree in writing, a record of the condition of the holding, though made during a previous tenant's occupancy, may be deemed to have been made during the tenant's occupancy and on the date specified in the agreement, and has effect subject to such modifications as may be so specified.[63] The amount of the compensation is " the cost, as at the date of the tenant's quitting the holding, of making good the dilapidation, or deterioration or damage ".[64] The landlord, instead of claiming compensation under the Act, may claim compensation under and in accordance with a written lease on the tenant's quitting the holding on the termination of the tenancy.[65] Compensation, however, cannot be claimed both under the Act and under the lease,[65] but in that connection any claim by the landlord in relation to fixed equipment[66] falls to be disregarded.[65] If the tenant has remained during two or more tenancies, the landlord is still entitled to his right to compensation though the tenancy in which the act or omission that in whole or part caused the dilapidation, etc. occurred was not the tenancy at the termination of which the tenant quits.[67] It has been held that there is nothing in the Act which excludes the right of the landlord to bring an action of damages at common law for breach of contract or covenant during the continuance of the lease.[68] The words " on the tenant quitting " may have been inserted, said Singleton, L. J.,[69] to cover the case where there have been several tenancies by the same tenant and to show that the right to compensation does not arise when one tenancy ends and another begins,

---

[60] s. 57 (1).
[61] s. 59 (1).
[62] See s. 17.
[63] s. 59 (2).
[64] s. 57 (2).
[65] s. 57 (3).
[66] s. 6 (1). See supra, p. 305.
[67] s. 59 (3).
[68] Kent v Conniff [1953] 1 Q.B. 361.
[69] Kent, supra, at 372.

but only when the tenant quits on the last of them. If the landlord proves that the tenant failed to fulfil his responsibilities to farm in accordance with the rules of good husbandry, then he can claim compensation under these provisions for the cost of restoring to a proper state fields which have not been manured.[70]

Compensation for General Deterioration of a Holding. A landlord may claim compensation from his tenant on the tenant quitting a holding on the termination of the tenancy if he proves that the value of the holding generally has been reduced by reason of any dilapidation or deterioration of, or damage to, any part of the holding or anything in or on the holding, or otherwise, due to the non-fulfilment by the tenant of his responsibilities to farm the holding in accordance with the rules of good husbandry.[71] The landlord, however, must not have been compensated already under the compensation provisions[72] for deterioration etc. of part of the holding.[71] The amount is " an amount equal to the decrease attributable thereto in the value of the holding ".[71] These provisions cover, among others, the case where as a result of the specific failures by the tenant, which are subject to the claims made under the provisions in regard to deterioration of parts of a holding,[73] the landlord can also prove a general depreciation of his farm as a whole, that claim being, however, as above stated, subject to the limitation that he must always in the kind of case where there is also a claim under the provisions in regard to deterioration of parts of a holding[73] bring into account anything he recovered under them so that he does not in any case recover twice over.[74]

There are similar rules to those in the case of the provisions in regard to deterioration of parts of a holding[73] to the effect that the landlord must notify the tenant of his intention to claim compensation not later than three months before the termination of the tenancy[75] and that there must be a record of the holding[76] and that where the tenant has remained during two or more tenancies the landlord can claim though the act or omission occurred during the tenancy other than the tenancy at the termination of which the tenant quits.[77]

Rights of compensation conferred by the 1949 Act are in lieu of rights to compensation conferred by any former Act relating to agricultural holdings.[78]

[70] *Evans* v *Jones* [1955] 2 Q.B. 58.
[71] s. 58.
[72] s. 57 (1), (3). See *supra*, p. 346.
[73] s. 57.
[74] *Evans, supra*, at 64 *per* Evershed, M. R.
[75] s. 59 (1). See *supra*, p. 346.
[76] s. 59 (2). See *supra*, p. 346.
[77] s. 59 (3). See *supra*, p. 346.
[78] s. 99 (10).

CONTRACTING OUT OF STATUTORY COMPENSATION

General prohibition of Contracting Out. Save as expressly provided in the Act, in any case where apart from the particular section of the Act[79] the provisions of the Act provide for compensation, a tenant or a landlord is entitled to compensation in accordance with these provisions and not otherwise and notwithstanding any agreement to the contrary;[79] but where landlord and tenant enter a written agreement for any such variation of the terms of the lease as could be made by direction or order[80] reducing the amount of permanent pasture, the agreement may provide for the exclusion of compensation.[81] It has been held (under previous Acts) that the right to claim compensation for improvements so far as statutory which the tenant can make without the landlord's consent is not affected by a clause in the lease providing for notice of intention to claim one month prior to the determination of the tenancy instead of at any time up to the determination,[82] but that in cases where the landlord's consent is necessary in order to carry out an improvement, since that consent may be refused or made conditionally, it is competent to contract that the right to claim compensation shall be limited to where a claim is made not later than a certain date prior to expiry of the lease or that no compensation shall be due at all.[83] And where a clause entitled a landlord to resume possession without notice and without compensation, thus preventing the tenant from giving notice and claiming compensation, it was held,[84] under provisions in the 1908 Act somewhat similar to those in the 1949 Act, to be void, while a clause entitling the landlord to resume without notice and paying compensation only for growing crops, but not providing for compensation for disturbance or a special system of farming and abating the rent in respect of part resumed, was also held ineffective.[85] It only gave a limited right to compensation. The landlord's contractual right must give way to the tenant's statutory right. It is impossible to give effect to such a clause without invading to some extent the tenant's rights under the Act. The effect of the Act[86] is to make unenforceable any provision in an agreement the effect of which is to deprive or curtail any right to compensation or necessarily to result in such. The effect of the Act[86] is that neither tenant nor landlord can have any other remedy than compensation under the Act in any case for which the Act provides for compensation and avoids any agreement to the contrary.[87]

---

[79] s. 64 (1).
[80] Under s. 9.
[81] s. 64 (1), *proviso.*
[82] *Cathcart* v *Chalmers,* 1911 S.C. 292.
[83] *Turnbull* v *Millar,* 1942 S.C. 521.
[84] *Re Disraeli Agreement* [1938] 4 All E.R. 658.
[85] *Coates* v *Diment* [1951] 1 All E.R. 890.
[86] s. 64 (1).
[87] *Kent* v *Conniff* [1953] 1 Q.B. 361.

Nothing in the provisions of the Act, apart from the foregoing provision of the Act,[86] is to be construed as disentitling a tenant or a landlord to compensation in any case for which the provisions of the Act do not provide for compensation, but a claim for compensation in any such case must be in writing in order to be enforceable.[88]

RESPONSIBILITIES OF LANDLORD AND OF TENANT

Responsibilities of Landlord. For the purpose of determining for the Agriculture (Scotland) Act 1948, whether the owner of agricultural land is fulfilling his responsibilities to manage it in accordance with the rules of good estate management, such rules were laid down in that Act and these have effect for the purposes of the 1949 Act[89] as for those of the 1948 Act. These rules are:

(1) For the purposes of the Act, the owner of agricultural land shall be deemed to fulfil his responsibilities to manage it in accordance with the rules of good estate management in so far as his management of the land and (so far as it affects the management of that land) of other land managed by him is such as to be reasonably adequate, having regard to the character and situation of the land and other relevant circumstances, to enable an occupier of the land reasonably skilled in husbandry to maintain efficient production as respects both the kind of produce and the quality and quantity thereof.

(2) In determining whether the management of land is such as aforesaid regard shall be had, but without prejudice to the generality of the provisions of the last foregoing paragraph, to the extent to which the owner is making regular muirburn in the interests of sheep stock, exercising systematic control of vermin on land not in the control of a tenant, and undertaking the eradication of bracken, whins and broom as far as is reasonably practicable, and to the extent to which the owner is fulfilling his responsibilities in relation to the provision, improvement, replacement and renewal of the fixed equipment on the land in so far as is necessary to enable an occupier reasonably skilled in husbandry to maintain efficient production as aforesaid.

Responsibilities of Tenant. For the purposes of determining for the purposes of the 1948 Act whether an occupier of agricultural land is fulfilling his responsibilities to farm in accordance with the rules of good husbandry, rules of good husbandry were laid down in the Act[90] and these have effect for the purposes of the 1949 Act as for the purposes of the 1948 Act.[88] While an obligation to conform to the rules of good

---

[88] s. 64 (2).
[89] s. 93 (2). The sanctions were repealed by the 1958 Act, s. 1 (2).
[90] See *supra*, p. 314.

husbandry was implied at common law,[91] the duty came as a result of the 1948 and 1949 Acts to be one owed to the nation and it must now be regarded as an express condition of every agricultural lease.[92]

MISCELLANEOUS PROVISIONS OR INCIDENTS OF LEASE

Freedom of Cropping or Disposal of Produce.　A tenant, notwithstanding any custom of the country or the terms of any lease or agreement as to the disposal of crops or the method of cropping arable land, can, without incurring any penalty, forfeiture or liability, dispose of the produce (which includes anything whether alive or dead produced in the course of agriculture)[93] of the holding other than the manure produced thereon, and practise any system of cropping of the arable land on the holding.[94] The general obligation to follow the rules of good husbandry still, of course, applies. It should be noted that " custom of the country " does not imply an immemorial or universal usage but only the prevalent usage of the neighbourhood where the land lies which has subsisted for a reasonable length of time.[95] While it may vary between different parts of a county, it is the custom prevailing throughout the particular district, and not that of a particular estate or property.[96] Before exercising these rights or as soon as may be after exercising them, the tenant must have made " suitable and adequate provision ", in the case of disposal of produce, to return to the holding the full equivalent manurial value to the holding of all crops sold off or removed from it in breach of the custom, contract, or agreement (that is, he must restore the fertility of the land, leaving it as it would have been if the crops had not been removed), and in the case of the practice of a system of cropping, to protect the holding from injury or deterioration.[97] Arable land does not include land in grass which by the terms of the lease is to be retained in the same condition throughout the tenancy;[98] that is, the tenant cannot break up permanent pasture. The reference to the terms of the lease is construed as one to the terms as so modified where the Secretary of State[99] or an arbiter[1] has directed that the lease is to have effect subject to modifications.[2]

These rights to freedom do not apply, in case of a tenancy from year to year, as respects the year before the tenant quits or any period after he has given or received notice to quit which results in his quitting, or, in any other case, as respects the year before the expiry of the lease.[3]

---

[91] Rankine, 415.
[92] See 1963 S.L.T. (News) 69.
[93] s. 93.
[94] s. 12 (1).
[95] *Williams* v *Lewis* [1915] 3 K.B. 493 at 494, *per* Bray, J.
[96] Halsbury, *Laws of England,* 3rd ed., I. 257.
[97] s. 12 (1), *proviso.*
[98] s. 12 (5).
[99] Under s. 9, or under s. 12 of the Agriculture (Scotland) Act 1948.
[1] Under s. 9.
[2] s. 12 (5), as amended by 1958 Act, Schedule First, Part II, para. 33.
[3] s. 12 (4). This includes a break : see *Alston's Trs.* v *Muir,* 1919 2 S.L.T. 8.

If the tenant, of course, follows the terms of the lease or custom, the common law rules apply. If the tenant exercises these rights of freedom in such a manner as to, or as to be likely to, injure or deteriorate the holding, the landlord has certain, "but no other", remedies.[4] If the case so requires, he can obtain an interdict, restraining the exercise of the tenant's rights in that manner,[5] and in any case, on the tenant quitting, can recover damages for any injury or deterioration of the holding attributable to the tenant's exercise of his rights.[4] The damages are the injury to the reversion on the determination of the tenancy, that is, the diminution of the rent which the landlord can get on re-letting.[6] Acquiescence may bar claims.[7] For the purposes of interdict the question whether the tenant is exercising or has exercised his rights in such a manner as to injure or deteriorate the holding or is likely to do so, is determined by arbitration, and the arbiter's certificate as to his determination in the matter is conclusive proof of the facts in his certificate for any proceedings under this part[8] of the Act.[9] An arbiter, it has been said,[10] should not hold a tenant liable for compensation for removing produce merely because he is infringing thereby the rules of good husbandry. Whether the tenant's freedom extends to a right to cease cropping or to lay down grass on a large scale over almost all of the holding is not decided.[11]

Prohibition of Removal by Tenant of Manure Compost, Hay, Straw or Roots. If either party has given notice to quit, the tenant, subject to any agreement to the contrary, cannot at any time after the date of the notice, sell or remove from the holding any manure, or compost, or any hay or straw or roots grown in the last year of his tenancy unless and until he has given to the landlord or the incoming tenant a reasonable opportunity of agreeing to purchase such manure, etc., on the termination of the tenancy at the fair market value or at such other value as is provided by the lease.[12] Possibly, on the analogy of a claim for compensation for disturbance, the tenant need not notify the landlord before advertising for sale.[13]

Right of Tenant to Remove Fixtures and Buildings. The tenant's rights to remove fixtures and buildings erected by him are extended beyond those which he has at common law. Where, without being under any obligation to do so, he has affixed to a holding any engine, machinery,

---

[4] s. 12 (2).
[5] See Connell, *op. cit.*, 5th ed., p. 47, and *infra*, p. 366 as to the effect on this of the wide terms of the arbitration clause, s. 74.
[6] *Williams, supra;* Walker, *Law of Damages*, pp. 351-2.
[7] Walker, *op. cit.*, p. 351 and cases cited.
[8] s. 12.
[9] s. 12 (3), as amended by 1958 Act, Schedule First, Part II, para. 33.
[10] Connell, *op. cit.*, 5th ed., p. 114.
[11] *Ibid.*, p. 114.
[12] s. 13.
[13] *Barbour* v *McDouall*, 1914 S.C. 844.

fencing or other fixture, or has erected any building other than one in respect of which he is under the Act or otherwise entitled to compensation, and the fixture or the building was not affixed or erected instead of a fixture or building belonging to the landlord, the tenant can remove these at any time during the continuance of the tenancy, or before the expiry of six months, or such longer period as may be agreed from the termination of the tenancy, and such are his property as long as he may remove them.[14] It is necessary, however, that before he does remove them he has paid all rent which he owes and performed or satisfied all his other obligations to the landlord in respect of the holding, and also has at least one month before the exercise of the right and the termination of the tenancy given written notice to the landlord of his intention to remove the fixture or building.[15] Further, in the removal he must not do any avoidable damage to any other building or other part of the holding; and all damage that is so done due to the removal he must make good immediately after the removal.[16] At any time before the expiry of the notice, the landlord may give to the tenant a written counter-notice electing to buy a fixture or a building comprised in the notice; the price to be paid by the landlord is " the fair value thereof to an incoming tenant ".[17] A fixture is anything annexed to heritable property, that is, fastened to or connected with it.[18] The tenant may at any time during the tenancy require the making of a record of any fixtures or buildings which under the Act he is entitled to remove.[19] An engine, machinery, fencing or temporary structure, removeable by a tenant at common law, can apparently be removed apart from the Act.[20]

Sale to Landlord or Incoming Tenant of Implements, etc.   Where a tenant has entered into an agreement, or it is a term of the lease that on quitting the holding the tenant will sell to the landlord or the incoming tenant any implements of husbandry, fixtures, farm produce or farm stock on or used in connection with the holding, it is deemed, despite anything to the contrary in the agreement or the lease, to be a condition of that agreement or lease (a) that the property in the goods shall not pass to the buyer till the price is paid, and (b) that payment shall be made within a month after the tenant has quitted the holding or within a month after delivery of the award in the valuation where the price is to be ascertained by valuation.[21] If payment is not so made, the

[14] s. 14 (1).
[15] s. 14 (2).
[16] s. 14 (4).
[17] s. 14 (3). See re market gardens, *infra,* p. 360.
[18] See Gloag & Henderson, *Introduction to the Law of Scotland,* 6th ed., pp. 451, 452; Smith, *A Short Commentary,* p. 500; Rankine, p. 286.
[19] s. 17 (1).
[20] Connell, *op. cit.,* 5th ed., p. 118. See too s. 100.
[21] s. 22 (1).

outgoing tenant is entitled to sell or remove the goods, and receive from the landlord or the incoming tenant as the case may be by whom the price was payable compensation of an amount equal to any loss or expense unavoidably incurred by the outgoing tenant upon or in connection with such sale or removal, together with any expenses reasonably incurred by him in the preparation of his claim for compensation.[22] Any question as to the amount of compensation is determined by arbitration.[23]

Landlord's Right to Penal Rent or Liquidated Damages. Despite any provision in a lease by which the tenant is made liable to pay a higher rent or other liquidated damages in the event of a breach or non-fulfilment of any of the terms or conditions in the lease, the landlord cannot recover any sum in consequence of a breach or non-fulfilment in excess of the damage suffered by him in consequence thereof.[24] Thus, where a clause in a lease requires payment of a penalty of two or three years' rent for breach or non-fulfilment of provisions as to cultivation, the landlord can only recover his actual loss. The landlord, however, can enforce penalties not stated in sterling or a clause of irritancy or a clause entitling him to withdraw certain rights and privileges.[25]

Record of Holding. The landlord or the tenant may, at any time during the tenancy, require the making of a record of the condition of the fixed equipment on, and of the cultivation of, the holding.[26] The tenant may also, at any time during the tenancy, require the making of a record of existing improvements carried out by him, or in respect of the carrying out of which he has with the landlord's written consent paid compensation to an outgoing tenant,[27] and of any fixtures or buildings which he is under the Act[28] entitled to remove.[26] In regard to such a record (1) it must be made by a person appointed by the Secretary of State,[29] whose remuneration shall be such a sum as the Secretary of State may fix[30] and is recoverable by that person from either party, who can in turn recover from the other party any excess over his due proportion of the costs of the record;[31] (2) it must be in the prescribed form;[29] (3) its cost, in the absence of agreement between landlord and tenant, must be borne equally by them;[32] any expenses,

---

[22] s. 22 (2).
[23] s. 22 (3).
[24] s. 16.
[25] Connell, *op. cit.*, 5th ed., p. 12. The landlord can remove a tenant whose estate has been sequestrated or who has by failure to pay rent or otherwise incurred an irritancy of the lease or other liability to be removed: s. 24 (5).
[26] s. 17 (1).
[27] See ss. 46, 55, *supra*.
[28] s. 14.
[29] s. 17 (2).
[30] s. 17 (7).
[31] s. 17 (8).
[32] s. 17 (3).

23

other than the remuneration of the party making the record, of and incidental to the making of it are to be taxed by the Sheriff Court auditor, subject to review by the Sheriff[30] and any part of those expenses paid by either party in excess of his due proportion can be recovered by him from the other party;[31] and (4) it must show any consideration or allowances made by one party to the other.[33]

A record may be made, if landlord or tenant so requires, of part only of a holding or of fixed equipment only.[34]

Any question or difference between landlord and tenant arising out of the making of a record, e.g. as to fixtures or buildings that the tenant can remove, is on the application of either party to be referred to the Land Court, which is to determine the question or difference.[35]

The making of a record of the condition of the fixed equipment on the holding is obligatory in a new lease, that is, where a lease has been entered into for the letting of a holding, and it must be made forthwith.[36] When it is made it is deemed part of the lease.[36] The provisions of the Act above mentioned[37] apply to the making of this record and to its cost.[36] The Act does not state whose responsibility it is for having the record made and it provides no penalties for failure to have it made. If the record is not made, however, certain rights to compensation of landlord and tenant cannot be claimed and enforced; records are essential for the tenant's claim in respect of the continuous adoption of a special standard or system of farming,[38] and the landlord's claim for dilapidations, deterioration, etc.[39]

Power of Landlord to Enter on Holding. The landlord or any person authorised by him may at all reasonable times enter on the holding in order to view the state of the holding, to fulfil his responsibilities to manage the holding in accordance with the rules of good estate management set forth in the 1948 Act,[40] and to provide, improve, replace or renew fixed equipment on the holding otherwise than in fulfilment of his responsibilities to manage in accordance with the rules of good estate management.[41]

Entry on and Inspection of Land on Behalf of Secretary of State. A person authorised by the Secretary of State can at all reasonable times enter into and inspect any land in order to determine whether, and if so in what manner, any of the powers conferred on the Secretary of State under the Act are to be exercised in relation to the land, or

---

[33] s. 17 (4).
[34] s. 17 (5).
[35] s. 17 (6).
[36] s. 5 (1).
[37] s. 17.
[38] s. 56.
[39] ss. 57, 58, 59.
[40] Schedule Fifth; 1949 Act, s. 93 (2).
[41] s. 18.

whether, and if so in what manner, any direction given under any such power has been complied with.[42] If required, he must produce some duly authenticated document showing his authority to act.[43] Twenty-four hours' notice too must be given to the occupier if admission is demanded as of right to land used for residential purposes,[44] and in other cases notice that it is proposed to enter during a period specified not exceeding fourteen days and beginning at least twenty-four hours after the giving of the notice.[45]

Removal of Tenant for Non-Payment of Rent. If the rent is six months in arrear, that is six months' rent is " due and unpaid ", the landlord may raise an action of removing against the tenant in the Sheriff Court, concluding for his removal at the next ensuing term of Whitsunday or Martinmas.[46] The landlord can bring the action without any warning and with the usual *induciae;* forty days' notice or forty days' *induciae* are not necessary.[47] If the arrears are not paid up or if security is not found for the arrears and one year's rent further, the Sheriff must decree the tenant's removal and may eject him at the next ensuing term as if the lease were determined and the tenant had been legally warned to remove.[46] If the tenant pleads, *e.g.,* a right of retention of rent, the action must be sisted for arbitration on that issue.[48] A tenant so removed has the rights of an outgoing tenant as if his tenancy had terminated naturally at that term.[49] He will be presumably entitled to compensation for improvements but not, of course, for disturbance. It is not decided what the position is if there are different terms of entry under the lease.

Application by Landlord of Sums recovered under Fire Insurance Policy. Where a tenant is liable, in case of a lease entered into before 1st November 1948, for the whole or a part of a fire insurance policy premium in the landlord's name over any buildings or other subjects included in the lease and the landlord recovers a sum under the policy in respect of the destruction of or damage to the buildings or other subjects by fire, then, unless the tenant otherwise agrees, the landlord must expend that sum on the rebuilding, repair or restoration of the buildings or subjects so destroyed or damaged in the manner that is agreed by the parties or, if they fail to agree, that is decided by the Secretary of State.[50]

[42] s. 89 (1). Cp. Agriculture (Scotland) Act 1948, ss. 47, 82.
[43] s. 89 (2).
[44] s. 89 (3).
[45] s. 89 (4).
[46] s. 19. In a lease entered into on or after 1st November 1948, these terms are 28th May and 28th November.
[47] *Ballantyne* v *Brechin* (1893) 1 S.L.T. 306.
[48] *Brodie* v *Ker*, 1952 S.C. 216.
[49] s. 19 (2). See s. 19 (3) as to procedure.
[50] s. 23.

SUCCESSION TO LEASE

Bequest of Lease. A tenant may by will or other testamentary writing bequeath his lease to his son-in-law or daughter-in-law, or any one of the persons who would be, or would in any circumstances have been, entitled to succeed to the estate on intestacy under the Succession (Scotland) Act 1964.[51] The legatee, if he accepts the legacy, must notify the landlord within twenty-one days after the tenant's death or, if he is prevented by some unavoidable cause from doing so, as soon as possible thereafter.[52] If notice is given this imports acceptance of the lease and, unless the landlord gives a counter-notice, the lease is binding on the landlord and the legatee as landlord and tenant as from the date of the tenant's death.[53]

The landlord may give, within one month after the legatee has given notice, counter-notice of objection to receive him as tenant.[54] In that event, the tenant may apply to the Land Court for an order declaring him tenant as from the date of the tenant's death.[55] If the tenant delays unduly to apply, the landlord, it has been held by the Land Court, may apply to have the legacy made null and void.[56] The Court must make the order, unless they find established to their satisfaction, after a hearing, any reasonable ground of objection by the landlord, when they must declare the bequest null and void.[57] Probably any objection must be personal to the legatee, *e.g.,* lack of sufficient capital or skill, or being of a disreputable character. That the legatee is a woman is probably not sufficient objection.[58] In the interim, whilst such proceedings are pending, the legatee with the consent of the executor in whom the lease is vested under the Succession (Scotland) Act[59] is entitled to possession unless the Court on cause shown direct otherwise.[60] If the landlord seeks to challenge the validity of the bequest, he must do so by proceedings in the ordinary courts.[61]

Where the legatee does not accept the bequest or where the Land Court hold the bequest null and void on the landlord's objection to the legatee, the right to the lease is treated as intestate estate of the

[51] 1949 Act, s. 20 (1) as amended by 1958 Act, s. 6 (1), as substituted by Succession (Scotland) Act, 1964, Schedule 2, para. 19.

[52] 1949 Act, s. 20 (2). See *Irving* v *Church of Scotland General Trustees* (1960) 48 S.L.C.R. 16, where a widow was held to have intimated timeously by telephone. In *Mackinnon* v *Martin* (1958) 46 S.L.C.R. 19, a legatee who had been unable to find the will until more than twenty one days after the testator's death was held to have been prevented by unavoidable cause.

[53] s. 20 (2).

[54] s. 20 (3).

[55] s. 20 (4).

[56] *Marquis of Lothian's Trs.* v *Wight* (1952) 40 S.L.C.R. 22.

[57] s. 20 (5).

[58] It was so held by the Land Court in *Fraser* v *Murray's Trs.* (1954) 42 S.L.C.R. 10. In *Service* v *Duke of Argyll,* 1951 S.L.T. (Sh. Ct.) 2, an objection to a woman as unfit or incapable was on the facts rejected. A widow was accepted as a suitable person in *Irving, supra.*

[59] s. 14 (1); that is the ordinary executor in moveable estate.

[60] s. 20 (6), as amended by Succession (Scotland) Act 1964, Schedule 2, para. 20.

[61] *Mackenzie* v *Cameron* (1894) 21 R. 427.

deceased tenant in accordance with Part I of the Succession (Scotland) Act 1964.[62] Where there is a valid bequest by the deceased, the fact that the lease or the deceased's interest in it is vested in the executor under the Succession (Scotland) Act 1964 does not prevent the operation in relation to the legatee of the foregoing provisions.[62a]

These provisions do not apply where there is an express exclusion of legatees in the lease. So where there was a clause in a lease expressly excluding assignees, legal or conventional, sub-tenants, legatees under the Agricultural Holdings Acts and heirs portioners, it was held that the provisions of the Act did not apply.[63] The section of the Act, said Lord President Clyde,[64] eliminated the common law rule that the absence of an express power to assign prevented any assignation and implied a power to assign where none such was expressly given, but it did not go further and empower the tenant to assign where he has expressly agreed not to in his lease. It was quite natural to infer that Parliament meant to alter the law as to the effect of the absence of reference to assignation, but very clear words were necessary to justify the deletion of express terms in an existing contract. The provisions thus apply where there is only an implied prohibition or exclusion of assignation, and are not affected by the Succession (Scotland) Act 1964 giving the power to bequeath to any one entitled on intestacy notwithstanding an implied prohibition of assignation.[65]

Though the point did not need to be decided, the Lord President expressed the opinion[66] that " a specified bequest of the lease to a definite individual " was " primarily what the section had in view ", and so he was not satisfied that where trustees held the residue of an estate for a widow in liferent and others in fee this amounted to a bequest to any person of the lease of the holding. Thus, it is not decided if trustees or legatees under the section are the proper applicants.[67]

Objection to Successors. The acquirer of the lease[68] must give notice of the acquisition to the landlord within twenty-one days after the date of the acquisition, or if prevented by some unavoidable cause from doing so as soon as possible thereafter, and unless the landlord as aforementioned gives counter-notice, the lease is binding on the landlord and the acquirer as landlord and tenant respectively from the

[62] s. 20 (7) as substituted by Succession (Scotland) Act 1964, Schedule 2, para. 21.
[62a] Succession (Scotland) Act 1964, s. 16 (8). The provisions referred to are s. 20 (2)-(7).
[63] *Kennedy* v *Johnstone*, 1956 S.C. 39.
[64] *Kennedy, supra*, at 44.
[65] s. 29 (1) (2).
[66] *Kennedy, supra*, at 46. See to the same effect, Johnston, *Agricultural Holdings (Scotland) Acts* (1909), p. 56.
[67] See opinions in *Kennedy, supra;* and cp. *Linton's Trs.* v *Wemyss Landed Estates Co.* (1953) 41 S.L.C.R. 14.
[68] " acquirer " means any person to whom the lease is transferred under Succession (Scotland) Act 1964, s. 16. See as to this 1949 Act, s. 21 (6) as introduced by Succession (Scotland) Act 1964, Schedule 2, para. 22.

date of the acquisition.[69] Where the acquirer has duly given notice to the landlord, the landlord may within one month after the giving of the notice give the acquirer a counter-notice of objection to receive him as tenant and may, but not before the expiry of one month from the giving of the counter-notice, apply to the Land Court for an order terminating the lease.[70] The Court must make the order terminating the lease, which will take effect from such term of Whitsun or Martinmas as the Court may specify if they are satisfied that any reasonable ground of objection has been established.[71] While proceedings are pending, the acquirer with the executor's consent is to have possession, unless the Land Court on cause shown order otherwise.[72] Where the lease is terminated in the above way, that termination is treated as termination of the acquirer's tenancy for the purpose of the compensation provisions other than those for disturbance, which are not applicable as compensation for disturbance is not payable.[73]

Where an interest of a tenant under a lease[74] in a deceased person's estate vested in his executor is an interest under a lease and the subject of a valid bequest but the bequest is declared null and void, and where among the conditions of the lease is one prohibiting assignation, the executor can transfer that interest to anyone of those entitled to succeed to the deceased's intestate estate, or to claim legal rights or the prior rights of a surviving spouse in or towards satisfaction of that person's entitlement or claim; he cannot, however, without the landlord's consent transfer that interest to any other person.[75]

If the executor at any time is satisfied that the interest cannot be disposed of according to law and if he informs the landlord accordingly, or the interest is not disposed of within a year, or such a longer period as is agreed between landlord and executor, or, if they cannot agree, by the Sheriff on summary application by the executor, in the case of an interest under a lease which is the subject of an application to the Land Court under the Act,[76] from the date of determination or withdrawal of the petition, or, as the case may be, of the application, either the landlord or the executor may on giving due notice[77] to the other, terminate the lease so far as it relates to that interest despite any

[69] s. 21 (1), as substituted by Succession (Scotland) Act 1964, Schedule 2, para. 22.
[70] s. 21 (2), as substituted, *supra.*
[71] s. 21 (3), as substituted, *supra.* The objection must be made on grounds personal to the heir, and so an heir though he had no farming experience but was a man of ability and financial standing could not reasonably be objected to: *Marquis of Lothian's Trs.* v *Johnston,* 1952 L.C., Roxburgh (R.N. 92). Note that s. 21 (3) was s. 21 (2) in the 1949 Act.
[72] s. 21 (4), as substituted, *supra.*
[73] s. 21 (5), as substituted, *supra,* the original sub-section having been (3).
[74] 1964 Act, s. 16 (9).
[75] *Ibid.,* s. 16 (2).
[76] 1949 Act, s. 20.
[77] 1964 Act, s. 16 (4): the period is such as may be agreed, or failing agreement not less than one year and not more than two years ending with the term of Whitsun or Martinmas specified in the lease.

provision in it or any enactment or rule to the contrary.[78] But any claim of any party to the lease for compensation or damages in respect of the termination of the lease or any rights under it is not prejudiced;[79] and such an award of compensation or damages in respect of termination by the executor is enforceable only against the deceased's estate and not against the executor personally.[79]

MARKET GARDENS

Introductory: Meaning of Term. There are a number of special provisions in relation to market gardens. Almost all the provisions of the Act, *e.g.*, compensation, apply equally to market gardens as to ordinary agricultural holdings. Thus, the improvements for which compensation may be claimed are the same, with the addition of certain others. A "market garden" is defined as "a holding, cultivated, wholly or mainly, for the purpose of the trade or business of market gardening".[80] Land used as an orchard with rhubarb and other crops grown underneath the trees, the fruit crops being sold, is held to be " a market garden ".[81] Where the lessee of ten acres of ground planted the whole of the area with raspberry bushes and sold the fruit to jam makers and fruit dealers, it was held that this was " a market garden ", and a typical instance of such, even though the lease had stipulated that the area was not to be treated for compensation or removal as a market garden.[82] On the other hand, where a holding was let on condition that it was not to be deemed to be let or treated as a market garden, it was held that compensation could not be claimed by the tenant.[83] A lease of buildings and ground for the purpose of growing bulbs, an experimental station for the growing of bulbs, was also held not to be " a market garden ".[84] Lord President Clyde said[85] that the term must be interpreted according to the ordinary meaning in popular language. The trade or business of a market gardener was one that produced the goods characteristic of a greengrocer's shop and which in the ordinary course reached the shop *via* the early morning market where such goods are disposed of wholesale, no doubt including small fruit and possibly flowers, but not the highly specialised industry of growing bulbs. Lord Sands and Lord Blackburn in the same case thought a garden near a town devoted wholly or mainly to the growing of flowers for market might be a market garden. But " an occupier of residential property who sells his surplus fruit and vegetables does not thereby become a market gardener ".[86]

[78] *Ibid.*, s. 16 (3).
[79] *Ibid.*, s. 16 (5).
[80] s. 93 (1). The same definition appears in the 1908 and 1923 Acts.
[81] *Lowther* v *Clifford* [1927] 1 K.B. 130.
[82] *Grewar* v *Moncur's Curator Bonis*, 1916 S.C. 764.
[83] *Masters and Duveen* [1923] 2 K.B. 729.
[84] *Watters* v *Hunter*, 1927 S.C. 310.
[85] *Watters, supra*, at 317.
[86] *Bickerdike* v *Lucy* [1920] 1 K.B. 707, at 711, *per* Avory, J.

Fixtures and Buildings. Where it is agreed by a written agreement made on or after 1st January 1898 that a holding shall be let or treated as a market garden, the provisions of the Act[87] as to the tenant's right to remove fixtures and buildings are to extend to every fixture or building erected by the tenant to or upon the holding or acquired by him since 31st December 1900 " for the purposes of his trade or business as a market gardener ".[88] It was held in one case that where there was a lease of a market garden which reserved right to the landlord to work minerals, and where glasshouses, which were tenant's fixtures and were in existence at the commencement of the lease, having been erected by the previous tenant and being known to the landlord, were destroyed by mineral workings, the tenant was entitled to compensation and that the loss fell to be measured by the cost of reinstatement, the tenant also being entitled to damages for loss of stock and loss of custom.[89]

Removal of Fruit Trees and Fruit Bushes. Where it is agreed as above stated that a holding shall be let or treated as a market garden, the tenant may remove all fruit trees and fruit bushes planted by him in the holding and not permanently set out, but, if he does not remove them before the termination of the tenancy, they remain the landlord's property and the tenant does not receive any compensation for them.[90]

Where the land to which the agreement relates is part of a holding only, these provisions apply as if that part were a separate holding.[91]

Improvements. Where it is agreed as above that a holding[92] shall be let or treated as a market garden, the provisions of the Act are to apply as if improvements of the kind specified in the Fourth Schedule (i) if begun before 31st July 1931, were among those specified in the Second Schedule, Part III; (ii) if begun on or after that date and before 1st November 1948, were among those specified in the Third Schedule, Part III; and (iii) if begun on or after 1st November 1948 were among those specified in the First Schedule, Part III.[93]

An incoming tenant of a market garden can claim compensation for the whole or a part of an improvement which he has purchased even though the landlord has not consented in writing to the purchase.[94] This is a modification of the provision[95] as to the right of a tenant on quitting to claim compensation for the whole or part of an old improvement for which he has on his entry paid the outgoing tenant.

---

[87] s. 14.
[88] s. 65 (1) (3).
[89] *Gibson* v *Farie*, 1918 1 S.L.T. 404.
[90] s. 65 (1) (c).
[91] s. 65 (3). See *Taylor* v *Steel Maitland*, 1913 S.C. 562.
[92] See s. 65 (3); *Taylor, supra.*
[93] s. 65 (1) (a).
[94] s. 65 (1) (d).
[95] s. 46. See *supra*, p. 333.

If under a lease current on 1st January 1898 the holding was then
with the landlord's knowledge in use or cultivation as a market garden,
and the tenant had then[96] carried out, without any written notice of
dissent from the landlord prior to carrying it out, an improvement (other
than such an alteration of a building as did not constitute an enlargement
thereof), the provisions of the Act[97] apply as if there had been a written
agreement after 1st January 1898 that the holding should be let or
treated as a market garden and that the improvements in respect of
which compensation is payable under the provisions of the Act will
include improvements carried out before or after that date.[98] If the
tenancy was from year to year, the compensation is such, if any, as
could have been claimed if the Act had not been passed.[99] Where the
land so used and cultivated consists of part of a holding only, the
provisions apply as if that part were a separate holding.[1]

Where the alteration of a building, not being an alteration constituting an enlargement of the building, was begun before 1st November
1948 no right to compensation is available.[2]

Where a compulsory rights order under the Opencast Coal Act 1958
has been made as to market gardens, compensation is due[3] to a tenant for
certain improvements[4] as if the tenant had quitted at the date of entry;
but where land immediately before the date of entry was occupied by a
tenant, then this right to compensation is not to apply to those improvements unless they are improvements to which the provision of the 1949
Act[5] as to fixtures and buildings has effect by agreement or under a
direction[6] of the Land Court.[7]

Power of Land Court to Treat a Holding as a Market Garden. The
improvements which a tenant of a market garden could and still can
make without consent of or notice to the landlord include the erection
or enlargement of buildings for the purpose of the trade or business of a
market gardener.[8] The effect was that the landlord might have to pay
considerable compensation at the end of a lease or tenancy, and this led
landlords to refuse to let holdings as or for market gardens and also,

---

[96] This has been defined or interpreted as " hereafter ": *Smith* v *Callander* (1901)
3 F. (H.L.) 28; see *Taylor, supra.*
[97] s. 65.
[98] s. 65 (2).
[99] s. 66 (2), *proviso.*
[1] s. 65 (3).
[2] s. 65 (4).
[3] As under s. 26 of the Opencast Coal Act.
[4] Those in Schedule Fourth, Part VI, are to be included among those in that
Schedule, Part IV; they are the same as those in the 1949 Act, Schedule Fourth:
see *supra,* p. 360. By s. 28 (5) if under the 1949 Act, s. 79, the Secretary of State
varies the provisions of the Fourth Schedule, he may make a corresponding
variation in the provisions of Part VI.
[5] s. 65 (1) (b), *supra,* p. 360.
[6] s. 66 (1), *infra,* p. 362.
[7] Opencast Coal Act, s. 28 (1), (2), (3), (6).
[8] 1908 Act, s. 29 (1), and Schedule Third; 1949 Act, Schedule Fourth; s. 65 (1) (a).

if they did so let them, to do so at high rents. This resulted in the introduction of provisions based on what was called the "Evesham custom"[9] into Scotland under the 1920 Act, and the law is now contained in the 1949 Act as amended by the 1958 Act.[10] Where a tenant of a holding wishes to make on it or on any part of it any of the improvements that may be made by tenants of market gardens, that is an improvement specified in the Fourth Schedule, and intimates in writing to the landlord to that effect and the landlord refuses or within a reasonable time fails to agree in writing that the holding or that part of it shall be treated as a market garden, the tenant may apply to the Land Court, and the Court, after being satisfied that the holding or that part of it is suitable for the purposes of market gardening, may direct that the holding or that part of it shall be treated as a market garden either in respect of all or of some of the improvements specified in the Fourth Schedule, and the provisions of the Act above mentioned[11] will apply as regards any improvement carried out after the date of the direction.[12] Thus, any claim for compensation will be limited to these improvements. The direction of the Court may be made subject to conditions for the landlord's protection which the Court thinks fit to attach to it.[13] If it relates only to part of the holding it may be, on the landlord's application, made on the condition that the tenant consents to the division of the holding into two parts, of which one is the part to which the direction relates, to be held at rents agreed by parties or determined in default of agreement by arbitration, but otherwise on the terms and conditions so far as applicable on which the holding is held.[13] Thus, one holding is made into two distinct and separate holdings, both under the terms and conditions of the lease but one also under the conditions attached by the Court and under the Act. If such a direction is given and if the tenancy is later determined by notice to quit given by the tenant or by his becoming notour bankrupt or executing a trust deed for creditors, he is not entitled to compensation in respect of the developments mentioned in the direction, unless (1) not later than one month after the date when the notice is given or the date of the bankruptcy[14] or the execution of the trust deed or such later date as is agreed, he produces to the landlord a written offer by a "substantial and otherwise suitable" person which is to hold good for three months from the date of its production to the landlord to accept a tenancy of the holding from the termination of the tenant's tenancy on the terms and conditions of that tenancy so far as applicable and to pay to the outgoing tenant all compensation payable under the Act (that is, not merely market gar-

---

[9] Halsbury, *Laws of England*, 3rd ed., I. 319, note (9).
[10] s. 66 (2), (3).
[11] s. 65, *supra*, p. 360.
[12] s. 66 (1), as amended by 1958 Act, s. 8 (1), and Schedule First, Part II, para. 43.
[13] s. 66 (4), as amended, *supra*.
[14] The date of the first deliverance on the petition. Bankruptcy (Scotland) Act 1913, s. 41.

den improvement compensation) or the lease, and (2) the landlord fails to accept the offer within three months of its production to him.[15] If, however, the landlord accepts the offer, the incoming tenant must pay to the landlord on demand all sums payable to him by the outgoing tenant on the termination of the tenancy in respect of rent or breach of contract or otherwise in respect of the holding.[16] The sums may be deducted by the incoming tenant from any compensation he has to pay to the outgoing tenant, subject to any agreement between the two tenants.[16] Such a new tenancy is deemed not to be a new tenancy for the purpose of the provisions[17] relating to the variation of rent and arbitration as to rent.[18]

Agreement regarding Market Garden Compensation. Substituted compensation (compensation in place of that provided under the Act) may be made under a written agreement securing to the tenant for an improvement under the Fourth Schedule " fair and reasonable " compensation " having regard to the circumstances existing at the time of making the agreement ".[19] Where landlord and tenant have agreed that a holding be let or treated as a market garden, they may by a written agreement substitute for the compensation provisions that would apply if it was not a market garden the compensation provisions contained in the Act[20] where the Court have given a direction that a holding is to be treated as a market garden.[21] Thus, substituted compensation for market garden improvements under the Fourth Schedule is not limited as in other cases of substituted compensation to cases where the lease was entered before 1st January 1921.

ARBITRATION AND SETTLEMENT OF CLAIMS

Introductory. The great principle of the Acts has been arbitration. From first to last the policy of Parliament has been to narrow the ambit of the court's functions, and to expand that of various competing tribunals.[22] It is not proposed in the succeeding paragraphs to deal with matters covered by the general law of arbitration, which can be studied in the relevant books on that subject, but it is proposed to confine the statements of the law and decisions to those directly given in or under the Acts. Where an Act such as the 1949 Act gives a fairly detailed code of procedure, that code must, of course, be adhered to in proceedings under the Act, but except in so far as modified or altered in the Act the arbiter's powers, rights and duties are those of an arbiter under

[15] s. 66 (2).
[16] s. 66 (3).
[17] s. 7.
[18] s. 66 (5).
[19] s. 67 (1).
[20] s. 66 (2), (3).
[21] s. 67 (2).
[22] *Brodie* v *Ker,* 1952 S.C. 216, *per* consulted judges at 222.

a common law submission. Any provision of the 1923 Act or Part I of the 1948 Act or of any other enactment which has the effect of requiring an improvement to be determined by arbitration under the 1923 Act is construed as having the effect of requiring that matter to be determined by arbitration under the 1949 Act, and an arbitration under the 1923 Act uncompleted on 24th November 1949 may be carried on and completed as if begun under the 1949 Act; but in the application of the provisions of the 1949 Act regarding arbitration[23] to an arbitration for the purposes of the Acts repealed by the 1949 Act so far as continued by the 1949 Act the provision[24] as to compensation by agreement instead of under the Act refers to those repealed Acts instead of the 1949 Act.[25]

Whatever the advantages of arbitration, it has undoubtedly resulted in a restriction of the number of authoritative decisions on the Acts.

Settlement by Arbitration. It is provided by the 1949 Act[26] that, without prejudice to any other provision of the Acts, any claim of whatever nature by the tenant or the landlord of a holding against the other which arises under the Act or any custom or agreement and on or out of the termination of the tenancy of the whole or part of the holding is to be determined by arbitration. The claim must not arise on or out of the termination of a tenancy before 1st November 1948.[27] Before the expiry of two months from the termination of the tenancy (if the tenant lawfully remains in occupation of part of the holding after the termination of the tenancy, which means the termination of the occupation[28]) the claimant must have served written notice on the other party of his intention to claim; and that notice must specify the nature of the claim, it being sufficient if it refers to the statutory provision, custom, or term of the agreement under which the claim is made.[29] At this stage it is not necessary under the Act (as it was under previous Acts) to give particulars. Where a notice was by error given in the name as landlord of the landlord's son who had been acting as his father's agent to the tenant's knowledge, it was held that since the ambiguity or error in the notice was purely technical and had not affected the tenant's rights or understanding of the proceedings, the notice was valid.[30] The Court take an indulgent view where the party cannot reasonably mistake what is meant; and here the tenant was not

---

[23] Schedule Sixth.
[24] *Ibid.*, para. 12.
[25] s. 99 (5).
[26] s. 68 (1).
[27] s. 68 (6).
[28] s. 68 (5). This applies only where the landlord has allowed the tenant to retain possession of part of a holding after the ish in terms of a new agreement. *Coutts* v *Barclay-Harvey*, 1956 S.L.T. (Sh. Ct.) 54. See Opencast Coal Act 1958, s. 24, *supra*, p. 339.
[29] s. 68 (2).
[30] *Frankland* v *Capstick* [1959] 1 All E.R. 209.

in any way deceived or under any misapprehension as to who the land-lord was; there was merely *falsa demonstratio*. Landlord and tenant may within four months of the termination of the tenancy (or termina-tion of occupation[31]) settle the claim by written agreement. The Secretary of State can on application of either party within the four months extend the period by two months and, on a further application within the two months, for another two months.[32] If there is no settlement within the original period or the extended period, the claim becomes unenforce-able unless, within a month of the end of the period and its extension or within such longer time as the Secretary of State may in special circumstances allow, an arbiter is appointed by agreement of parties under the Act or an application for the appointment of an arbiter under the Act has been made by either party.[33] A mere agreement to appoint a certain person as arbiter is not enough and does not satisfy the words " appointed by agreement ".[34] There must be a written document under the hands of parties (or it may be their agents) appointing a named arbiter to determine a specified dispute. One of the manifest purposes of this part of the Act was to apply the most powerful compulsitor on the claimant to pursue his claims with the utmost expedition,[35] and the section read in the light of the provisions of the Sixth Schedule that the appointment of an arbiter must be in writing, which is obviously different from evidence of consent to an appointment in written correspondence, shows that there must be an appointment.[36] " I cannot imagine," said Lord Keith,[37] " that the legislature intended that a mere agreement to appoint a certain person arbiter, locked within the bosoms of the parties to the agreement and never communicated, would be a sufficient appointment."

Matters to be referred to Arbitration. Unless as otherwise expressly provided in the Act, " any question or difference of any kind whatso-ever " between the landlord and the tenant of an agricultural holding " arising out of the tenancy or in connection with the holding (not being a question or difference as to liability for rent) " is whether arising during the currency or on the termination of the tenancy to be deter-mined by arbitration.[38] This provision must be read along with the provision already referred to.[39] It has been held by a Court of Seven

---

[31] See note 5, *supra.*
[32] s. 68 (3).
[33] s. 68 (4). See *Crawford's Trs.* v *Smith*, 1952 S.L.T. (Notes) 5, where it was held that in granting an application made to him seven days after the expiry of the original period the Secretary of State need not state the special circumstances that weighed with him; on the facts, in any event, the circum-stances there were very special.
[34] *Chalmers Property Investment Co.* v *MacColl*, 1951 S.C. 24.
[35] *Chalmers, supra* at 29, *per* L.P. Cooper.
[36] *Chalmers, supra* at 31, *per* Lord Keith.
[37] *Chalmers, supra* at 30.
[38] s. 74.
[39] s. 68 (1), *supra*, p. 364.

Judges[40] that, where in an action of removal in enforcement of a conventional irritancy for non-payment of rent, the tenant pleaded a right of retention in respect of failure by the landlord to perform certain obligations in the lease and where, in another action of removal, the tenant pleaded that a notice to quit was inept in respect of failure to comply with certain statutory formalities, both these issues fell to be determined by arbitration, being neither expressly provided for in the Act under the provisions as to notices to quit nor questions or differences as to liability for rent. The section of the Act, said Lord Jamieson,[41] is wide in its terms and, apart from these two exceptions, any question or difference of any kind between a landlord and a tenant arising out of the tenancy must go to arbitration and the jurisdiction of the Court is ousted. The consulted judges reserved their opinion, though inclining to the affirmative view, whether questions as to whether subjects were holdings, parties landlord and tenant or whether the question or difference did not arise out of something extraneous to the tenancy would be for the Court; but pointing out that to give the words " question or difference as to liability for rent " the widest popular meaning would go far to deprive the scheme of the Act of any intelligible purpose, they considered the words were confined to cases where liability to pay the rent sued for was disputed upon grounds which, if sustained, in law extinguished liability, e.g., where it was alleged the rent had been in whole or in part paid, perhaps to an agent or a factor held out by the landlord as authorised, or where liability for the rent sued for was alleged to have been discharged by some transaction personal to the parties and wholly extraneous to the lease and to the relationship of landlord and tenant. On the other hand, when retention is pleaded, liability is admitted; the Court is simply asked to exercise its discretionary equitable power and the issue is not one of " liability for rent ". The exception of " liability for rent " must be construed in the strict legal sense of questions or differences whether liability for rent exists or has been extinguished; in retention, however, the obligation to pay is not extinguished but postponed.[42] An argument that the sufficiency of the counter-notice, whether a letter from the tenant's solicitors to the landlord's solicitors constituted a counter-notice, was not within the Act as arising only out of an attempted termination of the tenancy was rejected. The issue was held to be covered by the very wide terms of the Act.[43] But it has been questioned[44] whether these wide terms affected the landlord's right to interdict under the Act[45] against threatened injury to or deterioriation of a holding by a tenant, and it has

[40] *Brodie* v *Ker,* and *McCallum* v *Macnair,* 1952 S.C. 216; *McCallum* was followed in *Sheriff* v *Christie* (1953) 69 Sh. Ct. Rep. 88.
[41] *Brodie, supra* at 236.
[42] *Brodie, supra, per* Lord Patrick at 239.
[43] *Brodie, supra.*
[44] Connell, *op. cit.,* 5th ed., p. 47.
[45] s. 12 (2).

been suggested[46] that a Sheriff would only award interim interdict and sist the cause for the arbiter to decide whether the tenant has exercised his rights in a way likely to cause injury or deterioration. It has been held under the 1923 Act that a dispute between landlord and tenant as to whether the former could retain the agreed value of sheep stock taken over by him at waygoing against a claim for damages against the tenant, being a question or difference as to the existence of a right of retention, was to be determined by arbitration.[47] But the jurisdiction of the Court is not to be taken to be excluded unless there is clear language in the Act alleged to have that effect.[48] The right of the subject to invoke the jurisdiction of the Courts is only to be taken away by express provision or clear implication in a contract or an Act, and the 1949 Act[49] reaffirms this.[50] And so a question as to the applicability of a section as contrasted with its operation is not excluded from the Courts.[51] The question whether a lease has terminated is a question precedent to, going to the root of, the existence of any statutory claim for improvements and is fundamental to the exclusive statutory jurisdiction of the arbiter; it is one for the Court, and the arbiter is not judge of what is a legal or a competent claim under the Act.[52] It was held under the 1908 Act that the question as to the validity of a notice to quit was to be determined by the arbiter.[53] But under an analogous provision in the 1931 Act it was held[54] that, where parties were in dispute as to the constitution of the contract of tenancy, the landlord maintaining that the contract was founded on a draft lease, the tenant that it was founded on informal writings between the parties, the issue, *viz.*, the basis of the contract, did not come within the arbitration provision, for the " tenancy " in the provision meant one known to and accepted by the parties, not one the basis of which was in dispute between them.

The question has been raised whether it is for the Court to determine the " relevance " of the claim alleged to have been by the Act remitted to the arbiter. It is not enough that the party claiming arbitration simply asserts that a question for arbitration has arisen; he must also satisfy the Court from his pleadings that a question or difference " between the landlord and the tenant of an agricultural holding arising out of the tenancy or in connection with the holding " really exists and a live question too as contrasted with a purely academic controversy.[55] As

[46] Connell, *op. cit.*, 5th ed., p. 47.
[47] *Galbraith* v *Ardnacross Farming Co.*, 1953 S.L.T. (Notes) 30, following *Brodie, supra.*
[48] *Goldsack* v *Shore* [1950] 1 K.B. 708, *per Evershed*, M.R. at 712.
[49] s. 100.
[50] *Brodie, supra, per* consulted judges at 224.
[51] *Goldsack* v *Shore, supra.*
[52] *Donaldson's Hospital Trs.* v *Esslemont*, 1925 S.C. 199, and 1926 S.C. (H.L.) 68 where the point was acquiesced in.
[53] *Viscountess Cowdray* v *Ferries*, 1919 S.C. (H.L.) 27.
[54] *Fairholme's Trs.* v *Graham*, 1943 S.L.T. 158.
[55] *Brodie, supra, per* consulted judges at 227.

long as the averments show that such a question or difference arises or exists, the Court must send the determination of such a question or difference to an arbiter.[56] The function of the Court is to determine whether the pleadings disclose that a genuine question or difference between the parties exists, and, if so, any questions of law must be for the arbiter, who can seek the Court's opinion.[57]

The questions, differences, or claims must be between landlord and tenant[58] in order that the Act may apply. If the issues are between outgoing and incoming tenant or outgoing tenant and prospective landlord, the Act does not apply and there must in these cases be common law arbitration or resort to the Courts.[59]

Matters Expressly Referred to Arbitration. Although the provisions just mentioned are wide in their terms and scope, in a number of sections in the Act it is stated that the matters mentioned in the sections are to be or may be referred to arbitration, sometimes failing agreement. *E.g.,* compensation for damage by game unless agreement is made after the damage has been sustained,[60] and the right of the landlord who has not a right to kill and take the game to indemnification by the person who has this right;[61] variation of rent;[62] reduction of rent where part of a holding is quitted or the landlord resumes possession of it;[63] increase of rent in respect of certain improvements by the landlord;[64] questions as to the operation of the provision for treating as a lease from year to year a let for less than a year;[65] settlement of the terms of a lease;[66] liabilities of landlord and tenant for the provision and maintenance of fixed equipment;[67] where liability for maintaining or repair of fixed equipment is transferred to the one party, the other party's claim for compensation for failure by the former to maintain or repair;[68] the value of fixtures;[69] rents where division of a holding occurs following a direction by the Land Court that part of a holding is to be treated as a market garden;[70] the amount of compensation to the outgoing tenant for loss, expenses, etc. incurred on the sale or removal of imple-

[56] *Brodie, supra,* per L.J.C. Thomson at 229. See too *Galbraith, supra.*
[57] *Brodie, supra,* per Lord Jamieson at 238.
[58] See *Cunningham* v *Fife County Council,* 1948 S.C. 439, where it was held that a purchaser from the original landlord, as an assignee, was a landlord for this purpose. The relationship between the tenant and the assignee who undertook the burden of compensation under the missives brought the Act into operation. Cp. *Secretary of State for Scotland* v *Prentice,* 1963 S.L.T. (Sh. Ct.) 48.
[59] *Cameron* v *Nicol,* 1930 S.C. 1; *Roger* v *Hutcheson,* 1922 S.C. (H.L.) 140.
[60] s. 15 (2).
[61] s. 15 (3).
[62] s. 7.
[63] s. 34.
[64] s. 8 (4).
[65] s. 2 (2).
[66] s. 4.
[67] s. 5 (5).
[68] s. 6.
[69] s. 14.
[70] s. 66.

ments, etc. where there is a failure by the landlord or incoming tenant to implement an agreement to purchase the same;[71] the question whether the tenant has exercised or is exercising rights as to freedom of cropping and disposal of produce in a manner such as to be likely to injure or to deteriorate the holding.[72]

Matters Expressly Excluded from Arbitration. The Act provides that the general provision[73] for arbitration is not to apply to valuations of sheep stocks, dung, fallow, straw, crops, fences and other specific things the property of an outgoing tenant, agreed under a lease to be taken over from him at the termination of a tenancy by the landlord or the incoming tenant, or to any questions which it may be necessary to determine in order to ascertain the sum to be paid in pursuance of such agreement, and that whether or not such valuations and questions are under the lease referred to arbitration.[74]

Arbiter. Any matter arising before or after 1st August 1948 that under the Act or Regulations made under the Act or under a lease must be determined by arbitration is to be determined, even though an agreement under the lease or otherwise provides for a different method, by a single arbiter in accordance with the provisions[75] of the Act.[76] The Arbitration (Scotland) Act 1894 does not apply to these arbitrations.

Appointment of Arbiter. There is a panel of such numbers of persons as may be appointed by the Lord President after consultation with the Secretary of State, and from this panel the arbiter to be appointed must be selected unless in the case where an appointment is by agreement.[77] Any person holding office or acting or serving under or by virtue of a former Act relating to holdings is to continue to hold his office or act or serve as if appointed by or by virtue of the corresponding provision of the Act.[78] The panel must be revised by the Lord President after consultation with the Secretary of State at intervals of not more than five years as the Lord President and the Secretary of State may agree.[79] A person agreed on between the parties (who need not be from the panel) or in default of agreement appointed under the written application[80] of either of them by the Secretary of State from among the mem-

[71] s. 22.
[72] s. 12 (3).
[73] s. 74.
[74] s. 75 (4).
[75] Schedule Sixth. See *infra.*
[76] s. 75 (1).
[77] s. 76 (1).
[78] s. 99 (9).
[79] s. 76 (2).
[80] The form is in S.I. 1960 No. 1337, Schedule 2, Form A in cases other than an issue as to rent, Form B in issues as to rent.

bers of the panel is to be appointed arbiter.[81] An agreement to appoint a named arbiter is not an appointment, which must be in writing in a written document appointing a named arbiter to determine a specified dispute.[82] An interdict against the Secretary of State prohibiting the appointment of an arbiter is not competent, but the Court may make a declaratory order declaring the rights of the party applicant.[83] It has been held[84] under the 1923 Act that the Department of Agriculture for Scotland (which at the time made the appointment from a panel) acted in appointing arbiters in an administrative capacity and that its selection of an arbiter from the panel could not be challenged. It had been alleged that material facts had been withheld from the Department and that the arbiter was an interested party. Lord Mackay observed "I have looked in vain and sought help in vain from the statute for anything to indicate that the Department, when applied to in order to nominate, is arbitral in its acting, need afford any party hearing at all, or would be right in having a sederunt to consider what parties had to say . . . There is a panel selected by the higher authority, and out of that panel it must select." The Department was chosen as selector because of its presumed knowledge of the necessary facets of the problem and has already given its advisory consent to the names put upon the panel. It was said that the Department would always refuse to constitute themselves a legal tribunal to find if the claim is a proper one or not but would appoint someone to act as arbiter and leave parties to work out the question in the arbitration.[85] If the Secretary of State is a party to any question or difference which under the Act is to be determined by arbitration or by an arbiter appointed under the Act, the arbiter must be appointed by the Land Court.[86]

If the person appointed dies, or is incapable of acting, or for seven days after the notice to him from either party requiring him to act fails to act, a new arbiter may be appointed as if no arbiter had been appointed.[87]

Neither party can revoke an appointment without the other's consent.[88] Every appointment, revocation or notice or consent must be in writing,[89] though the writing need not be holograph or tested.[90]

Removal for Misconduct. Where an arbiter has misconducted himself the Sheriff may remove him and may set aside his award.[91] This would

---

[81] Schedule Sixth, para. 1.
[82] *Chalmers Property Investment Co.* v *MacColl*, 1951 S.C. 24. See *supra*, p. 365.
[83] Crown Proceedings Act 1947, s. 21 (1) (a), 43 (a).
[84] *Ramsay* v *McLaren*, 1936 S.L.T. 35.
[85] *Christison's Trs.* v *Callender-Brodie* (1906) 8 F. 928 at 931, *per* L.P. Dunedin.
[86] s. 77.
[87] Schedule Sixth, para. 2.
[88] *Ibid.*, para. 3.
[89] *Ibid.*, para. 4.
[90] s. 85.
[91] Schedule Sixth, paras. 21, 22.

occur if he disregarded or refused to follow the opinion of the Sheriff or on appeal from the Sheriff the decision of the Court of Session on a case stated by him,[92] for he would thereby convict himself of open disregard of the judicial obligations which he assumed when he allowed himself to be nominated as arbiter.[93]

Remuneration of Arbiter. The fixing of the amount of the arbiter's remuneration is dependent on the mode of appointment. If he is appointed by the Secretary of State, it is such an amount as the Secretary of State fixes.[94] If he is appointed by the parties, then they may agree the amount; if they do not or cannot agree, then on the application of either of them or of the arbiter it is fixed by the auditor of the Sheriff Court with a right of appeal to the Sheriff against the auditor's decision.[94] The arbiter in all these cases can recover the amount from either party, and if one party pays an amount in excess of the amount directed by the arbiter's award to be paid by him in respect of the expenses of the award he can recover it from the other party.[95] If the arbiter is appointed by the Land Court, the amount is such as the Land Court fixes.[96]

Proceedings in Arbitration. Each party must within twenty-eight days from the appointment of the arbiter deliver to him a statement of his case and all necessary particulars.[97] This is peremptory and the arbiter cannot receive and adjudicate on a claim that has not been timeously lodged.[98] Unless the arbiter consents, no amendment or addition to the statement or particulars delivered can be made after the twenty-eight days.[97] The particulars under the previous Acts, it was held, must be clear and intelligible, affording fair notice of the basis of the claim with sufficient specification to enable the other party to form at least a provisional judgment whether the claim is a valid one in whole or in part. [99] It was held[1] that the words " cost of the loss occasioned by selling and through diminished value of implements rendered wholly or partially surplus to requirements by resumption " were sufficient in that case. But the term " all necessary particulars " may mean that something more even than the particulars required under former law are necessary,[2] and it has been held that " the statement of the

---

[92] *Mitchell Gill* v *Buchan*, 1921 S.C. 390, *per* L.P. Clyde at 395 and Lord Skerrington at 397. See *infra*, p. 376.
[93] *Mitchell Gill, supra, per* L.P. at 396.
[94] s. 76 (3).
[95] s. 76 (4).
[96] s. 77.
[97] Schedule Sixth, para. 5, as amended by Agriculture (Miscellaneous Provisions) Act 1963, s. 20.
[98] *Jamieson* v *Clark* (1951) 67 Sh. Ct. Rep. 17.
[99] *Adam* v *Smythe*, 1948 S.C. 445; also *Simpson* v *Henderson*, 1944 S.C. 365, where the particulars merely repeated the words of the Act.
[1] *Edinburgh Corporation* v *Gray*, 1948 S.C. 538.
[2] Connell, *op. cit.*, 5th ed., p. 57.

case ", while probably not implying a condescendence and pleas in law, means a document with short averments or statements of fact setting out the nature of the claim, and whether it is founded on contractual or statutory obligations, and that, thus, a mere note of claim setting out particulars under headings along with correspondence did not comply with the statutory provision.[3]

The arbiter must ascertain that there is a relevant claim and also assure himself that he has jurisdiction, and if he considers the claim not to be relevant or that there is no jurisdiction the arbiter must decide accordingly.[4] Indeed, if the arbiter were to proceed to deal with an irrelevant claim he might be interdicted.[5]

At the hearing before the arbiter each party is confined to the matters alleged in the statement and particulars and any amendment or addition that has been allowed.[6] It has been pointed out[7] that no specific provision is made in the Act for answers, but presumably they may be ordered if the arbiter thinks them necessary, and indeed they are impliedly permitted as they are referred to elsewhere.[8] Probably, it is suggested, there should be consent of parties to answers.[9] The parties and all claiming through them must, subject to any legal objection, submit to examination by the arbiter on oath or affirmation as to the matters in dispute.[10] The arbiter is empowered to administer oaths and to take the affirmation of parties and witnesses, and witnesses, if the arbiter thinks fit, are to be examined on oath or affirmation.[11] The arbiter has a discretion whether the parties should be examined on oath or affirmation.[12] Subject also to any legal objection, the parties must produce before the arbiter all samples, books, deeds, papers, accounts, writings and documents within their possession or power which may be required or called for and must do all other things which the arbiter may require during the proceedings.[10] The arbiter need not hear expert evidence on issues on which he is himself sufficiently expert.[13] Any forms for the proceedings specified by statutory instrument made by the Secretary of State are, if used, sufficient.[14]

[3] *Robertson's Trs.* v *Cunningham*, 1951 S.L.T. (Sh. Ct.) 89.
[4] *Christison's Trs.* v *Callender-Brodie* (1906) 8 F. 928 at 931, *per* L.P. Dunedin. See too *Brodie-Innes* v *Brown*, 1917 1 S.L.T. 49.
[5] *Donaldson's Hospital Trs.* v *Esslemont*, 1926 S.C. (H.L.) 68; *Hoth* v *Cowan*, 1926 S.C. 58. See *Glasgow, Yoker & Clydebank Rly. Co.* v *Lidgerwood* (1895) 23 R. 195; *Christison's Trs., per* L.P., *supra.*
[6] Schedule Sixth, para. 5.
[7] Connell, *op. cit.,* 5th ed., p. 218.
[8] Schedule Sixth, para. 18.
[9] See Connell, *op. cit.,* 5th ed., pp. 218, 245, 253.
[10] Schedule Sixth, para. 6.
[11] *Ibid.,* para. 7.
[12] *Maclean* v *Chalmers Property Investment Co.,* 1951 S.L.T. (Sh. Ct.) 71.
[13] *Fletcher* v *Robertson*, 1918, 1 S.L.T. 68.
[14] Schedule Sixth, para. 23.

Where the Secretary of State is the landlord or the tenant of a holding, the provisions of the Act as to arbitration apply with the substitution of the Land Court for the Secretary of State.[15]

Award of Arbiter. The arbiter must make and sign his award within two months of his appointment or such longer period as is, either before or after the expiry of the two months, agreed in writing by parties, or fixed by the Secretary of State.[16] The Secretary of State can issue regulations to expedite arbitrations.[17] The form of application to him to extend the time for making an award is in a statutory instrument.[18] The arbiter's obligation to issue the award timeously is absolute and a failure to do so is misconduct.[19] The award must be in the form prescribed by the Secretary of State under statutory instruments.[20] In the award the arbiter must state separately the amounts which he awards in respect of the several claims before him and, if either party so asks, must specify the amount he awards in respect of any particular improvement or any particular matter the subject of the award.[21] If compensation under an agreement is under the Act substituted for compensation under the Act in respect of improvements, the arbiter must award compensation in accordance with the agreement and not in accordance with the Act.[22] A date not later than one month after delivery of the award must be fixed in the award for payment of money awarded as compensation, expenses or otherwise.[23] The award is held delivered when signed and put in the clerk's hands for delivery to the parties.[24] The arbiter may correct in an award any clerical mistake or error due to an accidental slip or omission.[25] An arbiter normally in practice gives a note of his proposed findings,[26] on which parties may make representations; he also usually in practice gives a note of his reasons for his decision along with his award (and his proposed findings), but now under the Tribunal and Inquiries Act 1958,[27] if he is appointed by the Secretary of State, he must furnish a statement of his reasons if requested to do so on or before giving or notifying his decision by one of the parties.[28]

---

[15] s. 87 (2).
[16] Schedule Sixth, para. 8.
[17] s. 75 (2).
[18] S.I. 1960, No. 1337, Schedule 2, Form C.
[19] *Halliday* v *Semple,* 1960 S.L.T. (Sh. Ct.) 11.
[20] Schedule Sixth, para. 10. This is now S.I. 1960, No. 1337, Schedule 1.
[21] *Ibid.,* para. 11.
[22] *Ibid.,* para. 12.
[23] *Ibid.,* para. 13.
[24] *McQuaker* v *Phoenix Assurance Co.* (1859) 21 D. 794.
[25] Schedule Sixth, para. 15. *Quaere* whether this is competent after the issue of the award: Connell, *op. cit.,* 5th ed., p. 76.
[26] The Court in a stated case will not entertain representations that may be made to an arbiter against his own proposed findings, especially if these have not been made to the arbiter; *Chalmers Property Investment Co.* v *Bowman,* 1953 S.L.T. (Sh. Ct.) 38.
[27] s. 12; First Schedule, Part II, para. 24.
[28] The statement is part of the decision and is incorporated in the record, s. 12 (3). See in England, *Re Poyser and Mills' Arbitration* [1964] 2 Q.B. 467, that if the reasons given are not proper adequate reasons there is error in law on the face of the award and the High Court can set the award aside.

An award is final and binding on the parties and those claiming under them.[29] The arbiter may, if he thinks fit, make an interim award for payment of any sum on account of the sum to be finally awarded.[30] The award must be probative.[31] It has, however, been held in a Sheriff Court case that if it is not probative the claimant can sue on it on proof that it was in fact the arbiter's award.[32]

An alternative award such as one giving different sums in different circumstances may possibly be made.[33]

Endorsement of Award. An award or agreement under the Act as to compensation, expenses or otherwise may, if any sum payable under it is not paid within one month after the date on which it becomes payable, be recorded for execution in the Books of Council and Session or in the Sheriff Court books and is enforceable in like manner as a recorded decree-arbitral.[34]

Expenses of Arbitration. The expenses of and incidental to the arbitration and award are in the arbiter's discretion.[35] On general principles he must act judicially and legally in exercising that discretion.[36] He may direct to and by whom and in what manner the whole or any part of the expenses are to be paid.[35] In awarding expenses, he must take into consideration the reasonableness or unreasonableness of either party's claim in respect of amount or otherwise, and any unreasonable demand for particulars or refusal to supply particulars, and generally all the circumstances of the case.[37] Where he thinks expenses have been unnecessarily incurred, including the expenses of any witness whom he considers has been called unnecessarily, he may disallow these items.[37] There cannot be included in the expenses or charged against any party the remuneration or expenses of any person appointed by the arbiter to act as clerk or otherwise to assist him in the arbitration unless the appointment was made after the submission to him of the claim and answers and with consent of parties or the sanction of the Sheriff.[38]

Expenses when determined by the arbiter are subject to taxation, on the application of either party, by the Auditor of the Sheriff Court, and his taxation can in turn be appealed to and reviewed by the Sheriff.[39]

The Secretary of State may (by statutory instrument, which can be annulled by either House of Parliament), make such provision as he

[29] Schedule Sixth, para. 14.
[30] *Ibid.*, para. 9.
[31] See form of award in S.I. 1960, No. 1337, Schedule 1.
[32] *Cameron* v *MacKay* (1938) 54 Sh. Ct. Rep. 276.
[33] *Glendinning* v *Board of Agriculture*, 1918 S.C. (H.L.) 56.
[34] s. 69.
[35] Schedule Sixth, para. 16.
[36] *Breslin* v *Barr & Thornton*, 1923 S.C. 90, a case in relation to the Workmens' Compensation Acts.
[37] Schedule Sixth, para. 17.
[38] *Ibid.*, para. 18.
[39] *Ibid.*, para. 16.

thinks desirable for expediting or reducing the expenses of arbitration proceedings under the Act by means of rules, which must not be inconsistent with the statutory rules in the Act.[40]

Stated Case. The arbiter may at any stage of the proceedings—and must, if so directed by the Sheriff, whose direction may be given on the application of either party—state a case for the opinion of the Sheriff on any question of law arising in the course of the arbitration.[41] The arbiter has been held entitled to refuse to state a case as to the competency of the arbitration and the conduct of the arbitration procedure.[42] A stated case, however, cannot be made after the final award is issued, for it is guidance *ab ante* that is provided by this method; the Court is not entitled to recall or reverse the arbiter's decision, and when his final award is issued, he is *functus*.[43] If an arbiter who is asked to state a case refuses to do so because he thinks that there is no question of law, either party may apply to the Sheriff to have the arbiter ordered to state a case, and the Sheriff may direct him to do so.[41] Where the landlord had asked an arbiter who had issued proposed findings to state a case but parties did not agree on its terms and the arbiter stated the case and the landlord then sued the arbiter and the tenant in the Sheriff Court to state some questions of law which he desired, it was held[44] that, on the assumption that appeal on the point to the Court of Session was competent,[45] the action was not competent as amounting to an unlawful attempt to get round and enlarge the scope of the arbitration. The code of procedure under the Act is specially designed to be as final as possible on fact, and to allow just a limited measure of appeal on points of law.[46] The provision for stating a case " has a plain but limited scope . . . The actual statement of the case is the arbiter's affair. The parties cannot dictate or compel either the form of the findings in fact or the form of the questions in law ". A party can only try to influence these in two ways, *viz.,* by persuasion at adjustment of the case, or by persuading the Sheriff that there are proper grounds for putting some pressure on the arbiter to simplify or explicate the original case, and this the Sheriff can do by remit.[46] As Lord Patrick observed,[47] the landlord could have applied to the Sheriff in the process of the stated case to have further or different questions stated and the Sheriff might or might not have assented as he thought the questions were ones that properly arose in the arbitration. But before resort is made to the

---

[40] s. 75 (2), (3).
[41] Schedule Sixth, para. 19.
[42] *Broxburn Oil Co.* v *Earl of Buchan* (1926) 42 Sh. Ct. Rep. 300.
[43] *Hendry* v *Fordyce* (1953) 69 Sh. Ct. Rep. 191. See in relation to other similar Acts, *e.g., Johnston's Trs.* v *Glasgow Corporation,* 1912 S.C. 300; *McNamara* v *Scottish Catholic Insurance Society,* 1929 S.C. 55.
[44] *Forsyth-Grant* v *Salmon,* 1961 S.C. 54.
[45] Lord Mackintosh at 58 thought that appeal was not competent.
[46] *Forsyth-Grant, supra, per* L.J.C. Thomson at 57.
[47] *Forsyth-Grant, supra,* at 57.

common law jurisdiction of the courts the statutory process must be followed out and exhausted. If the Sheriff's jurisdiction is exercised by the Sheriff Substitute, there is no appeal to the Sheriff.[48] The Sheriff's opinion is final, unless in accordance with the provisions of an Act of Sederunt either party appeals to the. Court of Session against the opinion.[49] An Act of Sederunt has been passed operating as from 15th June, 1965.[50] The proper procedure under that Act for such an appeal is regulated by express provisions in the Rules[50a] of Court and under these Rules[50b] the appeal must be made within twenty-one days to the Inner House. This Act of Sederunt confirms and applies the decision reached by the Second Division[51] under the previous Rules that the procedure is the same as that in the Rules regulating ordinary appeals from the Sheriff Court. The Court of Session is final, and no appeal lies from its decision.[52] The arbiter is bound to act in accordance with the opinion of the Sheriff or the decision of the Court of Session.[53] That opinion and decision are binding on him. Machinery is provided under the Act " through the authoritative legal tribunals for the ascertainment of what the law is on the question which has arisen in the course of the arbitration—in a form which is final for the purposes of the arbitration. Once the arbiter is furnished with the final answer to the question of law, he is no more entitled to disregard it, or to substitute a different answer more to his liking, than he would be to disregard or subvert the facts on which his award is asked, however little to his taste their complexion might be ".[54] An arbiter is no more above the law than any other subject of the Crown or any other judicial officer: on the contrary he is bound by it.[54] An arbiter under the Act is bound by the final answer in law which he gets from the appropriate tribunal appointed in the Act to determine any incidental question of law which he submits or is required to submit to that tribunal.[54] To act contrary to that final answer is misconduct and open disregard of the judicial obligation which he assumed when he allowed himself to be nominated as arbiter.[54] The decision is not the same as advice received from his clerk or a private individual, but is an effective adjudication on the issue for the purposes

---

[48] s. 91.
[49] Schedule Sixth, para. 20. The status of the Land Court in relation to the Sheriff Court has not been the subject of judicial decision but decisions of the Land Court deserve great respect, if they are not binding on the Sheriff: *Halliday* v *Fergusson & Sons,* 1961 S.L.T. 176 at 180, *per* Sheriff Principal (Kidd, Q.C.).
[50] A.S. (Rules of Court, Consolidation and Amendment) 1964 (S.I. 1965, No. 321), as amended by A.S. (Rules of Court Amendment No. 1) 1965.
[50a] Rules 267-273.
[50b] Rule 268, formerly 277.
[51] *Macnab of Macnab* v *Willison,* 1960 S.C. 83. These Rules were 276-282, but not expressly applied to appeal under Agricultural Holdings (Scotland) Act 1949, s. 75 and Schedule Sixth.
[52] Schedule Sixth, para. 20.
[53] *Mitchell Gill* v *Buchan,* 1921 S.C. 390. See also *Kennedy* v *Johnstone,* 1956 S.L.T. 73, as to the similar duty of the Land Court, *infra,* pp. 377, 487.
[54] *Mitchell Gill, supra, per* L.P. Clyde at 396.

of the arbitration; and this adjudication is an ingredient in the arbiter's award which he must accept and act upon.[55]

The expenses of a stated case must be dealt with by the Sheriff, not by the arbiter, for when an Act directs a question to go by stated case or otherwise to a Court of law it means that the ordinary incidents of Court should follow, that it must dispose of the question according to the usual rules of procedure, that is, *inter alia*, that the Court should have power of disposing of expenses of proceedings before it according to the discretion of the judge.[56] And, of course, if there is an appeal to the Court of Session, that Court deals with the expenses of the appeal to it. But the arbiter deals with the other expenses.[57]

Setting Aside an Award. The Sheriff may set aside an award where the arbiter has misconducted himself or where an arbitration or award has been improperly procured.[58] An example of misconduct justifying the setting aside of an award is the failure of the arbiter to issue his award timeously—a breach of an absolute obligation.[59] The award may also be set aside by reduction at common law, or under the Act of Regulations 1695. In the latter case the grounds are corruption, bribery, and falsehood, and in the former such grounds as acting *ultra vires*,[60] the failure of the award to exhaust the reference, misconduct or improper conduct of the arbiter, an award which is bad on the face of it or ambiguous or improperly executed or obtained by fraud of one of the parties.[61]

REFERENCE TO LAND COURT

Jurisdiction of Land Court. Any question or difference between the landlord and the tenant of a holding which by or under the Act or under the lease falls to be determined by arbitration may by agreement of the landlord and the tenant be referred to and determined by the Land Court.[62] On the joint application of parties the Land Court must determine such questions or differences.[62] While a stated case to the Sheriff or an appeal to the Court of Session is not available, parties may have a special case stated on any question of law for the opinion of the Court of Session.[63] The Land Court must loyally carry out and follow the opinion given by the Court of Session in such a stated case.[64]

Again, where any matter is referred under the Act to the decision of the Secretary of State and he is himself the landlord or the tenant of

[55] *Mitchell Gill, supra, per* Lord Cullen at 399.
[56] *McQuater* v *Fergusson*, 1911 S.C. 640.
[57] *Thomson* v *Earl of Galloway*, 1919 S.C. 611.
[58] Schedule Sixth, para. 22. See in England, *Re Poyser & Mills' Arbitration*, [1964] 2 Q.B. 467, that the High Court there would have jurisdiction.
[59] *Halliday* v *Semple*, 1960 S.L.T. (Sh. Ct.) 11.
[60] See *Chalmers Property Investment Co.* v *Bowman*, 1953 S.L.T. (Sh. Ct.) 38.
[61] See in England, *Re Poyser & Mills' Arbitration, supra.*
[62] s. 78. See as to the Land Court, *infra, pp.* 482 *et seq.*
[63] Land Court Rules Nos. 102-8.
[64] *Kennedy* v *Johnstone, supra.* See *infra,* p. 487.

the holding, then in place of the Secretary of State the matter must be referred to the decision of the Land Court.[65] In such event, therefore, any provision for an appeal to an arbiter from the decision of the Secretary of State does not apply.[65]

Procedure. The provisions of the Small Landholders (Scotland) Acts 1886-1931 with regard to the Land Court apply with any necessary modifications for the purpose of determining any matter which they are required by or under the 1949 Act to determine in like manner as these provisions apply for the purpose of the determination by the Court of matters referred to them under these Acts.[66] Thus, under the 1911 Act[67] three members of the Land Court are a quorum, and an order in an application for consent to a notice to quit by a tribunal of only two members, following the death of the third member before judgment was pronounced, despite a joint minute by both the parties asking for a decision by the two in the circumstances, which was inept—for it implied that both members would take the same view, which, as they had disagreed, they had not done—was not a valid exercise of the Court's statutory function.[68] The Land Court is a statutory body. It is bound to act within the sphere laid down for it by the Legislature, and even the consent of all the parties in a case before it cannot confer on it powers which Parliament has not given to it, nor relieve it of limitations which Parliament has seen fit to impose on it.[69]

ARBITRATIONS AND VALUATIONS OUTSIDE THE ACT

Introductory. As already stated[70] the provisions of the Act as to arbitrations do not apply to valuations of sheep stocks, dung, fallow, straw, crops, fences and other specific things the property of an outgoing tenant, agreed under a lease to be taken over from him at the termination of a tenancy by the landlord or the incoming tenant, or any questions which it may be necessary to determine in order to ascertain the sum to be paid in pursuance of such agreement, and that whether such valuations and questions are referred to arbitration under the lease or not.[71] Thus, the away-going valuations that normally arise take place not under the Act but at common law. And so, with the exception of sheep stock etc. taken over by the owner of an entailed estate under the Entail (Scotland) Act 1914, these are decided by an arbiter, or two arbiters and an

---

[65] s. 87 (1).
[66] s. 73. The Land Court Rules No. 120, provides that where there is no provision in an Act or in the Rules the Court is to have regard to the general practice of Courts, and so it was held in *Carnegie* v *Davidson,* 1966 S.L.T. (Land Ct.) 3, that it was too late, in accordance with the general practice, to move for certification of two skilled witnesses two months after the proof.
[67] s. 25 (5). See *infra,* p. 490.
[68] *McCallum* v *Arthur,* 1955 S.C. 188.
[69] *McCallum, supra,* per L.P. Clyde at 195.
[70] *Supra,* p. 369.
[71] s. 75 (4).

oversman, as the parties so decide, without any appeal or stated case, unless under the Sheep Stocks Valuation (Scotland) Act 1937 or the Hill Farming Act 1946.[72] As the Act says, questions incidental to the valuation but necessary to the making of the valuation are excluded from the arbitrations, and thus they can be determined by the valuer. Having regard to the terms of the reference, Lord Ormidale in one case held that arbiters appointed to value the *bona fide* sheep stock on a farm in order to determine the sum payable by the landlord to the outgoing tenant had jurisdiction to determine what was the *bona fide* stock of the farm,[73] but in the Inner House, while the view was expressed that on the facts the party was barred from objecting, the Lord Justice Clerk and Lord Dundas also took the view that the issue had not under the reference been submitted to the arbiters, who had accepted the position that the stock put before them was the *bona fide* stock of the farm.[74]

Subject-matter of Valuations or Common Law Arbitrations. While under the Act[75] agreements between landlord and incoming tenant made after 1st November 1948 providing for the latter to pay compensation under the Act to the outgoing tenant are null and void, agreements are allowed[76] which provide for the incoming tenant paying up to a certain sum compensation for certain temporary improvements,[77] such as the unexhausted value of manure and feeding stuffs. Agreements between outgoing and incoming tenant with the landlord's consent are apparently valid. An incoming tenant, of course, need not take over anything, including sheep stocks, at valuation, unless he is expressly under obligation to do so, except grass seeds sown with the last white crop of the away-going tenant and the cost of harrowing and rolling them; land left in bare fallow for which the away-going tenant is entitled to receive payment; and dung, generally such dung as is lawfully withheld from application to the land and made after the sowing of the green crop.[78]

Appointment of Arbiters and Oversman. The normal practice is a submission to two arbiters mutually chosen and to an oversman appointed by the arbiters when and should they differ in their opinion on the valuation, the arbiters having power under the Arbitration (Scotland) Act 1894[79] to name an oversman unless the agreement to refer provides otherwise. The Court can under that Act appoint an arbiter if a party refuses to name an arbiter and there is no provision made for that in

[72] *Infra*, p. 383.
[73] *Fletcher* v *Robertson*, 1918 1 S.L.T. 68.
[74] *Fletcher* v *Robertson*, 1919 1 S.L.T. 260.
[75] s. 11 (1).
[76] s. 11 (2).
[77] Schedule First, Part III. See *supra*, p. 334, note 56.
[78] Rankine, 429, *et seq.*
[79] s. 4.

the reference.[80] The reference may be to one arbiter only, and again the Court can under that Act appoint if a party refuses to concur in the nomination and there is no provision for that in the reference.[81] The arbiters are more correctly called valuers, but are often referred to as arbiters.[82]

Procedure. This may be provided for in a Minute of Submission or in the lease or be left to local custom. Not being strictly arbitrations, these valuations, which are " left to the speedy determination of those skilled in rustic matters ",[83] are not subjected to strict scrutiny or enforcement of the rules of arbitration. The Court thus will not reduce an award or valuation on the ground of irregularity or informality of form or procedure. In agricultural arbitrations, it has been said,[84] where the question is the value of such things as an away-going crop or dung on a farm and where the arbiters are chosen because of their experience in such matters which enables them to value by inspecting the subjects, it is desirable that there should be as few formalities as possible and in such arbitrations mere irregularities of procedure will not vitiate an award, even if they are of the kind that would be fatal in other classes of submission where the duties of the arbiters are more of a judicial character. It has also been said [85] that such submissions " are not to be too strictly dealt with as regards procedure ", although relaxation of rules of sound procedure must not be carried too far. Where only details are concerned, mere technicalities may not be enough to set aside an award.[85] In the case[86] where these observations were made, the majority of the Court held that an award that bore to be the award of " the arbiters and oversman " went beyond a mere irregularity or informality and was one of substance and the award must be reduced. And where an award did not comply with the imperative statutory direction of the Sheep Stocks Valuation Act 1937 by showing within its four corners the basis of valuation of each class of stock, this was held[87] to be not an informality but an important and essential part of the arbiter's duty. Parties were entitled to assume and expect that the statutory directions would be given effect to in the award, not as a mere technical rule of procedure but as a condition precedent to the due performance of the valuer's duty. There is thus a distinction between an arbitration and an agricultural valuation, where custom has sanctioned an informal method of fixing the valuation by men of experience in agricultural

[80] s. 3.
[81] s. 2.
[82] *Davidson v Logan,* 1908 S.C. 350, *per* Lords Low and Stormonth Darling.
[83] *McLaren v Aikman,* 1939 S.C. 222, *per* Lord Carmont at 231.
[84] *Davidson, supra, per* Lord Low at 366.
[85] *Davidson, supra, per* L.J.C. Macdonald at 369.
[86] *Davidson, supra.* But cp. *Cameron v Nicol,* 1930 S.C. 1.
[87] *Dunlop v Mundell,* 1943 S.L.T. 286.

matters, and where thus the procedure need not be as strictly formal as in an ordinary formal arbitration.[88]

Where a question of the value of sheep stock is referred to an arbiter, then not less than twenty-eight days before the determination of the question, the outgoing tenant must submit to the arbiter a statement of the sales of sheep from the stock (a) in the case where the valuation is in respect of a tenancy that ends at Whitsunday, during the preceding three years and (b) in the case where the valuation is in respect of a tenancy that ends at Martinmas, during the current year and in each of the two preceding years.[89] He must also submit such sale-notes and other evidence as may be required by the arbiter to vouch the accuracy of his statement.[89] These provisions have been held to be peremptory and an arbiter must apply them.[90] All the documents which the one party submits are open to the inspection of the other party.[89]

Principles of Valuation and the Award. There are various principles of valuation such as market value, consuming value, value as going concern, break up value, market value at a particular market and others adopted by valuers and recognised in practice in respect of crops, manure, etc., but in the case of sheep stocks the matter is regulated by statute. It has been laid down by the Court of Session that it " is the duty of the arbiter to value the sheep upon the basis of their value to an occupant of the farm in view of the arbiter's estimate of the return to be realised by such occupant from them in accordance with the course of prudent management in lambs' wool and price when ultimately sold, and not upon the basis either (1) of market value only, or (2) of the cost and loss which would be involved in the restocking of the farm with a like stock if the present sheep stock were removed. The arbiter is entitled to take into account both current market prices and the special qualities of the sheep, both in themselves and in their relation to the ground, which, in his opinion, will tend either to enhance or to diminish the return to be realised from them by an occupant of the farm ".[91] Excessive and uneconomic prices for these had, however, come to be fixed by arbiters or valuers, who had made too high allowances for hefting and acclimatisation,[92] and to put an end to this practice the Sheep Stocks Valuation (Scotland) Act 1937 was passed. It provided[93] that in all valuations under all leases entered into either before or after the passing of the Act on 10th June 1937 where the tenant is bound at the termination of the tenancy to leave the sheep stock on the holding

[88] *McLaren, supra,* at 229, *per* Lord Wark, cp. L.J.C. Aitchison at 228. See also *Cameron, supra; Nivison* v *Howat* (1883) 11 R. 182; *McGregor* v *Stevenson* (1847) 9 D. 1056; *Stewart* v *Williamson,* 1910 S.C. (H.L.) 47.
[89] Hill Farming Act 1946, s. 30.
[90] *Chapman* v *Lockhart,* 1950 C.L. 4508.
[91] *Williamson* v *Stewart,* 1912 S.C. 235.
[92] *Pott's Judicial Factor* v *Glendinning,* 1949 S.C. 200 at 204, *per* L.P. Cooper.
[93] s. 1 (1). See *Bell* v *Simpson, infra.*

to be taken over by the landlord or the incoming tenant at a price or valuation to be fixed by arbitration, the arbiter must show in his award the basis of valuation of each class of stock and state separately any amounts included in respect of acclimatisation or hefting or of any other consideration or factor for which he has made special allowance. If he fail to do so, the award can be set aside by the Sheriff. In an important decision[94] Lord Russell held that the term " basis of valuation " was well known to all who concerned themselves with the transfer or valuation of sheep stock. It did not need definition and was adopted by the Court in *Williamson's* case. In the case decided by Lord Russell it was provided in the submission as " sale price by auction at Lanark plus ten shillings a head as acclimatisation value ". " Each class of stock " described, said Lord Russell, each distinctive group into which the individual members of the stock are normally divided by reference to sex, age and other recognised attributes for the purpose of determining the value or price as between buyer and seller of the individual member of that group. The award there, however, failed to show the basis of valuation of each class of stock as it merely said, *e.g.,* " ewes 40/- " and the basis must be shown within the four corners of the award and could not be derived from the preamble that referred to the submission. There arose, however, an unsatisfactory and unfair practice of stocks being taken over at fixed prices or an unequally unsatisfactory practice of stipulating for the prices at an auction mart in the area, where there might not be regular sales. There was, therefore, passed the Hill Farming Act 1946,[95] which made important changes and provided that in any arbitration in pursuance of a lease entered into after the commencement of the Act on 6th November 1946 as to the value of sheep stock to be taken over by landlord or incoming tenant, the arbiter must fix the value in accordance with the provisions of the Second Schedule to the Act,[96] in the case of a valuation in respect of a tenancy ending at Whitsunday in accordance with the provisions of Part I, in the case where the tenancy ends at Martinmas in accordance with the provisions of Part II.[97] The Second Schedule in both parts contains detailed and technical provisions as to the course to be adopted by the valuer in making the valuation, including rules to be applied in valuing different classes of stock.[97] In the case of such arbitrations, the arbiter need no longer show

---

[94] *Dunlop* v *Mundell,* 1943 S.L.T. 286.
[95] See s. 31 of this Act, by which ss. 28-30 and Schedule Second of the Act are to be construed as one with the Sheep Stocks Valuation (Scotland) Act 1937, and may be cited with that Act as the Sheep Stocks Valuation (Scotland) Acts 1937 and 1946.
[96] As amended by Agriculture (Miscellaneous Provisions) Act 1963, s. 21, which provides that certain limits and amounts shall be expressed as certain percentages instead of as sums of money, this amendment not affecting valuations made in respect of a lease entered into before the commencement of the Act on 15th May 1963.
[97] s. 28 (1).

the basis of valuation, etc., but must instead show separately the particulars set forth in Part III of the Schedule.[98] These are as follows:—

1. The three-year average price for ewes and the three-year average price for lambs ascertained under Part I, or the mean of the average prices calculated under Part II, of this Schedule, as the case may be.

2. Any amount added or taken away by way of adjustment for the purpose of fixing the basic ewe value or the basic lamb value, and the grounds on which such adjustment was made.

3. The number of each class of stock value (ewes and gimmers of all ages with lambs being taken as one class, and eild ewes and eild gimmers being taken as separate classes at a Whitsunday valuation, and ewes and gimmers of all ages being taken as one class at a Martinmas valuation) and the value placed on each class.

4. Any amount added or taken away by way of adjustment in fixing the value of ewe hoggs at a Whitsunday valuation, or the value of ewe lambs at a Martinmas valuation, and the grounds on which such adjustment was made.

Interim Award. Where any question under the 1937 or the 1946 Acts is submitted for the Sheriff's decision, if the arbiter is satisfied that whatever that decision is the sum ultimately found due will be not less than a particular amount, he can, pending the decision, make an order directing payment to the outgoing tenant of such sum not exceeding that amount, as he may think fit, to account of the sum ultimately to be awarded by him.[99]

Stated Case. As already stated, there is no provision or power for a stated case on a question of law in a common law arbitration or valuation except in the case of sheep stock valuations under the Sheep Stocks Valuation (Scotland) Act 1937 or the Hill Farming Act 1946.[95] Under the former Act,[1] in any arbitration in pursuance of a lease entered into after the passing of the Act on 10th June 1937 as to the price or value of sheep stock to be taken over at the termination of the tenancy by the landlord or the incoming tenant, the arbiter may, at any stage of the proceedings, and must, if so directed by the Sheriff, whose direction may be given on the application of either party, submit in the form of a stated case for the decision of the Sheriff any question of law arising in the course of the arbitration. "Arbiter" includes an oversman and any person required to determine the value or price of sheep stock in pursuance of any provision in the lease of an agricultural holding, and the term " arbitration " is construed

---

[98] s. 28 (2).
[99] 1937 Act, s. 2 (3).
[1] s. 2 (1).

accordingly.[2] It has been held[3] that this provision as to a stated case applies, as its language sets out, only to arbitrations in pursuance of leases entered into after the passing of the Act and that the words " entered into " qualify " lease " and not " arbitration ". Not only was there, said the Court, a clear express contrast with the rest of the Act but a contrary decision would have involved hardship as interfering with current contracts and giving possibly to the incoming tenant less at his ish than the inflated value he had paid at entry.

The Sheriff's decision is final unless in accordance with the provisions of an Act of Sederunt either party appeals to the Court of Session. Such an Act of Sederunt has been passed.[4] The Court of Session is final.[5] The arbiter is, of course, bound by the decision of the Sheriff or the Court of Session and must act in accordance with it.[6]

Pending the decision on the stated case the arbiter, as already stated, may make an interim award.[7]

Setting Aside Award or Valuation.   Apart from the ordinary grounds for reduction at common law or under the Act of Regulations 1695, an award or valuation may be set aside by the Sheriff under the 1937 Act in respect of the arbiter's failure to comply with any of the requirements either of that Act[8] as to the details that must be set out in his award,[9] or of the 1946 Act.[9a] The jurisdiction given to the Sheriff under the 1937 Act is permissive and not privative and exclusive, and the Court of Session's otherwise privative jurisdiction in reductions is not derogated from at all.[10] The opinion has been reserved as to whether the Sheriff's jurisdiction is limited to setting aside *ope exceptionis* in any defended proceeding.[11]

Reference to Land Court.   Under the 1937 Act it is provided[12] that if both parties agree, any question or difference as to the value or price of sheep stock required under a lease to be taken over at the termination of the tenancy by landlord or incoming tenant, whether the lease be entered into before or after 10th June 1937, may be referred to the Land Court instead of determined by a valuer or valuers under the lease.

[2] *Ibid.,* s. 4.
[3] *Pott's J.F.* v *Glendinning,* 1949 S.C. 200.
[4] *Supra,* p. 376.
[5] s. 2 (2).
[6] See *supra,* p. 371.
[7] See *supra,* 374.
[8] s. 1 (1). Where there was no written lease and the tenant signed a minute of agreement with the incoming tenant agreeing that the sheep stock be taken over at valuation it was held that an arbiter's award could not be set aside by the Court, which in the absence of an obligation in a lease (as the Act provided for) had no jurisdiction. *Bell* v *Simpson,* 1965 S.L.T. (Sh. Ct.) 9.
[9] s. 1 (2).
[9a] The 1946 Act is to be read with the 1937 Act: 1946 Act, s. 31.
[10] *Dunlop, supra.*
[11] *Dunlop, supra,* at 287-8, *per* Lord Russell.
[12] s. 3 (1).

The Court on the joint application of parties must determine that question or difference accordingly. The 1946 Act, however, provided[13] that in leases entered into after the commencement of that Act the application need no longer be joint: either party may require it, and the Court must determine the issue on that party's application, and in accordance with the provisions of the Second Schedule to the Act.[14] The Court, however, is not bound to determine the value under that Schedule where the lease was entered into before the 1946 Act came into operation.[15]

Procedure on Reference. The outgoing tenant must, not later than twenty-eight days before the determination of the question, submit to the Court a statement of the sales of sheep from the stock (a) during the preceding three years in case of a valuation in respect of a tenancy ending at Whitsunday, (b) during the current year and each of the two preceding years in case of a valuation where the tenancy ends at Martinmas.[16] He must also submit such sale-notes and other evidence as may be required by the Court to vouch the accuracy of the foregoing statement.[16] Any documents he so submits to the Court are open to the other party's inspection.[16]

The provisions of the Small Landholders (Scotland) Acts 1886-1931 with regard to the Land Court apply with any necessary modifications to the determining of any issues or questions which the Court is required to determine under the 1937 and 1946 Acts in the like manner as they do for the purpose of determining questions under the 1886-1931 Acts.[17]

CONTRACTING OUT OF THE ACTS

In contrast to the Rent Restrictions Acts it is competent to contract out of certain provisions of the Agricultural Holdings Acts and not competent to do so in the case of other provisions.

Cases where Contracting Out of Acts Competent. It appears to be competent to contract out of the provisions[18] regarding the tenant's rights to remove buildings and fixtures. There is no express provision to the contrary, and in England under a similar provision in the English 1908 Act it was held competent to contract out.[19] It has been held that by implication from the contrast with other provisions excluding the right, the Act permits contracting out of the provisions[20] relating to the bequest of a lease.[21] Probably, it is competent to do so as to the

---

[13] s. 29 (1).
[14] s. 29 (2).
[15] *Stewart* v *Watter's Reps.* (1955) 43 S.L.C.R. 27.
[16] 1946 Act, s. 30.
[17] 1937 Act, s. 3 (2); 1946 Act, s. 39 (2). See *infra*, p. 484.
[18] s. 14.
[19] *Premier Dairies* v *Garlick* [1920] 2 Ch. 17.
[20] s. 20, as amended by 1958 Act, s. 6.
[21] *Kennedy* v *Johnstone*, 1956 S.C. 39.

provisions for arbitration regarding rent.[22] If a tenant renounce or agree to end the tenancy he may possibly be entitled to agree to renounce his claim for compensation.[23]

Cases where Contracting Out of Acts Not Competent. This is often shown by words such as " notwithstanding anything in an agreement to the contrary ". It is not competent to contract out of the provision of the Act in regard to continuation of a tenancy by tacit relocation;[24] the provisions as to compensation for damage by game,[25] except as to the amount of compensation after damage has been sustained;[26] the provisions as to notice to quit;[27] the provisions[28] as to provision of and maintenance of fixed equipment;[29] the affording of opportunity to the landlord or the incoming tenant to buy manure, compost, hay, or straw or roots grown in the last year of the tenancy;[30] where an agreement or a clause in a lease provides that the tenant on quitting will sell to the landlord or the incoming tenant implements of husbandry, fixtures, farm produce, etc., the provision that the property of the goods shall not pass to the buyer until the price is paid and that the price shall be paid within one month after quitting or after delivery of the award if there is a valuation;[31] the provisions for arbitration;[32] those for compensation for landlord and tenant save as expressly provided in the Act and except for a written agreement as to permanent pasture;[33] the provisions for compensation for disturbance;[34] the provisions as to absence of compensation for anything done in pursuance of an order or direction[35] varying the lease in respect of a direction reducing the area of land to be maintained as permanent pasture;[36] the provisions as to assessing compensation where land is ploughed up in pursuance[37] of a direction;[36] the absence of compensation for certain old and new improvements;[38] the absence of compensation for old improvements which the tenant was required to carry out under a lease dated before 1st January 1921.[39]

[22] s. 7.
[23] *Roger* v *Hutcheson*, 1921 S.C. 787 at 805, *per* Lord Salvesen.
[24] s. 3 (2).
[25] s. 64 (1).
[26] s. 15 (2).
[27] s. 24 (1).
[28] s. 5 (2).
[29] *Secretary of State for Scotland* v *Sinclair* (1960) 48 S.L.C.R. 10.
[30] s. 13.
[31] s. 22 (1).
[32] s. 74. *Brodie* v *Ker*, 1952 S.C. 216, approving *Houison-Craufurd's Trs.* v *Davies*, 1951 S.C. 1.
[33] s. 64 (1). See *supra*, p. 324.
[34] s. 35 (5).
[35] s. 9 (2) (b).
[36] s. 63 (1).
[37] s. 9.
[38] s. 63 (2): *i.e.*, the old improvements in Schedule Second, Part III and Schedule Third, Part III or the new ones in Schedule First, Part III carried out for purposes of the 1923 Act, s. 35 (1) *proviso* or the 1949 Act, s. 12 (1) *proviso*.
[39] s. 37 (1), *proviso*.

CHAPTER XIX

THE CROFTERS AND SMALL LANDHOLDERS ACTS

INTRODUCTION

Object of Acts.[1] "A large proportion of the agricultural and pastoral land in Scotland is held under the provisions of the Small Landholders Acts."[2] The purpose of these Acts is to ameliorate the condition of the crofting population in the Highlands and Islands and to encourage and improve the small holdings industry, and in that respect (a) to afford security of tenure and prevent arbitrary eviction and (b) to secure a fair rent for crofters and landholders and prevent the requiring or demanding of rack rents from humble cultivators of small areas of land, these being the two main objects, and (c) to prevent the crofter from being deprived of his improvements or unreasonably refused additional land. The effect is to give a right to crofters and landholders that, though it is really a right *sui generis,* is declared to be equivalent to a lease.[3] The first Act in 1886 followed a long agitation for improvement of the condition of crofters, arising from the discontent and distress in the Highlands, especially the West Highlands, which had developed from the adverse soil and climate of the area, the overcrowding, the lack of opportunity of industrial employment and the harsh estate management that sometimes was present. These unsatisfactory conditions had culminated in evictions, the trial of some crofters in the Court of Session in 1883 for breach of interdict, the report—known as the Napier Report— of a Royal Commission appointed also in 1883 to inquire into the condition of the crofter population in the Highlands, the return of crofter members of Parliament for the Northern constituencies in December 1885 and the breakdown in Skye and Lewis of estate management and local administration.[4]

History of Legislation. There has been a long series of Acts, commencing with the Crofters Holdings (Scotland) Act 1886 and ending with the Crofters (Scotland) Act 1961. These Acts, which are hereinafter referred to by the date (or year) of the Act alone, *e.g.,* " 1886 Act ", are as follows: the Crofters Holdings (Scotland) Act 1886; the Crofters

---

[1] The chief textbooks are—Johnston, *The Crofters Holdings (Scotland) Acts* (1887, 1888, 1901); do., *The Small Landholders (Scotland) Acts, 1886-1911* (1912, 1914); Connell, *Small Landholders (Scotland) Act, 1911* (1912); Rankine, *Law of Leases in Scotland,* 3rd ed., Chapter XXIII, and Scott, *Law of Small-holdings in Scotland* (1933).
[2] Gloag & Henderson, *Introduction to Scots Law,* 6th ed., 383.
[3] Crofters Holdings (Scotland) Act, 1886, s. 19.
[4] See *e.g.,* Cockburn, *Circuit Journeys,* 355.

Holdings (Scotland) Act 1887; the Crofters Commission (Delegation of Powers) Act 1888; the Crofters Common Grazings Regulation Act 1891; the Congested Districts (Scotland) Act 1897; the Crofters Common Grazings Regulation Act 1908; the Small Landholders (Scotland) Act 1911; the Land Settlement (Scotland) Act 1919;[5] the Small Landholders and Agricultural Holdings (Scotland) Act 1931; the Land Settlement (Scotland) Act 1934; the Scottish Land Court Act 1938; the Agriculture (Scotland) Act 1948; the Crofters (Scotland) Act 1955; and the Crofters (Scotland) Act 1961.[6]

The first Act, that of 1886, applied only to what came to be known as the Seven Crofting Counties—Argyll, Inverness, Caithness, Sutherland, Ross and Cromarty, Orkney and Shetland—and only to such parishes therein as were declared to be "crofting parishes"—and to tenants occupying on a yearly tenancy holdings in such parishes of which the rent did not exceed £30 per annum. It applied only to persons who were called "crofters" and persons known as "cottars". To these persons it afforded security of tenure, the right to a fair rent fixed by a judicial tribunal and to a septennial revision of that rent and compensation for permanent improvements made by themselves or by their predecessors in the same family, and it also provided the crofter with a limited right of bequeathing his holding to members of his family. A body, called the Crofters Commission, was set up under the Act to deal with all questions relating to the tenancies of the crofters' holdings, having power, inter alia, to enlarge the area of holdings. The Act was slightly amended in 1887 in relation to the sale of crofters' effects under a decree for payment of rent which had been overdue; and in 1888 in relation to the right of the Commission to delegate their powers to some of their number.

Next, in 1891 an Act was passed to bring under statutory control the management and regulation of common grazings attached to holdings, by which crofters were empowered to appoint a committee to make regulations concerning the exercise of rights of common grazing, subject to approval of the Crofters Commission. If the crofters did not appoint such a committee, the Commission was authorised to do so.

The Congested Districts (Scotland) Act 1897, though it generally appears in the textbooks on the subject, is not strictly part of the Small Landholders Acts. It was concerned with aid to congested districts in the Highlands and Islands. It, therefore, is not treated in the 1911 Act as one of the Landholders Acts.[7] The purpose and object of the Act was to improve the congested districts in the Highlands and Islands, that is,[8] any crofting parish or crofting parishes or any area in a crofting

---

[5] There were also three wartime Acts in 1916 and 1918, which are referred to later.

[6] In addition, there are the Reorganisation of Offices (Scotland) Acts 1928 and 1939, and the Rent Act 1965, s. 30.

[7] ss. 31, 36.

[8] s. 10.

parish or crofting parishes defined by the Commissioners under the Act, which they, having regard to the population and valuation thereof, should determine to be a congested district. A Congested Districts Board set up under the Act was authorised to provide, equip and adapt land for occupation by crofters and fishermen, to whom loans and grants could be given, to assist crofters in migrating from these districts, to develop and improve the agriculture and fishing industries and to develop spinning, weaving and other rural industries. This was in the crofting parishes only. The Board could use part of a fund set up under the Act to acquire available land for enlarging holdings or constituting new ones, this being a wider power than that possessed by the Crofters Commission under the 1886 Act, which could only take available land as defined and could not pay compensation on any enlargements being made. For the purpose of the 1897 Act, the landward parts of certain parishes in Argyll, Inverness and Ross and Cromarty were deemed by the Agriculture (Scotland) Act 1948[9] to be congested districts.

Under the Crofting Common Grazings Regulation Act 1908 the Crofters Commission was empowered to appoint a committee without any application therefor having been made by crofters.

The 1911 Act, designed to "encourage the formation of small agricultural holdings in Scotland, and to amend the law relating to the tenure of such holdings", made provision for the creation of new holdings with the authority of the Land Court, in the absence of agreement by the landlord, and provided a new system of tenure for existing holdings. It applied, in contrast to the earlier Acts, to the whole of Scotland and it raised the qualifying limits to a rent not exceeding £50 or an area not exceeding 50 acres whatever the rent, except in the case of the Island of Lewis, where the limits were made £30 rent or an area of 30 acres.[10] Accordingly, statutory smallholdings now included, with certain exceptions and qualifications, all holdings where the rent was not more than £50 and all holdings, though the rent was over £50, of which the area did not, exclusive of common grazings (grazing or hill pasture land held by two or more tenants in common), exceed 50 acres. The Act also made an important and valuable development in providing for the compulsory constitution of new holdings. The term "crofters" was dropped and a material and vital distinction was made between holders by a division of holders into two classes, called "landholders" and "statutory small tenants" respectively, the former being those who or whose predecessors in the same family had provided or paid for the buildings and permanent improvements on the holding while the latter were those who or whose predecessors in the same family had not done so. The rights of the former class were much more exten-

[9] s. 79. The landward parts were defined in Schedule Seventh of the 1948 Act.
[10] ss. 26, 27.

sive than those of the latter. A new body, the Land Court, was set up in lieu of the Crofters Commission, while the Congested Districts Board was replaced by the Board of Agriculture. Provision was made for a record of the condition of a holding and the buildings etc. thereon to be appended by the Land Court, on application, to an order fixing a fair rent for a holding.

Next came three war-time Acts during the First World War, two[11] of which empowered the Board of Agriculture to acquire by agreement, by purchase or lease, up to 20,000 acres, for experimental smallholding colonies, of which three-quarters was to consist of land suitable for utilisation as arable land, the third[12] allowing the Board to accept gifts of land for ex-sailor and ex-soldier settlements.

The 1919 Act extended the powers and duties of the Board of Agriculture, authorising it to purchase land and to acquire land anywhere in Scotland by agreement or compulsorily for land settlement without restriction and to assist the provision of equipment and the adaptation of land acquired for settlement. The Board was also empowered to make orders for the constitution of holdings without reference to the Land Court. The Act excluded some compensation claims which had been allowed under the 1911 Act but which had been found, in practice, to be too expensive. In the settling of land the Board was, until 1921, to give preference to ex-servicemen. Advances were authorised to be made by the Board to holders settled under the Act for the purchase of livestock, seeds, fertilisers or implements.

By the Reorganisation of Offices (Scotland) Act 1928,[13] the functions of the Board of Agriculture were transferred to a new body—the Department of Agriculture for Scotland—as from an appointed day, viz., 1st January 1929.[14]

Under the 1931 Act, a number of important alterations were made. The Act was not retrospective.[15] Doubts about the power of the Department of Agriculture (which had in 1929 succeeded the Board of Agriculture) to continue loans to incoming tenants who were not statutory successors of the outgoing tenants were removed. Landlords had to give information to the Department in regard to leases, etc., of lands which the Department proposed to take over for purposes of land settlement. The Act made new provision for the removal of a landholder by the Land Court for breach of the statutory conditions. It also provided that the Department or the Land Court could terminate a tenant's right to a holding where a new holder failed to occupy, cultivate and equip a holding. It made amendments, too, in the law and practice in regard to cases of vacant holdings and schemes for enlargement of holdings.

---

[11] Small Holding Colonies Act 1916 and the Small Holding Colonies (Amendment) Act 1918.
[12] Sailors and Soldiers (Gifts for Land Settlement) Act 1916.
[13] s. 1 (1), (4) (a).
[14] S.R. & O. 1928/958.
[15] See *Smith* v *Smith* (1932) 20 S.L.C.R. 30.

A record of the holding could now be made by the Land Court at any time, and not merely when a fair rent was being fixed. It restricted the landlord's right of resumption by providing that occupation of a holding by a landlord for personal residence where it was his only landed estate was not to be regarded as a "reasonable purpose" for resumption. The right to compensation for improvements was extended to the case where these had been made under a specific written obligation provided that fair consideration had not been received for them. Compensation for disturbance was authorised in the case of a statutory small tenant whose holding was resumed. An option was given to a statutory small tenant to become a landholder. Contracting out of the Act was, unless the Land Court approved, prohibited in terms more stringent than those which were contained in the Agricultural Holdings (Scotland) Act 1923. The duty of the Department to erect fences was limited and its power to assist landholders by gift was extended to dwellinghouses or other buildings.

The powers of the Department of Agriculture in regard to compulsory purchase of land under the 1919 Act[16] for the purposes of the war-time 1916 and 1918 Acts were made permanent by the Agricultural Land (Utilisation) Act 1931,[17] which is, of course, strictly not one of the Landholders Acts. The Land Settlement (Scotland) Act 1934 authorised the payment of a certain sum to the Agriculture Fund for certain purposes under the 1911 and 1919 Acts.

Next came the Scottish Land Court Act 1938, which made new provision in regard to the tenure of office and superannuation of members other than the Chairman of the Court—overruling or setting aside the decision in *Mackay and Esslemont* v *Lord Advocate*[18] that such members held office for life or until removed from office by the Secretary of State for inability or misbehaviour.

Under the Reorganisation of Offices (Scotland) Act 1939[19] the powers, duties and functions of the Department of Agriculture were transferred to the Secretary of State for Scotland on an appointed day, *viz.*, 4th September 1939.[20] Since that Act, the Department of Agriculture has no longer been a statutory department with a separate *persona* but is a department of the Secretary of State, acting in his name and under his direction.

The 1955 Act, which followed a Report of a Commission of Enquiry into Crofting Conditions, called the Taylor Commission,[21] was designed to provide for the "reorganisation, development and regulation of crofting in the crofting counties of Scotland" and to "re-enact the

[16] s. 1.
[17] s. 24 (i).
[18] 1937 S.C 860.
[19] ss. 1 (1); (6) (b). McLarty, *A Source Book and History of Administrative Law in Scotland*, 1956, Chapter III, p. 42, by Sir Patrick R. Laird.
[20] S.R. & O. 1939/865.
[21] 1954, Cmd. 9091.

provisions of the Landholders Acts with respect to cottars " and to authorise the making of grants and loans to develop agriculture on crofts, and the provision of houses and buildings for crofters and cottars. It restored the crofting counties and set up a code for these areas, provided for the establishment of a new Crofters Commission for these areas and generally re-enacted the existing law as to the tenure of crofters. It, however, made provision for a register of crofts, in regard to the terminating of the tenancies of absentee crofters, and compensation to cottars for improvements, and also, in general, re-enacted the law in relation to common grazings. It repealed the Acts of 1887, 1891 and 1908 in relation to the crofting counties.

The Crofters (Scotland) Act 1961 amended the 1955 Act and made further provision for regulating, developing and reorganising crofting in the crofting counties, including an increase in the permitted size of new crofts, and the giving of a right to a crofter to erect buildings or execute works which are regarded as permanent improvements for a subsidiary or auxiliary occupation if these do not interfere with the normal working of the croft. It also altered the basis of valuation of permanent improvements, amended the law regarding absentee crofters, and gave a crofter power to sublet and provided for subletting by the crofter or the Commission if the crofter has not used the croft adequately; and it further repealed the provisions in the 1955 Act for dispossession on failure to work the croft in accordance with the rules of good husbandry. The Act also provided for a Register of Crofts and increased the powers of the Land Court.

SUBJECTS

Situation. The subjects affected by the Crofters and Landholders Acts must be considered from two aspects, first, the part of the country in which they are situated and, second, the necessary characteristics of a holding under the Acts. First, the part of the country. The original Act of 1886 applied only to certain counties, which came to be called the crofting counties,[22] *viz.*, Argyll, Caithness, Inverness, Ross and Cromarty, Sutherland, and Orkney and Shetland, and further, only to such portions of these counties as the Crofters Commission determined to be " crofting parishes ".[22] A crofting parish was one in which there were at 25th June 1886, or had been within the previous eighty years, holdings consisting of arable land, with a right of pasturage in common with one another, and in which there were at that date tenants of holdings from year to year who resided on their holdings, the annual rent of which did not exceed £30 at that date.[23] Nearly all the parishes were found by the Commission to be crofting parishes. The 1911 Act extended the provisions of the 1886 Act as amended by it to the whole country[24]

[22] 1886 Act, s. 19.
[23] *Ibid.*, s. 34.
[24] s. 1.

and repealed the provisions in regard to and the definition of crofting parishes.[25] In the crofting etc. Acts, " crofting parish " was to mean a parish to which the Crofters Acts applied at 1st April 1912.[26] But the 1955 Act (along with the 1961 Act) has now made a new and special code for the crofting counties.[27]

Necessary Characteristics of a Holding. The 1886 Act[28] defined a holding as " any piece of land held by a crofter, consisting of arable or pasture land or of land partly arable and partly pasture, and which has been occupied and used as arable or pasture land (whether such pasture land is held by the crofter alone or in common with others) immediately preceding the passing of the Act, including the site of his dwellinghouse and any offices or other conveniences connected therewith " but not " garden ground only, appurtenant to a house ". This definition has to be read in conjunction with the definition under that Act of a " crofter ",[29] which provided that the annual rent of a holding must not exceed £30 in money. The Act did not exclude a holding because it was within the boundaries of a burgh. That definition of a holding was repealed under the 1911 Act,[30] and the 1911 Act divided holdings into (i) existing holdings and (ii) new holdings.[31]

Existing Holdings. The 1911 Act did not define holdings except indirectly by reference to the Agricultural Holdings Act[32] but laid down[31] that in the Crofters Acts and the 1911 Act the word " holding " meant and included (a) all holdings that were crofter holdings under the 1886 Act; (b) all holdings held by a tenant from year to year who resided on or within two miles from the holding, and by himself and his family cultivated the holding with or without hired labour, who or his predecessor in the same family has provided or paid for the whole or the greater part of the buildings or other permanent improvements on the holding without receiving from the landlord or any predecessor in title, payment or fair consideration therefor; (c) as from the termination of the lease, all holdings held under a lease for a term longer than a year by such a tenant as in (b), who is referred to as a " leaseholder ". In cases (a) and (b) the crofter became a leaseholder when the 1911 Act came into operation, *viz.*, 1st April 1912,[33] and in the case of (c) when the lease expired. In cases (b) and (c) the present rent must not exceed £50, unless the land, exclusive of any common

---

[25] s. 39 and Schedule Second.
[26] 1911 Act, s. 31 (2).
[27] 1955 Act, s. 37. See *infra*, pp. 404 *et seq.*
[28] s. 34. Where a lease of a croft in 1909 reserved to a landlord " all plantations and woods " it was held scrub oak and birch of natural origin were not included. *Marquis of Bute* v *Baxter*, 1966 S.L.T. (Land Ct.) 9.
[29] s. 34. See *infra*, p. 406.
[30] Schedule Second.
[31] s. 2 (1).
[32] *Malcolm* v *McDougall*, 1916 S.C. 283 at 289, *per* Lord Johnston.
[33] s. 38.

pasture or grazing land held or to be held therewith, did not exceed 50 acres, though the Land Court could fix a rent exceeding £50.[34] In the case of the Island of Lewis these figures were made £30 and 30 acres;[10] Lewis, however, now comes under the 1955 and 1961 Acts. If the subjects would have been a holding but for the existence of a second house, which is used for summer letting only and not in connection with the agricultural or pastoral occupation of the holding, the Acts apply only to the part other than this second house, which can be excised from the holding, leaving the rest of the holding a " holding " under the Acts.[35] The term " holding " also includes the holding of a statutory small tenant, that is, a tenant or landholder who or whose predecessor in the same family did not provide or pay for the buildings or other permanent improvements, etc., at 31st July 1931, if the statutory small tenant has applied by written notice to the landlord to become a landholder, and he will then so become on expiry of the period of tenancy current when the notice was served.[36]

A holding is deemed to include any rights in pasture or grazing land held or to be held by the landholder alone or in common with others, and the site of any dwellinghouse erected or to be erected on the holding or held or to be held therewith, and of any offices or other conveniences connected with such dwellinghouse;[37] but the holding of tenants or leaseholders, that is, those in (b) and (c) above, is not deemed to include any lands or heritages at 1st April 1912 forming part of such holding and occupied by a subtenant of such tenant or leaseholder, whether or not paying rent.[38] Where a house on a holding was sublet for a year from Martinmas to Martinmas except July and August, it was held that this let was for less than a year and the subtenant was not a subtenant within the Act.[35]

Exclusions from Existing Holdings. There were excluded[39] in the case of tenants and leaseholders, (a) holdings where the rent exceeded £50 and the land exceeded 50 acres as above mentioned, (b) land that was garden ground only, appurtenant to a house, or any land to which, as the site of or as required for the protection of or for access to an ancient monument or other object of historical or archaeological interest the Land Court determine that the Landholders Act should not apply; (c) any land within the parliamentary, police or municipal boundary of any burgh or police burgh; (d) any land that was a market garden within the Agricultural Holdings (Scotland) Act 1908;[40] (e) any land being

---

[34] s. 26 (3).
[35] *McNeill* v *Duke of Hamilton's Trs.*, 1918 S.C. 221.
[36] 1931 Act, s. 14.
[37] 1911 Act, s. 26 (1). This re-enacted the definition in the 1886 Act so far as common grazings are concerned. It applies to a statutory small tenant—1911 Act, s. 32 (14).
[38] *Ibid.*, s. 26 (6).
[39] *Ibid.*, s. 26 (3).
[40] s. 35, re-enacted in the Agricultural Holdings (Scotland) Act 1949, s. 93 (1).

or forming part of a glebe, or any smallholding under the Small Holdings Act 1892 or any allotment; (f) any land that was not a holding under the Agricultural Holdings (Scotland) Act 1908;[41] (g) any land that was a woodland or which was or formed part of the home farm of any estate, or of any policy or park, or of any pleasure ground or other land used for the amenity or convenience of any residence or farm-steading or which was permanent grass park held for the purposes of a business or calling not primarily agricultural or pastoral, including that of a butcher, cattledealer and the like; (h) any land *bona fide* held and used for purposes of public recreation; and (i) any land acquired by agreement or compulsorily for any public undertaking under any Act or any order having the force of an Act. In construing these provisions it was held that subjects being within the royalty of a burgh, that is within the charter boundary, though outwith the parliamentary and police boundaries thereof, were within the municipal boundary of a burgh and were thus excluded.[42] Where a dairyman was tenant of a grass park on which he grazed five cows and which was all in permanent pasture, there being no buildings on the holding, and where he sold milk of the five cows, and bought and sold to customers milk of ten other cows of neighbouring farmers, his business was held to be primarily pastoral and within the Acts.[43] " The exception to which the 26th section (3) (g) applies is, I think, the case of a man carrying on the business of butcher, who hires grass fields in the vicinity of his slaughter-house into which he temporarily turns cattle on their way from the grazing to the slaughter-house, for custody or keeping, or feeding, as the case may be—a purpose which is strictly subordinate to and incidental to his business as a butcher. But when a man grazes cows upon a field and sells the milk, whether it be from a dairy on or off the holding, and whether it be milk from cows grazed elsewhere as well as from cows grazed on the holding, it appears to me that he is using his field for a purely pastoral purpose."[44] Lotted lands, that is lands which were laid out or lotted by an estate for the individual agricultural use of householders in villages or burghs of barony on the estate, held on lease usually from year to year, no particular lot being in practice let in connection with a particular house in the particular case, were held to form a holding.[45] Three acres of land, a dwellinghouse of eight rooms, a byre and other offices and garden were held to form a holding,[46] as were also a cottage with a plot of garden ground and a byre, one rood of arable (potato) land at some distance and a fifteenth share of a

[41] The definition in this Act, s. 35, was repealed and re-enacted by the Agricultural Holdings (Scotland) Act 1923, s. 49. See the new definition in the Agricultural Holdings (Scotland) Act 1949, s. 1 (1); *supra,* p. 295; and see as to this, *infra,* p. 396.
[42] *Clark* v *Fraser* and *Mackenzie* v *Wallace's Trs.,* 1919 S.C. 201.
[43] *Howatson* v *McClymont,* 1914 S.C. 159.
[44] *Ibid.,* at 161, *per* L.P. Strathclyde.
[45] *Countess of Seafield's Trs.* v *McCurrach,* 1914 S.C. 174.
[46] *Hamilton* v *Duke of Hamilton's Trs.,* 1918 S.C. 282.

common grazing of 58 acres, the Act not prescribing any ratio of the value of the house to the land,[47] and also land for growing hay and pasturing, milk being sold at a dairy;[48] but a blacksmith's shop, a dwellinghouse and about five and a half acres of land were held not to form a holding, as neither wholly agricultural nor wholly pastoral nor in part one and in part the other.[49] These decisions were all, of course, under or in relation to the definition of " holding " in the Agricultural Holdings (Scotland) Act 1908, which was re-enacted in the 1923 Act. The Agricultural Holdings (Scotland) Act 1949 has made a radically new definition,[41] and it provides[50] that references in other Acts to a holding within the 1923 Act are to be construed as a reference to a holding in accordance with that definition.

Under the 1886 Act[51] there were three further exclusions and these were applied by the 1911 Act[52] to landholders other than crofters. They were (a) any holding or building let to any person during his continuance in any office, appointment, or employment of the landlord or of any tenant; (b) any holding or building let at a nominal rent or without rent, as a pension for former service or on account of old age or poverty; (c) any holding or building let to a person during his tenure of any office such as that of clergyman or schoolmaster or to any innkeeper or tradesman placed in the district by the landlord for the benefit of the neighbourhood. The words " placed in the district by the landlord for the benefit of the neighbourhood " apply to an innkeeper as well as a tradesman.[53] " Placed " means that the landlord builds premises adapted for the particular purpose of the trade, and lets them to the tradesman who carries on his business there.[54] The placing need not be by express act: if premises are placed, the landlord has impliedly placed the innkeeper or tradesman. " Placing the shop there, he also placed the blacksmith there."[55] Innkeeping involves the provision of lodging for customers and not merely the supply of liquor or other refreshments, and so a crofter who carried on a small alehouse (having a licence to sell porter and ale) on his croft, subsidiary to the crofting and carried on a small amount of such business with occasional customers was held not to be an innkeeper.[56] But the carrying on of a blacksmith's shop[57] or a ferry[58] takes the holding outwith the Acts. And where a holding was on 1st April 1912 let to a tradesman, viz., a tailor, the son and

[47] *Malcolm* v *McDougall*, 1916 S.C. 283.
[48] *Howatson, supra.*
[49] *Stormonth-Darling* v *Young*, 1915 S.C. 44.
[50] s. 95 (1).
[51] s. 33.
[52] s. 26 (7).
[53] *Taylor* v *Fordyce*, 1918 S.C. 824 at 832-3, *per* L.P. Strathclyde.
[54] *Stormonth-Darling, supra*, at 51, *per* Lord Salvesen.
[55] *Ibid.*, at 53, *per* Lord Guthrie.
[56] *Taylor* v *Fordyce*, 1918 S.C. 824.
[57] *Stormonth-Darling* v *Young*, 1915 S.C. 44.
[58] *Breadalbane* v *Orr* (1896) 4 S.L.T. 75.

successor of the original tailor, placed in the district by the landlord for the benefit of the neighbourhood, the holding was held to be one outwith the Acts.[59]

Certain subsidiary forms of occupation or employment are allowed by the Acts to be carried on,[60] in order to enable the landholder to obtain a livelihood, only a few large holdings being of sufficient size to permit a living being obtained from them alone.

New Holdings. The Acts before 1911 provided for enlargement of holdings only. The 1911 Act, being designed " to encourage the formation of small agricultural holdings ", however, provided for the first time for the creation of new holdings. The term " holding " means and includes every holding which is constituted by registration of an applicant in terms of the provisions of the 1911 Act respecting the constitution of new holdings.[61] A new holding may be formed or constituted by agreement between the landlord and the tenant for the creation and equipment of a holding, the tenant applying to the Land Court for registration as a new holder; on his registration the new holding is constituted,[62] and the new holder acquires the full status of a landholder.[63]

Alternatively, an agreement may be made between the Secretary of State and a landlord for the creation and equipment of holdings, that is, by adjustment and registration of a scheme for registration by agreement of a holder or holders.[64] The Secretary's predecessor, the Board of Agriculture, was indeed set up in 1912 to create new holdings. Where the Secretary of State has entered into an agreement with the landlord, tenant or other person for or in connection with the constitution of a new holding or new holdings on land in which the landlord, tenant or other person is interested, the Secretary of State may pay to any person so interested such compensation, if any, as the Secretary of State thinks equitable and consistent with the provisions of the 1911 Act in respect of any damage or injury done to him in consequence of and directly attributable to the constitution of new holdings, and it may be a term of such agreement by the Secretary of State with the landlord that the provisions of the 1911 Act, section 17, in regard to vacant holdings apply in regard to such holding as if the holding was constituted otherwise than by agreement, and in that case that section applies accordingly.[64] There is also provision for compulsory procedure, failing such agreement between the Secretary of State and the landlord. Where the Secretary of State is satisfied (and he must be satisfied), that there is a

[59] *Lynch* v *Blair College Trs.* (1949) 37 S.L.C.R. 27.
[60] See " Security of Tenure ", *infra,* pp. 416, 418.
[61] 1911 Act, s. 2 (1) (iv).
[62] *Ibid.,* s. 7 (1).
[63] *Ibid.,* s. 2 (2).
[64] *Ibid.,* s. 7 (11) (f), as substituted by 1919 Act, s. 9.

demand for small holdings and that suitable land is available for that purpose, then he must prepare a scheme for the constitution of one or more new holdings on such land to be occupied by new holders on such terms and conditions not inconsistent with the Landholders Acts as he thinks reasonable.[65] The scheme must show the situation and total area of the land on which holdings are to be constituted, the number and respective situations and areas of the new holdings, any existing buildings to be used for the new holdings, details of the water supply for each holding, the situation and share of any common pasture or grazing to be occupied in connection with the holdings and the rent of each holding;[66] and, where necessary, the scheme will also include provision for water supply from any part of the estate.[67] Where the Secretary of State intends to prepare such a scheme, he must give notice to the landlord of any land to be comprised in it, and, when the landlord has received such a notice, he may not then let or agree to let the land or any part of it without the Secretary of State's consent until the Secretary of State has made an order confirming the scheme or has abandoned it.[68] This restriction must not be for more than twelve months,[69] and compensation is to be paid by the Secretary of State, as agreed on or, failing agreement, as determined by the Land Court on either party's application, in respect of any loss sustained by a landlord, tenant or occupier thereby.[70] The Secretary of State may require the landlord (subject to a penalty for failure without reasonable cause) to give certain information, as to occupiers and terms of tenancies, with a view to ascertaining the suitability and availability of any land for small holdings.[71] The Secretary of State must intimate the prepared scheme to the landlord, tenant and occupier and must give an opportunity to these parties to consider the scheme and make representations to him, and thereafter, after giving all interested persons an opportunity of being heard, he may make an order confirming the scheme in whole or in part with or without modification, or he may abandon it.[72] The Order is recorded in the Landholders Holdings Book and is then enforceable like an order of the Land Court.[73] The Secretary of State must then notify the landlord, tenant and occupier.[74] Compensation is payable by the Secretary of State to these three parties for any damage and injury done to them in consequence of and directly attributable to the constitution of the new holdings, including any damage or injury done

---

[65] *Ibid.*, s. 7 (8) (a), as substituted by 1919 Act, s. 9.
[66] *Ibid.*, s. 7 (8) (b), as substituted by 1919 Act, s. 9.
[67] *Ibid.*, s. 7 (8) (c), as substituted by 1919 Act, s. 9.
[68] *Ibid.*, s. 7 (9), as substituted by 1919 Act, s. 9.
[69] *Ibid.*, s. 7 (9) proviso (a), as substituted by 1919 Act, s. 9, and as further amended by 1931 Act, s. 16 (1).
[70] *Ibid.*, s. 7 (9) proviso (b), as substituted by 1919 Act, s. 9.
[71] 1931 Act, s. 2 (1).
[72] 1911 Act, s. 7 (10), as substituted by 1919 Act, s. 9, and as amended by Reorganisation of Offices (Scotland) Act 1939, Schedule.
[73] *Ibid.*, s. 7 (11) (e) (ii), as substituted by 1919 Act, s. 9.
[74] *Ibid.*, s. 7 (11) (a), as substituted by 1919 Act, s. 9.

to a landlord in respect of an obligation to take over sheep stock at a valuation.[74] The amount is such as may be agreed or, failing agreement, determined by the Land Court after giving all interested an opportunity of being heard and leading evidence.[74] Compensation does not include any allowance on account of the constitution being compulsory, or any compensation for injury to or depreciation in the selling value of the land or of any estate of which the land forms part, except in so far as it arises from injury to or depreciation in the letting value of the land or estate, or compensation for injury done to the value of the sporting rights in excess of the estimated value of these rights if the land or estate was put to the full reasonable use to which it could be let under an ordinary lease of ordinary agricultural or pastoral land.[75] Any benefit or relief enhancing the letting value of the land or estate resulting to a landlord or other person in consequence of or directly attributable to the constitution of new holdings under the scheme must be set off against any damage or injury done.[76] Tenant's compensation is fixed having regard to the duration of the lease but with no allowance for loss of tenant's profits for a period exceeding three years.[77] A claim for compensation must be initiated within twenty-eight days of the notification of the order confirming the scheme, unless the Land Court certify that the failure to do so was, in the circumstances, due to reasonable cause.[78]

At any time within two months after the Land Court have fixed and awarded compensation, the Secretary of State can resolve to abandon the scheme and withdraw the order on payment of such expenses reasonably incurred by the parties in connection with the making of the order or the claim for compensation as may be agreed or, failing agreement, determined by the Land Court.[79]

Any landlord interested can represent to the Secretary of State against a prepared scheme being confirmed by the Secretary of State, and the Secretary of State may, before he consents to the scheme, refer it to the Land Court for inquiry and report.[80]

The Secretary of State may make the order effective by entering on the land, carrying out works, and otherwise as may be required, due compensation being made for any surface damage at an amount agreed on or, failing agreement, determined by the Land Court, and he can negotiate with one or more duly qualified applicants with a view to their registration as new holders in respect of the land.[81] The landlord remains owner and receives each year in perpetuity the fair rents fixed by the Secretary of State, revisable every seven years by the Land Court.

[75] *Ibid.*, s. 7 (11) (b), as substituted by 1919 Act, s. 9.
[76] *Ibid.*, s. 7 (11) (c), as substituted by 1919 Act, s. 9.
[77] *Ibid.*, s. 7 (11) (d), as substituted by 1919 Act, s. 9.
[78] 1931 Act, s. 16 (2).
[79] 1911 Act, s. 7 (11) (e) (i), as substituted by 1919 Act, s. 9.
[80] *Ibid.*, s. 7 (11) (g), as substituted by 1919 Act, s. 9.
[81] *Ibid.*, s. 7 (13).

He is consulted as to the choice of tenants, who are, of course, his tenants, his views receiving preferential treatment.[82]

When the Board of Agriculture (the Secretary of State's predecessor) took over an estate for small holdings, they were in the practice of taking over existing buildings, which they made available to new holders. These had often to be extensively adapted and subdivided. The Board were in the practice of paying to the landlord the value of the buildings and of using them for the scheme, new holders being given loans from the Board to enable them to pay a price to the Board. The rent was for the land alone, and, in assessing compensation to the owner, an element was included based on the present structural value of the buildings; and as between the Board and the new holders, all buildings that were capable of adaptation were treated for use in the occupation as the equivalent of so much financial assistance by the Board to the new holders to enable them to equip their holdings. These existing buildings became improvements, for which the landlord paid compensation to the outgoing holder or tenant or to the Board. But in a case where for the first time the Board had changed their practice and the rent now included rent for the buildings, it was held[83] that, in fixing the rent, the Board were entitled to regard it as including any buildings comprised within it and thus that the value of the buildings could be included in the rent, and that the landholder and the Board could adapt or structurally alter the buildings without the landlord's consent though they had not been taken over. And, while the Board was not bound to buy the buildings, paying the purchase price to the landlord, there might be a relevant and competent claim for compensation in respect of the buildings taken over,[84] the landlord being entitled to compensation for the diminished value of the buildings, even though the value of them was included in the rent. " It is elementary that, under these Acts, no property whatever is transferred from the owner to anyone—neither the land, nor anything on it, nor under it. His property may be, and often is, most prejudicially affected, and the injury thus done to him is met, more or less, by the statutory compensation. But the property of the land remains with him, and the property of every " improvement " which is put up by the landholder becomes his because the land is his. No doubt he may be made to pay for these " improvements " afterwards if the holder gives up his holding; and no doubt, meanwhile, he is reduced to the position of a titular or rent charger with certain restricted statutory rights. But nothing whatever is *taken* from him in property (in the sense in which an ordinary undertaker takes), and accordingly nothing in the shape of price can be demanded from the Board. The Board exercises its statutory powers merely by stepping in and removing

[82] Scott, *Law of Smallholdings*, p. 191.
[83] *Stair Estates* v *Board of Agriculture*, 1926 S.C. 553.
[84] Because of the terms of the 1911 Act, s. 7 (11), as substituted by the 1919 Act, s. 9; *ibid., per* L.P. Clyde at p. 561.

the owner and his tenants from the lands which they respectively own and occupy, and turning these lands to the purpose of planting upon them smallholders who will be under none of the obligations to the owner which are incumbent on common-law tenants, and who will pay to him only such rent as the Land Court thinks from time to time it is proper that they should pay. In the owner's claim for compensation in the present case he made, as matter of fact, no claim for the *price* of his buildings as on a sale, but merely included among the particulars of his claim an item representing the *value* of the buildings interfered with. There was nothing incompetent or wrong about this—quite the contrary."[85] If the buildings are in fact taken over, there can be set off against the sum awarded for the loss of letting value the capitalised value of a return on the sum allowed to the landlords for buildings.[86] So where part of a farm was taken for holdings and the value of the remainder depreciated in letting value, compensation for which was awarded, and the rent of the new holding was fixed as for land unequipped with buildings, and the buildings on the holding were taken over on payment of compensation, it was held that interest on the compensation for the buildings fell to be taken into account in assessing damages for injury to the letting value of the farm, and that the capitalised value of that interest fell to be deducted from the compensation for the depreciation in letting value.[87] Where a whole farm was taken, it was held[88] that, in estimating the compensation payable under the 1911 Act[89] to the tenants, compensation for loss of annual profits was payable only for the period that might reasonably be expected to elapse before the tenants could acquire another farm of similar class and quality and not for the rest of the lease subject to deduction for the contingency of the lease being terminated at one of the breaks; and that in estimating annual profits there could be deducted from receipts a sum representing the value of the tenants' own labour on the farm, without making any corresponding award in their favour for possible loss due to their being deprived of their situations on their farm; and, further, that from annual profits interest at five per cent. on the tenants' capital embarked in the farm could be deducted. The tenants were not entitled to a sum for estimated loss on realisation of stock if the Board finally determined to go on with the scheme. " But here the whole farm is taken. The tenants have to leave, but when they do so they are free. They are not tethered to the remainder of the farm. It is at once open to them to take another, or seek other means of making a livelihood. To treat them as entitled to be compensated by a payment of compensation based on loss of average profits for the whole remaining years of the lease, even with a deduction

[85] *Ibid., per* L.P. Clyde at 560-1.
[86] *Macdonald* v *Board of Agriculture,* 1915 S.C. 1127 (O.H.).
[87] *Macdonald, supra.*
[88] *MacIntyre* v *Board of Agriculture,* 1916 S.C. 983 (O.H.).
[89] 1911 Act, s. 7 (11). See, however, s. 7 (11) (e) as later substituted by the 1919 Act, s. 9.

in respect of the contingency of the lease being foreshortened at the break would be equivalent to saying that they were entitled to have an annuity based on their former average profits paid to them for the years of the estimated endurance of the lease. For that there is no justification. The tenants are not entitled to sit down, fold their hands and enjoy themselves at the expense of the Board of Agriculture—that is, of the national taxpayer—for the remaining years of their lease. Like the servant prematurely dismissed, they are bound in equity to minimise the loss as far as they can by seeking another or other employment. It is, therefore, for the arbiter to consider the circumstances of the district, and that in a pretty wide sense, and to estimate the prospects in matter of time of the claimants finding another suitable farm, fairly similar in class and quality to that from which they are being ousted, and to award the compensation on that basis."[90] In the case of new buildings, the Secretary of State gives loans for the purpose of their erection.[91] The Secretary of State also provides, usually by gift, new roads, fences, etc.[91] At outgoing, each holder can claim compensation for permanent improvements suitable to the holding and executed or paid for by him.

Exclusions from New Holdings. The same limit as to rent and acreage[92] applies in the case of new holdings as in the case of existing holdings.[93] The exclusions under the 1886 Act[94] apply to new holdings except where the holder is registered by agreement, in which case they do not apply to him or his statutory successors.[95] Some of the exclusions in the 1911 Act apply to new holdings,[96] others only by agreement,[97] and a person cannot be registered as a new holder in respect of any holding which is not either wholly agricultural or wholly pastoral, or in part agricultural and as to the residue pastoral,[98] but a person is admissible to registration as a new holder in respect of land within the Parliamentary or police boundary of any burgh or police burgh situated in the counties of Argyll, Inverness, Ross and Cromarty, Sutherland, Caithness, Orkney and Shetland.[99] A new holder can be registered (or a holding enlarged) in respect of land comprised in a deer forest or otherwise kept or preserved mainly or exclusively for sporting

90 *MacIntyre, supra,* at 986, *per* Lord Johnston.
91 See *infra,* p. 412.
92 1911 Act, s. 26 (3) (a), (4).
93 *Board of Agriculture & Ors.* (1929) 17 S.L.C.R. 65.
94 s. 33.
95 1911 Act, s. 26 (7).
96 *Ibid.,* s. 26 (3) (a) to (e), (4).
97 *Ibid.,* s. 26 (3) (g) to (i), (4).
98 *Ibid.,* s. 26 (4).
99 1919 Act, s. 15, as amended by 1931 Act, s. 21.

purposes.[1] Further, there are excluded (a) land which is or forms part of a farm not exceeding 150 acres occupied by a person who has no personal interest in any other farm, or, in the case of a farm so occupied which exceeds 150 acres but is wholly or mainly pastoral, not exceeding an annual value in the Valuation Roll of £80; but two or more new holders can be registered otherwise than by agreement in respect of the whole of such farm, not being a farm wholly or mainly pastoral, where no other land is available in the neighbourhood of any existing village or township;[2] and (b) land which is or forms part of a farm occupied subject to a lease in force at Whitsunday 1911 or in the case of land in the crofting counties at Whitsunday 1906, so long as the lease is in force.[2]

One Holding. Under the 1886 Act, it was held that a tenant could not be a crofter in respect of more than one holding except by consent of the landlord. In the 1911 Act, it was provided[3] that a person could not be admitted to registration as a new holder in respect of land belonging to more than one landlord or in respect of more than one holding, and a person is not held an existing yearly tenant or qualified landholder in respect of land belonging to more than one landlord or of more than one holding, unless such land or holdings have been worked as one holding. Whether holdings are worked as one is a question of fact in each case, to be determined by proof by way of evidence and inspection. So where the subjects comprised a dwellinghouse, offices, stable and garden ground with certain grazing rights in an adjacent pasture, and also a field of three acres, less than two miles distant and held by the same tenant on a separate tenancy, it was held that the separate subjects, in the circumstances there, had been worked as one holding and were, therefore, a " holding ".[4] " Subjects held under different and distinct tenures may, for convenience, or for any reason, be worked together; but that fact will not alter their respective characters in law."[5] So where a crofter in 1886 was a tenant of a holding with a varied right of grazing on other land, and ten years later got from the same landlord the tenancy of a barn and stable and separate rents were paid and receipts granted for the original holding, the grazing right and the barn and stable, it was held[6] that, though these were all

---

[1] 1911 Act, s. 26 (5); this is subject to ss. 7 and 16 of the 1911 Act. See Johnston, *Small Landholders Acts*, 2nd ed., p. 60, that the subsection is awkwardly expressed and must authorise something the Act does not elsewhere authorise; in the case of an enlargement there is too a complication in that s. 16 adopts all restrictions elsewhere in the Act. Under the 1886 Act, s. 13 (3) (e), land in a deer forest cannot be taken for enlargement if the use of the rest as a deer forest would be seriously impaired and the prosperity of the local inhabitants injured. See Scott, *Law of Smallholdings*, p. 216.
[2] 1911 Act, s. 7 (16).
[3] s. 26 (2).
[4] *Fullarton* v *Duke of Hamilton's Trs.*, 1918 S.C. 292.
[5] *Murray* v *Pilkington*, 1919 S.C. 156, at 161, *per* Lord Dundas.
[6] *Murray, supra.*

in fact worked as one holding, in the circumstances the grazing right and the barn and stable were separate tenancies and not part of the holding. The original croft had never been enlarged to comprise the grazing and the barn and stable.

Purchase by Secretary of State. Prior to 1919 the Congested Districts Board had bought lands but only to a limited amount. Under the 1919 Act[7] the Board (and later the Department) was authorised with the consent of the Secretary of State and the Treasury to acquire land anywhere on which schemes are carried out later by agreement or compulsorily for the purposes of the Small Holding Colonies Acts 1916 and 1918. Arbitration for fixing compensation was abolished and certain classes of claims for compensation were excluded. The code for this method, one which the Department came generally to use in establishing new holdings, is in the 1919 Act, Part I, as amended by the Statute Law Revision Act 1927 and the Agricultural Land (Utilisation) Act 1931 (which extended the Department's powers under the 1916 and 1918 Acts). Since the 1939 Act, of course, it is the Secretary of State (with the Treasury's consent) who is authorised to acquire such land.[8] It is outside and not part of the Landholders Acts.[9] The Secretary of State can also acquire land by feuing or leasing, though, in the latter case, holders are not landholders but only subtenants. After notice to the landlord and occupiers, and under penalty for obstruction, the Secretary of State can enter and inspect land, with a view to ascertaining if it is suitable land for the purpose.[10] Certain subjects are excluded from acquisition, *viz.,* lands forming part of a park or of any home farm attached to a mansion-house if the land is required for the amenity or the convenience of the mansion-house or any land forming part of a garden or pleasure ground or woodland.[11]

Holdings outwith the Acts. Holdings may be constituted and equipped and let outside the Acts.[12]

Crofts under the 1955 and 1961 Acts. The 1955 Act, as already mentioned, reintroduced crofts and established a new code for the seven crofting counties. This has subsequently been amended by the 1961 Act. A croft is defined[13] as meaning (a) as from the date of commencement

[7] Part I.
[8] 1939 Act, s. 1 and Schedule, amending the 1919 Act to this effect.
[9] 1919 Act, s. 33.
[10] *Ibid.,* s. 8.
[11] *Ibid.,* s. 3 (2).
[12] See *infra,* p. 495, " Contracting Out ".
[13] 1955 Act, s. 3 (1), as amended by 1961 Act, Schedule First, paras. 9 (a) and (b). This definition covers the 1961 Act, any reference in the 1955 Act to the 1955 Act including, unless the context otherwise requires, a reference to the 1961 Act: 1961 Act, Schedule First, para. 8.

of the 1955 Act[14] every holding, whether occupied by a landholder or not, situate in the crofting counties which was immediately before the commencement of the Act a holding to which the provisions of the Landholders Acts in relation to landholders applied; (b) as from that date every holding situate in these counties which immediately before the commencement of the Act was a holding to which the provisions of these Acts in relation to statutory small tenants applied; (c) as from the date of registration every holding situate in these counties which was before the commencement of the 1961 Act[15] constituted a croft by the registration of the tenant thereof as a crofter under the 1955 Act;[16] and (d) as from the date of the direction every holding situated as aforesaid to which the Secretary of State has directed under the 1961 Act[17] that it be a croft. For the purposes of the Acts any right in pastoral or grazing land held or to be held by the tenant of a croft, alone or in common with others, is deemed part of the croft.[18] But this does not (according to a Divisional Land Court decision, the Full Court reserving their opinion) apply to grazing let outwith the Acts, as, *e.g.*, a hill grazing let to a crofter on a year to year basis.[19] And where the tenant of one croft was also tenant of grazing lands about a mile away from the croft, it was held that the rights in pasture or grazing land must be enjoyed in association with the holding and form a pertinent of it, and could not be real rights in and to separate lands, as in that case.[20] Where a croft is vacant, the Secretary of State may direct that it shall cease to be a croft.[21]

New Crofts. The landlord and the tenant of a holding in the crofting counties, the area of which does not exceed seventy-five acres (exclusive of any common pasture or grazing held therewith) or the annual rent of which does not exceed £50, and which is not a croft, may apply to the Secretary of State for a direction that the holding be a croft and he may give the direction if he thinks fit;[22] the holding then becomes a croft under the Acts from the date of his direction.[22] He must inform the Commission of his direction.[23] References in the Landholders Acts to registration of a tenant as a crofter—a system repealed by the 1961 Act[24]—are construed in the crofting counties as references to the giving

[14] 1st October 1955—Crofters (Scotland) Act 1955 Commencement Order 1955 (No. 1201) (c. 9).
[15] 27th August 1961—1961 Act, s. 19 (2).
[16] s. 4, which section is repealed by 1961 Act, s. 2 (6). Mere noting for registration does not justify an application for compensation on renunciation. *Wallace* v *Stewart* (1961) 49 S.L.C.R. 18.
[17] 1961 Act, s. 2 (1). See *infra*.
[18] 1955 Act, s. 3 (5); 1961 Act, Schedule First, para. 8.
[19] *Campbell* v *Secretary of State for Scotland* (1960) 48 S.L.C.R. 41.
[20] *Ross* v *Graesser*, 1962 S.C. 66.
[21] 1955 Act, s. 16. See *infra*, p. 467.
[22] 1961 Act, s. 2 (1).
[23] *Ibid.*, s. 2 (5).
[24] *Ibid.*, s. 2 (6).

of such a direction.[25] Apart from these provisions, the provisions of the Landholders Acts as to new holdings including common grazings apply with amendments.[26] Where a person to whom a new holding has been allocated or let by the Secretary of State fails without reasonable cause within three months of the term of entry to occupy, cultivate and proceed to equip the holding, the Secretary of State may, after considering any objections by that person, terminate his right to the holding and allocate or let it to another person.[27]

Crown Land. The Acts of 1955 and 1961 apply to land an interest in which belongs to Her Majesty in right of the Crown or a Government Department or which is held in trust for Her Majesty for the purposes of a Government Department, subject to any modifications prescribed by regulations made by the Secretary of State.[28]

PERSONS

Crofter under the 1886 Act. A crofter was defined in the 1886 Act[29] as any person who, at the passing of the Act, was tenant of a holding (being arable or pasture land other than garden ground) from year to year who resided on his holding, the annual rent of which did not exceed £30 in money and which was situated in a crofting parish, and the successors of such person in the holding being his heirs or legatees. The Act applied only to crofters (and their successors) in possession at the date of the Act: the Act was intended to assist and protect those only who in the circumstances at that time were occupying under unfavourable conditions. Thus, new holders after the date of the Act were not included: they were not to be encouraged or favoured.

Landholders. The 1911 Act abolished the term " crofter " and in lieu created the class known as " landholders ",[30] of which there were four categories.[31] A smallholder who became a landholder by virtue of the 1911 Act had to be in one or other of these categories. First, an existing crofter as at 1st April 1912; second, a new holder, that is, a person established on a holding constituted by agreement or under the schedule or purchase provisions of the Acts and registered as such; third, an existing yearly tenant—the tenant on 1st April 1912 from year to year of a " holding " who resided on or within two miles thereof and who by himself and the members of his family cultivated it with or without hired labour; fourth, a qualified leaseholder—the tenant on 1st April 1912, under a lease for more than a year, with the same

25 *Ibid.*, s. 2 (7).
26 1955 Act, s. 38 (2), (3), (4), Schedule Sixth.
27 1931 Act, s. 4, as applied by 1961 Act, s. 2 (6).
28 1955 Act, ss. 37 (1), 38 (1); 1961 Act, Schedule First, para. 8.
29 1886 Act, s. 34. This was repealed by 1911 Act, Schedule Second.
30 s. 1.
31 *Ibid.*, s. 2 (1), (2).

qualities as an existing yearly tenant as to residence and cultivation. The existing crofter became a landholder when the 1911 Act came into operation, on 1st April 1912; the new holder from the date of registration; the existing yearly tenant became, as from 1st April 1912, a landholder or a statutory small tenant; and the leaseholder became as from the termination of the lease a landholder or a statutory small tenant. The crofter's tenancy was, unless inconsistent with any of the provisions of the Act, deemed to be a continuance of his crofting tenancy under the 1886 Act and all deeds and contracts were construed accordingly.[32] An occupant of land for less than a year and a person who did not satisfy the conditions as to residence and cultivation are thus not within the provisions of the Acts.

The distinction between a landholder and a statutory small tenant is that if the existing yearly tenant (or the qualified leaseholder) or his predecessor in the same family had provided or paid for the whole or the greater part of the buildings or other permanent improvements on the holding without receiving from the landlord or any predecessor in title payment or fair consideration therefor, he is, unless disqualified under the Act, a landholder: and if he or his predecessor in the same family had not so provided or paid he is, unless disqualified under the Act,[33] a statutory small tenant.[34] The statutory small tenant has not the same degree of security of tenure as the landholder.

The distinction only applies to existing yearly tenants and qualified leaseholders. No similar provision occurred in the 1886 Act as to crofters, while the 1911 and 1919 Acts did not make any such provision in the case of new holders. The term " predecessor in the same family " was not defined in the 1911 Act, but it was held that a deceased husband as a subtenant was not a predecessor,[35] that a father-in-law and a brother-in-law were not predecessors,[36] and that the term was not confined to immediate predecessors.[37] The 1931 Act, however, gave a definition of the phrase, which applies to improvements[38]—" the wife or husband of such landholder or cottar, and any person to whom such landholder or cottar, or the wife or husband of such landholder or cottar might, failing nearer heirs, have succeeded in case of intestacy."

The term " landholder " includes " the successors of every such person (that is, every one of the four classes) in the holding being his heirs and legatees ".[39]

[32] *Ibid.*, s. 26 (9).
[33] *Ibid.*, s. 26.
[34] *Ibid.*, s. 2 (1), (2).
[35] *Hamilton* v *Duke of Hamilton's Trs.*, 1918 S.C. 282.
[36] *Kidd* v *Morison*, 1916 S.C. 759.
[37] *Irvine* v *Fordyce*, 1927 S.C. 72.
[38] s. 9. See *infra*, p. 422.
[39] 1911 Act, s. 2 (2).

Statutory Small Tenants.   They are a class created by the 1911 Act,
and created apparently to cover the case of holdings in the Lowlands,
there being far fewer instances in the rest of the country where the
landlord had provided the permanent improvements. As already stated,
the statutory small tenant is an existing yearly tenant or a qualified
leaseholder who or whose predecessor in the same family has not
provided or paid for the whole or the greater part of the buildings or
other permanent improvements on the holding without receiving from
the landlord or any predecessor in title payment or fair consideration
therefor.[40] The term means and includes[41] a tenant from year to year
or leaseholder, not otherwise disqualified in terms of the 1911 Act, in
regard to whom the Act provides that he shall not be held an existing
yearly tenant or a qualified leaseholder, and the successors of such
tenant or leaseholder in the holding, being his heirs, legatees (if within
the relationship specified in the 1886 Act) or assignees, if assignation
is permitted under the lease.[42] A person is not a statutory small tenant
if he is disqualified from being an existing yearly tenant or a qualified
leaseholder.[43] In the event of a dispute as to whether a person is a
statutory small tenant, the Land Court can determine that matter summarily.[44] There are outside the Highlands not many such tenants. A
special code was made for these tenants,[45] to whom the provisions of
the Acts do not apply except as specially provided.[46]

A statutory small tenant can become a landholder and be included
in the definition thereof. Thus, where on the renewal of the tenancy
the landlord fails to provide such buildings as will enable the tenant
to cultivate the holding according to the terms of the lease or agreement,
or fails at any time to maintain the buildings or permanent improvements required for the cultivation and reasonable equipment of the
holding, in so far as the tenant is not by common law or express written
agreement bound to do so, the tenant may apply to the Land Court,
and the Court may, after giving the landlord an opportunity to remedy
his failure, declare the tenant a landholder.[47] The statutory small tenant
too may opt to become a landholder if within a month prior to the
expiry of any period of the tenancy current at or subsequent to the
commencement of the 1931 Act he serves written notice to that effect
on the landlord; but if the landlord, within a month after that notice
has been served on him, gives to the Land Court a written undertaking
that the tenant shall have the same compensation rights for permanent
improvements as if he were a landholder, the Court, after intimation

---

[40] *Ibid.,* s. 2 (1).
[41] *Ibid.,* s. 32 (1).
[42] *Ibid.,* s. 16, as amended by 1919 Act, s. 13.
[43] *Ibid.,* s. 26 (10).
[44] *Ibid.,* s. 32 (13).
[45] *Ibid.,* s. 32, as amended by 1931 Act, ss. 13, 18.
[46] *Ibid.,* s. 32 (2).
[47] *Ibid.,* s. 32 (11).

to the tenant, may order that undertaking to be recorded in the Landholders' Holdings Book, and the tenant is then deemed a landholder but to that limited extent only.[48]

New Holders. A new holder is not qualified for registration otherwise than by agreement who does not satisfy the Secretary of State as to his ability to fulfil the obligations incumbent on him.[49] Reasonable consideration must be given by the Secretary of State to any objections by a landlord to an applicant, and preference, other things being equal, must be given to applicants preferred by the landlord.[50] The Secretary of State must here consider whether the circumstances justify him in refusing to give preference to applicants tendered by the landlord.[51] (For two years after the 1919 Act came into operation, preference had to be given to suitable persons who had served in the forces of the Crown in the 1914-18 War or any previous war).[52]

Effect of Alteration of Tenancy. If a tenant became a landholder or a statutory small tenant on 1st April 1912, that is, on the 1911 Act coming into operation, his rights as such are not lost by a later agreement by him with the landlord whereby he accepts a lease for less than a year.[53] Thus, the acceptance, by the tenant, *currente termino,* of missives altering the conditions of the tenancy, altering the tenancy to a monthly let for a house and a seasonal let for grazings, so as to take him out of the category of a statutory small tenant, were held not to prevent him demanding a renewal of the original tenancy as from its natural termination. The circumstances, however, were very special; the missives had been prepared by the landlord and accepted and signed by the tenant, both parties being in ignorance of the statutory incidents of the tenancy, there had been no subsequent change in the parties' relationship and the tenant made the demand for renewal before the natural termination of the lease.[54] The statutory small tenant is entitled, on determination of the tenancy, to a renewal of it on certain terms and conditions, notwithstanding an agreement to the contrary, unless the landlord satisfies the Land Court that there is a reasonable ground of objection to him,[55] and these missives were an agreement to the contrary and void, the 1911 Act having as its purpose the securing of fixity of tenure at a fair rent to those who satisfy its requirements and, in this particular provision, to protect a statutory small tenant against himself.[54]

[48] 1931 Act, s. 14.
[49] 1911 Act, s. 7 (14).
[50] *Ibid.,* s. 7 (15).
[51] *Department of Agriculture* v *Cameron* (1931) 19 S.L.C.R. 9.
[52] 1919 Act, s. 28.
[53] *Clelland* v *William Baird & Son,* 1923 S.C. 370.
[54] *Clelland, supra.* See *Cheyne* v *Paterson,* 1929 S.C. 119 at 128, *per* L.P. Clyde.
[55] 1911 Act, s. 32 (4).

Joint Holders. Existing crofters, existing yearly tenants and quali-fied leaseholders can be joint tenants, but one person only can be registered as a new holder.[56] A joint tenancy can be continued by statutory successors, but where after 1st April 1912 a holding is held by one landholder or a joint holding ceases to be such, only one person can be landholder of the holding.[56] The Acts apply to joint tenancies by statutory small tenants at 1st April 1912.[57]

Subtenants. Privileges and rights are provided only as against landlords, and " landlord " is defined by reference to the Agricultural Holdings Acts.[58] A subtenant is not a crofter[59] but there might be cases where the crofters might remain tenants, holding from the landlord and thus be crofters under the Act. The croft might fall within the bounds of a large farm separately let, and the occupier of the croft might be a tenant of the proprietor, though the rents are paid to the farm tenant.[60] The 1911 Act excluded a subtenant; it provided[61] that any lands or heritages forming, as at 1st April 1912, part of a holding and occupied at that date by a subtenant, whether or not paying rent, of an existing yearly tenant or a qualified leaseholder was not to be deemed to be included within the holding; and this applied also to statutory small tenants.[62] The Acts do not apply to a subtenant under a long lease no matter how long the lease and whether or not a registered lease.[63] In the case of crofters under the 1955 and 1961 Acts, a subtenant under a sublease is not a crofter or a tenant of a holding under the Agricultural Holdings (Scotland) Act 1949;[64] but if under a sublease of a croft a right in any common grazing is let under the sublease[65] the subtenant will come into the crofter's place as to any matters concerning such right and any grazing regulations will apply to the subtenant.[66]

Crofters under 1955 and 1961 Acts. The 1955 Act abolished the distinction between landholders and statutory small tenants in the counties of Argyll, Caithness, Inverness, Orkney, Ross and Cromarty, Sutherland and Shetland and reintroduced the class known as "crofters".[67]

---

[56] *Ibid.,* s. 26 (8).
[57] *Carmichaels* v *Maccoll,* 1913 S.C. 916.
[58] 1886 Act, s. 34. See *infra,* p. 412.
[59] *McDougall* v *McAlister* (1890) 17 R. 555; *Livingstone* v *Beattie* (1891) 18 R. 735; *Dalgleish* v *Livingston* (1895) 22 R. 646.
[60] *Livingstone, supra,* per Lords Kinnear at 743 and McLaren at 744. But see *Dalgleish, supra,* and opinions therein.
[61] s. 26 (6). See *Morrison* v *Nicolson* (1913) 1 S.L.C.R. 89, that the subsection is not limited to subtenancies which are *not* consented to by the landlord. See too Scott, *Law of Smallholdings,* p. 136; Johnston, *The Small Landholders (Scotland) Acts 1886-1911,* 2nd ed., p. 61.
[62] s. 26 (10).
[63] *Macdonald* v *Bennet* (1949) 37 S.L.C.R. 24.
[64] 1961 Act, s. 13 (1).
[65] Being one in terms of s. 11 (1) (a) or (b) or (4) or (7) or granted with the Commission's consent.
[66] *Ibid.,* s. 13 (2).
[67] 1955 Act, s. 3 (2); 1961 Act, s. 17 (1), Schedule First, para. 8.

A crofter is defined for the purpose of the 1955 and the 1961 Acts as meaning the tenant of a croft.[68] Parties may agree whether a tenant is a crofter or the Land Court may decide the issue, and if there is agreement[68a] the landlord, or if the Court decide then the Court, must notify the Crofters Commission accordingly; if neither of these events occurs, the Crofters Commission may decide the matter.[69] The tenancy of a crofter under the two Acts who was a person who at the commencement of the 1955 Act became a crofter is deemed so far as is consistent with the Acts to be a continuance of his tenancy as a landholder or a statutory small tenant and all contracts and other deeds are construed accordingly.[70] "Landlord" means any person who for the time being is entitled to receive the rent and profits, or to take possession of a croft.[71]

Cottars. The 1886 Act referred to and had provisions in favour of persons called "cottars". These were defined[72] as either the occupier of a dwellinghouse situated in a crofting parish with or without land, who pays no rent to the landlord—that is, squatters who had built houses on bare tolerance from the landlord—or the tenant from year to year of a dwellinghouse situated in a crofting parish who resides therein and who pays to the landlord therefor an annual rent not exceeding £6, whether with or without garden ground but without arable or pasture land—those who are tenants of houses without land. Thus, some pay rent, others do not do so. Some have built their own houses, others live in houses belonging to their landlord. The dwellinghouse is the principal subject for the cottar.[73] The cottar, who is of a special class within the general crofting class, must hold from a landlord. If any person holds or occupies without the owner's knowledge or consent he is not a cottar.[74] A subtenant is not a cottar, any more than he is a crofter.[75] The 1955 Act repealing the provision of the 1886 Act[76] redefined the cottar in the same terms.[77]

---

[68] 1955 Act, s. 3 (2). See definition of "croft" *supra,* p. 404.
[68a] Where a landlord had intimated to the Commission, on being required by the Commission to give information for the Register, that the tenant was a crofter this was held not to be an agreement. *Elder* v *Manson,* 1964 S.L.T. (Land Ct.) 15.
[69] *Ibid.,* s. 15 (3), (4). See *infra,* p. 492.
[70] *Ibid.,* s. 39 (1). See 1961 Act, Schedule First, para. 8. In *Marquis of Bute* v *Baxter,* 1966 S.L.T. (Land Ct.) 9, it was held that a lease in 1909 providing for compensation for resumption, by abatement of rent, of rough ground was inconsistent with the provisions of the 1955 Act.
[71] *Ibid.,* s. 37 (1).
[72] 1886 Act, s. 34.
[73] *McDougall* v *McAlister* (1890) 17 R. 555.
[74] *Macinnes* v *Lady Strathcona* (1926) 14 S.L.C.R. 39.
[75] *Macvicar* v *Cameron* (1931) 19 S.L.C.R. 63.
[76] 1955 Act, s. 38 (3), Schedule Sixth.
[77] *Ibid.,* s. 28 (4).

"*Landlord*" *and* "*Tenant*". These are defined in the Agricultural Holdings Acts,[78] and under the 1955 Act[79] the term "landlord" is specifically defined in the same terms as in the Agricultural Holdings (Scotland) Act 1949.

ASSISTANCE IN AND FENCING OF NEW HOLDINGS

Assistance to Landholders. The Secretary of State may assist a landholder, whether he be registered by agreement or otherwise, by loans of money, or gifts of money, subject to any conditions he may prescribe, for the equipment of new holdings, that is, for dividing fencing or otherwise preparing or adapting the land, making occupation roads, or executing other works such as works for the provision of drainage or water supply or erecting or adapting a dwellinghouse or houses or other buildings or any similar purpose,[80] or by grants towards the provision of houses and other buildings in certain cases.[81] The Secretary of State may, too, make or guarantee advances to land banks or co-operative or credit societies for the assistance of the Secretary of State's tenants, landholders or statutory small tenants or to associations having as their object or one of their objects the taking over and management of sheep stocks on common grazings.[82] In the event of failure of a statutory successor taking place or being deemed to take place under the 1911 Act,[83] the landlord is liable to repay to the Secretary of State the amount of any outstanding liability in respect of a loan under the 1911 Act,[84] but the Secretary of State cannot recover from him any sum in excess of an amount agreed on, or in the event of a dispute, assessed by the Land Court, as the amount due by the landlord by way of compensation for permanent improvements if the holding had been renounced when the failure of the statutory successor took place or is deemed to have taken place.[85]

Fences. Where an order is made for the constitution of new holdings the Secretary of State must, if requested by the landlord, erect and maintain or cause to be erected and maintained such march fence or fences as the normal and reasonable practice of agriculture and estate management may require in the conditions.[86] This obligation, however, arises only where the intrusion of new holders on an estate alters the existing conditions to such an extent that it would not be

[78] 1886 Act, s. 34.
[79] s. 37 (1).
[80] 1911 Act, s. 7 (7), as amended by 1919 Act, s. 32, and Schedule Fourth, and 1931 Act, ss. 15, 41 (2) and Schedule Second.
[81] Agriculture (Scotland) Act 1948, s. 77.
[82] 1919 Act, s. 16; 1931 Act, s. 20; 1939 Act, Schedule.
[83] s. 22.
[84] s. 7.
[85] 1911 Act, s. 8 (2), as added by the Agriculture (Scotland) Act 1948, s. 66. (The original s. 8 (2) had been repealed by the 1931 Act, s. 3 (2)).
[86] 1919 Act, s. 10, as amended by 1931 Act, s. 19.

fair to require the landlord to bear the added burden.[87] If there is any dispute about the necessity for or adequacy of the fence or fences, it must be settled by agreement, or, failing agreement, by the Land Court.[86]

PROVISIONS IN RELATION TO SMALL LANDHOLDERS

General. The landholder has security of tenure as against the landlord and a right to a fair or judicial rent. He is bound to the landlord only as a yearly tenant; he can leave at the end of the year. He can be removed for breach of certain statutory conditions, which amount to an irritancy. The landlord can resume possession of the holding for certain reasons. The landholder cannot assign the holding but he can bequeath it or, in case of personal infirmity, bequeath it in anticipation to a relative.

Rent. The rent payable annually by the landholder is the " present rent ", that is, the rent, including money and any prestations other than money, (a) in the case of an existing crofter when the 1911 Act was passed payable for the year current on the passing of the 1886 Act or where the rent so payable has been altered under that Act payable for the year current at the commencement of the 1911 Act, (b) in the case of an existing yearly tenant payable for the year current when the 1911 Act commenced, and (c) in the case of a qualified leaseholder or a statutory small tenant becoming a landholder subsequently and in the case of new holders or of landholders whose holdings are enlarged, the rent payable or fixed for the last year of the lease or tenancy or at the date of registration or of the enlargement.[88] That is the rent, unless and until the " present rent " is altered under the Acts.[88] A proportion of an insurance premium paid by the tenant on a fire policy over buildings in the holding was held not to be an item to be taken into account in computing the " present rent ".[89]

Both parties may voluntarily agree to alter the rent to such an amount and for such a period as may be agreed on, and that remains the rent so long as the agreement exists, and also after expiry of the agreement so long as the Land Court have not fixed a different rent or a new agreement has not been made.[90] Alternatively, either the landlord or the small landholder may apply to the Land Court to fix a fair rent for the holding,[91] but unless by agreement neither party can apply to the Court for revision of the rent if the subject of the let is unaltered.[92] The existence of missives does not prevent an application to the Court to fix a fair rent. The rent that is fixed by the Court is the rent payable by the landholder as from the first term of Whitsunday or Martinmas

[87] *Board of Agriculture* v *Sinclair's Trs.* (1923) 11 S.L.C.R. 50.
[88] 1911 Act, s. 13.
[89] *Marquis of Breadalbane* v *Robertson,* 1914 S.C. 215.
[90] 1886 Act, s. 5.
[91] *Ibid.,* s. 6 (1).
[92] *Ibid.,* ss. 5, 7.

after the date when it is fixed; if the rent fixed is less than the rent hitherto paid, the reduction takes effect from the date of the application to the Court, up to the first term of Whitsunday or Martinmas next following the date when the rent is fixed,[93] and the landholder can deduct the amount overpaid for that period.[94]

In fixing the rent the Land Court must consider " all the circumstances of the case, holding and district ", and particularly any permanent or unexhausted improvements on the holding, and suitable thereto which have been executed or paid for by the landholder or his " predecessors in the same family[95] ".[96] The Court should consider only a fair division of profits between landlord and tenant, ignoring the open market rent and any grant to which the tenant is entitled.[97] The potential and not the actual return should be examined, and competition and inefficient management ignored.[98] Consideration of the sporting value of the land is not to govern the fixing of the rent.[99] Nor, it has been held,[1] is the fact that the tenant has received a loan from his landlord (in the case, the Department of Agriculture) to enable him to build a house on the holding to affect the fixing of the rent; if it were allowed to do so, it would directly contradict the statutory character and qualities of the loan, which operate towards permanent improvement of the holding, and the loan must be deemed to have been wholly expended for his benefit. Nor again is loss to the tenant as a contingent seller of the house in respect of the difference between the cost of erection and the present value to be considered.[1] The state of repair of buildings which are tenant's improvements and deterioration of buildings due to non-cultivation by the tenant are not relevant factors in fixing the rent.[2] And the tenant cannot credit himself with a labour charge of a standard wage for himself.[3] But the Court is entitled to take into account special circumstances affecting the holding such as the return derived by the landholder from summer letting to holiday visitors,[4] or the fact that the situation of the holding is such that there is a risk of damage to crops from game or deer, thereby diminishing the letting value.[5] And it was held that the Court are not bound to exclude from consideration improvements executed by the landholder or his predecessors in the same

---

[93] *Ibid.*, s. 6 (2).
[94] *Ibid.*, s. 6 (3).
[95] See as to this term, *supra*, p. 407, *infra*, p. 422.
[96] 1886 Act, s. 6 (1). See as to principles, Johnston, *The Crofters Holding Acts*, 3rd ed., 5-6; Scott, *Law of Smallholdings*, 73-4; Crofters Commission Report, 1886, p. 102. See *infra*, p. 416.
[97] *Secretary of State for Scotland* v *Murray* (1962) 50 S.L.C.R. 3.
[98] *Lochiel Estate Trs.* v *Stewart* (1961) 49 S.L.C.R. App. 44.
[99] See 1886 Act, s. 11.
[1] *Department of Agriculture* v *Burnett*, 1937 S.C. 367. The loan was under 1911 Act, s. 7 (7).
[2] *Harrold* v *Secretary of State for Scotland* (1953) 41 S.L.C.R. 37.
[3] *Secretary of State for Scotland* v *Ramage* (1952) 40 S.L.C.R. 29.
[4] *McNeill* v *Duke of Hamilton's Trs.*, 1918 S.C. 221; *Fullarton* v *Duke of Hamilton's Trs.*, 1918 S.C. 292; *Sinclair* v *Campbell*, 1919 S.C. 341.
[5] *McKelvie* v *Duke of Hamilton's Trs.*, 1918 S.C. 301.

family in implement of a specific written agreement or obligation if fair consideration for the improvements has not been received by the landholder or his predecessors;[6] this applies also to a statutory small tenant.[7]

Once the rent has been fixed by the Court—and when so fixed it is payable as from the first term after the Court's decision—it cannot be altered except by agreement, for the next seven years.[8] In the case of a person registered as a new holder by agreement, the rent so agreed between landlord and landholder cannot, if agreed for a specified period, be altered by the Land Court during that period, and in any event it cannot be so altered for seven years from the time when it first becomes payable.[9] The same applies to the case of a new holding constituted under a scheme under the 1911 Act.[10]

With a view to giving a fresh start to those who are burdened by long-standing arrears or relieving those whose arrears are caused by back rents beyond their ability to pay, the Land Court has absolute powers to deal with any arrears of rent.[11] Thus, it can, on a review and consideration of the circumstances that led to the arrears of rent arising, cancel the arrears in whole or in part, or it may determine that the arrears must be paid in full or in part, and it may order payment to be made by instalments or in one sum.[11] Though a landholder has granted a bill or promissory note to the landlord for the arrears at the landlord's request, the Court can still deal with these arrears.[12] The effect of the Acts, however, is not to suspend or postpone the power of the ordinary courts to pronounce decree for payment of arrears.[13]

On an application to it to fix a fair rent or another application by the landholder, the Land Court may pronounce an order which will sist or suspend proceedings depending in any Court for removal of the landholder for non-payment of rent till the application is finally determined and on such terms as to payment of rent or otherwise as they shall think fit.[14] And the Land Court can, on the landholder's application, before the *induciae* in the action in the other Court have expired, prohibit the sale of the landholder's effects on the holding under proceedings for recovery of rent till the application to fix the rent has been finally determined, on such terms as to payment of rent or otherwise as they shall think fit, if the Land Court are satisfied that the sale would defeat the intention of the 1886 Act.[15]

---

[6] *MacKinnon* v *Duke of Hamilton's Trs.*, 1918 S.C. 274. See 1931 Act, s. 12, *infra*, p. 422.
[7] *Wilkie* v *Hill*, 1916 S.C. 892.
[8] 1886 Act, s. 6 (2).
[9] 1911 Act, s. 7 (6).
[10] 1919 Act, s. 17, Schedule Second.
[11] 1886 Act, s. 6 (5).
[12] 1887 Act, s. 12.
[13] *Fraser* v *Macdonald* (1886) 14 R. 181; *Stuart & Stuart* v *Macleod* (1891) 19 R. 223.
[14] 1886 Act, s. 6 (4).
[15] 1887 Act, s. 2, as amended by 1911 Act, s. 39.

THE CROFTERS AND SMALL LANDHOLDERS ACTS

Security of Tenure. The landholder has a perpetual tenure provided that he fulfils certain conditions. He can only be removed from the tenancy of the holding on certain statutory grounds, which are called " statutory conditions ". He must be in breach of one or more of these statutory conditions. They are:

(1) the landholder shall pay his rent at the terms at which it is due and payable;[16]

(2) the landholder shall not execute any deed purporting to assign his tenancy;[17]

(3) the landholder shall not, to the prejudice of the interest of the landlord, persistently injure the holding by the dilapidation of buildings or, after notice has been given by the landlord to the landholder not to commit, or to desist from, the particular injury specified in such notice, by the deterioration of the soil;[18] " buildings " include those erected by the landlord as well as those erected by the landholder or his predecessors.[19]

(4) The landholder shall not, without the consent of the landlord in writing, subdivide his holding or sublet it or any part of it or erect or suffer to be erected on the holding any dwellinghouse otherwise than in substitution for those already upon the holding at the time of the passing of the 1886 Act[20] or, in the case of landholders other than crofters, the date when the Landholders Act first applied to the holding;[21] nothing, however, is to be construed as debarring subletting of the dwellinghouse to holiday visitors.[21] And probably subletting for a period less than a year is permissible.[22] Not every let will infer subletting.[23] The prohibition moreover only applies to subletting after the time when the Acts applied to the holding. If the subletting was prior to the Acts applying to the holding, the sublet part, of course, falls outside the Acts for the tenant does not carry with him as landholder the subjects in a subtenancy; the subjects of the subtenancy revert to the landlord unfettered, the subtenant not being a landholder; and the Land Court on application to fix a fair and equitable rent must exclude the sublet part, and can, failing agreement, adjust the rent excluding the sublet part.[24] The provision as

---

[16] 1886 Act, s. 1 (1).
[17] *Ibid.*, s. 1 (2). If he is unable to work the holding through illness, old age, or infirmity, the Land Court may give leave to his assigning his holding to a member of his family: 1911 Act, s. 21; 1919 Act, s. 13. See *infra*, p. 425.
[18] *Ibid.*, s. 1 (3).
[19] *MacKenzie's Tr.* v *MacKenzie* (1905) 7 F. 505.
[20] 1886 Act, s. 1 (4). A landholder was held not to be in breach of this provision where he sublet for potato growing five years previously and then for a limited and temporary right of grazing stock to consume the grass: *Little* v *McEwan* (1964) 52 S.L.C.R. 3, 1965 S.L.T. (Land Ct.) 3.
[21] 1911 Act, s. 10 (2).
[22] *McNeill* v *Duke of Hamilton's Trs.*, 1918 S.C. 221.
[23] Scott, *Law of Smallholdings*, p. 137.
[24] *Ibid.*, p. 136; Johnston, *The Small Landholders (Scotland) Acts 1886-1911*, 2nd ed., p. 61. See *supra*, p. 414.

to the erection of dwellinghouses does not apply to a new holder but a new holder, established by the Secretary of State or his predecessors, or statutory successors of that new holder must have or have had the written consent of the landlord and the Secretary of State or his predecessors, in order to be entitled to erect or suffer to be erected on the holding more than one dwellinghouse.[21] Where there were joint tenants in a holding and a dwellinghouse for each, one small and old, the other larger and recently built in substitution for a previous one, and while the joint tenancy continued both were suitable to and reasonably required for the holding, it was held that neither house was an " extra dwellinghouse ".[25] An additional house can be excised from a holding.[22]

(5) The landholder shall not persistently violate any written condition signed by him for the protection of the interest of the landlord or of neighbouring crofters which is legally applicable to the holding, and which the Land Court shall find to be reasonable;[26] whether a residence clause or condition is reasonable depends on the circumstances of the case, and so where a holding was very small in extent, viz. 2·3 acres of arable land and one-sixth of 123·7 acres of common grazing and also grazing of an island of 4 acres, it was held that it was not reasonable to order removal of the holder for breach of a condition of residence.[27]

(6) The landholder shall not do any act whereby he becomes notour bankrupt within the meaning of the Bankruptcy (Scotland) Act 1886, and the Debtors (Scotland) Act 1880,[28] and shall not execute a trust deed for behoof of creditors;[29] a landholder in whose favour an order has been made prohibiting the sale of his effects till an application to fix a fair rent for the holding has been finally determined[30] is not to be held notour bankrupt by reason of decree or diligence before or during the subsistence of the order and for the rent to which the order relates, but this does not apply after the decision on arrears in relation to decrees and diligence not invalidated by the decision.[31]

(7) The landlord or any person or persons authorised by him in that behalf (he or they making reasonable compensation for any damage to be done or occasioned thereby), shall have the right to enter upon the holding for any of the purposes following (that is to say)—mining or taking minerals, or digging or searching

[25] Mackinnon v Duke of Hamilton's Trs., 1918 S.C. 274.
[26] 1886 Act, s. 1 (5).
[27] Secretary of State for Scotland v Mackenzie (1951) 39 S.L.C.R. 19.
[28] These two Acts were repealed by the Bankruptcy (Scotland) Act 1913, which defines " notour bankruptcy " in ss. 5 and 6.
[29] 1886 Act, s. 1 (6). See Secretary of State for Scotland v Black, 1965 S.L.T. (Land Ct.) 2.
[30] Supra, p. 413.
[31] 1887 Act, s. 3.

27

for minerals, quarrying or taking stone, marble, gravel, sand, clay, slate or other workable mineral, cutting or taking timber or peats, excepting timber and other trees planted by the landholder or his predecessors in the holding, being of the same family, or that may be necessary for ornament or shelter, and excepting also such peats as may be required for the use of the holding, opening or making roads, fences, drains, and water-courses, passing and repassing to and from the shore of the sea or any loch with or without horses and carriages for exercising any right of property or other right belonging to the landlord, viewing or examining at all reasonable times the state of the holding and all buildings and improvements thereon, hunting, shooting, fishing or taking game or fish, wild birds, or vermin (" game " meaning deer, hares, rabbits, pheasants, partridges, quails, landrails, grouse, black-game, capercailzie, ptarmigan, woodcock, snipe, wild duck, widgeon and teal). The landholder shall not obstruct the landlord, or any person or persons authorised by him in that behalf as aforesaid, in the exercise of any rights reserved or conferred by this subsection.[32] This right of the landlord does not affect a landholder's right to recover any compensation for damage by game under the Agricultural Holdings Acts to which he is entitled.[33]

(8) The landholder shall not on his holding, without the consent of his landlord, open any house for the sale of intoxicating liquors;[34] but if, at the commencement of the 1886 or 1911 Acts or the termination of the lease as leaseholder under the 1911 Act, the landholder is using any house for the sale of intoxicating liquor, then he is not excluded from being a landholder or prohibited from continuing so to use the house without the landlord's consent, for he does not in that case " open " a house.[35]

(9) The landholder shall, by himself or his family, with or without hired labour, cultivate his holding without prejudice to his right given by the 1911 Act[36] to make such use thereof for subsidiary or ancillary occupations as in the case of dispute the Land Court may find to be reasonable and not inconsistent with the cultivation of the holding, " cultivate " here including the use of a holding for horticulture or for any purpose of husbandry, inclusive of the keeping or breeding of livestock, poultry, or bees, and the growth of fruit, vegetables and like.[36] Such subsidiary occupations include the carrying on of a small alehouse on the

[32] 1886 Act, s. 1 (7).
[33] 1911 Act, s. 10 (3). See supra, p. 324.
[34] 1886 Act, s. 1 (8).
[35] Johnston, Small Landholders Acts 1886-1911, 2nd ed., 80, n. 19.
[36] 1911 Act, s. 10 (1). A landholder was held not to be in breach of this rule by merely growing grass. Little v McEwan, supra.

croft[37] but not the carrying on of a weaving mill[38] or a black-smith's smithy.[39]

If the landholder fails to pay one year's rent or breaks any other statutory condition he can be removed by order of the Land Court on application by the landlord to the Court and after the Court have considered any objections by the landholder.[40] And the Land Court can also make an order for removal on application by the Secretary of State and after considering any objections by the landholder, in a case where the landholder, his rights to compensation for permanent improvements having been, in respect of a loan, transferred in whole or in part to the Secretary of State under the 1911 Act,[41] abandons his holding or breaks any statutory condition other than one as to payment of rent or breaks any condition of repayment of a loan under that Act.[40] Where an application for removal in the case of an interest vested in an executor is made to the Land Court, the Court must not make an order for removal unless the Court is satisfied that it is reasonable to do so, having regard to the fact that the interest is vested in the executor in his capacity as executor.[42] Again, where a person to whom a new holding has been allocated or let by the Secretary of State fails without reason-able cause, within three months of the term of entry, to occupy, cultivate or proceed to equip the holding, the Secretary of State can, after considering any objections by the holder, terminate his right to the holding and allocate or let it to some other person; and when a person has been registered by order of the Land Court as a landholder in respect of a holding and he fails without any reasonable cause within three months of the registration to occupy, cultivate or proceed to equip the holding, the Secretary of State or the landlord may apply to the Land Court, which may, after giving the parties an opportunity of being heard, cancel the registration and terminate the landholder's right to the holding, and the Secretary of State can then allocate or let it to another person.[43]

Residence was taken as necessary in the case of a crofter under the 1886 Act which defined him as one " who resides on the holding ", but that definition was repealed in the 1911 Act.[44] Though residence on the holding was, however, necessary for existing yearly tenants and qualified leaseholders at the commencement of the 1911 Act, on 1st April 1912, it is not a continuing statutory condition, and so where an existing yearly tenant bequeathed the holding to his heir and the heir did not propose to reside on or within two miles of the holding, it was held

[37] *Taylor* v *Fordyce*, 1918 S.C. 824.
[38] *Yool* v *Shepherd*, 1914 S.C. 689.
[39] *Stormonth-Darling* v *Young*, 1915 S.C. 44.
[40] 1931 Act, s. 3 (1). See, *e.g.*, *Secretary of State for Scotland* v *Black*, 1965 S.L.T. (Land Ct.) 2. See Rent Act 1965, s. 30.
[41] s. 8.
[42] Succession (Scotland) Act 1964, s. 16 (6).
[43] 1931 Act, s. 4.
[44] s. 39, Schedule Second.

that, though that was a necessary qualification or condition at the commencement of the Act, it was not a continuing condition and the heir was a landholder.[45] In the case of new holders, residence is not necessary at any stage.

Under the 1886 Act[46] and the 1911 Act the remedy where there were arrears of rent or the breach of some other statutory condition was an action of removing or an action of declarator of irritancy and removing before the Sheriff. Summary ejection was not competent.[47] Under the 1931 Act,[48] however, as already stated, the Land Court on application can order removal for failure to pay a year's rent or breach of any other statutory condition, etc.

A landholder can be dispossessed by the Secretary of State on the ground of bad husbandry.[49]

On his removal from the holding a landholder is entitled to his rights under the Agricultural Holdings Acts, and also, on certain conditions, to compensation for permanent improvements.[50]

Resumption by Landlord. If the landlord applies to the Land Court and satisfies the Court that he desires to resume possession of the whole or a part of the holding (though the tenant has fulfilled the statutory conditions), " for some reasonable purpose, having relation to the good of the holding or of the estate, including the using, letting or feuing of land proposed to be resumed, for the building of dwellings, or for small allotments, or for harbours, piers, boat-shelters, or other buildings, or for churches or other places of religious worship, or for schools, or for planting, or for roads practicable for carriages from the holding or holdings to the high road or the sea shore, the protection of an ancient monument or other object of historical or archaeological interest from destruction or injury ", the Land Court may authorise resumption by the landlord on such terms and conditions as it thinks fit.[51] The Court may require the holder to surrender the whole or the part of the holding on the landlord making adequate compensation to him by letting to him other land of equivalent value in the neighbourhood, or by reduction of rent or compensation in money or otherwise as the Court determine.[51] It is in accordance with principle and the practice of the Court for the landlord to make a capital payment for the loss of the statutory tenure and loss of profits as well as a reduction of rent for

---

[45] *Rogerson* v *Chilston*, 1917 S.C. 453.
[46] s. 3.
[47] *MacKenzie* v *Munro* (1891), 22 R. 45.
[48] s. 3 (1). By 1931 Act, s. 3 (2), the 1886 Act, s. 3 and 1911 Act, s. 8 (2), which authorised removal by the Land Court for breach of conditions of repayment of a loan, were repealed; s. 3 (2) of the 1931 Act was itself repealed by the Statute Law Revision Act 1950, s. 1, Schedule First.
[49] Agriculture (Scotland) Act 1948, s. 32.
[50] See *infra*, p. 422.
[51] 1886 Act, s. 2, as amended by 1911 Act, ss. 19, 31 (2), Schedule Second, and 1931 Act, s. 8 (1), (2).

loss of land, in a case of resumption of part of the arable land of a holding.[52] The terms and conditions of resumption are directed to safeguard the tenant's rights in the subjects let and remaining after the resumption has been authorised.[53] It is also " a well-established principle of law that when in such a case the statutory requirements for resumption are fulfilled the Court *must* grant compensation ".[53]

The occupation by a landlord of a holding, being his only landed estate, for the purpose of personally residing thereon is not a " reasonable purpose " in respect of which the Court may authorise resumption.[54] It has been held that resumption of part of a holding for quarrying by the landlord is a " reasonable purpose ", and an application to that effect was granted by the Court subject to an obligation on the landlord to erect a fence.[55] Though the general power of feuing[56] has been repealed,[57] the original limited power of feuing under the 1886 Act[58] remains.[59]

The important amendments which were made in the 1931 Act[60] as to what amounted to a " reasonable purpose " were caused by the sale at high prices after the 1914-18 War of small holdings on the break-up of estates, and the new owners of the holdings resuming the holdings and, not being bound to reside there, often leaving the holding vacant or letting it to a tenant under the ordinary law and so defeating the object of security of tenure of landholders.

Renunciation by Landholder. A landholder may renounce his holding as at any term of Whitsunday or Martinmas if he gives one month's written notice to the landlord.[61] In the case of a new holder or his statutory successor the term of outgo under the notice must be similar to the term of ingo or entry; thus, *e.g.,* if the term of entry is Whitsunday, he can renounce only at Whitsunday.[62] The notice of renunciation is, however, not, without the Land Court's consent, effective unless within two months from the date of the notice the landlord or the landholder intimates it in writing to the Secretary of State.[63] The landholder too cannot, unless by agreement with the Secretary of State, renounce his holding without the Land Court's consent, so long as any liability to the Secretary of State is not wholly discharged.[63] On renuncia-

---

[52] *Macdonald* v *Macdonald* (1950) 38 S.L.C.R. 14.
[53] *Stornoway Trust* v *Sandwick Landholders* (1949) 37 S.L.C.R. 3.
[54] 1931 Act, s. 8 (1).
[55] *Cameron* v *MacLaren* (1949) 37 S.L.C.R. 32.
[56] 1911 Act, s. 19.
[57] 1931 Act, s. 8 (2).
[58] s. 2.
[59] *Duke of Argyll* v *Macdonald* (1933) 21 S.L.C.R. 16, where the Land Court pointed out the absurdity and incomprehensibility of the legislation.
[60] s. 8.
[61] 1886 Act, s. 7.
[62] 1931 Act, s. 22.
[63] 1911 Act, s. 18.

tion, the landholder is entitled to his rights under the Agricultural Holdings Acts and also on certain conditions to compensation for permanent improvements.

Compensation for Improvements. Where a landholder is removed from his holding or where he renounces his holding, he is entitled on removal or renunciation to his rights under the Agricultural Holdings Acts[64] and also to compensation for any permanent improvements which are suitable to the holding and which have been executed or paid for by himself or his predecessors in the same family, and even if these were executed in virtue of a specific written agreement under which he was bound to make them, provided he has not received fair consideration for them by way of reduction of rent or otherwise.[65] Thus, unless he has paid or given fair consideration for them, the landlord cannot acquire the benefit of improvements which have been made by the landholder and must pay compensation to take that benefit. " Predecessor in the same family " is now defined[66] as " the wife or husband of such landholder or cottar, and any person to whom such landholder or cottar or the wife or husband of such landholder or cottar might, failing nearer heirs, have succeeded in case of intestacy ". " Permanent improvements ", which include most of those under the Agricultural Holdings Acts,[67] are as follows: [68] Dwellinghouse; farm offices; subsoil or other drains; walls and fences; deep trenching; clearing the ground; planting trees; making piers and landing-stages; roads practicable for carriages from the holding or holdings to the public road or the sea shore; all other improvements which, in the judgment of the Land Court, shall add to the value of the holding to the incoming tenant. These provisions as to compensation do not apply to any buildings erected by a landholder in violation of any interdict or other judicial order.[69] Where a lease provided that all buildings and other permanent improvements were the property of the proprietors, it was held that this was not inconsistent with the landlord's liability to pay compensation, to defeat which an express discharge was necessary.[70] While consent of or notice to the landlord is required under the Agricultural Holdings Acts for certain improvements, there are no such provisions in the Landholders Acts.

Improvements are valued by the Land Court at such a sum as represents their value to an incoming tenant, under deduction of the value of any assistance or consideration given by the landlord or his

[64] Failing agreement, the compensation is assessed by the Land Court: 1886 Act, s. 31.
[65] 1886 Act, s. 8, as amended by 1931 Act, s. 12.
[66] 1931 Act, s. 9.
[67] *Supra,* pp. 325 *et seq.*
[68] 1886 Act, Schedule.
[69] 1886 Act, s. 9.
[70] *Macdonald* v *Douglas* (1948) 36 S.L.C.R. 13.

predecessors to the landholder in respect of the improvements and of the value of any deterioration permitted or committed by the tenant during the previous four years.[71] The Court can consider all the facts and circumstances as shown by inspection and can use their own expert knowledge.[72] The valuation is a matter for experts and there is no one single formula which is the sole principle of valuation.[73] The fact that buildings are in a state of disrepair does not render them unfit to be valued nor does their condition make them not "suitable to the holding".[73] Where notice of renunciation has been given and become effective on the joint application of landholder and landlord, or where the landholder's rights to compensation for permanent improvements have been transferred to the Secretary of State under the 1911 Act,[74] on the joint application of the Secretary of State and the landlord, the Land Court may assess, prior to renunciation, the amount due by the landlord on renunciation in respect of compensation for permanent improvements under the 1886 Act as amended by the 1931 Act, and that amount is the amount due on renunciation.[75] The landlord can set off all rent due or to become due against any sums found due by him for improvements on the holding.[76]

The effect of an agreement for assistance to a landholder by a loan under the 1911 Act,[77] recorded in the Landholders Holding Book, is to transfer to the Secretary of State all rights of the landholder and his statutory successors to compensation for permanent improvements up to the amount of any outstanding liability owing to the Secretary of State. In the event of a dispute, the amount of that compensation is assessed by the Land Court, and any amount due to the Secretary of State by a landlord under the 1911 Act may, if the Secretary of State on the landlord's application so determines, be deemed a loan to the landlord secured on the holding and any buildings thereon.[78] In the case of resumption or of an existing yearly tenant or qualified lease-holder or a statutory small tenant becoming a landholder, the rights of interested parties so far as affected by the 1911 Act at the date of resumption or of becoming a landholder are, in the event of dispute, adjusted by order of the Land Court on the application of any party interested.[79]

An incoming holder may pay the compensation to the outgoing holder with consent of the landlord and agree with the Secretary of State to assume any outstanding liability to the Secretary of State of

[71] 1886 Act, s. 10.
[72] *Smith* v *Marquis of Aberdeen's Trs.*, 1916 S.C. 905.
[73] *Wight* v *Morison*, Court of Session (1922) 10 S.L.C.R. 91, affirming 10 S.L.C.R. 53.
[74] s. 8.
[75] 1931 Act, s. 11.
[76] 1911 Act, s. 23.
[77] *Ibid.*, s. 7.
[78] *Ibid.*, s. 8 (1).
[79] *Ibid.*, s. 14.

the outgoing holder in respect of a loan to him; he is then deemed to have executed or paid for the improvements and on renunciation or removal is entitled to compensation at his outgoing.[80] A loan can run with the tenure, for the Secretary of State may provide assistance to a new holder by loans to enable him to pay compensation to the outgoing holder,[81] and where the outgoing holder is liable to the Secretary of State in respect of a loan, the Secretary of State and the incoming holder may agree that he assume such liability, and the amount is then deemed a loan to the incoming holder.[82] In any case where the landlord has not paid the compensation due to the outgoing holder or the Secretary of State or has not applied to the Secretary of State to determine that any compensation due to the Secretary of State shall be deemed a loan to him, he is deemed to have given consent.[82] Where a new holder or the Secretary of State for him has paid to a landlord a sum representing the value to the holder of the existing buildings, he is deemed to have executed or paid for the buildings, and can claim compensation accordingly, and any loan granted to him to enable him to do so or any such payment by the Secretary of State is deemed a loan by the Secretary of State under the 1911 Act.[83]

Notwithstanding a discharge of claims, the tenant will be entitled to the compensation under the Acts in so far as payment or fair consideration has not been given.[84]

Though there is no specific provision, it is clearly implied that the Land Court is the body that has jurisdiction in relation to compensation and that the jurisdiction of the ordinary courts is excluded.[85] Where compensation for improvements is sought under the Agricultural Holdings Acts, the improvements are to be valued by the Land Court, unless parties otherwise agree.[86]

A distant legatee or heir can claim compensation for improvements if the Land Court allow the holding to be added to a neighbouring holding for enlargement.[87]

Under the Open-Cast Coal Act 1958,[88] where immediately before an authorisation under that Act[89] came into operation, any of the land comprised in the authorisation consisted of or included the whole or a part of a holding, that Act in relation to the land has effect to the extent that references to an agricultural holding or the tenant of such or the Agricultural Holdings (Scotland) Act 1949 include references to a

---

[80] 1931 Act, s. 1 (1). In view of 1886 Act, s. 8 (b), s. 1 (1) of 1931 seems unnecessary.
[81] *Ibid.*, s. 1 (2).
[82] *Ibid.*, s. 1 (1).
[83] *Ibid.*, s. 1 (3).
[84] *Smith* v *Marquis of Aberdeen's Trs.*, 1916 S.C. 905.
[85] *McDougall* v *McAlister* (1890) 17 R. 555.
[86] 1886 Act, s. 31. See *infra*, p. 486.
[87] *Ibid.*, s. 16.
[88] s. 52 (5).
[89] s. 1.

holding and a landholder and to the Landholders Acts, references to the appropriate sections in the 1949 Act[90] being substituted by appropriate references to the 1886 Act.[91] For the purposes of the 1958 Act, in regard to compensation for diminution in the value of a holding, an improvement to the holding for which a holder would be entitled on termination of a tenancy to compensation under the Landholders Acts is treated as a separate holding, and any compensation payable under the 1958 Act[92] for the improvements is payable to the holder as if he were the owner.[93] Any dispute as to the right to compensation under the 1958 Act of a holder or the owner of a holding or as to the amount of compensation and any matter arising in relation to a holding which is referable to arbitration under the 1958 Act is to be determined by the Land Court under and in terms of the Landholders Acts.[93]

Assignation of Holding. A landholder has in general no right to assign his holding or to execute any deed purporting to assign it.[94] It has been questioned whether any assignee, even one with consent of the landlord, is a landholder,[95] but the Land Court have expressed the opinion that the prohibition against assignation must be construed as subject to the right of the landlord to give his consent to an assignation.[96] If a landholder, however, is unable to work the holding because of illness, old age or infirmity, he may apply to the Land Court for authority to assign it to " his son-in-law, or any one of the persons who would be, or would in any circumstances have been, entitled to succeed to the estate on intestacy by virtue of the Succession (Scotland) Act 1964 ", and if, after intimation to the landlord or any other party interested and after such hearing or inquiry as the Court think necessary, the Court think the assignation is reasonable and proper, it may authorise the assignation on such terms and conditions, if any, as it deems fit.[97] If a condition imposed by the Court is that the former tenant continue to reside on the holding, he must be treated as in a privileged position, and, if the assignee abuse the condition, the Court may recall the authority to assign.[98]

Succession: Bequest of Holding. A landholder has a right to bequeath by will or other testamentary writing his right to his holding to one person, being his son-in-law, or any one of the persons who

[90] ss. 57, 58. See *supra*, pp. 346-7.
[91] s. 10.
[92] s. 23.
[93] s. 52 (5). Ss. 24 and 25 of the 1958 Act relating to compensation for improvements do not apply to any improvement in respect of which compensation is payable under s. 23.
[94] 1886 Act, s. 1 (2).
[95] *Encyclopaedia of Scots Law*, Vol. 14, p. 139.
[96] *Campbell* v *Board of Agriculture* (1928) 16 S.L.C.R. 27.
[97] 1911 Act, s. 21, as amended by Succession (Scotland) Act 1964, Schedule 2, para. 15.
[98] *McDonald* v *Uig Crofters Ltd.* (1950) 38 S.L.C.R. 11.

would be, or would in any circumstances have been, entitled to succeed
to the estate on intestacy by virtue of the Succession (Scotland) Act
1964, on conditions which are very similar to those applicable to
bequests under the Agricultural Holdings (Scotland) Acts.[99] The right
exists despite any implied prohibition of assignation in the lease.[1] The
legatee must intimate the bequest to the landlord or his agent within
two months after the landholder's death, or if he is unavoidably prevented from doing so, as soon as possible thereafter. That intimation
imports or implies acceptance of the bequest by the legatee. Within
one month after the intimation has been made, the landlord can in
turn intimate to the legatee that he objects to receive him as a landholder; if he does not do so, the legatee becomes landholder as from
the date of death of the testator or predecessor. If, however, the landlord
does object to him and intimates to that effect to him, the legatee may
present a petition to the Land Court for declarator that he is the
landholder from the date of the deceased's death, and the landlord
can then state his objection to the Land Court. If the Court, exercising
a fair discretion, consider the objection to be a reasonable one, the
Court will declare the bequest to be null and void.[99] The Court proceed
on the general lines on which objections to bequests are sustained or
repelled under the Agricultural Holdings (Scotland) Acts.[2] The Court's
decision is final, and must be intimated by the landlord to the executor
of the deceased tenant.[3] Pending the proceedings on the petition, the
legatee, with the consent of the executor in whom the tenancy is vested
under the Succession (Scotland) Act 1964, has possession unless the
Court otherwise directs on cause shown.[4] If the legatee accepts the
bequest and the bequest is not declared null and void, the legatee is
entitled to possess on the same terms and conditions as if he was the
nearest heir.[4a]

If the bequest is set aside as null and void and the legatee is thus
refused as successor, or if the legatee declines to accept the bequest,
then the right to the holding is treated as intestate estate of the deceased
tenant in accordance with the Succession (Scotland) Act 1964 Part I,
and where a tenancy is transferred under that Act the executor of the
deceased tenant must as soon as possible furnish particulars of the
transferee to the landlord, who is bound to accept the transferee as
tenant.[5]

---

[99] 1886 Act, s. 16, as amended by 1911 Act, s. 20 and Succession (Scotland) Act,
1964, Schedule 2, para. 9.
[1] Succession (Scotland) Act 1964, s. 29 (1), (2).
[2] See *supra*, p. 356.
[3] 1886 Act, s. 16, as amended by 1911 Act, s. 20 and Succession (Scotland) Act,
1964, Schedule 2, para. 10.
[4] 1886 Act, s. 16, as amended by 1911 Act, s. 20 and Succession (Scotland) Act
1964, Schedule 2, para. 11.
[4a] 1886 Act, s. 16 (g).
[5] 1886 Act, s. 16, as amended by Succession (Scotland) Act, 1964, Schedule 2,
para. 12.

The fact that the interest which is the subject of a valid bequest is vested in the executor under the Succession (Scotland) Act 1964 does not prevent the operation of the foregoing provisions.[6]

Where the interest of a tenant under a lease comprised in a deceased person's estate vested in the deceased's executor is the subject of a valid bequest but the bequest is declared null and void under the foregoing provisions, and among the conditions of the lease is one prohibiting assignation, the executor may transfer the interest to anyone of those entitled to succeed to the deceased's intestate estate or to claim legal rights or the prior rights of a surviving spouse in or towards satisfaction of that person's entitlement to claim, but he may not without the landlord's consent transfer the interest to any other person.[6a] If at any time the executor is satisfied that the interest cannot be disposed of according to law and so informs the landlord or the interest is not disposed of within a year or such longer period as may be fixed by agreement between the landlord and himself, or, failing such agreement, by the Sheriff on summary application made by the executor,[6b] either the landlord or the executor may, on giving due notice to the other, terminate the lease so far as it relates to that interest, despite any provisions in the lease or any enactment or rule of law to the contrary effect;[7] the period of notice must be either such as is agreed on, or failing agreement not less than one year and not more than two years ending with such term of Whitsunday or Martinmas as may be specified in the lease.[8] The last provision[7] does not prejudice any claim by any party to the lease for compensation or damages in respect of the termination of the lease or any rights under it in pursuance of that provision. Any such award of compensation or damages is enforceable only against the deceased's estate and is not enforceable against the executor personally.[9]

Succession: Intestate Succession to Holding. Where there is no bequest, or again in the case of a bequest which the legatee does not accept, a holding passes on the tenant's or holder's death to his heirs according to the ordinary rules of intestate succession.[10] This is implied in the term " landholder ", which includes " the successors of any such person in the holding, being his heirs or legatees ".[11]

---

[6] Succession (Scotland) Act 1964, s. 16 (8).
[6a] *Ibid.,* s. 16 (2).
[6b] In the case of an interest that is the subject of petition to the Land Court under 1886 Act, s. 16 (or application under the Agricultural Holdings (Scotland) Act 1949, s. 20) from the date of determination or withdrawal thereof.
[7] *Ibid.,* s. 16 (3).
[8] *Ibid.,* s. 16 (4).
[9] *Ibid.,* s. 16 (5).
[10] See Succession (Scotland) Act 1964, Part I.
[11] 1911 Act, s. 2 (2). The 1886 Act applied to every crofter and to his heirs and legatees in the same manner as if the tenancy were a lease: s. 19.

The claim must be made timeously;[12] the successor must so exercise his rights; if he " does not choose to come forward and go through the operation which is equivalent to what we would call taking up the lease where there is a lease, he must be held to have abandoned his rights ".[13]

Statutory successor is defined[14] as " any person who in terms of the Landholders Act as the case may be has succeeded or may succeed to a holding whether as a person to whom the lease is transferred under the Succession (Scotland) Act 1964[15] or the executor or heir-at-law or legatee of his immediate predecessor being a crofter or landholder in occupation of the holding ".

Compulsory Enlargement of Holdings. The provisions on this subject were passed because crofters often had holdings that were insufficient even with their other callings to support them and their families and they could not get from their landlords lets of additional land which was available and which they were able and willing to take and to stock. A landholder or two or more landholders resident on neighbouring holdings in a parish may, if the landlord on being applied to refuses to let to them available land which they are willing to take on lease on reasonable terms for enlarging their holdings, apply to the Secretary of State setting out the facts.[16] Reasonable terms are such terms as are usually obtained in the letting of land of the like quality and similarly situated in the same district for other purposes than that of a deer forest, or of a grouse moor or other sporting purpose.[16]

The procedure thereafter is the same as in the case of the creating of new holdings as regards acquisition of the land, compensation and assistance to equipment.[17] Intimation is made to the landlord or landlords,[18] and to tenants, and any others in the occupation of the land, and notice is given of the time and place of any hearing of parties.[19] The Secretary of State may visit the place and call in assessors or valuers.[19] Opportunity is afforded to both parties to be heard and an inquiry may be ordered.[18] Before awarding additional land to the landholder or landholders the Secretary of State must be satisfied that there is land available for enlarging holdings in the parish or in an adjacent parish which the landlord refuses to let for that purpose on reasonable terms.[18] Land is not to be deemed available for the purpose of enlarging holdings otherwise than by agreement (a) which is land in respect

---

[12] *MacIver* v *MacIver*, 1909 S.C. 639, a decision on the 1886 Act. See *per* Lord McLaren at 643-4 as to the reluctance or refusal of elder sons to succeed.
[13] *Ibid.*, at 642, *per* L.P. Dunedin.
[14] 1911 Act, s. 31, as amended by Succession (Scotland) Act 1964, Schedule 2, para. 16.
[15] s. 16. See *supra*, p. 425.
[16] 1886 Act, s. 11, as amended by 1911 Act, s. 16 (1), and Schedule Second, and 1919 Act, s. 11.
[17] 1911 Act, s. 16 (1) *proviso*, as replaced and amended by 1919 Act, s. 11.
[18] 1886 Act, s. 12, as amended by 1911 Act, s. 16 (1) *proviso* and 1919 Act, s. 11.
[19] 1886 Act, s. 21, as amended by 1911 Act, s. 16 (1) and 1919 Act, s. 11.

of which a person would not be admissible to registration otherwise than by agreement as a new holder under the 1911 Act;[20] (b) if it is arable land, unless it lies contiguous or next to land already in the occupancy of the holder making the application, that is to the holding to which it is to be added:[20] (c) if its addition to the existing holding would make the rent or acreage of the holding exceed the statutory limits of rent or acreage for a new holding under the 1911 Act;[20] (d) if it is let as a deer forest and its assignation would seriously impair the use of the remainder as a deer forest and would act injuriously upon the prosperity of the inhabitants generally of the district in which the deer forest is situated.[21] Thus, it will be noted, the Secretary of State is limited in enlargement of holdings by the statutory restrictions on the rent and the area of holdings. He must also be satisfied that the tenants are able and willing to pay a fair rent and properly, so far as it is pastoral, to stock and, so far as it is arable, to cultivate the additional land.[22]

If he is so satisfied as to the land and the tenants, he may make an order which lets, and thus adds, the additional land or such part or parts of it as is thought proper to the holdings of the applicants, or of one or more of them, at a fair rent and on such terms and conditions as he considers to be just.[22] When the order confirming the scheme has been made, the Secretary of State may make whatever order is necessary for assigning the land to the landholders.[23] The land of one proprietor can be taken to enlarge a holding on the estate of another proprietor; it is available land for enlarging a holding otherwise than by agreement,[24] for under the 1911 Act[25] it could be taken for a new holding, and the enlargement provisions of the 1886 Act[26] do not limit the choice of land to land of the same proprietor. On enlargement a holding as enlarged becomes a *unum quid*.[27] The land assigned is deemed to be part of the holding or holdings to which it is so assigned and is subject to the provisions of the Acts.[28] In the order confirming a scheme, the names of the applicants or the areas or the rents of their existing holdings need not be included if the order specifies the locality from which the application is received and the land which is available.[23]

Instead, however, of giving to each landholder a piece of additional land for himself, the Secretary of State may, if he thinks it just and expedient, assign to the body of landholders who have applied such a piece of land with rights of common pasturage among themselves; he

[20] 1911 Act, s. 16 (2).
[21] 1886 Act, s. 13 (3) (e).
[22] 1886 Act, s. 12, as amended by 1911 Act, s. 16 (1) and 1919 Act, s. 11.
[23] 1931 Act, s. 7.
[24] *Von Schroder's Trs.* v *Board of Agriculture*, 1915 S.C. 1.
[25] s. 16 (2).
[26] ss. 11, 12.
[27] *McColl* v *Carmichael* (1922) 10 S.L.C.R. 18.
[28] 1886 Act, s. 15, as amended by 1911 Act, s. 16 (1) and 1919 Act, s. 11.

may also admit the applicants to a share of rights of common pasturage enjoyed by other landholders.[29] The Land Court may also let new holdings with a share of a common pasture or grazing.[30]

Where land is assigned by the Secretary of State for enlarging holdings, he may make such orders and directions as to the erection and maintenance of the fencing of this land as he considers necessary or expedient, and may decern that the cost thereof be paid by the person or persons interested as he thinks just having regard to the advantage accruing to the party or parties interested from the fencing of the land.[31]

Vacant Holdings: Rights of Landlord. A holding may become vacant because, for example, of the death of the holder and the failure of a statutory successor, or of renunciation by or removal of the holder. In order to prevent, in such a situation, the landlord re-letting under another tenure, it is provided that where a holding (whether existing or new) becomes or is about to become vacant through failure of a statutory successor or renunciation or removal, the landlord must intimate this forthwith to the Secretary of State in writing and the landlord cannot let the holding, without the Secretary of State's consent, otherwise than to a neighbouring landholder for enlargement of his holding or to a new holder.[32] He can thus let it without consent only to a neighbouring holder as an enlargement or to a new holder. The Secretary of State, in the case where the landlord has not agreed to let as a landholder's holding (that is, to a neighbouring holder for enlargement or a new holder), has the same powers in regard to the holding as if it had been included in a confirmed scheme under the 1911 Act[33] at such rent as the Secretary of State fixes, and the Secretary of State must pay such compensation, in lieu of that provided for in the 1911 Act, as failing agreement the Land Court may determine in respect of any damage or injury arising out of any alteration in the rent or the terms and conditions of occupancy of the holding.[34] Where, under the Acts, the holding was otherwise than by agreement constituted as a new holding or enlarged, the Land Court, on the landlord's application and after hearing the Secretary of State, must assess any damage or injury done by the constitution or enlargement of the holding, as the case may be, to the landlord through non-payment of rent or depreciation in the

---

[29] 1886 Act, s. 12, as amended by 1911 Act, s. 16 (1) and 1919 Act, s. 11.
[30] 1911 Act, s. 24 (5) (b), as substituted by 1919 Act, s. 14.
[31] 1886 Act, s. 21, as amended by 1911 Act, s. 16 (1) and 1919 Act, s. 11. Where on enlargement of common grazings, under a finding of the Crofters Commission in 1886 the crofters were to be liable for one-half of the cost of repairing a boundary fence erected on that enlargement, the Land Court was held to have no power to order the crofters to join with the landlord in carrying out the repairs. *Vestey* v *Inverkirkaig & Strathan Crofters* (1961) 49 S.L.C.R. App. 57.
[32] 1911 Act, s. 17 as amended by 1919 Act, s. 12 and 1931 Act, s. 6.
[33] s. 7, as amended by 1919 Act, s. 9.
[34] 1931 Act, s. 6.

letting value of land in the holding or the imposition of liabilities in respect of, or the payment of compensation for, permanent improvements on the holding and require the Secretary of State to pay compensation to the landlord in respect of that damage or injury to such amount as the Court determine.[35] This does not apply to a holding ceasing to be held by a landholder because of resumption by the landlord or of a sale of the holding to the landholder.[35]

If the landlord does let without the Secretary of State's consent to a neighbouring holder as an enlargement or to a new holder (as he is entitled to do), he suffers no loss and has no claim, but he may have a claim, if he can prove additional damage or injury, for loss of rent, or depreciation in the letting value or compensation for improvements on the new holding or enlargement becoming and remaining for some time vacant.[36]

If the landlord lets a holding otherwise than in compliance with the provisions of the Acts, the Secretary of State can declare the let null and void and can treat the holding, without payment of compensation, as if it had been duly constituted as a new holding, or assign the holding for enlargement of a neighbouring holding or holdings.[37]

Additional Conditions. In addition to the statutory conditions, breach of which by the landholder entitles the landlord to have him removed, there are other conditions of tenancy of a holding. Thus, the landholder can recover compensation for damage by game such as a tenant under the Agricultural Holdings (Scotland) Acts can claim and his claim for compensation is, failing agreement, determined by the Land Court.[38] The Land Court, on the application of landholders or others concerned, may draw up a scheme regulating the use by landholders on the same estate of seaweed for the reasonable purposes of their holdings, peat bogs, and heather or grass used for thatching purposes, and include the charge for all these in the fixed rent.[39]

On payment of compensation for any surface damage, the landlord can use for any estate purpose any springs of water rising on a holding and not required for the use of it. This, however, does not affect the rights of any persons other than the landlord and the landholder. Any dispute as to the requirements of the holding or the amount of compensation are determined by the Land Court.[40]

Record of Holding. A record of the condition of the cultivation of the holding and of the buildings and other permanent improvements on it, and of those by whom the permanent improvements have been

[35] 1911 Act, s. 17 *proviso*, as amended by 1919 Act, s. 32, Schedule Fourth.
[36] Scott, *Law of Smallholdings*, p. 133.
[37] 1919 Act, s. 12.
[38] 1911 Act, s. 10 (3).
[39] 1886 Act, s. 12, as amended by 1911 Act, s. 28.
[40] 1911 Act, s. 12.

executed or paid for must be made by the Land Court on the application of the Secretary of State or the landlord or the landholder,[41] the application being intimated by the Court to others concerned and each party being given an opportunity of being heard on any matter affecting the record.[42] This is an extension of the original statutory provision[43] under which on any such application the Land Court had to append to their order fixing a fair rent for a holding such a record and which thus limited the making of a record to such an occasion. The record had to be appended to the order; an application four months after the order was held to be too late.[44] The record's value lies mainly where the situation as to permanent improvements by both parties is a complicated one.

Landholder's Holdings Book. A Landholder's Holdings Book must be kept in the Sheriff Clerk's office of every county or judicial district of a county, in which the Sheriff Clerk or, in the case of a district, the Clerk or his depute, must record all Land Court applications and the orders following on these applications, and any other proceedings in the case which the Court think necessary to be recorded. The Land Court must send these applications and orders to the Sheriff Clerk for recording.[45] All agreements for loans given by the Secretary of State or his predecessors to new holders under the 1911 Act must also be recorded, and the effect of recording is to transfer to the Secretary of State the landholder's rights and those of his statutory successor to compensation for permanent improvements.[46] Orders by the Land Court constituting the registration of new holders under the 1911 Act and the relative applications must be recorded,[47] as also orders by the Secretary of State for the constitution of new holdings, which are enforceable like orders of the Land Court.[48]

Register of Smallholdings. The Secretary of State must from time to time revise a Register of Smallholdings (whether held by landholders or statutory small tenants or not) throughout Scotland (ordered by the 1911 Act to be compiled by the Board of Agriculture) in a form and containing such particulars as may be approved by the Secretary of State.[49] A smallholding in this connection is a holding within the Agricultural Holdings Acts which does not exceed fifty acres in extent or, if exceeding that area, is of an annual value as entered in the Valuation Roll of not

[41] 1931 Act, s. 10 (1).
[42] *Ibid.*, s. 10 (2).
[43] 1911 Act, s. 8 (4).
[44] *Bridges* v *Mackie* (1915) 3 S.L.C.R. 67.
[45] 1886 Act, s. 27, as amended by 1911 Act, ss. 1, 28 (1).
[46] 1911 Act, s. 8.
[47] *Ibid.*, s. 15 (2).
[48] 1919 Act, s. 9 (11) (e) (ii).
[49] 1911 Act, s. 33 (1). This no longer applies in the crofting counties under the 1955 Act, s. 38, Schedule Sixth; in the case of crofts in those counties there is instead a Register of Crofts, 1961 Act, s. 3. See *infra*, p. 467.

more than £50.[50] A person is not held to be a landholder or a statutory small tenant merely because he is entered as such in the Register; the mere entry does not determine that issue.[51] Agreements between landlord and tenant, or orders of the Land Court, that a tenant is a landholder or a statutory small tenant within the meaning of the Landholders' Acts must be communicated by the landlord and tenant and the Land Court respectively to the Secretary of State for the purposes of the Register.[51]

Common Grazings. There are a number of statutory provisions which regulate the numerous common grazings which are found in the Highlands and Islands. It is provided[52] that the Secretary of State may, if it appears to him just and expedient, by order provide for admitting landholders, who have applied to lease land available for enlargement which the landlord has refused to let, to participate in common pasture occupied by other landholders or for conferring on the applicants rights of pasturage common as among themselves over available land specified in the order on such terms and conditions as the Secretary of State determines. The first Act regulating these grazings was the Crofters Common Grazings Regulation Act 1891; there followed the Crofters Common Grazings Regulation Act 1908, which amended the 1891 Act in important respects, and the 1911 Act. Landholders sharing a common grazing are, at a public meeting of shareholders or others claiming interest in the common, to appoint a Committee to make regulations as to the number of stock each landholder can put on the grazing and any other matters affecting the fair exercise of their joint rights by the landholders.[53] If the shareholders or others do not appoint a committee, the Land Court at the request of two landholders interested or the landlord or landlords can do so,[54] and, if the Land Court think fit, they can appoint a committee and make regulations without any request from a landlord or crofters interested.[55] The Land Court can appoint or provide for the appointment of members in place of others after their suspension or removal by the Court on the ground that they are not properly carrying out the regulations made.[56] If those interested in a common pasture or grazing decline to act on such a committee, the Land Court can appoint any persons in the neighbourhood whether or not landholders.[56] If the Land Court think that a grazing constable instead of a committee should be appointed for any township or townships or persons interested, they may make provision accordingly, and regulations providing for this are deemed regulations under the Act which the

[50] *Ibid.*, s. 33 (2).
[51] *Ibid.*. s. 33 (3).
[52] 1886 Act, s. 12, as amended by 1919 Act, s. 11, and the 1928 and 1939 Acts.
[53] 1891 Act, s. 2, as amended by 1911 Act, s. 24 (4). The Committee was to remain in office for three years. 1891 Act, s. 3.
[54] *Ibid.*, s. 4.
[55] 1908 Act, s. 2.
[56] 1911 Act, s. 24 (4). The Land Court replaced the former Commission as from 1st April, 1912. 1911 Act, s. 28 (1).

constable may enforce.[56] A person appointed by the Court can summon and attend a committee meeting in order to advise the committee and can otherwise assist in the administration of the Act.[57]

The regulations must be intimated to the Land Court, which in turn must give reasonable notice to the landlord and, if asked, hear the parties and, if necessary, hold an inquiry and can approve, with or without alteration, or refuse approval of the regulations. In considering the regulations made, the Court must have regard to any existing custom in the matters affected, whether founded on estate rules or otherwise. When approved, the regulations come into force and they may be added to or altered by the committee with the Land Court's approval.[58] Regulations approved by the Court are an order of the Court under the Acts, provisions of which for recording and enforcing orders etc. apply to the Regulations.[59] Signed conditions by all landholders interested, found by the Court to be reasonable, may be recorded and enforced as if regulations.[60]

The Land Court can themselves make such regulations as they think expedient as to the exercise of pasture, grazing or other rights held or to be held in common under the Landholders' Acts.[61] The Court must intimate this to any person or persons, landholders or not, using or claiming to use the pasture, grazing, etc., hear them if they have so applied and hold an inquiry if thought necessary.[62]

In the case of a breach or non-observance of the regulations a petition can be presented by the committee or any two crofters interested or the landlord to the Sheriff, who can make orders for enforcement by warrant for sale of surplus stock and the disposal of the proceeds, by penalties or otherwise.[63] A person committing a breach of the regulations can be summarily convicted by a Sheriff and fined.[64] A person convicted summarily by a Sheriff of a breach of regulations made by the Land Court under the 1911 Act or of regulations confirmed by the Crofters Commission under the 1955 Act may also be fined.[65] The regulations may provide for the removal by some person mentioned in them of any stock placed on the pasture or grazing in breach of the regulations.[66]

The Land Court, on the application of the landlord or landlords or any landholder, can on such terms and conditions as are considered by them to be equitable, apportion a common grazing or pasture into

[57] 1908 Act, s. 2. A grazings officer now acts on the Land Court staff.
[58] 1891 Act, s. 2.
[59] Ibid., s. 6.
[60] Ibid., s. 7.
[61] 1911 Act, s. 24 (1).
[62] Ibid., s. 24 (2).
[63] 1891 Act, s. 5.
[64] 1908 Act, s. 2, repealed by 1955 Act, Schedule Sixth, Part I, in regard to crofting counties.
[65] 1911 Act, s. 24 (3); 1955 Act, s. 27 (1) and Schedule Sixth, Part I.
[66] Ibid., s. 24 (2).

separate parts for the exclusive use of the several townships or persons interested as arable ground or as pasture or as sites for houses or other buildings if they are satisfied that this is for the good of the estate or estates and of the holdings or tenancies concerned.[67] The Land Court, on the like conditions, may admit new holders to participate in a common pasture or grazing occupied by existing landholders, statutory small tenants or others, or apportion a common pasture or grazing for the exclusive use of new holders in common or individually as arable ground or pasture, or as sites for houses or other buildings, if satisfied that such participation or apportionment is for the good of the estate or estates and of the holdings or tenancies concerned.[67a] The Land Court can also apportion lands held runrig.[68]

Grazings can be resumed by a landlord on the authority of the Land Court where such is reasonable and for the good of the holdings on the same conditions as holdings can be resumed.[69]

A holding is deemed to include any right to pasture a grazing land held by the tenant or landholder alone or in common with others;[70] and in determining whether a holding is within the limits of a smallholding, the land is taken " exclusive of any common pasture, or grazing, held or to be held therewith ".[71]

Landholders interested in a common grazing or part of one which has been apportioned under the 1911 Act[72] can appoint two or more of their number and authorise in writing one person *bona fide* employed by them for reward to kill and take ground game on the common grazing or part thereof, as the case may be.[73]

PROVISIONS IN RELATION TO STATUTORY SMALL TENANTS

General. As already stated, the provisions of the Landholders Acts, apart from section 32 of the 1911 Act do not apply to a statutory small tenant. The ordinary common law obligations of landlord and tenant in agricultural subjects still apply. He has, however, like the landholder the right to have a judicially fixed rent and to security of tenure, but while a landholder possesses under statutory conditions, the statutory small tenant will generally be under a lease for a term when the 1911 Act commenced and, whether or not, the conditions, pactional or common law or both, are not statutorily stereotyped. Unless with the landlord's consent, neither the tenant nor the Land Court can alter any conditions other than those relating to the amount of rent or the period of renewal. The terms and conditions, except as agreed to be varied, are those of the

---

[67] *Ibid.,* s. 24 (5), (a) as substituted by 1919 Act, s. 14.
[67a] *Ibid.,* s. 24 (5) (b) as substituted by 1919 Act, s. 14.
[68] *Ibid.,* s. 24 (6).
[69] 1886 Act, s. 2; 1911 Act, ss. 19, 26 (1); 1931 Act, s. 8. See Scott, *op. cit.,* p. 156, and *supra,* p. 420.
[70] 1911 Act, s. 26 (1). See *supra,* p. 394.
[71] *Ibid.,* s. 26 (3).
[72] *Ibid.,* s. 24 (5).
[73] 1931 Act. s. 23 (1).

determining tenancy as if it had been renewed by tacit relocation for the full period of renewal.[74] The tenant is entitled to renewal on these terms. A statutory small tenant cannot compel his landlord to provide or maintain buildings, nor can the Land Court order the landlord to that effect, but if the landlord does not provide or maintain buildings, the tenant can apply to the Land Court to be declared a landholder and have a fair rent fixed.[75]

Rent. A statutory small tenant or his landlord may, failing agreement, apply to the Land Court to fix an " equitable " rent, and the Court may determine the rent.[76] In determining the rent, the Court, so far as practicable, must " act on their own knowledge and experience, taking into consideration all the circumstances of the case, holding and district ", including the rent at which the holding has been let, the proposed conditions of the renewed tenancy, the improvements made by the landlord and the tenant respectively and their then condition and value, and must fix as the rent to be paid by the tenant the rent which in their opinion would be an equitable rent as between a willing lessor and a willing lessee, that is, such as might reasonably be looked for in the open market, but allowing no rent in respect of improvements made by or at the expense of the tenant or any of his predecessors in title and for which no payment or fair consideration has been received by him or his predecessor from the landlord or his predecessor.[77] It was held[78] that improvements made by a tenant under an obligation imposed upon him under the lease are tenant's improvements and that the landlord is not entitled to rent in respect of them except so far as the tenant has received payment or fair consideration for them from the landlord. The words of the Act were held to be absolute and unqualified. Revenue derived by a statutory small tenant from letting houses on the holding to summer visitors should be taken into account in fixing the equitable rent.[79] The procedure of the Court in fixing a " fair " rent in the case of landholders[80] is applied in fixing an " equitable " rent in the case of statutory small tenants.[81]

The rent can only be revised at the expiry of the agreed-upon term or the term fixed by the Court.

The Land Court cannot, as they can in the case of a landholder, deal with[82] or cancel arrears of rent.[83]

---

[74] 1911 Act, s. 32 (9).
[75] *Ibid.*, s. 32 (11); *supra* and *infra*, pp. 413, 486.
[76] *Ibid.*, s. 32 (7). See as to difference between " equitable rent " and " full rent ", Johnston, *The Small Landholders (Scotland) Acts, 1886-1911,* 2nd ed., p. 70.
[77] *Ibid.*, s. 32 (8).
[78] *Wilkie* v *Hill,* 1916 S.C. 892.
[79] *Fullarton* v *Duke of Hamilton's Trustees,* 1918 S.C. 292.
[80] 1886 Act, s. 20. See *infra,* p. 483.
[81] 1911 Act, s. 32 (14), applying 1886 Act, s. 20.
[82] *Steven* v *Henderson* (1913), 1 S.L.C.R. 64.
[83] *Rutherford* v *McCorquodale* (1934) 22 S.L.C.R. 53.

On the same conditions as in the case of a landholder, the Land Court can sist proceedings for removal of a tenant for non-payment of rent till an application to fix the rent is finally determined,[84] and can also stay proceedings for the sale of the tenant's effects.[84]

Security of Tenure. Subject to the provisions of the Agricultural Holdings Acts and the Landholders Acts, a landlord and a tenant may agree on the terms and conditions of a renewed tenancy.[85] Despite an agreement to the contrary, a statutory small tenant may obtain, on application to the Land Court, a renewal of his tenancy on the terms and conditions stated in the 1911 Act on the determination of the tenancy, unless the landlord can satisfy the Court that there is reasonable ground of objection to him.[86] It has been held by the Land Court that the withholding of rent by the statutory small tenant because of failure by the landlord to roof a byre was not a reasonable ground of objection to the renewal of the tenancy.[87] The Court will determine the period of renewal.[88] The fact that a notice to quit has been served on the tenant does not affect the tenant's right to a renewal,[89] which is a statutory right, but if he has given written notice to the landlord to terminate the tenancy, he is not entitled to renewal.[90] After the expiry he holds under the statutory renewal, of which the terms have still to be fixed.

The tenant, if he wishes renewal, must seek renewal before the tenancy has terminated.[91] " It may well be—although it is unnecessary now to express an opinion on the point—that if the tenant gives due notice of the termination of the tenancy, wishing (1) to prevent tacit relocation and (2) to get a renewal of the tenancy on new terms as regards rent and duration, he must demand the renewal and state the desired terms either within the period during which a valid notice of termination can be given under the Agricultural Holdings Acts—or at any rate before the landlord has acted on the notice. The section says nothing in express terms about this, but it is possible that the necessity for continuity in agricultural occupation and management which governs so many of the obligations of landlord and tenant may require such an interpretation of the provisions of the section. What, however, is certain is that a demand for renewal of the tenancy can only be made (1) by the person who is still statutory small tenant of the farm for the time being and (2) in relation to a tenancy which is still determining and not in relation to one which has actually terminated. A demand for renewal is too late if not made before the term at which the tenancy actually

---

[84] 1911 Act, s. 32 (14).
[85] *Ibid.,* s. 32 (6).
[86] *Ibid.,* s. 32 (4).
[87] *MacRobert Estates Trustees* v *Mason* (1948) 36 S.L.C.R. 33.
[88] 1911 Act, s. 32 (7).
[89] *Morison's Trustees* v *Grant,* 1913 S.C. 919.
[90] 1911 Act, s. 32 (4), as amended by 1931 Act, s. 18.
[91] *Cheyne* v *Paterson,* 1929 S.C. 119. The circumstances in this case had been left open in the earlier case of *Clyne, infra.*

terminated in accordance with due notice ".[92] So where the tenant had renounced the lease prior to the natural termination of the lease and then refused to remove at the agreed-on ish or under the renunciation, it was held[91] that the tenant was not entitled to a renewal on the ground that his claim was not made timeously. " Once more, it may well be " said the Lord President,[93] " that, as in the case of notice of termination by either landlord or tenant in the last year of the currency of a tenancy, so in the case of a renunciation of the tenancy during its currency, the tenant (if he desires to have his tenancy renewed as from the term at which the renunciation takes effect) must make his demand for renewal either at the same time as he renounces, or at any rate forthwith thereafter. But once more, it is not necessary for the purposes of the present case to express an opinion on the point. It is enough that the (tenant) in the present case made no demand for renewal until after his admittedly valid renunciation had taken effect and the tenancy had actually terminated ". If he had made a demand contemporaneously with his renunciation or before he had allowed the landlord to act upon it (which he had done by selling the farm) or at worst before the current tenancy had come to an end, a different situation might possibly have arisen. Lords Blackburn and Morison held that the right was excluded because it only emerged at the natural termination of the lease. Said Lord Blackburn[94] " The principal privilege which the Act (that is the 1911 Act) conferred upon such tenants was the right to demand a new lease from their landlord on the expiry of the existing lease. In the event of the landlord offering a new lease on terms which the statutory small tenant was prepared to accept, and might accept, the relations between him and his landlord were to continue to be regulated, as they had been before the expiry of the existing lease, by the terms of a bargain voluntarily entered into between them, and their rights arising thereunder were to be regulated by the common law. But, in the event of the statutory small tenant being dissatisfied on the expiry of his existing lease with the terms offered for the new lease, he had the right, under the Act, to apply to the Land Court to fix what the terms of the new lease were to be. Once these terms were fixed, the only change in the relations between the statutory small tenant and his landlord under the new lease arose from the fact that the terms of the lease as to rent, duration, and possibly some other matters, had been fixed by the Land Court and not by voluntary agreement. . . . There is no doubt that if the reclaimer (the tenant) was still in possession under the lease (adjusted by the Land Court) at its expiry, he would be entitled to a renewal, the terms of which might be adjusted either by mutual agreement or by the Land Court. But, during the currency of the lease, the Land Court has no

92 *Ibid.*, at 126, *per* L.P. Clyde.
93 *Ibid.*, at 127.
94 *Ibid.*, at 128-9.

jurisdiction to interfere in any questions which may arise between the parties to the lease as to their respective rights under the lease. Such questions are left to be settled by the common law. Nor has the Land Court power to introduce into a lease, adjusted by it on the application of a statutory small tenant, a clause prohibiting the parties to the new lease from putting an end to it by mutual consent if they so desire . . . (such) would be disastrous to tenant and landlord . . . the right given to a statutory small tenant on the determination of the tenancy to apply to the Land Court to adjust a new lease only arises on the natural termination of the lease under which he is in occupation of the subjects at the date of the application. Until a lease adjusted by the Land Court has come to its natural termination, the statutory small tenant has no right under the Act to demand the adjustment of a new lease . . . having himself renounced the lease and his renunciation having been accepted, the (tenant) has no legal right either at common law or under the statute to remain in occupation of the subjects ".

Where neither party gives notice of termination, then tacit relocation operates.[95] The tenant and his landlord will be presumed to have agreed to renewal on the existing conditions for a year and so from year to year, so long as no application is made to the Court. Where the tenant held on a lease renewed by tacit relocation yearly it was held that the Court could not make the renewal run from Martinmas 1913 when the last period of tacit relocation had begun and after which the tenant had made his application.[95] The earliest date from which renewal could run, since renewal is only " on any determination of the tenancy ", was when the current year of tenancy was completed.[95]

The tenant can thus remain indefinitely in the holding. He is bound, of course, for any agreed-upon term that the Land Court may think reasonable. His security of tenure is not affected by the Agricultural Holdings (Scotland) Act 1949, which gave a benefit to agricultural tenants and did not seek to take away benefits from those who already had security of tenure.[96]

The tenant may be removed for failure to pay rent or breach of conditions in his lease or at common law, which under the lease or at common law are sanctioned by an irritancy.

Except so far as varied by the Landholders Acts, the Agricultural Holdings (Scotland) Acts apply in the case of the tenancy of a statutory small tenant as if the tenancy were a lease, and for the purposes of these

---

[95] *Wilkie* v *Hill*, 1916 S.C. 892. An earlier case of *Clyne* v *Sharp's Trustees,* 1913 S.C. 907, where it was held that the tenant's right to a renewal was not affected by the fact that the lease had expired, was regarded as a very special one, referable only to its own particular circumstances, *viz.,* that the ish was at Whitsun 1912, the Act commenced on 1st April 1912, and the application was made on 16th August 1912, as soon as the Land Court was constituted. *Clyne* did not apply to a tenancy renewed by tacit relocation after the Act came into force.

[96] *Millar* v *Gibson* (1955) 43 S.L.C.R. 3.

latter Acts the tenancy as renewed from time to time is deemed to be a lease current for the period of renewal.[97]

As regards conditions, these are the ordinary conditions under the lease or at common law or under the provisions of the Landholders Acts, and the statutory provision entitling the landlord to use spring water rising on a holding on payment of compensation.[98]

Resumption by the Landlord. The landlord can resume under an agreement. Without prejudice to any agreement, however, the Land Court, on the landlord's application to it, if it is satisfied that he desires to resume possession of the holding or a part of it for building, planting or the protection of an ancient monument or other object of historical or archaeological interest from destruction or injury or some other reasonable purpose " having relation to the good of the holding or the estate ", can authorise the resumption by the landlord, on payment of compensation by him to the tenant in respect of improvements on or in connection with the land resumed to which the tenant would be entitled under the Agricultural Holdings Acts on determination of the tenancy ".[99] Where a part only of the holding is resumed, the tenant is entitled to a reduction of rent as agreed on or failing agreement is determined by the Land Court.[99] The landlord's intention to reside on the holding is not a ground of resumption.[1] In contrast to the case of a landholder, the landlord may resume for feuing without specification of purpose, the repeal of the provision regarding feuing in the 1911 Act[2] by the 1931 Act[3] having left the original general and absolute power of feuing unresolved.[4] Prior to the 1931 Act the Land Court authorised resumption of the whole of a holding for feuing.[5] The Court cannot make actual payment of compensation a condition precedent to resumption.[6]

Compensation for Improvements. A statutory small tenant is entitled, if the landlord resumes, to such compensation for disturbance as would be payable under the Agricultural Holdings (Scotland) Acts to a tenant to whom notice to quit or of resumption of a part of the holding had been given,[7] and to compensation for improvements on or in connection with the land resumed, to which a tenant under the Agricultural Holdings Acts would be entitled on termination of the tenancy.[8] He can obtain the same rights of compensation as a landholder if he gives written

---

[97] 1911 Act, s. 32 (5).
[98] 1911 Act, s. 32 (14), applying 1911 Act, s. 12.
[99] 1911 Act, s. 32 (15), as amended by 1931 Act, s. 8 (2).
[1] 1931 Act, s. 8 (1).
[2] s. 19.
[3] s. 8 (2).
[4] *Duke of Argyll* v *Macdonald* (1933) 21 S.L.C.R. 16, where the absurdity of the 1931 Act, s. 8 (2) in this connection is pointed out.
[5] *Fergusson* v *McCulloch* (1921) 9 S.L.C.R. 44.
[6] *Whyte* v *Stewart,* 1914 S.C. 675.
[7] 1931 Act, s. 13.
[8] 1911 Act, s. 32 (15).

notice one month before the expiry of the tenancy to the landlord of his desire to become a landholder, and if, within a month after service of that notice, the landlord lodges with the Land Court a written under- taking that the tenant shall have the same rights as if he were a land- holder to compensation for permanent improvements.[9] Unless the tenant has given that notice he, therefore, obtains such compensation only as he is entitled to receive under the Agricultural Holdings (Scotland) Acts. If he becomes a landholder, the rights of interested parties so far as affected by the 1911 Act at the date of his becoming a landholder are, in the event of dispute, to be adjusted by order of the Land Court on the application of any party interested.[10]

Where again both parties agree, the issue of compensation may be submitted by them for determination to the Land Court.[11] If, however, they do not so agree, the issue is settled by arbitration under the Agricul- tural Holdings (Scotland) Act;[12] where the parties are not agreed on an arbiter, the arbiter is appointed by the Land Court, and in that case his remuneration is paid by the Court.[13]

Subletting of Holding.   A statutory small tenant is not prohibited by the Acts from subletting the holding but he may be prohibited by the terms and conditions of his lease. The question is otherwise determined by the common law of leases.

Assignation of Holding.   A statutory small tenant is not entitled to assign his lease unless the lease permits it;[14] there is no statutory pro- vision authorising assignation. Nor can he apply in case of illness, old age or infirmity to the Land Court for authority to assign to any person to whom he could bequeath the holding.

Succession: *Bequest of Holding.*   Unless there are express provi- sions in the lease empowering him to bequeath to a wider extent, the statutory small tenant can only bequeath to a member of his family[15] as defined in the Acts.[16] This limited right has been held not to be affected, and thus extended, by the provisions[17] of the Agricultural Hold- ings (Scotland) Act 1949.[18]

Succession: *Intestate Succession.*   There is a right of succession to a statutory small tenant to the same extent as in the case of a land-

[9] 1931 Act, s. 14.
[10] 1911 Act, s. 14.
[11] 1931 Act, s. 34.
[12] 1911 Act, s. 32 (5).
[13] *Ibid.*, s. 32 (10).
[14] *Ibid.*, s. 32 (1).
[15] *Ibid.*, s. 32 (1).
[16] See *supra*, p. 425.
[17] s. 20.
[18] *Alexander* v *Anstruther* (1955) 43 S.L.C.R. 5.

holder.[19] The successors of the statutory small tenant are referred to as " the successors of such tenant or leaseholder in the holding, being his heirs, legatees " (if within the relationship specified in the Acts) or assignees (if assignation is permitted by the lease) ".[15] There is, however, no provision, as in the case of landholders, for devolution from an heir to those next in succession, so that if the immediate heir does not take up the succession, the tenancy falls to the landlord.[20] A statutory small tenant legitimated *per subsequens matrimonium* and brought up as his grandfather's heir was held to have a clear title to succeed to the grandfather's holding,[21] but a first cousin of the deceased mother of an illegitimate person was held not entitled to succeed as heir-at-law.[22]

Enlargement of Holding. A statutory small tenant is not entitled to a compulsory enlargement of his holding; the statutory provisions apply only to landholders. He can, however, be given an extension of his holding as a new holding.

Vacant Holdings: Rights of Landlord. When a holding of a statutory small tenant becomes vacant, it cannot be retained within the Acts as it can in the case of a holding of a landholder. Nor can it be merged in or amalgamated with any other agricultural holding under the Agricultural Holdings (Scotland) Acts except with the sanction of the Secretary of State.[23] There is, however, no obligation on the landlord to let it under any particular form of tenure.

Record of Holding. The statutory provisions in regard to a record of the holding in the case of a landholder's holding apply also in the case of a holding of a statutory small tenant.[24]

Landholders' Holdings Book. This Book is applicable in the case of statutory small tenants and the recording in it of Land Court applications, orders and other proceedings applies equally in the case of holdings of statutory small tenants.[25] Written undertakings by a landlord that a statutory small tenant shall have the same rights to compensation for permanent improvements as if a landholder must be recorded in the Book, and the recording constitutes the tenant a landholder as regards these rights alone.[26]

Register of Smallholdings. This includes the holdings of statutory small tenants and the provisions previously mentioned apply in such cases too.[27]

19 *Supra*, p. 427.
20 *Sim* v *Gordon* (1919) 7 S.L.C.R. 3.
21 *MacKenzie* v *Grant* (1948) 36 S.L.C.R. 40.
22 *Grant* v *Macdonald* (1948) 36 S.L.C.R. 7.
23 1911 Act, s. 32 (3).
24 *Ibid.*, s. 32 (14). See *supra*, p. 431.
25 *Ibid.*, s. 32 (14), applying 1886 Act, s. 27.
26 1931 Act, s. 14.
27 *Supra*, p. 432.

PROVISIONS IN RELATION TO CROFTERS

THE CROFTERS ACTS 1955 AND 1961

General. As has already been mentioned,[28] the 1955 Act created a new and separate code for crofters in the crofting counties, that is, the counties of Argyll, Caithness, Inverness, Orkney, Ross and Cromarty, Sutherland and Zetland.[29] The code for these counties is thus now contained in the 1955 Act, as later amended by the 1961 Act, and in the provisions of the Landholders Acts 1886-1931 as modified in their application to the crofting counties.[30] The 1955 Act uses the old name " crofter " for holders in these parts instead of " landholders " and abolishes the distinction in these counties between landholders and statutory small tenants. There is, thus, a third set or class of holder—the crofter in the crofting counties.

Rent. The rent payable as one of the statutory conditions is the yearly rent, including money and any prestations other than money, payable for the year current at the commencement of the 1955 Act (that is, on 1st October 1955) or in the case of a croft let thereafter fixed at the date of the letting, unless and until the rent is altered.[31] The rent may be altered by written agreement between landlord and crofter to such an amount and for such a period as may be agreed on by them, and in that event that rent is the rent payable so long as the agreement subsists and then so long as no new agreement is made between landlord and crofter or no different rent has been fixed by the Land Court under the Act.[32]

On application either of the crofter or of the landlord,[33] the Land Court may determine what is a fair rent to be paid for the croft and order accordingly, and such rent is then the rent payable as from the first term of Whitsunday or Martinmas next succeeding the Land Court's decision.[34] In fixing the fair rent the Court must hear the parties and take into consideration " all the circumstances of the case, of the croft and of the district ", and, in particular, " any permanent or unexhausted improvements on the croft and suitable thereto which have been executed or paid for by the crofter or his predecessors in the tenancy ".[35] Where

---

[28] See *supra*, pp. 404, 410.

[29] s. 37 (1). Unless otherwise indicated, the section and schedule references are to the 1955 Act, which modifies certain provisions of certain Acts in their application to these counties and directs that others are not to apply (Schedule Sixth). It provides for entry on and inspection of land on behalf of the Secretary of State and the Crofters Commission: s. 30.

[30] 1955 Act, s. 38 (2)-(4) and Schedule Sixth.

[31] s. 5 (1).

[32] s. 5 (2).

[33] Where the crofter was in fact proprietor of the whole holding under her disposition, the application was held not competent. *Grant* v *Pearson* (1959) 49 S.L.C.R. 37.

[34] s. 5 (3).

[35] s. 5 (4).

the rent is fixed by the Court, it cannot be altered for seven years from the term at which it first became payable unless by mutual agreement between landlord and crofter.[36] Where, however, the rent payable for a croft which was immediately before the commencement of the 1955 Act a holding to which the Landholders Acts in relation to statutory small tenants applied was last fixed by the Land Court before that date, it can be altered by the Court at any time after that date.[37] If the croft is first let after the commencement of the Acts, the Land Court cannot alter the rent agreed upon for seven years from the term when it first became payable or such longer period as the landlord and the crofter may agree upon.[38]

There are provisions as to the amount of the rent in a sublease granted by the Commission, with a right to the Land Court to vary the rent on application by the crofter.[39] And there are provisions as to the fixing by the Land Court of the rents of crofts under a reorganisation scheme and as to the variation of such rents.[40] Where a landlord is entitled at common law and under the terms of the let to discontinue a private water supply system to certain crofts, he must on discontinuance allow an abatement of the rent.[41]

Security of Tenure. A crofter may not be removed from a croft of which he is the tenant unless one year's rent is unpaid or there is a breach of one or more of the statutory conditions other than the condition as to payment of rent or in pursuance of any enactment contained in the Acts.[42] The statutory conditions are as follows : [43]

1. The crofter shall pay his rent at the terms at which it is due and payable.

2. The crofter shall not, except in accordance with the provisions of " this " Act, execute any deed purporting to assign his tenancy.

3. The crofter shall, by himself or his family, with or without hired labour, cultivate his croft, without prejudice to the right by the Act conferred on him to make such use thereof for subsidiary or auxiliary occupations as, in case of dispute, the Land Court may find to be reasonable and not inconsistent with the cultivation of the croft. " Cultivate " includes the use of a croft for horticulture or for any purpose of husbandry, including the keeping or breed-

---

[36] s. 5 (3), *proviso* (a).
[37] s. 39 (3).
[38] s. 5 (3), *proviso* (b).
[39] 1961 Act, s. 12 (12); see *infra*, pp. 456, 486.
[40] *Ibid.*, s. 9 (3), (4), (5); see *infra*, p. 471.
[41] *Secretary of State for Scotland* v *Mackay*, 1964, S.L.T. (Land Ct.) 2. The County Council were prepared to connect up to the public system on payment of the usual water rates.
[42] s. 3 (3). See Rent Act 1965, s. 30.
[43] Schedule Second, as amended by 1961 Act, Schedule First, para. 20. " This " Act refers to the 1955 Act. See 1955 Act, s. 37 (1).

ing of livestock, poultry or bees, and the growing of fruit, vegetables and the like.

3. (A) The crofter shall provide such fixed equipment on his croft as may be necessary to enable him to cultivate the croft.

4. The crofter shall not, to the prejudice of the interest of the landlord, persistently injure the croft by the dilapidation of buildings or, after notice in writing has been given by the landlord to the crofter not to commit, or to desist from, the particular injury specified in the notice, by the deterioration of the soil.

5. The crofter shall not sublet his croft or any part thereof otherwise than with the consent in writing of the Commission and in accordance with such conditions (which shall not include conditions relating to rent) as the Commission in giving their consent may impose. But nothing in this paragraph is to be construed as debarring a crofter from subletting any dwellinghouse or other buildings forming part of his croft to holiday visitors.

6. The crofter shall not, except in accordance with the provisions of " this " Act, subdivide his croft.

7. The crofter shall not, without the consent in writing of the landlord, erect or suffer to be erected on the croft any dwellinghouse otherwise than in substitution for a dwellinghouse which at the commencement of " this " Act was already on the croft; but if at the commencement of " this " Act there was no dwellinghouse on the croft, the crofter may erect one dwellinghouse thereon.

8. The crofter shall not persistently violate any written condition signed by him for the protection of the interest of the landlord or of neighbouring crofters which is legally applicable to the croft and which the Land Court shall find to be reasonable.

9. The crofter shall not do any act whereby he becomes bankrupt within the meaning of the Bankruptcy (Scotland) Act 1913, and shall not execute a trust deed for creditors.

10. The crofter shall permit the landlord or any person authorised by the landlord in that behalf to enter upon the croft for the purpose of exercising (subject always to the payment of such compensation as in case of dispute the Land Court may find to be reasonable in respect of any damage done or occasioned thereby) any of the following rights, and shall not obstruct the landlord or any person authorised as aforesaid in the exercise of any of such rights, that is to say :

    (a) mining or taking minerals, or digging or searching for minerals;

    (b) quarrying or taking stone, marble, gravel, sand, clay, slate or other workable mineral;

(c) Using for any estate purpose any springs of water rising on the croft and not required for the use thereof;[44]

(d) cutting or taking timber or peats, excepting timber and other trees planted by the crofter or any of his predecessors in the tenancy, or which may be necessary for ornament, or shelter, and excepting also such peats as may be required for the use of the croft;

(e) opening or making roads, fences, drains and water-courses;

(f) passing and repassing to and from the shore of the sea or any loch with or without vehicles for the purpose of exercising any right of property or other right belonging to the landlord;

(g) viewing or examining at reasonable times the state of the croft and all buildings or improvements thereon;[44a]

(h) hunting, shooting, fishing or taking game or fish, wild birds or vermin;

but nothing in this paragraph precludes the crofter from recovering any compensation for damage by game which is recoverable under section fifteen of the Agricultural Holdings (Scotland) Act 1949, by a tenant, and that section applies, accordingly, with the substitution, however, of the Land Court for arbitration. " Game " means deer, hares, rabbits, pheasants, partridges, grouse, blackgame, capercailzie, ptarmigan, woodcock, snipe, wild duck, widgeon and teal.

11. The crofter shall not on his croft, without the consent in writing of the landlord, open any house for the sale of intoxicating liquors.

When a year's rent is unpaid or the crofter has broken one or more of the statutory conditions other than as to payment of rent, then, on the landlord's application, the Land Court may, after considering any objections by the crofter, make an order for his removal.[45] If a crofter whose rights to compensation for permanent improvements have been transferred in whole or in part to the Secretary of State in respect of a loan from the Secretary of State[46] has abandoned his croft or broken any of the statutory conditions other than as to payment of rent or any of the conditions of repayment of the loan in the loan agreement, again, on the Secretary of State's application, the Land Court can, after hearing

---

[44] See *MacColl* v *Downie's Trs.* (1962) 50 S.L.C.R. 28. In *Secretary of State for Scotland* v *Greig* (1963) 51 S.L.C.R. 3, it was held that where the Board had been ordered by the Land Court in 1914 to carry out certain drainage works and maintain them, the Secretary of State had no power or duty to carry them out, but only such power as the landlords of the ground granted him (which they were entitled to do).

[44a] A crofter is, in the absence of agreement to the contrary, entirely responsible for maintenance of buildings whether these are provided by his landlord or himself. *Holman* v *Henderson,* 1965 S.L.T. (Land Ct.) 13.

[45] 1955 Act, s. 13 (1).

[46] ss. 22, 23.

any objections by the crofter and the landlord, make an order for the crofter's removal.[47]

If the crofter is removed, the landlord can set off all rent due or to become due against any sum found to be due by the landlord to the crofter or to the Secretary of State in respect of permanent improvements made on the croft.[48]

Where the Crofters' Commission find that a crofter is not ordinarily resident on or within ten miles of the croft, that is, is an absentee crofter, and that it is in the interest of the crofting community in the district where the croft is situated that the tenancy be terminated and the croft let to another or others, they may make an order terminating his tenancy and requiring him to give up occupation at a term of Whitsunday or Martinmas not earlier than three months after the making of the order.[49] The Commission must, however, before they make the order, take into consideration " all the circumstances of the case, including the extent, if any, to which the croft is being worked, and, where the croft is being worked by a member of the crofter's family, the nature of the arrangements under which it is being worked "; they must also notify the crofter and the landlord, not less than six months before the term when the proposed order will take effect, that they propose to make the order, and they must also give both parties an opportunity to make representations against the proposed order.[50] They must further notify both parties of the making of the order not less than three months before the term when the order takes effect.[50] If the crofter does not give up occupation on or before the date when the order takes effect, the Sheriff must, on the Commission's application, grant warrant, unless cause to the contrary is shown, for the crofter's ejection, and the Commission can recover from the crofter their expenses in the application and in the execution of the warrant.[51] If the Commission are satisfied that the crofter or any of his predecessors in the tenancy (that is, those who before him have been tenants of the croft since it was last vacant)[52] either provided or paid for the whole or the greater part of the dwelling-house and that on the termination of the tenancy he is entitled to compensation for it as an improvement, the Commission must notify the crofter and the landlord accordingly; and the crofter, on giving notice not later than a month before the term when the order takes effect, is entitled to a conveyance in feu (under reservation of the minerals) of the dwellinghouse and such suitable garden ground and rights of access as the Commission consider reasonable and on such terms in regard to feu-duty or otherwise as either the parties agree upon or the Land

[47] s. 13 (2).
[48] s. 13 (3), as amended by 1961 Act, Schedule First, para. 3.
[49] s. 17 (1), as amended by 1961 Act, s. 7 (1).
[50] s. 17 (2). See as to procedure for such representations, including, whether or not they are made, the requiring of an opportunity to be heard: s. 33.
[51] s. 17 (3).
[52] s. 37 (1).

Court determine in the case of feu-duty, and in any other case the Commission determine, to be reasonable.[53] If the landlord so requires, the conveyance must contain a clause giving the superior a right of pre-emption over the subjects on the first occasion when the subjects are offered for sale after the grant of the conveyance.[54]

If the landlord does not execute and deliver at his own expense to the Commission the necessary conveyance within a period which the Commission consider reasonable, the Commission must prepare the conveyance and submit it to the landlord for execution.[55] Similarly, they must prepare it and submit it to him if he requests them to prepare it.[55] If, within one month after the conveyance has been submitted to him, he does not execute and return it to the Commission, the Commission can execute it, and it will then have the same force and effect as if executed by the landlord.[55]

The conveyance is recorded in the Register of Sasines on behalf of the crofter.[55] And the effect of the recording there is that any existing heritable security as defined in the 1955 Act over the subjects before the execution of the conveyance no longer burdens the *dominium utile* but only the superiority.[56] The Commission may insist on delivery from the landlord or any other possessor of them of any documents they consider necessary for preparing the conveyance, and if they are not delivered in obedience to this demand the Sheriff can order their delivery.[57]

In the case both of the provisions for executing and recording the conveyance and of the provisions for delivery of documents, if some person other than the landlord is infeft in the property, references to the landlord are construed as references to the landlord and that other person for their respective interests.[57]

The consideration due by the crofter in respect of the conveyance is, in addition to any feu-duty, such sum as the crofter and the landlord may agree on or is determined by the Land Court (if they do not agree) to be the value as at the termination of the tenancy of any assistance or consideration given by the landlord or any predecessor in respect of the dwellinghouse.[58] The crofter too cannot get from the landlord on the termination of the tenancy any compensation for the dwelling-house as an improvement[59] but otherwise has the same rights and is subject to the same liabilities in respect of compensation as if he had renounced the tenancy at the term when the order takes effect.[60] Further, if there is a loan from the Secretary of State, the amount of any liability

[53] s. 17 (4), as amended by 1961 Act, s. 7 (2) and (3).
[54] 1961 Act, s. 7 (4).
[55] s. 17 (5).
[56] s. 17 (7).
[57] s. 17 (6).
[58] s. 17 (8), as amended by 1961 Act, Schedule First, para. 6.
[59] *Ibid.*
[60] s. 17 (9).

thereunder at the tenancy's termination is, if the Secretary of State on the crofter's application so determines, deemed from the date of recording to be a loan from the Secretary of State.[61] If the crofter requests them to do so, the Commission are to act for him in any matter connected with the grant of the conveyance in feu and the recording of it.[62] Any expenses the Commission so incur in acting for the crofter are payable by them and not recoverable from any other person.[63]

Where an order has been made terminating a tenancy because of the crofter's absence[64] and the croft then becomes vacant, and it remains unlet for six months from the date of vacancy, the Secretary of State must, if the landlord within three months of the expiry of the six months requires the Secretary of State to do so, declare that the croft shall cease to be a croft.[65] The Secretary of State must then purchase the buildings on the croft, and he is deemed authorised to do so compulsorily and to have served a notice to treat on the date when the notice was given.[66] The provisions of the Acts then no longer apply to the croft but that is without prejudice to a later exercise of any statutory powers as to the constitution of new crofts or the enlarging of existing ones.[67]

Resumption by Landlord. If the landlord applies to them and satisfies them that he desires to resume the whole or a part of the croft " for some reasonable purpose having relation to the good of the croft or of the estate or to the public interest ", the Land Court may authorise the resumption by him on such terms and conditions as they think fit, and they may require the crofter to surrender his croft in whole or in part to the landlord, on the landlord making adequate compensation to the crofter by letting to him other land of equivalent value in the neighbourhood or by payment of compensation in money or by way of adjustment of rent or in such other manner as the Land Court may determine.[68] " Reasonable purpose " includes[69] " the using, letting or feuing of the land proposed to be resumed for the building of dwellings, or for small allotments, or for harbours, piers, boat shelters or other like buildings, or for churches or other places of religious worship, or for schools, or for halls or community centres, or for planting, or for

[61] s. 17 (10). The provisions of Schedule Third apply to the loan: *Ibid.*
[62] 1961 Act, s. 7 (5).
[63] *Ibid.*, s. 7 (6).
[64] See *supra*, p. 447.
[65] s. 16 (7).
[66] s. 16 (8).
[67] s. 16 (9). See *Murray's Trs.* v *Ross*, 1964 S.L.T. (Land Ct.) 9.
[68] s. 12 (1). In *Secretary of State for Scotland* v *Macdonald* (1961) 49 S.L.C.R. 42 it was held that an application to resume part of common grazings should be approved, and compensation was awarded in terms agreed by all parties. See *Marquess of Bute* v *Baxter*, 1966 S.L.T. (Land Ct.), 9, where it was held compensation for resumption must be fixed under s. 12, as the original lease providing for resumption of part of the land on abatement of rent was inconsistent with the 1955 Act. The Court left undecided the question whether an application under s. 12 was a bar to the lease terms if the lease was not inconsistent.
[69] s. 12 (2), as amended by 1961 Act, Schedule First, para. 11.

roads practicable for vehicular traffic from the croft or township to the public road or to the seashore, or for any other purpose likely to provide employment for crofters and others in the locality, and the protection of an ancient monument or other object of historical or archaeological interest from injury or destruction ". Resumption of common grazings for quarrying in connection with a guided missile site has been held to be for " a reasonable purpose ", the Court considering that it would not affect a certain statue in the area.[70]

If, with the consent of a majority of those sharing in a common grazing and with the approval of the Crofters' Commission, application is made for authority to resume any land that forms part of the common grazing " for the purpose of using, letting or other disposing of it for the planting of trees ", the Land Court must not withhold authority for the resumption.[71]

On land being resumed in pursuance of an order of the Land Court authorising its resumption, the provisions of the 1955 and 1961 Acts cease to apply to it but this, however, is without prejudice to the subsequent exercise of any powers conferred by any Act for the constitution of new crofts or the enlargement of existing crofts.[72]

Renunciation of Holding. On giving one year's notice in writing to the landlord a crofter is entitled to renounce his tenancy as at any term of Whitsunday or Martinmas.[73] If he renounces, the landlord can set off all rent due or to become due against any sum found due by the landlord to the crofter or the Secretary of State by way of compensation for permanent improvements made on the croft.[74] If the Commission are satisfied, on a crofter applying to them and after consulting the landlord, that the crofter is unable by reason of illness or old age or infirmity properly to work his croft and that he is willing to renounce the tenancy subject to the conditions that he retain the occupation of

---

[70] *Andreae* v *Mackay* (1959) 47 S.L.C.R. 30. See *Bray* v *MacAuslane* (1961) 49 S.L.C.R. App. 105, that resumption of part containing ruined buildings to create holiday accommodation was for a reasonable purpose; *Russell* v *Murray* (1961) 49 S.L.C.R. App. 123, that a subtenant of part who had carried on business there for twenty-seven years should be allowed to resume the part purchased; *Brocket's Trs.* v *Holdgson* (1961) 49 S.L.C.R. 25, where resumption of part, so that the local authority could erect six double houses on the part held, was not a reasonable purpose; *Sutherland's Trustees* v *Mackay* (1961) 49 S.L.C.R. 33, where resumption of part was allowed on the landlord erecting fences and paying compensation adjusted to the high wintering value of the part; *Murray's Trs.* v *Ross,* 1964 S.L.T. (Land Ct.) 9, where it was held that, even though the tenant consented, an application to resume a croft except for a house and garden in order to fence the land for building but no building contract to feu had been entered into nor had the landlord any specific proposals was not for a reasonable purpose.
[71] s. 12 (3).
[72] s. 12 (4), as added by 1961 Act, Schedule First, para. 11 (b).
[73] s. 7 (1). Crofters, it has been held, cannot renounce part of their crofts in order to avoid liability to repair a boundary fence on common grazings under an order of the Commission in 1886: *Vestey* v *Inverkirkaig & Strathan Crofters* (1961) 49 S.L.C.R. App. 57.
[74] s. 7 (2), as amended by 1961 Act, Schedule First, para. 1.

the house on the croft and that he become the owner of it and that it is in the general interest of the crofting community in the district where the croft is situated that he should be authorised to renounce on these conditions, he may be authorised by the Crofters Commission to renounce.[75] The Commission must notify the landlord of their authorisation.[75] Thereafter, if the crofter applies to the Commission and the landlord by notice not later than one month before the date when the renunciation takes effect, he is entitled to obtain a conveyance in feu (under reservation of the minerals) of the dwellinghouse together with such suitable garden ground and such rights of access as the Commission may determine to be reasonable and on such terms as to feu-duty or otherwise as may be agreed between the landlord and the crofter or, failing agreement, the Commission determine to be reasonable.[76] The provisions of the 1955 Act[77] in regard to a conveyance to a crofter where an order has been made terminating the tenancy because of his absence apply with the necessary modifications here.[76] And where a conveyance in feu has been granted, the grantee and his or her wife or husband are, so long as either continues to occupy the subjects, not liable to pay any higher sum for local rates than if the subjects had remained part of the croft, but liability for the domestic water rate under the Water (Scotland) Act 1949 is not affected;[78] and, so long again as either of them continues to occupy, they continue to enjoy any right they had when the authorisation was given to cut and take peats.[79] The correct procedure on renunciation is to apply to the Secretary of State for an order that the croft, being vacant, is no longer a croft.[79a]

Compensation for Improvements. Where a crofter renounces his tenancy or is removed from his croft, he is entitled to compensation for any permanent improvements. These are[80]

1. Dwellinghouse.
2. Farm offices.
3. Subsoil and other drains.
4. Walls and fences.
5. Deep trenching.
6. Clearing the ground.
7. Planting trees.
8. Making piers or landing stages.
9. Roads practicable for vehicles from the croft to the public road or the sea shore.

[75] s. 18 (1). See *McLean* v *Roger*, 1964 S.L.T. (Land Ct.) 11.
[76] s. 18 (2). See *McLean* v *Roger, supra.*
[77] s. 17 (5)-(10), as amended by 1961 Act, Schedule First, para. 6. See *supra*, p. 448.
[78] s. 18 (3).
[79] s. 18 (4).
[79a] Under s. 16 (9) *supra.* See *Murray's Trs. (supra).*
[80] Schedule Fifth, as amended by 1961 Act, Schedule First, para. 21. A peat road nearly three-quarters of a mile long leading to the croft has been held to be an improvement on the croft and compensation given so far as suitable to the holding: *Mackenzie* v *Roger*, 1964 S.L.T. (Land Ct.) 8.

10. All other improvements which, in the judgment of the Land Court, will add to the value of the croft as an agricultural subject.
11. Buildings or other structures erected under section five of the Crofters (Scotland) Act 1961, being buildings or structures which are fixtures on the land; or works executed under the said section five.

but no building or other structure, however, erected on a croft is to be held to be a permanent improvement unless it is a fixture on the land.[81] The permanent improvement must have been made on the croft, be suitable to the croft and have been executed or paid for by the crofter or any of his predecessors in the tenancy (that is, those who before him have been tenants of the croft since it was last vacant[82]), and either been executed otherwise than in pursuance of a specific written agreement under which the crofter was bound to execute it or, if it has been executed in pursuance of such an agreement, the crofter has not received, by way of reduction of rent or otherwise, fair consideration for the improvement.[83] The tenant cannot apply for compensation if he has assigned the croft.[84] Where the holding is merely noted for registration there can be no claim.[85] If he has applied before his death, his widow can prosecute his claim.[86] He has a right to claim before quitting the holding.[87] This right to compensation does not apply in respect of buildings erected by a crofter in contravention of any interdict or other judicial order.[88] Any buildings or other structures erected, if fixtures on the land, or any works executed on his croft by a crofter which are reasonably required to enable him to make use of the croft for any subsidiary or auxiliary occupation and which will not interfere substantially with the use of the croft as an agricultural subject are permanent improvements deemed suitable to the croft,[89] and this applies to such buildings or other structures erected or works executed before the commencement of the 1961 Act.[90] But the crofter must not have renounced his tenancy or been removed from his croft before the commencement of that Act.[91] Where the tenancy is ended by the Commission because the crofter is an absentee and he dies before the

---

[81] s. 37 (1), as amended by 1961 Act, Schedule First, para. 18.
[82] s. 37 (1).
[83] s. 14 (1). See as to the effect of delay in claiming compensation after renouncing, *Macleod* v *Vestey* (1962) 50 S.L.C.R. 23. No compensation is due for surveying and laying out a croft in fields, but is, *inter alia*, due for renewing a landlord's fence, making a silage pit and temporary pasture. *Fraser* v *Secretary of State for Scotland* (1961) 49 S.L.C.R. App. 148.
[84] *MacLean* v *Secretary of State for Scotland* (1961) 49 S.L.C.R. App. 141.
[85] *Wallace* v *Stewart* (1961) 49 S.L.C.R. 18.
[86] *Davidson's Exrx.* v *Stewart*, 1964 S.L.T. (Land Ct.) 6.
[87] *Davidson's Exrx.*, *supra*, approving *Kerr* v *Duke of Hamilton's Trs.* (1919) 7 S.L.C.R. 92.
[88] s. 14 (3).
[89] 1961 Act, s. 5 (2).
[90] *Ibid.*, s. 5 (3).
[91] *Ibid.*, s. 5 (3), *proviso*.

notice lapses, his executors have a vested right to compensation and the deceased's interest in a sheep club.[92]

A crofter is deemed to have executed or paid for an improvement where on becoming tenant (a) he has with the landlord's consent paid to the outgoing tenant any compensation due to him in respect of any permanent improvement and has agreed with the Secretary of State to assume any outstanding liability to the Secretary of State of the outgoing tenant in respect of a loan to him, or (b) the Secretary of State on his behalf has paid to the landlord a sum representing the value to such person of an existing improvement on the croft.[93] And a landlord is deemed to have given his consent to the payment to the outgoing tenant where the landlord has not paid the compensation due to the outgoing tenant or the Secretary of State and has not applied to the Secretary of State to determine[94] that any amount due by him to the Secretary of State under the loan provisions of the 1955 Act[95] shall be deemed to be a loan to him by the Secretary of State.[93]

The amount of compensation where the renunciation or the removal is after the commencement of the 1961 Act is a sum equal to (a) the value of the improvement as at the date of renunciation or of removal calculated in accordance with the rule aftermentioned, less (b) the value of any assistance or consideration which may be proved to have been given by the landlord of the croft or any of his predecessors in title in respect of the improvement.[96] The value of the improvement is the amount, if any, which, having regard to the location of the croft and of any other circumstances which might affect the demand for the tenancy of the croft, the landlord might reasonably be expected to receive in respect of the improvement from a person who might reasonably be expected to obtain the tenancy of the croft if it were offered on the open market for letting as a separate croft with entry at the date of renunciation or removal.[97] Where renunciation was notified because of illness etc., subject to the grant of a conveyance in feu of the dwellinghouse and its pertinents, it was held that when valuing the improvements (claimed

---

[92] *MacIntosh's Exrs.* v *Secretary of State for Scotland* (1961) 49 S.L.C.R. App. 142.
[93] 1955 Act, s. 14 (2).
[94] Under s. 23 (4).
[95] s. 23 (3).
[96] 1961 Act, s. 6 (1). See *Thompson* v *Fraser* (1961) 49 S.L.C.R. App. 157.
[97] 1961 Act, s. 6 (2). See opinion reserved as to the construction of this subsection in *Thompson, supra.* Open market value should be fixed on relevant evidence and the court's knowledge and experience of locality and crofting conditions generally. *Balfour* v *Couper* (1963) 51 S.L.C.R. 13. In *Jeromson* v *Cromarty* (1963) 51 S.L.C.R. 6, it was held that improvements should be valued on an open market basis and this was market value measured by a consideration of current prices in the open market for comparable subjects. Where land was resumed for road widening, it was held that the tenants should get a capital sum related to their net loss of profits over a long period of years. *Secretary of State for Scotland* v *Kennedy* (1961) 49 S.L.C.R. App. 111.

excluding the house and its pertinents) regard must be taken, *inter alia*, of the landlord's inability to include the house with the croft.[98]

In the case where the compensation has become payable by termination of the tenancy before the commencement of the Act,[99] the amount of compensation is fixed, failing agreement, by the Land Court,[1] and is fixed after taking into account and there is deducted from the compensation, the value of any assistance or consideration which may be proved to have been given by the landlord or any of his predecessors in title in respect of any of the improvements.[2] An improvement is valued at the sum that fairly represents its value to an incoming tenant.[3] Against the compensation can be set off compensation due to the landlord for deterioration or damage.[4] Where a crofter has given notice of renunciation of his tenancy, the Land Court may assess prior to the renunciation the amount which on the renunciation will become due for compensation for permanent improvements as well as the amount that will become due on renunciation for compensation for deterioration or damage, on the application of the crofter and the landlord, or, where the crofter's rights to compensation have been transferred in whole or in part to the Secretary of State under the 1955 Act the Secretary of State, and the amounts so assessed will become due on renunciation.[5]

The provisions of the Agricultural Holdings (Scotland) Act 1949 regarding payment to outgoing tenants of compensation for improvements are not affected by the 1955 and 1961 Acts[6] but compensation is not payable under the 1949 Act for an improvement for which it is payable under the 1955 and 1961 Acts.[7] Where improvements are valued under the 1949 Act with a view to payment of compensation to a crofter, the valuation, unless landlord and tenant otherwise agree in writing, must be made by the Land Court.[8]

A crofter who immediately before the commencement of the 1955 Act was a statutory small tenant or the statutory successor of such a croft is not entitled to any compensation for permanent improvements made or begun before the commencement of the Act to which he would not have been entitled had his tenancy expired immediately before the commencement of the Act.[9] " Statutory successor " is any person who

---

[98] *McLean* v *Roger*, 1964 S.L.T. (Land Ct.) 11, which was distinguished by the Court in *Greig* v *McIntyre*, 1965 S.L.T. (Land Ct.) 7, where it was laid down that the Court should consider the possibility of the open market as if each croft existing before the scheme came into force had been offered for letting in turn at the moment when renunciation was deemed to have taken effect, *viz.*, as the Court would do normally in case of a voluntary renunciation.

[99] 1961 Act, s. 6 (6).

[1] 1955 Act, s. 14 (8).

[2] s. 14 (5).

[3] s. 14 (4). See also *McLean* v *Roger* (*supra*).

[4] s. 14 (7); 1961 Act, Schedule First, para. 4.

[5] s. 14 (9).

[6] s. 14 (10); 1961 Act, Schedule First, para. 8.

[7] s. 14 (10), *proviso* (b). 1961 Act, *supra*.

[8] s. 14 (10), *proviso* (a).

[9] s. 14 (11).

under the 1955 Act has succeeded or may succeed to a croft, whether as heir-at-law, legatee or assignee of his immediate predecessor, being a crofter in occupation of the croft.[10]

Where a crofter's tenancy is terminated by the Commission because of his absence he has the same rights and liabilities in regard to compensation as if he had renounced at the term when the Commission's order of termination takes effect,[11] but where under the Act the dwelling-house is conveyed to him following such an order, he cannot get compensation from the landlord for the house as for an improvement.[12]

The Opencast Coal Act 1958 contains provisions regarding compensation for improvements affected by such coal workings.[13] These provisions have been already referred to and they apply with the substitution for " holding " and " holder " of the words " croft " and " crofter ", and for " the Landholders Acts " of the Crofters Act 1955.[14]

Where compensation is assessed[15] by the Land Court[16] then, if the crofter's tenancy began before the commencement of the 1961 Act or he holds the tenancy as statutory successor to his immediate predecessor in the tenancy and each of whose predecessors (the tenancy of each of whom began after the commencement of the 1961 Act) held the tenancy as statutory successor to his immediate predecessor,[17] the crofter may request the Land Court to determine the amount that would have been payable for compensation in respect of the improvement as if the 1961 Act had not been passed, and, if that amount is greater than the amount assessed by the Court, the Secretary of State must pay the difference to him, less any amount due to the Secretary of State by him in respect of any loan made by the Secretary of State or his predecessors under the 1911[18] or 1955[19] Acts.[20] These provisions do not, however, apply where compensation for the improvement has been previously assessed.[21]

Erection of Buildings etc. by Crofter. A crofter can erect any buildings or other structures or execute any works which are reasonably required to enable him to make use of the croft for any subsidiary or auxiliary occupation[22] and will not interfere substantially with the use of the croft as an agricultural subject.[23]

---

[10] s. 37 (1).
[11] s. 17 (9).
[12] s. 17 (8).
[13] See *supra*, p. 424.
[14] Including for " 1886 Act, s. 10 " of " 1955 Act, s. 14 ".
[15] Under 1961 Act, s. 6 (1) and (2).
[16] Under 1955 Act, ss. 14 (8) or 19 (9) (a), or 1961 Act, s. 9 (3) (a).
[17] 1961 Act, s. 6 (4).
[18] ss. 7, 9.
[19] s. 22 (2), (3).
[20] 1961 Act, s. 6 (3).
[21] *Ibid.*, s. 6 (3), *proviso* (b).
[22] 1955 Act, Schedule Second, para. 3.
[23] 1961 Act, s. 5 (1).

Assignation of Holding. A crofter can assign his croft but only with the written consent of the Crofters Commission.[24] If he assigns without that consent, the assignation and any deed purporting to assign the croft are null and void, and the Commission may declare the croft vacant.[25] Where he had arranged with his landlords to transfer the tenancy to his wife and the subject had been assigned or re-let to her but the Crofters Commission's sanction had not been obtained, it was held that she was not a crofter and so on outgoing no compensation was due.[26] When he desires to assign his croft he must apply to the Commission for their consent,[27] and the Commission must notify the landlord and, before deciding whether to give or withhold consent, they must give the crofter and the landlord an opportunity of making representations to them.[28] They must, in considering the application, take into account " the family and other circumstances of the crofter and of the proposed assignee " and " the general interest of the township in which the croft is situated ".[29]

Where the Commission have given consent to an assignation, the assignation takes effect at the term of Whitsunday or Martinmas first occurring not less than two months after the date when the consent was intimated to the crofter, unless before the term the crofter or his heir or legatee jointly give written notice to the Commission that they do not intend to proceed with the assignation.[30]

Subdivision of Croft. A crofter is not entitled to subdivide his croft without the consent in writing of his landlord and of the Crofters Commission. If he does subdivide without these consents, the subdivision is null and void.[31]

Subletting. Notwithstanding any enactment or rule of law, a crofter can after the commencement of the 1961 Act[32] sublet his croft (or part of his croft[33]) without the consent of the landlord,[34] but only with the consent in writing of the Commission.[35] In applying to the Commission for their consent, he must furnish the Commission with such information as to the proposed sublease as they require, including the subtenant's

---

[24] 1955 Act, s. 8 (1).
[25] s. 8 (5), as amended by 1961 Act, Schedule First, para. 10 (d).
[26] *MacPhee* v *Westminster (Liverpool) Trust Co. Ltd.* (1962) 50 S.L.C.R. 33.
[27] s. 8 (2), as amended by 1961 Act, Schedule First, para. 10 (a).
[28] s. 8 (3), as amended by 1961 Act, Schedule First, para. 10 (b). See as to procedure for such representations, including, whether or not such are made, the requiring of opportunity to be heard: s. 33.
[29] s. 8 (4), as amended by 1961 Act, Schedule First, para. 10 (c).
[30] s. 8 (6), as added by 1961 Act, Schedule First, para. 10 (e).
[31] s. 9.
[32] 27th August, 1961.
[33] 1961 Act, s. 13 (4): note that in all provisions in regard to subletting, a reference to a croft includes a reference to a part.
[34] 1961 Act, s. 11 (2).
[35] *Ibid.,* s. 11 (3).

name, the duration of the sublease and its terms and conditions other than as to rent;[36] and the Commission must serve notice on the landlord of the application, specifying the subtenant's name and designation.[37] In determining whether or not to consent, the Commission must have regard to any observations made by the landlord within fourteen days of the service of the notice on him,[37] and, if they consent, they may impose any conditions they think fit other than as to rent.[38] Any sublease without such consent is null and void,[35] unless it is a subletting of a dwellinghouse or other building that is part of a croft to holiday visitors, in which case the Commission's consent is not required.[39]

Where a sublease was entered into before the commencement of the 1961 Act without the landlord's consent, it is held valid from the date of the joint intimation of it by the landlord and the crofter to the Commission, with the name of the subtenant and its duration, provided the intimation was made within six months of the commencement of the Act.[40] If such a sublease was entered into with the landlord's written consent it is null and void after six months from the commencement of the Act, unless before the six months have expired the crofter intimates it to the Commission with the subtenant's name and the duration of the sublease.[41]

Compulsory Subletting. Where the Commission consider a crofter is not making adequate use of his croft (that is, such use of it for agriculture as having regard to its nature and location a tenant reasonably skilled in husbandry might be expected to make of it[42]) they may serve a notice on him, called a preliminary notice, of their opinion to that effect and informing him that unless he satisfies them within a year after service of the notice that he is making adequate use, they may require him to sublet;[43] they can, however, withdraw this preliminary notice at any time.[43]

If he does not satisfy them within that year, the Commission may within a month thereafter serve notice on him that, after a month from service of the notice or such longer period as the notice specifies, the croft will become subject to a requirement that it be sublet.[44] The crofter can at any time before that month or period ends refer to the Secretary of State the question whether he is making adequate use of the croft.[45]

[36] *Ibid.,* s. 11 (4).
[37] *Ibid.,* s. 11 (5).
[38] *Ibid.,* s. 11 (6).
[39] *Ibid.,* s. 11 (3), *proviso.*
[40] *Ibid.,* s. 11 (1) (a).
[41] *Ibid.,* s. 11 (1) (b).
[42] *Ibid.,* s. 12 (16).
[43] *Ibid.,* s. 12 (1). The provisions of s. 12 do not come into force until a day appointed by the Secretary of State subject to affirmative resolution of both Houses: s. 19 (2).
[44] *Ibid.,* s. 12 (2).
[45] *Ibid.,* s. 12 (3).

The Secretary of State must then afford the crofter an opportunity of making representations and, unless the crofter objects, must consult any grazings committee in respect of common grazings in the township where the croft lies.[45] He may then annul or confirm the notice.[45] If there is no appeal to the Secretary of State or if on the reference to him he confirms the notice, the Commission may serve on the crofter another notice requiring him within three months of service of the notice to submit for their approval his proposals (other than as to rent) for subletting:[46] the notice must be served on him within a month from the last date for a reference or from the date of confirmation of the notice.[47] When the proposals are submitted to them, the Commission must notify the landlord of the proposals with the name and designation of the subtenant, and any observations made by the landlord within fourteen days of the service of the notice on him must be regarded by the Commission in deciding whether or not to approve the proposals.[48] Approval may be subject to any conditions other than as to rent which the Commission think fit to impose.[49] When proposals are not submitted by the crofter timeously, or though submitted are not approved or the crofter does not in effect sublet in accordance with the proposals, the Commission may themselves sublet to anyone they think fit,[50] but they must first consult any appropriate grazings committee; and thereafter, if they propose to sublet, they must inform the landlord and the crofter, specifying the subtenant's name and designation and must have regard to any observations which the landlord or the crofter make within fourteen days of service of the notice on them.[51] Further, when they grant the sublease they must forthwith give the landlord and the crofter and the subtenant intimation of the granting of the sublease with the subtenant's name, the duration of the sublease and its terms and conditions.[52] Such a sublease by the Commission has effect in all respects as if it had been granted by the crofter in accordance with his proposals approved by the Commission.[53]

As to the subjects of the sublease, the sublease, whether by the crofter or the Commission, does not include, unless the crofter so wishes, any dwellinghouse or garden ground that is part of the croft; any buildings or other structures erected or works executed on the croft which are permanent improvements;[54] such part of the croft as the Commission determine, being a part which taken together with the site of such a dwellinghouse, garden ground, buildings, structures, or works extends

46 *Ibid.*, s. 12 (4).
47 *Ibid.*, s. 12 (4).
48 *Ibid.*, s. 12 (5).
49 *Ibid.*, s. 12 (6).
50 *Ibid.*, s. 12 (7).
51 *Ibid.*, s. 12 (8).
52 *Ibid.*, s. 12 (9). The Commission must also make a record of the condition of the fixed equipment. See *infra*, p. 467.
53 *Ibid.*. s. 12 (11).
54 Under 1961 Act, s. 5 (2), (3). See *supra*, p. 451.

to an acre; and any right pertaining to the tenancy of the croft to cut or take peat.[55]

As to the rent in a sublease by the Commission, if the sublease is of the whole croft or a whole croft other than any subjects which are not included under the Act, the rent is a sum equal to one and one-quarter times the rent payable to the landlord by the crofter; in any other case it is such proportion of that sum as the Commission determine.[56] But the Land Court may vary that rent and substitute such other rent as the Court think just in all the circumstances, where the crofter applies for variation within six months from the date when notice of the granting of the sublease was given to him.[57] The rent that the Land Court so fix is payable from the date of entry under the sublease.[57]

As to the duration of a sublease by the Commission, this is such number of years, not exceeding five, as the Commission determine,[58] but the Commission may terminate the sublease before its due expiry where the subtenant has broken one or more of its terms and conditions,[59] and also where the crofter or the subtenant represent to the Commission that the circumstances of either have so materially altered that it is reasonable that it be terminated.[60] The Commission then serve notice of termination on a date stated in the notice not later than a year from the date of service of the notice.[60]

There are certain terms and conditions under which a sublease by the Commission must be granted.[58] There may or may not be others but these are compulsory. They are as follows. The subtenant must make adequate use as above defined of the land comprised in the sublease; he must maintain any permanent improvements that are on the land at the commencement of the sublease in as good a state of repair as they were in at that date, and, if he does not do so, he must on the termination of the sublease pay to the crofter the cost (which, failing agreement between the subtenant and the crofter, is to be determined by the Land Court), at that termination, of making good any deterioration of or damage to such improvements due to his failure; and he must not make any permanent improvements on the land in the sublease other than the following—subsoil and other drains; walls and fences; deep trenching; and clearing the ground, and the crofter is not held responsible for the maintenance of any permanent improvements erected by the subtenant without the crofter's consent.[61] If the Commission are satisfied that the subtenant has broken one or more of the terms or conditions of the sublease, they may serve on the crofter and the subtenant a written notice terminating the sublease on a date mentioned in the

[55] 1961 Act, s. 12 (10). See previous paragraph.
[56] *Ibid.*, s. 12 (12).
[57] *Ibid.*, s. 12 (12), *proviso.*
[58] *Ibid.*, s. 12 (13).
[59] *Ibid.*, s. 12 (14) (a). See *infra.*
[60] *Ibid.*, s. 12 (14) (b).
[61] *Ibid.*, s. 12 (13).

notice, which is to be not later than a year from the date of service of the notice.[62]

If a person occupies a croft but has ceased to be entitled to do so under these provisions in regard to subletting where a croft is not adequately used, or if a subtenant of a croft has had the croft sublet by the crofter after the date when a further notice was served on the crofter by the Commission under these provisions and otherwise than in accordance with proposals approved by the Commission, the Commission can by written notice require him to give up occupation on or before such date as may be specified in the notice, not less than a month from the date of the service of the notice.[63] If he fails to do so, he must be ejected from his croft by warrant of the Sheriff on the Commission's application, unless cause to the contrary is shown, and the Commission may recover their expenses of the application and of the execution of the warrant from him.[64]

A subtenant under a sublease is not a crofter nor a tenant under the Agricultural Holdings (Scotland) Act 1949.[65] Where under a sublease a right in any common grazing is let to the subtenant (whether the sublease is one existing at the commencement of the 1961 Act and intimated to the Commission, or one granted by a crofter after the commencement of that Act with the consent of the Commission and in accordance with any conditions they have imposed, or one granted by a crofter or the Commission in accordance with the provisions in relation to subleasing of crofts not adequately used), the subtenant comes into the crofter's place in relation to any matter that concerns that right, and any grazings regulations that apply to that common grazing apply to the subtenant.[66]

On the termination of a tenancy of a croft, any existing sublease comes to an end;[67] but if the subtenant applies to the Commission within a month from the date when it came to an end, the Commission can make an order allowing the subtenant to continue to occupy the croft for a period not exceeding a year from that date and subject to conditions.[68] No proceedings for removal of the subtenant can be taken by the owner of the croft before the expiry of the month or, if an application has been made to the Commission for permission to remain, before the date which the Commission determine.[68]

Compensation to Landlord for Deterioration. Where a crofter renounces the tenancy or is removed from the croft the landlord can recover from him compensation for any deterioration of, or damage to, any fixed equipment (which has the same meaning as in the Agricultural

---

[62] *Ibid.,* s. 12 (14) (a).
[63] *Ibid.,* s. 12 (15).
[64] *Ibid.,* s. 12 (15), applying 1955 Act, s. 17 (3).
[65] *Ibid.,* s. 13 (1).
[66] *Ibid.,* s. 13 (2).
[67] *Ibid.,* s. 13 (3).
[68] *Ibid.,* s. 13 (3), *proviso.*

Holdings (Scotland) Act 1949[69]) provided by the landlord, which has been committed or permitted by the crofter.[70] The amount of the compensation is the cost as at the date of the crofter's quitting of making good the deterioration or damage.[71] The landlord can set off the amount of that compensation against any compensation payable by him in respect of permanent improvements.[71] Failing agreement, the amount of compensation is fixed by the Land Court.[72] Where a crofter has given a notice of renunciation, the Land Court can assess, prior to renunciation, the amount which will be due on renunciation taking effect for compensation for deterioration or damage as well as the amount which will be due on renunciation for compensation for permanent improvements, on the application of the crofter and the landlord, or where the crofter's rights to compensation for permanent improvements have been transferred in whole or part to the Secretary of State under the loan provisions of the 1955 Act on the application of the Secretary of State and the landlord, and the amounts so assessed become due on renunciation.[73]

Bequest of Croft. A crofter may by will or other testamentary writing bequeath his tenancy of his croft to any one person, but if the legatee is not a member of the crofter's family (that is, the wife or husband of the crofter or his son-in-law or daughter-in-law or any person who, failing nearer heirs, would be entitled to succeed in case of intestacy to the tenancy[74]) it is necessary to obtain the approval of the Crofters Commission, otherwise the bequest is null and void.[75] If the legatee accepts the bequest, however, he must notify the landlord of the bequest within two months of the crofter's death, or, if he is prevented from doing so by some unavoidable cause, within a further four weeks; if no such notice is given by him, the bequest is null and void.[76] By giving the notice the legatee impliedly accepts the bequest.[76] The landlord may within one month of the giving of notice intimate to the Crofters Commission an objection to receiving the legatee as the tenant, giving the grounds of his objection.[77] Unless the landlord has stated an objection, the legatee comes into the crofter's place as from the date of death of the crofter, and the landlord must so notify the Commission.[76] If the landlord states an objection the Crofters Commission will decide on the objection. They must first give the legatee and the landlord an opportunity to make representations. If thereafter they are satisfied that the objection is reasonable they must declare the legacy null and void, and

[69] s. 37 (1).
[70] s. 14 (6).
[71] s. 14 (7), as amended by 1961 Act, Schedule First, para. 4.
[72] s. 14 (8).
[73] s. 14 (9).
[74] s. 10 (7).
[75] s. 10 (2).
[76] s. 10 (2).
[77] s. 10 (3).

inform parties accordingly,[78] but if they are not satisfied that the objection is a reasonable one, they must notify parties, and the legatee then takes the place of the deceased crofter as from the date of the deceased crofter's death.[78]

Where a legacy becomes null and void because it is to one not a member of the crofter's family and the Commission have not given their approval or because notice has not been given by the legatee to the landlord or because the Commission uphold the landlord's objection to the legatee as reasonable, the right to the croft passes to the heir-at-law of the deceased crofter;[79] and in a case where the tenant has died before the commencement of the 1955 Act the right passes as if the Act had not been passed.[80]

Any question as to the validity or the effect of a bequest is determined by any Court that has jurisdiction to determine the validity and effect of the whole testamentary writings of the deceased.[81]

The right of any person to succeed to the tenancy by virtue of a bequest by the tenant, where the tenant died before the commencement of the Act, is to be determined as if the Act had not been passed.[82]

Succession to Croft. Where the crofter has not bequeathed the croft, or a bequest of it does not receive effect, his heir-at-law is entitled to the right to the tenancy and, if the heir, being a person who, failing nearer heirs, would be entitled to succeed to the tenancy, makes application to the landlord to be accepted as tenant within three months of the right devolving upon him, the landlord must accept him as the successor, and notify the Commission to that effect, if he is satisfied (and he must be satisfied) that there is no nearer heir who desires to succeed.[83] The term " heir-at-law " includes any person entitled to succeed to the tenancy by virtue of the Intestate Husbands' Estate (Scotland) Acts 1911 and 1919 and the Law Reform (Miscellaneous Provisions) (Scotland) Act 1940.[84] If the successors (heirs-at-law) are heirs portioners the eldest is entitled to succeed to the tenancy without division.[85] If the landlord is not satisfied as to any matter on which he must be satisfied or if any dispute arises as to the right of any person to be accepted as successor, the Crofters Commission are empowered to decide the issue, on a reference by the land-

---

[78] s. 10 (4). See as to the procedure for such representations, including, whether or not such are made, the requiring of an opportunity of being heard: s. 33.
[79] s. 10 (5); see note 83, *infra.*
[80] s. 39 (4).
[81] s. 10 (6).
[82] s. 39 (4).
[83] s. 11 (1). Nothing in the Succession (Scotland) Act 1964, applies to the tenancy of a croft within the 1955 Act, s. 3 (1), or affects the succession or devolution thereof: s. 37 (1) (b). It was undecided under the 1886 Act whether the heir by renouncing could propel the succession to the next succeeding heir. *Balfour* v *Hutchison* (1899) 7 S.L.T. 82 (O.H.).
[84] s. 11 (8).
[85] s. 11 (9). On the failure of the eldest, it was held that the holding passed to her heir or representative and not to the next heir portioner, *Balfour, supra.*

lord, who must refer the question, or by any person having an interest, who may do so.[86]

Prior to the Succession (Scotland) Act 1964, crofting tenancies were treated as in the case of ordinary leases as subject to collation[86a] and it has been considered that the exception to collation laid down[86b] where a lease excluded assignees and subtenants on the ground that the heir then took in his own right did not apply to crofting tenancies in view of the crofter's power of bequest.[86c] As the Act does not apply to such tenancies, and collation is thus not "inconsistent with" the Act and, having regard to its equitable nature, the view has been expressed that collation still applies; indeed that it would be inequitable if it did not apply,[86c] even possibly if the successor were some person lower in the order of succession owing to nearer heirs not accepting the succession.

Where at the end of three months from the date when the right devolved on the heir-at-law, no person has been accepted by the landlord as successor, the landlord must notify the Commission;[87] and, whether or not the landlord has notified them, if it appears to them at the end of the three months that no person has been accepted by the landlord as successor, the Commission must give notice by advertisement or otherwise, as they may think proper, to persons who may claim to be entitled to succeed to the tenancy, requiring them if they desire so to succeed to give intimation to the Commission to that effect before such date as is specified in the notice, not earlier than six months after the date when the right devolved on the heir-at-law.[88] The Commission then must nominate as successor the person from among those who have given intimation who appears to them to be the nearest heir.[88] The Commission must not before the date specified in their notice nominate any person as successor unless they are satisfied that there is no nearer heir who desires to succeed.[89] They must notify the landlord of the heir nominated by them, and the landlord must accept him as successor.[88]

If there is no person duly nominated as successor, the Commission must declare the croft to be vacant and notify the landlord to that effect.[90] The landlord is then liable, if the crofter was at his death under any liability to the Secretary of State in respect of a loan, to pay to the Secretary of State the whole or so much of "the value of the improvements on the croft"—that is, such sum as may be agreed or as, failing agreement, may be determined by the Land Court to be the sum which would have been due by the landlord by way of compensation for per-

[86] s. 11 (2).
[86a] A doubt was expressed in 1965 S.L.T. (News) 59.
[86b] *Paterson's Judicial Factor* v *Paterson*, 1956 S.L.T. 223.
[86c] M. C. Meston, " Collation of Crofting Tenancies ", 1965 S.L.T. (News) 209.
[87] s. 11 (3).
[88] s. 11 (4).
[89] s. 11 (4), *proviso*.
[90] s. 11 (5).

manent improvements if the deceased crofter had immediately before his death renounced the tenancy—as will discharge the liability of the deceased crofter, and to pay to his executor if a claim is made by him not later than twelve months after the date when the croft was declared vacant, any balance of the value; if the crofter was not under any such liability and a claim is made by the executor, the landlord must pay to the executor the value of the improvements on the croft as above defined.[91] Where the croft is declared vacant following on the death after the commencement of the 1961 Act of a crofter who immediately before his death was " qualified "—that is, whose tenancy of the croft began before the commencement of the 1961 Act or who held the tenancy as statutory successor to his immediate predecessor in the tenancy and each of whose predecessors (being in each case a person whose tenancy began after the commencement of the 1961 Act) held such tenancy as statutory successor to his immediate predecessor[92]— and where the value of the improvements is determined by the Land Court, the crofter's executor may ask the Court to determine what would have been their value if the 1961 Act had not been passed, and if that value is more than the value previously determined by the Court, the Secretary of State must pay the difference to the executor,[93] being, however, entitled to set off against such difference any amount due to him by the crofter at his death in respect of a loan under the 1911 or 1955 Acts.[94]

If the Commission have either nominated a successor or the croft has been declared vacant, the rights of all heirs other than any heir so nominated to succeed to the tenancy are extinguished.[95]

The right of any person to succeed to the tenancy by virtue of the right having devolved on the heir-at-law of the tenant, where the tenant died before the commencement of the 1955 Act, is determined as if the Act had not been passed.[96]

Enlargement of Crofts. The provisions of the 1886 Act in this connection as amended apply here.[97] If the owner of any land not itself a croft and not part of a croft agrees to grant a tenancy of it to a crofter and both the owner and the crofter agree that it will form part of any croft of which the crofter is tenant, then, provided that the area of the croft (exclusive of any common pasture or grazing) and of the land and the rent of the croft and the rent under the tenancy do not exceed the limits mentioned below, it forms part of the croft from the date of

[91] s. 11 (7). See Highlands and Islands Development Act 1965.
[92] s. 11 (7B), as added by 1961 Act, Schedule First, para. 2.
[93] s. 11 (7A), as added by 1961 Act, Schedule First, para. 2.
[94] s. 11 (7A), *proviso,* as added, *supra.*
[95] s. 11 (6).
[96] s. 39 (4).
[97] s. 38 (2), (3). *Supra,* p. 428.

entry under the tenancy and comes under the Acts.[98] The owner of the land must notify the Commission of the enlargement.[99] Where, however, though the owner and the crofter agree, the area of the original croft (exclusive of any common pasture or grazing held therewith) together with the area of the land exceeds seventy five acres and the rent of the croft and the rent under the tenancy together exceed £50, the owner and the crofter must jointly apply to the Secretary of State to direct that the land form part of the croft, and then from the later of the date of the direction or the date of entry under the tenancy the land forms part of the croft and comes under the Acts.[1] The Secretary of State must notify the Commission of his direction.[2]

Vacant Croft: Rights of Landlord. The provisions in regard to this matter apply in relation to a part of a croft as to a whole croft.[3] Where the landlord of a croft receives a notice of renunciation of the croft from the crofter or gets an order for his removal from the Land Court or where for any other reason a croft is vacant, the landlord must notify the Crofters Commission (under a penalty of a fine not exceeding £10 for failure to do so[4]) within a month from receipt of the notice of renunciation or from the date when the Land Court made the order of removal or the vacancy came to his knowledge.[5] This does not apply to a croft declared vacant by the Commission in the exercise of any power conferred on them by the Act.[6] Except with the written consent of the Commission, or, if they do not consent, with the Secretary of State's consent, the landlord cannot let the whole or any part of the vacant croft to any person: if he does let it without such consent, the lease is null and void.[7] Where any person occupies a croft under such a null and void letting, the Commission may by written notice require him to give up occupation on or before a day specified in the notice not less than one month from the date of service of the notice.[8] If he does not

---

[98] 1961 Act, s. 2 (2) (a).
[99] *Ibid.*, s. 2 (5).
[1] *Ibid.*, s. 2 (2) (b).
[2] *Ibid.*, s. 2 (5).
[3] 1955 Act, s. 16 (13), as added by 1961 Act, Schedule First, para. 12 (d).
[4] s. 16 (10).
[5] s. 16 (1). Provision was made for notice to the Commission (under penalty of failure to do so as above) within three months of the commencement of the Act in the case where at the commencement of the Act a croft was vacant or was subject to a notice of renunciation or a Land Court order that had not taken effect: s. 16 (2). This did not apply to a croft declared vacant by the Commission in the exercise of any power conferred on them by the Act: s. 16 (12). A croft was held vacant at the commencement of the Act though it was occupied otherwise than by a crofter and the consent of the Secretary of State to the occupation had not been obtained: s. 16 (11); and for the purposes of s. 16 a croft is taken as vacant though it is occupied if it is occupied otherwise than by the tenant of the croft: s. 16 (11A), as added by 1961 Act, Schedule First, para. 12 (c).
[6] s. 16 (12).
[7] s. 16 (3). See *MacPhee* v *Westminster (Liverpool) Trust Co. Ltd.* (1962) 50 S.L.C.R. 33.
[8] s. 16 (3A), as added by 1961 Act, Schedule First, para. 12 (a).

30

give up the occupation, then the same rule applies with necessary modifications as applies where a crofter fails to give up occupation of a croft[8]—that is, the Sheriff on the Commission's application must give warrant for his ejection unless cause to the contrary is shown.[9] But where a croft is vacant at any time after the expiry of one month from the occurrence of the vacancy,[10] the Commission may give notice to the landlord to submit to them his proposals for reletting the croft, whether as a separate croft or as an enlargement of another, and if he does not submit any proposals within two months from the giving of the notice or the Commission does not approve of the proposals that he has duly submitted, then, if they think fit, they can themselves let the croft to any person or persons and on such terms and conditions, including conditions as to rent, as the Commission after consulting the landlord may fix.[11] Such a let is effective in all respects as if the landlord had himself granted it.[11] The landlord may, within a month from the date of the letting by the Commission, apply to the Land Court for a variation of the terms and conditions of the letting, and if the Land Court make a variation it is effective from the date of the letting.[12] The Commission, however, must not let the croft while the Secretary of State is considering an application by the landlord for consent to let or for a direction that the croft shall cease to be a croft.[13] Where the letting by the Commission is as an enlargement of another croft and any buildings on the vacant croft are no longer required because of the enlargement in connection with the occupation of the croft, the Commission must notify the landlord to that effect. The buildings then cease to form part of the croft and the landlord may at any time within six months of the giving of the notice notify the Secretary of State requiring him to buy the buildings,[14] and the Secretary of State is then deemed to be authorised to buy them compulsorily and to have served notice to treat on the date when the notice was given;[15] the price payable is such sum as the landlord and the Secretary of State may agree, or failing agreement the Land Court may determine, to be equal to the amount that an outgoing tenant who had erected or paid for the erection of the buildings would have been entitled to receive from the landlord as com-

---

[9] s. 17 (3). See *supra*, p. 460.

[10] If the vacancy had been at the commencement of the Act, at any time after a month from the date when notice of the vacancy is given by the landlord to the Commission or after four months from the commencement of the Act, whichever was the earlier.

[11] s. 16 (4).

[12] s. 16 (5).

[13] s. 16 (4), *proviso*.

[14] s. 16 (6). See s. 32 (1) in relation to the application of the Lands Clauses Acts, etc.

[15] s. 16 (8). See s. 32 (1), *supra*, and also s. 32 (2), as amended by 1961 Act, Schedule First, para. 16, that the power to withdraw a notice to treat under the Acquisition of Land (Assessment of Compensation) Act 1919, s. 5 (2) does not apply here.

pensation for permanent improvements in respect of the buildings at the date when notice was given to the Secretary of State requiring him to purchase.[16]

Where a croft is vacant, the landlord may apply to the Secretary of State to direct that it shall cease to be a croft, and if the Secretary of State directs to that effect, the provisions of the Act cease to apply to the croft, but, of course, without prejudice to the subsequent exercise of any statutory powers for the constitution of new crofts or the enlargement of existing ones; and the Secretary of State must intimate to the Commission any such direction he has given.[17]

Record of Crofts. On the application of the landlord or the crofter, the Land Court must make a record of the condition of the cultivation of a croft and of the buildings and other permanent improvements[18] thereon and by whom these improvements have been executed or paid for.[19] The application must be intimated by the Court to the other party concerned and each party must be given an opportunity of being heard on any matter affecting the record.[20] The Crofters Commission, when they grant a sublease, must make a record of the condition at the date of entry to the sublease of the fixed equipment let under the sublease.[21]

Crofters Holdings Book. In the Crofting Counties the Landholders Holdings Book kept under the 1886 Act[22] is called the Crofters Holdings Book.[23] The Crofters Commission must send to the sheriff clerk to be recorded in the Book every order, determination, consent, authorisation or other proceeding of the Commission which they may think proper to be recorded in it[24] and the relevant provisions of the 1886 Act[25] apply as they apply in regard to orders of the Land Court.[26] A loan agreement in respect of a loan by the Secretary of State must be recorded in the Book.[27]

Register of Crofts. The Crofters Commission must compile, and maintain, a register called the Register of Crofts,[28] in which are to be entered the name, location, rent and extent of every croft, the name of the tenant and of the landlord thereof and such other matters relating to each croft as the Commission with the Secretary of State's approval

[16] s. 16 (8), *proviso*, as amended by 1961 Act, Schedule First, para. 5.
[17] s. 16 (9), as amended by 1961 Act, Schedule First, para. 12 (b).
[18] Schedule Fifth. See *supra*, p. 451.
[19] s. 6 (1).
[20] s. 6 (2).
[21] 1961 Act, s. 12 (9).
[22] 1955 Act, s. 27. See *supra*, p. 432.
[23] *Ibid.*, ss. 37 (1), 39 (2).
[24] *Ibid.*, s. 2 (3).
[25] s. 27.
[26] 1955 Act, s. 2 (3). See *supra*, p. 432.
[27] *Ibid.*, s. 23 (3).
[28] 1961 Act, s. 3 (1).

decide are proper to be entered. The Commission must from time to time insert new entries or alter or omit entries so far as necessary to ensure the accuracy of the Register. They must send a copy of any new entry and of any altered entry to the landlord and the tenant of the particular croft, and, if an entry is omitted, must intimate the omission to the owner and the tenant of the land.[29]

The Commission can by notice[30] to the owner or occupier of any croft require him to furnish them with such information as is specified in the notice as to the acreage, rent and the tenure of the croft and such other matters regarding the ownership or the occupation of the croft as they may reasonably require for the execution of their functions under the Act.[31] A penalty of a fine not exceeding £10 is imposed on an owner or an occupier who without reasonable cause fails within three months of service of the notice to give the information asked for, or knowingly or recklessly gives information false in a material particular.[32] If a request for an extract of an entry is made to the Commission by a person whom they consider " has good reason for desiring " it, the Commission must furnish an extract duly certified by their secretary.[33] A document purporting to be an extract and certified by the secretary is sufficient evidence that the Register contains such an entry.[33] Entry in the Register is not conclusive; it does not necessarily mean that the holding is a croft.[33a]

The Register compiled under the 1955 Act (which is repealed by the 1961 Act) so far as having particulars required by the 1961 Act[34] is to be deemed compiled under the 1961 Act.[35]

Reorganisation of Crofting Townships. Either of their own accord or on representations being made to them by a crofter who is the tenant of a croft in a township or the landlord of such a croft or a grazings committee appointed under the 1955 Act in respect of common grazings shared in by the crofter, the Crofters Commission, after such inquiries and after such consultation with the tenants and the landlords of crofts in the township and any such grazings committee as they think fit, may, if they are satisfied that the township ought to be reorganised in order to secure the preservation or better development of it, prepare a draft reorganisation scheme.[36] The scheme must provide for the reallocation of the land in the township in such a way as the Commission think will

---

[29] *Ibid.,* s. 3 (2).
[30] See as to such, 1955 Act, s. 29.
[31] 1955 Act, s. 15 (1). See *Elder* v *Manson,* 1964 S.L.T. (Land Ct.) 15.
[32] s. 15 (5).
[33] 1961 Act, s. 3 (3). See *Elder* (*infra*) where there was no such extract or other evidence of entry produced.
[33a] *Wallace* v *Stewart* (1961) 49 S.L.C.R. 18, approved in *Elder* v *Manson,* 1964 S.L.T. (Land Ct.) 15. In *Wallace* the holding had merely been noted for registration.
[34] *Ibid.,* s. 3 (2).
[35] *Ibid.,* s. 3 (4).
[36] *Ibid.,* s. 8 (1).

be " most conducive to the proper and efficient use " of the land and " to the general benefit of the township ", so that under the scheme each crofter who is the tenant of a croft in the township and who so wishes will be given the tenancy of a croft, which, if he wishes, shall include any dwellinghouse which was part of the croft of which he was tenant immediately before the date when the scheme was put into effect and be of a value not less than that of the croft of which he was tenant.[37]

In addition, a scheme may provide, if the Commission thinks fit, as to all or any of the following matters[38]—(a) the inclusion of any land in the vicinity of the township, being land to which the 1955[39] and 1961 Acts do not apply, which the Commission think should be used for the enlargement of crofts in the township or of common grazings used exclusively or shared in by the township; (b) the admission into the township of new crofters and the allocation to them of shares in the common grazings; (c) the apportionment of part of any common grazings in which it shares for the exclusive use of the township; (d) the inclusion in any croft formed under the scheme of a part of the common grazings or of any lands held runrig; (e) the grant to any crofter (not being a person who under the scheme becomes the tenant of a croft) who so wishes, of a conveyance in feu (under a reservation of minerals) of the dwellinghouse which formed part of the croft of which he was tenant immediately before the date when the scheme was put into effect with the like pertinents, on the like terms and conditions, and in the like manner, as if an order terminating the tenancy had been made by the Commission[40] and a notice had been given to the crofter and his landlord by the Commission and to the Commission and the landlord by the crofter;[41] and (f) any other matter incidental to or consequential on the provisions of the scheme.

The Commission must also prepare such maps and plans as are necessary to indicate the general effect of the scheme and its effect on each of the crofts in the township.[42] They must serve on each crofter who is the tenant of a croft in the township a copy of the scheme and a notice of the place within the locality of the township where the maps and plans may be inspected at all reasonable hours and requesting the crofter within four months of such service to intimate in writing to the Commission whether or not he is in favour of the scheme: if he does not reply, he is deemed to have intimated that he is in favour of the scheme.[43]

---

[37] *Ibid.*, s. 8 (2).
[38] *Ibid.*, s. 8 (3).
[39] Where such land is included in a confirmed scheme then as from the date when the scheme is put into effect, the 1955 and 1961 Acts apply to that land: 1961 Act, s. 2 (3).
[40] Under 1955 Act, s. 17 (1).
[41] Under *ibid.*, s. 17 (4); s. 17 (5)-(10) of that Act apply here with any necessary modifications: 1961 Act, s. 8 (3).
[42] 1961 Act, s. 8 (4).
[43] *Ibid.*, s. 8 (5).

If within the four months a majority of the crofters so served intimate that they are in favour of the scheme, the draft scheme with the maps and plans and such information as is deemed necessary by the Commission or required by the Secretary of State for informing him as to the general purport and effect of the scheme and a statement of the Commission's views on the prospects of the development of agricultural and other industries in the township and in the locality in which the township is situated must be submitted by the Commission to the Secretary of State,[44] who may confirm it with or without modification.[45] Before confirming it, he must serve on every owner and occupier of land to which it applies a copy of the scheme and a notice of the place in the locality where the land is situated where a copy of the maps and plans can be inspected and informing the owner or occupier that he may within twenty-eight days of service of the notice object to the scheme or any provision in it.[46] He must also publish in two successive weeks in one or more newspapers in the locality of the land a notice that the draft scheme has been submitted to him, specifying the land affected, the place where a copy of the scheme, maps, etc., can be inspected and the time and manner for lodging objections.[47] If no objections are made or all are withdrawn, the Secretary of State may approve the draft scheme with or without modification.[48] If any objection is not withdrawn, the Secretary of State, before he decides whether to confirm the draft scheme, must order a public local enquiry to be held;[49] and, after considering the objection and the report of the person who held the enquiry, may confirm the draft scheme with or without modification.[50] He can require any one who has objected to put his objection in writing.[51] He may disregard it if he thinks it frivolous or if it relates only to assessment of any sum which the Land Court must fix or relates to assessment of compensation for the compulsory purchase of land.[51] Where he proposes any modification (whether there has or has not been an enquiry) he must, before he confirms the draft scheme, further serve on every owner and occupier of land affected and any other person whom he thinks may be substantially affected by the modification a notice of the modification and of the right to make representations to him within fourteen days, and he must consider any such representations.[52]

---

[44] *Ibid.*, s. 8 (6).
[45] *Ibid.*, s. 8 (7).
[46] *Ibid.*, Schedule Second, para 1 (a).
[47] *Ibid.*, para. 1 (b).
[48] *Ibid.*, para. 2.
[49] The provisions of s. 355 (2)-(9) of the Local Government (Scotland) Act 1947, apply to such an enquiry.
[50] 1961 Act, Schedule Second, para. 3.
[51] *Ibid.*, para. 5.
[52] *Ibid.*, para. 4. See as to the procedure for representations, including the requiring of an opportunity to be heard: 1955 Act, s. 33.

When the Secretary of State has confirmed the draft scheme, he must forthwith serve on every person who is owner or occupier of land affected and any other person whom he thinks is substantially affected by the scheme a notice that the scheme has been confirmed,[53] and must publish in one or more newspapers in the locality of the land a similar notice, which must also name a place in the locality where a copy of the scheme, maps and plans can be inspected.[54] If any one is aggrieved by a scheme and wants to contest the validity of it as *ultra vires* or because some statutory requirement of the 1961 Act has not been complied with, he can apply to the Court of Session within six weeks of the first publication of the newspaper notice, and if the Court is satisfied that it is *ultra vires* or that his interests have been substantially prejudiced by a failure to comply with a statutory requirement, the Court may quash the scheme generally or so far as affecting his property or person; but only by this procedure can a scheme be questioned.[55]

Putting of Reorganisation Scheme into Effect. It is the Commission's duty to put a confirmed scheme into effect,[56] on such date as they appoint, and there may be different dates for different provisions of the scheme.[57] Subject to any directions by the Secretary of State, the Commission may do all such things as are necessary for putting the scheme into effect.[56] On the confirmation of a scheme the Commission must remit it to the Land Court so that the Court can fix the sums payable on its being put into effect, *viz.*, (a) to each person who immediately before the date was the tenant of a croft in the township, by way of compensation for permanent improvements because of the termination of his tenancy as aftermentioned; (b) by each person (whether or not immediately before that date a tenant of a croft in the township) who under the scheme becomes the tenant of a croft in respect of permanent improvements on the croft, and (c) by way of rent in respect of each croft formed under the scheme.[58] In fixing the rents the Land Court must proceed so that the aggregate of the rents fixed, so far as attributable to subjects that were part of the crofts in the township at the date of confirmation of the scheme, does not exceed the aggregate of the rents of those subjects at that date and is fairly apportioned among those subjects.[59] The rent fixed by the Court for any croft cannot be altered for seven years from the term when it first became payable, unless by agreement.[60]

[53] *Ibid.*, para. 7 (a).
[54] *Ibid.*, para. 7 (b).
[55] *Ibid.*, Schedule Second, para. 8.
[56] *Ibid.*, s. 9 (1).
[57] *Ibid.*, s. 9 (2).
[58] *Ibid.*, s. 9 (3). See *Greig v McIntyre*, 1965 S.L.T. (Land Ct.) 7, as to assessment of compensation.
[59] *Ibid.*, s. 9 (4).
[60] *Ibid.*, s. 9 (5).

In order to put a scheme into effect the Commission must also serve on the tenant and the landlord of every croft affected and every person other than a tenant who is under the scheme to become a tenant of a croft a notice of the date when the scheme is to be put into effect.[61] Where such notices have been served, every such tenant is deemed to have given notice of renunciation of his tenancy immediately before that date, and every person who is to become tenant of a croft becomes the tenant of that croft on that date.[61] If there is included in the scheme land in the vicinity of the township, the Secretary of State must, on confirming the scheme, serve on the owner of that land a notice requiring him to undertake that he will let the land on the date when the scheme is put into effect in accordance with the scheme; and on the occupier who is not owner a copy of the scheme and a notice ending his interest in the land on the expiry of three months from the date when the notice was served on him.[62] The Secretary of State is then where the occupier's interest is so terminated deemed authorised to purchase compulsorily and to have served notice to treat on the date when the interest terminated.[63]

Where the owner does not within two months from the date of service of the notice on him enter into the undertaking required or, having entered into it, does not let the land in accordance with the scheme on the date when the scheme comes into operation, or if the owner of any land to which a scheme applies within two months of service on him of notice of confirmation of the scheme gives to the Secretary of State notice requiring him to buy the land, the Secretary of State is deemed authorised to buy the land compulsorily and to have served notice to treat immediately before the date when the scheme is put into effect.[64] Any such purchase is deemed completed immediately before the date when the scheme is put into effect, and, as landlord, the Secretary of State is liable to pay compensation and entitled to receive sums for permanent improvements which became payable on that date[65] and any sum payable then for compensation[66] for deterioration of or damage to the fixed equipment.[67]

If on the scheme being put into effect any buildings on land subject to the scheme are no longer required in connection with the occupation of the land, the Commission must, on the scheme being confirmed, notify the landlord accordingly and of the effect of this provision of the 1961 Act in relation to the buildings, and thereupon the provisions of the 1955 Act[68] under which the Secretary of State may be required to

---

[61] *Ibid.*, s. 9 (6).
[62] *Ibid.*, s. 9 (8).
[63] *Ibid.*, s. 9 (9).
[64] *Ibid.*, s. 9 (10).
[65] Under *ibid.*, s. 9 (3), (4).
[66] Under 1955 Act, s. 14 (6).
[67] 1961 Act, s. 9 (10).
[68] 1955 Act, s. 16 (6), (8). See *supra*, p. 466.

purchase buildings on certain crofts apply to those buildings as if the notice had been one given by the Commission to the landlord immediately before the date of putting the scheme into effect.[69]

Unless the context so requires otherwise, the provisions of the 1961 Act apply in relation to a group of neighbouring townships as they apply to a township.[70]

Reorganisation Schemes submitted for Confirmation before the 1961 Act. The provisions of the 1955 Act apply to reorganisation schemes submitted for confirmation to the Secretary of State before the commencement of the 1961 Act.[71] As any such schemes will presumably have been dealt with at the date of publication of this book it is not proposed to deal with those provisions of the 1955 Act,[72] which have now been repealed by the 1961 Act.[73]

Financial Assistance to Crofters. The Secretary of State, after consultation with the Crofters Commission and subject to Treasury approval, is empowered to make schemes for giving grants and loans to crofters, to occupiers of crofts who are also the owners of their crofts and who in the Secretary of State's opinion are of substantially the same economic status as a crofter, to occupiers of holdings, other than crofts, in the crofting counties, the area of which does not exceed 75 acres (exclusive of any common pasture or grazing held therewith) or the annual rent of which if they were crofts let to crofters under the 1955 and the 1961 Acts would not in the Secretary of State's opinion exceed £50 and who are in his opinion of substantially the same economic status as a crofter, and to subtenants of crofts or parts of crofts in terms of the provisions of the 1961 Act, for the purpose of aiding and developing agricultural production on crofts, including holdings and other crofts as above mentioned and parts of crofts, and to administer these schemes through the agency of the Commission.[74] The scheme must be in a statutory instrument laid before Parliament.[74] A grant cannot be given in respect of buildings if a grant or subsidy has already been made under any other Act.[75] With Treasury approval, the Secretary of State may assist (a) by grants or loans or the supply for payment in cash of building and other materials towards the erection or improvement or rebuilding of dwellinghouses and other buildings for crofters,[76] or (b) by loan to an incoming tenant to enable him to pay to the outgoing tenant or the landlord the compensation for permanent improvements due

[69] 1961 Act, s. 9 (7).
[70] *Ibid.*, s. 9 (11).
[71] *Ibid.*, s. 9 (12).
[72] ss. 19, 20, 37 (2).
[73] Schedule Third.
[74] 1955 Act, s. 22 (1), as amended by 1961 Act, s. 14 (1). See S.I. 1965, No. 1519.
[75] *Ibid.*, s. 22 (5), (8).
[76] s. 22 (2).

to the outgoing tenant.[77] If the outgoing tenant is liable to the Secretary of State in respect of a loan to him, the incoming tenant may by agreement with the Secretary of State assume the liability, and the amount of it is deemed a loan to him.[78] The Secretary of State must inform the landlord of the giving of any such assistance by loan.[79]

In the case of a grant towards the erection of dwellinghouses, regulations must be made by the Secretary of State for securing *inter alia* (a) that conditions as to occupation and maintenance apply for a period not exceeding forty years from completion of the work and (b) that on a breach of any of them he may recover a sum proportionate to the grant as the time between the breach and the expiry of the period bears to the whole period, and (c) that the conditions shall cease on payment to him of a certain sum, and (d) that such conditions shall be contained in a notice to be recorded in the Register of Sasines and further that when they cease to apply a similar notice will be recorded to that effect in that Register.[80] These regulations have been made by the Secretary of State.[81] The Secretary of State may by regulation provide that the conditions applied to a dwellinghouse by these regulations shall not apply to a dwellinghouse in the circumstances and to the extent stated in the regulation.[82]

Where the assistance is by loan, the loan agreement must be recorded in the Crofters Holdings Book, and, as recorded, it has the effect of transferring to the Secretary of State all rights of the crofter and his statutory successors to compensation for permanent improvements up to the amount of any outstanding liability to the Secretary of State,[83] which, if the Secretary of State so determines on the application of the landlord, may be deemed to be a loan from the Secretary of State to the landlord,[84] and then the following provisions apply: —

1. The loan shall be secured by a bond which shall be a charge on the land in favour of the Secretary of State.
2. The loan shall either be repaid by half-yearly instalments of principal with such interest and within such period (not exceeding such period as may be fixed by the Treasury) from the date of the loan, or at such date after the date of the loan not exceeding eighteen months as may be agreed on, or shall be repaid with such interest and within such period by a terminable annuity payable by half-yearly instalments.
3. The amount for the time being unpaid may at any time be discharged, and any such terminable annuity may at any time be redeemed in accordance with tables fixed by the Secretary of State.

[77] s. 22 (3).
[78] s. 23 (5).
[79] s. 23 (2).
[80] s. 22 (4). See also Agriculture (Scotland) Act 1948, s. 77 (3).
[81] S.I. 56/13138.
[82] 1961 Act, s. 14 (2). See S.I. 1965, No. 2153.
[83] 1955 Act, s. 23 (3).
[84] *Ibid.*, s. 23 (4).

4. A certificate by the Secretary of State that the whole of the loan has been repaid or that such terminable annuity has been redeemed shall, without any other instrument, operate as a discharge of the loan or extinction of the terminable annuity, as the case may be, and the recording of such certificate in the appropriate Register of Sasines shall be equivalent to the recording of a discharge of the said bond.

5. The Secretary of State shall cause to be prepared and duly recorded all deeds, writs and instruments necessary for securing the payment of any loan over land made by him, and shall include in the loan the cost so incurred, or to be incurred, in accordance with scales set forth in tables fixed by the Secretary of State.[85]

A person is not disqualified from receiving assistance as above mentioned[86] towards the erection, etc., of dwellinghouses and other buildings because he has become owner of the croft after the Secretary of State has undertaken to provide the assistance.[87] An occupier of a holding under the 1897 Act on land acquired by the Congested Districts (Scotland) Commissioners, who is also the owner of the holding, is deemed to be a crofter for the purpose of the provision of assistance[86] towards the erection, etc., of dwellinghouses and other buildings.[88] In the case of loans in these two cases the provisions of the Third Schedule of the 1955 Act also apply.[89] So too where a holding in the crofting counties does not exceed fifty acres in area or the annual value of it does not exceed £50 and it is occupied by the owner of it, who is in the Secretary of State's opinion of substantially the same economic status as a crofter,[90] the Secretary of State can provide assistance to the owner by loan, grant and the supply of building or other materials for the erection, etc., of buildings other than a dwellinghouse as in the case of a crofter, and in such a case the provisions of the 1955 Act[91] apply also.[92]

Common Grazings. In this connection and for the purposes of the 1955 and 1961 Acts, a person who is not a crofter but is entitled to share in a common grazing along with crofters is included in the term ' crofter '.[93] A Grazings Committee may be appointed from time to time at a public meeting of the crofters who share in a common grazing and

[85] 1955 Act, Schedule Third.
[86] s. 22 (2).
[87] s. 22 (7).
[88] s. 22 (6).
[89] s. 23 (6).
[90] s. 31 (2).
[91] s. 22 (2), (4), (5) and Schedule Third.
[92] ss. 31 (1), (3).
[93] 1961 Act, s. 15 (6). See *Crofters Commission,* 1961 S.L.T. (Sh. Ct.) 20, decided under the similar s. (27 (6)) of 1955 Act, that persons who *de facto* shared common grazings without title to do so were not crofters within the meaning of the subsection.

shall be of such a number as the meeting shall decide.[94] Notice of the meeting may be given by any two crofters interested in the common grazing by notice in each of two successive weeks in one or more newspapers circulating in the district or by notice posted for two successive weeks in a public place or places in that district approved by the Commission, any dispute as to the sufficiency of the notice being determined by the Commission.[95] A person may be appointed a member of a committee though he is not a crofter.[96] If the crofters do not appoint this committee, the Commission may do so, after such enquiry as they deem necessary.[97] The term of office of the members of a committee is three years, and a new committee must be appointed in the same way at the end of the three years, the retiring members being eligible for re-election.[98] The quorum is the majority, and a casual vacancy can be filled by the rest of the committee.[99] The committee, or where the Commission have appointed the committee the Commission, must appoint a clerk, who may be a member of the committee.[1] A member or all the members or the clerk can be removed from office by the Commission, should the Commission be satisfied after such enquiry, if any, as they deem necessary, that the member or all the members or the clerk are not carrying out their duties under the Act, and the Commission may appoint or provide for the appointment of others, who need not be crofters, in his or their place.[2]

Alternatively to appointing a committee, the Commission may appoint a grazings constable,[3] whose term of office is that specified in his instrument of appointment, and whose annual remuneration, fixed by the Commission, is defrayed by assessment on the crofters who share in the common grazing.[4]

The powers and duties of a grazings committee, whether appointed by a meeting or by the Commission, and those of a grazings constable are the same.[3] It is the committee's duty to maintain the common grazings, and to provide and maintain and, if necessary, replace the fixed equipment (which has the same meaning as in the Agricultural Holdings (Scotland) Act 1949[5]) required in connection with the grazings,[5a] and to carry out, but only with the consent of a majority of the crofters ordinarily resident in the township and with the approval of the Commission, works for the improvement of such grazings and equip-

94 1955 Act, s. 24 (1).
95 Ibid., s. 24 (2), as amended by 1961 Act, Schedule First, para. 13.
96 1961 Act, s. 15 (1).
97 1955 Act, s. 24 (3).
98 s. 24 (4).
99 s. 24 (5).
1 s. 24 (6).
2 s. 24 (8).
3 s. 24 (3).
4 s. 24 (7).
5 s. 37 (1); see 1949 Act, s. 93 (1).
5a See ss. 25 (1) (a), 26 (2) (a), as amended by 1961 Act, s. 18 (1), Schedule First, paras. 14, 15.

ment.[6] Where under the existing system each crofter maintained only the part of a township access road *ex adverso* of his croft, an application to decide whether the crofters were bound to contribute work and materials towards its repair was dismissed as unnecessary as the committee had no power to alter that system for the road did not serve the common grazings.[7] The committee have a duty to maintain, repair and, if necessary, replace existing fences and dykes separating holdings of individual crofters from the common grazings regardless of when, or by whom, or with what original intention the fences were erected, and they were held to have power in terms of the regulations made for these grazings to recover the cost of the maintenance, repair and replacement from all the shareholders in the common grazings in proportions corresponding to their respective rights in the grazings as such proportions were fixed by the committee, whose decision was final.[8] A person appointed by the Commission may summon and attend a meeting of a committee to advise and otherwise assist them in performing their duties.[9]

Every committee must, as soon as possible and in any event within six months after being required by the Commission to do so, make regulations as to the management and use of the common grazings and submit them to the Commission for confirmation.[10] These may be confirmed without modification by the Commission, and the Commission may fix the date for their coming into operation; if they do not do so, they come into operation on the expiry of one month from the date of confirmation.[11] The Commission may refuse to confirm them.[11] Unless they are confirmed after consultation with the landlord[12] by the Commission they are of no effect.[11] If the committee fail timeously to make and submit regulations or if they make and submit regulations which the Commission think are not sufficient and satisfactory, the Commission may, after consultation with the landlord,[13] make regulations which will have the same force and effect as if made by the committee and confirmed by the Commission.[14] The committee must administer these regulations with a view to their due observance.[15] *Inter alia*, these regulations must provide for the following matters[16]: —

(a) the recovery by the grazings committee from the crofters sharing in the common grazings of all expenses incurred by the committee

---

[6] s. 25 (1), as amended by 1961 Act, Schedule First, para. 14.
[7] *MacDonald* v *Greig*, 1964 S.L.T. (Land Ct.) 5.
[8] *Crofters Commission* v *Cameron of Garth*, 1964 S.L.T. 276.
[9] 1955 Act, s. 25 (2).
[10] ss. 25 (1) (c), 26 (1).
[11] s. 26 (3).
[12] s. 26 (6).
[13] s. 26 (6): a copy of the regulations confirmed or made or amended by the Commission must be sent to the landlord and the committee.
[14] s. 26 (4).
[15] s. 25 (1) (c).
[16] s. 26 (2), as amended by 1961 Act, Schedule First, para. 15, and s. 15 (2).

in maintaining the common grazings and in providing, maintaining or replacing any fixed equipment[17] required in connection therewith;

(b) the recovery by the grazings committee from the crofters consenting to the carrying out of works for the improvement of the common grazings or the fixed equipment[17] required in connection therewith of the expenses incurred by the grazings committee in carrying out such works and the levying on and recovery from the crofters sharing in the common grazings or consenting to the carrying out of such works in such proportions as specified in the regulations of such sums as in the committee's opinion are necessary to enable the committee to meet any expenses they may incur in this or the preceding paragraph;[18]

(c) the number and the kind of stock which each crofter is entitled to put on the common grazings;

(d) the alteration of individual soumings where works for the improvement of the common grazings or the fixed equipment required in connection therewith have been carried out and all the crofters have not contributed to the expenses incurred in carrying out such works;

(e) where appropriate, the cutting of peats and the collection of seaweed;

(f) subject to the provisions of the Acts, the summoning of meetings of the grazings committee and the procedure and conduct of business at such meetings.

The regulations may restrict the use of any part of the common grazings on which works of improvement have been carried out to crofters who contribute to the expenses incurred by the committee in carrying out the works, and in that case may regulate the number and kinds of stock which each contributing crofter can put on that part and which each crofter, whether or not contributing, can put on the rest.[19]

The committee may from time to time, and, if the Commission so requires, must within the time appointed by the Commission, make further amending regulations, also subject to confirmation and to the power of the Commission to make them (after consulting the landlord) themselves, if the committee fail to make and submit them timeously or make and submit insufficient and unsatisfactory regulations.[20] Regulations for the time being in force are of effect despite anything contrary thereto or inconsistent therewith in any lease or other agreement, whether that is entered into before or after they come into force.[21] A person who contravenes or fails to comply with a regulation is liable

17 *Supra*, p. 476.
18 See *Crofters Commission* v *Cameron, supra.*
19 1961 Act, s. 15 (3).
20 1955 Act, s. 26 (5).
21 s. 26 (7).

to a fine on summary conviction of up to 40/-, and a further fine per day in case of a continuing offence.[22]

Where the owner of any land to which the 1955 and 1961 Acts do not apply agrees to grant rights in any pasture or grazing land to the crofters sharing in any common grazing, and the owner and the crofters agree that that land will form part of the common grazing, then as from the date when the rights are first exercisable by the crofters, the land will form part of the common grazing, and the Acts will apply to the common grazing as so enlarged.[23]

A person sharing in a common grazing is not entitled to a right of access over part of the common grazing as a pertinent of his croft.[24] And while crofters in a common grazing are entitled to water their stock from the supply there they may not use that supply for domestic purposes.[25]

Where regulations prescribe that a crofter's right to share is conditional on his making his croft available during the winter season for the accommodation of any stock belonging to other persons sharing in such grazings, he may apply to the committee for consent to the exclusion of such stock from his croft or part of it.[26] The committee, if they give consent, may give it subject to any conditions which they think proper.[26] From the committee's decision the crofter can appeal to the Commission, who may, if they consent, give their consent subject to any conditions which they think fit.[26]

On the application of any crofters interested the Commission, after consulting the committee, can apportion a common grazing that is shared by two or more townships into separate parts for the exclusive use of one of the several townships, or may apportion a part of such grazing for the exclusive use of one of the townships;[27] and, on the application of any crofter interested and after a similar consultation, may apportion a part of a common grazing for the exclusive use of that crofter.[28] In either of these cases the Commission may make the apportionment subject to such conditions including those as to fencing or draining of the apportioned part as they think fit.[29]

Liability to maintain a fence between two common grazings has been held to fall to be shared equally between the townships concerned;[30] failing agreement or regulations otherwise, responsibility for such matters must be determined by custom.[30]

---

[22] s. 27 (1).
[23] 1961 Act, s. 2 (4).
[24] *Macdonald* v *Barvas Estates Ltd.* (1961) 49 S.L.C.R. App. 55.
[25] *MacColl* v *Downie's Trs.* (1962) 50 S.L.C.R. 28.
[26] 1955 Act, s. 27 (2).
[27] s. 27 (3), as amended by 1961 Act, s. 15 (4).
[28] s. 27 (4).
[29] 1961 Act, s. 15 (5).
[30] *Totescore Common Grazings Committee* v *Indrigill Common Grazings Committee* (1961) 49 S.L.C.R. 44.

Again, on the application of any interested crofter or a landlord, the Commission may apportion lands held runrig among the holders in such manner as the Commission think just and expedient.[31] Further, crofters interested in the whole or part of a common grazing may appoint not more than two of themselves, and authorise in writing one person *bona fide* employed by them for reward, to kill and take ground game on the whole or a part of the common grazing as the case may be, and a person so authorised is deemed the occupier but cannot authorise any other person to kill and take ground game.[32]

Miscellaneous. The provisions of the Landholders Acts in regard to the right of the Secretary of State to require information about holdings and as to the erection of fences apply to crofts.[33]

PROVISIONS IN RELATION TO COTTARS
(a) Under the pre-1955 legislation

General. The statutory definition of a cottar has already been given.[34] It will be noted that, though the 1911 Act extended the Acts to the whole of Scotland, the limitation of cottars to the crofting parishes in the 1886 Act was not repealed and remained.[35]

Tenure and Rent. A cottar has no security of tenure and he is not entitled to apply for the fixing of a fair or equitable rent.

Compensation for Improvements. This is the main statutory right given to a cottar. When a cottar, if he is not paying rent, is removed from his dwelling and any land or buildings occupied by him in connection therewith, or, if he is paying rent, renounces his tenancy or is removed, he is entitled to compensation for permanent improvements, if suitable to the holding, executed or paid for by him or his predecessors in the same family[36] and if, though executed in virtue of any written agreement under which he was bound to execute them, he has not received by way of reduction of rent or otherwise fair consideration for them.[37] This right does not apply to buildings erected by the cottar in violation of an interdict or other judicial order.[38]

Succession. There is at common law or by statute no right of succession either as heir or as legatee to a cottar,[39] and the executor has no claim.[40]

[31] 1955 Act, s. 27 (7).
[32] s. 27 (5).
[33] *Supra*, pp. 398, 412. 1955 Act, s. 38 (2) (3).
[34] *Supra*, p. 411.
[35] Scott, *Law of Smallholdings*, p. 153. It remains under the 1955, 1961 Acts.
[36] *Supra*, pp. 407, 422.
[37] 1886 Act, s. 9, as amended by 1931 Act, s. 12.
[38] *Ibid.*, s. 9.
[39] *Sutherland* v *Earl of Ronaldshay* (1920) 8 S.L.C.R. 17; *McInnes, infra,* at 47, approving Rankine, 622; *White* v *Cameron,* 1966 S.L.T. (Land Ct.) 7.
[40] *McInnes* v *Lady Strathcona* (1926) 14 S.L.C.R. 39.

Loans. The Secretary of State, if he is of opinion that assistance should be provided for the improvement or rebuilding of dwellinghouses or other buildings of cottars, may provide assistance by way of loans, subject to the same conditions and incidents as loans made by him to landholders[41] on the constitution of new holdings.[42] The assistance may include the erection of new buildings in replacement of existing ones or otherwise,[43] and the Secretary of State can supply by payment in cash building or other materials to cottars to be used by them for the aforesaid purposes.[44]

Common Grazings. The Land Court, on the application of the Secretary of State and on such conditions as they think equitable, may grant pasture or grazing rights on a common pasture or grazing to cottars who have been in use to pasture or graze stock thereon.[45]

(b) Under the 1955 and 1961 Acts

Compensation for Improvements. If a cottar who does pay rent is removed from his dwelling and any land or buildings occupied by him in connection therewith, or if a cottar who pays rent is removed or renounces his tenancy, he is entitled to compensation for any permanent improvement,[46] if the improvement is suitable to the subject and was executed or paid for by him or any of his predecessors in the same family (that is, the wife or husband of the cottar and any person to whom the cottar or the husband or wife of the cottar might, failing nearer heirs, have succeeded in case of intestacy)[47] and, if it was executed in pursuance of a specific agreement under which he was bound to execute it, he has not received by way of reduction of rent or otherwise fair consideration for it.[48] This does not apply to any buildings erected by the cottar in contravention of any interdict or other judicial order.[49] The amount of compensation is, failing agreement, fixed by the Land Court.[49] Where a cottar renounced the tenancy or was removed before the commencement of the 1961 Act, the provisions of the 1955 Act[50] as to compensation to crofters for improvements apply as they do to a crofter whose tenancy was determined before the commencement of the 1961 Act,[51] and where he renounces or is removed after that commencement, certain provisions of the 1955[52] and 1961[53] Acts relating to compensation

---

[41] 1911 Act, s. 7.
[42] *Ibid.*, s. 9.
[43] 1931 Act, s. 5 (1).
[44] *Ibid.*, s. 5 (2).
[45] 1911 Act, s. 24 (5) (c), as substituted by 1919 Act, s. 14.
[46] 1955 Act, Schedule Fifth. See *supra*, p. 451.
[47] *Ibid.*, s. 28 (4).
[48] *Ibid.*, s. 28 (1).
[49] *Ibid.*, s. 28 (2), as substituted by 1961 Act, s. 6 (5), Schedule First, para. 7.
[50] s. 14 (3), (4), (5). See *supra*, p. 452.
[51] s. 28 (2) (a), as substituted by 1961 Act, s. 6 (5) and Schedule First, para. 7.
[52] s. 14 (3). *Supra.*
[53] s. 6 (1), (2). *Supra.*

31

for improvements apply to the cottars.[54] Where compensation is to be assessed under the 1961 Act[53] in respect of any permanent improvement and the Land Court fix the amount of it, then the cottar, if he is " qualified "—that is, a cottar whose occupation of the subject began before the commencement of the 1961 Act or who occupies the subject as heir-at-law, legatee or assignee of his immediate predecessor as occupier of the subject, and each of whose predecessors (being in each case a person whose occupation began after the commencement of the 1961 Act) occupied the subject as heir-at-law, legatee or assignee of his immediate predecessor[55]—may request the Land Court to assess the amount that would have been payable as compensation in respect of the improvement had the 1961 Act not been passed, and if that amount is greater than the amount previously fixed by the Court, the Secretary of State must pay the difference to the cottar,[56] the Secretary of State being entitled to set off against that difference any amount due by the cottar in respect of a loan under the 1955 and 1961 Acts.[57] This provision does not apply where compensation in respect of the improvement has previously been assessed under the 1961 Act.[53]

Succession. In the absence of a clear indication to the contrary in the 1955 and 1961 Acts, the presumption is against such a substantial alteration in the law in these Acts.[57a]

Assistance to Cottars. The Secretary of State can make loans or grants or supply building or other materials for the erection, improvement or rebuilding of dwellinghouses and other buildings for cottars as in the case of crofters[58] and the provisions of the Act thereanent[59] apply to such assistance to cottars.[58]

JUDICIAL AND ADMINISTRATIVE AUTHORITIES
LAND COURT

Introduction. The Land Court, which is the judicial tribunal for administering the Acts, was created by the 1911 Act and replaced the Crofters Commission set up under the 1886 Act,[60] taking over the judicial functions that were held by that Commission, and it is a Court for statutory small tenants as well as landholders.[61] The Crofters Commission consisted of three members appointed by the Crown (who also

[54] s. 28 (2B), as added by 1961 Act, s. 6 (5), Schedule First, para. 7.
[55] s. 28 (2B) as added by 1961 Act. This provision is based on a misapprehension or erroneous view of the existing law at its date. *White* v *Cameron,* 1966 S.L.T. (Land Ct.) 7.
[56] s. 28 (2A), as added by 1961 Act, Schedule First, para. 7.
[57] s. 2 (2A), *proviso,* as added by 1961 Act, Schedule First, para. 7.
[57a] *White* v *Cameron, supra.*
[58] 1955 Act, s. 28 (3).
[59] *Ibid.,* s. 22 (2), (4), (5), (7). See *supra,* p. 473.
[60] s. 17.
[61] 1911 Act, s. 32 (14), applying 1911 Act, s. 25.

appointed to any vacancies), of whom one had to be a person who could speak the Gaelic language and another had to be an advocate of not less than ten years' standing.[60] They could delegate their powers to one or more of their number assisted by two valuers or assessors, but in such a case the decision of this body was subject to review by the whole Commission on appeal.[62] The Commission held sittings in the districts covered by the Act.[61] It could appoint officers, including assessors, valuers, clerks, etc.[61] Parties could demand, and the Commission could order, that evidence be taken on oath.[63] The Commission could award expenses.[63] Their powers, which were to deal with all questions regarding tenancies of crofts, included such matters as fixing a fair rent, authorising a landlord to resume holdings, the enlargement of holdings, questions of arrears of rent, the valuation of improvements, the allocation of pasturage and the regulation of common grazings. The decision of the Commission was final;[64] but it was held that, as they had no jurisdiction to determine questions of law arising on the construction of the Acts, e.g., whether a man was a crofter, except incidentally so far as that was necessary to enable them to explicate their own jurisdiction, in fixing a fair rent or fixing boundaries, their determination of any such questions as a substantive fact could be set aside in an action of reduction by the courts.[65] Thus, the decision of the Commission was final only on administrative or discretionary matters such as a fair rent, the value of improvements, etc. They could make rules for their own procedure,[66] and Rules were so made. They had to intimate to those interested all applications for a fair rent[67] or for the enlargement of holdings[68] and to notify the time and place of a hearing to parties.[69] They could appoint in such cases valuers or assessors specially qualified by legal knowledge.[70] Not being a court of law, however, the Commission could not directly enforce its own orders, and a decree conform of the Sheriff was necessary.[71]

Constitution. The Land Court consists of not more than seven members namely, a chairman, who must be an advocate of the Scottish Bar of ten years' standing and who as chairman has the rank and tenure of office of a Senator of the College of Justice, that is, a Judge of the Court of Session, and six other members, usually agriculturalists, one of

[62] Crofters Commission (Delegation of Powers) Act 1888, amending 1886 Act, s. 23.
[63] 1886 Act, s. 24.
[64] *Ibid.*, s. 25.
[65] *Sitwell v McLeod* (1899) 1 F. 950.
[66] 1886 Act, s. 29.
[67] *Ibid.*, s. 20.
[68] *Ibid.*, s. 21.
[69] *Ibid.*, ss. 20, 21.
[70] *Ibid.*, ss. 20, 21.
[71] *Ibid.*, s. 28.

whom must be familiar with Gaelic.[72] The tenure of office of these other members was held[73] at one time to be for life or till they were removed by the Secretary of State for Scotland for inability or misbehaviour, so that the insertion in a member's commission or appointment of an age limit (65 years) was illegal; but under the Scottish Land Court Act 1938 every such other member appointed on and after 2nd June 1938 must vacate office on attaining 65 years of age and, if he held office on that date, had to vacate office on attaining 65 years of age or, if he was already of that age before that date, on that date. The Secretary of State can remove any member other than the chairman for inability or misbehaviour but only after his order of removal has lain before both Houses of Parliament for not less than 30 days or if neither House has passed a resolution against it.[74] If and when the chairman is temporarily unable to attend or the office of chairman is vacant, the Crown can appoint a temporary chairman.[75]

There is a Principal Clerk of Court and there are three Legal Assessors, qualified solicitors experienced in agricultural law. The Principal Clerk is appointed by the Crown, the Assessors by the Court.

The Court is a body corporate with a common seal.[76] All Courts of Justice must take judicial notice of its corporate seal, and any order or other instrument purporting to be signed with it must be received as evidence without further proof.[76']

Powers of Court. It may be noted at the outset that the provisions of the Landholders Acts 1886-1931 in regard to the Court apply, with the necessary modifications, to the determination of any matter which they have jurisdiction under the 1955 and 1961 Acts to determine, as these provisions apply to the determination of matters referred to the Court under the Landholders Acts 1886-1931.[77] The Court, which has all the powers of the former Crofters Commission and the additional powers given by the 1911 and later Acts, is a court of law[78] and has the ordinary powers of a court for regulating its own procedure. The Court may ascertain the facts in any case by hearing parties and examining witnesses, or by means of affidavits, or by such other mode of enquiry as they may deem appropriate, and may require the production of all books, papers, plans and documents relating to the case, and may summon and examine on oath such witnesses as they think fit to call or allow to appear before them.[79] They may determine the amount of expenses of any proceedings before them and the proportion to be borne

---

[72] 1911 Act, s. 3 (1)-(3), as amended by Agriculture (Scotland) Act 1948 s. 70 (1). The number is at present, in fact, five.
[73] *Mackay and Esslemont* v *Lord Advocate*, 1937 S.C. 860 (O.H.).
[74] 1911 Act, s. 3 (4).
[75] *Ibid.*, s. 3 (5).
[76] *Ibid.*, s. 25 (1).
[77] 1955 Act, s. 34 (1), as amended by 1961 Act, Schedule First, paras. 8 and 17.
[78] *Matheson* v *Board of Agriculture for Scotland*, 1917 S.C. 145.
[79] 1911 Act, s. 25 (3).

by the different parties.[80] There must, however, be a decree conform of
the Sheriff of the County where the holding is situated in order that
decrees or orders on which execution and diligence can proceed may be
enforced.[81] The uplifting of a consigned sum must be by an order of the
Sheriff and not of the Land Court.[82]

The Court may, when sitting in open court, report in writing to a
Lord Ordinary any person who has been guilty of contempt of Court
and he may punish that person as if the contempt had been committed
in his own Court.[83] When the chairman is sitting in open court, he
has the same power to punish.[83] So where there is contempt of Court
the chairman can convict and sentence, though doubt has been expressed
whether the chairman can act alone.[84] But it " has been said over and
over again that the greatest restraint and discretion should be used by
the Court in dealing with contempt of Court, lest a process, the purpose
of which is to prevent interference with the administration of justice,
should degenerate into an oppressive or vindictive use of the Court's
powers . . . The Court should never forget that disappointed litigants
sometimes feel aggrieved and some of them are ill-tempered and that
they may say or write things which are foolish and reprehensible. The
Court should be on its guard against putting an overstrained construction upon such utterances, and above all it should not be too ready to
find in them an attempt to interfere with the administration of justice
and to visit them with the penal consequence of contempt of Court ".[85]
And so the Court of Session held that a letter written to the Clerk of
the Land Court by a dissatisfied party was only an intimation of dislike
of the 1911 Act legislation, which the writer desired altered by appropriate means, and was not a complaint against previous decisions in
connection with affairs in relation to tenants and not an intimation of
threats against the Court nor an attempt to interfere with the administration of justice.[84] A fine imposed by the Land Court was, therefore,
ordered to be repaid. Apart from cases of contempt of Court the Court
has no power to impose penalties. Any member of the Court or any
person authorised by the Court can for the purpose of the Acts enter
on and inspect any lands or buildings at all reasonable hours on any
lawful day after notice to the owner and the occupier:[86] this covers
holdings of statutory small tenants.[87]

---

[80] *Ibid.*, s. 25 (4). See *Munro* v *Margrave Estates Ltd.* (1961) 49 S.L.C.R. App.
194, where a Full Court held a Divisional Court finding on expenses should
not be disturbed.
[81] *Ibid.*, s. 25 (6). See as to the procedure for obtaining a decree conform, 1958
S.L.T. (News) 135. The Sheriff is acting only in a ministerial respect. *Duke of
Argyll* v *Cameron* (1888) 16 R. 139.
[82] *Pearson* v *MacDonald* (1961) 49 S.L.C.R. App. 184.
[83] 1911 Act, s. 25 (3).
[84] *Milburn*, 1946 S.C. 301.
[85] *Ibid.*, at 315, *per* L.P. Normand.
[86] 1911 Act, s. 7 (19).
[87] *Ibid.*, s. 32 (14).

Jurisdiction. The jurisdiction of the Court in relation to the Land-holders and the Crofters Acts includes the following matters—the determination of who are landholders and statutory small tenants, the fixing of the rents of landholders and statutory small tenants on applica-tion, questions of common grazings, of buildings and duration of leases in regard to statutory small tenants, questions in relation to renunciation by holders, resumption by landlords, bequests, assignations, vacant hold-ings, compensation for improvements, questions as to compensation and fencing in regard to the compulsory creation of new holdings and the enlargement of holdings, differences between landlord and tenant of an agricultural holding if they jointly so agree,[88] actions for removal of landholders,[89] disputes as to the existence and maintenance and extent of rights and privileges which are, or are claimed as, incidents, accessory or appurtenant to a holding or other subjects to which the Acts apply, such as water supply, access,[89a] etc.; and questions as to the value of sheep stocks.[90] Matters which are otherwise referable to the Secretary of State in regard to holdings of less than 50 acres or of which the rent is under £50 of which the Secretary of State is landlord are to be referred to the Land Court for determination.[91]

The Court can determine all incidental issues, and so, in connection with succession to a holding, the Court will determine the validity of a will,[92] or accept a plea against a will, or whether an alleged will is a testamentary document, even though it covers moveable as well as heritable property,[93] by way of exception.[94]

The Court can determine any question of fact or law under the 1955 or the 1961 Acts, whether arising before or after the commence-ment of the 1961 Act, including whether a holding is a croft, or who is tenant of a croft, or as to the boundaries of a croft or any pasture or grazing land a right in which forms part of a croft, whether any land is or is part of a common pasture or grazing to which the 1955 and 1961 Acts apply,[95] but the Court cannot determine any question which the 1955 and the 1961 Acts reserve for another Court or any question other than one of law decided by the Secretary of State or the Com-mission under their functions under these Acts.[96]

---

[88] Agricultural Holdings (Scotland) Act 1949, s. 78. See *supra*, p. 377.
[89] 1931 Act, s. 3. Under the 1886 Act, s. 3, these came within the Sheriff's juris-diction.
[89a] *e.g.*, whether there was a right of access as claimed in relation to an access that passed through land occupied by the crofter's former landlord and had existed for many years as a pertinent and the crofter claimed a right to use, widen and improve it; but entry on an adjoining proprietor's land to carry out works on that land cannot be authorised. *Maclean* v *Fletcher*, 1965 S.L.T. (Land Ct.) 5.
[90] See *supra*, p. 384.
[91] 1931 Act, s. 35 (1).
[92] *MacCuish* v *Hitchcock* (1947) 35 S.L.C.R. 3; *Campbell* v *Duke of Argyll* (1947) 35 S.L.C.R. 24.
[93] *Elder* v *Murray and Pilkington* (1949) 37 S.L.C.R. 7.
[94] *Macdonald* v *Macdonald* (1941) 29 S.L.C.R. 70.
[95] 1961 Act, s. 4 (1).
[96] *Ibid.*, s. 4 (1), *proviso*.

Appeal. For the purposes of the Landholders Acts, the Land Court has full power and jurisdiction to hear and determine all matters, of law or of fact, and no other court can review the orders or determinations of the Land Court.[97] The Court is thus final on all questions of fact,[98] but the Court may, if they think fit, and must on any party's request, state a special case on any question of law arising in the proceedings before them for the opinion of either Division of the Court of Session, who are in turn authorised finally to determine the same.[97] If the Land Court refuse to state a case because they consider that no question of law is involved, an application can be made to the Court of Session for an order on the Land Court to state a case.[99] Appeal from the Land Court is thus only by a stated case on a question of law to the Court of Session. There is no further appeal to the House of Lords. The appeal by stated case may be from a decision of a single member, it not being necessary to submit the order first to a full Bench of the Land Court.[1] These statutory provisions as to a stated case apply to proceedings in the Land Court under any enactments other than the Landholders Acts, *e.g.,* the Crofters Acts 1955 and 1961.[2]

Where exclusion or inclusion of evidence is objected to by a party, he should ask for a specific question to be put in the special case.[3] And the Court of Session have held that the Land Court are entitled to refuse to state a case on what is a question of fact, in the particular case whether a written condition of a let requiring a tenant to repair and maintain waterworks was reasonable, the landlord having applied for allocation of responsibilities.[4]

The Land Court must loyally accept and obey an opinion of the Court of Session in a special stated case.[5] After the Court of Session had decided a question of law in a special case the chairman of the Land Court at a diet to consider the form of order to be pronounced by the Land Court, refused to pronounce an order giving effect to the Court of Session decision, observing that the decision was *ultra vires,* contrary to law and of no legal force and effect, and that there would in future be no appeal to the Court of Session in cases, as this one was, of bequests under the Agricultural Holdings (Scotland) Act 1949. The landlord in whose favour the decision had been given presented a petition to the *nobile officium* of the Court of Session claiming a remit to the Land Court to give effect to the determination of the Court of Session but before it was heard an order giving effect to the Court of

[97] 1911 Act, s. 25 (2).
[98] *Pottinger* v *Hay* (1928) 16 S.L.C.R. 58.
[99] Johnston, *The Small Landholders Acts,* 2nd ed., p. 56, quoted in Scott, *Law of Landholdings,* p. 252. The question must be one of law: *Grant* v *Seafield's Trs.* (1934) 22 S.L.C.R. 76.
[1] *Strachan* v *Hunter,* 1916 S.C. 901.
[2] 1961 Act, s. 4 (3).
[3] *Sinclair* v *Campbell,* 1919 S.C. 341.
[4] *Secretary of State for Scotland* v *Petrie* (1953) 41 S.L.C.R. 30.
[5] *Kennedy* v *Johnstone,* 1956 S.L.T. 73.

Session's determination and dealing with expenses in a manner agreed by the parties was issued by the Land Court, signed by two lay members, a note by the chairman being appended in which he agreed as to the question of expenses but expressed a formal dissent on the main issue. The petition was not proceeded with, but in view of the publicity caused by the chairman's attitude the Court of Session delivered an opinion[5] that under the 1911 Act[6] the Land Court was bound on the request of any party to state a case to either Division on a question of law, and that, when the Division answered the question, the Land Court was bound to give effect to that answer. Otherwise, said the Court, the right of bringing a question of law by stated case would be futile and ineffective. Moreover, the Land Court Rules bound the Land Court to bring their decision into conformity with the Court of Session's opinion, and to take any necessary steps for that purpose. The chairman's statement, too, prejudged a litigant's right to require the Land Court to state a case, which was a statutory right of a litigant, and involved a disregard of the duties imposed on the Land Court by Parliament.

Appeal may be made to the Court of Session against a conviction for contempt of Court.[7] The appeal is a quasi-criminal proceeding to which the principles of the procedure of the High Court of Justiciary apply.[7] The law administered in the High Court of Justiciary " is applicable in the Court of Session when it is dealing with an appeal against conviction for contempt of Court, which is a quasi-criminal proceeding. The interest of the appellant in such a case is to get rid of the conviction and not merely to recover any money which he has paid in satisfaction of a fine. There is no similarity to an appeal to the Court of Session or to a reclaiming motion in the Court of Session in a civil cause after the payment has been made in implement of a decree."[8] Payment of a fine imposed by the Land Court does not bar the appeal. " Suspension is not rendered incompetent or barred through the sentence having been obtempered by imprisonment or payment of the fine imposed."[9] In a quasi-criminal proceeding the appellant is not concerned with another private party. No embarrassing difficulties can arise from an order to repay a fine paid over to public custody.[8]

A party may obtain a rehearing from the Land Court, but he must apply for it within three months from the date of receipt by the Sheriff Clerk of a final judgment or order, unless all parties concur, or leave is given by the Court on special cause being shown to the Court.[10] The Land Court ought to consider and decide on an application for a rehearing after final judgment has been given, notwithstanding an appli-

---

[6] This would equally apply under the 1955 and 1961 Acts: 1961 Act, s. 4 (3).
[7] *Milburn*, 1946 S.C. 301.
[8] *Ibid.*, at 313, *per* L.P. Normand.
[9] Trotter, *Summary Criminal Jurisdiction*, p. 66; Renton & Brown, *Criminal Procedure*, 3rd ed., p. 315.
[10] Land Court Rules Nos. 90, 94. Special cause was held shown in *Garenin Grazings Committee* v *Garenin Tenants* (1950), 38 S.L.C.R. 16.

cation for a special case by the appellant.[11] " It is the duty of the Land Court to consider on its merits a motion for a rehearing and it is not a good ground of refusal that there stands unwithdrawn a requisition for a special case."[12]

The grounds for a rehearing are[13] (1) that the order or orders, sought to be varied, recalled or annulled (a) proceeded upon essential error, either shared by all the parties, or induced by one or more of the opposing parties; or (b) were obtained or procured by fraud or fabrication of documents, or subordination of perjury, or other like misconduct on the part of one or more of the opposing parties in course of the application; (2) that pertinent and important evidence as to disputed matters of fact had been tendered and erroneously rejected or disallowed at the hearing of the application; (3) that the party moving was prepared to adduce pertinent and important evidence of the tenor set forth in his statement, which was unknown to, or could not reasonably have been discovered by, him before the hearing of the application or which because of want of means to prepare his case or his absence from Scotland, or other excusable cause he had been unable to adduce at the proper time; (4) that the opposing party or parties had, without reasonable excuse, failed substantially to fulfil or comply with the conditions imposed in the interest of the party moving by the order or orders sought to be varied or recalled; (5) any other ground essential to the justice of the case. If the Court are satisfied that if the order or orders in question were allowed to stand a substantial wrong or miscarriage of justice, which cannot by any other process be so conveniently remedied or set right, would be likely to be occasioned thereby, they may order a rehearing before answer or otherwise in whole or in part and in such manner and on such terms and conditions as they think just,[14] and may on such rehearing vary, recall or annul the order or orders in whole or in part or as to some parties only and may make further orders.[15] A ground for rehearing may be that competent and essential evidence was not led at a previous hearing.[16] It was held that the Court could not rehear a decision of the original Crofters Commission as such would not have been competent under the Commission's Rules, which did not provide for a rehearing.[17]

Procedure. The Court can from time to time make rules for conducting the business of the Court.[18] The Court " is a Court of law, and consequently has power to regulate its own procedure. . . . To stay

[11] *McColl* v *Beresford's Trs.*, 1920 S.C. 394.
[12] *Ibid.*, at 397, *per* Lord Skerrington.
[13] Land Court Rules No. 95.
[14] *Ibid.*, No. 98.
[15] *Ibid.*, No. 101.
[16] *Baird's Trs.* v *Rendall* (1920) 8 S.L.C.R. 74.
[17] *Mackenzie* v *Mackenzie* (1921) 9 S.L.C.R. 1; *Wight* v *Morison* (1922) 10 S.L.C.R. 53, 91.
[18] 1911 Act, s. 3 (12).

procedure is to regulate procedure, and therefore to grant a sist is inherent in any court of law, including the Land Court."[19] The Court has framed and issued Rules of Court.[20]

The quorum of the Court is three[21] and important cases are usually taken by the Full Court. An Order by a tribunal of two members only, following the death of the third member before judgment was pronounced, although there was a joint minute by both parties calling for a decision by the two in the circumstances, was held inept and not a valid exercise of the Court's statutory function.[22] The Court, however, generally works in Divisions—usually one member with a legal assessor being a Division; and these Divisions go on circuit to particular parts of the country. From a judgment or order of a Division a party dissatisfied with that judgment or order may appeal to the Full Court of three or more members, including, where it is of the quorum of three, not more than one member who was a party to the judgment or order, of whom one must be the chairman of the Court.[21] It has been held[23] that it is sufficient that an appeal to the Full Court is intimated timeously —that is, within a month from receipt by the Sheriff Clerk of the order[24] —to the Land Court and it is not a relevant objection that notice of appeal has not been lodged with the Sheriff Clerk but has been given to the Land Court direct; the substance of the Rules[25] (that any appeal to the Full Court is by signed note and that the note may be an application below the order or on a separate paper to the Sheriff Clerk) is that the Land Court be notified of the appeal.

All relevant objections to documents can be dealt with *ope exceptionis*, even if the document is the basis of the action or of the defence.[26]

The Court can deal with or determine all incidental issues, *e.g.*, whether an alleged will is a testamentary document, even though it covers moveable as well as heritable property, and this can be done *ope exceptionis*.[27]

All orders and determinations must be in writing.[28] The Court must intimate to the Crofters Commission their determination of any question under the Landholders Acts in relation to the crofting counties or the 1955 or the 1961 Acts.[29]

---

[19] *Matheson* v *Board of Agriculture*, 1917 S.C. 145, at 150, *per* L.P. Strathclyde.
[20] Rules of Scottish Land Court, S.R.& 0., 1912, No. 1750 (s. 109), as amended in 1932. They are to be found also in the *Parliament House Book*, Division L. See also 1958 S.L.T. (News) 134.
[21] 1911 Act, s. 25 (5). A Divisional Court finding on expenses should not be disturbed, the Full Court held in *Munro* v *Margrave Estates* (1961) 49 S.L.C.R. App. 194.
[22] *McCallum* v *Arthur*, 1955 S.C. 188. See *supra*, p. 378.
[23] *Macpherson* v *Secretary of State for Scotland* (1958) 46 S.L.C.R. 3. Land Court Rules Nos. 80, 81.
[24] Land Court Rules No. 83.
[25] *Ibid.*, Nos. 80, 81.
[26] *Ibid.*, No. 56.
[27] *Elder* v *Murray and Pilkington* (1949) 37 S.L.C.R. 7. See *supra*, p. 486.
[28] 1911 Act, s. 25 (1).
[29] 1961 Act, s. 4 (2).

ARBITRATION

Where in any proceeding under the Acts the Land Court or the Crofters Commission is empowered to pronounce an order, the landlord and the landholder or crofter may agree to accept the decision of an arbiter mutually chosen instead of the decision of the Court or the Commission, and in that event any order pronounced by the arbiter is when recorded in the Landholders Holding Book or Crofters Holding Book along with the agreement to accept his decision as effectual as an order of the Court or the Commission, and all regulations applicable to the Court or the Commission and to the orders pronounced by them apply to a sole arbiter and the orders pronounced by him.[30]

THE NEW CROFTERS COMMISSION

Introduction. The 1955 Act, as already stated, set up a new code for the seven crofting counties and, as recommended in the Report of a Commission called the Taylor Commission,[31] re-established the Crofters Commission[32] for those counties which, as has been seen,[33] had been set up by the 1886 Act and merged in the Land Court by the 1911 Act.

Constitution. The Commission, which is a body corporate with a common seal,[34] consists of not more than nine members appointed by the Secretary of State, of whom one is appointed by the Secretary of State as chairman.[35] The members must include persons with a knowledge of crofting conditions, and at least one member must be able to speak the Gaelic language.[36] The members hold and vacate office in accordance with the terms of the instrument of their appointment but any member can resign by notice to the Secretary of State, and a member ceasing to hold office can be re-appointed.[37] A member may be an M.P.[38] The quorum is three or such larger number as the Commission may from time to time determine.[39] A vacancy in the membership or a defect in any appointment does not invalidate proceedings,[40] and the chairman on an equal division of votes has a casting vote.[41] The Commission may refer to one or more of their members to report and recommend such matters as the Commission may determine and may delegate to one or more members such of their functions to such extent and subject to such conditions or restrictions as may, with the approval

[30] 1886 Act, s. 30, as amended by 1911 Act, s. 28; 1955 Act, ss. 38 (2), (3), 39 (2).
[31] Cmd. 9091.
[32] 1955 Act, s. 1 (1).
[33] *Supra,* p. 390.
[34] 1955 Act, Schedule First, para. 1.
[35] *Ibid.,* s. 1 (3), as amended by 1961 Act, s. 1.
[36] *Ibid.,* s. 1 (4).
[37] *Ibid.,* Schedule First, para. 2.
[38] House of Commons Disqualification Act, 1957, Schedule Fourth, Part I, repealing 1955 Act, Schedule First, para. 3.
[39] 1955 Act, Schedule First, para. 5.
[40] *Ibid.,* Schedule First, para. 6.
[41] *Ibid.,* Schedule First, para. 7.

of the Secretary of State, be so determined.[42] To assist them in the local execution of their functions under the Act the Commission can appoint a panel of suitable persons resident in the crofting counties to act as assessors, when so required by the Commission.[43] The Commission has an office in the crofting counties at which notices etc. are to be received.[44] The Secretary of State may provide the services of such officers and servants as the Commission may require.[45]

Powers. The functions of the Commission are the reorganising, developing and regulating of crofting in the crofting counties, the promoting of the interests of crofters there and the keeping under review of matters relating to crofting and such other functions as are conferred on them by or under the Act.[46] In carrying out these functions they must act in accordance with any general directions given by the Secretary of State and must have regard to local circumstances and conditions.[47] They must further,[48] (a) keep under general review all matters relating to crofts and crofting conditions, including land settlement, the improvement of land and livestock, the planting of trees, the supply of agricultural equipment and requisites, the marketing of agricultural produce, experimental work on crofting methods, the provision of demonstration crofts, the needs of the crofting communities for public services of all kinds, the provision of social amenities and the need for industries to provide supplementary occupations for crofters or work for their families; and make such recommendations as they may think fit on any of these matters; (b) collaborate so far as their powers and duties permit with any body or person in the carrying out of any measures for the economic development and social improvement of the crofting counties; (c) advise the Secretary of State on any matter relating to crofts and crofting conditions which he may refer to them, or on which they may think fit to submit advice to him, and (d) exercise the powers conferred on them by the 1955 and 1961 Acts in such manner as may seem to them desirable in each case. They can collect information about holdings from owners and occupiers, must compile and revise a Register of Crofts and decide whether a tenant is a crofter where neither agreement nor decision of the Court in that connection exists.[49] They must make an annual report to the Secretary of State for Scotland on the exercise and performance of their functions under the Acts.[50]

[42] *Ibid.*, Schedule First, para. 8.
[43] *Ibid.*, s. 2 (2).
[44] *Ibid.*, Schedule First, para. 11.
[45] *Ibid.*, Schedule First, para. 12.
[46] *Ibid.*, s. 1 (1).
[47] *Ibid.*, s. 1 (2).
[48] *Ibid.*, s. 2 (1).
[49] *Ibid.*, s. 15. See *supra*, p. 467.
[50] *Ibid.*, s. 2 (4).

Procedure. The Commission have power to regulate their own procedure and make rules for that purpose.[51] They can order that evidence be taken on oath.[52] The Commission is a tribunal within the Tribunals and Inquiries Act 1958 and must comply with the provisions of that Act, *e.g.*, in regard to awards.[53]

THE SECRETARY OF STATE FOR SCOTLAND

History. The Board of Agriculture for Scotland was set up under the 1911 Act[54] as the administrative body and office for small holdings. It replaced in powers, duties and property the Congested Districts (Scotland) Commissioners under the Congested Districts (Scotland) Act 1897[55] and also took over some of the powers and duties previously exercised and carried out by the Board of Agriculture and Fisheries of which the Secretary for Scotland was a member, set up under the Board of Agriculture Act 1889.[56] It consisted of not more than three persons, who did not require any specific qualifications, and who were appointed by the Crown on the recommendation of the Secretary for Scotland and who held office during His Majesty's pleasure, one of whom was chairman of the Board while another member was Commissioner for Small Holdings.[57] The Board was in 1929 abolished and was succeeded by the Department of Agriculture for Scotland under the Reorganisation of Offices (Scotland) Act 1928,[58] and to the Department there were transferred all the powers, duties, functions and property of the Board. The Department, which acted under the control and direction of the Secretary of State for Scotland, consisted of a Secretary and such other officers and servants as the Secretary of State, with Treasury approval, appointed. There were four assistant Secretaries, one of whom was in charge of the Small Holdings Division of the Department, for which Division Scotland was divided into three Districts, in each of which there was a Divisional Land Officer. Finally, under the Reorganisation of Offices (Scotland) Act 1939,[59] the Department was abolished as a statutory department, and the powers, duties, functions and property of the Department were transferred to the Secretary of State for Scotland and these are carried out or held by a department of the Secretary of State, acting in his name and under his direction, known as the Department of Agriculture. The Schedule to that Act of 1939

[51] *Ibid.*, Schedule First, para. 10; 1886 Act, s. 29.
[52] *Ibid.*, Schedule First, para. 9.
[53] s. 12 (1), (3).
[54] s. 4.
[55] 1911 Act, ss. 28 (1), 29.
[56] These were specified in the 1911 Act, Schedule First, or were in a local Act or could be added to by Order in Council: s. 4 (12); see also s. 28 (2).
[57] *Ibid.*, s. 4 (6). This office was abolished by the 1919 Act, Schedule Fourth.
[58] s. 1 (1).
[59] s. 1.

contains the consequential amendments in cases for example where loans had to have the consent of the Secretary of State under the 1886 and 1897 Acts.

Powers and Duties. These include, as already mentioned, the creation and equipment of small holdings, the enlargement of holdings, the making of gifts, grants, loans, etc., to holders for buildings, with a power of entry on and inspection of land and buildings,[60] the duty of promoting the interests of agriculture, and other rural industries in Scotland, and exercising any powers and duties conferred on or transferred to the Board under the 1911 Act,[61] of promoting aid and developing instruction in agriculture and other rural industries,[62] and of taking such steps as are thought proper for the promotion and development of agricultural organisation and co-operation,[63] and of submitting an annual report of their proceedings to be laid before Parliament.[61] The Secretary of State can undertake the collection and preparation of statistics relating to agriculture and other rural industries, and make or aid in making such enquiries, experiments and research and collect or aid in collecting such information relating thereto as may be thought advisable.[64] He can sell or let land acquired under the 1916 and 1918 Acts: a tenant can be given an option to buy, and tenants on the estates now held by the Secretary of State are entitled to buy their holdings if they have been in occupation for not less than six years.[65] He can erect, repair or improve dwellinghouses and other buildings on any land acquired by them and can execute any other improvement on or in connection with and for the benefit of any such land.[66]

CONTRACTING OUT OF ACTS

1886 Act. The original Act of 1886 had no provisions which excluded agreements or contracts that involved contracting out of the Act. The Act allowed parties to agree that a sole arbiter mutually chosen should act in place of the Crofters Commission and to accept his decision instead of the Commission's decision.[67] His decision was treated as equivalent to and as effectual to all intents and purposes as an order of the Commission, and all regulations applicable to the Commission and their orders were applied to his orders.[67]

---

[60] 1911 Act, s. 7 (19); 1955 Act, s. 30.
[61] 1911 Act, s. 4 (2), as amended by the Reorganisation of Offices (Scotland) Act 1928, s. 1 (4) and Schedule. The Board's powers and duties under this section originally included forestry but these were transferred to the Forestry Commission under the Forestry Act 1919, s. 3.
[62] *Ibid.,* s. 4 (4).
[63] *Ibid.,* s. 4 (5).
[64] *Ibid.,* s. 4 (3).
[65] 1919 Act, s. 6.
[66] *Ibid.,* s. 7.
[67] s. 30.

Landholders Acts. In general, contracting out of the Acts is not allowed. Any contract or agreement made by a landholder which deprives him of any right conferred on him by any provision of the Acts is to that extent void unless the contract or agreement is approved by the Land Court.[68] A landowner, however, can constitute and equip a holding and let it by voluntary agreement at such rent, for such period and on such terms and conditions as may be agreed on; such a contract is outside the Acts, under conditions governed by the contract as interpreted by the ordinary law,[69] and none of the statutory provisions apply unless by joint consent of parties. If, however, land is comprised in a scheme for new holdings referred to in an intimation to the landlord under the 1911 Act,[70] it is not competent to contract out while the scheme is under consideration, without the Secretary of State's consent.[71] Except in those circumstances, a landlord and a landholder cannot by mutual agreement take a holding outwith the Acts.[72] Unless the landlord satisfies the Land Court that there is reasonable ground of objection to a statutory small tenant and the Court find accordingly, the tenant for the time being is, notwithstanding any agreement to the contrary, entitled on any such determination to a renewal of the tenancy on the terms and conditions specified[73] in the Act,[74] provided that he has not given written notice to the landlord that he is to terminate the tenancy. It was held by the Court of Session[75] that a clause in a lease discharging past and future claims did not debar the Court from considering whether payment or fair consideration had been made or received for improvements or from assessing compensation therefor so far as payment or fair consideration had not been received.

1955 and 1961 Acts. Contracting out is forbidden under these Acts unless the Land Court approve; any contract or agreement by a crofter by virtue of which he is deprived of any rights conferred on him by any provision of the 1955 and 1961 Acts is to that extent void unless the contract or agreement is approved by the Land Court.[76]

---

[68] 1931 Act, s. 25.
[69] 1911 Act, s. 35.
[70] *Ibid.*, s. 7 (9), as amended by 1919 Act, s. 17.
[71] *Ibid.*, s. 35 *proviso*, as amended by 1919 Act, s. 17, Schedule Second.
[72] See *Whyte* v *Garden's Trs.* (1925) 13 S.L.C.R. 99.
[73] 1911 Act, s. 32.
[74] *Ibid.*, s. 32 (4). See *supra*, p. 437.
[75] *Smith* v *Marquis of Aberdeen's Trs.*, 1916 S.C. 905. Note other views in later Land Court cases: *Gillies* v *Board of Agriculture* (1926) 14 S.L.C.R. 84; *Ross* v *Reid* (1930), 18 S.L.C.R. 82.
[76] 1955 Act, s. 3 (4); 1961 Act, Schedule First, para. 8.

CHAPTER XX

THE RENT RESTRICTIONS ACTS

INTRODUCTION

History. By a series of Acts commencing in 1915, some now repealed in whole or in part, Parliament has created limitations or restrictions on the amount of rent which a landlord can charge, or the amount by which he can increase the rent of certain dwellinghouses, and on the right of a landlord to obtain possession of such houses, that is, on his right to obtain from the court a decree of removal of a tenant. In short, the main purpose of the Acts is achieved " by abrogating the common law rights of the landlords of dwellinghouses to which the Acts apply and maintaining the tenants in possession ".[1] The Acts were passed owing to the scarcity of houses and to avoid the exaction of excessive rents that might have occurred if letting had been left to unregulated competition.[2] " One main purpose of the Rent Acts is to mitigate the hardships inherent in a period of shortage of dwellinghouses."[3] Their object thus has been to protect the home and they began in order to protect humble occupiers from being turned out of their homes or having rents heavily raised against them.[4] More recently, provisions have been introduced to protect residential occupiers from harassment and from eviction without due process of law.[5] The purpose of the Acts and the mischief they were intended to remedy is a significant guide to the interpretation of them.[6] The Acts also dealt with and restricted the amount of interest chargeable on a mortgage or heritable security and the right of the bondholder or security holder to obtain repayment of his loan in cases where the security was over certain dwellinghouses; this part of the legislation is, however, not within the scope of this work.

The first Act was the Increase of Rent and Mortgage Interest (War Restrictions) Act 1915. It was, as the title implies, passed as an intended temporary war-time measure in the Great War of 1914-18 to meet the acute housing shortage that then prevailed. The shortage has continued in varying degrees till the present day, but was always, until the 1965 Act, in the legislation treated as temporary or of an emergency nature;

---

[1] *Alex. Cowan & Sons* v *Acton,* 1952 S.C. 73 at 91, *per* Lord Patrick.
[2] *Menzies* v *Mackay,* 1938 S.C. 74 at 78, *per* L.J.C. Aitchison.
[3] *Alex. Cowan & Sons, supra,* at 90-91, *per* Lord Patrick.
[4] *Reidy* v *Walker* [1933] 2 K.B. 266 at 272, *per* Goddard, J.
[5] 1965 Act, ss. 30, 32; the provision against eviction without due process of law does not apply to tenancies protected by the Rent Acts and is discussed, *supra,* in Chapter XVII.
[6] *Stewart* v *Mackay,* 1947 S.C. 287 at 296, *per* L.P. Cooper.

hence the earlier Acts were always more or less framed and treated as temporary legislation. Some Acts have been kept in force only by Expiring Laws Continuance Acts; and the " principal " Acts 1920-25, as amended, up to the 1939 Act, were under the Act[7] to continue until six months after such date as by Order-in-Council the emergency that occasioned the passing of the 1939 Act was declared to be at an end. Since the Increase of Rent and Mortgage Interest (Restrictions) Act 1920, which at the time repealed all prior Acts and consolidated and amended the law, no attempt at a consolidation Act has been made, though with the appointment of Law Reform Commissions in 1965 this long-overdue step seems more imminent, and many of the Acts subsequent to 1920 have referred back to the 1920 Act as the " principal Act " with consequent confusion and lack of clarity and an enormous mass of not always consistent case-law. The 1920 Act was until 1933 called the " principal Act " but since then it is the 1920 to 1925 Acts that are referred to as " the principal Acts ".[8] Some of the Acts may be cited collectively as the Rent and Mortgage Interest Restrictions Acts 1920-39.[9] There are various other groupings, and some Acts even are to be construed as one.[10] Lord Justice Mackinnon was well justified in referring to the legislation as " that chaos of verbal darkness "[11] and again as " that welter of chaotic verbiage which may be cited together as the Rent Restrictions Acts ".[12] Many other justifiably uncomplimentary observations have been made by other judges and legal advisers called on to decide or advise in a jungle of legislation and decision that a consolidation Act could have largely cleared away. The Acts are full of difficulties, which have been added to by the mass of case-law, and have " become a byword for confused draftsmanship ".[13] " Hard cases, invidious distinctions and anomalies can scarcely be avoided in legislation which is designed to alleviate the hardships of an abnormal situation by a partial departure from the normal system of law."[14]

The Acts in force in Scotland at the present time are: the Increase of Rent and Mortgage Interest (Restrictions) Act 1920; Rent Restrictions (Notices of Increase) Act 1923; Rent and Mortgage Interest Restrictions Act 1923; Prevention of Eviction Act 1924; Rent and Mortgage Interest (Restrictions Continuation) Act 1925; Rent and Mortgage Interest Restrictions (Amendment) Act 1933; Increase of Rent and Mortgage Interest (Restrictions) Act 1935; Increase of Rent and Mortgage Interest (Restrictions) Act 1938; Rent and Mortgage Interest Restrictions Act

---

[7] s. 1.
[8] 1933 Act, s. 1; 1933 Act, s. 8 (2) and 1939 Act, s. 7 (1).
[9] 1939 Act, s. 9 (1).
[10] 1924 Act, s. 3.
[11] *Winchester Court* v *Miller* [1944] K.B. 734 at 744.
[12] *Vaughan* v *Shaw* [1945] K.B. 400 at 401.
[13] *Joint Properties* v *Williamson*, 1945 S.C. 68 at 74, *per* L.P. Normand.
[14] *Ibid.*, at 74-5, *per* L.P. Normand.

1939;[15] Rent of Furnished Houses Control (Scotland) Act 1943; Landlord and Tenant (Rent Control) Act 1949; Reserve and Auxiliary Forces (Protection of Civil Interests) Act 1951; Crown Lessees (Protection of Sub-Tenants) Act 1952; Housing (Repairs and Rents) (Scotland) Act 1954; Rent Act 1957; Landlord and Tenant (Temporary Provisions) Act 1958, and Landlord and Tenant (Furniture and Fittings) Act 1959; and the Rent Act 1965.[16] They will be referred to hereafter simply by the year and the word "Act".

The effect of the Rent Acts in general is as follows. If the tenancy or lease is one to which the Acts apply, the rent that can be charged is limited to what is called the standard rent or the rent limit, as the case may be,[17] and increases in that rent may only be made in certain limited cases. The landlord's right to recover possession is removed, except in certain limited circumstances. If the tenant dies, his widow or some member of his family residing with him on the premises may succeed to the tenancy, and such a person may be succeeded in his turn by a similar successor. During the currency of the lease the contract determines the rights of parties subject to these restrictions; if the contract period ends, the lease may be renewed by tacit relocation, unless the landlord gives notice of removal or to quit. If he does give such notice, the tenant need not leave, except in certain clearly-defined circumstances, but may remain in occupation by invoking the protection of the Acts; the tenancy then becomes what is called a statutory tenancy, the tenant a statutory tenant, that is "a tenant who by virtue of the provisions of this Act retains possession of any dwelling house to which this Act applies", in the words of the 1920 Act.[18] Again, a landlord may not charge a premium in respect of the grant, renewal or assignation of a tenancy or lease to which the principal Acts apply. The terms and conditions of the tenancy or lease are restricted in that, for instance, no new burden can be put on the tenant unless there is a proportionate reduction in the rent.

It has been said in a number of cases that the Acts put a status on a house,[19] e.g., in respect that the standard rent or rent limit is binding on all future landlords and tenants. The 1920 Act[20] provides that where the Act has become applicable to any dwellinghouse it shall continue to do so, whether or not the dwellinghouse continues to be one to which, by reason of its rateable value or otherwise, the Act applies; but the Acts apply only to dwellinghouses, and a house originally used

---

[15] The Rent and Mortgage Interest Restrictions Acts 1920-1939 are referred to as "the Rent Acts" by the Rent Act 1965, s. 47 (1), and this terminology has been adopted here.

[16] Although s. 5 of the Protection from Eviction Act 1964 remains in force, it has no application in Scotland.

[17] "Standard rent" in the case of controlled tenancies, "rent limit" in the case of regulated tenancies; see infra, pp. 530 et seq., 551 et seq.

[18] s. 15 (1).

[19] E.g. Brown v Robins [1943] 1 All E.R. 548 at 551, per Scott, L.J.

[20] s. 12 (6).

as a dwellinghouse is no longer protected if it is subsequently let for business purposes or as business premises[21] or, in the case of regulated tenancies, is used for retail trade.[22] Another aspect of status was said to be that if a tenant sublets for business purposes the Acts no longer apply to the premises,[23] while if the tenancy is outside the Acts, a sublet will not change this and it is also outside them,[24] unless in certain cases where statutory protection is given to subtenants. The exclusion by the 1957 Act from control of new leases or tenancies of houses rated at £40 or under unless where the tenant has been occupying the premises or part of them under a controlled tenancy may have modified this view.

It has been pointed out that the terms " landlord " and " tenant ", though used and defined in the Acts, are not strictly correct terms when one is dealing with the Acts, which in large measure fence the contractual capacity of the parties by statutory provisions. " It seems quite clear that neither in the Act of 1920 nor in that of 1923 is the word ' landlord ' used in the technical sense of a person between whom and the tenant a contractual relation of landlord and tenant exists."[25] It is significant that the term " residential occupier " has been adopted in certain sections of the 1965 Act.[26]

The Rent Acts apply only to dwelling-houses, but their protection does not extend to every dwellinghouse or every residential occupier. Nor in the cases where they do apply, is there yet a uniform pattern of protection and control. The structure of what may be called in general terms rent control is complicated, particularly in matters of detail; and the 1965 Act, by superimposing a new tier of rent control with its own system of regulation of rents, has added greatly to the complication. It is essential at the outset to master the classification; to this end the remainder of this introductory section is devoted to a close examination of the premises and persons protected by the Acts, the several categories of rent control and the ways in which premises may be released from such control.

Premises Protected by the Acts. The premises or subjects of lettings must, to be entitled to protection, be such as are covered by the Rent Acts. This involves a consideration of whether (a) they are of the character or class of property intended by the Acts to be protected, and (b) the premises fall within what are generally referred to as the economic or financial limits set by the Acts for control or regulation. There is a presumption that the Acts apply to premises, and if the question arises in any proceedings whether the Acts do apply to a particular dwellinghouse, it is deemed to

---

[21] *Williams* v *Perry* [1924] 1 K.B. 936; *Phillips* v *Hallahan* [1925] 1 K.B. 756.
[22] *Infra*, p. 503.
[23] *Gidden* v *Mills* [1925] 2 K.B. 713; *Haskins* v *Lewis* [1931] 2 K.B. 1.
[24] *Rudler* v *Franks* [1947] K.B. 530.
[25] *Lloyd* v *Cook* [1929] 1 K.B. 103 at 135, *per* Greer, L.J.
[26] *E.g.*, ss. 30, 32; note in particular s. 32 (2) for an extension of the term " tenant ".

be one covered by the Acts unless the contrary is shown.[27] It is, however, always necessary to show that the premises are in fact a dwellinghouse.[28] The presumption is of limited scope. It only shows that at the date of the dispute the premises come within the Acts[29] It does not, for instance, operate in favour of old as against new control or of new as against old control[30] nor does it include a presumption that the house was let at a particular rent at any time.[31] The tenant, if he claims repayment of overpaid rent under new control, must show that old control was applicable.[32] It was provided[33] that, if the Acts become applicable to a dwellinghouse, they continue to apply whether or not the house continues to be one to which they apply (unless the house has lost its identity or become part of another subject or become a house to which the Acts do not apply). Though the meaning of this provision has been considered ambiguous,[34] it has been thought that it means that if premises have been within the Acts and become outside the Acts and then become premises to which the Acts apply, the Acts are applicable to the premises again.[35] The status of the house at the time the question is raised is a material factor. Thus, a previous business or furnished let is irrelevant if the house is at the time let unfurnished.[36] And a sublet is the material tenancy.[37] The Act, it is said, operates in rem, not in personam, on property and not on persons.[38] This rule is well settled,[39] and it may be much too late to question it, but the quality of being exempt from the provisions of the Acts does not apply until there is a tenancy invoking an occupying tenant.[40] " I must confess that I find these expressions more confusing than helpful nor do they seem to me to be really accurate descriptions of the operation of the Acts. Of course the Acts deal with houses below a certain value and the house must come within the class of dwellings to which the Acts apply. But it is a letting that brings them into effect ... It is not accurate to say the Acts are not concerned with persons, for instance assignees are not protected unless in certain limited cases."[41] So in Critchley v Clifford,[42] where there was a let of a farm and cottage and

---

[27] 1938 Act, s. 7 (1).
[28] Wright v Arnold [1947] K.B. 280.
[29] Stirling v Gilbert [1952] 2 All E.R. 153 at 158, per Jenkins, L.J.
[30] Stirling, supra.
[31] Ford v Langford [1949] 1 All E.R. 483.
[32] Keane v Clarke [1951] 2 K.B. 732.
[33] 1920 Act, s. 12 (6). See supra, p. 498.
[34] Prout v Hunter [1924] 2 K.B. 736 at 743, per Scrutton, L.J.
[35] Phillips v Hallahan [1925] 1 K.B. 756 at 760, per Greer, J.
[36] Ebner v Lascelles [1928] 2 K.B. 486; Leslie & Co. v Cumming [1926] 2 K.B. 417 at 424-5, per Mackinnon, J. The time may be the service of notice to quit. Alex. Cowan & Sons, infra.
[37] Prout, supra, at 741-2, per Bankes, L.J., at 745, per Sargant, L.J.
[38] Prout, supra, at 744, per Sargant, L.J.; Fraser, Rent Acts in Scotland, 2nd ed., 8; Megarry, Rent Acts, 9th ed., 17 et seq.; Halsbury, Laws of England, 3rd ed., XXIII p. 721.
[39] Critchley v Clifford [1962] 1 Q.B. 131 at 142, per Willmer, L.J.
[40] Critchley, supra, at 141, per Ormerod, L.J.
[41] Critchley, supra, at 148, per Danckwerts, L.J.
[42] [1962] 1 Q.B. 131; see infra, p. 593.

the farm was not within the Rent Acts but was covered by the Agricultural Holdings Acts and the cottage was sublet within the Rent Acts' limits and the subtenant was not employed on the farm, it was held that he was protected under the Rent Acts. The status of the cottage fell to be looked at after the material letting, which was that to the occupying tenant, and it was the subtenant's position when possession was claimed that had to be regarded.

(a) The subject of the let must, for the tenant to be entitled to the protection of the Rent Acts, be a dwellinghouse. The term " dwellinghouse " is defined, for the purposes of the Acts, as " a house let as a separate dwelling or a part of a house being a part so let ".[43] Rooms in a dwellinghouse subject to a separate letting wholly or partly as a dwelling are regarded as part of a dwellinghouse let as a separate dwelling.[44] There must be a letting. The occupier must be a tenant.[45] But for some purposes, e.g., the paying of an excess price for furniture as a condition of a grant of a lease, subjects may be a dwellinghouse within the Acts though they are not actually let at the time of the offence.[46] The subjects must be a house and be let as a dwelling, which is a separate dwelling. " Dwelling " means that the subjects are suitable for all the major activities of residential life such as sleeping, cooking and feeding, and are actually being so used.[47] The subjects may be one room.[48] The dwelling need not be a self-contained unit. Rooms let together need not be a physical unit, e.g., on one floor; they may be scattered, provided the dwelling is a separate dwelling, that is, provided it is let as a single letting of subjects to be occupied as a unit.[49] If, e.g., two flats are let as one and each would be within the Act but the whole is outside the Act, it is the whole that is regarded.[49] Two semi-detached houses originally let as a unit may be a separate dwelling though there is no means of intercommunication and one of the houses has been sublet by the tenant.[50]

(b) Shared Accommodation. Where part of the accommodation is shared, and that part amounts to essential living accommodation such as a kitchen, there is not a letting as a separate dwelling and thus not a protected tenancy.[51] The sharing of a bathroom and lavatory, however, does not prevent the premises being a separate dwelling.[52] If a

---

[43] 1933 Act, s. 16 (1), which amended 1920 Act, s. 12 (2). See Schaffer v Ross [1940] 1 K.B. 418, that " let as a separate dwelling " qualifies ' house' and ' part of a house '.
[44] 1920 Act, s. 12 (8).
[45] See supra.
[46] Minns v Moore [1950] 1 K.B. 241.
[47] Curl v Angelo [1948] 2 All E.R. 189; Wimbush v Cibulia [1949] 2 K.B. 564.
[48] Curl, supra.
[49] Langford Property Co. v Goldrich [1949] 1 K.B. 511.
[50] Whitty v Scott-Russell [1950] 2 K.B. 32.
[51] Neale v Del Soto [1945] K.B. 144, where two rooms were let and the kitchen was shared as well as the bathroom, lavatory, coalhouse and garage.
[52] Cole v Harris [1945] K.B. 474.

tenancy is of the whole subjects less the kitchen and the tenant is given a right to use it with the landlord, the tenant is not protected, but if the let is of the whole subjects and the tenant gives the landlord a right to use an essential living room such as the kitchen, the tenant is protected, for there is in that case a let of a separate dwelling.[53] And so with a subtenancy, if the tenant sublets and gives a right to use the kitchen, the tenant is protected but the subtenant is not protected apart from the 1949 Act. The Acts do not protect a tenant of part of a house who shares some of the living accommodation with the landlord or other persons. If then the tenant shares the kichen accommodation with a subtenant he is still protected,[54] but the subtenant is held not to be protected apart from the Act.[55] But while the questions as to whether there is a " sharing " and whether the accommodation shared is " living accommodation " remain as above stated, the law has been altered by the special provisions of the 1949 Act, which modifies the law, distinguishing between a sharing with the landlord and a sharing with another or others, and continues the protection of the Acts as modified by the 1949 Act to the tenant if he shares with someone other than the landlord, by providing that if the tenant has exclusive occupation of any accommodation but under the tenancy shares or has the use of other living accommodation with another or others than the landlord, the separate accommodation is deemed a dwelling-house to which the Acts apply.[56] While, however, it excludes the protection of the Acts if the tenant shares living accommodation with the landlord or the landlord and others, it gives such a tenant protection as if he were a tenant of a furnished letting under the 1943 Act by providing[57] that if the tenant has exclusive occupation of any accommodation but has under the tenancy a share of or the use of other accommodation with the landlord or with the landlord and others, then he is to be treated as if he were the tenant of a furnished letting under the 1943 Act even though the rent does not include payment for the use of furniture or for services. And in the case of a subtenant sharing with the tenant, the fact that the tenant has sublet part of the premises to a subtenant on terms that include the sharing of living accommodation by the subtenant, or by two or more subtenants, does not deprive the tenant of the protection of the Acts as against his landlord,[58] and the subtenant is protected against the tenant's landlord,[59] where the subtenant is otherwise not protected.[58] Where the subtenant shares with the tenant he is not protected, however, against the tenant's landlord if the landlord has obtained possession against the tenant.[59] Each case must be decided

[53] *Rogers* v *Hyde* [1951] 2 K.B. 923.
[54] *Baker* v *Turner* [1950] A.C. 401, where there was a sublet of a furnished bedroom and a share of the use of the kitchen.
[55] *Shackleton* v *Greenhalgh* [1951] 1 K.B. 725.
[56] s. 8.
[57] s. 7.
[58] s. 9.
[59] *Shackleton, supra.*

on its own facts in the light of the whole arrangements and the surrounding circumstances.[60] The tenant is protected where he shares living accommodation with persons other than the landlord from a term of the contract of tenancy which modifies or terminates his right to use shared living accommodation other than a provision for variation in the identity or increase in the number of persons entitled to use such accommodation; such a term is void.[61] The Sheriff under the Act[62] may, on the landlord's application, make such an order or otherwise as is thought just to terminate the tenant's right to use the whole or part of the shared accommodation other than living accommodation or to modify the tenant's right to use the whole or any part of the shared accommodation, living or non-living, by varying the persons or increasing the number of persons entitled to use the accommodation.

(c) Business Premises. The Rent Acts do not apply to a let of premises for business purposes[63] or for retail trade,[64] for the reason that the premises are not then let as a dwelling. If they are let as business premises they are not protected, even though they are in fact used as a dwellinghouse,[65] unless a new agreement in accordance with the change of use is made.[66] On the other hand, a temperance hotel[67] has been held to be a dwellinghouse, as also a guest-house where rooms are reserved for the tenant's occupation.[68] If part only of the subjects is used as a shop or office or for business, trade or professional purposes, then, in the case of controlled tenancies, the Acts still apply;[69] accordingly, where there is a let to the same tenant of a shop with living or residential accommodation above it, the tenant will be protected.[70] In the case of regulated tenancies, however, the fact that the Tenancy of Shops (Scotland) Acts 1949 and 1964 apply to a tenancy would appear to exclude the premises from the Rent Acts, and even a partial use as a shop would deprive the premises of the higher measure of protection afforded to dwellings.[71]

The residential accommodation need not be a substantial or the main part of the subjects.[72] The whole subjects, of course, must be in the

[60] *Goodrich* v *Paisner* [1957] A.C. 65.
[61] s. 8 (6).
[62] s. 8 (8).
[63] Such premises are, in England only, protected by Part II of the Landlord and Tenant Act, 1954.
[64] But see the Tenancy of Shops (Scotland) Acts 1949 and 1964, discussed *infra*, Ch. XXI.
[65] *Williams* v *Perry* [1924] 1 K.B. 736; *Barrett* v *Hardy Bros.* [1925] 2 K.B. 220 at 227, *per* Scrutton, L.J.; *Macmillan* v *Rees* (1946) 62 T.L.R. 331.
[66] *Levermore* v *Jobey* [1956] 2 All E.R. 362.
[67] *Falconer* v *Chisholm's Trs.*, 1925 S.C. 742.
[68] *Colls* v *Parnham* [1922] 1 K.B. 325; *Vickery, infra.*
[69] 1920 Act, s. 12 (2), *proviso* (ii); 1939 Act, s. 3 (3).
[70] *Greig* v *Francis & Campion* (1922) 38 T.L.R. 519.
[71] This seems to be the effect of s. 1 (3) of the 1965 Act, taken with Schedule 1, para. 1 (1), which omits *proviso* (ii) of s. 12 (2) of the 1920 Act for the purpose of determining whether a tenancy is a regulated tenancy.
[72] *Vickery* v *Martin* [1944] K.B. 679.

tenant's exclusive occupation[73] and he must use the residential part as his home.[74] If premises are let for residence and the tenant sublets for business purposes, the Acts cease any longer to apply: the premises are no longer protected.[75] If the whole subjects are let and adapted for business purposes, residence in them will not make them a dwellinghouse,[76] in the absence of a new contract of tenancy or a modification of the existing one.[76] If the business premises are in fact and in occupation completely separate from the residential part so that they are held not to be or form part of the house, notwithstanding that they are let in the one let at one rent, forming a complex unit of location, they will not be protected, as in a case where a house and a room used as and constructed for a shop having separate entrances but internal communication were let in one lease and at one rent, the Court pointing out that each could be separately let.[77]

The test where part is used for business purposes, and no purpose is stated in the lease, whether the subjects are a dwellinghouse is not whether the business part is unsubstantial or the residential accommodation is a substantial part of the whole[78] nor, unless in marginal cases, the main or predominant use of the premises.[77] It is a question of the facts of the particular case.[78] Is it a dwellinghouse?[79] The considerations are different where the issue is under later parts of the sub-section, in which event the predominant use or letting is material.[79] So where there is a let of composite subjects, if in substance the let is one of business premises to which the dwellinghouse is a mere adjunct, then the Acts do not apply.[80] The nature and character of the subjects have to be considered, and the mere fact of the presence of a dwellinghouse in a composite let is not sufficient.[81] The familiar example is the caretaker's house.[82] These principles were applied in two Scottish cases. Where there was a let of premises to a coal merchant, consisting of a dwellinghouse where he and his family lived and a coal ree, garage, etc. for his business, the area of the house being comparatively small, it was held that the dominant purpose of the let was to carry on the business of a coal merchant and not the provision of a dwellinghouse.[83] And where a

---

[73] *Gidden* v *Mills* [1925] 2 K.B. 713; *Haskins* v *Lewis* [1931] 2 K.B. 1, where it was said that possession of the whole should have been given in *Gidden*.
[74] *Vickery, supra.*
[75] *Gidden, supra; Haskins, supra.*
[76] *Court* v *Robinson* [1951] 2 K.B. 60; *Macmillan & Co.* v *Ross* (1946) 62 T.L.R. 331.
[77] *Whiteley* v *Wilson* [1953] 1 Q.B. 77. This is on the 1939 Act, s. 3 (3), first part.
[78] *Vickery, supra,* where the Court approved at 682 and 684, *per* Lord Greene, M.R., *Epsom Grand Stand Association (infra)* and *Hicks* v *Snook* (1928) 93 J.P. 55.
[79] *Whiteley, supra,* at 83, *per* Lord Evershed, M.R.
[80] *Cargill* v *Phillips,* 1951 S.C. 67; *Pender* v *Reid,* 1948 S.C. 381. These cases were based really on s. 3 (3) second part, *infra. Pender* was followed in *Feyereisel* v *Turnidge* [1952] 2 Q.B. 29.
[81] *Pender, supra,* at 384-5, *per* L.J.C. Thomson.
[82] *Cargill, supra,* at 72, *per* Lord Patrick.
[83] *Pender, supra.*

dwellinghouse, stable, byre and cartshed formerly in a dairyman's occupation were let, the subjects to be used for no other purposes, the area of the house being much smaller than that of the rest, and the tenant converted with the landlord's consent an outhouse into a butcher's shop and store and carried on business for thirty years, later transferring the business to his son but continuing to live there, it was held,[84] on a consideration of the character of the premises and the area respectively occupied by the house and the remainder, the history of the subjects, the terms of the lease and the later agreement and the tenant's actings, that the primary purpose of the letting was business.

Where the original user is altered in a sublet, as in a let unfurnished and a subletting furnished, or a let of a house and a subletting of it for business purposes, then as between the original landlord and the tenant it is the letting to the occupying tenant that must be regarded.[85] The character of the premises can, of course, be changed by agreement, express or implied, of landlord and tenant.[86] If there is a stipulation by the tenant that he will not use the subjects or any part of them except as a shop for a particular business, this does not generally prevent the tenant living in the subjects if part is adapted for that purpose.[87] A stipulation not to use the subjects other than as a hotel or boarding-house is not breached by the tenant sleeping in the premises.[88] But if there is a breach of a lease or agreement, the use in the breach will not alter the character of the premises,[89] unless it can be said that in face of clear and unambiguous contrary use the landlord has waived the breach.[90]

In considering whether premises are a dwelling-house or otherwise the lease or agreement must, in the first place, be considered, and in construing it the Court must have regard to the surrounding circumstances with reference to which it was entered into, including the nature of the subject matter of the letting; the actual use is irrelevant in the absence of a new agreement.[91] In the absence of any written lease or agreement, or where the lease or agreement is inconclusive in its terms, the Court must examine the purposes for which the subjects are in fact being used.[92] And so on a review of a composite let of a house and shop, a shop with a house above and behind it, it was held,[93] proceeding on the nature and character of the subjects, the terms of the lease and the use made of the premises, that the letting was one for professional purposes

---

[84] Cargill, supra.
[85] Prout v Hunter [1924] 2 K.B. 736; Gidden, supra; Haskins, supra.
[86] Williams v Perry, supra.
[87] R. v Brighton Area Rent Tribunal [1954] 1 Q.B. 446.
[88] Vickery, supra; Kitchen's Tr. v Madders [1950] Ch. 134. See Court v Robinson, supra.
[89] Epsom Grand Stand Assoc. v Clarke (1919) 35 T.L.R. 525 at 526, per Bankes, L.J.
[90] Hyman v Steward (1925) 41 T.L.R. 501; Court, supra.
[91] Levermore v Jobey [1956] 2 All E.R. 362, at 364, 365, per Jenkins, L.J.
[92] Alex. Cowan & Sons v Acton, 1952 S.C. 73; Levermore, supra, at 364. See also McClymont's Trs. v Ross, 1929 S.C. 585 at 589, per L.P. Clyde.
[93] Alex. Cowan & Sons, supra.

and not as a dwellinghouse. The Court differed as to the point of time at which the character of the premises fell to be considered.[94]

Under the Reserve and Auxiliary Forces (Protection of Civil Interests) Act 1951[95] a serviceman can apply for renewal of the tenancy of business premises to the Sheriff, who can renew for up to four months beyond expiry of the period of service.

Premises Excluded. Certain categories of dwellinghouse which would otherwise be covered by the Acts are expressly excluded from them by statutory provision. The exclusion in these cases enumerated below is a general one, from control and regulation alike.[96]

(a) Furnished Lettings. Where a dwelling-house is *bona fide* let at a rent which includes payments in respect of board, attendance or use of furniture, that house is, provided that the amount of rent attributable to the attendance or use of furniture forms " a substantial portion " of the whole rent, classed as a furnished house[97] and now dealt with separately under its own legislation.[98]

(b) Licensed Premises, that is, any dwellinghouse which consists of or comprises premises licensed for the sale of intoxicating liquor for consumption on the premises.[99]

(c) Houses let with land or other premises. Here there is a distinction between old and new control, the new control position applicable to regulated tenancies. In the case of old control, if a house is let together with land or premises and if the land or other premises let separately would have a rateable value of a quarter or more of the rateable value of the house, then the whole subjects are not protected under old control,[1] but if the rateable value would be less than a quarter, the land or other premises are regarded as part of the house.[1] Save in such a case the Acts do not apply to a house let with land other than its site.[1] The rateable value is the yearly value in the Valuation Roll for the year ending 15th May 1915, or, if the house was first assessed thereafter, the rateable value at which it was first assessed.[2] The house includes its site and probably a garden and outbuildings.[3] In the case of new control,[4] if a

---

[94] L.J.C. Thomson took, without taking it as necessarily the crucial date, the time of service of the notice to quit, Lord Patrick the date of expiry of the notice, being that of termination of the contractual tenancy.
[95] ss. 38, 39.
[96] For the application of these exclusions to regulated tenancies, see 1965 Act, s. 1 (2).
[97] 1920 Act, s. 12 (2), *proviso* (i); 1939 Act, s. 3 (2).
[98] *Infra*, pp. 608 *et seq.*
[99] 1933 Act, s. 1 (3); 1920 Act, s. 12 (2), *proviso* (ii); the latter excluded only " off " licence premises; 1939 Act, s. 3 (2) (a); 1965 Act, Schedule I, Part I, para. 2.
[1] 1920 Act, s. 12 (2), *proviso* (iii).
[2] 1920 Act, ss. 12 (1) (e), 18 (1) (a). Where land is rated only after the house, see *Davies* v *Gilbert* [1955] 1 All E.R. 415.
[3] *Wellersley* v *White* [1921] 2 K.B. 204 at 210, *per* Lush, J.
[4] The 1939 Act alone applies here: 1939 Act, s. 3 (1), Schedule First.

house is let with land or other premises consisting of agricultural land[5] of more than two acres in extent the subjects are excluded.[6] The land or premises are thus, unless it or they so consist, treated as part of the house;[6] but, save in such a case, new control does not apply to a dwellinghouse let together with land other than its site.[6] Under the 1939 Act, it will be noted, the rateable value formula disappears.[7] The house includes the site and probably a garden and outbuildings.[8] One let[9] or one rent are not necessary for a letting together if the subjects are held together at the material time, and the subjects need not be contiguous or adjacent or related in any way.[10] So whether they are " let together " is a question of the facts.[9] The land or premises must be an adjunct to the house: if the house is an adjunct only to the land or the premises as where it is a mere adjunct to business premises, where the let is in substance one of business premises, the dominant purpose being business, the house is not protected.[11] The question is, of course, a different one from the question whether, where part of a single subject or structure is used as living accommodation, the subject is a dwellinghouse, for where there is no issue of " let with " or dominant purpose or use, different considerations apply.

(d) Crown property. A tenant is not protected if the landlord is the Crown, as the Acts do not expressly refer to the Crown.[12] The Crown in this context includes the Crown's agents such as a government department[13] or a Territorial Army Association,[14] but not the British Transport Commission,[15] for in terms of the Transport Act 1947, including the extent of ministerial control thereunder, it is not a servant or agent of the Crown but its own master, a public authority or statutory corporation but not a government department, having none of the privileges or immunities of the Crown, its servants not civil servants, its property not that of the Crown. A subtenant of a Crown tenant was also held not to be protected as the Acts operate in rem;[16] but the protection of the Acts

---

[5] 1939 Act, s. 8 (c): " land used for agricultural or pastoral purposes only or as woodlands, market gardens, orchards, allotments or allotment gardens and any lands exceeding one-quarter of an acre used for the purpose of poultry farming ", but not " any land occupied together with a house as a park, garden or pleasure ground or any land kept or preserved mainly or exclusively for sporting purposes ".

[6] Ibid., s. 3 (3), In Pender, supra, L.J.C. Thomson said the subsection was a telescoped and revised version of two provisos in s. 12 (2) of the 1920 Act and was not easy to construe.

[7] Pender, supra, at 384, per L.J.C. Thomson.

[8] Pender, supra, at 391, per Lord Mackay.

[9] Mann v Merrill [1945] 1 All E.R. 708.

[10] Falconer v Chisholm's Trs., 1925 S.C. 742.

[11] Feyereisel v Turnidge [1952] 2 Q.B. 29; Pender, supra; Cargill, supra.

[12] Wirral Estates v Shaw [1932] 2 K.B. 247.

[13] Tamlin v Hannaford [1950] 1 K.B. 18.

[14] London County Territorial and Auxiliary Forces Association v Nichols [1949] 1 K.B. 35.

[15] Tamlin, supra. Now the British Railways Board: Transport Act 1962.

[16] Rudler v Franks [1947] K.B. 530; Clark v Downes (1931) 145 L.T. 20.

has now by statute[17] been given as from 1st September 1952 to such subtenants,[18] but not to tenants.[19] If an order or judgment made before that date had not been executed, the tenant could apply to the Court to rescind it and the Court could make such rescission or variation as was necessary to carry out the statutory provision[20] It should be noted, however, that the 1965 Act's provision against eviction without due process of law is expressly made binding on the Crown.[21]

(e) Houses in an agricultural holding in England. A dwellinghouse comprised in an agricultural holding and occupied by the person responsible for control, whether as tenant, or as servant or agent of the tenant, of the farming of the holding is not in England included within the scope or protection of the Acts.[22] Where part of such subjects is sublet the subtenant is also not protected[23] on the principle that the Acts do not apply to subjects let which are only a part of premises that are not within the Acts.[24] This exemption of houses in agricultural holdings does not, however, apply in Scotland.

(f) Lettings at a rent less than two-thirds of the rateable value. The Acts were intended to apply only where there were lettings at an economic rent. The Acts do not apply to that rent or tenancy if the rent payable in respect of any tenancy is less than two-thirds of the rateable value appropriate to the form of control which would otherwise apply, but apply to the house as if no such tenancy existed or had ever existed.[25] A house let at no rent at all is covered by this exception.[26] The tenant is not protected in possession for he is not a tenant under the Acts.[27] Rent means the whole rent including rates if these are to be paid by the tenant or are included in the rent actually paid to the landlord.[28] If it is in kind, however, by way of goods and services and this is quantified by the parties in money value, this is the rent.[29] Where the rent in the lease is under two-thirds but a lump sum paid as consideration for the grant of the lease falls to be treated as commuted rent and added to the rent in the lease and the effect is to make the rent more than two-thirds of the rateable value, the exception does not apply and the tenancy is controlled.[30] The rent payable when exemption is sought, whatever date is

17 Crown Lessees (Protection of Subtenants) Act 1952.
18 Ibid., s. 1 (1).
19 Ibid., s. 1 (2).
20 Ibid., s. 2 (4).
21 Ibid., s. 36.
22 Agricultural Holdings Act 1948, s. 95, Schedule Seventh.
23 Sherwood v Moody [1952] 1 All E.R. 389.
24 Cow v Casey [1949] 1 K.B. 474.
25 1920 Act, s. 12 (7); 1965 Act, Schedule 1, para. 1 (3). Rateable value is annual value in the Valuation Roll—1920 Act, s. 18 (1) (a). It has been held that entry in the Valuation Roll is conclusive as to whether a dwelling house is subject to the Acts: W. C. Galbraith & Jones v Allan (1963) 79 Sh. Ct. Rep. 169.
26 Ecclesiastical Commissioners v Hilder (1920) 36 T.L.R. 771.
27 Bracey v Pales [1927] 1 K.B. 818.
28 Mackworth v Hellard [1921] 2 K.B. 755.
29 Montague v Browning [1954] 2 All E.R. 601 at 604, per Denning, L.J.
30 Samrose Props. v Gibbard [1958] 1 All E.R. 502.

regarded as material, is the material rent.[31] If the rent is variable the tenancy may at times be protected when the rent rises above the two-thirds limit; it will be protected when the rent rises[32] and not protected when it falls.[33] In a let at a progressive rent the relevant rent is not that in fact payable at the material date but the rent provided for under the tenancy current at that date.[34] The tenancy is exempt here and not the premises,[35] so that any new letting of the premises at an economic rent will be protected by the Acts.[35] A sublet above the two-thirds limit will be protected even if the tenant who has granted it is exempted by his rent being less than two-thirds. If a dwelling is provided or improved with the aid of an improvement grant and is at a time when certain statutory conditions must be observed let to someone in consequence of his employment by the landlord, and the rent is less than two-thirds, the landlord is nevertheless entitled to possession only in accordance with the Rent Acts.[36] On the termination of the contractual period of such a tenancy the landlord is free to raise the rent, and so bring the premises within the ambit of the Acts as a regulated tenancy. The extent to which the rent may be raised depends upon whether the dwellinghouse was within the previous three years the subject of another regulated tenancy;[37] if this is the case, the previous rent limit will apply, but otherwise, subject to the rent officer's review, the landlord is free to set his own figure.[38]

(g) Letting by exempted authorities. This at one time meant local authority houses, that is any dwellinghouse being or forming part of a house or dwelling in respect of which the local authority had under the Housing Acts,[39] for the purpose of providing housing accommodation, to keep a housing revenue account and which had not been sold or disposed of;[40] such houses were exempted from new control. And the exemption extended to some houses, e.g., under the Housing (Rural Workers) Act 1926, of which the local authority was not landlord. It was held that where a tenant of a house under the Rent Acts voluntarily removed from it as it was considered by the local authority to be overcrowded under the Housing Acts and became a tenant of a local authority

---

[31] J. & F. Stone Lighting & Radio v Levitt [1947] A.C. 209 at 215, per Lord Thankerton, at 217-8, per Lord Porter.
[32] Mackworth, supra.
[33] J. & F. Stone, supra.
[34] Woozley v Woodall Smith [1950] 1 K.B. 325, where there was a let at a progressive rent and the rent on 1st September 1939 was less than two thirds but the maximum was more than that and it was held that the tenancy came within the Act, for in cases of progressive rent the maximum is the standard rent under the 1920 Act, s. 12 (1) (a) and, reading that as amended by the 1939 Act, Schedule First, the rent payable under the lease or at which the property was let on 1st September 1939 was the standard rent and so that must be the maximum rent.
[35] Waller & Son v Thomas [1921] 1 K.B. 541.
[36] Housing (Scotland) Act 1950, s. 120.
[37] 1965 Act, s. 3 (3).
[38] See infra, p. 552.
[39] Housing (Scotland) Act 1935, s. 39, later, Housing (Scotland) Act 1950, s. 137. See also Housing (Scotland) Act 1925, Part III.
[40] 1939 Act, ss. 3 (2) (c) and 8 (d).

house, which was exempt from the Rent Acts, he could not claim the
" security of tenure " provided for by the Housing Acts as this operated
only if there had been eviction by Order of Court, even if it could be held
to include equivalent protection to that of the Rent Acts.[41] Though old
control was not in law excluded, it was in fact excluded because the
majority of such houses had been erected after 2nd April 1919 and, thus,
were in any event as new houses excluded from old control.[42] Under the
1954 Act[43] and thus also under the 1965 Act,[44] however, all local
authority houses are excluded from the Rent Acts.

Houses of five classes of authorities are now comprised in this
exception. First, local authorities, joint board or joint committees under
the Local Government (Scotland) Act 1947 or the common good of a
burgh or any trust under the control of a local authority;[45] second,
development corporations established under statutory authority (New
Towns Act 1946);[46] third, housing associations in relation to which
certain requirements are fulfilled;[47] fourth, Scottish Special Housing
Association or any housing trust in existence on 13th November 1953 or
any authorised society within the Housing Act 1914;[48] the executive
councils under the National Health Service (Scotland) Act 1947.[49]
Tenancies, including subtenancies, where the landlord is one of such
authorities, are not protected and are not deemed to be the interests of
tenants of dwellinghouses to which control applies.[50]

The present exemption is wider than the former one of local
authorities only, for under the former exemption it was held that
subtenants were not protected against their own landlord,[51] whereas under
the 1954 Act there are provisions for extending the protection to subtenants, in that, the exemption now applying to the tenancy and not to
the house, subtenants though not protected against the local authority
where the tenancy comes to an end are still protected against their own
landlord[52] In the case of servicemen the protection of the Rent Acts
still applies though the house is one of the five classes of authority
houses.[53]

(h) Letting to servicemen. A certain protection is given to persons
serving, whether voluntarily or by call-up, otherwise than as regulars

[41] Glasgow Corporation v Bruce, 1942 S.C. 81.
[42] 1920 Act, s. 12 (9).
[43] This is by s. 25 (1), repealing the 1939 Act, s. 3 (2) (c), 8 (d).
[44] 1965 Act, s. 1 (2).
[45] 1954 Act, s. 25 (1) (a).
[46] Ibid., s. 25 (1) (b).
[47] Ibid., s. 25 (1) (c). The conditions are in s. 25 (2), as amended by 1957 Act,
Schedule Sixth, para. 32.
[48] Ibid., s. 25 (1) (d).
[49] Ibid., s. 25 (1) (e).
[50] Ibid., s. 25 (1).
[51] Percy G. Moore v Stretch [1951] 1 All E.R. 228.
[52] 1954 Act, s. 25 (5).
[53] Ibid., s. 25 (4).

in the Armed Forces of the Crown in regard to their families' residences where the Acts would not otherwise apply. This is by special statute.[54] The object is to protect the rights and interests of such men and their dependants while absent from home on service in their rented family homes. The provisions are too detailed to discuss here and may be found treated of in the undernoted authorities.[55] The general effect, however, is to protect up to four months after the period of service and to allow eviction or possession by the landlord only in certain exceptional circumstances. From the provisions only two premises are excluded—dwelling houses consisting of or comprising premises licensed for the sale of intoxicating liquor for consumption on the premises, and premises *bona fide* let at a rent that includes payment for board.

(i) *Formerly Exempted or Decontrolled Premises.* At one time houses of which the landlord had obtained actual possession after 31st July 1923[56] and houses let for over two years[57] were exempted, but these exemptions were repealed in 1938 and 1939.[58] Under the 1933 Act decontrol by actual possession on the grant of a lease was limited after 18th July 1933 to houses rented between £26. 5. 0. and £45;[59] houses rented under £26. 5. 0. decontrolled before that date and let at that date continued to be decontrolled only if there was registration of the house as decontrolled with the local authority.[60] A failure by the landlord to register a house as decontrolled resulted in the house still being controlled;[61] but an error in a date in the application for registration did not affect the application.[62] Under the 1938 Act, however, after 28th May 1938 houses rented between £26. 5. 0. and £35 (the new limit under that Act) were no longer decontrolled by actual possession or the grant of a lease[63] but if at that date let and the landlord claimed they were already decontrolled at that date, he had to register the house with the local authority as decontrolled.[64] The system of decontrol by registration ended in 1939.[65] And houses of which the rent did not exceed 3/- a week and of which the landlord had had possession were exempted also from the landlord's right to possession,[66] but this again was repealed in 1939.[67]

---

[54] Reserve and Auxiliary Forces (Restriction of Civil Interests) Act 1951, ss. 14, 16-20, 23, 25, as amended by Rent Act 1957, s. 26 (3), Schedule Eighth, Part II.
[55] Halsbury, *Laws of England*, 3rd ed., XXIII, pp. 761 *et seq.*; Megarry, *op. cit.*, 9th ed., p. 12.
[56] 1923 Act, s. 2 (1).
[57] 1923 Act, s. 2 (2); 1925 Act, s. 1 (3) (b).
[58] Partly in 1938, s. 3 (1), and wholly in 1939 Act, ss. 2, 9 (3), Schedule Second.
[59] 1933 Act, s. 2 (1).
[60] *Ibid.,* s 2 (2).
[61] *Tibber* v *Upcott* [1940] 1 K.B. 618.
[62] *Holt* v *Dawson* [1940] 1 K.B. 46.
[63] s. 3 (1).
[64] s. 4 (1).
[65] 1939 Act, s. 9 (3), Schedule Second.
[66] 1933 Act, s. 5.
[67] 1939 Act, s. 5.

And houses not let immediately before 18th July 1933[68] or 26th May 1938[69] were also decontrolled: this decontrol also ended in 1939.[70]

Controlled and Regulated Tenancies. Since the 1965 Act it has become necessary to distinguish between lettings of dwellinghouses which were subject to rent control before the commencement date of that Act, known as " controlled tenancies ", and those of dwellinghouses which became subject to rent regulation by virtue of that Act. This distinction is fundamental to the existing legislation, because the position of the new category of regulated tenancy is in many respects different, both as regards rent control and security of tenure, from that of the controlled tenancy, which was unaltered by the 1965 Act. Controlled tenancies in their turn must be distinguished according to whether they were subject to control before the commencement date of the 1939 Act, that is as " old control " houses, or became controlled under the provisions of the 1939 Act as " new control " houses. These categories are the result of the see-saw of rent control, the reimposition of restrictions after periods of gradual decontrol. As will be shown later, it is foreseeable that the category of controlled tenancies will vanish altogether, and that all lettings of houses below the current economic limit will be subject to the Rent Acts and the 1965 Act as regulated tenancies.

(a) " Old control " houses are those which were still subject to the Rent Acts immediately before 2nd September 1939, the commencement date of the 1939 Act. Under the 1920 Act[71] it had been provided that the Acts were to apply to a letting of a dwellinghouse where the annual amount of the standard rent or the rateable value of the house did not exceed £90 per annum.[72] The expression " standard rent " meant[73] the rent at which the house was let at 3rd August 1914, or where the house was not let on that date the rent at which it was last let before that date, or where the house was first let after 3rd August 1914 the rent at which it was first let. The expression " rateable value " meant[74] the yearly value in the valuation roll for the year ending 15th May 1915, or if first assessed thereafter the value at which it was first assessed. The 1923 Act[75] introduced a system of creeping decontrol, houses becoming decontrolled on the landlord's subsequently coming into actual possession or granting a lease to the sitting tenant for not less than two years. The 1933 Act reduced the ceiling for control, or the economic limit as it is called, to £45, that is as from 28th November 1933 where the recoverable rent (the maximum rent which under the Acts could be recovered from the tenant) or the rateable value on 16th May 1931 did not exceed £45,

---

[68] 1933 Act, s. 1 (2).
[69] 1938 Act, s. 2 (1).
[70] 1939 Act, ss. 3, 9 (3), Schedule Second.
[71] s. 12 (1) (2).
[72] For London the figure was £105.
[73] s. 12 (1) (a).
[74] s. 12 (1) (c), 18 (1) (a).
[75] s. 2.

and discontinued the 1923 Act's system of decontrol for houses rated at
£26. 5. 0. or under. The economic limit was further reduced by the 1938
Act, houses becoming decontrolled as from 28th November 1938 where
the rateable value on 16th May 1931 exceeded £35; the 1938 Act
put an end, however, to the 1923 Act's system of creeping decontrol.
Thus, it was the figure of £35 which was finally established as the
economic limit for rent control before the emergence of the new level
and slightly altered pattern of "new control". A house could be
controlled immediately before 2nd September 1939, and, thus, an "old
control" house, only if (a) its rateable value at 16th May 1931 did not
exceed £35; (b) it had not been decontrolled under the 1923 Act, before
2nd September 1939; (c) it had been built before 2nd April 1919;[76] and
(d) it had not been reconstructed since 1919 by being converted into two
or more separate and self-contained flats.[76]

(b) The 1939 Act[77] ended all forms of decontrol as from 2nd
September 1939, and by raising the economic limit for Scotland once
more to £90[78] brought many new houses under rent control and recontrolled many which had formerly been released from control. These
houses, known as "new control" houses, were in a slightly different
position as regards rent control;[79] "old control" houses were unaffected.
There the position rested until 1954, when in altered political and
economic circumstances decontrol was again introduced. The 1954 Act
decontrolled, as well as lettings by local authorities and certain other
public bodies,[80] houses consisting of premises erected after 30th August
1954, or produced after that date by the conversion into separate and
self-contained dwellings of other premises with or without the addition
of new premises,[81] unless the conversion or the erection had been effected
with the aid of an improvement grant; the relevant date was the date of
the completion, not of the commencement, of the work. A more sweeping
decontrol was introduced by the 1957 Act, reducing the economic limit
from £90 to £40;[82] as from 6th July 1957 any dwellinghouse the rateable
value of which exceeded £40 on 7th November 1956 was at once, subject
to certain transitional provisions,[83] freed from control. In addition a
measure of "creeping decontrol" was reintroduced, in that tenancies
created by leases or agreements coming into operation on or after 6th
July 1957 were, irrespective of the 1956 rateable value, to be outside
control.[84] Provision was also made for the control of houses inside the
limit by an order of the Secretary of State reducing the economic limit
to a new level, but this facility, never in fact made use of, was removed

[76] 1920 Act, s. 12 (9).
[77] s. 3 (1), 8 (a).
[78] For London the figure was £100, and for elsewhere in England and Wales, £75.
[79] See *infra*, p. 540.
[80] See *supra*, p. 510.
[81] s. 27.
[82] s. 11 (1); £40 for London, £30 for elsewhere in England and Wales.
[83] See *infra*, p. 527.
[84] s. 11 (2).

33

and replaced by the 1965 Act.[85] Two sets of tenancy were excluded from the Act's decontrol provisions: the case where the person to whom the new tenancy was granted was immediately before the grant the tenant under a controlled tenancy of the same premises,[86] and if the tenancy ends by reason of the landlord obtaining possession on grounds of over-crowding under the Housing (Scotland) Acts 1950[87] or the 1954 Act[88] the decontrol provisions do not apply to the first subsequent tenancy of the whole or any part of the premises which are not decontrolled by having a new tenant.[89]

Thus, at the commencement date of the 1965 Act only tenancies of the following premises were still subject to control: (a) where the dwelling-house had not been erected or produced by conversion after 30th August 1954; (b) where the rateable value at 7th November 1956 did not exceed £40; and (c) where the lease had come into operation before 6th July 1957.

(c) The 1965 Act reimposed the security of tenure provisions of the Rent Acts and introduced rent regulation to all those tenancies of dwelling-houses whose rateable value does not exceed £200[90] which would have been controlled tenancies but for one of the following reasons only:[91]

    (i)   that the dwellinghouse was erected or produced by conversion after 30th August, 1954; or

    (ii) that the 1956 rateable value exceeded the limit of £40 set for decontrol by the 1957 Act; or

    (iii) that the tenancy was created by a lease or agreement coming into operation at or after 6th July, 1957.

Tenancies covered by the 1965 Act are termed "regulated tenancies",[92] while controlled tenancies were left unaffected by the new category.[93] The broad effect of the 1965 Act was thus to catch in the fire of rent regulation those tenancies which had escaped from the frying pan of control. As controlled tenancies become entitled to decontrol by reason of the 1957 Act[94] they are automatically[95] converted into regulated tenancies as the pool into which lettings fall as they escape control. A similar translation occurs on the succession of the "second successor" to the "first successor".[96] Provision is also made in the 1965 Act[97] for a more sweeping extension of the system of rent regulation to those tenancies which will remain controlled under the old system. This is to

[85] s. 11 (3); see 1965 Act, s. 11, and *infra*, p. 527.
[86] s. 11 (2), *proviso*.
[87] 1950 Act, s. 35.
[88] 1954 Act, s. 11.
[89] s. 11 (6).
[90] For Greater London the figure is £400.
[91] 1965 Act, s. 1 (1), (2).
[92] s. 1 (4).
[93] s. 1 (7).
[94] s. 11 (2), which was not repealed by the 1965 Act.
[95] This is the effect of s. 1 (2) (c).
[96] Under s. 13; see *infra*, p. 596.
[97] s. 11. See *infra*, p. 528.

be effected in due course by means of a release from control order issued by the Secretary of State, similar to that formerly available for a different reason under the 1957 Act; again, as the rateable value limit of control is lowered, so the tenancies released from control become regulated tenancies. It is by this method that the category of controlled tenancy may before long be eliminated.

The rateable value to which regard must be had for the purposes of the 1965 Act's economic limit of £200 is the figure shown in the valuation roll as at 23rd March 1965, that is, the 1964 rateable value.[98] Where the figure shown was subsequently altered, by reason of an appeal to the valuation committee for instance, and the alteration takes effect from a date not later than 23rd March 1965 it is the altered figure that is taken into account.[99] In the case of houses first assessed after 23rd March 1965, the rateable value taken is the value at which it was first assessed.[1] Where the premises form only part of the lands and heritages shown on the roll, the rateable value of the premises is taken to be such proportion of the rateable value of those lands and heritages as may be agreed as being a proper apportionment, or as may in the event of dispute be decided by the Sheriff, whose decision is final.[2]

Contractual and Statutory Tenancies. From the date when a contractual tenancy ends as at the expiry of a notice to quit, the former tenant is either a person with no right to occupy the premises or he is a statutory tenant.[3] A contractual tenancy is one where no notice to quit or remove or statutory notice of increase of rent has been given or where such a notice has been given and a new contract has been entered into. A contractual tenant is thus a person whose possession is controlled and determined by the lease or tenancy agreement, subject, however, to the restrictions contained in the Acts. A tenant is thus a contractual tenant and holds under a contractual tenancy if he holds his house under a lease that is current or one that has been followed by tacit relocation. A change of tenant, unless on the death of a former tenant, since the last increase, means a new agreement or contract and then, unless the tenancy is made statutory by notice to remove or of increase of rent to the new tenant, the tenancy is again contractual. No increase in rent may be brought into effect until after the determination of the current let. The landlord cannot increase the rent while the tenancy is contractual even to the extent of the permitted increases, but the contractual tenant can have the rent reduced to the sum authorised by the Acts. Such a reduction or an apportionment does not avoid the lease or make the tenant a statutory tenant.[4] Notice

[98] s. 43 (1), (3).
[99] s. 43 (4).
[1] See 1920 Act, s. 12 (1) (e).
[2] s. 43 (1) (a), (2).
[3] *Alex. Cowan & Sons* v *Acton*, 1952 S.C. 73, at 80, *per* Lord Patrick.
[4] *Fumasoli* v *Comyn and Fish* (1924) 132 L.T. 490.

of an intended increase (which operates as a notice to quit) must be given
at the time when it would be competent to serve a notice to remove or
quit and the increased rent comes into effect at the date when but for the
Acts the tenant would have had to remove.[5] A statutory tenancy is one
where notice to quit or notice of increase of rent has been given to the
tenant or where the tenant has died and his widow or a member of his
family has succeeded to the tenancy since the house was first subject to
the Acts and no new contract has been entered into.[6] A statutory tenant
(a term which prior to the 1954 Act was only given as a marginal heading
to a section[7] of the 1920 Act) is defined in the 1954 Act[8] as a tenant, as
defined by the 1920 Act,[9] " who retains possession by virtue of the Rent
Acts and not as being entitled to a tenancy ". The statutory tenant, then,
is one whose possession or occupation depends wholly upon the Acts,
apart from which he has no right to be there; he holds his house under a
statutory tenancy by virtue of the Acts if he is a tenant on whom notice
to quit has been served[10] or one who holds his house by virtue of the
statutory succession provisions. No new notice to remove is necessary as
a condition of recovering possession[11] or of increasing the rent.[12] Where
then a contractual tenancy is converted into a statutory tenancy by notice
to quit or notice of intention to increase the rent, the landlord can recover
possession if the court is satisfied that he is entitled to get possession and
can increase the rent to a certain amount. Where a notice to quit has
been served by the landlord, acceptance of rent for no more than three
months from the expiry of the notice is not to be deemed to prejudice any
right of possession.[13] Acceptance of rent for over three months does not
impliedly make a new notice necessary;[14] it may bar an action of removal[15]
but does not imply a new contract[16]

The distinction between a contractual and a statutory tenancy is of
importance, in the case of regulated tenancies, before a rent for the
dwellinghouse has been registered, with regard to the limit on recoverable
rent and the way that increases may be made.[17] In addition, certain
results flow from a statutory tenancy, some of which are statutory, others
derived from case-law. Neither Parliament nor the draftsmen of the
Acts appear to have thought out the nature of the rights they were giving

---

[5] 1920 Act, s. 3 (1); Rent Restrictions (Notices of Increase) Act 1923, s. 1 (1),
   following *Kerr* v *Bryde*, 1923 S.C. (H.L.) 12.
[6] *Shuter* v *Hersch* [1922] 1 K.B. 438; *Felce* v *Hill* (1923) 92 L.J. K.B. 974; *Wolff* v
   Smith [1923] 2 Ch. 393.
[7] s. 15.
[8] s. 39 (1).
[9] s. 12 (1) (g).
[10] See *supra* that this operates as a notice to quit.
[11] 1920 Act, s. 15 (1); *Aston* v *Smith* [1924] 2 K.B. 143.
[12] *Shuter, supra.*
[13] 1920 Act, s. 16 (3). See *Davies* v *Bristow* [1920] 3 K.B. 428 at 438, *per* Lush, J.
[14] *Shuter, supra,* at 446, 450.
[15] 1920 Act, s. 16 (3), *supra.*
[16] *Davies* v *Bristow, supra; Penrhos College* v *Butler* [1920] 3 K.B. 428; *Kerr,
   supra,* at 25, *per* Lord Wrenbury.
[17] See *infra,* pp. 555 *et seq.*

to tenants, whether it was a sum assignable or bequeathable or a right of property; and the courts have had to go slowly and with caution.[18] " This case, like all cases in my experience under the Rent Restriction Acts, is of a most bewildering character. The reason for that bewilderment comes, I think, from this, that when the Acts were drafted—and I think this applies practically to all the Acts that have so far been passed— those who drafted them and those who passed them had not made up their minds what was the nature of the privilege they were conferring on the tenant. One view to be taken was that the tenant was to be given something in the nature of property which he could pass on to other people; another view was that he was not being given a property but a personal privilege which he could not pass on to other people. The construction of the Acts by the Courts is made difficult by the fact that when temporary difficulties, difficulties which only raise some small point, have been called to the attention of those framing amending Acts, clauses have been put in the amending Acts to meet those difficulties without considering whether they fit into one theory or the other. . . . The Acts have been passed without those framing them having any clear idea whether they were conferring property on the tenant or whether they were conferring a privilege of personal occupation, and the Courts have very slowly—and I do not think that they have finished yet—been trying to frame a consistent theory of what must happen."[19] The position of the statutory tenant, as the law now stands, is as follows :

(a) The terms of the contractual tenancy which is now ended must still be observed. The statutory tenant must, so long as he retains possession, observe and is entitled to the benefit of all the terms and conditions of the original contract of tenancy so far as the same are consistent with the provisions of the Act.[20] "The ' original contract of tenancy ' means the lease under which the tenant possessed immediately before he converted himself into a statutory tenant by asserting his rights to retain possession in defiance of a notice to quit."[21] So a term affecting the amount of rent that is payable, as a term under which the rent is to be reduced below the standard rent or rent limit on punctual payment is not consistent with the Act;[22] or one under which the tenant is entitled to pay less than the standard rent or rent limit.[23] The common law right of retention of rent, an equitable remedy based on mutual contracts, is not a " term and condition " of the lease and even if it were, it is inconsistent with provisions for suspension of statutory permitted increases, and thus a tenant's right to withhold payment of rent in respect that the house is

18 *Skinner, infra,* at 558, *per* Scrutton, L.J.
19 *Haskins* v *Lewis* [1931] 2 K.B. 1 at 9, *per* Scrutton, L.J.
20 1920 Act, s. 15 (1).
21 *Stobbs & Sons, infra, per* L.P. Cooper at 222.
22 *Regional Properties* v *Oxley* [1945] A.C. 347.
23 *Capital & Counties Properties* v *Butler* [1944] K.B. 730.

not wind and water tight is not carried over to the statutory tenancy.[24] The tenant cannot retain possession under the Acts and retain the rent at common law. But an obligation to provide hot water and heating is not inconsistent with the Acts,[25] nor is a purely personal obligation that does not bind the tenant *qua* tenant.[26] It follows, too, as the Act provides, that the statutory tenant can give up possession only if he gives such notice as the original contract required or, if that was silent on the point, at least three months' notice.[27] He is not allowed to, and is guilty of an offence if he does it and liable to a fine, ask or receive, as a condition or inducement to leave, money or any other consideration from any person other than the landlord.[28]

(b) The statutory tenant's protection exists only if he is actually occupying the premises personally.[29] By contrast, a contractual tenant is entitled to possession, though not actually occupying.

(c) The statutory tenant cannot contract out of the Acts. If he does so, the contract or agreement is not enforceable.[30]

(d) The statutory tenant's right is that of personal occupation of the premises as a residence; that is indeed the object of his becoming a statutory tenant. Thus, even if the contract does not prohibit assignation, he cannot assign the lease.[31]

(e) He may sublet part of the subjects, provided his lease does not prohibit subletting.[32] A sublet of the whole of the premises, however, is a nullity,[33] and the tenant loses the protection of the Acts.[34] If he regains possession his statutory tenancy may revive if he is held not to have abandoned the premises.[35] The fact that there is a sublet of part does not necessarily imply abandonment of possession, particularly if the sublet is not let as a separate dwelling.[36]

---

[24] *Stobbs & Sons* v *Hislop*, 1948 S.C. 216.
[25] *Engvall* v *Ideal Flats* [1945] K.B. 205.
[26] *R.M.R. Housing Society* v *Combs* [1951] 1 K.B. 486.
[27] 1920 Act, s. 15 (1).
[28] *Ibid.*, s. 15 (2).
[29] *Infra*, p. 520.
[30] *Barton* v *Fincham* [1921] 2 K.B. 291; *Brown* v *Draper* [1944] K.B. 309. See *infra*, p. 626.
[31] *Keeves* v *Dean* [1924] 1 K.B. 685; *Lovibond* v *Vincent* [1929] 1 K.B. 687. See *Joint Properties* v *Williamson*, 1945 S.C. 68 at 80, *per* Lord Russell.
[32] *Roe* v *Russell* [1928] 2 K.B. 117; *Baker* v *Turner* [1950] A.C. 401; *Lewis* v *Reeves* [1952] 1 K.B. 19.
[33] Halsbury, *Laws of England*, 3rd ed., XXIII p. 806; see *Oak Property Co.* v *Chapman* [1947] K.B. 886.
[34] 1933 Act, Schedule First (d). See *infra*, p. 591.
[35] *Wigley* v *Leigh* [1950] 2 K.B. 305.
[36] *Berkeley* v *Papadoyannis* [1954] 2 Q.B. 149; *Baker* v *Turner*, *supra*.

(f) He cannot transmit his rights by will,[37] or an *inter vivos* trust deed.[38] The tenancy does not pass to his trustee in bankruptcy.[39]

(g) The tenancy on his death does not pass on intestacy,[37] but a widow or member of his family may succeed to it[40] as first or second successor.

(h) As long as he occupies the premises as a residence and is thus protected by the Acts, his possession is good against the whole world except only a person who claims under a title superior to that of the landlord and to whom the tenant is only a trespasser.[41] Hence, as against a mortgagee or heritable creditor the statutory tenant is not protected if the landlord, the debtor, had not power under the security deed to lease.[42]

(i) He may be entitled to the benefit of an option to renew in the original tenancy.[43]

Persons Protected by the Acts. The occupier of the premises, in order to obtain the benefits of the provisions of the Acts as to possession, must establish that he is of the class of persons whom the Acts were intended to protect, that his occupancy is lawful and that it is derived or flows from a tenancy or lease. He must have his possession on a contract of tenancy. He must be a tenant. It must be a lease or letting, not a licence or personal privilege, although, of course, the 1965 Act's provisions against harassment and eviction without due process of law apply generally to all residential occupiers.[44] In determining whether in any case it is a lease or a licence, the intention of the parties is the determining factor,[45] not the words used by them.[46] Exclusive possession and payment of rent may point equally one way or the other.[47] So where a managing director was given the use of a flat at a rent by his company and he remained after expiry of the lease and even after he had later resigned, it was held in the circumstances there that the residence after his resignation was a mere personal privilege or licence.[48] The tenant if claiming to be a statutory tenant must show that there was at some time a contractual tenancy, from which he derives the statutory tenancy on which he now founds. In other words, the statutory tenancy must originate in a contractual tenancy. The tenant must be able to found his

---

[37] *Infra*, p. 595. The right of a surviving spouse in a dwellinghouse under the Succession (Scotland) Act 1964, does not apply to tenancies under the Rent Acts : Succession (Scotland) Act 1964, s. 8 (6).
[38] *Wilkins* v *Carlton Shoe Co.* (1930) 46 T.L.R. 415.
[39] *Sutton* v *Dorf* [1932] 2 K.B. 304. There is no Scots decision.
[40] *Infra*, p. 596.
[41] *Dudley Building Society* v *Emerson* [1949] 2 All E.R. 252.
[42] *Dudley, supra; Kitchen's Tr.* v *Madders* [1950] Ch. 134.
[43] *McIlroy Ltd.* v *Clements* [1923] W.N. 81.
[44] 1965 Act, s. 32 (2), (3).
[45] *Booker* v *Palmer* [1942] 2 All E.R. 674 at 676-7, per Lord Greene, M.R.
[46] *Taylor* v *Caldwell* (1863) 3 B. & S. 826.
[47] *Murray Bull & Co.* v *Murray* [1953] 1 Q.B. 211; *Marcroft Wagons, infra.*
[48] *Murray Bull & Co., supra.* See too *Piper* v *Muggleton* [1956] 2 Q.B. 569.

possession on a contract of tenancy.[49] He must, therefore, not be a trespasser. He must retain possession in order to be protected;[50] so he must be in possession when his contractual tenancy expires and continue without interruption to be in possession.[51] He must not be a person allowed temporarily to remain on tenancy without a title, as *e.g.,* a daughter allowed to remain on after the statutory tenant's death at a rent.[52]

The occupation must be as tenant, under the contractual relationship of landlord and tenant. So in the case of a servant occupying premises at a rent approved by his master, it is necessary to enquire whether the occupation is as a tenant or as a servant. The occupation will be held to be as a servant only, where it is necessary for the due performance of his duties or he is required to occupy the premises so as to perform his duties better or more satisfactorily;[53] but if he is merely permitted to occupy premises of his employer for his own purposes he will be held to be a tenant. So a gamekeeper occupying for the purposes of his employment[54] and a schoolmaster occupying a house belonging to an Education Authority in virtue of his office[55] have been held to occupy as servants and not as tenants. So too a caretaker,[56] a motor mechanic,[57] or a gardener[58] will not be held to be tenants. Occupation rent-free is not generally protected by the Acts, which are intended to cover tenancies in respect of which or where rent is paid.[59] It is immaterial whether the lease is for a term of years or periodic from year to year. So a tenant at sufferance has been held to be protected[60] and a tenant at will at a rent is also held to be protected.[61]

A statutory tenant for the purposes of security of possession must be occupying the premises personally;[62] the purpose of the Acts is to afford security of possession to a tenant residing in a house. Protection of the home is indeed the whole policy and intention of the Acts,[63] so they do not include where a person gives a license, for example, to his sister-in-

---

[49] *Marquis of Bute, infra,* at 284, *per* L.P. Clyde; *Pollock, infra,* at 283, *per* Lord Hunter.
[50] 1920 Act, s. 15 (1).
[51] *John M. Brown Ltd.* v *Bestwick* [1951] 1 K.B. 21.
[52] *Marcroft Wagons* v *Smith* [1951] 2 K.B. 496.
[53] Note, however, that a service occupier is deemed to be a tenant for the purposes of the 1965 Act's provision against eviction without due process of law: s. 32 (2); see special protection of agricultural employees: s. 33.
[54] *Marquis of Bute* v *Prenderleith,* 1921 S.C. 281.
[55] *Pollock* v *Inverness Assessor,* 1923 S.L.T. 282.
[56] *Ecclesiastical Commissioners* v *Hilder* (1920) 36 T.L.R. 771.
[57] *National Steam Car Co.* v *Barham* (1919) 122 L.T. 315.
[58] *Ford* v *Langford* [1949] 1 All E.R. 483.
[59] *Bracey* v *Pales* [1927] 1 K.B. 818; *Milne* v *Darroch* (1937), 53 Sh. Ct. Rep. 1 at 12. Where payment is in kind or services, see *Montague* v *Browning* [1954] 2 All E.R. 601.
[60] *Dobson* v *Richards* [1919] W.N. 166; *Artizans, Labourers & General Dwellings Co.* v *Whitaker* [1919] 2 K.B. 301. Halsbury, 3rd ed., XXIII, p. 743.
[61] *Chamberlain* v *Farr* [1942] 2 All E.R. 567.
[62] *Menzies* v *Mackay,* 1938 S.C. 74; *Skinner* v *Geary* [1931] 2 K.B. 546; *Keeves, supra.*
[63] *Temple* v *Mitchell,* 1956 S.C. 267, *per* Lord Mackintosh at 281, *Menzies, supra, per* L.J.C. Aitchison, at 80; *Reidy* v *Walker* [1933] 2 K.B. 266, at 272, *per* Goddard, J.

law or sister to occupy his house.[64] In the leading Scottish case[65] a man tenanted two controlled houses, one in Glasgow, the other in a sea-side resort near Glasgow—Largs. He ordinarily occupied the Glasgow house; the Largs house he kept closed in the winter but sublet for part of the summer, occupying it with his family for a few weeks as a holiday house. He intended eventually to retire there and live there in his later years. He was held, following an English case,[66] not to be a statutory tenant of the Largs house. To be protected, said Lord Justice Clerk Aitchison, the premises must be, and must continue to be, in the personal occupation of the tenant, and personal occupation must be reasonably judged of. There must be occupation in a substantial sense and, as Lord Wark observed, in this case there was not occupation in any substantial sense as a home of the house in Largs. The statutory tenant has only a personal right to retain possession of the house as his home,[67] a statutory right, it has been said, of irremovability.[68] It is not a right of property and so he cannot assign[69] nor can the right pass to his trustee in bankruptcy.[70] For this reason (that it cannot occupy a house as a dwellinghouse, that is, reside in a domestic sense) a limited company cannot be a statutory tenant,[71] but it may enjoy the benefit of the financial provisions of the Acts during a contractual tenancy, for a right to standard rent, it has been held, is a right *in rem*.[72]

In the ordinary case there must be substantial occupation of the premises by the statutory tenant.[73] If he abandons the premises without intention to return or in such circumstances that his return is very unlikely or remotely possible, he ceases to have the protection of the Acts.[74] Also, if he inverts his possession, uses the subjects for other purposes than residence, *e.g.*, business or retail trade, his security is lost. Temporary absence does not amount to abandonment,[75] but if the absence is prolonged or sufficiently unintermittent it may raise a presumption of abandonment and the onus then falls on the tenant to rebut that presumption by proving an intention to return—*animus revertendi*—and some act or acts of a formal visible and physical nature, such as leaving furniture or putting in a caretaker as licensee and so preserving the premises for his ultimate home-coming, showing that he

---

[64] *Skinner, supra.* See too *S.L. Dando, infra.*

[65] *Menzies, supra.*

[66] *Skinner, supra.*

[67] *Roe v Russell* [1928] 2 K.B. 117 at 131, *per* Sargant, L.J.; *Skinner, supra,* at 539, *per* Scrutton, L.J.; *Carter, infra,* at 291, *per* Lord Greene, M.R.

[68] *Marcroft Wagons v Smith* [1951] 2 K.B. 496 at 501, *per* Lord Evershed, M.R., who added " a new *monstrum horrendum, informe, ingens* ".

[69] *Supra,* p. 518; *infra,* p. 590.

[70] *Sutton v Dorf* [1932] 2 K.B. 304. There is no Scots authority.

[71] *Hiller v United Dairies* [1934] 1 K.B. 57; *Reidy v Walker* [1933] 2 K.B. 266. See *G. E. Stevens (High Wycombe) v High Wycombe Corp.* (1961) 2 All E.R. 738.

[72] *Carter v S.U. Carburettor Co.* [1942] 2 K.B. 288.

[73] *Menzies, Skinner, Keeves, supra.*

[74] *Cove v Flick, infra.*

[75] *Wigley v Leigh* [1950] 2 K.B. 305; *Hallwood Estates v Flack* [1950] W.N. 268.

intends to and is continuing occupation.[76] The fact that he has been convicted and sentenced to imprisonment puts him for that matter in no better position than if his absence had been voluntary.[77] If, however, the caretaker moves out or the furniture is removed otherwise than temporarily, then the protection ceases, whether or not the tenant wills or desires the moving and removal.[78] Where a lease provided that the tenant or his present manager should reside, the tenant was held not protected where the manager and his family resided but the tenant had never done so and never intended to reside.[79] And where the tenant took the house intending it as a residence for his father, mother and sister and himself and he later married and left and did not mean to return, there was no protection under the Act.[80] The fact that he has not personally resided in the house for some considerable time is not neces- sarily conclusive that he has ceased to retain possession, if he intends to resume personal occupation, and the fact of leaving his wife or some other agent in occupation or his furniture are relevant considerations. If he is absent for business or other reasons but intends eventually to return and uses the house meantime as a residence for his family, he is still a statutory tenant.[81] Thus, even prolonged temporary absence, as in the case of a man at sea, is not necessarily inconsistent with his being a statutory tenant of his home.[82] If he is absent, leaving a licensee residing, but has no intention of returning, however, he ceases to be protected. Normal occupation by a wife will be sufficient to support an alleged intention to return.[83]

The position of a deserted wife has caused difficulty, and conflicting decisions in Scotland and in England have not helped the solution of the problem. In Scotland[84] a husband, who was a statutory tenant, departed from his home and left his wife and family and the furniture in the house. The wife paid the next half year's rent, his whereabouts being unknown, and this was accepted by the landlord from her as his agent, but when she tendered at the next three half-terms the respective

---

[76] *Brown* v *Brash* [1948] 2 K.B. 247; *Old Gate Estates, infra; Wigley, supra,* where a wife, statutory tenant, was held protected where she had gone to Ireland for health reasons, and intended to return when her health improved and had left a man servant, who kept up the place, and certain improvements were carried out; *Dixon* v *Tommis* [1952] 1 All E.R. 725, where the tenant had been absent a short time and intended to return within three years, his son occupying in the interval, he was held protected. The question was one of degree and the Court followed the views in *Brown, supra.* Where the tenant aged 73 had left the premises because of mental illness without intention to abandon she was held still protected so long as there was a real hope of return and the practical possibility of fulfilment of that hope within a reasonable time. *Tickner* v *Hearn* [1961] 1 All E.R. 65.
[77] *Brown, supra,* where his mistress had later left the home.
[78] *Brown, supra,* at 254-5, *per* the Court.
[79] *S.L. Dando* v *Hitchcock* [1954] 2 Q.B. 317.
[80] *Cove* v *Flick* [1954] 2 Q.B. 326.
[81] *Skinner, supra.*
[82] *Menzies, supra,* at 78, *per* L.J.C. Aitchison; *Skinner, supra,* at 562, *per* Scrutton, L.J.
[83] *Brown* v *Draper* [1944] K.B. 309; *Smith* v *Penny* [1947] K.B. 230.
[84] *Temple* v *Mitchell,* 1956 S.C. 267.

half-terms' rents, acceptance of them was refused. Notice to quit was served on husband and wife and an action of removing raised against the husband tenant, the wife being later made a party to the action. It was held that the landlord was entitled to succeed and that the wife was not protected. It was pointed out that in the absence of an intention to return the husband must be taken to have given up possession. If he is not personally in occupation, the tenant must show an intention to return. No mandate had been given to the wife and, as he must have been taken to have given up possession through lack of intention to return, he could not give her any more than any other person a right to remain on in the house. " He cannot ", said Lord Justice Clerk Thomson, " confer on her a right to vindicate a tenancy which he himself is not in a position to vindicate ". Had such an intention been proved, Lord Patrick said, it would, of course, have altered the position. Lord Mackintosh, however, dissented, holding that by common law a wife could vicariously possess,[85] and he agreed with the English decisions, which were not out of accord with Scots law, and in the interests of uniformity should, he said, be followed. Possession could be by servants, family, etc. on the tenant's behalf[85] without his permanent, or even occasional, residence, " family " clearly including wife and children. There was nothing in the common law of Scotland to stand in the way of it being held that a tenant's possession could be retained by his leaving his wife and family in it though he went away. When he could have had them ejected, the fair inference was that they were there with his tacit permission, especially when he left his furniture there. So " retains possession " in the 1920 Act could be so construed that the wife's possession is the husband's possession.

Continued residence by a wife after divorce will not give her a protected tenancy,[86] but in the case of desertion in England the Courts have taken a different attitude to the Scots Courts in respect of the different position of the wife under English Law. A wife in England is entitled to remain in the house, having an independent right attaching to her as wife under the Married Women's Property Acts by virtue of the consortium, and, if she is deserted, that right of occupation cannot be taken away while she resides there, and by and through her occupation her husband continues as statutory tenant; in Scotland the husband or wife who owns or occupies a house can eject the other spouse on grounds of property or possession.[87] In one case[88] it was held that the husband who had left furniture in the house was still in possession and that in order to get possession the landlord must make the tenant a party to the action. The wife's possession was to be treated as her husband's and was not unlawful as long as he had a right to claim

[85] Rankine, *Leases,* 3rd ed., 234.
[86] *Robson* v *Headland* (1948) 64 T.L.R. 596.
[87] Gloag & Henderson, *Introduction to Scots Law,* 6th ed., 606 and cases cited.
[88] *Brown* v *Draper* [1944] K.B. 309.

the protection of the Acts. And in another case,[89] where the husband who had deserted had written to the landlords saying that he was giving up possession, and he ceased to pay rent, and later gave them a document purporting to revoke any leave he might have given his wife to occupy and between the raising and the hearing of an action by the landlords against both husband and wife he returned to live with her, it was held that, the material time being that of the raising of the action, as she was then with his furniture in the house, he was still in possession as a statutory tenant. The Courts in England have held that, even if the wife is guilty of misconduct and thus is not entitled to reside *vis-à-vis* the husband, possession can be taken away from her only if her husband withdraws the right of the wife to occupy.[90] He must have revoked her licence to occupy, and probably under the authority or order of the Court.[91]

There cannot be a statutory tenancy, if through the house having been destroyed or seriously damaged it is not possible to occupy it or reside in it.[92] Habitability is not, however, the test. The test is identity. Has the building ceased to exist, has the identity been destroyed? Thus, where though uninhabitable it was temporarily used as business premises, the house remaining substantially the original building in the tenant's occupation, and the tenant though so using it was waiting to return and live in it when it was repaired, it was held to have retained its statutory protection.[93] If it is temporarily unusable, therefore, the protection is not lost.[93]

Cases arise where a tenant has more than one house. In that event there can be protection for each house if each is used substantially and genuinely by the tenant as a home or residence.[94] Two houses may be in different places and yet in the personal occupation of the same person.[94] There is nothing to prevent a person having a house in one locality from having another in another locality of which he is a tenant also protected by the Acts.[94] Where a man has a house in the country but, since he carries on business in London, has a flat there, then as a matter of commonsense and fact it can be fairly and truthfully said that both places are each the man's home.[95] The true test is whether the premises of which possession is sought by the landlord were in the personal occupation of the tenant as his home or, if he had more than one home, as one of his homes. There must be both a true *animus* or intention and *corpus;* it is not enough to leave furniture and a caretaker

[89] *Old Gate Estates* v *Alexander* [1950] 1 K.B. 311. See also *Middleton* v *Baldock* [1950] 1 K.B. 657.
[90] *Middleton, supra,* at 714, *per* Denning, L.J.
[91] *Wabe* v *Taylor* [1952] 2 Q.B. 735.
[92] *Ellis & Sons Amalgamated Properties* v *Sisman* [1948] 1 K.B. 653, *East End Dwellings Co.* v *Finsbury Borough Council* [1952] A.C. 109.
[93] *Morleys (Birmingham)* v *Slater* [1950] 1 K.B. 506.
[94] *Menzies, supra, per* L.J.C. Aitchison, at 78; *Langford Property Co.* v *Tureman* [1949] 1 K.B. 29; *Beck* v *Scholz* [1953] 1 Q.B. 570.
[95] *Beck, supra,* at 574, *per* Lord Evershed, M.R.

and to have a desire to retain possession because it is found convenient to visit the house occasionally.[96] Where the tenant had a flat in London where he worked and where he slept two nights a week it was held he was not deprived of protection because he had a cottage in the country where he resided with his wife and family.[97] Where a person had a house let to him as a dwellinghouse and part of it was used as a dwelling-house, and then he bought another house and lived there with his family, and one room in the former house was used twice a week for sleeping in, it was held that the premises were originally let as a dwelling-house and it was for the landlord to show that the later use did not entitle them to protection.[98] But the Court, it has been said, ought to be somewhat cautious in giving the protection of the Acts to what have been called " two home men ";[99] and should look critically at cases which, if they were extended repeatedly, would go far to defeat one of the main purposes of the Acts, which is to make the best use of the unfortunately limited housing resources.[99] In one case,[1] where the tenant had only temporarily left his former home, leaving his son and his furniture there and said that he intended to return on retirement in three years' time, the Court with some difficulty gave protection to the old home. In another,[2] where furniture was left in a London flat and two caretakers kept it available for occasional visits by the tenant and her husband, who both lived in Luton, the tenant sleeping about four or five times a year, the husband about once every two months, in the flat, the Court remitted to the lower Court to state whether in the common sense the flat was personally occupied by the tenant as a home or had been abandoned. Thus, the Court of Session have refused to protect what was really a short holiday house at a seaside resort where the owner had his home in a nearby city.[3] In the latest case,[4] where a dentist had been let premises comprising a shop and a house above and behind the shop and had at first used the shop and the kitchen for his business, and two years later and for four years used the house as a residence for his family and himself, and the family then removed to another house a quarter of a mile away which he had bought, but he continued to sleep there in the original house from time to time, and where, at the expiry of a notice to quit, he then owned the house, which he was trying to sell, and had leased another, it was held that the basic point was that the premises were let for professional purposes and had reverted to that

[96] *Ibid.*, at 575, 576, *per* Lord Evershed, M.R.
[97] *Langford Property Co.*, *supra.*
[98] *Green* v *Coggins* [1949] 2 All E.R. 815, especially at 816, *per* Lord Evershed. M.R.
[99] *Dixon* v *Tommis* [1952] 1 All E.R. 725 at 727, *per* Lord Evershed, M.R.: *Megarry, op. cit.*, 9th ed., 169, the similar statement in the 6th ed. being approved in *Beck, supra, per* M.R. at 575.
[1] *Dixon, supra.*
[2] *Beck* v *Scholz* [1953] 1 Q.B. 570.
[3] *Menzies* v *Mackay, supra.*
[4] *Alex Cowan & Sons* v *Acton*, 1952 S.C. 73. The Court expressed views as to the *tempus* for determining this issue.

state and were not protected. " Domesticity being the keynote of the Acts I cannot persuade myself that the Acts are intended to allow a professional man to protect premises which while they may be capable of being used for housing purposes are in fact used by him as business premises, by the single expedient of sleeping away from his own family home, however convenient that may be in the interests of his profession."[5] Cases where a man is protected in respect of two separate houses are cases " where by reason of the necessities of his calling a man had to have two dwellinghouses at separate points ".[6] Where a statutory tenancy of one house was being claimed when the tenant was already entitled to occupy two other houses and so little needing the three that he was trying to sell one, to apply the Acts would be to abrogate the landlord's right merely to enable the tenant to sell a home he already had.[6]

The mere fact of subletting part of the premises does not imply that the tenant has abandoned possession of that part or, as it has been put, the application of the " *Skinner* v *Geary* " principle.[7] By the mere fact of non-residence and subletting the tenant does not lose his protection; but previous occupation and intention to re-occupy at the close of the sublet are vital. Even a sublet of the whole does not *per se* imply abandonment.[8] The tenant may suspend a decision as to whether he will or will not re-occupy, if the subtenant should go, the whole or any part of the premises sublet.[9] And so where the tenant had never occupied at any material time any part of the premises sublet nor had any intention of occupying them at any future time, there was held to be no protection under the Acts.[10]

Where the tenant dies, if he was a contractual tenant, the lease passes at common law to his heir;[11] whether he was a contractual tenant or a statutory tenant it may, however, pass to one of the class allowed by the Acts to succeed him.[12]

Decontrol and Release from Regulation. Although the gradual process of decontrol which had been carried on before the war was ended in 1939, decontrol was reintroduced in regard to new dwellinghouses in 1954 and more especially by the 1957 Act in regard to new leases and dwellinghouses over £40 in rateable value.[13] The 1957 Act contained

---

[5] *Ibid.*, at 83, *per* L.J.C. Thomson.
[6] *Ibid.*, at 91, *per* Lord Patrick.
[7] *Berkeley, infra; Megarry, op. cit.*, 9th ed., 168.
[8] *Megarry, op. cit.*, 9th ed., 167-8.
[9] *Berkeley* v *Papadoyannis* [1954] 2 Q.B. 149.
[10] *Crowhurst* v *Maidment* [1953] 1 Q.B. 23.
[11] Rankine, *Leases*, 3rd ed., 157; Fraser, *Rent Acts*, 2nd ed., 8. See Succession (Scotland) Act 1964.
[12] See, *infra*, p. 594. The right of the surviving spouse in a dwellinghouse under the Succession (Scotland) 1964, is not applicable to tenancies under the Rent Acts: Succession (Scotland) Act 1964, ss. 8 (6).
[13] See *supra*, p. 513.

transitional provisions[14] designed to soften the impact of decontrol on sitting tenants, that is, those who though remaining in occupation under the existing contractual or statutory tenancy would lose protection by reason of the lowering of the economic limit.[15] The intention was to provide them with a period of grace in which they could either negotiate new tenancies or make other arrangements for their accommodation. These provisions included a standstill on removal for at least fifteen months, during which time the tenant was entitled to retain possession in the like circumstances, to the like extent and subject to the like provisions as if the Rent Acts had not ceased to apply to the dwelling-house.[16] During the standstill period the rent remained frozen at the figure recoverable from the tenant for the last rental period before decontrol.[17] If, on the other hand, the landlord agreed with the tenant to grant him a new tenancy of the premises (as opposed to insisting on his removal) which was to last for at least three years, those transitional provisions ceased to apply.[18] The 1957 Act also introduced a new principle, that the tenant of a decontrolled house was entitled to claim compensation at any time before giving up possession for improvements made by him and completed after 15th August 1945 which added to the value of the house;[19] on the other hand, no compensation was payable if the person by whom the improvement was made was under an obligation to make it in pursuance of a contract entered into for valuable consideration, or if it was made in breach of the terms of the lease, or if the landlord had objected in writing to the improvement before it was completed.[20]

As has been explained above,[21] the 1965 Act did not put an end to decontrol; rather it made use of it, by allowing for the gradual conversion of decontrolled premises into regulated tenancies. Although the 1957 Act's transitional provisions were not repealed, they have, in effect, fallen into abeyance since the Secretary of State's power to release tenancies from control has been replaced by a new power, to convert existing controlled tenancies into regulated tenancies.[22] This latter power, the means whereby the process of conversion from control to regulation can be accelerated, is exercisable by statutory instrument, which must be approved by a resolution of each House of Parliament.[23] The mechanism for the conversion is that of lowering the economic limit within which the Rent Acts'

[14] Contained in Schedule Fourth.
[15] Either by reason of s. 11 (1), or under an order made by the Secretary of State under s. 11 (3).
[16] Schedule 4, para. 2; note that a person who retained possession under this provision was not a statutory tenant: *Cheesman* v *Bagnall* [1962] 2 All E.R. 195.
[17] *Ibid.*, paras. 3, 15 (a).
[18] *Ibid.*, para. 4.
[19] *Ibid.*, para. 5.
[20] *Ibid.*, para. 5 (4).
[21] *Supra*, p. 514.
[22] 1965 Act, s. 11.
[23] s. 11 (8).

provisions for rent control apply in any area in Scotland; tenancies
released from control by such an order are to be treated as regulated
tenancies.[24] The main significance of such a conversion is, of course, the
possibility of an increase in rent, but here the tenant of the former controlled tenancy is well protected. Until an application is made for the
registration of a fair rent for the dwellinghouse the recoverable rent for
both contractual and statutory periods remains frozen at its former limit
for the last rental period before decontrol, subject to the permitted
increases where these apply.[25] Once the fair rent has been determined and
registered the statutory tenant is still protected against a sudden large
rise in rent; a notice of increase served after the limit on recoverable
rent has been raised after registration will only be valid if the rent
specified in the notice does not exceed by more than 15 per cent. the
controlled rent payable for the rental period beginning twelve months
before the notice takes effect.[26]

The 1965 Act is unusual among those Acts which have re-imposed
rent control in that it contains a built-in provision for release from rent
regulation.[27] Such a release can be effected by the Secretary of State
by statutory instrument, which must be approved by a resolution of each
House of Parliament.[28] In order that he may make such an order the
Secretary of State must be satisfied with respect to every part of the area
to which the order applies that the demand for tenancies of dwellinghouses over the specified rateable value, or of the specified class or
description of dwellinghouse, or dwellinghouses of that class or
description over the specified rateable value, does not substantially
exceed the supply.[29] The making of transitional provisions, including
those to avoid or mitigate hardship, is left to the Secretary of State,[30]
but such provisions would probably resemble those found in the 1957
Act.[31]

CONTROL AND REGULATION OF RENT

Introductory. As has already been stated, one of the main objects of
the Rent Acts has always been to limit the amount that can be charged
to a tenant in respect of basic rent, and at the same time to restrict the
making of increases to that rent to certain circumstances and amounts.
The mechanism whereby this object has been achieved is undoubtedly
the most complex aspect of these Acts; and the position is made even
more involved because there is no uniform method of control, different

[24] s. 11 (3).
[25] s. 11 (5).
[26] s. 11 (6).
[27] s. 12.
[28] s. 12 (3).
[29] s. 12 (1).
[30] s. 12 (2).
[31] See 1957 Act, Schedule 4; *supra*, p. 527.

provisions being applied to different categories of tenancy.[32] In the case of controlled tenancies, the standard rent of old and new control houses must be ascertained under separate provisions, subject now to the 1957 Act. Regulated tenancies, on the other hand, are to be distinguished according to whether the rent payable in respect of the dwelling-house has been registered under Part II of the 1965 Act, where Part II is in force in the local registration area; until it has been registered, a system of rent regulation not unlike that applied to controlled tenancies operates, administered by the Courts. Thereafter, the new system of rent regulation administered by rent officers and rent assessment committees will apply.

Prior to the 1965 Act rent control had always taken the severe form of a rent freeze; in other words, the basic or standard rent, once ascertained, was fixed for all time at its original level, subject to limited increases in certain clearly defined circumstances but not to the element attributable to rent. The 1965 Act, in the first instance, imposed a similar standstill on all rents payable under regulated tenancies; but the new system of registration of rents which is being extended to local authority areas by statutory instrument is intended to break away from this fierce form of restriction, which has been the cause of the see-saw of control and decontrol since rent restriction was first introduced. The keynote of the new system is flexibility. Rent fixing is no longer to be the responsibility of the Courts, but is transferred to local rent assessment officials; hence the new system is marked by a new-found simplicity of language which preserves the element of discretion appropriate to governmental control. The term "fair rent", which is the basis of the rent payable once registration has come into force, is loosely defined;[33] an increase in the element attributable to rent is now a possibility, should the rent assessment committee choose to interpret this term so as to give the landlord a fair return on his property, which will fluctuate with the national growth rate or, perhaps, the fall in the value of the pound.

As has been explained above,[34] provision is made in the 1965 Act for the wholesale conversion by statutory instrument of controlled tenancies into regulated tenancies, and it is likely that this will be done before very long. The "fair rent" system is accordingly the only one of the four systems presently in operation which is likely to be permanent. However, for the present it is not possible to ignore the other forms of control, and this chapter contains a separate discussion of all four, in chronological order.

---

[32] For a discussion of the different categories of tenancy covered by the Rent Acts, see *supra*, pp. 512 *et seq.*
[33] 1965 Acts, s. 27; see *infra*, p. 558.
[34] *Supra*, p. 527.

34

A. *Controlled Tenancies*

Old Control. It will be recalled that the 1920 Act applied to houses of which the standard rent or rateable value[35] did not exceed £90 *per annum*. The standard rent[36] was the rent at which the premises were *bona fide* let on 3rd August 1914, or, if they were not then let, the rent at which they were last let before that date, or, if they were let for the first time after that date, the rent at which they were first let. It was the rent at which the house was last let, no matter how long ago and how uneconomic.[37] And the let for the first time must be an unfurnished let.[38] The rateable value, too, was the yearly value in the Valuation Roll for the year ending 15th May 1915, or where the house was first assessed after that date the rateable value at which it was first assessed.[39] If the rateable value in the Valuation Roll was greater then the standard rent at the date by reference to which the standard rent was fixed, then the rateable value at that date was the standard rent.[40] In the case of a let at a progressive rent it was the maximum rent payable under the lease that formed the standard rent.[40] The term " progressive rent " was not statutorily defined, but it has been judicially stated to be " a rent under one single tenancy and a rent which automatically rises during the continuance of that tenancy ".[41] Alterations in the rateable value after the appropriate day or the day of first assessment did not affect the application of the Acts.[42] The standard rent applied to the existing let and any subsequent let, though a decision as to the standard rent did not create an estoppel or bar as against later tenants.[43] In determining the standard rent it is not every or any previous letting that can be considered, for the nature and terms of the letting must be ascertained. Thus, *e.g.,* a business let, a letting for business purposes,[44] or a furnished letting,[45] will not be considered, nor will the rent under a let originally agreed as a furnished let but on proof found to be not such in terms of the Acts on the ground of lack of " substantiality " under the 1923 Act, for such a let is not to be regarded as a let unfurnished with reference to which the standard rent can be fixed.[46] A let by the Crown, however, though excluded from the Acts, will be looked at.[47] It is the rent paid by the occupying tenant, including a subtenant; that is, it is in such a case

---

[35] The yearly value according to the Valuation Roll, 1920 Act, s. 18 (1) (a).
[36] 1920 Act, s. 12 (1) (a).
[37] *Davies* v *Warwick* [1943] K.B. 329.
[38] *Signy* v *Abbey National Building Society* [1944] K.B. 449.
[39] 1920 Act, ss. 12 (1) (e), 18 (1) (a).
[40] 1920 Act, s. 12 (1) a), *proviso*.
[41] *Wheeler* v *Wirral Estates* [1935] 1 K.B. 294 at 300, *per* Lord Wright, M.R.
[42] *Eyre* v *Haynes* [1946] 1 All E.R. 225; *R.* v *Sidmouth Rent Tribunal* [1951] 1 K.B. 778.
[43] *Lazarus-Barlow* v *Regent Estates* [1949] 2 K.B. 465.
[44] *Macmillan Ltd.* v *Rees* [1946] 1 All E.R. 675.
[45] *Signy* v *Abbey National Building Society* [1944] K.B. 449.
[46] *Di Mascio* v *Munro*, 1956 S.C. 245.
[47] *Clarke* v *Downes* (1931) 145 L.T. 20.

the subrent that governs.[48] The tenancy of the occupying tenant, therefore, is the one to be considered.[48] If there has been a reconstruction so that loss of identity has occurred, the standard rent is held to be lost and the standard rent is the rent at which the first let took place after reconstruction.[49] The standard rent, too, must not have been fixed collusively at too high a rate, otherwise no effect will be given to it[50] and the motive in fixing it, e.g., friendship or reward for services, will not be considered unless the rent is obviously a complete sham.[51] The Sheriff Court can determine on application by the landlord or the tenant any question as to the amount of the rent, or standard rent or net rent.[52] Where the rent was under two-thirds of the rateable value the standard rent was the rateable value or an earlier rent.[53] If it is not reasonably practicable to obtain sufficient evidence of the standard rent, the Court can determine it as of such amount as might be thought proper, having regard to the standard rents of similar houses in the neighbourhood.[54]

The rent is the rent payable in money and does not include other obligations by the tenant, such as giving the landlord the use of a part of the house,[55] or the covenant of a tenant of tied licensed premises[56] or discount on liquor supplied by the landlord to the tenant.[56] It includes payment for cleaning expenses or the services of a housekeeper[57] and occupier's rates if the landlord by agreement under the House Letting and Rating Acts 1911 and 1920 paid these items.[58]

If requested in writing, the landlord must, under penalty of a fine for failure, give the tenant a written statement of the amount of the standard rent.[59] Where rent is payable weekly, the landlord has to provide a rent book or other similar document containing certain matters specified in Regulations[60] under penalty of a fine on the landlord and anyone who on his behalf demands or receives rent.[61] If the book or document does not conform to the prescribed requirements and is used, the landlord is liable to a fine.[62] The 1938 Act introduced the *need* for such a book, that is, made it compulsory in such cases. And in other cases than weekly tenants, if a rent book or similar document is used by the landlord or on his behalf it must contain a notice in a form

[48] *Glossop* v *Ashley* [1922] 1 K.B. 1.
[49] *Phillips* v *Barnet* [1921] 2 K.B. 799; *Sinclair* v *Powell* [1922] 1 K.B. 393.
[50] *Conqueror Properties Trust* v *Barnes Corporation* [1944] K.B. 96.
[51] *Insall* v *Nottingham Corporation* [1949] 1 K.B. 261.
[52] 1923 Act, s. 11 (1).
[53] *Brakspear & Sons* v *Barton* [1924] 2 K.B. 88 at 99, 100, *per* McCardie, J.
[54] 1933 Act, s. 6.
[55] *Hornsby* v *Maynard* [1925] 1 K.B. 514.
[56] *Glossop, supra; Brakspear & Sons, supra,* at 102, *per* McCardie, J.
[57] *Woods & Co.* v *City and West End Properties* (1921) 38 T.L.R. 98.
[58] *Westminster and General Properties and Investment Co.* v *Simmons* (1919) 35 T.L.R. 669. See the Valuation and Rating (Scotland) Act 1956, s. 16 (3).
[59] 1920 Act, s. 11.
[60] 1938 Act, s. 6 (1); 1933 Act, s. 14 (1); S.I. 1957 No. 1044, as amended by S.I. 1964 No. 1207, and 1965 No. 2043.
[61] *Ibid.,* s. 6 (2).
[62] 1933 Act, s. 14 (3); 1957 Act, s. 26 (1), Schedule Sixth, para. 20.

prescribed by Regulations.[63] Any entry in such a book showing the tenant in arrears in respect of a sum that is irrecoverable by statute renders the maker of the entry liable to a fine, unless he proves that the landlord has a *bona fide* claim that the sum was recoverable.[64] If the Court determines the reasonable rent, the book may be corrected.[65]

Apportionment. If the house the standard rent or rateable value of which falls to be determined is part of larger premises and the Acts apply to the house and the premises, then the standard rent or rateable value of the house can be ascertained by apportioning the standard rent or rateable value in respect of the letting of the whole premises.[66] That is, where a dwellinghouse or other premises was let as a whole on 3rd August 1914 or the other appropriate date and the subjects have been later divided and the parts let as separate dwellings or houses, the Sheriff can on the application of either party make such apportionment as he thinks just, and his decision is final and conclusive.[66] The Court must consider the size, accessibility and aspect and other physical advantages and amenity values enjoyed by the tenant as compared with those of the rest of the comprising property, but not amenities enjoyed at the landlord's expense, *e.g.* gas or telephone.[67] Apportionment was designed to determine the current statutory rent for the part and to determine whether the standard rent of the part brings the part within the Acts. If the whole premises were within the Acts, the part was necessarily also within the Acts. But the whole premises did not need to be within the Acts in respect of rent or character.[68] Apportionment can be made even though the comprising property is not within the Acts.[68] The house or the part must have been still substantially in the form in which it was let; there must not have been any substantial alteration since the appropriate date otherwise there cannot be an apportionment,[69] and this holds even though the part has not lost its identity.[70] So where an alteration or reconstruction only affects part, there can be no apportionment of the reconstructed part, whose standard rent is that at which it was first let after conversion.[71] But apportionment of a part not

---

[63] 1933 Act, s. 14; S.I. 1957 No. 1044, as amended by S.I. 1964 No. 1207, and 1965 No. 2043.
[64] 1920 Act, s. 14 (2); 1933 Act, s. 8 (2); 1938 Act, s. 7 (7), Schedule Second; 1957 Act, s. 26 (1), Schedule Sixth, para. 17.
[65] 1933 Act, s. 8 (1).
[66] 1920 Act, s. 12 (3); 1938 Act, s. 5.
[67] *Bainbridge* v *Congdon* [1925] 2 K.B. 261.
[68] *Capital & Provincial Property Trust* v *Rice* [1952] A.C. 142; *Woodhead* v *Putnam* [1923] 1 K.B. 252 *per* the Court at 256; *Joy* v *Eppner* [1925] 1 K.B. 362 at 370, *per* Salter, J., where the whole premises were described as " the comprising property "; *Barrett* v *Hardy Bros.* [1925] 2 K.B. 220; *Upsons* v *Herne* [1946] K.B. 591.
[69] *Marchbank* v *Campbell* [1923] 1 K.B. 245; *Sinclair* v *Powell* [1922] 1 K.B. 393 at 407, *per* Atkin, L.J.
[70] *Stockham* v *Easton* [1924] 1 K.B. 52; *Abrahart* v *Webster* [1925] 1 K.B. 563 at 571-2, *per* Atkin, L.J.
[71] *Sinclair* v *Powell* [1922] 1 K.B. 393.

affected by alteration is competent,[72] unless that part has or acquires some benefits from alterations to other parts.[73] If the whole property has never had a standard rent because it has never been let as a whole (for example, has been reconstructed) there cannot be any apportionment.[74] A tenancy at a rent less than two-thirds of the rateable value is not considered for purposes of apportionment.[75]

The tenant has only to prove that the comprising property was let on the appropriate date; it lies with the landlord to prove that apportionment is not necessary as the house was separately let on that date.[76]

Overpayments before the date of apportionment are recoverable,[77] though ascertained only after the apportionment has taken place.[78]

Permitted Increases of Standard Rent. Certain increases could be made to the basic or standard rent, and that rent with the addition of these increases was the " recoverable rent " but these increases were allowed only during a statutory tenancy, a period, that is, during which the tenant continues in possession under the Acts and but for the Acts the landlord would be entitled to obtain possession.[79] These increases were :

(a) Six per cent. expenditure on improvements or structural alterations, excluding decoration or repairs, incurred between 4th August 1914 and 2nd July 1920, and 8 per cent. of such expenditure if incurred after 2nd July 1920.[80] Expenditure on additional or improved fixtures or fittings (not decoration or repairs) was deemed expenditure on improvements.[81] Repairs meant repairs required to keep the house " in good and tenantable repair ".[82] The amount of expenditure incurred or any liability incurred to a local authority by a landlord or a superior landlord after 6th July 1957 in carrying out street works in a street to which a house subject to a controlled tenancy has access in compliance with the local authority's requirements under various Acts—any of the Acts referred to in the Local Government (Street Works) Act 1956 or the corresponding provisions of any local Act—is under the 1957 Act[83] to be treated as expenditure on improvements for the purpose of this provision of the 1920 Act, whether

[72] *Abrahart, supra.*
[73] *Stockham, supra.*
[74] *Lelyveld* v *Peppercorn* [1924] 2 K.B. 638.
[75] 1920 Act, s. 12 (7); *Joy* v *Eppner* [1925] 1 K.B. 362.
[76] *Platman* v *Frohman* [1929] 1 K.B. 376.
[77] 1920 Act, s. 14 (1). These are retrospective and the tenant can counter claim: *Kimm* v *Cohen* (1923) 40 T.L.R. 123.
[78] *Field* v *Gover* [1944] K.B. 200.
[79] 1920 Act, s. 3 (1).
[80] *Ibid.*, ss. 2 (1) (a), 5.
[81] 1933 Act, s. 7 (1).
[82] 1920 Act, s. 2 (5).
[83] s. 18.

or not apart from the section it would be so treated.[84] If the same landlord or superior landlord has other premises in the same street and benefit accrues from the works to the other premises, the amount to be treated as incurred for a house is the proportion thereof as may be determined by written agreement between landlord and tenant or, failing such, as determined by the Sheriff as properly apportionable to the house, having regard to the benefit accruing to the house and the other premises.[85]

(b) A sum equal to the difference between owner's rates in respect of the rating year 1919-1920 and such rates in respect of the year 1914-1915.[86] That is, any increase in the rates (including increased yearly or rateable value)[87] as between these two rating years. Rates mean rates, charges and assessments imposed, assessed or levied by an assessing authority, the proceeds of which are applicable to public local purposes and which are leviable in respect of the yearly value of lands and heritages,[88] and include water rents and charges.[89] The landlord of a small house can recover increases of occupier's rates paid between Whitsun and October.[90] No increase can be made for rates payable by the landlord other than occupiers' rates for which he is responsible under the House Letting and Rating (Scotland) Acts 1911, 1920.[91] It has been held that if the rates have decreased the rent must be decreased accordingly.[92]

(c) Fifteen per cent. of the net rent.[93] The net rent is the standard rent less occupier's rates if these are paid by the landlord at the time by reference to which the standard rent is calculated under the House Letting and Rating Acts. It means, where the landlord at the time by reference to which the standard rent is fixed paid the rates chargeable on, or which but for the provisions of any Act would be chargeable on the occupier, the standard rent less these rates, and in any other case the standard rent.[94] Where the burden of these rates fell on the landlord under an Act it was held that the full amount of the occupier's rates must be deducted, any statutory allowance to the landlord for the cost

---

[84] s. 18 (1), (2).
[85] s. 18 (2), proviso.
[86] 1920 Act, ss. 2 (1) (b), 18 (1) (a) and (b). No increase of owner's rates was allowed after the year ending Whitsun 1920, s. 18 (1) (b).
[87] Steel v Mahoney (1918) 34 T.L.R. 327.
[88] House Letting and Rating (Scotland) Act 1911, s. 1; 1920 Act, s. 18 (1) (a).
[89] 1920 Act, s. 12 (1) (d).
[90] 1923 Act, s. 19 (b). House Letting and Rating (Scotland) Acts 1911, 1920.
[91] 1920 Act, s. 18 (1) (b).
[92] Strickland v Palmer [1924] 2 K.B. 572.
[93] 1920 Act, s. 2 (1) (c).
[94] Ibid., s. 12 (1) (c).

of collection, as under the House Letting and Rating Acts, being ignored.[95] This is now statutory also.[96]

(d) Twenty-five per cent. of the net rent where the landlord is responsible for the whole of the repairs or a corresponding proportion of the repairs.[97] Repairs are any repairs required to keep the premises " in good and tenantable repair ".[98] The landlord is deemed liable for all repairs for which the tenant is not expressly liable,[99] and, subject to this, he is deemed liable for any repairs which he is expressly liable to carry out and any other repairs from time to time required to secure that the house is in good and tenantable repair, not being repairs which the tenant is under express liability to carry out; while the tenant is deemed responsible for any repairs which he is expressly liable to carry out only, and the extent of the landlord's liability is determined by comparing the respective burdens of responsibility. The amount of the liability must be settled by agreement or by the Court before any increase can be made;[97] and the amount cannot be determined in the action in which the increase is sued for.[1]

Certain addition is allowed in the case of railway employees' houses,[2] and the landlord can add to the rent of a house if it comes within the House Letting and Rating (Scotland) Acts 1911, 1920 the full amount of the occupier's rates for which he is liable.[3] Again, if part of a house to which the Act applies is sublet and that part is a dwellinghouse to which the Act applies, the subtenant's rent can be increased by 10 per cent. of the net subrent and the principal tenant's by 5 per cent. of that net rent.[4] If the tenant's interest is determined and the subtenant becomes the tenant, the increase is reduced from 10 per cent. to 5 per cent.[5] The tenant, if asked by the landlord in writing, must give the landlord written particulars of any sublet.[6]

No increase is due or recoverable for any period prior to the expiry of four clear weeks, or where the increase is for rates, one clear week, after service of notice by the landlord on the tenant of an intention to increase the rent.[7] This applies despite any contrary agreement.[7] An error or omission if material, as opposed to a trifling mistake, renders the notice invalid.[8] Not only may a notice be valid though it does not

[95] *Strood Estates* v *Gregory* [1938] A.C. 118.
[96] 1938 Act, s. 7 (2).
[97] 1920 Act, s. 2 (1) (d).
[98] *Ibid.*, s. 2 (5).
[99] *Ibid.*, s. 2 (5); 1954 Act, s. 23.
[1] *Bourne* v *Litton* [1924] 2 K.B. 10.
[2] 1920 Act, s. 2 (1) (e).
[3] See the Valuation and Rating (Scotland) Act 1956, s. 16 (3).
[4] 1923 Act, s. 7 (1).
[5] *Ibid.*, s. 7 (1), amended by 1938 Act, s. 7 (7), Schedule Second.
[6] *Ibid.*, s. 7 (2). He must give notice of the subletting: 1933 Act, s. 4 (4).
[7] 1920 Act, s. 3 (2).
[8] *E.g.*, *Penfold* v *Newman* [1922] 1 K.B. 645, *Hill* v *Hasler* [1921] 3 K.B. 643.

exactly comply with the form in the Regulations provided it is substantially to the same effect but it is not vitiated by some small errors (as in the amount of increases of rent so small as not to affect the amount of increased rent), provided it is not false or misleading in any material respect.[9] A landlord can correct an error by a new notice provided this is served before any increased rent is paid or demanded under the erroneous notice.[10]

If the rent is increased and the increase exceeds the standard rent plus the permitted increases the excess is not recoverable.[11] Where the rent stipulated for exceeds the standard rent, the excess cannot be recovered even though the rent is less than when the house was first let.[12] That is, in order to justify recovery of overpayment there must be an increase of the contractual rent since the prescribed date above the standard rent and not of the contractual rent above some pre-existing figure.[12] So where there is a let of a part at a rent less than that obtained before the house became a controlled house, the rent may still be in excess of the standard rent and overpayment be claimable.[12] If the contractual rent is less than the standard rent with the permitted increases, then when the contractual tenancy ends, the rent may be increased to the amount of the recoverable rent, viz., the standard rent plus increases.[13]

Any excess sum paid as rent irrecoverable by the landlord under the Acts can be recovered from the landlord or his representatives within two years of the payment[14] and any such sum and any sum that the tenant can recover can even be deducted by the tenant from the rent[14] within the two years.[15]

The benefit of the restriction on increase passes with the house to a new tenant.[16] So, unless the proper notice was given to a former tenant, it has to be given when the house is being let to a new tenant.[16] But a landlord in possession who is entitled to make an increase may by notice served on a prospective tenant that the rent will be an increased rent make the increase, and if the prospective tenant takes the house the increase operates at once.[17]

Where there is letting subsequent to the letting which determined the standard rent and the terms of this new let differ materially from the letting that determined the standard rent, if the tenant has had transferred to him a burden or liability previously borne by the landlord,

---

[9] *Fredco Estates* v *Bryant* [1961] 1 All E.R. 34. Though it is signed by agents and this is not stated it is valid if the signers are well known to the tenant as the landlord's agents. *Fredco Estates* (*supra*).

[10] *McKellar* v *McMaster*, 1926 S.C. 754 at 758-9, *per* L.J.C. Alness.

[11] 1920 Act, s. 1.

[12] *Field* v *Gover* [1944] K.B. 200.

[13] *Regional Properties* v *Oxley* [1945] A.C. 347.

[14] 1920 Act, s. 14 (1); 1923 Act, s. 8 (2); 1938 Act, s. 7 (6).

[15] *Bayley* v *Walker* [1925] 1 K.B. 447.

[16] 1920 Act, s. 3 (2); *Schmit* v *Christy* [1922] 2 K.B. 60.

[17] 1938 Act, s. 7 (4).

this is deemed an increase of rent, whether or not the sum payable by way of rent is increased, if the new terms are on the whole less favourable to him than the previous terms.[18] If, however, a burden or liability previously borne by the tenant is transferred to the landlord and as a result the terms on which any house is held are on the whole not less favourable to the tenant than the previous terms, then an appropriate increase of rent can be made and is not to be deemed an increase of rent for the purposes of the Acts.[18] A burden will be held to be transferred if the landlord undertakes an obligation to do something which he, though not previously obliged to do, as for example, to supply hot water, would in fact normally do.[19] So where a tenant agreed to keep the premises in repair but in fact the landlord did the repairs of the exterior and also supplied free hot water and removed refuse and on a new tenancy agreed to keep the exterior in repair and to arrange for a supply of hot water and for the removal of refuse, the House of Lords held that there had been a transfer of a burden of liability in regard to the repairs and a transfer of a burden in respect of the hot water and the refuse. It was enough that a greater burden or liability was imposed on the landlord by the terms of a letting than was imposed by the letting under which the standard rent was fixed.[19] The cessation of voluntary services is not a transfer[20] nor are trading arrangements as to discount on liquor transactions a transfer of liability.[21] The amount of the increase or decrease must, failing agreement, be settled by the Court and if there have been overpayments these can be recovered[22] within two years.[23] Rent is not to be deemed increased if liability for rates is transferred from landlord to tenant, provided a corresponding reduction is made in rent.[24] Previous terms under the Act mean the terms of a previous tenancy which determined the standard rent.[25]

Under the 1954 Act[26] where there is a let under a contractual tenancy and the house is occupied by a statutory tenant and the standard rent is the rent at which the house was let at the beginning on or before 1st September 1939, or an amount ascertainable by apportionment of a rent, and services for the tenant are to be provided under the terms of the letting or are provided by the landlord, and an agreement in relation to these services is made after 30th August 1954 between the landlord and the tenant or a former tenant that the landlord is entitled to a specified increase of rent in respect of the rise in the cost of services in the period after 3rd September 1939 and ending with 30th August

[18] 1920 Act, s. 2 (3). *E.g.*, an increase in the tenant's obligation to repair. *Ebner* v *Lascelles* [1928] 2 K.B. 486 at 500, *per* Salter, J.
[19] *Asher* v *Seaford Estates* [1950] A.C. 508.
[20] *First National Housing Trust* v *Chesterfield R.D.C.* [1948] 2 K.B. 351.
[21] *Brakspear* v *Barton* [1924] 2 K.B. 88.
[22] 1920 Act, s. 14 (1).
[23] *Ibid.*, s. 8 (2); 1938 Act, s. 7 (6).
[24] 1920 Act, s. 2 (3).
[25] *Winchester Court* v *Miller* [1944] K.B. 734.
[26] s. 31 (1), (2).

1954 or a Tribunal under the 1943 Act has, on the landlord's application, determined that it is just that there should be a specified increase, the landlord can recover the amount of that increase; where there is such an agreement or determination as to services which that landlord is not liable to provide under the letting, then any withholding or restoration of them in whole or in part is treated as a transfer from the landlord or the tenant of a burden previously borne by him.[27]

A proper notice of increase must be given by the landlord and has permanent effect on future tenants.[28] The notice of increase, which is not necessary in certain cases,[29] has to be in a form specified in Regulations and state certain matters, including the amounts of increases under separate heads and the dates from which they are to take effect.[30] The Sheriff can amend a notice if he is satisfied that any error or omission in it was due to the landlord's *bona fide* mistake, and can order that, as amended, it is to be deemed to have had effect as a valid notice.[31] Under the Rent Restriction (Notices of Increase) Act 1923,[32] where the tenancy is a periodic one and only determinable by notice to quit, notice of increase takes effect automatically as a valid notice to quit on the day immediately before the day from which the increase is to take effect or on the earliest day thereafter on which if it had been a notice to quit it would have been effective. This reversed a House of Lords decision[33] that if the landlord did not give notice to quit he could not resume possession and thus could not increase the rent. The common law had not been altered by the 1920 Act and the tenant remained by tacit relocation a contractual tenant and the rent in the absence of the notice could not be raised.

Suspension of Permitted Increases. The right to some of the increases depends upon keeping the house in proper repair. An increase for repairs or the 15 per cent. increase can be suspended if the house is "not in all respects reasonably fit for human habitation or is otherwise not in a reasonable state of repair."[34] At any time not less than three months after the date of any increase permitted in respect of repairs, the tenant or the sanitary authority[35] (that is, the local authority under the Public Health Acts) on behalf of the tenant may apply to the Sheriff for an order suspending any such increase and any increase of 15 per cent. of net rent on the ground that the house is not in all respects reasonably

---

[27] s. 31 (3).
[28] 1920 Act, s. 3 (2). It can be given to a prospective tenant. 1938 Act, s. 7 (4).
[29] *E.g.*, the subletting increase: 1923 Act, s. 7 (1).
[30] 1920 Act, s. 3 (2). S.I. 1957 No. 1044.
[31] 1923 Act, s. 6 (1). The tenant was liable for the increase since the date when, if valid, notice would have had effect but not more than six months before the Sheriff's order: s. 8 (1). If the tenant had paid, the excess was repayable to him only in respect of the preceding six months: s. 8 (2).
[32] s. 1.
[33] *Kerr* v *Bryde*, 1923 S.C. (H.L.) 12.
[34] 1920 Act, s. 2 (2); 1923 Act, ss. 5 (1), 18 (1).
[35] *Glasgow Corporation* v *Mickel*, 1922 S.C. 228.

fit for human habitation or is otherwise not in a reasonable state of repair, and, if the Sheriff is satisfied on the production of a certificate of the sanitary authority or otherwise that any such ground is established and the condition of the house is not due to the tenant's neglect or default or breach of express agreement, he must order suspension of the increase until he is satisfied, on the report of the sanitary authority or otherwise, that the necessary repairs (other than those for which the tenant is liable) have been made.[36] And his decision is final.[37] The house is deemed in a reasonable state of repair if it is " in good and tenantable repair ".[38] The authority, on the landlord's application, if satisfied that the necessary repairs have been made, must issue to him an appropriate report on payment of a fee.[39] The right of suspension is in addition to or in place of the common law right to retain the rent of an uninhabitable house.

If the tenant too has got from the sanitary authority a certificate that the house is not in a reasonable state of repair or that it cannot be put into that state at a reasonable expense,[40] and served a copy on the landlord then he has a good defence to the landlord's claim for the 15 per cent. and the repairs increases in respect of any subsequent rental period that the house was not during that period in a reasonable state of repair.[41] The certificate takes effect in the next rental period after its issue. The sanitary authority are bound on the tenant's application to issue the certificate if they are satisfied that the house is not in a reasonable state of repair, or not capable of being put into a reasonable state of repair at reasonable expense;[42] the certificate must state the repairs that are necessary.[43] The condition of the property must not, of course, have been due to the tenant's default or breach of agreement. But where a statutory tenant had served on the landlord a certificate of a local authority that the house was not in a reasonable state of repair and the landlord reduced the rent by the amount of the 40 per cent. increase it was held that the tenant could not also retain the rent till the repairs were carried out, as the common law right of a tenant to retain had been superseded by the statutory remedy of suspension.[44] Lord Russell expressed the opinion that in the case of a contractual tenant he could retain the rent.[45] An increase for an improvement or structural alteration may be suspended or reduced by the Sheriff on the tenant's application because the expenditure was wholly or partly unnecessary—if he was tenant when it was incurred and has not given written consent to it and the expenditure or, if the first

[36] 1920 Act, s. 2 (2).
[37] *Ibid.*, s. 2 (6); *Glasgow Corporation, supra.*
[38] 1920 Act, s. 2 (5).
[39] 1923 Act, s. 5 (2).
[40] 1938 Act, s. 8 (3) (d).
[41] 1923 Act, s. 5 (1).
[42] 1933 Act, s. 12.
[43] 1923 Act, s. 18 (1); 1938 Act, s. 8 (3) (d).
[44] *Stobbs & Sons* v *Hislop*, 1948 S.C. 216.
[45] *Ibid.*, at 20.

tenant after it was incurred the landlord having been in possession when the expenditure was incurred, he became tenant without notice of the alteration or improvement, the amount of the expenditure and the amount of the maximum increase of rent.[46]

Reduction of Rent and Increases under Valuation and Rating (Scotland) Act 1956. Under the Valuation and Rating (Scotland) Act 1956, all recoverable rents under the 1920 and 1923 Acts were reduced by the amount of owner's rates paid in the year 1956-7, in May 1957 as from 16th May 1957 (or other date in certain cases) as a result of the abolition of owner's rates, and the provision that all rates thereafter were to be levied on occupiers;[47] and the standard rents and permitted increases were reduced correspondingly by a fraction representing the poundage of owner's rates for 1956-7.[48]

New Control. The basic element of new control or re-controlled houses was fixed by the 1939 Act,[49] passed when the Second World War was imminent, as a rateable value at or less than £90 and as from 2nd September 1939. Rateable value is the value shown on the appropriate day, 16th May 1939, in the Valuation Roll as the rateable value or, if this is different, the net annual value.[50] If the first assessment was after the appropriate day, the rateable value (or the net annual value if that differed from the rateable value) is that on the day on which the house was first assessed.[51] This rule applied also to houses not already at that time subject to control under the 1920 Act, including some houses which had never before been subject to control such as houses erected after 2nd April 1919[52] and some of which had been decontrolled[53] prior to the 1939 Act.[54] The standard rent is that at which the house was *bona fide* let on 1st September 1939, or the rent at which it was last previously let or the rent at which it is first let thereafter.[55] When it is not reasonably practicable to obtain sufficient evidence of the standard rent, the Court can determine it as of such amount as might be thought proper having regard to the standard rents of similar houses in the neighbourhood.[56] If the rent is progressive, the standard rent is the maximum amount.[57] But rateable value is now the only relevant consideration in determining whether a house falls within the scope of the 1939 Act; rent is irrelevant.[58] In the

[46] 1920 Act, s. 2 (1) (a); 1933 Act, s. 7 (2).
[47] s. 16 (1).
[48] s. 16 (2), Schedule Third.
[49] ss. 3 (1), 8 (a), Schedule First.
[50] 1939 Act, s. 7 (1) and Schedule First, amending 1920 Act, s. 12 (1) (e).
[51] *Ibid.*, s. 7 (3) and Schedule First, amending 1920 Act, s. 12 (1) (e).
[52] 1920 Act, s. 12 (9).
[53] *Supra,* p. 511.
[54] 1939 Act, s. 3.
[55] 1920 Act, s. 12 (1) (a), as amended by 1939, Schedule First.
[56] 1933 Act, s. 6, as amended by 1939 Act, Schedule First.
[57] 1920 Act, s. 12 (1) (a), as amended by 1939 Act, Schedule First.
[58] *Yeate's Trs.* v *Gilfillan,* 1949 S.L.T. (Notes) 19.

case of a letting at a rent less than two-thirds of the rateable value, the standard rent is the rateable value or an earlier rent.[59] Where two houses hitherto separately assessed are let as a single dwellinghouse, it was held that the aggregate of the two separate assessments is a separate assessment for determining the rateable value on the appropriate day.[60]

Apportionment. The provision already dealt with as to this matter applied with the substitution of 16th May 1939 for 3rd August 1914.[61]

Permitted Increases of Rent under New Control. The 1939 Act allowed the following two increases *only* for 1939 or new control houses :
(i) 8 per cent. of the amount spent on improvements or structural alterations where since 2nd September 1939 the landlord has incurred expenditure on such improvements or structural alterations;[62] in the case of any expenditure or costs incurred after 3rd July 1962 the figure is now 12½ per cent. [63]
(ii) The amount of any increase of rates where the rent included occupier's rates for which the landlord is responsible under the House Letting and Rating (Scotland) Acts 1911, 1920,[64] that is, the full amount of the rates which the landlord is responsible for under these Acts.
An increase could also take place if there was a transfer of a burden or obligation under the provisions of the 1920 Act previously referred to.[65]

Rent under 1949 Act and 1954 Act. The standard rent of a new control house might be determined by a letting subsequent to 1st September 1939, and, in line with the general increase in the cost of living since then, rents had risen, sometimes heavily, so that the standard rent might be a very large sum. The Landlord and Tenant (Rent Control) Act 1949, was, therefore, passed, by which the standard rent of a house let for the first time since 1st September 1939, can be referred to a Rent Tribunal set up under the 1943 Act,[66] which is empowered to approve the rent or to reduce it to a sum that the Tribunal think reasonable having regard to the terms and conditions, other than those fixing the amount of rent, of the letting at the time of the application.[67] It cannot be increased. Thus, the standard rent in such cases is not the amount of rent on the first letting but the reasonable rent as determined by the Tribunal. If this is less than what would be the standard rent, it is the

---

[59] *Supra,* p. 531.
[60] *Langford Property Co.* v *Goldrich* [1949] 1 K.B. 511.
[61] 1939 Act, ss. 7 (2), 8 (a).
[62] 1920 Act, s. 2 (1) (a), as amended by 1939 Act, Schedule First.
[63] Housing (Scotland) Act 1962, s. 16.
[64] Fraser, *Rent Acts in Scotland,* 2nd ed., p. 74.
[65] *Supra,* p. 537.
[66] *Infra,* p. 617.
[67] s. 1 (1) (4).

standard rent,[68] if more, the standard rent is not affected by the Act. The
" reasonable rent " becomes the standard rent if and only if it was less
than the standard rent. The rent must be entered in the Register of the
Tribunal prepared and kept by the Local Authority.[69] Any premium
paid for this grant, continuance or renewal of the tenancy is disregarded,[70]
but if paid before 2nd June 1949, and if the tenant so requires, it is
deducted in instalments from the standard rent in the form of a " rental
equivalent ". The premium is divided up and deducted from the whole
rent in instalments called " rental equivalents " until repaid to the tenant
or his successor.[71] In determining the reasonable rent, the Tribunal must
decide how far to take into account the landlord's return on his outlay
or capital, though this is not conclusive.[72] If the Tribunal thinks the
limit imposed by the principal Acts on the recoverable rent exceeds what
would be the standard rent apart from the provisions[73] of the Act, it has
to determine the amount of the excess and if the rent determined as
reasonable by the Tribunal, reduced by the excess, is less than what would
be the standard rent apart from the provisions of the Act[73] the rent so
determined and reduced is from the date of the Tribunal's determination
the standard rent.[74]

Houses under the management of a housing association under the
Housing (Scotland) Act 1950 or houses where the rent was otherwise
limited by an Act were excluded from the scope of the 1949 Act,[75] but
this exemption was ended under the 1954 Act.[76]

The Tribunal must be satisfied by proof that the dwellinghouse is
within the rateable value limits of the Acts.[77] If it is part of larger
premises and was not rated separately, proof of apportionment by the
Court is necessary.[78] The Tribunal cannot act if the application is withdrawn before it makes its decision;[79] and it cannot entertain a second
application after a decision.[80]

The Tribunal has jurisdiction to determine questions appropriate to
the Courts such as forgery, or the validity of the contract or whether a
contract existed, only if these are collateral questions, and it must follow
the principles applied in the courts on such issues.[81] And it can decide
on a " reasonable rent " on its own knowledge and information, though

[68] s. 1 (2).
[69] s. 5.
[70] s. 1 (5).
[71] Schedule First, Part I.
[72] R. v Brighton Rent Tribunal [1950] 2 K.B. at 416-7, per Lord Goddard L.C.J.
[73] s. 1.
[74] s. 1 (3).
[75] s. 1 (7).
[76] s. 28 (4).
[77] R. v Sidmouth Rent Tribunal [1951] 1 K.B. 778.
[78] R. v Fulham Rent Tribunal [1951] 2 K.B. 1.
[79] R. v Hampstead Rent Tribunal [1951] 1 K.B. 541.
[80] R. v Brighton Rent Tribunal [1950] 2 K.B. 410. 1949 Act, s. 1 (1).
[81] R. v Fulham Rent Tribunal, supra; R. v London Rent Tribunal [1951] 1 K.B.
641.

if it notes certain material facts from its own observation, the party affected must be given an opportunity of being heard on it.[82] Expenses cannot be awarded by the Tribunal.

The 1954 Act[83] empowered the Tribunal to increase the rent to an appropriate reasonable figure; this did not apply to new houses built under licence as the licence would fix the rent.[84] The rent determined by the Tribunal if it *differed from* (was even greater than) the standard rent became the new standard rent. The provisions of the 1949 Act[85] for where the reasonable rent is less than the standard rent are changed to provisions for where it *differs* from the standard rent.[86] This applies whether the determination is made before or after 30th August 1954.[87] But an increase of rent by a determination made before 30th August 1954 is not to operate till a date specified in a notice served by the landlord on the tenant and the date must not be earlier than four clear weeks after service of the notice.[88] Where a determination as to a house made before 30th August 1954 has effect under the 1954 Act,[89] any apportionment necessary to determine the standard rent of a house comprised in the first mentioned house, being an apportionment before the coming into operation of the increase of rent under the determination may, without prejudice to the provision of the 1949 Act[90] for variation of apportionments made before a determination, be varied so as to accord with the determination.[91] The provisions for fixing a reasonable rent do not apply to a standard rent fixed under the 1954 Act[92] when the exemption of an authority ceases.[93]

Increase under the 1954 Act. Increases hitherto permitted were not large and the cost of upkeep and repairs had, with the increased cost of materials, wages, etc., risen considerably, by about 20 per cent., discouraging or preventing repairs being carried out and so causing properties to deteriorate. To meet this situation the 1954 Act allowed an increase in rent (a repairs increase) of two-fifths of the rent recoverable before 30th August 1954 of a house let under a controlled tenancy or occupied by a statutory tenant, if the landlord was wholly responsible for repairs, (or a proportion thereby if he was only partly responsible,[94]) and if the house was in good and tenantable repair and not in other respects unfit

---

[82] *R. v Paddington and St. Marylebone Rent Tribunal* [1949] 1 K.B. 666.
[83] s. 28.
[84] Building Materials & Housing Act 1945, s. 7 (1), as amended by Housing (Scotland) Act 1949, s. 38.
[85] s. 1 (2), (3).
[86] s. 28 (1).
[87] s. 28 (2).
[88] s. 28 (2), *proviso.*
[89] s. 28.
[90] s. 4.
[91] s. 28 (3).
[92] s. 26.
[93] s. 28 (5).
[94] s, 16 (2).

for human habitation, and work of repair and maintenance had been carried out by the landlord to a certain value.[95] The landlord was deemed to be wholly liable for repairs unless the tenant was expressly liable.[96] The landlord must give notice of the increase in the prescribed form;[97] this under the 1954 Act could be given to a prospective tenant,[98] but with the Acts no longer applying to new lettings the 1957 Act repealed this provision.[99] Work the cost of which the landlord can count towards a repairs increase is work required for securing that premises used for human habitation are in good and tenantable repair and are not in any other respect unfit for human habitation.[1] The increase may be passed on to a subtenant, for the increase paid by a tenant or a just proportion if the sublet was of part only, may be recovered from a subtenant:[2] notice must be served on the subtenant.[3] The tenant can also, of course, in his own right as landlord claim the repairs increase from the subtenant but the two increases must not exceed the maximum amount of the repairs increase.[4]

In determining whether a house is in good and tenantable repair, any defect due to any act, neglect or default or breach of agreement by the tenant or anyone claiming under him is ignored.[5]

Certain houses are excluded from the provisions;[6] (a) those first let after 1st September 1939 of which the standard rent has been fixed by the Tribunal under the 1949 Act; (b) those provided by conversion or improved, with the aid of a grant, under the Housing (Scotland) Act 1950 Part VII and the rents of which have been fixed by the local authority under Section 113 of that Act, not having been let within five years before the application for the grant, and (c) those provided for agricultural workers with the aid of a grant under the Housing (Scotland) Act 1952[7] and where the local authority has fixed the rent under that Act. Those in respect of which the standard rent is in the future fixed by the local authority under the 1954 Act,[8] being houses that have ceased to belong by sale etc. to an exempted authority under the Rent Acts, were excluded under the 1954 Act, but this provision has been repealed by the 1957 Act[9] as new lettings are now excluded.

---

[95] s. 16 (1). For repairs increase, see ss. 16-24, Schedule First.
[96] s. 23 (1). Repairs include maintenance but not improvements or structural alterations or additional or improved fixtures or fittings: s. 39 (1).
[97] s. 17. The date in the notice must be not less than eight weeks after service of the notice: s. 17 (2).
[98] s. 34 (1).
[99] s. 26 (3); Schedule Eighth, Part II.
[1] Schedule First, para. 10.
[2] s. 21 (1) (2).
[3] s. 21 (5).
[4] s. 21 (3).
[5] s. 24 (1).
[6] s. 16 (3).
[7] s. 3.
[8] s. 26.
[9] s. 26 (3); Schedule Eighth, Part II.

In the case of certain classes of house a repairs increase will only be granted if certain conditions are complied with and subject to certain special procedure,[10] namely, houses which have been subject to one of the statutory procedures during a specified period available for dealing with houses in disrepair—(a) those in respect of which there were in force at any time between 13th November 1953 (the date of publication of the Bill) and 30th August 1954 (the date of commencement of the Act) certificates by the sanitary authorities granted under the Rent Restrictions Acts that the houses were not in reasonable repair or orders of courts under the Acts suspending the increase of 40 per cent. provided for under the 1920 Act;[11] (b) those in respect of which notice was given or served by a local authority under the Public Health (Scotland) Act 1897 or in respect of which notices under the Act were in force during the same period in respect of a nuisance arising from any want or defect of a structural character; (c) those in respect of which notices under the Housing (Scotland) Act 1950[12] were in force at any time during the period, requiring landlords to carry out works on houses unfit because of disrepair or sanitary defects.[13] And these provisions are applicable even though the certificates or notices have been complied with or withdrawn.[14]

In order to qualify for the repairs increase, to justify an increase of rent on this ground, it must be shown, first, that the house is in good and tenantable repair and that it is not otherwise unfit for human habitation.[15] For the purposes of the Act the local authority must[16] apply the definition of the Housing (Scotland) Act 1950[17] and have regard to " the extent, if any, to which by reason of disrepair or sanitary defects the house falls short of the provisions of any building regulations in operation in the district ". If the house comes to deteriorate so that that test can no longer be applied the increase is suspended until it is put into proper condition. In the case of a house which is part of a larger building, it is not to be regarded as in good and tenantable repair unless every part of the building which the tenant of the house requires to use in connection with his occupation is also in good and tenantable repair. There must also, secondly, be produced by the landlord satisfactory evidence of the amount spent by the landlord on repair of the house in the appropriate period[18] as laid down in the Act.[19] In the twelve months before service of the notice of increase, work of not less than three-fifths

---

[10] Schedule Second. The landlord must obtain a certificate of repair from the local authority. *Ibid.*, para. 1.
[11] s. 2 (1) (c) or (d).
[12] s. 7.
[13] s. 20, Schedule Second.
[14] See 1954 S.L.T. (News) 165.
[15] s. 16 (1) (a).
[16] s. 39 (2).
[17] s. 184 (2).
[18] s. 16 (1) (b).
[19] Schedule First.

35

in value of the rent recoverable immediately before 30th August 1954 must have been carried out on the house.[20] Notice may be served at any time after the carrying out of the work but for six months from 30th August 1954 the landlord could show at his option that in any continuous period of three years falling within four years immediately preceding service of the notice of increase he has spent six-fifths of the 1954 rent.[21] The expenditure test is a once and for all one when the increase is claimed so that once a house qualifies for the increase, the landlord need not spend the amount of the repairs increase or any minimum sum on the maintenance of the property. All expenditure on a building consisting of more than one house, whether work is carried out on all or any of the houses or on the building or so as to enure for the benefit of all or any of the houses is, in assessing whether an increase is justified for one house, added together and apportioned between the houses owned by the landlord on the basis of their rateable value or floor space.[22]

Notice of the increase must be given[23] and must[24] specify a date for the coming into operation of the increase that is not less than eight clear weeks from the date of service of the notice.

The tenant can appeal against the notice. If he says that the landlord has not spent the minimum sum, he can appeal to the Sheriff,[25] or where it is necessary to determine the extent to which the landlord is responsible for repairs to the house,[25] or whether the house is one in respect of which a repairs increase is recoverable, or as to the amount of rent recoverable before 30th August 1954; proceedings are to be in the same manner as small debt proceedings[26] and the Sheriff's decision is final and conclusive.[26] If he maintains that the house is not habitable, he must apply to the local authority for a certificate that an increase of rent is not justified as either or both conditions have not been fulfilled, that is, a disrepair certificate, which replaces certificates of sanitary authorities under older Acts and if that is issued,[27] the notice is suspended and no increase can be demanded unless and until the local authority, on being satisfied that the house has been put into a proper state of repair, withdraw the notice.[28] On being satisfied that the necessary work has been done by the landlord, the local authority may revoke the certificate on the landlord's application.[29] In old control houses, not only the repairs increase but those of the 40 per cent. increases under the 1920 Act[30]

---

[20] Schedule First, para. 1.
[21] Ibid., para. 2.
[22] Ibid., para. 7 (3).
[23] s. 17 (1).
[24] s. 17 (2). The form of the notice is set out in Regulations: S.I. 1957, No. 1044.
[25] Schedule First, para. 4.
[26] s. 41 (1).
[27] s. 18 (1). The subtenant can also apply to the local authority: s. 21 (4).
[28] s. 18 (3), (4).
[29] s. 18 (4).
[30] s. 2 (1) (c), (d).

will be suspended by a certificate of disrepair[31] but the 1957 Act[32] repealed this provision, except where a certificate was granted before 6th July 1957 or after that in pursuance of a previous application, and only the 1954 Act increase (or the 1957 Act increase) is now suspended unless as above stated. In determining whether to grant or to revoke the local authority must disregard the cause of the defect; the provision[33] that defects due to the act, neglect or default or breach of agreement of the tenant are to be disregarded does not have effect in determining such questions.[33] The local authority must, on the landlord's application, revoke that order if the necessary work has been done to their satisfaction.[34] Within twenty-one days of service on him of a copy of the certificate of disrepair or of notice of the local authority's refusal to revoke, the landlord may appeal to the Sheriff against the issue of the certificate or a refusal to revoke a certificate.[35] The procedure in this case is summary and appeal to the Court of Session by stated case is competent.[36] The tenant cannot appeal against a refusal to issue a certificate but, if he can satisfy the court that a certificate should have been granted, no repairs increase or increase under the 1920 Act will be payable.[37]

The repairs increase may be suspended. If there is in force at 30th August 1954 a certificate of the sanitary authority under the Rent Acts that the house is not in a reasonable state of repair, this is treated as a certificate of disrepair, or if there is an order of the court under[38] the 1920 Act.[39] And if the local authority serves a notice under the Housing (Scotland) Act 1950[40] requiring the execution of works on a house where a notice of repairs increase has been served, then as soon as the Housing Act notice becomes operative the authority must issue a certificate and serve a copy on both parties, and from its service on the landlord it operates as a certificate of disrepair;[41] and so long as it is in force the repairs increase is not recoverable.[42] If on service of a notice of repairs or at any later time the tenant considers the landlord is not entitled to the increase for the statutory reasons, he can apply to the local authority for a certificate of disrepair[42] and if the authority are satisfied that this is so, they must issue a certificate to that effect of disrepair and so long as it is in force the repairs increase is not payable.[43]

[31] s. 19 (1).
[32] s. 9 (3).
[33] s. 24 (1).
[34] s. 18 (4).
[35] s. 18 (6).
[36] s. 41 (2).
[37] s. 18 (5). The subtenant can also withhold the landlord's increase and the tenant's increase: s. 21 (4).
[38] s. 2 (1) (c), (d).
[39] s. 19 (2).
[40] s. 7.
[41] s. 18 (2).
[42] s. 18 (1).
[43] s. 18 (3).

In the case of the special classes of house abovementioned,[44] the landlord must satisfy the local authority that the house now fulfils both of these conditions which justify an increase and get a certificate of repair from the authority.[45] He must then get from the tenant a written agreement that work of the minimum sum necessary to qualify has been done: if the tenant will not agree, the landlord can apply to the authority for a declaration that it has been done.[46] If the local authority refuse to give such a certificate and issue a certificate of refusal, the refusal is treated as a certificate of disrepair.[47] Copies must be served on both parties,[47] and the landlord can appeal to the Sheriff as against a certificate of disrepair granted on the tenant's application.[48] If the Sheriff revokes the certificate of refusal, the local authority must forthwith grant a certificate of repair.[48] If a certificate or order which causes the inclusion of the house in the special class procedure was in force at 30th August, 1954 and the landlord successfully applies to the local authority for a certificate of repair, the earlier certificate is automatically revoked.[49]

Increase in Cost of Services. Where a dwellinghouse is let under a controlled tenancy or occupied by a statutory tenant and the standard rent is the rent at which the house was let under a letting beginning on or before 1st September 1939 or, if the house is part of a larger property, is an amount ascertainable by apportionment of a rent under such a letting and if services (including attendance, the provision of heating or lighting, the supply of hot water and any other privilege or facility connected with the occupancy of a dwellinghouse[50]) are either under the terms of the letting or in fact provided by the landlord,[51] an increase can be claimed in respect of an increase in the cost of services, in terms of an agreement in writing made after 30th August 1954 between the landlord and the tenant or a former tenant as to the right of the landlord to an increase of a specified amount or in terms of an order of a Rent Tribunal on the landlord's application, in respect of the rise over the period beginning on 3rd September 1939 and ending on 30th August 1954 in the cost of the provision of the services.[52] This increase, of which no notice is necessary, runs from the date stated in the agreement or of the Tribunal's determination.[53] The Tribunal must make such inquiries as they think fit and give both parties an opportunity of being heard or, if they (the parties) prefer, of submitting written representations.[54] Both

---

[44] *Supra*, p. 545.
[45] Schedule Second, para. 1.
[46] *Ibid.*, para. 5.
[47] *Ibid.*, para. 2.
[48] *Ibid.*, para. 4.
[49] *Ibid.*, para. 1.
[50] s. 39 (1).
[51] s. 31 (1).
[52] s. 31 (2).
[53] s. 31 (4).
[54] s. 31 (5).

the repairs increase and the cost of services increase can be made during a contractual tenancy.[55] But where the letting was before 30th August 1954 and under the agreement the tenant was obliged to pay a repairs increase where such was permitted under general legislation, then the tenant is relieved of that obligation but the statutory increase can be claimed.[56] The owner's liability for rates on houses subject to a repairs increase was limited,[57] but this has been repealed by the Valuation and Rating (Scotland) Act 1956.[58]

Increases under 1957 Act. The rents of certain controlled houses may be increased in accordance with the provisions of this Act, which came into operation on 6th July 1957.[59] First, the repairs increase under the 1954 Act is enlarged to one half instead of two-fifths of the rent recoverable immediately before the passing of the 1954 Act, that is on 30th August, 1954 with a view to including the further increase in repair costs since 30th August 1954;[60] if that rent included occupier's rates or the provision of services or the use of furniture, these are deducted from it in calculating the recoverable rent. If the two-fifths increase is in operation, the tenant or the subtenant must get eight weeks' notice of the increase to one-half in prescribed form as provided in Regulations and this is not recoverable until the period of the notice has expired.[61] Second, a landlord who is wholly responsible for repairs can increase the rent of a controlled house by one-quarter of the 1954 recoverable rent, that is, the rent recoverable immediately before 30th August 1954 and not that rent as reduced under the Valuation and Rating (Scotland) Act 1956 if the house is in good and tenantable repair and is not otherwise unfit for human habitation,[62] and if the house is not a house in respect of which an increase under the 1954 Act is recoverable.[63] The expenditure test does not now apply in this case. If he is responsible for only part of the repairs, the amount of the increase is to be reduced proportionately.[64] Any question whether the landlord is responsible for repairs or the amount of the aforesaid reduction must be determined, failing written agreement between landlord and tenant, by the Sheriff.[65] The increase may be passed on to a subtenant.[66] The landlord is entitled to the 1954 Act increase, though there is already a 1957 Act increase, but no 1957 increase can take effect while the 1954 Act increase is

[55] s. 16 (1).
[56] s. 22.
[57] s. 35-36.
[58] Schedule Seventh, Parts III and IV.
[59] s. 27 (2).
[60] s. 9 (1).
[61] s. 9 (2).
[62] s. 7 (1), (2).
[63] s. 7 (3) (b).
[64] s. 7 (2), *proviso.*
[65] s. 7 (4).
[66] s. 8 (1).

recoverable.[67] The 1957 Act is thus alternative to the repairs increase and cannot be charged for any period for which a repairs increase is recoverable.[67] If the tenant thinks that either or both of the conditions justifying an increase are not fulfilled he can after service of a notice upon it apply to the local authority for a certificate of disrepair; if this is granted, the increase is not payable while it is in force.[66] Where the 1957 increase has been claimed, four months must elapse before the 1954 Act increase can be claimed in substitution; that is, a further notice in respect of the 1954 Act increase cannot be served until four months after service of the notice in respect of the 1957 Act increase.[68]

The provisions of the 1954 Act as to service of notices of increase, granting or refusing of certificates of disrepair and passing on increases to subtenants,[69] and the provisions of the Act as to certificates or notices of local authorities or orders of a Sheriff as to the state of repair of property are applied to the 1957 Act increase,[70] and those as to applications and appeals to the Sheriff, which are to be under small debt procedure and final and conclusive, are also applied to that increase.[69] The effect of the 1954 Act[71] provisions on a certificate of disrepair suspending the permitted increases under the 1920 Act[72] has been repealed,[73] and a tenant thus can no longer withhold payment of the 1920 Act increases in the event of disrepair.

The four classes of house excluded from the repairs increase in the 1954 Act are likewise excluded from the 1957 Act increase.[74] The houses, also, which are subject to special procedure under the 1954 Act are subject to that procedure in regard to the 1957 Act increase.[75]

The increase may be claimed during the currency of an existing tenancy without terminating that tenancy.[76] It is claimable notwithstanding anything in the terms of the tenancy or of any Act.[76]

A notice of increase of eight clear weeks is necessary under the 1957 Act.[77] The provisions of the 1923 Act[78] in relation to amendment of an erroneous notice by the Court are applied to the 1957 notices of increase.[79] There are modifications of the 1954 Act in relation to the 1957 Act increases. Thus, the declaration required by the 1954 Act[80] is omitted, and there is now a provision that notice of intention to increase the rent by the 1957 increase is not to be served under the section of the 1954

[67] s. 8 (2).
[68] s. 9 (5).
[69] s. 8 (1). The form of notice for the 1957 Act increase is prescribed by S.I. 1957 No. 1044.
[70] s. 8 (3).
[71] s. 19 (1).
[72] s. 2 (1) (c), (d).
[73] 1957 Act, s. 9 (3). *Supra*, pp. 534 *et seq.*
[74] s. 7 (3).
[75] s. 8 (1).
[76] s. 7 (1).
[77] s. 8 (1).
[78] ss. 6 (1), 8 (1). See *supra*, p. 538.
[79] 1957 Act, Schedule Sixth, para. 2.
[80] Schedule First.

Act[81] in respect of a house at any time within four months after a notice to increase the rent by way of repairs increase has been served in respect of the house and any notice served in contravention is to be void.[82]

The rules previously stated[83] as contained in the earlier legislation in relation to recovery of overpayments are applied by the 1957 Act to sums made irrecoverable by that Act.[84] Decontrol of premises does not affect the recovery of former overpayments.[85]

The landlord of certain private subsidiary houses[86]—houses built with Government contributions in agricultural parishes, rural workers' and agricultural workers' houses for which assistance has been given under local authority schemes and houses in respect of which improvement grants have been made by a local authority—can charge the 1954 Act or the 1957 Act increase despite conditions imposed by one of the four Acts or an agreement or undertaking entered into under those Acts limiting the rents.[87] These conditions are to have effect as if they limited the rent to that fixed under the conditions plus the 1954 or 1957 Act increases.[87]

B. Regulated Tenancies

Regulation of Rents. The 1965 Act provides that the rent which is to be payable under a regulated tenancy is, instead of being controlled by the Rent Acts, to be regulated in accordance with separate and entirely new provisions contained in Parts I and II of that Act.[88] Thus, it is the system of rent regulation which especially marks out the new class of tenancy from those lettings which were already subject to control. The critical figure in the case of the controlled dwellinghouse is the " standard rent "; in the case of the regulated tenancy it is the " rent limit ", that is, the limit on contractual rent or on the rent recoverable during statutory periods.[89] The method by which this limit is ascertained takes one or other of two forms, depending on whether the rent payable for the dwellinghouse in question has been registered in the Register of Rents under Part II of the 1965 Act. Until the rent has been registered, it is to be fixed by temporary provisions contained in Part I of the Act,[90] which follow closely the existing pattern for rent control as applied to England by the 1957 Act. Once the rent for the dwellinghouse has been registered,

---

[81] s. 17.
[82] Schedule Third, adding to s. 17 (1) (b).
[83] *Supra.*
[84] s. 26 (1), Schedule Sixth, para. 1.
[85] Schedule Fourth, para. 8.
[86] Houses under the Housing (Scotland) Act 1950, ss. 101, 114 (1) (c) (ii), Housing (Financial Provisions) Act 1924, s. 2, and the Housing (Rural Workers) Act 1926, s. 3.
[87] s. 10.
[88] s. 2. See Rent Regulation (Forms, etc.) (Scotland) Regulations 1965 No. 2042, prescribing the forms to be used in Scotland for the purposes of the 1965 Act.
[89] See ss. 3 and 5; compare the "rent limit " in 1957 Act, s. 1, for England only.
[90] s. 3 (3).

however, the registered rent replaces the previous figure as the limit on rent recoverable for the tenancy.[91]

A distinction is drawn by the 1965 Act between the contractual and statutory periods of a regulated tenancy[89] During the contractual period the limit represents the figure beyond which any excess is irrecoverable from the tenant, whatever may have been stipulated for in the contract; the landlord is not entitled to claim that figure unless he has contracted for it, and he cannot claim for more whatever the terms of the contract. In the case of the statutory period, on the other hand, the limit becomes the rent for the dwellinghouse, all of which the landlord can claim by service on the tenant of the appropriate notice of increase where necessary. This distinction is of importance with regard to the permitted variation on the rent limit, and is considered again in context below.

Limit on Contractual Rent. The limit on the landlord's power to stipulate for increased rent during the currency of the lease is ascertained in the following way. In the case of an agreement made before 8th December 1965, the limit is the amount of rent which was payable under that agreement, allowing for any variation agreed on by the parties before that date.[92] Where the agreement was entered into on or after that date it is the rent fixed by that agreement;[92] at first sight, the landlord will enjoy a certain measure of freedom in arriving at the rent which he will demand from a tenant under the lease, but he must bear in mind that the figure will be subject to review before it is registered and, if it is thought to be too high, will be replaced. Where a regulated tenancy changes hands and a new regulated tenancy is created, the limit remains that amount of rent which was payable for the last rental period of any previous regulated tenancy which existed over the house within the last three years, or the latest if there was more than one.[93] The landlord is thus prevented from raising the rent limit at the end of a tenancy without leaving the premises empty during this period or occupying them himself. This reference back, it should be noticed, applies only for a period of three years, and only where the dwellinghouse was previously let as a regulated tenancy; in other cases, *e.g.,* where the house was previously let as a shop or as business premises, the landlord is free to proceed on the basis that it is a new agreement. Where a tenancy has been released from control subsequent to 8th December 1965 and the rent is accordingly maintained at an artificially low level,[94] or where a controlled tenancy was converted into a regulated tenancy by a second

[91] s. 3 (2).
[92] s. 3 (3) (b).
[93] s. 3 (3) (a): compare the three-year period mentioned in Schedule 3, para. 3 and Schedule 4, para. 1 (b) outside which a fresh application for registration, not based on alteration of circumstances, may be made.
[94] Under s. 11 (6); see *infra,* p. 553.

transmission on death,[95] the reference back likewise does not apply;[96] similarly, where the rents of subsidised private houses have been fixed by a local authority, these " artificial " rents are not to be treated as the basis for the calculation of the new rent limit once these houses are released from such control.[97] Once again the landlord in either case, on the emergence of a new unfettered regulated tenancy, may proceed as if it were a new agreement. The landlord is bound to supply the tenant, if requested by him in writing to do so, with a written statement of the rent which was payable for the last rental period of the previous regulated tenancy, subject to certain penalties if he fails to comply with the request without reasonable excuse.[98]

Adjustment of the limit set upon the rent for which the landlord may ask under the contract, enabling him to stipulate for an increase, is allowed for in similar situations as those already discussed in relation to new control.[99] During the contractual period the rent limit will be increased or decreased as the case may be if the amount of rent which it is reasonable to charge is affected in the following circumstances only:

(a) *Repairs, Services, Furniture*: Where under the terms of the tenancy there is any difference as regards the responsibility for repairs, the provision of services by the landlord or the use of furniture by the tenant as compared with the terms of the previous tenancy. If the difference is such that the amount of rent which it is reasonable to charge is affected, the limit will be increased by an appropriate amount.[1]

(b) *Rates*: Where for any contractual period there is a difference in the rates payable by the landlord in respect of the dwellinghouse and the amount so borne during the last rental period of the previous tenancy, or, as the case may be, the first rental period for which the previous terms were agreed.[2] Where the rating and rental periods are of different lengths, the necessary adjustment must be made in the calculation; the Act provides that for the purposes of such an adjustment a period of one month shall be treated as equivalent to one-twelfth of a year and a period of a week as equivalent to one fifty-second of a year.[3]

(c) *Services*: Where for any contractual period there is an increase in the cost of the provision of any services provided for the

[95] By s. 13, which provides, in subsection (3) that the rent limit is nevertheless to remain at the existing level of control.
[96] s. 11 (5).
[97] s. 18 (2).
[98] s. 19. See Rent Book (Forms of Notice) (Scotland) Regulations 1965 No. 2043, as to the form of notice in rent books, in the case of regulated tenancies.
[99] s. 4.
[1] s. 4 (2).
[2] s. 4 (3).
[3] s. 8.

tenant by the landlord compared with the cost at the time when the previous terms or rent for the previous tenancy were agreed.[4]

(d) *Improvements*: Where an improvement has been effected in the dwellinghouse.[5] The word "improvement" is defined in the Act[6] in exactly the same terms as in the 1957 Act, that is, that it includes "structural alteration, extension or addition and the provision of additional fixtures or fittings, but does not include anything done by way of decoration or repair". Provided that the improvement was completed after the time as from which the rent for the previous tenancy or the previous terms were agreed, and in any event after 8th December 1965, the limit on recoverable rent will be increased by $12\frac{1}{2}$ per cent. per annum[7] of the amount expended on the improvement by the landlord or any superior landlord or by any person from whom either of them derives title.[5]

Once a situation has arisen in which such an adjustment applies, the landlord is free to stipulate for the appropriate increase to be paid by the tenant. No notice of increase is necessary, but the landlord may only, as a matter of common law, recover increased rent from his tenant so far as this is consistent with the terms of the lease. If the previous terms of the lease already provided for a variation of the rent in any of the circumstances stated above, however, the landlord is not entitled by the Act to a further variation by reason of the same circumstances.[8]

The amount of any increase under circumstances (a) and (c) may be called in question by either party. In the event of such a dispute the amount of the increase or decrease, or the question whether the limit falls to be altered at all, will be determined by the Sheriff. Such a determination may be made so as to relate to past rental periods, and will in any case continue to have effect until revoked or varied by a fresh determination by him.[9] It will be noticed that the criterion upon which the decision of whether an alteration is justified in circumstances (a) and (c) is based is not simply whether there has been an alteration in circumstances, but rather whether the amount of rent which it is reasonable to charge has been affected; it is in these cases that the determination of the Sheriff may be invoked. In the case of an alteration in respect of a variation in the rates or an improvement effected by the landlord no such question arises.

---

[4] s. 4 (4).
[5] s. 4 (5); *cp. supra*, pp. 533, 541, for controlled tenancies.
[6] s. 17 (1).
[7] The figure of $12\frac{1}{2}$ per cent. is the same as that applied in the case of new control to improvements effected after 3rd July 1962, by s. 16 of the Housing (Scotland) Act 1962.
[8] s. 4 (6).
[9] s. 4 (7).

Limit of Rent during Statutory Periods. When the contractual period is superseded by the statutory period[10] the limit on the recoverable rent remains unchanged; the landlord is still restricted to that rent which was recoverable for the last contractual period of the tenancy.[11] In the case of any subsequent variation of that limit, however, certain important differences arise.

Variation of the limit of recoverable rent during the statutory period is competent in the following circumstances only:

(a) *Rates*: Where any rates are, or were during the last contractual period, borne by the landlord in respect of the dwellinghouse, by the amount of any difference for any statutory period from the rates payable for the last contractual period.[12] The Second Schedule of the 1957 Act, which previously had no application in Scotland as the rates increase in the case of controlled dwellinghouses in this country is still to be ascertained under the Rent Acts,[13] is extended to Scotland for the purpose of calculating the amount of rates for this provision.[14] That Schedule provides[15] that the amount of rates for any rental period shall for the purposes of the Act be taken to be that part of the total rates payable for the rating period which includes the rental period in question, bearing the same relation to the total rates for the rating period as the rental period bears to the rating period. Where these periods are of different lengths the 1965 Act provides that for the purposes of the necessary adjustment for calculations of the rates variation a period of one month shall be treated as equivalent to one-twelfth of a year and a period of a week as equivalent to one fifty-second of a year.[16] Thus, if the rating period is a year and the rental period one month, the rates to be included in the rent limit will be a twelfth of the total for the rating period.

Any discount or allowance made under any enactment relating to allowances given where the rates are paid by the owner instead of by the occupier are left out of account.[17] The landlord may levy an increase on his statutory tenant in this situation whether or not he was entitled to do so under the contract, which is now superseded; but no increase may take effect except in pursuance of a notice of increase served by the landlord on the tenant.[18]

---

[10] See *supra,* pp. 515, 516.
[11] s. 5.
[12] s. 6 (2); compare s. 3 (1) of the 1957 Act, which applies to England only.
[13] 1920 Act, s. 2 (1) (b); see *supra,* p. 534.
[14] s. 47 contains certain modifications to Schedule 2 of the 1957 Act in its application to Scotland.
[15] Schedule 2, para. 1.
[16] 1965 Act, s. 8.
[17] 1957 Act, Schedule 2, para. 5.
[18] s. 6 (2).

The notice must specify the amount of the increase, and the date from which it is to take effect, and must take the prescribed form.[19] The date cannot be earlier than six months before the service of the notice, and if the date is earlier than the date of service the unpaid rent does not become due from the tenant until the day after such service.[20]

(b) *Services, Furniture*: Where there is, for any statutory period, any difference as respects the provision of services for the tenant by the landlord or the use of furniture by the tenant, or any circumstances relating thereto, as compared with the last contractual period.[21] The criterion of materiality of any such difference is, as in the case of the contractual period, whether the amount of rent which it is reasonable to charge is affected; if so, the rent limit is decreased or increased by an appropriate amount.[21] This provision is designed especially to meet the case where the landlord withdraws services or furniture from the tenant at the end of the contractual period, although, of course, it operates equally well the other way. It should be noticed that no notice of increase is required in this case should the landlord provide additional services and seek to charge for them by increasing the rent. Questions as to the amount of any such increase or decrease, or whether any such variation of the rent limit is justified by the circumstances, are in the first instance to be determined by agreement in writing between the landlord and the tenant; failing such agreement, determination of the question will be made by the Sheriff.[22] Any such determination may be made so as to relate to past statutory periods, and will continue to have effect until revoked or varied by agreement of the parties or by the Sheriff.[22]

(c) *Improvements*: Where improvements have been effected in the dwellinghouse by the landlord or superior landlord.[23] In order to qualify for this variation, which will naturally take the form of an increase in the rent limit, the improvements in question must have been completed after the time as from which the rent for the previous tenancy was agreed, and in any event after 8th December 1965. The amount of the increase allowed is, as for the contractual period, 12½ per cent. per annum of the amount expended on the improvement by the landlord or any superior landlord or by any person from whom either of them derives

---

[19] s. 9 (1); note that where a notice of increase is served during the contractual period and the tenancy could, by a notice to quit served by the landlord at the same time, have been brought to an end before the date specified in the notice of increase, that notice has the double effect of converting the tenancy from that date and marking the date as from which the increase takse effect: s. 9 (3).

[20] s. 6 (3).

[21] s. 6 (4).

[22] s. 6 (5).

[23] s. 6 (6); for the definition of " improvement " see s. 17 (1), and *supra*, p. 554.

title. It is essential in this case for the landlord to serve a notice of increase in the prescribed form[24] on the tenant before he is able to recover the increased amount from the tenant; the notice must specify the amount of the increase and the date from which it is to take effect, which in the case of the repairs increase cannot be any date before the service of the notice.[25]

As in the case of the improvements increase allowable in relation to new control houses,[26] the statutory tenant of a regulated tenancy is protected against unnecessary improvements or the expenditure by the landlord of an unreasonable amount. He is entitled to apply to the Sheriff within one month of the service upon him of the notice of increase for an order cancelling or reducing the increase on either of these grounds; in special cases the Sheriff may allow a late application.[27] Where, however, the tenant had himself consented in writing to the improvement and had acknowledged, in whatever terms, that the rent could be increased on account of that improvement, he is barred from making such an application; similarly, no such application may be made where the local authority has approved of or required the making of the improvement,[28] either by making a grant for the purpose[29] or by directing[30] the landlord to carry out street works.

Where a grant has been made by the local authority to the landlord for carrying out an improvement in the dwellinghouse,[29] the amount of that grant is to be subtracted from the landlord's expenditure in order to ascertain his expenditure on the improvement for the purposes of the improvement variation.[31] Money expended by the landlord on works carried out on a street under directions given by the local authority[30] is treated for the purposes of this variation as an improvement effected on the dwellinghouse;[32] but where benefit accrued from the carrying out of these works to other premises of the landlord not occupied by the tenant this must be taken into account and the appropriate deduction made as may be determined by agreement in writing between the parties or, failing agreement, by the Sheriff.[33] Similarly where a grant or contribution has been made towards the cost of the street works under an enactment, this too must be taken into account in computing the landlord's true expenditure in the dwellinghouse.[34]

[24] See note 88, *supra*.
[25] s. 6 (6).
[26] *Supra*, p. 541.
[27] s. 6 (7).
[28] ss. 6 (7), 17 (5).
[29] Under the Housing (Scotland) Act 1950, s. 111.
[30] Under any of the enactments referred to in s. 1 of the Local Government (Street Works) (Scotland) Act 1956, which relate to private streets.
[31] s. 17 (2).
[32] s. 17 (3).
[33] s. 17 (4) (a).
[34] s. 17 (4) (b).

Proceedings before Registration. In some cases the ascertainment of the amount of any alteration or variation in the rent limit is automatic, and there is no room for dispute; for instance, where there is a fluctuation in the amount of rates borne by the landlord, the appropriate limit will be altered without more ado.[35] In the majority of the circumstances discussed above, however, there is an element of uncertainty both as regards whether in a particular case any variation is justified and as to the amount of such a variation. The determination of all such questions is, at this stage, to be made, failing agreement, by the Sheriff.

The Act directs[36] that where an application is made to the Sheriff for such a determination or for an order (*e.g.,* cancelling or reducing an improvements increase on the ground that the improvement was unnecessary or the amount expended was excessive[37]) under its provisions, it shall be made by way of summary application. The application is to be conducted and disposed of in like manner as proceedings brought under the Small Debt (Scotland) Acts 1837 to 1889, and the Sheriff's determination on any such application is to be final.

Registration of Rents. The system of registration of rents, the most important innovation made by the 1965 Act, and the new method of arriving at the rent limit for a dwellinghouse which goes with it, is designed to replace the old system of the rent freeze, in selected urban areas at first but eventually over the whole country. The central figure in this new system is the rent officer. It is his task to determine the " fair rent " for a dwellinghouse[38] on the application of either landlord or tenant or both where they have failed to agree; his determination is subject to review by the local rent assessment committee, whose decision can be appealed on a point of law to the Court of Session but is not otherwise subject to review by the Courts.[39] Where the fair rent has been determined and, if determined by agreement between the parties, approved by the rent officer, it is his task to register that figure, with certain adjustments,[40] in the Register of Rents which he keeps for the purpose. Once registered it becomes the rent limit for that dwellinghouse, replacing any previous limit set before registration was resorted to.[41] Thereafter the registered rent is subject to review by the rent officer or the rent assessment committee, but always the criterion remains that of what is a fair rent in the circumstances.

The provisions of Part I of the 1965 Act which deal with rent regulation before registration are, like those applicable to controlled dwellinghouses, highly complex. This is complexity born of necessity,

---

[35] See ss. 4 (3), 6 (2).
[36] s. 45; see *infra,* p. 624.
[37] s. 6 (7).
[38] s. 27.
[39] Tribunals and Inquiries (Rent Assessment Committees) Order 1965 No. 2151.
[40] s. 28.
[41] s. 3 (2).

since the arbiter of rent fixing in such cases is the Sheriff, and the prime need is for certainty, even at the expense of clarity. The system of registration of rents contained in Part II is the very opposite of this; the provisions which deal with the method of fixing the rent limit, in particular the section which defines the " fair rent ", are simple, indeed deceptively so. For, as will be seen below,[42] the term " fair rent " is not precisely defined; in the end of the day it can only mean what in the rent officials' eyes is the proper rent in the circumstances. This obscurity is consistent with the transmission of rent fixing to the State; it would be a mistake to expect any objectivity which would limit the State's discretion to control the pattern of the rise in rent levels in a given area as it thinks fit.

At the time of writing, the 1965 Act having only recently passed into law, few rent assessment committees have yet been constituted and the system has barely begun to operate. What follows can only be an outline of the provisions of the Act; little can be said of that all-important matter, what in practice the rent officials' policy will be. For it is to this practice, and in particular to the decisions of the rent assessment committees, that the parties must look for guidance when attempting to agree, as in the first instance they are entitled to do, the fair rent which is to form the basis for the rent limit for the dwellinghouse with which they are concerned.

The Machinery of Registration. Rent officers and rent assessment committees are being set up on a regional basis, by registration areas. The registration areas for this purpose are local authority areas; that is, large burghs and counties, or in some cases groupings of such areas;[43] each have or will have their own hierarchy of rent officials. Both rent officers and the members of the rent assessment committees are to be appointed by the Secretary of State. In the case of the rent officers for the area, however, the appointment is to be made after consultation with the local authority;[43] they are, in effect, local government officials, paid by the central government[44] but entitled to be ranked as local authority officers for superannuation and other purposes.[45] The qualifications for the post of rent officer have been left deliberately vague; there is no requirement, for instance, that they should be experienced in valuation work or otherwise professionally equipped for the job. The intention was that they should be, in a sense, amateurs, people capable of arriving at a common sense, man in the street, view of what a fair rent should be; in practice, few of them are likely to be newcomers to housing problems. There is no set number of rent officers for these areas; the number to be appointed is left to the Secretary of State.[46]

---

[42] *Infra,* pp. 559, 561.
[43] s. 24 (2).
[44] s. 24 (3).
[45] s. 24 (4).
[46] s. 24 (2).

The members of the rent assessment committees are to be drawn from a central panel of persons appointed for the purpose by the Secretary of State;[47] consultation with the local authority at this level is not required by the Act. The panel is the medium of state control, and it is through the decisions of the rent assessment committees that a measure of uniformity of decision, or otherwise as may be thought desirable, will be achieved throughout the country. Two of the members of the panel act as president and vice-president on the nomination of the Secretary of State,[48] and it is generally speaking their task to determine the number of rent assessment committees to act for any registration area and their constitution.[49] Each committee is to consist of a chairman and one or two other members, all, of course, drawn from the panel;[50] in certain cases, if the president of the panel thinks fit, he may direct that the chairman of the committee sitting alone may exercise the functions of the whole committee, where the parties consent.[51] Once again there is nothing in the Act limiting the Secretary of State's discretion in selecting members of the panel; it is natural, however, that he will look for trained lawyers and valuers to carry out the functions of rent fixing at this level. The committees are under the supervision of the Council on Tribunals set up under the Tribunals and Inquiries Act 1958.[52]

The preparation and day to day administration of the Register of Rents in a given area is the responsibility of the local rent officer.[53] The register is to contain, in addition to the figure which represents the rent limit for the dwellinghouse, a specification of the dwellinghouse (probably in general terms, such as the address, the number of rooms, the character of essential services and its gross annual and rateable values) and certain particulars with regard to the tenancy as prescribed by order of the Secretary of State.[54] The rent officer is directed to make the register available for public inspection; the precise details of this facility are again left to the Secretary of State to prescribe.[55] The register will thus provide a useful guide to parties as to the level of the rents in their area for a particular standard of dwellinghouse. Copies of entries in the register may be obtained, on payment of a fee, and are sufficient evidence of that entry, when certified under the hand of the rent officer or any person duly authorised by him, in proceedings in Court or elsewhere.[56]

[47] s. 25; Schedule 2, para. 10 (a).
[48] Schedule 2, para. 10 (d).
[49] Ibid., para. 10 (e).
[50] Ibid., para. 10 (f).
[51] Ibid., para. 6.
[52] Tribunals and Inquiries (Rent Assessment Committees) Order 1965 No. 2151.
[53] s. 26 (1).
[54] s. 26 (2).
[55] s. 26 (1).
[56] s. 26 (3).

Ascertainment of the Amount to be Registered as Rent. The key section of the Act,[57] avoiding any precise definition, directs that in determining what the " fair rent " for a dwellinghouse should be, " regard shall be had to all the circumstances other than personal circumstances ", that is, of the landlord or tenant such as relative means (clearly a mere change of landlord or tenant would not constitute an altered circumstance in this context), " and in particular to the age, character and locality of the dwellinghouse and to its state of repair ". At the same time it is to be assumed that there is no *substantial* shortage of such letting accommodation in the locality,[58] in other words, that the supply and demand of accommodation for letting are equally balanced. No regard, on the other hand, may be had to any disrepair or defect attributable to the failure of a tenant or any predecessor in title of his in that lease to comply with its terms, or to any improvement which he or his predecessor may have carried out on their own account which the tenant was not required to make by those terms;[59] thus evidence of such defects or improvements presented by either tenant or landlord in support of his application will be irrelevant.

Accordingly, in assessing the fair rent the rent officer is required by the Act to take the following considerations into account:

   (a)   the age of the dwellinghouse;

   (b)   its character, *e.g.,* the number of rooms, size, whether on ground or upper floors;

   (c)   its locality, in particular the general standard of accommodation in the area;

   (d)   its state of repair, on the assumption[59] that the tenant has fulfilled his obligations, but only those obligations, under the lease.

Taken by themselves these considerations, it may be thought, give little guidance as to the general level of value which should be taken as a starting point before taking individual factors into account. Naturally, the gross annual value of the house will give some indication, but this should only be taken as a general guide. There is no suggestion in the Act that the fair rent should bear a close relation to the gross annual value, which necessarily grows progressively out of date following the year of assessment. The determinations of rent officials in the early cases have shown that this is in practice not to be the case; if it were, of course, their appointment might well be considered an unnecessary duplication. A better guide, it is suggested, is the figure which would represent a fair return on the landlord's capital—for this is what " fairness " so far as he is concerned must entail. Fairness *quoad* the tenant will, no doubt, ensure that the landlord's return is not excessive having regard to the four

---

[57] s. 27.

[58] s. 27 (2). For a similar direction in relation to valuation for rating, see Valuation and Rating (Scotland) Act 1956, s. 6 (4).

[59] s. 27 (3).

considerations noted above, and that scarcity value is minimised; but fairness *quoad* the landlord must involve securing for him a return on his property which will present a reasonable alternative to an outright sale. That this balance must be struck is clearly necessary if private property for letting is to be kept available. The point is most sharply raised in an application for a certificate of fair rent,[60] which is made where a prospective landlord still has the chance to sell and is merely " testing the market ", but the figure for a fair rent must, in principle, be the same at whatever stage the application is made. It is suggested, therefore, that a landlord could relevantly put forward details of either the current capital value of the dwellinghouse (on the basis of an open market price; a discount for scarcity value would not, it is submitted, be a proper deduction here since it is only with regard to the fixing of the rent itself and in relation to " the number of dwellinghouses in the locality which are available for letting " that the Act[58] directs that such a discount must be made), or of his capital costs (on maintenance, fixed charges, depreciation or interest on capital, etc.) upon which an income return is required. What will constitute a proper return on the capital thus employed will then be a matter for decision in each case.

The procedure for deciding on the fair rent and for its registration is stated in full in Schedule 3 of the Act. It is invoked by an application to the rent officer for the registration of a rent for the dwellinghouse;[61] in addition to being in the prescribed form and containing certain prescribed particulars, the application should state the figure which the applicant considers is the appropriate figure for the premises in question.[62] The application may be made by either landlord or tenant, or by both jointly on the basis of an agreed figure; the rent officer has no power to review rents *ex proprio motu,* but until such an application is made and a rent registered for the dwellinghouse the rent freeze imposed by Part I of the Act remains in force.[63]

In the first place, the figure of the fair rent may be agreed upon between the parties themselves, and a joint application made on that basis; the clearest guidance to the parties at the stage of negotiation will no doubt, once the system is well under way, be afforded by the Register of Rents. If the application is made jointly, or if no objection is made by the other party in the case of an application by one party only, the figure stated in the application may be registered by the rent officer, if he approves of it, without more ado. If, however, one of the parties objects to the figure in the case of an application by the other party alone and makes representations to the rent officer to this effect within a

[60] See *infra,* p. 562.
[61] Note that no such application will be entertained where a condition as to rent has been imposed on the dwellinghouse by the local authority as being a subsidised dwellinghouse, Schedule 3, para. 18, or one improved with local authority assistance, *ibid.*, para. 17.
[62] For applications supported by certificates of fair rent, see *infra,* p. 565.
[63] See s. 3 (3).

specified period,[64] or the rent officer for his part is not satisfied that the figure stated in the application is a fair rent (whether or not the application was made jointly), the rent officer is given power, after consulting with the parties, to determine for himself what the fair rent is to be and register that as the rent for the dwellinghouse. The consultation procedure is informal and the general aim is presumably that objections should be fully aired in the parties' presence and agreement, if possible, reached between them; in the end, however, it is the rent officer's responsibility, whether or not agreement is reached, to decide on the fair rent figure.[65]

Once the rent officer has reached his decision and has notified the parties accordingly, either party has an opportunity to object to it in writing within twenty-eight days. If such an objection is made the matter is referred to the rent assessment committee for the registration area. The committee may call for further information from either party,[66] and may receive representations in writing or hear oral representations by either party or by a solicitor or counsel on their behalf. They have power, after making such inquiry as they think fit and considering the information before them, to confirm the figure already registered as being a fair rent or to substitute a figure of their own. Their decision on the matter is final in fact, but is appealable on a point of law to the Court of Session.[67]

When the fair rent for the dwellinghouse has been determined, it becomes the basis for the figure which is registered as the rent for that house. The actual amount entered on the register must include any sums payable by the tenant to the landlord for the use of furniture or services,[68] whether or not those sums are payable under separate agreements. Where the rates for the dwellinghouse are borne by the landlord that fact is noted on the register, although the registered amount may not include anything in respect of the rates; instead, an extra charge may be levied by the landlord for the amount of the rates paid by him for any rental period,[69] no notice of increase being required as the rates subsequently alter.[70] Provision is also made for the entry of any sums payable to the landlord by the tenant which are by their nature subject to fluctuation; provided that the terms of the fluctuating amount are reasonable in the opinion of the rent officer or the committee, the amount registered may be entered as being an amount variable in accordance with those terms, and further recourse to the rent officer for variation is considered.[71] It will be observed that there is at this stage available to the parties a built-in provision for variation, without the expense and delay of further applica-

[64] See Schedule 3, para. 5.
[65] Schedule 3, para. 8.
[66] See s. 29 for the penalties for failure to give information to the committee when required to do so.
[67] Tribunals and Inquiries (Rent Assessment Committees) Order 1965 No. 2151.
[68] s. 28 (1).
[69] Ascertained in accordance with Schedule 2 of the 1957 Act as applied to Scotland by the 1965 Act, s. 47 (2); see *supra*, p. 555.
[70] s. 28 (2).
[71] s. 28 (3).

tion to the rent officer, in those cases where variation of the rent limit will most often be desired.

The Effect of Registration. Where a rent for the dwellinghouse has been registered under the Act it becomes the limit on contractual rent, or, as the case may be, on the rent recoverable during a statutory period.[72] The limit set by the registered amount takes effect as from the date of the application for the registration, unless otherwise directed by the rent officer or the committee, that date being entered on the register.[73] From that date any previous registration ceases to have effect,[74] or if registration is being made for the first time in respect of the dwellinghouse, the limit set by Part I of the Act is replaced. If a valid notice of increase has been served on the tenant and is intercepted by registration so that the amount of the increase is reduced in consequence, that notice is not invalidated but has effect, as from the date from which the registration takes effect, as if it specified such part only of the increase as has not become irrecoverable.[75]

If in consequence of the rent officials' review before making registration the rent limit for the dwellinghouse is raised, the landlord is free, within the terms of the lease, to levy an increase in the rent paid by the tenant up to the new level.[76] During the statutory period, if the rent payable for that period would exceed the registered rent, the amount of the excess will, notwithstanding anything in any agreement, be irrecoverable from the tenant.[77] Where, however, the registered rent represents an increase in the level of the former rent limit, the rent payable by the tenant may be increased up to the new level by a notice of increase.[78] The notice, which must be in the prescribed form, must specify the date as from which the increase is to take effect; that date cannot be earlier than four weeks before the service of the notice, and in any event not earlier than the date on which the rent constituting the new limit was registered.

Once the rent has been registered, it remains the rent limit for the dwellinghouse until subsequently replaced by the rent officer. No application by either party alone for the registration of a different rent can be entertained, with one important exception, for the next three years.[79]

Variation of the Registered Rent. As was noticed above,[80] the Act enables certain entries to be made in the register by the rent officer which will allow the landlord to vary the rent payable by the tenant in respect of variations in the rates or other naturally fluctuating payments made by

---

[72] s. 3 (2).
[73] Schedule 3, para. 13.
[74] *Ibid.,* para. 14.
[75] *Ibid.,* para. 15.
[76] See s. 3 (2).
[77] s. 7 (a).
[78] s. 7 (b).
[79] Schedule 3, para. 3.
[80] *Supra,* p. 563.

him under the terms of the lease without the necessity of further recourse to the rent officer. These variations do not, of course, involve any alteration in the figure entered in the register. That figure can be altered in the following three circumstances, and then only by a fresh application to the rent officer.[81]

(a) The general rule that no application by either party alone for the registration of a different rent can be entertained before the expiration of a period of three years from the date of the last application is subject to this exception.[82] Such an application will be entertained if it is made on the following ground only, that " since that date there has been such a change in the condition of the dwellinghouse (including the making of any improvements therein), the terms of the tenancy or any other circumstances taken into consideration when the rent was registered or confirmed as to make the registered rent no longer a fair rent ". This exception is broadly framed, and makes refreshing reading when compared with the loopholes of variation contained in earlier legislation and in Part I of the Act. In fact, of course, it merely reflects the wide terms of the criteria provided for the determination of the fair rent; the discretion of the rent officials, both as to whether to allow an alteration in the registered rent in the circumstances and as to the amount of the alteration, is complete. A mere change of landlord or tenant would not constitute an altered circumstance for this purpose, since personal considerations are irrelevant in arriving at a fair rent.[83]

(b) If agreement is reached between the parties, however, joint application within the three year period will be entertained.[79] It will be necessary for agreement to have been reached both as to the necessity for an alteration and as to the amount. The figure arrived at by agreement is, nevertheless, still subject to the rent officer's approval as being, in the altered circumstances, a fair rent.

(c) Once the triennium has expired, an *ex parte* application may be made. The Act does not indicate the grounds upon which such a fresh application should be based. Although, of course, an application based on some change of circumstance will still be appropriate, there is no need to await such a change before making a further application once the three year period has elapsed. For this is the stage at which the rent officials are empowered to allow an increase in the basic element, the element attributable to rent. There is, it should be noticed, no express direction on the rent officer to allow such an increase, and no indication of what rate of increase would be permitted; the matter rests entirely at the discretion of the rent officer or the committee. It is not yet possible to predict how such a triennial increase in the basic rent would operate; it is essentially a matter for government control, and it may be expected that rises will be permitted in some areas where letting accommodation

---

[81] The procedure is the same as that outlined *supra,* p. 562; see generally Schedule 3.
[82] Schedule 3, para. 3 (b).
[83] s. 27 (1).

is in short supply—whatever may be said in the "fair rent" section[84]—in order to assure the prospective landlord that he will get a fair return for his capital in releasing his heritable property for occupation by a regulated tenant. Economic factors may well operate too; a steeper rise may be permitted in some years than in others. At any rate, it is clear that, although a permanent rent freeze is not intended by the Act, there is no escape from state control.

If the application is entertained by the rent officer the usual procedure is followed.[85] In this case the rent officer or the rent assessment committee has power to determine a new fair rent, if they think the application justified, and register it as the rent for the dwellinghouse in place of the former figure; if, however, in their view the circumstances disclosed in the application do not invalidate the registered rent as a fair rent, they will confirm the rent for the time being registered and will note that confirmation on the register. Where a fresh registration is made, the new limit operates from the date of the application unless the rent officer or the committee determine that it shall take effect as from a later date. Once again, three years must elapse from the date on which the registration took effect, or the date of the application if the rent already registered was merely confirmed, before a fresh application by one party alone will be entertained.

Certificates of Fair Rent. The lack of objectivity in the definition of the term "fair rent" may raise doubts in the minds of prospective landlords or landlords who contemplate making improvements in the dwellinghouse. In such situations, however, a certificate, known as a certificate of fair rent, may be sought from the rent officer, specifying a rent which in his opinion would be a fair rent under a regulated tenancy of that house or after the improvements are carried out. If within three years of the date of the certificate the house is in fact let on a regulated tenancy or the specified improvements are completed, then the rent officer, on application, will register the rent for the dwellinghouse in accordance with the certificate.[86]

The persons who may apply for a certificate of fair rent are landlords or prospective landlords who intend to provide a dwellinghouse by the erection or conversion of any premises, to make any improvements in a dwellinghouse, or to let on a regulated tenancy a dwellinghouse not at the time being subject to such a tenancy; the last case is subject to the proviso that either no rent for it is registered under the Act or that three years at least have elapsed since the date as from which the rent was last registered or confirmed. Such a person is required to submit an application in the prescribed form, stating the rent which the applicant thinks should be specified in the certificate as well as the terms of the tenancy

---

[84] s. 27.
[85] See Schedule 3; *supra*, p. 562.
[86] See Schedule 4 and Schedule 3, para. 16.

or prospective tenancy; where the conversion or erection of premises is contemplated or the making of improvements, the application must be accompanied by plans and specifications of the works to be carried out. Accuracy in the statement of these details is essential, as they are the basis for the fair rent to be specified in the certificate; if in the event the works are not carried out conform to those plans or the tenancy is let on different terms the certificate will be disregarded.[87]

The procedure whereby such applications are dealt with is similar to that which is followed in the case of applications for registration.[88] If the information supplied in the application is thought by the rent officer, or the rent committee if the matter is referred to them, to be insufficient, no certificate of fair rent will be issued. Otherwise a certificate must be issued specifying the rent stated in the application or such other figure which in the rent officer or the rent committee's view represents a fair rent in the circumstances set out in the application.

Where an application for a certificate of fair rent is made with respect to a dwellinghouse which it is intended to improve and the dwellinghouse is subject to a regulated tenancy the tenant will be notified at each step in the proceedings.[89] He will have the right to make representations, to request a reference to the rent assessment committee and to be present or represented in the same way as the applicant. If a certificate of fair rent is issued in pursuance of the application a copy of that certificate must be sent to him.

The certificate remains valid for three years. If within that period the works are carried out in accordance with the certificate, it may be used in support of an application for the registration of a rent for the dwellinghouse by the landlord or the prospective landlord. Provided that the rent officer, or, if the matter is referred to them, the rent assessment committee, are satisfied that the works have been carried out in accordance with the plans and specifications, or that the dwellinghouse is in the same condition as at the date of the certificate, the rent will be registered in accordance with the certificate without further consideration. If they are not satisfied, the application will be refused; but such a refusal will not prevent the landlord who has executed improvements from seeking an alteration in the registered rent in the normal way.[90] In the case of an application by a prospective landlord, the registration will remain provisional until the regulated tenancy is granted; such a tenancy should be granted within one month of the date of the registration, unless the rent officer has allowed a longer time.

[87] See Schedule 3, para. 16 (2).
[88] For the details see Schedule 4.
[89] Schedule 4, para. 13.
[90] See Schedule 3, para. 3.

C. Miscellaneous

Transitional Provisions. Where an existing controlled tenancy[91] is released from control by order of the Secretary of State, and so becomes subject to rent regulation, the sitting tenant is protected against the large increase in the rent limit which would probably arise if a fair rent were determined for the dwellinghouse and registered. A notice of increase served following upon such a raising of the limit will only be valid if the rent specified in it does not exceed by more than 15 per cent. of the controlled rent the rent payable for the rental period beginning twelve months before the notice takes effect.[92] Successive increases over a long period may thus be necessary to bring the rent payable up to the new limit set under Part II of the 1965 Act. Where, however, the increase can be attributed to the provision of additional or improved services or furniture or the carrying out of an improvement, this restriction does not apply; it is aimed only at the element attributable to rent. Likewise, in ascertaining the amount of the rent payable for any rental period for this purpose, any amount payable in respect of rates borne by the landlord or a superior landlord must be disregarded.

The 1957 Act provided[93] that where a decontrol order could be served under that Act, the rent payable after the time of decontrol was to be fixed at the rent recoverable at that time; it could not be increased so long as the tenancy continued or the tenant retained possession under the transitional provisions. The 1965 Act, while allowing for release from rent regulation by order of the Secretary of State, does not itself contain provision for such a standstill period, leaving it to the Secretary of State to make such transitional provisions to avoid or mitigate hardship as he may think desirable.

Advance Rents. In many districts there was a practice to provide in leases where rent was payable quarterly but not in advance that the rent was to be paid on the first day of the month on the 28th day of which the quarter ended; the effect of this was to make the rent payable in advance.[94] The 1957 Act prohibited this practice in the case of a grant, continuance or renewal of a tenancy of a dwellinghouse which had been decontrolled under that Act[95] for a period of three years after 6th July 1957. It provided[96] that where there was a requirement that the rent was to be payable before the beginning of the rental period, or earlier than six months before the end of the rental period if that period was more than six months long, that provision should be unenforceable,

---

[91] As defined by s. 11 (1) of the 1965 Act.
[92] s. 11 (6); note that the rent remains frozen at its former level until an application is made for registration, s. 11 (5).
[93] Schedule 4, paras. 3, 15 (a); see *supra*, p. 527.
[94] 73 S.L.R. 132.
[95] Under ss. 11 (1) and (2); *supra*, p. 513.
[96] s. 15.

whether the requirement was imposed as a condition of the grant, renewal or continuance of the tenancy or under the terms of the lease. The rent for any rental period to which this requirement related was to be irrecoverable from the tenant, and a person purporting to impose such a requirement was liable to certain penalties and could be ordered to repay the rent.

This protective provision is extended by the 1965 Act to cover regulated tenancies in the same circumstances.[97] The effect of this is that a person may not, as a condition of the grant, continuance or renewal of a regulated tenancy, require the payment of rent in advance; in the case of a yearly let, it would be illegal to require rent to be paid yearly in advance, though not six months in advance.

A " rental period " is defined[98] as a period in respect of which a payment for rent falls to be made. A letting on a yearly basis, it has been suggested,[99] is not affected if the tenancy were one from Whitsun to Whitsun and the rent declared to be payable at the usual terms; a letting on a yearly basis from 28th May to 28th May may be affected if the rent is to be payable quarterly in advance at the usual legal terms, while a stipulation for payment of a year's rent in advance in a yearly tenancy certainly would be.

SECURITY OF TENURE

Introductory. Security of tenure for the tenant of a dwellinghouse has always been one of the principal objects of the Rent Acts. It is the necessary counterpart to rent restriction; without the inter-action of these two safeguards the social purpose of the legislation could not be achieved. The effect of the Acts is to invest the tenant with a most valuable right, probably the most important he has under this legislation—*viz.*: to remain in occupation of the dwellinghouse, except in certain clearly defined circumstances; equally, the Acts seriously restrict the right of a landlord to recover possession from his tenant. During the period of a contractual tenancy, the terms of the contract of lease rule and the landlord can only obtain possession as against the tenant on the ordinary grounds at common law, that is, for breach of the terms of the lease creating a legal or conventional irritancy; in other words, the tenant is during the currency of this period protected in his occupation of the dwellinghouse by the terms of his contract with the landlord. Where, however, a contractual tenancy has been lawfully determined or terminated, whether by service of a notice to quit at the end of the contractual period or by an irritancy or forfeiture, the contractual protection is ended. It is at this point that the Rent Acts operate to maintain him in occupation of the dwellinghouse; the tenant, if he is within the definition of " tenant "[1] and occupies a house subject to the Rent Acts,

97 1965 Act, s. 38.
98 1957 Act, s. 25 (1).
99 73 S.L.R. 132-3.
1 See 1920 Act, s. 12 (i) (g).

is entitled to hold over, as it is said, after the expiry of the contractual tenancy and to become a statutory tenant. Provided that he remains in occupation, the statutory tenant can only be deprived of possession by the landlord in certain limited circumstances. Even if these circumstances are proved to exist, the Court, that is the Sheriff Court, has a discretion based on reasonableness, with which an appeal court will rarely interfere.

A tenancy to which the Rent Acts apply is, as a " protected tenancy ", outwith the coverage of the 1965 Act's provision against unlawful eviction.[2] That Act's provision against the harassment of a residential occupier[3] is of general application, however, and a statutory tenant holding over under the Rent Acts is protected against such interference just like any other residential occupier. Indeed that protection is of greater significance in his case, since his continuance as tenant depends upon his remaining in occupation of the premises and exercising his rights under the Acts.

An important alteration in the framework of the law was made, in the case of regulated tenancies only, by the 1965 Act. This is the introduction of certain categories of letting where the security of tenure provisions do not apply;[4] in other words, not only are there now circumstances in which, should they arise, the tenant of any protected letting may be evicted, but there are also categories of tenancy where from the outset the landlord has the right to recover possession for certain purposes whether or not these circumstances have arisen. This evident relaxation was motivated by different considerations in the three categories recognised at present by that Act, not the least of which was the encouragement of the offering of letting accommodation by former owner-occupiers for relatively short periods. Whatever the considerations in 1965, however, it is a device which could well be extended in the future.

Restriction on Landlord's Rights to Recover Possession. The law is contained in the 1933 Act,[5] which replaced the security of tenure provisions in previous Acts,[6] and the legislation has been evolved by the method of trial and error.[7] Having regard to the difference in the terms of phraseology of the provisions in the previous Acts, decisions on one of these Acts are not helpful and indeed may be misleading in construing the 1933 Act.[8] The position of recontrolled or new control houses is the same as that of controlled or old control houses; that is, the 1939 Act

[2] ss. 32, 34.
[3] s. 30 (2).
[4] See, in the case of owner-occupied houses, s. 14, of houses held for occupation by a minister, s. 15, or by a person employed in agriculture, s. 16; *infra,* pp. 588 *et seq.*
[5] ss. 3, 4 (1) and Schedule First as amended by 1939 and 1957 Acts.
[6] 1920 Act, s. 5 (1); 1923 Act, s. 4.
[7] *Stewart, infra,* at 292, per L.P. Cooper.
[8] *Barclay* v *Hannah,* 1947 S.C. 245 at 249, *per* L.P. Cooper at 250, *per* Lord Carmont; *Stewart* v *Mackay,* 1947 S.C. 287 at 292, *per* L.P., and at 296, *per* Lord Carmont.

did not alter the existing law, which applies to both classes of house.[9] The existing law is also applied to regulated tenancies, but in their case certain small amendments are made.[10]

While normally the conditions or circumstances concerned must exist at the date of an order, in questions of possession under the 1933 Act the Court may consider the situation at the date of commencement of proceedings or in the course of the hearing of the case. So where possession is sought for the non-payment of rent the material date is that when proceedings commenced[11] so that payment later is too late, and tender of payment in Court during the proceedings does not necessarily prevent the Court making the order, but it will not normally be reasonable for the Court so to act.[12] And where the ground is the requirement of the house by the landlord for a whole-time employee, the employee must be in his employment at the date of the hearing.[13] Alternative accommodation, however, need only be available when the order takes effect.[14]

Condition for Making Order for Possession. No order for the recovery of possession (except in the case of an owner-occupied house, or a house held for occupation by a minister or by a person employed in agriculture[15]) can be made by the Court unless it is satisfied that it is reasonable to do so.[16] This primary prohibition addressed to the Court, couched as it is in negative form, is an imperative direction to the Court to exercise a judicial function on the question of reasonableness.[17] But though the Court is charged with a judicial duty to consider all the circumstances of the application for possession in each case, the power of the Court is purely a discretionary power. The Court is not compelled, it is only empowered, to make the order.[18] This overriding discretion is very wide,[19] entitling the Court to take into account all the circumstances at the date of the hearing[20] in a broad commonsense way as a man of the world, all the circumstances that may affect the interest of the landlord or of the tenant in the premises, including financial hardship to the tenant,[21] the conduct of the parties[22] and the interest of the

[9] Except for certain dates in some of the grounds in the case of new control houses. 1939 Act, Schedule First and see *infra*.
[10] 1965 Act, c. 1 (6); Schedule 1, Part II.
[11] *Bird* v *Hildage* [1948] 1 K.B. 91.
[12] *Dellenty* v *Pellow* [1951] 2 K.B. 858; *Brewer* v *Jacobs* [1923] 1 K.B. 528.
[13] *Benninga (Mitcham)* v *Bijstra* [1946] K.B. 58.
[14] 1933 Act, s. 3 (1) (b).
[15] 1965 Act, ss. 14, 15 and 16; see *infra*, pp. 588 *et seq.*
[16] 1933 Act, ss. 3 (1), 4 (1).
[17] *Barclay, supra*, at 248, per L.P.
[18] *Barclay, supra*, at 249, *per* Lord Moncrieff.
[19] *Cresswell, infra*; *Bell, London & Provincial Properties* v *Reuben* [1947] K.B. 157.
[20] *Nevile* v *Hardy* [1921] 1 Ch. 404; *Benninga, supra*.
[21] *Williamson* v *Pallart* [1924] 2 K.B. 173; *Cuming* v *Danson* [1942] 2 All E.R. 653; *Warren* v *Austen* [1947] 2 All E.R. 185; *Cresswell* v *Hodgson* [1951] 2 K.B. 92.
[22] *Bell, London & Provincial Props, supra*.

public.[23] The reasonableness to be proved by the landlord may be less in relation to the burden or onus of proof where alternative accommodation is offered by the landlord.[24] It is too wide a proposition to say that it is never reasonable to make an order if a tenant threatens or intends to continue the breach of the agreement;[22] for instance, an order was refused in a case where the tenant intended to continue the breach, namely, keeping a dog on the premises.[22] The discretion must be exercised judicially.[25] Once, however, suitability of alternative accommodation is determined it cannot be taken into consideration on the issue of reasonableness.[26] But the question of remuneration from an occupation as, e.g., taking in lodgers on the premises, has been in Scotland treated as irrelevant.[27] Where the ground for the application has been breach of an obligation the Court will regard it as unreasonable to make an order if the breach is of a minor nature or has been induced by the landlord.[28] With such a very wide discretion in the Sheriff Court, the Court of Session will be slow to interfere, and will usually do so only on very strong grounds where the discretion has been exercised on wrong considerations such as a wrong principle of law or the inclusion of some irrelevant factor or the exclusion of some relevant or material factor.[29]

Circumstances justifying Making of Order for Possession. Before, however, the Court considers the issue of reasonableness, it must be satisfied or find proved either (a) that there is suitable alternative accommodation available for the tenant, or (b) that one or other of a number of specified grounds or circumstances exist justifying or entitling the Court to make an order giving the landlord possession.[30] These specified grounds, which are considered *seriatim* below, and are all (except (9)) contained in the First Schedule to the 1933 Act, are as follows : —

(1) that any rent lawfully due from the tenant has not been paid, or any other obligation of the tenancy (whether under the contract of tenancy or under the principal Acts), so far as the obligation is consistent with the provisions of the principal Acts, has been broken or not performed;

(2) that the tenant or any person residing or lodging with him or being his subtenant has been guilty of conduct which is a nuisance or

[23] *Cresswell, supra,* at 97, *per* Denning, L.J.
[24] *Cumming, supra,* at 657, *per* Scott, L.J. In *Briddon, infra,* Morton, L.J. at 614 reserved his opinion.
[25] *Chiverton* v *Ede* [1921] 2 K.B. 30 at 44, *per* McCardie, J.
[26] *Burgh of Paisley* v *Bamford,* 1950 S.L.T. 200.
[27] *Burgh of Paisley, supra,* at 208, *per* Lord Jamieson, *Stewart* v *Mackay, supra.* Contra in England, in *Warren, supra.*
[28] *Upjohn* v *Macfarlane* [1922] 2 Ch. 256.
[29] *Kemp* v *Ballachulish Estate Co.,* 1933 S.C. 478 at 492, *per* Lord Anderson; *Kerrigan* v *Nelson,* 1946 S.C. 388; *Darnell* v *Millwood* [1951] 1 All E.R. 88 at 90, per Lord Evershed, M.R.; *Cresswell, supra.*
[30] 1933 Act, ss. 3 (1), 4 (1). See Reorganisation of Offices (Scotland) Act 1939.

annoyance to adjoining occupiers, or has been convicted of using the premises or allowing the premises to be used for an immoral or illegal purpose, or the condition of the dwellinghouse has, in the opinion of the court, deteriorated owing to acts of waste by, or the neglect or default of, the tenant or any such person, and, where such person is a lodger or subtenant, the court is satisfied that the tenant has not, before the making or giving of the order or judgment, taken such steps as he ought reasonably to have taken for the removal of the lodger or subtenant;

(3) that the tenant has given notice to quit, and, in consequence of that notice, the landlord has contracted to sell or let the dwellinghouse or has taken any other steps as a result of which he would, in the opinion of the Court, be seriously prejudiced if he could not obtain possession;

(4) that the tenant without the consent of the landlord has at any time after 8th December 1965 (or, for controlled dwellinghouses, 31st July 1923 in the case of old control and 1st September 1939 in the case of new control) assigned or sublet the whole of the dwellinghouse or sublet part of the dwellinghouse, the remainder being already sublet;

(5) (in the case of controlled dwellinghouses only, such premises being excluded from regulated tenancies[31]) that the dwellinghouse consists of or includes premises licensed for the sale of intoxicating liquor not to be consumed on the premises, and the tenant has committed an offence as holder of the licence or has not conducted the business to the satisfaction of the licensing justices or the police authority, or has carried it on in a manner detrimental to the public interest, or the renewal of the licence has for any reason been refused;

(6) that the dwellinghouse is so overcrowded as to be dangerous or injurious to the health of the inmates, and the court is satisfied that the overcrowding could have been abated by the removal of any lodger or subtenant (not being a parent or child of the tenant) whom it would, having regard to all the circumstances of the case, including the question whether other accommodation is available for him have been reasonable to remove, and that the tenant has not taken such steps as he ought reasonably to have taken for his removal;

(7) that the dwellinghouse is reasonably required by the landlord for occupation as a residence for some person engaged in his whole-time employment or in the whole-time employment of some tenant of his or with whom, conditional on housing accommodation being provided, a contract for such employment has been entered into, and either—

---

[31] See 1965 Act, Schedule 1, Part I, para. 2.

(i) the tenant was in the employment of the landlord or a former landlord, and the dwellinghouse was let to him in consequence of that employment and he has ceased to be in that employment; or

(ii) the Court is satisfied by a certificate of the county agricultural committee, or where there is no such county committee, of the Secretary of State for Scotland, that the person for whose occupation the dwellinghouse is required by the landlord is, or is to be, employed on work necessary for the proper working of an agricultural holding or as an estate workman on the maintenance and repair of the buildings, plant, or equipment, of agricultural holdings comprised in the estate;

(8) that the dwellinghouse is reasonably required by the landlord (not being a landlord who has become landlord by purchasing the dwellinghouse or any interest therein after 23rd March 1965, or in the case of a controlled dwellinghouse 7th November 1956[32]) for occupation as a residence for (i) himself, or (ii) any son or daughter of his over eighteen years of age, or (iii) his father or mother or (in the case of regulated tenancies only) the father or mother of his spouse. The proviso is added to this ground that an order or judgment may not be made or given if the Court is satisfied that having regard to all the circumstances of the lease, including the question whether other accommodation is available for the landlord or the tenant, greater hardship would be caused by granting than by refusing to grant the order or judgment;

(9) that[33] the Court is satisfied that the rent charged after 18th July 1933 by the tenant for any sublet part of the dwellinghouse which is also a dwellinghouse to which the principal Acts apply was in excess of the recoverable rent of that part.

Circumstances (a) and (b) are alternative, so that if the landlord is offering suitable alternative accommodation the specified grounds are not relevant;[34] in such a case the only questions which the Court must consider are whether the alternative accommodation offered is suitable, and whether in the circumstances it is reasonable to grant the order. If no alternative accommodation is offered, conversely, the Court is limited to granting an order for possession on one or more of the specified grounds only.[35]

(a) *Suitable Alternative Accommodation.* This involves the establishing to the satisfaction of the Court that suitable alternative accom-

---

[32] This date was substituted by the 1957 Act, 6th Schedule, para. 21 for the previous dates of 6th September, 1937 (old control) and 1st September, 1939 (new control).
[33] This ground is contained in s. 4 (1) of the 1933 Act, not Schedule First.
[34] *Briddon* v *George* [1946] 1 All E.R. 609.
[35] *Barton* v *Fincham* [1921] 2 K.B. 291 at 295, *per* Bankes, L.J.; see also *Goodwin* v *Rhodes* [1921] 2 K.B. 182.

modation is available for the tenant or will be available for him when
the order or judgment takes effect.[36] The onus of availability is on the
landlord.[37] The fact that accommodation was available and was refused
by the tenant is not sufficient; it must be available at the relevant time.[38]
And if it is not available at the hearing but will be available later, the
proceedings may be adjourned till it is available.[39] The onus of suitability is on the landlord too.[37] A certificate of the housing authority
for the area where the house is situated certifying that the authority
will provide suitable alternative accommodation for the tenant by a
date specified in the certificate is conclusive evidence that such accommodation will be available for him by that date.[40] The certificate is
absolutely conclusive and settles the issue once and for all, and the
Court cannot reopen the issue or reconsider it when it comes to deal
with reasonableness.[41] It is not, however, conclusive of the suitability
of alternative accommodation;[42] and so where there was a considerable
difference between the rentals of the accommodation offered by the
landlord and of the council house in the authority's certificate, it was
held that in the absence of further evidence to produce a basis of
comparison the case must be determined on the issue of suitability to
the means of the tenant and his family as regards extent and character.[42]
Where there is no such certificate produced to the Court, accommodation
is to be deemed to be suitable if it consists of a dwellinghouse to which
the principal Acts apply or of premises to be let as a separate dwellinghouse on terms which in the Court's opinion (i) will afford security of
tenure reasonably equivalent to the security afforded by the principal
Acts in the case of dwellinghouses to which the Acts apply[43]—this will
not cover a council house as opposed to a controlled or regulated house[44]
—and (ii) is reasonably suitable to the needs of the tenant and his
family as regards proximity to their places of work and either (i) similar
as regards rental and extent to the accommodation afforded by houses
provided in the neighbourhood by a housing authority for persons
whose needs as regards extent are, in the Court's opinion, similar to
those of the tenant and his family, or (ii) otherwise reasonably suitable
to the means of the tenant and the needs of himself and his family as
regards extent and character. For the foregoing purpose any certificates
of a housing authority stating the extent of accommodation afforded by
dwellinghouses provided by it for the needs of tenants with families

---

[36] 1933 Act, s. 3 (1) (b).
[37] *Nevile* v *Hardy, supra.*
[38] *Kimpson* v *Markham* [1921] 2 K.B. 157. The time is when the case comes before
the Court.
[39] *Lees* v *Duley* [1921] W.N. 283.
[40] 1933 Act, s. 3 (2).
[41] *Burgh of Paisley* v *Bamford,* 1950 S.L.T. 200.
[42] *Turner* v *Keiller,* 1950 S.C. 43.
[43] 1933 Act, s. 3 (3). This is regarded as exhaustive of the forms of accommodation
to be considered suitable, apart from those in s. 3 (2). *Sheehan* v *Cutler* [1946]
K.B. 339 at 343-4, *per* Morton, L.J.
[44] *Sills* v *Watkins* [1956] 1 Q.B. 250.

of such number as specified in the certificate and the amount of rent charged by it for such dwellinghouse is conclusive of these facts.[45] " Family " must be those persons permanently residing with the tenant, who have in other words made their home with him and would be regarded by the ordinary person as a member of the family.[46] A lodger as a relative living permanently there may be a member of the family[47] and so may a housekeeper.[48] The landlord need not provide the alternative accommodation himself.[49]

The following points may be noted:

(1) Alternative accommodation may be suitable though it consist of part of the accommodation in the original tenancy, part that is, of the subjects already occupied by the tenant.[50]

(2) Alternative accommodation is residential accommodation for the tenant and his family, and its unsuitability for, or the fact that it does not provide for, the tenant's business or occupation, or that he used the original house for business purposes, is an irrelevant factor.[51] And the absence of a garage is likewise an irrelevant consideration.[52]

(3) The accommodation must generally be under one roof. Where it comprises a house and a room, the room may not be held as part of a separate dwelling, including where it is under the same roof.[53] There must not be a sharing of accommodation.[54]

(4) Alternative accommodation is not to be deemed suitable if the result of occupation of it by the tenant and his family would be overcrowding under the Housing (Scotland) Act 1950.[55]

(5) Where the tenant has two houses, the second one may not be taken as alternative accommodation if his use of it, e.g., for health purposes, is justified.[56]

(b) The scheduled grounds will now be considered in more detail.

(1) *Non-payment of Rent or Breach of Agreement.* This is the first of the scheduled grounds, *viz.,* that rent lawfully due has not been paid, or any other obligation of the tenancy (whether under the contract of tenancy or the Act), so far as it is consistent with the provisions of the Acts, has been broken or not performed.[57] In the case of members of

---

45 1933 Act, s. 3 (4).
46 *Standingford* v *Probert* [1950] 1 K.B. 377.
47 *Stewart* v *Mackay, supra; Standingford, supra.*
48 *Darnell* v *Millward* [1951] 1 All E.R. 88.
49 *Bazalgette* v *Hampson* [1920] W.N. 59, 89 L.J. K.B. 476.
50 *Thompson* v *Rolls* [1926] 2 K.B. 426; *Parmee* v *Mitchell* [1950] 2 K.B. 199.
51 *M.C.C.* v *Hall* [1929] 2 K.B. 110; *Stewart* v *MacKay, supra.* In England it would seem a broader view was taken in *Warren* v *Austen, supra.* See *Burgh of Paisley, supra, per* Lord Jamieson at 209.
52 *Briddon, supra.*
53 *Sheehan* v *Cutler* [1946] K.B. 339; *Standingford, supra.* Fraser, 2nd ed., 103.
54 *Barnard* v *Towers* [1953] 2 All E.R. 877.
55 1938 Act, s. 7 (3).
56 *Dakyns* v *Pace* [1948] 1 K.B. 22.
57 1933 Act, Schedule First (a).

the Reserve or Auxiliary Forces leave of the Court to enforce the judgment or order is necessary by special Statute.[58] The material date of non-payment is the date when proceedings commenced;[59] and so if the rent, though not paid on the lawful or due date, is paid before proceedings are raised the action is irrelevant.[59] A tender of payment after proceedings are raised even at the hearing will not prevent an order being made but it may be generally unreasonable in the circumstances to make the order.[60] Unless the circumstances amount to personal bar or show an alteration in the terms of the lease, the fact that the landlord has habitually accepted the rent at a later date than the due date of payment will not change the date and make the rent due on other than that day of payment.[59] In determining whether rent has or has not been paid where it is payable in advance, any sums paid by the tenant in satisfaction of a decree or decrees for rent and expenses must, if the action in which the decree was obtained was raised before the expiry of the period in respect of which the rent was due, be imputed wholly to rent and not to expenses.[61]

The obligation must be one of the tenancy, arising out of the tenancy, and not a purely personal obligation unconnected with the use of the premises, e.g., to remain in the employment of a third party.[62] So where a tenant left his employment voluntarily for a new job, the Court held that an express obligation in the tenancy agreement on the tenant to remain in the employment of a certain company was not an obligation of the tenancy as it was not binding on the tenant as tenant but was personal and collateral to the tenancy agreement and did not relate to the subject matter of the tenancy.[62] The Court of Appeal rejected[63] the obiter dictum of the Lord President in the Marquis of Bute v Prenderleith[64] that an obligation of the tenancy included any obligation laid down in the lease by which the tenancy was created, whether relating to the subject let or any other matter, and so even if the occupier in that case had been held to be a tenant, he neither did, nor could any longer, perform the condition on which alone he had any right to occupy. Examples of obligations are to fire and keep a house aired, prohibition of subletting, prohibition of keeping a dog;[65] where the lease provided that the tenant was not to use the premises for any trade or business but was to keep them as a private dwelling-house only, it was held that the taking in of lodgers or paying guests was a breach of the obligation.[66] The breach may be before the hearing

[58] Reserve and Auxiliary Forces (Protection of Civil Interests) Act 1951, s. 4 (2).
[59] Bird v Hildage [1948] 1 K.B. 91.
[60] Dellenty v Pellow [1951] 2 K.B. 858
[61] 1933 Act, s. 15 (g).
[62] R.M.R. Housing Socy. v Coombs [1951] 1 K.B. 486.
[63] Ibid., at 494, per Lord Evershed, M.R.
[64] 1921 S.C. 281 at 284.
[65] Bell, London & Provincial Props. v Reuben [1947] K.B. 157.
[66] Tendler v Sproule [1947] 1 All E.R. 193.

37

of the case.[67] Where the tenant is alleged to be in breach of an obligation to repair, or *e.g.*, to cultivate a garden, the onus is on him to show that the condition falls within an exception of " fair wear and tear ".[68] If the landlord accepts rent in the knowledge of the breach, he may not be barred from seeking possession.[69]

(2) *Nuisance or Annoyance on the Premises or Abuse of or Damage to the Premises.* This is the second ground, *viz.,* that the tenant or any other person residing or lodging with him or being his subtenant has been guilty of conduct which is a nuisance or annoyance to adjoining occupiers, or has been convicted of using the premises or allowing them to be used for an immoral or illegal purpose, or the condition of the dwellinghouse has, in the opinion of the Court, deteriorated owing to acts of waste or the neglect or default of the tenant or any such person, and where such person is a lodger or subtenant, the Court is satisfied that the tenant has not, before the making or giving of the order or judgment, taken such steps as he ought reasonably to have taken for the removal of the lodger or the subtenant.[70] Annoyance is a wider term than ' nuisance' and is anything that would disturb the reasonable peace of mind of an ordinary sensible person though it does not form a physical detriment to comfort;[71] and thus it relates more to personal conduct. The use of premises for prostitution would generally be a nuisance;[72] but the judge has been held to have a discretion.[73] The standard of the " adjoining occupier " is that of the ordinary reasonable person.[72]

As regards conviction for use of premises for an immoral or illegal purpose, there is held to be such a conviction if the tenant has availed himself or taken advantage of his tenancy of the premises and the opportunity it affords him to commit the offence, as if, for example, he is convicted of receiving stolen goods and has used the premises for keeping such goods.[74] The fact that the subjects are merely the scene of the crime or offence is not enough.[74] Frequent or continuous use, however, is not necessary.[75] A single conviction may or may not be enough. A single conviction for assault on the premises would probably not be enough,[76] and a single offence of selling intoxicating liquor within prohibited hours on licensed premises is not enough, for there must be the putting to an improper use to carry out an unlawful purpose,

---

[67] *Brown, infra,* at 122, 123, 128, *per* Lord Evershed, M.R. and at 132, *per* Romer, L.J.
[68] *Brown* v *Davis* [1958] 1 Q.B. 117.
[69] *Oak Property Co.* v *Chapman* [1947] K.B. 886.
[70] 1933 Act, Schedule First (b).
[71] *Tod-Heatly* v *Benham* (1888) 40 Ch. D. 80 at 98, *per* Bowen, L.J.
[72] *Frederick Platts Co.* v *Grigor* (1950) 66 T.L.R. (Pt. 1) 859.
[73] *Yates* v *Morris* [1951] 1 K.B. 77.
[74] *S. Schneiders & Sons* v *Abrahams* [1925] 1 K.B. 301; *Waller & Son* v *Thomas* [1921] 1 K.B. 541.
[75] *Hodson* v *Jones* [1951] W.N. 127; *S. Schneiders & Sons, supra.*
[76] *S. Schneiders & Sons, supra, per* Bankes, L.J. at 307 and Atkin, L.J., at 311.

not an isolated illegal act in carrying out a lawful purpose.[77] A single instance of use for the deposit of stolen goods is, however, sufficient.[78]

" Waste " is an English law term,[79] and has so far not been construed in Scotland.

(3) *Notice to Quit given by the Tenant.* This ground is that the tenant has given notice to quit and, in consequence of the notice, the landlord has contracted to sell or let the dwellinghouse or has taken any other steps as a result of which he would, in the Court's opinion, be seriously prejudiced if he could not obtain possession.[80] The notice need not be formal. It may be verbal in the case of a yearly tenancy.[81] According to English authority, there must be a notice to quit or an agreement that can be regarded as such; a mere agreement or under- taking to leave or give up possession is not enough.[82] Nor is it sufficient for the ground to apply that the tenant leave the premises without notice.[83] And, again in England, it has been held that possession can be obtained against a subtenant though notice has been given by the tenant, who has later sublet.[84] The landlord must have contracted to sell or let or taken other steps; the mere intention to sell in the absence of a binding contract is not enough.[85]

(4) *Assignation or Subletting of Premises.* The fourth ground is that without the consent of the landlord the tenant has at any time after 8th December 1965[86] (or, for controlled dwellinghouses, 31st July 1923 in the case of old control and 1st September 1939 in the case of new control[87]) assigned or sublet the whole of the house or sublet part of it, the rest being already sublet.[88] " Tenant includes a contractual tenant,[89] and indeed in the case of an assignation it is only the assignation of a contractual tenancy that is referred to, as a statutory tenant has nothing to assign.[90] The landlord's consent must be actual, expressly or impliedly, and the implied common law right of a tenant to sublet is not implied consent for this purpose so that the subtenant can claim that the landlord has consented for that is an implied right of a tenant and there is at common law no implied consent of the landlord to every urban sublet. The landlord must thus have been given notice or had

---

[77] *Waller & Son, supra,* at 553, *per* McCardie, J.
[78] *S. Schneiders & Sons, supra.*
[79] Halsbury, *Laws of England,* 3rd ed., XXIII, pp. 566-7.
[80] 1933 Act, Schedule First (c).
[81] *Craighall Cast Stone Co.* v *Wood Bros.,* 1931 S.C. 66.
[82] *De Vries* v *Sparks* (1927) 43 T.L.R. 448, 137 L.T. 441. *Cp.* in Scotland, *Stark* v *Forrester* (1920) 36 Sh. Ct. Rep. 262.
[83] *Standingford* v *Bruce* [1926] 1 K.B. 466.
[84] *Hylton* v *Heal* [1921] 2 K.B. 438. But a different view has been expressed by writers in Scotland—see Fraser, *Rent Acts,* 2nd ed., p. 113.
[85] *Barton* v *Fincham* [1921] 2 K.B. 291.
[86] 1933 Act, Schedule First, as applied to regulated tenancies by 1965 Act, Schedule 1, Part II, para. 12.
[87] 1939 Act, Schedule First.
[88] 1933 Act, Schedule First (d).
[89] *Regional Properties* v *Frankenschwerth* [1951] 1 K.B. 631.
[90] *Skinner* v *Geary, supra.* See *infra,* p. 590.

knowledge of the sublet.[91] Consent may be given after the assignation but before proceedings are raised.[92] The date for determining whether there is a lawful sublet is that of the raising of the action of ejection.[93] Where the statutory tenant of premises consisting of four rooms had each room equipped as a flatlet and let the rooms as and when he could but the subtenants did not occupy the whole premises at one time for more than a period of about a month, it was held[94] that an order could be made for possession because of the subletting without consent of the whole premises, notwithstanding that when the action for possession was begun each room in the premises was not shown to be sublet and that the period of subletting of the whole was of such short duration, and in the circumstances too the Court thought it reasonable to make the order. The tenant was carrying on a regular course of business as a boarding house and letting rooms when he could; and the fact that every room was not let on every day was irrelevant. If a tenant unlawfully sublets the whole, or part " the remainder being already sublet ", the Court can, assuming reasonableness, order possession to be given up even though the subtenancy is determined and the tenant back in possession before proceedings are started.[95] Thus, where a house was subdivided into four flats and these were sublet without consent and later the tenant resumed possession of one, an order for possession was made.[95]

(5) *Licensed Premises.* The ground in this case, which applies only in the case of controlled tenancies[96] (licensed premises being excluded from the category of regulated tenancies[97]) is that a dwellinghouse consists of or includes premises licensed for the sale of excisable liquor not to be consumed on the premises and the tenant has committed an offence as holder of the licence or has not conducted the business to the satisfaction of the licensing court or the police authority or has carried it on in a manner detrimental to the public interest or the renewal of the licence has for any reason been refused.[98] The Act thus relates to what are called " off-licence " premises, where the house is partly used for business.

(6) *Overcrowding.* This ground is that the dwellinghouse is so overcrowded as to be dangerous or injurious to the health of the inmates and the Court is satisfied that the overcrowding could have been abated by the removal of any lodger or subtenant (not being a parent or child of the tenant) whom it would, having regard to all the circumstances of the case, including the question whether other accommodation is

---

91 *Dalrymple's Trs.* v *Brown*, 1945 S.C. 190; *Regional Properties, supra.*
92 *Hyde* v *Pimley* [1952] 2 Q.B. 506; *Dalrymple's Trs., supra.*
93 *Oak Property Co.* v *Chapman* [1947] K.B. 886.
94 *Finkle* v *Strzelczyk* [1961] 3 All E.R. 409.
95 *Ibid.,* distinguishing *Oak Property Co., supra.*
96 See 1965 Act, Schedule 1, Part II, para. 2 (2).
97 *Ibid.,* Part I, para. 2.
98 1933 Act, Schedule First (e) as interpreted by s. 15 (c).

available for him, have been reasonable to remove and the tenant has not taken such steps as he might reasonably have taken for his removal.[99] The landlord has somewhat similar rights under the Housing Acts[1] where it is provided that where a dwellinghouse is overcrowded in circumstances that render the occupier guilty of an offence, nothing in the Rent Acts is to prevent the landlord obtaining possession.[2] The question of reasonableness does not enter into the Housing Acts' provision, and thus the Rent Act provision is not now used; and indeed in England it was repealed in the 1938 Act in view of the provision of the Housing Act.

(7) *House required for Employee.* The seventh ground is that the dwellinghouse is reasonably required by the landlord for occupation as a residence for some person engaged in his whole-time employment or in the whole-time employment of some tenant of his or with whom, conditional on housing accommodation being provided, a contract for such employment had been entered into, and either (a) the tenant was in the employment of the landlord or a former landlord and the house was let to him in consequence of that employment and he has ceased to be in that employment, or (b) the Court is satisfied by a certificate of the Secretary of State for Scotland[3] that the person for whose occupation the house is required is or is to be employed on work necessary for the proper working of an agricultural holding or as an estate workman on the maintenance and repair of the buildings, plant or equipment of agricultural holdings comprised in the estate.[4] It is essential that the employee is actually in the landlord's employment and is not merely prospectively engaged; thus, " engaged " means he is actually in the employment of the landlord.[5] He need not be actually carrying out work but must be contractually bound prior to the date of the hearing;[5] and even if then he is unable to work, he is still regarded as " engaged ".[6] The house at the time of the hearing must be reasonably required.[5] The tenant must be the original tenant, not the successor of a deceased tenant.[7] The occupier must prove that his possession is based on a tenancy;[5] there must have been a letting and not a mere service occupation.[8] The landlord must next prove that the letting was in consequence of employment.[5] The employment must be exclusively

---

[99] *Ibid.,* Schedule First (f).
[1] Housing (Scotland) Act 1950, s. 55 (1); formerly Housing (Scotland) Act 1935, s. 8.
[2] The date is that of the hearing: *Zbytniewski* v *Broughton* [1956] 2 Q.B. 673.
[3] The Act (*infra*) says the Department of Agriculture, but by the Reorganisation of Offices (Scotland) Act 1939, the Secretary of State for Scotland is substituted for the Department of Agriculture.
[4] 1933 Act, Schedule First (g).
[5] *Benninga (Mitcham)* v *Bijstra* [1946] K.B. 58.
[6] *Fuggle Ltd.* v *Gadsden* [1948] 2 K.B. 236.
[7] *Bolsover Colliery Co.* v *Abbott* [1946] K.B. 8.
[8] *Marquis of Bute* v *Prenderleith,* 1921 S.C. 281. See *supra,* p. 520. In *Macgregor* v *Dunnett,* 1949 S.C. 510, the L.P. (Cooper) at p. 515 thought that there might be a case there under (g).

that of the landlord. So where a person was employed as a ploughman by the landlord and two other persons as *pro indiviso* owners and joint occupiers of a farm, it was held that he was not in the exclusive whole-time employment of the landlord, the Court saying it was too dangerous to depart from the strict letter of the Schedule in view of the obscurity as to its spirit and intention.[9] What was in the mind of the landlord is relevant; the knowledge or mental attitude of the tenant is not relevant.[10]

The onus is on the landlord to prove that he reasonably requires the house.[11] And he must have a continuing present need for the house at the time of the action.[12]

It is not necessary to prove that the nature of the employment was such that the letting was necessary or that the employment has not changed in character.[13] Thus, it may be any kind of employment and not the particular job undertaken at the first engagement.[13] The fact that the person continues for a time in occupation or possession after his employment has ceased does not infer a new tenancy.[14] The termination of the contractual tenancy is the material date.[15]

Where a certificate is issued by the Secretary of State for Scotland, it is conclusive only that the person is within the classes provided for, that is, that the person is employed in work of a certain type and to that extent is qualified as a prospective occupant, or in other words is a qualified occupant.[16] It is not conclusive as to whether the house was reasonably required or whether it is reasonable to make the order; that is for the Court to determine under its judicial duty in terms of the Act.[16] The employee need not be named or otherwise identified in the certificate but it is desirable, though not essential, that his category should be specified.[17] The certificate is valid for a successor of the worker.[18]

(8) *House required for the Landlord, etc.* The eighth ground is that the dwellinghouse is reasonably required by the landlord (not being a landlord who has become such by purchasing the dwellinghouse or any interest therein after 23rd March 1965,[19] or in the case of controlled tenancies 7th November 1956[20]) for occupation as a residence for himself,

---

[9] *Grimond* v *Duncan*, 1949 S.C. 195.
[10] *Braithwaite & Co.* v *Elliot* [1947] K.B. 177; *Royal Crown Derby Porcelain Co.* v *Russell* [1949] 2 K.B. 417.
[11] *Lees* v *Duley* [1921] W.N. 283.
[12] *Nevile* v *Hardy, supra; Benninga (supra).*
[13] *Munro* v *Daw* [1948] 1 K.B. 125.
[14] *Benninga, supra.*
[15] *Read* v *Gordon* [1941] 1 K.B. 495.
[16] *Barclay* v *Hannah,* 1947 S.C. 245; *Harris* v *Brent* [1945] 1 All E.R. 386; *Pickford* v *Mace* [1943] K.B. 623.
[17] *Pickford, supra.*
[18] *Harris* v *Rowley* [1949] 2 K.B. 697.
[19] 1965 Act, Schedule 1, Part II, para. 12 (3).
[20] 1957 Act, s. 26 (1) and Schedule Sixth, para. 21, amending 1933 Act, Schedule First (h). Prior to this Act the date was 6th December 1937 in the case of old control (1938 Act, s. 7 (7) and Schedule Second) and 1st September 1939 in the case of new control (1939 Act, Schedule First).

any son or daughter of his over eighteen years of age or his father or mother[20] or, in the case of regulated tenancies only,[19] the father or mother of his spouse; provided that no order or judgment is to be made if the Court is satisfied that, having regard to all the circumstances of the case including the question whether other accommodation is available for the landlord or the tenant, greater hardship would be caused by granting the order or judgment than by refusing to grant it.[21]

In deciding the issue of whether the house is " reasonably required " all the circumstances affecting the interest of landlord or tenant must be considered, including financial hardship to the tenant by having to remove.[22] The fact that the landlord is living elsewhere is not relevant.[23] The landlord requires the house only if it will be used as part of one household with his own, not as a separate household as when he proposed to put in as tenants of the upper floor (of which possession was being required) a married couple who could then more easily look after him in the lower flat.[24]

The restriction that the landlord must not have become landlord by purchasing after 7th November 1956 applies only if the tenant was in the house at the date of the purchase, not a tenant whose let was subsequent to the purchase.[25] " Purchase " is taken in its ordinary as opposed to its technical conveyancing meaning[26] and hence where the landlord has taken a lease subject to the rights of the sitting tenant the restriction is inoperative.[27] He is held to have purchased a house as a residence for himself if his wife and family are to live there, though he may have for business reasons to live elsewhere.[28] There is held to be a " purchase " at the date of a binding contract rather than at the date of completion.[29] The term " landlord " includes a person who is successor to his interest on his death,[30] and so a person deriving title from a landlord who has become landlord by purchase is in no better position than the original landlord.[30] The restriction is not available to trustees if they have not a beneficial interest,[31] but it may be available to an executor[32] for executors beneficially interested if all of them require to occupy the premises are " landlords " within the Act.[33] Pro indiviso or joint beneficial owners are landlords and may sue if all concur in

---

[21] 1933 Act, Schedule First (h), which is not repealed by the new para. (h) in the 1957 Act, s. 26 (1) and Schedule Sixth, para. 21. Piper v Harvey [1958] 1 All E.R. 454.
[22] Williamson v Pallant [1924] 2 K.B. 173.
[23] Nevile v Hardy, supra.
[24] Richter v Wilson [1963] 2 Q.B. 426.
[25] Epps v Rothnie [1945] K.B. 562; Fowle v Bell [1947] K.B. 242; Newton v Biggs [1953] 2 Q.B. 211.
[26] Baker v Lewis, infra.
[27] Powell v Cleland [1948] 1 K.B. 262.
[28] Smith v Penny [1947] K.B. 230.
[29] Emberson v Robertson [1953] 2 All E.R. 755.
[30] Littlechild v Holt [1950] 1 K.B. 1; Lucas v Lineham [1950] 1 K.B. 548.
[31] Parker v Rosenberg [1947] K.B. 371.
[32] Baker v Lewis [1947] K.B. 186.
[33] Sharpe v Nicholls [1945] K.B. 382.

the action and the house is reasonably required for a residence for them all and for any child of theirs.[34] The restriction does not apply, thus, if the landlord has succeeded under a will.[32]

The onus lies on the tenant to show greater hardship,[35] and thus the Court will grant the order unless satisfied that there would be greater hardship by making the order than by refusing it, and in determining that issue the Court must consider not merely the conditions at the date of the hearing but future circumstances as well.[36] The Court must consider all the circumstances, such as the position of relatives and dependants of the parties with due regard to their proximity to the landlord or tenant.[37] The existence of alternative accommodation on both sides is a material element, as is the fact that the tenant would have to sell or store furniture or has no other accommodation available;[38] but hardship to third parties is irrelevant, unless the third party is a relative or a close friend residing in the house.[37] The issue of hardship is one for the judge of first instance[39]—the Sheriff—and the Court of Session will be slow to interfere where he has applied his mind to the problem.[40] The Court, it has been said, in England will only upset the judge's decision on hardship where there is no evidence on which he could have properly based his decision.[41] If he has refused an order, the Court must on appeal consider any changes of circumstances subsequent to the date of the original hearing and up to the date of the appeal hearing.[42] A new application may be made to the judge if changes of circumstances occur after the date of the hearing by the judge.[43]

(9) *Excessive Rent for Sublet.* Under this ground, which is contained in section 4 (1) of the 1933 Act and not in the First Schedule, the Court may make an order for possession if it is satisfied that the rent charged by the tenant for any sublet part of the house which is also a dwellinghouse to which the Rent Acts apply was in excess of the recoverable rent for that part. The recoverable rent is the maximum rent recoverable under the Acts,[44] including the 1965 Act. Failing any previous determination of the recoverable rent for the part in question, it can be ascertained by the Court in the proceedings for the recovery of possession by the process of appropriation or otherwise determined.[45] This ground does not apply if the sublet is outwith the Rent Acts, such

---

[34] *Baker, supra* at 193 *per* Asquith, L.J.; *McIntyre* v *Hardcastle* [1948] 2 K.B. 82.
[35] *Kerrigan* v *Nelson,* 1946 S.C. 388; *Sims, infra.*
[36] *Bumstead* v *Wood* (1946) 62 T.L.R. 272; *Sims* v *Wilson* [1946] 2 All E.R. 261.
[37] *Harte* v *Frampton* [1948] 1 K.B. 73.
[38] *Sims, supra,* at 265, *per* Morton, L.J.
[39] *Sims, supra; Smith, supra,* at 233, *per* Somervell, L.J.; *Kerrigan, supra.*
[40] *Kerrigan, supra.*
[41] *Sims, supra.*
[42] *King* v *Taylor* [1955] 1 Q.B. 150.
[43] *Burman* v *Woods* [1948] 1 K.B. 111.
[44] 1933 Act, s. 16 (1).
[45] *Ibid.,* s. 4 (2).

as a sharing of accommodation between the tenant and an alleged sub-tenant.[46]

Decree by Misrepresentation. Where an order or judgment has been made under the seventh and eighth grounds abovementioned[47] and it is subsequently made to appear to the Court that the order or judgment was obtained by misrepresentation or the concealment of material facts, the Court may order the landlord to pay to the former tenant such a sum as appears sufficient to compensate him for the damage or loss sustained by the tenant as a result of the order or judgment.[48] The order to pay compensation may be made though the tenant believing that the statements in the misrepresentation were true, that the true position was as represented by the landlord, consented to the order for possession.[49] The tenant must, however, prove beyond reasonable doubt that it was owing to misrepresentation or concealment that the order or judgment for possession was made.[50]

Temporary Restrictions on Right to Possession. The 1957 Act[51] placed certain temporary restrictions upon the right of the landlord of a house decontrolled under that Act to recover possession. The purpose of these restrictions was to provide for the transition from a situation where the tenant was fully protected to one where the landlord's common law rights were wholly revived. It was provided that the tenant should be entitled to retain possession of the house and to have full protection until a date specified in a notice served on him by the landlord; and that that date was to be at least six months after the date of service of the notice, and in any case at least fifteen months after decontrol.[52]

Although this provision was not repealed by the 1965 Act, it has no application to any decontrolled dwellinghouse after the commence-ment of the Act; as has already been explained,[53] the effect of decontrol is no longer a release from the Rent Acts, since a regulated tenancy, with continued protection, arises in its place. Under the law which now obtains, the only means of release from regulation is an order to that effect by the Secretary of State releasing dwellinghouses above a certain rateable value from the category of regulated tenancies.[54] In such a case, the framing of such transitional provisions as may be necessary to avoid or mitigate hardship is left to the Secretary of State, and such provisions as he thinks desirable may be contained in the order.[55]

---

[46] *Kenyon* v *Walker* [1946] 2 All E.R. 595.
[47] 1933 Act, Schedule First (g) and (h) as amended.
[48] 1920 Act, s. 5 (6), (7); 123 Act, s. 4; 1933 Act, s. 17 (1) and Schedule Second; 1939 Act, Schedule First; 1957 Act, s. 26 (3) and Eighth Schedule, Part II.
[49] *Thorne* v *Smith* [1947] K.B. 307.
[50] *Hurd* v *Hicks* (1948) 98 L.J. 430.
[53] *Supra*, p. 527.
[52] 1957 Act, Fourth Schedule, para. 2.
[51] *Supra*, p. 527.
[54] 1965 Act, s. 12 (1).
[55] *Ibid.*, s. 12 (2).

Suspension of Order for Possession. At the time of making the application for or the making or giving of any order or judgment for the recovery of possession of any controlled dwellinghouse or the ejection of a tenant or where any such order or judgment has been made or given but has not been executed, the Court has wide powers to adjourn the application, or stay or suspend execution of any such order or decree, or postpone the date of possession, for such period or periods and subject to such conditions, if any, in regard to payment of arrears of rent as it thinks fit; and, if such conditions are compiled with, the Court may, if it thinks fit, discharge or rescind any such order or decree.[56] If the order is made unconditionally but is suspended, and the tenant dies during the time of the suspension, then no member of his family can succeed to the tenancy under the statutory provisions for succession,[57] for the order ends all rights under the statute or as otherwise of the tenant.[58] If, however, it is made conditionally, then, if the tenant dies and whether his death was before or after default in compliance with the order, a member of the family can avail himself of the succession provisions,[57] for the order ends the tenant's statutory right;[59] the first or second successor, however, as a result of and in terms of the 1920 or the 1965 Act[60] is bound by the terms of the order.[59] Wide use is made of these powers in postponing the date of possession or suspending an order, *e.g.,* on condition that the current rent and part of the arrears is paid[61] or on condition that the nuisance ceases.[62] Even if a decree or order has been made by consent of parties, the Court may suspend it on a later application by the tenant.[63] The Court is not bound to grant suspension and postpone the issue indefinitely, and it will, therefore, not grant it if it thinks the effect would be to allow an unsatisfactory tenant to remain.[64] The Court has no power to discharge an absolute order,[65] but it can convert an absolute into a conditional order by making a subsequent order postponing the date of possession on conditions, and, if the conditions are fulfilled, it can discharge the original order.[66] The two orders—that for possession and that for postponement—may be in one order.[66] The application for suspension of the unconditional order should not constitute a retrial of the whole case.[67]

---

[56] 1920 Act, s. 5 (2); 1923 Act, s. 4; 1939 Act, s. 3 (1).
[57] 1920 Act, s. 12 (1) (g); 1965 Act, s. 13.
[58] *American Economic Laundry* v *Little* [1951] 1 K.B. 400.
[59] *Sherrin* v *Brand* [1956] 1 Q.B. 403. This question had been resolved in *American Economic Laundry* (*supra*) and in *Mills* v *Allen, infra.*
[60] 1920 Act, ss. 12 (1) (g) and 15 (1); 1965 Act, s. 13.
[61] *Mills* v *Allen* [1953] 2 Q.B. 341.
[62] *Yates* v *Morris* [1951] 1 K.B. 77.
[63] *Rossiter* v *Langley* [1925] 1 K.B. 741.
[64] *Kelly* v *White; Penn-Gaskell* v *Roberts* [1920] W.N. 220.
[65] *American Economic Laundry, supra,* at 406, *per* Somervell, L.J.; *Payne* v *Cooper* [1958] 1 Q.B. 174 at 183-4, *per* Lord Evershed, M.R.
[66] *Payne* v *Cooper* [1958] 1 Q.B. 174.
[67] *Goldthorpe* v *Bain* [1952] 2 Q.B. 455.

The Court's powers of suspension, etc., apply until the tenant has actually been removed. In the case of orders or judgments made before the 1920, 1939 or 1965 Acts came into operation but not executed, if the Court is of opinion that the order or judgment would not have been made if those Acts respectively had been in force at the time when the order or judgment was made, the Court, on the tenant's application, can rescind or vary the order or judgment as the Court think fit to give effect to the Acts.[68]

Statutory Exclusion of Restrictions on Possession. In certain cases under housing legislation the restrictions on the landlord's right to possession have been removed. So where a dwellinghouse is overcrowded in such circumstances that the occupier is guilty of an offence,[69] the date is that of the hearing.[70] Where before the appointed day under the Housing Act a house is overcrowded and has been so for at least six months, nothing in the Rent Acts is to prevent the making of an order for the recovery of possession or ejection if the Court is satisfied that it is reasonable to make an order and suitable alternative accommodation has been offered to and is available for the occupier.[71] The local authority can take any such steps for ending the tenancy or for the recovery of possession as the landlord could have taken, but the Court must be satisfied as to the reasonableness of the order and the offer and availability of suitable alternative accommodation before making an order on the authority's application.[71] Again, where possession is taken by a local authority under the Housing Acts of a house in respect of which a demolition order or a closing order or a clearance order has been made, the Rent Acts do not apply.[72] Nothing in these Acts is to prevent the obtaining of possession where a house is required for the purpose of enabling a local authority to exercise its powers under any Act relating to the housing of the working classes, or where possession of a house is required for the purpose of securing compliance with any bye-laws for the prevention of overcrowding or for the purpose of carrying out a redevelopment plan.[72] Possession can also be obtained of a house which is unfit for human habitation, is not capable of being made so at reasonable expense and is a house in respect of which the owner has given an undertaking that it will not be used for human habitation until it is rendered fit.[72] In these cases the Court is bound to grant the order or decree; no obligation is imposed upon the local authority to show that alternative accommodation is available for the tenant.[73]

In the case of regulated tenancies only, the 1965 Act has introduced an immunity from the security of tenure provisions of the Rent Acts

[68] 1920 Act, s. 5 (3); 1939 Act, s. 4; 1965 Act, s. 20.
[69] Housing (Scotland) Act 1950, s. 55 (1), (2).
[70] *Zbytniewski* v *Broughton* [1956] 2 Q.B. 673.
[71] Housing (Scotland) Act 1950, s. 55 (3).
[72] *Ibid.,* s. 158.
[73] *Parry* v *Harding* [1925] 1 K.B. 111.

in favour of certain private landlords.[74] The circumstances in which this immunity applies are in each case closely defined, but where it does apply the landlord of the dwellinghouse is from the outset entitled to recover possession from the tenant whether or not the Sheriff would have power to grant such an order under the 1933 Act.[75] No higher right is conferred on the landlord by this immunity than he would enjoy under contract or at common law; he is merely exempted, in this respect, from the restrictive provisions of the Rent Acts. This exemption arises in the following cases only : —

(a) *Owner-occupied Houses.*[76] Where an owner-occupier, that is, a person who has previously occupied the dwellinghouse as his residence, has let the dwellinghouse on a regulated tenancy and a situation has arisen where by contract or at common law he would be entitled to recover possession of the dwellinghouse (*e.g.,* the expiry of the period of the lease), then, provided certain conditions are satisfied, he is entitled to do so whether or not the tenant could be evicted under the 1933 Act. There are, in effect, three conditions which must be satisfied before the owner-occupier can benefit by this provision. It is only where the dwellinghouse is required as a residence (*i.e.,* not merely for temporary occupation) for the owner-occupier himself, or for any member of his family[77] who was residing with him when he last occupied the dwellinghouse as a residence, that the Court is entitled to disregard the 1933 Act. The nature of the claimant's residence must be residence as a home; absence of a temporary nature will not disqualify him, but where his residence with the owner was merely temporary or where he was a subtenant this condition will not be satisfied.[78] Secondly, the landlord must give the tenant notice in writing not later than the commencement of the tenancy that possession may be recovered under this provision. Finally, if at any time after the commencement of the 1965 Act the dwellinghouse has been let by the owner-occupier on a regulated tenancy in respect of which the tenant was not given such notice, the owner-occupier loses the right to benefit from this provision. This closely-guarded exemption, it is clear, is intended to benefit only those landlords who are prepared to make their property available during a temporary absence and who would otherwise be discouraged from doing so; but it is essential that due notice be given to the tenant that the lease is

[74] 1965 Act, s. 14, 15 and 16.
[75] *I.e.,* under s. 3 of the 1933 Act.
[76] s. 14.
[77] See 1920 Act, s. 12 (1) (g), discussed *supra,* p. 582.
[78] See *Middleton* v *Bull* [1951] 2 T.L.R. 1010; *Collier* v *Stoneman* [1957] 3 All E.R. 20.

not one in respect of which he can remain in occupation under the Rent Acts.

(b) *Dwellinghouses Held for Occupation by a Minister.*[79] This exemption is intended to benefit ministers or full-time lay missionaries of any religious denominations.[80] Where a dwellinghouse is held for occupation by such a person as a residence from which to perform the duties of his office and it is let on a regulated tenancy (in this case, whether or not it is let as such to a minister), possession of that dwellinghouse can be recovered so that it may be let to a minister (or another minister, for instance the present incumbent's successor) whether or not the tenant could be evicted under the 1933 Act. Again, certain conditions must be satisfied before the Court is entitled to disregard the 1933 Act. The tenant must be given notice in writing not later than the commencement of the tenancy that possession may be recovered under this provision. Secondly, the dwellinghouse must be required for occupation by a minister as a residence from which to perform the duties of his office. In this case, it may be noticed, it is no bar to the operation of this provision that the premises may have at some stage after the commencement of the 1965 Act been let to a tenant to whom such written notice was not given; further, it does not appear to be necessary that the premises should previously have been occupied by a minister. The effect is to enable a religious body which leases dwellinghouses to its ministers to benefit from this provision from the very first letting of that house.

(c) *Dwellinghouses Held for Occupation by a Person Employed in Agriculture.*[81] This exception is intended to overcome the situation which would otherwise arise where a farmer owns a cottage which has come into his possession as a result of one of his workers leaving his employment. Until he is able to replace that worker with another employee, or during a period when for some reason he can operate the farm without a replacement, the probability would be that, but for this exception, the cottage would remain empty; the farmer would be unwilling to let the cottage to an outsider without the assurance that he could recover possession when he required the use of it again for an agricultural employee. This provision enables him to do so, provided, of course, he is entitled to recover possession under the terms of the lease at common law. Again, certain conditions are laid down which

---

[79] s. 15.
[80] Note that a Jehovah's Witness has been held not to be a "regular minister" for the purposes of the National Service Act, 1948; *Walsh* v *Lord Advocate*, 1956 S.C. (H.L.) 126.
[81] s. 16.

must be satisfied before the 1933 Act may be disregarded. The cottage must previously have been occupied by a person who was employed in agriculture under the terms of his employment. It must have been let on a regulated tenancy to someone else, that is, to someone who was not at any time so employed or the widow of such a person. Due notice in writing must have been served on the tenant not later than the commencement of the tenancy that possession might be recovered under this provision. Finally, the cottage must now be required for occupation by a person already employed or to be employed by the landlord in agriculture.

ASSIGNATION, SUBLETTING AND TRANSMISSION ON DEATH

Assignation. As has already been mentioned, a statutory tenant, whether of a controlled or a regulated tenancy, cannot assign the tenancy; he has no estate or property in the dwellinghouse, but only a personal right to retain possession, which is not a term or condition of the original tenancy but merely an incident of it under the original contract.[82] The term " tenant " is defined as including " any person from time to time deriving title under the original landlord, tenant, mortgagee, or mortgagor ";[83] this is confined to persons deriving title from the holder of the tenancy while his estate under the original contract of tenancy subsists. " Tenant ", that is, means contractual tenant in this context.[82] So, on the other hand, " tenant " will include an assignee deriving title from the original tenant during his contractual tenancy.[82] But if the assignee is to be protected as a statutory tenant then the landlord must have knowledge of the assignation and expressly or impliedly consent to it.[84] Assignation without the landlord's consent is a ground for recovery of possession,[85] and this applies to an assignation from a contractual tenant before the expiry of the contractual tenancy.[86] Even where under the terms of the lease the tenant can assign without asking the consent of the landlord, such consent is nevertheless required by the Acts, as it is fair that the Court have power to make an order for possession against an assignee unknown to and not approved of by the landlord.[86]

Exchange of Statutory Tenancy. Under the 1957 Act, however, there can be a voluntary exchange of houses held on a statutory tenancy; if there is an agreement in writing between a statutory tenant and an incoming tenant (who may or may not be the tenant of a controlled house), a person, that is, who proposes to occupy the house, the incom-

---

[82] *Keeves* v *Dean* [1924] 1 K.B. 685; *Joint Properties* v *Williamson*, 1945 S.C. 68; *Regional Properties, infra.*
[83] 1920 Act, s. 12 (1) (f).
[84] *Dalrymple's Trs.* v *Brown*, 1945 S.C. 190.
[85] 1933 Act, Schedule First (d). *Supra*, p. 579.
[86] *Regional Properties* v *Frankenschwerth* [1951] 1 K.B. 631, following L.P.'s opinion in *Dalrymple's Trs., supra.*

ing tenant is deemed from such date as is specified in the agreement to be the date of exchange to be the tenant under the statutory tenancy.[87] The landlord, and also a superior landlord (in the case of a subletting) if his consent would have been required to an assignation of the tenancy on the coming to an end of which the statutory tenancy arose, must be a party to the agreement otherwise the agreement does not have effect.[88] Thus, a statutory tenant (a contractual tenant cannot arrange an exchange under the Act) may, with his landlord's consent, assign his statutory tenancy to an incoming tenant, who will get the protection of the Acts. The assigning statutory tenant may not and need not get in exchange a controlled tenancy, e.g., an exchange with an owner-occupier who is prepared to let.

Subletting. A tenant of urban subjects is entitled, in the absence of a prohibition in the lease, to sublet the subjects; if he does so, however, there is no privity of contract between landlord and subtenant so that when the tenant's interest comes to an end the subtenant's right also terminates.[89] The subtenant will be protected under the Acts only if the landlord knows of the subletting and has consented, expressly or impliedly, to the sublet.[90] The provision in the Acts[91] entitling the landlord to seek recovery of possession in the event of a breach or non-performance of an obligation of the tenancy is not confined to the statutory tenancy between landlord and subtenant but covers the original contractual tenancy also. Thus, if there is a breach of an obligation in this contract the landlord can recover against the subtenant;[92] if, however, the breach is an innocent or a minor one or has been induced by the landlord, the Court will regard it as not reasonable to make the order.[93] A subletting by a contractual tenant is determined immediately before the determination of the main lease.[94] A sublet by a contractual tenant may be of the whole premises.[95] The expression "tenant" is defined as including for the purposes of the Acts a subtenant.[96] Where the original tenancy did not prohibit subletting, a statutory tenant may, without the landlord's consent, sublet part[97] but not the whole of the premises,[98] for his right as statutory tenant remains so long only as he retains possession. The part he retains remains protected.[99] He must

---

[87] s. 17 (1).
[88] s. 17 (2).
[89] *Supra,* pp. 149, 166.
[90] *Dalrymple's Trs., supra.*
[91] 1933 Act, Schedule First (a). See *supra,* p. 576.
[92] *Chapman* v *Hughes* (1923) 129 L.T. 223, 39 T.L.R. 260.
[93] *Upjohn* v *Macfarlane* [1922] 2 Ch. 256.
[94] *Norman, infra.*
[95] *Gidden* v *Mills* [1925] 2 K.B. 713, *Hyde* v *Pimley* [1952] 2 Q.B. 506 at 514-5, *per* the Court.
[96] 1920 Act, s. 12 (1) (f) and (g).
[97] *Roe* v *Russell, infra; Lewis* v *Reeves, infra.*
[98] Halsbury, *Laws of England,* 3rd ed., XXIII p. 806. *Oak Property Co., infra; Hyde, supra,* at 514, *per* the Court.
[99] *Campbell* v *Lill* (1926) 42 T.L.R. 397.

inform the landlord and give him particulars of the subtenancy, including rent, within fourteen days, otherwise if, without reasonable cause, he does not do so or he supplies a statement false in a material particular, he is liable to a fine.[1] An order against a tenant for recovery of possession does not affect the right of any subtenant to whom the premises or part thereof are lawfully sublet before proceedings for possession are taken, nor is it in any way operative against such tenant.[2] So, if the subtenant is lawfully and in fact in possession, the landlord must institute separate proceedings against the subtenant and the latter can then plead matters personal as between himself and the landlord as to the reasonableness of the landlord's demand for possession,[3] or the landlord must make the subtenant a party to the proceedings against the tenant when the Court must consider whether it is reasonable to make the order against the subtenant. If the statutory tenant has sublet the whole or a part of the premises and the landlord is given an order for possession against him or the tenancy ends for any other reason, a subtenant to whom the premises or a part of them have been lawfully sublet is deemed, subject to the provisions of the Acts, to become the tenant of the landlord on the same terms as if the tenancy had continued.[4] This is a wider provision than the previous one, but the two provisions to some extent overlap.[5] They protect a lawful subtenant where possession is sought against the tenant. If the subtenant is a protected subtenant, then when the tenant goes out, he becomes a direct tenant of the head landlord on the same terms as he held before; if previously a protected statutory or contractual subtenant he becomes a protected head tenant, statutory or contractual.[6] The words " any other reason " are held to include the voluntary giving up of the premises or departure without notice[7] or the death of the statutory tenant.[8]

For the Acts to apply and the subtenant to be protected, the subletting must be lawful; the premises must have been lawfully sublet.[9] The sublet must not be contrary to the terms of the lease or agreement.[10] Where there is no prohibition, there must be knowledge and express or implied consent by the landlord.[11] The material date is the date when the action of ejection is raised.[12] The provisions apply both to dwellinghouses of which the tenant is a contractual tenant and dwellinghouses

---

[1] 1933 Act, s. 4 (4); 1939 Act, s. 3 (1), Schedule First.
[2] 1920 Act, s. 5 (5); 1923 Act, s. 4 (5); 1939 Act, s. 3 (1); Schedule First.
[3] *Hylton* v *Heal* [1921] 2 K.B. 438 at 449, *per* Rowlatt, J.
[4] 1920 Act, s. 15 (3); *Haskins* v *Lewis* [1931] 2 K.B. 1.
[5] *Roe, infra,* at 128, *per* Scrutton, L.J.
[6] *Stanley* v *Compton* [1951] 1 All E.R. 859 at 863, *per* Denning, L.J.
[7] *Barton* v *Fincham* [1921] 2 K.B. 291; *Standingford* v *Bruce* [1926] 1 K.B. 466; *Watson* v *Saunders-Roe* [1947] K.B. 437.
[8] *Lewis* v *Reeves* [1952] 1 k.B. 19.
[9] *Roe* v *Russell* [1928] 2 K.B. 117.
[10] *Ward* v *Larkins* (1923) 130 L.T. 184.
[11] 1933 Act, Schedule First (d); *Dalrymple's Trs., supra; Regional Properties, supra.*
[12] *Oak Property Co.* v *Chapman* [1947] K.B. 886 at 895, 896, *per* the Court.

of which he is a statutory tenant.[9] If notice to quit is given by the tenant and he then sublets, the subtenant is not protected.[13] The premises let to the subtenant must be a separate dwellinghouse within the Acts and not involve a sharing of accommodation with the tenant.[14] So a subtenant must prove not only that the subletting is lawful but that both the lease and the sublease are within the provisions of the Acts. When the tenant's right ends, the subtenant comes in his place but the tenancy is subject to the terms of the original contract of subtenancy with certain exceptions as to increase of the rent.

In determining whether the Acts apply the position of the subtenant when possession is claimed is material.[15] So where there was a let of a farm and a cottage and the farm was within the Agricultural Holdings Acts (and so not within the Rent Restrictions Acts), and there was a sublet of the cottage within the limits of rateable value under the latter Acts and the subtenant was not employed on the farm, it was held[16] that the subtenant was entitled to the protection of those Acts, for the determining factor was the letting of the cottage, not the farm. The object of the Acts is *prima facie* to protect the occupying tenant and the material letting is that under which the occupying tenant holds. It follows that the status of the house must be looked at as it was after the material letting, otherwise it would be impossible in the vast majority of cases to apply the Acts at all, for till the premises are let, no question as to the application of the Acts arises. But where in such a case as the above, the lease of the farm is surrendered, then the subtenant is no longer protected against the landlord.[17]

Where a subletting is originally unlawful as in breach of contract, it can become lawful if the landlord consents to it and that consent may be implied from the landlord's acceptance of rent from the subtenant in knowledge of the breach.[18] In the case of a statutory tenant, waiver by acceptance has been regarded as a question of fact in each case.[19] The waiver makes the subletting lawful only as from the date of the waiver.[20] If the sublet thus becomes lawful, the subtenant is protected provided that it has become lawful at any time before the tenant's right is terminated,[21] including the case where the tenant himself terminates

[13] *Hylton, supra.*
[14] *Stanley* v *Compton* [1951] 1 All E.R. 859.
[15] *Glossop* v *Ashley* [1922] 1 K.B. 1; *Prout* v *Hunter* [1924] 2 K.B. 736.
[16] *Critchley* v *Clifford* [1962] 1 Q.B. 131, following *Prout, supra.*
[17] *Cow* v *Casey* [1949] 1 K.B. 474; *Legge* v *Matthews* [1960] 2 Q.B. 37. This was altered in England by the Housing and Repairs Act 1954, s. 41, provided the original subjects of the main letting are " premises ", *e.g.,* a dwellinghouse, and not a farm. *Hobhouse* v *Wall* [1963] 2 Q.B. 124.
[18] *Norman* v *Simpson* [1946] K.B. 158; *Wright & Bowers* v *Arnold* [1947] K.B. 280; *Watson* v *Saunders-Roe* [1947] K.B. 437; *Oak Property Co., supra,* at 899, *per* the Court.
[19] *Oak Property Co., supra.*
[20] *Muspratt* (*infra*).
[21] *Norman* and *Watson, supra; Muspratt* v *Johnston* [1963] 2 Q.B. 383.

it.[22] The tenant is not liable to the landlord.[22] Where the subletting is in breach of the lease or contract, both tenant and subtenant are not protected.[23]

The subtenant is not protected against the landlord if the tenancy of the tenant is one outwith the Acts—the Acts[24] apply only where the principal tenant is tenant of a dwellinghouse to which the Acts apply —as e.g., where the tenancy is not within the relevant rateable value[25] or, at one time, if the tenancy was at a rent less than two-thirds of the rateable value;[26] but the latter restriction of the rent being not less than two-thirds of the rateable value is now, under the 1954 Act, disregarded for this purpose.[27]

Shared Accommodation. Where a tenant of premises, being a house or a part of a house, has sublet a part but not the whole, no part of the premises is against the landlord or a superior landlord to be treated as not being a dwellinghouse protected by the Acts by reason only that the terms on which any person claiming under the tenant holds any part of the premises include the use of accommodation in common with other persons.[28] This provision is, however, declared to be without prejudice to the rights and liabilities of and against each other of the tenant and anyone claiming under him.[28]

Position of Subtenant vis-à-vis the Tenant (his own Landlord). If the tenant claims possession against the subtenant then the provisions of the Acts as to recovery of possession by a landlord apply, for " landlord " includes a tenant who has sublet to a subtenant.[29] The question whether the subtenant holds under a controlled or a regulated tenancy will be determined in the normal way. The distinction is of significance, since the provisions in favour of owner-occupiers and of landlords (including principal tenants) of houses held for occupation by ministers of religion or persons employed in agriculture apply only to the latter.[30] Unless, however, there are such grounds for recovery of possession the subtenant is protected against the tenant so long as he remains tenant notwithstanding that the subletting is unlawful or is outside control.[31]

Transmission on Death of Tenant. Where a contractual tenant dies, the lease or tenancy will, in accordance with the ordinary law,[32] pass

---

[22] *Watson, supra.*
[23] *Dick* v *Jacques* (1920) 36 T.L.R. 773; *Chapman* v *Hughes* (1923) 39 T.L.R. 260.
[24] 1920 Act, ss. 15 (3), 5 (5); 1933 Act, s. 4 (5); 1939 Act, s. 3 (1).
[25] *Cow* v *Casey* [1949] 1 K.B. 474; *Knight* v *Olive* [1954] 1 Q.B. 514.
[26] *Knightsbridge Estates Trust* v *Deeley* [1950] 2 K.B. 228.
[27] s. 32 (1).
[28] 1949 Act, s. 9 (a).
[29] 1920 Act, s. 12 (1) (g). *Logan* v *Fair*, 1922 S.C. 76; *Lloyd* v *Cook*, [1929] 1 K.B. 103.
[30] 1965 Act, ss. 14, 15, 16.
[31] *Knight, supra,* at 519, *per* Jenkins, L.J. Under the Crown Lessees (Rights of Subtenants) Act, 1952, subtenants of Crown property are now protected.
[32] See now Succession (Scotland) Act 1964. *Supra,* pp. 177, 179.

under his will if he has died testate, or to his heir if he has died intestate. The heir, if he is in possession before the expiry of the contractual tenancy, being a contractual tenant under the Act,[33] as a person deriving title under the original tenant, becomes on the expiry a statutory tenant and is entitled to the protection of the Acts.[34] The Rent Acts, however, provide for a limited statutory right of succession in certain persons,[35] and, while it was for a long time considered[36] that this statutory right applied only to the case of a statutory tenant (see next paragraph), it has now been authoritatively decided[37] that the statutory provisions apply also to a contractual tenant. The result of this decision is that the legatee's or the heir's right in law is suspended until the statutory successors, the persons entitled under the Acts to succeed, have by death or otherwise ceased in turn to be tenants. Where an original contractual tenant had died, leaving his whole estate to his widow and she continued to occupy and pay rent but never intimated the legacy to the landlord, and after her death her son, who was the original tenant's son and heir and had resided in the house continuously since before the tenant's death, continued to occupy the house, it was held[38] on the facts that the widow's occupation was to be attributed to her statutory right of succession under the Acts and not to the legacy to her. And though she had not perfected her testamentary right by intimation to the landlord, that right had passed to her, for there was a mere failure to turn the testamentary right to account in a question with the landlord and not a failure in succession; she had never renounced the succession. Thus, as legatee she excluded the heir at law. In other cases, however, where the legatee is not one with a statutory right, if a contractual tenancy still subsists on the husband's death and devolves on someone other than the widow or other member, it is not destroyed but the rights and obligations that would ordinarily devolve on the successor in title of the contractual tenancy are suspended so long as the widow or other member and his or her second successor as defined in the 1965 Act[39] retains possession of the dwellinghouse.[40]

Where a statutory tenant dies, the lease or tenancy cannot be disposed of by his or her will nor will it pass on intestacy.[41] Under the Acts, however, by virtue of the definition of the expression "tenant" certain persons are given a limited right of succession; two transmissions are, since the 1965 Act, possible, to a first successor and a second

[33] 1920 Act, s. 12 (1) (f).
[34] *Harrison* v *Hopkins* [1950] 1 K.B. 124; *Lawrence* v *Hartwell* [1946] K.B. 553 at 558, *per* Morton, L.J.
[35] *Infra*, p. 596.
[36] See *e.g., Thynne* v *Salmon* [1948] 1 K.B. 482; *Smith* v *Mather* [1948] 2 K.B. 212.
[37] *Moodie* v *Hosegood* [1952] A.C. 61.
[38] *Grant's Trs.* v *Arrol*, 1954 S.C. 306.
[39] s. 13 (4).
[40] *Moodie* (*supra*), at 74, *per* Lord Morton.
[41] *Lovibond* v *Vincent* [1929] 1 K.B. 687.

successor respectively. If the tenant leaves a widow residing on the premises with him at his death, she is entitled to succeed as first successor to the lease or tenancy and becomes a tenant for the purposes of the Acts.[42] If he leaves no such widow or if the tenant is a woman, the lease or tenancy passes to such member of the family residing with him on the premises at his death and who has resided with him or her for not less than six months immediately before his or her death as in default of agreement the Sheriff Court may decide.[43] Formerly, on the death of the tenant's widow or other member of his family to whom the tenancy had transmitted, the statutory right of succession came to an end and the dwellinghouse, in the absence of any other person to whom the statutory tenancy could lawfully pass, reverted to the landlord; only one transmission was allowed.[44] The 1965 Act, in order to prevent undue hardship, in particular to the children of a widow whose death might follow quickly on that of her husband, introduced a second succession right and extended the definition of " tenant " accordingly;[45] this right to retain possession of the tenancy is granted to a relative, defined in exactly the same terms as before, of the first successor, and in effect merely allows a double operation of the former law. There is one difference, however; where the original tenant held under a controlled tenancy and his first successor was likewise a controlled tenant, on the transmission of the tenancy to the second successor the tenancy becomes a regulated tenancy.[46] The significance of this alteration is principally that the means whereby the rent is restricted alters, for the second successor retains, with minor alterations, full security of tenure; the rent previously payable under the controlled tenancy will be disregarded for the purposes of ascertaining the new limit on contractual rent.[47] Apart from this minor difference, however, the 1965 Act's provision of a second succession right cannot be regarded as having altered the recognised rule that once the successors allowed by the law have died all statutory rights of succession come to an end.

Where someone is left at the deceased's death living in the house who is capable of being a " tenant " within the succession provisions, and, without any assertion of right, that person remains and pays rent, the proper inference is that he or she is remaining or occupying as a

[42] 1920 Act, s. 12 (1) (g), as amended by 1935 Act, s. 1, which deleted the words " dying intestate " after " tenant ". The right of the surviving spouse in a dwellinghouse under the Succession (Scotland) Act 1964 does not apply to tenancies under the Rent Acts: Succession (Scotland) Act 1964, s. 8 (6).
[43] 1920 Act, s. 12 (1) (g), as amended by 1933 Act, s. 13, and 1954 Act, s. 33. Prior to the 1954 Act there was no right of succession to a member of the family if there was a widow not residing with the deceased; *Tinkham* v *Perry* [1951] 1 K.B. 547.
[44] *Summers* v *Donohue* [1945] K.B. 376; *Pain* v *Cobb* (1931) 47 T.L.R. 596; *Phillips* v *Welton* [1848] 2 All E.R. 845; *Campbell* v *Wright*, 1952 S.C. 240.
[45] s. 13.
[46] s. 13 (3).
[47] s. 13 (3) (b).

statutory tenant by virtue of these provisions.[48] If the successor is provided with alternative accommodation by the landlord, a new contractual tenancy will arise, and with it the possibility of further succession.[49] If on the death of the second successor a further successor is allowed, although not entitled under the Acts, to remain in occupation of the dwellinghouse and pays rent to the landlord, it is a question of fact whether a new contractual tenancy is to be inferred—and this is an inference which the Court will not readily make.[50] The statutory rights of succession, it should be noticed, operate only in favour of one of the persons who fulfil the necessary qualifications, not to a number of persons jointly.[51]

The Court can only decide between rival claims of members of the family.[52] The words " residing with " must be given their ordinary and popular significance; the successor must have been fairly and truly speaking residing with the predecessor.[53] The word " family " is broadly construed. It is used in a sense " base, common and popular ".[54] It is in each case a question of whether the person would in ordinary language be said to be a member of the family.[55] While it is usually referred to as a question of fact, it has been suggested that it is in truth a question of construction of the paragraph.[56] There must be a family relationship of some kind, de iure or de facto, between the survivor and the deceased statutory tenant;[57] but the existence of such a relationship is not always in itself enough: the way in which parties acted is also to be taken into account.[58] Thus, a niece by marriage,[59] a husband,[60] married sons and their wives,[61] and brothers and sisters,[62] and adopted children even if not adopted under the Adoption Acts,[63] and probably illegitimate children[64] have been held to be included. First cousins, however, are not included.[65] A mistress or an " unmarried " husband may be if there are children so that they can be said to be all living together,[66] and a lodger

---

[48] Phillips, supra.
[49] Strutt v Panter [1953] 1 Q.B. 397.
[50] Marcroft Wagons v Smith [1951] 2 K.B. 496.
[51] Dealex Properties Ltd. v Brooks [1965] 1 All E.R. 1080.
[52] Butler v Hudson [1953] 2 Q.B. 407.
[53] Collier v Stoneman [1957] 3 All E.R. 20.
[54] Langdon, infra, at 669, per Lord Evershed, M.R.
[55] Brock, infra, at 394, per Cohen, L.J.; Standingford, infra, at 383, per Cohen, L.J.
[56] Langdon, infra, at 670, per Lord Evershed, M.R.
[57] Ross v Collins [1964] 1 All E.R. 861.
[58] Ibid., at 865, per Pearson, L.J.
[59] Jones v Whitehill [1950] 2 K.B. 204.
[60] Salter v Lask [1925] 1 K.B. 584.
[61] Standingford v Probert [1950] 1 K.B. 377, per Cohen, L.J. at 383.
[62] Price v Gould (1930) 143 L.T. 333.
[63] Brock v Wollans [1949] 2 K.B. 388.
[64] Brock, supra, at 394, per Bucknill, L.J., at 396, per Denning, L.J.
[65] Langdon v Horton [1951] 1 K.B. 666.
[66] Gammans v Ekins [1950] 2 K.B. 328; Perry v Dembowski [1951] 2 K.B. 420; Hawes v Evenden [1953] 2 All E.R. 737.

may be held a member of the family.[67] A housekeeper is not such nor are a housekeeper and her husband and child members of the family.[68] The question is primarily one for the Sheriff, the judge of first instance, for the policy of the Court is to leave to the Court of first instance the determination of the numerous difficult problems and questions under the Acts requiring the application of a broad, commonsense, man-of-the-world view.[69]

The letting to either of these statutory successors is subject to the same limitations as affected the original tenant's right.[70] A statutory tenant by succession is, however, not liable for his predecessor's arrears of rent, and an order for possession will not be made because of the predecessor's default.[71] He can sublet and the subtenant will be protected after his own death.[72]

Existence of Suspended Order for Possession. Where a tenant, that is a statutory tenant, dies during the currency of an unconditional suspended order for possession, no one can succeed. The Acts do not apply.[73] If the order is conditional, and whether or not the tenant has observed the conditions before his death, the Acts apply and there can be a statutory succession, but any successor is bound by the terms of the order.[74]

Exchange of Statutory Tenancy. Where there is an exchange of statutory tenancy as provided for in the 1957 Act,[75] then the question whether the statutory provisions regarding succession can be effective in the event of the death of the incoming tenant must be determined generally according as these provisions have or have not had effect already in regard to the statutory tenancy; that is, if succession to a second successor has already taken place (the outgoing tenant being himself the second successor), no further right of succession can occur on the death of the incoming tenant. If the outgoing tenant was the original contractual tenant (that is, the original statutory tenant) then the statutory rights of succession will arise on the death of the incoming tenant during the controlled tenancy, and the incoming tenant thus replaces the outgoing tenant vis-à-vis succession under the Acts.[75] The exchange agreement, however, may provide that the provisions are to be capable of having effect in the event of the death of the incoming tenant notwithstanding that they have already had effect in favour of the previous

[67] *Brock, supra,* at 394, *per* Cohen, L.J.; *Standingford, supra,* at 385, *per* Cohen, L.J. See *Stewart* v *Mackay,* 1947 S.C. 287.
[68] *Ross (supra); Darnell* v *Millwood* [1951] 1 All E.R. 88.
[69] *Langdon, supra,* at 670, *per* Lord Evershed, M.R.
[70] *Bolsover Colliery Co.* v *Abbott* [1946] K.B. 8; *Mills* v *Allen* [1953] 2 Q.B. 341.
[71] *Tickner* v *Clifton* [1929] 1 K.B. 207.
[72] *Lewis* v *Reeves* [1952] 1 Q.B. 19.
[73] *American Economic Laundry* v *Little* [1951] 1 K.B. 400.
[74] *Sherrin* v *Brand* [1956] 1 Q.B. 403. See *supra,* p. 586.
[75] s. 17 (1). See *supra,* p. 590.

tenant.[76] The statutory rights of succession may thus be made to devolve in the case of the deceased incoming tenant though the outgoing tenant had already succeeded to the tenancy. The landlord, and a superior landlord in the case of a sublet, if his consent would have been required to an assignation of the tenancy on the coming to an end of which the statutory tenancy arose, must be parties to the agreement.[77]

Decontrol and Release from Regulation. References in the 1957 Act[78] to the tenant, include, in relation to any time after the time of decontrol, any other person who would have been entitled to succeed him as statutory tenant under the statutory succession provisions if the house had remained controlled.[79] This provision is of little significance since the 1965 Act, however, because dwellinghouses decontrolled under the 1957 Act remain protected by the Rent Acts as regulated tenancies. It is likely that where an order for release from regulation is made by the Secretary of State under the 1965 Act,[80] the transitional provisions which he may make[81] will include a similar direction.

PREMIUMS AND OTHER CONSIDERATIONS

Prohibition of Premium on Grant, Renewal or Continuance of Tenancy. The position here has to be looked at in three stages: prior to and after 2nd June 1949 (for though the Act of 1949 repealed the prior legislation and amended and re-enacted it, it saved transactions, that is, anything done prior to that date[82]), and after 8th December 1965, the date on which certain amendments made by the 1965 Act came into force.

i) 1920 Act: It was provided by this Act that a person shall not as a condition of the grant, renewal or continuance of a tenancy or subtenancy require payment of any fine, premium[83] or other like sum, or the giving of any pecuniary consideration, in addition to the rent.[84] If it was paid or given, the tenant could recover it, while the person requiring the payment was liable to a fine not exceeding £100 sterling.[85] The prohibition did not apply to the grant, renewal or continuance of a tenancy for fourteen years or upwards,[86] and this applied even if there was a break provided the break was not exercised.[87] The statutory provision, being of a penal nature, was strictly construed. It was thus held

---

[76] *Ibid.*, s. 17 (3).
[77] *Ibid.*, s. 17 (2).
[78] Schedule Fourth.
[79] *Ibid.*, para. 14.
[80] s. 12 (1).
[81] s. 12 (2).
[82] 1949 Act, s. 2 (7).
[83] Colloquially called " Key money ".
[84] 1920 Act, s. 8 (1).
[85] *Ibid.*, s. 8 (2).
[86] *Ibid.*, s. 8 (3).
[87] *Bishop* v *Paisley Assessor,* 1910 S.C. 821.

that " grant " means the creation of a tenancy and does not cover an assignation[88] or a surrender.[89] And for a landlord to require a premium for permitting his tenant to make a sublet was held not to be a breach of the prohibition.[90] It was limited to a landlord, including a sub-lessor.[91] If the premium so called was really rent, then it was treated as such and irrecoverable,[92] but the cessation of the benefit of a discount on liquor supplied by the landlord to the tenant of licensed premises was not a fine or premium.[93] Where the purchase of any furniture or other articles[94] was required as a condition of a grant, renewal or continuance of a tenancy or subtenancy, the price, if so requested by the tenant or subtenant, had to be stated in writing, and, if it exceeded the reasonable price of the articles, the excess was treated as a fine or premium.[95] It was not an exception that the dwellinghouse was being let for the first time.[96] The Court could order repayment of the amount paid or the value of the consideration to the payer.[85] The 1939 Act extended these provisions to new control houses.[97]

A statutory tenant could not, as a condition of giving up possession, ask or receive any sum or the giving of any other consideration from any person other than the landlord; if he did so, he was liable to a fine and the Court could order repayment.[98] This rule has been regarded as showing that such a tenant has no right to assign his tenancy.[99] It was applied also to excessive charges for furniture or other articles to be taken over.[1] There was no restriction on asking or receiving a sum from the landlord. It should be noticed that the prohibition was applied, in terms of the section of the Act, only to a statutory, not a contractual, tenant.[2] The 1939 Act extended the provisions to new control houses.[3]

ii) 1949 Act: The provisions of the 1920 Act were repealed by this Act,[4] which to a large extent repeated the earlier law as regards cases where the premium had been given subsequent to 2nd June 1949;[5] in effect, therefore, the provisions discussed above still applied, and are, subject to the 1965 Act, still in force. The penalty remains a fine of £100.[6]

---

[88] *Mason, Herring & Brooks* v *Harris* [1921] 1 K.B. 653.
[89] *Remmington* v *Larchin* [1921] 3 K.B. 404.
[90] *Strathern* v *Beaton*, 1923 J.C. 59.
[91] *Remmington, supra.*
[92] *Rush* v *Matthews* [1926] 1 K.B. 492.
[93] *Brakspear* v *Barton* [1924] 2 K.B. 88.
[94] In *Daly* v *Cannon* [1954] 1 All E.R. 315 under the Public Health Act 1936, " article " was held to be some inanimate object.
[95] 1923 Act, s. 9 (1).
[96] *Minns* v *Moore* [1950] 1 K.B. 241.
[97] 1939 Act, s. 3 (1), Schedule First.
[98] 1920 Act, s. 15 (2).
[99] *Keeves* v *Dean, supra,* at 693, *per* Bankes, L.J., at 695, *per* Scrutton, L.J.
[1] 1923 Act, s. 9 (2).
[2] *Mason, supra.*
[3] s. 3 (1).
[4] s. 2 (7).
[5] s. 2 (1).
[6] s. 2 (6).

The exception previously made in respect of leases of fourteen years or more was abolished, but still holds good for leases made before 2nd June, 1949.[7] Where a premium is made a condition of the grant of a fourteen year lease made before 2nd June 1949 (and is thus lawful), and it is payable in instalments, the demand for instalments is not regarded as the requirement of a premium as a condition of continuance of the lease or tenancy; the landlord is only enforcing a personal obligation that was when it was created valid in law.[8] A premium can be recovered and a Court in imposing a fine can order repayment;[9] this is alternative to the right of the party to recover by ordinary process.[10] A third party who has paid it can also recover.[10] The two year limitation imposed under the 1923 and 1938 Acts[11] does not apply to the recovery of premiums.[12] A premium, however, which was lawful before the Act but is made unlawful by the Act can be recovered by the payer if it was paid under an agreement subsequent to 25th March 1949;[13] and where there is an agreement made since 25th March 1949 but before 2nd June 1949 providing for a premium, which could lawfully be required under the 1920 Act but under the 1949 Act is recoverable, the agreement is voidable at the option of either party.[14] But a tenancy does not become invalid because the premium has been unlawfully required in contravention of the Act.[15] Where a premium is paid at the tenant's request instead of a sum of rent, this does not involve a breach of the Act.[16] The previous provision in the 1923 Act in regard to payment of an excessive price by way of a premium for furniture is repealed[17] and substantially re-enacted,[18] the provision being now extended expressly to fittings,[18] and the paying of an excessive price for furniture or fittings or other articles as a condition of assignation of a tenancy.[18] A fine of £10 was imposed here as a penalty,[19] for failure, without reasonable cause, to give a written statement of the price when such was demanded or for giving knowingly a false statement, but this was repealed by the 1959 Act.[20] The provisions as to premiums demanded by a tenant now apply to all tenants, contractual and statutory.[21] A reasonable price is not a fixed standard: it is the price which it is reasonable to expect that a willing incoming tenant who is ready to take the articles would agree

---

[7] s. 2 (7). Second Schedule.
[8] *Regor Estates* v *Wright* [1951] 1 K.B. 689.
[9] 1949 Act, s. 2 (6).
[10] *Temple* v *Lewis* [1954] 1 Q.B. 22.
[11] 1923 Act, s. 8 (2); 1938 Act, s. 7 (6).
[12] *Collen-Jones* v *Davis* (1951) 101 L.J. 235.
[13] s. 2 (5).
[14] s. 2 (5), *proviso*.
[15] *Grace Rymer Investments* v *Waite* [1958] 1 All E.R. 138.
[16] *Woods* v *Wise* [1955] 2 K.B. 29.
[17] 1949 Act, s. 3 (3), without prejudice to the effect of statements of the price of articles already given before 2nd June, 1949.
[18] *Ibid.*, s. 3 (1).
[19] *Ibid.*, s. 3 (2).
[20] s. 2 (3). *Infra*, p. 607.
[21] *Ibid.*, s. 2 (2).

to pay to a willing outgoing tenant who is ready to leave them there. The market value, if any, will indicate the reasonable price but is not necessarily conclusive. All the circumstances relevant as to the value of the furniture in the premises must be looked at, excluding, however, any inflation of value due to extraneous circumstances, such as the desire of the tenant to get the tenancy.[22]

iii) 1965 Act: This Act made two alterations to the law already existing under the 1949 Act. In the first place, it amended the 1949 Act so as to prohibit not only the requiring of any premium but also the receipt of a premium in connection with a grant, renewal or continuance of a tenancy;[23] even " voluntary " payments, it appears, are now illegal. Secondly, it extended the 1949 Act's provisions to cover regulated tenancies, but it makes special rules for the ascertainment of the date before which a premium will be allowed, on the assignation of a tenancy, when a premium has previously been paid on its grant, continuance or renewal.[24]

Premium. A premium is defined in the 1949 Act as including " any fine or other like sum and any other pecuniary consideration in addition to rent ".[25] The provisions of the 1949 Act are also strictly construed as being of a penal nature.[26] The consideration must be to the landlord, and so a payment to a third party, someone who is not the landlord, *e.g.*, a builder with whom the tenant has been required to contract, is not struck at.[27] Every payment is not affected. Whether a sum is a premium is to be determined by looking at the whole transaction, and extrinsic evidence is admissible if it does not contradict the written agreement or lease.[28]

A payment or contribution by the tenant to the landlord towards work done by the landlord for which the tenant is not responsible and put in by the tenant to limit his liability, he having previously agreed to complete the work himself, is not, it has been held, a pecuniary consideration in addition to rent within the definition of a premium.[29] Whether or not the payment was a premium within the Act, the Court have held that a payment for the genuine purchase or the goodwill of a business made to the seller, who entered into an obligation or restrictive covenant not to carry on a similar business, was not made in respect

---

[22] *Eales* v *Dale* [1954] 1 Q.B. 539, see *per* Lord Evershed, M.R. at 544 and Denning, L.J. at 548.
[23] 1965 Act, s. 37 and 5th Schedule, Parts I & II.
[24] 1965 Act, *Ibid.*, Part III; *infra*, p. 605.
[25] 1949 Act, s. 18 (2).
[26] *Minns, supra*, at 250, *per* Lord Evershed, M.R.
[27] *R.* v *Birmingham West Rent Tribunal* [1951] 2 K.B. 54.
[28] *Woods, supra*, at 39-41, *per* Lord Evershed, M.R.; *Regor Estates, supra*, at 698, *per* Cohen, L.J.
[29] *R.* v *Fulham Rent Tribunal* [1950] 2 All E.R. 211. It was also held that where the tenant agreed to pay the landlord one half of the profit on any assignation he made, this was a premium in respect of the grant, though it was not paid when the lease was granted and might never become payable.

of the grant of a tenancy and was thus not within the Act.[30] But a payment for the goodwill of a business carried on in the premises when in fact no business was carried on there was a premium,[31] as was a sum paid as advance rent.[32] The landlord will be liable if an agent acting in the course of his employment as agent and within the scope of his authority has demanded a premium.[33] An illegal premium can be recovered, unless on order under the 1920 Act,[34] by the tenant though he has aided and abetted the commission of a criminal offence, for it is not contrary to public policy for the Courts to give effect to the provisions[35] allowing recovery, even though there has been connivance.[36]

Premium on Assignation. The 1949 Act made an innovation by prohibiting the assignation of a tenancy as a means of exacting a premium. Prior to this, a contractual tenant could demand a premium, on an assignation, from the landlord,[37] though not from a prospective new tenant.[38] Under the 1949 Act, however, a person may not as a condition of the assignation of a tenancy to which the Act applies require payment of a premium or in connection with such an assignation receive any premium.[39] A tenancy to which the Act applies is one of a dwellinghouse, " being a tenancy to which the principal Acts apply such that when the dwellinghouse is let under the tenancy it is a dwellinghouse to which the principal Acts apply ".[40] If the tenancy when granted is one to which the Acts apply, it is immaterial that at the date when the premium was demanded the dwellinghouse was not subject to the Acts.[41] The provision applies to controlled and regulated tenancies and to both the contractual and statutory periods. An excessive price for furniture, fittings or other articles as a condition of an assignation is also struck at by the Act.[42] The price asked must, at the request of the person on whom the demand is made, be stated in writing, and failure without reasonable cause to give it or knowingly giving a false statement renders the person required to make it liable to a fine.[43] A tenant assignor can require or receive payment from his assignee, if so entitled by contract or general law, of outgoings discharged or paid by the assignor for a period after the assignment; sums reasonably spent by the assignor on structural alterations or the provision or improvement of fixtures which the tenant cannot

[30] *R.* v *Barnet Rent Tribunal* [1950] 2 K.B. 506.
[31] *Lower* v *Porter* [1956] 1 Q.B. 325.
[32] *Grace Rymer Investments, supra.*
[33] *Barker* v *Levinson* [1951] 1 K.B. 342.
[34] s. 15 (2).
[35] 1949 Act, s. 2 (5).
[36] *Gray* v *Southouse* [1949] 2 All E.R. 1019.
[37] *Mason, supra.* A statutory tenant cannot assign his tenancy. See *supra,* p. 590.
[38] 1920 Act, s. 15 (2).
[39] s. 2 (2), as amended by 1965 Act, 5th Schedule, Part I, para. 2.
[40] s. 2 (3).
[41] See *Minns, supra; Lower, supra.*
[42] s. 3 (1).
[43] s. 3 (2).

remove as against the landlord; where the assignor became tenant by assignation a sum not exceeding any reasonable amount paid by the assignor to his assignor for expenditure incurred by that assignor or any previous assignor in carrying out any such alteration or providing or improving such fixtures; and where part of a dwellinghouse is used as a shop or office or for business, trade or professional purposes, a reasonable amount in respect of any goodwill of the business, trade or profession, being goodwill transferred to the assignee in connection with the assignation or accruing to him in consequence thereof.[44] A tenant can pass on to his assignee a proportion of any premiums he lawfully paid on the previous grant, renewal or continuance of a tenancy.[45] The provisions of the 1949 Act in regard to the recovery or receipt of illegal premiums and penalties[46] are extended to premiums required on an assignation;[47] but it is not an offence that payment for outgoings is referable to a period before assignation, or that expenditure on alterations, etc., was not reasonably incurred or the sum is not a reasonable amount where incurred by a prior assignee, or that the amount for goodwill is not a reasonable amount.[48]

The 1954 Act,[49] however, allowed within limits a premium on an assignation where a premium had been lawfully charged on an assignation before the 1949 Act: the amount is the amount which bears to the premium paid on the earlier assignation the same proportion as the period of the tenancy still to run at the time of the later assignation bears to the period of the tenancy still to run at the time of the earlier assignation.[50] Where before the 1949 Act a premium was paid on more than one occasion on the assignation of the same tenancy, any of these assignations except the last is to be disregarded for the purposes of the 1954 Act,[51] and a premium paid on an assignation before the 1949 Act recovered under the 1949 Act[52] is to be treated as not paid, also for the purposes of the 1954 Act.[53] If the premium paid on the grant, continuance, renewal or assignation of a tenancy consisted only of such outgoings, sum for improvements or amount for goodwill as specified in the 1949 Act[54] it is to be treated as not paid for the purposes of the 1949[55] and 1954[56] Acts;[57] and if it included any such outgoings, sum for

---

[44] s. 2 (4).
[45] Schedule First, Part II.
[46] s. 2 (5), (6).
[47] s. 2 (2).
[48] 1954 Act, s. 30 (2).
[49] s. 29 (1).
[50] s. 29 (2).
[51] s. 29 (3).
[52] s. 2 (5).
[53] s. 29 (4).
[54] s. 2 (4).
[55] Schedule First, Part II.
[56] s. 29.
[57] s. 30 (1) (a).

improvements or amount of goodwill, it is to be treated for such purposes as if only the residue had been paid.[58]

Where a premium has lawfully been required and paid or received in respect of the grant, renewal or continuance of a tenancy before the commencement date of the Act,[59] which extended these provisions to cover that class of tenancy, a measure of relief is allowed on any assignation of that tenancy or any subsequent tenancy of the same dwelling-house.[60] It is a condition of this relief that since that grant, renewal or continuance the landlord has not granted a tenancy under which, as against the landlord, a person became entitled to possession other than the person entitled to possession of the dwellinghouse immediately before that tenancy began. In these circumstances a premium may be required or received, but it may not exceed a certain proportion of the premium previously paid.

Position of Crown. The Crown, not being bound by the Acts, can require a premium for the grant, renewal or continuance of a tenancy[61] and an immediate or direct tenant of the Crown can demand a premium on the assignation of a tenancy,[62] but a tenant of the Crown cannot require a premium on the grant, renewal or continuance of a subtenancy from him, nor a subtenant on an assignation where it would otherwise be unlawful.

Special Provisions in Relation to Decontrolled Premises. The provisions of the 1949 Act[63] are applied in regard to the grant, renewal, continuance or assignation of a tenancy at any time during the three years beginning with 6th July 1957 of a tenancy excluded from control by reason of the provisions of the 1957 Act that decontrolled on 6th July 1957 dwellinghouses whose rateable value exceeded certain limits or of the provisions that decontrolled tenancies granted on or after that date; or of a tenancy excluded from control by reason only of those provisions and the provision of the 1920 Act[64] excluding tenancies where the rent is less than two-thirds of the rateable value.[65] This did not affect the assignation after 6th July 1957 of a tenancy granted before that date and not renewed or continued thereafter, being a tenancy to which the 1920 Act provision[64] applies.[66] An order of the Secretary of State providing

---

[58] s. 30 (1) (b).
[59] In the case of a subtenancy of the Crown the relevant date is 1st September 1952 (Crown Lessees (Protection of Subtenants) Act 1952, s. 2 (1), *proviso* (31) (b.); in the case of a regulated tenancy the date is to be ascertained in accordance with the provision contained in the 1965 Act, Sched. 5, Part III; in all other cases the relevant date is 2nd June 1949.
[60] 1949 Act, First Schedule, Part II, para. 5 (1) and (2).
[61] Crown Lessees (Protection of Subtenants) Act 1952, s. 1 (3) (a).
[62] *Ibid.*, s. 1 (3) (b).
[63] s. 2.
[64] s. 12 (7).
[65] 1957 Act, s. 13 (1).
[66] *Ibid.*, s. 13 (1), *proviso*.

for decontrol by reference to rateable values may direct that the provision of the 1957 Act shall apply to such order with the substitution for the three years of whatever period of not less than three years beginning with the date when the order excludes control as is specified.[67] Contravention of the provisions involves on summary conviction a fine not exceeding £100 and the Court may order repayment in full or in part.[68]

Where a tenancy is granted, renewed or continued in such circumstances that the restrictions on premiums in relation to decontrolled premises apply, then any requirement that the rent is to be payable in advance before the beginning of the rental period in respect of which it is payable or earlier than six months before the end of the period, if that is more than six months long, is void whether the requirement is imposed as a condition of the grant, renewal or continuance thereof or under the terms thereof.[69] The rent is not recoverable from the tenant, who can recover any rent he has paid.[70] There is a penalty of a fine of £100 and the Court may order recovery or repayment.[71]

The statutory provisions[72] in regard to the prohibition of premiums and penalties for a breach thereof have been extended to the requiring of the making of any loan, whether secured or unsecured, as a condition of the grant, continuance, renewal or assignation of a tenancy as they apply to the requiring of a premium.[73] And an agreement for the making of a loan or a security issued in pursuance of such an agreement is not invalidated, but any sum lent in circumstances involving a contravention of the prohibition in the 1949 Act[74] is repayable to the lender on demand, notwithstanding anything in the agreement.[75]

In the case of a statutory exchange of a statutory tenancy under the 1957 Act[76] payment of any pecuniary consideration cannot be required for entering an agreement for exchange[77] (and, if required and made, it is recoverable by proceedings or deduction from the rent[78] and the person requiring it is liable to a fine of up to £100 and the Court may order payment[79]), except that the outgoing tenant may make charges in respect of outgoings, improvements and goodwill of a business, trade or profession,[80] as under the 1949 Act.[81]

---

[67] *Ibid.*, s. 13 (2).
[68] 1949 Act, s. 2 (6).
[69] 1957 Act, s. 15 (1), extended to regulated tenancies by 1965 Act, s. 38.
[70] *Ibid.*, ss. 15 (1), 26 (1), Schedule Sixth, para. 1, applying 1920 Act, s. 14.
[71] *Ibid.*, s. 15 (2).
[72] 1949 Act, s. 2 (1), (2), (6).
[73] 1957 Act, s. 14 (1).
[74] s. 2.
[75] 1957 Act, s. 14 (2).
[76] s. 17 (1). See *supra*, p. 590.
[77] s. 17 (4).
[78] s. 17 (4) (a).
[79] s. 17 (4) (b).
[80] s. 17 (4), *proviso*.
[81] s. 2 (4) of which is applied.

Excessive Prices for Purchase of Furniture and Fittings. Under the 1959 Act the range of prohibitions of premiums or sums in the nature of premiums has been extended and a loophole in the law closed. A person cannot, and is guilty of an offence if he does so, offer furniture (including fittings and other articles[82]) in connection with the proposed grant, renewal, continuance or assignation of a tenancy to which for the time being the relevant section of the 1949 Act,[83] or that section as extended by the relevant section of the 1957 Act,[84] applies, where the terms require the purchase of furniture (including fittings and other articles[85]), at a price he knows or ought to know is unreasonably high or otherwise seeks to obtain such a price for it whether or not a contract is actually concluded.[86] It is also an offence for a person to fail to furnish to any person seeking to obtain or retain accommodation whom he provides with particulars of the tenancy, a written inventory of the furniture (including fittings and other articles) specifying the price required for each item.[86] The penalty in each case is a maximum fine of £100.[87]

The local authority is given special powers. It can publish information about the Act for the assistance of anyone offering or seeking tenancies.[88] It can also enforce the Act, for if a local authority have reasonable grounds to suspect that an offence of offering furniture including as above at an unreasonably high price has taken place as regards a tenancy or a proposed tenancy of the premises, they may give notice to the person entitled to possession that on a certain date specified in the notice (not earlier than twenty-four hours from the date of the giving of notice or, if the premises are unoccupied, than the expiry of such period after the giving of notice as may be reasonable in the circumstances), facilities will be required for entry on the premises and inspection of furniture including fittings and other articles therein.[89] Warrant to enter premises and inspect the furniture as above defined can be obtained, on sworn written information from a Sheriff or a magistrate or a J.P. having jurisdiction in the place where the premises are, if facilities are not given after the date in the notice.[90] If a person acting under a warrant is wilfully obstructed, an offence is created, and the person so obstructing is liable to a maximum fine of £20 or, on a second or later occasion, of £50.[91]

Consideration for Exchange of Statutory Tenancy. It is unlawful to require payment of any pecuniary consideration for entering into an

[82] s. 1 (8).
[83] s. 2.
[84] s. 13.
[85] s. 1 (8).
[86] s. 1 (1).
[87] s. 1 (1).
[88] s. 1 (7).
[89] s. 1 (2).
[90] s. 1 (3).
[91] s. 1 (5).

agreement for the exchange of a statutory tenancy under the 1957 Act.[92] Again the fine is £100 and the Court may order recovery of the considera- tion, which also may be recovered in the ordinary way or if made to the landlord by deduction from the rent.[92] The outgoing tenant may obtain from the incoming tenant a certain portion of outgoings, improvements or alterations and the goodwill of a business, trade or profession.[93]

FURNISHED HOUSES

Introductory. As was mentioned above,[94] the Rent Acts do not apply to leases of houses where the amount of rent which is fairly attributable to attendance or the use of the furniture forms a substantial portion of the whole rent.[95] The tenant of a furnished letting had at one time the right to have his rent restricted if it could be said to be excessive, but it was not until 1943, with the passing of the Rent of Furnished Houses Control (Scotland) Act of that year, that any real control was put upon the rents payable under such lettings. The Furnished Houses (Rent Con- trol) Act 1946, applying only to England, combined rent control with a measure of security of tenure; similar security of tenure provisions were extended to Scottish furnished leases in the Landlord and Tenant (Rent Control) Act 1949. The 1943 Act applies generally to any house let in consideration of a rent which includes payment for the use of furniture or for services.[96] There are thus separate definitions of a furnished letting for the purposes of the Rent Acts and of the 1943 Act; these will be enlarged upon below. Suffice it to say at this stage that there was until 1965 a potential overlap in that a letting might not be a furnished letting to the extent of losing the protection of the Rent Acts, yet come within the definition of a furnished house for the purposes of the 1943 Act. Since 1965, however, any letting in any area in which Part II (Registration of Rents) of the 1965 Act is in force which is a regulated tenancy within the meaning of that Act[97] is excluded from being a furnished house for the purposes of the 1943 Act.[98]

Exclusion from the Rent Acts. The 1920 Act provided[99] that it should not apply "to a dwellinghouse *bona fide* let at a rent which includes payments in respect of board, attendance or use of furniture." This definition was soon seen to be too broad, for clearly even a trifling amount of furniture was sufficient to exclude the letting from the Acts,[1] and in the 1923 Act[2] the following delimitation was made: "A dwelling-

---

[92] 1957 Act, s. 17 (4).
[93] *Ibid.,* s. 17 (4), *proviso,* applying 1949 Act, s. 2 (4).
[94] *Supra,* p. 506.
[95] See 1920 Act, s. 12 (2) (i); 1923 Act, s. 10 (1).
[96] See 1943 Act, s. 2 (1).
[97] 1965 Act, s. 1 (4).
[98] *Ibid.,* s. 39 (5) (a).
[99] s. 12 (2) (i).
[1] *E.g., Wilkes* v *Goodwin* [1923] 2 K.B. 86.
[2] s. 10 (1).

house shall not be deemed to be *bona fide* let at a rent which includes payments in respect of attendance or the use of furniture unless the amount of rent which is fairly attributable to the attendance or the use of furniture, regard being had to the value of the same to the tenant, forms a substantial portion of the whole rent." The temptation to be more specific has been resisted, and it is to these definitions which apply to regulated and controlled tenancies alike, as interpreted by judicial decision,[3] that the landlord (upon whom the onus lies[4] to prove that the exception applies) must turn.

The following points have been established: —

(a) the words "*bona fide*" cover the whole of the phrase and represent a stipulation that the rent to be paid genuinely includes payments in respect of board, attendance and the use of furniture.[5] They mean genuine and not a colourable use of words.[5] The letting may be *bona fide* where the landlord has not furniture and buys it for the tenant in order to make such a let.[6] The purchase of the furniture by the tenant may or may not avoid the statutory provisions according to the circumstances of the particular case.[7] It may not be a sufficiently fundamental matter as to change the character of the tenancy.[7]

(b) The character of the letting is fixed at the date of the original contract and changes in the quantity or value of the furniture provided or the amount of the rent will not affect the character of the letting, unless of course, there has been a fundamental change of circumstances or a new contract.[8] So if no furniture is provided at the commencement of the letting or where furniture is provided,[9] if the amount of rent is varied,[10] this will not generally affect the original character, unless there is a fundamental change.

(c) There must be an actual use of furniture, not a mere right to demand delivery of it[11]

(d) "Rent" is all the payments under the letting, including, *e.g.*, for attendance, even though the other payments are provided for separately.[12] There is a presumption that the rent includes an element attributable to the furniture and that the furniture is of some value to the tenant.[13]

---

[3] Notably *Palser* v *Grinling* [1948] A.C. 291, in which each phrase is examined in detail.

[4] *Palser, supra.*

[5] *Palser, supra*, at 310, *per* Viscount Simon.

[6] *Maclay* v *Dixon* [1944] 1 All E.R. 22.

[7] *Stagg, infra; Welch* v *Nagy* [1950] 1 K.B. 455 at 461-2, *per* Asquith, L.J. In *Stagg*, the purchase was held not to be so fundamental a change of circumstances as to change the character of the letting.

[8] *Jozwiak* v *Hierowski* [1948] 2 All E.R. 9; *Stagg* v *Brickett* [1951] 1 K.B. 648 at 657-8, *per* Denning, L.J.

[9] *R.* v *Fulham Rent Tribunal* [1951] 2 K.B. 1 at 6, *per* Lord Goddard, L.C.J.

[10] *Bowness* v *O'Dwyer* [1948] 2 K.B. 219; *Stagg, supra*, at 657, *per* Denning, L.J.

[11] *Brown* v *Robins* [1943] 1 All E.R. 548.

[12] *Artillery Mansions* v *Macartney* [1949] 1 K.B. 164; *Alliance Property Co.* v *Shaffer* [1949] 1 K.B. 367.

[13] *Seabrook* v *Mervyn* [1947] 1 All E.R. 295.

(e) " Board " is any board provided and not only full board.[14] "Attendance " is service personal to the tenant performed by an attendant provided by the landlord in accordance with his covenant for the benefit or convenience of the individual tenant in his use or enjoyment of the premises. " Service " is a wider word than " attendance ". Attendance, being personal in its nature, may be dispensed with by an individual tenant at his pleasure, though it is not on that account excluded from what the tenant pays for when the landlord has covenanted to supply it.[15] The attendance must be an attendance provided for in the lease or contract of letting and not in a collateral arrangement nor given as an obligement.[16] It must be contracted for and supplied in relation to the subjects.[17] The following have been held to be attendance : an agreement or obligation to remove refuse,[18] to clean the outside of windows at intervals, to provide the services of a caretaker to carry wood, coal, etc.;[19] the following, on the other hand, have been held not to be attendance : an obligation to keep clean the common hall and staircase of a block of flats,[20] to provide a porter,[20] to provide central heating or piped hot water,[21] to maintain a system of electric bells, or a gas-cooker, or a dustbin at the rear of the house.[19] Where attendance is by a servant of the landlord, his wages must be apportioned among the tenants, if there is more than one, to whom the service is given after deducting any part of his wages which is not paid in respect of attendance proper.[22]

(f) In regard to furniture, on the question as to what articles are " furniture " the terms of the lease or contract are not conclusive. The word has a defined meaning. The articles must be commonly so regarded; articles which were at the outset of the letting part of the house are, therefore, not within the term.[23] The landlord must have a proprietory right in them as against the tenant.[23] They must, further, be provided for the use or enjoyment of the particular dwellinghouse and not for common use outside the subjects let, as in the hall of a block of flats. A fixture, something attached to the fabric of the house, may constitute furniture if it is commonly so regarded and can be detached without appreciable injury to or alteration of the fabric or itself.[23] Thus, a fitted bath, a corner seat fitted solidly into a corner, built-in wardrobes and cupboards, a table fixed to a wall

---

[14] *Wilkes* v *Goodwin* [1923] 2 K.B. 86 at 93, *per* Bankes, L.J., at 96, *per* L.J. Scrutton. See *Ibid., per* Younger, L.J., at 110.
[15] *Palser, supra,* at 310, *per* Viscount Simon.
[16] *Michael* v *Phillips* [1924] 1 K.B. 16.
[17] *King* v *Millen* [1922] 2 K.B. 647.
[18] *Nye* v *Davis* [1922] 2 K.B. 56; *Engvall* v *Ideal Flats* [1945] K.B. 205.
[19] *Engvall, supra.*
[20] *Palser, supra,* at 318, *per* Viscount Simon.
[21] *Wood* v *Carwardine* [1923] 2 K.B. 185; *Palser, supra,* at 318, *per* Viscount Simon.
[22] *Palser, supra,* at 318, 319, *per* Viscount Simon.
[23] *Palser, supra,* at 312-3, *per* Viscount Simon.

and depending for support on a wall-bracket, and a built-in kitchen cabinet are not held to be furniture.[24] Nor are a bath fixture,[25] or an electric panel fire.[26] On the other hand, a refrigerator plugged to the wall, linoleum and rubber floor covering, if detachable, and a fitted medical chest are held to be furniture.[27]

(g) The amount of rent is the portion of the whole rent.[28] The whole rent is to be divided actually or notionally into a portion which is rent for the dwellinghouse and a portion which is fairly attributable to the use of furniture and which must be substantial.[29] The whole rent is the entire contractual sum payable, including rates if paid by the landlord.[30]

(h) In construing "fairly attributable", the value in the lease is not necessarily to be taken. The chief consideration is that if the landlord did not provide it, the tenant would have to provide it for himself.[31]

(i) The words "regard being had to the value of the same to the tenant" involve the exercise of a broad judgment and any arithmetical calculations must be qualified by what is fair and reasonable.[32] It is the value of services to the original tenant; in determining what proportion of the rent is fairly attributable to attendance, regard, therefore, is to be had to the value to the original tenant of the service.[33] The tenant is thus the actual tenant and not a hypothetical or average tenant.[34] The value in the lease is *prima facie* to be accepted,[35] and the value must be calculated at the time of the original contract unless there is a new contract[35] other than a new contract made on a reduction of rent by a Rent Tribunal.[36] The fact that the amount of furniture is more than necessary is an item in valuing, and the value of the excess must be discounted.[37]

(j) "Substantial portion" involves comparison with the whole rent and is equivalent to "not insubstantial". It means considerable. It is a question of circumstances, a question of fact in each case, and percentages are only a guide and thus the Court should not apply a fixed percentage. The onus of showing it is a "substantial portion" lies on the landlord.[38] What is a substantial portion is taken *prima*

---

[24] *Palser, supra*, at 313, 314, 319, 320, *per* Viscount Simon.
[25] *Gray* v *Fidler* [1943] K.B. 694.
[26] *R.* v *Blackpool Rent Tribunal* [1948] 2 K.B. 277.
[27] *Palser, supra*, at 319-20, *per* Viscount Simon.
[28] *Palser, supra*, at 314, *per* Viscount Simon.
[29] *Palser, supra*, at 312, *per* Viscount Simon.
[30] *Palser, supra*, at 317, *per* Viscount Simon; *Artillery Mansions, supra*.
[31] *Palser, supra*, at 315, *per* Viscount Simon.
[32] *Palser, supra*, at 315-6, *per* Viscount Simon.
[33] *Palser, supra*, at 314, *per* Viscount Simon; *Artillery Mansions, supra*.
[34] *Palser, supra*, at 309, 310, *per* Viscount Simon; *Artillery Mansions, supra*.
[35] *Artillery Mansions, supra*.
[36] *Bowness* v *O'Dwyer* [1948] 2 K.B. 219.
[37] *Palser, supra*.
[38] *Palser, supra*, at 317, *per* Viscount Simon; *Hern* v *Palmer* [1955] 1 All E.R. 396.

facie at the date of the lease or letting.[39] Where both a payment for attendance and a payment for the use of furniture are included in the rent, then in determining a " substantial portion ", the two payments are added together and are not considered separately.[40] It is sufficient if the sum total, therefore is a " substantial portion " of the whole rent. The judge does not need to quantify the amount of " substantial portion."[41]

Though furnished lettings as defined in the Acts were excluded from the control provisions both as regards rent and as regards the landlord's right to possession, there were provisions designed to secure protection for tenants in such lettings against excessive rents. So where a person let a dwelling house at a rent which included payment in respect of the use of furniture and it was proved to the satisfaction of the Sheriff on the tenant's application that the rent charged yielded or would yield to the landlord a profit more than 25% in excess of the normal profit, the Sheriff could order the excess to be irrecoverable and any excess paid was to be repaid to the tenant.[42] " Normal profit " meant the profit which might reasonably have been expected from a similar letting in the year ending 3rd August 1914 in the case of old control houses,[43] and in the year ending 1st September 1939 in the case of new control houses,[44] but in the case of new control houses the 25% limit was omitted.[45] The overpayment could be recovered though the rent was not excessive at the date of the application.[46] It did not matter that the rent was in part in respect of attendance or other extra.[47] If the rent yielded a profit that was in all the circumstances of the case extortionate, the landlord was liable to a fine not exceeding £100 and the Court could order the excess to be irrecoverable and any excess paid to be repaid.[48] Extortion necessarily involved unfairness or oppression or similar conduct of a blameworthy character on the part of the landlord.[49] There had thus to be clear and proper evidence of extortion; mere evidence of a high rate of profit in the case of new control houses was not in itself sufficient proof of extortion[50] under the 1920 Act as amended by the 1939 Act. Prior to the amendment in 1939 the reference to the allowed margin of profit enabled the excess over that margin to be sufficient proof of extortion. These

---

[39] *Bowness, supra; Stagg, supra.*
[40] *Palser, supra*, at 310, *per* Viscount Simon.
[41] *Roppel* v *Bennett* [1949] 1 K.B. 115.
[42] 1920 Act, s. 9 (1), as amended by 1923 Act, s. 10 (2).
[43] 1920 Act, s. 9 (2).
[44] 1939 Act, s. 3 (1), Schedule First.
[45] 1939 Act, Schedule First.
[46] *Robbel* v *Bennet* [1949] 1 K.B. 115.
[47] *Lederer* v *Parker*, [1950] 1 K.B. 90.
[48] 1920 Act, s. 10, as amended by 1923 Act, s. 10 (2), 1939 Act, s. 3 (1), Schedule First.
[49] *Binnie, infra*, at 124, *per* Lord Fleming.
[50] *Binnie* v *Morris*, 1943 J.C. 119.

provisions applied to new control as well as old control houses,[51] but were eventually repealed by the 1957 Act.[52]

Application of 1943 Act. The law was radically altered in favour of the tenant of the furnished letting by the 1943 Act. This Act was at first a temporary one, being continued by yearly Expiring Laws Continuance Acts, but the 1965 Act made it a permanent measure.[53] The 1965 Act also greatly extended its application, which had been restricted by the 1957 Act[54] to tally with the provisions for the decontrol of unfurnished lettings. The 1943 Act now extends to cover all contracts relating to dwellings in Scotland let furnished the rateable value of which did not on the appropriate day exceed £200;[55] in other words, its coverage remains co-extensive with that of the Rent Acts over unfurnished dwellinghouses. The 1965 Act contains a decontrol provision similar to that made for regulated tenancies; decontrol may be effected by the Secretary of State by order reducing the upper limit of the rateable value of houses to which the 1943 Act applies.[56]

A lease becomes a furnished letting for the purposes of the Act where the right to occupy a house or part of a house " as a residence "[57] is granted " in consideration of a rent which includes payment for the use of furniture or for services, whether or not, in the case of such a contract with regard to part of a house, the lessee is entitled, in addition to exclusive occupation thereof, to the use in common with any other person of other rooms or accommodation in the house."[58] Provided exclusive occupation is enjoyed, even a lodger in a single room may be entitled to the protection of the Act.[59] The expression " services " in this context is defined[60] as including " attendance, the provision of heating or lighting, the supply of hot water and any other privilege or facility connected with the occupancy of a house or part of a house." The question of whether a house is let furnished depends to some extent on the terms of the contract; it has been held that, in the absence of any contractual obligation on the landlord to provide services, the rent cannot be said to include payment for services even though services are in fact provided.[61] However, it is not possible, in the case of furniture, to escape from the Act by omitting all reference to it in the lease.[62] The word " furniture " is used in its

---

[51] 1939 Act, s. 3 (1), Schedule First, which also amended 1920 Act, s. 10.
[52] s. 26 (3); 6th Schedule, para. 16.
[53] s. 39 (1).
[54] s. 12 (1) and (7).
[55] s. 39 (2) (a); for the expression " the appropriate day " see s. 43 (3); for Greater London the figure is £400.
[56] s. 39 (2) (b).
[57] For a discussion of the expression " residence " see *supra,* p. 520.
[58] 1943 Act, s. 2 (1).
[59] *R.* v *Battersea, etc. Rent Tribunal* [1957] 1 All E.R. 352.
[60] s. 9 (1).
[61] *R.* v *Paddington Rent Tribunal* [1948] 2 K.B. 413.
[62] *R.* v *Blackpool Rent Tribunal* [1948] 2 K.B. 277.

ordinary everyday meaning, and it has been held that a gas cooker and a water heater are not furniture within the meaning of this Act.[62]

Two important exclusions must be mentioned. Firstly, the Act does not apply to a house or part of a house let at a rent which includes payment in respect of board, provided that it can be said that the value of such board to the lessee forms a substantial proportion of the whole rent.[63] Secondly, the right to occupy a house or part of a house for a holiday is expressly excluded from the scope of this Act.[64] On the other hand, it is not possible to avoid the Act by putting the contract into two or more documents, the one providing for payment for occupation and the other for services and the like; the expression " rent " for the purposes of the Act's definition covers the aggregate of all such payments, which are deemed to be included in one contract.[65] Although a dwelling-house can conceivably be the subject of a controlled tenancy and of a furnished letting within the 1943 Act's definition at the same time, any tenancy in an area in which registration of rents has been introduced under Part II of the 1965 Act which is a regulated tenancy is expressly excluded from the 1943 Act.[66]

Rent Control. The object of the 1943 Act was to introduce provisions for the control of rents payable under furnished lettings. In order to do this, it provided for the constitution in local authority areas of Rent Tribunals, to serve the whole or part of such area or several of them;[67] these tribunals were set up gradually over Scotland as the Act was extended to each area by order of the Secretary of State.[68] Once constituted, it became the function of these Tribunals to determine on application what was a reasonable rent for the contract in question,[69] and to enter in a Register set up for the purpose any rent that had been approved, reduced or increased as a result of such application.[70] At the same time the Act directed that the provisions of the 1920 Act against excessive rents were not to apply to the rent of any letting which had been registered after the date of its registration.[71] The Act thus introduced informal proceedings and a more flexible criterion in place of the formality of rent-fixing by the Court, which existed at that time in the case of unfurnished lettings.

A reference of a contract to the Rent Tribunal may be made by the landlord or the tenant, and in certain circumstances by the local authority;[72] in this last case some prior complaint or inquiry is required—

---

[63] s. 9 (3).
[64] 1965 Act, s. 39 (11).
[65] s. 9 (2).
[66] 1965 Act, s. 39 (5) (a).
[67] s. 1 (2).
[68] Under s. 1 (1).
[69] s. 2 (2).
[70] s. 2 (4).
[71] s. 5.
[72] s. 2 (1).

" it was never intended that this Act should be used as a general rent-fixing Tribunal throughout a district. It is to deal with individual cases where hardship exists or may be reasonably supposed to exist."[73] Thereafter the Tribunal makes such inquiry as it thinks fit and allows each party (including the local authority, if the house is one where there is an obligation to keep a Revenue Account under the Housing Acts) an opportunity of being heard or making written representations. At the conclusion of these proceedings it is the duty of the Tribunal to approve the rent payable under the contract or to reduce it to such sum as it thinks reasonable in all the circumstances; alternatively it may dismiss the reference altogether.[74] In either case it must notify the parties and the local authority of its decision.[74] It has been held that once a furnished letting has been referred to a Tribunal, it has jurisdiction to fix the rent even though the letting has ended before the reference is held.[75]

Although the determination of what is a reasonable rent in all the circumstances is essentially a matter for the discretion of the Rent Tribunal, a number of points illustrating some limit on this discretion may be made. It was held, in a case under the 1946 Act, that when the Rent Tribunal is considering the case of a dwellinghouse to which the Rent Acts apply but which is nevertheless a furnished house for the purposes of the 1946 Act, the Tribunal has no power to reduce the rent below the " standard rent " which is payable under the Rent Acts.[76] The 1965 Act provides that where a dwellinghouse constitutes a regulated tenancy, then, in an area in which registration of rents under Part II of the Act is in force, the 1943 Act does not apply;[77] it also provides that if a rent has been registered for a dwellinghouse under the 1965 Act and the house is subsequently let under a contract which makes it a furnished letting to the exclusion of the Rent Acts (and so for the 1965 Act), the Tribunal may not reduce the rent below the amount which would be recoverable from the tenant under a regulated tenancy of that house.[78] The Tribunal, in considering all the circumstances, can take into account any non-contractual services provided or the cessation of such services.[79] It has been held that it is not sufficient, for a valid exercise by a Tribunal of its discretion, that there should be a contract of tenancy in existence; the Tribunal must know, at the time when they come to their decision, who are the parties to that contract, since it is necessary that it should be aware of all the circumstances in the case.[80]

[73] R. v Paddington & St. Marylebone Rent Tribunal [1949] 1 K.B. 666, at p. 680.
[74] s. 2 (2).
[75] R. v West London Rent Tribunal [1965] 2 All E.R. 734.
[76] R. v Paddington Rent Tribunal [1948] 2 K.B. 413.
[77] s. 39 (5) (a).
[78] s. 39 (5) (b).
[79] R. v Paddington & St. Marylebone Rent Tribunal, supra.
[80] R. v Paddington & St. Marylebone Rent Tribunal and Ors. [1961] 3 All E.R. 1047.

The Tribunal is required to keep a register, and to enter in that register the prescribed particulars[81] of a contract which has been referred to it and under which the rent has been approved, reduced or increased.[82] Once the "reasonable rent" has been determined and registered by the Tribunal, only the registered amount can be demanded as rent.[83] To require or receive a rent or sums in excess of the registered rent is an offence, punishable by fine or imprisonment;[84] an excess or overpayments can be recovered by the tenant.[85] On the other hand, a rent in excess of the registered rent of the unit of letting may be received for part of the original unit, but the tenant may, of course, apply to have the rent of the new unit separately determined and registered; until this is done there is no offence.[86] Where the rent has been entered on the register, no fresh application can be entertained by the Tribunal from either party in the absence of any change in the circumstances relating to the contract. Where change of circumstance can be shown, the landlord or the tenant or the local authority may make a fresh application for reconsideration of the registered rent; in this case the Tribunal may approve the rent as it stands, reduce it or even increase it.[87] A change of tenant does not, it has been held, constitute change of circumstances.[88]

Under the 1954 Act, in the case of a pre-1939 letting, where services are provided or are to be provided by the landlord under the terms of the lease, the landlord may recover the amount of the increase in the cost thereof as agreed with the tenant or determined by the Tribunal to be just.[89] If the agreement or determination is made in respect of services that the landlord is not liable to provide, however, any withholding or restoration of those services in whole or in part is to be treated for this purpose as a transfer from the landlord or the tenant, as the case may be, of a burden previously borne by him.[90]

Where a contract is referred to it, the Tribunal may by written notice to the landlord require him to give within a certain period of not less than seven days from the date of service of the notice such information as it may reasonably require regarding such of the prescribed particulars relating to the contract as are specified in the notice.[91] The particulars prescribed[92] are the following: accommodation, furniture and services provided by the landlord, and the payments contracted to be made by the tenant in respect thereof; if the landlord refuses or fails without reasonable cause to comply with this requirement he is liable to a fine

[81] S.R.O., 1943, 1774 S. 62, s. 10, Second Schedule.
[82] s. 2 (4); 1949 Act, Second Schedule.
[83] s. 3 (1) (a).
[84] s. 7 (1).
[85] s. 3 (2).
[86] *Gluchowska* v *Tottenham Borough Council* [1954] 1 Q.B. 439.
[87] s. 2 (3).
[88] *R.* v *Fulham Rent Tribunal* [1951] 2 All E.R. 1030.
[89] 1954 Act, s. 31 (1), (2).
[90] s. 31 (3).
[91] s. 2 (1), as amended by 1949 Act, Second Schedule.
[92] S.R.O., 1943, 1774 S. 62, s. 9, First Schedule.

of up to £50, and on a second or subsequent conviction to a fine not exceeding £100.[93]

Where there is a weekly let, the landlord must provide a rent book.[94]

The Rent Tribunal. The Tribunal in any area consists of a chairman and two other members; they are appointed under the 1943 Act by the Secretary of State.[95] There is no formal mechanism for co-ordination between it and the Rent Assessment Committee for that area, as there is in England; but since both bodies are closely linked to the Secretary of State it is to be expected that they will work together in arriving at figures which are related to each other's views as to what is reasonable or fair.

The Rent Tribunal is not a Court of Law, and its procedure is not subject to the ordinary rules of procedure or hearing of evidence;[96] nor is it limited to acting solely on the evidence heard by it or bound by any particular principles. It has, in short, complete discretion to act, subject to the rules of natural justice,[97] on its own views, impressions, knowledge and opinions;[98] its procedure is such as it itself may direct.[99] There is no appeal from the decisions on fact.[1] On point of law, however, provision is made under the Tribunals and Inquiries Act 1958[2] for an appeal to the Court of Session; and under the 1957 Act[3] the Sheriff has jurisdiction to determine any question which may arise as to the application of the 1943 Act, including the jurisdiction of the Tribunal, to any contract, or as to any matter which may be material for determining any such question.

Security of Tenure. The 1943 Act made no provision for the tenant's security of tenure, but this was soon remedied by the 1949 Act which introduced security of a limited nature on the pattern of that afforded to English tenants by the 1946 Act. The mechanism is the comparatively simple one of extending any period of notice on the service by the landlord of a notice to quit, and although each extension is limited to six months it is possible under certain circumstances to obtain repeated extensions of notice of an unlimited number. This remedy can, however, on a strict reading of the sections concerned,[4] only be invoked by a tenant

---

[93] s. 7 (2), as amended by 1965 Act, s. 39 (10).
[94] 1957 Act, s. 12 (6), (7), S.I. 1957 No. 1044, as amended by 1965 No. 2043.
[95] 1943 Act, s. 1 (2); 1st Schedule. The appointment of the chairman is made from a panel of persons appointed by the Lord President: Tribunals & Inquiries Act 1958, s. 3.
[96] *R. v Brighton Rent Tribunal* [1950] 2 K.B. 410.
[97] *R. v Kingston-upon-Hull Rent Tribunal* [1949] 1 All E.R. 260.
[98] *R. v Brighton Rent Tribunal, supra; R. v Paddington North, etc. Rent Tribunal* [1956] 1 Q.B. 229.
[99] S.R.O., 1943, 1774 S. 62, para. 6 (2).
[1] *R. v Paddington Rent Tribunal* [1947] 1 All E.R. 448, *per* Lord Goddard, L.C.J. at p. 449.
[2] ss. 9 and 16.
[3] s. 19 (2).
[4] 1949 Act, ss. 11 (1), 17 (6).

where a notice to quit has been served on him. Where the contract determines by effluxion of time[5] and not by a notice to quit, he would appear not to be entitled to apply for the right to hold over in possession.[6]

The first extension of notice is an automatic one: where the lease has been referred by the landlord or the local authority to the Rent Tribunal for the fixing or reconsideration of the rent payable for the furnished letting, a notice to quit served on the tenant at any time before the Tribunal gives its decision or within six months thereafter has no effect until a period of six months has expired from the date of its decision.[7] It is always open to the Tribunal to direct, if they think fit, that a shorter period shall be substituted for the standard six months' extension.[8] However, it is for the landlord to make representations to the Tribunal if he seeks a reduction of the standard six months period.

The 1965 Act, which greatly increased the coverage of these provisions by raising the rateable values of dwellinghouses over which the Tribunal has jurisdiction, introduced in addition certain specific circumstances in which the Tribunal may, on the lessor's application, direct that any period of extension of notice shall be reduced so as to end at a specified date.[9] These circumstances, similar to some of those enumerated in Schedule 1 of the 1933 Act in which the sheriff may grant decree of removing against the tenant of an unfurnished dwellinghouse without proof of alternative accommodation, are as follows: —

(i) where the lessee has not complied with the terms of the contract;

(ii) where he or any person residing or lodging with him has been guilty of conduct which is a nuisance or annoyance to adjoining occupiers;

(iii) where such a person has been convicted of using the dwelling or allowing it to be used for an immoral or illegal purpose; or

(iv) where the condition of the dwelling has deteriorated owing to any act or neglect of the lessee or any such person.[10]

If at any time during the period pending the Tribunal's decision the reference to the Tribunal is withdrawn, the extended period of notice expires seven days after the withdrawal is made.[11] It should be observed that in order to benefit the tenant under this provision, the lease may be referred to the Tribunal either before or after the service of the notice

---

[5] In order for this to be so, the fixed period must be for less than one year, otherwise a notice to quit will be required by the Sheriff Courts (Scotland) Act 1907, s. 37.

[6] See *Langford Property Co. Ltd.* v *Goodman* [1954] 163 Estates Gazette 324 (G.B.); this proposition was not disputed when the 1965 Bill was being scrutinised by Parliament.

[7] 1949 Act, s. 17 (6), as amended by 1965 Act, s. 39 (8).

[8] s. 17 (6), *proviso* (a).

[9] 1965 Act, s. 39 (7).

[10] *Ibid.*, see *supra*, pp. 576 *et seq.*

[11] 1949 Act, s. 17 (6), *proviso* (b).

to quit.[12] The notice, where served after such a reference, should, for this provision to apply, have been served within six months of the Tribunal's decision, since it is with reference to the date of that decision that the vital extension is granted. If the notice would normally have expired within the six month period, it will expire at the end of it.[13]

The tenant is thereafter entitled to apply for extensions of the automatic period discussed above for further periods of six months on the service of subsequent notices to quit, whether they are served before or after the reference.[14] An application for such an extension may be made any number of times, and will be entertained provided that the existing period of notice, whether by virtue of the contract or the statutory provisions, has not yet expired and that the Tribunal have not already substituted a shorter period than the standard six months or made a direction under the 1965 Act.[15] An application may be made even if the original six months period after the Tribunal's decision has expired.[16]

On an application the notice to quit has not, unless the application has been withdrawn, effect before the determination of the application,[17] and the Tribunal, after making such enquiry as they think fit and giving each party an opportunity of being heard or, at his option, of submitting representations in writing, may direct that the notice to quit is not to have effect until the end of such period not exceeding three months from the date at which the notice would have effect apart from the direction as may be specified in the direction;[18] that is, a further extension up to six months or extensions up to six months each can be made. If the Tribunal refuse a direction, the notice to quit does not have effect before the expiry of seven days from the determination of the application.[19] And if the direction is refused on such an application,[20] no subsequent application can be made in relation to the same notice.[21]

As has been mentioned above, extensions of notice may not be granted where the lease of the furnished dwelling was for a fixed period. The 1965 Act reinforced the position of the owner-occupier by a similar provision to that already discussed in relation to regulated tenancies.[22] Provided that the owner-occupier, that is a person who has previously occupied the dwelling as a residence, has given notice in writing to the lessee, at or before the time when the lessee was granted the right to occupy the dwelling (or, in the case of leases granted before 8th December 1965,

---

[12] 1965 Act, s. 39 (6), which reversed the decision in *R. v Folkestone Rent Tribunal* [1952] 1 K.B. 54, approved by Lord Porter in *Preston and Area Rent Tribunal v. Pickavance* [1953] A.C. 562.
[13] *Alexander v Springate* [1951] 1 K.B. 803.
[14] 1949 Act, s. 11 (1), as amended by 1965 Act, s. 39 (8).
[15] s. 11 (1), *proviso*, as amended, and as applied to Scotland by s. 19 (7).
[16] *Preston and Area Rent Tribunal, supra.*
[17] s. 11 (2) (a).
[18] 1949 Act, s. 11 (2) (b).
[19] *Ibid.*, s. 11 (2) (c).
[20] That is under s. 11 (1).
[21] s. 11 (4).
[22] s. 40

within six months of that date), that he is the owner-occupier, and that he does not occupy any other part of the house as a residence, the security of tenure provisions contained in the 1949 Act will not apply to a notice to quit served by him. It is essential, however, that at the time the notice is to take effect the dwelling should be required as a residence for him or any member of his family who resided with him when he last occupied the dwelling as a residence.[22]

Furnished Sublettings. Prior to the 1949 Act, if a tenant sublet furnished the whole or a part of the premises the landlord could recover possession. Under that Act, however, the tenant of a house or part of a house may sublet part of the premises furnished and still retain the protection of the Rent Acts, for the protection remains though the rent includes payments in respect of board, attendance or the use of furniture.[23] But the subtenant is not protected against the tenant,[23] and if the tenant gives up possession is not protected against the landlord.[24] If there is a furnished sublet of the whole premises at the time when an action for possession has been raised there is no protection even though the original let to the tenant was unfurnished.[25] This, however, applies only to contractual tenancies.[26] Where the subtenant of the whole of furnished premises applies to the Rent Tribunal[27] for an extension of security of tenure, he gets a statutory security of tenure as against the tenant in respect that during the period of that security the dwellinghouse is not regarded as sublet furnished and the tenant is still protected by the Acts.[26] In the case in question the landlord claimed possession on the ground that the sublet of the whole was still in existence in terms of the 1949 Act,[28] but the Court, rejecting the literal interpretation of the Act, held that the sublease had expired when the notice to quit expired and the subtenant had only a statutory security of tenure.[26] It is not competent to raise an action for possession on the ground that the whole premises have been sublet furnished where the period of subletting has terminated and the tenant is in possession at the time of the action.[29]

Premiums on Assignation. In the case of furnished lettings, if the rent payable for a furnished house has been entered on the Register under the 1943 Act, then, unless the rent is fixed for a limited period and that period has expired, it is illegal for a person as a condition of a grant, renewal, continuance or assignation of rights under the contract to which the 1943 Act applies to require or to receive payment of a premium.[30]

---

[22] s. 9.
[24] *Shackleton* v *Greenhalgh* [1951] 1 K.B. 725.
[25] *Prout* v *Hunter* [1924] 2 K.B. 736.
[26] *Francis Jackson Developments* v *Hall* [1951] 2 K.B. 488.
[27] 1949 Act, s. 11. See *supra*, p. 619.
[28] s. 11 (2).
[29] *Leslie & Co.* v *Cumming* [1926] 2 K.B. 417.
[30] 1949 Act, s. 12 (1), (2).

This provision does not, however, make it illegal to require payment of
so much of any outgoings paid by the grantor or assignor as is referable
to any period after the grant or assignation takes effect, or to require
payment of a reasonable amount in respect of the goodwill of a business,
trade or profession, being goodwill transferred to the grantee or assignee
in connection with the grant or assignation or accruing to him in consequence thereof.[31] The provisions of the 1943 Act [32] which are repealed
by the 1949 Act are repealed without prejudice to their operation as to
anything done before the commencement of that Act.[33] The provisions
of the 1949 Act as to recovery of an unlawful premium, as to penalties
and as to an excessive price asked for furniture, etc. are applied to
furnished houses.[34] The prohibition, however, does not apply to a
subtenant of the Crown unless the premium was required under an
agreement before 8th February 1952.[35]

LEGAL PROCEEDINGS UNDER THE ACTS

Introductory. The lynchpin of the judicial administration of the Acts
in Scotland is, and has always been, the Sheriff Court; its counterpart
in England is the County Court, but in some respects the jurisdiction of
these Courts is dissimilar. The importance of the Sheriff Court in these
matters is underlined by the fact that in a number of cases its determination is final and conclusive, and also because there is, unlike the County
Court, no upward monetary limit on its jurisdiction.

In the past the Sheriff Court was required to deal with matters arising
in connection with rent restriction—that is, the fixing or variation of
standard rents—as well as, in dealing with actions of removing or other
such applications, to apply the security of tenure provisions contained in
the Acts. Under the 1943 Act, however, Rent Tribunals were set up in
local authority areas to deal with the rents of furnished houses and with
the provisions of a measure of security of tenure to the tenants of such
houses. Their jurisdiction was subsequently extended by the 1949 and
1954 Acts[36] to the giving of approval to, or increasing or reducing as the
case might be, the standard rent of unfurnished houses subject to " new "
control. More recently the 1965 Act, by providing new machinery for the
regulation of the rents of regulated tenancies, has made more significant
inroads into the jurisdiction of the Sheriff Court. Once registration of
rents has been brought into force in a given local authority area it is
the rent officers and the rent assessment committee for that area who
administer the new " fair rent " system. Eventually, therefore, rent fixing
will fall outside the jurisdiction of the Sheriff Court altogether.

---

[31] *Ibid.,* s. 12 (2), *proviso.*
[32] s. 3 (1) (b), which prohibited the requiring or receiving of a fine or premium
as a condition of the grant, renewal or continuance of a contract of let of
furnished premises.
[33] 1949 Act, s. 12 (4) and *proviso,* 17 (2).
[34] *Ibid.,* s. 12 (3).
[35] Crown Lessees (Protection of Subtenants) Act 1952.
[36] 1949 Act, ss. 1, 6 : 1954 Act, s. 28.

The structure and functioning of Rent Tribunals, Rent Assessment Committees and Rent Officers has already been discussed,[37] and is not within the scope of this section.

Sheriff Court. Broadly speaking, any dispute arising under the Rent Acts and their attendant legislation, and not one which it is competent for a Rent Tribunal or Rent Assessment Committee to deal with, may be referred to the Sheriff Court. Under the 1920 Act[38] the Sheriff Court was given jurisdiction to deal with any claims or other proceedings arising out of that Act or any of its provisions, although not otherwise within its jurisdiction. This provision was applied to claims and proceedings for the recovery of any sums of money recoverable by virtue of the 1949 Act,[39] and to any claims made under the 1957[40] or 1958[41] Acts. These provisions did not, it may be noticed, give exclusive jurisdiction to the Sheriff Court, but this has been in practice the Court normally resorted to.[42] Similarly, any applications required to be made for an order or determination under the 1965 Act are to be made to the Sheriff Court; in this case, however, such applications must be made in like manner as proceedings brought under the Small Debt Acts,[43] and it does not appear to be open to the litigant to proceed elsewhere.

No useful purpose would be served by rehearsing in this context all the situations in which applications for orders or determinations under the Acts require to be made. They are many and very varied, and have been noted in the appropriate passages throughout this chapter. As an indication of the breadth of the scope of the Sheriff Court's jurisdiction, however, the following instances may be mentioned:

(i) Questions as to the applicability of the Acts. Under the 1957 Act[44] the Sheriff Court has jurisdiction in the case of proceedings relating to a dwelling[45] or any application made for the purpose by the landlord or the tenant, to determine any question as to the applicability of the Rent Acts or of the Rent of Furnished Houses Control (Scotland) Act 1943, or as to any matter which is or may become material for the determination of any such question. This replaces, so far as the 1943 Act is concerned, the rule that it was for the Rent Tribunal to decide whether it had jurisdiction, its decision being open to review in the Court of Session. Questions arising as to the applicability of the 1965 Act would appear to be covered by the 1957 provision, but where registration of rents under Part II of that Act is in force it seems that it is a matter for the Rent Officer or Rent Assessment Committee to decide whether a given property

---

[37] *Supra*, pp. 559, 617.
[38] s. 17 (2).
[39] s. 13.
[40] ss. 19 (3), 27 (3).
[41] s. 4 (1). This Act, which was temporary, has now expired.
[42] See Megarry, *Rent Acts*, 9th ed., p. 23.
[43] s. 45.
[44] s. 19 (2).
[45] Defined in s. 25 (1).

is within its jurisdiction; the applicability of the Acts is, however, a question of law upon which appeals from Rent Assessment Committees to the Court of Session will be competent under the Tribunals and Inquiries Act 1958.[46]

(ii) Questions as to the proper apportionment or aggregation of rateable values for the purposes of the 1957 Act (controlled tenancies)[47] and the 1965 Act (regulated tenancies and furnished houses).[48]

(iii) The determination, failing agreement, of the successor[49] or the second successor[50] to a statutory tenant.

(iv) Rents. The amount of the rent, standard rent or net rent payable under a controlled tenancy,[51] and of any permitted increases;[52] in the case of regulated tenancies, before the rent for the dwellinghouse has been registered under Part II of the 1965 Act, any question whether, or by what amount, the limit set by that Act[53] should be increased or decreased.[54]

(v) Repairs. Any question whether the landlord is responsible for repairs, or the amount of any reduction in the repairs increase where the landlord is only in part liable for repairs;[55] the just proportion of a repairs increase to be passed on to a subtenant,[56] whether the necessary repairs work has been carried out in order to justify a repairs increase.[57]

(vi) Improvements. Questions arising as to whether compensation is payable by the landlord for improvements made by the tenant, the amount of such compensation and as to the recovery of compensation in the case of subtenants from a superior landlord;[58] whether any improvement in respect of which a notice of increase has been served on the statutory tenant of a regulated tenancy was unnecessary, or whether a greater amount was expended on it than was reasonable;[59] whether benefit has accrued from the carrying out of the improvements to other premises of the landlord or superior landlord, and the apportionment of the amount between such premises and the subjects occupied by the tenant.[60]

(vii) Various. Questions arising in respect of the 1957 increase;[61] questions as to the termination of the right to use shared accommodation

[46] s. 9 of the 1958 Act has been extended to them by the Tribunals and Inquiries (Rent Assessment Committees) Order 1965 No. 2151.
[47] 1957 Act, Fifth Schedule, Part 1, para. 5 (a).
[48] 1965 Act, s. 43.
[49] 1920 Act, s. 12 (1) (g), as amended.
[50] 1965 Act, s. 13.
[51] 1923 Act, s. 11 (1); cp. 1954 Act, s. 39 (3).
[52] 1920 Act, s. 2 (6); 1923 Act, s. 11 (1).
[53] In s. 3 (3).
[54] ss. 4 (7), 6 (5).
[55] 1954 Act, s. 16 (4); 1957 Act, s. 7 (4).
[56] 1954 Act, s. 21 (2).
[57] 1954 Act, 1st Schedule, para. 4 (1).
[58] 1957 Act, Fourth Schedule, paras. 5 (5), (6), 15 (b).
[59] 1965 Act, s. 6 (7).
[60] 1965 Act, s. 17 (4).
[61] 1957 Act, s. 8 (1).

other than living accommodation or the modification of rights regarding shared accommodation.[62] In addition, the security of tenure provisions embodied in the Acts[63] will frequently be in issue in actions of removing or of ejection heard before a Sheriff.

Procedure. There are three forms of procedure available appropriate to particular cases or circumstances. These are (1) an ordinary action, either small debt, summary or ordinary; (2) an application; and (3) a reference to the Sheriff as arbitrator or arbiter. An action for removal of a tenant or recovery of possession may be either by ordinary action or by an application. In many classes of cases the proceedings are by application. Applications are by initial writ or by minute, the former being treated as a summary application. Provision is made for questions under the Acts to be referred with consent of parties for determination by the Sheriff sitting as arbitrator or instead of the Sheriff someone appointed by the Sheriff,[64] by the process of initial writ or minute in any depending action or cause.[65] The Court of Session could provide for this by Act of Sederunt,[64] and has done so.[65] In certain cases there is specific reference to the procedure to be adopted. For instance, under the 1954 Act[66] and in particular under the 1965 Act[67] applications made to the Sheriff under certain situations for orders or determinations are to be conducted and disposed of as proceedings under the Small Debt Acts. The 1954 Act[68] also provides that any appeal to the Sheriff by an aggrieved landlord against the granting by a local authority of a certificate of disrepair, or the refusal of the authority to revoke such a certificate in connection with the condition of a house, is to be made under certain provisions of the Housing (Scotland) Act 1950;[69] these provisions are similarly applied to appeals by the landlord under the 1954 Act against a certificate by the local authority that an increase of rent is not justified. In questions as to permitted increases of rent, summary application to the Sheriff is required,[70] and the Sheriff may determine such questions raised by initial writ under the Sheriff Courts Acts or by minute in a depending process, the initial writ being treated as a summary application.[71]

The 1920 Act[72] empowered the Court of Session to make rules and to give directions by Act of Sederunt to carry out the 1920 Act. This

---

[62] 1949 Act, ss. 8 (8), 17 (2).
[63] In particular, 1920 Act, s. 5; 1933 Act, s. 3 and First Schedule; 1965 Act, ss. 14-16, 33.
[64] 1920 Act, s. 11 (2).
[65] A.S. 14th December, 1923, as amended by A.S. 17th November, 1925.
[66] s. 41 (1).
[67] s. 45.
[68] s. 41 (2).
[69] 1950 Act, s. 166 (1), (2), (5).
[70] 1920 Act, s. 2 (6); *Glasgow Corporation* v *Mickel,* 1922 S.C. 228; 1923 Act, s. 11 (1).
[71] A.S. 14th December, 1923, as amended by A.S. 17th November, 1925.
[72] ss. 17 (1), 18 (1) (a).

provision is applied by the 1957 Act;[73] and is applied to the 1958 Act.[74] The Court, acting under the powers of the 1920 Act, passed two Acts of Sederunt[75] to regulate proceedings in Court.

Under the 1958 Act[76] the Sheriff in proceedings for recovery of possession or applications to extend the period of suspension of an order for possession may not order expenses unless where he exercises his discretion to refuse or revoke suspension on any ground on which an order for possession can be made under the Rent Acts, or where it appears to him, having regard to the conduct of the parties respectively in and in connection with the proceedings, that there are special reasons for making an order for possession.

Appeal. In the case of ordinary actions dealing with questions under the Acts, where such an action is competent the ordinary methods of appeal appropriate to that action are competent also. In cases where procedure under the Small Debt Acts is required,[77] however, the determination of the Sheriff is declared to be final and conclusive; a similar restriction on appeal is made in certain other limited situations by sections of the 1920,[78] 1949[79] and 1957[80] Acts.

Appeal lies in all cases from the Sheriff-Substitute to the Sheriff-Principal,[81] even where the Sheriff is declared final.[82] Where the Sheriff Court is declared final and conclusive, however, then, even where the Sheriff has misdirected himself and applied a wrong principle of law, appeal is not competent from the Sheriff Court.[83] If, however, a point arises incidentally in such a case as an incident of an ordinary process, appeal is competent on that point.[84] In the case where the provisions of the Housing (Scotland) Act 1950 are to apply,[85] the Sheriff in terms of that Act may state during the proceedings a case on a question of law for the Court of Session and must do so if directed by the Court of Session.[86] Where the Sheriff or some other person is sitting as arbitrator, his decision is, of course, final.

CONTRACTING OUT OF OR INTO ACTS

Prohibition of Contracting out of or into the Acts. The provisions of the Acts are mandatory and a tenant cannot contract out of them; there

[73] s. 19 (3).
[74] s. 4 (1).
[75] 14th December, 1923, and 17th November, 1925.
[76] s. 4 (2).
[77] 1954 Act, s. 41 (1); 1965 Act, s. 45.
[78] s. 2 (6).
[79] s. 8 (9).
[80] ss. 19 (4), 18 (2).
[81] *Glasgow Corporation, supra; Bain* v *Ormiston,* 1928 S.C. 764.
[82] Fraser, *Rent Acts,* 2nd ed., p. 139.
[83] *Field* v *Gover* [1944] K.B. 200 at 207, *per* Scott, L.J.; *Glasgow Corporation, supra.* See, however, *Haldane* v *Sinclair,* 1927 S.C. 562 at 567, *per* L.P. Clyde.
[84] *Purves* v *Graham,* 1924 S.C. 477; *Strickland* v *Palmer* [1924] 2 K.B. 572.
[85] See *supra,* p. 624.
[86] s. 166 (2).

40

is equally no right to contract into the Acts.[87] "No contract and *a fortiori* no mere statement of his wishes or intentions can deprive him of the statutory protection. . . . He cannot contract to give up his right to claim protection."[88] "It has been laid down . . . that parties to a tenancy cannot so contract that although the conditions are present which Parliament has declared cause the Acts to apply to the premises, nevertheless those Acts shall not apply."[89] Parliament has definitely determined that the Court shall exercise its jurisdiction only in certain circumstances and in no others; the Legislature has restricted the jurisdiction of the Court and no agreement of parties can give the Court a jurisdiction that Parliament has said it is not to exercise.[90] The tenant, therefore, cannot undertake to pay more than the recoverable rent, and an agreement with a new tenant will not permit the landlord to recover rent in excess of the standard rent and permitted increases without the necessary notice of increase,[91] nor can there be in a lease a provision for possession on a ground that is a personal obligation of the tenant only and unconnected with the use of the premises, *e.g.*, that his possession is conditional on his remaining in his employment with a third party.[92] The only Scottish authorities here are *dicta* by Lords Mackenzie and Guthrie in a case under the original 1915 Act, that they thought contracting out was not permissible, Lord Dundas, however, reserving his opinion.[93] It does not matter that the tenant has agreed or undertaken to vacate; the landlord must, if he refuses to do so, establish the necessary ground for possession under the Act and obtain the authority of the Court, even if valuable consideration is given by the tenant,[94] unless perhaps the contract or undertaking to quit can be construed as amounting to a notice by the tenant to quit, which is a ground for possession by the landlord.[95] On the other hand, an agreement between a landlord and a tenant that the tenant will vacate the premises on a future date, the landlord undertaking to pay the tenant a sum for giving up possession or vacating, has been held not to be void on the ground of public policy or want of maturity or as amounting to an attempt to contract out of the Acts.[96]

It is specifically provided that the repairs increase under the 1954 Act[97] and the cost of services increase under that Act[98] and the 1957 Act

---

[87] *Hitchinson* v *Gray* (1964) 108 S.J. 197.
[88] *Brown* v *Draper* [1944] K.B. 309 at 313, *per* Lord Greene, M.R.
[89] *R.M.R. Housing Socy., infra*, at 493, *per* Lord Evershed, M.R. See also *Middleton* v *Baldock* [1950] 1 All E.R. 708.
[90] *Barton, infra*, at 295-6, *per* Bankes, L.J.
[91] *Schmit* v *Christy* [1922] 2 K.B. 60.
[92] *R.M.R. Housing Socy.* v *Combs* [1951] 1 K.B. 486.
[93] *Smith* v *Barclay*, 1919 57 S.L.R. 93 at 99, 97; 1920 1 S.L.T. 13 at 18, 19 and 17.
[94] *Barton* v *Fincham* [1921] 2 K.B. 291; *Brown* v *Draper* [1944] K.B. 309.
[95] *Infra*, p. 627. See *Flannagan* v *Shaw* [1920] 3 K.B. 96 at 108, *per* Duke, L.J., and *Smith, supra, per* Lord Dundas at 97-98.
[96] *Rajbenback* v *Mamon* [1955] 1 Q.B. 283, the judge stating that in *Barton* (*supra*) public policy was not discussed.
[97] s. 16 (1).
[98] s. 31 (2).

rent increase[99] are recoverable notwithstanding anything in the terms of the tenancy or statutory tenancy or any enactment. And a sum lent in contravention of the provisions against requiring the making of any loan as a condition of the grant, renewal, continuance or assignation of a tenancy is repayable to the lender on demand, notwithstanding anything in the agreement for the loan.[1] Similarly, the 1965 Act provides that rent in excess of the rent limit for a regulated tenancy is to be irrecoverable from the tenant, notwithstanding anything in any agreement.[2]

" There is nothing to prevent parties from so arranging matters that there is nothing to which the Acts can apply, provided that the transaction in question is a genuine transaction and not a mere sham."[3] Parties may therefore so arrange it that a lease is outside the Acts.[4] The substance and scope and not the mere form of the lease or transaction must here be examined. The Court must ask whether the transaction as a whole and according to substance is in truth one which is on that side of the line which frees the premises from the Acts or is within the mischief the Acts were designed to avoid.[5] And so a lump sum in a year's lease in addition to the rent was held to be in truth rent despite an agreement that the lease was not to be within the Acts.[18] But an arrangement by which a lease ceased or was surrendered and the tenant was allowed to remain in occupation rent-free was upheld as being on the facts a genuine surrender.[6]

It has been held that a statutory tenant may by agreement turn his statutory tenancy into a contractual one, in a case where a widow who was a statutory tenant by succession was held to have become a contractual one because the landlord had offered her a tenancy on new conditions and rent had been paid and accepted on that basis.[7] On the other hand, it is not competent by agreement to bring under the protection of the Acts premises which are by reason of statutory exception[8] excluded from control or regulation.[9]

---

[99] s. 7 (1).
[1] 1957 Act, s. 14 (2).
[2] ss. 3 (1), 5, 7.
[3] Megarry, *Rent Acts*, 9th ed., p. 15, approved from a prior edition by Lord Evershed, M.R., in *Foster* v *Robinson* [1951] 1 K.B. 149 at 158. See also *Maclay, infra*, at 23, *per* Scott, L.J. and *Samrose, infra*, at 503-4, *per* Lord Evershed, M.R. and at 508-9, *per* Morris, L.J.
[4] *Maclay* v *Dixon* [1944] 1 All E.R. 22; Megarry, *supra*.
[5] *Samrose Props.* v *Gibbard* [1958] 1 All E.R. 502.
[6] *Foster, supra; Turner* v *Watts* (1928) 44 T.L.R. 337.
[7] *Bungalows (Maidenhead)* v *Mason* [1954] 1 All E.R. 1002.
[8] See *supra*, p. 506.
[9] *Rogers* v *Hyde* [1951] 2 K.B. 923.

CHAPTER XXI

THE TENANCY OF SHOPS (SCOTLAND) ACTS

Introduction. Just as the Rent Restrictions Acts are intended to protect and afford security of tenure to tenants of dwellinghouses, the Agricultural Holdings Acts and the Crofters and Small Landholders Acts to protect tenants of agricultural holdings, small holdings and crofts respectively, so the Tenancy of Shops (Scotland) Act 1949 was designed to afford security of tenure to a tenant of premises consisting of a shop. The Act was a temporary Act until 31st December 1950[1] to meet what was expected to be a temporary situation, but it was continued by numerous Expiring Laws Continuance Acts until 31st December 1964,[2] and its provisions except for one subsection were made permanent by the Tenancy of Shops (Scotland) Act 1964. In its comparative brevity the "Act is more reminiscent of earlier legislation which laid down a principle and left the Courts to apply that principle to the infinite variety of individual cases than to the more modern legislation which by meticulous codification seems to provide for every contingency ".[3]

Subjects. The subject of the Act is a " shop ", which is defined[4] as including " any shop within the meaning of the Shops Acts 1912-36 or any of those Acts ". These Acts were consolidated by the Shops Act 1950, which provides[5] that a " shop " includes " any premises where any retail trade or business is carried on "; " retail trade or business " includes " the business of a barber or hairdresser, the sale of refreshments or intoxicating liquors, the business of lending books or periodicals when carried on for the purpose of gain, and retail sales, but does not include the sale of programmes and catalogues and other similar sales at theatres and places of amusement ". The Act also applies to such premises where the interest of the landlord or the tenant belongs to Her Majesty in right of the Crown or a Government Department or is held on behalf of Her Majesty for the purposes of a Government Department.[6] Whether any premises are a shop must be judged by the character of the business rather than by the area occupied by each of the various components.[7] It has thus been held that premises where secondhand cars, petrol and motor accessories were sold and cars garaged and

---

[1] s. 3 (3).
[2] Expiring Laws Continuance Act 1963 being the last Act.
[3] *Loudon* v *St. Paul's Parish Church,* 1949 S.L.T. (Sh. Ct.) 54 at 55.
[4] s. 3 (2).
[5] s. 74 (1). See formerly 1912 Act, s. 19 (1).
[6] s. 2.
[7] *Thom* v *British Transport Commission,* 1954 S.L.T. (Sh. Ct.) 21 at 22.

repaired were a shop;[8] and that a garage where cars were garaged and repaired with a retail business of the sale of petrol, oil, spare parts, tyres and motor accessories, the garage occupying the larger part, was a shop,[9] the premises being considered to have the character of and to be used as a shop, though a garage may in some cases not properly be able to be regarded as a shop from its type of business; that a sub post-office was in view of the sale of stamps therein a shop,[10] and that premises occupied by an optician in which he did not sell anything but carried out ophthalmic dispensing and supplied spectacles,[10a] were a shop.

Parties. These must be " landlord " and " tenant ", but the Act, in contrast to the Rent Restrictions Act 1920 and the Agricultural Holdings Act 1949 has no definitions of these terms. The Act is not applicable to a subtenant,[11] for not only are the references always to " tenancies " and " tenants " but there is the absence of definition, and certain public bodies in possession of shops in the exercise of special powers are deemed to be tenants, and the provisions of the Act are clearly not designed for subtenants. Purchasers of the premises under missives are not " landlords " and so they cannot use a notice to quit given by the sellers;[12] nor are lessees under a long lease " landlords ".[13]

Protection to Tenant by Renewal of Tenancy. This is the purpose of the Act. If a landlord of any premises consisting of a shop and occupied by a tenant gives or has given notice of termination of the tenancy to the tenant, that is notice to quit, taking effect after the passing of the Act, and the tenant is unable to get a renewal of the tenancy from the landlord on terms satisfactory to him, he may apply to the Sheriff for renewal of the tenancy at any time before the notice takes effect and not later than the expiry of twenty-one days after its service or the passing of the Act.[14] The Sheriff may determine that there should be a renewal of the tenancy for a period that must not exceed one year at such rent and on such terms and conditions as he thinks in all the circumstances reasonable,[15] and in that event parties are deemed to have entered into a new lease for that period, at that rent and on these terms and conditions.[15] The renewal dates from the expiry of the notice to quit.[16] If the Sheriff is satisfied that it will not be possible to dispose of the application by the tenant finally before notice of termination takes effect, that is before the notice to quit expires, he may make an

---

[8] *Grosvenor Garages (Glasgow) Ltd.* v *St. Mungo Property Co.* (1955), 71 Sh. Ct. Rep. 155.
[9] *Thom, supra.*
[10] *King* v *Cross Fisher Properties,* 1956 S.L.T. (Sh. Ct.) 79.
[10a] *Craig* v *Saunders & Connor,* 1962 S.L.T. (Sh. Ct.) 85.
[11] *Ashley Wallpaper Co.* v *Morrisons Associated Cos.,* 1952 S.L.T. (Sh. Ct.) 25.
[12] *Cuthbertson* v *Orr's Trs.* (1954), 70 Sh. Ct. Rep. 273.
[13] *James Craig (Glasgow) Ltd.* v *Wood & Selby,* (1953), 69 Sh. Ct. Rep. 164.
[14] s. 1 (1).
[15] s. 1 (2).
[16] *Hill* v *McCaskill's Trs.,* 1951 S.L.T. (Sh. Ct.) 41.

interim order authorising the tenant to continue in occupation for a period not exceeding three months at such rent and on such terms and conditions as he thinks fit.[17] On the other hand, the Sheriff may determine that there should not be a renewal; he may refuse the application for renewal. If, in all the circumstances, he thinks it reasonable to do so, he may, therefore, dismiss the application.[18] He must not determine in favour of renewal if he is satisfied on one or other of six matters:—

(a) that the tenant is in breach of any condition of his tenancy which in the opinion of the Sheriff is material.[18] Where a condition of a let was that the premises " shall be used by the tenant exclusively as a newsagents and stationers and for no other purpose whatsoever " it was held that the selling of cigarettes and tobacco was a breach of a material condition;[19]

(b) that the tenant is notour bankrupt or is divested of his estate by a trust deed for creditors or, being a company, is unable to pay its debts;[18]

(c) that the landlord has offered to sell[20] the premises to the tenant at such price as may, failing agreement, be fixed by a single arbiter agreed on by parties, or, failing agreement by them thereon, appointed by the Sheriff;[18]

(d) that the landlord has offered to afford to the tenant, on terms and conditions which in the Sheriff's opinion are reasonable, alternative accommodation[20a] which in the Sheriff's opinion is suitable for the purposes of the business carried on by the tenant in the premises;[18]

(e) that the tenant has given notice of termination of the tenancy and in consequence of this notice the landlord has contracted to sell or let the premises or has taken any other steps as a result of which he would in the opinion of the Sheriff be seriously prejudiced if he could not obtain possession of the premises;[18]

(f) that, having regard to all the circumstances of the case, greater hardship would be caused by determining that the tenancy shall be renewed than by refusing so to do.[18] Hardship must be read in a wide and liberal sense and includes the case of a limited company[21] or of a co-operative society[22] and also the case of

---

[17] s. 1 (5).
[18] s. 1 (3).
[19] *McCallum* v *Glasgow Corporation* (1955), 71 Sh. Ct. Rep. 178.
[20] See *MacDonald* v *Taylor's Trs.* (1954), 70 Sh. Ct. Rep. 275, which held there was no *bona fide* offer to sell by the landlord where buyers under missives entitling them to oppose the tenant's application in name of the sellers offered to sell on behalf of the sellers and the buyers. (See also *Hunter* v *Bruce*, 1949 S.L.T. (Sh. Ct.) 57.)
[20a] See *Hurry* v *McLaughlan* (1953), 69 Sh. Ct. Rep. 305, where it was held that the interests of third parties were irrelevant but that the alternative accommodation was not reasonable as it involved the loss of passing trade.
[21] *Loudon* v *St. Paul's Parish Church*, 1949 S.L.T. (Sh. Ct.) 54.
[22] *MacLeod* v *MacTavish*, 1952 S.L.T. (Sh. Ct.) 20; *White* v *Paisley Co-operative Society*, 1956 S.L.T. (Sh. Ct.) 95. Cp. *St. George Co-operative Society* v *Burnett's Trs.* (1953), 69 Sh. Ct. Rep. 325.

trustees.[23] Hardship on a private individual, it has been said, is on a different plane from any hardship on an impersonal concern such as a public corporation and it may be often extremely difficult to find any basis for comparison.[23a] In considering the issue the age and financial situation of the tenant are, *inter alia*, factors of importance.[24] But the Act is designed to give temporary relief to tenants of shops who would suffer hardship if required to remove at once, but, given a reasonable extension of tenure, would have a reasonable expectation of making arrangements, whether financial or by obtaining other business, for alleviating the hardship. It was not designed to cover a case where the tenant says he cannot afford to pay the reasonable economic rent demanded and there is no prospect that he will ever be able to do so.[25] Some examples of greater hardship on a landlord[26] and on a tenant[27] are noted below.

Further Applications for Renewal. Where a tenancy has been renewed by the Sheriff, then before the period of the renewal ends the tenant may apply to the Sheriff for a further period of renewal.[28] If the tenancy is renewed, the provisions of the Act apply to a tenancy so further renewed as to one renewed for the first time.[28] Each application must stand or fall without any necessary reference to matters previously raised between the parties, and, thus, an argument by a tenant making his third application that the landlords could not succeed unless they could point to the emergence of some new consideration which would throw fresh light on their need for possession of the property was rejected, it being observed that refusal of possession to a landlord for several years might be regarded both on the question of reasonableness and on that of relevant hardship.[29]

In order, however, that an application for further renewal may be made, a fresh notice to remove must have been served by the landlord. Where no further notice had been served by the landlord, it was held

---

[23] *MacLeod, supra; McDowall* v *Thomson* (1950), 66 Sh. Ct. Rep. 101.
[23a] *Thom* v *British Transport Commission* (1952), 68 Sh. Ct. Rep. 290.
[24] *McDowall, supra.*
[25] *Stenhouse* v *East Kilbride Development Corporation*, 1962 S.L.T. (Sh. Ct.) 35 at 37.
[26] *St. George Co-operative Society, supra*—desire of a trustee to sell the whole property. Cp. *Craig* v *Saunders & Connor*, 1962 S.L.T. (Sh. Ct.) 85; *Anderson* v *National Bank of Scotland* (1957), 73 Sh. Ct. Rep. 10—the tenant had known for years of the landlord's proposals for rebuilding and made no effort to buy or lease other available shops in the neighbourhood. Continued exclusion may possibly in time become a hardship; *White, supra.*
[27] *Skelton* v *Paterson* (1954), 70 Sh. Ct. Rep. 287, where the tenant had invested his savings in a shop and the landlord wished to expand his existing business; *Thom, supra*, where the tenant depended for his livelihood on the business and the landlord could otherwise overcome a garaging problem.
[28] s. 1 (4).
[29] *Wallace* v *Bute Gift Co.*, 1954 S.L.T. (Sh. Ct.) 55.

that as the original notice had lapsed when the tenancy was renewed and no further notice had been served, the application was incompetent.[30] In any event, an application for renewal must be made not later than the expiry of twenty-one days after service of the notice of removal.[31] Provided, however, a fresh notice is served, a new application can be made after expiry of the period of renewal.[32]

Where a tenant does not apply for further renewal, or has applied but his application has been refused, a new notice to remove must be served in order to secure his removal.[33]

Proceedings. The application for renewal is conducted and disposed of in a summary manner as proceedings under the Small Debt (Scotland) Acts 1837-89.[34] The decision of the Sheriff is final and not subject to appeal or review.[34] Procedure is thus judicial and not administrative, and the Sheriff can award expenses, and any award ought to approximate to what would be given in the Small Debt Court.[35]

---

[30] *Scottish Gas Board* v *Kerr's Trs.,* 1956 S.L.T. (Sh. Ct.) 69. The Sheriff followed *Pow* v *Fraser and Carmichael,* 1953 S.L.T. (Sh. Ct.) 20 where the basis of the decision was put on tacit relocation, which the Sheriff thought was not necessary, and did not follow a contrary decision in *Hill* v *McCaskill's Trs.,* 1951 S.L.T. (Sh. Ct.) 41. See too *White* v *Paton* (1953), 69 Sh. Ct. Rep. 176.
[31] s. 1 (1), *supra.*
[32] *Pow, supra.*
[33] *Scottish Gas Board, supra.*
[34] s. 1 (7).
[35] *Lennon* v *Craig,* 1949 S.L.T. (Sh. Ct.) 56; *MacLeod* v *MacTavish, supra.*

CHAPTER XXII

THE ALLOTMENTS ACTS

Introduction. Sir John Rankine in 1916[1] described the first Act on the subject, of 1892, as not having been a success and said that the subject would, therefore, be dealt with briefly in his book on *The Law of Leases.*[2] There has been an entire absence of reported decisions upon the 1892 and the later Acts. Whether or not the Acts have been successful, the subject is not one of major importance and, therefore, does not require a detailed survey.

The first Act is the Allotments (Scotland) Act, 1892, which was designed to make provision for allotments for the labouring population or classes in Scotland, imposed powers and duties in that connection upon local authorities, *viz.,* town councils and county councils. The Act was amended materially by several later statutes. The first of these was the Local Government (Scotland) Act 1894, Part IV, which in creating Parish Councils provided that these Councils were to have the same power of making representations as to allotments that had been given by the 1892 Act to parliamentary electors[3] and that a Parish Council should exercise and perform in a parish the powers and duties of allotment managers under the 1892 Act as to allotments provided by the parish, without any appointment.[4] It made detailed provisions as to the leasing by parish councils of land for allotments or common pasture.[5]

Next came the Land Settlement (Scotland) Act 1919, Part III, which removed the restriction of the provision of allotments to the labouring population and so extended the scope of the legislation to cover all classes of the community,[6] It not only transferred to parish councils all the powers and duties of county councils as to allotments, providing too that the provisions of the 1894 Act should apply as to the exercise and performance of powers and duties transferred to or imposed on parish councils by the 1919 Act as if imposed by the 1894 Act,[7] but also made *inter alia* provision for compulsory purchase of land for allotments, the appointment in burghs of consultative committees, and the temporary use of land by a local authority which had been acquired for other purposes, and the sale of fruit trees &c. or the hire of imple-

---

[1] *Leases,* 3rd ed., p. 39. There are no text-books on the subject.
[2] *Op. cit.,* pp. 39-40.
[3] s. 24 (4), later repealed by 1919 Act, Schedule Fourth.
[4] *Ibid.,* later repealed by 1922 Act, Schedule First.
[5] s. 26, later repealed by 1922 Act, Schedule First.
[6] s. 32, Schedule Fourth.
[7] s. 18 (1).

ments to cultivators if there were inadequate facilities for the purchase or hire of such respectively from a co-operative society. It enabled the Board of Agriculture for Scotland to apply sums out of the Agriculture (Scotland) Fund with the Secretary of State's approval to a certain amount (not exceeding £4,000) in a year for encouraging and developing the provision of allotments throughout Scotland as they might think fit.[8]

The Allotments (Scotland) Act 1922 made many important changes in the law, introducing a category of allotments called allotment gardens and making important provisions as to the termination of tenancies of allotment gardens, the payment of compensation for crops and manure to tenants of these gardens on termination of their tenancies, and restrictions on the tenancy of such gardens, and provisions as to land leased for allotments, as to common pasture, the establishment of burgh allotments committees for allotment gardens and the abolition of consultative committees, the use by local authorities of unoccupied ground, the amendment of the provisions regarding compulsory purchase, the provision of arbitration where land is proposed to be resumed by a local authority or association's landlord and restrictions on expenditure and on rents &c.

The Allotments (Scotland) Act 1926, of two sections, dealt with the expenses of a local authority, modifying a restriction thereon in the 1922 Act that the expenses of proceedings must come out of receipts.[9] By the Local Government (Scotland) Act 1929[10] the powers of parish councils, which bodies were abolished by that Act, were transferred to district councils.

A temporary special set of provisions for eight years from 31st July 1931 to 31st July 1939 was made by the Agricultural Land (Utilisation) Act 1931, Part II, for the providing of allotments by the Department of Agriculture for Scotland for persons who were unemployed wholly or in part-time employment, for the defraying of the losses of local authorities if they provided allotments for such persons, the making of grants by the Department to local authorities to assist them in providing seeds, fertilisers and equipment for these tenants. It changed in the application of the 1931 Act the purposes for which under the 1919 Act[11] sums might be applied out of the Agriculture (Scotland) Fund to the provision of allotments and allotment gardens and the purchase or leasing or equipment of land therefor; and the making of grants to local authorities or societies or associations for providing allotments or allotment gardens in aid of expenditure by these authorities, societies or associations in connection with the provision of allotments or allotment gardens.[12] The Local Government (Scotland) Act

[8] s. 18 (3).
[9] This Act was repealed by the Local Government (Scotland) Act 1947, s. 381, Schedule Fourteenth.
[10] s. 1 (2).
[11] s. 18 (3), supra.
[12] s. 24 (j).

1947 also made a number of amendments, chiefly as to expenditure and the acquiring of land.

The Allotments (Scotland) Act 1950 both amended the existing law and made entirely new provisions. It extends the minimum period of a notice to remove from allotments, removes restrictions on a tenant's rights to compensation on termination for crops and manure and restricts the obligations of some authorities to provide allotments to allotment gardens. It gives a tenant of an allotment garden a right to compensation for disturbance and the landlord of such a tenant a right to compensation for deterioration; and it authorises a local authority to provide information and prizes. Finally, the Local Government and Miscellaneous Financial Provisions (Scotland) Act 1958 abolished the obligation on local authorities to establish allotments committees.

The steps by which the Board of Agriculture for Scotland was succeeded by the Department of Agriculture for Scotland and the Department in turn by the Secretary of State for Scotland will be found in the chapter on the Crofters and Small Landholders Acts.

SUBJECTS

Allotment. An allotment was originally defined in the 1892 Act as including a field garden;[13] this definition was later repealed in the 1922 Act.[14] The only other indication given in that Act of 1892 was as to size.[15] One person cannot hold any allotment or allotments exceeding one acre;[15] but where land is acquired on lease by a local authority for use as allotments, it may let to one person an allotment or allotments (not being an allotment garden or allotment gardens[16]) exceeding one acre.[17] Where, however, the land is acquired on lease compulsorily, the allotment or allotments must either not exceed in the whole four acres of pasture or one acre of arable and three acres of pasture or £4 in annual value.[17] Unless in the case of certain provisions of the 1892 Act,[18] " allotment " includes, provided the context does not otherwise require, an " allotment garden."[19]

Allotment Garden. This category of allotment was introduced by the 1922 Act and is an area not exceeding forty poles which is wholly or mainly cultivated by the occupier for the production of vegetable crops for consumption by himself or his family and is not let to the occupier during his continuance in office, appointment, or employment held under the landlord or let along with any dwellinghouse.[20] Where land is used

---

[13] s. 16.
[14] Schedule First.
[15] s. 7 (3).
[16] As to these, see *infra*.
[17] 1922 Act, s. 6 (1).
[18] s. 7 (3) as to size, s. 7 (6) as to removal of fruit trees and s. 8 (2) *proviso* as to payment of compensation under that Act.
[19] 1922 Act, s. 19 (2).
[20] 1922 Act, s. 19 (1). The term has the same meaning for the purposes of the 1950 Act, 1950 Act, s. 13.

by a tenant as an allotment garden, then for the purposes of the 1922 and 1950 Acts it is deemed to have been let to him to be used as such unless the contrary is proved,[21] and where the land has been sublet to him by a local authority or association holding the land under a lease the land is deemed let to the authority or association for subletting for that purpose unless the contrary is proved.[21] A local authority may let to one person two or more allotment gardens if their aggregate extent is not in excess of fifty poles but otherwise one person cannot hold more than one garden.[22]

Common Pasture. A local authority, if satisfied that, having regard to the wants and circumstances of the population of the burgh or district as the case may be, it is desirable to acquire land for affording common pasture, may acquire land which is suitable for that purpose by purchase or lease, whether within or without their area, and the provisions of the Allotments Acts apply so far as applicable as if the word " allotments " in the Acts included common pasture.[23] If the land, however, has been compulsorily leased by the local authority it must not at one time exceed twenty acres.[24] Rent is held to include a charge for turning out an animal.[25]

PROVISION OF ALLOTMENTS AND OF LAND THEREFOR

Authorities. Two sets of authorities may obtain, or if they have it already may use, land and provide allotments on it. These are (a) local authorities. A local authority is in a burgh a town council and elsewhere a district council.[26] The 1950 Act[27] defines a local authority as meaning for the purpose of that Act a town council or a district council acting under the 1892-1926 Acts. Upon these two authorities the powers and duties as to allotments is primarily and principally laid. The other body is (b) an association, which is defined as an association formed for the purposes of creating or promoting the creation of allotments.[28] Associations were first introduced in the 1922 Act and were a consequence of the development and use of allotments in the first Great War of 1914-18. There are no statutory obligations laid upon these associations, which act on a purely non-obligatory basis.

An obligation is placed upon a local authority to provide allotments in certain circumstances. If six registered parliamentary electors or ratepayers in a burgh or district make written representation to the relevant

21 1922 Act, s. 19 (3); 1950 Act, s. 7.
22 *Ibid.,* s. 5.
23 *Ibid.,* s. 7.
24 *Ibid.,* s. 7, *proviso* (b).
25 *Ibid.,* s. 7.
26 1892 Act, s. 15, as amended by the 1919 Act, Schedule Third, and the Local Government (Scotland) Act 1929, s. 1 (2).
27 s. 13.
28 1922 Act, s. 19 (1); 1950 Act, s. 13.

local authority that it is the duty of that authority to take proceedings under the Acts to provide allotments, the local authority must take that representation into consideration, and, if they are of opinion, after enquiry or otherwise, that there is a demand for allotments, they must acquire by purchase or lease any suitable land which may be available within or without their area adequate to provide a sufficient number of allotments and let these allotments to applicants for them.[29] But, except in the case of a town council of a burgh whose population is, according to the last published census for the time being, ten thousand or upwards, the obligation of a local authority is limited to the provision of allotment gardens and in that exceptional case to the provision of such gardens not exceeding twenty poles in extent.[30]

In addition to being satisfied as to the demand for allotments, the local authority must also be satisfied in every case before taking proceedings that in their opinion their expenses incurred under the provisions of the Acts other than those expenses referred to in the next paragraph may reasonably be expected, after the proceedings are taken, to be defrayed out of the receipts of the authority under these provisions.[31] The expenditure so incurred or payable by a town council or a district council so far as falling to be defrayed out of the rate or any grant under the Local Government (Scotland) Act 1929 Part III must be such as in the council's opinion may reasonably be expected not to exceed the produce of a penny per pound calculated on the gross annual valuation of the burgh or the district according to the valuation roll for the year corresponding as nearly as may be to the financial year immediately preceding that to which the expenditure relates.[32] The expenses and receipts are calculated in the case of a town council and in the case of a district council as the Secretary of State for Scotland[33] directs.[34]

Expenses are not to include[35]:—

(a) expenses in relation to the acquisition of land other than the price,

---

[29] 1892 Act, s. 2 (1), as amended by 1922 Act, Schedule First. See Electoral Registers Act 1953, Schedule that " parliamentary electors " does not include during the period beginning 16th February and ending 1st October in any year a person so registered by s. 2 of the Electoral Registers Act 1949 (that is, one coming of age during the currency of the register on 15th June) unless where the part of the register in which his name appears is a part continued in force by s. 1 (6) of the 1949 Act.

[30] 1950 Act, s. 9. Previously the restriction was that the obligation of a town council of a burgh, whose population was ten thousand or upwards, was limited to providing allotment gardens not exceeding twenty poles in extent: 1922 Act, s. 12, repealed by 1950 Act.

[31] 1922 Act, s. 16 (1).

[32] Local Government (Scotland) Act 1947, ss. 191 (4), 192, repealing in Schedule Fourteenth the Allotments (Scotland) Act 1926.

[33] Originally the Scottish Board of Health, from 1st January 1929 the Department of Health for Scotland and from 4th September 1939 the Secretary of State. See Reorganisation of Offices (Scotland) Acts 1928, 1939, and S.R. & O. 1928/959 and 1939/865.

[34] 1922 Act, s. 16 (2).

[35] Ibid., s. 16 (2), proviso.

feu-duty, ground annual or rent, or other compensation payable in respect of the land;

(b) expenses incurred in making roads to be used by the public;

(c) sinking fund charges in respect of loans raised in connection with the purchase of land.

All expenses incurred by a town council under the 1892 Act are defrayed out of the burgh rate or out of moneys borrowed on the security of that rate subject to the provisions of the Public Health (Scotland) Acts.[36] A local authority can borrow money for the purposes of the Allotments Acts.[37]

Allotments Committees. Prior to 16th May 1959 a council of a burgh with a population of ten thousand or upwards had, unless exempted by the Secretary of State, to establish an Allotments Committee, to which was referred all the matters relating to the exercise and performance by the council of their powers and duties under the Acts as to the provision of allotment gardens, except the power of raising a rate or borrowing money.[38] The council before exercising any such powers had, unless the particular matter was in their opinion urgent, to receive and consider the committee's report as to the particular matter. The council could delegate to the committee with or without restrictions, any of their powers except the two above referred to.[38] A committee comprised persons who were occupiers of allotment gardens other than members of the council, representative of the interests of occupiers of allotment gardens in the burgh, but not being more than a third or less than two or one-fifth of the total number of the members of the Committee whichever was the larger number.[39] The committee's accounts under the delegated powers were treated as accounts of the council and were made up and audited accordingly.[40] This obligation to establish such a committee was abolished as from 16th May 1959.[41] Any committee appointed by a local authority to carry out its functions under the 1922 Act may to an extent not exceeding one-third of the membership consist of persons who are not members of the local authority having responsibilities and experience in regard to the functions for the purposes for which they are appointed.[42]

Provision of Land. A local authority can obtain or acquire land for the purposes of the Acts by various methods:

[36] 1919 Act, s. 18 (2), as amended by Local Government (Scotland) Act 1947, ss. 224, 261.
[37] Local Government (Scotland) Act 1947, s. 258 repealing 1922 Act, s. 18.
[38] 1922 Act, s. 9 (1).
[39] *Ibid.,* s. 9 (2).
[40] *Ibid.,* s. 9 (3).
[41] Local Government and Miscellaneous Financial Provisions (Scotland) Act 1958, s. 13, Schedule Fifth, para. 1.
[42] Local Government (Scotland) Act 1947, s. 115 (3), as added by 1958 Act, *supra,* Schedule Fifth, para. 18.

(a) by purchase. This may be by agreement or by compulsory acquisition. If the purchase is by agreement, the provisions of the Local Government (Scotland) Act 1947 apply[43] and the purchase may be with consent of the Secretary of State though the land is not immediately required for the purpose.[43] If the local authority cannot purchase by agreement suitable land for allotments at a reasonable price, they may apply to the Secretary of State for an order providing for the compulsory acquisition of that land by purchase.[44] The Secretary of State must not, however, make an order for purchase in respect of (a) any park, garden, playing ground or other land required for the amenity or convenience of a dwellinghouse, or (b) any land which, being the property of a railway or canal company, is required for the purposes of that undertaking.[45] The Secretary of State must also have regard to the extent of land in the neighbourhood held by any owner and to the convenience of other property belonging to the same owner.[45] He must too avoid taking an undue or inconvenient quantity of land from any one owner.[45]

(b) by lease.[46] Where land is acquired by them on lease, the local authority must not, without the written consent of the landlord,[47] break up or permit to be broken up, any permanent pasture on the land so leased, unless they are entitled to do so in terms of the lease; but if land is leased after 4th August 1922, the local authority may be authorised by the Secretary of State without the landlord's written consent to break up or permit to be broken up such permanent pasture if the Secretary of State is satisfied that no other land equally suitable for allotments is reasonably available.[48]

If land which the local authority has acquired on lease is at any time during the authority's tenancy shown to the satisfaction of the Secretary of State for Scotland to be required by the landlord for the purpose of working and winning the mines, minerals or surface minerals under it or for feuing for building, or for any road or work to be used in connection with such working, winning or

---

[43] Local Government (Scotland) Act 1947, ss. 156-8. These sections repeal 1892 Act, s. 3 (1). 1947 Act, s. 381, Schedule Fourteenth.

[44] 1919 Act, s. 20, as substituted by 1922 Act, s. 8 (3). The 1919 Act had by Schedule IV repealed the previous provisions in the 1892 Act, ss. 3 (2)-(4) amd. 4. The procedure is regulated by the 1919 Act, Schedule First, as amended by the 1922 Act, Schedule Second. See too Local Government (Scotland) Act 1947, ss. 159, 161.

[45] 1892 Act, s. 3 (5), as amended by 1919 Act, Schedule Third. Para. (b) in the text, of course, falls to be read in the light of the modern Transport Acts 1947, etc.

[46] Local Government (Scotland) Act 1947, s. 156. Land may be acquired by agreement with consent of the Secretary of State though it is not immediately required for the purpose: s. 157.

[47] For the purpose of the 1922 Act, s. 6 (1), infra, a landlord is the person for the time being entitled to receive the rent of the land acquired on lease by the local authority.

[48] 1922 Act, s. 6 (1) (c).

feuing, the landlord can resume possession on giving the authority twelve months' notice in writing and on resumption of the land paying to the authority and the existing allotment holders such compensation for loss as is agreed between landlord and tenant or failing agreement determined under the Agricultural Holdings Acts.[49] If the letting has been for allotment gardens then the foregoing sentence has effect subject to the provisions as to termination of tenancies of allotment gardens, compensation on removing and the determination of questions arising on resumption.[49]

Where land is let to a local authority to be let by the authority for use as allotment gardens the provisions as to termination by notice to remove or by resumption of possession are the same[50] in respect of the tenancy of the authority as in the case of the tenancies of subtenants, that is of allotment holders.[51] And where under a lease entered into after 4th August 1922 land is let to a local authority or an association for the purpose of being sublet for use as allotment gardens, the compensation provisions regarding crops and manure of the 1922 Act as amended[52] apply to the tenancy of the local authority or association even though the crops have been grown and the manure applied by the subtenants.[53] And where land is let before or after 26th November 1950, to a local authority or association for subletting to a tenant for use as an allotment garden and the tenancy is terminated as to the whole or part of the land by resumption of possession for certain purposes[54] or where the lessor's right of tenancy is terminated, the compensation provisions for disturbance [55] apply.[56]

If land is acquired compulsorily under a compulsory leasing order for use as allotments the order must not authorise the compulsory taking on lease of any mines or minerals or confer the right to make, sell, or carry away any stone, gravel, sand or clay.[57] The lease must be for a period of not less than ten and not more than thirty-five years.[58] On the termination of the tenancy any compensation due by the landlord for improvements or by the authority for depreciation is, failing agreement, determined by arbitration under the Agricultural Holdings Acts.[59]

---

[49] Ibid., s. 6 (1) (d).
[50] See infra, pp. 646, 648.
[51] 1922 Act, s. 1 (2).
[52] See infra, p. 650.
[53] 1922 Act, s. 2 (4).
[54] Ibid., s. 1 (1) (b) and (c).
[55] 1950 Act, s. 3.
[56] Ibid., s. 3 (1).
[57] 1922 Act, s. 6 (2) (c).
[58] Ibid., s. 6 (2) (a). The procedure is as in the 1919 Act, Schedule First, as amended by the 1922 Act, Schedule Second.
[59] Ibid., s. 6 (2) (b).

Land already owned or occupied as a small holding cannot be acquired on lease by an authority.[60]

(c) Where land belonging to a local authority is not immediately required for the purpose for which it was acquired and is in the local authority's opinion suitable for temporary use in the form of allotments, the authority may with the consent of the Secretary of State make it available for that purpose subject to any necessary conditions and restrictions as to tenure or otherwise.[61]

(d) The Secretary of State may let land which he or his predecessors (the Board or the Department) has acquired for small holdings to a local authority for use by subletting for allotments.[62]

(e) A local authority may, after giving fourteen days' written notice to the owner in the same manner as notices given to an owner under the compulsory leasing provisions,[63] enter for the purpose of providing allotment gardens on any unoccupied land—land in respect of which no person is entered as tenant or occupier in the valuation roll in force at the date of the notice and which has not been let and occupied after the roll was made up and before the date of the notice[64]—may adapt any such land for use for the purposes of providing allotment gardens, let any such land for use by the tenant as an allotment garden or let it to any association for the purpose of subletting for that use[65] but any tenancy created by an authority or an association will terminate when the local authority's occupation is terminated.[65] The right of occupation may be terminated (a) by the local authority by not less than six months' written notice by the local authority to the owner expiring on or before 1st May or on or after 1st November or (b) by the owner by not less than one month's notice to the local authority where the land is required for any purpose other than use for agriculture.[66] On the termination of its right of occupation, the local authority must remove any erection or work of adaptation, making good any injury to the land caused by the removal.[67] Any person " interested " in any such land so entered and who thereby suffers loss is entitled, if he claims not later than a year after the termination of the occupation, to payment of the amount of his loss as that is determined by agreement or, failing agreement, by an arbiter appointed, failing agreement, by the Secretary of State.[68]

[60] *Ibid.*, s. 6 (3).
[61] 1919 Act., s. 21. See too Local Government (Scotland) Act 1947, s. 163.
[62] 1922 Act, s. 14.
[63] *Ibid.*, s. 10 (2).
[64] *Ibid.*, s. 10 (6).
[65] *Ibid.*, s. 10 (1).
[66] 1922 Act, s. 10 (3).
[67] *Ibid.*, s. 10 (1).
[68] *Ibid.*, s. 10 (5).

41

The amount of the loss may be paid in periodical payments and a periodical payment of compensation in the nature of rent must not exceed the rental value of the land, that is,[69] the annual value which a tenant might reasonably be expected to pay for the land if the land had remained in the same condition as at the date of entry.[70]

The provisions as to entry on unoccupied land do not apply to land which has been acquired by any corporation or company for a railway, dock, canal, water or other public undertaking or to land which is or forms part of any area dedicated or appropriated as a public park, garden, or pleasure ground, or for use for the purposes of public recreation.[71]

(f) By feu.[72]

(g) By excambion.[73]

An association can acquire land, e.g. by lease, for the purpose of being sublet for use as allotment gardens.[74] The Secretary of State may let land to an association for subletting for use as allotments.[75] Where land is let to an association for subletting for use as allotment gardens the provisions regarding the termination of such a tenancy or the resumption of possession are the same[76] as in the case of tenancies of the sub-tenants.[77]

The Secretary of State may let land which he or his predecessors have acquired for the purpose of small holdings for use by the tenant as an allotment.[78]

Lessor. This term is defined as any person for the time being entitled to receive the rent or resume possession of the land.[79]

Letting by Local Authority. A local authority can let land belonging to them for a term up to seven years without consent but if the term is one of over seven years only by public roup or with the consent of the Secretary of State.[80]

TERMS OF LETTING

General. The local authority may from time to time make such regulations as are necessary and proper for regulating the terms on which

---

[69] *Ibid.,* s. 10 (6).
[70] *Ibid.,* s. 10 (5), *proviso.*
[71] *Ibid.,* s. 10 (7).
[72] Local Government (Scotland) Act 1947, s. 156.
[73] *Ibid.,* ss. 156, 167.
[74] See 1922 Act, ss. 1 (2), 2 (4), (11).
[75] *Ibid.,* s. 14.
[76] See *infra,* pp. 646, 648.
[77] 1922 Act, s. 1 (2).
[78] *Ibid.,* s. 14.
[79] *Ibid.,* s. 19 (1); 1950 Act, s. 13.
[80] Local Government (Scotland) Act 1947, s. 165.

allotments, which include allotment gardens,[81] are to be let and for preventing undue preference in letting and for carrying out the provisions of the Acts.[82] They may revoke or vary the regulations.[82] The regulations may define the persons eligible to be tenants and the notices to be given for letting and the size of allotments, including allotment gardens, the conditions under which they are to be cultivated and the rent to be paid,[82] They must provide for reasonable notice to be given to a tenant of the determination of his tenancy of an allotment.[82] They must require that access to allotments and allotment gardens be only by roads or paths provided by them.[83] Such regulations are of no force unless and until they are confirmed by the Secretary of State for Scotland after such publication and inquiry and with such modifications as he may determine.[82] They bind everyone, and the local authority are to make them known in such manner as they think fit to all those interested.[84]

In the case of common pasture these regulations may extend to the regulation of the turning out of animals on the common pasture, to the defining of the persons, that is persons resident within the burgh or district, entitled to turn them out, the number of animals to be turned out, and the conditions under which animals may be turned out, and to the fixing of the charges to be made for each animal, and otherwise to the regulation of the common pasture.[85]

Allotment Managers. The local authority may appoint allotment managers.[86] These may consist either partly of members of the authority and partly of other persons or wholly of other persons: the other persons must reside in the locality and contribute to the rate or assessment out of which expenses of the Acts are paid.[86] The local authority can remove allotment managers.[86] The proceedings and powers of managers are those prescribed by the local authority subject always to the provisions of the Acts.[87] They may be empowered by the local authority to do anything in management which the authority are authorised to do and may incur expenses to the amount prescribed by the authority.[87]

Agreement for Letting or Lease. If the rent under the agreement or lease for letting an allotment garden, whether provided by the local authority or otherwise, is under ten shillings per annum and no other consideration is paid the agreement or lease does not require a stamp.[88]

[81] 1922 Act, s. 19 (2).
[82] 1892 Act, s. 6 (1).
[83] 1922 Act, s. 15.
[84] 1892 Act, s. 6 (2). Any inhabitant of a burgh or district can, on demand, get a free copy.
[85] 1922 Act, s. 7, *proviso* (a).
[86] 1892 Act, s. 6 (3). See as to use of a schoolroom free of charge for their election, etc., s. 15.
[87] *Ibid.*, s. 6 (4).
[88] 1919 Act, s. 22 (3).

Rent. Land let by a local authority for use as an allotment or allotment garden is to be let at the fair rent for such use.[89] If, however, the local authority are satisfied that there are special circumstances affecting a person which render it proper for them to let land to him at a rent less than the fair rent they may let land to him for use as an allotment or allotment garden at such a reduced rent.[90] Not more than a quarter's rent for land let by a local authority for use as an allotment or allotment garden can be required to be paid in advance,[91] unless in a case where the yearly rent is twenty shillings or less.[91] If an allotment or allotment garden cannot be let in accordance with the Acts and regulations, it can be let to any person whatever at the best annual rent which can be got for the same and on such terms as may enable the local authority to resume possession within not more than twelve months if it should at any time be required to be let.[92]

RIGHTS AND DUTIES OF LANDLORD AND TENANT DURING CURRENCY OF LEASE

Rights and Duties of Landlord. Two important duties are laid on local authorities. First, it is the duty of a local authority providing allotments and allotment gardens to make provision for access to the allotments and allotment gardens by suitable roads or paths, where such means of access are not already available and by regulations under the Acts to require that access to the allotments and allotment gardens be had only by such roads or paths.[93] Second, it is the duty of an authority to keep a Register of particulars of the tenancy, acreage and rent of allotments and allotment gardens let and of those unlet, and to make up within one month after 15th May in each year accounts of receipts and expenditure for the year ending on that day and of liabilities at that day.[94] Both the Register and the accounts must be open to inspection by the ratepayers, who may take copies.[94]

A local authority may improve land acquired by it and adapt it for letting in allotments or allotment gardens by, *inter alia,* draining and fencing it, and dividing it, acquiring approaches, making roads and otherwise as they think fit, and they may from time to time do whatever is necessary to maintain drains, fencing, approaches and roads or otherwise for maintaining allotments in proper condition.[95] The authority may purchase and sell to the holder or cultivator of an allotment garden, whether or not the garden has been provided by the authority, fruit trees, seeds, plants, fertilisers or implements required, or may hire out

[89] 1950 Act, s. 10 (1).
[90] *Ibid.,* s. 10 (1), *proviso.*
[91] *Ibid.,* s. 10 (2).
[92] 1892 Act, s. 7 (4).
[93] 1922 Acts, ss. 15, 19 (2).
[94] 1892 Act, s. 14.
[95] *Ibid.,* s. 5, 1922 Act, s. 19 (2).

implements at a price or charge sufficient to cover the cost of purchase, if in the authority's opinion facilities for purchase or hire from a co-operative society are inadequate,[96]

A local authority may borrow money and there are provisions in that connection regarding the maximum date of repayment.[97]

In order to promote the proper cultivation of allotments and allotment gardens in their area, a local authority may incur or contribute towards expenses of (a) the dissemination—whether by lectures, cinematograph shows, exhibitions or otherwise—of information on questions regarding allotments and (b) the award of prizes in connection with the cultivation and maintenance of allotments.[98]

If a local authority are levying the assessment they can resolve, and if another authority is levying the assessment they can require, that they be entered as occupiers in the valuation roll.[99] An association can also require that they be entered as occupiers but the authority imposing the assessment must agree.[1]

A local authority has the powers of an ordinary landlord in regard to the recovery of rent and possession.[2]

Rights and Duties of Tenant. An important restriction upon the tenant is that in the case both of allotments[3] and of allotment gardens[4] provided by a local authority he cannot sublet the allotment or allotment garden. He is entitled to erect on his allotment or allotment garden[5] a tool-house, shed, greenhouse, fowl-house or pigsty but no other building.[6] The local authority can pull down any other building and sell or dispose of the materials and the proceeds of the sale or disposal are applicable as in the case of rent.[7] Where the tenant is tenant of an allotment on land acquired by a local authority on lease—but not in the case of the tenancy of an allotment garden—he may, if permitted by the local authority, erect a stable, byre or barn.[8] The tenant must not reside more than one mile out of the burgh or district, otherwise the local authority may serve notice ending his tenancy.[8a]

[96] 1919 Act, s. 22 (1).
[97] Local Government (Scotland) Act 1947, ss. 258 etc., Schedule Sixth. These repeal 1922 Act, s. 18 : 1947 Act, Schedule Fourteenth.
[98] 1950 Act, s. 11.
[99] 1922 Act, s. 17 (1).
[1] *Ibid.,* s. 17 (2).
[2] 1892 Act, s. 8 (1).
[3] *Ibid.,* s. 7 (3).
[4] 1922 Act, s. 5.
[5] *Ibid.,* s. 19 (2).
[6] 1892 Act, s. 7 (5).
[7] *Ibid.,* s. 7 (5).
[8] 1922 Act, s. 6 (1) (b).
[8a] 1892 Act, s. 8 (2).

TERMINATION OF TENANCY

Methods of Termination of Tenancy of Allotment. If an allotment falls within the definition of an agricultural holding,[9] the law in regard to such holdings[10] applies.[11] Regulations made by a local authority as to allotments must provide for reasonable notice of termination being given to the tenant.[12] If a tenant of an allotment fails to pay rent or to obey the local authority's regulations the tenancy may be terminated, for, if the rent is in arrear for not less than forty days or if it appears to the local authority that the tenant of an allotment not less than three months after the commencement of the tenancy has not duly observed the regulations affecting the allotment or is resident more than a mile out of the burgh or the district of the allotment, the authority may serve on the tenant, or, if he is so residing out of the burgh or the district, leave at his last known place of abode in the burgh or the district or fix in some conspicuous manner on the allotment written notice determining the tenancy at the expiry of one month after the notice has been so served or affixed and the tenancy then determines accordingly.[13] If land is acquired on lease by a local authority and it is shown to the satisfaction of the Secretary of State to be required by the landlord for the purpose of working and winning the mines, minerals, or surface minerals thereunder, or for feuing for building, or for any road or work to be used in connection with such working or winning or feuing, the landlord can resume possession on giving the local authority twelve months' previous written notice of his intention to do so.[14]

Methods of Termination of Tenancy of Allotment Gardens. Where land is let by an authority or an association or any other person for use as an allotment garden the tenancy of that land or any part of it cannot be terminated by the landlord by notice to remove unless the notice is in writing and is one of twelve months or longer expiring on or before 1st May or on or after 1st November in any year.[15] The tenancy cannot be terminated by the landlord by resumption of possession unless (1) by resumption of possession after three months' or longer written notice to the tenant under a power contained in or affecting the lease, " on account of the land being required for building, mining, or any other industrial purpose, or for roads or sewers necessary in connection with any of those purposes ";[16] or (2) by resumption of possession under

---

[9] See *supra*, p. 295.
[10] See *supra*, Ch. XVIII.
[11] See 1892 Act, s. 8 (2).
[12] 1892 Act, s. 6 (1).
[13] *Ibid.*, s. 8 (2).
[14] 1922 Act, s. 6 (1) (d).
[15] *Ibid.*, s. 1 (1) (a), as amended by 1950 Act, s. 1 (1). The amendment in the 1950 Act did not apply to notices prior to 26th November 1950: s. 1 (2); nor to land let by a local authority under Defence Regulations 1939, Regulation 62A.
[16] 1922 Act, s. 1 (1) (b).

a power of resumption in the lease in the case of land let by a corporation or company who are owners or lessees of a railway, dock, canal, water or other public undertaking on account of the land being required by the corporation or company for any purpose (not being the use of the land for agriculture) for which it was acquired or held by the corporation or company or appropriated under any statutory provision, or in the case of land let by a local authority within the Housing (Scotland) Acts 1890-1921[17] (being land acquired by the authority under those Acts before the passing of the 1922 Act, that is before 4th August 1922) on account of the land being required by the authority for the purposes of those Acts;[18] or (3) by resumption of possession because of an irritancy of the lease by the tenant or his breach of the regulations made by a local authority under the Allotments Acts.[19]

Where land is let to a local authority or to an association for subletting for use as allotment gardens, or is occupied by a local authority under their powers of entry on unoccupied ground and the lessor or the person who but for that occupation would be entitled to possession, proposes in terms of the 1922 Act to resume possession for any particular purpose (other than resumption required by a corporation or company who are the owners or lessees of a railway, dock, canal, water, or other public undertaking[20]), written notice must be given of the purpose to the local authority or association;[21] and the authority or association may serve a counter-notice on the person requiring possession within ten days after receipt of the notice demanding that the question whether resumption of possession is required in good faith for the purpose specified be determined by arbitration under and in accordance with the Agricultural Holdings (Scotland) Act, 1949.[22] Till these ten days have expired or the question has been determined possession cannot be resumed.[23]

These provisions do not apply to land held by or on behalf of the Admiralty, War Department, Air Council[24] or Minister of Supply[25] and let for use as an allotment garden when possession is required for naval, military or air force purposes, or for purposes of the Ministry of Supply as the case may be.[26] Apart from these cases they apply to land vested in a government department for public purposes.[27] Also

---

[17] These Acts were almost entirely repealed by the Housing (Scotland) Act 1925 and replaced by that and later Housing Acts.
[18] 1922 Act, s. 1 (1) (c).
[19] *Ibid.*, s. 1 (1) (d). There was a saving clause in respect of notices, resumption or proceedings for resumption before 4th August 1922: s. 1 (3) (a).
[20] *Ibid.*, s. 11 (4).
[21] *Ibid.*, s. 11 (1).
[22] *Ibid.*, s. 11 (2).
[23] *Ibid.*, s. 11 (3).
[24] These three departments are now amalgamated into the Ministry of Defence: S.I. 1964/487-8.
[25] Now Minister of Aviation; S.I. 1959/1768 and see too S.I. 1959/1827, 1975.
[26] *Ibid.*, s. 1 (4), as amended by 1950 Act, s. 8 (1).
[27] *Ibid.*, s. 3, as applied to 1950 Act by 1950 Act, s. 7 (2).

they do not apply to any land of which possession was taken by or on behalf of any government department under the Acts relating to the Defence of the Realm or regulations made thereunder, and possession of which has been continued by any Act or to any land forming part of a royal park.[27]

Where under a lease entered into before 4th August 1922 the tenancy of an allotment garden is by express provision or implication made terminable by the landlord by notice to remove expiring on a date between 1st May and 1st November, the tenancy is terminable on 1st November, and any such notice given in accordance with the lease has the effect of a notice to remove at that date.[28]

A tenancy of a tenant to whom unoccupied land is let by an authority or association for use as an allotment garden is terminated if the authority's right of occupation is terminated.[29]

Where land is let to a local authority or to an association for subletting for use as allotment gardens the same rules as to termination apply as in the case of the tenancies of the subtenants.[30] And where land is let to a local authority or an association and is sublet by the authority or the association, notice from the lessor to the authority or the association has effect as notice at the same time to every subtenant affected thereby, but the authority or the association must serve forthwith by post intimation of the notice on each subtenant.[31]

A tenancy of an allotment garden may be terminated in the same way as that of an allotment if the rent is in arrear for not less than forty days or the tenant has not duly observed the regulations or is resident more than a mile from the burgh or district of the allotment garden.[32]

RIGHTS OF PARTIES ON TERMINATION OTHER THAN TO COMPENSATION

Allotments. The tenant of an allotment[33] is entitled to remove before the expiry of his tenancy, that is, on the termination of the tenancy, fruit and other trees and bushes planted by him or acquired by him for which he has no claim for compensation.[34] He can also remove before the expiry of the tenancy any tool-house, shed, greenhouse, fowl-house or pigsty which he has erected; if he does not do so, the local authority may after the expiry pull down the building or buildings and dispose of the materials and apply the proceeds as if the building had been prohibited to be erected.[35] And where a tenant has paid compensation to an outgoing tenant for any fruit trees or bushes he has the same

[28] *Ibid.*, s. 1 (3) (b).
[29] *Ibid.*, s. 10 (1) (c), (4).
[30] *Ibid.*, s. 1 (2).
[31] *Ibid.*, s. 2 (11) (b).
[32] 1892 Act, s. 8 (2); 1922 Act, s. 19 (2). See *supra*, p. 645.
[33] This does not include an allotment garden: 1922 Act s. 19 (2) (b).
[34] 1892 Act, s. 7 (16).
[35] *Ibid.*, s. 7 (5).

right of removal of these trees or bushes as he would have had under the Acts had he provided and planted them.[36] If he has been permitted by the local authority to erect on the allotment a stable, byre or barn in a case where the land has been leased by the authority he can remove it on termination of the tenancy.[37]

Allotment Gardens.   A tenant of land let to him by a local authority, an association or any other person for use by him as an allotment garden may, before the termination of his tenancy, remove any fruit trees or bushes provided and planted by the tenant and any erection, fencing or other improvement erected or made by the tenant, making good any injury caused by such removal.[38] Where unoccupied land is occupied by a local authority or an association under the Acts[39] and the tenancy of a tenant to whom such land is let by the authority or association is terminated by the termination of the authority's right of occupation, he has the same rights as regards the removal of fruit trees or bushes or improvements as if his tenancy had been terminated by a notice to remove given by the authority or association.[40]

COMPENSATION PROVISIONS

(a) Allotments

Compensation for Disturbance.   The tenant of an allotment[41] whose tenancy is determined because of his failure to pay the rent or failure to observe duly the regulations affecting the allotment or of his being resident more than a mile from the burgh or district of the allotment[42] is entitled to receive compensation, which, in default of agreement between incoming and outgoing tenant, the local authority must pay to the outgoing tenant on demand.[43] The compensation is assessed by an arbiter appointed by the local authority or, if the tenant so elects, by a reference under the Agricultural Holdings (Scotland) Act 1949.[43] The Court ordering his ejection may on ejectment stay proceedings till payment of the compensation due to the tenant has been made or secured to the court's satisfaction.[44] Further, where land is acquired on lease by a local authority and it is proved to the Secretary of State's satisfaction that the landlord requires the land for certain purposes[45] the landlord can resume possession but he must pay to the local authority's tenants compensation for loss arising to them directly from

[36] 1922 Act, s. 4.
[37] *Ibid.,* s. 6 (1) (b).
[38] *Ibid.,* s. 2 (8).
[39] 1922 Act, s. 10. See *supra,* p. 641.
[40] *Ibid.,* s. 10 (4).
[41] This does not include an allotment garden: 1922 Act, s. 19 (2) (b).
[42] 1892 Act, s. 8 (2). *Supra,* p. 645.
[43] *Ibid.,* s. 8 (2), *proviso.*
[44] *Ibid.,* s. 8 (3).
[45] 1922 Act, s. 6 (1) (d).

the resumption as the same is agreed between the landlord and the local authority or, failing that, under and in terms of the Agricultural Holdings (Scotland) Acts.[45]

(b) Allotment Gardens

Compensation for Crops and Manure. Notwithstanding any agreement to the contrary, where land is let by a local authority, an association or any other person for use by the tenant as an allotment garden, the tenant is entitled at the termination of the tenancy, on removing from the land, to recover from his landlord compensation for crops growing on the land in the ordinary course of the cultivation of the land as an allotment garden and for manure applied to the land.[46] Compensation is based on the value of the growing crops and manure to an incoming tenant.[46] This right exists whether the termination is by notice or removal given by the authority or association or person or because the tenancy of the authority, association or person has been terminated.[47] It is recoverable only if the tenancy is terminated by the tenant's landlord by notice to remove or by resumption of possession[48] by his landlord under a power to do so in the lease for certain purposes.[49] Compensation is payable whether the termination of the tenancy is of the whole or any part of the land which is the subject of a lease.[50]

The tenant's right to compensation was until the 1950 Act limited to the compensation above provided or any compensation provided by the lease and the provisions of the Agricultural Holdings Acts did not apply.[51] The 1950 Act, as will be seen, has extended his rights.

The amount of compensation, whether as above provided or under the lease, is in the absence of agreement between the parties determined by an arbiter who, failing agreement, is appointed by the sheriff having jurisdiction in the place where the allotment garden is situated on an application by letter from either or any of the parties.[52] The agreement or the determination can, if the sum due is not paid within fourteen days of the agreement or determination, be registered for execution in the Books of Council and Session or the Sheriff Court Books and is then enforceable as a recorded decree arbitral.[53] The expenses of the arbitration may be awarded by the arbiter against any or all of the parties

---

[46] *Ibid.*, s. 2 (1). The section applied to a tenancy current at 4th August 1922, but did not affect anything done before then: s. 2 (5). It did not apply to a tenancy terminated before 4th August 1922, or where notice to remove has been given or proceedings for resumption have commenced or resumption taken place before then: s. 2 (10).

[47] *Ibid.*, s. 2 (2).

[48] *Ibid.*, s. 2 (3), as substituted by 1950 Act, s. 2 (1). The amendment did not affect a tenancy terminated by a notice to remove given before the passing of the 1950 Act: *Ibid.*, s. 2 (2).

[49] *Ibid.*, s. 1 (1) (b) (c). *Supra,* pp. 646-7.

[50] *Ibid.*, s. 2 (6).

[51] *Ibid.*, s. 2 (7).

[52] *Ibid.*, s. 2 (9) (a).

[53] *Ibid.*, s. 2 (9) (b)

and in such proportions as he directs: he can recover it from any of the parties, and any party paying an excess over his due share or proportion can recover it from the other party or parties; and it may be deducted from the compensation due to that party.[54]

Compensation for Disturbance. Where a tenancy under which land is let, whether before or after the passing of the 1950 Act on 26th October 1950, by a local authority, an association or any other person for use by the tenant as an allotment garden is terminated in respect of the whole or any part of the land comprised in the tenancy (a) by resumption of possession for certain purposes,[55] or (b) by termination of the tenancy of the local authority or association, or (c) by termination of the right of occupation by the authority of unoccupied land where a local authority or association have let out such land, the tenant is entitled, on removing from the land or part of it, to compensation from the landlord for disturbance.[56] This right exists despite any agreement to the contrary.[57] Thus, as in the case of compensation for crops and manure, contracting out is not allowed.

The amount of the compensation is in the case of termination of the tenancy of the whole land an amount equal to a year's rent of the land at the rate at which rent was payable immediately before the termination of the tenancy;[57] and in the case of the termination of a tenancy of part of the land an amount bearing to the year's rent (as above defined) of the whole the same proportion that the area of the part bears to the area of the whole land.[57]

This right of compensation is in addition to any compensation payable for crops and manure.[58] Where a tenancy terminated before 26th October 1950 or has terminated thereafter in consequence of a notice given or legal proceedings begun before that date, the right of compensation for disturbance is excluded.[59] The provisions of the 1922 Act[60] regarding the determination of and the recovery of compensation for crops and manure apply to the determination of and the recovery of compensation for disturbance.[61]

Right of Set-off. Out of any money payable by a landlord[62] to a tenant by way of compensation for crops and manure or for disturbance the landlord can deduct any sum due to him by the tenant under or in respect of the tenancy including any sum due to the landlord by way of compensation for depreciation,[63] in terms of the next paragraph.

[54] *Ibid.*, s. 2 (9) (c).
[55] *Ibid.*, s. 1 (1) (b), (c).
[56] 1950 Act, s. 3 (1).
[57] *Ibid.*, s. 3 (2).
[58] *Ibid.*, s. 3 (3).
[59] *Ibid.*, s. 3 (4).
[60] s. 2 (9). See *supra*, p. 650.
[61] 1950 Act, s. 7.
[62] Referred to as " the lessor " in the section.
[63] 1950 Act, s. 5 (1).

Compensation to Landlord for Depreciation. Where the tenant of land let, whether before or after 26th October 1950, for use by him as an allotment garden removes from the land on the termination of his tenancy, the landlord[62] is entitled to compensation from the tenant in respect of any deterioration of the land caused by the failure of the tenant to maintain it clean and in a good state of cultivation and fertility.[64] The right exists despite any agreement to the contrary: thus, contracting out is forbidden here also.[64]

The amount of the compensation is the cost, as at the date of the tenant removing from the land, of making good the deterioration.[65]

Where the tenant has remained in the land during two or more tenancies, the landlord is not deprived of his right to this compensation by reason only that the tenancy during which an act or omission occurred which in whole or in part caused the deterioration was a tenancy other than the one at the termination of which the tenant removes from the land;[66] but the right is excluded where the tenancy terminated before 26th October 1950 or terminated after that date in consequence of a notice given or legal proceedings prior to that date.[67] Here also the provisions of the 1922 Act[68] as to the determination of and the recovery by a tenant of compensation for crops and manure apply.[69]

Right of Set-off. A tenant is entitled to deduct out of any money due by him to the landlord under or in respect of the tenancy, including any money due by way of compensation for deterioration, any sum that is payable to him by the landlord by way of compensation for crops and manure or for disturbance.[70]

Exclusion of Wartime Allotment Gardens. The provisions above mentioned in regard to compensation for disturbance and for deterioration and in regard to the right of set-off do not apply to land let by a local authority under the Defence Regulations 1939, Regulation 62A, and in any document which embodies an arrangement for the cultivation or use of land made in pursuance of the Cultivation of Lands (Allotments) (Scotland) Order 1939 as originally made or as amended by the Cultivation of Lands (Allotments) (Scotland) (Amendment) Order 1941, any reference to compensation which a person would have been entitled to if the arrangement had been a letting under a contract of tenancy of land for use as an allotment garden or for subletting in allotment gardens is to be construed in the same manner as

64 *Ibid.,* s. 4 (1).
65 *Ibid.,* s. 4 (2).
66 *Ibid.,* s. 4 (3).
67 *Ibid.,* s. 4 (4).
68 s. 2 (9). See *supra,* p. 650.
69 1950 Act, s. 7.
70 *Ibid.,* s. 5 (2).

if the provisions for compensation for disturbance or for deterioration had not been made.[71]

Exclusion of certain Crown Lands. The provisions as to compensation for crops and manure, for disturbance and for deterioration do not apply to any land of which possession was taken by or on behalf of any government department under the Acts relating to the Defence of the Realm or the regulations made thereunder, and possession of which has been continued by virtue of any Act or to any land forming part of a royal park.[72]

Expenses of and Receipts of Crown. Any expenses incurred by a minister of the Crown or by a government department (other than the Crown Estate Commissioners[73]) in paying compensation under the provisions relating to compensation for disturbance or for deterioration are to be defrayed out of moneys provided by Parliament and any sums received by a minister of the Crown or a government department (other than the Crown Estate Commissioners) by way of compensation under these provisions are to be paid into the Exchequer.[74]

Open Cast Coal Act, 1958. Under this Act[75] a tenancy of an allotment ends on the date of entry under a compulsory order[76] and there are provisions[77] for compensation, including loss arising from a forced sale of trees, bushes, structures, improvements, etc. which the tenant has removed from the land.

[71] *Ibid.,* s. 6
[72] 1922 Act, s. 3; 1950 Act, s. 7.
[73] Formerly the Commissioners of Crown Lands: Crown Estate Acts 1956 and 1961.
[74] 1950 Act, s. 12 (1).
[75] s. 41 (1), (3), Schedule Eighth.
[76] Schedule Eighth, para. 2.
[77] *Ibid.,* paras. 3-9.

INDEX

42

42A